THE MODERN LIBRARY
of the World's Best Books

THE COMPLETE WORKS
AND LETTERS
OF
CHARLES LAMB

≫≫≫≫≫≫≫≫≫≫≫≫≫≫≫≫≫≫≫≫≫≫≫≫≫≫≫≫≫≫≫≫►

The publishers will be pleased to send, upon request, an illustrated folder setting forth the purpose and scope of THE MODERN LIBRARY, *and listing each volume in the series. Every reader of books will find titles he has been looking for, handsomely printed, in unabridged editions, and at an unusually low price.*

≫≫≫≫≫≫≫≫≫≫≫≫≫≫≫≫≫≫≫≫≫≫≫≫≫≫≫≫≫≫≫≫►

THE
COMPLETE WORKS AND LETTERS
OF
CHARLES LAMB

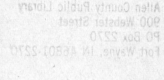

BENNETT A. CERF · DONALD S. KLOPFER
THE MODERN LIBRARY
NEW YORK

THE MODERN LIBRARY

IS PUBLISHED BY

RANDOM HOUSE, INC.

BENNETT A. CERF · DONALD S. KLOPFER · ROBERT K. HAAS

Manufactured in the United States of America
By H. Wolff

CONTENTS

LETTERS

CHAPTER I

1796–1800

LETTERS TO COLERIDGE, SOUTHEY, ROBERT LLOYD, AND MANNING

CHAPTER II

1800–1809

Letters to Coleridge, Manning, and Others

CHAPTER III

1809–1816

Letters to Manning, Coleridge, Wordsworth, and Others

CHAPTER IV

1817–1823

LETTERS TO THE WORDSWORTHS, BERNARD BARTON, AND OTHERS

CHAPTER V

1824–1827

Letters to Bernard Barton and Others

CHAPTER VI

1828–1834

LETTERS TO BERNARD BARTON, COWDEN CLARKE, PROCTER, MOXON, AND OTHERS

INTRODUCTION

In a letter to John Taylor, his publisher, Charles Lamb insisted that the friendly and discriminating reader of his works has no need of an explanatory preface. The Essays themselves, he contended, were *all preface,* since introductions generally, being "nothing but a talk with the reader," add little to what his own writings reveal of the author. Especially in Lamb are confidences, sometimes thinly disguised, entrusted to the reader, by means of which a complete biography can be constructed. His Essays, blending fact with fiction, tell of his family, his boyhood and youth, the tragedy that befell his sister Mary and continued for thirty-eight years of Lamb's life, his servitude as a clerk, his friends, his literary and critical encounters and achievements, the outward characteristics and the inner meanings of a life quite as illustrious as it was deliberately and by circumstance obscure. One of the Essays even provides a thumb-nail autobiography in which the main dates and facts are recorded, the physical peculiarities described and the habits of a lifetime confessed. It even directs, in the bantering humor by which he is commonly known, curious bibliophiles to his "true works" in the ledger archives safeguarded by the East India Company. And if the Essays alone do not lay bare the facts, the Letters leave little unrevealed of the events of his life and their emotional consequences. Together, they constitute a self-portrait as well as an autobiography, the story of a spirit as saintly and a judgment as penetrative as ever adorned English literature.

Averse as Charles Lamb was to a biographical preface, as always mere talk, elaborating unnecessarily upon what the text itself undertakes to reveal, an introduction to his complete works is essential for the guidance of those readers who would have facts separated from the Lambian chaff. Besides, it was impossible, with all his self-revealing candor, to provide the estimate that his contemporaries and his successors placed upon his unique contribution to letters. Nor could he, even with his supreme critical perception, pass the objective judgment on his own work that the reader with a hundred-year historical perspective can afford it. The facts of his life, gleaned from the Essays and Letters, as well as from numerous biographers and commentators, have taken on the qualities of a legend to the English-speaking world.

On the 10th of February, 1775, Charles Lamb was born in Crown Office Row, Inner Temple. At the time, his father, John Lamb, was a clerk and general servant to Samuel Salt, a member of Parliament. His mother, born Elizabeth Field, was the daughter of a housekeeper who served in Blakesware, in Hertfordshire, disguised as Blakesmoor in the Essays. Of the seven children born to his parents, only three survived. These were John, Mary Anne, known to the world as Mary, and Charles, the youngest. It is important to remember, in view of the most tragic single circumstance of Charles Lamb's life, that Mary was ten years older than Charles.

The Essay, *The Old Benchers of the Inner Temple,* commemorates his father under the pseudonym of Lovel, the faithful servant and versatile, if somewhat frustrated, artist. That John Lamb had difficulties in making ends meet is only too apparent, but provision was found for the education of his children under the tutelage of a Mr. Bird, also given unexpected immortality in one of the Essays. It was to Samuel Salt, however, that Charles Lamb, then eight years old, owed his admission into the charitable educational institution, Christ's Hospital. Of his school days, there remains a record, part fact, part fancy, of incomparable grace and poignancy. It tells of a "poor, friendless boy" who was destined to exercise quite as profound an influence over English letters as he exercised for almost a half century over Charles Lamb. His name was Samuel Taylor Coleridge.

The seven years Lamb spent at Christ's Hospital were, on the whole, happy and profitable. Here he gained some knowledge of Greek and Latin, and was made a deputy Grecian. His reading, presumably guided by Coleridge, who was three years his senior, included Virgil, Sallust, Terence and Xenophon. It is known that Coleridge received the first impulse to write verse under the inspiration of the sonnets of William Lisle Bowles. That he communicated his enthusiasm to Lamb is established by their correspondence. The seeds of literary aspiration were planted in him by Coleridge; growth was postponed by the blight of poverty. Charles Lamb had to leave school.

Thoughts of entering the Church were out of the question because of an impediment in his speech. At the time, his brother John, now twenty-six, was employed as a clerk in the South Sea House, thanks to the sponsorship of Samuel Salt. A debonair young man-about-town and dilettante in the arts, John gave little thought to the plight of his family. The mother, wearied by the birth of seven children, had little understanding of their needs. The father was in failing health; consequently Charles and Mary were flung together and they found a haven in Samuel Salt's library, where they browsed at will.

An hereditary taint of insanity in the family cast a sombre shadow over their lives. One way or another, and in a wide degree of intensity, it touched the three children. By his own admission, Charles Lamb himself was committed in a madhouse at Hoxton, a sufferer from the family malady. In a letter to Coleridge, written in 1796, he says: "I am got somewhat rational now and don't bite any one. But mad I was! Coleridge, it may convince you of my regards for you when I tell you my head ran on you in my madness, as much almost as on another person. . . ."

One of the last services rendered to the Lambs by Samuel Salt before his death was to use his influence in having Charles Lamb promoted to a clerkship in the accountant's office of the East India Company. From one point of view, this post might be considered a sinecure, for it lasted thirty-three years. From another, it made him a "prisoner to the desk ... almost grown to the wood." At any rate, it afforded him an annual holiday of a single week, usually spent in Hertfordshire or at one of the two English universities. At Cambridge it was possible to renew friendship with Coleridge and escape the drudgery of the desk to the realm of poetry.

Lamb's first appearance in print was under the aegis of Coleridge. If they reveal nothing else, these first poems throw light on an early love affair with the "fair-haired" Alice W——n. All references to her in the Essays and Letters are extremely reticent. There is some reason for belief that his temporary derangement and commitment may have been caused by his disappointment in love.

An event of frightful consequences made it imperative that Charles Lamb have at his command all the resources of reason. Mary, who contributed to the family support by doing needlework, suffered a mental collapse. Without any warning, she snatched a knife, pursued an inoffensive servant-girl, and, finally, even before Charles could wrest the instrument from her, she stabbed her mother to death. In the mêlée she wounded the now senile father. At the subsequent inquest a verdict of insanity was rendered and Mary was sent to a madhouse. It is little wonder that such a catastrophe should put all thoughts of poetry out of Charles Lamb's mind. Thenceforward his life was to be devoted to the care of his sister who had only periodic respites from insanity. It is a curious phenomenon that, following Mary's murderous assault, Charles never again suffered a relapse into mania. It is even more curious that for the ten years that Mary survived Charles her psychosis was abated.

It was to Coleridge that Lamb turned for assuagement of his grief. His Letters of this period to the author of *The Ancient Mariner* indicate how Lamb sought solace in Shakspearean study. Thereafter he became so immersed in the Elizabethan dramatists and poets that he established himself as one of the foremost authorities on sixteenth and seventeenth century literature. Friendships with Southey, Lloyd and the Wordsworths were formed at this period and were destined to last a lifetime. But for a single interlude of animosity, when Southey attacked one of his essays, *Witches, and Other Night Fears*, the amenities of their relationship were as rare as any in the annals of literary history.

Two years after the murder of his mother, Lamb wrote his best-known lyric, *The Old Familiar Faces*. So effectively does it blend lyric poignancy with reference to his own misfortunes that it is accepted now as a personal document as well as a heartrending song. At this time, too, he was occupied with his first venture into novel writing. *Rosamund Gray* is a romance that appealed to readers of the last decade of the eighteenth century. To them it was redolent with a sad, nostalgic charm; it had sweetness, purity and delicacy. Even Shelley said of it: "What a lovely thing is his *Rosamund Gray!* How much knowledge of the sweetest and deepest part of our nature in it! When I think of such a mind as Lamb's, when I see how unnoticed remain things of such exquisite and complete perfection, what should I hope for myself, if I had not higher objects in view than fame?" For us, a novel like *Rosamund Gray* must have only the charm to be found in a period piece. It exudes virtue and villainy. The gratuitous strictures volunteered by the author seem sententious and ludicrous, rather than of the highest moral purpose. None the less, a real feeling of calamity pervades the story and the student of Lamb can find in it evidence of those qualities which have made Lamb so beloved by his compeers. *Rosamund Gray* was only a fair success and earned him very little money.

The years of enslavement to his ledgers were not especially conducive to prolific literary labors. "Why the devil am I never to have a chance of scribbling my own free thoughts, verse or prose, again? Why must I write of tea and drugs, and price goods and the bales of indigo?" The office, where he was confined by day, at home where he was confined by night, tending Mary, were the zones of his existence. Occasionally Mary got better, and then the attacks would recur with increased severity. "We are in a manner *marked,*" Lamb cries out.

With the turn of the century, Lamb was eking out his salary as a clerk by writing for the newspapers. He tells of the drudgery of supplying paragraphs on order. But high ambition dominated him. He undertook a drama in blank verse, *John Woodvil*. It was submitted to John Kemble of Drury Lane. After a year had elapsed, Lamb made inquiries as to the fate of his manuscript, only to be told that it was lost. The re-submission of a copy only gained for it a rejection slip. If *John Woodvil* is lacking in dramatic and structural merits, it at least indicates Lamb's constant preoccupation with the Elizabethan and Restoration periods. Faltering as it must be considered as a drama, yet it is a tentative step toward the achievement upon which his fame rests most securely—the actual revival of interest in the writers of the sixteenth and seventeenth centuries.

The virus of writing for the theatre had entered Lamb's blood. And by 1806 he had completed the farce, *Mr. H——*. If he was disappointed by the rejection of *John Woodvil*, the acceptance and ultimate fate of *Mr. H——* was cause for even greater chagrin. The play was actually produced at Drury Lane with one of the best light comedians, Elliston, in the title rôle. Lamb himself attended the opening night and sat through the performance not only an auditor of the hisses which greeted his play, but actually a participant in the hisses himself. When at long last the curtain fell, Lamb knew all the discomfiture that can possibly befall a dramatic author. Naturally, he had hoped for success, but his own critical insight failed him and he would not accept what should have been obvious, that *Mr. H——* was too tenuous a play for public acceptance. To expect an audience to be amused and mystified through a whole evening by a mere surname, however objectionable, is to put too great a strain on the patience of a public gathering. Little wonder that Lamb himself joined in the hissing!

In the same year he undertook with his sister a project that has since been one of the great boons to children the world over, as well as a source of immense profit to publishers and booksellers. How the *Tales from Shakspeare* profited Charles and Mary Lamb is told in one of his letters. William Godwin, the father-in-law of Shelley, was a bookseller then. He promised to bring out the Shakspeare plays in a juvenile version. Mary condensed such dramas as *The Tempest, The Winter's Tale, A Midsummer Night's Dream, Much Ado About Nothing, Two Gentlemen of Verona,* and *Cymbeline.* Charles simplified *Othello, Macbeth, Hamlet, King Lear* and the other tragedies. The task appealed to him for the reason that he thought it would be popular among children. Besides, he was in great need of money. For the entire undertaking they earned the sum of sixty guineas, $300 in American money! To attempt to compute the earnings of *Tales from Shakspeare* to publishers is well-nigh impossible.

Encouraged by the success of their joint authorship, Mary, with the help of Charles, compiled *Poetry for Children* and a collection of short stories for girls, *Mrs. Leicester's School.* There followed juvenile abridgments, *The Adventures of Ulysses* and *The Adventures of Telemachus.* None of these condensations properly belongs in Lamb's works and must be omitted from this volume because of Mary's share in them.

When Leigh Hunt established his quarterly review, *The Reflector,* Lamb had a medium in which to publish critical articles on Shakspeare, and it was here the famous Essay on Hogarth appeared. These forays into criticism are incomparable for their ingenuity, grace and perception. Too often, however, Lamb enthusiasts place emphasis on his wit, his gentle nature, and his martyrdom, at the expense of his invaluable contributions to the art of criticism. These latter, it cannot be too strongly stressed, are the foundations for the whole edifice of his reputation.

With the improvement in his economic situation, due to his rise as an employee of the East India Company, Lamb could now indulge himself with his friends. To his house came Hazlitt, Coleridge, Wordsworth, Cary, the translator of Dante, Southey and the whole illustrious company of early nineteenth century literature. At this time, too, Lamb could afford to satisfy his passion for the theatre and for those London sights, smells and street cries to which he was so firmly attached. The stage had a never-failing enchantment for him. The theatre was always a place for escape from reality. The then growing tendency for making the drama akin to life only drew forth expressions of contempt. He did not want to recognize "ourselves, our brothers, our aunts, kinsfolk, allies, patrons, enemies—the same as in life." Why carry our everyday cares to the theatre with us? The stage meant illusion, and it must, in defiance of reality, be the platform from which sonorous phrases and noble periods are declaimed.

The improvement in the condition of his servitude did not, however, release new springs of creative or critical writing in Lamb. For a period of nine years there was a hiatus, during which he played whist, drank and smoked, according to his own testimony, more than was good for him. With the establishment of the *London Magazine* in 1820, Lamb began, under the pseudonym of Elia, that series of Essays by which he won his most lasting fame. The *nom de plume* was derived from a fellow-clerk in the South Sea House, an Italian. At the time, John Lamb was working there, and Charles, fearing that John might not like certain allusions, merely appropriated the name of the unwitting Italian. When Charles Lamb went to confess to the original Elia his usurpation of the name, he discovered that his fellow-clerk had died a year before of consumption, totally unaware of the stir created by the Essays written over his name.

In wealth of content and in varied modulation of style, these Essays display the rich qualities of Lamb's mind and heart. They are gay, bantering, whimsical; at the same time they are full of quaint and rambling allusions, unimpeachable erudition and that unerring critical perception by which Lamb is always distinguished. They cannot fail to arouse a deep personal affection for the man.

When Lamb published his poems, it was natural that he should dedicate them to Samuel Taylor Coleridge. To him it would be "a kind of disloyalty to offer to any one but yourself a volume containing the early pieces." In this dedication he calls attention to a charge which has frequently been made against him—the over-use of an archaic style. Throughout Lamb's works there appear unfamiliar, outmoded words. His love for reviving obsolete terms amounted almost to an affectation. When his sister Mary brought the same charge against him, saying it was entirely against the spirit of the age, Lamb replied: "Damn the age! I will write for antiquity!"

In April, 1825, Lamb summoned the courage to apply for retirement from his employment with the East India Company on a pension. After thirty-three years on the treadmill his new-found freedom made him feel "like a disembodied soul in this, my eternity." His description of his emancipation in that most moving of all Essays, *The Superannuated Man,* indicated how deeply the chains of drudgery had pressed into his spirit. To beguile the heavy hours of his freedom, he established "office hours" in the British Museum, where he went each day on schedule to do his stint of reading in obscure folios of sixteenth and seventeenth century dramatists.

In the meantime, Charles was constantly haunted by the fear of the recurrence of Mary's insanity. Her mental condition grew steadily worse. Long periods of confinement were followed by a brief and melancholy convalescence, then temporary restoration of sanity—and then the blow fell again. Charles's writings became more and more desultory. In fact, his literary work can be considered finished at this period in his life. Only an occasional bit of poetry, *Album Verses,* came from his pen.

A new attachment came to Charles and Mary during the twilight of their lives. Emma Isola was adopted by them and became their protégée and companion. When she was married to Moxon, the publisher of *The Last Essays of Elia,* a sense of loss presaging a far more serious loss befell the Lambs. Coleridge died. When the news came to Charles Lamb he wrote: "I feel how great a part he was of me. His great and dear spirit haunts me. I cannot think a thought, I cannot make a criticism on men or books, without an ineffectual turning and reference to him. He was the proof and touchstone of all my cogitations." The link between Charles Lamb and Samuel Taylor Coleridge in life was so strong that it was almost inevitable that Elia should follow close upon the author of *Kubla Khan* to the grave. In December, 1834, while walking, Lamb suffered an accidental fall. His face was scratched. An attack of erysipelas ensued. Within five days, on December 24, 1834, he died.

Charles Lamb has been compared to such essayists as Montaigne, Addison, Steele and others of equal renown. There is definitely a kinship with Montaigne in their simplicity and clarity of vision. As a commentator, he was perhaps a little more personal and intimate. The chief difference appears in the manner in which Lamb combined gentleness with a penetrating critical acumen.

Lamb's own estimate of his contemporaries is worthy of note. What he felt toward Coleridge has been made apparent. He considered Blake as "one of the most extraordinary persons of the age." It is not surprising that, steeped in the writings of Marlowe, he should look with disparagement upon the then recently completed *Faust* of Goethe. He had no great admiration for Sir Walter Scott, but considered De Foe one of the notable novelists of the time. Nor did he share in the general fanfare of acclaim accorded Voltaire. Although we know from a letter written by Benjamin R. Haydon, the English painter, that Lamb spent some time in the company of Keats, no mention of him is ever made in the Essays or correspondence. Of Byron, Lamb wrote: "I have a thorough aversion to his character, and a very moderate admiration of his genius. He is great in so little a way." Lamb's animus toward Shelley might possibly be traced to some unfortunate disagreements with Shelley's father-in-law, William Godwin, an avowed atheist. Of Shelley, Lamb said: "For his theories and nostrums, they are oracular enough; but I either comprehend 'em not, or there is 'miching malice' and mischief in 'em, but, for the most part, ringing with their own emptiness." Not at all in accord with our present-day romantic conception of Shelley is Lamb's description of the poet's voice. "Shelley I saw once. His voice is the most obnoxious squeak I ever was tormented with, ten thousand times worse than the Laureate's, whose voice is the worst part about him, except his Laureateship." Lamb's own profession of religion is not entirely explicit in his writings. Frequently he adverts to the seriousness of demeanor and the intransigency of spirit of the Quakers. He extols their virtues and gives instances of their exemplary conduct.

In spite of such occasional barbs at men like Shelley and Byron, his gentleness made him beloved by the foremost personalities of his time. It is true that Carlyle, in a splenetic mood, uttered some derogatory fulminations against Lamb. But the tributes paid him by Wordsworth, Coleridge, Hazlitt, Southey, the English Laureate, and others are little short of idolatrous. We have his physical likeness conveyed to us by his own hand: "Below the middle stature; cast of face slightly Jewish, with no Judaic tinge in his complexional religion; stammers abominably, and is therefore apt to discharge his occasional conversation in a quaint aphorism or a poor quibble, than in set and edifying speeches; has consequently been libelled as a person always aiming at wit; which, as he told a dull fellow that charged him with it, is at least as good as aiming at dulness. A small eater, but not drinker; confesses a partiality for the production of the juniper-berry; was a fierce smoker of tobacco, but may be resembled to a volcano burnt out, emitting only now and then a casual puff."

In the hundred and one years that have elapsed since Lamb's death, every facet of his life and work has been illuminated by such commentators as Sir Thomas Noon Talfourd, who, out of consideration for the sensibilities of Mary, suppressed many details of the family tragedy while she was still alive; Canon Alfred Ainger, recognized as the most authoritative editor and biographer of Lamb; and our own eminent contemporary, E. V. Lucas, who enshrined Lamb in a recent book as St. Charles. Each has brought to his task a love for the gentle clerk of Leadenhall Street. Each has paid tribute to his charm, his wit, and, above all, to his monumental achievement of reviving for posterity the Golden Age of English letters.

This volume contains the complete writings of Charles Lamb, grouped into essays, dramas, poetry and translations, rather than in the strict chronological order in which they were produced. The Letters, of which four hundred and sixty-seven are here offered, are those which were arranged by Canon Alfred Ainger and have appended to them the Notes compiled by him. It is possible that there are some letters written by Lamb still unrevealed. Hastily scribbled notes which made casual engagements have been omitted by Canon Ainger as being inconsequential, and of no importance except for the autograph. The Modern Library edition brings together for the first time in a single volume the complete essays, plays, poetry, translations and letters of that obscure clerk who signed himself Elia or Charles Lamb.

SAXE COMMINS

July, 1935.

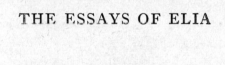

THE ESSAYS OF ELIA

THE ESSAYS OF ELIA

THE SOUTH-SEA HOUSE

READER, in thy passage from the Bank—where thou hast been receiving thy half-yearly dividends (supposing thou art a lean annuitant like myself)—to the Flower Pot, to secure a place for Dalston, or Shacklewell, or some other thy suburban retreat northerly,—didst thou never observe a melancholy-looking, handsome brick and stone edifice, to the left—where Threadneedle Street abuts upon Bishopsgate? I dare say thou hast often admired its magnificent portals ever gaping wide, and disclosing to view a grave court, with cloisters, and pillars, with few or no traces of goers-in or comers-out—a desolation something like Balclutha's.[1]

This was once a house of trade,—a centre of busy interests. The throng of merchants was here—the quick pulse of gain—and here some forms of business are still kept up, though the soul be long since fled. Here are still to be seen stately porticos; imposing staircases; offices roomy as the state apartments in palaces—deserted, or thinly peopled with a few straggling clerks; the still more sacred interiors of court and committee-rooms, with venerable faces of beadles, doorkeepers—directors seated in form on solemn days (to proclaim a dead dividend), at long worm-eaten tables, that have been mahogany, with tarnished gilt-leather coverings, supporting massy silver inkstands long since dry;—the oaken wainscots hung with pictures of deceased governors and sub-governors, of Queen Anne, and the two first monarchs of the Brunswick dynasty:—huge charts, which subsequent discoveries have antiquated; dusty maps of Mexico, dim as dreams,—and soundings of the Bay of Panama! The long passages hung with buckets, appended, in idle row, to walls, whose substance might defy any, short of the last, conflagration;—with vast ranges of cellarage under all, where dollars and pieces-of-eight once lay, an "unsunned heap," for Mammon to have solaced his solitary heart withal,—long since dissipated, or scattered into air at the blast of the breaking of that famous BUBBLE.——

Such is the SOUTH-SEA HOUSE. At least, such it was forty years ago, when I knew it,—a magnificent relic! What alterations may have been made in it since, I have had no opportunities of verifying. Time, I take for granted, has not freshened it. No wind has resuscitated the face of the

---

[1] I passed by the walls of Balclutha, and they were desolate.—OSSIAN.

3

sleeping waters. A thicker crust by this time stagnates upon it. The moths, that were then battering upon its obsolete ledgers and daybooks, have rested from their depredations, but other light generations have succeeded, making fine fretwork among their single and double entries. Layers of dust have accumulated (a superfœtation of dirt!) upon the old layers, that seldom used to be disturbed, save by some curious finger, now and then, inquisitive to explore the mode of book-keeping in Queen Anne's reign; or, with less hallowed curiosity, seeking to unveil some of the mysteries of that tremendous HOAX whose extent the petty peculators of our day look back upon with the same expression of incredulous admiration, and hopeless ambition of rivalry, as would become the puny face of modern conspiracy contemplating the Titan size of Vaux's superhuman plot.

Peace to the manes of the BUBBLE! Silence and destitution are upon thy walls, proud house, for a memorial!

Situated as thou art, in the very heart of stirring and living commerce, —amid the fret and fever of speculation—with the Bank, and the 'Change, and the India House about thee, in the hey-day of present prosperity, with their important faces, as it were, insulting thee, their *poor neighbour out of business*—to the idle and merely contemplative,—to such as me, old house! there is a charm in thy quiet: a cessation—a coolness from business—an indolence almost cloistral—which is delightful! With what reverence have I paced thy great bare rooms and courts at eventide! They spoke of the past:—the shade of some dead accountant, with visionary pen in ear, would flit by me, stiff as in life. Living accounts and accountants puzzle me. I have no skill in figuring. But thy great dead tomes, which scarce three degenerate clerks of the present day could lift from their enshrining shelves—with their old fantastic flourishes, and decorative rubric interlacings—their sums in triple columniations, set down with formal superfluity of ciphers—with pious sentences at the beginning, without which our religious ancestors never ventured to open a book of business, or bill of lading—the costly vellum covers of some of them almost persuading us that we are got into some *better library,*—are very agreeable and edifying spectacles. I can look upon these defunct dragons with complacency. Thy heavy odd-shaped ivory-handled penknives (our ancestors had everything on a larger scale than we have hearts for) are as good as anything from Herculaneum. The pounce-boxes of our days have gone retrograde.

The very clerks which I remember in the South-Sea House—I speak of forty years back—had an air very different from those in the public offices that I have had to do with since. They partook of the genius of the place!

They were mostly (for the establishment did not admit of superfluous salaries) bachelors. Generally (for they had not much to do) persons of a curious and speculative turn of mind. Old-fashioned, for a reason mentioned before. Humourists, for they were of all descriptions; and, not having been brought together in early life (which has a tendency to assimilate the members of corporate bodies to each other), but, for the most part, placed in this house in ripe or middle age, they necessarily carried into it their separate habits and oddities, unqualified, if I may so speak, as into a common stock. Hence they formed a sort of Noah's ark. Odd fishes. A lay-monastery. Domestic retainers in a great house, kept more for show than use. Yet pleasant fellows, full of chat—and not a few among them had arrived at considerable proficiency on the German flute.

The cashier at that time was one Evans, a Cambro-Briton. He had something of the choleric complexion of his countrymen stamped on his visage, but was a worthy sensible man at bottom. He wore his hair, to the last, powdered and frizzed out, in the fashion which I remember to have seen in caricatures of what were termed, in my young days, *Maccaronies*. He was the last of that race of beaux. Melancholy as a gib-cat over his counter all the forenoon, I think I see him, making up his cash (as they call it) with tremulous fingers, as if he feared every one about him was a defaulter; in his hypochondry ready to imagine himself one; haunted, at least, with the idea of the possibility of his becoming one; his tristful visage clearing up a little over his roast neck of veal at Anderton's at two (where his picture still hangs, taken a little before his death by desire of the master of the coffee-house, which he had frequented for the last five-and-twenty years), but not attaining the meridian of its animation till evening brought on the hour of tea and visiting. The simultaneous sound of his well-known rap at the door with the stroke of the clock announcing six, was a topic of never-failing mirth in the families which this dear old bachelor gladdened with his presence. Then was his *forte*, his glorified hour! How would he chirp, and expand, over a muffin! How would he dilate into secret history! His countryman, Pennant himself, in particular, could not be more eloquent than he in relation to old and new London—the site of old theatres, churches, streets gone to decay—where Rosamond's Pond stood—the Mulberry gardens—and the Conduit in Cheap—with many a pleasant anecdote, derived from paternal tradition, of those grotesque figures which Hogarth has immortalised in his picture of *Noon*,—the worthy descendants of those heroic confessors, who, flying to this country, from the wrath of Louis the Fourteenth and his dragoons, kept alive the flame of pure religion in the sheltering obscurities of Hog Lane, and the vicinity of the Seven Dials!

Deputy, under Evans, was Thomas Tame. He had the air and stoop of a nobleman. You would have taken him for one, had you met him in one of the passages leading to Westminster Hall. By stoop, I mean that gentle bending of the body forwards, which, in great men, must be supposed to be the effect of an habitual condescending attention to the applications of their inferiors. While he held you in converse, you felt strained to the height in the colloquy. The conference over, you were at leisure to smile at the comparative insignificance of the pretensions which had just awed you. His intellect was of the shallowest order. It did not reach to a saw or a proverb. His mind was in its original state of white paper. A sucking-babe might have posed him. What was it then? Was he rich?

Alas, no! Thomas Tame was very poor. Both he and his wife looked outwardly gentlefolks, when I fear all was not well at all times within. She
had a neat meagre person, which it was evident she had not sinned in
over-pampering; but in its veins was noble blood. She traced her
descent, by some labyrinth of relationship, which I never thoroughly
understood,—much less can explain with any heraldic certainty at this
time of day,—to the illustrious, but unfortunate house of Derwentwater.
This was the secret of Thomas's stoop. This was the thought—the sentiment—the bright solitary star of your lives,—ye mild and happy pair,—
which cheered you in the night of intellect, and in the obscurity of your
station! This was to you instead of riches, instead of rank, instead of
glittering attainments: and it was worth them all together. You insulted
none with it; but while you wore it as a piece of defensive armour only,
no insult likewise could reach you through it. *Decus et solamen.*

Of quite another stamp was the then accountant, John Tipp. He
neither pretended to high blood, nor, in good truth, cared one fig about
the matter. He "thought an accountant the greatest character in the
world, and himself the greatest accountant in it." Yet John was not without his hobby. The fiddle relieved his vacant hours. He sang, certainly,
with other notes than to the Orphean lyre. He did, indeed, scream and
scrape most abominably. His fine suite of official rooms in Threadneedle
Street, which, without anything very substantial appended to them, were
enough to enlarge a man's notions of himself that lived in them (I know
not who is the occupier of them now), resounded fortnightly to the notes
of a concert of "sweet breasts," as our ancestors would have called them,
culled from club-rooms and orchestras—chorus-singers—first and second
violoncellos—double-basses—and clarionets—who ate his cold mutton,
and drank his punch, and praised his ear. He sate like Lord Midas among
them. But at the desk Tipp was quite another sort of creature. Thence all
ideas, that were purely ornamental, were banished. You could not speak
of anything romantic without rebuke. Politics were excluded. A newspaper was thought too refined and abstracted. The whole duty of man
consisted in writing off dividend warrants. The striking of the annual
balance in the company's books (which, perhaps, differed from the balance of last year in the sum of £25:1:6) occupied his days and nights for
a month previous. Not that Tipp was blind to the deadness of *things* (as
they call them in the city) in his beloved house, or did not sigh for a
return of the old stirring days when South-Sea hopes were young—(he
was indeed equal to the wielding of any of the most intricate accounts of
the most flourishing company in these or those days):—but to a genuine
accountant the difference of proceeds is as nothing. The fractional farthing is as dear to his heart as the thousands which stand before it. He is
the true actor, who, whether his part be a prince or a peasant, must act it
with like intensity. With Tipp form was everything. His life was formal.
His actions seemed ruled with a ruler. His pen was not less erring than
his heart. He made the best executor in the world; he was plagued with
incessant executorships accordingly, which excited his spleen and soothed

his vanity in equal ratios. He would swear (for Tipp swore) at the little orphans, whose rights he would guard with a tenacity like the grasp of the dying hand that commended their interests to his protection. With all this there was about him a sort of timidity—(his few enemies used to give it a worse name)—a something which in reverence to the dead, we will place, if you please, a little on this side of the heroic. Nature certainly had been pleased to endow John Tipp with a sufficient measure of the principle of self-preservation. There is a cowardice which we do not despise, because it has nothing base or treacherous in its elements; it betrays itself, not you: it is mere temperament; the absence of the romantic and the enterprising; it sees a lion in the way, and will not, with Fortinbras, "greatly find quarrel in a straw," when some supposed honour is at stake. Tipp never mounted the box of a stage-coach in his life; or leaned against the rails of a balcony; or walked upon the ridge of a parapet; or looked down a precipice; or let off a gun; or went upon a water-party; or would willingly let you go, if he could have helped it: neither was it recorded of him, that for lucre, or for intimidation, he ever forsook friend or principle.

Whom next shall we summon from the dusty dead, in whom common qualities become uncommon? Can I forget thee, Henry Man, the wit, the polished man of letters, the *author,* of the South-Sea House? who never enteredst thy office in a morning, or quittedst it in mid-day—(what didst *thou* in an office?)—without some quirk that left a sting! Thy gibes and thy jokes are now extinct, or survive but in two forgotten volumes, which I had the good fortune to rescue from a stall in Barbican, not three days ago, and found thee terse, fresh, epigrammatic, as alive. Thy wit is a little gone by in these fastidious days—thy topics are staled by the "new-born gauds" of the time:—but great thou used to be in Public Ledgers, and in Chronicles, upon Chatham, and Shelburne, and Rockingham, and Howe, and Burgoyne, and Clinton, and the war which ended in the tearing from Great Britain her rebellious colonies,—and Keppel, and Wilkes, and Sawbridge, and Bull, and Dunning, and Pratt, and Richmond,—and such small politics.——

A little less facetious, and a great deal more obstreperous, was fine rattling, rattle-headed Plumer. He was descended,—not in a right line, reader (for his lineal pretensions, like his personal, favoured a little of the sinister bend)—from the Plumers of Hertfordshire. So tradition gave him out; and certain family features not a little sanctioned the opinion. Certainly old Walter Plumer (his reputed author) had been a rake in his days, and visited much in Italy, and had seen the world. He was uncle, bachelor-uncle, to the fine old whig still living, who has represented the county in so many successive parliaments, and has a fine old mansion near Ware. Walter flourished in George the Second's days, and was the same who was summoned before the House of Commons about a business of franks, with the old Duchess of Marlborough. You may read of it in Johnson's Life of Cave. Cave came off cleverly in that business. It is certain our Plumer did nothing to discountenance the rumour. He rather seemed pleased whenever it was, with all gentleness, insinuated. But, besides his family pretensions, Plumer was an engaging fellow, and sang gloriously.——

Not so sweetly sang Plumer as thou sangest, mild, child-like, pastoral M——; a flute's breathing less divinely whispering than thy Arcadian melodies, when, in tones worthy of Arden, thou didst chant that song sung by Amiens to the banished Duke, which proclaims the winter wind more lenient than for a man to be ungrateful. Thy sire was old surly M——, the unapproachable churchwarden of Bishopsgate. He knew not what he did, when he begat thee, like spring, gentle offspring of blustering winter:—only unfortunate in thy ending, which should have been mild, conciliatory, swan-like.——

Much remains to sing. Many fantastic shapes rise up, but they must be mine in private:—already I have fooled the reader to the top of his bent;—else could I omit that strange creature Woollett, who existed in trying the question, and *bought litigations?*—and still stranger, inimitable, solemn Hepworth, from whose gravity Newton might have deduced the law of gravitation. How profoundly would he nib a pen— with what deliberation would he wet a wafer!——

But it is time to close—night's wheels are rattling fast over me—it is proper to have done with this solemn mockery.

Reader, what if I have been playing with thee all this while?—peradventure the very *names,* which I have summoned up before thee, are fantastic—insubstantial—like Henry Pimpernel, and old John Naps of Greece:——

Be satisfied that something answering to them has had a being. Their importance is from the past.

OXFORD IN THE VACATION

Casting a preparatory glance at the bottom of this article—as the wary connoisseur in prints, with cursory eye (which, while it reads, seems as though it read not), never fails to consult the *quis sculpsit* in the corner, before he pronounces some rare piece to be a Vivares, or a Woollet—— methinks I hear you exclaim, reader, *Who is Elia?*

Because in my last I tried to divert thee with some half-forgotten humours of some old clerks defunct, in an old house of business, long since gone to decay, doubtless you have already set me down in your mind as one of the self-same college—a votary of the desk—a notched and cropt scrivener—one that sucks his sustenance, as certain sick people are said to do, through a quill.

Well, I do agnize something of the sort. I confess that it is my humour, my fancy—in the forepart of the day, when the mind of your man of letters requires some relaxation—(and none better than such as at first sight seems most abhorrent from his beloved studies)—to while away some good hours of my time in the contemplation of indigos, cottons, raw silks, piece-goods, flowered or otherwise. In the first place * * * * and then it sends you home with such increased appetite to your books * * * not to say, that your outside sheets, and waste wrappers of foolscap, do receive into them, most kindly and naturally, the impression of sonnets, epigrams, *essays*—so that the very parings of a counting-house are, in some sort, the settings up of an author. The enfranchised quill, that has plodded all the morning among the cart-rucks of figures and ciphers, frisks and curvets so at its ease over the flowery carpet-ground of a midnight dissertation.—It feels its promotion. * * * So that you see, upon the whole, the literary dignity of *Elia* is very little, if at all, compromised in the condescension.

Not that, in my anxious detail of the many commodities incidental to the life of a public office, I would be thought blind to certain flaws, which a cunning carper might be able to pick in this Joseph's vest. And here I must have leave, in the fulness of my soul, to regret the abolition, and doing away-with altogether, of those consolatory interstices and sprinklings of freedom, through the four seasons,—the *red-letter days,* now become, to all intents and purposes, *dead-letter days.* There was Paul, and Stephen, and Barnabas—

Andrew and John, men famous in old times

—we were used to keep all their days holy as long back as I was at school at Christ's. I remember their effigies, by the same token, in the old Basket Prayer-Book. There hung Peter in his uneasy posture—holy Bartlemy in the troublesome act of flaying, after the famous Marsyas by Spagnoletti.——I honoured them all, and could almost have wept the defalcation of Iscariot—so much did we love to keep holy memories sacred:—only methought I a little grudged at the coalition of the *better Jude* with Simon—clubbing (as it were) their sanctities together to make up one poor gaudy-day between them—as an economy unworthy of the dispensation.

These were bright visitations in a scholar's and a clerk's life "far off their coming shone."—I was as good as an almanac in those days. I could have told you such a saint's day falls out next week, or the week after. Peradventure the Epiphany, by some periodical infelicity, would, once in six years, merge in a Sabbath. Now am I little better than one of the profane. Let me not be thought to arraign the wisdom of my civil superiors, who have judged the further observation of these holy tides to be papistical, superstitious. Only in a custom of such long standing, methinks, if their Holinesses the Bishops had, in decency, been first sounded——but I am wading out of my depths. I am not the man to decide the limits of civil and ecclesiastical authority——I am plain Elia—no Selden, nor Archbishop Usher—though at present in the thick of their books, here in the heart of learning, under the shadow of the mighty Bodley.

I can here play the gentleman, enact the student. To such a one as myself, who has been defrauded in his young years of the sweet food of academic institution, nowhere is so pleasant, to while away a few idle weeks at, as one or other of the Universities. Their vacation, too, at this time of the year, falls in so pat with *ours*. Here I can take my walks unmolested, and fancy myself of what degree or standing I please. I seem admitted *ad eundem*. I fetch up past opportunities. I can rise at the chapel-bell, and dream that it rings for *me*. In moods of humility I can be a Sizar, or a Servitor. When the peacock vein rises, I strut a Gentleman Commoner. In graver moments I proceed Master of Arts. Indeed I do not think I am much unlike that respectable character. I have seen your dim-eyed vergers, and bed-makers in spectacles, drop a bow or a curtsy, as I pass, wisely mistaking me for something of the sort. I go about in black, which favours the notion. Only in Christ Church reverend quadrangle, I can be content to pass for nothing short of a Seraphic Doctor.

The walks at these times are so much one's own,—the tall trees of Christ's, the groves of Magdalen! The halls deserted, and with open doors inviting one to slip in unperceived, and pay a devoir to some Founder, or noble or royal Benefactress (that should have been ours), whose portrait seems to smile upon their overlooked beadsman, and to adopt me for their own. Then, to take a peep in by the way at the butteries, and sculleries, redolent of antique hospitality: the immense caves of kitchens, kitchen fireplaces, cordial recesses; ovens whose first pies were baked four centuries ago; and spits which have cooked for Chaucer! Not the meanest minister among the dishes but is hallowed to me through his imagination, and the Cook goes forth a Manciple.

Antiquity! thou wondrous charm, what art thou? that, being nothing, art everything! When thou *wert*, thou wert not antiquity—then thou wert nothing, but hadst a remoter *antiquity*, as thou calledst it, to look back to with blind veneration; thou thyself being to thyself flat, jejune, *modern!* What mystery lurks in this retroversion? or what half Januses[1] are we, that cannot look forward with the same idolatry with which we for ever revert! The mighty future is as nothing, being everything! the past is everything, being nothing!

What were thy *dark ages?* Surely the sun rose as brightly then as now, and man got him to his work in the morning. Why is it we can never hear mention of them without an accompanying feeling as though a palpable obscure had dimmed the face of things, and that our ancestors wandered to and fro groping!

Above all thy rarities, old Oxenford, what do most arride and solace me, are thy repositories of mouldering learning, thy shelves——

What a place to be in is an old library! It seems as though all the souls of all the writers, that have bequeathed their labours to these Bodleians, were reposing here, as in some dormitory, or middle state. I do not want

---

[1] Januses of one face—Sir Thomas Browne.

to handle, to profane the leaves, their winding-sheets. I could as soon dislodge a shade. I seem to inhale learning, walking amid their foliage; and the odour of their old moth-scented coverings is fragrant as the first bloom of those sciential apples which grew amid the happy orchard.

Still less have I curiosity to disturb the elder repose of MSS. Those *variæ lectiones,* so tempting to the more erudite palates, do but disturb and unsettle my faith. I am no Herculanean raker. The credit of the three witnesses might have slept unimpeached for me. I leave these curiosities to Porson, and to G. D.—whom, by the way, I found busy as a moth over some rotten archive, rummaged out of some seldom-explored press, in a nook at Oriel. With long poring he is grown almost into a book. He stood as passive as one by the side of the old shelves. I longed to new-coat him in russia, and assign him his place. He might have mustered for a tall Scapula.

D. is assiduous in his visits to these seats of learning. No inconsiderable portion of his moderate fortune, I apprehend, is consumed in journeys between them and Clifford's Inn—where, like a dove on the asp's nest, he has long taken up his unconscious abode, amid an incongruous assembly of attorneys, attorneys' clerks, apparitors, promoters, vermin of the law, among whom he sits "in calm and sinless peace." The fangs of the law pierce him not—the winds of litigation blow over his humble chambers—the hard sheriff's officer moves his hat as he passes— legal nor illegal discourtesy touches him—none thinks of offering violence or injustice to him—you would as soon "strike an abstract idea."

D. has been engaged, he tells me, through a course of laborious years, in an investigation into all curious matter connected with the two Universities; and has lately lit upon a MS. collection of charters, relative to C——, by which he hopes to settle some disputed points—particularly that long controversy between them as to priority of foundation. The ardour with which he engages in these liberal pursuits, I am afraid, has not met with all the encouragement it deserved, either here, or at C——. Your caputs, and heads of colleges, care less than anybody else about these questions.—Contented to suck the milky fountains of their Alma Maters, without inquiring into the venerable gentlewomen's years, they rather hold such curiosities to be impertinent—unreverend. They have their good glebe lands *in manu,* and care not much to rake into the title-deeds. I gather at least so much from other sources, for D. is not a man to complain.

D. started like an unbroke heifer when I interrupted him. *A priori* it was not very probable that we should have met in Oriel. But D. would have done the same, had I accosted him on the sudden in his own walks in Clifford's Inn, or in the Temple. In addition to a provoking short-sightedness (the effect of late studies and watchings at the midnight oil) D. is the most absent of men. He made a call the other morning at our friend M.'s in Bedford Square; and, finding nobody at home, was ushered into the hall, where, asking for pen and ink, with great exactitude of purpose he enters me his name in the book—which ordinarily lies about in such places, to record the failures of the untimely or unfortunate visitor—and takes his leave with many ceremonies and professions of regret. Some two or three hours after, his walking destinies returned him into the same neighbourhood again, and again the quiet image of the fireside circle at M.'s—Mrs. M. presiding at it like a Queen Lar, with pretty A. S. at her side—striking irresistibly on his fancy, he makes another call (forgetting that they were "certainly not to return from the country before that day week"), and disappointed a second time, inquires for pen and paper as before: again the book is brought, and in the line just above that in which he is about to print his second name (his re-script)—his first name (scarce dry) looks out upon him like another Sosia, or as if a man should suddenly encounter his own duplicate!—The effect may be conceived. D. made many a good resolution against any such lapses in future. I hope he will not keep them too rigorously.

For with G. D.—to be absent from the body is sometimes (not to speak it profanely) to be present with the Lord. At the very time when, personally encountering thee, he passes on with no recognition——or, being stopped, starts like a thing surprised—at that moment, reader, he is on Mount Tabor—or Parnassus—or co-sphered with Plato—or, with Harrington, framing "immortal commonwealths"—devising some plan of amelioration to thy country, or thy species——peradventure meditating some individual kindness or courtesy, to be done to *thee thyself,* the returning consciousness of which made him to start so guiltily at thy obtruded personal presence.

D. is delightful anywhere, but he is at the best in such places as these. He cares not much for Bath. He is out of his element at Buxton, at Scarborough, or Harrowgate. The Cam and the Isis are to him "better than all the waters of Damascus." On the Muses' hill he is happy, and good, as one of the Shepherds on the Delectable Mountains; and when he goes about with you to show you the halls and colleges, you think you have with you the Interpreter at the House Beautiful.

CHRIST'S HOSPITAL FIVE-AND-THIRTY YEARS AGO

In Mr. Lamb's "Works," published a year or two since, I find a magnificent eulogy on my old school,[1] such as it was, or now appears to him to have been, between the years 1782 and 1789. It happens very oddly that my own standing at Christ's was nearly corresponding with his; and, with all gratitude to him for his enthusiasm for the cloisters, I think he has contrived to bring together whatever can be said in praise of them, dropping all the other side of the argument most ingeniously.

---

[1] Recollections of Christ's Hospital.

I remember L. at school, and can well recollect that he had some peculiar advantages, which I and others of his schoolfellows had not. His friends lived in town, and were near at hand; and he had the privilege of going to see them almost as often as he wished, through some invidious distinction, which was denied to us. The present worthy sub-treasurer to the Inner Temple can explain how that happened. He had his tea and hot rolls in a morning, while we were battening upon our quarter of a penny loaf—our *crug*—moistened with attenuated small beer, in wooden piggins, smacking of the pitched leathern jack it was poured from. Our Monday's milk porritch, blue and tasteless, and the pease soup of Saturday, coarse and choking, were enriched for him with a slice of "extraordinary bread and butter," from the hot loaf of the Temple. The Wednesday's mess of millet, somewhat less repugnant— (we had three banyan to four meat days in the week)—was endeared to his palate with a lump of double-refined, and a smack of ginger (to make it go down the more glibly) or the fragrant cinnamon. In lieu of our *half-pickled* Sundays, or *quite fresh* boiled beef on Thursdays (strong as *caro equina*), with detestable marigolds floating in the pail to poison the broth—our scanty mutton scrags on Friday—and rather more savoury, but grudging, portions of the same flesh, rotten-roasted or rare, on the Tuesdays (the only dish which excited our appetites, and disappointed our stomachs, in almost equal proportion)—he had his hot plate of roast veal, or the more tempting griskin (exotics unknown to our palates), cooked in the paternal kitchen (a great thing), and brought him daily by his maid or aunt! I remember the good old relative (in whom love forbade pride) squatting down upon some odd stone in a by-nook of the cloisters, disclosing the viands (of higher regale than those cates which the ravens ministered to the Tishbite); and the contending passions of L. at the unfolding. There was love for the bringer; shame for the thing brought, and the manner of its bringing; sympathy for those who were too many to share in it; and, at top of all, hunger (eldest, strongest of the passions!) predominant, breaking down the stony fences of shame, and awkwardness, and a troubling over-consciousness.

I was a poor friendless boy. My parents, and those who should care for me, were far away. Those few acquaintances of theirs, which they could reckon upon being kind to me in the great city, after a little forced notice, which they had the grace to take of me on my first arrival in town, soon grew tired of my holiday visits. They seemed to them to recur too often, though I thought them few enough; and, one after another, they all failed me, and I felt myself alone among six hundred playmates.

O the cruelty of separating a poor lad from his early homestead! The yearnings which I used to have towards it in those unfledged years! How, in my dreams, would my native town (far in the west) come back, with its church, and trees, and faces! How I would wake weeping, and in the anguish of my heart exclaim upon sweet Calne in Wiltshire!

To this late hour of my life, I trace impressions left by the recollections of those friendless holidays. The long warm days of summer never return but they bring with them a gloom from the haunting memory of those *whole-day leaves*, when, by some strange arrangement, we were turned out for the live-long day, upon our own hands, whether we had friends to go to or none. I remember those bathing excursions to the New River which L. recalls with such relish, better, I think, than he can—for he was a home-seeking lad, and did not much care for such water pastimes:—How merrily we would sally forth into the fields; and strip under the first warmth of the sun; and wanton like young dace in the streams; getting us appetites for noon, which those of us that were penniless (our scanty morning crust long since exhausted) had not the means of allaying—while the cattle, and the birds, and the fishes were at feed about us and we had nothing to satisfy our cravings—the very beauty of the day, and the exercise of the pastime, and the sense of liberty, setting a keener edge upon them! How faint and languid, finally, we would return, towards night-fall, to our desired morsel, half-rejoicing, half-reluctant, that the hours of our uneasy liberty had expired!

It was worse in the days of winter, to go prowling about the streets objectless—shivering at cold windows of print-shops, to extract a little amusement; or haply, as a last resort in the hopes of a little novelty, to pay a fifty-times repeated visit (where our individual faces should be as well known to the warden as those of his own charges) to the Lions in the Tower—to whose levee, by courtesy immemorial, we had a prescriptive title to admission.

L.'s governor (so we called the patron who presented us to the foundation) lived in a manner under his paternal roof. Any complaint which he had to make was sure of being attended to. This was understood at Christ's, and was an effectual screen to him against the severity of masters, or worse tyranny of the monitors. The oppressions of these young brutes are heart-sickening to call to recollection. I have been called out of my bed, and *waked for the purpose,* in the coldest winter nights—and this not once, but night after night—in my shirt, to receive the discipline of a leathern thong, with eleven other sufferers, because it pleased my callow overseer, when there has been any talking heard after we were gone to bed, to make the six last beds in the dormitory, where the youngest children of us slept, answerable for an offence they neither dared to commit nor had the power to hinder. The same execrable tyranny drove the younger part of us from the fires, when our feet were perishing with snow; and, under the cruellest penalties, forbade the indulgence of a drink of water when we lay in sleepless summer nights fevered with the season and the day's sports.

There was one H——, who, I learned, in after days was seen expiating some maturer offence in the hulks. (Do I flatter myself in fancying that this might be the planter of that name, who suffered—at Nevis, I think, or St. Kitts—some few years since? My friend Tobin was the benevolent instrument of bringing him to the gallows.) This petty Nero actually branded a boy who had offended him with a red-hot iron; and nearly starved forty of us with exacting contributions, to the one half of our bread, to pamper a young ass, which, incredible as it may seem, with the connivance of the nurse's daughter (a young flame of his) he had contrived to smuggle in, and keep upon the leads of the *ward*, as they called our dormitories. This game went on for better than a week, till the foolish beast, not able to fare well but he must cry roast meat—happier than Caligula's minion, could he have kept his own counsel—but, foolisher, alas! than any of his species in the fables—waxing fat, and kicking, in the fulness of bread, one unlucky minute would needs proclaim his good fortune to the world below; and, laying out his simple throat, blew such a ram's-horn blast, as (toppling down the walls of his own Jericho) set concealment any longer at defiance. The client was dismissed, with certain attentions, to Smithfield; but I never understood that the patron underwent any censure on the occasion. This was in the stewardship of L.'s admired Perry.

Under the same *facile* administration, can L. have forgotten the cool impunity with which the nurses used to carry away openly, in open platters, for their own tables, one out of two of every hot joint, which the careful matron had been seeing scrupulously weighed out for our dinners? These things were daily practised in that magnificent apartment which L. (grown connoisseur since, we presume) praises so highly for the grand paintings "by Verrio, and others," with which it is "hung round and adorned." But the sight of sleek, well-fed blue-coat boys in pictures was, at that time, I believe, little consolatory to him, or us, the living ones, who saw the better part of our provisions carried away before our faces by harpies; and ourselves reduced (with the Trojan in the hall of Dido)

> To feed our mind with idle portraiture.

L. has recorded the repugnance of the school to *gags*, or the fat of fresh beef boiled; and sets it down to some superstition. But these unctuous morsels are never grateful to young palates (children are universally fat-haters), and in strong, coarse, boiled meats, *unsalted*, are detestable. A *gag-eater* in our time was equivalent to a *goule*, and held in equal detestation. —— suffered under the imputation:

> . . . . 'Twas said
> He ate strange flesh.

He was observed, after dinner, carefully to gather up the remnants left at his table (not many nor very choice fragments, you may credit me)—and, in an especial manner, these disreputable morsels, which he would convey away and secretly stow in the settle that stood at his bedside. None saw when he ate them. It was rumoured that he privately devoured them in the night. He was watched, but no traces of such midnight practices were discoverable. Some reported that on leave-days he had been seen to carry out of the bounds a large blue check handkerchief, full of something. This then must be the accursed thing. Conjecture next was at work to imagine how he could dispose of it. Some said he sold it to

the beggars. This belief generally prevailed. He went about moping.
None spake to him. No one would play with him. He was excommu-
nicated; put out of the pale of the school. He was too powerful a boy to
be beaten, but he underwent every mode of that negative punishment
which is more grievous than many stripes. Still he persevered. At length
he was observed by two of his schoolfellows, who were determined to get
at the secret, and had traced him one leave-day for the purpose, to enter
a large worn-out building, such as there exist specimens of in Chancery
Lane, which are let out to various scales of pauperism, with open door
and a common staircase. After him they silently slunk in, and followed
by stealth up four flights, and saw him tap at a poor wicket, which was
opened by an aged woman, meanly clad. Suspicion was now ripened into
certainty. The informers had secured their victim. They had him in their
toils. Accusation was formally preferred, and retribution most signal was
looked for. Mr. Hathaway, the then steward (for this happened a little
after my time), with that patient sagacity which tempered all his conduct, determined to investigate the matter before he proceeded to sentence. The result was that the supposed mendicants, the receivers or purchasers of the mysterious scraps, turned out to be the parents of ——, an
honest couple come to decay—whom this seasonable supply had, in all
probability, saved from mendicancy; and that this young stork, at the
expense of his own good name, had all this while been only feeding the
old birds!—The governors on this occasion, much to their honour, voted
a present relief to the family of ——, and presented him with a silver
medal. The lesson which the steward read upon RASH JUDGMENT, on the
occasion of publicly delivering the medal to ——, I believe would not be
lost upon his auditory.—I had left school then, but I well remember
——. He was a tall, shambling youth, with a cast in his eye, not at all
calculated to conciliate hostile prejudices. I have since seen him carrying a baker's basket. I think I heard he did not do quite so well by himself as he had done by the old folks.

I was a hypochondriac lad; and the sight of a boy in fetters, upon the
day of my first putting on the blue clothes, was not exactly fitted to
assuage the natural terrors of initiation. I was of tender years, barely
turned of seven; and had only read of such things in books, or seen them
but in dreams. I was told he had *run away*. This was the punishment for
the first offence.—As a novice I was soon after taken to see the dungeons.
These were little, square, Bedlam cells, where a boy could just lie at his
length upon straw and a blanket—a mattress, I think, was afterwards
substituted—with a peep of light, let in askance, from a prison-orifice at
top, barely enough to read by. Here the poor boy was locked in by himself all day, without sight of any but the porter who brought him his
bread and water—who *might not speak to him;*—or of the beadle, who
came twice a week to call him out to receive his periodical chastisement,
which was almost welcome, because it separated him from a brief interval
from solitude:—and here he was shut up by himself *of nights* out of the
reach of any sound, to suffer whatever horrors the weak nerves, and

superstition incident to his time of life, might subject him to.[1] This was the penalty for the second offence. Wouldst thou like, reader, to see what became of him in the next degree?

The culprit, who had been a third time an offender, and whose expulsion was at this time deemed irreversible, was brought forth, as at some solemn *auto da fe*, arrayed in uncouth and most appalling attire—all trace of his late "watchet weeds" carefully effaced, he was exposed in a jacket resembling those which London lamplighters formerly delighted in, with a cap of the same. The effect of this divestiture was such as the ingenious devisers of it could have anticipated. With his pale and frighted features, it was as if some of those disfigurements in Dante had seized upon him. In this disguisement he was brought into the hall (*L.'s favourite state-room*), where awaited him the whole number of his schoolfellows, whose joint lessons and sports he was thenceforth to share no more; the awful presence of the steward, to be seen for the last time; of the executioner beadle, clad in his state robe for the occasion; and of two faces more, of direr import, because never but in these extremities visible. These were governors; two of whom by choice, or charter, were always accustomed to officiate at these *Ultima Supplicia;* not to mitigate (so at least we understood it), but to enforce the uttermost stripe. Old Bamber Gascoigne, and Peter Aubert, I remember, were colleagues on one occasion, when the beadle turning rather pale, a glass of brandy was ordered to prepare him for the mysteries. The scourging was, after the old Roman fashion, long and stately. The lictor accompanied the criminal quite round the hall. We were generally too faint, with attending to the previous disgusting circumstances, to make accurate report with our eyes of the degree of corporal suffering inflicted. Report, of course, gave out the back knotty and livid. After scourging, he was made over, in his *San Benito*, to his friends, if he had any (but commonly such poor runagates were friendless), or to his parish officer, who, to enhance the effect of the scene, had his station allotted to him on the outside of the hall gate.

These solemn pageantries were not played off so often as to spoil the general mirth of the community. We had plenty of exercise and recreation *after* school hours; and, for myself, I must confess, that I was never happier than *in* them. The Upper and the Lower Grammar Schools were held in the same room; and an imaginary line only divided their bounds. Their character was as different as that of the inhabitants on the two sides of the Pyrenees. The Rev. James Boyer was the Upper Master; but the Rev. Matthew Field presided over that portion of the apartment of which I had the good fortune to be a member. We lived a life as careless as birds. We talked and did just what we pleased, and nobody molested

---

[1] One or two instances of lunacy, or attempted suicide, accordingly, at length convinced the governors of the impolicy of this part of the sentence, and the midnight torture to the spirits was dispensed with.—This fancy of dungeons for children was a sprout of Howard's brain; for which (saving the reverence due to Holy Paul) methinks I could willingly spit upon his statue.

us. We carried an accidence, or a grammar, for form; but, for any trouble it gave us, we might take two years in getting through the verbs deponent, and another two in forgetting all that we had learned about them. There was now and then the formality of saying a lesson, but if you had not learned it, a brush across the shoulders (just enough to disturb a fly) was the sole remonstrance. Field never used the rod; and in truth he wielded the cane with no great good-will—holding it "like a dancer." It looked in his hands rather like an emblem than an instrument of authority; and an emblem, too, he was ashamed of. He was a good, easy man, that did not care to ruffle his own peace, nor perhaps set any great consideration upon the value of juvenile time. He came among us, now and then, but often stayed away whole days from us; and when he came it made no difference to us—he had his private room to retire to, the short time he stayed, to be out of the sound of our noise. Our mirth and uproar went on. We had classics of our own, without being beholden to "insolent Greece or haughty Rome," that passed current among us—Peter Wilkins—the Adventures of the Hon. Captain Robert Boyle—the Fortunate Bluecoat Boy—and the like. Or we cultivated a turn for mechanic and scientific operations; making little sundials of paper; or weaving those ingenious parentheses called *cat-cradles;* or making dry peas to dance upon the end of a tin pipe; or studying the art military over that laudable game "French and English," and a hundred other such devices to pass away the time—mixing the useful with the agreeable—as would have made the souls of Rousseau and John Locke chuckle to have seen us.

Matthew Field belonged to that class of modest divines who affect to mix in equal proportion the *gentleman,* the *scholar,* and the *Christian;* but, I know not how, the first ingredient is generally found to be the predominating dose in the composition. He was engaged in gay parties, or with his courtly bow at some episcopal levee, when he should have been attending upon us. He had for many years the classical charge of a hundred children, during the four or five first years of their education, and his very highest form seldom proceeded further than two or three of the introductory fables of Phædrus. How things were suffered to go on thus, I cannot guess. Boyer, who was the proper person to have remedied these abuses, always affected, perhaps felt, a delicacy in interfering in a province not strictly his own. I have not been without my suspicions, that he was not altogether displeased at the contrast we presented to his end of the school. We were a sort of Helots to his young Spartans. He would sometimes, with ironic deference, send to borrow a rod of the Under Master, and then, with Sardonic grin, observe to one of his upper boys, "how neat and fresh the twigs looked." While his pale students were battering their brains over Xenophon and Plato, with a silence as deep as that enjoyed by the Samite, we were enjoying ourselves at our ease in our little Goshen. We saw a little into the secrets of his discipline, and the prospect did but the more reconcile us to our lot. His thunders rolled innocuous for us: his storms came near, but never touched us; contrary to Gideon's miracle, while all around were drenched, our fleece was dry.[1] His boys turned out the better scholars; we, I suspect, have the advantage in temper. His pupils cannot speak of him without something of terror allaying their gratitude; the remembrance of Field comes back with all the soothing images of indolence, and summer slumbers, and work like play, and innocent idleness, and Elysian exemptions, and life itself a "playing holiday."

Though sufficiently removed from the jurisdiction of Boyer, we were near enough (as I have said) to understand a little of his system. We occasionally heard sounds of the *Ululantes,* and caught glances of Tartarus. B. was a rabid pedant. His English style was crampt to barbarism. His Easter anthems (for his duty obliged him to those periodical flights) were grating as scrannel pipes.[2]—He would laugh, ay, and heartily, but then it must be at Flaccus's quibble about *Rex* —— or at the *tristis serveritas in vultu,* or *inspicere in patinas,* of Terence—thin jests, which at their first broaching could hardly have had *vis* enough to move a Roman muscle.—He had two wigs, both pedantic, but of different omen. The one serene, smiling, fresh powdered, betokening a mild day. The other, an old, discoloured, unkempt, angry caxon, denoting frequent and bloody execution. Woe to the school, when he made his morning appearance in his *passy,* or *passionate wig.* No comet expounded surer.—J. B. had a heavy hand. I have known him double his knotty fist at a poor trembling child (the maternal milk hardly dry upon its lips) with a "Sirrah, do you presume to set your wits at me?"—Nothing was more common than to see him make a headlong entry into the schoolroom, from his inner recess, or library. and, with turbulent eye, singling out a lad, roar out, "Od's my life, sirrah" (his favourite adjuration), "I have a great mind to whip you,"—then, with as sudden a retracting impulse, fling back into his lair—and, after a cooling lapse of some minutes (during which all but the culprit had totally forgotten the context) drive headlong out again, piecing out his imperfect sense, as if it had been some Devil's Litany, with the expletory yell—*"and I* WILL, *too."*—In his gentler moods, when the *rabidus furor* was assuaged, he had resort to an ingenious method, peculiar, for what I have heard, to himself, of whipping the boy, and reading the Debates, at the same time; a paragraph, and a lash between; which in those times, when parliamentary oratory was most at a height and flourishing in these realms, was not calculated to impress the patient with a veneration for the diffuser graces of rhetoric.

Once, and but once, the uplifted rod was known to fall ineffectual

---

[1] Cowley.

[2] In this and everything B. was the antipodes of his coadjutor. While the former was digging his brains for crude anthems, worth a pig-nut, F. would be recreating his gentlemanly fancy in the more flowery walks of the Muses. A little dramatic effusion of his, under the name of Vertumnus and Pomona, is not yet forgotten by the chroniclers of that sort of literature. It was accepted by Garrick, but the town did not give it their sanction.—B. used to say of it, in a way of half-compliment, half-irony, that it was *too classical for representation.*

from his hand—when droll squinting W—— having been caught putting the inside of the master's desk to a use for which the architect had clearly not designed it, to justify himself, with great simplicity averred, that *he did not know that the thing had been forewarned*. This exquisite irrecognition of any law antecedent to the *oral* or *declaratory,* struck so irresistibly upon the fancy of all who heard it (the pedagogue himself not excepted)—that remission was unavoidable.

L. has given credit to B.'s great merits as an instructor. Coleridge, in his literary life, has pronounced a more intelligible and ample encomium on them. The author of the Country Spectator doubts not to compare him with the ablest teachers of antiquity. Perhaps we cannot dismiss him better than with the pious ejaculation of C.—when he heard that his old master was on his deathbed: "Poor J. B.!—may all his faults be forgiven; and may he be wafted to bliss by little cherub boys all head and wings, with no *bottoms* to reproach his sublunary infirmities."

Under him were many good and sound scholars bred.—First Grecian of my time was Lancelot Pepys Stevens, kindest of boys and men, since Co-grammar-master (and inseparable companion) with Dr. T——e. What an edifying spectacle did this brace of friends present to those who remembered the anti-socialities of their predecessors!—You never met the one by chance in the street without a wonder, which was quickly dissipated by the almost immediate sub-appearance of the other. Generally arm-in-arm, these kindly coadjutors lightened for each other the toilsome duties of their profession, and when, in advanced age, one found it convenient to retire, the other was not long in discovering that it suited him to lay down the fasces also. Oh, it is pleasant, as it is rare, to find the same arm linked in yours at forty, which at thirteen helped it to turn over the *Cicero De Amicitiâ,* or some tale of Antique Friendship, which the young heart even then was burning to anticipate!—Co-Grecian with S. was Th——, who has since executed with ability various diplomatic functions at the Northern courts. Th—— was a tall, dark, saturnine youth, sparing of speech, with raven locks.—Thomas Fanshaw Middleton followed him (now Bishop of Calcutta), a scholar and a gentleman in his teens. He has the reputation of an excellent critic; and is author (besides the Country Spectator) of a Treatise on the Greek Article, against Sharpe. M. is said to bear his mitre high in India, where the *regni novitas* (I dare say) sufficiently justifies the bearing. A humility quite as primitive as that of Jewel or Hooker might not be exactly fitted to impress the minds of those Anglo-Asiatic diocesans with a reverence for home institutions, and the church which those fathers watered. The manners of M. at school, though firm, were mild and unassuming.—Next to M. (if not senior to him) was Richards, author of the Aboriginal Britons, the most spirited of the Oxford Prize Poems; a pale, studious Grecian.—Then followed poor S——, ill-fated M——! of these the Muse is silent.

> Finding some of Edward's race
> Unhappy, pass their annals by.

Come back into memory, like as thou wert in the day-spring of thy fancies, with hope like a fiery column before thee—the dark pillar not yet turned—Samuel Taylor Coleridge—Logician, Metaphysician, Bard! —How have I seen the casual passer through the Cloisters stand still, entranced with admiration (while he weighed the disproportion between the *speech* and the *garb* of the young Mirandula), to hear thee unfold, in thy deep and sweet intonations, the mysteries of Jamblichus, or Plotinus (for even in those years thou waxedst not pale at such philosophic draughts), or reciting Homer in his Greek, or Pindar——while the walls of the old Grey Friars re-echoed to the accents of the *inspired charity-boy!*—Many were the "wit-combats" (to dally awhile with the words of old Fuller) between him and C. V. Le G——, "which two I behold like a Spanish great galleon, and an English man-of-war; Master Coleridge, like the former, was built far higher in learning, solid, but slow in his performances. C. V. L., with the English man-of-war, lesser in bulk, but lighter in sailing, could turn with all tides, tack about, and take advantage of all winds, by the quickness of his wit and invention."

Nor shalt thou, their compeer, be quickly forgotten, Allen, with the cordial smile, and still more cordial laugh, with which thou wert wont to make the old Cloisters shake, in thy cognition of some poignant jest of theirs; or the anticipation of some more material, and, peradventure practical one, of thine own. Extinct are those smiles, with that beautiful countenance, with which (for thou wert the *Nireus formosus* of the school), in the days of thy maturer waggery, thou didst disarm the wrath of infuriated town-damsel, who, incensed by provoking pinch, turning tigress-like round, suddenly converted by thy angel-look, exchanged the half-formed terrible "*bl*——," for a gentler greeting— "*bless thy handsome face!*"

Next follow two, who ought to be now alive, and the friends of Elia— the junior Le G—— and F——; who impelled, the former by a roving temper, the latter by too quick a sense of neglect—ill capable of enduring the slights poor Sizars are sometimes subject to in our seats of learning—exchanged their Alma Mater for the camp; perishing, one by climate, and one on the plains of Salamanca:—Le G——, sanguine, volatile, sweet-natured; F——, dogged, faithful, anticipative of insult, warmhearted, with something of the old Roman height about him.

Fine, frank-hearted Fr——, the present master of Hertford, with Marmaduke T——, mildest of Missionaries—and both my good friends still—close the catalogue of Grecians in my time.

THE TWO RACES OF MEN

THE human species, according to the best theory I can form of it, is composed of two distinct races, *the men who borrow, and the men who lend*. To these two original diversities may be reduced all those impertinent classifications of Gothic and Celtic tribes, white men, black men, red men. All the dwellers upon earth, "Parthians, and Medes, and Elamites," flock hither, and do naturally fall in with one or other of these primary distinctions. The infinite superiority of the former, which I choose to designate as the *great race,* is discernible in their figure, port, and a certain instinctive sovereignty. The latter are born degraded. "He shall serve his brethren." There is something in the air of one of this cast, lean and suspicious; contrasting with the open, trusting, generous manners of the other.

Observe who have been the greatest borrowers of all ages—Alcibiades —Falstaff—Sir Richard Steele—our late incomparable Brinsley—what a family likeness in all four!

What a careless, even deportment hath your borrower! what rosy gills! what a beautiful reliance on Providence doth he manifest,—taking no more thought than lilies! What contempt for money,—accounting it (yours and mine especially) no better than dross! What a liberal confounding of those pedantic distinctions of *meum* and *tuum!* or rather, what a noble simplification of language (beyond Tooke), resolving these supposed opposites into one clear, intelligible pronoun adjective!—What near approaches doth he make to the primitive *community,*—to the extent of one half of the principle at least.

He is the true taxer who "calleth all the world up to be taxed"; and the distance is as vast between him and *one of us,* as subsisted between the Augustan Majesty and the poorest obolary Jew that paid it tribute-pittance at Jerusalem!—His exactions, too, have such a cheerful, voluntary air! So far removed from your sour parochial or state-gatherers,— those ink-horn varlets, who carry their want of welcome in their faces! He cometh to you with a smile, and troubleth you with no receipt; confining himself to no set season. Every day is his Candlemas, or his Feast of Holy Michael. He applieth the *lene tormentum* of a pleasant look to your purse,—which to that gentle warmth expands her silken leaves, as naturally as the cloak of the traveller, for which sun and wind contended! He is the true Propontic which never ebbeth! The sea which taketh handsomely at each man's hand. In vain the victim, whom he delighteth to honour, struggles with destiny; he is in the net. Lend therefore cheerfully, O man ordained to lend—that thou lose not in the end, with thy worldly penny, the reversion promised. Combine not preposterously in thine own person the penalties of Lazarus and of Dives!— but, when thou seest the proper authority coming, meet it smilingly, as it were half-way. Come, a handsome sacrifice! See how light *he* makes of it! Strain not courtesies with a noble enemy.

Reflections like the foregoing were forced upon my mind by the death of my old friend, Ralph Bigod, Esq., who parted this life, on Wednesday evening; dying, as he had lived, without much trouble. He boasted himself a descendant from mighty ancestors of that name, who heretofore held ducal dignities in this realm. In his actions and sentiments he belied not the stock to which he pretended. Early in life he found himself invested with ample revenues; which, with that noble disinterestedness which I have noticed as inherent in men of the *great race,* he took almost immediate measures entirely to dissipate and bring to nothing: for there is something revolting in the idea of a king holding a private purse; and the thoughts of Bigod were all regal. Thus furnished by the very act of disfurnishment; getting rid of the cumbersome luggage of riches, more apt (as one sings)

> To slacken virtue, and abate her edge,
> Than prompt her to do aught may merit praise,—

he set forth, like some Alexander, upon his great enterprise, "borrowing and to borrow!"

In his periegesis, or triumphant progress throughout this island, it has been calculated that he laid a tythe part of the inhabitants under contribution. I reject this estimate as greatly exaggerated:—but having had the honour of accompanying my friend divers times, in his perambulations about this vast city, I own I was greatly struck at first with the prodigious number of faces we met who claimed a sort of respectful acquaintance with us. He was one day so obliging as to explain the phenomenon. It seems, these were his tributaries; feeders of his exchequer; gentlemen, his good friends (as he was pleased to express himself), to whom he had occasionally been beholden for a loan. Their multitudes did no way disconcert him. He rather took a pride in numbering them; and, with Comus, seemed pleased to be "stocked with so fair a herd."

With such sources, it was a wonder how he contrived to keep his treasury always empty. He did it by force of an aphorism, which he had often in his mouth, that "money kept longer than three days stinks." So he made use of it while it was fresh. A good part he drank away (for he was an excellent toss-pot); some he gave away, the rest he threw away, literally tossing and hurling it violently from him—as boys do burrs, or as if it had been infectious,—into ponds, or ditches, or deep holes, inscrutable cavities of the earth;—or he would bury it (where he would never seek it again) by a river's side under some bank, which (he would facetiously observe) paid no interest—but out away from him it must go peremptorily, as Hagar's offspring into the wilderness, while it was sweet. He never missed it. The streams were perennial which fed his fisc. When new supplies became necessary, the first person that had the felicity to fall in with him, friend or stranger, was sure to contribute to the deficiency. For Bigod had an *undeniable* way with him. He had a cheerful, open exterior, a quick jovial eye, a bald forehead, just touched with grey (*cana fides*). He anticipated no excuse, and found none. And, waiving for a while my theory as to the *great race,* I would put it to the most untheorising reader, who may at times have disposable coin in his pockets, whether it is not more repugnant to the kindliness of his nature to refuse such a one as I am describing, than to say *no* to a poor petitionary rogue (your bastard borrower), who, by his mumping visnomy, tells you, that he expects nothing better; and, therefore, whose preconceived notions and expectations you do in reality so much less shock in the refusal.

When I think of this man; his fiery glow of heart; his swell of feeling; how magnificent, how *ideal* he was; how great at the midnight hour; and when I compare with him the companions with whom I have associated since, I grudge the saving of a few idle ducats, and think that I am fallen into the society of *lenders,* and *little* men.

To one like Elia, whose treasures are rather cased in leather covers than closed in iron coffers, there is a class of alienators more formidable than that which I have touched upon; I mean your *borrowers of books*— those mutilators of collections, spoilers of the symmetry of shelves, and creators of odd volumes. There is Comberbatch, matchless in his depredations!

That foul gap in the bottom shelf facing you, like a great eye-tooth knocked out—(you are now with me in my little back study in Bloomsbury, reader!)——with the huge Switzer-like tomes on each side (like the Guildhall giants, in their reformed posture, guardant of nothing), once held the tallest of my folios, *Opera Bonaventuræ,* choice and massy divinity, to which its two supporters (school divinity also, but of a lesser calibre,—Bellarmine, and Holy Thomas), showed but as dwarfs,—itself an Ascapart!—*that* Comberbatch abstracted upon the faith of a theory he holds, which is more easy, I confess, for me to suffer by than to refute, namely, that "the title to property in a book (my Bonaventure, for instance), is in exact ratio to the claimant's powers of understanding and appreciating the same." Should he go on acting upon this theory, which of our shelves is safe?

The slight vacuum in the left-hand case—two shelves from the ceiling —scarcely distinguishable but by the quick eye of a loser—was whilom the commodious resting-place of Browne on Urn Burial. C. will hardly allege that he knows more about that treatise than I do, who introduced it to him, and was indeed the first (of the moderns) to discover its beauties—but so have I known a foolish lover to praise his mistress in the presence of a rival more qualified to carry her off than himself. Just below, Dodsley's dramas want their fourth volume, where Vittoria Corombona is! The remainder nine are as distasteful as Priam's refuse sons when the Fates *borrowed* Hector. Here stood the Anatomy of Melancholy, in sober state. There loitered the Compleat Angler; quiet as in life, by some stream side. In yonder nook, John Buncle, a widower-volume, with "eyes closed," mourns his ravished mate.

One justice I must do my friend, that if he sometimes, like the sea, sweeps away a treasure, at another time, sea-like, he throws up as rich an equivalent to match it. I have a small under-collection of this nature (my friend's gatherings in his various calls), picked up, he has forgotten at what odd places, and deposited with as little memory at mine. I take in these orphans, the twice-deserted. These proselytes of the gate are welcome as the true Hebrews. There they stand in conjunction;

natives, and naturalised. The latter seem as little disposed to inquire out their true lineage as I am.—I charge no warehouse-room for these deodands, nor shall ever put myself to the ungentlemanly trouble of advertising a sale of them to pay expenses.

To lose a volume to C. carries some sense and meaning in it. You are sure that he will make one hearty meal on your viands, if he can give no account of the platter after it. But what moved thee, wayward, spiteful K., to be so importunate to carry off with thee, in spite of tears and adjurations to thee to forbear, the Letters of that princely woman, the thrice noble Margaret Newcastle?—knowing at the time, and knowing that I knew also, thou most assuredly wouldst never turn over one leaf of the illustrious folio:—what but the mere spirit of contradiction, and childish love of getting the better of thy friend?—Then, worst cut of all! to transport it with thee to the Gallican land—

> Unworthy land to harbour such a sweetness,
> A virtue in which all ennobling thoughts dwelt,
> Pure thoughts, kind thoughts, high thoughts, her sex's wonder!

——hadst thou not thy play-books, and books of jests and fancies, about thee, to keep thee merry, even as thou keepest all companies with thy quips and mirthful tales? Child of the Green-room, it was unkindly done of thee. Thy wife, too, that part-French, better-part Englishwoman!— that *she* could fix upon no other treatise to bear away, in kindly token of remembering us, than the works of Fulke Greville, Lord Brook—of which no Frenchman, nor woman of France, Italy, or England, was ever by nature constituted to comprehend a tittle!—*Was there not Zimmerman on Solitude?*

Reader, if haply thou art blest with a moderate collection, be shy of showing it; or if thy heart overfloweth to lend them, lend thy books; but let it be to such a one as S. T. C.—he will return them (generally anticipating the time appointed) with usury; enriched with annotations tripling their value. I have had experience. Many are these precious MSS. of his—(in *matter* oftentimes, and almost in *quantity* not unfrequently, vying with the originals) in no very clerky hand—legible in my Daniel; in old Burton; in Sir Thomas Browne; and those abstruser cogitations of the Greville, now, alas! wandering in Pagan lands. I counsel thee, shut not thy heart, nor thy library, against S. T. C.

NEW YEAR'S EVE

EVERY man hath two birthdays: two days, at least, in every year, which set him upon revolving the lapse of time, as it affects his mortal duration. The one is that which in an especial manner he termeth *his*. In the gradual desuetude of old observances, this custom of solemnising our proper birthday hath nearly passed away, or is left to children, who reflect nothing at all about the matter, nor understand anything in it beyond cake and orange. But the birth of a New Year is of an interest too wide to be pretermitted by king or cobbler. No one ever regarded the first of January with indifference. It is that from which all date their time, and count upon what is left. It is the nativity of our common Adam.

Of all sound of all bells—(bells, the music nighest bordering upon heaven)—most solemn and touching is the peal which rings out the Old Year. I never hear it without a gathering-up of my mind to a concentration of all the images that have been diffused over the past twelve-month; all I have done or suffered, performed or neglected—in that regretted time. I begin to know its worth, as when a person dies. It takes a personal colour; nor was it a poetical flight in a contemporary, when he exclaimed,

> I saw the skirts of the departing Year.

It is no more than what in sober sadness every one of us seems to be conscious of, in that awful leave-taking. I am sure I felt it, and all felt it with me, last night; though some of my companions affected rather to manifest an exhilaration at the birth of the coming year, than any very tender regrets for the decease of its predecessor. But I am none of those who

> Welcome the coming, speed the parting guest.

I am naturally, beforehand, shy of novelties; new books, new faces, new years,—from some mental twist which makes it difficult in me to face the prospective. I have almost ceased to hope; and am sanguine only in the prospects of other (former) years. I plunge into foregone visions and conclusions. I encounter pell-mell with past disappointments. I am armour-proof against old discouragements. I forgive, or overcome in fancy, old adversaries. I play over again *for love,* as the gamesters phrase it, games, for which I once paid so dear. I would scarce now have any of those untoward accidents and events of my life reversed. I would no more alter them than the incidents of some well-contrived novel. Methinks it is better that I should have pined away seven of my goldenest years, when I was thrall to the fair hair, and fairer eyes of Alice W—n, than that so passionate a love-adventure should be lost. It was better that our family should have missed that legacy, which old Dorrell cheated us of, than that I should have at this moment two thousand pounds *in banco,* and be without the idea of that specious old rogue.

In a degree beneath manhood, it is my infirmity to look back upon those early days. Do I advance a paradox, when I say, that, skipping over the intervention of forty years, a man may have leave to love *himself,* without the imputation of self-love?

If I know aught of myself, no one whose mind is introspective—and mine is painfully so—can have a less respect for his present identity than I have for the man Elia. I know him to be light, and vain, and humoursome; a notorious * * * ; addicted to * * * * ; averse from counsel, neither taking it nor offering it;— * * * besides; a stammering buffoon; what you will; lay it on, and spare not: I subscribe to it all, and much more than thou canst be willing to lay at his door;— but for the child Elia, that "other me," there, in the background—I must take leave to cherish the remembrance of that young master—with as little reference, I protest, to this stupid changeling of five-and-forty, as if it had been a child of some other house, and not of my parents. I can cry over its patient small-pox at five, and rougher medicaments. I can lay its poor fevered head upon the sick pillow at Christ's, and wake with it in surprise at the gentle posture of maternal tenderness hanging over it, that unknown had watched its sleep. I know how it shrank from any the least colour of falsehood. God help thee, Elia, how art thou changed!—Thou art sophisticated.—I know how honest, how courageous (for a weakling) it was—how religious, how imaginative, how hopeful! From what have I not fallen, if the child I remember was indeed myself, —and not some dissembling guardian, presenting a false identity, to give the rule to my unpractised steps, and regulate the tone of my moral being!

That I am fond of indulging, beyond a hope of sympathy, in such retrospection, may be the symptom of some sickly idiosyncrasy. Or is it owing to another cause: simply, that being without wife or family, I have not learned to project myself enough out of myself; and having no off-spring of my own to dally with, I turn back upon memory, and adopt my own early idea, as my heir and favourite? If these speculations seem fantastical to thee, reader (a busy man perchance), if I tread out of the way of thy sympathy, and am singularly conceited only, I retire, im-penetrable to ridicule, under the phantom cloud of Elia.

The elders, with whom I was brought up, were of a character not likely to let slip the sacred observance of any old institution; and the ringing out of the Old Year was kept by them with circumstances of peculiar ceremony.—In those days the sound of those midnight chimes, though it seemed to raise hilarity in all around me, never failed to bring a train of pensive imagery into my fancy. Yet I then scarce conceived what it meant, or thought of it as a reckoning that concerned me. Not childhood alone, but the young man till thirty, never feels practically that he is mortal. He knows it indeed, and, if need were, he could preach a homily on the fragility of life; but he brings it not home to himself, any more than in a hot June we can appropriate to our imagination the freezing days of December. But now, shall I confess a truth?—I feel these audits but too powerfully. I begin to count the probabilities of my duration, and to grudge at the expenditure of moments and shortest periods, like misers' farthings. In proportion as the years both lessen and shorten, I set more count upon their periods, and would fain lay my ineffectual finger upon the spoke of the great wheel. I am not content to pass away "like a weaver's shuttle." Those metaphors solace me not, nor sweeten the unpalatable draught of mortality. I care not to be carried with the tide, that smoothly bears human life to eternity; and reluct at the inevitable course of destiny. I am in love with this green earth; the face of town and country; the unspeakable rural solitudes, and the sweet security of streets. I would set up my tabernacle here. I am content to stand still at the age to which I am arrived; I, and my friends: to be no younger, no richer, no handsomer. I do not want to be weaned by age; or drop, like mellow fruit, as they say, into the grave.—Any alteration, on this earth of mine, in diet or in lodging, puzzles and discomposes me. My household-gods plant a terrible fixed foot, and are not rooted up without blood. They do not willingly seek Lavinian shores. A new state of being staggers me.

Sun, and sky, and breeze, and solitary walks, and summer holidays, and the greenness of fields, and the delicious juices of meats and fishes, and society, and the cheerful glass, and candle-light, and fireside conversations, and innocent vanities, and jests, and *irony itself*—do these things go out with life?

Can a ghost laugh, or shake his gaunt sides, when you are pleasant with him?

And you, my midnight darlings, my Folios! must I part with the intense delight of having you (huge armfuls) in my embraces? Must knowledge come to me, if it come at all, by some awkward experiment of intuition, and no longer by this familiar process of reading?

Shall I enjoy friendships there, wanting the smiling indications which point me to them here,—the recognisable face—the "sweet assurance of a look"?—

In winter this intolerable disinclination to dying—to give it its mildest name—does more especially haunt and beset me. In a genial August noon, beneath a sweltering sky, death is almost problematic. At those times do such poor snakes as myself enjoy an immortality. Then we expand and burgeon. Then we are as strong again, as valiant again, as wise again, and a great deal taller. The blast that nips and shrinks me, puts me in thoughts of death. All things allied to the insubstantial, wait upon that master feeling; cold, numbness, dreams, perplexity; moonlight itself, with its shadowy and spectral appearances,—that cold ghost of the sun, or Phœbus' sickly sister, like that innutritious one denounced in the Canticles:—I am none of her minions—I hold with the Persian.

Whatsoever thwarts, or puts me out of my way, brings death into my mind. All partial evils, like humours, run into that capital plague-sore. —I have heard some profess an indifference to life. Such hail the end of their existence as a port of refuge; and speak of the grave as of some soft arms, in which they may slumber as on a pillow. Some have wooed death——but out upon thee, I say, thou foul, ugly phantom! I detest, abhor, execrate, and (with Friar John) give thee to six score thousand devils, as in no instance to be excused or tolerated, but shunned as an universal viper; to be branded, proscribed, and spoken evil of! In no way can I be brought to digest thee, thou thin, melancholy *Privation,* or more frightful and confounding *Positive!*

Those antidotes, prescribed against the fear of thee, are altogether frigid and insulting, like thyself. For what satisfaction hath a man, that he shall "lie down with kings and emperors in death," who in his lifetime never greatly coveted the society of such bed-fellows?—or, forsooth, that "so shall the fairest face appear"?—why, to comfort me, must Alice W—n be a goblin? More than all, I conceive disgust at those impertinent and misbecoming familiarities inscribed upon your ordinary tombstones. Every dead man must take upon himself to be lecturing me with his odious truism, that "Such as he now is I must shortly be." Not so shortly, friend, perhaps as thou imaginest. In the meantime I am alive. I move about. I am worth twenty of thee. Know thy betters! Thy New Years' days are past. I survive, a jolly candidate for 1821. Another cup of wine—and while that turncoat bell, that just now mournfully chanted the obsequies of 1820 departed, with changed notes lustily rings in a successor, let us attune to its peal the song made on a like occasion, by hearty, cheerful Mr. Cotton.

THE NEW YEAR

Hark, the cock crows, and yon bright star
Tells us, the day himself's not far;
And see where, breaking from the night,
He gilds the western hills with light.
With him old Janus doth appear,
Peeping into the future year,
With such a look as seems to say,
The prospect is not good that way.
Thus do we rise ill sights to see,
And 'gainst ourselves to prophesy;
When the prophetic fear of things
A more tormenting mischief brings,
More full of soul-tormenting gall
Than direst mischiefs can befall.
But stay! but stay! methinks my sight,
Better inform'd by clearer light,
Discerns sereneness in that brow,
That all contracted seem'd but now.
His revers'd face may show distaste,
And frown upon the ills are past;
But that which this way looks is clear,
And smiles upon the New-born Year.
He looks too from a place so high,
The year lies open to his eye;
And all the moments open are
To the exact discoverer.
Yet more and more he smiles upon
The happy revolution.
Why should we then suspect or fear
The influences of a year,
So smiles upon us the first morn,
And speaks us good so soon as born?
Plague on't! the last was ill enough,
This cannot but make better proof;
Or, at the worst, as we brush'd through

The last, why so we may this too;
And then the next in reason shou'd
Be superexcellently good:
For the worst ills (we daily see)
Have no more perpetuity
Than the best fortunes that do fall;
Which also bring us wherewithal
Longer their being to support,
Than those do of the other sort:
And who has one good year in three,
And yet repines a destiny,
Appears ungrateful in the case,
And merits not the good he has.
Then let us welcome the New Guest
With lusty brimmers of the best:
Mirth always should Good Fortune meet,
And renders e'en Disaster sweet:
And though the Princess turn her back,
Let us but line ourselves with sack,
We better shall by far hold out,
Till the next Year she face about.

How say you, reader—do not these verses smack of the rough magnanimity of the old English vein? Do they not fortify like a cordial; enlarging the heart, and productive of sweet blood, and generous spirits, in the concoction? Where be those puling fears of death, just now expressed or affected?—Passed like a cloud—absorbed in the purging sunlight of clear poetry—clean washed away by a wave of genuine Helicon, your only Spa for these hypochondries—And now another cup of the generous! and a merry New Year, and many of them to you all, my masters!

MRS. BATTLE'S OPINIONS ON WHIST

"A CLEAR fire, a clean hearth, and the rigour of the game." This was the celebrated *wish* of old Sarah Battle (now with God), who, next to her devotions, loved a good game of whist. She was none of your lukewarm gamesters, your half-and-half players, who have no objection to take a hand, if you want one to make up a rubber; who affirm that they have no pleasure in winning; that they like to win one game and lose another; that they can while away an hour very agreeably at a card-table, but are indifferent whether they play or no; and will desire an adversary, who has slipped a wrong card, to take it up and play another. These insufferable triflers are the curse of a table. One of these flies will spoil a whole pot. Of such it may be said that they do not play at cards, but only play at playing at them.

Sarah Battle was none of that breed. She detested them, as I do, from her heart and soul, and would not, save upon a striking emergency, willingly seat herself at the same table with them. She loved a thorough-paced partner, a determined enemy. She took, and gave, no concessions. She hated favours. She never made a revoke, nor ever passed it over in her adversary without exacting the utmost forfeiture. She fought a good fight: cut and thrust. She held not her good sword (her cards) "like a dancer." She sate bolt upright; and neither showed you her cards, nor desired to see yours. All people have their blind side—their superstitions; and I have heard her declare, under the rose, that hearts was her favourite suit.

I never in my life—and I knew Sarah Battle many of the best years of it—saw her take out her snuff-box when it was her turn to play; or snuff a candle in the middle of a game; or ring for a servant, till it was fairly over. She never introduced, or connived at, miscellaneous conversation during its process. As she emphatically observed, cards were cards; and if I ever saw unmingled distaste in her fine last-century countenance, it was at the airs of a young gentleman of a literary turn, who had been with difficulty persuaded to take a hand; and who, in his excess of candour, declared, that he thought there was no harm in unbending the mind now and then, after serious studies, in recreations of that kind! She could not bear to have her noble occupation, to which she wound up her faculties, considered in that light. It was her business, her duty, the thing she came into the world to do,—and she did it. She unbent her mind afterwards over a book.

Pope was her favourite author: his Rape of the Lock her favourite work. She once did me the favour to play over with me (with the cards) his celebrated game of Ombre in that poem; and to explain to me how far it agreed with, and in what points it would be found to differ from, tradrille. Her illustrations were apposite and poignant; and I had the pleasure of sending the substance of them to Mr. Bowles; but I suppose they came too late to be inserted among his ingenious notes upon that author.

Quadrille, she has often told me, was her first love; but whist had engaged her maturer esteem. The former, she said, was showy and specious, and likely to allure young persons. The uncertainty and quick shifting of partners—a thing which the constancy of whist abhors; the dazzling supremacy and regal investiture of Spadille—absurd, as she justly observed, in the pure aristocracy of whist, where his crown and garter gave him no proper power above his brother-nobility of the Aces;—the giddy vanity, so taking to the inexperienced, of playing alone; above all, the overpowering attractions of a *Sans Prendre Vole*,—to the triumph of which there is certainly nothing parallel or approaching, in the contingencies of whist;—all these, she would say, make quadrille a game of captivation to the young and enthusiastic. But whist was the *solider* game: that was her word. It was a long meal; not, like quadrille, a feast of snatches. One or two rubbers might co-extend in duration with an evening. They gave time to form rooted friendships, to cultivate steady enmities. She despised the chance-started, capricious, and ever-fluctuating alliances of the other. The skirmishes of quadrille, she would say, reminded her of the petty ephemeral embroilments of the little Italian states, depicted by Machiavel: perpetually changing postures and connexions; bitter foes to-day, sugared darlings to-morrow; kissing and scratching in a breath;—but the wars of whist were comparable to the long, steady, deep-rooted, rational antipathies of the great French and English nations.

A grave simplicity was what she chiefly admired in her favourite game. There was nothing silly in it, like the nob in cribbage—nothing super-fluous. No *flushes*—that most irrational of all pleas that a reasonable being can set up:—that any one should claim four by virtue of holding cards of the same mark and colour, without reference to the playing of the game, or the individual worth or pretensions of the cards themselves! She held this to be a solecism; as pitiful an ambition at cards as allitera-tion is in authorship. She despised superficiality, and looked deeper than the colours of things.—Suits were soldiers, she would say, and must have an uniformity of array to distinguish them: but what should we say to a foolish squire, who should claim a merit from dressing up his tenantry in red jackets, that never were to be marshalled—never to take the field?—She even wished that whist were more simple than it is; and, in my mind, would have stripped it of some appendages, which, in the state of human frailty, may be venially, and even commendably, allowed of. She saw no reason for the deciding of the trump by the turn of the card. Why not one suit always trumps?—Why two colours, when the mark of the suits would have sufficiently distinguished them without it?—

"But the eye, my dear Madam, is agreeably refreshed with the variety. Man is not the creature of pure reason—he must have his senses delight-fully appealed to. We see it in Roman Catholic countries, where the music and the paintings draw in many to worship, whom your Quaker spirit of unsensualising would have kept out.—You yourself have a pretty collection of paintings—but confess to me, whether, walking in your gallery at Sandham, among those clear Vandykes, or among the Paul Potters in the ante-room, you ever felt your bosom glow with an elegant delight, at all comparable to *that* you have it in your power to experience most evenings over a well-arranged assortment of the court-cards?—the pretty antic habits, like heralds in a procession—the gay triumph-assuring scarlets—the contrasting deadly-killing sables—the 'hoary ma-jesty of spades'—Pam in all his glory!—

"All these might be dispensed with; and with their naked names upon the drab pasteboard, the game might go on very well pictureless. But the *beauty* of cards would be extinguished for ever. Stripped of all that is imaginative in them, they must degenerate into mere gambling. Imagine a dull deal board, or drum head, to spread them on, instead of that nice verdant carpet (next to nature's), fittest arena for those courtly com-batants to play their gallant jousts and turneys in!—Exchange those delicately-turned ivory markers—(work of Chinese artist, unconscious of their symbol,—or as profanely slighting their true application as the arrantest Ephesian journeyman that turned out those little shrines for the goddess)—exchange them for little bits of leather (our ancestors' money) or chalk and a slate!"—

The old lady, with a smile, confessed the soundness of my logic; and to her approbation of my arguments on her favourite topic that evening, I have always fancied myself indebted for the legacy of a curious crib-bage-board, made of the finest Sienna marble, which her maternal uncle (old Walter Plumer, whom I have elsewhere celebrated) brought with him from Florence:—this, and a trifle of five hundred pounds, came to me at her death.

The former bequest (which I do not least value) I have kept with religious care; though she herself, to confess a truth, was never greatly taken with cribbage. It was an essentially vulgar game, I have heard her say,—disputing with her uncle, who was very partial to it. She could never heartily bring her mouth to pronounce *"Go"*—or *"That's a go."* She called it an ungrammatical game. The pegging teased her. I once knew her to forfeit a rubber (a five-dollar stake) because she would not take advantage of the turn-up knave, which would have given it her, but which she must have claimed by the disgraceful tenure of declaring *"two for his heels."* There is something extremely genteel in this sort of self-denial. Sarah Battle was a gentlewoman born.

Piquet she held the best game at the cards for two persons, though she would ridicule the pedantry of the terms—such as pique—repique—the capot—they savoured (she thought) of affectation. But games for two, or even three, she never greatly cared for. She loved the quadrate, or square. She would argue thus:—Cards are warfare: the ends are gain with glory. But cards are war, in disguise of a sport: when single adver-saries encounter, the ends proposed are too palpable. By themselves it is too close a fight; with spectators it is not much bettered. No looker-on can be interested, except for a bet, and then it is a mere affair of money; he cares not for your luck *sympathetically,* or for your play.—Three are still worse; a mere naked war of every man against every man, as in cribbage, without league or alliance; or a rotation of petty and con-tradictory interests, a succession of heartless leagues, and not much more hearty infractions of them, as in tradrille.—But in square games (*she meant whist*), all that is possible to be attained in card-playing is accom-plished. There are the incentives of profit with honour, common to every species—though the *latter* can be but very imperfectly enjoyed in those other games, where the spectator is only feebly a participator. But the parties in whist are spectators and principals too. They are a theatre to themselves, and a looker-on is not wanted. He is rather worse than noth-ing, and an impertinence. Whist abhors neutrality, or interests beyond its sphere. You glory in some surprising stroke of skill or fortune, not because a cold—or even an interested—bystander witnesses it, but because your *partner* sympathises in the contingency. You win for two. You triumph for two. Two are exalted. Two again are mortified; which divides their disgrace, as the conjunction doubles (by taking off the invidiousness) your glories. Two losing to two are better reconciled, than one to one in that close butchery. The hostile feeling is weakened by multiplying the channels. War becomes a civil game. By such reasonings as these the old lady was accustomed to defend her favourite pastime.

No inducement could ever prevail upon her to play at any game, where chance entered into the composition, *for nothing*. Chance, she would argue—and here again, admire the subtlety of her conclusion;—chance is nothing, but where something else depends upon it. It is obvious that cannot be *glory*. What rational cause of exultation could it give to a man to turn up size ace a hundred times together by himself? or before spectators, where no stake was depending. Make a lottery of a hundred thousand tickets with but one fortunate number—and what possible principle of our nature, except stupid wonderment, could it gratify to gain that number as many times successively, without a prize? Therefore she disliked the mixture of chance in backgammon, where it was not played for money. She called it foolish, and those people idiots, who were taken with a lucky hit under such circumstances. Games of pure skill were as little to her fancy. Played for a stake, they were a mere system of over-reaching. Played for glory, they were a mere setting of one man's wit—his memory, or combination-faculty rather—against another's; like a mock-engagement at a review, bloodless and profitless. She could not conceive a *game* wanting the spritely infusion of chance, the handsome excuses of good fortune. Two people playing at chess in a corner of a room, while whist was stirring in the centre, would inspire her with insufferable horror and ennui. Those well-cut similitudes of Castles, and Knights, the *imagery* of the board, she would argue (and I think in this case justly), were entirely misplaced and senseless. Those hard head-contests can in no instance ally with the fancy. They reject form and colour. A pencil and dry slate (she used to say) were the proper arena for such combatants.

To those puny objectors against cards, as nurturing the bad passions, she would retort, that man is a gaming animal. He must be always trying to get the better in something or other:—that this passion can scarcely be more safely expended than upon a game at cards: that cards are a temporary illusion; in truth, a mere drama; for we do but *play* at being mightily concerned, where a few idle shillings are at stake, yet, during the illusion, we *are* as mightily concerned as those whose stake is crowns and kingdoms. They are a sort of dream-fighting; much ado; great battling, and little bloodshed; mighty means for disproportioned ends; quite as diverting, and a great deal more innoxious, than many of those more serious *games* of life, which men play, without esteeming them to be such.—

With great deference to the old lady's judgment in these matters, I think I have experienced some moments in my life, when playing at cards *for nothing* has even been agreeable. When I am in sickness, or not in the best spirits, I sometimes call for the cards, and play a game at piquet *for love* with my cousin Bridget—Bridget Elia.

I grant there is something sneaking in it; but with a tooth-ache, or a sprained ankle,—when you are subdued and humble,—you are glad to put up with an inferior spring of action.

There is such a thing in nature, I am convinced, as *sick whist*.

I grant it is not the highest style of man—I deprecate the manes of Sarah Battle—she lives not, alas! to whom I should apologise.

At such times, those *terms* which my old friend objected to, come in as something admissible.—I love to get a tierce or a quatorze, though they mean nothing. I am subdued to an inferior interest. Those shadows of winning amuse me.

That last game I had with my sweet cousin (I capotted her)—(dare I tell thee, how foolish I am?)—I wished it might have lasted for ever, though we gained nothing, and lost nothing, though it was a mere shade of play: I would be content to go on in that idle folly for ever. The pipkin should be ever boiling, that was to prepare the gentle lenitive to my foot, which Bridget was doomed to apply after the game was over: and, as I do not much relish appliances, there it should ever bubble. Bridget and I should be ever playing.

A CHAPTER ON EARS

I HAVE no ear.—

Mistake me not, reader—nor imagine that I am by nature destitute of those exterior twin appendages, hanging ornaments, and (architecturally speaking) handsome volutes to the human capital. Better my mother had never borne me.—I am, I think, rather delicately than copiously provided with those conduits; and I feel no disposition to envy the mule for his plenty, or the mole for her exactness, in those ingenious labyrinthine inlets—those indispensable side-intelligencers.

Neither have I incurred, or done anything to incur, with Defoe, that hideous disfigurement, which constrained him to draw upon assurance—to feel "quite unabashed," and at ease upon that article. I was never, I thank my stars, in the pillory; nor, if I read them aright, is it within the compass of my destiny, that I ever should be.

When therefore I say that I have no ear, you will understand me to mean—*for music*. To say that this heart never melted at the concord of sweet sounds, would be a foul self-libel. *"Water parted from the sea"* never fails to move it strangely. So does *"In infancy."* But they were used to be sung at her harpsichord (the old-fashioned instrument in vogue in those days) by a gentlewoman—the gentlest, sure, that ever merited the appellation—the sweetest—why should I hesitate to name Mrs. S——, once the blooming Fanny Weatheral of the Temple—who had power to thrill the soul of Elia, small imp as he was, even in his long coats; and to make him glow, tremble, and blush with a passion, that not faintly indicated the dayspring of that absorbing sentiment which was afterwards destined to overwhelm and subdue his nature quite for Alice W——n.

I even think that *sentimentally* I am disposed to harmony. But *organically* I am incapable of a tune. I have been practising *"God save the King"* all my life; whistling and humming of it over to myself in solitary corners; and am not yet arrived, they tell me, within many quavers of it. Yet hath the loyalty of Elia never been impeached.

I am not without suspicion, that I have an undeveloped faculty of music within me. For thrumming, in my wild way, on my friend A.'s piano, the other morning, while he was engaged in an adjoining parlour, —on his return he was pleased to say, *"he thought it could not be the maid!"* On his first surprise at hearing the keys touched in somewhat an airy and masterful way, not dreaming of me, his suspicions had lighted on *Jenny*. But a grace, snatched from a superior refinement, soon convinced him that some being—technically perhaps deficient, but higher informed from a principle common to all the fine arts—had swayed the keys to a mood which Jenny, with all her (less cultivated) enthusiasm, could never have elicited from them. I mention this as a proof of my friend's penetration, and not with any view of disparaging Jenny.

Scientifically I could never be made to understand (yet have I taken some pains) what a note in music is; or how one note should differ from another. Much less in voices can I distinguish a soprano from a tenor. Only sometimes the thorough-bass I contrive to guess at, from its being supereminently harsh and disagreeable. I tremble, however, for my mis-application of the simplest terms of *that* which I disclaim. While I profess my ignorance, I scarce know what to *say* I am ignorant of. I hate, perhaps, by misnomers. *Sostenuto* and *adagio* stand in the like relation of obscurity to me; and *Sol, Fa, Mi, Re,* is as conjuring as *Baralipton*.

It is hard to stand alone in an age like this,—(constituted to the quick and critical perception of all harmonious combinations, I verily believe, beyond all preceding ages, since Jubal stumbled upon the gamut,) to remain, as it were, singly unimpressible to the magic influences of an art, which is said to have such an especial stroke at soothing, elevating, and refining the passions.—Yet, rather than break the candid current of my confessions, I must avow to you, that I have received a great deal more pain than pleasure from this so cried-up faculty.

I am constitutionally susceptible of noises. A carpenter's hammer, in a warm summer noon, will fret me into more than midsummer madness. But those unconnected, unset sounds are nothing to the measured malice of music. The ear is passive to those single strokes; willingly enduring stripes while it hath no task to con. To music it cannot be passive. It will strive—mine at least will—spite of its inaptitude, to thrid the maze; like an unskilled eye painfully poring upon hieroglyphics. I have sat through an Italian Opera, till, for sheer pain, and inexplicable anguish, I have rushed out into the noisiest places of the crowded streets, to solace myself with sounds, which I was not obliged to follow, and get rid of tne distracting torment of endless, fruitless, barren attention! I take refuge in the unpretending assemblage of honest common-life sounds;—and the purgatory of the Enraged Musician becomes my paradise.

I have sat at an Oratorio (that profanation of the purposes of the cheerful playhouse) watching the faces of the auditory in the pit (what a contrast to Hogarth's Laughing Audience!) immovable, or affecting some faint emotion—till (as some have said, that our occupations in the next world will be but a shadow of what delighted us in this) I have imagined myself in some cold Theatre in Hades, where some of the *forms* of the earthly one should be kept up, with none of the *enjoyment;* or like that

> ——Party in a parlour
> All silent, and all DAMNED.

Above all, those insufferable concertos, and pieces of music, as they are called, do plague and embitter my apprehension.—Words are something; but to be exposed to an endless battery of mere sounds; to be long a dying; to lie stretched upon a rack of roses; to keep up languor by unintermitted effort; to pile honey upon sugar, and sugar upon honey, to an interminable tedious sweetness; to fill up sound with feeling, and strain ideas to keep pace with it; to gaze on empty frames, and be forced to make the pictures for yourself; to read a book, *all stops,* and be obliged to supply the verbal matter; to invent extempore tragedies to answer to the vague gestures of an inexplicable rambling mime—these are faint shadows of what I have undergone from a series of the ablest-executed pieces of this empty *instrumental music.*

I deny not, that in the opening of a concert, I have experienced something vastly lulling and agreeable:—afterwards followeth the languor and the oppression.—Like that disappointing book in Patmos; or, like the comings on of melancholy, described by Burton, doth music make her first insinuating approaches:—"Most pleasant it is to such as are melancholy given to walk alone in some solitary grove, betwixt wood and water, by some brook side, and to meditate upon some delightsome and pleasant subject, which shall affect him most, *amabilis insania,* and *mentis gratissimus error.* A most incomparable delight to build castles in the air, to go smiling to themselves, acting an infinite variety of parts, which they suppose, and strongly imagine, they act, or that they see done.—So delightsome these toys at first, they could spend whole days and nights without sleep, even whole years, in such contemplations, and fantastical meditations, which are like so many dreams, and will hardly be drawn from them—winding and unwinding themselves as so many clocks, and still pleasing their humours, until at the last the SCENE TURNS UPON A SUDDEN, and they being now habitated to such meditations and solitary places, can endure no company, can think of nothing but harsh and distasteful subjects. Fear, sorrow, suspicion, *subrusticus pudor,* discontent, cares, and weariness of life, surprise them on a sudden and they can think of nothing else; continually suspecting, no sooner are their eyes open, but this infernal plague of melancholy seizeth on them, and terrifies their souls, representing some dismal object to their minds; which now, by no means, no labour, no persuasions, they can avoid, they cannot be rid of, they cannot resist."

Something like this "SCENE TURNING" I have experienced at the evening parties, at the house of my good Catholic friend *Nov*——; who, by the aid of a capital organ, himself the most finished of players, converts his drawing-room into a chapel, his week days into Sundays, and these latter into minor heavens.[1]

When my friend commences upon one of those solemn anthems, which peradventure struck upon my heedless ear, rambling in the side aisles of the dim Abbey, some five-and-thirty years since, waking a new sense, and putting a soul of old religion into my young apprehension—(whether it be *that,* in which the Psalmist, weary of the persecutions of bad men, wisheth to himself dove's wings—or *that other,* which, with a like measure of sobriety and pathos, inquireth by what means the young man shall best cleanse his mind)—a holy calm pervadeth me.—I am for the time

> ——rapt above earth,
> And possess joys not promised at my birth.

But when this master of the spell, not content to have laid a soul prostrate, goes on, in his power, to inflict more bliss than lies in her capacity to receive,—impatient to overcome her "earthly" with his "heavenly,"—still pouring in, for protracted hours, fresh waves and fresh from the sea of sound, or from that inexhausted *German* ocean, above which, in triumphant progress, dolphin-seated, ride those Arions *Haydn* and *Mozart,* with their attendant Tritons, *Bach, Beethoven,* and a countless tribe, whom to attempt to reckon up would but plunge me again in the deeps,—I stagger under the weight of harmony, reeling to and fro at my wits' end;—clouds, as of frankincense, oppress me—priests, altars, censers, dazzle before me—the genius of *his* religion hath me in her toils —a shadowy triple tiara invests the brow of my friend, late so naked, so ingenuous—he is Pope,—and by him sits, like as in the anomaly of dreams, a she-Pope too,—tri-coroneted like himself!—I am converted, and yet a Protestant;—at once *malleus hereticorum,* and myself grand heresiarch: or three heresies centre in my person:—I am Marcion, Ebion, and Cerinthus—Gog and Magog—what not?—till the coming in of the friendly supper-tray dissipates the figment, and a draught of true Lutheran beer (in which chiefly my friend shows himself no bigot) at once reconciles me to the rationalities of a purer faith; and restores to me the genuine unterrifying aspects of my pleasant-countenanced host and hostess.

[1] I have been there, and still would go;
'Tis like a little heaven below.—DR. WATTS.

ALL FOOLS' DAY

THE compliments of the season to my worthy masters, and a merry first of April to us all!

Many happy returns of this day to you—and you—and *you,* Sir— nay, never frown, man, nor put a long face upon the matter. Do not we know one another? what need of ceremony among friends? we have all a touch of *that same*—you understand me—a speck of the motley. Beshrew the man who on such a day as this, the *general festival,* should affect to stand aloof. I am none of those sneakers. I am free of the corporation, and care not who knows it. He that meets me in the forest to-day, shall meet with no wise-acre, I can tell him. *Stultus sum.* Translate me that, and take the meaning of it to yourself for your pains. What! man, we have four quarters of the globe on our side, at the least computation.

Fill us a cup of that sparkling gooseberry—we will drink no wise, melancholy, politic port on this day—and let us troll the catch of Amiens —*duc ad me*—*duc ad me*—how goes it?

> Here shall he see
> Gross fools as he.

Now would I give a trifle to know, historically and authentically, who was the greatest fool that ever lived. I would certainly give him in a bumper. Marry, of the present breed, I think I could without much difficulty name you the party.

Remove your cap a little further, if you please: it hides my bauble. And now each man bestride his hobby, and dust away his bells to what tune he pleases. I will give you, for my part,

> ————The crazy old church clock,
> And the bewildered chimes.

Good master Empedocles, you are welcome. It is long since you went a salamander-gathering down Ætna. Worse than samphire-picking by some odds. 'Tis a mercy your worship did not singe your mustachios.

Ha! Cleombrotus! and what salads in faith did you light upon at the bottom of the Mediterranean? You were founder, I take it, of the disinterested sect of the Calenturists.

Gebir, my old free-mason, and prince of plasterers at Babel, bring in your trowel, most Ancient Grand! You have claim to a seat here at my right hand, as patron of the stammerers. You left your work, if I remember Herodotus correctly, at eight hundred million toises, or thereabout, above the level of the sea. Bless us, what a long bell you must have pulled, to call your top workmen to their nuncheon on the low grounds of Shinar. Or did you send up your garlic and onions by a rocket? I am a rogue if I am not ashamed to show you our Monument on Fish Street Hill, after your altitudes. Yet we think it somewhat.

What, the magnanimous Alexander in tears?—cry, baby, put its finger in its eye, it shall have another globe, round as an orange, pretty moppet!

Mister Adams——'odso, I honour your coat—pray do us the favour to read to us that sermon, which you lent to Mistress Slipslop—the twenty and second in your portmanteau there—on Female Incontinence —the same—it will come in most irrelevantly and impertinently seasonable to the time of the day.

Good Master Raymund Lully, you look wise. Pray correct that error.——

Duns, spare your definitions. I must fine you a bumper, or a paradox. We will have nothing said or done syllogistically this day. Remove those logical forms, waiter, that no gentleman break the tender shins of his apprehension stumbling across them.

Master Stephen, you are late.—Ha! Cokes, is it you?—Aguecheek, my dear knight, let me pay my devoir to you.—Master Shallow, your worship's poor servant to command.—Master Silence, I will use few words with you.—Slender, it will go hard if I edge not you in somewhere. —You six will engross all the poor wit of the company to-day.—I know it, I know it.

Ha! honest R——, my fine old Librarian of Ludgate, time out of mind, art thou here again? Bless thy doublet, it is not over-new, threadbare as thy stories:—what dost thou flitting about the world at this rate? —Thy customers are extinct, defunct, bed-rid, have ceased to read long ago.—Thou goest still among them, seeing if, peradventure, thou canst hawk a volume or two.—Good Granville S——, thy last patron, is flown.

> King Pandion, he is dead,
> All thy friends are lapt in lead.—

Nevertheless, noble R——, come in, and take your seat here, between Armado and Quisada; for in true courtesy, in gravity, in fantastic smiling to thyself, in courteous smiling upon others, in the goodly ornature of well-apparelled speech, and the commendation of wise sentences, thou art nothing inferior to those accomplished Dons of Spain. The spirit of chivalry forsake me for ever, when I forget thy singing the song of Macheath, which declares that he might be *happy with either,* situated between those two ancient spinsters—when I forget the inimitable formal love which thou didst make, turning now to the one, and now to the other, with that Malvolian smile—as if Cervantes, not Gay, had written it for his hero; and as if thousands of periods must revolve, before the mirror of courtesy could have given his invidious preference between a pair of so goodly-propertied and meritorious-equal damsels. * * * *

To descend from these altitudes, and not to protract our Fools' Banquet beyond its appropriate day,—for I fear the second of April is not many hours distant—in sober verity I will confess a truth to thee, reader. I love a *Fool*—as naturally, as if I were of kith and kin to him. When a child, with child-like apprehensions, that dived not below the surface of the matter, I read those *Parables*—not guessing at the involved wisdom —I had more yearnings towards that simple architect, that built his house upon the sand, than I entertained for his more cautious neighbour: I grudged at the hard censure pronounced upon the quiet soul that kept his talent; and—prizing their simplicity beyond the more provident, and, to my apprehension, somewhat *unfeminine* wariness of their competitors —I felt a kindliness, that almost amounted to a *tendre,* for those five thoughtless virgins.—I have never made an acquaintance since, that lasted: or a friendship, that answered; with any that had not some tincture of the absurd in their characters. I venerate an honest obliquity of understanding. The more laughable blunders a man shall commit in your company, the more tests he giveth you, that he will not betray or overreach you. I love the safety which a palpable hallucination warrants; the security which a word out of season ratifies. And take my word for this, reader, and say a fool told it you, if you please, that he who hath not a dram of folly in his mixture, hath pounds of much worse matter in his composition. It is observed, that "the foolisher the fowl or fish,—woodcocks—dotterels—cods'-heads, etc., the finer the flesh thereof," and what are commonly the world's received fools, but such whereof the world is not worthy? and what have been some of the kindliest patterns of our species, but so many darlings of absurdity, minions of the goddess, and her white boys?—Reader, if you wrest my words beyond their fair construction, it is you, and not I, that are the *April Fool.*

A QUAKERS' MEETING

> Still-born Silence! thou that art
> Flood-gate of the deeper heart!
> Offspring of a heavenly kind!
> Frost o' the mouth, and thaw o' the mind!
> Secrecy's confidant, and he
> Who makes religion mystery!
> Admiration's speaking'st tongue!
> Leave, thy desert shades among,
> Reverend hermits' hallow'd cells,
> Where retired devotion dwells!
> With thy enthusiasms come,
> Seize our tongues, and strike us dumb! [1]

READER, would'st thou know what true peace and quiet mean; would'st thou find a refuge from the noises and clamours of the multitude; would'st thou enjoy at once solitude and society; would'st thou possess the depth of thine own spirit in stillness, without being shut out from the consolatory faces of thy species; would'st thou be alone and yet accompanied; solitary, yet not desolate; singular, yet not without some to keep thee in countenance; a unit in aggregate; a simple in composite:—come with me into a Quakers' Meeting.

Dost thou love silence deep as that "before the winds were made"? go

[1] From *Poems of all Sorts,* by Richard Fleckno, 1653.

not out into the wilderness, descend not into the profundities of the earth; shut not up thy casements; nor pour wax into the little cells of thy ears, with little-faith'd self-mistrusting Ulysses.—Retire with me into a Quakers' Meeting.

For a man to refrain even from good words, and to hold his peace, it is commendable; but for a multitude it is great mastery.

What is the stillness of the desert compared with this place? what the uncommunicating muteness of fishes?—here the goddess reigns and revels.—"Boreas, and Cesias, and Argestes loud," do not with their interconfounding uproars more augment the brawl—nor the waves of the blown Baltic with their clubbed sounds—than their opposite (Silence her sacred self) is multiplied and rendered more intense by numbers, and by sympathy. She too hath her deeps, that call unto deeps. Negation itself hath a positive more and less; and closed eyes would seem to obscure the great obscurity of midnight.

There are wounds which an imperfect solitude cannot heal. By imperfect I mean that which a man enjoyeth by himself. The perfect is that which he can sometimes attain in crowds, but nowhere so absolutely as in a Quakers' Meeting.—Those first hermits did certainly understand this principle, when they retired into Egyptian solitudes, not singly, but in shoals, to enjoy one another's want of conversation. The Carthusian is bound to his brethren by this agreeing spirit of incommunicativeness. In secular occasions, what so pleasant as to be reading a book through a long winter evening, with a friend sitting by—say, a wife—he, or she, too (if that be probable), reading another, without interruption, or oral communication?—can there be no sympathy without the gabble of words?—away with this inhuman, shy, single, shade-and-cavern-haunting solitariness. Give me, Master Zimmermann, a sympathetic solitude.

To pace alone in the cloisters or side aisles of some cathedral, time-stricken;

> Or under hanging mountains,
> Or by the fall of fountains;

is but a vulgar luxury compared with that which those enjoy who come together for the purposes of more complete, abstracted solitude. This is the loneliness "to be felt."—The Abbey Church of Westminster hath nothing so solemn, so spirit-soothing, as the naked walls and benches of a Quakers' Meeting. Here are no tombs, no inscriptions.

> ————Sands, ignoble things,
> Dropt from the ruined sides of kings—

but here is something which throws Antiquity herself into the foreground—Silence—eldest of things—language of old Night—primitive discourser—to which the insolent decays of mouldering grandeur have but arrived by a violent, and, as we may say, unnatural progression.

> How reverend is the view of these hushed heads,
> Looking tranquillity!

Nothing-plotting, nought-caballing, unmischievous synod! convocation without intrigue! parliament without debate! what a lesson dost thou read to council, and to consistory!—if my pen treat of you lightly— as haply it will wander—yet my spirit hath gravely felt the wisdom of your custom, when sitting among you in deepest peace, which some out-welling tears would rather confirm than disturb, I have reverted to the times of your beginnings, and the sowings of the seed by Fox and Dewesbury.—I have witnessed that which brought before my eyes your heroic tranquillity, inflexible to the rude jests and serious violence of the insolent soldiery, republican or royalist, sent to molest you—for ye sate betwixt the fires of two persecutions, the outcast and offscouring of church and presbytery.—I have seen the reeling sea-ruffian, who had wandered into your receptacle with the avowed intention of disturbing your quiet, from the very spirit of the place receive in a moment a new heart, and presently sit among ye as a lamb amidst lambs. And I remember Penn before his accusers, and Fox in the bail-dock, where he was lifted up in spirit, as he tells us, and "the Judge and the Jury became as dead men under his feet."

Reader, if you are not acquainted with it, I would recommend to you, above all church-narratives, to read Sewel's History of the Quakers. It is in folio, and is the abstract of the journals of Fox and the primitive Friends. It is far more edifying and affecting than anything you will read of Wesley and his colleagues. Here is nothing to stagger you, nothing to make you mistrust, no suspicion of alloy, no drop or dreg of the worldly or ambitious spirit. You will here read the true story of that much-injured, ridiculed man (who perhaps hath been a by-word in your mouth)—James Naylor: what dreadful sufferings, with what patience, he endured, even to the boring through of his tongue with red-hot irons, without a murmur; and with what strength of mind, when the delusion he had fallen into, which they stigmatised for blasphemy, had given way to clearer thoughts, he could renounce his error, in a strain of the beautifullest humility, yet keep his first grounds, and be a Quaker still!—so different from the practice of your common converts from enthusiasm, who, when they apostatize, *apostatize all*, and think they can never get far enough from the society of their former errors, even to the renunciation of some saving truths, with which they had been mingled, not implicated.

Get the writings of John Woolman by heart; and love the early Quakers.

How far the followers of these good men in our days have kept to the primitive spirit, or in what proportion they have substituted formality for it, the Judge of Spirits can alone determine. I have seen faces in their assemblies upon which the dove sate visibly brooding. Others, again, I have watched, when my thoughts should have been better engaged, in which I could possibly detect nothing but a blank inanity. But quiet was in all, and the disposition to unanimity, and the absence of the fierce controversial workings.—If the spiritual pretensions of the Quakers have abated, at least they make few pretences. Hypocrites they certainly are not, in their preaching. It is seldom, indeed, that you shall see one get up amongst them to hold forth. Only now and then a trembling, female, generally *ancient*, voice is heard—you cannot guess from what part of the meeting it proceeds—with a low, buzzing, musical sound, laying out a few words which "she thought might suit the condition of some present," with a quaking diffidence, which leaves no possibility of supposing that anything of female vanity was mixed up, where the tones were so full of tenderness, and a restraining modesty.—The men, for what I have observed, speak seldomer.

Once only, and it was some years ago, I witnessed a sample of the old Foxian orgasm. It was a man of giant stature, who, as Wordsworth phrases it, might have danced "from head to foot equipt in iron mail." His frame was of iron, too. But *he* was malleable. I saw him shake all over with the spirit—I dare not say of delusion. The strivings of the outer man were unutterable—he seemed not to speak, but to be spoken from. I saw the strong man bowed down, and his knees to fail—his joints all seemed loosening—it was a figure to set off against Paul preaching—the words he uttered were few, and sound—he was evidently resisting his will—keeping down his own word-wisdom with more mighty effort than the world's orators strain for theirs. "He had been a WIT in his youth," he told us, with expressions of a sober remorse. And it was not till long after the impression had begun to wear away that I was enabled, with something like a smile, to recall the striking incongruity of the confession—understanding the term in its worldly acceptation—with the frame and physiognomy of the person before me. His brow would have scared away the Levities—the Jocos Risus-que—faster than the Loves fled the face of Dis at Enna.—By *wit*, even in his youth, I will be sworn he understood something far within the limits of an allowable liberty.

More frequently the Meeting is broken up without a word having been spoken. But the mind has been fed. You go away with a sermon not made with hands. You have been in the milder caverns of Trophonius; or as in some den, where that fiercest and savagest of all wild creatures, the TONGUE, that unruly member, has strangely lain tied up and captive. You have bathed with stillness.—O, when the spirit is sore fretted, even tired to sickness of the janglings and nonsense-noises of the world, what a balm and a solace it is to go and seat yourself for a quiet half-hour upon some undisputed corner of a bench, among the gentle Quakers!

Their garb and stillness conjoined, present a uniformity, tranquil and herd-like—as in the pasture—"forty feeding like one." —

The very garments of a Quaker seem incapable of receiving a soil; and cleanliness in them to be something more than the absence of its contrary. Every Quakeress is a lily; and when they come up in bands to their Whitsun-conferences, whitening the easterly streets of the metropolis, from all parts of the United Kingdom, they show like troops of the Shining Ones.

THE OLD AND THE NEW SCHOOLMASTER

My reading has been lamentably desultory and immethodical. Odd, out of the way, old English plays, and treatises, have supplied me with most of my notions, and ways of feeling. In everything that relates to *science,* I am a whole Encyclopædia behind the rest of the world. I should have scarcely cut a figure among the franklins, or country gentlemen, in King John's days. I know less geography than a school-boy of six weeks' standing. To me a map of old Ortelius is as authentic as Arrowsmith. I do not know whereabout Africa merges into Asia; whether Ethiopia lie in one or other of these great divisions; nor can form the remotest conjecture of the position of New South Wales, or Van Diemen's Land. Yet do I hold a correspondence with a very dear friend in the first-named of these two Terræ Incognitæ. I have no astronomy. I do not know where to look for the Bear, or Charles's Wain; the place of any star; or the name of any of them at sight. I guess at Venus only by her brightness—and if the sun on some portentous morn were to make his first appearance in the West, I verily believe, that, while all the world were gasping in apprehension about me, I alone should stand unterrified, from sheer incuriosity and want of observation. Of history and chronology I possess some vague points, such as one cannot help picking up in the course of miscellaneous study; but I never deliberately sat down to a chronicle, even of my own country. I have most dim apprehensions of the four great monarchies; and sometimes the Assyrian, sometimes the Persian, floats as *first,* in my fancy. I make the widest conjectures concerning Egypt and her shepherd kings. My friend *M.,* with great painstaking, got me to think I understood the first proposition in Euclid, but gave me over in despair at the second. I am entirely unacquainted with the modern languages; and, like a better man than myself, have "small Latin and less Greek." I am a stranger to the shapes and texture of the commonest trees, herbs, flowers—not from the circumstance of my being town-born—for I should have brought the same inobservant spirit into the world with me, had I first seen it "on Devon's leafy shores,"—and am no less at a loss among purely town-objects, tools, engines, mechanic processes.—Not that I affect ignorance —but my head has not many mansions, nor spacious; and I have been obliged to fill it with such cabinet curiosities as it can hold without aching. I sometimes wonder, how I have passed my probation with so little discredit in the world, as I have done, upon so meagre a stock. But the fact is, a man may do very well with a very little knowledge, and scarce be found out, in mixed company; everybody is so much more ready to produce his own, than to call for a display of your acquisitions. But in a *tête-à-tête* there is no shuffling. The truth will out. There is nothing which I dread so much, as the being left alone for a quarter of an hour with a sensible, well-informed man, that does not know me. I lately got into a dilemma of this sort.—

In one of my daily jaunts between Bishopsgate and Shacklewell, the coach stopped to take up a staid-looking gentleman, about the wrong side of thirty, who was giving his parting directions (while the steps were adjusting), in a tone of mild authority, to a tall youth, who seemed to be neither his clerk, his son, nor his servant, but something partaking of all three. The youth was dismissed, and we drove on. As we were the sole passengers, he naturally enough addressed his conversation to me; and we discussed the merits of the fare, the civility and punctuality of the driver; the circumstance of an opposition coach having been lately set up, with the probabilities of its success—to all which I was enabled to return pretty satisfactory answers, having been drilled into this kind of etiquette by some years' daily practice of riding to and fro in the stage aforesaid—when he suddenly alarmed me by a startling question, whether I had seen the show of prize cattle that morning in Smithfield? Now, as I had not seen it, and do not greatly care for such sort of exhibitions, I was obliged to return a cold negative. He seemed a little mortified, as well as astonished, at my declaration, as (it appeared) he was just come fresh from the sight, and doubtless had hoped to compare notes on the subject. However, he assured me that I had lost a fine treat, as it far exceeded the show of last year. We were now approaching Norton Folgate, when the sight of some shop-goods *ticketed* freshened him up into a dissertation upon the cheapness of cottons this spring. I was now a little in heart, as the nature of my morning avocations had brought me into some sort of familiarity with the raw material; and I was surprised to find how eloquent I was becoming on the state of the India market—when, presently, he dashed my incipient vanity to the earth at once, by inquiring whether I had ever made any calculations as to the value of the rental of all the retail shops in London. Had he asked of me, what song the Syrens sang, or what Achilles assumed when he hid himself among women, I might, with Sir Thomas Browne, have hazarded a "wide solution." [1] My companion saw my embarrassment, and, the almshouses beyond Shoreditch just coming in view, with great good-nature and dexterity shifted his conversation to the subject of public charities; which led to the comparative merits of provisions for the poor in past and present times, with observations on the old monastic institutions, and charitable orders; but, finding me rather dimly impressed with some glimmering notions from old poetic associations, than strongly fortified with any speculations reducible to calculation on the subject, he gave the matter up; and, the country beginning to open more and more upon us, as we approached the turnpike at Kingsland (the destined termination of his journey), he put a home thrust upon me, in the most unfortunate position he could have chosen, by advancing some queries relative to the North Pole Expedition. While I was muttering out something about the Panorama of those strange regions (which I had actually seen), by way of parrying the question, the coach stopping relieved me from any further apprehensions.

[1] Urn Burial.

My companion getting out, left me in the comfortable possession of my ignorance; and I heard him, as he went off, putting questions to an outside passenger, who had alighted with him, regarding an epidemic disorder, that had been rife about Dalston, and which my friend assured him had gone through five or six schools in that neighbourhood. The truth now flashed upon me, that my companion was a schoolmaster; and that the youth, whom he had parted from at our first acquaintance, must have been one of the bigger boys, or the usher.—He was evidently a kind-hearted man, who did not seem so much desirous of provoking discussion by the questions which he put, as of obtaining information at any rate. It did not appear that he took any interest, either, in such kind of inquiries, for their own sake; but that he was in some way bound to seek for knowledge. A greenish-coloured coat, which he had on, forbade me to surmise that he was a clergyman. The adventure gave birth to some reflections on the difference between persons of his profession in past and present times.

Rest to the souls of those fine old Pedagogues; the breed, long since extinct, of the Lilys, and the Linacres: who believing that all learning was contained in the languages which they taught, and despising every other acquirement as superficial and useless, came to their task as to a sport! Passing from infancy to age, they dreamed away all their days as in a grammar-school. Revolving in a perpetual cycle of declensions, conjugations, syntaxes, and prosodies; renewing constantly the occupations which had charmed their studious childhood; rehearsing continually the part of the past; life must have slipped from them at last like one day. They were always in their first garden, reaping harvests of their golden time, among their *Flori* and their *Spici-legia;* in Arcadia still, but kings; the ferule of their sway not much harsher, but of like dignity with that mild sceptre attributed to king Basileus; the Greek and Latin, their stately Pamela and their Philoclea; with the occasional duncery of some untoward tyro, serving for a refreshing interlude of a Mopsa, or a clown Damœtas!

With what a savour doth the Preface to Colet's, or (as it is sometimes called) Paul's Accidence, set forth! "To exhort every man to the learning of grammar, that intendeth to attain the understanding of the tongues, wherein is contained a great treasury of wisdom and knowledge, it would seem but vain and lost labour; for so much as it is known, that nothing can surely be ended, whose beginning is either feeble or faulty; and no building be perfect whereas the foundation and groundwork is ready to fall, and unable to uphold the burden of the frame." How well doth this stately preamble (comparable to those which Milton commendeth as "having been the usage to prefix to some solemn law, then first promulgated by Solon or Lycurgus") correspond with and illustrate that pious zeal for conformity, expressed in a succeeding clause, which would fence about grammar-rules with the severity of faith-articles!—"as for the diversity of grammars, it is well profitably taken away by the king majesties wisdom, who foreseeing the inconvenience, and favourably providing the remedie, caused one kind of grammar by sundry learned men to be diligently drawn, and so to be set out, only everywhere to be taught for the use of learners, and for the hurt in changing of schoolmaisters." What a *gusto* in that which follows: "wherein it is profitable that he [the pupil] can orderly decline his noun and his verb." *His* noun!

The fine dream is fading away fast; and the least concern of a teacher in the present day is to inculcate grammar-rules.

The modern schoolmaster is expected to know a little of everything, because his pupil is required not to be entirely ignorant of anything. He must be superficially, if I may so say, omniscient. He is to know something of pneumatics; of chemistry; of whatever is curious or proper to excite the attention of the youthful mind; an insight into mechanics is desirable, with a touch of statistics; the quality of soils, etc., botany, the constitution of his country, *cum multis aliis*. You may get a notion of some part of his expected duties by consulting the famous Tractate on Education, addressed to Mr. Hartlib.

All these things—these, or the desire of them—he is expected to instil, not by set lessons from professors, which he may charge in the bill, but at school intervals, as he walks the streets, or saunters through green fields (those natural instructors), with his pupils. The least part of what is expected from him is to be done in school-hours. He must insinuate knowledge at the *mollia tempora fandi*. He must seize every occasion— the season of the year—the time of the day—a passing cloud—a rainbow —a waggon of hay—a regiment of soldiers going by—to inculcate something useful. He can receive no pleasure from a casual glimpse of Nature, but must catch at it as an object of instruction. He must interpret beauty into the picturesque. He cannot relish a beggar-man, or a gipsy, for thinking of the suitable improvement. Nothing comes to him, not spoiled by the sophisticating medium of moral uses. The Universe— that Great Book, as it has been called—is to him, indeed, to all intents and purposes, a book out of which he is doomed to read tedious homilies to distasting schoolboys.—Vacations themselves are none to him, he is only rather worse off than before; for commonly he has some intrusive upper-boy fastened upon him at such times; some cadet of a great family; some neglected lump of nobility, or gentry; that he must drag after him to the play, to the Panorama, to Mr. Bartley's Orrery, to the Panopticon, or into the country, to a friend's house, or his favourite watering-place. Wherever he goes this uneasy shadow attends him. A boy is at his board, and in his path, and in all his movements. He is boy-rid, sick of perpetual boy.

Boys are capital fellows in their own way, among their mates; but they are unwholesome companions for grown people. The restraint is felt no less on the one side than on the other.—Even a child, that "plaything for an hour," tires *always*. The noises of children, playing their own fancies—as I now hearken to them, by fits, sporting on the green before my window, while I am engaged in these grave speculations at my neat surburban retreat at Shacklewell—by distance made more sweet—inexpressibly take from the labour of my task. It is like writing to music. They seem to modulate my periods. They ought at least to do so—for in the voice of that tender age there is a kind of poetry, far unlike the harsh prose-accents of man's conversation.—I should but spoil their sport, and diminish my own sympathy for them, by mingling in their pastime.

I would not be domesticated all my days with a person of very superior capacity to my own—not, if I know myself at all, from any considerations of jealousy or self-comparison, for the occasional communion with such minds has constituted the fortune and felicity of my life—but the habit of too constant intercourse with spirits above you, instead of raising you, keeps you down. Too frequent doses of original thinking from others, restrain what lesser portion of that faculty you may possess of your own. You get entangled in another man's mind, even as you lose yourself in another man's grounds. You are walking with a tall varlet, whose strides out-pace yours to lassitude. The constant operation of such potent agency would reduce me, I am convinced, to imbecility. You may derive thoughts from others; your way of thinking, the mould in which your thoughts are cast, must be your own. Intellect may be imparted, but not each man's intellectual frame.—

As little as I should wish to be always thus dragged upward, as little (or rather still less) is it desirable to be stunted downwards by your associates. The trumpet does not more stun you by its loudness, than a whisper teases you by its provoking inaudibility.

Why are we never quite at our ease in the presence of a schoolmaster? —because we are conscious that he is not quite at his ease in ours. He is awkward, and out of place, in the society of his equals. He comes like Gulliver from among his little people, and he cannot fit the stature of his understanding to yours. He cannot meet you on the square. He wants a point given him, like an indifferent whist-player. He is so used to teaching, that he wants to be teaching *you*. One of these professors, upon my complaining that these little sketches of mine were anything but methodical, and that I was unable to make them otherwise, kindly offered to instruct me in the method by which young gentlemen in *his* seminary were taught to compose English themes. The jests of a schoolmaster are coarse, or thin. They do not *tell* out of school. He is under the restraint of a formal or didactive hypocrisy in company, as a clergyman is under a moral one. He can no more let his intellect loose in society than the other can his inclinations.—He is forlorn among his coevals; his juniors cannot be his friends.

"I take blame to myself," said a sensible man of this profession, writing to a friend respecting a youth who had quitted his school abruptly, "that your nephew was not more attached to me. But persons in my situation are more to be pitied than can well be imagined. We are surrounded by young, and, consequently, ardently affectionate hearts, but *we* can never hope to share an atom of their affections. The relation of master and scholar forbids this. *How pleasing this must be to you, how I envy your feelings!* my friends will sometimes say to me, when they see young men whom I have educated return after some years' absence from school, their eyes shining with pleasure, while they shake hands with their old master, bringing a present of game to me, or a toy to my wife, and thanking me in the warmest terms for my care of their education. A holiday is begged for the boys; the house is a scene of happiness; I, only, am sad at heart.—This fine-spirited and warm-hearted youth, who fancies he repays his master with gratitude for the care of his boyish years—this young man—in the eight long years I watched over him with a parent's anxiety, never could repay me with one look of genuine feeling. He was proud, when I praised; he was submissive, when I reproved him; but he did never *love* me—and what he now mistakes for gratitude and kindness for me, is but the pleasant sensation which all persons feel at revisiting the scenes of their boyish hopes and fears; and the seeing on equal terms the man they were accustomed to look up to with reverence. My wife, too," this interesting correspondent goes on to say, "my once darling Anna, is the wife of a schoolmaster.—When I married her—knowing that the wife of a schoolmaster ought to be a busy notable creature, and fearing that my gentle Anna would ill supply the loss of my dear bustling mother, just then dead, who never sat still, was in every part of the house in a moment, and whom I was obliged some-times to threaten to fasten down in a chair, to save her from fatiguing herself to death—I expressed my fears that I was bringing her into a way of life unsuitable to her; and she, who loved me tenderly, promised for my sake to exert herself to perform the duties of her new situation. She promised, and she has kept her word. What wonders will not woman's love perform?—My house is managed with a propriety and decorum unknown in other schools; my boys are well fed, look healthy, and have every proper accommodation; and all this performed with a careful economy, that never descends to meanness. But I have lost my gentle *helpless* Anna! When we sit down to enjoy an hour of repose after the fatigue of the day, I am compelled to listen to what have been her useful (and they are really useful) employments through the day, and what she proposes for her to-morrow's task. Her heart and her features are changed by the duties of her situation. To the boys, she never appears other than the *master's wife,* and she looks up to me as the *boys' master;* to whom all show of love and affection would be highly improper, and unbecoming the dignity of her situation and mine. Yet *this* my gratitude forbids me to hint to her. For my sake she submitted to be this altered creature, and can I reproach her for it?"—For the communication of this letter I am indebted to my cousin Bridget.

IMPERFECT SYMPATHIES

> I am of a constitution so general, that it consorts and sympathizeth with all things; I have no antipathy, or rather idiosyncrasy in anything. Those natural repugnancies do not touch me, nor do I behold with prejudice the French, Italian, Spaniard, or Dutch.—*Religio Medici.*

THAT the author of the Religio Medici, mounted upon the airy stilts of abstraction, conversant about notional and conjectural essences; in whose categories of Being the possible took the upper hand of the actual; should have overlooked the impertinent individualities of such poor concretions as mankind, is not much to be admired. It is rather to be wondered at, that in the genus of animals he should have condescended to distinguish that species at all. For myself—earth-bound and fettered to the scene of my activities,—

> Standing on earth, not rapt above the sky,

I confess that I do feel the differences of mankind, national or individual, to an unhealthy excess. I can look with no indifferent eye upon things or persons. Whatever is, is to me a matter of taste or distaste; or when once it becomes indifferent, it begins to be disrelishing. I am, in plainer words, a bundle of prejudices—made up of likings and dislikings—the variest thrall to sympathies, apathies, antipathies. In a certain sense, I hope it may be said of me that I am a lover of my species. I can feel for all indifferently, but I cannot feel towards all equally. The more purely-English word that expresses sympathy, will better explain my meaning. I can be a friend to a worthy man, who upon another account cannot be my mate or *fellow.* I cannot *like* all people alike.[1]

[1] I would be understood as confining myself to the subject of *imperfect sympathies.* To nations or classes of men there can be no direct antipathy. There may be individuals born and constellated so opposite to another individual nature, that the same sphere cannot hold them. I have met with my moral antipodes, and can believe the story of two persons meeting (who never saw one another before in their lives) and instantly fighting.

> ————We by proof find there should be
> 'Twixt man and man such an antipathy,
> That though he can show no just reason why
> For any former wrong or injury,
> Can neither find a blemish in his fame,
> Nor aught in face or feature justly blame,
> Can challenge or accuse him of no evil,
> Yet notwithstanding hates him as a devil.

The lines are from old Heywood's "Hierarchie of Angels," and he subjoins a curious story in confirmation, of a Spaniard who attempted to assassinate a King Ferdinand of Spain, and being put to the rack could give no other reason for the deed but an inveterate antipathy which he had taken to the first sight of the King.

> ————The cause which to that act compell'd him
> Was, he ne'er loved him since he first beheld him.

I have been trying all my life to like Scotchmen, and am obliged to desist from the experiment in despair. They cannot like me—and in truth, I never knew one of that nation who attempted to do it. There is something more plain and ingenuous in their mode of proceeding. We know one another at first sight. There is an order of imperfect intellects (under which mine must be content to rank) which in its constitution is essentially anti-Caledonian. The owners of the sort of faculties I allude to, have minds rather suggestive than comprehensive. They have no pretences to much clearness or precision in their ideas, or in their manner of expressing them. Their intellectual wardrobe (to confess fairly) has few whole pieces in it. They are content with fragments and scattered pieces of Truth. She presents no full front to them—a feature or side-face at the most. Hints and glimpses, germs and crude essays at a system, is the utmost they pretend to. They beat up a little game peradventure—and leave it to knottier heads, more robust constitutions, to run it down. The light that lights them is not steady and polar, but mutable and shifting: waxing, and again waning. Their conversation is accordingly. They will throw out a random word in or out of season, and be content to let it pass for what it is worth. They cannot speak always as if they were upon their oath—but must be understood, speaking or writing, with some abatement. They seldom wait to mature a proposition, but e'en bring it to market in the green ear. They delight to impart their defective discoveries as they arise, without waiting for their full development. They are no systematizers, and would but err more by attempting it. Their minds, as I said before, are suggestive merely. The brain of a true Caledonian (if I am not mistaken) is constituted upon quite a different plan. His Minerva is born in panoply. You are never admitted to see his ideas in their growth—if, indeed, they do grow, and are not rather put together upon principles of clock-work. You never catch his mind in an undress. He never hints or suggests anything, but unlades his stock of ideas in perfect order and completeness. He brings his total wealth into company, and gravely unpacks it. His riches are always about him. He never stoops to catch a glittering something in your presence to share it with you, before he quite knows whether it be true touch or not. You cannot cry *halves* to anything that he finds. He does not find, but bring. You never witness his first apprehension of a thing. His understanding is always at its meridian—you never see the first dawn, the early streaks.—He has no falterings of self-suspicion. Surmises, guesses, misgivings, half-intuitions, semi-consciousnesses, partial illuminations, dim instincts, embryo conceptions, have no place in his brain, or vocabulary. The twilight of dubiety never falls upon him. Is he orthodox—he has no doubts. Is he an infidel—he has none either. Between the affirmative and the negative there is no border-land with him. You cannot hover with him upon the confines of truth, or wander in the maze of a probable argument. He always keeps the path. You cannot make excursions with him—for he sets you right. His taste never fluctuates. His morality never abates. He cannot compromise, or understand middle actions. There can be but a right and a wrong. His conversation is as a book. His affirmations have the sanctity of an oath. You must speak upon the square with him. He stops a metaphor like a suspected person in an enemy's country. "A healthy book!"—said one of his countrymen to me, who had ventured to give that appellation to John Buncle,—"Did I catch rightly what you said? I have heard of a man in health, and of a healthy state of body, but I do not see how that epithet can be properly applied to a book." Above all, you must beware of indirect expressions before a Caledonian. Clap an extinguisher upon your irony, if you are unhappily blest with a vein of it. Remember you are upon your oath. I have a print of a graceful female after Leonardo da Vinci, which I was showing off to Mr. * * * * After he had examined it minutely, I ventured to ask him how he liked MY BEAUTY (a foolish name it goes by among my friends)—when he very gravely assured me, that "he had considerable respect for my character and talents" (so he was pleased to say), "but had not given himself much thought about the degree of my personal pretensions." The misconception staggered me, but did not seem much to disconcert him.—Persons of this nation are particularly fond of affirming a truth—which nobody doubts. They do not so properly affirm, as annunciate it. They do indeed appear to have such a love of truth (as if, like virtue, it were valuable for itself) that all truth becomes equally valuable, whether the proposition that contains it be new or old, disputed, or such as is impossible to become a subject of disputation. I was present not long since at a party of North Britons, where a son of Burns was expected; and happened to drop a silly expression (in my South British way), that I wished it were the father instead of the son—when four of them started up at once to inform me, that "that was impossible, because he was dead." An impracticable wish, it seems, was more than they could conceive. Swift has hit off this part of their character, namely their love of truth, in his biting way, but with an illiberality that necessarily confines the passage to the margin.[1] The tediousness of these people is certainly provoking. I wonder if they ever tire one another!—In my early life I had a passionate fondness for the poetry of Burns. I have sometimes foolishly hoped to ingratiate myself with his countrymen by expressing it. But I have always found that a true Scot resents your admiration of his compatriot, even more than he would your contempt of him. The latter he imputes to your "imperfect acquaintance with many of the words which he uses"; and the same objection makes it a presumption in you to suppose that you can admire him.—Thomson

---

[1] There are some people who think they sufficiently acquit themselves, and entertain their company, with relating facts of no consequence, not at all out of the road of such common incidents as happen every day; and this I have observed more frequently among the Scots than any other nation, who are very careful not to omit the minutest circumstances of time or place; which kind of discourse, if it were not a little relieved by the uncouth terms and phrases, as well as accent and gesture, peculiar to that country, would be hardly tolerable.—*Hints towards an Essay on Conversation.*

they seem to have forgotten. Smollett they have neither forgotten nor forgiven, for his delineation of Rory and his companion, upon their first introduction to our metropolis.—Speak of Smollett as a great genius, and they will retort upon you Hume's History compared with *his* Continuation of it. What if the historian had continued Humphrey Clinker?

I have, in the abstract, no disrespect for Jews. They are a piece of stubborn antiquity, compared with which Stonehenge is in its nonage. They date beyond the pyramids. But I should not care to be in habits of familiar intercourse with any of that nation. I confess that I have not the nerves to enter their synagogues. Old prejudices cling about me. I cannot shake off the story of Hugh of Lincoln. Centuries of injury, contempt, and hate, on the one side,—of cloaked revenge, dissimulation, and hate, on the other, between our and their fathers, must and ought to affect the blood of the children. I cannot believe it can run clear and kindly yet; or that a few fine words, such as candour, liberality, the light of a nineteenth century, can close up the breaches of so deadly a disunion. A Hebrew is nowhere congenial to me. He is least distasteful on 'Change—for the mercantile spirit levels all distinctions, as all are beauties in the dark. I boldly confess that I do not relish the approximation of Jew and Christian, which has become so fashionable. The reciprocal endearments have, to me, something hypocritical and unnatural in them. I do not like to see the Church and Synagogue kissing and congeeing in awkward postures of an affected civility. If *they* are converted, why do they not come over to us altogether? Why keep up a form of separation, when the life of it is fled? If they can sit with us at table, why do they keck at our cookery? I do not understand these half convertites. Jews christianizing—Christians judaizing—puzzle me. I like fish or flesh. A moderate Jew is a more confounding piece of anomaly than a wet Quaker. The spirit of the synagogue is essentially *separative*. B—— would have been more in keeping if he had abided by the faith of his forefathers. There is a fine scorn in his face, which nature meant to be of——Christians. The Hebrew spirit is strong in him, in spite of his proselytism. He cannot conquer the Shibboleth. How it breaks out, when he sings, "The Children of Israel passed through the Red Sea!" The auditors, for the moment, are as Egyptians to him, and he rides over our necks in triumph. There is no mistaking him. B—— has a strong expression of sense in his countenance, and it is confirmed by his singing. The foundation of his vocal excellence is sense. He sings with understanding, as Kemble delivered dialogue. He would sing the Commandments, and give an appropriate character to each prohibition. His nation, in general, have not oversensible countenances. How should they?—but you seldom see a silly expression among them.—Gain, and the pursuit of gain, sharpen a man's visage. I never heard of an idiot being born among them.—Some admire the Jewish female-physiognomy. I admire it—but with trembling. Jael had those full dark inscrutable eyes.

In the Negro countenance you will often meet with strong traits of benignity. I have felt yearnings of tenderness towards some of these faces—or rather masks—that have looked out kindly upon one in casual encounters in the streets and highways. I love what Fuller beautifully calls—these "images of God cut in ebony." But I should not like to associate with them, to share my meals and my good-nights with them —because they are black.

I love Quaker ways, and Quaker worship. I venerate the Quaker principles. It does me good for the rest of the day when I meet any of their people in my path. When I am ruffled or disturbed by any occurrence, the sight, or quiet voice of a Quaker, acts upon me as a ventilator, lightening the air, and taking off a load from the bosom. But I cannot like the Quakers (as Desdemona would say) "to live with them." I am all over sophisticated—with humours, fancies, craving hourly sympathy. I must have books, pictures, theatres, chit-chat, scandal, jokes, ambiguities, and a thousand whim-whams, which their simpler taste can do without. I should starve at their primitive banquet. My appetites are too high for the salads which (according to Evelyn) Eve dressed for the angel, my gusto too excited

> To sit a guest with Daniel at his pulse.

The indirect answers which Quakers are often found to return to a question put to them may be explained, I think, without the vulgar assumption, that they are more given to evasion and equivocating than other people. They naturally look to their words more carefully, and are more cautious of committing themselves. They have a peculiar character to keep up on his head. They stand in a manner upon their veracity. A Quaker is by law exempted from taking an oath. The custom of resorting to an oath in extreme cases, sanctified as it is by all religious antiquity, is apt (it must be confessed) to introduce into the laxer sort of minds the notion of two kinds of truth—the one applicable to the solemn affairs of justice, and the other to the common proceedings of daily intercourse. As truth bound upon the conscience by an oath can be but truth, so in the common affirmations of the shop and the market-place a latitude is expected, and conceded upon questions wanting this solemn covenant. Something less than truth satisfies. It is common to hear a person say, "You do not expect me to speak as if I were upon my oath." Hence a great deal of incorrectness and inadvertancy, short of falsehood, creeps into ordinary conversation; and a kind of secondary or laic-truth is tolerated, where clergy-truth—oath-truth, by the nature of the circumstances, is not required. A Quaker knows none of this distinction. His simple affirmation being received, upon the most sacred occasions, without any further test, stamps a value upon the words which he is to use upon the most indifferent topics of life. He looks to them, naturally, with more severity. You can have of him no more than his word. He knows, if he is caught tripping in a casual expression, he forfeits, for himself at least, his claim to the invidious exemption. He knows that his syllables are weighed—and how far a consciousness of this particular watchfulness, exerted against a person, has a tendency to produce indirect answers, and a diverting of the question by honest means, might be illustrated, and the practice justified, by a more sacred example than is proper to be adduced upon this occasion. The admirable presence of mind, which is notorious in Quakers upon all contingencies, might be traced to this imposed self-watchfulness—if it did not seem rather an humble and secular scion of that old stock of religious constancy, which never bent or faltered, in the Primitive Friends, or gave way to the winds of persecution, to the violence of judge or accuser, under trials and racking examinations. "You will never be the wiser, if I sit here answering your questions till midnight," said one of those upright Justicers to Penn, who had been putting law-cases with a puzzling subtlety. "Thereafter as the answers may be," retorted the Quaker. The astonishing composure of this people is sometimes ludicrously displayed in lighter instances.—I was travelling in a stage-coach with three male Quakers, buttoned up in the straitest nonconformity of their sect. We stopped to bait at Andover, where a meal, partly tea apparatus, partly supper, was set before us. My friends confined themselves to the tea-table. I in my way took supper. When the landlady brought in the bill, the eldest of my companions discovered that she had charged for both meals. This was resisted. Mine hostess was very clamorous and positive. Some mild arguments were used on the part of the Quakers, for which the heated mind of the good lady seemed by no means a fit recipient. The guard came in with his usual peremptory notice. The Quakers pulled out their money and formally tendered it—so much for tea—I, in humble imitation, tendering mine—for the supper which I had taken. She would not relax in her demand. So they all three quietly put up their silver, as did myself, and marched out of the room, the eldest and gravest going first, with myself closing up the rear, who thought I could not do better than follow the example of such grave and warrantable personages. We got in. The steps went up. The coach drove off. The murmurs of mine hostess, not very indistinctly or ambiguously pronounced, became after a time inaudible—and now my conscience, which the whimsical scene had for a while suspended, beginning to give some twitches, I waited, in the hope that some justification would be offered by these serious persons for the seeming injustice of their conduct. To my great surprise not a syllable was dropped on the subject. They sat as mute as at a meeting. At length the eldest of them broke silence, by inquiring of his next neighbour, "Hath thee heard how indigos go at the India House?" and the question operated as a soporific on my moral feeling as far as Exeter.

WITCHES, AND OTHER NIGHT FEARS

WE are too hasty when we set down our ancestors in the gross for fools, for the monstrous inconsistencies (as they seem to us) involved in their creed of witchcraft. In the relations of this visible world we find them to have been as rational, and shrewd to detect an historic anomaly, as ourselves. But when once the invisible world was supposed to be opened, and the lawless agency of bad spirits assumed, what measures of probability, of decency, of fitness, or proportion—of that which distinguishes the likely from the palpable absurd—could they have to guide them in the rejection or admission of any particular testimony?—That maidens pined away, wasting inwardly as their waxen images consumed before a fire—that corn was lodged, and cattle lamed—that whirlwinds uptore in diabolic revelry the oaks of the forest—or that spits and kettles only danced a fearful innocent vagary about some rustic's kitchen when no wind was stirring—were all equally probable where no law of agency was understood. That the prince of the powers of darkness, passing by the flower and pomp of the earth, should lay preposterous siege to the weak fantasy of indigent eld—has neither likelihood nor unlikelihood *a priori* to us, who have no measure to guess at his policy, or standard to estimate what rate those anile souls may fetch in the devil's market. Nor, when the wicked are expressly symbolised by a goat, was it to be wondered at so much, that *he* should come sometimes in that body, and assert his metaphor.—That the intercourse was opened at all between both worlds was perhaps the mistake—but that once assumed, I see no reason for disbelieving one attested story of this nature more than another on the score of absurdity. There is no law to judge of the lawless, or canon by which a dream may be criticised.

I have sometimes thought that I could not have existed in the days of received witchcraft; that I could not have slept in a village where one of those reputed hags dwelt. Our ancestors were bolder, or more obtuse. Amidst the universal belief that these wretches were in league with the author of all evil, holding hell tributary to their muttering, no simple Justice of the Peace seems to have scrupled issuing, or silly Headborough serving, a warrant upon them—as if they should subpœna Satan!—Prospero in his boat, with his books and wand about him, suffers himself to be conveyed away at the mercy of his enemies to an unknown island. He might have raised a storm or two, we think, on the passage. His acquiescence is in exact analogy to the non-resistance of witches to the constituted powers.—What stops the Fiend in Spenser from tearing Guyon to pieces—or who had made it a condition of his prey that Guyon must take assay of the glorious bait—we have no guess. We do not know the laws of that country.

From my childhood I was extremely inquisitive about witches and witch-stories. My maid, and more legendary aunt, supplied me with good store. But I shall mention the accident which directed my curiosity

originally into this channel. In my father's book-closet the History of the
Bible by Stackhouse occupied a distinguished station. The pictures with
which it abounds—one of the ark, in particular, and another of Solomon's temple, delineated with all the fidelity of ocular admeasurement,
as if the artist had been upon the spot—attracted my childish attention.
There was a picture, too, of the Witch raising up Samuel, which I wish
that I had never seen. We shall come to that hereafter. Stackhouse is in
two huge tomes—and there was a pleasure in removing folios of that
magnitude, which, with infinite straining, was as much as I could manage,
from the situation which they occupied upon an upper shelf. I have not
met with the work from that time to this, but I remember it consisted of
Old Testament stories, orderly set down, with the *objection* appended to
each story, and the *solution* of the objection regularly tacked to that.
The *objection* was a summary of whatever difficulties had been opposed
to the credibility of the history, by the shrewdness of ancient or modern
infidelity, drawn up with an almost complimentary excess of candour.
The *solution* was brief, modest, and satisfactory. The bane and antidote
were both before you. To doubts so put, and so quashed, there seemed to
be an end for ever. The dragon lay dead, for the foot of the veriest babe
to trample on. But—like as was rather feared than realised from that
slain monster in Spenser—from the womb of those crushed errors young
dragonets would creep, exceeding the prowess of so tender a Saint George
as myself to vanquish. The habit of expecting objections to every passage set me upon starting more objections, for the glory of finding a solution of my own for them. I became staggered and perplexed, a sceptic in
long-coats. The pretty Bible stories which I had read, or heard read in
church, lost their purity and sincerity of impression, and were turned into
so many historic or chronologic theses to be defended against whatever
impugners. I was not to disbelieve them, but—the next thing to that—I
was to be quite sure that some one or other would or had disbelieved
them. Next to making a child an infidel is the letting him know that
there are infidels at all. Credulity is the man's weakness, but the child's
strength. O, how ugly sound scriptural doubts from the mouth of a babe
and a suckling!—I should have lost myself in these mazes, and have
pined away, I think, with such unfit sustenance as these husks afforded,
but for a fortunate piece of ill-fortune which about this time befell me.
Turning over the picture of the ark with too much haste, I unhappily
made a breach in its ingenious fabric—driving my inconsiderate fingers
right through the two larger quadrupeds—the elephant and the camel—
that stare (as well they might) out of the two last windows next the
steerage in that unique piece of naval architecture. Stackhouse was
henceforth locked up, and became an interdicted treasure. With the
book, the *objections* and *solutions* gradually cleared out of my head, and
have seldom returned since in any force to trouble me.—But there was
one impression which I had imbibed from Stackhouse which no lock or
bar could shut out, and which was destined to try my childish nerves
rather more seriously.—That detestable picture!

I was dreadfully alive to nervous terrors. The night-time, solitude, and the dark, were my hell. The sufferings I endured in this nature would justify the expression. I never laid my head on my pillow, I suppose, from the fourth to the seventh or eighth year of my life—so far as memory serves in things so long ago—without an assurance, which realised its own prophecy, of seeing some frightful spectre. Be old Stackhouse then acquitted in part, if I say, that to his picture of the Witch raising up Samuel—(O that old man covered with a mantle!)—I owe—not my midnight terrors, the hell of my infancy—but the shape and manner of their visitation. It was he who dressed up for me a hag that nightly sate upon my pillow—a sure bedfellow, when my aunt or my maid was far from me. All day long, while the book was permitted me, I dreamed waking over his delineation, and at night (if I may use so bold an expression) awoke into sleep, and found the vision true. I durst not, even in the day-light, once enter the chamber where I slept, without my face turned to the window, aversely from the bed where my witch-ridden pillow was. Parents do not know what they do when they leave tender babes alone to go to sleep in the dark. The feeling about for a friendly arm—the hoping for a familiar voice—when they wake screaming—and find none to soothe them—what a terrible shaking it is to their poor nerves! The keeping them up till midnight, through candle-light and the unwholesome hours, as they are called,—would, I am satisfied, in a medical point of view, prove the better caution.—That detestable picture, as I have said, gave the fashion to my dreams—if dreams they were—for the scene of them was invariably the room in which I lay. Had I never met with the picture, the fears would have come self-pictured in some shape or other—

Headless bear, black man, or ape—

but, as it was, my imaginations took that form.—It is not book, or picture, or the stories of foolish servants, which create these terrors in children. They can at most but give them a direction. Dear little T. H., who of all children has been brought up with the most scrupulous exclusion of every taint of superstition—who was never allowed to hear of goblin or apparition, or scarcely to be told of bad men, or to read or hear of any distressing story—finds all this world of fear, from which he has been so rigidly excluded *ab extra,* in his own "thick-coming fancies"; and from his little midnight pillow, this nurse-child of optimism will start at shapes, unborrowed of tradition, in sweats to which the reveries of the cell-damned murderer are tranquillity.

Gorgons, and Hydras, and Chimæras dire—stories of Celæno and the Harpies—may reproduce themselves in the brain of superstition—but they were there before. They are transcripts, types—the archetypes are in us, and eternal. How else should the recital of that, which we know in a waking sense to be false, come to affect us at all?—or

——Names, whose sense we see not,
Fray us with things that be not?

Is it that we naturally conceive terror from such objects, considered in their capacity of being able to inflict upon us bodily injury?—O, least of all! These terrors are of older standing. They date beyond body—or, without the body, they would have been the same. All the cruel, tormenting, defined devils in Dante—tearing, mangling, choking, stifling, scorching demons—are they one half so fearful to the spirit of a man, as the simple idea of a spirit unembodied following him—

> Like one that on a lonesome road
> Doth walk in fear and dread,
> And having once turn'd round, walks on
> And turns no more his head;
> Because he knows a frightful fiend
> Doth close behind him tread.[1]

That the kind of fear here treated of is purely spiritual—that it is strong in proportion as it is objectless upon earth—that it predominates in the period of sinless infancy—are difficulties, the solution of which might afford some probable insight into our ante-mundane condition, and a peep at least into the shadowland of pre-existence.

My night-fancies have long ceased to be afflictive. I confess an occasional nightmare; but I do not, as in early youth, keep a stud of them. Fiendish faces, with the extinguished taper, will come and look at me; but I know them for mockeries, even while I cannot elude their presence, and I fight and grapple with them. For the credit of my imagination, I am almost ashamed to say how tame and prosaic my dreams are grown. They are never romantic, seldom even rural. They are of architecture and of buildings—cities abroad, which I have never seen and hardly have hoped to see. I have traversed, for the seeming length of a natural day, Rome, Amsterdam, Paris, Lisbon—their churches, palaces, squares, market-places, shops, suburbs, ruins, with an inexpressible sense of delight—a map-like distinctness of trace—and a daylight vividness of vision, that was all but being awake.—I have formerly travelled among the Westmoreland fells—my highest Alps,—but they are objects too mighty for the grasp of my dreaming recognition; and I have again and again awoke with ineffectual struggles of the inner eye, to make out a shape, in any way whatever, of Helvellyn. Methought I was in that country, but the mountains were gone. The poverty of my dreams mortifies me. There is Coleridge, at his will can conjure up icy domes, and pleasure-houses for Kubla Khan, and Abyssinian maids, and songs of Abara, and caverns,

> Where Alph, the sacred river, runs,

to solace his night solitudes—when I cannot muster a fiddle. Barry Cornwall has his tritons and his nereids gamboling before him in nocturnal visions, and proclaiming sons born to Neptune—when my stretch of imaginative activity can hardly, in the night season, raise up the ghost of a fish-wife. To set my failures in somewhat a mortifying light—

[1] Mr. Coleridge's Ancient Mariner.

it was after reading the noble Dream of this poet, that my fancy ran strong upon these marine spectra; and the poor plastic power, such as it is, within me set to work, to humour my folly in a sort of dream that very night. Methought I was upon the ocean billows at some sea nuptials, riding and mounted high, with the customary train sounding their conchs before me (I myself, you may be sure, the *leading god*), and jollily we went careering over the main, till just where Ino Leucothea should have greeted me (I think it was Ino) with a white embrace, the billows gradually subsiding, fell from a sea roughness to a sea calm, and thence to a river motion, and that river (as happens in the familiarisation of dreams) was no other than the gentle Thames, which landed me in the wafture of a placid wave or two, alone, safe and inglorious, somewhere at the foot of Lambeth palace.

The degree of the soul's creativeness in sleep might furnish no whimsical criterion of the quantum of poetical faculty resident in the same soul waking. An old gentleman, a friend of mine, and a humourist, used to carry this notion so far, that when he saw any stripling of his acquaintance ambitious of becoming a poet, his first question would be,— "Young man, what sort of dreams have you?" I have so much faith in my old friend's theory, that when I feel that idle vein returning upon me, I presently subside into my proper element of prose, remembering those eluding nereids, and that inauspicious inland landing.

VALENTINE'S DAY

Hail to thy returning festival, old Bishop Valentine! Great is thy name in the rubric, thou venerable Archflamen of Hymen! Immortal Gobetween; who and what manner of person art thou? Art thou but a *name*, typifying the restless principle which impels poor humans to seek perfection in union? or wert thou indeed a mortal prelate, with thy tippet and thy rochet, thy apron on, and decent lawn sleeves? Mysterious personage! like unto thee, assuredly, there is no other mitred father in the calendar; not Jerome, nor Ambrose, nor Cyril; nor the consigner of undipt infants to eternal torments, Austin, whom all mothers hate; nor he who hated all mothers, Origen; nor Bishop Bull, nor Archbishop Parker, nor Whitgift. Thou comest attended with thousands and ten thousands of little Loves, and the air is

> Brush'd with the hiss of rustling wings.

Singing Cupids are thy choristers and thy precentors; and instead of the crosier, the mystical arrow is borne before thee.

In other words, this is the day on which those charming little missives, ycleped Valentines, cross and intercross each other at every street and turning. The weary and all forspent twopenny postman sinks beneath a load of delicate embarrassments, not his own. It is scarcely credible to what an extent this ephemeral courtship is carried on in this loving town, to the great enrichment of porters, and detriment of knockers and bell-wires. In these little visual interpretations, no emblem is so common as the *heart,*—that little three-cornered exponent of all our hopes and fears, —the bestuck and bleeding heart; it is twisted and tortured into more allegories and affectations than an opera-hat. What authority we have in history or mythology for placing the headquarters and metropolis of God Cupid in this anatomical seat rather than in any other, is not very clear; but we have got it, and it will serve as well as any other. Else we might easily imagine, upon some other system which might have pre-vailed for anything which our pathology knows to the contrary, a lover addressing his mistress, in perfect simplicity of feeling, "Madam, my *liver* and fortune are entirely at your disposal"; or putting a delicate question, "Amanda, have you a *midriff* to bestow?" But custom has settled these things, and awarded the seat of sentiment to the aforesaid triangle, while its less fortunate neighbours wait at animal and ana-tomical distance.

Not many sounds in life, and I include all urban and all rural sounds, exceed in interest a *knock at the door.* It "gives a very echo to the throne where hope is seated." But its issues seldom answer to this oracle within. It is so seldom that just the person we want to see comes. But of all the clamorous visitations the welcomest in expectation is the sound that ushers in, or seems to usher in, a Valentine. As the raven himself was hoarse that announced the fatal entrance of Duncan, so the knock of the postman on this day is light, airy, confident, and be-fitting one that bringeth good tidings. It is less mechanical than on other days; you will say, "That is not the post, I am sure." Visions of Love, of Cupids, of Hymens!—delightful eternal common-places, which "hav-ing been will always be"; which no school-boy nor school-man can write away; having your irreversible throne in the fancy and affections—what are your transports, when the happy maiden, opening with careful finger, careful not to break the emblematic seal, bursts upon the sight of some well-designed allegory, some type, some youthful fancy, not without verses—

> Lovers all,
> A madrigal,

or some such device, not over abundant in sense—young Love disclaims it,—and not quite silly—something between wind and water, a chorus where the sheep might almost join the shepherd, as they did, or as I apprehend they did, in Arcadia.

All Valentines are not foolish; and I shall not easily forget thine, my kind friend (if I may have leave to call you so) E. B.—E. B. lived op-posite a young maiden whom he had often seen, unseen, from his parlour window in C—e Street. She was all joyousness and innocence, and just of an age to enjoy receiving a Valentine, and just of a temper to bear the disappointment of missing one with good-humour. E. B. is an artist of no common powers; in the fancy parts of designing, perhaps inferior to none; his name is known at the bottom of many a well-executed vignette in the way of his profession, but no further; for E. B. is modest, and the world meets nobody half-way. E. B. meditated how he could repay this young maiden for many a favour which she had done him unknown; for when a kindly face greets us, though but passing by, and never knows us again, nor we it, we should feel it as an obligation: and E. B. did. This good artist set himself at work to please the damsel. It was just before Valentine's day three years since. He wrought, unseen and unsuspected, a wondrous work. We need not say it was on the finest gilt paper with borders—full, not of common hearts and heartless allegory, but all the prettiest stories of love from Ovid, and older poets than Ovid (for E. B. is a scholar). There was Pyramus and Thisbe, and be sure Dido was not forgot, nor Hero and Leander, and swans more than sang in Cayster, with mottoes and fanciful devices, such as beseemed—a work, in short, of magic. Iris dipt the woof. This on Valentine's eve he commended to the all-swallowing indiscriminate orifice—(O ignoble trust!)—of the common post; but the humble medium did its duty, and from his watchful stand, the next morning he saw the cheerful messenger knock, and by and by the precious charge delivered. He saw, unseen, the happy girl unfold the Valentine, dance about, clap her hands, as one after one the pretty emblems unfolded themselves. She danced about, not with light love, or foolish expectations, for she had no lover; or, if she had, none she knew that could have created those bright images which delighted her. It was more like some fairy present; a God-send, as our familiarly pious ancestors termed a benefit received where the benefactor was unknown. It would do her no harm. It would do her good for ever after. It is good to love the unknown. I only give this as a specimen of E. B. and his modest way of doing a concealed kindness.

Good morrow to my Valentine, sings poor Ophelia; and no better wish, but with better auspices, we wish to all faithful lovers, who are not too wise to despise old legends, but are content to rank themselves humble diocesans of old Bishop Valentine and his true church.

MY RELATIONS

I AM arrived at that point of life at which a man may account it a blessing, as it is a singularity, if he have either of his parents surviving. I have not that felicity—and sometimes think feelingly of a passage in Browne's Christian Morals, where he speaks of a man that hath lived sixty or seventy years in the world. "In such a compass of time," he says, "a man may have a close apprehension what it is to be forgotten, when he hath lived to find none who could remember his father, or scarcely the friends of his youth, and may sensibly see with what a face in no long time OBLIVION will look upon himself."

I had an aunt, a dear and good one. She was one whom single blessedness had soured to the world. She often used to say, that I was the only thing in it which she loved; and, when she thought I was quitting it, she grieved over me with mother's tears. A partiality quite so exclusive my reason cannot altogether approve. She was from morning till night poring over good books, and devotional exercises. Her favourite volumes were, Thomas à Kempis, in Stanhope's translation; and a Roman Catholic Prayer Book, with the *matins* and *complines* regularly set down,—terms which I was at that time too young to understand. She persisted in reading them, although admonished daily concerning their Papistical tendency; and went to church every Sabbath as a good Protestant should do. These were the only books she studied; though, I think at one period of her life, she told me, she had read with great satisfaction the Adventures of an Unfortunate Young Nobleman. Finding the door of the chapel in Essex Street open one day—it was in the infancy of that heresy—she went in, liked the sermon, and the manner of worship, and frequented it at intervals for some time after. She came not for doctrinal points, and never missed them. With some little asperities in her constitution, which I have above hinted at, she was a steadfast, friendly being, and a fine *old Christian*. She was a woman of strong sense, and a shrewd mind—extraordinary at a *repartee;* one of the few occasions of her breaking silence—else she did not much value wit. The only secular employment I remember to have seen her engaged in, was, the splitting of French beans, and dropping them into a china basin of fair water. The odour of those tender vegetables to this day comes back upon my sense, redolent of soothing recollections. Certainly it is the most delicate of culinary operations.

Male aunts, as somebody calls them, I had none—to remember. By the uncle's side I may be said to have been born an orphan. Brother, or sister, I never had any—to know them. A sister, I think, that should have been Elizabeth, died in both our infancies. What a comfort, or what a care, may I not have missed in her!—But I have cousins sprinkled about in Hertfordshire—besides *two*, with whom I have been all my life in habits of the closest intimacy, and whom I may term cousins *par excellence*. These are James and Bridget Elia. They are older than myself by twelve, and ten, years; and neither of them seems disposed, in matters of advice and guidance, to waive any of the prerogatives which primogeniture confers. May they continue still in the same mind; and when they shall be seventy-five, and seventy-three, years old (I cannot spare them sooner), persist in treating me in my grand climacteric precisely as a stripling, or younger brother!

James is an inexplicable cousin. Nature hath her unities, which not every critic can penetrate: or, if we feel, we cannot explain them. The pen of Yorick, and of none since his, could have drawn J. E. entire— those fine Shandean lights and shades, which make up his story. I must limp after in my poor antithetical manner, as the fates have given me grace and talent. J. E. then—to the eye of a common observer at least—seemeth made up of contradictory principles. The genuine child of impulse, the frigid philosopher of prudence—the phlegm of my cousin's doctrine is invariably at war with his temperament, which is high sanguine. With always some fire-new project in his brain, J. E. is the systematic opponent of innovation, and crier down of everything that has not stood the test of age and experiment. With a hundred fine notions chasing one another hourly in his fancy, he is startled at the least approach to the romantic in others: and, determined by his own sense in everything, commends *you* to the guidance of common sense on all occasions.—With a touch of the eccentric in all which he does, or says, he is only anxious that *you* should not commit yourself by doing anything absurd or singular. On my once letting slip at table, that I was not fond of a certain popular dish, he begged me at any rate not to *say* so—for the world would think me mad. He disguises a passionate fondness for works of high art (whereof he hath amassed a choice collection), under the pretext of buying only to sell again—that his enthusiasm may give no encouragement to yours. Yet, if it were so, why does that piece of tender, pastoral Domenichino hang still by his wall?—is the ball of his sight much more dear to him?—or what picture-dealer can talk like him?

Whereas mankind in general are observed to warp their speculative conclusions to the bent of their individual humours, *his* theories are sure to be in diametrical opposition to his conclusions. He is courageous as Charles of Sweden, upon instinct; chary of his person upon principle, as a travelling Quaker. He has been preaching up to me, all my life, the doctrine of bowing to the great—the necessity of forms, and manner, to a man's getting on in the world. He himself never aims at either, that I can discover,—and has a spirit that would stand upright in the presence of the Cham of Tartary. It is pleasant to hear him discourse of patience —extolling it as the truest wisdom—and to see him during the last seven minutes that his dinner is getting ready. Nature never ran up in her haste a more restless piece of workmanship than when she moulded this impetuous cousin—and Art never turned out a more elaborate orator than he can display himself to be, upon his favourite topic of the advantages of quiet and contentedness in the state, whatever it be, that we are placed in. He is triumphant on this theme, when he has you safe in one of those short stages that ply for the western road, in a very obstructing manner, at the foot of John Murray's Street—where you get in when it is empty, and are expected to wait till the vehicle hath completed her just freight—a trying three-quarters of an hour to some people. He wonders at your fidgetiness,—"where could we be better than we are, *thus sitting, thus consulting?*"—"prefers, for his part, a state of rest to locomotion,"—with an eye all the while upon the coachman,—till at length, waxing out of all patience, at *your want of it,* he breaks out into a pathetic remonstrance at the fellow for detaining us so long over the time which he had professed, and declares peremptorily, that "the gentleman in the coach is determined to get out, if he does not drive on that instant."

Very quick at inventing an argument, or detecting a sophistry, he is incapable of attending *you* in any chain of arguing. Indeed, he makes wild work with logic; and seems to jump at most admirable conclusions by some process, not at all akin to it. Consonantly enough to this, he hath been heard to deny, upon certain occasions, that there exists such a faculty at all in man as *reason;* and wondereth how man came first to have a conceit of it—enforcing his negation with all the might of *reasoning* he is master of. He has some speculative notions against laughter, and will maintain that laughing is not natural to *him*—when peradventure the next moment his lungs shall crow like Chanticleer. He says some of the best things in the world—and declareth that wit is his aversion. It was he who said, upon seeing the Eton boys at play in their grounds—*What a pity to think, that these fine ingenuous lads in a few years will all be changed into frivolous Members of Parliament!*

His youth was fiery, glowing, tempestuous—and in age he discovereth no symptom of cooling. This is that which I admire in him. I hate people who meet Time half-way. I am for no compromise with that inevitable spoiler. While he lives, J. E. will take his swing.—It does me good, as I walk towards the street of my daily avocation, on some fine May morning, to meet him marching in a quite opposite direction, with a jolly handsome presence, and shining sanguine face, that indicate some purchase in his eye—a Claude—or a Hobbima—for much of his enviable leisure is consumed at Christie's and Phillips's—or where not, to pick up pictures, and such gauds. On these occasions he mostly stoppeth me, to read a short lecture on the advantage a person like me possesses above himself, in having his time occupied with business which he *must* do—assureth me that he often feels it hang heavy on his hands—wishes he had fewer holidays—and goes off—Westward Ho!—chanting a tune, to Pall Mall—perfectly convinced that he has convinced me—while I proceed in my opposite direction tuneless.

It is pleasant, again, to see this Professor of Indifference doing the honours of his new purchase, when he has fairly housed it. You must view it in every light, till *he* has found the best—placing it at this distance, and at that, but always suiting the focus of your sight to his own. You must spy at it through your fingers, to catch the aërial perspective—though you assure him that to you the landscape shows much more agreeable without that artifice. Woe be to the luckless wight who does not only not respond to his rapture, but who should drop an unseasonable intimation of preferring one of his anterior bargains to the present! —The last is always his best hit—his "Cynthia of the minute."—Alas! how many a mild Madonna have I known to *come in*—a Raphael!—keep its ascendancy for a few brief moons—then, after certain intermedial degradations, from the front drawing-room to the back gallery, thence to the dark parlour,—adopted in turn by each of the Carracci, under successive lowering ascriptions of filiation, mildly breaking its fall—consigned to the oblivious lumber-room, *go out* at last a Lucca Giordano, or plain Carlo Maratti!—which things when I beheld—musing upon the chances and mutabilities of fate below, hath made me to reflect upon the altered condition of great personages, or that woeful Queen of Richard the Second—

                    ————set forth in pomp,
            She came adorned hither like sweet May.
            Sent back like Hallowmass or shortest day.

With great love for *you*, J. E. hath but a limited sympathy with what you feel or do. He lives in a world of his own, and makes slender guesses at what passes in your mind. He never pierces the marrow of your habits. He will tell an old-established play-goer, that Mr. Such-a-one, of So-and-so (naming one of the theatres), is a very lively comedian— as a piece of news! He advertised me but the other day of some pleasant green lanes which he had found out for me, *knowing me to be a great walker*, in my own immediate vicinity—who have haunted the identical spot any time these twenty years!—He has not much respect for that class of feelings which goes by the name of sentimental. He applies the definition of real evil to bodily sufferings exclusively—and rejecteth all others as imaginary. He is affected by the sight, or the bare supposition, of a creature in pain, to a degree which I have never witnessed out of womankind. A constitutional acuteness to this class of sufferings may in part account for this. The animal tribe in particular he taketh under his especial protection. A broken-winded or spur-galled horse is sure to find an advocate in him. An over-loaded ass is his client for ever. He is the apostle to the brute kind—the never-failing friend of those who have none to care for them. The contemplation of a lobster boiled, or eels skinned *alive*, will wring him so, that "all for pity he could die." It will take the savour from his palate, and the rest from his pillow, for days and nights. With the intense feeling of Thomas Clarkson, he wanted only the steadiness of pursuit, and unity of purpose, of that "true yoke-fellow with Time," to have effected as much for the *Animal* as *he* hath done for the *Negro Creation*. But my uncontrollable cousin is but imperfectly formed for purposes which demand co-operation. He cannot wait. His amelioration plans must be ripened in a day. For this reason he has cut but an equivocal figure in benevolent societies, and combinations for the alleviation of human sufferings. His zeal constantly makes him to outrun, and put out, his coadjutors. He thinks of relieving, —while they think of debating. He was black-balled out of a society for the Relief of * * * * * * * * * *, because the fervour of his humanity toiled beyond the formal apprehension, and creeping processes, of his associates. I shall always consider this distinction as a patent of nobility in the Elia family!

Do I mention these seeming inconsistencies to smile at, or upbraid, my unique cousin? Marry, heaven, and all good manners, and the under-

standing that should be between kinsfolk, forbid!—With all the strange-
nesses of this *strangest of the Elias*—I would not have him in one jot or
tittle other than he is; neither would I barter or exchange my wild kinsman for the most exact, regular, and every way consistent kinsman
breathing.

In my next, reader, I may perhaps give you some account of my
cousin Bridget—if you are not already surfeited with cousins—and take
you by the hand, if you are willing to go with us, on an excursion which
we made a summer or two since, in search of *more cousins*—

Through the green plains of pleasant Hertfordshire.

MACKERY END, IN HERTFORDSHIRE

BRIDGET ELIA has been my housekeeper for many a long year. I have
obligations to Bridget, extending beyond the period of memory. We
house together, old bachelor and maid, in a sort of double singleness;
with such tolerable comfort, upon the whole, that I, for one, find in
myself no sort of disposition to go out upon the mountains, with the rash
king's offspring, to bewail my celibacy. We agree pretty well in our
tastes and habits—yet so, as "with a difference." We are generally in
harmony, with occasional bickerings—as it should be among near relations. Our sympathies are rather understood than expressed; and once,
upon my dissembling a tone in my voice more kind than ordinary, my
cousin burst into tears, and complained that I was altered. We are both
great readers in different directions. While I am hanging over (for the
thousandth time) some passage in old Burton, or one of his strange
contemporaries, she is abstracted in some modern tale, or adventure,
whereof our common reading-table is daily fed with assiduously fresh
supplies. Narrative teases me. I have little concern in the progress of
events. She must have a story—well, ill, or indifferently told—so there
be life stirring in it, and plenty of good or evil accidents. The fluctuations of fortune in fiction—and almost in real life—have ceased to interest, or operate but dully upon me. Out-of-the-way humours and opinions—heads with some diverting twist in them—the oddities of authorship, please me most. My cousin has a native disrelish of anything that
sounds odd or bizarre. Nothing goes down with her that is quaint, irregular, or out of the road of common sympathy. She "holds Nature more
clever." I can pardon her blindness to the beautiful obliquities of the
Religio Medici; but she must apologise to me for certain disrespectful
insinuations, which she has been pleased to throw out latterly, touching
the intellectuals of a dear favourite of mine, of the last century but one
—the thrice noble, chaste, and virtuous, but again somewhat fantastical
and original-brained, generous Margaret Newcastle.

It has been the lot of my cousin, oftener perhaps than I could have wished, to have had for her associates and mine, free-thinkers—leaders, and disciples, of novel philosophies and systems; but she neither wrangles with, nor accepts, their opinions. That which was good and venerable to her, when a child, retains its authority over her mind still. She never juggles or plays tricks with her understanding.

We are both of us inclined to be a little too positive; and I have observed the result of our disputes to be almost uniformly this—that in matters of fact, dates, and circumstances, it turns out, that I was in the right, and my cousin in the wrong. But where we have differed upon moral points; upon something proper to be done, or let alone; whatever heat of opposition, or steadiness of conviction, I set out with, I am sure always, in the long-run, to be brought over to her way of thinking.

I must touch upon the foibles of my kinswoman with a gentle hand, for Bridget does not like to be told of her faults. She hath an awkward trick (to say no worse of it) of reading in company: at which times she will answer *yes* or *no* to a question, without fully understanding its purport—which is provoking, and derogatory in the highest degree to the dignity of the putter of the said question. Her presence of mind is equal to the most pressing trials of life, but will sometimes desert her upon trifling occasions. When the purpose requires it, and is a thing of moment, she can speak to it greatly; but in matters which are not stuff of the conscience, she hath been known sometimes to let slip a word less seasonably.

Her education in youth was not much attended to; and she happily missed all that train of female garniture which passeth by the name of accomplishments. She was tumbled early, by accident or design, into a spacious closet of good old English reading, without much selection or prohibition, and browsed at will upon that fair and wholesome pasturage. Had I twenty girls, they should be brought up exactly in this fashion. I know not whether their chance in wedlock might not be diminished by it; but I can answer for it, that it makes (if the worst come to the worst) most incomparable old maids.

In a season of distress, she is the truest comforter; but in the teasing accidents, and minor perplexities, which do not call out the *will* to meet them, she sometimes maketh matters worse by an excess of participation. If she does not always divide your trouble, upon the pleasanter occasions of life she is sure always to treble your satisfaction. She is excellent to be at a play with, or upon a visit; but best, when she goes a journey with you.

We made an excursion together a few summers since, into Hertfordshire, to beat up the quarters of some of our less-known relations in that fine corn country.

The oldest thing I remember is Mackery End; or Mackarel End, as it is spelt, perhaps more properly, in some old maps of Hertfordshire; a farm-house,—delightfully situated within a gentle walk from Wheat-hampstead. I can just remember having been there, on a visit to a great-aunt, when I was a child, under the care of Bridget; who, as I have said, is older than myself by some ten years. I wish that I could throw into a heap the remainder of our joint existences; that we might share them in equal division. But that is impossible. The house was at that time in the occupation of a substantial yeoman, who had married my grandmother's sister. His name was Gladman. My grandmother was Bruton, married to a Field. The Gladmans and the Brutons are still flourishing in that part of the county, but the Fields are almost extinct. More than forty years had elapsed since the visit I speak of; and, for the greater portion of that period, we had lost sight of the other two branches also. Who or what sort of persons inherited Mackery End—kindred or strange folk— we were afraid almost to conjecture, but determined some day to explore.

By somewhat a circuitous route, taking the noble park at Luton in our way from St. Albans, we arrived at the spot of our anxious curiosity about noon. The sight of the old farm-house, though every trace of it was effaced from my recollection, affected me with a pleasure which I had not experienced for many a year. For though *I* had forgotten it, *we* had never forgotten being there together, and we had been talking about Mackery End all our lives, till memory on my part became mocked with a phantom of itself, and I thought I knew the aspect of a place, which, when present, O how unlike it was to *that*, which I had conjured up so many times instead of it!

Still the air breathed balmily about it; the season was in "the heart of June," and I could say with the poet,

> But thou, that didst appear so fair
> To fond imagination,
> Dost rival in the light of day
> Her delicate creation!

Bridget's was more a waking bliss than mine, for she easily remembered her old acquaintance again—some altered features, of course, a little grudged at. At first, indeed, she was ready to disbelieve for joy; but the scene soon re-confirmed itself in her affections—and she traversed every outpost of the old mansion, to the wood-house, the orchard, the place where the pigeon-house had stood (house and birds were alike flown)—with a breathless impatience of recognition, which was more pardonable perhaps than decorous at the age of fifty odd. But Bridget in some things is behind her years.

The only thing left was to get into the house—and that was a difficulty which to me singly would have been insurmountable; for I am terribly shy in making myself known to strangers and out-of-date kinsfolk. Love, stronger than scruple, winged my cousin in without me; but she soon returned with a creature that might have sat to a sculptor for the image of Welcome. It was the youngest of the Gladmans; who, by marriage with a Bruton, had become mistress of the old mansion. A comely brood are the Brutons. Six of them, females, were noted as the handsomest young women in the county. But this adopted Bruton, in my mind, was better than they all—more comely. She was born too late to have remembered me. She just recollected in early life to have had her cousin Bridget once pointed out to her, climbing a stile. But the name of kindred, and of cousinship, was enough. Those slender ties, that prove slight as gossamer in the rending atmosphere of a metropolis, bind faster, as we found it, in hearty, homely, loving Hertfordshire. In five minutes we were as thoroughly acquainted as if we had been born and bred up together; were familiar, even to the calling each other by our Christian names. So Christians should call one another. To have seen Bridget, and her—it was like the meeting of the two scriptural cousins! There was a grace and dignity, an amplitude of form and stature, answering to her mind, in this farmer's wife, which would have shined in a palace—or so we thought it. We were made welcome by husband and wife equally—we, and our friend that was with us.—I had almost forgotten him—but B. F. will not so soon forget that meeting, if peradventure he shall read this on the far distant shores where the kangaroo haunts. The fatted calf was made ready, or rather was already so, as if in anticipation of our coming; and, after an appropriate glass of native wine, never let me forget with what honest pride this hospitable cousin made us proceed to Wheathampstead, to introduce us (as some new-found rarity) to her mother and sister Gladmans, who did indeed know something more of us, at a time when she almost knew nothing.—With what corresponding kindness we were received by them also—how Bridget's memory, exalted by the occasion, warmed into a thousand half-obliterated recollections of things and persons, to my utter astonishment, and her own—and to the astoundment of B. F., who sat by, almost the only thing that was not a cousin there,—old effaced images of more than half-forgotten names and circumstances still crowding back upon her, as words written in lemon come out upon exposure to a friendly warmth,— when I forget all this, then may my country cousins forget me; and Bridget no more remember, that in the days of weakling infancy I was her tender charge—as I have been her care in foolish manhood since—in those pretty pastoral walks, long ago, about Mackery End, in Hertfordshire.

MY FIRST PLAY

At the north end of Cross Court there yet stands a portal, of some architectural pretensions, though reduced to humble use, serving at present for an entrance to a printing-office. This old door-way, if you are young, reader, you may not know was the identical pit entrance to old Drury— Garrick's Drury—all of it that is left. I never pass it without shaking some forty years from off my shoulders, recurring to the evening when I passed through it to see *my first play*. The afternoon had been wet, and the condition of our going (the elder folks and myself) was, that the rain should cease. With what a beating heart did I watch from the window the puddles, from the stillness of which I was taught to prognosticate the desired cessation! I seem to remember the last spurt, and the glee with which I ran to announce it.

We went with orders, which my godfather F. had sent us. He kept the oil shop (now Davies's) at the corner of Featherstone Buildings, in Holborn. F. was a tall grave person, lofty in speech, and had pretensions above his rank. He associated in those days with John Palmer, the comedian, whose gait and bearing he seemed to copy; if John (which is quite as likely) did not rather borrow somewhat of his manner from my godfather. He was also known to, and visited by, Sheridan. It was to his house in Holborn that young Brinsley brought his first wife on her elopement with him from a boarding-school at Bath—the beautiful Maria Linley. My parents were present (over a quadrille table) when he arrived in the evening with his harmonious charge. From either of these connexions it may be inferred that my godfather could command an order for the then Drury Lane theatre at pleasure—and, indeed, a pretty liberal issue of those cheap billets, in Brinsley's easy autograph, I have heard him say was the sole remuneration which he had received for many years' nightly illumination of the orchestra and various avenues of that theatre—and he was content it should be so. The honour of Sheridan's familiarity—or supposed familiarity—was better to my godfather than money.

F. was the most gentlemanly of oilmen; grandiloquent, yet courteous. His delivery of the commonest matters of fact was Ciceronian. He had two Latin words almost constantly in his mouth (how odd sounds Latin from an oilman's lips!), which my better knowledge since has enabled me to correct. In strict pronunciation they should have been sounded *vice versâ*—but in those young years they impressed me with more awe than they would now do, read aright from Seneca or Varro—in his own peculiar pronunciation, monosyllabically elaborated, or Anglicised, into something like *verse verse*. By an imposing manner, and the help of these distorted syllables, he climbed (but that was little) to the highest parochial honours which St. Andrew's has to bestow.

He is dead—and thus much I thought due to his memory, both for my first orders (little wondrous talismans!—slight keys, and insignificant to outward sight, but opening to me more than Arabian paradises!) and moreover that by his testamentary beneficence I came into possession of the only landed property which I could ever call my own—situate near the road-way village of pleasant Puckeridge, in Hertfordshire. When I journeyed down to take possession, and planted foot on my own ground, the stately habits of the donor descended upon me, and I strode (shall I confess the vanity?) with larger paces over my allotment of three-quarters of an acre, with its commodious mansion in the midst, with the feeling of an English freeholder that all betwixt sky and centre was my own. The estate has passed into more prudent hands, and nothing but an agrarian can restore it.

In those days were pit orders. Beshrew the uncomfortable manager who abolished them!—with one of these we went. I remember the waiting at the door—not that which is left—but between that and an inner door in shelter—O when shall I be such an expectant again!—with the cry of nonpareils, an indispensable play-house accompaniment in those days. As near as I can recollect, the fashionable pronunciation of the theatrical fruiteresses then was, "Chase some oranges, chase some numparels, chase a bill of the play";—chase *pro* chuse. But when we got in, and I beheld the green curtain that veiled a heaven to my imagination, which was soon to be disclosed—the breathless anticipations I endured! I had seen something like it in the plate prefixed to Troilus and Cressida, in Rowe's Shakspeare—the tent scene with Diomede—and a sight of that plate can always bring back in a measure the feeling of that evening.—The boxes at that time, full of well-dressed women of quality, projected over the pit: and the pilasters reaching down were adorned with a glistering substance (I know not what) under glass (as it seemed), resembling—a homely fancy—but I judged it to be sugarcandy—yet, to my raised imagination, divested of its homelier qualities, it appeared a glorified candy!—The orchestra lights at length arose, those "fair Auroras"! Once the bell sounded. It was to ring out yet once again—and, incapable of the anticipation, I reposed my shut eyes in a sort of resignation upon the maternal lap. It rang the second time. The curtain drew up—I was not past six years old, and the play was Artaxerxes!

I had dabbled a little in the Universal History—the ancient part of it—and here was the court of Persia.—It was being admitted to a sight of the past. I took no proper interest in the action going on, for I understood not its import—but I heard the word Darius, and I was in the midst of Daniel. All feeling was absorbed in vision. Gorgeous vests, gardens, palaces, princesses, passed before me. I knew not players. I was in Persepolis for the time, and the burning idol of their devotion almost converted me into a worshipper. I was awe-struck, and believed those significations to be something more than elemental fires. It was all enchantment and a dream. No such pleasure has since visited me but in dreams.—Harlequin's invasion followed; where, I remember, the transformation of the magistrates into reverend beldams seemed to me a piece of grave historic justice, and the tailor carrying his own head to be as sober a verity as the legend of St. Denys.

The next play to which I was taken was the Lady of the Manor, of which, with the exception of some scenery, very faint traces are left in my memory. It was followed by a pantomine, called Lun's Ghost—a satiric touch, I apprehend, upon Rich, not long since dead—but to my apprehension (too sincere for satire), Lun was as remote a piece of antiquity as Lud—the father of a line of Harlequins—transmitting his dagger of lath (the wooden sceptre) through countless ages. I saw the primeval Motley come from his silent tomb in a ghastly vest of white patchwork, like the apparition of a dead rainbow. So Harlequins (thought I) look when they are dead.

My third play followed in quick succession. It was the Way of the World. I think I must have sat at it as grave as a judge; for, I remember, the hysteric affectations of good Lady Wishfort affected me like some solemn tragic passion. Robinson Crusoe followed; in which Crusoe, man Friday, and the parrot were as good and authentic as in the story.— The clownery and pantaloonery of these pantomimes have clean passed out of my head. I believe, I no more laughed at them, than at the same age I should have been disposed to laugh at the grotesque Gothic heads (seeming to me then replete with devout meaning) that gape, and grin, in stone around the inside of the old Roman Church (my church) of the Templars.

I saw these plays in the season 1781-2, when I was from six to seven years old. After the intervention of six or seven other years (for at school all play-going was inhibited) I again entered the doors of a theatre. That old Artaxerxes evening had never done ringing in my fancy. I expected the same feelings to come again with the same occasion. But we differ from ourselves less at sixty and sixteen, than the latter does from six. In that interval what had I not lost! At the first period I knew nothing, understood nothing, discriminated nothing. I felt all, loved all, wondered all—

Was nourished, I could not tell how—

I had left the temple a devotee, and was returned a rationalist. The same things were there materially; but the emblem, the reference, was gone! —The green curtain was no longer a veil, drawn between two worlds, the unfolding of which was to bring back past ages to present a "royal ghost,"—but a certain quantity of green baize, which was to separate the audience for a given time from certain of their fellowmen who were to come forward and pretend those parts. The lights—the orchestra lights—came up a clumsy machinery. The first ring, and the second ring, was now but a trick of the prompter's bell—which had been, like the note of the cuckoo, a phantom of a voice, no hand seen or guessed at which ministered to its warning. The actors were men and women painted. I thought the fault was in them; but it was in myself, and the alteration which those many centuries—of six short twelvemonths—had wrought in me.—Perhaps it was fortunate for me that the play of the evening was but an indifferent comedy, as it gave me time to crop some unreasonable expectations, which might have interfered with the genuine emotions with which I was soon after enabled to enter upon the first appearance to me of Mrs. Siddons in Isabella. Comparison and retrospection soon yielded to the present attraction of the scene; and the theatre became to me, upon a new stock, the most delightful of recreations.

MODERN GALLANTRY

IN comparing modern with ancient manners, we are pleased to compliment ourselves upon the point of gallantry; a certain obsequiousness, or deferential respect, which we are supposed to pay to females, as females.

I shall believe that this principle actuates our conduct, when I can forget, that in the nineteenth century of the era from which we date our civility, we are but just beginning to leave off the very frequent practice of whipping females in public, in common with the coarsest male offenders.

I shall believe it to be influential, when I can shut my eyes to the fact, that in England women are still occasionally—hanged.

I shall believe in it, when actresses are no longer subject to be hissed off a stage by gentlemen.

I shall believe in it, when Dorimant hands a fish-wife across the kennel; or assists the apple-woman to pick up her wandering fruit, which some unlucky dray has just dissipated.

I shall believe in it, when the Dorimants in humbler life, who would be thought in their way notable adepts in this refinement, shall act upon it in places where they are not known, or think themselves not observed —when I shall see the traveller for some rich tradesman part with his admired box-coat, to spread it over the defenceless shoulders of the poor woman, who is passing to her parish on the roof of the same stage-coach with him, drenched in the rain—when I shall no longer see a woman standing up in the pit of a London theatre, till she is sick and faint with the exertion, with men about her, seated at their ease, and jeering at her distress; till one, that seems to have more manners or conscience than the rest, significantly declares "she should be welcome to his seat, if she were a little younger and handsomer." Place this dapper warehouseman, or that rider, in a circle of their own female acquaintance, and you shall confess you have not seen a politer-bred man in Lothbury.

Lastly, I shall begin to believe that there is some such principle influencing our conduct, when more than one-half of the drudgery and coarse servitude of the world shall cease to be performed by women.

Until that day comes, I shall never believe this boasted point to be anything more than a conventional fiction; a pageant got up between the sexes, in a certain rank, and at a certain time of life, in which both find their account equally.

I shall be even disposed to rank it among the salutary fictions of life, when in polite circles I shall see the same attentions paid to age as to youth, to homely features as to handsome, to coarse complexions as to clear—to the woman, as she is a woman, not as she is a beauty, a fortune, or a title.

I shall believe it to be something more than a name, when a well-dressed gentleman in a well-dressed company can advert to the topic of *female old age* without exciting, and intending to excite, a sneer:—when the phrases "antiquated virginity," and such a one has "overstood her market," pronounced in good company, shall raise immediate offence in man, or woman, that shall hear them spoken.

Joseph Paice, of Bread Street Hill, merchant, and one of the Directors of the South-Sea Company—the same to whom Edwards, the Shakspeare commentator, has addressed a fine sonnet—was the only pattern of consistent gallantry I have met with. He took me under his shelter at an early age, and bestowed some pains upon me. I owe to his precepts and example whatever there is of the man of business (and that is not much) in my composition. It was not his fault that I did not profit more. Though bred a Presbyterian, and brought up a merchant, he was the finest gentleman of his time. He had not *one* system of attention to females in the drawing-room, and *another* in the shop, or at the stall. I do not mean that he made no distinction. But he never lost sight of sex, or overlooked it in the casualties of a disadvantageous situation. I have seen him stand bareheaded—smile if you please—to a poor servant-girl, while she has been inquiring of him the way to some street—in such a posture of unforced civility, as neither to embarrass her in the acceptance, nor himself in the offer, of it. He was no dangler, in the common acceptation of the word, after women: but he reverenced and upheld, in every form in which it came before him, *womanhood*. I have seen him—nay, smile not—tenderly escorting a market-woman, whom he had encountered in a shower, exalting his umbrella over her poor basket of fruit, that it might receive no damage, with as much carefulness as if she had been a Countess. To the reverend form of Female Eld he would yield the wall (though it were to an ancient beggar-woman) with more ceremony than he can afford to show our grandams. He was the Preux Chevalier of Age; the Sir Calidore, or Sir Tristan, to those who have no Calidores or Tristans to defend them. The roses, that had long faded thence, still bloomed for him in those withered and yellow cheeks.

He was never married, but in his youth he paid his addresses to the beautiful Susan Winstanley—old Winstanley's daughter of Clapton—who dying in the early days of their courtship, confirmed in him the resolution of perpetual bachelorship. It was during their short courtship, he told me, that he had been one day treating his mistress with a profusion of civil speeches—the common gallantries—to which kind of thing she had hitherto manifested no repugnance—but in this instance with no effect. He could not obtain from her a decent acknowledgment in return. She rather seemed to resent his compliments. He could not set it down to caprice, for the lady had always shown herself above that littleness. When he ventured on the following day, finding her a little better humoured, to expostulate with her on her coldness of yesterday, she confessed, with her usual frankness, that she had no sort of dislike to his attentions; that she could even endure some high-flown compliments; that a young woman placed in her situation had a right to expect all sort of civil things said to her; that she hoped she could digest a dose of adulation, short of insincerity, with as little injury to her humility as most young women; but that—a little before he had commenced his compliments—she had overheard him by accident, in rather rough language, rating a young woman, who had not brought home his cravats quite to the appointed time, and she thought to herself, "As I am Miss Susan Winstanley, and a young lady—a reputed beauty, and known to be a fortune—I can have my choice of the finest speeches from the mouth of this very fine gentleman who is courting me,—but if I had been poor Mary Such-a-one (*naming the milliner*)—and had failed of bringing home the cravats to the appointed hour—though perhaps I had sat up half the night to forward them—what sort of compliments should I have received then?—And my woman's pride came to my assistance; and I thought, that if it were only to do *me* honour, a female, like myself, might have received handsomer usage: and I was determined not to accept any fine speeches, to the compromise of that sex, the belonging to which was after all my strongest claim and title to them."

I think the lady discovered both generosity, and a just way of thinking, in this rebuke which she gave her lover; and I have sometimes imagined, that the uncommon strain of courtesy, which through life regulated the actions and behaviour of my friend towards all of womankind indiscriminately, owed its happy origin to this seasonable lesson from the lips of his lamented mistress.

I wish the whole female world would entertain the same notion of these things that Miss Winstanley showed. Then we should see something of the spirit of consistent gallantry; and no longer witness the anomaly of the same man—a pattern of true politeness to a wife—of cold contempt, or rudeness, to a sister—the idolater of his female mistress— the disparager and despiser of his no less female aunt, or unfortunate— still female—maiden cousin. Just so much respect as a woman derogates from her own sex, in whatever condition placed—her hand-maid, or dependant—she deserves to have diminished from herself on that score; and probably will feel the diminution, when youth, and beauty, and advantages, not inseparable from sex, shall lose of their attraction. What a woman should demand of a man in courtship, or after it, is first—respect for her as she is a woman;—and next to that—to be respected by him above all other women. But let her stand upon her female character as upon a foundation; and let the attentions, incident to individual preference, to so many pretty additaments and ornaments—as many, and as fanciful, as you please—to that main structure. Let her first lesson be with sweet Susan Winstanley—to *reverence her sex*.

THE OLD BENCHERS OF THE INNER TEMPLE

I was born, and passed the first seven years of my life, in the Temple. Its church, its halls, its gardens, its fountain, its river, I had almost said —for in those young years, what was this king of rivers to me but a stream that watered our pleasant places?—these are of my oldest recollections. I repeat, to this day, no verses to myself more frequently, or with kindlier emotion, than those of Spenser, where he speaks of this spot.

> There when they came, whereas those bricky towers,
> The which on Themmes brode aged back doth ride,
> Where now the studious lawyers have their bowers,
> There whylome wont the Templer knights to bide,
> Till they decayed through pride.

Indeed, it is the most elegant spot in the metropolis. What a transition for a countryman visiting London for the first time—the passing from the crowded Strand or Fleet Street, by unexpected avenues, into its magnificent ample squares, its classic green recesses! What a cheerful, liberal look hath that portion of it, which, from three sides, overlooks the greater garden; that goodly pile

> Of building strong, albeit of Paper hight,

confronting with massy contrast, the lighter, older, more fantastically shrouded one, named of Harcourt, with the cheerful Crown Office Row (place of my kindly engendure), right opposite the stately stream, which washes the garden-foot with her yet scarcely trade-polluted waters, and seems but just weaned from her Twickenham Naïades! a man would give something to have been born in such places. What a collegiate aspect has that fine Elizabethan hall, where the fountain plays, which I have made to rise and fall, how many times! to the astoundment of the young urchins, my contemporaries, who, not being able to guess at its recondite machinery, were almost tempted to hail the wondrous work as magic! What an antique air had the now almost effaced sundials, with their moral inscriptions, seeming coevals with that Time which they measured, and to take their revelations of its flight immediately from heaven, holding correspondence with the fountain of light! How would the dark line steal imperceptibly on, watched by the eye of childhood, eager to detect its movement, never catched, nice as an evanescent cloud, or the first arrests of sleep!

> Ah! yet doth beauty like a dial hand
> Steal from his figure, and no pace perceived!

What a dead thing is a clock, with its ponderous embowelments of lead and brass, its pert or solemn dulness of communication, compared with the simple altar-like structure, and silent heart-language of the old dial! It stood as the garden god of Christian gardens. Why is it almost everywhere vanished? If its business-use be superseded by more elaborate inventions, its moral uses, its beauty, might have pleaded for its continuance. It spoke of moderate labours, of pleasures not protracted after sun-set, of temperance, and good hours. It was the primitive clock, the horologe of the first world. Adam could scarce have missed it in Paradise. It was the measure appropriate for sweet plants and flowers to spring by, for the birds to apportion their silver warblings by, for flocks to pasture and be led to fold by. The shepherd "carved it out quaintly in the sun"; and, turning philosopher by the very occupation, provided it with mottoes more touching than tomb-stones. It was a pretty device of the gardener, recorded by Marvell, who, in the days of artificial gardening, made a dial out of herbs and flowers. I must quote his verses a little higher up, for they are full, as all his serious poetry was, of a witty delicacy. They will not come in awkwardly, I hope, in a talk of fountains and sun-dials. He is speaking of sweet garden scenes:—

> What wondrous life is this I lead!
> Ripe apples drop about my head.
> The luscious clusters of the vine
> Upon my mouth do crush their wine.
> The nectarine, and curious peach,
> Into my hands themselves do reach.
> Stumbling on melons, as I pass,
> Insnared with flowers, I fall on grass.
> Meanwhile the mind from pleasure less
> Withdraws into its happiness.
> The mind, that ocean, where each kind
> Does straight its own resemblance find;
> Yet it creates, transcending these,
> Far other worlds and other seas;
> Annihilating all that's made
> To a green thought in a green shade.
> Here at the fountain's sliding foot,
> Or at some fruit-tree's mossy root,
> Casting the body's vest aside,
> My soul into the boughs does glide;
> There, like a bird, it sits and sings,
> Then wets and claps its silver wings,
> And, till prepared for longer flight,
> Waves in its plumes the various light.
> How well the skilful gardener drew,
> Of flowers and herbs, this dial new!
> Where, from above, the milder sun
> Does through a fragrant zodiac run:
> And, as it works, the industrious bee
> Computes its time as well as we.
> How could such sweet and wholesome hours
> Be reckon'd, but with herbs and flowers?[1]

The artificial fountains of the metropolis are, in like manner, fast vanishing. Most of them are dried up or bricked over. Yet, where one is left, as in that little green nook behind the South-Sea House, what a

[1] From a copy of verses entitled The Garden.

freshness it gives to the dreary pile! Four little winged marble boys used to play their virgin fancies, spouting out ever fresh streams from their innocent-wanton lips in the square of Lincoln's Inn, when I was no bigger than they were figured. They are gone, and the spring choked up. The fashion, they tell me, is gone by, and these things are esteemed childish. Why not, then, gratify children, by letting them stand? Lawyers, I suppose, were children once. They are awakening images to them at least. Why must everything smack of man and mannish? Is the world all grown up? Is childhood dead? Or is there not in the bosoms of the wisest and the best some of the child's heart left, to respond to its earliest enchantments? The figures were grotesque. Are the stiff-wigged living figures, that still flitter and chatter about that area, less Gothic in appearance? or is the splutter of their hot rhetoric one-half so refreshing and innocent as the little cool playful streams those exploded cherubs uttered?

They have lately gothicised the entrance to the Inner Temple, and the library front; to assimilate them, I suppose, to the body of the hall, which they do not at all resemble. What is become of the winged horse that stood over the former? a stately arms! and who has removed those frescoes of the Virtues, which Italianised the end of the Paper Buildings?—my first hint of allegory! They must account to me for these things, which I miss so greatly.

The terrace is, indeed, left, which we used to call the parade; but the traces are passed away of the footsteps which made its pavement awful! It is become common and profane. The old benchers had it almost sacred to themselves, in the forepart of the day at least. They might not be sided or jostled. Their air and dress asserted the parade. You left wide spaces betwixt you when you passed them. We walk on even terms with their successors. The roguish eye of J——ll, ever ready to be delivered of a jest, almost invites a stranger to vie a repartee with it. But what insolent familiar durst have mated Thomas Coventry?—whose person was a quadrate, his step massy and elephantine, his face square as the lion's, his gait peremptory and path-keeping, indivertible from his way as a moving column, the scarecrow of his inferiors, the browbeater of equals and superiors, who made a solitude of children wherever he came, for they fled his insufferable presence, as they would have shunned an Elisha bear. His growl was as thunder in their ears, whether he spake to them in mirth or in rebuke; his invitatory notes being, indeed, of all, the most repulsive and horrid. Clouds of snuff, aggravating the natural terrors of his speech, broke from each majestic nostril, darkening the air. He took it, not by pinches, but a palmful at once,—diving for it under the mighty flaps of his old-fashioned waistcoat pocket; his waistcoat red and angry, his coat dark rappee, tinctured by dye original, and by adjuncts, with buttons of obsolete gold. And so he paced the terrace.

By his side a milder form was sometimes to be seen; the pensive gentility of Samuel Salt. They were coevals, and had nothing but that and their benchership in common. In politics Salt was a whig, and Coventry a staunch tory. Many a sarcastic growl did the latter cast out—for Coventry had a rough spinous humour—at the political confederates of his associate, which rebounded from the gentle bosom of the latter like cannon-balls from wool. You could not ruffle Samuel Salt.

S. had the reputation of being a very clever man, and of excellent discernment in the chamber practice of the law. I suspect his knowledge did not amount to much. When a case of difficult disposition of money, testamentary or otherwise, came before him, he ordinarily handed it over, with a few instructions, to his man Lovel, who was a quick little fellow, and would despatch it out of hand by the light of natural understanding, of which he had an uncommon share. It was incredible what repute for talents S. enjoyed by the mere trick of gravity. He was a shy man; a child might pose him in a minute—indolent and procrastinating to the last degree. Yet men would give him credit for vast application, in spite of himself. He was not to be trusted with himself with impunity. He never dressed for a dinner party but he forgot his sword—they wore swords then—or some other necessary part of his equipage. Lovel had his eye upon him on all these occasions, and ordinarily gave him his cue. If there was anything which he could speak unseasonably, he was sure to do it.—He was to dine at a relative's of the unfortunate Miss Blandy on the day of her execution;—and L., who had a wary foresight of his probable hallucinations, before he set out schooled him, with great anxiety, not in any possible manner to allude to her story that day. S. promised faithfully to observe the injunction. He had not been seated in the parlour, where the company was expecting the dinner summons, four minutes, when, a pause in the conversation ensuing, he got up, looked out of window, and pulling down his ruffles—an ordinary motion with him—observed, "it was a gloomy day," and added, "Miss Blandy must be hanged by this time, I suppose." Instances of this sort were perpetual. Yet S. was thought by some of the greatest men of his time a fit person to be consulted, not alone in matters pertaining to the law, but in the ordinary niceties and embarrassments of conduct—from force of manner entirely. He never laughed. He had the same good fortune among the female world,—was a known toast with the ladies, and one or two are said to have died for love of him—I suppose, because he never trifled or talked gallantry with them, or paid them, indeed, hardly common attentions. He had a fine face and person, but wanted, methought, the spirit that should have shown them off with advantage to the women. His eye lacked lustre.—Not so, thought Susan P——; who, at the advanced age of sixty, was seen, in the cold evening time, unaccompanied, wetting the pavement of B——d Row, with tears that fell in drops which might be heard, because her friend had died that day—he, whom she had pursued with a hopeless passion for the last forty years—a passion which years could not extinguish or abate; nor the long-resolved, yet gently-enforced, puttings-off of unrelenting bachelorhood dissuade from its cherished purpose. Mild Susan P——, thou hast now thy friend in heaven!

Thomas Coventry was a cadet of the noble family of that name. He passed his youth in contracted circumstances, which gave him early those parsimonious habits which in after life never forsook him, so that with one windfall or another, about the time I knew him he was master of four or five hundred thousand pounds; nor did he look or walk worth a moidore less. He lived in a gloomy house opposite the pump in Serjeant's Inn, Fleet Street. J., the counsel, is doing self-imposed penance in it, for what reason I divine not, at this day. C. had an agreeable seat at North Cray, where he seldom spent above a day or two at a time in the summer; but preferred, during the hot months, standing at his window in this damp, close, well-like mansion, to watch, as he said, "the maids drawing water all day long." I suspect he had his within-door reasons for the preference. *Hic currus et arma fuêre.* He might think his treasures more safe. His house had the aspect of a strong-box. C. was a close hunks—a hoarder rather than a miser—or, if a miser, none of the mad Elwes breed, who have brought discredit upon a character which cannot exist without certain admirable points of steadiness and unity of purpose. One may hate a true miser, but cannot, I suspect, so easily despise him. By taking care of the pence he is often enabled to part with the pounds, upon a scale that leaves us careless generous fellows halting at an immeasurable distance behind. C. gave away £30,000 at once in his lifetime to a blind charity. His housekeeping was severely looked after, but he kept the table of a gentleman. He would know who came in and who went out of his house, but his kitchen chimney was never suffered to freeze.

Salt was his opposite in this, as in all—never knew what he was worth in the world; and having but a competency for his rank, which his indolent habits were little calculated to improve, might have suffered severely if he had not had honest people about him. Lovel took care of everything. He was at once his clerk, his good servant, his dresser, his friend, his "flapper," his guide, stop-watch, auditor, treasurer. He did nothing without consulting Lovel, or failed in anything without expecting and fearing his admonishing. He put himself almost too much in his hands, had they not been the purest in the world. He resigned his title almost to respect as a master, if L. could ever have forgotten for a moment that he was a servant.

I knew this Lovel. He was a man of an incorrigible and losing honesty. A good fellow withal, and "would strike." In the cause of the oppressed he never considered inequalities, or calculated the number of his opponents. He once wrested a sword out of the hand of a man of quality that had drawn upon him, and pommelled him severely with the hilt of it. The swordsman had offered insult to a female—an occasion upon which no odds against him could have prevented the interference of Lovel. He would stand next day bareheaded to the same person modestly to excuse his interference—for L. never forgot rank where something better was not concerned. L. was the liveliest little fellow breathing, had a face as gay as Garrick's, whom he was said greatly to

resemble (I have a portrait of him which confirms it), possessed a fine
turn for humorous poetry—next to Swift and Prior—moulded heads in
clay or plaster of Paris to admiration, by the dint of natural genius
merely; turned cribbage boards, and such small cabinet toys, to perfection; took a hand at quadrille or bowls with equal facility; made
punch better than any man of his degree in England; had the merriest
quips and conceits; and was altogether as brimful of rogueries and inventions as you could desire. He was a brother of the angle, moreover,
and just such a free, hearty, honest companion as Mr. Izaak Walton
would have chosen to go a-fishing with. I saw him in his old age and
the decay of his faculties, palsy-smitten, in the last sad stage of human
weakness—"a remnant most forlorn of what he was,"—yet even then his
eye would light up upon the mention of his favourite Garrick. He was
greatest, he would say, in Bayes—"was upon the stage nearly throughout the whole performance, and as busy as a bee." At intervals, too, he
would speak of his former life, and how he came up a little boy from
Lincoln, to go to service, and how his mother cried at parting with him,
and how he returned, after some years' absence, in his smart new livery,
to see her, and she blessed herself at the change, and could hardly be
brought to believe that it was "her own bairn." And then, the excitement subsiding, he would weep, till I have wished that sad second-
childhood might have a mother still to lay its head upon her lap. But
the common mother of us all in no long time after received him gently
into hers.

With Coventry, and with Salt, in their walks upon the terrace, most
commonly Peter Pierson would join to make up a third. They did not
walk linked arm-in-arm in those days—"as now our stout triumvirs
sweep the streets,"—but generally with both hands folded behind them
for state, or with one at least behind, the other carrying a cane. P. was a
benevolent, but not a prepossessing man. He had that in his face which
you could not term unhappiness; it rather implied an incapacity of being
happy. His cheeks were colourless, even to whiteness. His look was un-
inviting, resembling (but without his sourness) that of our great phi-
lanthropist. I know that he *did* good acts, but I could never make out
what he *was*. Contemporary with these, but subordinate, was Daines
Barrington—another oddity—he walked burly and square—in imitation, I think, of Coventry—howbeit he attained not to the dignity of his
prototype. Nevertheless, he did pretty well, upon the strength of being
a tolerable antiquarian, and having a brother a bishop. When the account of his year's treasurership came to be audited the following singular
charge was unanimously disallowed by the bench: "Item, disbursed Mr.
Allen, the gardener, twenty shillings for stuff to poison the sparrows, by
my orders." Next to him was old Barton—a jolly negation, who took
upon him the ordering of the bills of fare for the parliament chamber,
where the benchers dine—answering to the combination rooms at College—much to the easement of his less epicurean brethren. I know nothing more of him.—Then Read, and Twopeny—Read, good-humoured

and personable—Twopeny, good-humoured, but thin, and felicitous in jests upon his own figure. If T. was thin, Wharry was attenuated and fleeting. Many must remember him (for he was rather of later date) and his singular gait, which was performed by three steps and a jump regularly succeeding. The steps were little efforts, like that of a child beginning to walk; the jump comparatively vigorous, as a foot to an inch. Where he learned this figure, or what occasioned it, I could never discover. It was neither graceful in itself, nor seemed to answer the purpose any better than common walking. The extreme tenuity of his frame, I suspect, set him upon it. It was a trial of poising. Twopeny would often rally him upon his leanness, and hail him as Brother Lusty; but W. had no relish of a joke. His features were spiteful. I have heard that he would pinch his cat's ears extremely when anything had offended him. Jackson—the omniscient Jackson he was called—was of this period. He had the reputation of possessing more multifarious knowledge than any man of his time. He was the Friar Bacon of the less literate portion of the Temple. I remember a pleasant passage of the cook applying to him, with much formality of apology, for instructions how to write down *edge* bone of beef in his bill of commons. He was supposed to know, if any man in the world did. He decided the orthography to be—as I have given it—fortifying his authority with such anatomical reasons as dismissed the manciple (for the time) learned and happy. Some do spell it yet, perversely, *aitch* bone, from a fanciful resemblance between its shape and that of the aspirate so denominated. I had almost forgotten Mingay with the iron hand—but he was somewhat later. He had lost his right hand by some accident, and supplied it with a grappling-hook, which he wielded with a tolerable adroitness. I detected the substitute before I was old enough to reason whether it were artificial or not. I remember the astonishment it raised in me. He was a blustering, loud-talking person; and I reconciled the phenomenon to my ideas as an emblem of power—somewhat like the horns in the forehead of Michael Angelo's Moses. Baron Maseres, who walks (or did till very lately) in the costume of the reign of George the Second, closes my imperfect recollections of the old benchers of the Inner Temple.

Fantastic forms, whither are ye fled? Or, if the like of you exist, why exist they no more for me? Ye inexplicable, half-understood appearances, why comes in reason to tear away the preternatural mist, bright or gloomy, that enshrouded you? Why make ye so sorry a figure in my relation, who made up to me—to my childish eyes—the mythology of the Temple? In those days I saw Gods, as "old men covered with a mantle," walking upon the earth. Let the dreams of classic idolatry perish,—extinct be the fairies and fairy trumpery of legendary fabling, in the heart of childhood there will, for ever, spring up a well of innocent or wholesome superstition—the seeds of exaggeration will be busy there, and vital—from every-day forms educing the unknown and the uncommon. In that little Goshen there will be light when the grown world flounders about in the darkness of sense and materiality. While childhood, and while dreams, reducing childhood, shall be left, imagination shall not have spread her holy wings totally to fly the earth.

P. S.—I have done injustice to the soft shade of Samuel Salt. See what it is to trust to imperfect memory, and the erring notices of child-hood! Yet I protest I always thought that he had been a bachelor! This gentleman, R. N. informs me, married young, and losing his lady in childbed, within the first year of their union, fell into a deep melancholy, from the effects of which, probably, he never thoroughly recovered. In what a new light does this place his rejection (O call it by a gentler name!) of mild Susan P——, unravelling into beauty certain peculiari-ties of this very shy and retiring character! Henceforth let no one receive the narratives of Elia for true records! They are, in truth, but shadows of fact—verisimilitudes, not verities—or sitting but upon the remote edges and outskirts of history. He is no such honest chronicler as R. N., and would have done better perhaps to have consulted that gentleman before he sent these incondite reminiscences to press. But the worthy sub-treasurer—who respects his old and his new masters—would but have been puzzled at the indecorous liberties of Elia. The good man wots not, peradventure, of the licence which *Magazines* have arrived at in this plain-speaking age, or hardly dreams of their existence beyond the *Gentleman's*—his furthest monthly excursions in this nature having been long confined to the holy ground of honest *Urban's* obituary. May it be long before his own name shall help to swell those columns of un-envied flattery!—Meantime, O ye New Benchers of the Inner Temple, cherish him kindly, for he is himself the kindliest of human creatures. Should infirmities overtake him—he is yet in green and vigorous senility —make allowances for them, remembering that "ye yourselves are old." So may the Winged Horse, your ancient badge and cognisance, still flourish! so may future Hookers and Seldens illustrate your church and chambers! so may the sparrows, in default of more melodious quiristers, unpoisoned hop about your walks; so may the fresh-coloured and cleanly nursery-maid, who, by leave, airs her playful charge in your stately gar-dens, drop her prettiest blushing curtsy as ye pass, reductive of juvenes-cent emotion! so may the younkers of this generation eye you, pacing your stately terrace, with the same superstitious veneration with which the child Elia gazed on the Old Worthies that solemnised the parade before ye!

GRACE BEFORE MEAT

THE custom of saying grace at meals had, probably, its origin in the early times of the world, and the hunter-state of man, when dinners were precarious things, and a full meal was something more than a common blessing! when a belly-full was a wind-fall, and looked like a special providence. In the shouts and triumphal songs with which, after a season of sharp abstinence, a lucky booty of deer's or goat's flesh would naturally be ushered home, existed, perhaps, the germ of the modern grace. It is not otherwise easy to be understood, why the blessing of food—the act of eating—should have had a particular expression of thanksgiving annexed to it, distinct from that implied and silent gratitude with which we are expected to enter upon the enjoyment of the many other various gifts and good things of existence.

I own that I am disposed to say grace upon twenty other occasions in the course of the day besides my dinner. I want a form for setting out upon a pleasant walk, for a moonlight ramble, for a friendly meeting, or a solved problem. Why have we none for books, those spiritual repasts— a grace before Milton—a grace before Shakspeare—a devotional exercise proper to be said before reading the Faëry Queen?—but the received ritual having prescribed these forms to the solitary ceremony of manducation, I shall confine my observations to the experience which I have had of the grace, properly so called; commending my new scheme for extension to a niche in the grand philosophical, poetical, and perchance in part heretical, liturgy, now compiling by my friend Homo Humanus, for the use of a certain snug congregation of Utopian Rabelæsian Christians, no matter where assembled.

The form, then, of the benediction before eating has its beauty at a poor man's table, or at the simple and unprovocative repast of children. It is here that the grace becomes exceedingly graceful. The indigent man, who hardly knows whether he shall have a meal the next day or not, sits down to his fare with a present sense of the blessing, which can be but feebly acted by the rich, into whose minds the conception of wanting a dinner could never, but by some extreme theory, have entered. The proper end of food—the animal sustenance—is barely contemplated by them. The poor man's bread is his daily bread, literally his bread for the day. Their courses are perennial.

Again, the plainest diet seems the fittest to be preceded by the grace. That which is least stimulative to appetite, leaves the mind most free for foreign considerations. A man may feel thankful, heartily thankful, over a dish of plain mutton with turnips, and have leisure to reflect upon the ordinance and institution of eating; when he shall confess a perturbation of mind, inconsistent with the purposes of the grace, at the presence of venison or turtle. When I have sate (a *rarus hospes*) at rich men's tables, with the savoury soup and messes steaming up the nostrils, and moistening the lips of the guests with desire and a distracted choice, I have felt the introduction of that ceremony to be unseasonable. With the ravenous orgasm upon you, it seems impertinent to interpose a religious sentiment. It is a confusion of purpose to mutter out praises from a mouth that waters. The heats of epicurism put out the gentle flame of devotion. The incense which rises round is pagan, and the belly-god intercepts it for his own. The very excess of the provision beyond the needs, takes away all sense of proportion between the end and means. The giver is veiled by his gifts. You are startled at the injustice of returning thanks

—for what?—for having too much, while so many starve. It is to praise the Gods amiss.

I have observed this awkwardness felt, scarce consciously perhaps, by the good man who says the grace. I have seen it in clergymen and others —a sort of shame—a sense of the co-presence of circumstances which un-hallow the blessing. After a devotional tone put on for a few seconds, how rapidly the speaker will fall into his common voice! helping himself or his neighbour, as if to get rid of some uneasy sensation of hypocrisy. Not that the good man was a hypocrite, or was not most conscientious in the discharge of the duty; but he felt in his inmost mind the incom-patibility of the scene and the viands before him with the exercise of a calm and rational gratitude.

I hear somebody exclaim,—Would you have Christians sit down at table, like hogs to their troughs, without remembering the Giver?—no— I would have them sit down as Christians, remembering the Giver, and less like hogs. Or if their appetites must run riot, and they must pamper themselves with delicacies for which east and west are ransacked, I would have them postpone their benediction to a fitter season, when appetite is laid; when the still small voice can be heard, and the reason of the grace returns—with temperate diet and restricted dishes. Glut-tony and surfeiting are no proper occasions for thanksgiving. When Jeshurun waxed fat, we read that he kicked. Virgil knew the harpy-nature better, when he put into the mouth of Celæno anything but a blessing. We may be greatly sensible of the deliciousness of some kinds of food beyond others, though that is a meaner and inferior gratitude: but the proper object of the grace is sustenance, not relishes; daily bread, not delicacies; the means of life, and not the means of pampering the carcass. With what frame or composure, I wonder, can a city chaplain pronounce his benediction at some great Hall-feast, when he knows that his last concluding pious word—and that, in all probability, the sacred name which he preaches—is but the signal for so many impatient harpies to commence their foul orgies, with as little sense of true thankfulness (which is temperance) as those Virgilian fowl! It is well if the good man himself does not feel his devotions a little clouded, those foggy sensuous steams mingling with and polluting the pure altar sacrifice.

The severest satire upon full tables and surfeits is the banquet which Satan, in the "Paradise Regained," provides for a temptation in the wilderness:

> A table richly spread in regal mode
> With dishes piled, and meats of noblest sort
> And savour; beasts of chase, or fowl of game,
> In pastry built, or from the spit, or boiled,
> Gris-amber-steamed; all fish from sea or shore,
> Freshet or purling brook, for which was drained
> Pontus, and Lucrine bay, and Afric coast.

The Tempter, I warrant you, thought these cates would go down with-out the recommendatory preface of a benediction. They are like to be

short graces where the devil plays the host. I am afraid the poet wants
his usual decorum in this place. Was he thinking of the old Roman
luxury, or of a gaudy day at Cambridge? This was a temptation fitter
for a Heliogabalus. The whole banquet is too civic and culinary, and the
accompaniments altogether a profanation of that deep, abstracted holy
scene. The mighty artillery of sauces, which the cook-fiend conjures up, is
out of proportion to the simple wants and plain hunger of the guest. He
that disturbed him in his dreams, from his dreams might have been
taught better. To the temperate fantasies of the famished Son of God,
what sort of feasts presented themselves?—He dreamed indeed,

> ——As appetite is wont to dream,
> Of meats and drinks, nature's refreshment sweet.

But what meats?—

> Him thought, he by the brook of Cherith stood,
> And saw the ravens with their horny beaks
> Food to Elijah bringing even and morn;
> Though ravenous, taught to abstain from what they brought;
> He saw the prophet also how he fled
> Into the desert and how there he slept
> Under a juniper; then how awaked
> He found his supper on the coals prepared,
> And by the angel was bid rise and eat,
> And ate the second time after repose,
> The strength whereof sufficed him forty days:
> Sometimes, that with Elijah he partook,
> Or as a guest with Daniel at his pulse.

Nothing in Milton is finelier fancied than these temperate dreams of the
divine Hungerer. To which of these two visionary banquets, think you,
would the introduction of what is called the grace have been the most
fitting and pertinent?

Theoretically I am no enemy to graces; but practically I own that
(before meat especially) they seem to involve something awkward and
unseasonable. Our appetites, of one or another kind, are excellent spurs
to our reason, which might otherwise but feebly set about the great ends
of preserving and continuing the species. They are fit blessings to be contemplated at a distance with a becoming gratitude; but the moment of
appetite (the judicious reader will apprehend me) is, perhaps, the least
fit season for that exercise. The Quakers, who go about their business of
every description with more calmness than we, have more title to the use
of these benedictory prefaces. I have always admired their silent grace,
and the more because I have observed their applications to the meat and
drink following to be less passionate and sensual than ours. They are
neither gluttons nor wine-bibbers as a people. They eat, as a horse bolts
his chopped hay, with indifference, calmness, and cleanly circumstances.
They neither grease nor slop themselves. When I see a citizen in his bib
and tucker, I cannot imagine it a surplice.

I am no Quaker at my food. I confess I am not indifferent to the kinds of it. Those unctuous morsels of deer's flesh were not made to be received with dispassionate services. I hate a man who swallows it, affecting not to know what he is eating. I suspect his taste in higher matters. I shrink instinctively from one who professes to like minced veal. There is a physiognomical character in the tastes for food. C—— holds that a man cannot have a pure mind who refuses apple-dumplings. I am not certain but he is right. With the decay of my first innocence, I confess a less and less relish daily for those innocuous cates. The whole vegetable tribe have lost their gust with me. Only I stick to asparagus, which still seems to inspire gentle thoughts. I am impatient and querulous under culinary disappointments, as to come home at the dinner-hour, for instance, expecting some savoury mess, and to find one quite tasteless and sapidless. Butter ill melted—that commonest of kitchen failures—puts me beside my tenor.—The author of the Rambler used to make inarticulate animal noises over a favourite food. Was this the music quite proper to be preceded by the grace? or would the pious man have done better to postpone his devotions to a season when the blessing might be contemplated with less perturbation? I quarrel with no man's tastes, nor would set my thin face against those excellent things, in their way, jollity and feasting. But as these exercises, however laudable, have little in them of grace or gracefulness, a man should be sure, before he ventures so to grace them, that while he is pretending his devotions otherwhere, he is not secretly kissing his hand to some great fish—his Dagon—with a special consecration of no ark but the fat tureen before him. Graces are the sweet preluding strains to the banquets of angels and children; to the roots and severer repasts of the Chartreuse; to the slender, but not slenderly acknowledged, refection of the poor and humble man: but at the heaped-up boards of the pampered and the luxurious they become of dissonant mood, less timed and tuned to the occasion, methinks, than the noise of those better befitting organs would be which children hear tales of, at Hog's Norton. We sit too long at our meals, or are too curious in the study of them, or too disordered in our application to them, or engross too great a portion of those good things (which should be common) to our share, to be able with any grace to say grace. To be thankful for what we grasp exceeding our proportion, is to add hypocrisy to injustice. A lurking sense of this truth is what makes the performance of this duty so cold and spiritless a service at most tables. In houses where the grace is as indispensable as the napkin, who has not seen that never-settled question arise, as to *who shall say it?* while the good man of the house and the visitor clergyman, or some other guest belike of next authority, from years or gravity, shall be bandying about the office between them as a matter of compliment, each of them not unwilling to shift the awkward burthen of an equivocal duty from his own shoulders?

I once drank tea in company with two Methodist divines of different persuasions, whom it was my fortune to introduce to each other for the first time that evening. Before the first cup was handed round, one of these reverend gentlemen put it to the other, with all due solemnity, whether he chose to *say anything*. It seems it is the custom with some sectaries to put up a short prayer before this meal also. His reverend brother did not at first quite apprehend him, but upon an explanation, with little less importance he made answer that it was not a custom known in his church: in which courteous evasion the other acquiescing for good manners' sake, or in compliance with a weak brother, the supplementary or tea-grace was waived altogether. With what spirit might not Lucian have painted two priests, of *his* religion, playing into each other's hands the compliment of performing or omitting a sacrifice,—the hungry God meantime, doubtful of his incense, with expectant nostrils hovering over the two flamens, and (as between two stools) going away in the end without his supper.

A short form upon these occasions is felt to want reverence; a long one, I am afraid, cannot escape the charge of impertinence. I do not quite approve of the epigrammatic conciseness with which that equivocal wag (but my pleasant schoolfellow) C. V. L., when importuned for a grace, used to inquire, first slyly leering down the table, "Is there no clergyman here?"—significantly adding, "Thank G—." Nor do I think our old form at school quite pertinent, where we were used to preface our bald bread-and-cheese-suppers with a preamble, connecting with that humble blessing a recognition of benefits the most awful and overwhelming to the imagination which religion has to offer. *Non tunc illis erat locus.* I remember we were put to it to reconcile the phrase "good creatures," upon which the blessing rested, with the fare set before us, wilfully understanding that expression in a low and animal sense,—till some one recalled a legend, which told how, in the golden days of Christ's, the young Hospitallers were wont to have smoking joints of roast meat upon their nightly boards, till some pious benefactor, commiserating the decencies, rather than the palates, of the children, commuted our flesh for garments, and gave us—*horresco referens*—trousers instead of mutton.

DREAM CHILDREN: A REVERIE

CHILDREN love to listen to stories about their elders, when *they* were children; to stretch their imagination to the conception of a traditionary great-uncle, or grandame, whom they never saw. It was in this spirit that my little ones crept about me the other evening to hear about their great-grandmother Field, who lived in a great house in Norfolk (a hundred times bigger than that in which they and papa lived) which had been the scene—so at least it was generally believed in that part of the country—of the tragic incidents which they had lately become familiar with from the ballad of the Children in the Wood. Certain it is that the whole story of the children and their cruel uncle was to be seen fairly carved out in wood upon the chimney-piece of the great hall, the whole story down to the Robin Redbreasts; till a foolish rich person pulled it down to set up a marble one of modern invention in its stead, with no story upon it. Here Alice put out one of dear mother's looks, too tender to be called unbraiding. Then I went on to say, how religious and how good their great-grandmother Field was, how beloved and respected by everybody, though she was not indeed the mistress of this great house, but had only the charge of it (and yet in some respects she might be said to be the mistress of it too) committed to her by the owner, who preferred living in a newer and more fashionable mansion which he had purchased somewhere in the adjoining county; but still she lived in it in a manner as if it had been her own, and kept up the dignity of the great house in a sort while she lived, which afterwards came to decay, and was nearly pulled down, and all its old ornaments stripped and carried away to the owner's other house, where they were set up, and looked as awkward as if some one were to carry away the old tombs they had seen lately at the Abbey, and stick them up in Lady C.'s tawdry gilt drawing-room. Here John smiled, as much as to say, "that would be foolish indeed." And then I told how, when she came to die, her funeral was attended by a concourse of all the poor, and some of the gentry too, of the neighbour-hood for many miles round, to show their respect for her memory, because she had been such a good and religious woman; so good indeed that she knew all the Psaltery by heart, ay, and a great part of the Testament besides. Here little Alice spread her hands. Then I told what a tall, up-right, graceful person their great-grandmother Field once was; and how in her youth she was esteemed the best dancer—here Alice's little right foot played an involuntary movement, till, upon my looking grave, it desisted—the best dancer, I was saying, in the county, till a cruel disease, called a cancer, came, and bowed her down with pain; but it could never bend her good spirits, or make them stoop, but they were still upright, because she was so good and religious. Then I told how she was used to sleep by herself in a lone chamber of the great lone house; and how she believed that an apparition of two infants was to be seen at midnight gliding up and down the great staircase near where she slept, but she said "those innocents would do her no harm"; and how frightened I used to be, though in those days I had my maid to sleep with me, because I was never half so good or religious as she—and yet I never saw the in-fants. Here John expanded all his eyebrows and tried to look cou-rageous. Then I told how good she was to all her grandchildren, having us to the great house in the holydays, where I in particular used to spend many hours by myself, in gazing upon the old busts of the twelve Cæsars, that had been Emperors of Rome, till the old marble heads would seem to live again, or I to be turned into marble with them; how I never could be tired with roaming about that huge mansion, with its vast empty rooms, with their worn-out hangings, fluttering tapestry, and carved oaken panels, with the gilding almost rubbed out—sometimes in the spacious old-fashioned gardens, which I had almost to myself, unless when now and then a solitary gardening man would cross me—and how the nectarines and peaches hung upon the walls, without my ever offering to pluck them, because they were forbidden fruit, unless now and then,—and because I had more pleasure in strolling about among the old melancholy-looking yew-trees, or the firs, and picking up the red berries, and the fir-apples, which were good for nothing but to look at—or in lying about upon the fresh grass with all the fine garden smells around me—or basking in the orangery, till I could almost fancy myself ripening too along with the oranges and the limes in that grateful warmth— or in watching the dace that darted to and fro in the fish-pond, at the bottom of the garden, with here and there a great sulky pike hanging midway down the water in silent state, as if it mocked at their impertinent friskings,—I had more pleasure in these busy-idle diversions than in all the sweet flavours of peaches, nectarines, oranges, and such-like common baits of children. Here John slyly deposited back upon the plate a bunch of grapes, which, not unobserved by Alice, he had meditated dividing with her, and both seemed willing to relinquish them for the present as irrelevant. Then, in somewhat a more heightened tone, I told how, though their great-grandmother Field loved all her grandchildren, yet in an especial manner she might be said to love their uncle, John L——, because he was so handsome and spirited a youth, and a king to the rest of us; and, instead of moping about in solitary corners, like some of us, he would mount the most mettlesome horse he could get, when but an imp no bigger than themselves, and make it carry him half over the county in a morning, and join the hunters when there were any out—and yet he loved the old great house and gardens too, but had too much spirit to be always pent up within their boundaries—and how their uncle grew up to man's estate as brave as he was handsome, to the admiration of everybody, but of their great-grandmother Field most especially; and how he used to carry me upon his back when I was a lame-footed boy—for he was a good bit older than me—many a mile when I could not walk for pain;—and how in after life he became lame-footed too, and I did not always (I fear) make allowances enough for him when he was impatient, and in pain, nor remember sufficiently how considerate he had been to me when I was lame-footed; and how when he died, though he had not been dead an hour, it seemed as if he had died a great while ago, such a distance there is betwixt life and death; and how I bore his death as I thought pretty well at first, but afterwards it haunted and haunted me; and though I did not cry or take it to heart as some do, and as I think he would have done if I had died, yet I missed him all day long, and knew not till then how much I had loved him. I missed his kindness, and I missed his crossness, and wished him to be alive again, to be quarrelling with him (for we quarrelled sometimes), rather than not have him again, and was as uneasy without him, as he their poor uncle must have been when the doctor took off his limb.—Here the children fell a-crying, and asked if their little mourning which they had on was not for uncle John, and they looked up, and prayed me not to go on about their uncle, but to tell them some stories about their pretty dead mother. Then I told how for seven long years, in hope sometimes, sometimes in despair, yet persisting ever, I courted the fair Alice W——n; and, as much as children could understand, I explained to them what coyness, and difficulty, and denial, meant in maidens—when suddenly, turning to Alice, the soul of the first Alice looked out at her eyes with such a reality of re-presentment, that I became in doubt which of them stood there before me, or whose that bright hair was; and while I stood gazing, both the children gradually grew fainter to my view, receding, and still receding, till nothing at last but two mournful features were seen in the uttermost distance, which, without speech, strangely impressed upon me the effects of speech: "We are not of Alice, nor of thee, nor are we children at all. The children of Alice call Bartrum father. We are nothing; less than nothing, and dreams. We are only what might have been, and must wait upon the tedious shores of Lethe millions of ages before we have existence, and a name"——and immediately awaking, I found myself quietly seated in my bachelor arm-chair, where I had fallen asleep, with the faithful Bridget unchanged by my side—but John L. (or James Elia) was gone for ever.

DISTANT CORRESPONDENTS

IN A LETTER TO B. F., ESQ., AT SYDNEY, NEW SOUTH WALES

My dear F. When I think how welcome the sight of a letter from the world where you were born must be to you in that strange one to which you have been transplanted, I feel some compunctious visitings at my long silence. But, indeed, it is no easy effort to set about a correspondence at our distance. The weary world of waters between us oppresses the imagination. It is difficult to conceive how a scrawl of mine should ever stretch across it. It is a sort of presumption to expect that one's thoughts should live so far. It is like writing for posterity; and reminds me of one of Mrs. Rowe's superscriptions, "Alcander to Strephon in the shades." Cowley's Post-Angel is no more than would be expedient in such an intercourse. One drops a packet at Lombard Street, and in twenty-four hours a friend in Cumberland gets it as fresh as if it came in ice. It is only like whispering through a long trumpet. But suppose a tube let down from the moon, with yourself at one end and *the man* at the other; it would be some balk to the spirit of conversation, if you knew that the dialogue exchanged with that interesting theosophist would take two or three revolutions of a higher luminary in its passage. Yet, for aught I know, you may be some parasangs nigher that primitive idea—Plato's man— than we in England here have the honour to reckon ourselves.

Epistolary matter usually compriseth three topics; news, sentiment, and puns. In the latter, I include all non-serious subjects; or subjects serious in themselves, but treated after my fashion, non-seriously.—And first, for news. In them the most desirable circumstance, I suppose, is that they shall be true. But what security can I have that what I now send you for truth shall not, before you get it, unaccountably turn into a lie? For instance, our mutual friend P. is at this present writing—*my Now*—in good health, and enjoys a fair share of worldly reputation. You are glad to hear it. This is natural and friendly. But at this present reading—*your Now*—he may possibly be in the Bench, or going to be hanged, which in reason ought to abate something of your transport (*i.e.* at hearing he was well, etc.), or at least considerably to modify it. I am going to the play this evening, to have a laugh with Munden. You have no theatre, I think you told me, in your land of d——d realities. You naturally lick your lips, and envy me my felicity. Think but a moment, and you will correct the hateful emotion. Why, it is Sunday morning with you, and 1823. This confusion of tenses, this grand solecism of *two presents*, is in a degree common to all postage. But if I sent you word to Bath or Devizes, that I was expecting the aforesaid treat this evening, though at the moment you received the intelligence my full feast of fun would be over, yet there would be for a day or two after, as you would well know, a smack, a relish left upon my mental palate, which would give rational encouragement for you to foster a portion, at least, of the disagreeable passion, which it was in part my intention to produce. But ten months hence, your envy or your sympathy would be as useless as a passion spent upon the dead. Not only does truth, in these long intervals, un-essence herself, but (what is harder) one cannot venture a crude fiction, for the fear that it may ripen into a truth upon the voyage. What a wild improbable banter I put upon you, some three years since,——of Will Weatherall having married a servant-maid! I remember gravely consulting you how we were to receive her—for Will's wife was in no case to be rejected; and your no less serious replication in the matter; how tenderly you advised an abstemious introduction of literary topics before the lady, with a caution not to be too forward in bringing on the carpet matters more within the sphere of her intelligence; your deliberate judgment, or rather wise suspension of sentence, how far jacks, and spits, and mops, could, with propriety, be introduced as subjects; whether the conscious avoiding of all such matters in discourse would not have a worse look than the taking of them casually in our way; in what manner we should carry ourselves to our maid Becky, Mrs. William Weatherall being by; whether we should show more delicacy, and a truer sense of respect for Will's wife, by treating Becky with our customary chiding before her, or by an unusual deferential civility paid to Becky, as to a person of great worth, but thrown by the caprice of fate into a humble station. There were difficulties, I remember, on both sides, which you did me the favour to state with the precision of a lawyer, united to the tenderness of a friend. I laughed in my sleeve at your solemn pleadings, when lo! while I was valuing myself upon this flam put upon you in New South Wales, the devil in England, jealous possibly of any lie-children not his own, or working after my copy, has actually instigated our friend (not three days since) to the commission of a matrimony, which I had only conjured up for your diversion. William Weatherall has married Mrs. Cotterel's maid. But to take it in its truest sense, you will see, my dear F., that news from me must become history to you; which I neither profess to write, nor indeed care much for reading. No person, under a diviner, can, with any prospect of veracity, conduct a correspondence at such an arm's length. Two prophets, indeed, might thus interchange intelligence with effect; the epoch of the writer (Habakkuk) falling in with the true present time of the receiver (Daniel); but then we are no prophets.

Then as to sentiment. It fares little better with that. This kind of dish, above all, requires to be served up hot, or sent off in water-plates, that your friend may have it almost as warm as yourself. If it have time to cool, it is the most tasteless of all cold meats. I have often smiled at a conceit of the late Lord C. It seems that travelling somewhere about Geneva, he came to some pretty green spot, or nook, where a willow, or something, hung so fantastically and invitingly over a stream—was it?—or a rock?—no matter—but the stillness and the repose, after a weary journey, 'tis likely, in a languid moment of his Lordship's hot, restless life, so took his fancy that he could imagine no place so proper, in the event of his death, to lay his bones in. This was all very natural and excusable as a sentiment, and shows his character in a very pleasing light. But when from a passing sentiment it came to be an act; and when, by a positive testamentary disposal, his remains were actually carried all that way from England; who was there, some desperate sentimentalists excepted, that did not ask the question, Why could not his Lordship have found a spot as solitary, a nook as romantic, a tree as green and pendent, with a stream as emblematic to his purpose, in Surrey, in Dorset, or in Devon? Conceive the sentiment boarded up, freighted, entered at the Custom House (startling the tide-waiters with the novelty), hoisted into a ship. Conceive it pawed about and handled between the rude jests of tarpaulin ruffians—a thing of its delicate texture—the salt bilge wetting it till it became as vapid as a damaged lustring. Suppose it in material danger (mariners have some superstitution about sentiments) of being tossed over in a fresh gale to some propitiatory shark (spirit of Saint Gothard, save us from a quietus so foreign to the deviser's purpose!), but it has happily evaded a fishy consummation. Trace it then to its lucky landing—at Lyons shall we say?—I have not the map before me—jostled upon four men's shoulders—baiting at this town—stopping to refresh at t'other village—waiting a passport here, a license there; the sanction of the magistracy in this district, the concurrence of the ecclesiastics in that canton; till at length it arrives at its destination, tired out and jaded, from a brisk sentiment into a feature of silly pride or tawdry senseless affectation. How few sentiments, my dear F., I am afraid we can set down, in the sailor's phrase, as quite seaworthy.

Lastly, as to the agreeable levities, which, though contemptible in bulk, are the twinkling corpuscula which should irradiate a right friendly

epistle—your puns and small jests are, I apprehend, extremely circum-
scribed in their sphere of action. They are so far from a capacity of
being packed up and sent beyond sea, they will scarce endure to be
transported by hand from this room to the next. Their vigour is as the
instant of their birth. Their nutriment for their brief existence is the
intellectual atmosphere of the by-standers: or this last is the fine slime
of Nilus—the *melior lutus*—whose maternal recipiency is as necessary as
the *sol pater* to their equivocal generation. A pun hath a hearty kind of
present ear-kissing smack with it; you can no more transmit it in its
pristine flavour than you can send a kiss.—Have you not tried in some
instances to palm off a yesterday's pun upon a gentleman, and has it
answered? Not but it was new to his hearing, but it did not seem to
come new from you. It did not hitch in. It was like picking up at a
village ale-house a two-days'-old newspaper. You have not seen it before,
but you resent the stale thing as an affront. This sort of merchandise
above all requires a quick return. A pun, and its recognitory laugh,
must be co-instantaneous. The one is the brisk lightning, the other the
fierce thunder. A moment's interval, and the link is snapped. A pun is
reflected from a friend's face as from a mirror. Who would consult his
sweet visnomy, if the polished surface were two or three minutes (not
to speak of twelve months, my dear F.) in giving back its copy?

I cannot image to myself whereabout you are. When I try to fix it,
Peter Wilkins's island comes across me. Sometimes you seem to be in the
Hades of *Thieves*. I see Diogenes prying among you with his perpetual
fruitless lantern. What must you be willing by this time to give for the
sight of an honest man! You must almost have forgotten how *we* look.
And tell me what your Sydneyites do? are they th**v*ng all day long?
Merciful heaven! what property can stand against such a depredation!
The kangaroos—your Aborigines—do they keep their primitive simplicity un-Europe-tainted, with those little short fore pads, looking like a
lesson framed by nature to the pickpocket! Marry, for diving into fobs
they are rather lamely provided *a priori;* but if the hue and cry were
once up, they would show as fair a pair of hind-shifters as the expertest
loco-motor in the colony. We hear the most improbable tales at this distance. Pray is it true that the young Spartans among you are born with
six fingers, which spoils their scanning?—It must look very odd, but use
reconciles. For their scansion, it is less to be regretted; for if they take
it into their heads to be poets, it is odds but they turn out, the greater
part of them, vile plagiarists. Is there much difference to see, too, between the son of a th**f and the grandson? or where does the taint stop?
Do you bleach in three or in four generations? I have many questions
to put, but ten Delphic voyages can be made in a shorter time than it
will take to satisfy my scruples. Do you grow your own hemp?—What
is your staple trade,—exclusive of the national profession, I mean?
Your locksmiths, I take it, are some of your great capitalists.

I am insensibly chatting to you as familiarly as when we used to exchange good-morrows out of our old contiguous windows, in pump-

famed Hare Court in the Temple. Why did you ever leave that quiet corner?—Why did I?—with its complement of four poor elms, from whose smoke-dyed barks, the theme of jesting ruralists, I picked my first lady-birds! My heart is as dry as that spring sometimes proves in a thirsty August, when I revert to the space that is between us; a length of passage enough to render obsolete the phrases of our English letters before they can reach you. But while I talk I think you hear me—thoughts dallying with vain surmise—

> Aye me! while thee the seas and sounding shores
> Hold far away.

Come back, before I am grown into a very old man, so as you shall hardly know me. Come, before Bridget walks on crutches. Girls whom you left children have become sage matrons while you are tarrying there. The blooming Miss W—r (you remember Sally W—r) called upon us yesterday, an aged crone. Folks whom you knew die off every year. Formerly, I thought that death was wearing out,—I stood ramparted about with so many healthy friends. The departure of J. W., two springs back, corrected my delusion. Since then the old divorcer has been busy. If you do not make haste to return, there will be little left to greet you, of me, or mine.

THE PRAISE OF CHIMNEY-SWEEPERS

I LIKE to meet a sweep—understand me—not a grown sweeper—old chimney-sweepers are by no means attractive—but one of those tender novices, blooming through their first nigritude, the maternal washings not quite effaced from the cheek—such as come forth with the dawn, or somewhat earlier, with their little professional notes sounding like the *peep peep* of a young sparrow; or liker to the matin lark should I pronounce them, in their aërial ascents not seldom anticipating the sun-rise?

I have a kindly yearning toward these dim specks—poor blots—innocent blacknesses—

I reverence these young Africans of our own growth—these almost clergy imps, who sport their cloth without assumption; and from their little pulpits (the tops of chimneys), in the nipping air of a December morning, preach a lesson of patience to mankind.

When a child, what a mysterious pleasure it was to witness their operation! to see a chit no bigger than one's-self, enter, one knew not by what process, into what seemed the *fauces Averni*—to pursue him in imagination, as he went sounding on through so many dark stifling caverns, horrid shades! to shudder with the idea that "now, surely, he must be lost for ever!"—to revive at hearing his feeble shout of discovered daylight—and then (O fulness of delight!) running out of doors, to come just in time to see the sable phenomenon emerge in safety, the brandished weapon of his art victorious like some flag waved over a conquered citadel! I seem to remember having been told, that a bad sweep was once left in a stack with his brush, to indicate which way the wind blew. It was an awful spectacle certainly; not much unlike the old stage direction in Macbeth, where the "Apparition of a child crowned, with a tree in his hand, rises."

Reader, if thou meetest one of these small gentry in thy early rambles, it is good to give him a penny. It is better to give him twopence. If it be starving weather, and to the proper troubles of his hard occupation, a pair of kibed heels (no unusual accompaniment) be superadded, the demand on thy humanity will surely rise to a tester.

There is a composition, the ground-work of which I have understood to be the sweet wood yclept sassafras. This wood boiled down to a kind of tea, and tempered with an infusion of milk and sugar, hath to some tastes a delicacy beyond the China luxury. I know not how thy palate may relish it; for myself, with every deference to the judicious Mr. Read, who hath time out of mind kept open a shop (the only one he avers in London) for the vending of this "wholesome and pleasant beverage," on the south side of Fleet Street, as thou approachest Bridge Street—*the only Salopian house*—I have never yet adventured to dip my own particular lip in a basin of his commended ingredients—a cautious premonition to the olfactories constantly whispering to me, that my stomach must infallibly, with all due courtesy, decline it. Yet I have seen palates, otherwise not uninstructed in dietetical elegancies, sup it up with avidity.

I know not by what particular conformation of the organ it happens, but I have always found that this composition is surprisingly gratifying to the palate of a young chimney-sweeper—whether the oily particles (sassafras is slightly oleaginous) do attenuate and soften the fuliginous concretions, which are sometimes found (in dissections) to adhere to the roof of the mouth in these unfledged practitioners; or whether Nature, sensible that she had mingled too much of bitter wood in the lot of these raw victims, caused to grow out of the earth her sassafras for a sweet lenitive—but so it is, that no possible taste or odour to the senses of a young chimney-sweeper can convey a delicate excitement comparable to this mixture. Being penniless, they will yet hang their black heads over the ascending steam, to gratify one sense if possible, seemingly no less pleased than those domestic animals—cats—when they purr over a new-found sprig of valerian. There is something more in these sympathies than philosophy can inculcate.

Now albeit Mr. Read boasteth, not without reason, that his is the *only Salopian house;* yet be it known to thee, reader—if thou art one who keepest what are called good hours, thou art haply ignorant of the fact —he hath a race of industrious imitators, who from stalls, and under open sky, dispense the same savoury mess to humbler customers, at that dead time of the dawn, when (as extremes meet) the rake, reeling home from his midnight cups, and the hard-handed artisan leaving his bed to resume the premature labours of the day, jostle, not unfrequently to the manifest disconcerting of the former, for the honours of the pavement. It is the time when, in summer, between the expired and the not yet re-lumined kitchen-fires, the kennels of our fair metropolis give forth their least satisfactory odours. The rake, who wisheth to dissipate his o'ernight vapours in more grateful coffee, curses the ungenial fume, as he passeth; but the artisan stops to taste, and blesses the fragrant breakfast.

This is *saloop*—the precocious herb-woman's darling—the delight of the early gardener, who transports his smoking cabbages by break of day from Hammersmith to Covent Garden's famed piazzas—the delight, and oh! I fear, too often the envy, of the unpennied sweep. Him shouldst thou haply encounter, with his dim visage pendent over the grateful steam, regale him with a sumptuous basin (it will cost thee but three-halfpennies) and a slice of delicate bread and butter (an added half-penny)—so may thy culinary fires, eased of the o'er-charged secretions from thy worse-placed hospitalities, curl up a lighter volume to the wel-kin—so may the descending soot never taint thy costly well-ingredienced soups—nor the odious cry, quick-reaching from street to street, of the *fired chimney*, invite the rattling engines from ten adjacent parishes, to disturb for a casual scintillation thy peace and pocket!

I am by nature extremely susceptible of street affronts; the jeers and taunts of the populace; the low-bred triumph they display over the casual trip, or splashed stocking, of a gentleman. Yet can I endure the jocularity of a young sweep with something more than forgiveness.—In the last winter but one, pacing along Cheapside with my accustomed precipitation when I walk westward, a treacherous slide brought me upon my back in an instant. I scrambled up with pain and shame enough—yet outwardly trying to face it down, as if nothing had happened—when the roguish grin of one of these young wits encountered me. There he stood, pointing me out with his dusky finger to the mob, and to a poor woman (I suppose his mother) in particular, till the tears for the exquisiteness of the fun (so he thought it) worked themselves out at the corners of his poor red eyes, red from many a previous weeping, and soot-inflamed, yet twinkling through all with such a joy, snatched out of desolation, that Hogarth —— but Hogarth has got him already (how could he miss him?) in the March to Finchley, grinning at the pieman—there he stood, as he stands in the picture, irremovable, as if the jest was to last for ever—with such a maximum of glee, and minimum of mischief, in his mirth—for the grin of a genuine sweep hath absolutely no malice in it— that I could have been content, if the honour of a gentleman might en-dure it, to have remained his butt and his mockery till midnight.

I am by theory obdurate to the seductiveness of what are called a fine set of teeth. Every pair of rosy lips (the ladies must pardon me) is a casket presumably holding such jewels; but, methinks, they should take leave to "air" them as frugally as possible. The fine lady, or fine gentle-man, who show me their teeth, show me bones. Yet must I confess, that from the mouth of a true sweep a display (even to ostentation) of those white and shining ossifications, strikes me as an agreeable anomaly in manners, and an allowable piece of foppery. It is, as when

> A sable cloud
> Turns forth her silver lining on the night.

It is like some remnant of gentry not quite extinct; a badge of better days; a hint of nobility:—and, doubtless, under the obscuring darkness and double night of their forlorn disguisement, oftentimes lurketh good blood, and gentle conditions, derived from lost ancestry, and a lapsed pedigree. The premature apprenticements of these tender victims give but too much encouragement, I fear, to clandestine and almost infantile abductions; the seeds of civility and true courtesy, so often discernible in these young grafts (not otherwise to be accounted for) plainly hint at some forced adoptions; many noble Rachels mourning for their children, even in our days, countenance the fact; the tales of fairy-spiriting may shadow a lamentable verity, and the recovery of the young Montagu be but a solitary instance of good fortune out of many irreparable and hopeless *defiliations*.

In one of the state-beds at Arundel Castle, a few years since—under a ducal canopy—(that seat of the Howards is an object of curiosity to visitors, chiefly for its beds, in which the late duke was especially a connoisseur)—encircled with curtains of delicatest crimson, with starry coronets inwoven—folded between a pair of sheets whiter and softer than the lap where Venus lulled Ascanius—was discovered by chance, after all methods of search had failed, at noon-day, fast asleep, a lost chimney-sweeper. The little creature, having somehow confounded his passage among the intricacies of those lordly chimneys, by some unknown aperture had alighted upon this magnificent chamber; and, tired with his tedious explorations, was unable to resist the delicious invitement to repose, which he there saw exhibited; so creeping between the sheets very quietly, laid his black head upon the pillow, and slept like a young Howard.

Such is the account given to the visitors at the Castle.—But I cannot help seeming to perceive a confirmation of what I had just hinted at in this story. A high instinct was at work in the case, or I am mistaken. Is it probable that a poor child of that description, with whatever weariness he might be visited, would have ventured, under such a penalty as he would be taught to expect, to uncover the sheets of a duke's bed, and deliberately to lay himself down between them, when the rug, or the carpet, presented an obvious couch, still far above his pretensions—is this probable, I would ask, if the great power of nature, which I contend for, had not been manifested within him, prompting to the adventure? Doubtless this young nobleman (for such my mind misgives me that he must be) was allured by some memory, not amounting to full consciousness, of his condition in infancy, when he was used to be lapped by his mother, or his nurse, in just such sheets as he there found, into which he was now but creeping back as into his proper *incunabula*, and resting-place.—By no other theory than by this sentiment of a pre-existent state (as I may call it), can I explain a deed so venturous, and, indeed, upon any other system, so indecorous, in this tender, but unseasonable, sleeper.

My pleasant friend JEM WHITE was so impressed with a belief of metamorphoses like this frequently taking place, that in some sort to reverse the wrongs of fortune in these poor changelings, he instituted an annual feast of chimney-sweepers, at which it was his pleasure to officiate as host and waiter. It was a solemn supper held in Smithfield, upon the yearly return of the fair of St. Bartholomew. Cards were issued a week before to the master-sweeps in and about the metropolis, confining the invitation to their younger fry. Now and then an elderly stripling would get in among us, and be good-naturedly winked at; but our main body were infantry. One unfortunate wight, indeed, who, relying upon his dusky suit, had intruded himself into our party, but by tokens was providentially discovered in time to be no chimney-sweeper (all is not soot which look so), was quoited out of the presence with universal indignation, as not having on the wedding garment; but in general the greatest harmony prevailed. The place chosen was a convenient spot among the pens, at the north side of the fair, not so far distant as to be impervious to the agreeable hubbub of that vanity; but remote enough not to be obvious to the interruption of every gaping spectator in it. The guests assembled about seven. In those little temporary parlours three tables were spread with napery, not so fine as substantial, and at every board a comely hostess presided with her pan of hissing sausages. The nostrils of the young rogues dilated at the savour. JAMES WHITE, as head waiter, had charge of the first table; and myself, with our trusty companion BIGOD, ordinarily ministered to the other two. There was clambering and jostling, you may be sure, who should get at the first table—for Rochester in his maddest days could not have done the humours of the scene with more spirit than my friend. After some general expression of thanks for the honour the company had done him, his inaugural ceremony was to clasp the greasy waist of old dame Ursula (the fattest of the three), that stood frying and fretting, half-blessing, half-cursing "the gentleman," and imprint upon her chaste lips a tender salute, whereat the universal host would set up a shout that tore the concave, while hundreds of grinning teeth startled the night with their brightness. O it was a pleasure to see the sable younkers lick in the unctuous meat, with *his* more unctuous sayings—how he would fit the tit-bits to the puny mouths, reserving the lengthier links for the seniors —how he would intercept a morsel even in the jaws of some young desperado, declaring it "must to the pan again to be browned, for it was not fit for a gentleman's eating"—how he would recommend this slice of white bread, or that piece of kissing-crust, to a tender juvenile, advising them all to have a care of cracking their teeth, which were their best patrimony,—how genteelly he would deal about the small ale, as if it were wine, naming the brewer, and protesting, if it were not good, he should lose their custom; with a special recommendation to wipe the lip before drinking. Then we had our toasts—"The King,"—"the Cloth,"— which, whether they understood or not, was equally diverting and flattering;—and for a crowning sentiment, which never failed, "May the Brush supersede the Laurel!" All these, and fifty other fancies, which were rather felt than comprehended by his guests, would he utter, standing upon tables, and prefacing every sentiment with a "Gentlemen, give me leave to propose so and so," which was a prodigious comfort to those young orphans; every now and then stuffing into his mouth (for it did not do to be squeamish on these occasions) indiscriminate pieces of those reeking sausages, which pleased them mightily, and was the savouriest part, you may believe, of the entertainment.

> Golden lads and lasses must,
> As chimney-sweepers, come to dust—

JAMES WHITE is extinct, and with him these suppers have long ceased. He carried away with him half the fun of the world when he died—of my world at least. His old clients look for him among the pens; and, missing him, reproach the altered feast of St. Bartholomew, and the glory of Smithfield departed for ever.

A COMPLAINT OF THE DECAY OF BEGGARS

IN THE METROPOLIS

THE all-sweeping besom of societarian reformation—your only modern Alcides' club to rid the time of its abuses—is uplift with many-handed sway to extirpate the last fluttering tatters of the bugbear MENDICITY from the metropolis. Scrips, wallets, bags—staves, dogs, and crutches— the whole mendicant fraternity, with all their baggage, are fast posting out of the purlieus of this eleventh persecution. From the crowded crossing, from the corners of streets and turnings of alleys, the parting Genius of Beggary is "with sighing sent."

I do not approve of this wholesale going to work, this impertinent crusado, or *bellum ad exterminationem*, proclaimed against a species. Much good might be sucked from these Beggars.

They were the oldest and the honourablest form of pauperism. Their appeals were to our common nature; less revolting to an ingenuous mind than to be a suppliant to the particular humours or caprice of any fellow-creature, or set of fellow-creatures, parochial or societarian. Theirs were the only rates uninvidious in the levy, ungrudged in the assessment.

There was a dignity springing from the very depth of their desolation; as to be naked is to be so much nearer to the being a man, than to go in livery.

The greatest spirits have felt this in their reverses; and when Dionysius from king turned schoolmaster, do we feel anything towards him but contempt? Could Vandyke have made a picture of him, swaying a ferula for a sceptre, which would have affected our minds with the same heroic pity, the same compassionate admiration, with which we regard his Belisarius begging for an *obolum?* Would the moral have been more graceful, more pathetic?

The Blind Beggar in the legend—the father of pretty Bessy—whose story doggrel rhymes and alehouse signs cannot so degrade or attenuate but that some sparks of a lustrous spirit will shine through the disguisements—this noble Earl of Cornwall (as indeed he was) and memorable sport of fortune, fleeing from the unjust sentence of his liege lord, stript of all, and seated on the flowering green of Bethnal, with his more fresh and springing daughter by his side, illumining his rags and his beggary—would the child and parent have cut a better figure doing the honours of a counter, or expiating their fallen condition upon the three-foot eminence of some sempstering shop-board?

In tale or history your Beggar is ever the just antipode to your King. The poets and romancical writers (as dear Margaret Newcastle would call them), when they would most sharply and feelingly paint a reverse of fortune, never stop till they have brought down their hero in good earnest to rags and the wallet. The depth of the descent illustrates the height he falls from. There is no medium which can be presented to the imagination without offence. There is no breaking the fall. Lear, thrown from his palace, must divest him of his garments, till he answer "mere nature"; and Cresseid, fallen from a prince's love, must extend her pale arms, pale with other whiteness than of beauty, supplicating lazar arms with bell and clap-dish.

The Lucian wits knew this very well; and, with a converse policy, when they would express scorn of greatness without the pity, they show us an Alexander in the shades cobbling shoes, or a Semiramis getting up foul linen.

How would it sound in song, that a great monarch had declined his affections upon the daughter of a baker! yet do we feel the imagination at all violated when we read the "true ballad," where King Cophetua woos the beggar maid?

Pauperism, pauper, poor man, are expressions of pity, but pity alloyed with contempt. No one properly contemns a Beggar. Poverty is a comparative thing, and each degree of it is mocked by its "neighbour grice." Its poor rents and comings-in are soon summed up and told. Its pretences to property are almost ludicrous. Its pitiful attempts to save excite a smile. Every scornful companion can weigh his trifle-bigger purse against it. Poor man reproaches poor man in the street with impolitic mention of his condition, his own being a shade better, while the rich pass by and jeer at both. No rascally comparative insults a Beggar, or thinks of weighing purses with him. He is not in the scale of comparison. He is not under the measure of property. He confessedly hath none, any more than a dog or a sheep. No one twitteth him with ostentation above his means. No one accuses him of pride, or upbraideth him with mock humility. None jostle with him for the wall, or pick quarrels for precedency. No wealthy neighbour seeketh to eject him from his tenement. No man sues him. No man goes to law with him. If I were not the independent gentleman that I am, rather than I would be a retainer to the great, a led captain, or a poor relation, I would choose, out of the delicacy and the true greatness of my mind, to be a Beggar.

Rags, which are the reproach of poverty, are the Beggar's robes, and graceful *insignia* of his profession, his tenure, his full dress, the suit in which he is expected to show himself in public. He is never out of the fashion, or limpeth awkwardly behind it. He is not required to put on court mourning. He weareth all colours, fearing none. His costume hath undergone less change than the Quaker's. He is the only man in the universe who is not obliged to study appearances. The ups and downs of the world concern him no longer. He alone continueth in one stay. The price of stock or land affecteth him not. The fluctuations of agricultural or commercial prosperity touch him not, or at worst but change his customers. He is not expected to become bail or surety for any one. No man troubleth him with questioning his religion or politics. He is the only free man in the universe.

The Mendicants of this great city were so many of her sights, her lions. I can no more spare them than I could the Cries of London. No corner of a street is complete without them. They are as indispensable as the Ballad Singer; and in their picturesque attire as ornamental as the signs of old London. They were the standing morals, emblems, mementos, dial-mottos, the spital sermons, the books for children, the salutary checks and pauses to the high and rushing tide of greasy citizenry—

———Look
Upon that poor and broken bankrupt there.

Above all, those old blind Tobits that used to line the wall of Lincoln's Inn Garden, before modern fastidiousness had expelled them, casting up their ruined orbs to catch a ray of pity, and (if possible) of light, with their faithful Dog Guide at their feet,—whither are they fled? or into what corners, blind as themselves, have they been driven, out of the wholesome air and sun-warmth? immersed between four walls, in what withering poor-house do they endure the penalty of double darkness, where the chink of the dropt halfpenny no more consoles their forlorn bereavement, far from the sound of the cheerful and hope-stirring tread of the passenger? Where hang their useless staves? and who will farm their dogs?—Have the overseers of St. L— caused them to be shot? or were they tied up in sacks and dropt into the Thames, at the suggestion of B—, the mild rector of ——?

Well fare the soul of unfastidious Vincent Bourne, most classical, and at the same time, most English of the Latinists!—who has treated of this human and quadrupedal alliance, this dog and man friendship, in the sweetest of his poems, the *Epitaphium in Canem,* or, *Dog's Epitaph.*

Reader, peruse it; and say, if customary sights, which could call up such gentle poetry as this, were of a nature to do more harm or good to the moral sense of the passengers through the daily thoroughfares of a vast and busy metropolis.

Pauperis hic Iri requiesco Lyciscus, herilis,
Dum vixi, tutela vigil columenque senectæ,
Dux cæco fidus: nec, me ducente, solebat,
Prætenso hinc atque hinc baculo, per iniqua locorum
Incertam explorare viam; sed fila secutus,
Quæ dubios regerent passûs, vestigia tuta
Fixit inoffenso gressu; gelidumque sedile
In nudo nactus saxo, quâ prætereuntium
Unda frequens confluxit, ibi miserisque tenebras
Lamentis, noctemque oculis ploravit obortam.
Ploravit nec frustra; obolum dedit alter et alter,
Queis corda et mentem indiderat natura benignam.
Ad latus interea jacui sopitus herile,
Vel mediis vigil in somnis; ad herilia jussa
Auresque atque animum arrectus, seu frustula amicè
Porrexit sociasque dapes, seu longa diei
Tædia perpessus, reditum sub nocte parabat.
   Hi mores, hæc vita fuit, dum fata sinebant,
Dum neque languebam morbis, nec inerte senectâ;
Quæ tandem obrepsit, veterique satellite cæcum
Orbavit dominum: prisci sed gratia facti
Ne tota intereat, longos deleta per annos,
Exiguum hunc Irus tumulum de cespite fecit,
Etsi inopis, non ingratæ, munuscula dextræ;
Carmine signavitque brevi, dominumque canemque
Quod memoret, fidumque canem dominumque benignum.

Poor Irus' faithful wolf-dog here I lie,
That wont to tend my old blind master's steps,
His guide and guard; nor, while my service lasted,
Had he occasion for that staff, with which
He now goes picking out his path in fear
Over the highways and crossings; but would plant,
Safe in the conduct of my friendly string,
A firm foot forward still, till he had reach'd
His poor seat on some stone, nigh where the tide
Of passers by in thickest confluence flow'd:
To whom with loud and passionate laments
From morn to eve his dark estate he wail'd.
Nor wail'd to all in vain: some here and there,
The well-disposed and good, their pennies gave.
I meantime at his feet obsequious slept;
Not all-asleep in sleep, but heart and ear
Prick'd up at his least motion; to receive
At his kind hand my customary crumbs,
And common portion in his feast of scraps;
Or when night warn'd us homeward, tired and spent
With our long day and tedious beggary.
   These were my manners, this my way of life,
Till age and slow disease me overtook,
And sever'd from my sightless master's side.
But lest the grace of so good deeds should die,
Through tract of years in mute oblivion lost,

This slender tomb of turf hath Irus reared,
Cheap monument of no ungrudging hand,
And with short verse inscribed it, to attest,
In long and lasting union to attest,
The virtues of the Beggar and his Dog.

These dim eyes have in vain explored for some months past a well-known figure, or part of the figure of a man, who used to glide his comely upper half over the pavements of London, wheeling along with most ingenious celerity upon a machine of wood; a spectacle to natives, to foreigners, and to children. He was of a robust make, with a florid sailor-like complexion, and his head was bare to the storm and sunshine. He was a natural curiosity, a speculation to the scientific, a prodigy to the simple. The infant would stare at the mighty man brought down to his own level. The common cripple would despise his own pusillanimity, viewing the hale stoutness, and hearty heart, of this half-limbed giant. Few but must have noticed him; for the accident which brought him low took place during the riots of 1780, and he has been a groundling so long. He seemed earth-born, an Antæus, and to suck in fresh vigour from the soil which he neighboured. He was a grand fragment; as good as an Elgin marble. The nature, which should have recruited his reft legs and thighs, was not lost, but only retired into his upper parts, and he was half a Hercules. I heard a tremendous voice thundering and growling, as before an earthquake, and casting down my eyes, it was this mandrake reviling a steed that had started at his portentous appearance. He seemed to want but his just stature to have rent the offending quadruped in shivers. He was as the man-part of a centaur, from which the horse-half had been cloven in some dire Lapithan controversy. He moved on, as if he could have made shift with yet half of the body-portion which was left him. The *os sublime* was not wanting; and he threw out yet a jolly countenance upon the heavens. Forty-and-two years had he driven this out-of-door trade, and now that his hair is grizzled in the service, but his good spirits no way impaired, because he is not content to exchange his free air and exercise for the restraints of a poor-house, he is expiating his contumacy in one of those houses (ironically christened) of Correction.

Was a daily spectacle like this to be deemed a nuisance, which called for legal interference to remove? or not rather a salutary and a touching object to the passers-by in a great city? Among her shows, her museums, and supplies for ever-gaping curiosity (and what else but an accumulation of sights—endless sights—*is* a great city; or for what else is it desirable?) was there not room for one *Lusus* (not *Naturæ*, indeed, but) *Accidentium?* What if in forty-and-two-years' going about, the man had scraped together enough to give a portion to his child (as the rumour ran) of a few hundreds—whom had he injured?—whom had he imposed upon? The contributors had enjoyed their *sight* for their pennies. What if after being exposed all day to the heats, the rains, and the frosts of heaven—shuffling his ungainly trunk along in an elaborate and painful motion—he was enabled to retire at night to enjoy himself at a club of his fellow cripples over a dish of hot meat and vegetables, as the charge was gravely brought against him by a clergyman deposing before a House of Commons' Committee—was *this*, or was his truly paternal consideration, which (if a fact) deserved a statue rather than a whipping-post, and is inconsistent, at least, with the exaggeration of nocturnal orgies which he has been slandered with—a reason that he should be deprived of his chosen, harmless, nay edifying, way of life, and be committed in hoary age for a sturdy vagabond?—

There was a Yorick once, whom it would not have shamed to have sate down at the cripples' feast, and to have thrown in his benediction, ay, and his mite too, for a companionable symbol. "Age, thou hast lost thy breed."—

Half of these stories about the prodigious fortunes made by begging are (I verily believe) misers' calumnies. One was much talked of in the public papers some time since, and the usual charitable inferences deduced. A clerk in the Bank was surprised with the announcement of a five-hundred-pound legacy left him by a person whose name he was a stranger to. It seems that in his daily morning walks from Peckham (or some village thereabouts) where he lived, to his office, it had been his practice for the last twenty years to drop his halfpenny duly into the hat of some blind Bartimeus, that sate begging alms by the wayside in the Borough. The good old beggar recognised his daily benefactor by the voice only; and, when he died, left all the amassings of his alms (that had been half a century perhaps in the accumulating) to his old Bank friend. Was this a story to purse up people's hearts, and pennies, against giving an alms to the blind?—or not rather a beautiful moral of well-directed charity on the one part, and noble gratitude upon the other?

I sometimes wish I had been that Bank clerk.

I seem to remember a poor old grateful kind of creature, blinking, and looking up with his no eyes in the sun—

Is it possible I could have steeled my purse against him?

Perhaps I had no small change.

Reader, do not be frightened at the hard words imposition, imposture —*give, and ask no questions*. Cast thy bread upon the waters. Some have unawares (like this Bank clerk) entertained angels.

Shut not thy purse-strings always against painted distress. Act a charity sometimes. When a poor creature (outwardly and visibly such) comes before thee, do not stay to inquire whether the "seven small children," in whose name he implores thy assistance, have a veritable existence. Rake not into the bowels of unwelcome truth to save a halfpenny. It is good to believe him. If he be not all that he pretendeth, *give*, and under a personate father of a family, think (if thou pleasest) that thou hast relieved an indigent bachelor. When they come with their counterfeit looks, and mumping tones, think them players. You pay your money to see a comedian feign these things, which, concerning these poor people, thou canst not certainly tell whether they are feigned or not.

A DISSERTATION UPON ROAST PIG

Mankind, says a Chinese manuscript, which my friend M. was obliging enough to read and explain to me, for the first seventy thousand ages ate their meat raw, clawing or biting it from the living animal, just as they do in Abyssinia to this day. This period is not obscurely hinted at by their great Confucius in the second chapter of his Mundane Mutations, where he designates a kind of golden age by the term Chofang, literally the Cooks' Holiday. The manuscript goes on to say, that the art of roasting, or rather broiling (which I take to be the elder brother) was accidentally discovered in the manner following. The swine-herd, Ho-ti, having gone out into the woods one morning, as his manner was, to collect mast for his hogs, left his cottage in the care of his eldest son Bo-bo, a great lubberly boy, who being fond of playing with fire, as younkers of his age commonly are, let some sparks escape into a bundle of straw, which kindling quickly, spread the conflagration over every part of their poor mansion, till it was reduced to ashes. Together with the cottage (a sorry antediluvian make-shift of a building, you may think it), what was of much more importance, a fine litter of new-farrowed pigs, no less than nine in number, perished. China pigs have been esteemed a luxury all over the East, from the remotest periods that we read of. Bo-bo was in the utmost consternation, as you may think, not so much for the sake of the tenement, which his father and he could easily build up again with a few dry branches, and the labour of an hour or two, at any time, as for the loss of the pigs. While he was thinking what he should say to his father, and wringing his hands over the smoking remnants of one of those untimely sufferers, an odour assailed his nostrils, unlike any scent which he had before experienced. What could it proceed from?—not from the burnt cottage—he had smelt that smell before—indeed this was by no means the first accident of the kind which had occurred through the negligence of this unlucky young fire-brand. Much less did it resemble that of any known herb, weed, or flower. A premonitory moistening at the same time overflowed his nether lip. He knew not what to think. He next stooped down to feel the pig, if there were any signs of life in it. He burnt his fingers, and to cool them he applied them in his booby fashion to his mouth. Some of the crumbs of the scorched skin had come away with his fingers, and for the first time in his life (in the world's life indeed, for before him no man had known it) he tasted—*crackling!* Again he felt and fumbled at the pig. It did not burn him so much now, still he licked his fingers from a sort of habit. The truth at length broke into his slow understanding, that it was the pig that smelt so, and the pig that tasted so delicious; and surrendering himself up to the new-born pleasure, he fell to tearing up whole handfuls of the scorched skin with the flesh next it, and was cramming it down his throat in his beastly fashion, when his sire entered amid the smoking rafters, armed with retributory cudgel, and finding how affairs stood, began to rain blows upon the young rogue's shoulders, as thick as hailstones, which Bo-bo heeded not any more than if they had been flies. The tickling pleasure, which he experienced in his lower regions, had rendered him quite callous to any inconveniences he might feel in those remote quarters. His father might lay on, but he could not beat him from his pig, till he had fairly made an end of it, when, becoming a little more sensible of his situation, something like the following dialogue ensued.

"You graceless whelp, what have you got there devouring? Is it not enough that you have burnt me down three houses with your dog's tricks, and be hanged to you! but you must be eating fire, and I know not what —what have you got there, I say?"

"O father, the pig, the pig! do come and taste how nice the burnt pig eats."

The ears of Ho-ti tingled with horror. He cursed his son, and he cursed himself that ever he should beget a son that should eat burnt pig.

Bo-bo, whose scent was wonderfully sharpened since morning, soon raked out another pig, and fairly rending it asunder, thrust the lesser half by main force into the fists of Ho-ti, still shouting out, "Eat, eat, eat the burnt pig, father, only taste—O Lord!"—with such-like barbarous ejaculations, cramming all the while as if he would choke.

Ho-ti trembled every joint while he grasped the abominable thing, wavering whether he should not put his son to death for an unnatural young monster, when the crackling scorching his fingers, as it had done his son's, and applying the same remedy to them, he in his turn tasted some of its flavour, which, make what sour mouths he would for a pretense, proved not altogether displeasing to him. In conclusion (for the manuscript here is a little tedious), both father and son fairly set down to the mess, and never left off till they had despatched all that remained of the litter.

Bo-bo was strictly enjoined not to let the secret escape, for the neighbours would certainly have stoned them for a couple of abominable wretches, who could think of improving upon the good meat which God had sent them. Nevertheless, strange stories got about. It was observed that Ho-ti's cottage was burnt down now more frequently than ever. Nothing but fires from this time forward. Some would break out in broad day, others in the night-time. As often as the sow farrowed, so sure was the house of Ho-ti to be in a blaze; and Ho-ti himself, which was the more remarkable, instead of chastising his son, seemed to grow more indulgent to him than ever. At length they were watched, the terrible mystery discovered, and father and son summoned to take their trial at Pekin, then an inconsiderable assize town. Evidence was given, the obnoxious food itself produced in court, and verdict about to be pronounced, when the foreman of the jury begged that some of the burnt pig, of which the culprits stood accused, might be handed into the box. He handled it, and they all handled it; and burning their fingers, as Bo-bo and his father had done before them, and nature prompting to each of them the same remedy, against the face of all the facts, and the clearest charge which judge had ever given,—to the surprise of the whole court, townsfolk, strangers, reporters, and all present—without leaving the box, or any manner of consultation whatever, they brought in a simultaneous verdict of Not Guilty.

The judge, who was a shrewd fellow, winked at the manifest iniquity of the decision: and when the court was dismissed, went privily and bought up all the pigs that could be had for love or money. In a few days his lordship's town-house was observed to be on fire. The thing took wing, and now there was nothing to be seen but fire in every direction. Fuel and pigs grew enormously dear all over the district. The insurance-offices one and all shut up shop. People built slighter and slighter every day, until it was feared that the very science of architecture would in no long time be lost to the world. Thus this custom of firing houses continued, till in process of time, says my manuscript, a sage arose, like our Locke, who made a discovery that the flesh of swine, or indeed of any other animal, might be cooked (*burnt,* as they called it) without the necessity of consuming a whole house to dress it. Then first began the rude form of a gridiron. Roasting by the string or spit came in a century or two later, I forget in whose dynasty. By such slow degrees, concludes the manuscript, do the most useful, and seemingly the most obvious, arts make their way among mankind——

Without placing too implicit faith in the account above given, it must be agreed that if a worthy pretext for so dangerous an experiment as setting houses on fire (especially in these days) could be assigned in favour of any culinary object, that pretext and excuse might be found in ROAST PIG.

Of all the delicacies in the whole *mundus edibilis,* I will maintain it to be the most delicate—*princeps obsoniorum.*

I speak not of your grown porkers—things between pig and pork—those hobbydehoys—but a young and tender suckling—under a moon old—guiltless as yet of the sty—with no original speck of the *amor immunditæ,* the hereditary failing of the first parent, yet manifest—his voice as yet not broken, but something between a childish treble and a grumble—the mild forerunner or *præludium* of a grunt.

He must be roasted. I am not ignorant that our ancestors ate them seethed, or boiled—but what a sacrifice to the exterior tegument!

There is no flavour comparable, I will contend, to that of the crisp, tawny, well-watched, not over-roasted, *crackling,* as it is well called—the very teeth are invited to their share of the pleasure at this banquet in overcoming the coy, brittle resistance—with the adhesive oleaginous —O call it not fat! but an indefinable sweetness growing up to it—the tender blossoming of fat—fat cropped in the bud—taken in the shoot—in the first innocence—the cream and quintessence of the child-pig's yet pure food—the lean, no lean, but a kind of animal manna—or, rather, fat and lean (if it must be so) so blended and running into each other, that both together make but one ambrosian result or common substance.

Behold him, while he is "doing"—it seemeth rather a refreshing warmth, than a scorching heat, that he is so passive to. How equably he twirleth round the string!—Now he is just done. To see the extreme sensibility of that tender age! he hath wept out his pretty eyes—radiant jellies—shooting stars.—

See him in the dish, his second cradle, how meek he lieth!—wouldst thou have had this innocent grow up to the grossness and indocility which too often accompany maturer swinehood? Ten to one he would have proved a glutton, a sloven, an obstinate, disagreeable animal—wallowing in all manner of filthy conversation—from these sins he is happily snatched away—

> Ere sin could blight or sorrow fade,
> Death came with timely care—

his memory is odoriferous—no clown curseth, while his stomach half rejecteth, the rank bacon—no coal-heaver bolteth him in reeking sausages—he hath a fair sepulchre in the grateful stomach of the judicious epicure—and for such a tomb might be content to die.

He is the best of sapors. Pine-apple is great. She is indeed almost too transcendent—a delight, if not sinful, yet so like to sinning that really a tender-conscienced person would do well to pause—too ravishing for mortal taste, she woundeth and excoriateth the lips that approach her —like lovers' kisses, she biteth—she is a pleasure bordering on pain from the fierceness and insanity of her relish—but she stoppeth at the palate—she meddleth not with the appetite—and the coarsest hunger might barter her consistently for a mutton-chop.

Pig—let me speak his praise—is no less provocative of the appetite, than he is satisfactory to the criticalness of the censorious palate. The strong man may batten on him, and the weakling refuseth not his mild juices.

Unlike to mankind's mixed characters, a bundle of virtues and vices, inexplicably intertwisted, and not to be unravelled without hazard, he is—good throughout. No part of him is better or worse than another. He helpeth, as far as his little means extend, all around. He is the least envious of banquets. He is all neighbours' fare.

I am one of those, who freely and ungrudgingly impart a share of the good things of this life which fall to their lot (few as mine are in this kind) to a friend. I protest I take as great an interest in my friend's pleasures, his relishes, and proper satisfactions, as in mine own. "Presents," I often say, "endear Absents." Hares, pheasants, partridges, snipes, barndoor chickens (those "tame villatic fowl"), capons, plovers, brawn, barrels of oysters, I dispense as freely as I receive them. I love to taste them, as it were, upon the tongue of my friend. But a stop must be put somewhere. One would not, like Lear, "give everything." I make my stand upon pig. Methinks it is an ingratitude to the Giver of all good flavours to extra-domiciliate, or send out of the house slightingly (under pretext of friendship, or I know not what) a blessing so particularly adapted, predestined, I may say, to my individual palate—It argues an insensibility.

I remember a touch of conscience in this kind at school. My good old aunt, who never parted from me at the end of a holiday without stuffing a sweetmeat, or some nice thing into my pocket, had dismissed me one evening with a smoking plum-cake, fresh from the oven. In my way to school (it was over London Bridge) a grey-headed old beggar saluted me (I have no doubt, at this time of day, that he was a counterfeit). I had no pence to console him with, and in the vanity of self-denial and the very coxcombry of charity, schoolboy-like, I made him a present of —the whole cake! I walked on a little, buoyed up, as one is on such occasions, with a sweet soothing of self-satisfaction; but before I had got to the end of the bridge, my better feelings returned, and I burst into tears, thinking how ungrateful I had been to my good aunt, to go and give her good gift away to a stranger that I had never seen before, and who might be a bad man for aught I knew; and then I thought of the pleasure my aunt would be taking in thinking that I—I myself, and not another—would eat her nice cake—and what should I say to her the next time I saw her—how naughty I was to part with her pretty present! —and the odour of that spicy cake came back upon my recollection, and the pleasure and the curiosity I had taken in seeing her make it, and her joy when she sent it to the oven, and how disappointed she would feel that I had never had a bit of it in my mouth at last—and I blamed my impertinent spirit of alms-giving, and out-of-place hypocrisy of good-ness; and above all I wished never to see the face again of that insidious, good-for-nothing, old grey impostor.

Our ancestors were nice in their method of sacrificing these tender victims. We read of pigs whipt to death with something of a shock, as we hear of any other obsolete custom. The age of discipline is gone by, or it would be curious to inquire (in a philosophical light merely) what effect this process might have towards intenerating and dulcifying a sub-stance, naturally so mild and dulcet as the flesh of young pigs. It looks like refining a violet. Yet we should be cautious, while we condemn the inhumanity, how we censure the wisdom of the practice. It might impart a gusto.—

I remember an hypothesis, argued upon by the young students, when I was at St. Omer's, and maintained with much learning and pleasantry on both sides, "Whether, supposing that the flavour of a pig who ob-tained his death by whipping (*per flagellationem extremam*) superadded a pleasure upon the palate of a man more intense than any possible suf-fering we can conceive in the animal, is man justified in using that method of putting the animal to death?" I forget the decision.

His sauce should be considered. Decidedly, a few bread crumbs, done up with his liver and brains, and a dash of mild sage. But banish, dear Mrs. Cook, I beseech you, the whole onion tribe. Barbecue your whole hogs to your palate, steep them in shalots, stuff them out with plantations of the rank and guilty garlic; you cannot poison them, or make them stronger than they are—but consider, he is a weakling—a flower.

A BACHELOR'S COMPLAINT OF THE BEHAVIOUR OF MARRIED PEOPLE

As a single man, I have spent a good deal of my time in noting down the infirmities of Married People, to console myself for those superior pleasures, which they tell me I have lost by remaining as I am.

I cannot say that the quarrels of men and their wives ever made any great impression upon me, or had much tendency to strengthen in those anti-social resolutions, which I took up long ago upon more substantial considerations. What oftenest offends me at the houses of married persons where I visit, is an error of quite a different description;—it is that they are too loving.

Not too loving neither: that does not explain my meaning. Besides, why should that offend me? The very act of separating themselves from the rest of the world, to have the fuller enjoyment of each other's society, implies that they prefer one another to all the world.

But what I complain of is, that they carry this preference so undisguisedly, they perk it up in the faces of us single people so shamelessly, you cannot be in their company a moment without being made to feel, by some indirect hint or open avowal, that *you* are not the object of this preference. Now there are some things which give no offence, while implied or taken for granted merely; but expressed, there is much offence in them. If a man were to accost the first homely-featured or plain-dressed young woman of his acquaintance, and tell her bluntly, that she was not handsome or rich enough for him, and he could not marry her, he would deserve to be kicked for his ill manners; yet no less is implied in the fact, that having access and opportunity of putting the question to her, he has never yet thought fit to do it. The young woman understands this as clearly as if it were put into words; but no reasonable young woman would think of making this the ground of a quarrel. Just as little right have a married couple to tell me by speeches, and looks that are scarce less plain than speeches, that I am not the happy man,—the lady's choice. It is enough that I know I am not: I do not want this perpetual reminding.

The display of superior knowledge or riches may be made sufficiently mortifying; but these admit of a palliative. The knowledge which is brought out to insult me, may accidentally improve me; and in the rich man's houses and pictures,—his parks and gardens, I have a temporary usufruct at least. But the display of married happiness has none of these palliatives: it is throughout pure, unrecompensed, unqualified insult.

Marriage by its best title is a monopoly, and not of the least invidious sort. It is the cunning of most possessors of any exclusive privilege to keep their advantage as much out of sight as possible, that their less favoured neighbours, seeing little of the benefit, may the less be disposed to question the right. But these married monopolists thrust the most obnoxious part of their patent into our faces.

Nothing is to me more distasteful than that entire complacency and satisfaction which beam in the countenances of a new-married couple,—in that of the lady particularly: it tells you, that her lot is disposed of in this world: that *you* can have no hopes of her. It is true, I have none: nor wishes either, perhaps; but this is one of those truths which ought, as I said before, to be taken for granted, not expressed.

The excessive airs which those people give themselves, founded on the ignorance of us unmarried people, would be more offensive if they were less irrational. We will allow them to understand the mysteries belonging to their own craft better than we, who have not had the happiness to be made free of the company: but their arrogance is not content within these limits. If a single person presume to offer his opinion in their presence, though upon the most indifferent subject, he is immediately silenced as an incompetent person. Nay, a young married lady of my acquaintance, who, the best of the jest was, had not changed her condition above a fortnight before, in a question on which I had the misfortune to differ from her, respecting the properest mode of breeding oysters for the London market, had the assurance to ask with a sneer, how such an old Bachelor as I could pretend to know anything about such matters!

But what I have spoken of hitherto is nothing to the airs these creatures give themselves when they come, as they generally do, to have children. When I consider how little of a rarity children are,—that every street and blind alley swarms with them,—that the poorest people commonly have them in most abundance,—that there are few marriages that are not blest with at least one of these bargains,—how often they turn out ill, and defeat the fond hopes of their parents, taking to vicious courses, which end in poverty, disgrace, the gallows, etc.—I cannot for my life tell what cause for pride there can possibly be in having them. If they were young phœnixes, indeed, that were born but one in a year, there might be a pretext. But when they are so common——

I do not advert to the insolent merit which they assume with their husbands on these occasions. Let *them* look to that. But why *we*, who are not their natural-born subjects, should be expected to bring our spices, myrrh, and incense,—our tribute and homage of admiration,—I do not see.

"Like as the arrows in the hand of the giant, even so are the young children": so says the excellent office in our Prayer-book appointed for the churching of women. "Happy is the man that hath his quiver full of them": So say I; but then don't let him discharge his quiver upon us that are weaponless;—let them be arrows, but not to gall and stick us. I have generally observed that these arrows are double-headed: they have two forks, to be sure to hit with one or the other. As for instance, where you come into a house which is full of children, if you happen to take no notice of them (you are thinking of something else, perhaps, and turn a deaf ear to their innocent caresses), you are set down as untractable, morose, a hater of children. On the other hand, if you find them more than usually engaging,—if you are taken with their pretty manners, and set about in earnest to romp and play with them, some pretext or other is sure to be found for sending them out of the room; they are too noisy or boisterous, or Mr. —— does not like children. With one or other of these folks the arrow is sure to hit you.

I could forgive their jealousy, and dispense with toying with their brats, if it gives them any pain; but I think it unreasonable to be called upon to *love* them, where I see no occasion,—to love a whole family, perhaps eight, nine, or ten, indiscriminately,—to love all the pretty dears, because children are so engaging!

I know there is a proverb, "Love me, love my dog": that is not always so very practicable, particularly if the dog be set upon you to tease you or snap at you in sport. But a dog, or a lesser thing—any inanimate substance, as a keepsake, a watch or a ring, a tree, or the place where we last parted when my friend went away upon a long absence, I can make shift to love, because I love him, and anything that reminds me of him; provided it be in its nature indifferent, and apt to receive whatever hue fancy can give it. But children have a real character, and an essential being of themselves: they are amiable or unamiable *per se;* I must love or hate them as I see cause for either in their qualities. A child's nature is too serious a thing to admit of its being regarded as a mere appendage to another being, and to be loved or hated accordingly: they stand with me upon their own stock, as much as men and women do. Oh! but you will say, sure it is an attractive age,—there is something in the tender years of infancy that of itself charms us? This is the very reason why I am more nice about them. I know that a sweet child is the sweetest thing in nature, not even excepting the delicate creatures which bear them; but the prettier the kind of a thing is, the more desirable it is that it should be pretty of its kind. One daisy differs not much from another in glory; but a violet should look and smell the daintiest.—I was always rather squeamish in my women and children.

But this is not the worst: one must be admitted into their familiarity at least, before they can complain of inattention. It implies visits, and some kind of intercourse. But if the husband be a man with whom you have lived on a friendly footing before marriage—if you did not come in on the wife's side—if you did not sneak into the house in her train, but were an old friend in fast habits of intimacy before their courtship was so much as thought on,—look about you—your tenure is precarious—before a twelvemonth shall roll over your head, you shall find your old friend gradually grow cool and altered towards you, and at last seek opportunities of breaking with you. I have scarce a married friend of my acquaintance, upon whose firm faith I can rely, whose friendship did not commence *after the period of his marriage.* With some limitations, they can endure that; but that the good man should have dared to enter into a solemn league of friendship in which they were not consulted, though it happened before they knew him,—before they that are now man and wife ever met,—this is intolerable to them. Every long friendship, every old authentic intimacy, must be brought into their office to be new stamped with their currency, as a sovereign prince calls in the good old money that was coined in some reign before he was born or thought of, to be new marked and minted with the stamp of his authority, before he will let it pass current in the world. You may guess what luck generally befalls such a rusty piece of metal as I am in these *new mintings*.

Innumerable are the ways which they take to insult and worm you out of their husband's confidence. Laughing at all you say with a kind of wonder, as if you were a queer kind of fellow that said good things, *but an oddity,* is one of the ways;—they have a particular kind of stare for the purpose;—till at last the husband, who used to defer to your judgment, and would pass over some excrescences of understanding and manner for the sake of a general vein of observation (not quite vulgar) which he perceived in you, begins to suspect whether you are not altogether a humourist,—a fellow well enough to have consorted with in his bachelor days, but not quite so proper to be introduced to ladies. This may be called the staring way; and is that which has oftenest been put in practice against me.

Then there is the exaggerating way, or the way of irony; that is, where they find you an object of especial regard with their husband, who is not so easily to be shaken from the lasting attachment founded on esteem which he has conceived towards you, by never qualified exaggerations to cry up all that you say or do, till the good man, who understands well enough that it is all done in compliment to him, grows weary of the debt of gratitude which is due to so much candour, and by relaxing a little on his part, and taking down a peg or two in his enthusiasm, sinks at length to the kindly level of moderate esteem—that "decent affection and complacent kindness" towards you, where she herself can join in sympathy with him without much stretch and violence to her sincerity.

Another way (for the ways they have to accomplish so desirable a purpose are infinite) is, with a kind of innocent simplicity, continually to mistake what it was which first made their husband fond of you. If an esteem for something excellent in your moral character was that which riveted the chain which she is to break, upon any imaginary discovery of a want of poignancy in your conversation, she will cry, "I thought, my dear, you described your friend, Mr. ———, as a great wit?" If, on the other hand, it was for some supposed charm in your conversation that he first grew to like you, and was content for this to overlook some trifling irregularities in your moral deportment, upon the first notice of any of these she as readily exclaims, "This, my dear, is your good Mr. ———!" One good lady whom I took the liberty of expostulating with for not showing me quite so much respect as I thought due to her husband's old friend, had the candour to confess to me that she had often heard Mr.

———— speak of me before marriage, and that she had conceived a great desire to be acquainted with me, but that the sight of me had very much disappointed her expectations; for from her husband's representations of me, she had formed a notion that she was to see a fine, tall, officer-like-looking man (I use her very words), the very reverse of which proved to be the truth. This was candid; and I had the civility not to ask her in return, how she came to pitch upon a standard of personal accomplishments for her husband's friends which differed so much from his own; for my friend's dimensions as near as possible approximate to mine; he standing five feet five in his shoes, in which I have the advantage of him by about half an inch; and he no more than myself exhibiting any indications of a martial character in his air or countenance.

These are some of the mortifications which I have encountered in the absurd attempt to visit at their houses. To enumerate them all would be a vain endeavour; I shall therefore just glance at the very common impropriety of which married ladies are guilty,—of treating us as if we were their husbands, and *vice versâ*. I mean, when they use us with familiarity, and their husbands with ceremony. *Testacea,* for instance, kept me the other night two or three hours beyond by usual time of supping, while she was fretting because Mr. ———— did not come home, till the oysters were all spoiled, rather than she would be guilty of the impoliteness of touching one in his absence. This was reversing the point of good manners: for ceremony is an invention to take off the uneasy feeling which we derive from knowing ourselves to be less the object of love and esteem with a fellow-creature than some other person is. It endeavours to make up, by superior attentions in little points, for that invidious preference which it is forced to deny in the greater. Had *Testacea* kept the oysters back for me, and withstood her husband's importunities to go to supper, she would have acted according to the strict rules of propriety. I know no ceremony that ladies are bound to observe to their husbands, beyond the point of a modest behaviour and decorum: therefore I must protest against the vicarious gluttony of *Cerasia,* who at her own table sent away a dish of Morellas, which I was applying to with great good-will, to her husband at the other end of the table, and recommended a plate of less extraordinary gooseberries to my unwedded palate in their stead. Neither can I excuse the wanton affront of ————

But I am weary of stringing up all my married acquaintances by Roman denominations. Let them amend and change their manners, or I promise to record the full-length English of their names, to the terror of all such desperate offenders in future.

ON SOME OF THE OLD ACTORS

THE casual sight of an old Play Bill, which I picked up the other day—I know not by what chance it was preserved so long—tempts me to call to mind a few of the Players, who make the principal figure in it. It presents the cast of parts in the Twelfth Night, at the old Drury Lane Theatre two-and-thirty years ago. There is something very touching in these old remembrances. They make us think how we *once* used to read a Play Bill—not, as now peradventure, singling out a favourite performer, and casting a negligent eye over the rest; but spelling out every name, down to the very mutes and servants of the scene;—when it was a matter of no small moment to us whether Whitfield, or Packer, took the part of Fabian; when Benson, and Burton, and Phillimore—names of small account—had an importance, beyond what we can be content to attribute now to the time's best actors.—"Orsino, by Mr. Barrymore." —What a full Shakspearian sound it carries! how fresh to memory arise the image and the manner of the gentle actor!

Those who have only seen Mrs. Jordan within the last ten or fifteen years, can have no adequate notion of her performance of such parts as Ophelia; Helena, in All's Well that Ends Well; and Viola in this play. Her voice had latterly acquired a coarseness, which suited well enough with her Nells and Hoydens, but in those days it sank, with her steady, melting eye, into the heart. Her joyous parts—in which her memory now chiefly lives—in her youth were outdone by her plaintive ones. There is no giving an account how she delivered the disguised story of her love for Orsino. It was no set speech, that she had foreseen, so as to weave it into an harmonious period, line necessarily following line, to make up the music—yet I have heard it so spoken, or rather *read,* not without its grace and beauty—but, when she had declared her sister's history to be a "blank," and that she "never told her love," there was a pause, as if the story had ended—and then the image of the "worm in the bud," came up as a new suggestion—and the heightened image of "Patience" still followed after that, as by some growing (and not mechanical) process, thought springing up after thought, I would almost say, as they were watered by her tears. So in those fine lines—

> Right loyal cantos of contemned love—
> Hollow your name to the reverberate hills—

there was no preparation made in the foregoing image for that which was to follow. She used no rhetoric in her passion; or it was nature's own rhetoric, most legitimate then, when it seemed altogether without rule or law.

Mrs. Powel (now Mrs. Renard), then in the pride of her beauty, made an admirable Olivia. She was particularly excellent in her unbending scenes in conversation with the Clown. I have seen some Olivias—and those very sensible actresses too—who in these interlocutions have seemed to set their wits at the jester, and to vie conceits with him in downright emulation. But she used him for her sport, like what he was, to trifle a leisure sentence or two with, and then to be dismissed, and she to be the Great Lady still. She touched the imperious fantastic humour of the character with nicety. Her fine spacious person filled the scene.

The part of Malvolio has, in my judgment, been so often misunderstood, and the *general merits* of the actor, who then played it, so unduly appreciated, that I shall hope for pardon, if I am a little prolix upon these points.

Of all the actors who flourished in my time—a melancholy phrase if taken aright, reader—Bensley had most of the swell of soul, was greatest in the delivery of heroic conceptions, the emotions consequent upon the presentment of a great idea to the fancy. He had the true poetical enthusiasm—the rarest faculty among players. None that I remember possessed even a portion of that fine madness which he threw out in Hotspur's famous rant about glory, or the transports of the Venetian incendiary at the vision of the fired city. His voice had the dissonance, and at times the inspiriting effect, of the trumpet. His gait was uncouth and stiff, but no way embarrassed by affectation; and the thorough-bred gentleman was uppermost in every movement. He seized the moment of passion with greatest truth; like a faithful clock, never striking before the time; never anticipating or leading you to anticipate. He was totally destitute of trick and artifice. He seemed come upon the stage to do the poet's message simply, and he did it with as genuine fidelity as the nuncios in Homer deliver the errands of the gods. He let the passion or the sentiment do its own work without prop or bolstering. He would have scorned to mountebank it; and betrayed none of that *cleverness* which is the bane of serious acting. For this reason, his Iago was the only endurable one which I remember to have seen. No spectator, from his action, could divine more of his artifice than Othello was supposed to do. His confessions in soliloquy alone put you in possession of the mystery. There were no by-intimations to make the audience fancy their own discernment so much greater than that of the Moor—who commonly stands like a great helpless mark, set up for mine Ancient, and a quantity of barren spectators, to shoot their bolts at. The Iago of Bensley did not go to work so grossly. There was a triumphant tone about the character, natural to a general consciousness of power; but none of that petty vanity which chuckles and cannot contain itself upon any little successful stroke of its knavery—as is common with your small villains, and green probationers in mischief. It did not clap or crow before its time. It was not a man setting his wits at a child, and winking all the while at other children, who are mightily pleased at being let into the secret; but a consummate villain entrapping a noble nature into toils, against which no discernment was available, where the manner was as fathomless as the purpose seemed dark, and without motive. The part of Malvolio, in the Twelfth Night, was performed by Bensley, with a richness and a dignity, of which (to judge from some recent castings of that character) the very tradition must be worn out from the stage. No manager in those days would have dreamed of giving it to Mr. Baddeley, or Mr. Parsons; when Bensley was occasionally absent from the theatre, John Kemble thought it no derogation to succeed to the part. Malvolio is not essentially ludicrous. He becomes comic but by accident. He is cold, austere, repelling;

but dignified, consistent, and, for what appears, rather of an over-stretched morality. Maria describes him as a sort of Puritan; and he might have worn his gold chain with honour in one of our old roundhead families, in the service of a Lambert, or a Lady Fairfax. But his morality and his manners are misplaced in Illyria. He is opposed to the proper *levities* of the piece, and falls in the unequal contest. Still his pride, or his gravity (call it which you will), is inherent, and native to the man, not mock or affected, which latter only are the fit objects to excite laughter. His quality is at the best unlovely, but neither buffoon nor contemptible. His bearing is lofty, a little above his station, but probably not much above his deserts. We see no reason why he should not have been brave, honourable, accomplished. His careless committal of the ring to the ground (which he was commissioned to restore to Cesario), bespeaks a generosity of birth and feeling. His dialect on all occasions is that of a gentleman, and a man of education. We must not confound him with the eternal old, low steward of comedy. He is master of the household to a great princess; a dignity probably conferred upon him for other respects than age or length of service. Olivia, at the first in-dication of his supposed madness, declares that she "would not have him miscarry for half of her dowry." Does this look as if the character was meant to appear little or insignificant? Once, indeed, she accuses him to his face—of what?—of being "sick of self-love,"—but with a gentleness and considerateness, which could not have been, if she had not thought that this particular infirmity shaded some virtues. His rebuke to the knight, and his sottish revellers, is sensible and spirited; and when we take into consideration the unprotected condition of his mistress, and the strict regard with which her state of real or dissembled mourning would draw the eyes of the world upon her house-affairs, Malvolio might feel the honour of the family in some sort in his keeping; as it appears not that Olivia had any more brothers, or kinsmen, to look to it—for Sir Toby had dropped all such nice respects at the buttery-hatch. That Malvolio was meant to be represented as possessing estimable qualities, the expression of the Duke, in his anxiety to have him reconciled, almost infers: "Pursue him, and entreat him to a peace." Even in his abused state of chains and darkness, a sort of greatness seems never to desert him. He argues highly and well with the supposed Sir Topas, and philos-ophises gallantly upon his straw.[1] There must have been some shadow of worth about the man; he must have been something more than a mere vapour—a thing of straw, or Jack in office—before Fabian and Maria could have ventured sending him upon a courting-errand to Olivia. There was some consonancy (as he would say) in the undertaking, or the jest would have been too bold even for that house of misrule.

Bensley, accordingly, threw over the part an air of Spanish loftiness.

[1] CLOWN.   What is the opinion of Pythagoras concerning wild fowl?
MAL.   That the soul of our grandam might haply inhabit a bird.
CLOWN.   What thinkest thou of his opinion?
MAL.   I think nobly of the soul, and no way approve of his opinion.

He looked, spake, and moved like an old Castilian. He was starch, spruce, opinionated, but his superstructure of pride seemed bottomed upon a sense of worth. There was something in it beyond the coxcomb. It was big and swelling, but you could not be sure that it was hollow. You might wish to see it taken down, but you felt that it was upon an elevation. He was magnificent from the outset; but when the decent sobrieties of the character began to give way, and the poison of self-love, in his conceit of the Countess's affection, gradually to work, you would have thought that the hero of La Mancha in person stood before you. How he went smiling to himself! with what ineffable carelessness would he twirl his gold chain! what a dream it was! you were infected with the illusion, and did not wish that it should be removed! you had no room for laughter! if an unseasonable reflection of morality obtruded itself, it was a deep sense of the pitiable infirmity of man's nature, that can lay him open to such frenzies—but, in truth, you rather admired than pitied the lunacy while it lasted—you felt that an hour of such mistake was worth an age with the eyes open. Who would not wish to live but for a day in the conceit of such a lady's love as Olivia? Why, the Duke would have given his principality but for a quarter of a minute, sleeping or waking, to have been so deluded. The man seemed to tread upon air, to taste manna, to walk with his head in the clouds, to mate Hyperion. O! shake not the castles of his pride—endure yet for a season bright moments of confidence—"stand still, ye watches of the element," that Malvolio may be still in fancy fair Olivia's lord!—but fate and retribution say no—I hear the mischievous titter of Maria—the witty taunts of Sir Toby—the still more insupportable triumph of the foolish knight— the counterfeit Sir Topas is unmasked—and "thus the whirligig of time," as the true clown hath it, "brings in his revenges." I confess that I never saw the catastrophe of this character, while Bensley played it, without a kind of tragic interest. There was good foolery too. Few now remember Dodd. What an Aguecheek the stage lost in him! Lovegrove, who came nearest to the old actors, revived the character some few seasons ago, and made it sufficiently grotesque; but Dodd was *it*, as it came out of nature's hands. It might be said to remain *in puris naturalibus*. In expressing slowness of apprehension, this actor surpassed all others. You could see the first dawn of an idea stealing slowly over his countenance, climbing up by little and little, with a painful process, till it cleared up at last to the fulness of a twilight conception—its highest meridian. He seemed to keep back his intellect, as some have had the power to retard their pulsation. The balloon takes less time in filling than it took to cover the expansion of his broad moony face over all its quarters with expression. A glimmer of understanding would appear in a corner of his eye, and for lack of fuel go out again. A part of his forehead would catch a little intelligence, and be a long time in communicating it to the remainder.

I am ill at dates, but I think it is now better than five-and-twenty years ago, that walking in the gardens of Gray's Inn—they were then far finer than they are now—the accursed Verulam Buildings had not encroached upon all the east side of them, cutting out delicate green crankles, and shouldering away one of two of the stately alcoves of the terrace—the survivor stands gaping and relationless as if it remembered its brother—they are still the best gardens of any of the Inns of Court, my beloved Temple not forgotten—have the gravest character; their aspect being altogether reverend and law-breathing—Bacon has left the impress of his foot upon their gravel walks——taking my afternoon solace on a summer day upon the aforesaid terrace, a comely sad personage came towards me, whom, from his grave air and deportment, I judged to be one of the old Benchers of the Inn. He had a serious, thoughtful forehead, and seemed to be in meditations of mortality. As I have an instinctive awe of old Benchers, I was passing him with that sort of subindicative token of respect which one is apt to demonstrate towards a venerable stranger, and which rather denotes an inclination to greet him, than any positive motion of the body to that effect—a species of humility and will-worship which I observe, nine times out of ten, rather puzzles than pleases the person it is offered to—when the face turning full upon me, strangely identified itself with that of Dodd. Upon close inspection I was not mistaken. But could this sad thoughtful countenance be the same vacant face of folly which I had hailed so often under circumstances of gaiety; which I had never seen without a smile, or recognised but as the usher of mirth; that looked out so formally flat in Foppington, so frothily pert in Tattle, so impotently busy in Backbite; so blankly divested of all meaning, or resolutely expressive of none, in Acres, in Fribble, and a thousand agreeable impertinences? Was this the face—full of thought and carefulness—that had so often divested itself at will of every trace of either to give me diversion, to clear my cloudy face for two or three hours at least of its furrows? Was this the face—manly, sober, intelligent—which I had so often despised, made mocks at, made merry with? The remembrance of the freedoms which I had taken with it came upon me with a reproach of insult. I could have asked it pardon. I thought it looked upon me with a sense of injury. There is something strange as well as sad in seeing actors—your pleasant fellows particularly—subjected to and suffering the common lot;—their fortunes, their casualties, their deaths, seem to belong to the scene, their actions to be amenable to poetic justice only. We can hardly connect them with more awful responsibilities. The death of this fine actor took place shortly after this meeting. He had quitted the stage some months; and, as I learned afterwards, had been in the habit of resorting daily to these gardens, almost to the day of his decease. In these serious walks, probably, he was divesting himself of many scenic and some real vanities—weaning himself from the frivolities of the lesser and the greater theatre—doing gentle penance for a life of no very reprehensible fooleries—taking off by degrees the buffoon mask, which he might feel he had worn too long—and rehearsing for a more solemn cast of part. Dying, he "put on the weeds of Dominic." [1]

---

[1] Dodd was a man of reading, and left at his death a choice collection of old English literature. I should judge him to have been a man of wit. I know one

If few can remember Dodd, many yet living will not easily forget the pleasant creature who in those days enacted the part of the Clown to Dodd's Sir Andrew.—Richard, or rather Dicky Suett—for so in his lifetime he delighted to be called, and time hath ratified the appellation— lieth buried on the north side of the cemetery of Holy Paul, to whose service his nonage and tender years were dedicated. There are who do yet remember him at that period—his pipe clear and harmonious. He would often speak of his chorister days, when he was "cherub Dicky."

What clipped his wings, or made it expedient that he should exchange the holy for the profane state; whether he had lost his good voice (his best recommendation to that office), like Sir John, "with hallooing and singing of anthems"; or whether he was adjudged to lack something, even in those early years, of the gravity indispensable to an occupation which professeth to "commerce with the skies,"—I could never rightly learn; but we find him, after the probation of a twelvemonth or so, reverting to a secular condition, and become one of us.

I think he was not altogether of that timber out of which cathedral seats and sounding-boards are hewed. But if a glad heart—kind, and therefore glad—be any part of sanctity, then might the robe of Motley, with which he invested himself with so much humility after his deprivation, and which he wore so long with so much blameless satisfaction to himself and to the public, be accepted for a surplice—his white stole, and *albe*.

The first fruits of his secularisation was an engagement upon the boards of Old Drury, at which theatre he commenced, as I have been told, with adopting the manner of Parsons in old men's characters. At the period in which most of us knew him, he was no more an imitator than he was in any true sense himself imitable.

He was the Robin Goodfellow of the stage. He came in to trouble all things with a welcome perplexity, himself no whit troubled for the matter. He was known, like Puck, by his note—*Ha! Ha! Ha!*—sometimes deepening to *Ho! Ho! Ho!* with an irresistible accession, derived, perhaps, remotely from his ecclesiastical education, foreign to his prototype of —*O La!* Thousands of hearts yet respond to the chuckling *O La!* of Dicky Suett, brought back to their remembrance by the faithful transcript of his friend Mathews's mimicry. The "force of nature could no further go." He drolled upon the stock of these two syllables richer than the cuckoo.

Care, that troubles all the world, was forgotten in his composition. Had he had but two grains (nay, half a grain) of it, he could never have supported himself upon those two spider's strings, which served him (in

instance of an impromptu which no length of study could have bettered. My merry friend, Jem White, had seen him one evening in Aguecheek, and recognising Dodd the next day in Fleet Street, was irresistibly impelled to take off his hat and salute him as the identical Knight of the preceding evening with a "Save you, *Sir Andrew.*" Dodd, not at all disconcerted at this unusual address from a stranger, with a courteous half-rebuking wave of the hand, put him off with an "Away, *Fool.*"

the latter part of his unmixed existence) as legs. A doubt or a scruple must have made him totter, a sigh have puffed him down; the weight of a frown had staggered him, a wrinkle made him lose his balance. But on he went, scrambling upon those airy stilts of his, with Robin Goodfellow, "thorough brake, thorough briar," reckless of a scratched face or a torn doublet.

Shakspeare foresaw him, when he framed his fools and jesters. They have all the true Suett stamp, a loose and shambling gait, a slippery tongue, this last the ready midwife to a without-pain-delivered jest; in words, light as air, venting truths deep as the centre; with idlest rhymes tagging conceit when busiest, singing with Lear in the tempest, or Sir Toby at the buttery-hatch.

Jack Bannister and he had the fortune to be more of personal favourites with the town than any actors before or after. The difference, I take it, was this:—Jack was more *beloved* for his sweet, good-natured moral pretensions. Dicky was more *liked* for his sweet, good-natured, no pretensions at all. Your whole conscience stirred with Bannister's performance of Walter in the Children in the Wood—but Dicky seemed like a thing, as Shakspeare says of Love, too young to know what conscience is. He put us into Vesta's days. Evil fled before him—not as from Jack, as from an antagonist,—but because it could not touch him, any more than a cannon-ball a fly. He was delivered from the burthen of that death; and, when Death came himself, not in metaphor, to fetch Dicky, it is recorded of him by Robert Palmer, who kindly watched his exit, that he received the last stroke, neither varying his accustomed tranquillity, nor tune, with the simple exclamation, worthy to have been recorded in his epitaph—*O La! O La! Bobby!*

The elder Palmer (of stage-treading celebrity) commonly played Sir Toby in those days; but there is a solidity of wit in the jests of that half-Falstaff which he did not quite fill out. He was as much too showy as Moody (who sometimes took the part) was dry and sottish. In sock or buskin there was an air of swaggering gentility about Jack Palmer. He was a *gentleman* with a slight infusion of *the footman*. His brother Bob (of recenter memory), who was his shadow in everything while he lived, and dwindled into less than a shadow afterwards—was a *gentleman* with a little stronger infusion of the *latter ingredient;* that was all. It is amazing how a little of the more or less makes a difference in these things. When you saw Bobby in the Duke's Servant,[1] you said "What a pity such a pretty fellow was only a servant!" When you saw Jack figuring as Captain Absolute, you thought you could trace his promotion to some lady of quality who fancied the handsome fellow in his topknot, and had bought him a commission. Therefore Jack in Dick Amlet was insuperable.

Jack had two voices, both plausible, hypocritical, and insinuating; but his secondary or supplemental voice still more decisively histrionic than

---

[1] *High Life Below Stairs.*

his common one. It was reserved for the spectator; and the *dramatis personæ* were supposed to know nothing at all about it. The *lies* of Young Wilding, and the *sentiments* in Joseph Surface, were thus marked out in a sort of italics to the audience. This secret correspondence with the company before the curtain (which is the bane and death of tragedy) has an extremely happy effect in some kinds of comedy, in the more highly artificial comedy of Congreve or of Sheridan especially, where the absolute sense of reality (so indispensable to scenes of interest) is not required, or would rather interfere to diminish your pleasure. The fact is, you do not believe in such characters as Surface—the villain of artificial comedy—even while you read or see them. If you did, they would shock and not divert you. When Ben, in Love for Love, returns from sea, the following exquisite dialogue occurs at his first meeting with his father:—

SIR SAMPSON.   Thou has been many a weary league, Ben, since I saw thee.

BEN.   Ey, ey, been. Been far enough, an that be all.—Well, father how do all at home? how does brother Dick, and brother Val?

SIR SAMPSON.   Dick! body o' me, Dick has been dead these two years. I writ you word when you were at Leghorn.

BEN.   Mess, that's true; Marry, I had forgot. Dick's dead, as you say—well, and how?—I have a many questions to ask you—

Here is an instance of insensibility which in real life would be revolting, or rather in real life could not have co-existed with the warm-hearted temperament of the character. But when you read it in the spirit with which such playful selections and specious combinations rather than strict *metaphrases* of nature should be taken, or when you saw Bannister play it, it neither did, nor does, wound the moral sense at all. For what is Ben—the pleasant sailor which Bannister gives us—but a piece of satire—a creation of Congreve's fancy—a dreamy combination of all the accidents of a sailor's character—his contempt of money—his credulity to women—with that necessary estrangement from home which it is just within the verge of credibility to suppose *might* produce such an hallucination as is here described. We never think the worse of Ben for it, or feel it as a strain upon his character. But when an actor comes, and instead of the delightful phantom—the creature dear to half-belief —which Bannister exhibited—displays before our eyes a downright concretion of a Wapping sailor—a jolly warm-hearted Jack Tar—and nothing else—when instead of investing it with a delicious confusedness of the head, and a veering undirected goodness of purpose—he gives to it a downright daylight understanding, and a full consciousness of its actions; thrusting forward the sensibilities of the character with a pretence as if it stood upon nothing else, and was to be judged by them alone—we feel the discord of the thing; the scene is disturbed; a real man has got in among the *dramatis personæ*, and puts them out. We want the sailor turned out. We feel that his true place is not behind the curtain, but in the first or second gallery.

ON THE ARTIFICIAL COMEDY OF THE LAST CENTURY

THE artificial Comedy, or Comedy of manners, is quite extinct on our stage. Congreve and Farquhar show their heads once in seven years only; to be exploded and put down instantly. The times cannot bear them. Is it for a few wild speeches, an occasional licence of dialogue? I think not altogether. The business of their dramatic characters will not stand the moral test. We screw everything up to that. Idle gallantry in a fiction, a dream, the passing pageant of an evening, startles us in the same way as the alarming indications of profligacy in a son or ward in real life should startle a parent or guardian. We have no such middle emotions as dramatic interests left. We see a stage libertine playing his loose pranks of two hours' duration, and of no after consequence, with the severe eyes which inspect real vices with their bearings upon two worlds. We are spectators to a plot or intrigue (not reducible in life to the point of strict morality), and take it all for truth. We substitute a real for a dramatic person, and judge him accordingly. We try him in our courts, from which there is no appeal to the *dramatis personæ*, his peers. We have been spoiled with—not sentimental comedy—but a tyrant far more pernicious to our pleasures which has succeeded to it, the exclusive and all-devouring drama of common life; where the moral point is everything; where, instead of the fictitious half-believed personages of the stage (the phantoms of old comedy), we recognize ourselves, our brothers, aunts, kinsfolk, allies, patrons, enemies,—the same as in life,—with an interest in what is going on so hearty and substantial, that we cannot afford our moral judgment, in its deepest and most vital results, to compromise or slumber for a moment. What is *there* transacting, by no modification is made to affect us in any other manner than the same events or characters would do in our relationships of life. We carry our fire-side concerns to the theatre with us. We do not go thither, like our ancestors, to escape from the pressure of reality, so much as to confirm our experience of it; to make assurance double, and take a bond of fate. We must live our toilsome lives twice over, as it was the mournful privilege of Ulysses to descend twice to the shades. All that neutral ground of character, which stood between vice and virtue; or which in fact was indifferent to neither, where neither properly was called in question; that happy breathing-place from the burthen of a perpetual moral questioning—the sanctuary and quiet Alsatia of hunted casuistry—is broken up and disfranchised, as injurious to the interests of society. The privileges of the place are taken away by law. We dare not dally with images, or names, of wrong. We bark like foolish dogs at shadows. We dread infection from the scenic representation of disorder, and fear a painted pustule. In our anxiety that our morality should not take cold, we wrap it up in a great blanket surtout of precaution against the breeze and sunshine.

I confess for myself that (with no great delinquencies to answer for) I

am glad for a season to take an airing beyond the diocese of the strict
conscience,—not to live always in the precincts of the law-courts,—but
now and then, for a dream-while or so, to imagine a world with no meddling restrictions—to get into recesses, whither the hunter cannot follow me—

> ————Secret shades
> Of woody Ida's inmost grove,
> While yet there was no fear of Jove.

I come back to my cage and my restraint the fresher and more healthy
for it. I wear my shackles more contentedly for having respired the
breath of an imaginary freedom. I do not know how it is with others, but
I feel the better always for the perusal of one of Congreve's—nay, why
should I not add even of Wycherley's—comedies. I am the gayer at least
for it; and I could never connect those sports of a witty fancy in any
shape with any result to be drawn from them to imitation in real life.
They are a world of themselves almost as much as fairyland. Take one
of their characters, male or female (with few exceptions they are alike),
and place it in a modern play, and my virtuous indignation shall rise
against the profligate wretch as warmly as the Catos of the pit could
desire; because in a modern play I am to judge of the right and the
wrong. The standard of *police* is the measure of *political justice*. The
atmosphere will blight it; it cannot live here. It has got into a moral
world, where it has no business, from which it must needs fall headlong;
as dizzy, and incapable of making a stand, as a Swedenborgian bad spirit
that has wandered unawares into the sphere of one of his Good Men, or
Angels. But in its own world do we feel the creature is so very bad?—
The Fainalls and the Mirabels, the Dorimants and the Lady Touch-
woods, in their own sphere, do not offend my moral sense; in fact they
do not appeal to it at all. They seem engaged in their proper element.
They break through no laws, or conscientious restraints. They know
of none. They have got out of Christendom into the land—what shall
I call it?—of cuckoldry—the Utopia of gallantry, where pleasure is
duty, and the manners perfect freedom. It is altogether a speculative scene of things, which has no reference whatever to the world that
is. No good person can be justly offended as a spectator, because no
good person suffers on the stage. Judged morally, every character in
these plays—the few exceptions only are *mistakes*—is alike essentially vain and worthless. The great art of Congreve is especially shown
in this, that he has entirely excluded from his scenes—some little
generosities in the part of Angelica perhaps excepted—not only anything
like a faultless character, but any pretensions to goodness or good feelings whatsoever. Whether he did this designedly, or instinctively, the
effect is as happy, as the design (if design) was bold. I used to wonder
at the strange power which his Way of the World in particular possesses
of interesting you all along in the pursuits of characters, for whom you
absolutely care nothing—for you neither hate nor love his personages—
and I think it is owing to this very indifference for any, that you endure

the whole. He has spread a privation of moral light, I will call it, rather than by the ugly name of palpable darkness, over his creations; and his shadows flit before you without distinction or preference. Had he introduced a good character, a single gush of moral feeling, a revulsion of the judgment to actual life and actual duties, the impertinent Goshen would have only lighted to the discovery of deformities, which now are none, because we think them none.

Translated into real life, the characters of his, and his friend Wycherley's dramas, are profligates and strumpets,—the business of their brief existence, the undivided pursuit of lawless gallantry. No other spring of action, or possible motive of conduct, is recognised; principles which, universally acted upon, must reduce this frame of things to a chaos. But we do them wrong in so translating them. No such effects are produced, in *their* world. When we are among them, we are amongst a chaotic people. We are not to judge them by our usages. No reverend institutions are insulted by their proceedings—for they have none among them. No peace of families is violated—for no family ties exist among them. No purity of the marriage bed is stained—for none is supposed to have a being. No deep affections are disquieted, no holy wedlock bands are snapped asunder—for affection's depth and wedded faith are not of the growth of that soil. There is neither right nor wrong,—gratitude or its opposite,—claim or duty,—paternity or sonship. Of what consequence is it to Virtue, or how is she at all concerned about it, whether Sir Simon, or Dapperwit steal away Miss Martha; or who is the father of Lord Froth's or Sir Paul Pliant's children?

The whole is a passing pageant, where we should sit as unconcerned at the issues, for life or death, as at a battle of the frogs and mice. But, like Don Quixote, we take part against the puppets, and quite as impertinently. We dare not contemplate an Atlantis, a scheme, out of which our coxcombical moral sense is for a little transitory ease excluded. We have not the courage to imagine a state of things for which there is neither reward nor punishment. We cling to the painful necessities of shame and blame. We would indict our very dreams.

Amidst the mortifying circumstances attendant upon growing old, it is something to have seen the School for Scandal in its glory. This comedy grew out of Congreve and Wycherley, but gathered some allays of the sentimental comedy which followed theirs. It is impossible that it should be now *acted*, though it continues, at long intervals, to be announced in the bills. Its hero, when Palmer played it at least, was Joseph Surface. When I remember the gay boldness, the graceful solemn plausibility, the measured step, the insinuating voice—to express it in a word—the downright *acted* villainy of the part, so different from the pressure of conscious actual wickedness,—the hypocritical assumption of hypocrisy,—which made Jack so deservedly a favourite in there character, I must needs conclude the present generation of playgoers more virtuous than myself, or more dense. I freely confess that he divided the palm with me with his better brother; that, in fact, I liked him quite as well. Not but

there are passages,—like that, for instance, where Joseph is made to refuse a pittance to a poor relation,—incongruities which Sheridan was
forced upon by the attempt to join the artificial with the sentimental
comedy, either of which must destroy the other—but over these obstructions Jack's manner floated him so lightly, that a refusal from him no
more shocked you, than the easy compliance of Charles gave you in
reality any pleasure; you got over the paltry question as quickly as you
could, to get back into the regions of pure comedy, where no cold moral
reigns. The highly artificial manner of Palmer in this character counter-
acted every disagreeable impression which you might have received from
the contrast, supposing them real, between the two brothers. You did not
believe in Joseph with the same faith with which you believed in Charles.
The latter was a pleasant reality, the former a no less pleasant poetical
foil to it. The comedy, I have said, is incongruous; a mixture of Congreve with sentimental incompatibilities; the gaiety upon the whole is
buoyant; but it required the consummate art of Palmer to reconcile the
discordant elements.

A player with Jack's talents, if we had one now, would not dare to do
the part in the same manner. He would instinctively avoid every turn
which might tend to unrealise, and so to make the character fascinating.
He must take his cue from his spectators, who would expect a bad man
and a good man as rigidly opposed to each other as the death-beds of
those geniuses are contrasted in the prints, which I am sorry to say have
disappeared from the windows of my old friend Carrington Bowles, of
St. Paul's Churchyard memory—(an exhibition as venerable as the adjacent cathedral, and almost coeval) of the bad and good man at the hour
of death; where the ghastly apprehensions of the former,—and truly the
grim phantom with his reality of a toasting-fork is not to be despised,—
so finely contrast with the meek complacent kissing of the rod,—taking
it in like honey and butter,—with which the latter submits to the scythe
of the gentle bleeder, Time, who wields his lancet with the apprehensive
finger of a popular young ladies' surgeon. What flesh, like loving grass,
would not covet to meet half-way the stroke of such a delicate mower?
—John Palmer was twice an actor in this exquisite part. He was playing
to you all the while that he was playing upon Sir Peter and his lady.
You had the first intimation of a sentiment before it was on his lips. His
altered voice was meant to you, and you were to suppose that his fictitious co-flutterers on the stage perceived nothing at all of it. What
was it to you if that half reality, the husband, was over-reached by the
puppetry—or the thin thing (Lady Teazle's reputation) was persuaded
it was dying of a plethory? The fortunes of Othello and Desdemona
were not concerned in it. Poor Jack has passed from the stage in good
time, that he did not live to this our age of seriousness. The pleasant
old Teazle *King*, too, is gone in good time. His manner would scarce have
passed current in our day. We must love or hate—acquit or condemn—
censure or pity—exert our detestable coxcombry of moral judgment
upon everything. Joseph Surface, to go down now, must be a downright

revolting villain—no compromise—his first appearance must shock and give horror—his specious plausibilities, which the pleasurable faculties of our fathers welcomed with such hearty greetings, knowing that no harm (dramatic harm even) could come, or was meant to come, of them, must inspire a cold and killing aversion. Charles (the real canting person of the scene—for the hypocrisy of Joseph has its ulterior legitimate ends, but his brother's professions of a good heart centre in downright self-satisfaction) must be *loved*, and Joseph *hated*. To balance one disagreeable reality with another, Sir Peter Teazle must be no longer the comic idea of a fretful old bachelor bridegroom, whose teasings (while King acted it) were evidently as much played off at you, as they were meant to concern anybody on the stage,—he must be a real person, capable in law of sustaining an injury—a person towards whom duties are to be acknowledged—the genuine crim. con. antagonist of the villainous seducer Joseph. To realise him more, his sufferings under his unfortunate match must have the downright pungency of life—must (or should) make you not mirthful but uncomfortable, just as the same predicament would move you in a neighbour or old friend. The delicious scenes which give the play its name and zest, must affect you in the same serious manner as if you heard the reputation of a dear female friend attacked in your real presence. Crabtree and Sir Benjamin—those poor snakes that live but in the sunshine of your mirth—must be ripened by this hot-bed process of realisation into asps or amphisbænas; and Mrs. Candour—O! frightful!—become a hooded serpent. O! who that remembers Parsons and Dodd—the wasp and butterfly of the School for Scandal—in those two characters; and charming natural Miss Pope, the perfect gentlewoman as distinguished from the fine lady of comedy, in this latter part—would forego the true scenic delight—the escape from life—the oblivion of consequences—the holiday barring out of the pedant Reflection—those Saturnalia of two or three brief hours, well won from the world—to sit instead at one of our modern plays—to have his coward conscience (that forsooth must not be left for a moment) stimulated with perpetual appeals—dulled rather, and blunted, as a faculty without repose must be—and his moral vanity pampered with images of notional justice, notional beneficence, lives saved without the spectator's risk, and fortunes given away that cost the author nothing?

No piece was, perhaps, ever so completely cast in all its parts as this *manager's comedy*. Miss Farren had succeeded to Mrs. Abington in Lady Teazle; and Smith, the original Charles, had retired when I first saw it. The rest of the characters, with very slight exceptions, remained. I remember it was then the fashion to cry down John Kemble, who took the part of Charles after Smith; but, I thought, very unjustly. Smith, I fancy was more airy, and took the eye with a certain gaiety of person. He brought with him no sombre recollections of tragedy. He had not to expiate the fault of having pleased beforehand in lofty declamation. He had no sins of Hamlet or of Richard to atone for. His failure in these parts was a passport to success in one of so opposite a tendency. But, as far as I could judge, the weighty sense of Kemble made up for more personal incapacity than he had to answer for. His harshest tones in this part came steeped and dulcified in good-humour. He made his defects a grace. His exact declamatory manner, as he managed it, only served to convey the points of his dialogue with more precision. It seemed to head the shafts to carry them deeper. Not one of his sparkling sentences was lost. I remember minutely how he delivered each in succession, and cannot by any effort imagine how any of them could be altered for the better. No man could deliver brilliant dialogue—the dialogue of Congreve or Wycherley—because none understood it—half so well as John Kemble. His Valentine, in Love for Love, was, to my recollection, faultless. He flagged sometimes in the intervals of tragic passion. He would slumber over the level parts of an heroic character. His Macbeth has been known to nod. But he always seemed to me to be particularly alive to pointed and witty dialogue. The relaxing levities of tragedy have not been touched by any since him—the playful court-bred spirit in which he condescended to the players in Hamlet—the sportive relief which he threw into the darker shades of Richard—disappeared with him. He had his sluggish moods, his torpors —but they were the halting-stones and resting-place of his tragedy— politic savings, and fetches of the breath—husbandry of the lungs, where nature pointed him to be an economist—rather, I think, than errors of the judgment. They were, at worst, less painful than the eternal tormenting unappeasable vigilance,—the "lidless dragon eyes," of present fashionable tragedy.

ON THE ACTING OF MUNDEN

NOT many nights ago I had come home from seeing this extraordinary performer in Cockletop; and when I retired to my pillow, his whimsical image still stuck by me, in a manner as to threaten sleep. In vain I tried to divest myself of it, by conjuring up the most opposite associations. I resolved to be serious. I raised up the gravest topics of life; private misery, public calamity. All would not do:

>   ——There the antic sate
> Mocking our state——

his queer visnomy—his bewildering costume—all the strange things which he had raked together—his serpentine rod, swagging about in his pocket—Cleopatra's tear, and the rest of his relics—O'Keefe's wild farce, and *his* wilder commentary—till the passion of laughter, like grief in excess, relieved itself by its own weight, inviting the sleep which in the first instance it had driven away.

But I was not to escape so easily. No sooner did I fall into slumbers, than the same image, only more perplexing, assailed me in the shape of dreams. Not one Munden, but five hundred, were dancing before me, like the faces which, whether you will or no, come when you have been taking opium—all the strange combinations, which this strangest of all strange mortals ever shot his proper countenance into, from the day he came commissioned to dry up the tears of the town for the loss of the now almost forgotten Edwin. O for the power of the pencil to have fixed them when I awoke! A season or two since, there was exhibited a Hogarth gallery. I do not see why there should not be a Munden gallery. In richness and variety, the latter would not fall far short of the former.

There is one face of Farley, one face of Knight, one (but what a one it is!) of Liston; but Munden has none that you can properly pin down, and call *his*. When you think he has exhausted his battery of looks, in unaccountable warfare with your gravity, suddenly he sprouts out an entirely new set of features, like Hydra. He is not one, but legion; not so much a comedian, as a company. If his name could be multiplied like his countenance, it might fill a play-bill. He, and he alone, literally *makes faces:* applied to any other person, the phrase is a mere figure, denoting certain modifications of the human countenance. Out of some invisible wardrobe he dips for faces, as his friend Suett used for wigs, and fetches them out as easily. I should not be surprised to see him some day put out the head of a river-horse; or come forth a pewitt, or lapwing, some feathered metamorphosis.

I have seen this gifted actor in Sir Christopher Curry—in old Dornton—diffuse a glow of sentiment which has made the pulse of a crowded theatre beat like that of one man; when he has come in aid of the pulpit, doing good to the moral heart of a people. I have seen some faint approaches to this sort of excellence in other players. But in the grand grotesque of farce, Munden stands out as single and unaccompanied as Hogarth. Hogarth, strange to tell, had no followers. The school of Munden began, and must end, with himself.

Can any man *wonder*, like him? can any man *see ghosts*, like him? or *fight with his own shadow*—"SESSA"—as he does in that strangely-neglected thing, the Cobbler of Preston—where his alternations from the Cobbler to the Magnifico, and from the Magnifico to the Cobbler, keep the brain of the spectator in as wild a ferment, as if some Arabian Night were being acted before him. Who like him can throw, or ever attempted to throw, a preternatural interest over the commonest daily-life objects? A table or a joint-stool, in his conception, rises into a dignity equivalent to Cassiopeia's chair. It is invested with constellatory importance. You could not speak of it with more deference, if it were mounted into the firmament. A beggar in the hands of Michael Angelo, says Fuseli, rose the Patriarch of Poverty. So the gusto of Munden antiquates and ennobles what it touches. His pots and his ladles are as grand and primal as the seething-pots and hooks seen in old prophetic vision. A tub of butter, contemplated by him, amounts to a Platonic idea. He understands a leg of mutton in its quiddity. He stands wondering, amid the common-place materials of life, like primæval man with the sun and stars about him.

THE LAST ESSAYS OF ELIA

PREFACE

BY A FRIEND OF THE LATE ELIA

THIS poor gentleman, who for some months past had been in a declining way, hath at length paid his final tribute to nature.

To say truth, it is time he were gone. The humour of the thing, if ever there was much in it, was pretty well exhausted; and a two years' and a half existence has been a tolerable duration for a phantom.

I am now at liberty to confess, that much which I have heard objected to my late friend's writings was well-founded. Crude they are, I grant you—a sort of unlicked, incondite things villainously pranked in an affected array of antique modes and phrases. They had not been *his*, if they had been other than such; and better it is, that a writer should be natural in a self-pleasing quaintness, than to affect a naturalness (so called) that should be strange to him. Egotistical they have been pronounced by some who did not know, that what he tells us, as of himself, was often true only (historically) of another; as in a former Essay (to save many instances)—where under the *first person* (his favourite figure) he shadows forth the forlorn estate of a country-boy placed at a London school, far from his friends and connections—in direct opposition to his own early history. If it be egotism to imply and twine with his own identity the griefs and affections of another—making himself many, or reducing many unto himself—then is the skilful novelist, who all along brings in his hero or heroine, speaking of themselves, the greatest egotist of all; who yet has never, therefore, been accused of that narrowness. And how shall the intenser dramatist escape being faulty, who, doubtless, under cover of passion uttered by another, oftentimes gives blameless vent to his most inward feelings, and expresses his own story modestly?

My late friend was in many respects a singular character. Those who did not like him, hated him; and some, who once liked him, afterwards became his bitterest haters. The truth is, he gave himself too little concern what he uttered, and in whose presence. He observed neither time nor place, and would e'en out with what came uppermost. With the severe religionist he would pass for a free-thinker; while the other faction set him down for a bigot, or persuaded themselves that he belied his sentiments. Few understood him; and I am not certain that at all times he quite understood himself. He too much affected that dangerous figure —irony. He sowed doubtful speeches, and reaped plain, unequivocal hatred.—He would interrupt the gravest discussion with some light jest; and yet, perhaps, not quite irrelevant in ears that could understand it. Your long and much talkers hated him. The informal habit of his mind, joined to an inveterate impediment of speech, forbade him to be an orator; and he seemed determined that no one else should play that part when he was present. He was *petit* and ordinary in his person and appearance. I have seen him sometimes in what is called good company, but where he has been a stranger, sit silent, and be suspected for an odd fellow; till some unlucky occasion provoking it, he would stutter out some senseless pun (not altogether senseless perhaps, if rightly taken), which has stamped his character for the evening. It was hit or miss with him; but nine times out of ten, he contrived by this device to send away a whole company his enemies. His conceptions rose kindlier than his utterance, and his happiest *impromptus* had the appearance of effort. He has been accused of trying to be witty, when in truth he was but struggling to give his poor thoughts articulation. He chose his companions for some individuality of character which they manifested.—Hence, not many persons of science, and few professed *literati,* were of his councils. They were, for the most part, persons of an uncertain fortune; and, as to such people commonly nothing is more obnoxious than a gentleman of settled (though moderate) income, he passed with most of them for a great miser. To my knowledge this was a mistake. His *intimados,* to confess a truth, were in the world's eye a ragged regiment. He found them floating on the surface of society; and the colour, or something else, in the weed pleased him. The burrs stuck to him—but they were good and loving burrs for all that. He never greatly cared for the society of what are called good people. If any of these were scandalised (and offences were sure to arise) he could not help it. When he has been remonstrated with for not making more concessions to the feelings of good people, he would retort by asking, what one point did these good people ever concede to him? He was temperate in his meals and diversions, but always kept a little on this side of abstemiousness. Only in the use of the Indian weed he might be thought a little excessive. He took it, he would say, as a solvent of speech. Marry—as the friendly vapour ascended, how his prattle would curl up sometimes with it! the ligaments which tongue-tied him, were loosened, and the stammerer proceeded a statist!

I do not know whether I ought to bemoan or rejoice that my old friend is departed. His jests were beginning to grow obsolete, and his stories to be found out. He felt the approaches of age; and while he pretended to cling to life, you saw how slender were the ties left to bind him. Discoursing with him latterly on this subject, he expressed himself with a pettishness, which I thought unworthy of him. In our walks about his suburban retreat (as he called it) at Shacklewell, some children belonging to a school of industry had met us, and bowed and curtseyed, as he thought, in an especial manner to *him*. "They take me for a visiting governor," he muttered earnestly. He had a horror, which he carried to a foible, of looking like anything important and parochial. He thought that he approached nearer to that stamp daily. He had a general aversion from being treated like a grave or respectable character, and kept a wary eye upon the advances of age that should so entitle him. He herded always, while it was possible, with people younger than himself. He did not conform to the march of time, but was dragged along in the procession. His manners lagged behind his years. He was too much of the boy-man. The *toga virilis* never sate gracefully on his shoulders. The impressions of infancy had burnt into him, and he resented the impertinence of manhood. These were weaknesses; but such as they were, they are a key to explicate some of his writings.

THE LAST ESSAYS OF ELIA

BLAKESMOOR IN H——SHIRE

I DO not know a pleasure more affecting than to range at will over the deserted apartments of some fine old family mansion. The traces of extinct grandeur admit of a better passion than envy: and contemplations on the great and good, whom we fancy in succession to have been its inhabitants, weave for us illusions, incompatible with the bustle of modern occupancy, and vanities of foolish present aristocracy. The same difference of feeling, I think, attends us between entering an empty and a crowded church. In the latter it is chance but some present human frailty—an act of inattention on the part of some of the auditory—or a trait of affectation, or worse, vainglory on that of the preacher—puts us by our best thoughts, disharmonising the place and the occasion. But wouldst thou know the beauty of holiness?—go alone on some week-day, borrowing the keys of good Master Sexton, traverse the cool aisles of some country church: think of the piety that has kneeled there—the congregations, old and young, that have found consolation there—the meek pastor—the docile parishioner. With no disturbing emotions, no cross conflicting comparisons, drink in the tranquillity of the place, till thou thyself become as fixed and motionless as the marble effigies that kneel and weep around thee.

Journeying northward lately, I could not resist going some few miles out of my road to look upon the remains of an old great house with which I had been impressed in this way in infancy. I was apprised that the owner of it had lately pulled it down; still I had a vague notion that it could not all have perished, that so much solidity with magnificence could not have been crushed all at once into the mere dust and rubbish which I found it.

The work of ruin had proceeded with a swift hand indeed, and the demolition of a few weeks had reduced it to—an antiquity.

I was astonished at the indistinction of everything. Where had stood the great gates? What bounded the court-yard? Whereabout did the out-houses commence? A few bricks only lay as representatives of that which was so stately and so spacious.

Death does not shrink up his human victim at this rate. The burnt ashes of a man weigh more in their proportion.

Had I seen these brick-and-mortar knaves at their process of destruction, at the plucking of every panel I should have felt the varlets at my heart. I should have cried out to them to spare a plank at least out of the cheerful store-room, in whose hot window-seat I used to sit and read Cowley, with the grass-plot before, and the hum and flappings of that one solitary wasp that ever haunted it about me—it is in mine ears now, as oft as summer returns; or a panel of the yellow-room.

Why, every plank and panel of that house for me had magic in it. The tapestried bedrooms—tapestry so much better than painting—not adorning merely, but peopling the wainscots—at which childhood ever and anon would steal a look, shifting its coverlid (replaced as quickly) to exercise its tender courage in a momentary eye-encounter with those stern bright visages, staring reciprocally—all Ovid on the walls, in colours vivider than his descriptions. Actæon in mid sprout, with the unappeasable prudery of Diana; and the still more provoking, and almost culinary coolness of Dan Phœbus, eel-fashion, deliberately divesting of Marsyas.

Then, that haunted room—in which old Mrs. Battle died—whereinto I have crept, but always in the daytime, with a passion of fear; and a sneaking curiosity, terror-tainted, to hold communication with the past. —*How shall they build it up again?*

It was an old deserted place, yet not so long deserted but that traces of the splendour of past inmates were everywhere apparent. Its furniture was still standing—even to the tarnished gilt leather battledores, and crumbling feathers of shuttlecocks in the nursery, which told that children had once played there. But I was a lonely child, and had the range at will of every apartment, knew every nook and corner, wondered and worshipped everywhere.

The solitude of childhood is not so much the mother of thought, as it is the feeder of love, and silence, and admiration. So strange a passion for the place possessed me in those years, that, though there lay—I shame to say how few roods distant from the mansion—half hid by trees what I judged some romantic lake, such was the spell which bound me to the house, and such my carefulness not to pass its strict and proper precincts, that the idle waters lay unexplored for me; and not till late in life, curiosity prevailing over elder devotion, I found, to my astonishment, a pretty brawling brook had been the Lacus Incognitus of my infancy. Variegated views, extensive prospects—and those at no great distance from the house—I was told of such—what were they to me, being out of the boundaries of my Eden?—So far from a wish to roam, I would have drawn, methought, still closer the fences of my chosen prison; and have been hemmed in by a yet securer cincture of those excluding garden walls. I could have exclaimed with that garden-loving poet—

> Bind me, ye woodbines, in your twines;
> Curl me about, ye gadding vines;
> And oh so close your circles lace,
> That I may never leave this place;
> But, lest your fetters prove too weak,
> Ere I your silken bondage break,
> Do you, O brambles, chain me too,
> And, courteous briars, nail me through.

I was here as in a lonely temple. Snug fire-sides—the low-built roof—parlours ten feet by ten—frugal boards, and all the homeliness of home—these were the condition of my birth—the wholesome soil which I was planted in. Yet, without impeachment to their tenderest lessons, I am not sorry to have had glances at something beyond; and to have taken, if but a peep, in childhood, at the contrasting accidents of a great fortune.

To have the feeling of gentility, it is not necessary to have been born gentle. The pride of ancestry may be had on cheaper terms than to be obliged to an importunate race of ancestors; and the coatless antiquary in his unemblazoned cell, revolving the long line of a Mowbray's or De Clifford's pedigree, at those sounding names may warm himself into as gay a vanity as these who do inherit them. The claims of birth are ideal merely, and what herald shall go about to strip me of an idea? Is it trenchant to their swords? can it be hacked off as a spur can? or torn away like a tarnished garter?

What else were the families of the great to us? what pleasure should we take in their tedious genealogies, or their capitulatory brass monuments? What to us the uninterrupted current of their bloods, if our own did not answer within us to a cognate and correspondent elevation.

Or wherefore else, O tattered and diminished 'Scutcheon that hung upon the time-worn walls of thy princely stairs, BLAKESMOOR! have I in childhood so oft stood poring upon the mystic characters—thy emblematic supporters, with their prophetic "Resurgam"—till, every dreg of peasantry purging off, I received into myself Very Gentility? Thou wert first in my morning eyes; and of nights hast detained my steps from bedward, till it was but a step from gazing at thee to dreaming on thee.

This is the only true gentry by adoption; the veritable change of blood, and not, as empirics have fabled, by transfusion.

Who it was by dying that had earned the splendid trophy, I know not, I inquired not; but its fading rags, and colours cobweb-stained, told that its subject was of two centuries back.

And what if my ancestor at that date was some Damœtas—feeding flocks—not his own, upon the hills of Lincoln—did I in less earnest vindicate to myself the family trappings of this once proud Ægon? repaying by a backward triumph the insults he might possibly have heaped in his life-time upon my poor pastoral progenitor.

If it were presumption so to speculate, the present owners of the mansion had least reason to complain. They had long forsaken the old house of their fathers for a newer trifle; and I was left to appropriate to myself what images I could pick up, to raise my fancy, or to soothe my vanity.

I was the true descendant of those old W——s; and not the present family of that name, who had fled the old waste places.

Mine was that gallery of good old family portraits, which as I have gone over, giving them in fancy my own family name, one—and then another—would seem to smile, reaching forward from the canvas, to recognise the new relationship; while the rest looked grave, as it seemed, at the vacancy in their dwelling, and thoughts of fled posterity.

The Beauty with the cool blue pastoral drapery, and a lamb—that hung next the great bay window—with the bright yellow H——shire hair, and eye of watchet hue—so like my Alice!—I am persuaded she was a true Elia—Mildred Elia, I take it.

Mine, too, BLAKESMOOR, was thy noble Marble Hall, with its mosaic pavements, and its Twelve Cæsars—stately busts in marble—ranged round; of whose countenances, young reader of faces as I was, the frowning beauty of Nero, I remember, had most of my wonder: but the mild Galba had my love. There they stood in the coldness of death, yet freshness of immortality.

Mine, too, thy lofty Justice Hall, with its one chair of authority, high-backed and wickered, once the terror of luckless poacher, or self-forgetful maiden—so common since, that bats have roosted in it.

Mine, too,—whose else?—thy costly fruit-garden, with its sun-baked southern wall; the ampler pleasure-garden, rising backwards from the house in triple terraces, with flower-pots now of palest lead, save that a speck here and there, saved from the elements, bespake their pristine state to have been gilt and glittering; the verdant quarters backwarder still; and, stretching still beyond, in old formality, thy firry wilderness, the haunt of the squirrel, and the day-long murmuring wood-pigeon, with that antique image in the centre, God or Goddess I wist not; but child of Athens or old Rome paid never a sincerer worship to Pan or to Sylvanus in their native groves, than I to that fragmental mystery.

Was it for this, that I kissed my childish hands too fervently in your idol-worship, walks and windings of BLAKESMOOR! for this, or what sin of mine, has the plough passed over your pleasant places? I sometimes think that as men, when they die, do not die all, so of their extinguished habitations there may be a hope—a germ to be revivified.

POOR RELATIONS

A POOR RELATION—is the most irrelevant thing in nature,—a piece of impertinent correspondency,—an odious approximation,—a haunting conscience,—a preposterous shadow, lengthening in the noon-tide of our prosperity,—an unwelcome remembrancer,—a perpetually recurring mortification,—a drain on your purse, a more intolerable dun upon your pride,—a drawback upon success,—a rebuke to your rising,—a stain in your blood,—a blot on your 'scutcheon,—a rent in your garment,—a death's-head at your banquet,—Agathocles' pot,—a Mordecai in your gate, a Lazarus at your door,—a lion in your path,—a frog in your chamber,—a fly in your ointment,—a mote in your eye,—a triumph to your enemy, an apology to your friends,—the one thing not needful,—the hail in harvest,—the ounce of sour in a pound of sweet.

He is known by his knock. Your heart telleth you "That is Mr. ——." A rap, between familiarity and respect; that demands, and at the same time seems to despair of, entertainment. He entereth smiling and—embarrassed. He holdeth out his hand to you to shake, and—draweth it back again. He casually looketh in about dinner-time—when the table is full. He offereth to go away, seeing you have company—but is induced to stay. He filleth a chair, and your visitor's two children are accommodated at a side-table. He never cometh upon open days, when your wife says, with some complacency, "My dear, perhaps Mr. —— will drop in to-day." He remembereth birth-days—and professeth he is fortunate to have stumbled upon one. He declareth against fish, the turbot being small—yet suffereth himself to be importuned into a slice, against his first resolution. He sticketh by the port—yet will be prevailed upon to empty the remainder glass of claret, if a stranger press it upon him. He is a puzzle to the servants, who are fearful of being too obsequious, or not civil enough, to him. The guests think "they have seen him before." Every one speculateth upon his condition; and the most part take him to be—a tide-waiter. He calleth you by your Christian name, to imply that his other is the same with your own. He is too familiar by half, yet you wish he had less diffidence. With half the familiarity, he might pass for a casual dependant; with more boldness, he would be in no danger of being taken for what he is. He is too humble for a friend; yet taketh on him more state than befits a client. He is a worse guest than a country tenant, inasmuch as he bringeth up no rent—yet 'tis odds, from his garb and demeanour, that your guests take him for one. He is asked to make one at the whist table; refuseth on the score of poverty, and—resents being left out. When the company break up, he proffereth to go for a coach—and lets the servant go. He recollects your grandfather; and will thrust in some mean and quite unimportant anecdote of the family. He knew it when it was not quite so flourishing as "he is blest in seeing it now." He reviveth past situations, to institute what he calleth—favourable comparisons. With a reflecting sort of congratulation, he will inquire the price of your furniture; and insults you with a special commendation of your window-curtains. He is of opinion that the urn is the more elegant shape, but, after all, there was something more comfortable about the old tea-kettle—which you must remember. He dare say you must find a great convenience in having a carriage of your own, and appealeth to your lady if it is not so. Inquireth if you have had your arms done on vellum yet; and did not know, till lately, that such-and-such had been the crest of the family. His memory is unseasonable; his compliments perverse; his talk a trouble; his stay pertinacious; and when he goeth away, you dismiss his chair into a corner, as precipitately as possible, and feel fairly rid of two nuisances.

There is a worse evil under the sun, and that is—a female Poor Relation. You may do something with the other; you may pass him off tolerably well; but your indigent she-relative is hopeless. "He is an old humourist," you may say, "and affects to go threadbare. His circumstances are better than folks would take them to be. You are fond of having a Character at your table, and truly he is one." But in the indications of female poverty there can be no disguise. No woman dresses below herself from caprice. The truth must out without shuffling. "She is plainly related to the L——s; or what does she at their house?" She is, in all probability, your wife's cousin. Nine times out of ten, at least, this is the case.—Her garb is something between a gentlewoman and a beggar, yet the former evidently predominates. She is most provokingly humble, and ostentatiously sensible to her inferiority. He may require to be repressed sometimes—*aliquando sufflaminandus erat*—but there is no raising her. You send her soup at dinner, and she begs to be helped—after the gentlemen. Mr. —— requests the honour of taking wine with her; she hesitates between Port and Madeira, and chooses the former—because he does. She calls the servant *Sir;* and insists on not troubling him to hold her plate. The housekeeper patronises her. The children's governess takes upon her to correct her, when she has mistaken the piano for harpsichord.

Richard Amlet, Esq., in the play, is a notable instance of the disadvantages to which this chimerical notion of *affinity constituting a claim to acquaintance,* may subject the spirit of a gentleman. A little foolish blood is all that is betwixt him and a lady with a great estate. His stars are perpetually crossed by the malignant maternity of an old woman, who persists in calling him "her son Dick." But she has wherewithal in the end to recompense his indignities, and float him again upon the brilliant surface, under which it has been her seeming business and pleasure all along to sink him. All men, besides, are not of Dick's temperament. I knew an Amlet in real life, who, wanting Dick's buoyancy, sank indeed. Poor W—— was of my own standing at Christ's, a fine classic, and a youth of promise. If he had a blemish, it was too much pride; but its quality was inoffensive; it was not of that sort which hardens the heart, and serves to keep inferiors at a distance; it only sought to ward off derogation from itself. It was the principle of self-respect carried as far as it could go, without infringing upon that respect, which he would have every one else equally maintain for himself. He would have you to think alike with him on this topic. Many a quarrel have I had with him, when we were rather older boys, and our tallness made us more obnoxious to observation in the blue clothes, because I would not thread the alleys and blind ways of the town with him to elude notice, when we have been out together on a holiday in the streets of this sneering and prying metropolis. W—— went, sore with these notions, to Oxford, where the dignity and sweetness of a scholar's life, meeting with the alloy of a humble introduction, wrought in him a passionate devotion to the place, with a profound aversion from the society. The servitor's gown (worse than his school array) clung to him with Nessian venom. He thought himself ridiculous in a garb, under which Latimer must have walked erect, and in which Hooker, in his young days, possibly flaunted in a vein of no discommendable vanity. In the depth of college shades, or in his lonely chamber, the poor student shrunk from observation. He found shelter among books, which insult not; and studies. that ask no questions of a youth's finances. He was lord of his library, and seldom cared for looking out beyond his domains. The healing influence of studious pursuits was upon him, to soothe and to abstract. He was almost a healthy man; when the waywardness of his fate broke out against him with a second and worse malignity. The father of W—— had hitherto exercised the humble profession of house-painter at N——, near Oxford. A supposed interest with some of the heads of colleges had now induced him to take up his abode in that city, with the hope of being employed upon some public works which were talked of. From that moment I read in the countenance of the young man the determination which at length tore him from academical pursuits for ever. To a person unacquainted with our universities, the distance between the gownsmen and the townsmen, as they are called—the trading part of the latter especially—is carried to an excess that would appear harsh and incredible. The temperament of W——'s father was diametrically the reverse of his own. Old W—— was a little, busy, cringing tradesman, who, with his son upon his arm, would stand bowing and scraping, cap in hand, to any thing that wore the semblance of a gown—insensible to the winks and opener remonstrances of the young man, to whose chamber-fellow, or equal in standing, perhaps, he was thus obsequiously and gratuitously ducking. Such a state of things could not last. W—— must change the air of Oxford, or be suffocated. He chose the former; and let the sturdy moralist, who strains the point of the filial duties as high as they can bear, censure the dereliction; he cannot estimate the struggle. I stood with W——, the last afternoon I ever saw him, under the eaves of his paternal dwelling. It was in the fine lane leading from the High Street to the back of * * * * college, where W—— kept his rooms. He seemed thoughtful and more reconciled. I ventured to rally him—finding him in a better mood—upon a representation of the Artist Evangelist, which the old man, whose affairs were beginning to flourish, had caused to be set up in a splendid sort of frame over his really handsome shop, either as a token of prosperity or badge of gratitude to his saint. W—— looked up at the Luke, and, like Satan, "knew his mounted sign—and fled." A letter on his father's table, the next morning, announced that he had accepted a commission in a regiment about to embark for Portugal. He was among the first who perished before the walls of St. Sebastian.

I do not know how, upon a subject which I began with treating half seriously, I should have fallen upon a recital so eminently painful; but this theme of poor relationship is replete with so much matter for tragic as well as comic associations, that it is difficult to keep the account distinct without blending. The earliest impressions which I received on this matter, are certainly not attended with anything painful, or very humiliating, in the recalling. At my father's table (no very splendid one) was to be found, every Saturday, the mysterious figure of an aged gentleman, clothed in neat black, of a sad yet comely appearance. His deportment was of the essence of gravity; his words few or none; and I was not to make a noise in his presence. I had little inclination to have done so

—for my cue was to admire in silence. A particular elbow-chair was appropriated to him, which was in no case to be violated. A peculiar sort of sweet pudding, which appeared on no other occasion, distinguished the days of his coming. I used to think him a prodigiously rich man. All I could make out of him was, that he and my father had been schoolfellows, a world ago, at Lincoln, and that he came from the Mint. The Mint I knew to be a place where all the money was coined—and I thought he was the owner of all that money. Awful ideas of the Tower twined themselves about his presence. He seemed above human infirmities and passions. A sort of melancholy grandeur invested him. From some inexplicable doom I fancied him obliged to go about in an eternal suit of mourning; a captive—a stately being let out of the Tower on Saturdays. Often have I wondered at the temerity of my father, who, in spite of an habitual general respect which we all in common manifested towards him, would venture now and then to stand up against him in some argument, touching their youthful days. The houses of the ancient city of Lincoln are divided (as most of my readers know) between the dwellers on the hill and in the valley. This marked distinction formed an obvious division between the boys who lived above (however brought together in a common school) and the boys whose paternal residence was on the plain; a sufficient cause of hostility in the code of these young Grotiuses. My father had been a leading Mountaineer; and would still maintain the general superiority, in skill and hardihood, of the *Above Boys* (his own faction) over the *Below Boys* (so were they called), of which party his contemporary had been a chieftain. Many and hot were the skirmishes on this topic—the only one upon which the old gentleman was ever brought out—and bad blood bred; even sometimes almost to the recommencement (so I expected) of actual hostilities. But my father, who scorned to insist upon advantages, generally contrived to turn the conversation upon some adroit by-commendation of the old Minster; in the general preference of which, before all other cathedrals in the island, the dweller on the hill, and the plain-born, could meet on a conciliating level, and lay down their less important differences. Once only I saw the old gentleman really ruffled, and I remembered with anguish the thought that came over me: "Perhaps he will never come here again." He had been pressed to take another plate of the viand, which I have already mentioned as the indispensable concomitant of his visits. He had refused with a resistance amounting to rigour, when my aunt, an old Lincolnian, but who had something of this, in common with my cousin Bridget, that she would sometimes press civility out of season—uttered the following memorable application—"Do take another slice, Mr. Billet, for you do not get pudding every day." The old gentleman said nothing at the time—but he took occasion in the course of the evening, when some argument had intervened between them, to utter with an emphasis which chilled the company, and which chills me now as I write it—"Woman, you are superannuated!" John Billet did not survive long after the digesting of this affront; but he survived long enough to assure me that peace was actually restored! and, if I remember aright, another pudding was discreetly substituted in the place of that which had occasioned the offence. He died at the Mint (anno 1781), where he had long held, what he accounted, a comfortable independence; and with five pounds, fourteen shillings, and a penny, which were found in his escritoire after his decease, left the world, blessing God that he had enough to bury him, and that he had never been obliged to any man for a sixpence. This was—a Poor Relation.

DETACHED THOUGHTS ON BOOKS AND READING

To mind the inside of a book is to entertain one's self with the forced product of another man's brain. Now I think a man of quality and breeding may be much amused with the natural sprouts of his own.   *Lord Foppington, in the Relapse.*

AN ingenious acquaintance of my own was so much struck with this bright sally of his Lordship, that he has left off reading altogether, to the great improvement of his originality. At the hazard of losing some credit on this head, I must confess that I dedicate no inconsiderable portion of my time to other people's thoughts. I dream away my life in others' speculations. I love to lose myself in other men's minds. When I am not walking, I am reading; I cannot sit and think. Books think for me.

I have no repugnances. Shaftesbury is not too genteel for me, nor Jonathan Wild too low. I can read anything which I call *a book.* There are things in that shape which I cannot allow for such.

In this catalogue of *books which are no books—biblia a-biblia*—I reckon Court Calendars, Directories, Pocket Books, Draught Boards, bound and lettered on the back, Scientific Treatises, Almanacs, Statutes at Large: the works of Hume, Gibbon, Robertson, Beattie, Soame Jenyns, and generally, all those volumes which "no gentleman's library should be without": the Histories of Flavius Josephus (that learned Jew), and Paley's Moral Philosophy. With these exceptions, I can read almost anything. I bless my stars for a taste so catholic, so unexcluding.

I confess that it moves my spleen to see these *things in books' clothing* perched upon shelves, like false saints, usurpers of true shrines, intruders into the sanctuary, thrusting out the legitimate occupants. To reach down a well-bound semblance of a volume, and hope it some kind-hearted play-book, then, opening what "seem its leaves," to come bolt upon a withering Population Essay. To expect a Steele or a Farquhar, and find—Adam Smith. To view a well-arranged assortment of block-headed Encyclopædias (Anglicanas or Metropolitanas) set out in an array of russia, or morocco, when a tithe of that good leather would comfortably re-clothe my shivering folios—would renovate Paracelsus himself, and enable old Raymund Lully to look like himself again in the world. I never see these impostors, but I long to strip them, to warm my ragged veterans in their spoils.

To be strong-backed and neat-bound is the desideratum of a volume. Magnificence comes after. This, when it can be afforded, is not to be lavished upon all kinds of books indiscriminately. I would not dress a set of Magazines, for instance, in full suit. The dishabille, or half-binding (with russia backs ever) is *our* costume. A Shakspeare or a Milton (unless the first editions), it were mere foppery to trick out in gay apparel. The possession of them confers no distinction. The exterior of them (the things themselves being so common), strange to say, raises no sweet emotions, no tickling sense of property in the owner. Thomson's Seasons, again, looks best (I maintain it) a little torn and dog's-eared. How beautiful to a genuine lover of reading are the sullied leaves, and worn-out appearance, nay, the very odour (beyond russia), if we would not forget kind feelings in fastidiousness, of an old "Circulating Library" Tom Jones, or Vicar of Wakefield! How they speak of the thousand thumbs that have turned over their pages with delight!—of the lone sempstress, whom they may have cheered (milliner, or harder-working mantua-maker) after her long day's needle-toil, running far into midnight, when she has snatched an hour, ill spared from sleep, to steep her cares, as in some Lethean cup, in spelling out their enchanting contents! Who would have them a whit less soiled? What better condition could we desire to see them in?

In some respects the better a book is, the less it demands from binding. Fielding, Smollett, Sterne, and all that class of perpetually self-reproductive volumes—Great Nature's Stereotypes—we see them individually perish with less regret, because we know the copies of them to be "eterne." But where a book is at once both good and rare—where the individual is almost the species, and when *that* perishes,

> We know not where is that Promethean torch
> That can its light relumine,—

such a book, for instance, as the Life of the Duke of Newcastle, by his Duchess—no casket is rich enough, no casing sufficiently durable, to honour and keep safe such a jewel.

Not only rare volumes of this description, which seem hopeless ever to be reprinted, but old editions of writers, such as Sir Philip Sydney, Bishop Taylor, Milton in his prose works, Fuller—of whom we *have* reprints, yet the books themselves, though they go about, and are talked of here and there, we know have not endenizened themselves (nor possibly ever will) in the national heart, so as to become stock books— it is good to possess these in durable and costly covers. I do not care for a First Folio of Shakspeare. I rather prefer the common editions of Rowe and Tonson, without notes, and with *plates,* which, being so execrably bad, serve as maps or modest remembrancers, to the text; and without pretending to any supposable emulation with it, are so much better than the Shakspeare gallery *engravings,* which *did.* I have a community of feeling with my countrymen about his Plays, and I like those editions of him best which have been oftenest tumbled about and handled.—On the contrary, I cannot read Beaumont and Fletcher but in Folio. The Octavo editions are painful to look at. I have no sympathy with them. If they were as much read as the current editions of the other poet, I should prefer them in that shape to the older one. I do not know a more heartless sight than the reprint of the Anatomy of Melancholy. What need was there of unearthing the bones of that fantastic old great man, to expose them in a winding-sheet of the newest fashion to modern censure? what hapless stationer could dream of Burton ever becoming popular?—The wretched Malone could not do worse, when he bribed the sexton of Stratford church to let him whitewash the painted effigy of old Shakspeare, which stood there, in rude but lively fashion depicted, to the very colour of the cheek, the eye, the eyebrow, hair, the very dress he used to wear—the only authentic testimony we had, however imperfect, of these curious parts and parcels of him. They covered him over with a coat of white paint. By ——, if I had been a justice of peace for Warwickshire, I would have clapt both commentator and sexton fast in the stocks, for a pair of meddling sacrilegious varlets.

I think I see them at their work—these sapient trouble-tombs.

Shall I be thought fantastical if I confess that the names of some of our poets sound sweeter, and have a finer relish to the ear—to mine, at least—than that of Milton or of Shakspeare? It may be that the latter are more staled and rung upon in common discourse. The sweetest names, and which carry a perfume in the mention, are, Kit Marlowe, Drayton, Drummond of Hawthornden, and Cowley.

Much depends upon *when* and *where* you read a book. In the five or six impatient minutes, before the dinner is quite ready, who would think of taking up the Faëry Queen for a stop-gap, or a volume of Bishop Andrewes' sermons?

Milton almost requires a solemn service of music to be played before you enter upon him. But he brings his music, to which, who listens, had need bring docile thoughts, and purged ears.

Winter evenings—the world shut out—with less of ceremony the gentle Shakspeare enters. At such a season the Tempest, or his own Winter's Tale—

These two poets you cannot avoid reading aloud—to yourself, or (as it chances) to some single person listening. More than one—and it degenerates into an audience.

Books of quick interest, that hurry on for incidents, are for the eye to glide over only. It will not do to read them out. I could never listen to even the better kind of modern novels without extreme irksomeness.

A newspaper, read out, is intolerable. In some of the Bank offices it is the custom (to save so much individual time) for one of the clerks —who is the best scholar—to commence upon the "Times," or the "Chronicle," and recite its entire contents aloud, *pro bono publico*. With every advantage of lungs and elocution, the effect is singularly vapid.

In barbers shops and public-houses a fellow will get up and spell out a paragraph, which he communicates as some discovery. Another follows with *his* selection. So the entire journal transpires at length by piece-meal. Seldom-readers are slow readers, and, without this expedient, no one in the company would probably ever travel through the contents of a whole paper.

Newspapers always excite curiosity. No one ever lays one down without a feeling of disappointment.

What an eternal time that gentleman in black, at Nando's, keeps the paper! I am sick of hearing the waiter bawling out incessantly, "The 'Chronicle' is in hand, Sir."

Coming into an inn at night—having ordered your supper—what can be more delightful than to find lying in the window-seat, left there time out of mind by the carelessness of some former guest—two or three numbers of the old Town and Country Magazine, with its amusing *tête-à-tête* pictures—"The Royal Lover and Lady G——"; "The Melting Platonic and the old Beau,"—and such-like antiquated scandal? Would you exchange it—at that time, and in that place—for a better book?

Poor Tobin, who latterly fell blind, did not regret it so much for the weightier kinds of reading—the Paradise Lost, or Comus, he could have *read* to him—but he missed the pleasure of skimming over with his own eye a magazine, or a light pamphlet.

I should not care to be caught in the serious avenues of some cathedral alone, and reading *Candide*.

I do not remember a more whimsical surprise than having been once detected—by a familiar damsel—reclined at my ease upon the grass, on Primrose Hill (her Cythera), reading—*Pamela*. There was nothing in the book to make a man seriously ashamed at the exposure; but as she seated herself down by me, and seemed determined to read in company, I could have wished it had been—any other book. We read on very sociably for a few pages; and, not finding the author much to her taste, she got up, and—went away. Gentle casuist, I leave it to thee to conjecture, whether the blush (for there was one between us) was the property of the nymph or the swain in this dilemma. From me you shall never get the secret.

I am not much a friend to out-of-doors reading. I cannot settle my spirits to it. I knew a Unitarian minister, who was generally to be seen upon Snow Hill (as yet Skinner's Street *was not*), between the hours of ten and eleven in the morning, studying a volume of Lardner. I own this to have been a strain of abstraction beyond my reach. I used to admire how he sidled along, keeping clear of secular contacts. An illiterate encounter with a porter's knot, or a bread-basket, would have quickly put to flight all the theology I am master of, and have left me worse than indifferent to the five points.

There is a class of street-readers, whom I can never contemplate without affection—the poor gentry, who, not having wherewithal to buy or hire a book, filch a little learning at the open stalls—the owner, with his hard eye, casting envious looks at them all the while, and thinking when they will have done. Venturing tenderly, page after page, expecting every moment when he shall interpose his interdict, and yet unable to deny themselves the gratification, they "snatch a fearful joy." Martin B——, in this way, by daily fragments, got through two volumes of Clarissa, when the stall-keeper damped his laudable ambition, by asking him (it was in his younger days) whether he meant to purchase the work. M. declares, that under no circumstances in his life did he ever peruse a book with half the satisfaction which he took in those uneasy snatches. A quaint poetess of our day has moralised upon this subject in two very touching but homely stanzas.

> I saw a boy with eager eye
> Open a book upon a stall,
> And read, as he'd devour it all;
> Which, when the stall-man did espy,
> Soon to the boy I heard him call,
> "You Sir, you never buy a book,
> Therefore in one you shall not look."
> The boy pass'd slowly on, and with a sigh
> He wish'd he never had been taught to read,
> Then of the old churl's books he should have had no need.
>
> Of sufferings the poor have many,
> Which never can the rich annoy:
> I soon perceived another boy,
> Who look'd as if he had not any
> Food, for that day at least—enjoy
> The sight of cold meat in a tavern larder.
> This boy's case, then thought I, is surely harder,
> Thus hungry, longing, thus without a penny,
> Beholding choice of dainty-dressèd meat:
> No wonder if he wish he ne'er had learn'd to eat.

STAGE ILLUSION

A PLAY is said to be well or ill acted, in proportion to the scenical illusion produced. Whether such illusion can in any case be perfect, is not the question. The nearest approach to it, we are told, is, when the actor appears wholly unconscious of the presence of spectators. In tragedy—in all which is to affect the feelings—this undivided attention to his stage business seems indispensable. Yet it is, in fact, dispensed with every day by our cleverest tragedians; and while these references to an audience, in the shape of rant or sentiment, are not too frequent or palpable, a sufficient quantity of illusion for the purposes of dramatic interest may be said to be produced in spite of them. But, tragedy apart, it may be inquired whether, in certain characters in comedy, especially those which are a little extravagant, or which involve some notion repugnant to the moral sense, it is not a proof of the highest skill in the comedian when, without absolutely appealing to an audience, he keeps up a tacit understanding with them: and makes them, unconsciously to themselves, a

party in the scene. The utmost nicety is required in the mode of doing
this; but we speak only of the great artists in the profession.

The most mortifying infirmity in human nature, to feel in ourselves, or
to contemplate in another, is, perhaps, cowardice. To see a coward *done
to the life* upon a stage would produce anything but mirth. Yet we most
of us remember Jack Bannister's cowards. Could anything be more agreeable, more pleasant? We loved the rogues. How was this effected but by
the exquisite art of the actor in a perpetual subinsinuation to us, the
spectators, even in the extremity of the shaking fit, that he was not half
such a coward as we took him for? We saw all the common symptoms of
the malady upon him; the quivering lip, the cowering knees, the teeth
chattering; and could have sworn "that man was frightened." But we
forgot all the while—or kept it almost a secret to ourselves—that he
never once lost his self-possession; that he let out, by a thousand droll
looks and gestures—meant at *us,* and not at all supposed to be visible to
his fellows in the scene, that his confidence in his own resources had
never once deserted him. Was this a genuine picture of a coward; or not
rather a likeness, which the clever artist contrived to palm upon us
instead of an original; while we secretly connived at the delusion for the
purpose of greater pleasure, than a more genuine counterfeiting of the
imbecility, helplessness, and utter self-desertion, which we know to be
concomitants of cowardice in real life, could have given us?

Why are misers so hateful in the world, and so endurable on the stage,
but because the skilful actor, by a sort of sub-reference, rather than direct appeal to us, disarms the character of a great deal of its odiousness,
by seeming to engage *our* compassion for the insecure tenure by which
he holds his money-bags and parchments? By this subtle vent half of
the hatefulness of the character—the self-closeness with which in real
life it coils itself up from the sympathies of men—evaporates. The miser
becomes sympathetic; *i.e.,* is no genuine miser. Here again a diverting
likeness is substituted for a very disagreeable reality.

Spleen, irritability—the pitiable infirmities of old men, which produce
only pain to behold in the realities, counterfeited upon a stage, divert
not altogether for the comic appendages to them, but in part from an
inner conviction that they are *being acted* before us; that a likeness only
is going on, and not the thing itself. They please by being done under the
life, or beside it; not *to the life.* When Gattie acts an old man, is he angry
indeed? or only a pleasant counterfeit, just enough of a likeness to recognise, without pressing upon us the uneasy sense of a reality?

Comedians, paradoxical as it may seem, may be too natural. It was
the case with a late actor. Nothing could be more earnest or true than
the manner of Mr. Emery; this told excellently in his Tyke, and characters of a tragic cast. But when he carried the same rigid exclusiveness
of attention to the stage business, and wilful blindness and oblivion of
everything before the curtain into his comedy, it produced a harsh and
dissonant effect. He was out of keeping with the rest of the *Personæ
Dramatis.* There was as little link between him and them, as betwixt

himself and the audience. He was a third estate—dry, repulsive, and unsocial to all. Individually considered, his execution was masterly. But comedy is not this unbending thing; for this reason, that the same degree of credibility is not required of it as to serious scenes. The degrees of credibility demanded to the two things may be illustrated by the different sort of truth which we expect when a man tells us a mournful or a merry story. If we suspect the former of falsehood in any one tittle, we reject it altogether. Our tears refuse to flow at a suspected imposition. But the teller of a mirthful tale has latitude allowed him. We are content with less than absolute truth. 'Tis the same with dramatic illusion. We confess we love in comedy to see an audience naturalised behind the scenes—taken into the interest of the drama, welcomed as bystanders, however. There is something ungracious in a comic actor holding himself aloof from all participation or concern with those who are come to be diverted by him. Macbeth must see the dagger, and no ear but his own be told of it; but an old fool in farce may think he *sees something*, and by conscious words and looks express it, as plainly as he can speak, to pit, box, and gallery. When an impertinent in tragedy, an Osric, for instance, breaks in upon the serious passions of the scene, we approve of the contempt with which he is treated. But when the pleasant impertinent of comedy, in a piece purely meant to give delight, and raise mirth out of whimsical perplexities, worries the studious man with taking up his leisure, or making his house his home, the same sort of contempt expressed (however *natural*) would destroy the balance of delight in the spectators. To make the intrusion comic, the actor who plays the annoyed man must a little desert nature; he must, in short, be thinking of the audience, and express only so much dissatisfaction and peevishness as is consistent with the pleasure of comedy. In other words, his perplexity must seem half put on. If he repel the intruder with the sober set face of a man in earnest, and more especially if he deliver his expostulations in a tone which in the world must necessarily provoke a duel, his real-life manner will destroy the whimsical and purely dramatic existence of the other character (which to render it comic demands an antagonist comicality on the part of the character opposed to it), and convert what was meant for mirth, rather than belief, into a downright piece of impertinence indeed, which would raise no diversion in us, but rather stir pain, to see inflicted in earnest upon any unworthy person. A very judicious actor (in most of his parts) seems to have fallen into an error of this sort in his playing with Mr. Wrench in the farce of Free and Easy.

Many instances would be tedious; these may suffice to show that comic acting at least does not always demand from the performer that strict abstraction from all reference to an audience which is exacted of it; but that in some cases a sort of compromise may take place, and all the purposes of dramatic delight be attained by a judicious understanding, not too openly announced, between the ladies and gentlemen—on both sides of the curtain.

TO THE SHADE OF ELLISTON

JOYOUSEST of once embodied spirits, whither at length hast thou flown? to what genial region are we permitted to conjecture that thou hast flitted?

Art thou sowing thy WILD OATS yet (the harvest time was still to come with thee) upon casual sands of Avernus? or art thou enacting ROVER (as we would gladlier think) by wandering Elysian streams?

This mortal frame, while thou didst play thy brief antics amongst us, was in truth anything but a prison to thee, as the vain Platonist dreams of this *body* to be no better than a county gaol, forsooth, or some house of durance vile, whereof the five senses are the fetters. Thou knewest better than to be in a hurry to cast off those gyves; and had notice to quit, I fear, before thou wert quite ready to abandon this fleshy tenement. It was thy Pleasure-House, thy Palace of Dainty Devices: thy Louvre, or thy White-Hall.

What new mysterious lodgings dost thou tenant now? or when may we expect thy aërial house-warming?

Tartarus we know, and we have read of the Blessed Shades; now cannot I intelligibly fancy thee in either.

Is it too much to hazard a conjecture, that (as the schoolmen admitted a receptacle apart for Patriarchs and un-chrisom babes) there may exist—not far perchance from that store-house of all vanities, which Milton saw in vision—a LIMBO somewhere for PLAYERS? and that

> Up thither like aerial vapours fly
> Both all Stage things, and all that in Stage things
> Built their fond hopes of glory, or lasting fame?
> All the unaccomplished works of Authors' hands,
> Abortive, monstrous, or unkindly mixed,
> Damn'd upon earth, fleet thither—
> Play, Opera, Farce, with all their trumpery.—

There, by the neighbouring moon (by some not improperly supposed thy Regent Planet upon earth), mayst thou not still be acting thy managerial pranks, great disembodied Lessee? but Lessee still, and still a manager.

In Green Rooms, impervious to mortal eye, the muse beholds thee wielding posthumous empire.

Thin ghosts of Figurantes (never plump on earth) circle thee in endlessly, and still their song is *Fie on sinful Phantasy!*

Magnificent were thy capriccios on this globe of earth, ROBERT WILLIAM ELLISTON! for as yet we know not thy new name in heaven.

It irks me to think, that, stript of thy regalities, thou shouldst ferry over, a poor forked shade, in crazy Stygian wherry. Methinks I hear the old boatman, paddling by the weedy wharf, with raucid voice, bawling "SCULLS, SCULLS": to which, with waving hand, and majestic action, thou deignest no reply, other than in two curt monosyllables, "No: Oars."

But the laws of Pluto's kingdom know small difference between king and cobbler; manager and call-boy; and, if haply your dates of life were conterminant, you are quietly taking your passage, cheek by cheek (O ignoble levelling of Death) with the shade of some recently departed candle-snuffer.

But mercy! what strippings, what tearing off of histrionic robes, and private vanities! what denudations to the bone, before the surly Ferryman will admit you to set a foot within his battered lighter.

Crowns, sceptres; shield, sword, and truncheon; thy own coronation robes (for thou hast brought the whole property-man's wardrobe with thee, enough to sink a navy); the judge's ermine; the coxcomb's wig; the snuff-box *à la Foppington*—all must overboard, he positively swears —and that Ancient Mariner brooks no denial; for, since the tiresome monodrame of the old Thracian Harper, Charon, it is to be believed, hath shown small taste for theatricals.

Ay, now 'tis done. You are just boat-weight; *pura et puta anima.*

But, bless me, how *little* you look!

So shall we all look—kings and keysars—stripped for the last voyage.

But the murky rogue pushes off. Adieu, pleasant and thrice pleasant shade! with my parting thanks for many a heavy hour of life lightened by thy harmless extravaganzas, public or domestic.

Rhadamanthus, who tries the lighter causes below, leaving to his two brethren the heavy calendars—honest Rhadamanth, always partial to players, weighing their parti-coloured existence here upon earth,—making account of the few foibles, that may have shaded thy *real life,* as we call it (though substantially, scarcely less a vapour than thy idlest vagaries upon the boards of Drury), as but of so many echoes, natural repercussions, and results to be expected from the assumed extravagancies of thy *secondary* or *mock life,* nightly upon a stage—after a lenient castigation, with rods lighter than of those Medusean ringlets, but just enough to "whip the offending Adam out of thee," shall courteously dismiss thee at the right-hand gate—the o. p. side of Hades—that conducts to masques and merry-makings in the Theatre Royal of Proserpine.

PLAUDITO, ET VALETO.

ELLISTONIANA

My acquaintance with the pleasant creature, whose loss we all deplore, was but slight.

My first introduction to E., which afterwards ripened into an acquaintance a little on this side of intimacy, was over a counter in the Leamington Spa Library, then newly entered upon by a branch of his family. E., whom nothing misbecame—to auspicate, I suppose, the filial concern, and set it a-going with a lustre—was serving in person two damsels fair, who had come into the shop ostensibly to inquire for some new publication, but in reality to have a sight of the illustrious shopman, hoping some conference. With what an air did he reach down the volume, dispassionately giving his opinion of the worth of the work in question, and launching out into a dissertation on its comparative merits with those of certain publications of a similar stamp, its rivals! his enchanted customers fairly hanging on his lips, subdued to their authoritative sentence. So have I seen a gentleman in comedy *acting* the shopman. So Lovelace sold his gloves in King Street. I admired the histrionic art, by which he contrived to carry clean away every notion of disgrace, from the occupation he had so generously submitted to; and from that hour I judged him, with no after repentance, to be a person with whom it would be a felicity to be more acquainted.

To descant upon his merits as a Comedian would be superfluous. With his blended private and professional habits alone I have to do; that harmonious fusion of the manners of the player into those of everyday life, which brought the stage boards into streets, and dining-parlours, and kept up the play when the play was ended.—"I like Wrench," a friend was saying to him one day, "because he is the same, natural, easy creature, *on* the stage, that he is *off*." "My case exactly," retorted Elliston—with a charming forgetfulness, that the converse of a proposition does not always lead to the same conclusion—"I am the same person *off* the stage that I am *on*." The inference, at first sight, seems identical; but examine it a little, and it confesses only, that the one performer was never, and the other always, *acting*.

And in truth this was the charm of Elliston's private deportment. You had spirited performance always going on before your eyes, with nothing to pay. As where a monarch takes up his casual abode for a night, the poorest hovel which he honours by his sleeping in it, becomes *ipso facto* for that time a palace; so wherever Ellison walked, sate, or stood still, there was the theatre. He carried about with him his pit, boxes, and galleries, and set up his portable playhouse at corners of streets, and in the market-places. Upon flintiest pavements he trod the boards still; and if his theme chanced to be passionate, the green baize carpet of tragedy spontaneously rose beneath his feet. Now this was hearty, and showed a love for his art. So Apelles *always* painted—in thought. So G. D. *always* poetises. I hate a luke-warm artist. I have known actors—and some of them of Elliston's own stamp—who shall have agreeably been amusing you in the part of a rake or a coxcomb, through the two or three hours of their dramatic existence; but no sooner does the curtain fall with its leaden clatter, but a spirit of lead seems to seize on all their faculties. They emerge sour, morose persons, intolerable to their families, servants, etc. Another shall have been expanding your heart with generous deeds and sentiments, till it even beats with yearnings of universal sympathy; you absolutely long to go home and do some good action. The play seems tedious, till you can get fairly out of

the house, and realise your laudable intentions. At length the final bell
rings, and this cordial representative of all that is amiable in human
breasts steps forth—a miser. Elliston was more of a piece. Did he *play*
Ranger? and did Ranger fill the general bosom of the town with satisfaction? why should *he* not be Ranger, and diffuse the same cordial satisfaction among his private circles? with *his* temperament, *his* animal
spirits, *his* good-nature, *his* follies perchance, could he do better than
identify himself with his impersonation? Are we to like a pleasant rake,
or coxcomb, on the stage, and give ourselves airs of aversion for the
identical character, presented to us in actual life? or what would the
performer have gained by divesting himself of the impersonation? Could
the man Elliston have been essentially different from his part, even if he
had avoided to reflect to us studiously, in private circles, the airy brisk-
ness, the forwardness, and 'scape-goat trickeries of his protoype?

"But there is something not natural in this everlasting *acting;* we
want the real man."

Are you quite sure that it is not the man himself, whom you cannot,
or will not see, under some adventitious trappings, which, nevertheless,
sit not at all inconsistently upon him? What if it is the nature of some
men to be highly artificial? The fault is least reprehensible in *players.*
Cibber was his own Foppington, with almost as much wit as Vanbrugh
could add to it.

"My conceit of his person,"—it is Ben Jonson speaking of Lord Bacon,
—"was never increased towards him by his *place* or *honours.* But I have,
and do reverence him for the *greatness,* that was only proper to himself;
in that he seemed to me ever one of the *greatest* men, that had been in
many ages. In his adversity I ever prayed that Heaven would give him
strength; for *greatness* he could not want."

The quality here commended was scarcely less conspicuous in the subject of these idle reminiscences than in my Lord Verulam. Those who
have imagined that an unexpected elevation to the direction of a great
London Theatre affected the consequence of Elliston, or at all changed
his nature, knew not the essential *greatness* of the man whom they disparage. It was my fortune to encounter him near St. Dunstan's Church
(which, with its punctual giants, is now no more than dust and a
shadow), on the morning of his election to that high office. Grasping my
hand with a look of significance, he only uttered,—"Have you heard the
news?"—then, with another look following up the blow, he subjoined,
"I am the future Manager of Drury Lane Theatre."—Breathless as he
saw me, he stayed not for congratulation or reply, but mutely stalked
away, leaving me to chew upon his new-blown dignities at leisure. In
fact, nothing could be said to it. Expressive silence alone could muse his
praise. This was in his *great* style.

But was he less *great* (be witness, O ye Powers of Equanimity, that
supported in the ruins of Carthage the consular exile, and more recently
transmuted, for a more illustrious exile, the barren constableship of Elba
into an image of Imperial France), when, in melancholy after-years,

again, much near the same spot, I met him, when that sceptre had been wrested from his hand, and his dominion was curtailed to the petty managership, and part proprietorshop, of the small Olympic, *his Elba?* He still played nightly upon the boards of Drury, but in parts, alas! allotted to him, not magnificently distributed by him. Waiving his great loss as nothing, and magnificently sinking the sense of fallen *material* grandeur in the more liberal resentment of depreciations done to his more lofty *intellectual* pretensions, "Have you heard" (his customary exordium)—"have you heard," said he, "how they treat me? they put me in *comedy*." Thought I—but his finger on his lips forbade any verbal interruption—"where could they have put you better?" Then, after a pause—"Where I formerly played Romeo, I now play Mercutio,"—and so again he stalked away, neither staying, nor caring for, responses.

O, it was a rich scene,—but Sir A—— C——, the best of story-tellers and surgeons, who mends a lame narrative almost as well as he sets a fracture, alone could do justice to it,—that I was a witness to, in the tarnished room (that had once been green) of that same little Olympic. There, after his deposition from Imperial Drury, he substituted a throne. That Olympic Hill was his "highest heaven"; himself "Jove in his chair." There he sat in state, while before him, on complaint of prompter, was brought for judgment—how shall I describe her?—one of those little tawdry things that flirt at the tails of choruses—a probationer for the town, in either of its senses—the pertest little drab—a dirty fringe and appendage of the lamp's smoke—who, it seems, on some disapprobation expressed by a "highly respectable" audience,—had precipitately quitted her station on the boards, and withdrawn her small talents in disgust.

"And how dare you," said her manager,—assuming a censorial severity, which would have crushed the confidence of a Vestris, and disarmed that beautiful Rebel herself of her professional caprices—I verily believe, he thought *her* standing before him—"how dare you, Madam, withdraw yourself, without a notice, from your theatrical duties?" "I was hissed, Sir." "And you have the presumption to decide upon the taste of the town?" "I don't know that, Sir, but I will never stand to be hissed," was the subjoinder of young Confidence—when gathering up his features into one significant mass of wonder, pity, and expostulatory indignation —in a lesson never to have been lost upon a creature less forward than she who stood before him—his words were these: "They have hissed *me*."

'Twas the identical argument *a fortiori*, which the son of Peleus uses to Lycaon trembling under his lance, to persuade him to take his destiny with a good grace. "I too am mortal." And it is to be believed that in both cases the rhetoric missed of its application, for want of a proper understanding with the faculties of the respective recipients.

"Quite an Opera pit," he said to me, as he was courteously conducting me over the benches of his Surrey Theatre, the last retreat, and recess, of his everyday waning grandeur.

Those who knew Elliston, will know the *manner* in which he pronounced the latter sentence of the few words I am about to record. One proud day to me he took his roast mutton with us in the Temple, to which I had superadded a preliminary haddock. After a rather plentiful partaking of the meagre banquet, not unrefreshed with the humbler sort of liquors, I made a sort of apology for the humility of the fare, observing that for my own part I never ate but one dish at dinner. "I too never eat but one thing at dinner,"—was his reply—then after a pause—"reckoning fish as nothing." The manner was all. It was as if by one peremptory sentence he had decreed the annihilation of all the savoury esculents, which the pleasant and nutritious-food-giving Ocean pours forth upon poor humans from her watery bosom. This was *greatness*, tempered with considerate *tenderness* to the feelings of his scanty but welcoming entertainer.

Great wert thou in thy life, Robert William Elliston! and *not lessened* in thy death, if report speak truly, which says that thou didst direct that thy mortal remains should repose under no inscription but one of pure *Latinity*. Classical was thy bringing up! and beautiful was the feeling on thy last bed, which, connecting the man with the boy, took thee back to thy latest exercise of imagination, to the days when, undreaming of Theatres and Managerships, thou wert a scholar, and an early ripe one, under the roofs builded by the munificent and pious Colet. For thee the Pauline Muses weep. In elegies, that shall silence this crude prose, they shall celebrate thy praise.

THE OLD MARGATE HOY

I AM fond of passing my vacations (I believe I have said so before) at one or other of the Universities. Next to these my choice would fix me at some woody spot, such as the neighbourhood of Henley affords in abundance, on the banks of my beloved Thames. But somehow or other my cousin contrives to wheedle me, once in three or four seasons, to a watering-place. Old attachments cling to her in spite of experience. We have been dull at Worthing one summer, duller at Brighton another, dullest at Eastbourn a third, and are at this moment doing dreary penance at— Hastings!—and all because we were happy many years ago for a brief week at Margate. That was our first sea-side experiment, and many circumstances combined to make it the most agreeable holiday of my life. We had neither of us seen the sea, and we had never been from home so long together in company.

Can I forget thee, thou old Margate Hoy, with thy weather-beaten, sun-burnt captain, and his rough accommodations—ill exchanged for the foppery and fresh-water niceness of the modern steam-packet? To the winds and waves thou committedst thy goodly freightage, and didst ask no aid of magic fumes, and spells, and boiling caldrons. With the gales of heaven thou wentest swimmingly; or, when it was their pleasure, stoodest still with sailor-like patience. Thy course was natural, not forced, as in a hot-bed; nor didst thou go poisoning the breath of ocean with sulphureous smoke—a great sea chimera, chimneying and furnacing the deep; or liker to that fire-god parching up Scamander.

Can I forget thy honest, yet slender crew, with their coy reluctant responses (yet to the suppression of anything like contempt) to the raw questions, which we of the great city would be ever and anon putting to them, as to the uses of this or that strange naval implement? 'Specially can I forget thee, thou happy medium, thou shade of refuge between us and them, conciliating interpreter of their skill to our simplicity, comfortable ambassador between sea and land!—whose sailor-trousers did not more convincingly assure thee to be an adopted denizen of the former, than thy white cap, and whiter apron over them, with thy neat-figured practice in thy culinary vocation, bespoke thee to have been of inland nurture heretofore—a master cook of Eastcheap? How busily didst thou ply thy multifarious occupation, cook, mariner, attendant, chamberlain: here, there, like another Ariel, flaming at once about all parts of the deck, yet with kindlier ministrations—not to assist the tempest, but, as if touched with a kindred sense of our infirmities, to soothe the qualms which that untried motion might haply raise in our crude land-fancies. And when the o'erwashing billows drove us below deck (for it was far gone in October, and we had stiff and blowing weather), how did thy officious ministerings, still catering for our comfort, with cards, and cordials, and thy more cordial conversation, alleviate the closeness and the confinement of thy else (truth to say) not very savoury, nor very inviting, little cabin!

With these additaments to boot, we had on board a fellow-passenger, whose discourse in verity might have beguiled a longer voyage than we meditated, and have made mirth and wonder abound as far as the Azores. He was a dark, Spanish-complexioned young man, remarkably handsome, with an officer-like assurance and an insuppressible volubility of assertion. He was, in fact, the greatest liar I had met with then, or since. He was none of your hesitating, half-story-tellers (a most painful description of mortals) who go on sounding your belief, and only giving you as much as they see you can swallow at a time—the nibbling pick-pockets of your patience—but one who committed downright, daylight depredations upon his neighbour's faith. He did not stand shivering upon the brink, but was a hearty, thorough-paced liar, and plunged at once into the depths of your credulity. I partly believe, he made pretty sure of his company. Not many rich, not many wise, or learned, composed at that time the common stowage of a Margate packet. We were, I am afraid, a set of as unseasoned Londoners (let our enemies give it a worse name) as Aldermanbury, or Watling Street, at that time of day could have supplied. There might be an exception or two among us, but I scorn to make any invidious distinctions among such a jolly, companionable ship's company, as those were whom I sailed with. Something too must be conceded to the *Genius Loci*. Had the confident fellow told us half

the legends on land which he favoured us with on the other element, I
flatter myself the good sense of most of us would have revolted. But we
were in a new world, with everything unfamiliar about us, and the time
and place disposed us to the reception of any prodigious marvel whatsoever. Time has obliterated from my memory much of his wild fablings;
and the rest would appear but dull, as written, and to be read on
shore. He had been Aide-de-camp (among other rare accidents and fortunes) to a Persian Prince, and at one blow had stricken off the head of
the King of Carimania on horseback. He, of course, married the Prince's
daughter. I forget what unlucky turn in the politics of that court, combining with the loss of his consort, was the reason of his quitting Persia;
but, with the rapidity of a magician, he transported himself, along with
his hearers, back to England, where we still found him in the confidence
of great ladies. There was some story of a princess—Elizabeth, if I remember—having intrusted to his care an extraordinary casket of jewels,
upon some extraordinary occasion—but, as I am not certain of the name
or circumstance at this distance of time, I must leave it to the Royal
daughters of England to settle the honour among themselves in private.
I cannot call to mind half his pleasant wonders; but I perfectly remember, that in the course of his travels he had seen a phœnix; and he
obligingly undeceived us of the vulgar error, that there is but one of that
species at a time, assuring us that they were not uncommon in some parts
of Upper Egypt. Hitherto he had found the most implicit listeners. His
dreaming fancies had transported us beyond the "ignorant present." But
when (still hardying more and more in his triumphs over our simplicity)
he went on to affirm that he had actually sailed through the legs of the
Colossus at Rhodes, it really became necessary to make a stand. And
here I must do justice to the good sense and intrepidity of one of our
party, a youth, that had hitherto been one of his most deferential auditors, who, from his recent reading, made bold to assure the gentleman,
that there must be some mistake, as "the Colossus in question had been
destroyed long since"; to whose opinion, delivered with all modesty, our
hero was obliging enough to concede thus much, that "the figure was
indeed a little damaged." This was the only opposition he met with,
and it did not at all seem to stagger him, for he proceeded with his fables,
which the same youth appeared to swallow with still more complacency
than ever,—confirmed, as it were, by the extreme candour of that concession. With these prodigies he wheedled us on till we came in sight of
the Reculvers, which one of our own company (having been the voyage
before) immediately recognising, and pointing out to us, was considered
by us as no ordinary seaman.

All this time sat upon the edge of the deck quite a different character.
It was a lad, apparently very poor, very infirm, and very patient. His
eye was ever on the sea, with a smile; and, if he caught now and then
some snatches of these wild legends, it was by accident, and they seemed
not to concern him. The waves to him whispered more pleasant stories.
He was as one, being with us, but not of us. He heard the bell of dinner

ring without stirring; and when some of us pulled out our private stores —our cold meat and our salads—he produced none, and seemed to want none. Only a solitary biscuit he had laid in; provision for the one or two days and nights, to which these vessels then were oftentimes obliged to prolong their voyage. Upon a nearer acquaintance with him, which he seemed neither to court nor decline, we learned that he was going to Margate, with the hope of being admitted into the Infirmary there for sea-bathing. His disease was a scrofula, which appeared to have eaten all over him. He expressed great hopes of a cure; and when we asked him, whether he had any friends where he was going, he replied "he *had* no friends."

These pleasant, and some mournful passages, with the first sight of the sea, co-operating with youth, and a sense of holidays, and out-of-door adventure, to me that had been pent up in populous cities for many months before,—have left upon my mind the fragrance as of summer days gone by, bequeathing nothing but their remembrance for cold and wintry hours to chew upon.

Will it be thought a digression (it may spare some unwelcome comparisons), if I endeavour to account for the *dissatisfaction* which I have heard so many persons confess to have felt (as I did myself feel in part on this occasion), *at the sight of the sea for the first time?* I think the reason usually given—referring to the incapacity of actual objects for satisfying our preconceptions of them—scarcely goes deep enough into the question. Let the same person see a lion, an elephant, a mountain for the first time in his life, and he shall perhaps feel himself a little mortified. The things do not fill up that space which the idea of them seemed to take up in his mind. But they have still a correspondency to his first notion, and in time grow up to it, so as to produce a very similar impression: enlarging themselves (if I may say so) upon familiarity. But the sea remains a disappointment.—Is it not, that in *the latter* we had expected to behold (absurdly, I grant, but, I am afraid, by the law of imagination, unavoidably) not a definite object, as those wild beasts, or that mountain compassable by the eye, but *all the sea at once*, THE COMMENSURATE ANTAGONIST OF THE EARTH? I do not say we tell ourselves so much, but the craving of the mind is to be satisfied with nothing less. I will suppose the case of a young person of fifteen (as I then was) knowing nothing of the sea, but from description. He comes to it for the first time—all that he has been reading of it all his life, and *that* the most enthusiastic part of life,—all he has gathered from narratives of wandering seamen,—what he has gained from true voyages, and what he cherishes as credulously from romance and poetry,—crowding their images, and exacting strange tributes from expectation.—He thinks of the great deep, and of those who go down unto it; of its thousand isles, and of the vast continents it washes; of its receiving the mighty Plate, or Orellana, into its bosom, without disturbance, or sense of augmentation; of Biscay swells, and the mariner

> For many a day, and many a dreadful night,
> Incessant labouring round the stormy Cape;

of fatal rocks, and the "still-vexed Bermoothes"; of great whirlpools, and the water-spout; of sunken ships, and sumless treasures swallowed up in the unrestoring depths; of fishes and quaint monsters, to which all that is terrible on earth—

> Be but as buggs to frighten babes withal,
> Compared with the creatures in the sea's entral;

of naked savages, and Juan Fernandez; of pearls, and shells; of coral beds, and of enchanted isles; of mermaids' grots—

I do not assert that in sober earnest he expects to be shown all these wonders at once, but he is under the tyranny of a mighty faculty, which haunts him with confused hints and shadows of all these; and when the actual object opens first upon him, seen (in tame weather, too, most likely) from our unromantic coasts—a speck, a slip of sea-water, as it shows to him—what can it prove but a very unsatisfying and even diminutive entertainment? Or if he has come to it from the mouth of a river, was it much more than the river widening? and, even out of sight of land, what had he but a flat watery horizon about him, nothing comparable to the vast o'er-curtaining sky, his familiar object, seen daily without dread or amazement?—Who, in similar circumstances, has not been tempted to exclaim with Charoba, in the poem of Gebir,

> Is this the mighty ocean? is this *all?*

I love town or country; but this detestable Cinque Port is neither. I hate these scrubbed shoots, thrusting out their starved foliage from between the horrid fissures of dusty innutritious rocks; which the amateur calls "verdure to the edge of the sea." I require woods, and they show me stunted coppices. I cry out for the water-brooks, and pant for fresh streams, and inland murmurs. I cannot stand all day on the naked beach, watching the capricious hues of the sea, shifting like the colours of a dying mullet. I am tired of looking out at the windows of this island-prison. I would fain retire into the interior of my cage. While I gaze upon the sea, I want to be on it, over it, across it. It binds me in with chains, as of iron. My thoughts are abroad. I should not so feel in Staffordshire. There is no home for me here. There is no sense of home at Hastings. It is a place of fugitive resort, an heterogeneous assemblage of sea-mews and stock-brokers, Amphitrites of the town, and misses that coquet with the Ocean. If it were what it was in its primitive shape, and what it ought to have remained, a fair, honest fishing-town, and no more, it were something—with a few straggling fishermen's huts scattered about, artless as its cliffs, and with their materials filched from them, it were something. I could abide to dwell with Meshech; to assort with fisher-swains, and smugglers. There are, or I dream there are, many of this latter occupation here. Their faces become the place. I like a smuggler. He is the only honest thief. He robs nothing but the revenue,—an abstraction I never greatly cared about. I could go out with them in their mackerel boats, or about their less ostensible business, with some satisfaction. I can even tolerate those poor victims to monotony, who from day to day pace along the beach, in endless progress and recurrence, to watch their illicit countrymen—townsfolk or brethren perchance—whistling to the sheathing and unsheathing of their cutlasses (their only solace), who, under the mild name of preventive service, keep up a legitimated civil warfare in the deplorable absence of a foreign one, to show their detestation of run hollands, and zeal for Old England. But it is the visitants from town, that come here to *say* that they have been here, with no more relish of the seat than a pond-perch or a dace might be supposed to have, that are my aversion. I feel like a foolish dace in these regions, and have as little toleration for myself here as for them. What can they want here? if they had a true relish of the ocean, why have they brought all this land luggage with them? or why pitch their civilised tents in the desert? What mean these scanty book-rooms—marine libraries as they entitle them—if the sea were, as they would have us believe, a book "to read strange matter in"? what are their foolish concert-rooms, if they come, as they would fain be thought to do, to listen to the music of the waves? All is false and hollow pretension. They come, because it is the fashion, and to spoil the nature of the place. They are, mostly, as I have said, stock-brokers; but I have watched the better sort of them—now and then, an honest citizen (of the old stamp), in the simplicity of his heart, shall bring down his wife and daughters, to taste the sea breezes. I always know the date of their arrival. It is easy to see it in their countenance. A day or two they go wandering on the shingles, picking up cockle-shells, and thinking them great things; but, in a poor week, imagination slackens: they begin to discover that cockles produce no pearls, and then—O then!—if I could interpret for the pretty creatures (I know they have not the courage to confess it themselves) how gladly would they exchange their sea-side rambles for a Sunday walk on the green-sward of their accustomed Twickenham meadows!

I would ask of one of these sea-charmed emigrants, who think they truly love the sea, with its wild usages, what would their feelings be, if some of the unsophisticated aborigines of this place, encouraged by their courteous questionings here, should venture, on the faith of such assured sympathy between them, to return the visit, and come up to see—London. I must imagine them with their fishing-tackle on their back, as we carry our town necessaries. What a sensation would it cause in Lothbury? What vehement laughter would it not excite among

The daughters of Cheapside, and wives of Lombard Street!

I am sure that no town-bred or inland-born subjects can feel their true and natural nourishment at these sea-places. Nature, where she does not mean us for mariners and vagabonds, bids us stay at home. The salt foam seems to nourish a spleen. I am not half so good-natured as by the milder waters of my natural river. I would exchange these sea-gulls for swans, and scud a swallow for ever about the banks of Thamesis.

THE CONVALESCENT

A PRETTY severe fit of indisposition which, under the name of a nervous fever, has made a prisoner of me for some weeks past, and is but slowly leaving me, has reduced me to an incapacity of reflecting upon any topic foreign to itself. Expect no healthy conclusions from me this month, reader; I can offer you only sick men's dreams.

And truly the whole state of sickness is such; for what else is it but a magnificent dream for a man to lie a-bed, and draw daylight curtains about him; and, shutting out the sun, to induce a total oblivion of all the works which are going on under it? To become insensible to all the operations of life, except the beatings of one feeble pulse?

If there be a regal solitude, it is a sick bed. How the patient lords it there; what caprices he acts without control! how king-like he sways his pillow—tumbling, and tossing, and shifting, and lowering, and thumping, and flatting, and moulding it, to the ever-varying requisitions of his throbbing temples.

He changes sides oftener than a politician. Now he lies full length, then half-length, obliquely, transversely, head and feet quite across the bed; and none accuses him of tergiversation. Within the four curtains he is absolute. They are his Mare Clausum.

How sickness enlarges the dimensions of a man's self to himself! he is his own exclusive object. Supreme selfishness is inculcated upon him as his only duty. 'Tis the Two Tables of the Law to him. He has nothing to think of but how to get well. What passes out of doors, or within them, so he hear not the jarring of them, affects him not.

A little while ago he was greatly concerned in the event of a lawsuit, which was to be the making or the marring of his dearest friend. He was to be seen trudging about upon this man's errand to fifty quarters of the town at once, jogging this witness, refreshing that solicitor. The cause was to come on yesterday. He is absolutely as indifferent to the decision as if it were a question to be tried at Pekin. Peradventure from some whispering, going on about the house, not intended for his hearing, he picks up enough to make him understand that things went cross-grained in the court yesterday, and his friend is ruined. But the word "friend," and the word "ruin," disturb him no more than so much jargon. He is not to think of anything but how to get better.

What a world of foreign cares are merged in that absorbing consideration!

He has put on the strong armour of sickness; he is wrapped in the callous hide of suffering; he keeps his sympathy, like some curious vintage, under trusty lock and key, for his own use only.

He lies pitying himself, honing and moaning to himself; he yearneth over himself; his bowels are even melted within him, to think what he suffers; he is not ashamed to weep over himself.

He is for ever plotting how to do some good to himself; studying little stratagems and artificial alleviations.

He makes the most of himself; dividing himself, by an allowable fiction, into as many distinct individuals, as he hath sore and sorrowing members. Sometimes he meditates—as of a thing apart from him— upon his poor aching head, and that dull pain which, dozing or waking, lay in it all the past night like a log, or palpable substance of pain, not to be removed without opening the very skull, as it seemed, to take it thence. Or he pities his long, clammy, attenuated fingers. He compassionates himself all over; and his bed is a very discipline of humanity, and tender heart.

He is his own sympathiser; and instinctively feels that none can so well perform that office for him. He cares for few spectators to his tragedy. Only that punctual face of the old nurse pleases him, that announces his broths and his cordials. He likes it because it is so unmoved, and because he can pour forth his feverish ejaculations before it as unreservedly as to his bed-post.

To the world's business he is dead. He understands not what the callings and occupations of mortals are; only he has a glimmering conceit of some such thing, when the doctor makes his daily call: and even in the lines on that busy face he reads no multiplicity of patients, but solely conceives of himself as *the sick man*. To what other uneasy couch the good man is hastening, when he slips out of his chamber, folding up his thin douceur so carefully, for fear of rustling—is no speculation which he can at present entertain. He thinks only of the regular return of the same phenomenon at the same hour to-morrow.

Household rumours touch him not. Some faint murmur, indicative of life going on within the house, soothes him, while he knows not distinctly what it is. He is not to know anything, not to think of anything. Servants gliding up or down the distant staircase, treading as upon velvet, gently keep his ear awake, so long as he troubles not himself further than with some feeble guess at their errands. Exacter knowledge would be a burthen to him: he can just endure the pressure of conjecture. He opens his eye faintly at the dull stroke of the muffled knocker, and closes it again without asking "Who was it?" He is flattered by a general notion that inquiries are making after him, but he cares not to know the name of the inquirer. In the general stillness, and awful hush of the house, he lies in state, and feels his sovereignty.

To be sick is to enjoy monarchal prerogatives. Compare the silent tread, and quiet ministry, almost by the eye only, with which he is served —with the careless demeanour, the unceremonious goings in and out (slapping of doors, or leaving them open) of the very same attendants, when he is getting a little better—and you will confess, that from the bed of sickness (throne let me rather call it) to the elbow-chair of convalescence, is a fall from dignity, amounting to a deposition.

How convalescence shrinks a man back to his pristine stature! where is now the space, which he occupied so lately, in his own, in the family's eye?

The scene of his regalities, his sick room, which was his presence chamber, where he lay and acted his despotic fancies—how is it reduced to a common bedroom! The trimness of the very bed has something petty and unmeaning about it. It is *made* every day. How unlike to that wavy, many-furrowed, oceanic surface, which it presented so short a time since, when to *make* it was a service not to be thought of at oftener than three or four day revolutions, when the patient was with pain and grief to be lifted for a little while out of it, to submit to the encroachments of unwelcome neatness, and decencies which his shaken frame deprecated; then to be lifted into it again, for another three or four days' respite, to flounder it out of shape again, while every fresh furrow was an historical record of some shifting posture, some uneasy turning, some seeking for a little ease; and the shrunken skin scarce told a truer story than the crumpled coverlid.

Hushed are those mysterious sighs—those groans—so much more awful, while we knew not from what caverns of vast hidden suffering they proceeded. The Lernean pangs are quenched. The riddle of sickness is solved; and Philoctetes is become an ordinary personage.

Perhaps some relic of the sick man's dream of greatness survives in the still lingering visitations of the medical attendant. But how is he, too, changed with everything else! Can this be he—this man of news— of chat—of anecdote—of everything but physic—can this be he, who so lately came between the patient and his cruel enemy, as on some solemn embassy from Nature, erecting herself into a high mediating party?— Pshaw! 'tis some old woman.

Farewell with him all that made sickness pompous—the spell that hushed the household—the desertlike stillness, felt throughout its inmost chambers—the mute attendance—the inquiry by looks—the still softer delicacies of self-attention—the sole and single eye of distemper alonely fixed upon itself—world-thoughts excluded—the man a world unto himself—his own theatre—

What a speck is he dwindled into!

In this flat swamp of convalescence, left by the ebb of sickness, yet far enough from the terra firma of established health, your note, dear Editor, reached me, requesting—an article. In Articulo Mortis, thought I; but it is something hard—and the quibble, wretched as it was, relieved me. The summons, unseasonable as it appeared, seemed to link me on again to the petty businesses of life, which I had lost sight of; a gentle call to activity, however trivial; a wholesome meaning from that preposterous dream of self-absorption—the puffy state of sickness—in which I confess to have lain so long, insensible to the magazines and monarchies of the world alike; to its laws, and to its literature. The hypochondriac flatus is subsiding; the acres, which in imagination I had spread over—for the sick man swells in the sole contemplation of his single sufferings, till he becomes a Tityus to himself—are wasting to a span; and for the giant of self-importance, which I was so lately, you have me once again in my natural pretensions—the lean and meagre figure of your insignificant Essayist.

SANITY OF TRUE GENIUS

So far from the position holding true, that great wit (or genius, in our modern way of speaking) has a necessary alliance with insanity, the greatest wits, on the contrary, will ever be found to be the sanest writers. It is impossible for the mind to conceive of a mad Shakspeare. The greatness of wit, by which the poetic talent is here chiefly to be understood, manifests itself in the admirable balance of all the faculties. Madness is the disproportionate straining or excess of any one of them. "So strong a wit," says Cowley, speaking of a poetical friend,

> "——did Nature to him frame,
> As all things but his judgment overcame;
> His judgment like the heavenly moon did show,
> Tempering that mighty sea below."

The ground of the mistake is, that men, finding in the raptures of the higher poetry a condition of exaltation, to which they have no parallel in their own experience, besides the spurious resemblance of it in dreams and fevers, impute a state of dreaminess and fever to the poet. But the true poet dreams being awake. He is not possessed by his subject, but has dominion over it. In the groves of Eden he walks familiar as in his native paths. He ascends the empyrean heaven, and is not intoxicated. He treads the burning marl without dismay; he wins his flight without self-loss through realms of chaos "and old night." Or if, abandoning himself to that severer chaos of a "human mind untuned," he is content awhile to be mad with Lear, or to hate mankind (a sort of madness) with Timon, neither is that madness, nor this misanthropy, so unchecked, but that,—never letting the reins of reason wholly go, while most he seems to do so,—he has his better genius still whispering at his ear, with the good servant Kent suggesting saner counsels, or with the honest steward Flavius recommending kindlier resolutions. Where he seems most to recede from humanity, he will be found the truest to it. From beyond the scope of Nature if he summon possible existences, he subjugates them to the law of her consistency. He is beautifully loyal to that sovereign directress, even when he appears most to betray and desert her. His ideal tribes submit to policy; his very monsters are tamed to his hand, even as that wild sea-brood, shepherded by Proteus. He tames, and he clothes them with attributes of flesh and blood, till they wonder at themselves, like Indian Islanders forced to submit to European vesture. Caliban, the Witches, are as true to the laws of their own nature (ours with a difference), as Othello, Hamlet, and Macbeth. Herein the great and the little wits are differenced; that if the latter wander ever so little from nature or actual existence, they lose themselves and their readers. Their phantoms are lawless; their visions nightmares. They do not create, which implies shaping and consistency. Their imaginations are not active—for to be active is to call something into act and form—but passive, as men in sick dreams. For the super-natural, or something super-added to what we know of nature, they give you the plainly non-natural. And if this were all, and that these mental hallucinations were discoverable only in the treatment of subjects out of nature, or transcending it, the judgment might with some plea be pardoned if it ran riot, and a little wantonised: but even in the describing of real and every-day life, that which is before their eyes, one of these lesser wits shall more deviate from nature,—show more of that inconsequence, which has a natural alliance with frenzy,—than a great genius in his "maddest fits," as Withers somewhere calls them. We appeal to any one that is acquainted with the common run of Lane's novels,—as they existed some twenty or thirty years back,—those scanty intellectual viands of the whole female reading public, till a happier genius arose, and expelled for ever the innutritious phantoms,—whether he has not found his brain more "betossed," his memory more puzzled, his sense of when and where more confounded, among the improbable events, the incoherent incidents, the inconsistent characters, or no-characters, of some third-rate love-intrigue—where the persons shall be a Lord Glendamour and a Miss Rivers, and the scene only alternate between Bath and Bond Street—a more bewildering dreaminess induced upon him, than he has felt wandering over all the fairy-grounds of Spenser. In the productions we refer to, nothing but names and places is familiar; the persons are neither of this world nor of any other conceivable one; an endless stream of activities without purpose, or purposes destitute of motive:—we meet phantoms in our known walks; *fantasques* only christened. In the poet we have names which announce fiction; and we have absolutely no place at all, for the things and persons of the Faëry Queen prate not of their "whereabout." But in their inner nature, and the law of their speech and actions, we are at home, and upon acquainted ground. The one turns life into a dream; the other to the wildest dreams gives the sobrieties of everyday occurrences. By what subtle art of tracing the mental processes it is effected, we are not philosophers enough to explain, but in that wonderful episode of the cave of Mammon, in which the Money God appears first in the lowest form of a miser, is then a worker of metals, and becomes the god of all the treasures of the world; and has a daughter, Ambition, before whom all the world kneels for favours —with the Hesperian fruit, the waters of Tantalus, with Pilate washing his hands vainly, but not impertinently, in the same stream—that we should be at one moment in the cave of an old hoarder of treasures, at the next at the forge of the Cyclops, in a palace and yet in hell, all at once, with the shifting mutations of the most rambling dream, and our judgment yet all the time awake, and neither able nor willing to detect the fallacy,—is a proof of that hidden sanity which still guides the poet in the wildest seeming aberrations.

It is not enough to say that the whole episode is a copy of the mind's conceptions in sleep; it is, in some sort—but what a copy! Let the most romantic of us, that has been entertained all night with spectacle of some wild and magnificent vision, recombine it in the morning, and try it by his waking judgment. That which appeared so shifting, and yet so coherent, while that faculty was passive, when it comes under cool examination shall appear so reasonless and so unlinked, that we are ashamed to have been so deluded; and to have taken, though but in sleep, a monster for a god. But the transitions in this episode are every whit as violent as in the most extravagant dream, and yet the waking judgment ratifies them.

CAPTAIN JACKSON

Among the deaths in our obituary for this month, I observe with concern "At his cottage on the Bath road, Captain Jackson." The name and attribution are common enough; but a feeling like reproach persuades me, that this could have been no other in fact than my dear old friend, who some five-and-twenty years ago rented a tenement, which he was pleased to dignify with the appellation here used, about a mile from Westbourn Green. Alack, how good men, and the good turns they do us, slide out of memory, and are recalled but by the surprise of some such sad memento as that which now lies before us!

He whom I mean was a retired half-pay officer, with a wife and two grown-up daughters, whom he maintained with the port and notions of gentlewomen upon that slender professional allowance. Comely girls they were too.

And was I in danger of forgetting this man?—his cheerful suppers—the noble tone of hospitality, when first you set your foot in *the cottage* —the anxious ministerings about you, where little or nothing (God knows) was to be ministered.—Althea's horn in a poor platter—the power of self-enchantment, by which, in his magnificent wishes to entertain you, he multiplied his means to bounties.

You saw with your bodily eyes indeed what seemed a bare scrag, cold savings from the foregone meal—remnant hardly sufficient to send a mendicant from the door contented. But in the copious will—the revelling imagination of your host—the "mind, the mind, Master Shallow," whole beeves were spread before you—hecatombs—no end appeared to the profusion.

It was the widow's cruse—the loaves and fishes; carving could not lessen, nor helping diminish it—the stamina were left—the elemental bone still flourished, divested of its accidents.

"Let us live while we can," methinks I hear the open-handed creature exclaim; "while we have, let us not want," "here is plenty left"; "want for nothing"—with many more such hospitable sayings, the spurs of appetite, and old concomitants of smoking boards, and feast-oppressed chargers. Then sliding a slender ratio of Single Gloucester upon his wife's plate, or the daughters', he would convey the remanent rind into his own, with a merry quirk of "the nearer the bone," etc., and declaring that he universally preferred the outside. For we had our table distinctions, you are to know, and some of us in a manner sate above the salt. None but his guest or guests dreamed of tasting flesh luxuries at night, the fragments were _verè hospitibus sacra_. But of one thing or another there was always enough, and leavings: only he would sometimes finish the remainder crust, to show that he wished no savings.

Wine we had none; nor, except on very rare occasions, spirits; but the sensation of wine was there. Some thin kind of ale I remember— "British beverage," he would say! "Push about, my boys"; "Drink to your sweethearts, girls." At every meagre draught a toast must ensue, or a song. All the forms of good liquor were there, with none of the effects wanting. Shut your eyes, and you would swear a capacious bowl of punch was foaming in the centre, with beams of generous Port or Madeira radiating to it from each of the table corners. You got flustered, without knowing whence; tipsy upon words; and reeled under the potency of his unperforming Bacchanalian encouragements.

We had our songs—"Why, Soldiers, why,"—and the "British Grenadiers"—in which last we were all obliged to bear chorus. Both the daughters sang. Their proficiency was a nightly theme—the masters he had given them—the "no-expense" which he spared to accomplish them in a science "so necessary to young women." But then—they could not sing "without the instrument."

Sacred, and, by me, never-to-be-violated, secrets of Poverty! Should I disclose your honest aims at grandeur, your makeshift efforts of magnificence? Sleep, sleep, with all thy broken keys, if one of the bunch be extant; thrummed by a thousand ancestral thumbs; dear, cracked spinnet of dearer Louisa! Without mention of mine, be dumb, thou thin accompanier of her thinner warble! A veil be spread over the dear delighted face of the well-deluded father, who now haply listening to cherubic notes, scarce feels sincerer pleasure than when she awakened thy time-shaken chords responsive to the twitterings of that slender image of a voice.

We were not without our literary talk either. It did not extend far, but as far as it went, it was good. It was bottomed well; had good grounds to go upon. In _the cottage_ was a room, which tradition authenticated to have been the same in which Glover, in his occasional retirements, had penned the greater part of his Leonidas. This circumstance was nightly quoted, though none of the present inmates, that I could discover, appeared ever to have met with the poem in question. But that was no matter. Glover had written there, and the anecdote was pressed into the account of the family importance. It diffused a learned air through the apartment, the little side casement of which (the poet's study window), opening upon a superb view as far as the pretty spire of Harrow, over domains and patrimonial acres, not a rood nor square yard whereof our host could call his own, yet gave occasion to an immoderate expansion of—vanity shall I call it?—in his bosom, as he showed them in a glowing summer evening. It was all his, he took it all in, and communicated rich portions of it to his guests. It was a part of his largess, his hospitality; it was going over his grounds; he was lord for the time of showing them, and you the implicit lookers-up to his magnificence.

He was a juggler, who threw mists before your eyes—you had no time to detect his fallacies. He would say, "Hand me the *silver* sugar tongs"; and before you could discover it was a single spoon, and that *plated*, he would disturb and captivate your imagination by a misnomer of "the urn" for a tea-kettle; or by calling a homely bench a sofa. Rich men direct you to their furniture, poor ones divert you from it; he neither did one nor the other, but by simply assuming that everything was handsome about him, you were positively at a demur what you did, or did not see, at *the cottage*. With nothing to live on, he seemed to live on everything. He had a stock of wealth in his mind; not that which is properly termed *Content*, for in truth he was not to be *contained* at all, but overflowed all bounds by the force of a magnificent self-delusion.

Enthusiasm is catching; and even his wife, a sober native of North Britain, who generally saw things more as they were, was not proof against the continual collision of his credulity. Her daughters were rational and discreet young women; in the main, perhaps, not insensible to their true circumstances. I have seen them assume a thoughtful air at times. But such was the preponderating opulence of his fancy, that I am persuaded, not for any half-hour together did they ever look their own prospects fairly in the face. There was no resisting the vortex of his temperament. His riotous imagination conjured up handsome settlements before their eyes, which kept them up in the eye of the world too, and seem at last to have realised themselves; for they both have married since, I am told, more than respectably.

It is long since, and my memory waxes dim on some subjects, or I should wish to convey some notion of the manner in which the pleasant creature described the circumstances of his own wedding-day. I faintly remember something of a chaise-and-four, in which he made his entry into Glasgow on that morning to fetch the bride home, or carry her thither, I forget which. It so completely made out the stanza of the old ballad—

When we came down through Glasgow town,
We were a comely sight to see:

My love was clad in black velvet,
And I myself in cramasie.

I suppose it was the only occasion upon which his own actual splendour at all corresponded with the world's notions on that subject. In homely cart, or travelling caravan, by whatever humble vehicle they chanced to be transported in less prosperous days, the ride through Glasgow came back upon his fancy, not as a humiliating contrast, but as a fair occasion for reverting to that one day's state. It seemed an "equipage etern" from which no power of fate or fortune, once mounted, had power thereafter to dislodge him.

There is some merit in putting a handsome face upon indigent circumstances. To bully and swagger away the sense of them before strangers, may not be always discommendable. Tibbs, and Bobadil, even when detected, have more of our admiration than contempt. But for a man to put the cheat upon himself; to play the Bobadil at home; and, steeped in poverty up to the lips, to fancy himself all the while chin-deep in riches, is a strain of constitutional philosophy, and a mastery over fortune, which was reserved for my old friend Captain Jackson.

THE SUPERANNUATED MAN

Sera tamen respexit
Libertas.   VIRGIL.
A Clerk I was in London gay.—O'KEEFE.

IF peradventure, Reader, it has been thy lot to waste the golden years of thy life—thy shining youth—in the irksome confinement of an office; to have thy prison days prolonged through middle age down to decrepitude and silver hairs, without hope of release or respite; to have lived to forget that there are such things as holidays, or to remember them but as the prerogatives of childhood; then, and then only, will you be able to appreciate my deliverance.

It is now six-and-thirty years since I took my seat at the desk in Mincing Lane. Melancholy was the transition at fourteen from the abundant playtime, and the frequently-intervening vacations of school days, to the eight, nine, and sometimes ten hours' a day attendance at the counting-house. But time partially reconciles us to anything. I gradually became content—doggedly contented, as wild animals in cages.

It is true I had my Sundays to myself; but Sundays, admirable as the institution of them is for purposes of worship, are for that very reason the very worst adapted for days of unbending and recreation. In particular, there is a gloom for me attendant upon a city Sunday, a weight in the air. I miss the cheerful cries of London, the music, and the ballad-singers—the buzz and stirring murmur of the streets. Those eternal bells depress me. The closed shops repel me. Prints, pictures, all the glittering and endless succession of knacks and gewgaws, and ostentatiously displayed wares of tradesmen, which make a week-day saunter through the less busy parts of the metropolis so delightful—are shut out. No book-stalls deliciously to idle over—No busy faces to recreate the idle man who contemplates them ever passing by—the very face of business a charm by contrast to his temporary relaxation from it. Nothing to be seen but unhappy countenances—or half-happy at best—of emancipated 'prentices and little tradesfolks, with here and there a servant-maid that has got leave to go out, who, slaving all the week, with the habit has lost almost the capacity of enjoying a free hour; and livelily expressing the hollowness of a day's pleasuring. The very strollers in the fields on that day look anything but comfortable.

But besides Sundays, I had a day at Easter, and a day at Christmas, with a full week in the summer to go and air myself in my native fields of Hertfordshire. This last was a great indulgence; and the prospect of its recurrence, I believe, alone kept me up through the year, and made my durance tolerable. But when the week came round, did the glittering phantom of the distance keep touch with me? or rather was it not a series of seven uneasy days, spent in restless pursuit of pleasure, and a wearisome anxiety to find out how to make the most of them? Where was the quiet, where the promised rest? Before I had a taste of it, it was vanished. I was at the desk again, counting upon the fifty-one tedious weeks that must intervene before such another snatch would come. Still the prospect of its coming threw something of an illumination upon the darker side of my captivity. Without it, as I have said, I could scarcely have sustained my thraldom.

Independently of the rigours of attendance, I have ever been haunted with a sense (perhaps a mere caprice) of incapacity for business. This, during my latter years, had increased to such a degree, that it was visible in all the lines of my countenance. My health and my good spirits flagged. I had perpetually a dread of some crisis, to which I should be found unequal. Besides my daylight servitude, I served over again all night in my sleep, and would awake with terrors of imaginary false entries, errors in my accounts, and the like. I was fifty years of age, and no prospect of emancipation presented itself. I had grown to my desk, as it were; and the wood had entered into my soul.

My fellows in the office would sometimes rally me upon the trouble legible in my countenance; but I did not know that it had raised the suspicions of any of my employers, when, on the fifth of last month, a day ever to be remembered by me, L——, the junior partner in the firm, calling me on one side, directly taxed me with my bad looks, and frankly inquired the cause of them. So taxed, I honestly made confession of my infirmity, and added that I was afraid I should eventually be obliged to resign his service. He spoke some words of course to hearten me, and there the matter rested. A whole week I remained labouring under the impression that I had acted imprudently in my disclosure; that I had foolishly given a handle against myself, and had been anticipating my own dismissal. A week passed in this manner, the most anxious one, I verily believe, in my whole life, when on the evening of the 12th of April, just as I was about quitting my desk to go home (it might be about eight o'clock) I received an awful summons to attend the presence of the whole assembled firm in the formidable back parlour. I thought now my time is surely come, I have done for myself, I am going to be told that they have no longer occasion for me. L——, I could see, smiled at the terror I was in, which was a little relief to me,—when to my utter astonishment B——, the eldest partner, began a formal harangue to me on the length of my services, my very meritorious conduct during the whole of the time (the deuce, thought I, how did he find out that? I protest I never had the confidence to think as much). He went on to descant on the expediency of retiring at a certain time of life (how my heart panted!), and asking me a few questions as to the amount of my own property, of which I have a little, ended with a proposal, to which his three partners nodded a grave assent, that I should accept from the house, which I had served so well, a pension for life to the amount of two-thirds of my accustomed salary—a magnificent offer! I do not know what I answered between surprise and gratitude, but it was understood that I accepted their proposal, and I was told that I was free from that hour to leave their service. I stammered out a bow, and at just ten minutes after eight I went home—for ever. This noble benefit—gratitude forbids me to conceal their names—I owe to the kindness of the most munificent firm in the world—the house of Boldero, Merryweather, Bosanquet, and Lacy.

Esto perpetua!

For the first day or two I felt stunned, overwhelmed. I could only apprehend my felicity; I was too confused to taste it sincerely. I wandered about, thinking I was happy, and knowing that I was not. I was in the condition of a prisoner in the old Bastile, suddenly let loose after a forty years' confinement. I could scarce trust myself with myself. It was like passing out of Time into Eternity—for it is a sort of Eternity for a man to have his Time all to himself. It seemed to me that I had more time on my hands than I could ever manage. From a poor man, poor in Time, I was suddenly lifted up into a vast revenue; I could see no end of my possessions; I wanted some steward, or judicious bailiff, to manage my estates in Time for me. And here let me caution persons grown old in active business, not lightly, nor without weighing their own resources, to forego their customary employment all at once, for there may be danger in it. I feel it by myself, but I know that my resources are sufficient; and now that those first giddy raptures have subsided, I have a quiet home-feeling of the blessedness of my condition. I am in no hurry. Having all holidays, I am as though I had none. If Time hung heavy upon me, I could walk it away; but I do *not* walk all day long, as I used to do in those old transient holidays, thirty miles a day, to make the most of them. If Time were troublesome, I could read it away; but I do *not* read in that violent measure, with which, having no Time in my own but candlelight Time, I used to weary out my head and eyesight in bygone winters. I walk, read, or scribble (as now), just when the fit seizes me. I no longer hunt after pleasure; I let it come to me. I am like the man

——— that's born, and has his years come to him,
In some green desert.

"Years!" you will say; "what is this superannuated simpleton calculating upon? He has already told us he is past fifty."

I have indeed lived nominally fifty years, but deduct out of them the hours which I have lived to other people, and not to myself, and you will find me still a young fellow. For *that* is the only true Time, which a man can properly call his own, that which he has all to himself; the rest, though in some sense he may be said to live it, is other people's Time, not his. The remnant of my poor days, long or short, is at least multiplied for me threefold. My ten next years, if I stretch so far, will be as long as any preceding thirty. 'Tis a fair rule-of-three sum.

Among the strange fantasies which beset me at the commencement of my freedom, and of which all traces are not yet gone, one was, that a vast tract of time had intervened since I quitted the Counting House. I could not conceive of it as an affair of yesterday. The partners, and the clerks with whom I had for so many years, and for so many hours in each day of the year, been closely associated—being suddenly removed from them—they seemed as dead to me. There is a fine passage, which may serve to illustrate this fancy, in a Tragedy by Sir Robert Howard, speaking of a friend's death:—

——— 'Twas but just now he went away;
I have not since had time to shed a tear;
And yet the distance does the same appear
As if he had been a thousand years from me.
Time takes no measure in Eternity.

To dissipate this awkward feeling, I have been fain to go among them once or twice since; to visit my old desk-fellows—my co-brethren of the quill—that I had left below in the state militant. Not all the kindness with which they received me could quite restore to me that pleasant familiarity, which I had heretofore enjoyed among them. We cracked some of our old jokes, but methought they went off but faintly. My old desk; the peg where I hung my hat, were appropriated to another. I knew it must be, but I could not take it kindly. D——l take me, if I did not feel some remorse—beast, if I had not—at quitting my old compeers, the faithful partners of my toils for six-and-thirty years, that smoothed for me with their jokes and conundrums the ruggedness of my professional road. Had it been so rugged then, after all? or was I a coward simply? Well, it is too late to repent; and I also know that these suggestions are a common fallacy of the mind on such occasions. But my heart smote me. I had violently broken the bands betwixt us. It was at least not courteous. I shall be some time before I get quite reconciled to the separation. Farewell, old cronies, yet not for long, for again and again I

will come among ye, if I shall have your leave. Farewell, Ch——, dry,
sarcastic, and friendly! Do——, mild, slow to move, and gentlemanly!
Pl——, officious to do, and to volunteer, good services!—and thou,
thou dreary pile, fit mansion for a Gresham or a Whittington of old,
stately house of Merchants; with thy labyrinthine passages, and light-
excluding, pent-up offices, where candles for one-half the year supplied
the place of the sun's light; unhealthy contributor to my weal, stern
fosterer of my living, farewell! In thee remain, and not in the obscure
collection of some wandering bookseller, my "works"! There let them
rest, as I do from my labours, piled on thy massy shelves, more MSS. in
folio than ever Aquinas left, and full as useful! My mantle I bequeath
among ye.

A fortnight has passed since the date of my first communication. At
that period I was approaching to tranquillity, but had not reached it.
I boasted of a calm indeed, but it was comparative only. Something of
the first flutter was left; an unsettling sense of novelty; the dazzle to
weak eyes of unaccustomed light. I missed my old chains, forsooth, as
if they had been some necessary part of my apparel. I was a poor Carthusian, from strict cellular discipline suddenly by some revolution returned upon the world. I am now as if I had never been other than my
own master. It is natural to me to go where I please, to do what I please.
I find myself at eleven o'clock in the day in Bond Street, and it seems
to me that I have been sauntering there at that very hour for years past.
I digress into Soho, to explore a book-stall. Methinks I have been thirty
years a collector. There is nothing strange nor new in it. I find myself
before a fine picture in the morning. Was it ever otherwise? What is become of Fish Street Hill? Where is Fenchurch Street? Stones of old
Mincing Lane, which I have worn with my daily pilgrimage for six-and-
thirty years, to the footsteps of what toil-worn clerk are your everlasting
flints now vocal? I indent the gayer flags of Pall Mall. It is 'Change
time, and I am strangely among the Elgin marbles. It was no hyperbole
when I ventured to compare the change in my condition to a passing
into another world. Time stands still in a manner to me. I have lost
all distinction of season. I do not know the day of the week or of the
month. Each day used to be individually felt by me in its reference to
the foreign post days; in its distance from, or propinquity to, the next
Sunday. I had my Wednesday feelings, my Saturday nights' sensations.
The genius of each day was upon me distinctly during the whole of it,
affecting my appetite, spirits, etc. The phantom of the next day, with
the dreary five to follow, sate as a load upon my poor Sabbath recreations. What charm has washed that Ethiop white? What is gone of Black
Monday? All days are the same. Sunday itself—that unfortunate failure of a holiday, as it too often proved, what with my sense of its fugitiveness, and over-care to get the greatest quantity of pleasure out of it
—is melted down into a week day. I can spare to go to church now,
without grudging the huge cantle which it used to seem to cut out of the
holiday. I have Time for everything. I can visit a sick friend. I can

interrupt the man of much occupation when he is busiest. I can insult
over him with an invitation to take a day's pleasure with me to Windsor
this fine May-morning. It is Lucretian pleasure to behold the poor
drudges, whom I have left behind in the world, carking and caring; like
horses in a mill, drudging on in the same eternal round—and what is it
all for? A man can never have too much Time to himself, nor too little
to do. Had I a little son, I would christen him NOTHING-TO-DO; he
should do nothing. Man, I verily believe, is out of his element as long
as he is operative. I am altogether for the life contemplative. Will no
kindly earthquake come and swallow up those accursed cotton mills?
Take me that lumber of a desk there, and bowl it down

As low as to the fiends.

I am not longer * * * * *, clerk to the Firm of, etc. I am Retired Leisure. I am to be met with in trim gardens. I am already come to be
known by my vacant face and careless gesture, perambulating at no
fixed pace, nor with any settled purpose. I walk about; not to and from.
They tell me, a certain *cum dignitate* air, that has been buried so long
with my other good parts, has begun to shoot forth in my person. I grow
into gentility perceptibly. When I take up a newspaper, it is to read
the state of the opera. *Opus operatum est.* I have done all that I came
into this world to do. I have worked task-work, and have the rest of
the day to myself.

THE GENTEEL STYLE IN WRITING

IT is an ordinary criticism, that my Lord Shaftesbury, and Sir William
Temple, are models of the genteel style in writing. We should prefer
saying—of the lordly, and the gentlemanly. Nothing can be more unlike, than the inflated finical rhapsodies of Shaftesbury and the plain
natural chit-chat of Temple. The man of rank is discernible in both
writers; but in the one it is only insinuated gracefully, in the other it
stands out offensively. The peer seems to have written with his coronet
on, and his Earl's mantle before him; the commoner in his elbow-chair
and undress.—What can be more pleasant than the way in which the
retired statesman peeps out in his essays, penned by the latter in his delightful retreat at Shene? They scent of Nimeguen and the Hague.
Scarce an authority is quoted under an ambassador. Don Francisco de
Melo, a "Portugal Envoy in England," tells him it was frequent in his
country for men, spent with age and other decays, so as they could not
hope for above a year or two of life, to ship themselves away in a Brazil
fleet, and after their arrival there to go on a great length, sometimes of
twenty or thirty years, or more, by the force of that vigour they recovered with that remove. "Whether such an effect (Temple beautifully
adds) might grow from the air, or the fruits of that climate, or by ap-

proaching nearer the sun, which is the fountain of light and heat, when their natural heat was so far decayed: or whether the piecing out of an old man's life were worth the pains; I cannot tell: perhaps the play is not worth the candle." Monsieur Pompone, "French Ambassador in his (Sir William's) time at the Hague," certifies him, that in his life he had never heard of any man in France that arrived at a hundred years of age; a limitation of life which the old gentleman imputes to the excellence of their climate, giving them such a liveliness of temper and humour, as disposes them to more pleasures of all kinds than in other countries; and moralises upon the matter very sensibly. The "late Robert Earl of Leicester" furnishes him with a story of a Countess of Desmond, married out of England in Edward the Fourth's time, and who lived far in King James's reign. The "same noble person" gives him an account, how such a year, in the same reign, there went about the country a set of morrice-dancers, composed of ten men who danced, a Maid Marian, and a tabor and pipe; and how these twelve, one with another, made up twelve hundred years. "It was not so much (says Temple) that so many in one small county (Hertfordshire) should live to that age, as that they should be in vigour and in humour to travel and to dance." Monsieur Zulichem, one of his "colleagues at the Hague," informs him of a cure for the gout; which is confirmed by another "Envoy," Monsieur Serinchamps, in that town, who had tried it.—Old Prince Maurice of Nassau recommends to him the use of hammocks in that complaint; having been allured to sleep, while suffering under it himself, by the "constant motion or swinging of those airy beds." Count Egmont, and the Rhinegrave who "was killed last summer before Maestricht," impart to him their experiences.

But the rank of the writer is never more innocently disclosed, than where he takes for granted the compliments paid by foreigners to his fruit-trees. For the taste and perfection of what we esteem the best, he can truly say, that the French, who have eaten his peaches and grapes at Shene in no very ill year, have generally concluded that the last are as good as any they have eaten in France on this side Fontainebleau; and the first as good as any they have eat in Gascony. Italians have agreed his white figs to be as good as any of that sort in Italy, which is the earlier kind of white fig there; for in the later kind and the blue, we cannot come near the warm climates, no more than in the Frontignac or Muscat grape. His orange-trees, too, are as large as any he saw when he was young in France, except those of Fontainebleau; or what he has seen since in the Low Countries, except some very old ones of the Prince of Orange's. Of grapes he had the honour of bringing over four sorts into England, which he enumerates, and supposes that they are all by this time pretty common among some gardeners in his neighbourhood, as well as several persons of quality; for he ever thought all things of this kind "the commoner they are made the better." The garden pedantry with which he asserts that 'tis to little purpose to plant any of the best fruits, as peaches or grapes, hardly, he doubts, beyond Northamptonshire at the furthest northwards; and praises the "Bishop of Munster at Cosevelt," for attempting nothing beyond cherries in that cold climate; is equally pleasant and in character. "I may perhaps" (he thus ends his sweet Garden Essay with a passage worthy of Cowley) "be allowed to know something of this trade, since I have so long allowed myself to be good for nothing else, which few men will do, or enjoy their gardens, without often looking abroad to see how other matters play, what motions in the state, and what invitations they may hope for into other scenes. For my own part, as the country life, and this part of it more particularly, were the inclination of my youth itself, so they are the pleasure of my age; and I can truly say that, among many great employments that have fallen to my share, I have never asked or sought for any of them, but have often endeavoured to escape from them, into the ease and freedom of a private scene, where a man may go his own way and his own pace, in the common paths and circles of life. The measure of choosing well is whether a man likes what he has chosen, which, I thank God, has befallen me; and though among the follies of my life, building and planting have not been the least, and have cost me more than I have the confidence to own; yet they have been fully recompensed by the sweetness and satisfaction of this retreat, where, since my resolution taken of never entering again into any public employments, I have passed five years without ever once going to town, though I am almost in sight of it, and have a house there always ready to receive me. Nor has this been any sort of affectation, as some have thought it, but a mere want of desire or humour to make so small a remove; for when I am in this corner, I can truly say with Horace, *Me quoties reficit, etc.*"

> Me, when the cold Digentian stream revives,
> What does my friend believe I think or ask?
> Let me yet less possess, so I may live,
> Whate'er of life remains, unto myself.
> May I have books enough; and one year's store,
> Not to depend upon each doubtful hour:
> This is enough of mighty Jove to pray,
> Who, as he pleases, gives and takes away.

The writings of Temple are, in general, after this easy copy. On one occasion, indeed, his wit, which was mostly subordinate to nature and tenderness, has seduced him into a string of felicitous antitheses; which, it is obvious to remark, have been a model to Addison and succeeding essayists. "Who would not be covetous, and with reason," he says, "if health could be purchased with gold? who not ambitious, if it were at the command of power, or restored by honour? but, alas! a white staff will not help gouty feet to walk better than a common cane; nor a blue riband bind up a wound so well as a fillet. The glitter of gold, or of diamonds, will but hurt sore eyes instead of curing them; and an aching head will be no more eased by wearing a crown than a common nightcap." In a far better style, and more accordant wth his own humour of plainness, are the concluding sentences of his "Discourse upon Poetry."

Temple took a part in the controversy about the ancient and the modern learning; and, with that partiality so natural and so graceful in an old man, whose state engagements had left him little leisure to look into modern productions, while his retirement gave him occasion to look back upon the classic studies of his youth—decided in favour of the latter. "Certain it is," he says, "that, whether the fierceness of the Gothic humours, or noise of their perpetual wars, frighted it away, or that the unequal mixture of the modern languages would not bear it—the great heights and excellency both of poetry and music fell with the Roman learning and empire, and have never since recovered the admiration and applauses that before attended them. Yet, such as they are amongst us, they must be confessed to be the softest and the sweetest, the most general and most innocent amusements of common time and life. They still find room in the courts of princes, and the cottages of shepherds. They serve to revive and animate the dead calm of poor and idle lives, and to allay or divert the violent passions and perturbations of the greatest and the busiest men. And both these effects are of equal use to human life; for the mind of man is like the sea, which is neither agreeable to the beholder nor the voyager, in a calm or in a storm, but is so to both when a little agitated by gentle gales; and so the mind, when moved by soft and easy passions or affections. I know very well that many who pretend to be wise by the forms of being grave, are apt to despise both poetry and music, as toys and trifles too light for the use or entertainment of serious men. But whoever find themselves wholly insensible to their charms, would, I think, do well to keep their own counsel, for fear of reproaching their own temper, and bringing the goodness of their natures, if not of their understandings, into question. While this world lasts, I doubt not but the pleasure and request of these two entertainments will do so too; and happy those that content themselves with these, or any other so easy and so innocent, and do not trouble the world or other men, because they cannot be quiet themselves, though nobody hurts them." "When all is done (he concludes), human life is at the greatest and the best but like a froward child, that must be played with, and humoured a little, to keep it quiet, till it falls asleep, and then the care is over."

BARBARA S——

On the noon of the 14th of November, 1743 or 4, I forget which it was, just as the clock had struck one, Barbara S——, with her accustomed punctuality, ascended the long rambling staircase, with awkward interposed landing-places, which led to the office, or rather a sort of box with a desk in it, whereat sat the then Treasurer of (what few of our readers may remember) the Old Bath Theatre. All over the island it was the custom, and remains so I believe to this day, for the players to receive their weekly stipend on the Saturday. It was not much that Barbara had to claim.

This little maid had just entered her eleventh year; but her important station at the theatre, as it seemed to her, with the benefits which she felt to accrue from her pious application of her small earnings, had given an air of womanhood to her steps and to her behaviour. You would have taken her to have been at least five years older.

Till latterly she had merely been employed in choruses, or where children were wanted to fill up the scene. But the manager, observing a diligence and adroitness in her above her age, had for some few months past intrusted to her the performance of whole parts. You may guess the self-consequence of the promoted Barbara. She had already drawn tears in young Arthur; had rallied Richard with infantine petulance in the Duke of York; and in her turn had rebuked that petulance when she was Prince of Wales. She would have done the elder child in Morton's pathetic afterpiece to the life; but as yet the "Children in the Wood" was not.

Long after this little girl was grown an aged woman, I have seen some of these small parts, each making two or three pages at most, copied out in the rudest hand of the then prompter, who doubtless transcribed a little more carefully and fairly for the grown-up tragedy ladies of the establishment. But such as they were, blotted and scrawled, as for a child's use, she kept them all; and in the zenith of her after reputation it was a delightful sight to behold them bound up in costliest morocco, each single—each small part making a *book*—with fine clasps, gilt-splashed, etc. She had conscientiously kept them as they had been delivered to her; not a blot had been effaced or tampered with. They were precious to her for their affecting remembrancings. They were her principia, her rudiments; the elementary atoms; the little steps by which she pressed forward to perfection. "What," she would say, "could India-rubber, or a pumice-stone, have done for these darlings?"

I am in no hurry to begin my story—indeed I have little or none to tell—so I will just mention an observation of hers connected with that interesting time.

Not long before she died I had been discoursing with her on the quantity of real present emotion which a great tragic performer experiences during acting. I ventured to think, that though in the first instance such players must have possessed the feelings which they so powerfully called up in others, yet by frequent repetition those feelings must become deadened in great measure, and the performer trust to the memory of past emotion, rather than express a present one. She indignantly repelled the notion, that with a truly great tragedian the operation, by which such effects were produced upon an audience, could ever degrade itself into what was purely mechanical. With much delicacy, avoiding to instance in her *self*-experience, she told me, that so long ago as when she used to play the part of the Little Son to Mrs. Porter's Isabella (I think it was), when that impressive actress has been bending over her in some heart-rending colloquy, she has felt real hot tears come trickling from her, which (to use her powerful expression) have perfectly scalded her back.

I am not quite so sure that it was Mrs. Porter; but it was some great actress of that day. The name is indifferent; but the fact of the scalding tears I most distinctly remember.

I was always fond of the society of players, and am not sure that an impediment in my speech (which certainly kept me out of the pulpit) even more than certain personal disqualifications, which are often got over in that profession, did not prevent me at one time of life from adopting it. I have had the honour (I must ever call it) once to have been admitted to the tea-table of Miss Kelly. I have played at serious whist with Mr. Liston. I have chattered with ever good-humoured Mrs. Charles Kemble. I have conversed as friend to friend with her accomplished husband. I have been indulged with a classical conference with Macready; and with a sight of the Player-picture gallery, at Mr. Mathews's, when the kind owner, to remunerate me for my love of the old actors (whom he loves so much), went over it with me, supplying to his capital collection, what alone the artist could not give them—voice; and their living motion. Old tones, half-faded, of Dodd, and Parsons, and Baddeley, have lived again for me at his bidding. Only Edwin he could not restore to me. I have supped with ——; but I am growing a coxcomb.

As I was about to say—at the desk of the then treasurer of the old Bath theatre—not Diamond's—presented herself the little Barbara S——.

The parents of Barbara had been in reputable circumstances. The father had practised, I believe, as an apothecary in the town. But his practice, from causes which I feel my own infirmity too sensibly that way to arraign—or perhaps from that pure infelicity which accompanies some people in their walk through life, and which it is impossible to lay at the door of imprudence—was now reduced to nothing. They were in fact in the very teeth of starvation, when the manager, who knew and respected them in better days, took the little Barbara into his company.

At the period I commenced with, her slender earnings were the sole support of the family, including two younger sisters. I must throw a veil over some mortifying circumstances. Enough to say, that her Saturday's pittance was the only chance of a Sunday's (generally their only) meal of meat.

One thing I will only mention, that in some child's part, where in her theatrical character she was to sup off a roast fowl (O joy to Barbara!) some comic actor, who was for the night caterer for this dainty—in the misguided humour of his part, threw over the dish such a quantity of salt (O grief and pain of heart to Barbara!) that when she crammed a portion of it into her mouth, she was obliged sputteringly to reject it; and what with shame of her ill-acted part, and pain of real appetite at missing such a dainty, her little heart sobbed almost to breaking, till a flood of tears, which the well-fed spectators were totally unable to comprehend, mercifully relieved her.

This was the little starved, meritorious maid, who stood before old Ravenscroft, the treasurer, for her Saturday's payment.

Ravenscroft was a man, I have heard many old theatrical people besides herself say, of all men least calculated for a treasurer. He had no head for accounts, paid away at random, kept scarce any books, and summing up at the week's end, if he found himself a pound or so deficient, blest himself that it was no worse.

Now Barbara's weekly stipend was a bare half guinea.—By mistake he popped into her hand—a whole one.

Barbara tripped away.

She was entirely unconscious at first of the mistake: God knows, Ravenscroft would never have discovered it.

But when she had got down to the first of those uncouth landing-places, she became sensible of an unusual weight of metal pressing her little hand.

Now mark the dilemma.

She was by nature a good child. From her parents and those about her she had imbibed no contrary influence. But then they had taught her nothing. Poor men's smoky cabins are not always porticoes of moral philosophy. This little maid had no instinct to evil, but then she might be said to have no fixed principle. She had heard honesty commended, but never dreamed of its application to herself. She thought of it as something which concerned grown-up people, men and women. She had never known temptation, or thought of preparing resistance against it.

Her first impulse was to go pack to the old treasurer, and explain to him his blunder. He was already so confused with age, besides a natural want of punctuality, that she would have had some difficulty in making him understand it. She saw *that* in an instant. And then it was such a bit of money! and then the image of a larger allowance of butcher's-meat on their table next day came across her, till her little eyes glistened, and her mouth moistened. But then Mr. Ravenscroft had always been so good-natured, had stood her friend behind the scenes, and even recommended her promotion to some of her little parts. But again the old man was reputed to be worth a world of money. He was supposed to have fifty pounds a year clear of the theatre. And then came staring upon her the figures of her little stockingless and shoeless sisters. And when she looked at her own neat white cotton stockings, which her situation at the theatre had made it indispensable for her mother to provide for her, with hard straining and pinching from the family stock, and thought how glad she should be to cover their poor feet with the same—and how then they could accompany her to rehearsals, which they had hitherto been precluded from doing, by reason of their unfashionable attire,—in these thoughts she reached the second landing-place—the second, I mean, from the top—for there was still another left to traverse.

Now virtue support Barbara!

And that never-failing friend did step in—for at that moment a strength not her own, I have heard her say, was revealed to her—a reason above reasoning—and without her own agency, as it seemed (for she never felt her feet to move), she found herself transported back to the individual desk she had just quitted, and her hand in the old hand of Ravenscroft, who in silence took back the refunded treasure, and who had been sitting (good man) insensible to the lapse of minutes, which to her were anxious ages, and from that moment a deep peace fell upon her heart, and she knew the quality of honesty.

A year or two's unrepining application to her profession brightened up the feet and the prospects of her little sisters, set the whole family upon their legs again, and released her from the difficulty of discussing moral dogmas upon a landing-place.

I have heard her say that it was a surprise, not much short of mortification to her, to see the coolness with which the old man pocketed the difference, which had caused her such mortal throes.

This anecdote of herself I had in the year 1800, from the mouth of the late Mrs. Crawford,[1] then sixty-seven years of age (she died soon after); and to her struggles upon this childish occasion I have sometimes ventured to think her indebted for that power of rending the heart in the representation of conflicting emotions, for which in after years she was considered as little inferior (if at all so in the part of Lady Randolph) even to Mrs. Siddons.

THE TOMBS IN THE ABBEY

IN A LETTER TO R—— S——, ESQ.

THOUGH in some points of doctrine, and perhaps of discipline, I am diffident of lending a perfect assent to that church which you have so worthily *historified*, yet may the ill time never come to me, when with a chilled heart or a portion of irreverent sentiment, I shall enter her beautiful and time-hallowed Edifices. Judge, then, of my mortification when, after attending the choral anthems of last Wednesday at Westminster, and being desirous of renewing my acquaintance, after lapsed years, with the tombs and antiquities there, I found myself excluded; turned out, like a dog, or some profane person, into the common street, with feelings not very congenial to the place, or to the solemn service which I had been listening to. It was a jar after that music.

You had your education at Westminster; and doubtless among those dim aisles and cloisters, you must have gathered much of that devotional feeling in those young years, on which your purest mind feeds still—and may it feed! The antiquarian spirit, strong in you, and grace-

---

[1] The maiden name of this lady was Street, which she changed, by successive marriages, for those of Dancer, Barry, and Crawford. She was Mrs. Crawford, a third time a widow, when I knew her.

fully blending ever with the religious, may have been sown in you among those wrecks of splendid mortality. You owe it to the place of your education; you owe it to your learned fondness for the architecture of your ancestors; you owe it to the venerableness of your ecclesiastical establishment, which is daily lessened and called in question through these practices—to speak aloud your sense of them; never to desist raising your voice against them, till they be totally done away with and abolished; till the doors of Westminster Abbey be no longer closed against the decent, though low-in-purse, enthusiast, or blameless devotee, who must commit an injury against his family economy, if he would be indulged with a bare admission within its walls. You owe it to the decencies, which you wish to see maintained, in its impressive services, that our Cathedral be no longer an object of inspection to the poor at those times only, in which they must rob from their attendance on the worship every minute which they can bestow upon the fabric. In vain the public prints have taken up this subject,—in vain such poor, nameless writers as myself express their indignation. A word from you, sir,—a hint in your Journal—would be sufficient to fling open the doors of the Beautiful Temple again, as we can remember them when we were boys. At that time of life, what would the imaginative faculty (such as it is) in both of us, have suffered, if the entrance to so much reflection had been obstructed by the demand of so much silver!—If we had scraped it up to gain an occasional admission (as we certainly should have done) would the sight of those old tombs have been as impressive to us (while we have been weighing anxiously prudence against sentiment) as when the gates stood open as those of the adjacent Park; when we could walk in at any time, as the mood brought us, for a shorter or longer time, as that lasted? Is the being shown over a place the same as silently for ourselves detecting the genius of it? In no part of our beloved Abbey now can a person find entrance (out of service time) under the sum of *two shillings*. The rich and the great will smile at the anti-climax, presumed to lie in these two short words. But you can tell them, sir, how much quiet worth, how much capacity for enlarged feeling, how much taste and genius, may coexist, especially in youth, with a purse incompetent to this demand. A respected friend of ours, during his late visit to the metropolis, presented himself for admission to St. Paul's. At the same time a decently clothed man, with as decent a wife and child, were bargaining for the same indulgence. The price was only twopence each person. The poor but decent man hesitated, desirous to go in; but there were three of them, and he turned away reluctantly. Perhaps he wished to have seen the tomb of Nelson. Perhaps the Interior of the Cathedral was his object. But in the state of his finances, even sixpence might reasonably seem too much. Tell the Aristocracy of the country (no man can do it more impressively); instruct them of what value these insignificant pieces of money, these minims to their sight, may be to their humbler brethren. Shame these Sellers out of the Temple. Stifle not the suggestions of your better nature with the pretext, that an indiscriminate admission would expose the Tombs to violation. Remember your boy-days. Did you ever see, or hear, of a mob in the Abbey, while it was free to all? Do the rabble come there, or trouble their heads about such speculations? It is all that you can do to drive them into your churches; they do not voluntarily offer themselves. They have, alas! no passion for antiquities; for tomb of king or prelate, sage or poet. If they had, they would be no longer the rabble.

For forty years that I have known the Fabric, the only well-attested charge of violation adduced has been—a ridiculous dismemberment committed upon the effigy of that amiable spy, Major André. And is it for this—the wanton mischief of some schoolboy, fired perhaps with raw notions of Transatlantic Freedom—or the remote possibility of such a mischief occurring again, so easily to be prevented by stationing a constable within the walls, if the vergers are incompetent to the duty—is it upon such wretched pretences that the people of England are made to pay a new Peter's Pence, so long abrogated; or must content themselves with contemplating the ragged Exterior of their Cathedral? The mischief was done about the time that you were a scholar there. Do you know anything about the unfortunate relic?—

AMICUS REDIVIVUS

Where were ye, Nymphs, when the remorseless deep
Closed o'er the head of your loved Lycidas?

I DO not know when I have experienced a stranger sensation, than on seeing my old friend, G. D., who had been paying me a morning visit, a few Sundays back, at my cottage at Islington, upon taking leave, instead of turning down the right-hand path by which he had entered—with staff in hand, and at noonday, deliberately march right forwards into the midst of the stream that runs by us, and totally disappear.

A spectacle like this at dusk would have been appalling enough; but in the broad, open daylight, to witness such an unreserved motion towards self-destruction in a valued friend, took from me all power of speculation.

How I found my feet I know not. Consciousness was quite gone. Some spirit, not my own, whirled me to the spot. I remember nothing but the silvery apparition of a good white head emerging; nigh which a staff (the hand unseen that wielded it) pointed upwards, as feeling for the skies. In a moment (if time was in that time) he was on my shoulders; and I—freighted with a load more precious than his who bore Anchises.

And here I cannot but do justice to the officious zeal of sundry passers-by, who, albeit arriving a little too late to participate in the honours of the rescue, in philanthropic shoals came thronging to communicate their advice as to the recovery; prescribing variously the application, or non-application, of salt, etc., to the person of the patient. Life, meantime, was ebbing fast away, amidst the stifle of conflicting judgments, when one, more sagacious than the rest, by a bright thought, proposed sending for the Doctor. Trite as the counsel was, and impossible, as one should think, to be missed on,—shall I confess?—in this emergency it was to me as if an Angel had spoken. Great previous exertions—and mine had not been inconsiderable—are commonly followed by a debility of purpose. This was a moment of irresolution.

MONOCULUS—for so, in default of catching his true name, I choose to designate the medical gentleman who now appeared—is a grave, middle-aged person, who, without having studied at the college, or truckled to the pedantry of a diploma, hath employed a great portion of his valuable time in experimental processes upon the bodies of unfortunate fellow-creatures, in whom the vital spark, to mere vulgar thinking, would seem extinct and lost for ever. He omitteth no occasion of obtruding his services, from a case of common surfeit suffocation to the ignobler obstructions, sometimes induced by a too-wilful application of the plant *cannabis* outwardly. But though he declineth not altogether these drier extinctions, his occupation tendeth, for the most part, to water-practice; for the convenience of which, he hath judiciously fixed his quarters near the grand repository of the stream mentioned, where day and night, from his little watch-tower, at the Myddelton Head, he listeneth to detect the wrecks of drowned mortality—partly, as he saith, to be upon the spot—and partly, because the liquids which he useth to prescribe to himself and his patients, on these distressing occasions, are ordinarily more conveniently to be found at these common hostelries than in the shops and phials of the apothecaries. His ear hath arrived to such finesse by practice, that it is reported he can distinguish a plunge, at half a furlong distance; and can tell if it be casual or deliberate. He weareth a medal, suspended over a suit, originally of a sad brown, but which, by time and frequency of nightly divings, has been dinged into a true professional sable. He passeth by the name of Doctor, and is remarkable for wanting his left eye. His remedy—after a sufficient application of warm blankets, friction, etc., is a simple tumbler or more, of the purest Cognac, with water, made as hot as the convalescent can bear it. Where he findeth, as in the case of my friend, a squeamish subject, he condescendeth to be the taster; and showeth, by his own example, the innocuous nature of the prescription. Nothing can be more kind or encouraging than this procedure. It addeth confidence to the patient, to see his medical adviser go hand in hand with himself in the remedy. When the doctor swalloweth his own draught, what peevish invalid can refuse to pledge him in the potion? In fine, MONOCULUS is a humane, sensible man, who, for a slender pittance, scarce enough to sustain life, is content to wear it out in the endeavour to save the lives of others—his pretensions so moderate that with difficulty I could press a crown upon him, for the price of restoring the existence of such an invaluable creature to society as G. D.

It was pleasant to observe the effect of the subsiding alarm upon the nerves of the dear absentee. It seemed to have given a shake to memory, calling up notice after notice, of all the providential deliverances he had experienced in the course of his long and innocent life. Sitting up in my couch—my couch which, naked and void of furniture hitherto, for the salutary repose which it administered, shall be honoured with costly valance, at some price, and henceforth be a state-bed at Colebrook,—he discoursed of marvellous escapes—by carelessness of nurses—by pails of gelid, and kettles of the boiling element, in infancy—by orchard pranks, and snapping twigs, in schoolboy frolics—by descent of tiles at Trumpington, and of heavier tomes at Pembroke—by studious watchings, inducing frightful vigilance—by want, and the fear of want, and all the sore throbbings of the learned head.—Anon, he would burst out into little fragments of chanting—of songs long ago—ends of deliverance hymns, not remembered before since childhood, but coming up now, when his heart was made tender as a child's—for the *tremor cordis,* in the retrospect of a recent deliverance, as in the case of impending danger, acting upon an innocent heart, will produce a self-tenderness, which we should do ill to christen cowardice; and Shakspeare, in the latter crisis, has made his good Sir Hugh to remember the sitting by Babylon, and to mutter of shallow rivers.

Waters of Sir Hugh Myddelton—what a spark you were like to have extinguished for ever! Your salubrious streams to this City, for now near two centuries, would hardly have atoned for what you were in a moment washing away. Mockery of a river—liquid artifice—wretched conduit! henceforth rank with canals and sluggish aqueducts. Was it for this that, smit in boyhood with the explorations of that Abyssinian traveller, I paced the vales of Amwell to explore your tributary springs, to trace your salutary waters sparkling through green Hertfordshire, and cultured Enfield parks?—Ye have no swans—no Naiads—no river God—or did the benevolent hoary aspect of my friend tempt ye to suck him in, that ye also might have the tutelary genius of your waters?

Had he been drowned in Cam, there would have been some consonancy in it; but what willows had ye to wave and rustle over his moist sepulture?—or, having no *name,* besides that unmeaning assumption of *eternal novity,* did ye think to get one by the noble prize, and henceforth to be termed the STREAM DYERIAN?

> And could such spacious virtue find a grave
> Beneath the imposthumed bubble of a wave?

I protest, George, you shall not venture out again—no, not by daylight—without a sufficient pair of spectacles—in your musing moods especially. Your absence of mind we have borne, till your presence of body came to be called in question by it. You shall not go wandering into Euripus with Aristotle, if we can help it. Fie, man, to turn dipper at your years, after your many tracts in favour of sprinkling only!

I have nothing but water in my head o'nights since this frightful accident. Sometimes I am with Clarence in his dream. At others, I behold Christian beginning to sink, and crying out to his good brother Hopeful (that is, to me), "I sink in deep waters; the billows go over my head, all the waves go over me. Selah." Then I have before me Palinurus, just letting go the steerage. I cry out too late to save. Next follow—a mournful procession—*suicidal faces*, saved against their will from drowning; dolefully trailing a length of reluctant gratefulness, with ropy weeds pendent from locks of watchet hue—constrained Lazari—Pluto's half-subjects—stolen fees from the grave—bilking Charon of his fare. At their head Arion—or is it G. D.?—in his singing garments marcheth singly, with harp in hand, and votive garland, which Machaon (or Dr. Hawes) snatcheth straight, intending to suspend it to the stern God of Sea. Then follow dismal streams of Lethe, in which the half-drenched on earth are constrained to drown downright, by wharfs where Ophelia twice acts her muddy death.

And, doubtless, there is some notice in that invisible world when one of us approacheth (as my friend did so lately) to their inexorable precincts. When a soul knocks once, twice, at Death's door, the sensation aroused within the palace must be considerable; and the grim Feature, by modern science so often dispossessed of his prey, must have learned by this time to pity Tantalus.

A pulse assuredly was felt along the line of the Elysian shades, when the near arrival of G. D. was announced by no equivocal indications. From their seats of Asphodel arose the gentler and the graver ghosts—poet, or historian—of Grecian or of Roman lore—to crown with unfading chaplets the half-finished love-labours of their unwearied scholiast. Him Markland expected—him Tyrwhitt hoped to encounter—him the sweet lyrist of Peter House, whom he had barely seen upon earth,[1] with newest airs prepared to greet ——; and patron of the gentle Christ's boy—who should have been his patron through life—the mild Askew, with longing aspirations leaned foremost from his venerable Æsculapian chair, to welcome into that happy company the matured virtues of the man, whose tender scions in the boy he himself upon earth had so prophetically fed and watered.

SOME SONNETS OF SIR PHILIP SYDNEY

SYDNEY's Sonnets—I speak of the best of them—are among the very best of their sort. They fall below the plain moral dignity, the sanctity, and high yet modest spirit of self-approval, of Milton, in his compositions of a similar structure. They are in truth what Milton, censuring the Arcadia, says of that work (to which they are a sort of after-tune or application), "vain and amatorious" enough, yet the things in their kind (as he confesses to be true of the romance) may be "full of worth

---

[1] GRAIUM *tantum vidit.*

and wit." They savour of the Courtier, it must be allowed, and not of the Commonwealthsman. But Milton was a Courtier when he wrote the Masque at Ludlow Castle, and still more a Courtier when he composed the Arcades. When the national struggle was to begin, he becomingly cast these vanities behind him; and if the order of time had thrown Sir Philip upon the crisis which preceded the revolution, there is no reason why he should not have acted the same part in that emergency, which has glorified the name of a later Sydney. He did not want for plainness or boldness of spirit. His letter on the French match may testify he could speak his mind freely to Princes. The times did not call him to the scaffold.

The Sonnets which we oftenest call to mind of Milton were the compositions of his maturest years. Those of Sydney, which I am about to produce, were written in the very heyday of his blood. They are stuck full of amorous fancies—far-fetched conceits, befitting his occupation; for True Love thinks no labour to send out Thoughts upon the vast and more than Indian voyages, to bring home rich pearls, outlandish wealth, gums, jewels, spicery, to sacrifice in self-depreciating similitudes, as shadows of true amiabilities in the Beloved. We must be Lovers—or at least the cooling touch of time, the *circum præcordia frigus,* must not have so damped our faculties, as to take away our recollection that we were once so—before we can duly appreciate the glorious vanities, and graceful hyperboles, of the passion. The images which lie before our feet (though by some accounted the only natural) are least natural for the high Sydnean love to express its fancies by. They may serve for the loves of Tibullus, or the dear Author of the Schoolmistress; for passions that creep and whine in Elegies and Pastoral Ballads. I am sure Milton never loved at this rate. I am afraid some of his addresses (*ad Leonoram* I mean) have rather erred on the farther side; and that the poet came not much short of a religious indecorum, when he could thus apostrophise a singing-girl:--

> Angelus unicuique suus (sic credite gentes)
>   Obtigit æthereis ales ab ordinibus.
> Quid mirum, Leonora, tibi si gloria major,
>   Nam tua præsentem vox sonat ipsa Deum?
> Aut Deus, aut vacui certè mens tertia cœli,
>   Per tua secretò guttura serpit agens;
> Serpit agens, facilisque docet mortalia corda
>   Sensim immortali assuescere posse sono.
> QUOD SI CUNCTA QUIDEM DEUS EST, PER CUNCTAQUE FUSUS,
> IN TE UNA LOQUITUR, CÆTERA MUTUS HABET.

This is loving in a strange fashion; and it requires some candour of construction (besides the slight darkening of a dead language) to cast a veil over the ugly appearance of something very like blasphemy in the last two verses. I think the Lover would have been staggered if he had gone about to express the same thought in English. I am sure Sydney has no flights like this. His extravaganzas do not strike at the sky, though he takes leave to adopt the pale Dian into a fellowship with his mortal passions.

I

With how sad steps, O Moon, thou climb'st the skies;
How silently; and with how wan a face!
What! may it be, that even in heavenly place
That busy Archer his sharp arrow tries?
Sure, if that long-with-love-acquainted eyes
Can judge of love, thou feel'st a lover's case;
I read it in thy looks; thy languisht grace
To me, that feel the like, thy state descries.
Then, even of fellowship, O Moon, tell me,
Is constant love deem'd there but want of wit?
Are beauties there as proud as here they be?
Do they above love to be loved, and yet
Those lovers scorn, whom that love doth possess?
Do they call *virtue* there—*ungratefulness!*

The last line of this poem is a little obscured by transposition. He means, Do they call ungratefulness there a virtue?

II

Come, Sleep, O Sleep, the certain knot of peace,
The baiting-place of wit, the balm of woe,
The poor man's wealth, the prisoner's release,
The indifferent judge between the high and low;
With shield of proof shield me from out the prease [1]
Of those fierce darts despair at me doth throw;
O make in me those civil wars to cease:
I will good tribute pay if thou do so.
Take thou of me sweet pillows, sweetest bed;
A chamber deaf to noise, and blind to light;
A rosy garland, and a weary head.
And if these things, as being thine by right,
Move not thy heavy grace, thou shalt in me,
Livelier than elsewhere, STELLA'S image see.

III

The curious wits, seeing dull pensiveness
Bewray itself in my long-settled eyes,
Whence those same fumes of melancholy rise,
With idle pains, and missing aim, do guess.
Some, that know how my spring I did address,
Deem that my Muse some fruit of knowledge plies;
Others, because the Prince my service tries,
Think, that I think state errors to redress;
But harder judges judge, ambition's rage,
Scourge of itself, still climbing slippery place,
Holds my young brain captived in golden cage.
O fools, or over-wise! alas, the race
Of all my thoughts hath neither stop nor start,
But only STELLA'S eyes, and STELLA'S heart.

[1] Press.

IV

Because I oft in dark abstracted guise
Seem most alone in greatest company,
With dearth of words, or answers quite awry,
To them that would make speech of speech arise;
They deem, and of their doom the rumour flies,
That poison foul of bubbling *Pride* doth lie
So in my swelling breast, that only I
Fawn on myself, and others do despise;
Yet *Pride,* I think, doth not my soul possess,
Which looks too oft in his unflattering glass;
But one worse fault—*Ambition*—I confess,
That makes me oft my best friends overpass,
Unseen, unheard—while Thought to highest place
Bends all his powers, even unto STELLA's grace.

V

Having this day, my horse, my hand, my lance,
Guided so well that I obtained the prize,
Both by the judgment of the English eyes,
And of some sent from that *sweet enemy,*—France
Horsemen my skill in horsemanship advance;
Townsfolk my strength; a daintier judge applies
His praise to sleight, which from good use doth rise
Some lucky wits impute it but to chance;
Others, because of both sides I do take
My blood from them, who did excel in this.
Think Nature me a man of arms did make.
How far they shot awry! the true cause is,
STELLA looked on, and from her heavenly face
Sent forth the beams which made so fair my race.

VI

In martial sports I had my cunning tried,
And yet to break more staves did me address,
While with the people's shouts (I must confess)
Youth, luck, and praise, even fill'd my veins with pride—
When Cupid having me (his slave) descried
In Mars' livery, prancing in the press,
"What now, Sir Fool!" said he: "I would no less:
Look here, I say." I look'd, and STELLA spied,
Who hard by made a window send forth light.
My heart then quaked, then dazzled were mine eyes;
One hand forgot to rule, th' other to fight;
Nor trumpet's sound I heard, nor friendly cries
My foe came on, and beat the air for me—
Till that her blush made me my shame to see.

VII

No more, my dear, no more these counsels try;
O give my passions leave to run their race;
Let Fortune lay on me her worst disgrace;
Let folk o'ercharged with brain against me cry;
Let clouds bedim my face, break in mine eye;
Let me no steps, but of lost labour, trace;

Let all the earth with scorn recount my case—
But do not will me from my love to fly.
I do not envy Aristotle's wit,
Nor do aspire to Cæsar's bleeding fame;
Nor aught do care, though some above me sit;
Nor hope, nor wish, another course to frame,
But that which once may win thy cruel heart:
Thou art my wit, and thou my virtue art.

VIII

Love still a boy, and oft a wanton, is,
School'd only by his mother's tender eye;
What wonder, then, if he his lesson miss,
When for so soft a rod dear play he try?
And yet my Star, because a sugar'd kiss
In sport I suck'd, while she asleep did lie,
Doth lour, nay chide, nay threat, for only this.
Sweet, it was saucy Love, not humble I.
But no 'scuse serves; she makes her wrath appear
In Beauty's throne—see now who dares comes near
Those scarlet judges, threat'ning bloody pain?
O heav'nly Fool, thy most kiss-worthy face
Anger invests with such a lovely grace,
That anger's self I needs must kiss again.

IX

I never drank of Aganippe well,
Nor ever did in shade of Tempe sit,
And Muses scorn with vulgar brains to dwell;
Poor lay-man I, for sacred rites unfit.
Some do I hear of Poet's fury tell,
But (God wot) wot not what they mean by it;
And this I swear by blackest brook of hell,
I am no pick-purse of another's wit.
How falls it then, that with so smooth an ease
My thoughts I speak, and what I speak doth flow
In verse, and that my verse best wits doth please?
Guess me the cause—what is it thus?—fye, no.
Or so?—much less. How then? sure thus it is,
My lips are sweet, inspired with Stella's kiss.

X

Of all the kings that ever here did reign,
Edward, named Fourth, as first in praise I name,
Not for his fair outside, nor well-lined brain—
Although less gifts imp feathers oft on Fame.
Nor that he could, young-wise, wise-valiant, frame
His sire's revenge, join'd with a kingdom's gain;
And, gain'd by Mars could yet mad Mars so tame,
That Balance weigh'd what Sword did late obtain.
Nor that he made the Floure-de-luce so 'fraid,
Though strongly hedged of bloody Lions' paws,
That witty Lewis to him a tribute paid.
Nor this, nor that, nor any such small cause—
But only, for this worthy knight durst prove
To lose his crown rather than fail his love.

XI

O happy Thames, that didst my STELLA bear,
I saw thyself, with many a smiling line
Upon thy cheerful face, Joy's livery wear,
While those fair planets on thy streams did shine;
The boat for joy could not to dance forbear,
While wanton winds, with beauty so divine
Ravish'd, stay'd not, till in her golden hair
They did themelves (O sweetest prison) twine.
And fain those Æol's youth there would their stay
Have made; but, forced by nature still to fly,
First did with puffing kiss those locks display.
She, so dishevell'd, blush'd; from window I
With sight thereof cried out, O fair disgrace,
Let honour's self to thee grant highest place!

XII

Highway, since you my chief Parnassus be;
And that my Muse, to some ears not unsweet,
Tempers her words to trampling horses' feet,
More soft than to a chamber melody;
Now blessed You bear onward blessed Me
To Her, where I my heart safe left shall meet,
My Muse and I must you of duty greet
With thanks and wishes, wishing thankfully,
Be you still fair, honour'd by public heed,
By no encroachment wrong'd, nor time forgot;
Nor blamed for blood, nor shamed for sinful deed.
And that you know, I envy you no lot
Of highest wish, I wish you so much bliss,
Hundreds of years you STELLA's feet may kiss.

Of the foregoing, the first, the second, and the last sonnet, are my favourites. But the general beauty of them all is, that they are so perfectly characteristical. The spirit of "learning and of chivalry,"— of which union, Spenser has entitled Sydney to have been the "president,"—shines through them. I confess I can see nothing of the "jejune" or "frigid" in them; much less of the "stiff" and "cumbrous"— which I have sometimes heard objected to the Arcadia. The verse runs off swiftly and gallantly. It might have been tuned to the trumpet; or tempered (as himself expresses it) to "trampling horses' feet." They abound in felicitous phrases—

O heav'nly Fool, thy most kiss-worthy face—
                                            8th Sonnet.

———— Sweet pillows, sweetest bed;
A chamber deaf to noise, and blind to light;
A rosy garland, and a weary head.
                                            2nd Sonnet.

———— That sweet enemy,—France—
                                            5th Sonnet.

But they are not rich in words only, in vague and unlocalised feelings —the failing too much of some poetry of the present day—they are full, material, and circumstantiated. Time and place appropriates every one of them. It is not a fever of passion wasting itself upon a thin diet of dainty words, but a transcendent passion pervading and illuminating action, pursuits, studies, feats of arms, the opinions of contemporaries and his judgment of them. An historical thread runs through them, which almost affixes a date to them; marks the *when* and *where* they were written.

I have dwelt the longer upon what I conceive the merit of these poems, because I have been hurt by the wantonness (I wish I could treat it by a gentler name) with which W. H. takes every occasion of insulting the memory of Sir Philip Sydney. But the decisions of the Author of Table Talk, etc. (most profound and subtle where they are, as for the most part, just) are more safely to be relied upon, on subjects and authors he has a partiality for, than on such as he has conceived an accidental prejudice against. Milton wrote sonnets, and was a king-hater; and it was congenial perhaps to sacrifice a courtier to a patriot. But I was unwilling to lose a *fine idea* from my mind. The noble images, passions, sentiments, and poetical delicacies of character, scattered all over the Arcadia (spite of some stiffness and encumberment), justify to me the character which his contemporaries have left us of the writer. I cannot think with the "Critic," that Sir Philip Sydney was that *opprobrious thing* which a foolish nobleman in his insolent hostility chose to term him. I call to mind the epitaph made on him, to guide me to juster thoughts of him; and I repose upon the beautiful lines in the "Friend's Passion for his Astrophel," printed with the Elegies of Spenser and others.

> You knew—who knew not Astrophel?
> (That I should live to say I knew,
> And have not in possession still!)—
> Things known permit me to renew —
> Of him you know his merit such,
> I cannot say—you hear—too much.
>
> Within these woods of Arcady
> He chief delight and pleasure took;
> And on the mountain Partheny,
> Upon the crystal liquid brook,
> The Muses met him every day,
> That taught him sing, to write, and say.
>
> When he descended down the mount,
> His personage seemed most divine:
> A thousand graces one might count
> Upon his lovely cheerful eyne.
> To hear him speak, and sweetly smile,
> You were in Paradise the while.
>
> *A sweet attractive kind of grace;*
> *A full assurance given by looks;*

Continual comfort in a face,
The lineaments of Gospel books—
I trow that count'nance cannot lye,
Whose thoughts are legible in the eye.

     *   *   *   *   *

Above all others this is he,
Which erst approvèd in his song,
That love and honour might agree,
And that pure love will do no wrong.
    Sweet saints, it is no sin or blame
    To love a man of virtuous name.

Did never love so sweetly breathe
In any mortal breast before:
Did never Muse inspire beneath
A Poet's brain with finer store.
    He wrote of Love with high conceit,
    And Beauty rear'd above her height.

Or let any one read the deeper sorrows (grief running into rage) in
the Poem,—the last in the collection accompanying the above,—which
from internal testimony I believe to be Lord Brooke's—beginning with
"Silence augmenteth grief," and then seriously ask himself, whether the
subject of such absorbing and confounding regrets could have been *that
thing* which Lord Oxford termed him.

NEWSPAPERS THIRTY-FIVE YEARS AGO

Dan Stuart once told us, that he did not remember that he ever deliberately walked into the Exhibition at Somerset House in his life. He
might occasionally have escorted a party of ladies across the way that
were going in; but he never went in of his own head. Yet the office of
the Morning Post newspaper stood then just where it does now—we are
carrying you back, Reader, some thirty years or more—with its gilt-
globe-topt front facing that emporium of our artists' grand Annual Exposure. We sometimes wish that we had observed the same abstinence
with Daniel.

A word or two of D. S. He ever appeared to us one of the finest-
tempered of Editors. Perry, of the Morning Chronicle, was equally
pleasant, with a dash, no slight one either, of the courtier. S. was frank,
plain, and English all over. We have worked for both these gentlemen.

It is soothing to contemplate the head of the Ganges; to trace the first
little bubblings of a mighty river,

> With holy reverence to approach the rocks,
> Whence glide the streams renowned in ancient song.

Fired with a perusal of the Abyssinian Pilgrim's exploratory ramblings
after the cradle of the infant Nilus, we well remember on one fine summer holyday (a "whole day's leave" we called it at Christ's hospital) sal-

lying forth at rise of sun, not very well provisioned either for such an undertaking, to trace the current of the New River—Myddeltonian stream!—to its scaturient source, as we had read, in meadows by fair Amwell. Gallantly did we commence our solitary quest—for it was essential to the dignity of a DISCOVERY, that no eye of schoolboy, save our own, should beam on the detection. By flowery spots, and verdant lanes skirting Hornsey, Hope trained us on in many a baffling turn; endless, hopeless meanders, as it seemed; or as if the jealous waters had *dodged* us, reluctant to have the humble spot of their nativity revealed; till spent, and nigh famished, before set of the same sun, we sate down somewhere by Bowes Farm near Tottenham, with a tithe of our proposed labours only yet accomplished; sorely convinced in spirit, that that Brucian enterprise was as yet too arduous for our young shoulders.

Not more refreshing to the thirsty curiosity of the traveller is the tracing of some mighty waters up to their shallow fontlet, than it is to a pleased and candid reader to go back to the inexperienced essays, the first callow flights in authorship, of some established name in literature; from the Gnat which preluded to the Æneid, to the Duck which Samuel Johnson trod on.

In those days every Morning Paper, as an essential retainer to its establishment, kept an author, who was bound to furnish daily a quantum of witty paragraphs. Sixpence a joke—and it was thought pretty high too—was Dan Stuart's settled remuneration in these cases. The chat of the day, scandal, but, above all, *dress,* furnished the material. The length of no paragraph was to exceed seven lines. Shorter they might be, but they must be poignant.

A fashion of *flesh,* or rather *pink*-coloured hose for the ladies, luckily coming up at the juncture when we were on our probation for the place of Chief Jester to S.'s Paper, established our reputation in that line. We were pronounced a "capital hand." O the conceits which we varied upon *red* in all its prismatic differences! from the trite and obvious flower of Cytherea, to the flaming costume of the lady that has her sitting upon "many waters." Then there was the collateral topic of ankles. What an occasion to a truly chaste writer, like ourself, of touching that nice brink, and yet never tumbling over it, of a seemingly ever approximating something "not quite proper"; while, like a skilful posture-master, balancing betwixt decorums and their opposites, he keeps the line, from which a hair's-breadth deviation is destruction; hovering in the confines of light and darkness, or where "both seem either"; a hazy uncertain delicacy; Autolycus-like in the Play, still putting off his expectant auditory with "Whoop, do me no harm, good man!" But, above all, that conceit arrided us most at that time, and still tickles our midriff to remember, where, allusively to the flight of Astræa—*ultima Cœlestûm terras reliquist*—we pronounced—in reference to the stockings still—that MODESTY, TAKING HER FINAL LEAVE OF MORTALS, HER LAST BLUSH WAS VISIBLE IN HER ASCENT TO THE HEAVENS BY THE TRACT OF

THE GLOWING INSTEP. This might be called the crowning conceit: and was esteemed tolerable writing in those days.

But the fashion of jokes, with all other things, passes away; as did the transient mode which had so favoured us. The ankles of our fair friends in a few weeks began to reassume their whiteness, and left us scarce a leg to stand upon. Other female whims followed, but none methought so pregnant, so invitatory of shrewd conceits, and more than single meanings.

Somebody has said, that to swallow six cross-buns daily, consecutively for a fortnight, would surfeit the stoutest digestion. But to have to furnish as many jokes daily, and that not for a fortnight, but for a long twelvemonth, as we were constrained to do, was a little harder exaction. "Man goeth forth to his work until the evening"—from a reasonable hour in the morning, we presume it was meant. Now, as our main occupation took us up from eight till five every day in the City; and as our evening hours, at that time of life, had generally to do with anything rather than business, it follows, that the only time we could spare for this manufactory of jokes—our supplementary livelihood, that supplied us in every want beyond mere bread and cheese—was exactly that part of the day which (as we have heard of No Man's Land) may be fitly denominated No Man's Time; that is, no time in which a man ought to be up, and awake, in. To speak more plainly, it is that time of an hour, or an hour and a half's duration, in which a man, whose occasions call him up so preposterously, has to wait for his breakfast.

O those headaches at dawn of day, when at five, or half-past five in summer, and not much later in the dark seasons, we were compelled to rise, having been perhaps not above four hours in bed—(for we were no go-to-beds with the lamb, though we anticipated the lark ofttimes in her rising—we like a parting cup at midnight, as all young men did before these effeminate times, and to have our friends about us—we were not constellated under Aquarius, that watery sign, and therefore incapable of Bacchus, cold, washy, bloodless—we were none of your Basilian water-sponges, nor had taken our degrees at Mount Ague—we were right toping Capulets, jolly companions, we and they)—but to have to get up, as we said before, curtailed of half our fair sleep, fasting, with only a dim vista of refreshing bohea, in the distance—to be necessitated to rouse ourselves at the detestable rap of an old hag of a domestic, who seemed to take a diabolical pleasure in her announcement that it was "time to rise"; and whose chappy knuckles we have often yearned to amputate, and string them up at our chamber door, to be a terror to all such unseasonable rest-breakers in future——

"Facil" and sweet, as Virgil sings, had been the "descending" of the over-night, balmy the first sinking of the heavy head upon the pillow; but to get up, as he goes on to say,

—revocare gradus, superasque evadere ad auras—

and to get up, moreover, to make jokes with malice prepended—there was the "labour," there the "work."

No Egyptian taskmaster ever devised a slavery like to that, our slavery. No fractious operants ever turned out for half the tyranny which this necessity exercised upon us. Half a dozen jests in a day (bating Sundays too), why, it seems nothing! We make twice the number every day in our lives as a matter of course, and claim no Sabbatical exemptions. But then they come into our head. But when the head has to go out to them—when the mountain must go to Mahomet—

Reader, try it for once, only for one short twelvemonth.

It was not every week that a fashion of pink stockings came up; but mostly, instead of it, some rugged untractable subject; some topic impossible to be contorted into the risible; some feature, upon which no smile could play; some flint, from which no process of ingenuity could procure a scintillation. There they lay; there your appointed tale of brick-making was set before you, which you must finish, with or without straw, as it happened. The craving Dragon—*the Public*—like him in Bel's temple—must be fed; it expected its daily rations; and Daniel, and ourselves, to do us justice, did the best we could on this side bursting him.

While we were wringing out coy sprightlinesses for the Post, and writhing under the toil of what is called "easy writing," Bob Allen, our *quondam* schoolfellow, was tapping his impracticable brains in a like service for the Oracle. Not that Robert troubled himself much about wit. If his paragraphs had a sprightly air about them, it was sufficient. He carried this nonchalance so far at last, that a matter of intelligence, and that no very important one, was not seldom palmed upon his employers for a good jest; for example sake—*"Walking yesterday morning casually down Snow Hill, who should we meet but Mr. Deputy Humphreys! we rejoice to add, that the worthy Deputy appeared to enjoy a good state of health. We do not remember ever to have seen him look better."* This gentleman so surprisingly met upon Snow Hill, from some peculiarities in gait or gesture, was a constant butt for mirth to the small paragraphmongers of the day; and our friend thought that he might have his fling at him with the rest. We met A. in Holborn shortly after this extraordinary rencounter, which he told with tears of satisfaction in his eyes, and chuckling at the anticipated effects of its announcement next day in the paper. We did not quite comprehend where the wit of it lay at the time; nor was it easy to be detected, when the thing came out advantaged by type and letter-press. He had better have met anything that morning than a Common Council Man. His services were shortly after dispensed with, on the plea that his paragraphs of late had been deficient in point. The one in question, it must be owned, had an air, in the opening especially, proper to awaken curiosity; and the sentiment, or moral, wears the aspect of humanity and good neighbourly feeling. But somehow the conclusion was not judged altogether to answer to the magnificent promise of the premises. We traced our friend's pen afterwards in the True Briton, the Star, the Traveller,—from all which he was successively dismissed, the Proprietors having "no further occasion for his services." Nothing was easier than to detect him. When wit failed, or topics ran low, there constantly appeared the following:—"*It is not generally known that the three Blue Balls at the Pawnbrokers' shops are the ancient arms of Lombardy. The Lombards were the first money-brokers in Europe.*" Bob has done more to set the public right on this important point of blazonry, than the whole College of Heralds.

The appointment of a regular wit has long ceased to be a part of the economy of a Morning Paper. Editors find their own jokes, or do as well without them. Parson Este, and Topham, brought up the set custom of "witty paragraphs" first in the World. Boaden was a reigning paragraphist in his day, and succeeded poor Allen in the Oracle. But, as we said, the fashion of jokes passes away; and it would be difficult to discover in the biographer of Mrs. Siddons, any traces of that vivacity and fancy which charmed the whole town at the commencement of the present century. Even the prelusive delicacies of the present writer— the curt "Astræan allusion"—would be thought pedantic and out of date, in these days.

From the office of the Morning Post (for we may as well exhaust our Newspaper Reminiscences at once) by change of property in the paper, we were transferred, mortifying exchange! to the office of the Albion Newspaper, late Rackstrow's Museum, in Fleet Street. What a transition—from a handsome apartment, from rose-wood desks, and silver inkstands, to an office—no office, but a *den* rather, but just redeemed from the occupation of dead monsters, of which it seemed redolent— from the centre of loyalty and fashion, to a focus of vulgarity and sedition! Here in murky closet, inadequate from its square contents to the receipt of the two bodies of Editor and humble paragraph-maker, together at one time, sat in the discharge of his new editorial functions (the "Bigod" of Elia) the redoubted John Fenwick.

F., without a guinea in his pocket, and having left not many in the pockets of his friends whom he might command, had purchased (on tick doubtless) the whole and sole Editorship, Proprietorship, with all the rights and titles (such as they were worth) of the Albion from one Lovell; of whom we know nothing, save that he had stood in the pillory for a libel on the Prince of Wales. With this hopeless concern— for it had been sinking ever since its commencement, and could now reckon upon not more than a hundred subscribers—F. resolutely determined upon pulling down the Government in the first instance, and making both our fortunes by way of corollary. For seven weeks and more did this infatuated democrat go about borrowing seven-shilling pieces, and lesser coin, to meet the daily demands of the Stamp office, which allowed no credit to publications of that side in politics. An outcast from politer bread, we attached our small talents to the forlorn fortunes of our friend. Our occupation now was to write treason.

Recollections of feelings—which were all that now remained from our first boyish heats kindled by the French Revolution, when, if we were misled, we erred in the company of some who are accounted very good men now—rather than any tendency at this time to Republican doctrines—assisted us in assuming a style of writing, while the paper lasted, consonant in no very under tone to the right earnest fanaticism of F. Our cue was now to insinuate, rather than recommend, possible abdications. Blocks, axes, Whitehall tribunals, were covered with flowers of so cunning a periphrasis—as Mr. Bayes says, never naming the *thing* directly—that the keen eye of an Attorney General was insufficient to detect the lurking snake among them. There were times, indeed, when we sighed for our more gentleman-like occupation under Stuart. But with change of masters it is ever change of service. Already one paragraph, and another, as we learned afterwards from a gentleman at the Treasury, had begun to be marked at that office, with a view of its being submitted at least to the attention of the proper Law Officers—when an unlucky, or rather lucky epigram from our pen, aimed at Sir J——s M——h, who was on the eve of departing for India to reap the fruits of his apostasy, as F. pronounced it (it is hardly worth particularising), happening to offend the nice sense of Lord, or, as he then delighted to be called, Citizen Stanhope, deprived F. at once of the last hopes of a guinea from the last patron that had stuck by us; and breaking up our establishment, left us to the safe, but somewhat mortifying, neglect of the Crown Lawyers. It was about this time, or a little earlier, that Dan Stuart made that curious confession to us, that he had "never deliberately walked into an Exhibition at Somerset House in his life."

BARRENNESS OF THE IMAGINATIVE FACULTY IN THE PRODUCTIONS OF MODERN ART

HOGARTH excepted, can we produce any one painter within the last fifty years, or since the humour of exhibiting began, that has treated a story *imaginatively?* By this we mean, upon whom his subject has so acted, that it has seemed to direct *him*—not to be arranged by him? Any upon whom its leading or collateral points have impressed themselves so tyrannically, that he dared not treat it otherwise, lest he should falsify a revelation? Any that has imparted to his compositions, not merely so much truth as is enough to convey a story with clearness, but that individualising property, which should keep the subject so treated distinct in feature from every other subject, however similar, and to common apprehensions almost identical; so as that we might say, this and this part could have found an appropriate place in no other picture in the world but this? Is there anything in modern art—we will not demand that it should be equal—but in any way analogous to what Titian has effected, in that wonderful bringing together of two times in the Ariadne, in the National Gallery? Precipitous, with his reeling satyr rout about him, re-peopling and re-illuming suddenly the waste places, drunk with a new fury beyond the grape, Bacchus, born in fire, fire-like flings himself at the Cretan. This is the time present. With this telling of the story—an artist, and no ordinary one, might remain richly proud. Guido, in his harmonious version of it, saw no further. But from the depths of the imaginative spirit Titian has recalled past time, and laid it contributory with the present to one simultaneous effect. With the desert all ringing with the mad cymbals of his followers, made lucid with the presence and new offers of a god,—as if unconscious of Bacchus, or but idly casting her eyes as upon some unconcerning pageant— her soul undistracted from Theseus—Ariadne is still pacing the solitary shore in as much heart-silence, and in almost the same local solitude, with which she awoke at daybreak to catch the forlorn last glances of the sail that bore away the Athenian.

Here are two points miraculously co-uniting; fierce society, with the feeling of solitude still absolute; noonday revelations, with the accidents of the dull grey dawn unquenched and lingering; the *present* Bacchus, with the *past* Ariadne; two stories, with double Time; separate, and harmonising. Had the artist made the woman one shade less indifferent to the God; still more, had she expressed a rapture at his advent, where would have been the story of the mighty desolation of the heart previous? merged in the insipid accident of a flattering offer met with a welcome acceptance. The broken heart for Theseus was not lightly to be pieced up by a God.

We have before us a fine rough print, from a picture by Raphael in the Vatican. It is the Presentation of the new-born Eve to Adam by the Almighty. A fairer mother of mankind we might imagine, and a goodlier sire perhaps of men since born. But these are matters subordinate to the conception of the *situation,* displayed in this extraordinary production. A tolerably modern artist would have been satisfied with tempering certain raptures of connubial anticipation, with a suitable acknowledgment to the Giver of the blessing, in the countenance of the first bridegroom; something like the divided attention of the child (Adam was here a child-man) between the given toy, and the mother who had just blest it with the bauble. This is the obvious, the firstsight view, the superficial. An artist of a higher grade, considering the awful presence they were in, would have taken care to subtract something from the expression of the more human passion, and to heighten the more spiritual one. This would be as much as an exhibition-goer, from the opening of Somerset House to last year's show, has been encouraged to look for. It is obvious to hint at a lower expression yet, in a picture that, for respects of drawing and colouring, might be deemed not wholly inadmissible within these art-fostering walls, in which the raptures should be as ninety-nine, the gratitude as one, or perhaps zero! By neither the one passion nor the other has Raphael expounded the sit-

uation of Adam. Singly upon his brow sits the absorbing sense of
wonder at the created miracle. The *moment* is seized by the intuitive
artist, perhaps not self-conscious of his art, in which neither of the conflicting emotions—a moment how abstracted!—have had time to spring
up, or to battle for indecorous mastery.—We have seen a landscape of
a justly admired neoteric, in which he aimed at delineating a fiction,
one of the most severely beautiful in antiquity—the gardens of the
Hesperides. To do Mr. —— justice, he had painted a laudable orchard,
with fitting seclusion, and a veritable dragon (of which a Polypheme,
by Poussin, is somehow a fac-simile for the situation), looking over into
the world shut out backwards, so that none but a "still-climbing Hercules" could hope to catch a peep at the admired Ternary of Recluses.
No conventual porter could keep his eyes better than this custos with
the "lidless eyes." He not only sees that none *do* intrude into that
privacy, but, as clear as daylight, that none but *Hercules aut Diabolus*
by any manner of means *can*. So far all is well. We have absolute
solitude here or nowhere. *Ab extra* the damsels are snug enough. But
here the artist's courage seems to have failed him. He began to pity
his pretty charge, and, to comfort the irksomeness, has peopled their
solitude with a bevy of fair attendants, maids of honour, or ladies of the
bed-chamber, according to the approved etiquette at a court of the nineteenth century; giving to the whole scene the air of a *fête-champêtre*, if
we will but excuse the absence of the gentlemen. This is well, and
Watteauish. But what is become of the solitary mystery—the

> Daughters three
> That sing around the golden tree?

This is not the way in which Poussin would have treated this subject.

The paintings, or rather the stupendous architectural designs, of a
modern artist, have been urged as objections to the theory of our motto.
They are of a character, we confess, to stagger it. His towered structures are of the highest order of the material sublime. Whether they
were dreams, or transcripts of some elder workmanship—Assyrian ruins
old—restored by this mighty artist, they satisfy our most stretched
and craving conceptions of the glories of the antique world. It is a pity
that they were ever peopled. On that side, the imagination of the artist
halts, and appears defective. Let us examine the point of the story in
the Belshazzar's Feast. We will introduce it by an apposite anecdote.

The court historians of the day record, that at the first dinner given
by the late King (then Prince Regent) at the Pavilion, the following
characteristic frolic was played off. The guests were select and admiring; the banquet profuse and admirable; the lights lustrous and oriental; the eye was perfectly dazzled with the display of plate, among
which the great gold salt-cellar, brought from the regalia in the Tower
for this especial purpose, itself a tower! stood conspicuous for its magnitude. And now the Rev. * * * *, the then admired court Chaplain,
was proceeding with the grace, when, at a signal given, the lights were

suddenly overcast, and a huge transparency was discovered, in which glittered in gold letters—

"BRIGHTON—EARTHQUAKE—SWALLOW-UP ALIVE!"

Imagine the confusion of the guests; the Georges and garters, jewels, bracelets, moulted upon the occasion! The fans dropped, and picked up the next morning by the sly court-pages! Mrs. Fitz-what's-her-name fainting, and the Countess of * * * holding the smelling-bottle, till the good-humoured Prince caused harmony to be restored, by calling in fresh candles, and declaring that the whole was nothing but a pantomime *hoax,* got up by the ingenious Mr. Farley, of Covent Garden, from hints which his Royal Highness himself had furnished! Then imagine the infinite applause that followed, the mutual rallyings, the declarations that "they were not much frightened," of the assembled galaxy.

The point of time in the picture exactly answers to the appearance of the transparency in the anecdote. The huddle, the flutter, the bustle, the escape, the alarm, and the mock alarm; the prettinesses heightened by consternation; the courtier's fear which was flattery; and the lady's which was affectation; all that we may conceive to have taken place in a mob of Brighton courtiers, sympathising with the well-acted surprise of their sovereign; all this, and no more, is exhibited by the well-dressed lords and ladies in the Hall of Belus. Just this sort of consternation we have seen among a flock of disquieted wild geese at the report only of a gun having gone off!

But is this vulgar fright, this mere animal anxiety for the preservation of their persons,—such as we have witnessed at a theatre, when a slight alarm of fire has been given—an adequate exponent of a supernatural terror? the way in which the finger of God, writing judgments, would have been met by the withered conscience? There is a human fear, and a divine fear. The one is disturbed, restless, and bent upon escape. The other is bowed down, effortless, passive. When the spirit appeared before Eliphaz in the visions of the night, and the hair of his flesh stood up, was it in the thoughts of the Temanite to ring the bell of his chamber, or to call up the servants? But let us see in the text what there is to justify all this huddle of vulgar consternation.

From the words of Daniel it appears that Belshazzar had made a great feast to a thousand of his lords, and drank wine before the thousand. The golden and silver vessels are gorgeously enumerated, with the princes, the king's concubines, and his wives. Then follows—

"In the same hour came forth fingers of a man's hand, and wrote over against the candlestick upon the plaster of the wall of the king's palace; and the *king* saw the part of the hand that wrote. Then the *king's* countenance was changed, and his thoughts troubled him, so that the joints of his loins were loosened, and his knees smote one against another."

This is the plain text. By no hint can it be otherwise inferred, but that the appearance was solely confined to the fancy of Belshazzar, that his single brain was troubled. Not a word is spoken of its being seen by any else there present, not even by the queen herself, who merely undertakes for the interpretation of the phenomenon, as related to her, doubtless, by her husband. The lords are simply said to be astonished; *i.e.,* at the trouble and the change of countenance in their sovereign. Even the prophet does not appear to have seen the scroll, which the king saw. He recalls it only, as Joseph did the Dream to the King of Egypt. "Then was the part of the hand sent from him [the Lord], and this writing was written." He speaks of the phantasm as past.

Then what becomes of this needless multiplication of the miracle? this message to a royal conscience, singly expressed—for it was said, "Thy kingdom is divided,"—simultaneously impressed upon the fancies of a thousand courtiers, who were implied in it neither directly nor grammatically?

But admitting the artist's own version of the story, and that the sight was seen also by the thousand courtiers—let it have been visible to all Babylon—as the knees of Belshazzar were shaken, and his countenance troubled, even so would the knees of every man in Babylon, and their countenances, as of an individual man, have been troubled; bowed, bent down, so would they have remained, stupor-fixed, with no thought of struggling with that inevitable judgment.

Not all that is optically possible to be seen, is to be shown in every picture. The eye delightedly dwells upon the brilliant individualities in a Marriage at Cana, by Veronese, or Titian, to the very texture and colour of the wedding garments, the ring glittering upon the bride's fingers, the metal and fashion of the wine-pots; for at such seasons there is leisure and luxury to be curious. But in a "day of judgment," or in a "day of lesser horrors, yet divine," as at the impious feast of Belshazzar, the eye should see, as the actual eye of an agent or patient in the immediate scene would see, only in masses and indistinction. Not only the female attire and jewelry exposed to the critical eye of fashion, as minutely as the dresses in a Lady's Magazine, in the criticised picture,— but perhaps the curiosities of anatomical science, and studied diversities of posture, in the falling angels and sinners of Michael Angelo,—have no business in their great subjects. There was no leisure for them.

By a wise falsification, the great masters of painting got at their true conclusions; by not showing the actual appearances, that is, all that was to be seen at any given moment by an indifferent eye, but only what the eye might be supposed to see in the doing or suffering of some portentous action. Suppose the moment of the swallowing up of Pompeii. There they were to be seen—houses, columns, architectural proportions, differences of public and private buildings, men and women at their standing occupations, the diversified thousand postures, attitudes, dresses, in some confusion truly, but physically they were visible. But what eye saw them at that eclipsing moment, which reduces confusion to a kind of unity, and when the senses are upturned from their proprieties, when sight and hearing are a feeling only? A thousand years have passed, and we are at leisure to contemplate the weaver fixed standing at his shuttle, the baker at his oven, and turn over with antiquarian coolness the pots and pans of Pompeii.

"Sun, stand thou still upon Gibeon, and thou, Moon, in the valley of Ajalon." Who, in reading this magnificent Hebraism, in his conception, sees aught but the heroic son of Nun, with the outstretched arm, and the greater and lesser light obsequious? Doubtless there were to be seen hill and dale, and chariots and horsemen, on open plain, or winding by secret defiles, and all the circumstances and stratagems of war. But whose eyes would have been conscious of this array at the interposition of the synchronic miracle? Yet in the picture of this subject by the artist of the Belshazzar's Feast—no ignoble work either—the marshalling and landscape of the war is everything, the miracle sinks into an anecdote of the day; and the eye may "dart through rank and file traverse" for some minutes, before it shall discover, among his armed followers, *which is Joshua!* Not modern art alone, but ancient, where only it is to be found if anywhere, can be detected erring, from defect of this imaginative faculty. The world has nothing to show of the preternatural in painting, transcending the figure of Lazarus bursting his grave-clothes, in the great picture at Angerstein's. It seems a thing between two beings. A ghastly horror at itself struggles with newly-apprehending gratitude at second life bestowed. It cannot forget that it was a ghost. It has hardly felt that it is a body. It has to tell of the world of spirits.—Was it from a feeling, that the crowd of half-impassioned bystanders, and the still more irrelevant herd of passers-by at a distance, who have not heard, or but faintly have been told of the passing miracle, admirable as they are in design and hue—for it is a glorified work—do not respond adequately to the action—that the single figure of the Lazarus has been attributed to Michael Angelo, and the mighty Sebastian unfairly robbed of the fame of the greater half of the interest? Now that there were not indifferent passers-by within actual scope of the eyes of those present at the miracle, to whom the sound of it had but faintly, or not at all, reached, it would be hardihood to deny; but would they see them? or can the mind in the conception of it admit of such unconcerning objects; can it think of them at all? or what associating league to the imagination can there be between the seers, and the seers not, of a presential miracle?

Were an artist to paint upon demand a picture of a Dryad, we will ask whether, in the present low state of expectation, the patron would not, or ought not be fully satisfied with a beautiful naked figure recumbent under wide-stretched oaks? Dis-seat those woods, and place the same figure among fountains, and fall of pellucid water, and you have a—Naiad! Not so in a rough print we have seen after Julio Romano, we think—for it is long since—*there*, by no process, with mere change of scene, could the figure have reciprocated characters.

Long, grotesque, fantastic, yet with a grace of her own, beautiful in con-volution and distortion, linked to her connatural tree, co-twisting with its limbs her own, till both seemed either—these, animated branches; those, disanimated members—yet the animal and vegetable lives suffi-ciently kept distinct—*his* Dryad lay—an approximation of two natures, which to conceive, it must be seen; analogous to, not the same with, the delicacies of Ovidian transformations.

To the lowest subjects, and, to a superficial comprehension, the most barren, the Great Masters gave loftiness and fruitfulness. The large eye of genius saw in the meanness of present objects their capabilities of treatment from their relations to some grand Past or Future. How has Raphael—we must still linger about the Vatican—treated the humble craft of the shipbuilder, in *his* Building of the Ark? It is in that scriptural series, to which we have referred, and which, judging from some fine rough old graphic sketches of them which we possess, seem to be of a higher and more poetic grade than even the Cartoons. The dim of sight are the timid and the shrinking. There is a cowardice in modern art. As the Frenchman, of whom Coleridge's friend made the prophetic guess at Rome, from the beard and horns of the Moses of Michael Angelo collected no inferences beyond that of a He Goat and a Cornuto; so from this subject, of mere mechanic promise, it would in-stinctively turn away, as from one incapable of investiture with any grandeur. The dock-yards at Woolwich would object derogatory asso-ciations. The depôt at Chatham would be the mote and the beam in its intellectual eye. But not to the nautical preparations in the ship-yards of Civita Vecchia did Raphael look for instructions, when he imagined the building of the Vessel that was to be conservatory of the wrecks of the species of drowned mankind. In the intensity of the action, he keeps ever out of sight the meanness of the operation. There is the Patriarch, in calm forethought, and with holy prescience, giving directions. And there are his agents—the solitary but sufficient Three—hewing, sawing, every one with the might and earnestness of a Demiurgus; under some instinctive rather than technical guidance! giant-muscled; every one a Hercules, or liker to those Vulcanian Three, that in sounding caverns under Mongibello wrought in fire—Brontes, and black Steropes, and Pyracmon. So work the workmen that should repair a world!

Artists again err in the confounding of *poetic* with *pictorial subjects*. In the latter, the exterior accidents are nearly everything, the unseen qualities as nothing. Othello's colour—the infirmities and corpulence of a Sir John Falstaff—do they haunt us perpetually in the reading? or are they obtruded upon our conceptions one time for ninety-nine that we are lost in admiration of the respective moral or intellectual attributes of the character? But in a picture Othello is *always* a Blackamoor; and the other only Plump Jack. Deeply corporealised, and enchained hope-lessly in the grovelling fetters of externality, must be the mind, to which, in its better moments, the image of the high-souled, high-intelligenced Quixote—the errant Star of Knighthood, made more tender by eclipse—

has never presented itself divested from the unhallowed accompaniment of a Sancho, or a rabblement at the heels of Rosinante. That man has read his book by halves; he has laughed, mistaking his author's purport, which was—tears. The artist that pictures Quixote (and it is in this degrading point that he is every season held up at our Exhibitions) in the shallow hope of exciting mirth, would have joined the rabble at the heels of his starved steed. We wish not to see *that* counterfeited, which we would not have wished to see in the reality. Conscious of the heroic inside of the noble Quixote, who, on hearing that his withered person was passing, would have stepped over his threshold to gaze upon his forlorn habiliments, and the "strange bed-fellows which misery brings a man acquainted with"? Shade of Cervantes! who in thy Second Part could put into the mouth of thy Quixote those high aspirations of a super-chivalrous gallantry, where he replies to one of the shepherdesses, apprehensive that he would spoil their pretty net-works, and inviting him to be a guest with them, in accents like these: "Truly, fairest Lady, Actæon was not more astonished when he saw Diana bathing herself at the fountain, than I have been in beholding your beauty: I commend the manner of your pastime, and thank you for your kind offers; and, if I may serve you, so I may be sure you will be obeyed, you may command me: for my profession is this, To show myself thankful, and a doer of good to all sorts of people, especially of the rank that your person shows you to be; and if those nets, as they take up but a little piece of ground, should take up the whole world, I would seek out new worlds to pass through, rather than break them: and (he adds) that you may give credit to this my exaggeration, behold at least he that promiseth you this, is Don Quixote de la Mancha, if haply this name hath come to your hearing." Illustrious Romancer! were the "fine frenzies," which possessed the brain of thy own Quixote, a fit subject, as in this Second Part, to be exposed to the jeers of Duennas and Serving-men? to be monstered, and shown up at the heartless banquets of great men? Was that pitiable infirmity, which in thy First Part misleads him, *always from within*, into half-ludicrous, but more than half-compassionable and admirable errors, not infliction enough from heaven, that men by studied artifices must devise and practise upon the humour, to inflame where they should soothe it? Why, Goneril would have blushed to practise upon the abdicated king at this rate, and the she-wolf Regan not have endured to play the pranks upon his fled wits, which thou hast made thy Quixote suffer in Duchesses' halls, and at the hands of that unworthy nobleman.[1]

In the First Adventures, even, it needed all the art of the most consummate artist in the Book way that the world hath yet seen, to keep up in the mind of the reader the heroic attributes of the character without relaxing; so as absolutely that they shall suffer no alloy from the de-

---

[1] Yet from this Second Part, our cried-up pictures are mostly selected; the waiting-women with beards, etc.

basing fellowship of the clown. If it ever obtrudes itself as a dishar-
mony, are we inclined to laugh; or not, rather, to indulge a contrary
emotion?—Cervantes, stung, perchance, by the relish with which *his*
Reading Public had received the fooleries of the man, more to their
palates than the generosities of the master, in the sequel let his pen run
riot, lost the harmony and the balance, and sacrified a great idea to the
taste of his contemporaries. We know that in the present day the
Knight has fewer admirers than the Squire. Anticipating, what did
actually happen to him—as afterwards it did to his scarce inferior follower, the Author of "Guzman de Alfarache"—that some less knowing
hand would prevent him by a spurious Second Part; and judging that it
would be easier for his competitor to outbid him in the comicalities, than
in the *romance*, of his work, he abandoned his Knight, and has fairly set
up the Squire for his Hero. For what else has he unsealed the eyes of
Sancho? and instead of that twilight state of semi-insanity—the madness
at second-hand—the contagion, caught from a stronger mind infected—
that war between native cunning, and hereditary deference, with which
he has hitherto accompanied his master—two for a pair almost—does
he substitute a downright Knave, with open eyes, for his own ends only
following a confessed Madman; and offering at one time to lay, if not
actually laying, hands upon him! From the moment that Sancho loses his
reverence, Don Quixote is become—a treatable lunatic. Our artists
handle him accordingly.

THE WEDDING

I DO not know when I have been better pleased than at being invited
last week to be present at the wedding of a friend's daughter. I like to
make one at these ceremonies, which to us old people give back our youth
in a manner, and restore our gayest season, in the remembrance of our
own success, or the regrets, scarcely less tender, of our own youthful disappointments, in this point of a settlement. On these occasions I am sure
to be in good-humour for a week or two after, and enjoy a reflected
honeymoon. Being without a family, I am flattered with these temporary adoptions into a friend's family; I feel a sort of cousinhood, or
uncleship, for the season; I am inducted into degrees of affinity; and, in
the participated socialities of the little community, I lay down for a
brief while my solitary bachelorship. I carry this humour so far, that I
take it unkindly to be left out, even when a funeral is going on in the
house of a dear friend. But to my subject.——

The union itself had been long settled, but its celebration had been
hitherto deferred, to an almost unreasonable state of suspense in the
lovers by some invincible prejudices which the bride's father had unhappily contracted upon the subject of the too early marriages of females. He has been lecturing any time these five years—for to that

length the courtship has been protracted—upon the propriety of putting off the solemnity, till the lady should have completed her five-and-twentieth year. We all began to be afraid that a suit, which as yet had abated of none of its ardours, might at last be lingered on, till passion had time to cool, and love go out in the experiment. But a little wheedling on the part of his wife, who was by no means a party to these overstrained notions, joined to some serious expostulations on that of his friends, who, from the growing infirmities of the old gentleman, could not promise ourselves many years' enjoyment of his company, and were anxious to bring matters to a conclusion during his lifetime, at length prevailed; and on Monday last the daughter of my old friend, Admiral ———, having attained the *womanly* age of nineteen, was conducted to the church by her pleasant cousin J———, who told some few years older.

Before the youthful part of my female readers express their indignation at the abominable loss of time occasioned to the lovers by the preposterous notions of my old friend, they will do well to consider the reluctance which a fond parent naturally feels at parting with his child. To this unwillingness, I believe, in most cases may be traced the difference of opinion on this point between child and parent, whatever pretences of interest or prudence may be held out to cover it. The hardheartedness of fathers is a fine theme for romance writers, a sure and moving topic; but is there not something untender, to say no more of it, in the hurry which a beloved child is sometimes in to tear herself from the paternal stock, and commit herself to strange graftings? The case is heightened where the lady, as in the present instance, happens to be an only child. I do not understand these matters experimentally, but I can make a shrewd guess at the wounded pride of a parent upon these occasions. It is no new observation, I believe, that a lover in most cases has no rival so much to be feared as the father. Certainly there is a jealousy in *unparalleled subjects,* which is little less heartrending than the passion which we more strictly christen by that name. Mothers' scruples are more easily got over; for this reason, I suppose, that the protection transferred to a husband is less a derogation and a loss to their authority than to the paternal. Mothers, besides, have a trembling foresight, which paints the inconveniences (impossible to be conceived in the same degree by the other parent) of a life of forlorn celibacy, which the refusal of a tolerable match may entail upon their child. Mothers' instinct is a surer guide here, than the cold reasonings of a father on such a topic. To this instinct may be imputed, and by it alone may be excused the unbeseeming artifices, by which some wives push on the matrimonial projects of their daughters, which the husband, however approving, shall entertain with comparative indifference. A little shamelessness on this head is pardonable. With this explanation, forwardness becomes a grace, and maternal importunity receives the name of a virtue.—But the parson stays, while I preposterously assume his office; I am preaching, while the bride is on the threshold.

Nor let any of my female readers suppose that the sage reflections which have just escaped me have the obliquest tendency of application to the young lady, who, it will be seen, is about to venture upon a change in her condition, at a *mature and competent age,* and not without the fullest approbation of all parties. I only deprecate *very hasty marriages.*

It had been fixed that the ceremony should be gone through at an early hour, to give time for a little *déjeuné* afterwards, to which a select party of friends had been invited. We were in church a little before the clock struck eight.

Nothing could be more judicious or graceful than the dress of the bride-maids—the three charming Miss Foresters—on this morning. To give the bride an opportunity of shining singly, they had come habited all in green. I am ill at describing female apparel; but while *she* stood at the altar in vestments white and candid as her thoughts, a sacrificial whiteness, *they* assisted in robes, such as might become Diana's nymphs—Foresters indeed—as such who had not yet come to the resolution of putting off cold virginity. These young maids, not being so blest as to have a mother living, I am told, keep single for their father's sake, and live altogether so happy with their remaining parent, that the hearts of their lovers are ever broken with the prospect (so inauspicious to their hopes) of such uninterrupted and provoking home-comfort. Gallant girls! each a victim worthy of Iphigenia!

I do not know what business I have to be present in solemn places. I cannot divest me of an unseasonable disposition to levity upon the most awful occasions. I was never cut out for a public functionary. Ceremony and I have long shaken hands; but I could not resist the importunities of the young lady's father, whose gout unhappily confined him at home, to act as parent on this occasion, and *give away the bride.* Something ludicrous occurred to me at this most serious of all moments—a sense of my unfitness to have the disposal, even in imagination, of the sweet young creature beside me. I fear I was betrayed to some lightness, for the awful eye of the parson—and the rector's eye of Saint Mildred's in the Poultry is no trifle of a rebuke—was upon me in an instant, souring my incipient jest to the tristful severities of a funeral.

This was the only misbehaviour which I can plead to upon this solemn occasion, unless what was objected to me after the ceremony, by one of the handsome Miss T—— to be accounted a solecism. She was pleased to say that she had never seen a gentleman before me give away a bride, in black. Now black has been my ordinary apparel so long—indeed I take it to be the proper costume of an author—the stage sanctions it— that to have appeared in some lighter colour would have raised more mirth at my expense than the anomaly had created censure. But I could perceive that the bride's mother, and some elderly ladies present (God bless them!) would have been well content, if I had come in any other colour than that. But I got over the omen by a lucky apologue, which I remembered out of Pilpay, or some Indian author, of all the birds being invited to the linnet's wedding, at which, when all the rest came in their gayest feathers, the raven alone apologised for his cloak because "he had no other." This tolerably reconciled the elders. But with the young people all was merriment, and shaking of hands, and congratulations, and kissing away the bride's tears, and kissing from her in return, till a young lady, who assumed some experience in these matters, having worn the nuptial bands some four or five weeks longer than her friend, rescued her, archly observing, with half an eye upon the bridegroom, that at this rate she would have "none left."

My friend the Admiral was in fine wig and buckle on this occasion— a striking contrast to his usual neglect of personal appearance. He did not once shove up his borrowed locks (his custom ever at his morning studies) to betray the few grey stragglers of his own beneath them. He wore an aspect of thoughtful satisfaction. I trembled for the hour, which at length approached, when after a protracted *breakfast* of three hours —if stores of cold fowls, tongues, hams, botargoes, dried fruits, wines, cordials, etc., can deserve so meagre an appellation—the coach was announced, which was come to carry off the bride and bridegroom for a season, as custom has sensibly ordained, into the country; upon which design, wishing them a felicitous journey, let us return to the assembled guests.

> As when a well-graced actor leaves the stage,
> The eyes of men
> Are idly bent on him that enters next,

so idly did we bend our eyes upon one another, when the chief performers in the morning's pageant had vanished. None told his tale. None sipped her glass. The poor Admiral made an effort—it was not much. I had anticipated so far. Even the infinity of full satisfaction, that had betrayed itself through the prim looks and quiet deportment of his lady, began to wane into something of misgiving. No one knew whether to take their leaves or stay. We seemed assembled upon a silly occasion. In this crisis, betwixt tarrying and departure, I must do justice to a foolish talent of mine, which had otherwise like to have brought me into disgrace in the fore-part of the day; I mean a power, in any emergency, of thinking and giving vent to all manner of strange nonsense. In this awkward dilemma I found it sovereign. I rattled off some of my most excellent absurdities. All were willing to be relieved, at any expense of reason, from the pressure of the intolerable vacuum which had succeeded to the morning bustle. By this means I was fortunate in keeping together the better part of the company to a late hour; and a rubber of whist (the Admiral's favourite game) with some rare strokes of chance as well as skill, which came opportunely on his side—lengthened out till midnight—dismissed the old gentleman at last to his bed with comparatively easy spirits.

I have been at my old friend's various times since. I do not know a visiting place where every guest is so perfectly at his ease; nowhere, where harmony is so strangely the result of confusion. Everybody is at cross purposes, yet the effect is so much better than uniformity. Contradictory orders; servants pulling one way; master and mistress driving some other, yet both diverse; visitors huddled up in corners; chairs unsymmetrised; candles disposed by chance; meals at odd hours, tea and supper at once, or the latter preceding the former; the host and the guest conferring, yet each upon a different topic, each understanding himself, neither trying to understand or hear the other; draughts and politics, chess and political economy, cards and conversation on nautical matters, going on at once, without the hope, or indeed the wish, of distinguishing them, make it altogether the most perfect *concordia discors* you shall meet with. Yet somehow the old house is not quite what it should be. The Admiral still enjoys his pipe, but he has no Miss Emily to fill it for him. The instrument stands where it stood, but she is gone, whose delicate touch could sometimes for a short minute appease the warring elements. He has learnt, as Marvel expresses it, to "make his destiny his choice." He bears bravely up, but he does not come out with his flashes of wild wit so thick as formerly. His sea-songs seldomer escape him. His wife, too, looks as if she wanted some younger body to scold and set to rights. We all miss a junior presence. It is wonderful how one young maiden freshens up, and keeps green, the paternal roof. Old and young seem to have an interest in her, so long as she is not absolutely disposed of. The youthfulness of the house is flown. Emily is married.

REJOICINGS UPON THE NEW YEAR'S COMING OF AGE

THE *Old Year* being dead, and the *New Year* coming of age, which he does, by Calendar Law, as soon as the breath is out of the old gentleman's body, nothing would serve the young spark but he must give a dinner upon the occasion, to which all the *Days* in the year were invited. The *Festivals*, whom he deputed as his stewards, were mightily taken with the notion. They had been engaged time out of mind, they said, in providing mirth and good cheer for mortals below; and it was time they should have a taste of their own bounty. It was stiffly debated among them whether the *Fasts* should be admitted. Some said the appearance of such lean, starved guests, with their mortified faces, would pervert the ends of the meeting. But the objection was overruled by *Christmas Day*, who had a design upon *Ash Wednesday* (as you shall hear), and a mighty desire to see how the old Dominie would behave himself in his cups. Only the *Vigils* were requested to come with their lanterns, to light the gentlefolks home at night.

All the *Days* came to their day. Covers were provided for three hundred and sixty-five guests at the principal table; with an occasional knife and fork at the side-board for the *Twenty-Ninth of February*.

I should have told you that cards of invitation had been issued. The carriers were the *Hours;* twelve little, merry, whirligig foot-pages, as you should desire to see, that went all round, and found out the persons invited well enough, with the exception of *Easter Day, Shrove Tuesday*, and a few such *Moveables,* who had lately shifted their quarters.

Well, they all met at last, foul *Days*, fine *Days*, all sorts of *Days*, and a rare din they made of it. There was nothing but, Hail! fellow *Day*, well met—brother *Day*—sister *Day*—only *Lady Day* kept a little on the aloof, and seemed somewhat scornful. Yet some said *Twelfth Day* cut her out and out, for she came in a tiffany suit, white and gold, like a queen on a frost-cake, all royal, glittering, and *Epiphanous*. The rest came, some in green, some in white—but old *Lent and his family* were not yet out of mourning. Rainy *Days* came in, dripping; and sunshiny *Days* helped them to change their stockings. *Wedding Day* was there in his marriage finery, a little the worse for wear. *Pay Day* came late, as he always does; and *Doomsday* sent word—he might be expected.

April Fool (as my young lord's jester) took upon himself to marshal the guests, and wild work he made with it. It would have posed old Erra Pater to have found out any given *Day* in the year, to erect a scheme upon—good *Days*, bad *Days*, were so shuffled together, to the confounding of all sober horoscopy.

He had stuck the *Twenty-First of June* next to the *Twenty-Second of December*, and the former looked like a Maypole siding a marrow-bone. *Ash Wednesday* got wedged in (as was concerted) betwixt *Christmas* and *Lord Mayor's Days*. Lord! how he laid about him! Nothing but barons of beef and turkeys would go down with him—to the great greasing and detriment of his new sackcloth bib and tucker. And still *Christmas Day* was at his elbow, plying him with the wassail-bowl, till he roared, and hiccupp'd, and protested there was no faith in dried ling, but commended it to the devil for a sour, windy, acrimonious, censorious, hy-po-crit-crit-critical mess, and no dish for a gentleman. Then he dipt his fist into the middle of the great custard that stood before his *left-hand neighbour*, and daubed his hungry beard all over with it, till you would have taken him for the *Last Day in December*, it so hung in icicles.

At another part of the table, *Shrove Tuesday* was helping the *Second of September* to some cock broth,—which courtesy the latter returned with the delicate thigh of a hen pheasant—so there was no love lost for that matter. The *Last of Lent* was spunging upon *Shrovetide's* pancakes; which *April Fool* perceiving, told him he did well, for pancakes were proper to a good *fry-day*.

In another part, a hubbub arose about the *Thirtieth of January*, who, it seems, being a sour, puritanic character, that thought nobody's meat good or sanctified enough for him, had smuggled into the room a calf's head, which he had had cooked at home for that purpose, thinking to feast thereon incontinently; but as it lay in the dish, *March Many-weathers*, who is a very fine lady, and subject to the megrims, screamed out there was a "human head in the platter," and raved about Herodias' daughter to that degree, that the obnoxious viand was obliged to be removed; nor did she recover her stomach till she had gulped down a *Restorative*, confected of *Oak Apple*, which the merry *Twenty-Ninth of May* always carries about with him for that purpose.

The King's health[1] being called for after this, a notable dispute arose between the *Twelfth of August* (a zealous old Whig gentlewoman) and the *Twenty-Third of April* (a new-fangled lady of the Tory stamp), as to which of them should have the honour to propose it. *August* grew hot upon the matter, affirming time out of mind the prescriptive right to have lain with her, till her rival had basely supplanted her; whom she represented as little better than a *kept* mistress, who went about in *fine clothes*, while she (the legitimate BIRTHDAY) had scarcely a rag, etc.

April Fool, being made mediator, confirmed the right, in the strongest form of words, to the appellant, but decided for peace' sake that the exercise of it should remain with the present possessor. At the same time, he slyly rounded the first lady in the ear, that an action might lie against the Crown for *bi-geny*.

It beginning to grow a little duskish, *Candlemas* lustily bawled out for lights, which was opposed by all the *Days,* who protested against burning daylight. Then fair water was handed round in silver ewers, and the *same lady* was observed to take an unusual time in *Washing* herself.

May Day, with that sweetness which is peculiar to her, in a neat speech proposing the health of the founder, crowned her goblet (and by her example the rest of the company) with garlands. This being done, the lordly *New Year*, from the upper end of the table, in a cordial but somewhat lofty tone, returned thanks. He felt proud on an occasion of meeting so many of his worthy father's late tenants, promised to improve their farms, and at the same time to abate (if anything was found unreasonable) in their rents.

At the mention of this, the four *Quarter Days* involuntarily looked at each other, and smiled; *April Fool* whistled to an old tune of "New Brooms"; and a surly old rebel at the further end of the table (who was discovered to be no other than the *Fifth of November*) muttered out, distinctly enough to be heard by the whole company, words to this effect, that "when the old one is gone, he is a fool that looks for a better." Which rudeness of his, the guests resenting, unanimously voted his expulsion; and the malecontent was thrust out neck and heels into the cellar, as the properest place for such a *boutefeu* and firebrand as he had shown himself to be.

Order being restored—the young lord (who, to say truth, had been a little ruffled, and put beside his oratory) in as few, and yet as obliging words as possible, assured them of entire welcome; and, with a graceful turn, singling out poor *Twenty-Ninth of February*, that had sate all this while mumchance at the side-board, begged to couple his health with that of the good company before him—which he drank accordingly; observing that he had not seen his honest face any time these four years—with a number of endearing expressions besides. At the same time, removing the solitary *Day* from the forlorn seat which had been assigned him, he stationed him at his own board, somewhere between the *Greek Calends* and *Latter Lammas*.

---

[1] King George IV.

Ash Wednesday, being now called upon for a song, with his eyes fast stuck in his head, and as well as the Canary he had swallowed would give him leave, struck up a Carol, which *Christmas Day* had taught him for the nonce; and was followed by the latter, who gave "Miserere," in fine style, hitting off the mumping notes and lengthened drawl of *Old Mortification* with infinite humour. *April Fool* swore they had exchanged conditions; but *Good Friday* was observed to look extremely grave; and *Sunday* held her fan before her face that she might not be seen to smile.

Shrove-tide, Lord Mayor's Day, and *April Fool,* next joined in a glee—

Which is the properest day to drink?

in which all the *Days* chiming in, made a merry burden.

They next fell to quibbles and conundrums. The question being proposed, who had the greatest number of followers—the *Quarter Days* said, there could be no question as to that; for they had all the creditors in the world dogging their heels. But *April Fool* gave it in favour of the *Forty Days before Easter;* because the debtors in all cases outnumbered the creditors, and they kept *lent* all the year.

All this while *Valentine's Day* kept courting pretty *May,* who sate next him, slipping amorous *billets-doux* under the table, till the *Dog Days* (who are naturally of a warm constitution) began to be jealous, and to bark and rage exceedingly. *April Fool,* who likes a bit of sport above measure, and had some pretensions to the lady besides, as being but a cousin once removed,—clapped and halloo'd them on; and as fast as their indignation cooled, those mad wags, the *Ember Days,* were at it with their bellows, to blow it into a flame; and all was in a ferment; till old Madam *Septuagesima* (who boasts herself the *Mother of the Days*) wisely diverted the conversation with a tedious tale of the lovers which she could reckon when she was young; and of one Master *Rogation Day* in particular, who was for ever putting the *question* to her; but she kept him at a distance, as the chronicle would tell—by which I apprehend she meant the Almanack. Then she rambled on to the *Days that were gone,* the *good old Days,* and so to the *Days before the Flood*—which plainly showed her old head to be little better than crazed and doited.

Day being ended, the *Days* called for their cloaks and great-coats, and took their leaves. *Lord Mayor's Day* went off in a Mist, as usual; *Shortest Day* in a deep black Fog, that wrapt the little gentleman all round like a hedge-hog. Two *Vigils*—so watchmen are called in heaven— saw *Christmas Day* safe home—they had been used to the business before. Another *Vigil*—a stout, sturdy patrole, called the *Eve of St. Christopher*—seeing *Ash Wednesday* in a condition little better than he should be—e'en whipt him over his shoulders, pick-a-back fashion, and *Old Mortification* went floating home singing—

On the bat's back do I fly,

and a number of old snatches besides, between drunk and sober; but very few Aves or Penitentiaries (you may believe me) were among them. *Longest Day* set off westward in beautiful crimson and gold—the rest, some in one fashion, some in another; but *Valentine* and pretty *May* took their departure together in one of the prettiest silvery twilights a Lover's Day could wish to set in.

OLD CHINA

I HAVE an almost feminine partiality for old china. When I go to see any great house, I inquire for the china-closet, and next for the picture gallery. I cannot defend the order of preference, but by saying, that we have all some taste or other, of too ancient a date to admit of our remembering distinctly that it was an acquired one. I can call to mind the first play, and the first exhibition, that I was taken to; but I am not conscious of a time when china jars and saucers were introduced into my imagination.

I had no repugnance then—why should I now have?—to those little, lawless, azure-tinctured grotesques, that under the notion of men and women, float about, uncircumscribed by any element, in that world before perspective—a china tea-cup.

I like to see my old friends—whom distance cannot diminish—figuring up in the air (so they appear to our optics), yet on *terra firma* still— for so we must in courtesy interpret that speck of deeper blue,—which the decorous artist, to prevent absurdity, had made to spring up beneath their sandals.

I love the men with women's faces, and the women, if possible, with still more womanish expressions.

Here is a young and courtly Mandarin, handing tea to a lady from a salver—two miles off. See how distance seems to set off respect! And here the same lady, or another—for likeness is identity on tea-cups—is stepping into a little fairy boat, moored on the hither side of this calm garden river, with a dainty mincing foot, which in a right angle of incidence (as angles go in our world) must infallibly land her in the midst of a flowery mead—a furlong off on the other side of the same strange stream!

Farther on—if far or near can be predicated of their world—see horses, trees, pagodas, dancing the hays.

Here—a cow and rabbit couchant, and coextensive—so objects show, seen through the lucid atmosphere of fine Cathay.

I was pointing out to my cousin last evening, over our Hyson (which we are old-fashioned enough to drink unmixed still of an afternoon), some of these *speciosa miracula* upon a set of extraordinary old blue china (a recent purchase) which we were now for the first time using; and could not help remarking, how favourable circumstances had been to us of late years, that we could afford to please the eye sometimes with trifles of this sort—when a passing sentiment seemed to overshade the brows of my companion. I am quick at detecting these summer clouds in Bridget.

"I wish the good old times would come again," she said, "when we were not quite so rich. I do not mean, that I want to be poor; but there was a middle state"—so she was pleased to ramble on,—"in which I am sure we were a great deal happier. A purchase is but a purchase, now that you have money enough and to spare. Formerly it used to be a triumph. When we coveted a cheap luxury (and, O! how much ado I had to get you to consent in those times!)—we were used to have a debate two or three days before, and to weigh the *for* and *against,* and think what we might spare it out of, and what saving we could hit upon, that should be an equivalent. A thing was worth buying then, when we fel the money that we paid for it.

"Do you remember the brown suit, which you made to hang upon you, till all your friends cried shame upon you, it grew so threadbare—and all because of that folio Beaumont and Fletcher, which you dragged home late at night from Barker's in Covent Garden? Do you remember how we eyed it for weeks before we could make up our minds to the purchase, and had not come to a determination till it was near ten o'clock of the Saturday night, when you set off from Islington, fearing you should be too late—and when the old bookseller with some grumbling opened his shop, and by the twinkling taper (for he was setting bed-wards) lighted out the relic from his dusty treasures—and when you lugged it home, wishing it were twice as cumbersome—and when you presented it to me—and when we were exploring the perfectness of it (*collating,* you called it)—and while I was repairing some of the loose leaves with paste, which your impatience would not suffer to be left till daybreak—was there no pleasure in being a poor man? or can those neat black clothes which you wear now, and are so careful to keep brushed, since we have become rich and finical, give you half the honest vanity with which you flaunted it about in that overworn suit—your old corbeau—for four or five weeks longer than you should have done, to pacify your conscience for the mighty sum of fifteen—or sixteen shillings was it?—a great affair we thought it then—which you had lavished on the old folio. Now you can afford to buy any book that pleases you, but I do not see that you ever bring me home any nice old purchases now.

"When you came home with twenty apologies for laying out a less number of shillings upon that print after Lionardo, which we christened the 'Lady Blanch'; when you looked at the purchase, and thought of the money—and thought of the money, and looked again at the picture—was there no pleasure in being a poor man? Now, you have nothing to do but to walk into Colnaghi's, and buy a wilderness of Lionardos. Yet do you?

"Then, do you remember our pleasant walks to Enfield, and Potter's Bar, and Waltham. when we had a holyday—holydays, and all other fun, are gone now we are rich—and the little hand-basket in which I used to deposit our day's fare of savoury cold lamb and salad—and how you would pry about at noon-tide for some decent house, where we might go in and produce our store—only paying for the ale that you must call for —and speculate upon the looks of the landlady, and whether she was likely to allow us a table-cloth—and wish for such another honest hostess as Izaak Walton has described many a one on the pleasant banks of the Lea, when he went a-fishing—and sometimes they would prove obliging enough, and sometimes they would look grudgingly upon us—but we had cheerful looks still for one another, and would eat our plain food savourily, scarcely grudging Piscator his Trout Hall? Now—when we go out a day's pleasuring, which is seldom, moreover, we *ride* part of the way— and go into a fine inn, and order the best of dinners, never debating the expense—which, after all, never has half the relish of those chance country snaps, when we were at the mercy of uncertain usage, and a precarious welcome.

"You are too proud to see a play anywhere now but in the pit. Do you remember where it was we used to sit, when we saw the Battle of Hexham, and the Surrender of Calais, and Bannister and Mrs. Bland in the Children in the Wood—when we squeezed out our shillings apiece to sit three or four times in a season in the one-shilling gallery—where you felt all the time that you ought not to have brought me—and more strongly I felt obligation to you for having brought me—and the pleasure was the better for a little shame—and when the curtain drew up, what cared we for our place in the house, or what mattered it where we were sitting, when our thoughts were with Rosalind in Arden, or with Viola at the Court of Illyria. You used to say that the Gallery was the best place of all for enjoying a play socially—that the relish of such exhibitions must be in proportion to the infrequency of going—that the company we met there, not being in general readers of plays, were obliged to attend the more, and did attend, to what was going on, on the stage—because a word lost would have been a chasm, which it was impossible for them to fill up. With such reflections we consoled our pride then—and I appeal to you whether, as a woman, I met generally with less attention and accommodation than I have done since in more expensive situations in the house? The getting in indeed, and the crowding up those inconvenient staircases, was bad enough,—but there was still a law of civility to woman recognised to quite as great an extent as we ever found in the other passages—and how a little difficulty overcome heightened the snug seat and the play, afterwards! Now we can only pay our money and walk in. You cannot see, you say, in the galleries now. I am sure we saw, and heard too, well enough then—but sight, and all, I think, is gone with our poverty.

"There was pleasure in eating strawberries, before they became quite common—in the first dish of peas, while they were yet dear—to have them for a nice supper, a treat. What treat can we have now? If we were to treat ourselves now—that is, to have dainties a little above our means, it would be selfish and wicked. It is the very little more that we allow ourselves beyond what the actual poor can get at, that makes what I call a treat—when two people living together, as we have done, now and then indulge themselves in a cheap luxury, which both like; while each apologises, and is willing to take both halves of the blame to his single share. I see no harm in people making much of themselves, in that sense of the word. It may give them a hint how to make much of others. But now—what I mean by the word—we never do make much of ourselves. None but the poor can do it. I do not mean the veriest poor of all, but persons as we were, just above poverty.

"I know what you were going to say, that it is mighty pleasant at the end of the year to make all meet,—and much ado we used to have every Thirty-first Night of December to account for our exceedings—many a long face did you make over your puzzled accounts, and in contriving to make it out how we had spent so much—or that we had not spent so much—or that it was impossible we should spend so much next year— and still we found our slender capital decreasing—but then, betwixt ways, and projects, and compromises of one sort or another, and talk of curtailing this charge, and doing without that for the future—and the hope that youth brings, and laughing spirits (in which you were never poor till now), we pocketed up our loss, and in conclusion, with 'lusty brimmers' (as you used to quote it out of hearty cheerful Mr. Cotton, as you called him), we used to welcome in 'the coming guest.' Now we have no reckoning at all at the end of the old year—no flattering promises about the new year doing better for us."

Bridget is so sparing of her speech on most occasions, that when she gets into a rhetorical vein, I am careful how I interrupt it. I could not help, however, smiling at the phantom of wealth which her dear imagination had conjured up out of a clear income of poor —— hundred pounds a year. "It is true we were happier when we were poor but we were also younger, my cousin. I am afraid we must put up with the excess, for if we were to shake the superflux into the sea, we should not much mend ourselves. That we had much to struggle with, as we grew up together, we have reason to be most thankful. It strengthened and knit our compact closer. We could never have been what we have been to each other, if we had always had the sufficiency which you now complain of. The resisting power—those natural dilations of the youthful spirit, which circumstances cannot straiten—with us are long since passed away. Competence to age is supplementary youth, a sorry supplement indeed, but I fear the best that is to be had. We must ride where we formerly walked: live better and lie softer—and shall be wise to do so—than we had means to do in those good old days you speak of. Yet could those days return—could you and I once more walk our thirty miles a day— could Bannister and Mrs. Bland again be young, and you and I be young to see them—could the good old one-shilling gallery days return —they are dreams, my cousin, now—but could you and I at this moment, instead of this quiet argument, by our well-carpeted fireside, sitting on this luxurious sofa—be once more struggling up those inconvenient staircases, pushed about, and squeezed, and elbowed by the poorest rabble of poor gallery scramblers—could I once more hear those anxious shrieks of yours—and the delicious *Thank God, we are safe,* which always followed when the topmost stair, conquered, let in the first light of the whole cheerful theatre down beneath us—I know not the fathom line that ever touched a descent so deep as I would be willing to bury more wealth in than Crœsus had, or the great Jew R—— is supposed to have, to purchase it. And now do just look at that merry little Chinese waiter holding an umbrella, big enough for a bed-tester, over the head of that pretty insipid half Madonna-ish chit of a lady in that very blue summer-house."

THE CHILD ANGEL; A DREAM

I CHANCED upon the prettiest, oddest, fantastical thing of a dream the other night, that you shall hear of. I had been reading the "Loves of the Angels," and went to bed with my head full of speculations, suggested by that extraordinary legend. It had given birth to innumerable conjectures; and, I remember the last waking thought, which I gave expression to on my pillow, was a sort of wonder, "what could come of it."

I was suddenly transported, how or whither I could scarcely make out —but to some celestial region. It was not the real heavens neither—nor the downright Bible heaven—but a kind of fairy-land heaven, about which a poor human fancy may have leave to sport and air itself, I will hope, without presumption.

Methought—what wild things dreams are!—I was present—at what would you imagine?—at an angel's gossiping.

Whence it came, or how it came, or who bid it come, or whether it came purely of its own head, neither you nor I know—but there lay, sure enough, wrapt in its little cloudy swaddling-bands—a Child Angel.

Sun-threads—filmy beams—ran through the celestial napery of what seemed its princely cradle. All the winged orders hovered round, watching when the new-born should open its yet closed eyes; which, when it did, first one, and then the other—with a solicitude and apprehension, yet not such as, stained with fear, dim the expanding eyelids of mortal infants, but as if to explore its path in those its unhereditary palaces— what an inextinguishable titter that time spared not celestial visages! Nor wanted there to my seeming—O, the inexplicable simpleness of dreams!—bowls of that cheering nectar,

—which mortals *caudle* call below.

Nor were wanting faces of female ministrants,—stricken in years, as it might seem,—so dexterous were those heavenly attendants to counterfeit kindly similitudes of earth, to greet with terrestrial child-rites the young *present*, which earth had made to heaven.

Then were celestial harpings heard, not in full symphony, as those by which the spheres are tutored; but, as loudest instruments on earth speak oftentimes, muffled; so to accommodate their sound the better to the weak ears of the imperfect-born. And, with the noise of those subdued soundings, the Angelet sprang forth, fluttering its rudiments of pinions—but forthwith flagged and was recovered into the arms of those full-winged angels. And a wonder it was to see how, as years went round in heaven—a year in dreams is as a day—continually its white shoulders put forth buds of wings, but wanting the perfect angelic nutriment, anon was shorn of its aspiring, and fell fluttering—still caught by angel hands, for ever to put forth shoots, and to fall fluttering, because its birth was not of the unmixed vigour of heaven.

And a name was given to the Babe Angel, and it was to be called *Ge-Urania,* because its production was of earth and heaven.

And it could not taste of death, by reason of its adoption into immortal palaces: but it was to know weakness, and reliance, and the shadow of human imbecility; and it went with a lame gait; but in its goings it exceeded all mortal children in grace and swiftness. Then pity first sprang up in angelic bosoms; and yearnings (like the human) touched them at the sight of the immortal lame one.

And with pain did then first those Intuitive Essences, with pain and strife to their natures (not grief), put back their bright intelligences, and reduce their ethereal minds, schooling them to degrees and slower processes, so to adapt their lessons to the gradual illumination (as must needs be) of the half-earth-born; and what intuitive notices they could not repel (by reason that their nature is, to know all things at once) the half-heavenly novice, by the better part of its nature, aspired to receive into its understanding; so that Humility and Aspiration went on even-paced in the instruction of the glorious Amphibium.

But, by reason that Mature Humanity is too gross to breathe the air of that super-subtile region, its portion was, and is, to be a child for ever.

And because the human part of it might not press into the heart and inwards of the palace of its adoption, those full-natured angels tended it by turns in the purlieus of the palace, where were shady groves and rivulets, like this green earth from which it came; so Love, with Voluntary Humility, waited upon the entertainment of the new-adopted.

And myriads of years rolled round (in dreams Time is nothing), and still it kept, and is to keep, perpetual childhood, and is the Tutelar Genius of Childhood upon earth, and still goes lame and lovely.

By the banks of the river Pison is seen, lone sitting by the grave of the terrestrial Adah, whom the angel Nadir loved, a Child; but not the same which I saw in heaven. A mournful hue overcasts its lineaments; nevertheless, a correspondency is between the child by the grave, and that celestial orphan, whom I saw above: and the dimness of the grief upon the heavenly, is a shadow or emblem of that which stains the beauty of the terrestrial. And this correspondency is not to be understood but by dreams.

And in the archives of heaven I had grace to read, how that once the angel Nadir, being exiled from his place for mortal passion, upspringing on the wings of parental love (such power had parental love for a moment to suspend the else-irrevocable law) appeared for a brief instant in this station, and, depositing a wondrous Birth, straightway disappeared, and the palaces knew him no more. And this charge was the selfsame Babe, who goeth lame and lovely—but Adah sleepeth by the river Pison.

CONFESSIONS OF A DRUNKARD

DEHORTATIONS from the use of strong liquors have been the favourite topic of sober declaimers in all ages, and have been received with abundance of applause by water-drinking critics. But with the patient himself, the man that is to be cured, unfortunately their sound has seldom prevailed. Yet the evil is acknowledged, the remedy simple. Abstain. No force can oblige a man to raise the glass to his head against his will. 'Tis as easy as not to steal, not to tell lies.

Alas! the hand to pilfer, and the tongue to bear false witness, have no constitutional tendency. These are actions indifferent to them. At the first instance of the reformed will, they can be brought off without a murmur. The itching finger is but a figure in speech, and the tongue of the liar can with the same natural delight give forth useful truths with which it has been accustomed to scatter their pernicious contraries. But when a man has commenced sot——

O pause, thou sturdy moralist, thou person of stout nerves and a strong head, whose liver is happily untouched, and ere thy gorge riseth at the *name* which I have written, first learn what the *thing* is; how much of compassion, how much of human allowance, thou mayest virtuously mingle with thy disapprobation. Trample not on the ruins of a man. Exact not, under so terrible a penalty as infamy, a resuscitation from a state of death almost as real as that from which Lazarus rose not but by a miracle.

Begin a reformation, and custom will make it easy. But what if the beginning be dreadful, the first steps not like climbing a mountain but going through fire? what if the whole system must undergo a change violent as that which we conceive of the mutation of form in some insects? what if a process comparable to flaying alive be to be gone through? is the weakness that sinks under such struggles to be confounded with the pertinacity which clings to other vices, which have induced no constitutional necessity, no engagement of the whole victim, body and soul?

I have known one in that state, when he has tried to abstain but for one evening,—though the poisonous potion had long ceased to bring back its first enchantments, though he was sure it would rather deepen his gloom than brighten it,—in the violence of the struggle, and the necessity he has felt of getting rid of the present sensation at any rate, I have known him to scream out, to cry aloud, for the anguish and pain of the strife within him.

Why should I hesitate to declare, that the man of whom I speak is myself? I have no puling apology to make to mankind. I see them all in one way or another deviating from the pure reason. It is to my own nature alone I am accountable for the woe that I have brought upon it.

I believe that there are constitutions, robust heads and iron insides, whom scarce any excesses can hurt; whom brandy (I have seen them drink it like wine), at all events whom wine, taken in ever so plentiful a measure, can do no worse injury to than just to muddle their faculties, perhaps never very pellucid. On them this discourse is wasted. They would but laugh at a weak brother, who, trying his strength with them, and coming off foiled from the contest, would fain persuade them that such agonistic exercises are dangerous. It is to a very different description of persons I speak. It is to the weak, the nervous; to those who feel the want of some artificial aid to raise their spirits in society to what is no more than the ordinary pitch of all around them without it. This is the secret of our drinking. Such must fly the convivial board in the first instance, if they do not mean to sell themselves for term of life.

Twelve years ago I had completed my six-and-twentieth year. I had lived from the period of leaving school to that time pretty much in solitude. My companions were chiefly books, or at most one or two living ones of my own book-loving and sober stamp. I rose early, went to bed betimes, and the faculties which God had given me, I have reason to think, did not rust in me unused.

About that time I fell in with some companions of a different order. They were men of boisterous spirits, sitters up a-nights, disputants, drunken; yet seemed to have something noble about them. We dealt about the wit, or what passes for it after midnight, jovially. Of the quality called fancy I certainly possessed a larger share than my companions. Encouraged by their applause, I set up for a professed joker! I, who of all men am least fitted for such an occupation, having, in addition to the greatest difficulty which I experience at all times of finding words to express my meaning, a natural nervous impediment in my speech!

Reader, if you are gifted with nerves like mine, aspire to any character but that of a wit. When you find a tickling relish upon your tongue disposing you to that sort of conversation, especially if you find a preternatural flow of ideas setting in upon you at the sight of a bottle and fresh glasses, avoid giving way to it as you would fly your greatest destruction. If you cannot crush the power of fancy, or that within you which you mistake for such, divert it, give it some other play. Write an essay, pen a character or description,—but not as I do now, with tears trickling down your cheeks.

To be an object of compassion to friends, of derision to foes; to be suspected by strangers, stared at by fools; to be esteemed dull when you cannot be witty, to be applauded for witty when you know that you have been dull; to be called upon for the extemporaneous exercise of that faculty which no premeditation can give; to be spurred on to efforts which end in contempt; to be set on to provoke mirth which procures the procurer hatred; to give pleasure and be paid with squinting malice; to swallow draughts of life-destroying wine which are to be distilled into airy breath to tickle vain auditors; to mortgage miserable morrows for nights of madness; to waste whole seas of time upon those who pay it back in little inconsiderable drops of grudging applause,—are the wages of buffoonery and death.

Time, which has a sure stroke at dissolving all connexions which have no solider fastening than this liquid cement, more kind to me than my own taste or penetration, at length opened my eyes to the supposed qualities of my first friends. No trace of them is left but in the vices which they introduced, and the habits they infixed. In them my friends survive still, and exercise ample retribution for any supposed infidelity that I may have been guilty of towards them.

My next more immediate companions were and are persons of such intrinsic and felt worth, that though accidentally their acquaintance has proved pernicious to me, I do not know that if the thing were to do over again, I should have the courage to eschew the mischief at the price of forfeiting the benefit. I came to them reeking from the steams of my late over-heated notions of companionship; and the slightest fuel which they unconsciously afforded, was sufficient to feed my old fires into a propensity.

They were no drinkers, but, one from professional habits, and another from a custom derived from his father, smoked tobacco. The devil could not have devised a more subtle trap to re-take a backsliding penitent. The transition, from gulping down draughts of liquid fire to puffing out innocuous blasts of dry smoke, was so like cheating him. But he is too hard for us when we hope to commute. He beats us at barter; and when we think to set off a new failing against an old infirmity, 'tis odds but he puts the trick upon us of two for one. That (comparatively) white devil of tobacco brought with him in the end seven worse than himself.

It were impertinent to carry the reader through all the processes by which, from smoking at first with malt liquor, I took my degrees through thin wines, through stronger wine and water, through small punch, to those juggling compositions, which, under the name of mixed liquors, slur a great deal of brandy or other poison under less and less water continually, until they come next to none, and so to none at all. But it is hateful to disclose the secrets of my Tartarus.

I should repel my readers, from a mere incapacity of believing me, were I to tell them what tobacco has been to me, the drudging service which I have paid, the slavery which I have vowed to it. How, when I have resolved to quit it, a feeling as of ingratitude has started up; how it has put on personal claims and made the demands of a friend upon me. How the reading of it casually in a book, as where Adams takes his whiff in the chimney-corner of some inn in Joseph Andrews, or Piscator in the

Compleat Angler breaks his fast upon a morning pipe in that delicate room *Piscatoribus Sacrum,* has in a moment broken down the resistance of weeks. How a pipe was ever in my midnight path before me, till the vision forced me to realise it,—how then its ascending vapours curled, its fragrance lulled, and the thousand delicious ministerings conversant about it, employing every faculty, extracted the sense of pain. How from illuminating it came to darken, from a quick solace it turned to a negative relief, thence to a restlessness and dissatisfaction, thence to a positive misery. How, even now, when the whole secret stands confessed in all its dreadful truth before me, I feel myself linked to it beyond the power of revocation. Bone of my bone——

Persons not accustomed to examine the motives of their actions, to reckon up the countless nails that rivet the chains of habit, or perhaps being bound by none so obdurate as those I have confessed to, may recoil from this as from an overcharged picture. But what short of such a bondage is it, which in spite of protesting friends, a weeping wife, and a reprobating world, chains down many a poor fellow, of no original indisposition to goodness, to his pipe and his pot?

I have seen a print after Correggio, in which three female figures are ministering to a man who sits fast bound at the root of a tree. Sensuality is soothing him, Evil Habit is nailing him to a branch, and Repugnance at the same instant of time is applying a snake to his side. In his face is feeble delight, the recollection of past rather than perception of present pleasures, languid enjoyment of evil with utter imbecility to good, a Sybaritic effeminacy, a submission to bondage, the springs of the will gone down like a broken clock, the sin and the suffering co-instantaneous, or the latter forerunning the former, remorse preceding action—all this represented in one point of time.—When I saw this, I admired the wonderful skill of the painter. But when I went away, I wept, because I thought of my own condition.

Of *that* there is no hope that it should ever change. The waters have gone over me. But out of the black depths, could I be heard, I would cry out to all those who have but set a foot in the perilous flood. Could the youth, to whom the flavour of his first wine is delicious as the opening scenes of life or the entering upon some newly discovered paradise, look into my desolation, and be made to understand what a dreary thing it is when a man shall feel himself going down a precipice with open eyes and a passive will,—to see his destruction and have no power to stop it, and yet to feel it all the way emanating from himself; to perceive all goodness emptied out of him, and yet not to be able to forget a time when it was otherwise; to bear about the piteous spectacle of his own self-ruins:—could he see my fevered eye, feverish with last night's drinking, and feverishly looking for this night's repetition of the folly; could he feel the body of the death out of which I cry hourly with feebler and feebler outcry to be delivered,—it were enough to make him dash the sparkling beverage to the earth in all the pride of its mantling temptation; to make him clasp his teeth,

and not undo 'em
To suffer WET DAMNATION to run thro' 'em.

Yea, but (methinks I hear somebody object) if sobriety be that fine thing you would have us to understand, if the comforts of a cool brain are to be preferred to that state of heated excitement which you describe and deplore, what hinders in your instance that you do not return to those habits from which you would induce others never to swerve? if the blessing be worth preserving, is it not worth recovering?

Recovering!—O if a wish could transport me back to those days of youth, when a draught from the next clear spring could slake any heats which summer suns and youthful exercise had power to stir up in the blood, how gladly would I return to thee, pure element, the drink of children, and of child-like holy hermit! In my dreams I can sometimes fancy thy cool refreshment purling over my burning tongue. But my waking stomach rejects it. That which refreshes innocence only makes me sick and faint.

But is there no middle way betwixt total abstinence and the excess which kills you?—For your sake, reader, and that you may never attain to my experience, with pain I must utter the dreadful truth, that there is none, none that I can find. In my stage of habit (I speak not of habits less confirmed—for some of them I believe the advice to be most prudential), in the stage which I have reached, to stop short of that measure which is sufficient to draw on torpor and sleep, the benumbing apoplectic sleep of the drunkard, is to have taken none at all. The pain of the self-denial is all one. And what that is, I had rather the reader should believe on my credit, than know from his own trial. He will come to know it, whenever he shall arrive in that state, in which, paradoxical as it may appear, *reason shall only visit him through intoxication:* for it is a fearful truth, that the intellectual faculties by repeated acts of intemperance may be driven from their orderly sphere of action, their clear daylight ministeries, until they shall be brought at last to depend, for the faint manifestation of their departing energies, upon the returning periods of the fatal madness to which they owe their devastation. The drinking man is never less himself than during his sober intervals. Evil is so far his good.[1]

Behold me then, in the robust period of life, reduced to imbecility and decay. Hear me count my gains, and the profits which I have derived from the midnight cup.

Twelve years ago, I was possessed of a healthy frame of mind and body. I was never strong, but I think my constitution (for a weak one) was as happily exempt from the tendency to any malady as it was possible to be. I scarce knew what it was to ail anything. Now, except

---

[1] When poor M—— painted his last picture, with a pencil in one trembling hand, and a glass of brandy and water in the other, his fingers owed the comparative steadiness with which they were enabled to go through their task in an imperfect manner to a temporary firmness derived from a repetition of practices, the general effect of which had shaken both them and him so terribly.

when I am losing myself in a sea of drink, I am never free from those uneasy sensations in head and stomach, which are so much worse to bear than any definite pains or aches.

At that time I was seldom in bed after six in the morning, summer and winter. I awoke refreshed, and seldom without some merry thoughts in my head, or some piece of a song to welcome the new-born day. Now, the first feeling which besets me, after stretching out the hours of recumbence to their last possible extent, is a forecast of the wearisome day that lies before me, with a secret wish that I could have lain on still, or never awaked.

Life itself, my waking life, has much of the confusion, the trouble, and obscure perplexity, of an ill dream. In the day time I stumble upon dark mountains.

Business, which, though never very particularly adapted to my nature, yet as something of necessity to be gone through, and therefore best undertaken with cheerfulness, I used to enter upon with some degree of alacrity, now wearies, affrights, perplexes me. I fancy all sorts of discouragements, and am ready to give up an occupation which gives me bread, from a harassing conceit of incapacity. The slightest commission given me by a friend, or any small duty which I have to perform for myself, as giving orders to a tradesman, etc., haunts me as a labour impossible to be got through. So much the springs of action are broken.

The same cowardice attends me in all my intercourse with mankind. I dare not promise that a friend's honour, or his cause, would be safe in my keeping, if I were put to the expense of any manly resolution in defending it. So much the springs of moral action are deadened within me.

My favourite occupations in times past now cease to entertain. I can do nothing readily. Application for ever so short a time kills me. This poor abstract of my condition was penned at long intervals, with scarcely any attempt at connexion of thought, which is now difficult to me.

The noble passages which formerly delighted me in history or poetic fiction, now only draw a few weak tears, allied to dotage. My broken and dispirited nature seems to sink before anything great and admirable.

I perpetually catch myself in tears, for any cause, or none. It is inexpressible how much this infirmity adds to a sense of shame, and a general feeling of deterioration.

These are some of the instances, concerning which I can say with truth, that it was not always so with me.

Shall I lift up the veil of my weakness any further?—or is this disclosure sufficient?

I am a poor nameless egotist, who have no vanity to consult by these Confessions. I know not whether I shall be laughed at, or heard seriously. Such as they are, I commend them to the reader's attention, if he find his own case any way touched. I have told him what I am come to. Let him stop in time.

POPULAR FALLACIES

I.—THAT A BULLY IS ALWAYS A COWARD

THIS axiom contains a principle of compensation, which disposes us to admit the truth of it. But there is no safe trusting to dictionaries and definitions. We should more willingly fall in with this popular language, if we did not find *brutality* sometimes awkwardly coupled with *valour* in the same vocabulary. The comic writers, with their poetical justice, have contributed not a little to mislead us upon this point. To see a hectoring fellow exposed and beaten upon the stage, has something in it wonderfully diverting. Some people's share of animal 'spirits is notoriously low and defective. It has not strength to raise a vapour, or furnish out the wind of a tolerable bluster. These love to be told that huffing is no part of valour. The truest courage with them is that which is the least noisy and obtrusive. But confront one of these silent heroes with the swaggerer of real life, and his confidence in the theory quickly vanishes. Pretensions do not uniformly bespeak non-performance. A modest, inoffensive deportment docs not necessarily imply valour; neither does the absence of it justify us in denying that quality. Hickman wanted modesty —we do not mean *him* of Clarissa—but who ever doubted his courage? Even the poets—upon whom this equitable distribution of qualities should be most binding—have thought it agreeable to nature to depart from the rule upon occasion. Harapha, in the Agonistes, is indeed a bully upon the received notions. Milton has made him at once a blusterer, a giant, and a dastard. But Almanzor, in Dryden, talks of driving armies singly before him—and does it. Tom Brown had a shrewder insight into this kind of character than either of his predecessors. He divides the palm more equably, and allows his hero a sort of dimidiate pre-eminence: —"Bully Dawson kicked by half the town, and half the town kicked by Bully Dawson." This was true distributive justice.

II.—THAT ILL-GOTTEN GAIN NEVER PROSPERS

The weakest part of mankind have this saying commonest in their mouth. It is the trite consolation administered to the easy dupe, when he has been tricked out of his money or estate, that the acquisition of it will do the owner *no good*. But the rogues of this world—the prudenter part of them, at least,—know better; and if the observation had been as true as it is old, would not have failed by this time to have discovered it. They have pretty sharp distinctions of the fluctuating and the permanent. "Lightly come, lightly go," is a proverb, which they can very well afford to leave, when they leave little else, to the losers. They do not always find manors, got by rapine or chicanery, insensibly to melt away, as the poets will have it; or that all gold glides, like thawing snow, from the thief's hand that grasps it. Church land, alienated to lay uses, was formerly denounced to have this slippery quality. But some portions of it somehow always stuck so fast, that the denunciators have been fain to postpone the prophecy of refundment to a late posterity.

III.—THAT A MAN MUST NOT LAUGH AT HIS OWN JEST

The severest exaction surely ever invented upon the self-denial of poor human nature! This is to expect a gentleman to give a treat without partaking of it; to sit esurient at his own table, and commend the flavour of his venison upon the absurd strength of his never touching it himself. On the contrary, we love to see a wag *taste* his own joke to his party; to watch a quirk or a merry conceit flickering upon the lips some seconds before the tongue is delivered of it. If it be good, fresh, and racy—begotten of the occasion; if he that utters it never thought it before, he is naturally the first to be tickled with it; and any suppression of such complacence we hold to be churlish and insulting. What does it seem to imply but that your company is weak or foolish enough to be moved by an image or a fancy, that shall stir you not at all, or but faintly? This is exactly the humour of the fine gentleman in Mandeville, who, while he dazzles his guests with the display of some costly toy, affects himself to "see nothing considerable in it."

IV.—THAT SUCH A ONE SHOWS HIS BREEDING—THAT IT IS EASY TO PERCEIVE HE IS NO GENTLEMAN

A speech from the poorest sort of people, which always indicates that the party vituperated is a gentleman. The very fact which they deny is that which galls and exasperates them to use this language. The forbearance with which it is usually received is a proof what interpretation the bystander sets upon it. Of a kin to this, and still less politic, are the phrases with which, in their street rhetoric, they ply one another more grossly;—*He is a poor creature.—He has not a rag to cover*——*etc.;* though this last, we confess, is more frequently applied by females to females. They do not perceive that the satire glances upon themselves. A poor man, of all things in the world, should not upbraid an antagonist with poverty. Are there no other topics—as, to tell him his father was hanged—his sister, etc.——, without exposing a secret which should be kept snug between them; and doing an affront to the order to which they have the honour equally to belong? All this while they do not see how the wealthier man stands by and laughs in his sleeve at both.

V.—THAT THE POOR COPY THE VICES OF THE RICH

A smooth text to the letter; and, preached from the pulpit, is sure of a docile audience from the pews lined with satin. It is twice sitting upon velvet to a foolish squire to be told, that *he*—and not *perverse nature,* as the homilies would make us imagine, is the true cause of all the irregularities in his parish. This is striking at the root of free-will indeed, and denying the originality of sin in any sense. But men are not such implicit sheep as this comes to. If the abstinence from evil on the part of the upper classes is to derive itself from no higher principle than the apprehension of setting ill patterns to the lower, we beg leave to discharge them from all squeamishness on that score: they may even take their fill of pleasures, where they can find them. The Genius of Poverty, hampered and straitened as it is, is not so barren of invention, but it can trade upon the staple of its own vice, without drawing upon their capital. The poor are not quite such servile imitators as they take them for. Some of them are very clever artists in their way. Here and there we find an original. Who taught the poor to steal, to pilfer? They did not go to the great for schoolmasters in these faculties, surely. It is well if in some vices they allow us to be—no copyists. In no other sense is it true that the poor copy them, than as servants may be said to *take after* their masters and mistresses, when they succeed to their reversionary cold meats. If the master, from indisposition, or some other cause, neglect his food, the servant dines notwithstanding.

"O, but (some will say) the force of example is great." We knew a lady who was so scrupulous on this head, that she would put up with the calls of the most impertinent visitor, rather than let her servant say she was not at home, for fear of teaching her maid to tell an untruth; and this in the very face of the fact, which she knew well enough, that the wench was one of the greatest liars upon the earth without teaching; so much so, that her mistress possibly never heard two words of consecutive truth from her in her life. But nature must go for nothing: example must be everything. This liar in grain, who never opened her mouth without a lie, must be guarded against a remote inference, which she (pretty casuist!) might possibly draw from a form of words—literally false, but essentially deceiving no one—that under some circumstances a fib might not be so exceedingly sinful—a fiction, too, not at all in her own way, or one that she could be suspected of adopting, for few servant-wenches care to be denied to visitors.

This word *example* reminds us of another fine word which is in use upon these occasions—*encouragement*. "People in our sphere must not be thought to give encouragement to such proceedings." To such a frantic height is this principle capable of being carried, that we have known individuals who have thought it within the scope of their influence to sanction despair, and give *éclat* to—suicide. A domestic in the family of a county member lately deceased, from love, or some unknown cause, cut his throat, but not successfully. The poor fellow was otherwise much loved and respected; and great interest was used in his behalf, upon his recovery, that he might be permitted to retain his place; his word being first pledged, not without some substantial sponsors to promise for him, that the like should never happen again. His master was inclinable to keep him, but his mistress thought otherwise; and John in the end was dismissed, her ladyship declaring that she "could not think of encouraging any such doings in the county."

VI.—THAT ENOUGH IS AS GOOD AS A FEAST

Not a man, woman, or child, in ten miles round Guildhall, who really believes this saying. The inventor of it did not believe it himself. It was made in revenge by somebody, who was disappointed of a regale. It is a vile cold-scrag-of-mutton sophism; a lie palmed upon the palate, which knows better things. If nothing else could be said for a feast, this is sufficient, that from the superflux there is usually something left for the next day. Morally interpreted, it belongs to a class of proverbs which have a tendency to make us undervalue *money*. Of this cast are those notable observations, that money is not health; riches cannot purchase everything: the metaphor which makes gold to be mere muck, with the morality which traces fine clothing to the sheep's back, and denounces pearl as the unhandsome excretion of an oyster. Hence, too, the phrase which imputes dirt to acres—a sophistry so barefaced, that even the literal sense of it is true only in a wet season. This, and abundance of similar sage saws assuming to inculcate *content*, we verily believe to have been the invention of some cunning borrower, who had designs upon the purse of his wealthier neighbor, which he could only hope to carry by force of these verbal jugglings. Translate any one of these sayings out of the artful metonymy which envelops it, and the trick is apparent. Goodly legs and shoulders of mutton, exhilarating cordials, books, pictures, the opportunities of seeing foreign countries, independence, heart's ease, a man's own time to himself, are not *muck*—however we may be pleased to scandalise with that appellation the faithful metal that provides them for us.

VII.—OF TWO DISPUTANTS THE WARMEST IS GENERALLY IN THE WRONG

Our experience would lead us to quite an opposite conclusion. Temper, indeed, is no test of truth; but warmth and earnestness are a proof at least of a man's own conviction of the rectitude of that which he maintains. Coolness is as often the result of an unprincipled indifference to truth or falsehood, as of a sober confidence in a man's own side in a dispute. Nothing is more insulting sometimes than the appearance of this philosophic temper. There is little Titubus, the stammering law-stationer in Lincoln's Inn—we have seldom known this shrewd little fellow engaged in an argument where we were not convinced he had the best of it, if his tongue would but fairly have seconded him. When he has been spluttering excellent broken sense for an hour together, writhing and labouring to be delivered of the point of dispute—the very gist of the controversy knocking at his teeth, which like some obstinate iron-grating still obstructed its deliverance—his puny frame convulsed, and face reddening all over at an unfairness in the logic which he wanted articulation to expose, it has moved our gall to see a smooth portly fellow of an adversary, that cared not a button for the merits of the question, by merely laying his hand upon the head of the stationer, and desiring him to be

calm (your tall disputants have always the advantage), with a provoking sneer carry the argument clean from him in the opinion of all the
bystanders, who have gone away clearly convinced that Titubus must
have been in the wrong, because he was in a passion; and that Mr. ——,
meaning his opponent, is one of the fairest and at the same time one of
the most dispassionate arguers breathing.

VIII.—THAT VERBAL ALLUSIONS ARE NOT WIT, BECAUSE THEY WILL NOT BEAR A TRANSLATION

The same might be said of the wittiest local allusions. A custom is
sometimes as difficult to explain to a foreigner as a pun. What would become of a great part of the wit of the last age, if it were tried by this
test? How would certain topics, as aldermanity, cuckoldry, have sounded to a Terentian auditory, though Terence himself had been alive to
translate them? *Senator urbanus* with *Curruca* to boot for a synonym,
would but faintly have done the business. Words, involving notions, are
hard enough to render; it is too much to expect us to translate a sound,
and give an elegant version to a jingle. The Virgilian harmony is not
translatable, but by substituting harmonious sounds in another language
for it. To Latinise a pun, we must seek a pun in Latin that will answer
to it; as, to give an idea of the double endings in Hudibras, we must have
recourse to a similar practice in the old monkish doggerel. Dennis, the
fiercest oppugner of puns in ancient or modern times, professes himself
highly tickled with the "a stick," chiming to "ecclesiastic." Yet what
is this but a species of pun, a verbal consonance?

IX.—THAT THE WORST PUNS ARE THE BEST

If by worst be only meant the most far-fetched and startling, we agree
to it. A pun is not bound by the laws which limit nicer wit. It is a pistol
let off at the ear; not a feather to tickle the intellect. It is an antic
which does not stand upon manners, but comes bounding into the presence, and does not show the less comic for being dragged in sometimes
by the head and shoulders. What though it limp a little, or prove defective in one leg?—all the better. A pun may easily be too curious and
artificial. Who has not at one time or other been at a party of professors
(himself perhaps an old offender in that line), where, after ringing a
round of the most ingenious conceits, every man contributing his shot,
and some there the most expert shooters of the day; after making a poor
word run the gauntlet till it is ready to drop; after hunting and winding
it through all the possible ambages of similar sounds; after squeezing,
and hauling, and tugging at it, till the very milk of it will not yield a drop
further,—suddenly some obscure, unthought-of fellow in a corner, who
was never 'prentice to the trade, whom the company for very pity passed
over, as we do by a known poor man when a money-subscription is going
round, no one calling upon him for his quota—has all at once come out
with something so whimsical, yet so pertinent; so brazen in its preten-

sions, yet so impossible to be denied; so exquisitely good, and so de-
plorably bad, at the same time,—that it has proved a Robin Hood's
shot; anything ulterior to that is despaired of; and the party breaks up,
unanimously voting it to be the very worst (that is, best) pun of the
evening. This species of wit is the better for not being perfect in all its
parts. What it gains in completeness, it loses in naturalness. The more
exactly it satisfies the critical, the less hold it has upon some other faculties. The puns which are most entertaining are those which will least
bear an analysis. Of this kind is the following, recorded with a sort of
stigma, in one of Swift's Miscellanies.

An Oxford scholar, meeting a porter who was carrying a hare through
the streets, accosts him with this extraordinary question: "Prithee,
friend, is that thy own hare, or a wig?"

There is no excusing this, and no resisting it. A man might blur ten
sides of paper in attempting a defence of it against a critic who should
be laughter-proof. The quibble in itself is not considerable. It is only a
new turn given by a little false pronunciation, to a very common, though
not very courteous inquiry. Put by one gentleman to another at a dinner-
party, it would have been vapid; to the mistress of the house it would
have shown much less wit than rudeness. We must take in the totality of
time, place, and person; the pert look of the inquiring scholar, the desponding looks of the puzzled porter: the one stopping at leisure, the
other hurrying on with his burden; the innocent though rather abrupt
tendency of the first member of the question, with the utter and inextricable irrelevancy of the second; the place—a public street, not favourable to frivolous investigations; the affrontive quality of the primitive
inquiry (the common question) invidiously transferred to the derivative
(the new turn given to it) in the implied satire; namely, that few of that
tribe are expected to eat of the good things which they carry, they being
in most countries considered rather as the temporary trustees than owners of such dainties,—which the fellow was beginning to understand; but
then the *wig* again comes in, and he can make nothing of it; all put together constitute a picture: Hogarth could have made it intelligible on
canvas.

Yet nine out of ten critics will pronounce this a very bad pun, because
of the defectiveness in the concluding member, which is its very beauty,
and constitutes the surprise. The same person shall cry up for admirable
the cold quibble from Virgil about the broken Cremona[1]; because it is
made out in all its parts, and leaves nothing to the imagination. We venture to call it cold; because, of thousands who have admired it, it would
be difficult to find one who has heartily chuckled at it. As appealing to
the judgment merely (setting the risible faculty aside), we must pronounce it a monument of curious felicity. But as some stories are said
to be too good to be true, it may with equal truth be asserted of this bi-
verbal allusion, that it is too good to be natural. One cannot help suspecting that the incident was invented to fit the line. It would have been

[1] Swift.

better had it been less perfect. Like some Virgilian hemistichs, it has suffered by filling up. The *nimium Vicina* was enough in conscience; the *Cremonæ* afterwards loads it. It is, in fact, a double pun; and we have always observed that a superfœtation in this sort of wit is dangerous. When a man has said a good thing, it is seldom politic to follow it up. We do not care to be cheated a second time; or, perhaps the mind of man (with reverence be it spoken) is not capacious enough to lodge two puns at a time. The impression, to be forcible, must be simultaneous and undivided.

X.—THAT HANDSOME IS THAT HANDSOME DOES

Those who use this proverb can never have seen Mrs. Conrady.

The soul, if we may believe Plotinus, is a ray from the celestial beauty. As she partakes more or less of this heavenly light, she informs, with corresponding characters, the fleshly tenement which she chooses, and frames to herself a suitable mansion.

All which only proves that the soul of Mrs. Conrady, in her pre-existent state, was no great judge of architecture.

To the same effect, in a Hymn in honour of Beauty, divine Spenser *platonising,* sings:—

> ———Every spirit as it is more pure,
> And hath in it the more of heavenly light,
> So it the fairer body doth procure
> To habit in, and it more fairly dight
> With cheerful grace and amiable sight.
> For of the soul the body form doth take:
> For soul is form and doth the body make.

But Spenser, it is clear, never saw Mrs. Conrady.

These poets, we find, are no safe guides in philosophy; for here, in his very next stanza but one, is a saving clause, which throws us all out again, and leaves us as much to seek as ever:—

> Yet oft it falls, that many a gentle mind
> Dwells in deformed tabernacle drown'd,
> Either by chance, against the course of kind,
> Or through unaptness in the substance found,
> Which it assumed of some stubborn ground,
> That will not yield unto her form's direction,
> But is performed with some foul imperfection.

From which it would follow, that Spenser had seen somebody like Mrs. Conrady.

The spirit of this good lady—her previous *anima*—must have stumbled upon one of these untoward tabernacles which he speaks of. A more rebellious commodity of clay for a ground, as the poet calls it, no gentle mind—and sure hers is one of the gentlest—ever had to deal with.

Pondering upon her inexplicable visage—inexplicable, we mean, but by this modification of the theory—we have come to a conclusion that, if one must be plain, it is better to be plain all over, than amidst a tolerable residue of features, to hang out one that shall be exceptionable. No one can say of Mrs. Conrady's countenance that it would be better if she had but a nose. It is impossible to pull her to pieces in this manner. We have seen the most malicious beauties of her own sex baffled in the attempt at a selection. The *tout-ensemble* defies particularising. It is too complete—too consistent, as we may say—to admit of these invidious reservations. It is not as if some Apelles had picked out here a lip—and there a chin—out of the collected ugliness of Greece, to frame a model by. It is a symmetrical whole. We challenge the minutest connoisseur to cavil at any part or parcel of the countenance in question; to say that this, or that, is improperly placed. We are convinced that true ugliness, no less than is affirmed of true beauty, is the result of harmony. Like that, too, it reigns without a competitor. No one ever saw Mrs. Conrady, without pronouncing her to be the plainest woman that he ever met with in the course of his life. The first time that you are indulged with a sight of her face, is an era in your existence ever after. You are glad to have seen it—like Stonehenge. No one can pretend to forget it. No one ever apologised to her for meeting her in the street on such a day and not knowing her: the pretext would be too bare. Nobody can mistake her for another. Nobody can say of her, "I think I have seen that face somewhere, but I cannot call to mind where." You must remember that in such a parlour it first struck you—like a bust. You wondered where the owner of the house had picked it up. You wondered more when it began to move its lips—so mildly too! No one ever thought of asking her to sit for her picture. Lockets are for remembrance; and it would be clearly superfluous to hang an image at your heart, which, once seen, can never be out of it. It is not a mean face either; its entire originality precludes that. Neither is it of that order of plain faces which improve upon acquaintance. Some very good but ordinary people, by an unwearied perseverance in good offices, put a cheat upon our eyes; juggle our senses out of their natural impressions; and set us upon discovering good indications in a countenance, which at first sight promised nothing less. We detect gentleness, which had escaped us, lurking about an under lip. But when Mrs. Conrady has done you a service, her face remains the same; when she has done you a thousand, and you know that she is ready to double the number, still it is that individual face. Neither can you say of it, that it would be a good face if it were not marked by the small-pox—a compliment which is always more admissive than excusatory—for either Mrs. Conrady never had the small-pox; or, as we say, took it kindly. No, it stands upon its own merits fairly. There it is. It is her mark, her token; that which she is known by.

XI.—THAT WE MUST NOT LOOK A GIFT HORSE IN THE MOUTH

Nor a lady's age in the parish register. We hope we have more delicacy than to do either; but some faces spare us the trouble of these *dental* inquiries. And what if the beast, which my friend would force upon my acceptance, prove, upon the face of it, a sorry Rosinante, a lean, ill-favoured jade, whom no gentleman could think of setting up in his stables? Must I, rather than not be obliged to my friend, make her a companion to Eclipse or Lightfoot? A horse-giver, no more than a horse-seller, has a right to palm his spavined article upon us for good ware. An equivalent is expected in either case; and, with my own good-will, I would no more be cheated out of my thanks than out of my money. Some people have a knack of putting upon you gifts of no real value, to engage you to substantial gratitude. We thank them for nothing. Our friend Mitis carries this humour of never refusing a present, to the very point of absurdity—if it were possible to couple the ridiculous with so much mistaken delicacy, and real good-nature. Not an apartment in his fine house (and he has a true taste in household decorations), but is stuffed up with some preposterous print or mirror—the worst adapted to his panels that may be—the presents of his friends that know his weakness; while his noble Vandykes are displaced, to make room for a set of daubs, the work of some wretched artist of his acquaintance, who, having had them returned upon his hands for bad likenesses, finds his account in bestowing them here gratis. The good creature has not the heart to mortify the painter at the expense of an honest refusal. It is pleasant (if it did not vex one at the same time) to see him sitting in his dining parlour, surrounded with obscure aunts and cousins to God knows whom, while the true Lady Marys and Lady Bettys of his own honourable family, in favour to these adopted frights, are consigned to the staircase and the lumber-room. In like manner his goodly shelves are one by one stripped of his favourite old authors, to give place to a collection of presentation copies—the flour and bran of modern poetry. A presentation copy, reader—if haply you are yet innocent of such favours—is a copy of a book which does not sell, sent you by the author, with his foolish autograph at the beginning of it; for which, if a stranger, he only demands your friendship; if a brother author, he expects from you a book of yours, which does sell, in return. We can speak to experience, having by us a tolerable assortment of these gift-horses. Not to ride a metaphor to death —we are willing to acknowledge, that in some gifts there is sense. A duplicate out of a friend's library (where he has more than one copy of a rare author) is intelligible. There are favours, short of the pecuniary— a thing not fit to be hinted at among gentlemen—which confer as much grace upon the acceptor as the offerer; the kind, we confess, which is most to our palate, is of those little conciliatory missives, which for their vehicle generally choose a hamper—little odd presents of game, fruit, perhaps wine—though it is essential to the delicacy of the latter, that it be home-made. We love to have our friend in the country sitting thus at our table by proxy; to apprehend his presence (though a hundred miles may be between us) by a turkey, whose goodly aspect reflects to us his "plump corpusculum"; to taste him in grouse or woodcock; to feel him gliding down in the toast peculiar to the latter; to concorporate him in a slice of Canterbury brawn. This is indeed to have him within ourselves;

to know him intimately: such participation is methinks unitive, as the old theologians phrase it. For these considerations we should be sorry if certain restrictive regulations, which are thought to bear hard upon the peasantry of this country, were entirely done away with. A hare, as the law now stands, makes many friends. Caius conciliates Titius (knowing his *goût*) with a leash of partridges. Titius (suspecting his partiality for them) passes them to Lucius; who, in his turn, preferring his friend's relish to his own, makes them over to Marcius; till in their ever-widening progress, and round of unconscious circummigration, they distribute the seeds of harmony over half a parish. We are well-disposed to this kind of sensible remembrances; and are the less apt to be taken by those little airy tokens—impalpable to the palate—which, under the names of rings, lockets, keep-sakes, amuse some peoples' fancy mightily. We could never away with these indigestible trifles. They are the very kick-shaws and foppery of friendship.

XII.—THAT HOME IS HOME THOUGH IT IS NEVER SO HOMELY

Homes there are, we are sure, that are no homes; the home of the very poor man, and another which we shall speak to presently. Crowded places of cheap entertainment, and the benches of alehouses, if they could speak, might bear mournful testimony to the first. To them the very poor man resorts for an image of the home, which he cannot find at home. For a starved grate, and a scanty firing, that is not enough to keep alive the natural heat in the fingers of so many shivering children with their mother, he finds in the depths of winter always a blazing hearth, and a hob to warm his pittance of beer by. Instead of the clamours of a wife, made gaunt by famishing, he meets with a cheerful attendance beyond the merits of the trifle which he can afford to spend. He has companions which his home denies him, for the very poor man has no visitors. He can look into the goings on of the world, and speak a little to politics. At home there are no politics stirring, but the domestic. All interests, real or imaginary, all topics that should expand the mind of man, and connect him to a sympathy with general existence, are crushed in the absorbing consideration of food to be obtained for the family. Beyond the price of bread, news is senseless and impertinent. At home there is no larder. Here there is at least a show of plenty; and while he cooks his lean scrap of butcher's meat before the common bars, or munches his humbler cold viands, his relishing bread and cheese with an onion, in a corner, where no one reflects upon his poverty, he has a sight of the substantial joint providing for the landlord and his family. He takes an interest in the dressing of it; and while he assists in removing the trivet from the fire, he feels that there is such a thing as beef and cabbage, which he was beginning to forget at home. All this while he deserts his wife and children. But what wife, and what children? Prosperous men, who object to this desertion, image to themselves some clean contented family like that which they go home to. But look at the countenance of the poor wives who follow and persecute their good-man to the door of the public-house, which he is about to enter, when something like shame would restrain him, if stronger misery did not induce him to pass the threshold. That face, ground by want, in which every cheerful, every conversable lineament has been long effaced by misery,—is that a face to stay at home with? is it more a woman, or a wild cat? alas! it is the face of the wife of his youth, that once smiled upon him. It can smile no longer. What comforts can it share? what burthens can it lighten? Oh, 'tis a fine thing to talk of the humble meal shared together! But what if there be no bread in the cupboard? The innocent prattle of his children takes out the sting of a man's poverty. But the children of the very poor do not prattle. It is none of the least frightful features in that condition, that there is no childishness in its dwellings. Poor people, said a sensible old nurse to us once, do not bring up their children; they drag them up.

The little careless darling of the wealthier nursery, in their hovel is transformed betimes into a premature reflecting person. No one has time to dandle it, no one thinks it worth while to coax it, to soothe it, to toss it up and down, to humour it. There is none to kiss away its tears. If it cries, it can only be beaten. It has been prettily said, that "a babe is fed with milk and praise." But the aliment of this poor babe was thin, unnourishing; the return to its little baby-tricks, and efforts to engage attention, bitter ceaseless objurgation. It never had a toy, or knew what a coral meant. It grew up without the lullaby of nurses, it was a stranger to the patient fondle, the hushing caress, the attracting novelty, the costlier plaything, or the cheaper off-hand contrivance to divert the child; the prattled nonsense (best sense to it), the wise impertinences, the wholesome lies, the apt story interposed that puts a stop to present sufferings, and awakens the passions of young wonder. It was never sung to—no one ever told to it a tale of the nursery. It was dragged up, to live or to die as it happened. It had no young dreams. It broke at once into the iron realities of life. A child exists not for the very poor as any object of dalliance; it is only another mouth to be fed, a pair of little hands to be betimes inured to labour. It is the rival, till it can be the co-operator, for food with the parent. It is never his mirth, his diversion, his solace: it never makes him young again, with recalling his young times. The children of the very poor have no young times. It makes the very heart to bleed to overhear the casual street-talk between a poor woman and her little girl, a woman of the better sort of poor, in a condition rather above the squalid beings which we have been contemplating. It is not of toys, of nursery books, of summer holidays (fitting that age); of the promised sight, or play; of praised sufficiency at school. It is of mangling and clear-starching, of the price of coals, or of potatoes. The questions of the child, that should be the very outpourings of curiosity in idleness, are marked with forecast and melancholy providence. It has come to be a woman,—before it was a child. It has learned to go to market; it chaffers, it haggles, it envies, it murmurs; it is knowing, acute, sharpened; it never prattles. Had we not reason to say that the home of the very poor is no home?

There is yet another home, which we are constrained to deny to be one. It has a larder, which the home of the poor man wants; its fireside conveniences, of which the poor dream not. But with all this, it is no home. It is—the house of a man that is infested with many visitors. May we be branded for the veriest churl, if we deny our heart to the many noble-hearted friends that at times exchange their dwelling for our poor roof! It is not of guests that we complain, but of endless, purposeless visitants; droppers-in, as they are called. We sometimes wonder from what sky they fall. It is the very error of the position of our lodging; its horoscopy was ill calculated, being just situate in a medium—a plaguy suburban mid-space—fitted to catch idlers from town or country. We are older than we were, and age is easily put out of its way. We have fewer sands in our glass to reckon upon, and we cannot brook to see them drop in endlessly succeeding impertinences. At our time of life, to be alone sometimes is as needful as sleep. It is the refreshing sleep of the day. The growing infirmities of age manifest themselves in nothing more strongly, than in an inveterate dislike of interruption. The thing which we are doing, we wish to be permitted to do. We have neither much knowledge nor devices; but there are fewer in the place to which we hasten. We are not willingly put out of our way, even at a game of nine-pins. While youth was, we had vast reversions in time future; we are reduced to a present pittance, and obliged to economise in that article. We bleed away our moments now as hardly as our ducats. We cannot bear to have our thin wardrobe eaten and fretted into by moths. We are willing to barter our good time with a friend, who gives us in exchange his own. Herein is the distinction between the genuine guest and the visitant. This latter takes your good time, and gives you his bad in exchange. The guest is domestic to you as your good cat, or household bird; the visitant is your fly, that flaps in at your window, and out again, leaving nothing but a sense of disturbance, and victuals spoiled. The inferior functions of life begin to move heavily. We cannot concoct our food with interruptions. Our chief meal, to be nutritive, must be solitary. With difficulty we can eat before a guest; and never understood what the relish of public feasting meant. Meats have no sapor, nor digestion fair play, in a crowd. The unexpected coming in of a visitant stops the machine. There is a punctual generation who time their calls to the precise commencement of your dining-hour—not to eat—but to see you eat. Our knife and fork drop instinctively, and we feel that we have swallowed our latest morsel. Others again show their genius, as we have said, in knocking the moment you have just sat down to a book. They have a peculiar compassionate sneer, with which they "hope that they do not interrupt your studies." Though they flutter off the next moment, to carry their impertinences to the nearest student that they can call their friend, the tone of the book is spoiled; we shut the leaves, and with Dante's lovers, read no more that day. It were well if the effect of intrusion were simply co-extensive with its presence, but it mars all the good hours afterwards. These scratches in appearance leave an orifice that closes not hastily. "It is a prostitution of the bravery of friendship," says worthy Bishop Taylor, "to spend it upon impertinent people, who are, it may be, loads to their families, but can never ease my loads." This is the secret of their gaddings, their visits, and morning calls. They too have homes, which are—no homes.

XIII.— THAT YOU MUST LOVE ME AND LOVE MY DOG

"Good sir, or madam—as it may be—we most willingly embrace the offer of your friendship. We have long known your excellent qualities. We have wished to have you nearer to us; to hold you within the very innermost fold of our heart. We can have no reserve towards a person of your open and noble nature. The frankness of your humour suits us exactly. We have been long looking for such a friend. Quick—let us disburthen our troubles into each other's bosom—let us make our single joys shine by reduplication—But *yap, yap, yap!* what is this confounded cur? he has fastened his tooth, which is none of the bluntest, just in the fleshy part of my leg."

"It is my dog, sir. You must love him for my sake. Here, Test—Test —Test!"

"But he has bitten me."

"Ay, that he is apt to do, till you are better acquainted with him. I have had him three years. He never bites me."

Yap, yap, yap!—"He is at it again."

"Oh, sir, you must not kick him. He does not like to be kicked. I expect my dog to be treated with all the respect due to myself."

"But do you always take him out with you, when you go a friendship-hunting?"

"Invariably. 'Tis the sweetest, prettiest, best-conditioned animal. I call him my *test*—the touchstone by which to try a friend. No one can properly be said to love me, who does not love him."

"Excuse us, dear sir—or madam, aforesaid—if upon further consideration we are obliged to decline the otherwise invaluable offer of your friendship. We do not like dogs."

"Mighty well, sir,—you know the conditions—you may have worse offers. Come along, Test."

The above dialogue is not so imaginary, but that, in the intercourse of life, we have had frequent occasions of breaking off an agreeable intimacy by reason of these canine appendages. They do not always come in the shape of dogs; they sometimes wear the more plausible and human character of kinsfolk, near acquaintances, my friend's friend, his partner, his wife, or his children. We could never yet form a friendship—not to speak of more delicate correspondence—however much to our taste, without the intervention of some third anomaly, some impertinent clog affixed to the relation—the understood *dog* in the proverb. The good things of life are not to be had singly, but come to us with a mixture; like a schoolboy's holiday, with a task affixed to the tail of it. What a delightful companion is * * * *, if he did not always bring his tall cousin with him! He seems to grow with him; like some of those double births which we remember to have read of with such wonder and delight in the old "Athenian Oracle," where Swift commenced author by writing Pindaric Odes (what a beginning for him!) upon Sir William Temple. There is the picture of the brother, with the little brother peeping out at his shoulder; a species of fraternity, which we have no name of kin close enough to comprehend. When * * * * comes, poking in his head and shoulder into your room, as if to feel his entry, you think, surely you have now got him to yourself—what a three hours' chat we shall have!— but ever in the haunch of him, and before his diffident body is well disclosed in your apartment, appears the haunting shadow of the cousin, overpeering his modest kinsman, and sure to overlay the expected good talk with his insufferable procerity of stature, and uncorresponding dwarfishness of observation. Misfortunes seldom come alone. 'Tis hard when a blessing comes accompanied. Cannot we like Sempronia, without sitting down to chess with her eternal brother; or know Sulpicia, without knowing all the round of her card-playing relations?—must my friend's brethren of necessity be mine also? must we be hand and glove with Dick Selby the parson, or Jack Selby the calico-printer, because W. S., who is neither, but a ripe wit and a critic, has the misfortune to claim a common parentage with them? Let him lay down his brothers; and 'tis odds that we will cast him in a pair of ours (we have a superflux) to balance the concession. Let F. H. lay down his garrulous uncle; and Honorius dismiss his vapid wife, and superfluous establishment of six boys: things between boy and manhood—too ripe for play, too raw for conversation—that come in, impudently staring their father's old friend out of countenance; and will neither aid nor let alone, the conference; that we may once more meet upon equal terms, as we were wont to do in the disengaged state of bachelorhood.

It is well if your friend, or mistress, be content with these canicular probations. Few young ladies but in this sense keep a dog. But while Rutilia hounds at you her tiger aunt; or Ruspina expects you to cherish and fondle her viper sister, whom she has preposterously taken into her bosom, to try stinging conclusions upon your constancy; they must not complain if the house be rather thin of suitors. Scylla must have broken off many excellent matches in her time, if she insisted upon all, that loved her, loving her dogs also.

An excellent story to this moral is told of Merry, of Della Cruscan memory. In tender youth he loved and courted a modest appanage to the Opera—in truth a dancer,—who had won him by the artless contrast between her manners and situation. She seemed to him a native violet, that had been transplanted by some rude accident, into that exotic and artificial hotbed. Nor, in truth, was she less genuine and sincere than she appeared to him. He wooed and won this flower. Only for appearance' sake, and for due honour to the bride's relations, she craved that she might have the attendance of her friends and kindred at the approaching solemnity. The request was too amiable not to be conceded: and in this solicitude for conciliating the good-will of mere relations, he found a presage of her superior attentions to himself, when the golden shaft should have "killed the flock of all affections else." The morning came: and at the Star and Garter, Richmond—the place appointed for the breakfasting—accompanied with one English friend, he impatiently awaited what reinforcements the bride should bring to grace the ceremony. A rich muster she had made. They came in six coaches—the whole corps du ballet—French, Italian, men and women. Monsieur de B., the famous *pirouetter* of the day, led his fair spouse, but craggy, from the banks of the Seine. The Prima Donna had sent her excuse. But the first and second Buffa were there; and Signor Sc—, and Signora Ch—, and Madame V—, with a countless cavalcade besides of chorusers, figurantes! at the sight of whom Merry afterwards declared, that "then for the first time it struck him seriously, that he was about to marry—a dancer." But there was no help for it. Besides, it was her day; these were, in fact, her friends and kinsfolk. The assemblage, though whimsical, was all very natural. But when the bride—handing out of the last coach a still more extraordinary figure than the rest—presented to him as her *father*—the gentleman that was to *give her away*—no less a person than Signor Delpini himself—with a sort of pride, as much as to say, See what I have brought to do us honour!—the thought of so extraordinary a paternity quite overcame him; and slipping away under some pretence from the bride and her motley adherents, poor Merry took horse from the back yard to the nearest sea-coast, from which, shipping himself to America, he shortly after consoled himself with a more congenial match in the person of Miss Brunton; relieved from his intended clown father, and a bevy of painted buffas for bridesmaids.

XIV.—THAT WE SHOULD RISE WITH THE LARK

At what precise minute that little airy musician doffs his night-gear, and prepares to tune up his unseasonable matins, we are not naturalists enough to determine. But for a mere human gentleman—that has no orchestra business to call him from his warm bed to such preposterous exercises—we take ten, or half after ten (eleven, of course, during this Christmas solstice), to be the very earliest hour at which he can begin to think of abandoning his pillow. To think of it, we say; for to do it in earnest requires another half hour's good consideration. Not but there are pretty sun-risings, as we are told, and such like gawds, abroad in the world, in summer-time especially, some hours before what we have assigned; which a gentleman may see, as they say, only for getting up. But having been tempted once or twice, in earlier life, to assist at those ceremonies, we confess our curiosity abated. We are no longer ambitious of being the sun's courtiers, to attend at his morning levees. We hold the good hours of the dawn too sacred to waste them upon such observances; which have in them, besides, something Pagan and Persic. To say truth, we never anticipated our usual hour, or got up with the sun (as 'tis called), to go a journey, or upon a foolish whole day's pleasuring, but we suffered for it all the long hours after in listlessness and headaches; Nature herself sufficiently declaring her sense of our presumption in aspiring to regulate our frail waking courses by the measures of that celestial and sleepless traveller. We deny not that there is something sprightly and vigorous, at the outset especially, in these break-of-day excursions. It is flattering to get the start of a lazy world; to conquer death by proxy in his image. But the seeds of sleep and mortality are in us; and we pay usually, in strange qualms before night falls, the penalty of the unnatural inversion. Therefore, while the busy part of mankind are fast huddling on their clothes, are already up and about their occupations, content to have swallowed their sleep by wholesale; we choose to linger a-bed, and digest our dreams. It is the very time to recombine the wandering images, which night in a confused mass presented; to snatch them from forgetfulness; to shape, and mould them. Some people have no good of their dreams. Like fast feeders, they gulp them too grossly, to taste them curiously. We love to chew the cud of a foregone vision: to collect the scattered rays of a brighter phantasm, or act over again, with firmer nerves, the sadder nocturnal tragedies; to drag into day-light a struggling and half-vanishing night-mare; to handle and examine the terrors, or the airy solaces. We have too much respect for these spiritual communications, to let them go so lightly. We are not so stupid, or so careless as that Imperial forgetter of his dreams, that we should need a seer to remind us of the form of them. They seem to us to have as much significance as our waking concerns: or rather to import us more nearly, as more nearly we approach by years to the shadowy world, whither we are hastening. We have shaken hands with the world's business; we have done with it; we have discharged ourself of it. Why should we get up? we have neither suit to solicit, nor affairs to manage. The drama has shut in upon us at the fourth act. We have nothing here to expect, but in a short time a sick bed, and a dismissal. We delight to anticipate death by such shadows as night affords. We are already half acquainted with ghosts. We were never much in the world. Disappointment early struck a dark veil between us and its dazzling illusions. Our spirits showed grey before our hairs. The mighty changes of the world already appear as but the vain stuff out of which dramas are composed. We have asked no more of life than what the mimic images in play-houses present us with. Even those types have waxed fainter. Our clock appears to have struck. We are SUPERANNUATED. In this dearth of mundane satisfaction, we contract politic alliances with shadows. It is good to have friends at court. The abstracted media of dreams seem no ill introduction to that spiritual presence, upon which, in no long time, we expect to be thrown. We are trying to know a little of the usages of that colony; to learn the language, and the faces we shall meet with there, that we may be the less awkward at our first coming among them. We willingly call a phantom our fellow, as knowing we shall soon be of their dark companionship. Therefore, we cherish dreams. We try to spell in them the alphabet of the invisible world; and think we know already, how it shall be with us. Those uncouth shapes, which, while we clung to flesh and blood, affrighted us, have become familiar. We feel attenuated into their meagre essences, and have given the hand of half-way approach to incorporeal being. We once thought life to be something; but it has unaccountably fallen from us before its time. Therefore we choose to dally with visions. The sun has no purposes of ours to light us to. Why should we get up?

XV.—THAT WE SHOULD LIE DOWN WITH THE LAMB

We could never quite understand the philosophy of this arrangement, or the wisdom of our ancestors in sending us for instruction to these woolly bedfellows. A sheep, when it is dark, has nothing to do but to shut his silly eyes, and sleep if he can. Man found out long sixes,—Hail, candle-light! without disparagement to sun and moon, the kindliest luminary of the three—if we may not rather style thee their radiant deputy, mild viceroy of the moon!—We love to read, talk, sit silent, eat, drink, sleep, by candle-light. They are everybody's sun and moon. This is our peculiar and household planet. Wanting it, what savage unsocial nights must our ancestors have spent, wintering in caves and unillumined fastnesses! They must have lain about and grumbled at one another in the dark. What repartees could have passed, when you must have felt about for a smile, and handled a neighbour's cheek to be sure that he understood it? This accounts for the seriousness of the elder poetry. It has a sombre cast (try Hesiod or Ossian), derived from the tradition of those unlantern'd nights. Jokes came in with candles. We wonder how they saw to pick up a pin, if they had any. How did they sup? what a mélange of chance carving they must have made of it!—here one had got a leg of a goat, when he wanted a horse's shoulder—there another had dipped his scooped palm in a kid-skin of wild honey, when he meditated right mare's milk. There is neither good eating nor drinking in fresco. Who, even in these civilised times, has never experienced this, when at some economic table he has commenced dining after dusk, and waited· for the flavour till the lights came? The senses absolutely give and take reciprocally. Can you tell pork from veal in the dark? or distinguish Sherris from pure Malaga? Take away the candle from the smoking man; by the glimmering of the left ashes, he knows that he is still smoking, but he knows it only by an inference; till the restored light, coming in aid of the olfactories, reveals to both senses the full aroma. Then how he redoubles his puffs! how he burnishes!—there is absolutely no such thing as reading but by a candle. We have tried the affectation of a book at noon-day in gardens, and in sultry arbours; but it was labour thrown away. Those gay motes in the beam come about you, hovering and teasing, like so many coquettes, that will have you all to their self, and are jealous of your abstractions. By the midnight taper, the writer digests his meditations. By the same light we must approach to their perusal, if we would catch the flame, the odour. It is a mockery, all that is reported of the influential Phœbus. No true poem ever owed its birth to the sun's light. They are abstracted works—

> Things that were born, when none but the still night,
> And his dumb candle, saw his pinching throes.

Marry, daylight—daylight might furnish the images, the crude material; but for the fine shapings, the true turning and filing (as mine author hath it), they must be content to hold their inspiration of the candle. The mild internal light, that reveals them, like fires on the domestic hearth, goes out in the sunshine. Night and silence call out the starry fancies. Milton's Morning Hymn in Paradise, we would hold a good wager, was penned at midnight; and Taylor's rich description of a sun-rise smells decidedly of the taper. Even ourself, in these our humbler lucubrations, tune our best-measured cadences (Prose has her cadences) not unfrequently to the charm of the drowsier watchman, "blessing the doors"; or the wild sweep of winds at midnight. Even now a loftier speculation than we have yet attempted, courts our endeavours. We would indite something about the Solar System.—*Betty, bring the candles.*

XVI.—THAT A SULKY TEMPER IS A MISFORTUNE

We grant that it is, and a very serious one—to a man's friends, and to all that have to do with him; but whether the condition of the man himself is so much to be deplored may admit of a question. We can speak a little to it, being ourselves but lately recovered—we whisper it in confidence, reader,—out of a long and desperate fit of the sullens. Was the cure a blessing? The conviction which wrought it, came too clearly to leave a scruple of the fanciful injuries—for they were mere fancies— which had provoked the humour. But the humour itself was too self-pleasing, while it lasted—we know how bare we lay ourself in the confession—to be abandoned all at once with the grounds of it. We still brood over wrongs which we know to have been imaginary; and for our old acquaintance N——, whom we find to have been a truer friend than we took him for, we substitute some phantom—a Caius or a Titius—as like him as we dare to form it, to wreak our yet unsatisfied resentments on. It is mortifying to fall at once from the pinnacle of neglect; to forego the idea of having been ill-used and contumaciously treated by an old friend. The first thing to aggrandise a man in his own conceit, is to conceive of himself as neglected. There let him fix if he can. To undeceive him is to deprive him of the most tickling morsel within the range of self-complacency. No flattery can come near it. Happy is he who suspects his friend of an injustice; but supremely blest, who thinks all his friends in a conspiracy to depress and undervalue him. There is a pleasure (we sing not to the profane) far beyond the reach of all that the world calls joy—a deep, enduring satisfaction in the depths, where the superficial seek it not, of discontent. Were we to recite one half of this mystery,—which we were let into by our late dissatisfaction, all the world would be in love with disrespect; we should wear a slight for a bracelet, and neglects and contumacies would be the only matter for courtship. Unlike to that mysterious book in the Apocalypse, the study of this mystery is unpalatable only in the commencement. The first sting of a suspicion is grievous; but wait—out of that wound, which to flesh and blood seemed so difficult, there is balm and honey to be extracted. Your friend passed you on such or such a day,—having in his company one that you conceived worse than ambiguously disposed towards you,—passed you in the street without notice. To be sure, he is something short-sighted; and it was in your power to have accosted *him*. But facts and sane inferences are trifles to a true adept in the science of dissatisfaction. He must have seen you; and S——, who was with him, must have been the cause of the contempt. It galls you, and well it may. But have patience. Go home, and make the worst of it, and you are a made man from this time. Shut yourself up, and rejecting, as an enemy to your peace, every whispering suggestion that but insinuates there may be a mistake—reflect seriously upon the many lesser instances which you had begun to perceive, in proof of your friend's disaffection towards you. None of them singly was much to the purpose, but the aggregate weight is positive; and you have this last affront to clench them. Thus far the process is anything but agreeable. But now to your relief comes in the comparative faculty. You conjure up all the kind feelings you have had for your friend; what you have been to him, and what you would have been to him, if he would have suffered you; how you defended him in this or that place; and his good name—his literary reputation, and so forth, was always dearer to you than your own! Your heart, spite of itself, yearns towards him. You could weep tears of blood but for a restraining pride. How say you! do you not yet begin to apprehend a comfort?—some allay of sweetness in the bitter waters? Stop not here, nor penuriously cheat yourself of your reversions. You are on vantage ground. Enlarge your speculations, and take in the rest of your friends, as a spark kindles more sparks. Was there one among them who has not to you proved hollow, false, slippery as water? Begin to think that the relation itself is inconsistent with mortality. That the very idea of friendship, with its component parts, as honour, fidelity, steadiness, exists but in your single bosom. Image yourself to yourself, as the only possible friend in a world incapable of that communion. Now the gloom thickens. The little star of self-love twinkles, that is to encourage you through deeper glooms than this. You are not yet at the half point of your elevation. You are not yet, believe me, half sulky enough. Adverting to the world in general (as these circles in the mind will spread to infinity), reflect with what strange injustice you have been treated in quarters where (setting gratitude and the expectation of friendly returns aside as chimeras) you pretended no claim beyond justice, the naked due of all men. Think the very idea of right and fit fled from the earth, or your breast the solitary receptacle of it, till you have swelled yourself into at least one hemisphere; the other being the vast Arabia Stony of your friends and the world aforesaid. To grow bigger every moment in your own conceit, and the world to lessen; to deify yourself at the expense of your species; to judge the world—this is the acme and supreme point of your mystery—these the true PLEASURES of SULKINESS. We profess no more of this grand secret than what ourself experimented on one rainy afternoon in the last week, sulking in our study. We had proceeded to the penultimate point, at which the true adept seldom stops, where the consideration of benefit forgot is about to merge in the meditation of general injustice—when a knock at the door was followed by the entrance of the very friend whose not seeing of us in the morning (for we will now confess the case our own), an accidental oversight, had given rise to so much agreeable generalisation! To mortify us still more, and take down the whole flattering superstructure which pride had piled upon neglect, he had brought in his hand the identical S——, in whose favour we had suspected him of the contumacy. Asseverations were needless, where the frank manner of them both was convictive of the injurious nature of the suspicion. We fancied that they perceived our embarrassment; but were too proud or something else, to confess to the secret of it. We had been but too lately in the condition of the noble patient in Argos:—

> Qui se credebat miros audire tragœdos,
> In vacuo lætus sessor plausorque theatro—

and could have exclaimed with equal reason against the friendly hands that cured us—

> Pol, me occidistis, amici,
> Non servâstis, ait; cui sic extorta voluptas,
> Et demptus per vim mentis gratissimus error.

ROSAMUND GRAY

ROSAMUND GRAY

CHAPTER I

IT was noontide. The sun was very hot. An old gentlewoman sat spinning in a little arbour at the door of her cottage. She was blind; and her granddaughter was reading the Bible to her. The old lady had just left her work, to attend to the story of Ruth.

"Orpah kissed her mother-in-law; but Ruth clave unto her." It was a passage she could not let pass without a *comment*. The moral she drew from it was not very *new*, to be sure. The girl had heard it a hundred times before—and a hundred times more she could have heard it, without suspecting it to be tedious. Rosamund loved her grandmother.

The old lady loved Rosamund too; and she had reason for so doing. Rosamund was to her at once a child and a servant. She had only *her* left in the world. They two lived together.

They had once known better days. The story of Rosamund's parents, their failure, their folly, and distresses, may be told another time. Our tale hath grief enough in it.

It was now about a year and a half since Old Margaret Gray had sold off all her effects, to pay the debts of Rosamund's father—just after the mother had died of a broken heart; for her husband had fled his country to hide his shame in a foreign land. At that period the old lady retired to a small cottage in the village of Widford in Hertfordshire.

Rosamund, in her thirteenth year, was left destitute, without fortune or friends: she went with her grandmother. In all this time she had served her faithfully and lovingly.

Old Margaret Gray, when she first came into these parts, had eyes, and could see. The neighbours said, they had been dimmed by weeping: be that as it may, she was latterly grown quite blind. "God is very good to us, child; I can *feel* you yet." This she would sometimes say; and we need not wonder to hear, that Rosamund clave unto her grandmother.

Margaret retained a spirit unbroken by calamity. There was a principle *within*, which it seemed as if no outward circumstances could reach. It was a *religious* principle, and she had taught it to Rosamund; for the girl had mostly resided with her grandmother from her earliest years. Indeed she had taught her all that she knew herself; and the old lady's knowledge did not extend a vast way.

Margaret had drawn her maxims from observation; and a pretty long experience in life had contributed to make her, at times, a little *positive:* but Rosamund never argued with her grandmother.

Their library consisted chiefly in a large family Bible, with notes and expositions by various learned expositors, from Bishop Jewell downwards.

This might never be suffered to lie about like other books, but was kept constantly wrapt up in a handsome case of green velvet, with gold tassels—the only relic of departed grandeur they had brought with them to the cottage—everything else of value had been sold off for the purpose above mentioned.

This Bible Rosamund, when a child, had never dared to open without permission; and even yet, from habit, continued the custom. Margaret had parted with none of her *authority;* indeed it was never exerted with much harshness; and happy was Rosamund, though a girl grown, when she could obtain leave to read her Bible. It was a treasure too valuable for an indiscriminate use; and Margaret still pointed out to her granddaughter *where to read.*

Besides this, they had the "Compleat Angler, or Contemplative Man's Recreation," with cuts—"Pilgrim's Progress," the first part—a Cookery Book, with a few dry sprigs of rosemary and lavender stuck here and there between the leaves (I suppose to point to some of the old lady's most favourite receipts), and there was "Wither's Emblems," an old book, and quaint. The old-fashioned pictures in this last book were among the first exciters of the infant Rosamund's curiosity. Her contemplation had fed upon them in rather older years.

Rosamund had not read many books besides these; or if any, they had been only occasional companions: these were to Rosamund as old friends, that she had long known. I know not whether the peculiar cast of her mind might not be traced, in part, to a tincture she had received, early in life, from Walton and Wither, from John Bunyan and her Bible.

Rosamund's mind was pensive and reflective, rather than what passes usually for *clever* or *acute.* From a child she was remarkably shy and thoughtful—this was taken for stupidity and want of feeling; and the child has been sometimes whipt for being a *stubborn thing,* when her little heart was almost bursting with affection.

Even now her grandmother would often reprove her, when she found her too grave or melancholy; give her sprightly lectures about good-humour and rational mirth; and not unfrequently fall a-crying herself, to the great discredit of her lecture. Those tears endeared her the more to Rosamund.

Margaret would say, "Child, I love you to cry, when I think you are only remembering your poor dear father and mother;—I would have you think about them sometimes—it would be strange if you did not; but I fear, Rosamund, I fear, girl, you sometimes think too deeply about your own situation and poor prospects in life. When you do so, you do wrong—remember the naughty rich man in the parable. He never had any good thoughts about God, and his religion: and that might have been your case."

Rosamund, at these times, could not reply to her; she was not in the habit of *arguing* with her grandmother; so she was quite silent on these occasions—or else the girl knew well enough herself, that she had only been sad to think of the desolate condition of her best friend, to see her, in her old age, so infirm and blind. But she had never been used to make excuses, when the old lady said she was doing wrong.

The neighbours were all very kind to them. The veriest rustics never passed them without a bow, or a pulling off of the hat—some show of courtesy, awkward indeed, but affectionate—with a "Good-morrow, madam," or "young madam," as it might happen.

Rude and savage natures, who seem born with a propensity to express contempt for anything that looks like prosperity, yet felt respect for its declining lustre.

The farmers, and better sort of people (as they are called), all promised to provide for Rosamund when her grandmother should die. Margaret trusted in God and believed them.

She used to say, "I have lived many years in the world, and have never known people, *good people,* to be left without some friend; a relation, a benefactor, a *something.* God knows our wants—that it is not good for man or woman to be alone; and He always sends us a helpmate, a leaning place, a *somewhat.*" Upon this sure ground of experience, did Margaret build her trust in Providence.

CHAPTER II

ROSAMUND had just made an end of her story (as I was about to relate), and was listening to the application of the moral (which said application she was old enough to have made herself, but her grandmother still continued to treat her, in many respects, as a child, and Rosamund was in no haste to lay claim to the title of womanhood), when a young gentleman made his appearance and interrupted them.

It was young Allan Clare, who had brought a present of peaches, and some roses, for Rosamund.

He laid his little basket down on a seat of the arbour; and in a respectful tone of voice, as though he were addressing a parent, inquired of Margaret "how she did."

The old lady seemed pleased with his attentions—answered his inquiries by saying, that "her cough was less troublesome a-nights, but she had not yet got rid of it, and probably she never might; but she did not like to tease young people with an account of her infirmities."

A few kind words passed on either side, when young Clare, glancing a tender look at the girl, who had all this time been silent, took leave of them with saying, "I shall bring *Elinor* to see you in the evening."

When he was gone, the old lady began to prattle.

"That is a sweet-dispositioned youth, and I *do* love him dearly, I must say it—there is such a modesty in all he says or does—he should not come here so often, to be sure, but I don't know how to help it; there is so much goodness in him, I can't find it in my heart to forbid him. But, Rosamund, girl, I must tell you beforehand; when you grow older, Mr. Clare must be no companion for *you:* while you were both so young it was all very well—but the time is coming, when folks will think harm of it, if a rich young gentleman, like Mr. Clare, comes so often to our poor cottage.—Dost hear, girl? Why don't you answer? Come, I did not mean to say anything to hurt you—speak to me, Rosamund—nay, I must not have you be sullen—I don't love people that are sullen."

And in this manner was this poor soul running on, unheard and unheeded, when it occurred to her, that possibly the girl might not be *within hearing.*

And true it was, that Rosamund had slunk away at the first mention of Mr. Clare's good qualities: and when she returned, which was not till a few minutes after Margaret had made an end of her fine harangue, it is certain her cheeks *did* look very *rosy.* That might have been from the heat of the day or from exercise, for she had been walking in the garden.

Margaret, we know, was blind; and, in this case, it was lucky for Rosamund that she was so, or she might have made some not unlikely surmises.

I must not have my reader infer from this, that I at all think it likely, a young maid of fourteen would fall in love without asking her grandmother's leave—the thing itself is not to be conceived.

To obviate all suspicions, I am disposed to communicate a little anecdote of Rosamund.

A month or two back her grandmother had been giving her the strictest prohibitions, in her walks, not to go near a certain spot, which was dangerous from the circumstance of a huge overgrown oak-tree spreading its prodigious arms across a deep chalk-pit, which they partly concealed.

To this fatal place Rosamund came one day—female curiosity, we know, is older than the flood—let us not think hardly of the girl, if she partook of the sexual failing.

Rosamund ventured further and further—climbed along one of the branches—approached the forbidden chasm—her foot slipped—she was not killed—but it was by a mercy she escaped—other branches intercepted her fall—and with a palpitating heart she made her way back to the cottage.

It happened that evening, that her grandmother was in one of her best humours, caressed Rosamund, talked of old times, and what a blessing it was they two found a shelter in their little cottage, and in conclusion told Rosamund, "she was a good girl, and God would one day reward her for her kindness to her old blind grandmother."

· This was more than Rosamund could bear. Her morning's disobedience came fresh into her mind; she felt she did not deserve all this from

Margaret, and at last burst into a fit of crying, and made confession of her fault. The old gentlewoman kissed and forgave her.

Rosamund never went near that naughty chasm again.

Margaret would never have heard of this, if Rosamund had not told of it herself. But this young maid had a delicate moral sense, which would not suffer her to take advantage of her grandmother, to deceive her, or conceal anything from her, though Margaret was old, and blind, and easy to be imposed upon.

Another virtuous *trait* I recollect of Rosamund, and now I am in the vein will tell it.

Some, I know, will think these things trifles—and they are so—but if these *minutiæ* make my reader better acquainted with Rosamund, I am content to abide the imputation.

These promises of character, hints, and early indications of a *sweet nature*, are to me more dear, and choice in the selection, than any of those pretty wild-flowers, which this young maid, this virtuous Rosamund, has ever gathered in a fine May morning, to make a posy to place in the bosom of her old blind friend.

Rosamund had a very just notion of drawing, and would often employ her talent in making sketches of the surrounding scenery.

On a landscape, a larger piece than she had ever yet attempted, she had now been working for three or four months. She had taken great pains with it, given much time to it, and it was nearly finished. For *whose* particular inspection it was designed, I will not venture to conjecture. We know it could not have been for her grandmother's.

One day she went out on a short errand, and left her landscape on the table. When she returned, she found it *gone*.

Rosamund from the first suspected some mischief, but held her tongue. At length she made the fatal discovery. Margaret, in her absence, had laid violent hands on it; not knowing what it was, but taking it for some waste-paper, had torn it in half, and with one half of this elaborate composition had twisted herself up—a thread-paper!

Rosamund spread out her hands at sight of the disaster, gave her grandmother a roguish smile, but said not a word. She knew the poor soul would only fret, if she told her of it,—and when once Margaret was set a-fretting for other people's misfortunes, the fit held her pretty long.

So Rosamund that very afternoon began another piece of the same size and subject; and Margaret, to her dying day, never dreamed of the mischief she had unconsciously done.

CHAPTER III

ROSAMUND GRAY was the most beautiful young creature that eyes ever beheld. Her face had the sweetest expression in it—a gentleness—a modesty—a timidity—a certain charm—a grace without a name.

There was a sort of melancholy mingled in her smile. It was not the thoughtless levity of a girl—it was not the restrained simper of premature womanhood—it was something which the poet Young might have remembered, when he composed that perfect line,

> Soft, modest, melancholy, female, fair.

She was a mild-eyed maid, and everybody loved her. Young Allan Clare, when but a boy, sighed for her.

Her yellow hair fell in bright and curling clusters, like

> Those hanging locks
> Of young Apollo.

Her voice was trembling and musical. A graceful diffidence pleaded for her whenever she spake—and, if she said but little, that little found its way to the heart.

Young, and artless, and innocent, meaning no harm, and thinking none; affectionate as a smiling infant—playful, yet inobtrusive, as a weaned lamb—everybody loved her. Young Allan Clare, when but a boy, sighed for her.

The moon is shining in so brightly at my window, where I write, that I feel it a crime not to suspend my employment awhile to gaze at her.

See how she glideth, in maiden honour, through the clouds, who divide on either side to do her homage.

Beautiful vision!—as I contemplate thee, an internal harmony is communicated to my mind, a moral brightness, a tacit analogy of mental purity; a calm like *that* we ascribe in fancy to the favoured inhabitants of thy fairy regions, "argent fields."

I marvel not, O moon, that heathen people, in the "olden times," did worship thy deity—Cynthia, Diana, Hecate. Christian Europe invokes thee not by these names now—her idolatry is of a blacker stain: Belial is her God—she worships Mammon.

False things are told concerning thee, fair planet—for I will ne'er believe that thou canst take a perverse pleasure in distorting the brains of us, poor mortals. Lunatics! moonstruck! Calumny invented, and folly took up, these names. I would hope better things from thy mild aspect and benign influences.

Lady of Heaven, thou lendest thy pure lamp to light the way to the virgin mourner, when she goes to seek the tomb where her warrior lover lies.

Friend of the distressed, thou speakest only *peace* to the lonely sufferer, who walks forth in the placid evening, beneath thy gentle light, to chide at fortune, or to complain of changed friends, or unhappy loves.

Do I dream, or doth not even now a heavenly calm descend from thee into my bosom, as I meditate on the chaste loves of Rosamund and her Clare!

CHAPTER IV

Allan Clare was just two years older than Rosamund. He was a boy of fourteen, when he first became acquainted with her—it was soon after she had come to reside with her grandmother at Widford.

He met her by chance one day, carrying a pitcher in her hand, which she had been filling from a neighbouring well—the pitcher was heavy, and she seemed to be bending with its weight.

Allan insisted on carrying it for her—for he thought it a sin that a delicate young maid, like her, should be so employed, and he stand idle by.

Allan had a propensity to do little kind offices for everybody—but at the sight of Rosamund Gray, his first fire was kindled—his young mind seemed to have found an object, and his enthusiasm was from that time forth awakened. His visits, from that day, were pretty frequent at the cottage.

He was never happier than when he could get Rosamund to walk out with him. He would make her admire the scenes he admired—fancy the wildflowers he fancied—watch the clouds he was watching—and not unfrequently repeat to her poetry which he loved, and make her love it.

On their return, the old lady, who considered them yet as but children, would bid Rosamund fetch Mr. Clare a glass of her currant-wine, a bowl of new milk, or some cheap dainty which was more welcome to Allan than the costliest delicacies of a prince's court.

The boy and girl, for they were no more at that age, grew fond of each other—more fond than either of them suspected.

> They would sit, and sigh,
> And look upon each other, and conceive
> Not what they ail'd; yet something they did ail,
> And yet were well—and yet they were not well;
> And what was their disease, they could not tell.

And thus,

> In this first garden of their simpleness
> They spent their childhood.

A circumstance had lately happened, which in some sort altered the nature of their attachment.

Rosamund was one day reading the tale of "Julia de Roubigné"—a book which young Clare had lent her.

Allan was standing by, looking over her, with one hand thrown round her neck, and a finger of the other pointing to a passage in Julia's third letter.

"Maria! in my hours of visionary indulgence, I have sometimes painted to myself a *husband*—no matter whom—comforting me amidst the distresses which fortune had laid upon us. I have smiled upon him through my tears; tears, not of anguish, but of tenderness!—our children were playing around us, unconscious of misfortune; we had taught them to be humble, and to be happy; our little shed was reserved to us, and their smiles to cheer it.—I have imagined the luxury of such a scene, and affliction became a part of my dream of happiness."

The girl blushed as she read, and trembled—she had a sort of confused sensation, that Allan was noticing her—yet she durst not lift her eyes from the book, but continued reading, scarce knowing what she read.

Allan guessed the cause of her confusion. Allan trembled too—his colour came and went—his feelings became impetuous—and flinging both arms round her neck, he kissed his young favourite.

Rosamund was vexed and pleased, soothed and frightened, all in a moment—a fit of tears came to her relief.

Allan had indulged before in these little freedoms, and Rosamund had thought no harm of them; but from this time the girl grew timid and reserved—distant in her manner, and careful of her behaviour in Allan's presence—not seeking his society as before, but rather shunning it—delighting more to feed upon his idea in absence.

Allan too, from this day, seemed changed: his manner became, though not less tender, yet more respectful and diffident—his bosom felt a throb it had till now not known, in the society of Rosamund—and, if he was less familiar with her than in former times, that charm of delicacy had superadded a grace to Rosamund, which, while he feared, he loved.

There is a *mysterious character,* heightened, indeed, by fancy and passion, but not without foundation in reality and observation, which true lovers have ever imputed to the object of their affections. This character Rosamund had now acquired with Allan—something *angelic, perfect, exceeding nature.*

Young Clare dwelt very near to the cottage. He had lost his parents, who were rather wealthy, early in life; and was left to the care of a sister some ten years older than himself.

Elinor Clare was an excellent young lady—discreet, intelligent, and affectionate. Allan revered her as a parent, while he loved her as his own familiar friend. He told all the little secrets of his heart to her—but there was *one,* which he had hitherto unaccountably concealed from her —namely, the extent of his regard for Rosamund.

Elinor knew of his visits to the cottage, and was no stranger to the persons of Margaret and her grand-daughter. She had several times met them, when she had been walking with her brother—a civility usually passed on either side—but Elinor avoided troubling her brother with any unseasonable questions.

Allan's heart often beat, and he has been going to tell his sister *all*— but something like shame (false or true, I shall not stay to inquire) had hitherto kept him back;—still the secret, unrevealed, hung upon his conscience like a crime—for his temper had a sweet and noble frankness in it, which bespake him yet a virgin from the world.

There was a fine openness in his countenance—the character of it somewhat resembled Rosamund's—except that more fire and enthusiasm were discernible in Allan's; his eyes were of a darker blue than Rosamund's—his hair was of a chestnut colour—his cheeks ruddy, and tinged with brown. There was a cordial sweetness in Allan's smile, the like to which I never saw in any other face.

Elinor had hitherto connived at her brother's attachment to Rosamund. Elinor, I believe, was something of a physiognomist, and thought she could trace in the countenance and manner of Rosamund, qualities which no brother of hers need be ashamed to love.

The time was now come when Elinor was desirous of knowing her brother's favourite more intimately—an opportunity offered of breaking the matter to Allan.

The morning of the day in which he carried his present of fruit and flowers to Rosamund, his sister had observed him more than usually busy in the garden, culling fruit with a nicety of choice not common to him.

She came up to him, unobserved, and, taking him by the arm, inquired, with a questioning smile—"What are you doing, Allan? and who are those peaches designed for?"

"For Rosamund Gray"—he replied—and his heart seemed relieved of a burthen which had long oppressed it.

"I have a mind to become acquainted with your handsome friend—will you introduce me, Allan? I think I should like to go and see her this afternoon."

"Do go, do go, Elinor—you don't know what a good creature she is; and old blind Margaret, you will like *her* very much."

His sister promised to accompany him after dinner; and they parted. Allan gathered no more peaches, but hastily cropping a few roses to fling into his basket, went away with it half-filled, being impatient to announce to Rosamund the coming of her promised visitor.

CHAPTER V

When Allan returned home, he found an invitation had been left for him, in his absence, to spend that evening with a young friend, who had just quitted a public school in London, and was come to pass one night in his father's house at Widford, previous to his departure the next morning for Edinburgh University.

It was Allan's bosom friend—they had not met for some months—and it was probable a much longer time must intervene before they should meet again.

Yet Allan could not help looking a little blank when he first heard of the invitation. This was to have been an important evening. But Elinor soon relieved her brother by expressing her readiness to go alone to the cottage.

"I will not lose the pleasure I promised myself, whatever you may determine upon, Allan; I will go by myself rather than be disappointed."

"Will you, will you, Elinor?"

Elinor promised to go—and I believe, Allan, on a second thought, was not very sorry to be spared the awkwardness of introducing two persons to each other, both so dear to him, but either of whom might happen not much to fancy the other.

At times, indeed, he was confident that Elinor *must* love Rosamund, and Rosamund *must* love Elinor; but there were also times in which he felt misgivings—it was an event he could scarce hope for very joy!

Allan's *real presence* that evening was more at the cottage than at the house, where his *bodily semblance* was visiting—his friend could not help complaining of a certain absence of mind, a *coldness* he called it.

It might have been expected, and in the course of things predicted, that Allan would have asked his friend some questions of what had happened since their last meeting, what his feelings were on leaving school, the probable time when they should meet again, and a hundred natural questions which friendship is most lavish of at such times; but nothing of all this ever occurred to Allan—they did not even settle the method of their future correspondence.

The consequence was, as might have been expected, Allan's friend thought him much altered, and, after his departure, sat down to compose a doleful sonnet about a "faithless friend."—I do not find that he ever finished it—indignation, or a dearth of rhymes, causing him to break off in the middle.

CHAPTER VI

In my catalogue of the little library at the cottage, I forgot to mention a book of Common Prayer. My reader's fancy might easily have supplied the omission—old ladies of Margaret's stamp (God bless them!) may as well be without their spectacles, or their elbow chair, as their prayer-book—I love them for it.

Margaret's was a handsome octavo, printed by Baskerville, the binding red, and fortified with silver at the edges. Out of this book it was their custom every afternoon to read the proper psalms appointed for the day.

The way they managed was this: they took verse by verse—Rosamund *read* her little portion, and Margaret repeated hers in turn, from memory—for Margaret could say all the Psalter by heart, and a good part of the Bible besides. She would not unfrequently put the girl right when she stumbled or skipped. This Margaret imputed to giddiness—a quality which Rosamund was by no means remarkable for—but old ladies, like Margaret, are not in all instances alike discriminative.

They had been employed in this manner just before Miss Clare arrived at the cottage. The psalm they had been reading was the hundred and fourth—Margaret was naturally led by it into a discussion of the works of creation.

There had been *thunder* in the course of the day—an occasion of instruction which the old lady never let pass—she began—

"Thunder has a very awful sound—some say God Almighty is angry whenever it thunders—that it is the voice of God speaking to us; for my part, I am not afraid of it——"

And in this manner the old lady was going on to particularise, as usual, its beneficial effects, in clearing the air, destroying of vermin, etc., when the entrance of Miss Clare put an end to her discourse.

Rosamund received her with respectful tenderness—and, taking her grandmother by the hand, said, with great sweetness,—"Miss Clare is come to see you, grandmother."

"I beg pardon, lady—I cannot *see* you—but you are heartily welcome. Is your brother with you, Miss Clare?—I don't hear him."

"He could not come, madam, but he sends his love by me."

"You have an excellent brother, Miss Clare—but pray do us the honour to take some refreshment—Rosamund——"

And the old lady was going to give directions for a bottle of her currant wine—when Elinor, smiling, said, "She was come to take a cup of tea with her, and expected to find no ceremony."

"After tea, I promise myself a walk with *you*, Rosamund, if your grandmother can spare you." Rosamund looked at her grandmother.

"Oh, for that matter, I should be sorry to debar the girl from any pleasure—I am sure it's lonesome enough for her to be with *me* always—and if Miss Clare will take you out, child, I shall do very well by myself till you return—it will not be the first time, you know, that I have been left here alone—some of the neighbours will be dropping in by and by—or, if *not*, I shall take no harm."

Rosamund had all the simple manners of a child; she kissed her grandmother, and looked happy.

All tea-time the old lady's discourse was little more than a panegyric on young Clare's good qualities. Elinor looked at her young friend, and smiled. Rosamund was beginning to look grave—but there was a cordial sunshine in the face of Elinor, before which any clouds of reserve that had been gathering on Rosamund's soon broke away.

"Does your grandmother ever go out, Rosamund?"

Margaret prevented the girl's reply, by saying—"My dear young lady, I am an old woman, and very infirm—Rosamund takes me a few paces beyond the door sometimes—but I walk very badly—I love best to sit in our little arbour when the sun shines—I can yet feel it warm and cheerful—and, if I lose the beauties of the season, I shall be very happy if you and Rosamund can take delight in this fine summer evening."

"I shall want to rob you of Rosamund's company now and then, if we like one another. I had hoped to have seen *you*, madam, at our house. I don't know whether we could not make room for you to come and live with us—what say you to it? Allan would be proud to tend you, I am sure; and Rosamund and I should be nice company."

Margaret was all unused to such kindnesses, and wept—Margaret had a great spirit—yet she was not above accepting an obligation from a worthy person—there was a delicacy in Miss Clare's manner—she could have no interest but pure goodness, to induce her to make the offer—at length the old lady spake from a full heart.

"Miss Clare, this little cottage received us in our distress—it gave us shelter when we had *no home*—we have praised God in it—and, while life remains, I think I shall never part from it—Rosamund does everything for me——"

"And will do, grandmother, as long as I live";—and then Rosamund fell a-crying.

"You are a good girl, Rosamund; and if you do but find friends when I am dead and gone, I shall want no better accommodation while I live—but God bless you, lady, a thousand times, for your kind offer."

Elinor was moved to tears, and, affecting a sprightliness, bade Rosamund prepare for her walk. The girl put on her white silk bonnet; and Elinor thought she never beheld so lovely a creature.

They took leave of Margaret, and walked out together; they rambled over all Rosamund's favourite haunts—through many a sunny field—by secret glade or wood-walk, where the girl had wandered so often with her beloved Clare.

Who now so happy as Rosamund? She had oft-times heard Allan speak with great tenderness of his sister—she was now rambling, arm in arm, with that very sister, the "vaunted sister" of her friend, her beloved Clare.

Not a tree, not a bush, scarce a wild-flower in their path, but revived in Rosamund some tender recollection, a conversation perhaps, or some chaste endearment. Life, and a new scene of things, were now opening before her—she was got into a fairy land of uncertain existence.

Rosamund was too happy to talk much—but Elinor was delighted with her when she *did* talk:—the girl's remarks were suggested most of them by the passing scene—and they betrayed, all of them, the liveliness of present impulse;—her conversation did not consist in a comparison of vapid feeling, an interchange of sentiment lip-deep—it had all the freshness of young sensation in it.

Sometimes they talked of Allan.

"Allan is very good," said Rosamund, "very good *indeed* to my grandmother—he will sit with her, and hear her stories, and read to her, and try to divert her a hundred ways. I wonder sometimes he is not tired. She talks him to death!"

"Then you confess, Rosamund, that the old lady *does* tire *you* sometimes?"

"Oh, no, I did not mean *that*—it's very different—I am used to all her ways, and I can humour her, and please her, and I ought to do it, for she is the only friend I ever had in the world."

The new friends did not conclude their walk till it was late, and Rosamund began to be apprehensive about the old lady, who had been all this time alone.

On their return to the cottage, they found that Margaret had been somewhat impatient—old ladies, *good old ladies,* will be so at times—age is timorous and suspicious of danger, where no danger is.

Besides, it was Margaret's bed-time, for she kept very good hours—indeed, in the distribution of her meals, and sundry other particulars, she resembled the livers in the antique world, more than might well beseem a creature of this.

So the new friends parted for that night—Elinor having made Margaret promise to give Rosamund leave to come and see her the next day.

CHAPTER VII

Miss Clare, we may be sure, made her brother very happy, when she told him of the engagement she had made for the morrow, and how delighted she had been with his handsome friend.

Allan, I believe, got little sleep that night. I know not, whether joy be not a more troublesome bed-fellow than grief—hope keeps a body very wakeful, I know.

Elinor Clare was the best good creature—the least selfish human being I ever knew—always at work for other people's good, planning other people's happiness—continually forgetful to consult for her own personal gratifications, except indirectly, in the welfare of another;—while her parents lived, the most attentive of daughters—since they died, the kindest of sisters—I never knew but *one* like her. It happens that I have some of this young lady's *letters* in my possession—I shall present my reader with one of them. It was written a short time after the death of her mother, and addressed to a cousin, a dear friend of Elinor's, who was then on the point of being married to Mr. Beaumont, of Staffordshire, and had invited Elinor to assist at her nuptials. I will transcribe it with minute fidelity.

ELINOR CLARE TO MARIA LESLIE

Widford, *July the —, 17—*

Health, Innocence, and Beauty, shall be thy bridemaids, my sweet cousin. I have no heart to undertake the office. Alas! what have I to do in the house of feasting?

Maria! I fear lest my griefs should prove obtrusive. Yet bear with me a little—I have recovered already a share of my former spirits.

I fear more for Allan than myself. The loss of two such parents, within so short an interval, bears very heavy on him. The boy *hangs* about me from morning till night. He is perpetually forcing a smile into his poor pale cheeks—you know the sweetness of his smile, Maria.

To-day, after dinner, when he took his glass of wine in his hand, he burst into tears, and would not, or could not then, tell me the reason—afterwards he told me—"he had been used to drink Mamma's health after dinner, and *that* came into his head and made him cry." I feel the claims the boy has upon me—I perceive that I am living to *some end*—and the thought supports me.

Already I have attained to a state of complacent feelings—my mother's lessons were not thrown away upon her Elinor.

In the visions of last night her spirit seemed to stand at my bed-side—a light, as of noonday, shone upon the room—she opened my curtains—she smiled upon me with the same placid smile as in her lifetime. I felt no fear. "Elinor," she said, "for my sake take care of young Allan,"—and I awoke with calm feelings.

Maria! shall not the meeting of blessed spirits, think you, be something like this?—I think, I could even now behold my mother without dread—I would ask pardon of her for all my past omissions of duty, for all the little asperities in my temper, which have so often grieved her gentle spirit when living. Maria! I think she would not turn away from me.

Oftentimes a feeling, more vivid than memory, brings her before me—I see her sit in her old elbow chair—her arms folded upon her lap—a tear upon her cheek, that seems to upbraid her unkind daughter for some inattention—I wipe it away and kiss her honoured lips.

Maria! when I have been fancying all this, Allan will come in, with his poor eyes red with weeping, and taking me by the hand, destroy the vision in a moment.

I am prating to you, my sweet cousin, but it is the prattle of the heart, which Maria loves. Besides, whom have I to talk to of these things but you?—you have been my counsellor in times past, my companion, and sweet familiar friend. Bear with me a little—I mourn the "cherishers of my infancy."

I sometimes count it a blessing that my father did not prove the *survivor*. You know something of his story. You know there was a foul tale current—it was the busy malice of that bad man, S——, which helped to spread it abroad—you will recollect the active good-nature of our friends W—— and T——; what pains they took to undeceive people—with the better sort their kind labours prevailed; but there was still a party who shut their ears. You know the issue of it. My father's great spirit bore up against it for some time—my father never was a *bad* man—but that spirit was broken at the last—and the greatly-injured man was forced to leave his old paternal dwelling in Staffordshire—for the neighbours had begun to point at him. Maria! I have *seen* them *point* at him, and have been ready to drop.

In this part of the country, where the slander had not reached, he sought a retreat—and he found a still more grateful asylum in the daily solicitudes of the best of wives.

"An enemy hath done this," I have heard him say—and at such times my mother would speak to him so soothingly of forgiveness, and long-suffering, and the bearing of injuries with patience; would heal all his wounds with so gentle a touch;—I have seen the old man weep like a child.

The gloom that beset his mind, at times betrayed him into scepticism —he has doubted if there be a Providence! I have heard him say, "God has built a brave world, but methinks He has left His creatures to bustle in it *how they may.*"

At such times he could not endure to hear my mother talk in a religious strain. He would say, "Woman, have done—you confound, you perplex me, when you talk of these matters, and for one day at least unfit me for the business of life."

I have seen her look at him—O GOD, Maria! such a *look!* it plainly spake that she was willing to have shared her precious hope with the partner of her earthly cares—but she found a repulse—

Deprived of such a wife, think you, the old man could long have endured his existence? or what consolation would his wretched daughter have had to offer him, but silent and imbecile tears?

My sweet cousin, you will think me tedious—and I am so—but it does me good to talk these matters over. And do not you be alarmed for me —my sorrows are subsiding into a deep and sweet resignation. I shall soon be sufficiently composed, I know it, to participate in my friend's happiness.

Let me call her, while yet I may, my own Maria Leslie! Methinks, I shall not like you by any other name. Beaumont! Maria Beaumont! it hath a strange sound with it—I shall never be reconciled to this name —but do not you fear—Maria Leslie shall plead with me for Maria Beaumont. And now, my sweet Friend, God love you, and your

ELINOR CLARE.

I find in my collection several letters, written soon after the date of the preceding, and addressed all of them to Maria Beaumont.—I am tempted to make some short extracts from these—my tale will suffer interruption by them—but I was willing to preserve whatever memorials I could of Elinor Clare.

FROM ELINOR CLARE TO MARIA BEAUMONT

(AN EXTRACT)

—— I have been strolling out for half an hour in the fields; and my mind has been occupied by thoughts which Maria has a right to participate. I have been bringing my *mother* to my recollection. My heart ached with the remembrance of infirmities, that made her closing years of life so sore a trial to her.

I was concerned to think that our family differences have been one source of disquiet to her. I am sensible that *this last* we are apt to exaggerate after a person's death—and surely, in the main, there was considerable harmony among the members of our little family—still I was concerned to think that we ever gave her gentle spirit disquiet.

I thought on years back—on all my parents' friends—the H——s, the F——s, on D—— S——, and on many a merry evening, in the fireside circle, in that comfortable back parlour—it is never used now.—

O ye *Matravises* [1] of the age, ye know not what ye lose in despising these petty topics of endeared remembrance, associated circumstances of past times;—ye know not the throbbings of the heart, tender yet affectionately familiar, which accompany the dear and honoured names of *father* or of *mother*.

Maria! I thought on all these things; my heart ached at the review of them—it yet aches, while I write this—but I am never so satisfied with my train of thoughts, as when they run upon these subjects—the tears they draw from us, meliorate and soften the heart, and keep fresh within us that memory of dear friends dead, which alone can fit us for a readmission to their society hereafter.

FROM ANOTHER LETTER

—— I had a bad dream this morning—that Allan was dead—and who, of all persons in the world do you think, put on mourning for him? Why—*Matravis*. This alone might cure me of superstitious thoughts, if I were inclined to them; for why should Matravis *mourn* for us, or our family!—*Still* it was pleasant to awake, and find it but a dream.—Methinks something like an awaking from an ill dream shall the Resurrection from the Dead be.—Materially different from our accustomed scenes, and ways of life, the *World to come* may possibly not be—still it is represented to us under the notion of a *Rest,* a *Sabbath,* a state of bliss.

FROM ANOTHER LETTER

—— Methinks, you and I should have been born under the same roof, sucked the same milk, conned the same horn-book, thumbed the same Testament, together:—for we have been more than sisters, Maria! Something will still be whispering to me, that I shall one day be inmate of the same dwelling with my cousin, partaker with her in all the delights which spring from mutual good offices, kind words, attentions in sickness and in health,—conversation, sometimes innocently trivial, and at others profitably serious;—books read and commented on, together; meals ate, and walks taken, together,—and conferences, how we may best do good to this poor person or that, and wean our spirits from the world's *cares,* without divesting ourselves of its *charities.* What a picture I have drawn, Maria! and none of all these things may ever come to pass.

[1] This name will be explained presently.

—— Continue to write to me, my sweet cousin. Many good thoughts, resolutions, and proper views of things, pass through the mind in the course of the day, but are lost for want of committing them to paper. Seize them, Maria, as they pass, these Birds of Paradise, that show themselves and are gone,—and make a grateful present of the precious fugitives to your friend.

To use a homely illustration, just rising in my fancy,—shall the good housewife take such pains in pickling and preserving her worthless fruits, her walnuts, her apricots, and quinces—and is there not much *spiritual housewifery* in treasuring up our mind's best fruits—our heart's meditations in its most favoured moments?

This sad simile is much in the fashion of the old Moralisers, such as I conceive honest Baxter to have been, such as Quarles and Wither were with their curious, serio-comic, quaint emblems. But they sometimes reach the heart, when a more elegant simile rests in the fancy.

Not low and mean, like these, but beautifully familiarised to our conceptions, and condescending to human thoughts and notions, are all the discourses of our LORD—conveyed in parable, or similitude, what easy access do they win to the heart, through the medium of the delighted imagination! speaking of heavenly things in fable, or in simile, drawn from earth, from objects *common, accustomed*.

Life's business, with such delicious little interruptions as our correspondence affords, how pleasant it is!—why can we not paint on the dull paper our whole feelings, exquisite as they rise up?

—— I had meant to have left off at this place; but looking back, I am sorry to find too gloomy a cast tincturing my last page—a representation of life false and unthankful. Life is *not* all vanity and disappointment—it hath much of evil in it, no doubt; but to those who do not misuse it, it affords comfort, *temporary* comfort, much—much that endears us to it, and dignifies it—many true and good feelings, I trust, of which we need not be ashamed—hours of tranquillity and hope. But the morning was dull and overcast, and my spirits were under a cloud. I feel my error.

Is it no blessing that we two love one another so dearly—that Allan is left me—that you are settled in life—that wordly affairs go smooth with us both—above all, that our lot hath fallen to us in a Christian country? Maria! these things are not little. I will consider life as a long feast, and not forget to say grace.

—— Allan has written to me—you know, he is on a visit at his old tutor's in Gloucestershire—he is to return home on Thursday—Allan is a dear boy—he concludes his letter, which is very affectionate through-out, in this manner—

Elinor, I charge you to learn the following stanza by heart:—

> The monarch may forget his crown,
>   That on his head an hour hath been;
> The bridegroom may forget his bride
>   Was made his wedded wife yestreen;
> The mother may forget her child,
>   That smiles so sweetly on her knee:
> But I'll remember thee, Glencairn,
>   And all that thou hast done for me.

The lines are in Burns—you know, we read him for the first time to-gether at Margate—and I have been used to refer them to you, and to call you, in my mind, *Glencairn,*—for you were always very good to me. I had a thousand failings, but you would love me in spite of them all. I am going to drink your health.

I shall detain my reader no longer from the narrative.

CHAPTER VIII

THEY had but four rooms in the cottage. Margaret slept in the biggest room upstairs, and her granddaughter in a kind of closet adjoining, where she could be within hearing, if her grandmother should call her in the night.

The girl was often disturbed in that manner—two or three times in a night she has been forced to leave her bed, to fetch her grandmother's cordials, or do some little service for her—but she knew that Margaret's ailings were *real* and pressing, and Rosamund never complained—never suspected, that her grandmother's requisitions had anything unreason-able in them.

The night she parted with Miss Clare, she had helped Margaret to bed, as usual—and, after saying her prayers, as the custom was, kneeling by the old lady's bedside, kissed her grandmother, and wished her a good-night—Margaret blessed her, and charged her to go to bed directly. It was her customary injunction, and Rosamund had never dreamed of dis-obeying.

So she retired to her little room. The night was warm and clear—the moon very bright—her window commanded a view of *scenes* she had been tracing in the day-time with Miss Clare.

All the events of the day past, the occurrences of their walk arose in her mind. She fancied she should like to retrace those scenes—but it was now nine o'clock, a late hour in the village.

Still she fancied it would be very charming—and then her grand-mother's injunction came powerfully to her recollection—she sighed, and turned from the window—and walked up and down her little room.

Ever, when she looked at the window, the wish returned. It was not

so *very late*. The neighbours were yet about, passing under the window
to their homes—she thought, and thought again, till her sensations became vivid, even to painfulness—her bosom was aching to give them
vent.

The village clock struck ten!—the neighbours ceased to pass under
the window. Rosamund, stealing downstairs, fastened the latch behind
her, and left the cottage.

One, that knew her, met her, and observed her with some surprise.
Another recollects having wished her a good-night. Rosamund never
returned to the cottage.

An old man, that lay sick in a small house adjoining to Margaret's,
testified the next morning, that he had plainly heard the old creature
calling for her grand-daughter. All the night long she made her moan,
and ceased not to call upon the name of Rosamund. But no Rosamund
was there—the voice died away, but not till near daybreak.

When the neighbours came to search in the morning, Margaret was
missing! She had *straggled* out of bed, and made her way into Rosamund's room—worn out with fatigue and fright, when she found the girl
not there, she had laid herself down to die—and, it is thought, she died
praying—for she was discovered in a kneeling posture, her arms and face
extended on the pillow, where Rosamund had slept the night before—a
smile was on her face in death.

CHAPTER IX

FAIN would I draw a veil over the transactions of that night—but I cannot—grief, and burning shame, forbid me to be silent—black deeds are
about to be made public, which reflect a stain upon our common nature.

Rosamund, enthusiastic and improvident, wandered unprotected to a
distance from her guardian doors—through lonely glens, and wood walks,
where she had rambled many a *day* in safety—till she arrived at a shady
copse, out of the hearing of any human habitation.

Matravis met her.——"Flown with insolence and wine," returning
home late at night, he passed that way!

Matravis was a very ugly man. Sallow-complexioned! and if hearts
can wear that colour, his heart was sallow-complexioned also.

A young man with *gray* deliberation! cold and systematic in all his
plans; and all his plans were evil. His very lust was systematic.

He would brood over his bad purposes for such a dreary length of time
that, it might have been expected, some solitary check of conscience
must have intervened to save him from commission. But that *Light from
Heaven* was extinct in his dark bosom.

Nothing that is great, nothing that is amiable, existed for this unhappy man. He feared, he envied, he suspected; but he never loved.
The sublime and beautiful in nature, the excellent and becoming in
morals, were things placed beyond the capacity of his sensations. He

loved not poetry—nor ever took a lonely walk to meditate—never beheld virtue, which he did not try to disbelieve, or female beauty and innocence, which he did not lust to contaminate.

A sneer was perpetually upon his face, and malice *grinning* at his heart. He would say the most ill-natured things, with the least remorse, of any man I ever knew. This gained him the reputation of a wit—other *traits* got him the reputation of a villain.

And this man formerly paid his court to Elinor Clare!—with what success I leave my readers to determine. It was not in Elinor's nature to despise any living thing—but in the estimation of this man, to be rejected was to be *despised*—and Matravis *never forgave*.

He had long turned his eyes upon Rosamund Gray. To steal from the bosom of her friends the jewel they prized so much, the little ewe lamb they held so dear, was a scheme of delicate revenge, and Matravis had a twofold motive for accomplishing this young maid's ruin.

Often had he met her in her favourite solitudes, but found her ever cold and inaccessible. Of late the girl had avoided straying far from her own home, in the fear of meeting him—but she had never told her fears to Allan.

Matravis had, till now, been content to be a villain within the limits of the law—but, on the present occasion, hot fumes of wine, co-operating with his deep desire of revenge, and the insolence of an unhoped-for meeting, overcame his customary prudence, and Matravis rose, at once, to an audacity of glorious mischief.

Late at night he met her, a lonely, unprotected virgin—no friend at hand—no place near of refuge.

Rosamund Gray, my soul is exceeding sorrowful for thee—I loathe to tell the hateful circumstances of thy wrongs. Night and silence were the only witnesses of this young maid's disgrace—Matravis fled.

Rosamund, polluted and disgraced, wandered, an abandoned thing, about the fields and meadows till daybreak. Not caring to return to the cottage, she sat herself down before the gate of Miss Clare's house—in a stupor of grief.

Elinor was just rising, and had opened the windows of her chamber, when she perceived her desolate young friend. She ran to embrace her— she brought her into the house—she took Ler to her bosom—she kissed her—she spake to her; but Rosamund could not speak.

Tidings came from the cottage. Margaret's death was an event which could not be kept concealed from Rosamund. When the sweet maid heard of it, she languished, and fell sick—she never held up her head after that time.

If Rosamund had been a *sister*, she could not have been kindlier treated than by her two friends.

Allan had prospects in life—might, in time, have married into any of the first families in Hertfordshire—but Rosamund Gray, humbled though she was, and put to shame, had yet a charm for *him*—and he would

have been content to share his fortunes with her yet, if Rosamund would
have lived to be his companion.

But this was not to be—and the girl soon after died. She expired in
the arms of Elinor—quiet, gentle, as she lived—thankful that she died
not among strangers—and expressing, by signs rather than words, a
gratitude for the most trifling services, the common offices of humanity.
She died uncomplaining; and this young maid, this untaught Rosamund, might have given a lesson to the grave philosopher in death.

CHAPTER X

I WAS but a boy when these events took place. All the village remember
the story, and tell of Rosamund Gray, and old blind Margaret.

I parted from Allan Clare on that disastrous night, and set out for
Edinburgh the next morning, before the facts were commonly known—I
heard not of them—and it was four months before I received a letter
from Allan.

"His heart," he told me, "was gone from him—for his sister had died
of a frenzy fever!"—not a word of Rosamund in the letter—I was left
to collect her story from sources which may one day be explained.

I soon after quitted Scotland, on the death of my father, and returned
to my native village. Allan had left the place, and I could gain no
information, whether he were dead or living.

I passed the *cottage*. I did not dare to look that way, or to inquire
who lived there. A little dog, that had been Rosamund's, was yelping in
my path. I laughed aloud like one mad, whose mind had suddenly gone
from him—I stared vacantly around me, like one alienated from common perceptions.

But I was young at that time, and the impression became gradually
weakened as I mingled in the business of life. It is now *ten years* since
these events took place, and I sometimes think of them as unreal. Allan
Clare was a dear friend to me—but there are times when Allan and his
sister, Margaret and her grand-daughter, appear like personages of a
dream—an idle dream.

CHAPTER XI

STRANGE things have happened unto me—I seem scarce awake—but I
will recollect my thoughts, and try to give an account of what has befallen me in the last few weeks.

Since my father's death our family have resided in London. I am in
practice as a surgeon there. My mother died two years after we left
Widford.

A month or two ago, I had been busying myself in drawing up the
above narrative, intending to make it public. The employment had forced
my mind to dwell upon *facts*, which had begun to fade from it—the

memory of old times became vivid, and more vivid—I felt a strong desire to revisit the scenes of my native village—of the young loves of Rosamund and her Clare.

A kind of dread had hitherto kept me back; but I was restless now, till I had accomplished my wish. I set out one morning to walk—I reached Widford about eleven in the forenoon—after a slight breakfast at my inn—where I was mortified to perceive the old landlord did not know me again—(old Thomas Billet—he has often made angle-rods for me when a child)—I rambled over all my accustomed haunts.

Our old house was vacant, and to be sold. I entered, unmolested, into the room that had been my bedchamber. I kneeled down on the spot where my little bed had stood—I felt like a child—I prayed like one—it seemed as though old times were to return again—I looked round involuntarily, expecting to see some face I knew—but all was naked and mute. The bed was gone. My little pane of painted window, through which I loved to look at the sun when I awoke in a fine summer's morning, was taken out, and had been replaced by one of common glass.

I visited, by turns, every chamber—they were all desolate and unfurnished, one excepted, in which the owner had left a harpsichord, probably to be sold—I touched the keys—I played some old Scottish tunes, which had delighted me when a child. Past associations revived with the music—blended with a sense of *unreality,* which at last became too powerful—I rushed out of the room to give vent to my feelings.

I wandered, scarce knowing where, into an old wood, that stands at the back of the house—we called it the *Wilderness.* A well-known *form* was missing, that used to meet me in this place—it was thine—Ben Moxam—the kindest, gentlest, politest of human beings, yet was he nothing higher than a gardener in the family. Honest creature! thou didst never pass me in my childish rambles, without a soft speech, and a smile. I remember thy good-natured face. But there is one thing, for which I can never forgive thee, Ben Moxam—that thou didst join with an old maiden aunt of mine in a cruel plot, to lop away the hanging branches of the old fir-trees—I remember them sweeping to the ground.

I have often left my childish sports to ramble in this place—its glooms and its solitude had a mysterious charm for my young mind, nurturing within me that love of quietness and lonely thinking, which has accompanied me to maturer years.

In this *Wilderness* I found myself, after a ten years' absence. Its stately fir-trees were yet standing, with all their luxuriant company of underwood—the squirrel was there, and the melancholy cooings of the wood-pigeon—all was as I had left it—my heart softened at the sight—it seemed as though my character had been suffering a *change* since I forsook these shades.

My parents were both dead—I had no counsellor left, no experience of age to direct me, no sweet voice of reproof. The Lord had taken away my *friends,* and I knew not where He had laid them. I paced round the wilderness, seeking a comforter. I prayed that I might be restored to that *state of innocence,* in which I had wandered in those shades.

Methought my request was heard, for it seemed as though the stains of manhood were passing from me, and I were relapsing into the purity and simplicity of childhood. I was content to have been moulded into a perfect child. I stood still, as in a trance. I dreamed that I was enjoying a personal intercourse with my heavenly Father—and, extravagantly, put off the shoes from my feet—for the place where I stood, I thought, was holy ground.

This state of mind could not last long, and I returned with languid feelings to my inn. I ordered my dinner—green peas and a sweetbread— it had been a favourite dish with me in my childhood—I was allowed to have it on my birth-days. I was impatient to see it come upon table— but, when it came, I could scarce eat a mouthful—my tears choked me. I called for wine—I drank a pint and a half of red wine—and not till then had I dared to visit the churchyard, where my parents were interred.

The *cottage* lay in my way—Margaret had chosen it for that very reason, to be near the church—for the old lady was regular in her attendance on public worship—I passed on—and in a moment found myself among the tombs.

I had been present at my father's burial, and knew the spot again— my mother's funeral I was prevented by illness from attending—a plain stone was placed over the grave, with their initials carved upon it—for they both occupied one grave.

I prostrated myself before the spot—I kissed the earth that covered them—I contemplated, with gloomy delight, the time when I should mingle my dust with theirs—and kneeled, with my arms incumbent or the gravestone, in a kind of mental prayer—for I could not speak.

Having performed these duties, I arose with quieter feelings, and felt leisure to attend to indifferent objects.—Still I continued in the church-yard, reading the various inscriptions, and moralizing on them with that kind of levity, which will not unfrequently spring up in the mind, in the midst of deep melancholy.

I read of nothing but careful parents, loving husbands, and dutiful children. I said jestingly, where be all the *bad* people buried? Bad parents, bad husbands, bad children—what cemeteries are appointed for these?—do they not sleep in consecrated ground? or is it but a pious fiction, a generous oversight, in the survivors, which thus tricks out men's epitaphs when dead, who, in their lifetime, discharged the offices of life, perhaps, but lamely? Their failings, with their reproaches, now sleep with them in the grave. *Man wars not with the dead.* It is a *trait* of human nature, for which I love it.

I had not observed, till now, a little group assembled at the other end of the churchyard; it was a company of children, who were gathered round a young man, dressed in black, sitting on a gravestone.

He seemed to be asking them questions—probably, about their learning—and one little dirty ragged-headed fellow was clambering up his knees to kiss him. The children had been eating black cherries—for some of the stones were scattered about, and their mouths were smeared with them.

As I drew near them, I thought I discerned in the stranger a mild benignity of countenance, which I had somewhere seen before—I gazed at him more attentively.

It was Allan Clare! sitting on the grave of his sister.

I threw my arms about his neck. I exclaimed "Allan"—he turned his eyes upon me—he knew me—we both wept aloud—it seemed as though the interval since we parted had been as nothing—I cried out, "Come, and tell me about these things."

I drew him away from his little friends—he parted with a show of reluctance from the churchyard—Margaret and her grand-daughter lay buried there, as well as his sister—I took him to my inn—secured a room, where we might be private—ordered fresh wine—scarce knowing what I did, I danced for joy.

Allan was quite overcome, and taking me by the hand, he said, "This repays me for all."

It was a proud day for me—I had found the friend I thought dead— earth seemed to me no longer valuable, than as it contained *him;* and existence a blessing no longer than while I should live to be his comforter.

I began, at leisure, to survey him with more attention. Time and grief had left few traces of that fine *enthusiasm*, which once burned in his countenance—his eyes had lost their original fire, but they retained an uncommon sweetness, and whenever they were turned upon me, their smile pierced to my heart.

"Allan, I fear you have been a sufferer?" He replied not, and I could not press him further. I could not call the dead to life again.

So we drank and told old stories—and repeated old poetry—and sang old songs—as if nothing had happened. We sat till very late. I forgot that I had purposed returning to town that evening—to Allan all places were alike—I grew noisy, he grew cheerful—Allan's old manners, old enthusiasm, were returning upon him—we laughed, we wept, we mingled our tears, and talked extravagantly.

Allan was my chamber-fellow that night—and lay awake planning schemes of living together under the same roof, entering upon similar pursuits,—and praising GOD, that we had met.

I was obliged to return to town the next morning, and Allan proposed to accompany me. "Since the death of his sister," he told me, "he had been a wanderer."

In the course of our walk he unbosomed himself without reserve— told me many particulars of his way of life for the last nine or ten years, which I do not feel myself at liberty to divulge.

Once, on my attempting to cheer him, when I perceived him over thoughtful, he replied to me in these words:

"Do not regard me as unhappy when you catch me in these moods. I am never more happy than at times when, by the cast of my countenance, men judge me most miserable.

"My friend, the events which have left this sadness behind them are of no recent date. The melancholy which comes over me with the recollection of them is not hurtful, but only tends to soften and tranquillise my mind, to detach me from the restlessness of human pursuits.

"The stronger I feel this detachment, the more I find myself drawn heavenward to the contemplation of spiritual objects.

"I love to keep old friendships alive and warm within me, because I expect a renewal of them in the *World of Spirits*.

"I am a wandering and unconnected thing on the earth. I have made no new friendships, that can compensate me for the loss of the old—and the more I know mankind, the more does it become necessary for me to supply their loss by little images, recollections, and circumstances of past pleasures.

"I am sensible that I am surrounded by a multitude of very worthy people, plain-hearted souls, sincere and kind. But they have hitherto eluded my pursuit, and will continue to bless the little circle of their families and friends, while I must remain a stranger to them.

"Kept at a distance by mankind, I have not ceased to love them—and could I find the cruel persecutor, the malignant instrument of GOD's judgments on me and mine, I think I would forgive, and try to love him too.

"I have been a quiet sufferer. From the beginning of my calamities it was given to me, not to see the hand of man in them. I perceived a mighty arm, which none but myself could see, extended over me. I gave my heart to the Purifier, and my will to the Sovereign Will of the Universe. The irresistible wheels of destiny passed on in their everlasting rotation,—and I suffered myself to be carried along with them without complaining."

CHAPTER XII

ALLAN told me that for some years past, feeling himself disengaged from every personal tie, but not alienated from human sympathies, it had been his taste, his *humour* he called it, to spend a great portion of his time in *hospitals* and *lazar-houses*.

He had found a *wayward pleasure*, he refused to name it a virtue, in tending a description of people, who had long ceased to expect kindness or friendliness from mankind, but were content to accept the reluctant services, which the oftentimes unfeeling instruments and servants of these well-meant institutions deal out to the poor sick people under their care.

It is not medicine, it is not broths and coarse meats, served up at a stated hour with all the hard formalities of a prison—it is not the scanty dole of a bed to die on—which dying man requires from his species.

Looks, attentions, consolations,—in a word, *sympathies*, are what a man most needs in this awful close of mortal sufferings. A kind look, a smile, a drop of cold water to the parched lip—for these things a man shall bless you in death.

And these better things than cordials did Allan love to administer— to stay by a bedside the whole day, when something disgusting in a patient's distemper has kept the very nurses at a distance—to sit by, while the poor wretch got a little sleep—and be there to smile upon him when he awoke—to slip a guinea, now and then, into the hands of a nurse or attendant—these things have been to Allan as *privileges*, for which he was content to live; choice marks, and circumstances, of his Maker's goodness to him.

And I do not know whether occupations of this kind be not a spring of purer and nobler delight (certainly instances of a more disinterested virtue) than arises from what are called Friendships of Sentiment.

Between two persons of liberal education, like opinions, and common feelings, oftentimes subsists a Variety of Sentiment, which disposes each to look upon the other as the only being in the universe worthy of friend- ship, or capable of understanding it,—themselves they consider as the solitary receptacles of all that is delicate in feeling, or stable in attach- ment: when the odds are, that under every green hill, and in every crowded street, people of equal worth are to be found, who do more good in their generation, and make less noise in the doing of it.

It was in consequence of these benevolent propensities, I have been describing, that Allan oftentimes discovered considerable inclinations in favour of my way of life, which I have before mentioned as being that of a surgeon. He would frequently attend me on my visits to patients; and I began to think that he had serious intentions of making my pro- fession his study.

He was present with me at a scene—a *death-bed scene*—I shudder when I do but think of it.

CHAPTER XIII

I WAS sent for the other morning to the assistance of a gentleman, who had been wounded in a duel,—and his wounds by unskilful treatment had been brought to a dangerous crisis.

The uncommonness of the name, which was *Matravis*, suggested to me, that this might possibly be no other than Allan's old enemy. Under this apprehension, I did what I could to dissuade Allan from accom- panying me—but he seemed bent upon going, and even pleased himself with the notion, that it might lie within his ability to do the unhappy man some service. So he went with me.

When we came to the house, which was in Soho Square, we discovered that it was indeed the man—the identical Matravis, who had done all that mischief in times past—but not in a condition to excite any other sensation than pity in a heart more hard than Allan's.

Intense pain had brought on a delirium—we perceived this on first entering the room—for the wretched man was raving to himself—talking idly in mad unconnected sentences—that yet seemed, at times, to have a reference to *past facts*.

One while he told us his dream. "He had lost his way on a great heath, to which there seemed no end—it was cold, cold, cold—and dark, very dark—an old woman in leading-strings, *blind*, was groping about for a guide"—and then he frightened me,—for he seemed disposed to be *jocular*, and sang a song about "an old woman clothed in grey," and said "he did not believe in a devil."

Presently he bid us "not tell Allan Clare."—Allan was hanging over him at that very moment, sobbing.—I could not resist the impulse, but cried out, "*This* is Allan Clare—Allan Clare is come to see you, my dear Sir."—The wretched man did not hear me, I believe, for he turned his head away, and began talking of *charnel-houses*, and *dead men*, and "whether they knew anything that passed in their coffins."

Matravis died that night.

ESSAYS

ESSAYS

RECOLLECTIONS OF CHRIST'S HOSPITAL

To comfort the desponding parent with the thought that, without diminishing the stock which is imperiously demanded to furnish the more pressing and homely wants of our nature, he has disposed of one or more perhaps out of a numerous offspring, under the shelter of a care scarce less tender than the paternal, where not only their bodily cravings shall be supplied, but that mental *pabulum* is also dispensed, which HE hath declared to be no less necessary to our sustenance, who said, that, "not by bread alone man can live": for this Christ's Hospital unfolds her bounty. Here neither, on the one hand, are the youth lifted up above their family, which we must suppose liberal, though reduced; nor on the other hand, are they liable to be depressed below its level by the mean habits and sentiments which a common charity-school generates. It is, in a word, an Institution to keep those who have yet held up their heads in the world from sinking; to keep alive the spirit of a decent household, when poverty was in danger of crushing it; to assist those who are the most willing, but not always the most able, to assist themselves; to separate a child from his family for a season, in order to render him back hereafter, with feelings and habits more congenial to it, than he could even have attained by remaining at home in the bosom of it. It is a preserving and renovating principle, an antidote for the *res angusta domi*, when it presses, as it always does, most heavily upon the most ingenuous natures.

This is Christ's Hospital; and whether its character would be improved by confining its advantages to the very lowest of the people, let those judge who have witnessed the looks, the gestures, the behaviour, the manner of their play with one another, their deportment towards strangers, the whole aspect and physiognomy of that vast assemblage of boys on the London foundation, who freshen and make alive again with their sports the else mouldering cloisters of the old Grey Friars—which strangers who have never witnessed, if they pass through Newgate Street, or by Smithfield, would do well to go a little out of their way to see.

For the Christ's Hospital boy feels that he is no charity-boy; he feels it in the antiquity and regality of the foundation to which he belongs; in the usage which he meets with at school, and the treatment he is accustomed to out of its bounds; in the respect and even kindness, which his well-known garb never fails to procure him in the streets of the metrop-

olis; he feels it in his education, in that measure of classical attair
ments, which every individual at that school, though not destined to a
learned profession, has it in his power to procure, attainments which it
would be worse than folly to put in the reach of the labouring classes
to acquire: he feels it in the numberless comforts, and even magnifi-
cences, which surround him; in his old and awful cloisters, with their
traditions; in his spacious schoolrooms, and in the well-ordered, airy,
and lofty rooms where he sleeps; in his stately dining-hall, hung round
with pictures, by Verrio, Lely, and others, one of them surpassing in size
and grandeur almost any other in the kingdom[1]; above all, in the very
extent and magnitude of the body to which he belongs, and the consequent spirit, the intelligence, and public conscience, which is the result
of so many various yet wonderfully combining members. Compared with
this last-named advantage, what is the stock of information (I do not
here speak of book-learning, but of that knowledge which boy receives
from boy), the mass of collected opinions, the intelligence in common,
among the few and narrow members of an ordinary boarding-school?

The Christ's Hospital or Blue-coat boy has a distinctive character of
his own, as far removed from the abject qualities of a common charity-
boy as it is from the disgusting forwardness of a lad brought up at some
other of the public schools. There is *pride* in it, accumulated from the
circumstances which I have described, as differencing him from the former; and there is *a restraining modesty* from a sense of obligation and
dependence, which must ever keep his deportment from assimilating to
that of the latter. His very garb, as it is antique and venerable, feeds his
self-respect; as it is a badge of dependence, it restrains the natural petulance of that age from breaking out into overt acts of insolence. This
produces silence and a reserve before strangers, yet not that cowardly
shyness which boys mewed up at home will feel; he will speak up when
spoken to, but the stranger must begin the conversation with him. Within his bounds he is all fire and play; but in the streets he steals along
with all the self-concentration of a young monk. He is never known to
mix with other boys, they are a sort of laity to him. All this proceeds, I
have no doubt, from the continual consciousness which he carries about
him of the difference of his dress from that of the rest of the world; with
a modest jealousy over himself, lest, by over-hastily mixing with common and secular playfellows, he should commit the dignity of his cloth.
Nor let any one laugh at this; for, considering the propensity of the
multitude, and especially of the small multitude, to ridicule anything unusual in dress—above all, where such peculiarity may be construed by
malice into a mark of disparagement—this reserve will appear to be nothing more than a wise instinct in the Blue-coat boy. That it is neither
pride nor rusticity, at least that it has none of the offensive qualities of
either, a stranger may soon satisfy himself by putting a question to any

[1] By Verrio, representing James the Second on his throne, surrounded by his cour
tiers (all curious portraits), receiving the mathematical pupils at their annual prese·
tation: a custom still kept up on New-year's-day at Court.

of these boys: he may be sure of an answer couched in terms of plain civility, neither loquacious nor embarrassed. Let him put the same question to a parish-boy, or to one of the trencher-caps in the —— cloisters, and the impudent reply of the one shall not fail to exasperate any more than the certain servility, and mercenary eye to reward, which he will meet with in the other, can fail to depress and sadden him.

The Christ's Hospital boy is a religious character. His school is eminently a religious foundation; it has its peculiar prayers, its services at set times, its graces, hymns, and anthems, following each other in an almost monastic closeness of succession. This religious character in him is not always untinged with superstition. That is not wonderful, when we consider the thousand tales and traditions which must circulate, with undisturbed credulity, amongst so many boys, that have so few checks to their belief from any intercourse with the world at large; upon whom their equals in age must work so much, their elders so little. With this leaning towards an over-belief in matters of religion, which will soon correct itself when he comes out into society, may be classed a turn for romance above most other boys. This is to be traced in the same manner to their excess of society with each other, and defect of mingling with the world. Hence the peculiar avidity with which such books as the Arabian Nights' Entertainments, and others of a still wilder cast, are, or at least were in my time, sought for by the boys. I remember when some half-dozen of them set off from school, without map, card, or compass, on a serious expedition to find out *Philip Quarll's Island*.

The Christ's Hospital boy's sense of right and wrong is peculiarly tender and apprehensive. It is even apt to run out into ceremonial observances, and to impose a yoke upon itself beyond the strict obligations of the moral law. Those who were contemporaries with me at that school thirty years ago, will remember with what more than Judaic rigour the eating of the fat of certain boiled meats[1] was interdicted. A boy would have blushed as at the exposure of some heinous immorality, to have been detected eating that forbidden portion of his allowance of animal food, the whole of which, while he was in health, was little more than sufficient to allay his hunger. The same, or even greater, refinement was shown in the rejection of certain kinds of sweet-cake. What gave rise to these supererogatory penances, these self-denying ordinances, I could never learn[2]; they certainly argue no defect of the conscientious principle. A little excess in that article is not undesirable in youth, to make allowance for the inevitable waste which comes in maturer years. But in the less ambiguous line of duty, in those directions of the moral feelings

---

[1] Under the denomination of *gags*.

[2] I am told that the late steward [Mr. Hathaway] who evinced on many occasions a most praiseworthy anxiety to promote the comfort of the boys, had occasion for all his address and perseverance to eradicate the first of these unfortunate prejudices, in which he at length happily succeeded, and thereby restored to one-half of the animal nutrition of the school those honours which painful superstition and blind zeal had so long conspired to withhold from it.

which cannot be mistaken or depreciated, I will relate what took place in the year 1785, when Mr. Perry, the steward, died. I must be pardoned for taking my instances from my own times. Indeed, the vividness·of my recollections, while I am upon this subject, almost bring back those times; they are present to me still. But I believe that in the years which have elapsed since the period which I speak of, the character of the Christ's Hospital boy is very little changed. Their situation in point of many comforts is improved; but that which I ventured before to term the *public conscience* of the school, the pervading moral sense, of which every mind partakes and to which so many individual minds contribute, remains, I believe, pretty much the same as when I left it. I have seen, within this twelvemonth almost, the change which has been produced upon a boy of eight or nine years of age, upon being admitted into that school; how, from a pert young coxcomb, who thought that all knowledge was comprehended within his shallow brains, because a smattering of two or three languages and one or two sciences were stuffed into him by injudicious treatment at home, by a mixture with the wholesome society of so many schoolfellows, in less time than I have spoken of, he has sunk to his own level, and is contented to be carried on in the quiet orbit of modest self-knowledge in which the common mass of that unpresumptuous assemblage of boys seem to move: from being a little unfeeling mortal, he has got to feel and reflect. Nor would it be a difficult matter to show how, at a school like this, where the boy is neither entirely separated from home, nor yet exclusively under its influence, the best feelings, the filial for instance, are brought to a maturity which they could not have attained under a completely domestic education; how the relation of a parent is rendered less tender by unremitted association, and the very awfulness of age is best apprehended by some sojourning amidst the comparative levity of youth; how absence, not drawn out by too great extension into alienation or forgetfulness, puts an edge upon the relish of occasional intercourse, and the boy is made the better *child* by that which keeps the force of that relation from being felt as perpetually pressing on him; how the substituted paternity, into the care of which he is adopted, while in everything substantial it makes up for the natural, in the necessary omission of individual fondnesses and partialities, directs the mind only the more strongly to appreciate that natural and first tie, in which such weaknesses are the bond of strength, and the appetite which craves after them betrays no perverse palate. But these speculations rather belong to the question of the comparative advantages of a public over a private education in general. I must get back to my favourite school; and to that which took place when our old and good steward died.

And I will say, that when I think of the frequent instances which I have met with in children, of a hard-heartedness, a callousness, and insensibility to the loss of relations, even of those who have begot and nourished them, I cannot but consider it as a proof of something in the peculiar conformation of that school, favourable to the expansion of the best feelings of our nature, that, at the period which I am noticing, out of five hundred boys there was not a dry eye to be found among them, nor a heart that did not beat with genuine emotion. Every impulse to play, until the funeral day was past, seemed suspended throughout the school; and the boys, lately so mirthful and sprightly, were seen pacing their cloisters alone, or in sad groups standing about, few of them without some token, such as their slender means could provide, a black riband or something, to denote respect and a sense of their loss. The time itself was a time of anarchy, a time in which all authority (out of school hours) was abandoned. The ordinary restraints were for those days superseded; and the gates, which at other times kept us in, were left without watchers. Yet, with the exception of one or two graceless boys at most, who took advantage of that suspension of authorities to *skulk out,* as it was called, the whole body of that great school kept rigorously within their bounds, by a voluntary self-imprisonment; and they who broke bounds, though they escaped punishment from any master, fell into a general disrepute among us, and, for that which at any other time would have been applauded and admired as a mark of spirit, were consigned to infamy and reprobation; so much *natural government* have gratitude and the principles of reverence and love, and so much did a respect to their dead friends prevail with these Christ's Hospital boys, above any fear which his presence among them when living could ever produce. And if the impressions which were made on my mind so long ago are to be trusted, very richly did their steward deserve this tribute. It is a pleasure to me even now to call to mind his portly form, the regal awe which he always contrived to inspire, in spite of a tenderness and even weakness of nature that would have enfeebled the reins of discipline in any other master; a yearning of tenderness towards those under his protection, which could make five hundred boys at once feel towards him each as to their individual father. He had faults, with which we had nothing to do; but, with all his faults, indeed, Mr. Perry was a most extraordinary creature. Contemporary with him and still living, though he has long since resigned his occupation, will it be impertinent to mention the name of our excellent upper grammar-master, the Rev. James Boyer? He was a disciplinarian, indeed, of a different stamp from him whom I have just described; but, now the terrors of the rod, and of a temper a little too hasty to leave the more nervous of us quite at our ease to do justice to his merits in those days, are long since over, ungrateful were we if we should refuse our testimony to that unwearied assiduity with which he attended to the particular improvement of each of us. Had we been the offspring of the first gentry in the land, he could not have been instigated by the strongest views of recompense and reward to have made himself a greater slave to the most laborious of all occupations than he did for us sons of charity, from whom, or from our parents, he could expect nothing. He has had his reward in the satisfaction of having discharged his duty, in the pleasurable consciousness of having advanced the respectability of that institution to which, both man and boy, he was

attached; in the honours to which so many of his pupils have successfully aspired at both our Universities; and in the staff with which the
Governors of the Hospital, at the close of his hard labours, with the
highest expressions of the obligations the school lay under to him,
unanimously voted to present him.

I have often considered it among the felicities of the constitution of
this school, that the offices of steward and schoolmaster are kept distinct;
the strict business of education alone devolving upon the latter, while
the former has the charge of all things out of school, the control of the
provisions, the regulation of meals, of dress, of play, and the ordinary
intercourse of the boys. By this division of management, a superior respectability must attach to the teacher while his office is unmixed with
any of these lower concerns. A still greater advantage over the construction of common boarding-schools is to be found in the settled salaries of
the masters, rendering them totally free of obligation to any individual
pupil or his parents. This never fails to have its effect at schools where
each boy can reckon up to a hair what profit the master derives from
him, where he views him every day in the light of a caterer, a provider
for the family, who is to get so much by him in each of his meals. Boys
will see and consider these things; and how much must the sacred character of preceptor suffer in their minds by these degrading associations!
The very bill which the pupil carries home with him at Christmas, eked
out, perhaps, with elaborate though necessary minuteness, instructs him
that his teachers have other ends than the mere love to learning, in the
lessons which they give him; and though they put into his hands the fine
sayings of Seneca or Epictetus, yet they themselves are none of those
disinterested pedagogues to teach philosophy *gratis*. The master, too, is
sensible that he is seen in this light; and how much this must lessen that
affectionate regard to the learners which alone can sweeten the bitter labour of instruction, and convert the whole business into unwelcome and
uninteresting task-work, many preceptors that I have conversed with on
the subject are ready, with a sad heart, to acknowledge. From this inconvenience the settled salaries of the masters of this school in great
measure exempt them; while the happy custom of choosing masters (indeed every officer of the establishment) from those who have received
their education there, gives them an interest in advancing the character
of the school, and binds them to observe a tenderness and a respect to
the children, in which a stranger, feeling that dependence which I have
spoken of, might well be expected to fail.

In affectionate recollections of the place where he was bred up, in
hearty recognitions of old schoolfellows met with again after the lapse
of years, or in foreign countries, the Christ's Hospital boy yields to none;
I might almost say, he goes beyond most other boys. The very compass
and magnitude of the school, its thousand bearings, the space it takes up
in the imagination beyond the ordinary schools, impresses a remembrance, accompanied with an elevation of mind, that attends him through
life. It is too big, too affecting an object, to pass away quickly from his

mind. The Christ's Hospital boy's friends at school are commonly his intimates through life. For me, I do not know whether a constitutional imbecility does not incline me too obstinately to cling to the remembrances of childhood; in an inverted ratio to the usual sentiments of mankind, nothing that I have been engaged in since seems of any value or importance, compared to the colours which imagination gave to everything then. I belong to no *body corporate* such as I then made a part of. —And here, before I close, taking leave of the general reader, and addressing myself solely to my old schoolfellows, that were contemporaries with me from the year 1782 to 1789, let me have leave to remember some of those circumstances of our school, which they will not be unwilling to have brought back to their minds.

And first, let us remember, as first in importance in our childish eyes, the young men (as they almost were) who, under the denomination of *Grecians,* were waiting the expiration of the period when they should be sent, at the charges of the Hospital, to one or other of our universities, but more frequently to Cambridge. These youths, from their superior acquirements, their superior age and stature, and the fewness of their numbers (for seldom above two or three at a time were inaugurated into that high order), drew the eyes of all, and especially of the younger boys, into a reverent observance and admiration. How tall they used to seem to us! how stately would they pace along the cloisters! while the play of the lesser boys was absolutely suspended, or its boisterousness at least allayed, at their presence! Not that they ever beat or struck the boys— that would have been to have demeaned themselves—the dignity of their persons alone insured them all respect. The task of blows, of corporal chastisement, they left to the common monitors, or heads of wards, who, it must be confessed, in our time had rather too much licence allowed them to oppress and misuse their inferiors; and the interference of the Grecian, who may be considered as the spiritual power, was not unfrequently called for, to mitigate by its mediation the heavy unrelenting arm of this temporal power, or monitor. In fine, the Grecians were the solemn Muftis of the school. Æras were computed from their time;—it used to be said, such or such a thing was done when S—— or T—— was Grecian.

As I ventured to call the Grecians, the Muftis of the school, the King's boys,[1] as their character then was, may well pass for the Janissaries. They were the terror of all the other boys; bred up under that hardy sailor, as well as excellent mathematician, and co-navigator with Captain Cook, William Wales. All his systems were adapted to fit them for the rough element which they were destined to encounter. Frequent and severe punishments, which were expected to be born with more than Spartan fortitude, came to be considered less as inflictions of disgrace than as trials of obstinate endurance. To make his boys hardy, and to give them early sailor-habits, seemed to be his only aim; to this every-

---

[1] The mathematical pupils, bred up to the sea, on the foundation of Charles the Second.

thing was subordinate. Moral obliquities, indeed, were sure of receiving their full recompense, for no occasion of laying on the lash was ever let slip; but the effects expected to be produced from it were something very different from contrition or mortification. There was in William Wales a perpetual fund of humour, a constant glee about him, which heightened by an inveterate provincialism of north-country dialect, absolutely took away the sting from his severities. His punishments were a game at patience, in which the master was not always worst contented when he found himself at times overcome by his pupil. What success this discipline had, or how the effects of it operated upon the after-lives of these King's boys, I cannot say: but I am sure that, for the time, they were absolute nuisances to the rest of the school. Hardy, brutal, and often wicked, they were the most graceless lump in the whole mass; older and bigger than the other boys (for, by the system of their education they were kept longer at school by two or three years than any of the rest, except the Grecians), they were a constant terror to the younger part of the school; and some who may read this, I doubt not, will remember the consternation into which the juvenile fry of us were thrown, when the cry was raised in the cloisters, that *the First Order was coming*—for so they termed the first form or class of those boys. Still these sea-boys answered some good purposes in the school. They were the military class among the boys, foremost in athletic exercises, who extended the fame of the prowess of the school far and near; and the apprentices in the vicinage, and sometimes the butchers' boys in the neighboring market, had sad occasion to attest their valour.

The time would fail me if I were to attempt to enumerate all those circumstances, some pleasant, some attended with some pain, which, seen through the mist of distance, come sweetly softened to the memory. But I must crave leave to remember our transcending superiority in those invigorating sports, leap-frog, and basting the bear; our delightful excursions in the summer holidays to the New River, near Newington, where, like otters, we would live the long day in the water, never caring for dressing ourselves, when we had once stripped; our savoury meals afterwards, when we came home almost famished with staying out all day without our dinners; our visits at other times to the Tower, where, by ancient privilege, we had free access to all the curiosities; our solemn processions through the City at Easter, with the Lord Mayor's largess of buns, wine, and a shilling, with the festive questions and civic pleasantries of the dispensing Aldermen, which were more to us than all the rest of the banquet; our stately suppings in public, where the well-lighted hall, and the confluence of well-dressed company who came to see us, made the whole look more like a concert or assembly, than a scene of a plain bread and cheese collation; the annual orations upon St. Matthew's day, in which the senior scholar, before he had done, seldom failed to reckon up, among those who had done honour to our school by being educated in it, the names of those accomplished critics and Greek scholars, Joshua Barnes and Jeremiah Markland (I marvel they left out

Camden while they were about it). Let me have leave to remember our hymns and anthems, and well-toned organ; the doleful tune of the burial anthem chaunted in the solemn cloisters, upon the seldom-occurring funeral of some schoolfellow; the festivities at Christmas, when the richest of us would club our stock to have a gaudy day, sitting round the fire, replenished to the height with logs, and the pennyless, and he that could contribute nothing, partook in all the mirth, and in some of the substantialities of the feasting; the carol sung by night at that time of the year, which, when a young boy, I have so often lain awake to hear from seven (the hour of going to bed) till ten, when it was sung by the older boys and monitors, and have listened to it, in their rude chaunting, till I have been transported in fancy to the fields of Bethlehem, and the song which was sung at that season, by angels' voices to the shepherds.

Nor would I willingly forget any of those things which administered to our vanity. The hem-stitched bands and town-made shirts, which some of the most fashionable among us wore; the town-girdles, with buckles of silver, or shining stone; the badges of the sea-boys; the cots, or superior shoe-strings, of the monitors; the medals of the markers (those who were appointed to hear the Bible read in the wards on Sunday morning and evening), which bore on their obverse in silver, as certain parts of our garments carried, in meaner metal, the countenance of our Founder, that godly and royal child, King Edward the Sixth, the flower of the Tudor name—the young flower that was untimely cropt, as it began to fill our land with its early odours—the boy-patron of boys—the serious and holy child who walked with Cranmer and Ridley—fit associate, in those tender years, for the bishops, and future martyrs of our Church, to receive, or (as occasion sometimes proved), to give instruction.

> But, ah! what means the silent tear?
> Why, e'en 'mid joy, my bosom heave?
> Ye long-lost scenes, enchantments dear!
> Lo! now I linger o'er your grave.
>
> —Fly, then, ye hours of rosy hue,
> And bear away the bloom of years!
> And quick succeed, ye sickly crew
> Of doubts and sorrows, pains and fears!
>
> Still will I ponder Fate's unaltered plan,
> Nor, tracing back the child, forget that I am man.[1]

ON THE TRAGEDIES OF SHAKSPEARE

CONSIDERED WITH REFERENCE TO THEIR FITNESS FOR STAGE-REPRESENTATION

TAKING a turn the other day in the Abbey, I was struck with the affected attitude of a figure, which I do not remember to have seen before,

---

[1] Lines meditated in the cloisters of Christ's Hospital, in the "Poetics" of Mr. George Dyer.

and which upon examination proved to be a whole-length of the celebrated Mr. Garrick. Though I would not go so far with some good Cath-
olics abroad as to shut players altogether out of consecrated ground,
yet I own I was not a little scandalised at the introduction of theatrical
airs and gestures into a place set apart to remind us of the saddest realities. Going nearer, I found inscribed under this harlequin figure the
following lines:—

> To paint fair Nature, by divine command
> Her magic pencil in his glowing hand,
> A Shakspeare rose; then, to expand his fame
> Wide o'er this breathing world, a Garrick came.
> Though sunk in death the forms the Poet drew,
> The Actor's genius bade them breathe anew;
> Though, like the bard himself, in night they lay,
> Immortal Garrick called them back to day:
> And till Eternity with power sublime
> Shall mark the mortal hour of hoary Time,
> Shakspeare and Garrick like twin-stars shall shine,
> And earth irradiate with a beam divine.

It would be an insult to my readers' understanding to attempt anything like a criticism on this farrago of false thoughts and nonsense. But
the reflection it led me into was a kind of wonder, how, from the days of
the actor here celebrated to our own, it should have been the fashion to
compliment every performer in his turn, that has had the luck to please
the Town in any of the great characters of Shakspeare, with the notion
of possessing a *mind congenial with the poet's:* how people should come
thus unaccountably to confound the power of originating poetical images
and conceptions wth the faculty of being able to read or recite the same
when put into words[1]; or what connection that absolute mastery over the
heart and soul of man, which a great dramatic poet possesses, has with
those low tricks upon the eye and ear, which a player by observing a few
general effects, which some common passion, as grief, anger, etc., usually
has upon the gestures and exterior, can so easily compass. To know the
internal workings and movements of a great mind, of an Othello or a
Hamlet for instance, the *when* and the *why* and the *how far* they should
be moved; to what pitch a passion is becoming; to give the reins and to
pull in the curb exactly at the moment when the drawing in or the slack-
ening is most graceful; seems to demand a reach of intellect of a vastly
different extent from that which is employed upon the bare imitation of
the signs of these passions in the countenance or gesture, which signs
are usually observed to be most lively and emphatic in the weaker sort
of minds, and which signs can after all but indicate some passion, as I
said before, anger, or grief, generally; but of the motives and grounds of

---

[1] It is observable that we fall into this confusion only in *dramatic* recitations. We
never dream that the gentleman who reads Lucretius in public with great applause,
is therefore a great poet and philosopher; nor do we find that Tom Davis, the bookseller, who is recorded to have recited the Paradise Lost better than any man in
England in his day (though I cannot help thinking there must be some mistake in
this tradition) was therefore, by his intimate friends, set upon a level with Milton.

the passion, wherein it differs from the same passion in low and vulgar natures, of these the actor can give no more idea by his face or gesture than the eye (without a metaphor) can speak, or the muscles utter intelligible sounds. But such is the instantaneous nature of the impressions which we take in at the eye and ear at a play-house, compared with the slow apprehension oftentimes of the understanding in reading, that we are apt not only to sink the play-writer in the consideration which we pay to the actor, but even to identify in our minds, in a perverse manner, the actor with the character which he represents. It is difficult for a frequent play-goer to disembarrass the idea of Hamlet from the person and voice of Mr. K. We speak of Lady Macbeth, while we are in reality thinking of Mrs. S. Nor is this confusion incidental alone to unlettered persons, who, not possessing the advantage of reading, are necessarily dependent upon the stage-player for all the pleasure which they can receive from the drama, and to whom the very idea of *what an author is* cannot be made comprehensible without some pain and perplexity of mind: the error is one from which persons otherwise not meanly lettered, find it almost impossible to extricate themselves.

Never let me be so ungrateful as to forget the very high degree of satisfaction which I received some years back from seeing for the first time a tragedy of Shakspeare performed, in which those two great performers sustained the principal parts. It seemed to embody and realise conceptions which had hitherto assumed no distinct shape. But dearly do we pay all our life after for this juvenile pleasure, this sense of distinctness. When the novelty is past, we find to our cost that instead of realising an idea, we have only materialised and brought down a fine vision to the standard of flesh and blood. We have let go a dream, in quest of an unattainable substance.

How cruelly this operates upon the mind, to have its free conceptions thus cramped and pressed down to the measure of a strait-lacing actuality, may be judged from that delightful sensation of freshness, with which we turn to those plays of Shakspeare which have escaped being performed, and to those passages in the acting plays of the same writer which have happily been left out in the performance. How far the very custom of hearing anything *spouted,* withers and blows upon a fine passage, may be seen in those speeches from Henry the Fifth, etc., which are current in the mouths of schoolboys, from their being to be found in *Enfield's Speaker,* and such kind of books! I confess myself utterly unable to appreciate that celebrated soliloquy in Hamlet, beginning "To be or not to be," or to tell whether it be good, bad or indifferent, it has been so handled and pawed about by declamatory boys and men, and torn so inhumanly from its living place and principle of continuity in the play, till it is become to me a perfect dead member.

It may seem a paradox, but I cannot help being of opinion that the plays of Shakspeare are less calculated for performance on a stage, than those of almost any other dramatist whatever. Their distinguishing excellence is a reason that they should be so. There is so much in them, which comes not under the province of acting, with which eye, and tone, and gesture, have nothing to do.

The glory of the scenic art is to personate passion, and the turns of passion; and the more coarse and palpable the passion is, the more hold upon the eyes and ears of the spectators the performer obviously possesses. For this reason, scolding scenes, scenes where two persons talk themselves into a fit of fury, and then in a surprising manner talk themselves out of it again, have always been the most popular upon our stage. And the reason is plain, because the spectators are here most palpably appealed to, they are the proper judges in this war of words, they are the legitimate ring that should be formed round such "intellectual prize-fighters." Talking is the direct object of the imitation here. But in all the best dramas, and in Shakspeare above all, how obvious it is, that the form of *speaking*, whether it be in soliloquy or dialogue, is only a medium, and often a highly artificial one, for putting the reader or spectator into possession of that knowledge of the inner structure and workings of mind in a character, which he could otherwise never have arrived at *in that form of composition* by any gift short of intuition. We do here as we do with novels written in the *epistolary form*. How many improprieties, perfect solecisms in letter-writing, do we put up with in Clarissa and other books, for the sake of the delight which that form upon the whole gives us!

But the practice of stage representation reduces everything to a controversy of elocution. Every character, from the boisterous blasphemings of Bajazet to the shrinking timidity of womanhood, must play the orator. The love dialogues of Romeo and Juliet, those silver-sweet sounds of lovers' tongues by night! the more intimate and sacred sweetness of nuptial colloquy between an Othello or a Posthumus with their married wives, all those delicacies which are so delightful in the reading, as when we read of those youthful dalliances in Paradise—

> As beseem'd
> Fair couple link'd in happy nuptial league,
> Alone;

by the inherent fault of stage representation, how are these things sullied and turned from their very nature by being exposed to a large assembly; when such speeches as Imogen addresses to her lord, come drawling out of the mouth of a hired actress, whose courtship, though nominally addressed to the personated Posthumus, is manifestly aimed at the spectators, who are to judge of her endearments and her returns of love!

The character of Hamlet is perhaps that by which, since the days of Betterton, a succession of popular performers have had the greatest ambition to distinguish themselves. The length of the part may be one of their reasons. But for the character itself, we find it in a play, and therefore we judge it a fit subject of dramatic representation. The play itself abounds in maxims and reflections beyond any other, and therefore we consider it as a proper vehicle for conveying moral instruction. But Hamlet himself—what does he suffer meanwhile by being dragged forth as the public schoolmaster, to give lectures to the crowd! Why, nine parts in ten of what Hamlet does, are transactions between himself and his moral sense; they are the effusions of his solitary musings, which he retires to holes and corners and the most sequestered parts of the palace to pour forth; or rather, they are the silent meditations with which his bosom is bursting, reduced to *words* for the sake of the reader, who must else remain ignorant of what is passing there. These profound sorrows, these light-and-noise-abhorring ruminations, which the tongue scarce dares utter to deaf walls and chambers, how can they be represented by a gesticulating actor, who comes and mouths them out before an audience, making four hundred people his confidants at once! I say not that it is the fault of the actor so to do; he must pronounce them *ore rotundo;* he must accompany them with his eye; he must insinuate them into his auditory by some trick of eye, tone or gesture, or he fails. *He must be thinking all the while of his appearance, because he knows that all the while the spectators are judging of it.* And this is the way to represent the shy, negligent, retiring Hamlet!

It is true that there is no other mode of conveying a vast quantity of thought and feeling to a great portion of the audience, who otherwise would never earn it for themselves by reading, and the intellectual acquisition gained this way may, for aught I know, be inestimable; but I am not arguing that Hamlet should not be acted, but how much Hamlet is made another thing by being acted. I have heard much of the wonders which Garrick performed in this part; but as I never saw him, I must have leave to doubt whether the representation of such a character came within the province of his art. Those who tell me of him, speak of his eye, of the magic of his eye, and of his commanding voice: physical properties, vastly desirable in an actor, and without which he can never insinuate meaning into an auditory,—but what have they to do with Hamlet; what have they to do with intellect? In fact, the things aimed at in theatrical representation, are to arrest the spectator's eye upon the form and the gesture, and so to gain a more favourable hearing to what is spoken: it is not what the character is, but how he looks; not what he says, but how he speaks it. I see no reason to think that if the play of Hamlet were written over again by some such writer as Banks or Lillo, retaining the process of the story, but totally omitting all the poetry of it, all the divine features of Shakspeare, his stupendous intellect; and only taking care to give us enough of passionate dialogue, which Banks or Lillo were never at a loss to furnish; I see not how the effect could be much different upon an audience, nor how the actor has it in his power to represent Shakspeare to us differently from his representation of Banks or Lillo. Hamlet would still be a youthful accomplished prince, and must be gracefully personated; he might be puzzled in his mind, wavering in his conduct, seemingly cruel to Ophelia; he might see a ghost, and start at it, and address it kindly when he found it to be his father; all this in the poorest and most homely language of the servilest creeper after nature that ever consulted the palate of an audience; without troubling Shakspeare for the matter: and I see not but there would be room for all the power which an actor has, to display itself. All the passions and changes of passion might remain: for those are much less difficult to write or act than is thought; it is a trick easy to be attained, it is but rising or falling a note or two in the voice, a whisper with a significant foreboding look to announce its approach, and so contagious the counterfeit appearance of any emotion is, that let the words be what they will, the look and tone shall carry it off and make it pass for deep skill in the passions.

It is common for people to talk of Shakspeare's plays being *so natural;* that everybody can understand him. They are natural indeed, they are grounded deep in nature, so deep that the depth of them lies out of the reach of most of us. You shall hear the same persons say that George Barnwell is very natural, and Othello is very natural, that they are both very deep; and to them they are the same kind of thing. At the one they sit and shed tears, because a good sort of young man is tempted by a naughty woman to commit a *trifling peccadillo,* the murder of an uncle or so,[1] that is all, and so comes to an untimely end, which is *so moving;* and at the other, because a blackamoor in a fit of jealousy kills his innocent white wife; and the odds are that ninety-nine out of a hundred would willingly behold the same catastrophe happen to both the heroes, and have thought the rope more due to Othello than to Barnwell. For of the texture of Othello's mind, the inward construction marvellously laid open with all its strengths and weaknesses, its heroic confidences and its human misgivings, its agonies of hate springing from the depths of love, they see no more than the spectators at a cheaper rate, who pay their pennies a-piece to look through the man's telescope in Leicester Fields, see into the inward plot and topography of the moon. Some dim thing or other they see; they see an actor personating a passion, of grief, or anger, for instance, and they recognise it as a copy of the usual external effects of such passions; or at least as being true to *that symbol of the emotion which passes current at the theatre for it,* for it is often no more than that: but of the grounds of the passion, its correspondence to a great or heroic nature, which is the only worthy object of tragedy,— that common auditors know anything of this, or can have any such notions dinned into them by the mere strength of an actor's lungs,—that

[1] If this note could hope to meet the eye of any of the Managers, I would entreat and beg of them, in the name of both the Galleries, that this insult upon the morality of the common people of London should cease to be eternally repeated in the holiday weeks. Why are the 'Prentices of this famous and well-governed city, instead of an amusement, to be treated over and over again with a nauseous sermon of George Barnwell? Why *at the end of their vistas* are we to place the *gallows?* Were I an uncle, I should not much like a nephew of mine to have such an example placed before his eyes. It is really making uncle-murder too trivial to exhibit it as done upon such slight motives;—it is attributing too much to such characters as Millwood: —it is putting things into the heads of good young men, which they would never otherwise have dreamed of. Uncles that think anything of their lives, should fairly petition the Chamberlain against it.

apprehensions foreign to them should be thus infused into them by storm, I can neither believe, nor understand how it can be possible.

We talk of Shakspeare's admirable observation of life, when we should feel, that not from a petty inquisition into those cheap and everyday characters which surrounded him, as they surround us, but from his own mind, which was, to borrow a phrase of Ben Jonson's, the very "sphere of humanity," he fetched those images of virtue and of knowledge, of which every one of us recognising a part, think we comprehend in our natures the whole; and oftentimes mistake the powers which he positively creates in us, for nothing more than indigenous faculties of our own minds, which only waited the application of corresponding virtues in him to return a full and clear echo of the same.

To return to Hamlet.—Among the distinguishing features of that wonderful character, one of the most interesting (yet painful) is that soreness of mind which makes him treat the intrusions of Polonius with harshness, and that asperity which he puts on in his interviews with Ophelia. These tokens of an unhinged mind (if they be not mixed in the latter case with a profound artifice of love, to alienate Ophelia by affected discourtesies, so to prepare her mind for the breaking off of that loving intercourse, which can no longer find a place amidst business so serious as that which he has to do) are parts of his character, which to reconcile with our admiration of Hamlet, the most patient consideration of his situation is no more than necessary; they are what we *forgive afterwards*, and explain by the whole of his character, but *at the time* they are harsh and unpleasant. Yet such is the actor's necessity of giving strong blows to the audience, that I have never seen a player in this character, who did not exaggerate and strain to the utmost these ambiguous features,—these temporary deformities in the character. They make him express a vulgar scorn at Polonius which utterly degrades his gentility, and which no explanation can render palatable; they make him show contempt, and curl up the nose at Ophelia's father,—contempt in its very grossest and most hateful form; but they get applause by it: it is natural, people say; that is, the words are scornful, and the actor expresses scorn, and that they can judge of: but why so much scorn, and of that sort, they never think of asking.

So to Ophelia.—All the Hamlets that I have ever seen, rant and rave at her as if she had committed some great crime, and the audience are highly pleased, because the words of the part are satirical, and they are enforced by the strongest expression of satirical indignation of which the face and voice are capable. But then, whether Hamlet is likely to have put on such brutal appearances to a lady whom he loved so dearly, is never thought on. The truth is, that in all such deep affections as had subsisted between Hamlet and Ophelia, there is a stock of *supererogatory love* (if I may venture to use the expression), which in any great grief of heart, especially where that which preys upon the mind cannot be communicated, confers a kind of indulgence upon the grieved party to express itself, even to its heart's dearest object, in the language of a temporary alienation; but it is not alienation, it is a distraction purely, and so it always makes itself to be felt by that object: it is not anger, but grief assuming the appearance of anger,—love awkwardly counterfeiting hate, as sweet countenances when they try to frown: but such sternness and fierce disgust as Hamlet is made to show, is no counterfeit, but the real face of absolute aversion,—of irreconcileable alienation. It may be said he puts on the madman; but then he should only so far put on this counterfeit lunacy as his own real distraction will give him leave; that is, incompletely, imperfectly; not in that confirmed, practised way, like a master of his art, or as Dame Quickly would say, "like one of those harlotry players."

I mean no disrespect to any actor, but the sort of pleasure which Shakspeare's plays give in the acting seems to me not at all to differ from that which the audience receive from those of other writers; and, *they being in themselves essentially so different from all others,* I must conclude that there is something in the nature of acting which levels all distinctions. And, in fact, who does not speak indifferently of the Gamester and of Macbeth as fine stage performances, and praise the Mrs. Beverley in the same way as the Lady Macbeth of Mrs. S.? Belvidera, and Calista, and Isabella, and Euphrasia, are they less liked than Imogen, or than Juliet, or than Desdemona? Are they not spoken of and remembered in the same way? Is not the female performer as great (as they call it) in one as in the other? Did not Garrick shine, and was he not ambitious of shining, in every drawling tragedy that his wretched day produced,—the productions of the Hills, and the Murphys, and the Browns,—and shall he have that honour to dwell in our minds for ever as an inseparable concomitant with Shakspeare? A kindred mind! O who can read that affecting sonnet of Shakspeare which alludes to his profession as a player:—

> Oh for my sake do you with Fortune chide,
> The guilty goddess of my harmless deeds,
> That did not better for my life provide
> Than public means which public custom breeds—
> Thence comes it that my name receives a brand;
> And almost thence my nature is subdued
> To what it works in, like the dyer's hand.—

Or that other confession:—

> Alas! 'tis true, I have gone here and there,
> And made myself a motley to thy view,
> Gored mine own thoughts, sold cheap what is most dear—

Who can read these instances of jealous self-watchfulness in our sweet Shakspeare, and dream of any congeniality between him and one that, by every tradition of him, appears to have been as mere a player as ever existed; to have had his mind tainted with the lowest players' vices,— envy and jealousy, and miserable cravings after applause; one who in the exercise of his profession was jealous even of the women-performers that stood in his way; a manager full of managerial tricks and stratagems and finesse; that any resemblance should be dreamed of between him and Shakspeare,—Shakspeare who, in the plenitude and consciousness of his own powers, could with that noble modesty, which we can neither imitate nor appreciate, express himself thus of his own sense of his own defects:—

> Wishing me like to one more rich in hope,
> Featured like him, like him with friends possest;
> Desiring *this man's art, and that man's scope.*

I am almost disposed to deny to Garrick the merit of being an admirer of Shakspeare! A true lover of his excellences he certainly was not; for would any true lover of them have admitted into his matchless scenes such ribald trash as Tate and Cibber, and the rest of them, that

> With their darkness durst affront his light,

have foisted into the acting plays of Shakspeare? I believe it impossible that he could have had a proper reverence for Shakspeare, and have condescended to go through that interpolated scene in Richard the Third, in which Richard tries to break his wife's heart by telling her he loves another woman, and says, "if she survives this she is immortal." Yet I doubt not he delivered this vulgar stuff with as much anxiety of emphasis as any of the genuine parts: and for acting, it is as well calculated as any. But we have seen the part of Richard lately produce great fame to an actor by his manner of playing it, and it lets us into the secret of acting, and of popular judgments of Shakspeare derived from acting. Not one of the spectators who have witnessed Mr. C.'s exertions in that part, but has come away with a proper conviction that Richard is a very wicked man, and kills little children in their beds, with something like the pleasure which the giants and ogres in children's books are represented to have taken in that practice; moreover, that he is very close and shrewd, and devilish cunning, for you could see that by his eye. But is, in fact, this the impression we have in reading the Richard of Shakspeare? Do we feel anything like disgust, as we do at that butcher-like representation of him that passes for him on the stage? A horror at his crimes blends with the effect which we feel, but how is it qualified, how is it carried off, by the rich intellect which he displays, his resources, his wit, his buoyant spirits, his vast knowledge and insight into characters, the poetry of his part,—not an atom of all which is made perceivable in Mr. C.'s way of acting it. Nothing but his crimes, his actions, is visible; they are prominent and staring; the murderer stands out, but where is the lofty genius, the man of vast capacity,—the profound, the witty, accomplished Richard?

The truth is, the characters of Shakspeare are so much the objects of meditation rather than of interest or curiosity as to their actions, that while we are reading any of his great criminal characters,—Macbeth, Richard, even Iago,—we think not so much of the crimes which they commit, as of the ambition, the aspiring spirit, the intellectual activity, which prompts them to overleap these moral fences. Barnwell is a wretched murderer; there is a certain fitness between his neck and the rope; he is the legitimate heir to the gallows; nobody who thinks at all can think of any alleviating circumstances in his case to make him a fit object of mercy. Or to take an instance from the higher tragedy, what else but a mere assassin is Glenalvon? Do we think of anything but of the crime which he commits, and the rack which he deserves? That is all which we really think about him. Whereas in corresponding characters in Shakspeare, so little do the actions comparatively affect us, that while the impulses, the inner mind in all its perverted greatness, solely seems real and is exclusively attended to, the crime is comparatively nothing. But when we see these things represented, the acts which they do are comparatively everything, their impulses nothing. The state of sublime emotion into which we are elevated by those images of night and horror which Macbeth is made to utter, that solemn prelude with which he entertains the time till the bell shall strike which is to call him to murder Duncan,—when we no longer read it in a book, when we have given up that vantage ground of abstraction which reading possesses over seeing, and come to see a man in his bodily shape before our eyes actually preparing to commit a murder, if the acting be true and impressive, as I have witnessed it in Mr. K.'s performance of that part, the painful anxiety about the act, the natural longing to prevent it while it yet seems unperpetrated, the too close pressing semblance of reality, give a pain and an uneasiness which totally destroy all the delight which the words in the book convey, where the deed doing never presses upon us with the painful sense of presence: it rather seems to belong to history,—to something past and inevitable, if it has anything to do with time at all. The sublime images, the poetry alone, is that which is present to our minds in the reading.

So to see Lear acted,—to see an old man tottering about the stage with a walking-stick, turned out of doors by his daughters in a rainy night, has nothing in it but what is painful and disgusting. We want to take him into shelter and relieve him. That is all the feeling which the acting of Lear ever produced in me. But the Lear of Shakspeare cannot be acted. The contemptible machinery by which they mimic the storm which he goes out in, is not more inadequate to represent the horrors of the real elements, than any actor can be to represent Lear; they might more easily propose to personate the Satan of Milton upon a stage, or one of Michael Angelo's terrible figures. The greatness of Lear is not in corporal dimension, but in intellectual: the explosions of his passion are terrible as a volcano; they are storms turning up and disclosing to the bottom that sea, his mind, with all its vast riches. It is his mind which is laid bare. This case of flesh and blood seems too insignificant to be thought on; even as he himself neglects it. On the stage we see nothing but corporal infirmities and weakness, the impotence of rage; while we read it, we see not Lear, but we are Lear,—we are in his mind, we are sustained by a grandeur which baffles the malice of daughters and storms; in the aberrations of his reason, we discover a mighty irregular power of reasoning, immethodised from the ordinary purposes of life, but exerting its powers, as the wind blows where it listeth, at will upon the corruptions and abuses of mankind. What have looks, or tones, to do with that sublime identification of his age with that of the *heavens themselves*, when, in his reproaches to them for conniving at the injustice of his children, he reminds them that "they themselves are old"? What gesture shall we appropriate to this? What has the voice or the eye to do with such things? But the play is beyond all art, as the tamperings with it show: it is too hard and stony; it must have love-scenes, and a happy ending. It is not enough that Cordelia is a daughter, she must shine as a lover too. Tate has put his hook in the nostrils of this Leviathan, for Garrick and his followers, the show-men of the scene, to draw the mighty beast about more easily. A happy ending!—as if the living martyrdom that Lear had gone through,—the flaying of his feelings alive, did not make a fair dismissal from the stage of life the only decorous thing for him. If he is to live and be happy after, if he could sustain this world's burden after, why all this pudder and preparation,— why torment us with all this unnecessary sympathy? As if the childish pleasure of getting his gilt robes and sceptre again could tempt him to act over again his misused station—as if, at his years and with his experience, anything was left but to die.

Lear is essentially impossible to be represented on a stage. But how many dramatic personages are there in Shakspeare, which though more tractable and feasible (if I may so speak) than Lear, yet from some circumstance, some adjunct to their character, are improper to be shown to our bodily eye! Othello for instance. Nothing can be more soothing, more flattering to the nobler parts of our natures, than to read of a young Venetian lady of the highest extraction, through the force of love and from a sense of merit in him whom she loved, laying aside every consideration of kindred, and country, and colour, and wedding with a *coal-black Moor*—(for such he is represented, in the imperfect state of knowledge respecting foreign countries in those days, compared with our own, or in compliance with popular notions, though the Moors are now well enough known to be by many shades less unworthy of a white woman's fancy)—it is the perfect triumph of virtue over accidents, of the imagination over the senses. She sees Othello's colour in his mind. But upon the stage, when the imagination is no longer the ruling faculty, but we are left to our poor unassisted senses, I appeal to every one that has seen Othello played, whether he did not, on the contrary, sink Othello's mind in his colour; whether he did not find something extremely revolting in the courtship and wedded caresses of Othello and Desdemona; and whether the actual sight of the thing did not over-weigh all that beautiful compromise which we make in reading;—and the reason it should do so is obvious, because there is just so much reality presented to our senses as to give a perception of disagreement, with not enough of belief in the internal motives,—all that which is unseen,—to overpower and reconcile the first and obvious prejudices.[1] What we see upon a stage is body and bodily action; what we are conscious of in reading is almost exclusively the mind, and its movements; and this I think may sufficiently account for the very different sort of delight with which the same play so often affects us in the reading and the seeing.

It requires little reflection to perceive, that if those characters in Shakspeare which are within the precincts of nature, have yet something in them which appeals too exclusively to the imagination, to admit of their being made objects to the senses without suffering a change and a diminution,—that still stronger the objection must lie against representing another line of characters, which Shakspeare has introduced to give a wildness and a supernatural elevation to his scenes, as if to remove them still farther from that assimilation to common life in which their excellence is vulgarly supposed to consist. When we read the incantations of those terrible beings the Witches in Macbeth, though some of the ingredients of their hellish composition savour of the grotesque, yet is the effect upon us other than the most serious and appalling that can be imagined? Do we not feel spellbound as Macbeth was? Can any mirth accompany a sense of their presence? We might as well laugh under a consciousness of the principle of Evil himself being truly and really present with us. But attempt to bring these things on to a stage, and you turn them instantly into so many old women, that men and children are to laugh at. Contrary to the old saying, that "seeing is believing," the sight actually destroys the faith; and the mirth in which we indulge at their expense, when we see these creatures upon a stage, seems to be a sort of indemnification which we make to ourselves for the terror which they put us in when reading made them an object of belief,—when we surrendered up our reason to the poet, as children to their nurses and their elders; and we laugh at our fears as children, who thought they saw something in the dark, triumph when the bringing in of a candle discovers the vanity of their fears. For this exposure of supernatural agents upon a stage is truly bringing in a candle to expose their own delusiveness. It is the solitary taper and the book that generates a faith in these terrors: a ghost by chandelier light, and in good company, deceives no spectators,—a ghost that can be measured by the eye, and his human dimensions made out at leisure. The sight of a well-lighted house, and a well-dressed audience, shall arm the most nervous child against any apprehensions: as Tom Brown says of the impenetrable skin of Achilles

---

[1] The error of supposing that because Othello's colour does not offend us in the reading, it should also not offend us in the seeing, is just such a fallacy as supposing that an Adam and Eve in a picture shall affect us just as they do in the poem. But in the poem we for a while have Paradisaical senses given us, which vanish when we see a man and his wife without clothes in the picture. The painters themselves feel this, as is apparent by the awkward shifts they have recourse to, to make them look not quite naked; by a sort of prophetic anachronism, antedating the invention of fig-leaves. So in the reading of the play, we see with Desdemona's eyes: in the seeing of it, we are forced to look with our own.

with his impenetrable armour over it, "Bully Dawson would have fought the devil with such advantages."

Much has been said, and deservedly, in reprobation of the vile mixture which Dryden has thrown into the Tempest: doubtless without some such vicious alloy, the impure ears of that age would never have sate out to hear so much innocence of love as is contained in the sweet courtship of Ferdinand and Miranda. But is the Tempest of Shakspeare at all a subject for stage representation? It is one thing to read of an enchanter, and to believe the wondrous tale while we are reading it; but to have a conjurer brought before us in his conjuring-gown, with his spirits about him, which none but himself and some hundred of favoured spectators before the curtain are supposed to see, involves such a quantity of the *hateful incredible,* that all our reverence for the author cannot hinder us from perceiving such gross attempts upon the senses to be in the highest degree childish and inefficient. Spirits and fairies cannot be represented, they cannot even be painted,—they can only be believed. But the elaborate and anxious provision of scenery, which the luxury of the age demands, in these cases works a quite contrary effect to what is intended. That which in comedy, or plays of familiar life, adds so much to the life of the imitation, in plays which appeal to the higher faculties positively destroys the illusion which it is introduced to aid. A parlour or a drawing-room,—a library opening into a garden—a garden with an alcove in it,—a street, or the piazza of Covent Garden, does well enough in a scene; we are content to give as much credit to it as it demands; or rather, we think little about it,—it is little more than reading at the top of a page, "Scene, a garden"; we do not imagine ourselves there, but we readily admit the imitation of familiar objects. But to think by the help of painted trees and caverns, which we know to be painted, to transport our minds to Prospero, and his island and his lonely cell[1]; or by the aid of a fiddle dexterously thrown in, in an interval of speaking, to make us believe that we hear those super-natural noises of which the isle was full: the Orrery Lecturer at the Haymarket might as well hope, by his musical glasses cleverly stationed out of sight behind his apparatus, to make us believe that we do indeed hear the crystal spheres ring out that chime, which if it were to enwrap our fancy long, Milton thinks,

> Time would run back and fetch the age of gold,
> And speckled Vanity
> Would sicken soon and die,
> And leprous Sin would melt from earthly mould;
> Yea, Hell itself woud pass away,
> And leave its dolorous mansions to the peering day.

The garden of Eden, with our first parents in it, is not more impossible

---

[1] It will be said these things are done in pictures. But pictures and scenes are very different things. Painting is a world of itself, but in scene-painting there is the attempt to deceive: and there is the discordancy, never to be got over, between painted scenes and real people.

to be shown on a stage, than the Enchanted Isle, with its no less interesting and innocent first settlers.

The subject of Scenery is closely connected with that of the Dresses, which are so anxiously attended to on our stage. I remember the last time I saw Macbeth played, the discrepancy I felt at the changes of garment which he varied, the shiftings and reshiftings, like a Romish priest at mass. The luxury of stage-improvements, and the importunity of the public eye, require this. The coronation robe of the Scottish monarch was fairly a counterpart to that which our King wears when he goes to the Parliament House, just so full and cumbersome, and set out with ermine and pearls. And if things must be represented, I see not what to find fault with in this. But in reading, what robe are we conscious of? Some dim images of royalty—a crown and sceptre may float before our eyes, but who shall describe the fashion of it? Do we see in our mind's eye what Webb or any other robe-maker could pattern? This is the inevitable consequence of imitating everything, to make all things natural. Whereas the reading of a tragedy is a fine abstraction. It presents to the fancy just so much of external appearances as to make us feel that we are among flesh and blood, while by far the greater and better part of our imagination is employed upon the thoughts and internal machinery of the character. But in acting, scenery, dress, the most contemptible things, call upon us to judge of their naturalness.

Perhaps it would be no bad similitude, to liken the pleasure which we take in seeing one of these fine plays acted, compared with that quiet delight which we find in the reading of it, to the different feelings with which a reviewer, and a man that is not a reviewer, reads a fine poem. The accursed critical habit—the being called upon to judge and pronounce, must make it quite a different thing to the former. In seeing these plays acted, we are affected just as judges. When Hamlet compares the two pictures of Gertrude's first and second husband, who wants to see the pictures? But in the acting, a miniature must be lugged out; which we know not to be the picture, but only to show how finely a miniature may be represented. This showing of everything levels all things: it makes tricks, bows, and curtseys, of importance. Mrs. S. never got more fame by anything than by the manner in which she dismisses the guests in the banquet-scene in Macbeth: it is as much remembered as any of her thrilling tones or impressive looks. But does such a trifle as this enter into the imaginations of the readers of that wild and wonderful scene? Does not the mind dismiss the feasters as rapidly as it can? Does it care about the gracefulness of the doing it? But by acting, and judging of acting, all these non-essentials are raised into an importance, injurious to the main interest of the play.

I have confined my observations to the tragic parts of Shakspeare. It would be no very difficult task to extend the inquiry to his comedies; and to show why Falstaff, Shallow, Sir Hugh Evans, and the rest, are equally incompatible with stage representation. The length to which this Essay has run will make it, I am afraid, sufficiently distateful to the Amateurs of the Theatre, without going any deeper into the subject at present.

SPECIMENS FROM THE WRITINGS OF FULLER,

THE CHURCH HISTORIAN

THE writings of Fuller are usually designated by the title of quaint, and with sufficient reason; for such was his natural bias to conceits, that I doubt not upon most occasions it would have been going out of his way to have expressed himself out of them. But his wit is not always a *lumen siccum*, a dry faculty of surprising; on the contrary, his conceits are oftentimes deeply steeped in human feeling and passion. Above all, his way of telling a story, for its eager liveliness, and the perpetual running commentary of the narrator happily blended with the narration, is perhaps unequalled.

As his works are now scarcely perused but by antiquaries, I thought it might not be unacceptable to my readers to present them with some specimens of his manner, in single thoughts and phrases; and in some few passages of greater length, chiefly of a narrative description. I shall arrange them as I casually find them in my book of extracts, without being solicitous to specify the particular work from which they are taken.

Pyramids.—"The Pyramids themselves, doting with age, have forgotten the names of their founders."

Virtue in a short person.—"His soul had but a short diocese to visit, and therefore might the better attend the effectual informing thereof."

Intellect in a very tall one.—"Ofttimes such who are built four stories high, are observed to have little in their cock-loft."

Naturals.—"Their heads sometimes so little, that there is no room for wit; sometimes so long, that there is no wit for so much room."

Negroes.—"The image of God cut in ebony."

School-divinity.—"At the first it will be as welcome to thee as a prison, and their very solutions will seem knots unto thee."

Mr. Perkins the Divine.—"He had a capacious head, with angles winding and roomy enough to lodge all controversial intricacies."

The same.—"He would pronounce the word *Damn* with such an emphasis as left a doleful echo in his auditors' ears a good while after."

Judges in capital cases.—"O let him take heed how he strikes, that hath a dead hand."

Memory.—"Philosophers place it in the rear of the head, and it seems the mine of memory lies there, because there men naturally dig for it, scratching it when they are at a loss."

Fancy.—"It is the most boundless and restless faculty of the soul; for while the Understanding and the Will are kept, as it were, *in libera custodia* to their objects of *verum et bonum*, the Fancy is free from all engagements: it digs without spade, sails without ship, flies without wings, builds without charges, fights without bloodshed: in a moment striding from the centre to the circumference of the world; by a kind of omnipotency creating and annihilating things in an instant; and things divorced in Nature are married in Fancy as in a lawless place."

Infants.—"Some, admiring what motives to mirth infants meet with in their silent and solitary smiles, have resolved, how truly I know not, that then they converse with angels; as indeed such cannot among mortals find any fitter companions."

Music.—"Such is the sociableness of music, it conforms itself to all companies both in mirth and mourning; complying to improve that passion with which it finds the auditors most affected. In a word, it is an invention which might have beseemed a son of Seth to have been the father thereof: though better it was that Cain's great-grandchild should have the credit first to find it, than the world the unhappiness longer to have wanted it."

St. Monica.—"Drawing near her death, she sent most pious thoughts as harbingers to heaven, and her soul saw a glimpse of happiness through the chinks of her sickness-broken body." [1]

Mortality.—"To smell to a turf of fresh earth is wholesome for the body, no less are thoughts of mortality cordial to the soul."

Virgin.—"No lordling husband shall at the same time command her presence and distance; to be always near in constant attendance, and always to stand aloof in awful observance."

Elder Brother.—"Is one who made haste to come into the world to bring his parents the first news of male posterity, and is well rewarded for his tidings."

Bishop Fletcher.—"His pride was rather on him than in him, as only gait and gesture deep, not sinking to his heart, though causelessly condemned for a proud man, as who was a *good hypocrite,* and far more humble than he appeared."

Masters of Colleges.—"A little allay of dulness in a Master of a College makes him fitter to manage secular affairs."

The Good Yeoman.—"Is a gentleman in ore, whom the next age may see refined."

Good Parent.—"For his love, therein like a well-drawn picture, he eyes all his children alike."

Deformity in Children.—"This partiality is tyranny, when parents despise those that are deformed; *enough to break those whom God had bowed before.*"

Good Master.—"In correcting his servant he becomes not a slave to his own passion. Not cruelly making new *indentures* of the flesh of his apprentice. He is tender of his servant in sickness and age. If crippled in his service, his house is his hospital. Yet how many throw away those dry bones, out of the which themselves have sucked the marrow!"

[1] The soul's dark cottage, batter'd and decayed,
Lets in new lights through chinks which time has made.
WALLER.

Good Widow.—"If she can speak but little good of him [her dead husband] she speaks but little of him. So handsomely folding up her discourse, that his virtues are shown outwards, and his vices wrapt up in silence; as counting it barbarism to throw dirt on his memory, who hath mould cast on his body."

Horses.—"These are men's wings, wherewith they make such speed. A generous creature a horse is, sensible in some sort of honour; and made most handsome by that which deforms men most—pride."

Martyrdom.—"Heart of oak hath sometimes warped a little in the scorching heat of persecution. Their want of true courage herein cannot be excused. Yet many censure them for surrendering up their forts after a long siege, who would have yielded up their own at the first summons. —Oh! there is more required to make one valiant, than to call Cranmer or Jewel coward; as if the fire in Smithfield had been no hotter than what is painted in the Book of Martyrs."

Text of St. Paul.—"St. Paul saith, Let not the sun go down on your wrath, to carry news to the antipodes in another world of thy revengeful nature. Yet let us take the Apostle's meaning rather than his words, with all possible speed to depose our passion; not understanding him so literally, that we may take leave to be angry till sunset: then might our wrath lengthen with the days; and men in Greenland, where the day lasts above a quarter of a year, have plentiful scope for revenge." [1]

Bishop Brownrig.—"He carried learning enough *in numerato* about him in his pockets for any discourse, and had much more at home in his chests for any serious dispute."

Modest Want.—"Those that with diligence fight against poverty, though neither conquer till death makes it a drawn battle, expect not but prevent their craving of thee: for God forbid the heavens should never rain, till the earth first opens her mouth; seeing *some grounds will sooner burn than chap.*"

Death-bed Temptations.—"The devil is most busy on the last day of his term; and a tenant to be outed cares not what mischief he doth."

Conversation.—"Seeing we are civilised Englishmen, let us not be naked savages in our talk."

Wounded Soldier.—"Halting is the stateliest march of a soldier; and 'tis a brave sight to see the flesh of an ancient as torn as his colours."

Wat Tyler.—"A *misogrammatist;* if a good Greek word may be given to so barbarous a rebel."

Heralds.—"Heralds new mould men's names—taking from them, adding to them, melting out all the liquid letters, torturing mutes to make them speak, and making vowels dumb,—to bring it to a fallacious *ho-*

---

[1] This whimsical prevention of a consequence which no one would have thought of deducing,—setting up an absurdum on purpose to hunt it down,—placing guards as it were at the very outposts of possibility,—gravely giving out laws to insanity and prescribing moral fences to distempered intellects, could never have entered into a head less entertainingly constructed than that of Fuller, or Sir Thomas Browne, the very air of whose style the conclusion of this passage most aptly imitates.

monomy at the last, that their names may be the same with those noble
houses they pretend to."

Antiquarian Diligence.—"It is most worthy observation, with what
diligence he [Camden] inquired after ancient places, making hue and
cry after many a city which was run away, and by certain marks and
tokens pursuing to find it; as by the situation on the Roman highways,
by just distance from other ancient cities, by some affinity of name, by
tradition of the inhabitants, by Roman coins digged up, and by some
appearance of ruins. A broken urn is a whole evidence; or an old gate
still surviving, out of which the city is run out. Besides, commonly some
new spruce town not far off is grown out of the ashes thereof, which yet
hath so much natural affection as dutifully to own those reverend ruins
for her mother."

Henry de Essex.—"He is too well known in our English Chronicles,
being Baron of Raleigh, in Essex, and Hereditary Standard Bearer of
England. It happened in the reign of this king [Henry II.] there was a
fierce battle fought in Flintshire, at Coleshall, between the English and
Welsh, wherein this Henry de Essex *animum et signum simul abjecit,*
betwixt traitor and coward, cast away both his courage and banner together, occasioning a great overthrow of English. But he that had the
baseness to do, had the boldness to deny the doing, of so foul a fact;
until he was challenged in combat by Robert de Momford, a knight, eye-
witness thereof, and by him overcome in a duel. Whereupon his large inheritance was confiscated to the king, and he himself, *partly thrust,
partly going, into a convent, hid his head in a cowl, under which, betwixt
shame and sanctity, he blushed out the remainder of his life.*" [1]—
Worthies, article Bedfordshire.

Sir Edward Harwood, Knt.—"I have read of a bird, which hath a face
like, and yet will prey upon, a man: who coming to the water to drink,
and finding there by reflection, that he had killed one like himself, pineth
away by degrees, and never afterwards enjoyeth itself.[2] Such is in some

---

[1] The fine imagination of Fuller has done what might have been pronounced impossible: it has given an interest and a holy character to coward infamy. Nothing can
be more beautiful than the concluding account of the last days, and expiatory retirement, of poor Henry de Essex. The address with which the whole of this little story
is told is most consummate: the charm of it seems to consist in a perpetual balance of
antitheses not too violently opposed, and the consequent activity of mind in which
the reader is kept:—"Betwixt traitor and coward"—"baseness to do, boldness to
deny"—"partly thrust, partly going, into a convent"—"betwixt shame and sanctity."
The reader by this artifice is taken into a kind of partnership with the writer,—his
judgment is exercised in settling the preponderance,—he feels as if he were consulted
as to the issue. But the modern historian flings at once the dead weight of his own
judgment into the scale, and settles the matter.
[2] I do not know where Fuller read of this bird; but a more awful and affecting
story, and moralising of a story, in Natural History, or rather in that Fabulous Natural History where poets and mythologists found the Phœnix and the Unicorn, and
"other strange fowl," is nowhere extant. It is a fable which Sir Thomas Browne, if
he had heard of it, would have exploded among his Vulgar Errors; but the delight
which he would have taken in the discussing of its probabilities, would have shown
that the *truth of the fact,* though the avowed object of his search was not so much

sort the condition of Sir Edward. This accident, that he had killed one in a private quarrel, put a period to his carnal mirth, and was a covering to his eyes all the days of his life. No possible provocations could afterwards tempt him to a duel; and no wonder that one's conscience loathed that whereof he had surfeited. He refused all challenges with more honour than others accepted them; it being well known, that he would set foot as far in the face of his enemy as any man alive."—*Worthies,* article Lincolnshire.

Decayed Gentry.—"It happened in the reign of King James, when Henry Earl of Huntingdon was Lieutenant of Leicestershire, that a labourer's son in that country was pressed into the wars; as I take it, to go over with Count Mansfield. The old man at Leicester requested his son might be discharged, as being the only staff of his age, who by his industry maintained him and his mother. The Earl demanded his name, which the man for a long time was loath to tell (as suspecting it a fault for so poor a man to confess the truth), at last he told his name was Hastings. 'Cousin Hastings,' said the Earl, 'we cannot all be top branches of the tree, though we all spring from the same root; your son, my kinsman, shall not be pressed.' So good was the meeting of modesty in a poor, with courtesy in an honourable person, and gentry I believe in both. And I have reason to believe, that some who justly own the surnames and blood of Bohuns, Mortimers, and Plantagenets (though ignorant of their own extractions), are hid in the heap of common people, where they find that under a thatched cottage which some of their ancestors could not enjoy in a leaded castle,—contentment, with quiet and security."—*Worthies,* article Of Shire-Reeves or Shiriffes.

Tenderness of Conscience in a Tradesman.—"Thomas Curson, born in Allhallows, Lombard Street, armourer, dwelt without Bishopsgate. It happened that a stage-player borrowed a rusty musket, which had lain long leger in his shop: now though his part were comical, he therewith acted an unexpected tragedy, killing one of the standers-by, the gun casually going off on the stage, which he suspected not to be charged. Oh the difference of divers men in the tenderness of their consciences! some are scarce touched with a wound, whilst others are wounded with a touch therein. This poor armourer was highly afflicted therewith, though done against his will, yea, without his knowledge, in his absence, by another, out of mere chance. Hereupon he resolved to give all his estate to pious uses: no sooner had he gotten a round sum, but presently he posted with it in his apron to the Court of Aldermen, and was in pain till by their direction he had settled it for the relief of poor in his own and other parishes, and disposed of some hundreds of pounds accordingly, as I am credibly informed by the then churchwardens of the said parish. Thus

the motive which put him upon the investigation, as those hidden affinities and poetical analogies,—those *essential verities* in the application of strange fable, which made him linger with such reluctant delay among the last fading lights of popular tradition; and not seldom to conjure up a superstition, that had been long extinct, from its dusty grave, to inter it himself with greater ceremonies and solemnities of burial.

as he conceived himself casually (though at a great distance) to have occasioned the death of one, he was the immediate and direct cause of giving a comfortable living to many."

Burning of Wickliffe's Body by Order of the Council of Constance.— "Hitherto [A.D. 1428] the corpse of John Wickliffe had quietly slept in his grave about forty-one years after his death, till his body was reduced to bones, and his bones almost to dust. For though the earth in the chancel of Lutterworth, in Leicestershire, where he was interred, hath not so quick a digestion with the earth of Aceldama, to consume flesh in twenty-four hours, yet such the appetite thereof, and all other English graves, to leave small reversions of a body after so many years. But now such the spleen of the Council of Constance, as they not only cursed his memory as dying an obstinate heretic, but ordered that his bones (with this charitable caution,—if it may be discerned from the bodies of other faithful people) be taken out of the ground, and thrown far off from any Christian burial. In obedience hereunto, Richard Fleming, Bishop of Lincoln, Diocesan of Lutterworth, sent his officers (vultures with a quick sight, scent, at a dead carcass) to ungrave him. Accordingly to Lutterworth they come, Sumner, Commissary, Official, Chancellor, Proctors, Doctors, and their servants (so that the remnant of the body would not hold out a bone amongst so many hands), take what was left out of the grave, and burnt them to ashes, and cast them into Swift, a neighbouring brook, running hard by. *Thus this brook has conveyed his ashes into Avon, Avon into Severn, Severn into the narrow seas, they into the main ocean; and thus the ashes of Wickliffe are the emblem of his doctrine, which now is dispersed all the world over."* [1]—Church History.

---

[1] The concluding period of this most lively narrative I will not call a conceit: it is one of the grandest conceptions I ever met with. One feels the ashes of Wickliffe gliding away out of the reach of the Sumners, Commissaries, Officials, Proctors, Doctors, and all the puddering rout of executioners of the impotent rage of the baffled Council: from Swift into Avon, from Avon into Severn, from Severn into the narrow seas, from the narrow seas into the main ocean, where they become the emblem of his doctrine, "dispersed all the world over." Hamlet's tracing the body of Cæsar to the clay that stops a beer barrel is a no less curious pursuit of "ruined mortality"; but it is in an inverse ratio to this: it degrades and saddens us, for one part of our nature at least; but this expands the whole of our nature, and gives to the body a sort of ubiquity,—a diffusion as far as the actions of its partner can have reach or influence.

I have seen this passage smiled at, and set down as a quaint conceit of old Fuller. But what is not a conceit to those who read it in a temper different from that in which the writer composed it? The most pathetic parts of poetry to cold tempers seem and are nonsense, as divinity was to the Greeks foolishness. When Richard II., meditating on his own utter annihilation as to royalty, cries out,
              "O that I were a mockery king of snow,
              To melt before the sun of Bolingbroke,"
if we had been going on pace for pace with the passion before, this sudden conversion of a strong-felt metaphor into something to be actually realised in nature, like that of Jeremiah, "Oh! that my head were waters, and mine eyes a fountain of tears," is strictly and strikingly natural; but come unprepared upon it, and it is a conceit: and so is a "head" turned into "waters."

ON THE GENIUS AND CHARACTER OF HOGARTH;

WITH SOME REMARKS ON A PASSAGE IN THE WRITINGS OF THE LATE MR. BARRY

ONE of the earliest and noblest enjoyments I had when a boy, was in the contemplation of those capital prints by Hogarth, the Harlot's and Rake's Progresses, which, along with some others, hung upon the walls of a great hall in an old-fashioned house in ——shire, and seemed the solitary tenants (with myself) of that antiquated and life-deserted apartment.

Recollection of the manner in which those prints used to affect me has often made me wonder, when I have heard Hogarth described as a mere comic painter, as one of those whose chief ambition was to *raise a laugh*. To deny that there are throughout the prints which I have mentioned circumstances introduced of a laughable tendency, would be to run counter to the common notions of mankind; but to suppose that in their *ruling character* they appeal chiefly to the risible faculty, and not first and foremost to the very heart of man, its best and most serious feelings, would be to mistake no less grossly their aim and purpose. A set of severer Satires (for they are not so much Comedies, which they have been likened to, as they are strong and masculine Satires) less mingled with anything of mere fun, were never written upon paper, or graven upon copper. They resemble Juvenal, or the satiric touches in Timon of Athens.

I was pleased with the reply of a gentleman, who being asked which book he esteemed most in his library, answered,—"Shakspeare": being asked which he esteemed next best, replied, "Hogarth." His graphic representations are indeed books: they have the teeming, fruitful, suggestive meaning of *words*. Other pictures we look at,—his prints we read.

In pursuance of this parallel, I have sometimes entertained myself with comparing the Timon of Athens of Shakspeare (which I have just mentioned) and Hogarth's Rake's Progress together. The story, the moral, in both is nearly the same. The wild course of riot and extravagance, ending in the one with driving the Prodigal from the society of men into the solitude of the deserts, and in the other with conducting the Rake through his several stages of dissipation into the still more complete desolations of the mad-house, in the play and in the picture, are described with almost equal force and nature. The levee of the Rake, which forms the subject of the second plate in the series, is almost a transcript of Timon's levee in the opening scene of that play. We find a dedicating poet, and other similar characters, in both.

The concluding scene in the Rake's Progress is perhaps superior to the last scenes of Timon. If we seek for something of kindred excellence in poetry, it must be in the scenes of Lear's beginning madness, where the

King and the Fool and the Tom-o'-Bedlam conspire to produce such a
medley of mirth checked by misery, and misery rebuked by mirth;
where the society of those "strange bed-fellows" which misfortunes have
brought Lear acquainted with, so finely sets forth the destitute state of
the monarch; while the lunatic bans of the one, and the disjointed sayings and wild but pregnant allusions of the other, so wonderfully sympathise with that confusion, which they seem to assist in the production
of, in the senses of that "child-changed father."

In the scene in Bedlam, which terminates the Rake's Progress, we
find the same assortment of the ludicrous with the terrible. Here is desperate madness, the overturning of originally strong thinking faculties,
at which we shudder, as we contemplate the duration and pressure of
affliction which it must have asked to destroy such a building;—and
here is the gradual hurtless lapse into idiocy, of faculties, which at their
best of times never having been strong, we look upon the consummation
of their decay with no more of pity than is consistent with a smile. The
mad tailor, the poor driveller that has gone out of his wits (and truly he
appears to have had no great journey to go to get past their confines)
for the love of Charming Betty Careless,—these half-laughable, scarce-
pitiable objects, take off from the horror which the principal figure would
of itself raise, at the same time that they assist the feeling of the scene
by contributing to the general notion of its subject:—

> Madness, thou chaos of the brain,
> What art, that pleasure giv'st and pain?
> Tyranny of Fancy's reign!
> Mechanic Fancy, that can build
> Vast labyrinths and mazes wild,
> With rule disjointed, shapeless measure,
> Fill'd with horror, fill'd with pleasure!
> Shapes of horror, that would even
> Cast doubts of mercy upon heaven;
> Shapes of pleasure, that but seen,
> Would split the shaking sides of Spleen.[1]

Is it carrying the spirit of comparison to excess to remark, that in the
poor kneeling weeping female who accompanies her seducer in his sad
decay, there is something analogous to Kent, or Caius, as he delights
rather to be called, in Lear,—the noblest pattern of virtue which even
Shakspeare has conceived,—who follows his royal master in banishment,
that had pronounced *his* banishment, and, forgetful at once of his wrongs
and dignities, taking on himself the disguise of a menial, retains his
fidelity to the figure, his loyalty to the carcass, the shadow, the shell and
empty husk of Lear?

In the perusal of a book, or of a picture, much of the impression which
we receive depends upon the habit of mind which we bring with us to
such perusal. The same circumstance may make one person laugh, which
shall render another very serious; or in the same person the first im-

---

[1] Lines inscribed under the plate.

pression may be corrected by after-thought. The misemployed incongruous characters at the Harlot's Funeral, on a superficial inspection, provoke to laughter; but when we have sacrificed the first emotion to levity a very different frame of mind succeeds, or the painter has lost half his purpose. I never look at that wonderful assemblage of depraved beings, who, without a grain of reverence or pity in their perverted minds, are performing the sacred exteriors of duty to the relics of their departed partner in folly, but I am as much moved to sympathy from the very want of it in them, as I should be by the finest representation of a virtuous death-bed surrounded by real mourners, pious children, weeping friends,—perhaps more by the very contrast. What reflections does it not awake, of the dreadful heartless state in which the creature (a female too) must have lived, who in death wants the accompaniment of one genuine tear. That wretch who is removing the lid of the coffin to gaze upon the corpse with a face which indicates a perfect negation of all goodness or womanhood—the hypocrite parson and his demure partner —all the fiendish group—to a thoughtful mind present a moral emblem more affecting than if the poor friendless carcass had been depicted as thrown out to the woods, where wolves had assisted at its obsequies, itself furnishing forth its own funeral banquet.

It is easy to laugh at such incongruities as are met together in this picture,—incongruous objects being of the very essence of laughter,—but surely the laugh is far different in its kind from that thoughtless species to which we are moved by mere farce and grotesque. We laugh when Ferdinand Count Fathom, at the first sight of the white cliffs of Britain, feels his heart yearn with filial fondness towards the land of his progenitors, which he is coming to fleece and plunder,—we smile at the exquisite irony of the passage,—but if we are not led on by such passages to some more salutary feeling than laughter, we are very negligent perusers of them in book or picture.

It is the fashion with those who cry up the great Historical School in this country, at the head of which Sir Joshua Reynolds is placed, to exclude Hogarth from that school, as an artist of an inferior and vulgar class. Those persons seem to me to confound the painting of subjects in common or vulgar life with the being a vulgar artist. The quantity of thought which Hogarth crowds into every picture would alone *unvulgarise* every subject which he might choose. Let us take the lowest of his subjects, the print called Gin Lane. Here is plenty of poverty and low stuff to disgust upon a superficial view; and accordingly a cold spectator feels himself immediately disgusted and repelled. I have seen many turn away from it, not being able to bear it. The same persons would perhaps have looked with great complacency upon Poussin's celebrated picture of the Plague at Athens.[1] Disease and Death and bewildering Terror, in *Athenian garments*, are endurable, and come, as the delicate critics express it, within the "limits of pleasurable sensation." But the scenes of their own St. Giles's, delineated by their own countryman, are

[1] At the late Mr. Hope's, in Cavendish Square.

too shocking to think of. Yet if we could abstract our minds from the fascinating colours of the picture, and forget the coarse execution (in some respects) of the print, intended as it was to be a cheap plate, accessible to the poorer sort of people, for whose instruction it was done, I think we could have no hesitation in conferring the palm of superior genius upon Hogarth, comparing this work of his with Poussin's picture. There is more of imagination in it—that power which draws all things to one,—which makes things animate and inanimate, beings with their attributes, subjects, and their accessories, take one colour and serve to one effect. Everything in the print, to use a vulgar expression, *tells*. Every part is full of "strange images of death." It is perfectly amazing and astounding to look at. Not only the two prominent figures, the woman and the half-dead man, which are as terrible as anything which Michael Angelo ever drew, but everything else in the print, contributes to bewilder and stupefy,—the very houses, as I heard a friend of mine express it, tumbling all about in various directions, seem drunk—seem absolutely reeling from the effect of that diabolical spirit of frenzy which goes forth over the whole composition. To show the poetical and almost prophetical conception in the artist, one little circumstance may serve. Not content with the dying and dead figures, which he has strewed in profusion over the proper scene of the action, he shows you what (of a kindred nature) is passing beyond it. Close by the shell, in which, by direction of the parish beadle, a man is depositing his wife, is an old wall, which, partaking of the universal decay around it, is tumbling to pieces. Through a gap in this wall are seen three figures, which appear to make a part in some funeral procession which is passing by on the other side of the wall, out of the sphere of the composition. This extending of the interest beyond the bounds of the subject could only have been conceived by a great genius. Shakspeare, in his description of the painting of the Trojan War, in his Tarquin and Lucrece, has introduced a similar device, where the painter made a part stand for the whole:—

> For much imaginary work was there,
> Conceit deceitful, so compact, so kind,
> That for Achilles' image stood his spear,
> Grip'd in an armed hand; himself behind
> Was left unseen, save to the eye of mind:
> A hand, a foot, a face, a leg, a head,
> Stood for the whole to be imagined.

This he well calls *imaginary work*, where the spectator must meet the artist in his conceptions half-way; and it is peculiar to the confidence of high genius alone to trust so much to spectators or readers. Lesser artists show everything distinct and full, as they require an object to be made out to themselves before they can comprehend it.

When I think of the power displayed in this (I will not hesitate to say) sublime print, it seems to me the extreme narrowness of system alone, and of that rage for classification, by which, in matters of taste at least, we are perpetually perplexing, instead of arranging, our ideas, that would make us concede to the work of Poussin above mentioned, and deny to this of Hogarth, the name of a grand serious composition.

We are for ever deceiving ourselves with names and theories. We call one man a great historical painter, because he has taken for his subjects kings or great men, or transactions over which time has thrown a grandeur. We term another the painter of common life, and set him down in our minds for an artist of an inferior class, without reflecting whether the quantity of thought shown by the latter may not much more than level the distinction which their mere choice of subjects may seem to place between them; or whether, in fact, from that very common life a great artist may not extract as deep an interest as another man from that which we are pleased to call history.

I entertain the highest respect for the talents and virtues of Reynolds, but I do not like that his reputation should overshadow and stifle the merits of such a man as Hogarth, nor that to mere names and classifications we should be content to sacrifice one of the greatest ornaments of England.

I would ask the most enthusiastic admirer of Reynolds, whether in the countenances of his Staring and Grinning Despair, which he has given us for the faces of Ugolino and dying Beaufort, there be anything comparable to the expression which Hogarth has put into the face of his broken-down rake in the last plate but one of the Rake's Progress,[1] where a letter from the manager is brought to him to say that his play "will not do"? Here all is easy, natural, undistorted, but withal what a mass of woe is here accumulated!—the long history of a mis-spent life is compressed into the countenance as plainly as the series of plates before had told it; here is no attempt at Gorgonian looks, which are to freeze the beholder—no grinning at the antique bed-posts—no face-making, or consciousness of the presence of spectators in or out of the picture, but grief kept to a man's self, a face retiring from notice with the shame which great anguish sometimes brings with it,—a final leave taken of hope,—the coming on of vacancy and stupefaction,—a beginning alienation of mind looking like tranquillity. Here is matter for the mind of the beholder to feed on for the hour together,—matter to feed and fertilise the mind. It is too real to admit one thought about the power of the artist who did it. When we compare the expression in subjects which so fairly admit of comparison, and find the superiority so clearly to remain with Hogarth, shall the mere contemptible difference of the scene of it being laid, in the one case, in our Fleet or King's Bench Prison, and, in the other, in the State Prison of Pisa, or the bedroom of a cardinal,—or that the subject of the one has never been authenticated, and the other is matter of history,—so weigh down the real points of the

---

[1] The first perhaps in all Hogarth for serious expression. That which comes next to it, I think, is the jaded morning countenance of the debauchee in the second plate of the Marriage Alamode, which lectures on the vanity of pleasure as audibly as anything in Ecclesiastes.

comparison, as to induce us to rank the artist who has chosen the one
scene or subject (though confessedly inferior in that which constitutes
the soul of his art) in a class from which we exclude the better genius
(who has happened to make choice of the other) with something like
disgrace? [1]

The Boys under Demoniacal Possession of Raphael and Domenichino, by what law of classification are we bound to assign them to belong
to the great style in painting, and to degrade into an inferior class the
Rake of Hogarth when he is the Madman in the Bedlam scene? I am
sure he is far more impressive than either. It is a face which no one that
has seen can easily forget. There is the stretch of human suffering to the
utmost endurance, severe bodily pain brought on by strong mental
agony, the frightful obstinate laugh of madness,—yet all so unforced and
natural, that those who never were witness to madness in real life, think
they see nothing but what is familiar to them in this face. Here are no
tricks of distortion, nothing but the natural face of agony. This is high
tragic painting, and we might as well deny to Shakspeare the honours of
a great tragedian, because he has interwoven scenes of mirth with the
serious business of his plays, as refuse to Hogarth the same praise for
the two concluding scenes of the Rake's Progress, because of the Comic
Lunatics [2] which he has thrown into the one, or the Alchymist that he
has introduced in the other, who is paddling in the coals of his furnace,
keeping alive the flames of vain hope within the very walls of the prison
to which the vanity has conducted him, which have taught the darker

[1] Sir Joshua Reynolds, somewhere in his Lectures, speaks of the *presumption* of
Hogarth in attempting the grand style in painting, by which he means his choice of
certain Scripture subjects. Hogarth's excursions into Holy Land were not very numerous, but what he has left us in this kind have at least this merit, that they have
expression of *some sort or other* in them,—the Child Moses before Pharaoh's Daughter, for instance: which is more than can be said of Sir Joshua Reynolds's Repose in
Egypt, painted for Macklin's Bible, where for a Madonna he has substituted a sleepy,
insensible, unmotherly girl, one so little worthy to have been selected as the Mother
of the Saviour, that she seems to have neither heart nor feeling to entitle her to become a mother at all. But indeed the race of Virgin Mary painters seems to have
been cut up, root and branch, at the Reformation. Our artists are too good Protestants to give life to that admirable commixture of maternal tenderness with reverential awe and wonder approaching to worship, with which the Virgin Mothers of L.
da Vinci and Raphael (themselves by their divine countenances inviting men to worship) contemplate the union of the two natures in the person of their Heaven-born
Infant.

[2] There are of madmen, as there are of tame,
   All humour'd not alike. We have here some
   So apish and fantastic, play with a feather;
   And though 'twould grieve a soul to see God's image
   So blemish'd and defac'd, yet do they act
   Such antick and such pretty lunacies,
   That, spite of sorrow, they will make you smile.
   Others again we have, like angry lions,
   Fierce as wild bulls, untameable as flies.
                                             Honest Whore.

lesson of extinguished hope to the desponding figure who is the principal person of the scene.

It is the force of these kindly admixtures which assimilates the scenes of Hogarth and of Shakspeare to the drama of real life, where no such thing as pure tragedy is to be found; but merriment and infelicity, ponderous crime and feather-light vanity, like twi-formed births, disagreeing complexions of one intertexture, perpetually unite to show forth motley spectacles to the world. Then it is that the poet or painter shows his art, when in the selection of these comic adjuncts he chooses such circumstances as shall relieve, contrast with, or fall into, without forming a violent opposition to his principal object. Who sees not that the Grave-digger in Hamlet, the Fool in Lear, have a kind of correspondency to, and fall in with, the subjects which they seem to interrupt: while the comic stuff in Venice Preserved, and the doggerel nonsense of the Cook and his poisoning associates in the Rollo of Beaumont and Fletcher, are pure, irrelevant, impertinent discords,—as bad as the quarrelling dog and cat under the table of the Lord and the Disciples at Emmaus of Titian?

Not to tire the reader with perpetual reference to prints which he may not be fortunate enough to possess, it may be sufficient to remark, that the same tragic cast of expression and incident, blended in some instances with a greater alloy of comedy, characterises his other great work, the Marriage Alamode, as well as those less elaborate exertions of his genius, the prints called Industry and Idleness, the Distrest Poet, etc., forming, with the Harlot's and Rake's Progresses, the most considerable if not the largest class of his productions,—enough surely to rescue Hogarth from the imputation of being a mere buffoon, or one whose general aim was only to *shake the sides*.

There remains a very numerous class of his performances, the object of which must be confessed to be principally comic. But in all of them will be found something to distinguish them from the droll productions of Bunbury and others. They have this difference, that we do not merely laugh at, we are led into long trains of reflection by them. In this respect they resemble the characters of Chaucer's Pilgrims, which have strokes of humour in them enough to designate them for the most part as comic, but our strongest feeling still is wonder at the comprehensiveness of genius which could crowd, as poet and painter have done, into one small canvas so many diverse yet co-operating materials.

The faces of Hogarth have not a mere momentary interest, as in caricatures, or those grotesque physiognomies which we sometimes catch a glance of in the street, and, struck with their whimsicality, wish for a pencil and the power to sketch them down; and forget them again as rapidly,—but they are permanent abiding ideas. Not the sports of nature, but her necessary eternal classes. We feel that we cannot part with any of them, lest a link should be broken.

It is worthy of observation, that he has seldom drawn a mean or insignificant countenance.[1] Hogarth's mind was eminently reflective; and, as it has been well observed of Shakspeare, that he has transfused his own poetical character into the persons of his drama (they are all more or less *poets*) Hogarth has impressed a *thinking character* upon the persons of his canvas. This remark must not be taken universally. The exquisite idiotism of the little gentleman in the bag and sword beating his drum in the print of the Enraged Musician, would of itself rise up against so sweeping an assertion. But I think it will be found to be true of the generality of his countenances. The knife-grinder and Jew flute-player in the plate just mentioned, may serve as instances instead of a thousand. They have intense thinking faces, though the purpose to which they are subservient by no means required it; but indeed it seems as if it was painful to Hogarth to contemplate mere vacancy or insignificance.

This reflection of the artist's own intellect from the faces of his characters, is one reason why the works of Hogarth, so much more than those of any other artist, are objects of meditation. Our intellectual natures love the mirror which gives them back their own likenesses. The mental eye will not bend long with delight upon vacancy.

Another line of eternal separation between Hogarth and the common painters of droll or burlesque subjects, with whom he is often confounded, is the sense of beauty, which in the most unpromising subjects seems never wholly to have deserted him. "Hogarth himself," says Mr. Coleridge,[2] from whom I have borrowed this observation, speaking of a scene which took place at Ratzeburg, "never drew a more ludicrous distortion, both of attitude and physiognomy, than this effect occasioned: nor was there wanting beside it one of those beautiful female faces which the same Hogarth, *in whom the satirist never extinguished that love of beauty which belonged to him as a poet,* so often and so gladly introduces as the central figure in a crowd of humorous deformities, which figure (such is the power of true genius) neither acts nor is meant to act as a contrast; but diffuses through all and over each of the group a spirit of reconciliation and human kindness; and even when the attention is no longer consciously directed to the cause of this feeling, still blends its tenderness with our laughter: and *thus prevents the instructive merriment at the whims of nature, or the foibles or humours of our fellow-men, from degenerating into the heart-poison of contempt or hatred.*" To the beautiful females in Hogarth, which Mr. C. has pointed out, might be added, the frequent introduction of children (which Hogarth seems to have taken a particular delight in) into his pieces. They have a singular effect in giving tranquillity and a portion of their own innocence to the subject. The

---

[1] If there are any of that description, they are in his Strolling Players, a print which has been cried up by Lord Orford as the richest of his productions, and it may be, for what I know, in the mere lumber, the properties, and dead furniture of the scene, but in living character and expression it is (for Hogarth) lamentably poor and wanting; it is perhaps the only one of his performances at which we have a right to feel disgusted.

[2] *The Friend,* No. XVI.

baby riding in its mother's lap in the March to Finchley (its careless innocent face placed directly behind the intriguing time-furrowed countenance of the treason-plotting French priest), perfectly sobers the whole of that tumultuous scene. The boy mourner winding up his top with so much unpretending insensibility in the plate of the Harlot's Funeral (the only thing in that assembly that is not a hypocrite), quiets and soothes the mind that has been disturbed at the sight of so much depraved man and woman kind.

I had written thus far, when I met with a passage in the writings of the late Mr. Barry, which, as it falls in with the *vulgar notion* respecting Hogarth, which this Essay has been employed in combating, I shall take the liberty to transcribe, with such remarks as may suggest themselves to me in the transcription; referring the reader for a full answer to that which has gone before.

Notwithstanding Hogarth's merit does undoubtedly entitle him to an honourable place among the artists, and that his little compositions, considered as so many dramatic representations, abounding with humour, character, and extensive observations on the various incidents of low, faulty, and vicious life, are very ingeniously brought together, and frequently tell their own story with more facility than is often found in many of the elevated and more noble inventions of Raphael and other great men; yet it must be honestly confessed, that in what is called knowledge of the figure, foreigners have justly observed, that Hogarth is often so raw and unformed, as hardly to deserve the name of an artist. But this capital defect is not often perceivable, as examples of the naked and of elevated nature but rarely occur in his subjects, which are for the most part filled with characters that in their nature tend to deformity; besides his figures are small, and the jonctures, and other difficulties of drawing that might occur in their limbs, are artfully concealed with their clothes, rags, etc. But what would atone for all his defects, even if they were twice told, is his admirable fund of invention, ever inexhaustible in its resources; and his satire, which is always sharp and pertinent, and often highly moral, was (except in a few instances, where he weakly and meanly suffered his integrity to give way to his envy) seldom or never employed in a dishonest or unmanly way. Hogarth has been often imitated in his satirical vein, sometimes in his humorous: but very few have attempted to rival him in his moral walk. The line of art pursued by my very ingenious predecessor and brother Academician, Mr. Penny, is quite distinct from that of Hogarth, and is of a much more delicate and superior relish; he attempts the heart, and reaches it, whilst Hogarth's general aim is only to shake the sides; in other respects no comparison can be thought of, as Mr. Penny has all that knowledge of the figure and academical skill which the other wanted. As to Mr. Bunbury, who had so happily succeeded in the vein of humour and caricatura, he has for some time past altogether relinquished it, for the more amiable pursuit of beautiful nature: this, indeed, is not to be wondered at, when we recollect that he has, in Mrs. Bunbury, so admirable an exemplar of the most finished grace and beauty continually at his elbow. But (to say all that occurs to me on this subject) perhaps it may be reasonaby doubted, whether the being much conversant with Hogarth's method of exposing meanness, deformity, and vice, in many of his works, is not rather a dangerous, or, at least, a worthless pursuit; which, if it does not find a false relish and a love of and search after satire and buffoonery in the spectator, is at least not unlikely to give him one. Life is short; and the little leisure of it is much better laid out upon that species of art which is employed about the amiable and the admirable, as it is more likely to be attended with better and nobler consequences to ourselves. These two pursuits in art may be compared with two sets of people with whom we might associate; if we give ourselves up to the Footes, the Kenricks, etc., we shall be continually busied and paddling in whatever is ridiculous, faulty, and vicious in life; whereas there are those to be found with whom

we should be in the constant pursuit and study of all that gives a value and a dignity
to human nature. [Account of a Series of Pictures in the Great Room of the Society
of Arts, Manufactures, and Commerce, at the Adelphi, by James Barry, R.A., Professor of Painting to the Royal Academy; reprinted in the last quarto edition of his
works.]

—— It must be honestly confessed, that in what is called knowledge of the figure,
foreigners have justly observed, etc.

It is a secret well known to the professors of the art and mystery of
criticism, to insist upon what they do not find in a man's works, and to
pass over in silence what they do. That Hogarth did not draw the naked
figure so well as Michael Angelo might be allowed, especially as "examples of the naked," as Mr. Barry acknowledges, "rarely (he might almost
have said never) occur in his subjects"; and that his figures under their
draperies do not discover all the fine graces of an Antinoüs or an Apollo,
may be conceded likewise; perhaps it was more suitable to his purpose to
represent the average forms of mankind in the mediocrity (as Mr. Burke
expresses it) of the age in which he lived: but that his figures in general,
and in his best subjects, are so glaringly incorrect as is here insinuated, I
dare trust my own eye so far as positively to deny the fact. And there is
one part of the figure in which Hogarth is allowed to have excelled, which
these foreigners seem to have overlooked, or perhaps calculating from its
proportion to the whole (a seventh or an eighth, I forget which), deemed
it of trifling importance; I mean the human face; a small part, reckoning
by geographical inches, in the map of man's body, but here it is that the
painter of expression must condense the wonders of his skill, even at the
expense of neglecting the "jonctures and other difficulties of drawing in
the limbs," which it must be a cold eye that, in the interest so strongly
demanded by Hogarth's countenances, has leisure to survey and censure.

The line of art pursued by my very ingenious predecessor and brother Academician,
Mr. Penny.

The first impression caused in me by reading this passage was an eager
desire to know who this Mr. Penny was. This great surpasser of Hogarth
in the "delicacy of his relish," and the "line which he pursued," where is
he, what are his works, what has he to show? In vain I tried to recollect,
till by happily putting the question to a friend who is more conversant
in the works of the illustrious obscure than myself, I learnt that he was
the painter of a Death of Wolfe which missed the prize the year that the
celebrated picture of West on the same subject obtained it; that he also
made a picture of the Marquis of Granby relieving a Sick Soldier; moreover, that he was the inventor of two pictures of Suspended and Restored
Animation, which I now remember to have seen in the Exhibition some
years since, and the prints from which are still extant in good men's
houses. This then I suppose, is the line of subjects in which Mr. Penny
was so much superior to Hogarth. I confess I am not of that opinion.
The relieving of poverty by the purse, and the restoring a young man to
his parents by using the methods prescribed by the Humane Society, are

doubtless very amiable subjects, pretty things to teach the first rudiments of humanity; they amount to about as much instruction as the stories of good boys that give away their custards to poor beggar-boys in children's books. But, good God! is this *milk for babes* to be set up in opposition to Hogarth's moral scenes, his *strong meat for men?* As well might we prefer the fulsome verses upon their own goodness to which the gentlemen of the Literary Fund annually sit still with such shameless patience to listen, to the satires of Juvenal and Persius; because the former are full of tender images of Worth relieved by Charity, and Charity stretching out her hand to rescue sinking Genius, and the theme of the latter is men's crimes and follies with their black consequences—forgetful meanwhile of those strains of moral pathos, those sublime heart-touches, which these poets (in *them* chiefly showing themselves poets) are perpetually darting across the otherwise appalling gloom of their subject—consolatory remembrancers, when their pictures of guilty mankind have made us even to despair for our species, that there is such a thing as virtue and moral dignity in the world, that her unquenchable spark is not utterly out—refreshing admonitions, to which we turn for shelter from the too great heat and asperity of the general satire.

And is there nothing analogous to this in Hogarth? nothing which "attempts and reaches the heart"?—no aim beyond that of "shaking the sides"?—If the kneeling ministering female in the last scene of the Rake's Progress, the Bedlam scene, of which I have spoken before, and have dared almost to parallel it with the most absolute idea of Virtue which Shakspeare has left us, be not enough to disprove the assertion; if the sad endings of the Harlot and the Rake, the passionate heart-bleeding entreaties for forgiveness which the adulterous wife is pouring forth to her assassinated and dying lord in the last scene but one of the Marriage Alamode,—if these be not things to touch the ‚heart, and dispose the mind to a meditative tenderness: is there nothing sweetly conciliatory in the mild patient face and gesture with which the wife seems to allay and ventilate the feverish irritated feelings of her poor poverty-distracted mate (the true copy of the *genus irritabile*) in the print of the Distrest Poet? or if an image of maternal love be required, where shall we find a sublimer view of it than in that aged woman in Industry and Idleness (Plate V.) who is clinging with the fondness of hope not quite extinguished to her brutal vice-hardened child, whom she is accompanying to the ship which is to bear him away from his native soil, of which he has been adjudged unworthy: in whose shocking face every trace of the human countenance seems obliterated, and a brute beast's to be left instead, shocking and repulsive to all but her who watched over it in its cradle before it was so sadly altered, and feels it must belong to her while a pulse by the vindictive laws of his country shall be suffered to continue to beat in it. Compared with such things, what is Mr. Penny's "knowledge of the figure and academical skill which Hogarth wanted"?

With respect to what follows concerning another gentleman, with the congratulations to him on his escape out of the regions of "humour and

caricatura," in which it appears he was in danger of travelling side by
side with Hogarth, I can only congratulate my country, that Mrs. Hogarth knew *her* province better than, by disturbing her husband at his
palette, to divert him from that universality of subject, which has stamped
him perhaps, next to Shakspeare, the most inventive genius which this
island has produced, into the "amiable pursuit of beautiful nature," *i.e.*,
copying *ad infinitum* the individual charms and graces of Mrs. H.

Hogarth's method of exposing meanness, deformity, and vice, paddling in whatever
is ridiculous, faulty, and vicious.

A person unacquainted with the works thus stigmatised would be apt
to imagine that in Hogarth there was nothing else to be found but subjects of the coarsest and most repulsive nature. That his imagination was
naturally unsweet, and that he delighted in raking into every species of
moral filth. That he preyed upon sore places only, and took a pleasure
in exposing the unsound and rotten parts of human nature:—whereas,
with the exception of some of the plates of the Harlot's Progress, which
are harder in their character than any of the rest of his productions (the
Stages of Cruelty I omit as mere worthless caricaturas, foreign to his
general habits, the offspring of his fancy in some wayward humour),
there is scarce one of his pieces where vice is most strongly satirised, in
which some figure is not introduced upon which the moral eye may rest
satisfied; a face that indicates goodness, or perhaps mere good-hu-
mouredness and carelessness of mind (negation of evil) only, yet enough
to give a relaxation to the frowning brow of satire, and keep the general
air from tainting. Take the mild, supplicating posture of patient Poverty
in the poor woman that is persuading the pawnbroker to accept her
clothes in pledge, in the plate of Gin Lane, for an instance. A little does
it, a little of the *good* nature overpowers a world of *bad*. One cordial
honest laugh of a Tom Jones absolutely clears the atmosphere that was
reeking with the black putrefying breathings of a hypocrite Blifil. One
homely expostulating shrug from Strap warms the whole air which the
suggestions of a gentlemanly ingratitude from his friend Random had
begun to freeze. One "Lord bless us!" of Parson Adams upon the wickedness of the time, exorcises and purges off the mass of iniquity which
the world-knowledge of even a Fielding could cull out and rake together.
But of the severer class of Hogarth's performances, enough, I trust, has
been said to show that they do not merely shock and repulse; that there
is in them the "scorn of vice" and the "pity" too; something to touch
the heart, and keep alive the sense of moral beauty; the "lacrymæ rerum," and the sorrowing by which the heart is made better. If they be
bad things, then is satire and tragedy a bad thing; let us proclaim at
once an age of gold, and sink the existence of vice and misery in our
speculations: let us

—— wink, and shut our apprehensions up
From common sense of what men were and are:

let us *make believe* with the children, that everybody is good and happy; and, with Dr. Swift, write panegyrics upon the world.

But that larger half of Hogarth's works, which were painted more for entertainment than instruction (though such was the suggestiveness of his mind that there is always something to be learnt from them), his humorous scenes,—are they such as merely to disgust and set us against our species?

The confident assertions of such a man as I consider the late Mr. Barry to have been, have that weight of authority in them which staggers at first hearing, even a long preconceived opinion. When I read his pathetic admonition concerning the shortness of life, and how much better the little leisure of it were laid out upon "that species of art which is employed about the amiable and the admirable"; and Hogarth's "method," proscribed as a "dangerous or worthless pursuit," I began to think there was something in it; that I might have been indulging all my life a passion for the works of this artist, to the utter prejudice of my taste and moral sense; but my first convictions gradually returned, a world of good-natured English faces came up one by one to my recollection, and a glance at the matchless Election Entertainment, which I have the happiness to have hanging up in my parlour, subverted Mr. Barry's whole theory in an instant.

In that inimitable print (which in my judgment as far exceeds the more known and celebrated March to Finchley, as the best comedy exceeds the best farce that ever was written), let a person look till he be saturated, and when he has done wondering at the inventiveness of genius which could bring so many characters (more than thirty distinct classes of face) into a room and set them down at table together, or otherwise dispose them about, in so natural a manner, engage them in so many easy sets and occupations, yet all partaking of the spirit of the occasion which brought them together, so that we feel that nothing but an election time could have assembled them; having no central figure or principal group (for the hero of the piece, the Candidate, is properly set aside in the levelling indistinction of the day, one must look for him to find him), nothing to detain the eye from passing from part to part, where every part is alike instinct with life,—for here are no furniture-faces, no figures brought in to fill up the scene like stage choruses, but all *dramatis personæ:* when he shall have done wondering at all these faces so strongly charactered, yet finished with the accuracy of the finest miniature; when he shall have done admiring the numberless appendages of the scene, those gratuitous doles which rich genius flings into the heap when it has already done enough, the over-measure which it delights in giving, as if it felt its stores were exhaustless; the dumb rhetoric of the scenery—for tables, and chairs, and joint-stools in Hogarth are living and significant things; the witticisms that are expressed by words (all artists but Hogarth have failed when they have endeavoured to combine two mediums of expression, and have introduced words into their pictures), and the unwritten numberless little allusive pleasantries

that are scattered about; the work that is going on in the scene, and beyond it, as is made visible to the "eye of mind," by the mob which
chokes up the doorway, and the sword that has forced an entrance before its master; when he shall have sufficiently admired this wealth of
genius, let him fairly say what is the *result* left on his mind. Is it an
impression of the vileness and worthlessness of his species? or is it not
the general feeling which remains, after the individual faces have ceased
to act sensibly on his mind, a *kindly one in favour of his species?* was not
the general air of the scene wholesome? did it do the heart hurt to be
among it? Something of a riotous spirit to be sure is there, some worldly-
mindedness in some of the faces, a Doddingtonian smoothness which
does not promise any superfluous degree of sincerity in the fine gentleman who has been the occasion of calling so much good company together; but is not the general cast of expression in the faces of the good
sort? do they not seem cut out of the *good old rock*, substantial English
honesty? would one fear treachery among characters of their expression?
or shall we call their honest mirth and seldom-returning relaxation by
the hard names of vice and profligacy? That poor country fellow, that is
grasping his staff (which, from that difficulty of feeling themselves at
home which poor men experience at a feast, he has never parted with
since he came into the room), and is enjoying with a relish that seems to
fit all the capacities of his soul the slender joke, which that facetious
wag his neighbour is practising upon the gouty gentleman, whose eyes
the effort to suppress pain has made as round as rings—does it shock the
"dignity of human nature" to look at that man, and to sympathise with
him in the seldom-heard joke which has unbent his careworn, hard-
working visage, and drawn iron smiles from it? or with that full-hearted
cobbler, who is honouring with the grasp of an honest fist the unused
palm of that annoyed patrician, whom the licence of the time has seated
next him?

I can see nothing "dangerous" in the contemplation of such scenes as
this, or the Enraged Musician, or the Southwark Fair, or twenty other
pleasant prints which come crowding in upon my recollection, in which
the restless activities, the diversified bents and humours, the blameless
peculiarities of men, as they deserve to be called, rather than their "vices
and follies," are held up in a laughable point of view. All laughter is not
of a dangerous or soul-hardening tendency. There is the petrifying sneer
of a demon which excludes and kills Love, and there is the cordial laughter of a man which implies and cherishes it. What heart was ever made
the worse by joining in a hearty laugh at the simplicities of Sir Hugh
Evans or Parson Adams, where a sense of the ridiculous mutually kindles
and is kindled by a perception of the amiable? That tumultuous harmony of singers that are roaring out the words, "The world shall bow to
the Assyrian throne," from the opera of Judith, in the third plate of the
series called the Four Groups of Heads; which the quick eye of Hogarth
must have struck off in the very infancy of the rage for sacred oratorios
in this country, while "Music yet was young"; when we have done smil-

ing at the deafening distortions, which these tearers of devotion to rags and tatters, these takers of heaven by storm, in their boisterous mimicry of the occupation of angels, are making,—what unkindly impression is left behind, or what more of harsh or contemptuous feeling, than when we quietly leave Uncle Toby and Mr. Shandy riding their hobby-horses about the room? The conceited, long-backed Sign-painter, that with all the self-applause of a Raphael or Correggio (the twist of body which his conceit has thrown him into has something of the Correggiesque in it), is contemplating the picture of a bottle, which he is drawing from an actual bottle that hangs beside him, in the print of Beer Street,—while we smile at the enormity of the self-delusion, can we help loving the good-humour and self-complacency of the fellow? would we willingly wake him from his dream?

I say not that all the ridiculous subjects of Hogarth have, necessarily, something in them to make us like them; some are indifferent to us, some in their natures repulsive, and only made interesting by the wonderful skill and truth to nature in the painter; but I contend that there is in most of them that sprinkling of the better nature, which, like holy water, chases away and disperses the contagion of the bad. They have this in them, besides, that they bring us acquainted with the everyday human face,—they give us skill to detect those gradations of sense and virtue (which escape the careless or fastidious observer) in the countenances of the world about us; and prevent that disgust at common life, that *tædium quotidianarum formarum,* which an unrestricted passion for ideal forms and beauties is in danger of producing. In this, as in many other things, they are analogous to the best novels of Smollett or Fielding.

ON THE POETICAL WORKS OF GEORGE WITHER

THE poems of G. Wither are distinguished by a hearty homeliness of manner, and a plain moral speaking. He seems to have passed his life in one continued act of an innocent self-pleasing. That which he calls his Motto is a continued self-eulogy of two thousand lines, yet we read it to the end without any feeling of distaste, almost without a consciousness that we have been listening all the while to a man praising himself. There are none of the cold particles in it, the hardness and self-ends, which render vanity and egotism hateful. He seems to be praising another person, under the mask of self: or rather, we feel that it was indifferent to him where he found the virtue which he celebrates; whether another's bosom or his own were its chosen receptacle. His poems are full, and this in particular is one downright confession, of a generous self-seeking. But by self he sometimes means a great deal,—his friends, his principles, his country, the human race.

Whoever expects to find in the satirical pieces of this writer any of those peculiarities which pleased him in the satires of Dryden or Pope, will be grievously disappointed. Here are no high-finished characters, no nice traits of individual nature, few or no personalities. The game run down is coarse general vice, or folly as it appears in classes. A liar, a drunkard, a coxcomb, is *stript and whipt;* no Shaftesbury, no Villiers, or Wharton, is curiously anatomised, and read upon. But to a well-natured mind there is a charm of moral sensibility running through them, which amply compensates the want of those luxuries. Wither seems everywhere bursting with a love of goodness, and a hatred of all low and base actions. At this day it is hard to discover what parts of the poem here particularly alluded to, Abuses Stript and Whipt, could have occasioned the imprisonment of the author. Was Vice in High Places more suspicious than now? had she more power; or more leisure to listen after ill reports? That a man should be convicted of a libel when he named no names but Hate, and Envy, and Lust, and Avarice, is like one of the indictments in the Pilgrim's Progress, where Faithful is arraigned for having "railed on our noble Prince Beelzebub, and spoken contemptibly of his honourable friends, the Lord Old Man, the Lord Carnal Delight, and the Lord Luxurious." What unlucky jealousy could have tempted the great men of those days to appropriate such innocent abstractions to themselves?

Wither seems to have contemplated to a degree of idolatry his own possible virtue. He is for ever anticipating persecution and martyrdom; fingering, as it were, the flames, to try how he can bear them. Perhaps his premature defiance sometimes made him obnoxious to censures which he would otherwise have slipped by.

The homely versification of these Satires is not likely to attract in the present day. It is certainly not such as we should expect from a poet "soaring in the high region of his fancies, with his garland and his singing robes about him" [1]; nor is it such as he has shown in his Philarete, and in some parts of his Shepherds Hunting. He seems to have adopted this dress with voluntary humility, as fittest for a moral teacher, as our divines choose sober grey or black; but in their humility consists their sweetness. The deepest tone of moral feeling in them (though all throughout is weighty, earnest, and passionate) is in those pathetic injunctions against shedding of blood in quarrels, in the chapter entitled Revenge. The story of his own forbearance, which follows, is highly interesting. While the Christian sings his own victory over Anger, the Man of Courage cannot help peeping out to let you know, that it was some higher principle than *fear* which counselled this forbearance.

Whether encaged, or roaming at liberty, Wither never seems to have abated a jot of that free spirit which sets its mark upon his writings, as much as a predominant feature of independence impresses every page of our late glorious Burns; for the elder poet wraps his proof-armour closer about him, the other wears his too much outwards; he is thinking too much of annoying the foe to be quite easy within; the spiritual de-

---

[1] Milton.

fences of Wither are a perpetual source of inward sunshine, the magnanimity of the modern is not without its alloy of soreness, and a sense of injustice, which seems perpetually to gall and irritate. Wither was better skilled in the "sweet uses of adversity"; he knew how to extract the "precious jewel" from the head of the "toad," without drawing any of the "ugly venom" along with it. The prison notes of Wither are finer than the wood notes of most of his poetical brethren. The description in the Fourth Eclogue of his Shepherds Hunting (which was composed during his imprisonment in the Marshalsea) of the power of the Muse to extract pleasure from common objects, has been oftener quoted, and is more known, than any part of his writings. Indeed, the whole Eclogue is in a strain so much above not only what himself, but almost what any other poet has written, that he himself could not help noticing it; he remarks that his spirits had been raised higher than they were wont, "through the love of poesy." The praises of Poetry have been often sung in ancient and in modern times; strange powers have been ascribed to it of influence over animate and inanimate auditors; its force over fascinated crowds has been acknowledged; but, before Wither, no one ever celebrated its power *at home*, the wealth and the strength which this divine gift confers upon its possessor. Fame, and that too after death, was all which hitherto the poets had promised themselves from their art. It seems to have been left to Wither to discover that poetry was a present possession, as well as a rich reversion, and that the Muse had promise of both lives,—of this, and of that which was to come.

The Mistress of Philarete is in substance a panegyric protracted through several thousand lines in the mouth of a single speaker, but diversified, so as to produce an almost dramatic effect, by the artful introduction of some ladies, who are rather auditors than interlocutors in the scene; and of a boy, whose singing furnishes pretence for an occasional change of metre: though the seven-syllable line, in which the main part of it is written, is that in which Wither has shown himself so great a master, that I do not know that I am always thankful to him for the exchange.

Wither has chosen to bestow upon the lady whom he commends the name of Arete, or Virtue; and, assuming to himself the character of Philarete, or Lover of Virtue, there is a sort of propriety in that heaped measure of perfections which he attributes to this partly real, partly allegorical personage. Drayton before him had shadowed his mistress under the name of Idea, or Perfect Pattern, and some of the old Italian love-strains are couched in such religious terms as to make it doubtful whether it be a mistress, or Divine Grace, which the poet is addressing.

In this poem (full of beauties) there are two passages of pre-eminent merit. The first is where the lover, after a flight of rapturous commendation, expresses his wonder why all men that are about his mistress, even to her very servants, do not view her with the same eyes that he does.

Sometime I do admire
All men burn not with desire:
Nay, I muse her servants are not
Pleading love; but O! they dare not.
And I therefore wonder, why
They do not grow sick and die.
Sure they would do so, but that,
By the ordinance of fate,
There is some concealed thing,
So each gazer limiting,
He can see no more of merit,
Than beseems his worth and spirit.
For in her a grace there shines,
That o'er-daring thoughts confines,
Making worthless men despair
To be loved of one so fair.
Yea, the destinies agree,
Some *good judgments* blind should be,
And not gain the power of knowing
Those rare beauties in her growing.
Reason doth as much imply:
For, if every judging eye,
Which beholdeth her, should there
Find what excellences are,
All, o'ercome by those perfections,
Would be captive to affections.
So, in happiness unblest,
She for lovers should not rest.

The other is, where he has been comparing her beauties to gold, and stars, and the most excellent things in nature; and, fearing to be accused of hyperbole, the common charge against poets, vindicates himself by boldly taking upon him, that these comparisons are no hyperboles; but that the best things in nature do, in a lover's eye, fall short of those excellences which he adores in her.

What pearls, what rubies can
Seem so lovely fair to man,
As her lips whom he doth love,
When in sweet discourse they move,
Or her lovelier teeth, the while
She doth bless him with a smile?
Stars indeed fair creatures be;
Yet amongst us where is he
Joys not more the whilst he lies
Sunning in his mistress' eyes,
Than in all the glimmering light
Of a starry winter's night?
Note the beauty of an eye—
And if aught you praise it by
Leave such passion in your mind,
Let my reason's eye be blind.
Mark if ever red or white
Any where gave such delight,
As when they have taken place
In a worthy woman's face.

*   *   *   *

> I must praise her as I may,
> Which I do mine own rude way,
> Sometimes setting forth her glories
> By unheard of allegories—etc.

To the measure in which these lines are written the wits of Queen Anne's days contemptuously gave the name of Namby Pamby, in ridicule of Ambrose Philips, who has used it in some instances, as in the lines on Cuzzoni, to my feeling at least, very deliciously; but Wither, whose darling measure it seems to have been, may show, that in skilful hands it is capable of expressing the subtilest movements of passion. So true it is, which Drayton seems to have felt, that it is the poet who modifies the metre, not the metre the poet; in his own words, that

> It's possible to climb;
> To kindle, or to slake;
> Altho' in Skelton's rhime.[1]

[1] A long line is a line we are long repeating. In the *Shepherds Hunting* take the following:—

> If thy verse doth bravely tower,
> *As she makes wing, she gets power;*
> Yet the higher she doth soar,
> She's affronted still the more,
> Till she to the high'st hath past,
> Then she rests with fame at last.

What longer measure can go beyond the majesty of this! what Alexandrine is half so long in pronouncing or expresses *labour slowly but strongly surmounting difficulty* with the life with which it is done in the second of these lines? or what metre could go beyond these from *Philarete*—

> Her true beauty leaves behind
> Apprehensions in my mind
> Of more sweetness, than all art
> Or inventions can impart.
> *Thoughts too deep to be express'd,*
> *And too strong to be suppress'd.*

MISCELLANEOUS

ESSAYS AND SKETCHES

ESSAYS AND SKETCHES

TABLE TALK

FROM THE ATHENÆUM, 1834

IT is a desideratum in works that treat *de re culinariâ*, that we have no *rationale* of sauces, or theory of mixed flavours: as to show why cabbage is reprehensible with roast beef, laudable with bacon; why the haunch of mutton seeks the alliance of currant jelly, the shoulder civilly declineth it; why loin of veal (a pretty problem), being itself unctuous, seeketh the adventitious lubricity of melted butter,—and why the same part in pork, not more oleaginous, abhorreth from it; why the French bean sympathises with the flesh of deer; why salt fish points to parsnip, brawn makes a dead-set at mustard; why cats prefer valerian to heart's-ease, old ladies *vice versâ*,—though this is rather travelling out of the road of the dietetics, and may be thought a question more curious than relevant; why salmon (a strong sapor *per se*) fortifieth its condition with the mighty lobster sauce, whose embraces are fatal to the delicater relish of the turbot; why oysters in death rise up against the contamination of brown sugar, while they are posthumously amorous of vinegar; why the sour mango and the sweet jam by turns court and are accepted by the compliable mutton hash,—she not yet decidedly declaring for either. We are as yet but in the empirical stage of cookery. We feed ignorantly, and want to be able to give a reason of the relish that is in us; so that, if Nature should furnish us with a new meat, or be prodigally pleased to restore the phœnix, upon a *given* flavour, we might be able to pronounce instantly, on philosophical principles, what the sauce to it should be,—what the curious adjuncts.

The greatest pleasure I know is to do a good action by stealth, and to have it found out by accident.

'Tis unpleasant to meet a beggar. It is painful to deny him; and, if you relieve him, it is so much out of your pocket.

Men marry for fortune, and sometimes to please their fancy; but, much oftener than is suspected, they consider what the world will say of it,—how such a woman in their friends' eyes will look at the head of a table. Hence we see so many insipid beauties made wives of, that could not have struck the particular fancy of any man that had any fancy at all. These I call *furniture wives;* as men buy *furniture pictures,* because they suit this or that niche in their dining parlours.

Your universally cried-up beauties are the very last choice which a man of taste would make. What pleases all cannot have that individual charm which makes this or that countenance engaging to you, and to you only perhaps, you know not why. What gained the fair Gunnings titled husbands, who, after all, turned out very sorry wives? Popular repute.

It is a sore trial when a daughter shall marry against her father's approbation. A little hard-heartedness, and aversion to a reconcilement, is almost pardonable. After all, Will Dockwray's way is, perhaps, the wisest. His best-loved daughter made a most imprudent match; in fact, eloped with the last man in the world that her father would have wished her to marry. All the world said that he would never speak to her again. For months she durst not write to him, much less come near him. But, in a casual rencounter, he met her in the streets of Ware,— Ware, that will long remember the mild virtues of William Dockwray, Esq. What said the parent to his disobedient child, whose knees faltered under her at the sight of him? "Ha, Sukey! is it you?" with that benevolent aspect with which he paced the streets of Ware, venerated as an angel: "come and dine with us on Sunday." Then turning away, and again turning back, as if he had forgotten something, he added, "And, Sukey (do you hear?), bring your husband with you." This was all the reproof she ever heard from him. Need it be added, that the match turned out better for Susan than the world expected.

The vices of some men are magnificent. Compare the amours of Henry the Eighth and Charles the Second. The Stuart had mistresses: the Tudor *kept* wives.

"We read the Paradise Lost as a task," says Dr. Johnson. Nay, rather as a celestial recreation, of which the dullard mind is not at all hours alike recipient. "Nobody ever wished it longer," nor the moon rounder, he might have added. Why, 'tis the perfectness and completeness of it which makes us imagine that not a line could be added to it, or diminished from it, with advantage. Would we have a cubit added to the stature of the Medicean Venus? Do we wish her taller?

Amidst the complaints of the widespread of infidelity among us, it is consolatory that a sect has sprung up in the heart of the metropolis, and is daily on the increase, of teachers of that healing doctrine which Pope upheld, and against which Voltaire directed his envenomed wit: we mean those practical preachers of optimism, or the belief that *whatever is is best;* the cads of omnibuses, who from their little back pulpits, not once in three or four hours, as those proclaimers of "God and His prophet" in Mussulman countries, but every minute, at the entry or exit of a brief passenger, are heard, in an almost prophetic tone, to exclaim (Wisdom crying out, as it were, in the streets), "ALL'S RIGHT!"

Advice is not so commonly thrown away as is imagined. We seek it in difficulties; but in common speech we are apt to confound with it *admonition;* as when a friend reminds one that drink is prejudicial to the health, etc. We do not care to be told of that which we know better than the good man that admonishes. M—— sent to his friend L——, who is no water-drinker, a twopenny tract "Against the Use of Fermented Liquors." L—— acknowledged the obligation, as far as to *twopence.* Penotier's advice was the safest, after all:—
"I advised him—"
But I must tell you. The dear, good-meaning, no-thinking creature had been dumfounding a company of us with a detail of inextricable difficulties, in which the circumstances of an acquaintance of his were involved. No clew of light offered itself. He grew more and more misty as he proceeded. We pitied his friend, and thought,—

> God help the man so rapt in Error's endless maze!

when, suddenly brightening up his placid countenance like one that had found out a riddle, and looked to have the solution admired,—
"At last," said he, "I advised him—"
Here he paused, and here we were again interminably thrown back. By no possible guess could any of us aim at the drift of the meaning he was about to be delivered of.
"I advised him," he repeated, "to have some *advice* upon the subject."
A general approbation followed; it was unanimously agreed, that, under all the circumstances of the case, no sounder or more judicious counsel could have been given.

A laxity pervades the popular use of words.
Parson W—— is not quite so continent as Diana, yet prettily dissembleth his frailty. Is Parson W——, therefore, a *hyprocrite?* I think not. Where the concealment of a vice is less pernicious than the barefaced publication of it would be, no additional delinquency is incurred in the secrecy. Parson W—— is simply an immoral clergyman. But if Parson W—— were to be for ever haranguing on the opposite virtue; choosing for his perpetual text, in preference to all other pulpit-topics, the remarkable resistance recorded in the 39th of Exodus [Genesis?]; dwelling, moreover, and dilating upon it,—then Parson W—— might be reasonably suspected of hypocrisy. But Parson W—— rarely diverteth into such line of argument, or toucheth it briefly. His ordinary topics are fetched from "obedience to the powers that are," "submission to the civil magistrate in all commands that are not absolutely unlawful"; on which he can delight to expatiate with equal fervour and sincerity.
Again: to *despise* a person is properly to *look down* upon him with none or the least possible emotion; but when Clementina, who has lately

lost her lover, with bosom heaving, eyes flashing, and her whole frame in agitation, pronounces with a peculiar emphasis that she *"despises* the fellow," depend upon it he is not quite so despicable in her eyes as she would have us imagine.

One more instance: If we must naturalise that portentous phrase, *a truism,* it were well that we limited the use of it. Every commonplace or trite observation is not a truism. For example: A good name helps a man on in the world. This is nothing but a simple truth, however hackneyed. It has a distinct subject and predicate. But when the thing predicated is involved in the term of the subject, and so necessarily involved that by no possible conception they can be separated, then it becomes a truism; as to say, "A good name is a proof of a man's estimation in the world." We seem to be saying something, when we say nothing. I was describing to F—— some knavish tricks of a mutual friend of ours. "If he did so and so," was the reply, "he cannot be an honest man." Here was a genuine truism, truth upon truth, inference and proposition identical, or proposition identical, or rather a dictionary definition usurping the place of an inference.

We are ashamed at a sight of a monkey,—somehow as we are shy of poor relations.

A—— imagined a Caledonian compartment in Hades, where there should be fire without sulphur.

Absurd images are sometimes irresistible. I will mention two,—an elephant in a coach-office gravely coming to have his trunk booked; a mermaid over a fish-kettle cooking her own tail.

It is the praise of Shakspeare, with reference to the playwriters his contemporaries, that he has so few revolting characters. Yet he has one that is singularly mean and disagreeable,—the King in Hamlet. Neither has he characters of insignificance, unless the phantom that stalks over the stage as Julius Cæsar, in the play of that name, may be accounted one. Neither has he envious characters, excepting the short part of Don John, in Much Ado about Nothing. Neither has he unentertaining characters, if we except Parolles, and the little that there is of the Clown, in All's Well that Ends Well.

Is it possible that Shakspeare should never have read Homer, in Chapman's version at least? If he had read it, could he mean to *travesty* it in the parts of those big boobies, Ajax and Achilles? Ulysses, Nestor, and Agamemnon are true to their parts in the Iliad: they are gentlemen at least. Thersites, though unamusing, is fairly deducible from it. Troilus and Cressida are a fine graft upon it. But those two big bulks—

It would settle the dispute as to whether Shakspeare intended Othello for a jealous character, to consider how differently we are affected towards him and towards Leontes in the Winter's Tale. Leontes *is* that character. Othello's fault was simply credulity.

LEAR. Who are you?
Mine eyes are not o' the best. I'll tell you straight.
Are you not Kent?
KENT. The same; your servant Kent.
Where is your servant Caius?
LEAR. He's a good fellow, I can tell you that;
He'd strike, and quickly too: he's dead and rotten.
KENT. No, my good lord: I am the very man—
LEAR. I'll see that straight—
KENT. That from your first of difference and decay
Have follow'd your sad steps.
LEAR. You are welcome hither.
ALBANY. He knows not what he says; and vain is it
That we present us to him.
EDGAR. Look up, my lord.
KENT. Vex not his ghost. Oh! let him pass. He hates him,
That would upon the rack of this tough world
Stretch him out longer.

So ends King Lear, the most stupendous of the Shakspearian dramas; and Kent, the noblest feature of the conceptions of his divine mind. This is the magnanimity of authorship, when a writer, having a topic presented to him, fruitful of beauties for common minds, waives his privilege, and trusts to the judicious few for understanding the reason of his abstinence. What a pudder would a common dramatist have raised here of a reconciliation scene, a perfect recognition, between the assumed Caius and his master!—to the suffusing of many fair eyes, and the moistening of cambric handkerchiefs. The old dying king partially catching at the truth, and immediately lapsing into obliviousness, with the high-minded carelessness of the other to have his services appreciated,—as one that—

> Served not for gain,
> Or follow'd out of form,—

are among the most judicious, not to say heart-touching, strokes in Shakspeare.

Allied to this magnanimity it is, where the pith and point of an argument, the amplification of which might compromise the modesty of the speaker, is delivered briefly, and, as it were, *parenthetically;* as in those few but pregnant words, in which the man in the old "Nut-brown Maid" rather intimates than reveals his unsuspected high birth to the woman:—

> Now understand, to Westmoreland,
> *Which is my heritage,*
> I will you bring, and with a ring,
> By way of marriage,
> I will you take, and lady make.

Turn we to the version of it, ten times diluted, of dear Mat. Prior,— in his own way unequalled, and a poet nowadays too much neglected.

"In me," quoth Henry, addressing the astounded Emma,—with a flourish and an attitude, as we may conceive,—

> In me behold the potent Edgar's heir,
> Illustrious earl! him terrible in war,
> Let Loire confess.

And with a deal of skimble-skamble stuff, as Hotspur would term it, more, presents the lady with a full and true enumeration of his papa's rent-roll in the fat soil by Deva.

But, of all parentheses (not to quit the topic too suddenly), commend me to that most significant one, at the commencement of the old popular ballad of "Fair Rosamond":—

> When good King Henry ruled this land,
> The second of that name,

Now mark,—

> (Besides the queen) he dearly loved
> A fair and comely dame.

There is great virtue in this *besides*.

THE GENTLE GIANTESS

FROM THE "LONDON MAGAZINE," 1822

THE WIDOW BLACKET, of Oxford, is the largest female I ever had the pleasure of beholding. There may be her parallel upon the earth; but surely I never saw it. I take her to be lineally descended from the maid's aunt of Brainford, who caused Master Ford such uneasiness. She hath Atlantean shoulders; and, as she stoopeth in her gait,—with as few offences to answer for in her own particular as any of Eve's daughters,— her back seems broad enough to bear the blame of all the peccadilloes that have been committed since Adam. She girdeth her waist—or what she is pleased to esteem as such—nearly up to her shoulders; from beneath which, that huge dorsal expanse, in mountainous declivity, emergeth. Respect for her alone preventeth the idle boys, who follow her about in shoals, whenever she cometh abroad, from getting up, and riding. But her presence infallibly commands a reverence. She is indeed, as the Americans would express it, something awful. Her person is a burthen to herself no less than to the ground which bears her. To her mighty bone, she hath a pinguitude withal, which makes the depth of winter to her the most desirable season. Her distress in the warmer solstice is pitiable. During the months of July and August she usually renteth a cool cellar, where ices are kept, whereinto she descendeth when Sirius rageth. She dates from a hot Thursday,—some twenty-five years ago. Her apartment in summer is pervious to the four winds. Two doors, in north and south direction, and two windows, fronting the rising and

the setting sun, never closed, from every cardinal point, catch the contributory breezes. She loves to enjoy what she calls a quadruple draught.
That must be a shrew zephyr that can escape her. I owe a painful face-
ache, which oppresses me at this moment, to a cold caught, sitting by
her, one day in last July, at this receipt of coolness. Her fan, in ordinary,
resembles a banner spread, which she keepeth continually on the alert
to detect the least breeze. She possesseth an active and gadding mind, totally incommensurate with her person. No one delighteth more than herself in country exercises and pastimes. I have passed many an agreeable
holy-day with her in her favourite park at Woodstock. She performs
her part in these delightful ambulatory excursions by the aid of a portable garden chair. She setteth out with you at a fair foot-gallop, which
she keepeth up till you are both well breathed, and then she reposeth
for a few seconds. Then she is up again for a hundred paces or so, and
again resteth; her movement, on these sprightly occasions, being something between walking and flying. Her great weight seemeth to propel
her forward, ostrich-fashion. In this kind of relieved marching I have
traversed with her many scores of acres on those well-wooded and well-
watered domains. Her delight at Oxford is in the public walks and gardens, where, when the weather is not too oppressive, she passeth much
of her valuable time. There is a bench at Maudlin, or rather situated between the frontiers of that and ——'s College (some litigation, latterly,
about repairs, has vested the property of it finally in ——'s), where, at
the hour of noon, she is ordinarily to be found sitting,—so she calls it by
courtesy,—but, in fact, pressing and breaking of it down with her enormous settlement, as both those foundations, who, however, are good-
natured enough to wink at it, have found, I believe, to their cost. Here
she taketh the fresh air, principally at vacation times, when the walks
are freest from interruption of the younger fry of students. Here she
passeth her idle hours, not idly, but generally accompanied with a book,
—blessed if she can but intercept some resident Fellow (as usually there
are some of that brood left behind at these periods) or stray Master of
Arts (to most of whom she is better known than their dinner-bell), with
whom she may confer upon any curious topic of literature. I have seen
these shy gownsmen, who truly set but a very slight value upon female
conversation, cast a hawk's eye upon her from the length of Maudlin
Grove, and warily glide off into another walk,—true monks as they are,
and ungently neglecting the delicacies of her polished converse for their
own perverse and uncommunicating solitariness! Within doors her principal diversion is music, vocal and instrumental; in both which she is no
mean professor. Her voice is wonderfully fine; but, till I got used to it,
I confess it staggered me. It is, for all the world, like that of a piping
bullfinch; while, from her size and stature, you would expect notes to
drown the deep organ. The shake, which most fine singers reserve for
the close or cadence, by some unaccountable flexibility, or tremulousness
of pipe, she carrieth quite through the composition; so that her time, to
a common air or ballad, keeps double motion, like the earth,—running

the primary circuit of the tune, and still revolving upon its own axis. The effect, as I said before, when you are used to it, is as agreeable as it is altogether new and surprising. The spacious apartment of her outward frame lodgeth a soul in all respects disproportionate. Of more than mortal make, she evinceth withal a trembling sensibility, a yielding infirmity of purpose, a quick susceptibility to reproach, and all the train of diffident and blushing virtues, which for their nabitation usually seek out a feeble frame, an attenuated and meagre constitution. With more than man's bulk, her humours and occupations are eminently feminine. She sighs,—being six foot high. She languisheth,—being two feet wide. She worketh slender sprigs upon the delicate muslin, her fingers being capable of moulding a Colossus. She sippeth her wine out of her glass daintily,—her capacity being that of a tun of Heidelberg. She goeth mincingly with those feet of hers, whose solidity need not fear the black ox's pressure. Softest and largest of thy sex, adieu! By what parting attribute may I salute thee, last and best of the Titanesses,—Ogress, fed with milk instead of blood; not least, or least handsome, among Oxford's stately structures,—Oxford, who, in its deadest time of vacation, can never properly be said to be empty, having thee to fill it.

THE REYNOLDS GALLERY

FROM THE "EXAMINER", 1813

THE REYNOLDS GALLERY has, upon the whole, disappointed me. Some of the portraits are interesting. They are faces of characters whom we (middle-aged gentlemen) were born a little too late to remember, but about whom we have heard our fathers tell stories till we almost fancy to have seen them. There is a charm in the portrait of a Rodney or a Keppel, which even a picture of Nelson must want for me. I should turn away after a slight inspection from the best likeness that could be made of Mrs. Anne Clarke; but Kitty Fisher is a considerable personage. Then the dresses of some of the women so exactly remind us of modes which we can just recall; of the forms under which the venerable relationship of aunt or mother first presented themselves to our young eyes; the aprons, the coifs, the lappets, the hoods. Mercy on us! what a load of head ornaments seem to have conspired to bury a pretty face in the picture of Mrs. Long, *yet could not!* Beauty must have some "charmed life" to have been able to surmount the conspiracy of fashion in those days to destroy it.

The portraits which least pleased me were those boys, as infant Bacchuses, Jupiters, etc. But the artist is not to be blamed for the disguise. No doubt the parents wished to see their children deified in their lifetime. It was but putting a thunderbolt (instead of a squib) into young master's hands; and a whey-faced chit was transformed into the infant ruler of Olympus,—him who was afterward to shake heaven and earth with his black brow. Another good boy pleased his grandmamma by saying his prayers so well, and the blameless dotage of the good old woman imagined in him an adequate representative of the awful Prophet Samuel. *But the great historical compositions, where the artist was at liberty* to paint from *his own idea,—the Beaufort and the Ugolino:* why then, I must confess, pleading the liberty of table talk for my presumption, that they have not left any very elevating impressions on my mind. Pardon a ludicrous comparison. I know, madam, you admire them both; but placed opposite to each other as they are at the gallery, as if to set the one work in competition with the other, they did remind me of the famous contention for the prize of deformity, mentioned in the 173rd Number of the Spectator. The one stares, and the other grins; but is there common dignity in their countenances? Does anything of the history of their life gone by peep through the ruins of the mind in the face, like the unconquerable grandeur that surmounts the distortions of the Laocoön? The figures which stand by the bed of Beaufort are indeed happy representations of the plain unmannered old nobility of the English historical plays of Shakspeare; but, for anything else, give me leave to recommend those macaroons.

After leaving the Reynolds Gallery (where, upon the whole, I received a good deal of pleasure), not feeling that I had quite had my fill of paintings, I stumbled upon a picture in Piccadilly (No. 22, I think), which purports to be a portrait of Francis the First, by Leonardo da Vinci. Heavens, what a difference! It is but a portrait, as most of those I had been seeing; but, placed by them, it would kill them, swallow them up as Moses' rod the other rods. Where did these old painters get their models? I see no figures, not in my dreams, as this Francis, in the character, or rather with the attributes, of John the Baptist. A more than martial majesty in the brow and upon the eyelid; an arm muscular, beautifully formed; the long, graceful, massy fingers compressing, yet so as not to hurt, a lamb more lovely, more sweetly shrinking, than we can conceive that milk-white one which followed Una; the picture altogether looking as if it were eternal,—combining the truth of flesh with a promise of permanence like marble.

Leonardo, from the one or two specimens we have of him in England, must have been a stupendous genius. I can scarce think he has had his full fame,—he who could paint that wonderful personification of the Logos, or second person of the Trinity, grasping a globe, late in the possession of Mr. Troward of Pall Mall, where the hand was, by the boldest license, twice as big as the truth of drawing warranted; yet the effect, to every one that saw it, by some magic of genius was confessed to be not *monstrous,* but *miraculous* and *silencing.* It could not be gainsaid.

GUY FAUX

FROM THE "LONDON MAGAZINE," 1823

A VERY ingenious and subtle writer,[1] whom there is good reason for suspecting to be an ex-Jesuit, not unknown at Douay some five-and-twenty years since (he will not obtrude himself at M——th again in a hurry), about a twelvemonth back set himself to prove the character of the Powder-Plot conspirators to have been that of heroic self-devotedness and true Christian martyrdom. Under the mask of Protestant candour, he actually gained admission for his treatise into a London weekly paper [2] not particularly distinguished for its zeal towards either religion. But, admitting Catholic principles, his arguments are shrewd and incontrovertible. He says—

"Guy Faux was a fanatic; but he was no hypocrite. He ranks among *good haters*. He was cruel, bloody-minded, reckless of all considerations but those of an infuriated and bigoted faith; but he was a true son of the Catholic Church, a martyr, and a confessor, for all that. He who can prevail upon himself to devote his life for a cause, however we may condemn his opinions or abhor his actions, vouches at least for the honesty of his principles and the disinterestedness of his motives. He may be guilty of the worst practices; but he is capable of the greatest. He is no longer a slave, but free. The contempt of death is the beginning of virtue. The hero of the Gunpowder Plot was, if you will, a fool, a madman, an assassin; call him what names you please: still he was neither knave nor coward. He did not propose to blow up the Parliament, and come off, scot-free, himself: he showed that he valued his own life no more than theirs in such a cause, where the integrity of the Catholic faith and the salvation of perhaps millions of souls was at stake. He did not call it a murder, but a sacrifice, which he was about to achieve: he was armed with the Holy Spirit and with fire; he was the Church's chosen servant and her blessed martyr. He comforted himself as 'the best of cut-throats.' How many wretches are there that would have undertaken to do what he intended, for a sum of money, if they could have got off with impunity! How few are there who would have put themselves in Guy Faux's situation to save the universe! Yet, in the latter case, we affect to be thrown into greater consternation than at the most unredeemed acts of villainy; as if the absolute disinterestedness of the motive doubled the horror of the deed! The cowardice and selfishness of mankind are in fact shocked at the consequences to themselves if such examples are held up for imitation; and they make a fearful outcry against the violation of every principle of morality, lest they, too, should be called on for any such tremendous sacrifices; lest they, in their turn,

---

[1] William Hazlitt.
[2] The Examiner. then edited by Leigh Hunt.

should have to go on the forlorn hope of extra-official duty. *Charity begins at home* is a maxim that prevails as well in the courts of conscience as in those of prudence. We would be thought to shudder at the consequences of crime to others, while we tremble for them to ourselves. We talk of the dark and cowardly assassin; and this is well, when an individual shrinks from the face of an enemy, and purchases his own safety by striking a blow in the dark: but how the charge of cowardly can be applied to the public assassin, who, in the very act of destroying another, lays down his life as the pledge and forfeit of his sincerity and boldness, I am at a loss to devise. There may be barbarous prejudice, rooted hatred, unprincipled treachery, in such an act; but he who resolves to take all the danger and odium upon himself can no more be branded with cowardice, than Regulus devoting himself for his country, or Codrus leaping into the fiery gulf. A wily Father Inquisitor, coolly and with plenary authority condemning hundreds of helpless, unoffending victims to the flames, or to the horrors of a living tomb, while he himself would not suffer a hair of his head to be hurt, is, to me, a character without any qualifying trait in it. Again: the Spanish conqueror and hero, the favourite of his monarch, who enticed thirty thousand poor Mexicans into a large open building under promise of strict faith and cordial goodwill, and then set fire to it, making sport of the cries and agonies of these deluded creatures, is an instance of uniting the most hardened cruelty with the most heartless selfishness. His plea was, keeping no faith with heretics; this too was Guy Faux's: but I am sure at least that the latter kept faith with himself; he was in earnest in his professions. *His* was not gay, wanton, unfeeling depravity; he did not murder in sport: it was serious work that he had taken in hand. To see this arch-bigot, this heart-whole traitor, this pale miner in the infernal regions, skulking in his retreat with his cloak and dark lantern, moving cautiously about among his barrels of gunpowder loaded with death, but not yet ripe for destruction, regardless of the lives of others, and more than indifferent to his own, presents a picture of the strange infatuation of the human understanding, but not of the depravity of the human will, without an equal. There were thousands of pious Papists privy to and ready to applaud the deed when done: there was no one but our old Fifth of November friend, who still flutters in rags and straw on the occasion, that had the courage to attempt it. In him stern duty and unshaken faith prevailed over natural frailty."

It is impossible, upon Catholic principles, not to admit the force of this reasoning: we can only not help smiling (with the writer) at the simplicity of the gulled editor, swallowing the dregs of Loyola for the very quintessence of sublimated reason in England at the commencement of the nineteenth century. We will just, as a contrast, show what we Protestants (who are a party concerned) thought upon the same subject at a period rather nearer to the heroic project in question.

The Gunpowder Treason was the subject which called forth the earliest specimen which is left us of the pulpit eloquence of Jeremy Taylor. When he preached the sermon on that anniversary, which is printed at the end of the folio edition of his Sermons, he was a young man, just commencing his ministry under the auspices of Archbishop Laud. From the learning and mature oratory which it manifests, one should rather have conjectured it to have proceeded from the same person after he was ripened by time into a Bishop and Father of the Church. "And, really, these *Romano-barbari* could never pretend to any precedent for an act so barbarous as theirs. Adrammelech, indeed, killed a king; but he spared the people. Haman would have killed the people, but spared the king; but that both king and people, princes and judges, branch and rush and root, should die at once (as if Caligula's wish were actuated, and all England upon one head), was never known till now, that all the malice of the world met in this, as in a centre. The Sicilian evensong, the matins of St. Bartholomew, known for the pitiless and damned massacres, were but κάπνου σκίας ὄναρ, 'the dream of the shadow of smoke,' if compared with this great fire. *In tum occupato sæculo fabulas vulgares nequitia non invenit.* This was a busy age. Erostratus must have invented a more sublimed malice than the burning of one temple, or not have been so much as spoke of since the discovery of the powder treason. But I must make more haste; I shall not else climb the sublimity of this impiety. Nero was sometimes the *populare odium,* was popularly hated, and deserved it too: for he slew his master, and his wife, and all his family, once or twice over; opened his mother's womb; fired the city, laughed at it, slandered the Christians for it: but yet all these were but *principia malorum,* the very first 'rudiments of evil.' Add, then, to these, Herod's masterpiece at Ramah, as it was deciphered by the tears and sad threnes of the matrons in an universal mourning for the loss of their pretty infants; yet this of Herod will prove but an infant wickedness, and that of Nero the evil but of one city. I would willingly have found out an example, but I see I cannot, should I put into the scale the extract of all the old tyrants famous in antique stories,—

> "Bistonii stabulum regis, Busiridis aras,
> Antiphatæ mensas, et Taurica regna Thoantis;—

should I take for true story the highest cruelty as it was fancied by the most hieroglyphical Egyptian,—this alone would weigh them down, as if the Alps were put in scale against the dust of a balance. For, had this accursed treason prospered, we should have had the whole kingdom mourn for the inestimable loss of its chiefest glory, its life, its present joy, and all its very hopes for the future. For such was their destined malice, that they would not only have inflicted so cruel a blow, but have made it incurable, by cutting off our supplies of joy, the whole succession of the Line Royal. Not only the vine itself, but all the *gemmulæ,* and the tender olive branches, should either have been bent to their intentions, and made to grow crooked, or else been broken.

"And now, after such a sublimity of malice, I will not instance in the sacrilegious ruin of the neighbouring temples, which needs must have

perished in the flame; nor in the disturbing the ashes of our entombed
kings, devouring their dead ruins like sepulchral dogs; these are but
minutes in respect of the ruin prepared for the living temples.

"Stragem sed istam non tulit
Christus cadentum principum
Impune, ne forsan sui
Patris periret fabrica.
Ergo quæ poterit lingua retexere
Laudes, Christe, tuas, qui domitum struis
Infidum populum cum Duce perfido?"

In such strains of eloquent indignation did Jeremy Taylor's young
oratory inveigh against that stupendous attempt, which he truly says
had no parallel in ancient or modern times. A century and a half of
European crimes has elapsed since he made the assertion, and his position remains in its strength. He wrote near the time in which the nefari-
ous project had like to have been completed. Men's minds still were
shuddering from the recentness of the escape. It must have been within
his memory, or have been sounded in his ears so young by his parents,
that he would seem, in his maturer years, to have remembered it. No
wonder, then, that he describes it in words that burn. But to us, to
whom the tradition has come slowly down, and has had time to cool, the
story of Guido Vaux sounds rather like a tale, a fable, and an invention,
than true history. It supposes such gigantic audacity of daring, combined with such more than infantile stupidity in the motive,—such a
combination of the fiend and the monkey,—that credulity is almost
swallowed up in contemplating the singularity of the attempt. It has
accordingly, in some degree, shared the fate of fiction. It is familiarised
to us in a kind of serio-ludicrous way, like the story of *Guy of Warwick*,
or *Valentine and Orson*. The way which we take to perpetuate the
memory of this deliverance is well adapted to keep up this fabular
notion. Boys go about the streets annually with a beggarly scarecrow
dressed up, which is to be burnt indeed, at night, with holy zeal; but,
meantime, they beg a penny for *poor Guy*. This periodical petition,
which we have heard from our infancy, combined with the dress and
appearance of the effigy, so well calculated to move compassion, has the
effect of quite removing from our fancy the horrid circumstances of the
story which is thus commemorated; and in *poor Guy* vainly should we
try to recognise any of the features of that tremendous madman in
inquity, Guido Vaux, with his horrid crew of accomplices, that sought to
emulate earthquakes and bursting volcanoes in their more than mortal
mischief.

Indeed, the whole ceremony of burning Guy Faux, or *the Pope,* as he
is indifferently called, is a sort of *Treason Travestie,* and admirably
adapted to lower our feelings upon this memorable subject. The printers
of the little duodecimo *Prayer Book,* printed by T. Baskett,[1] in 1749,

[1] The same, I presume, upon whom the clergyman in the song of the "Vicar and
Moses," not without judgment, passes this memorable censure:—

which has the effigy of his sacred majesty George II. piously prefixed, have illustrated the service (a very fine one in itself) which is appointed for the anniversary of this day, with a print, which is not very easy to describe; but the contents appear to be these: The scene is a room, I conjecture, in the king's palace. Two persons—one of whom I take to be James himself, from his wearing his hat, while the other stands bareheaded—are intently surveying a sort of speculum, or magic mirror, which stands upon a pedestal in the midst of a room, in which a little figure of Guy Faux with his dark lantern, approaching the door of the Parliament House, is made discernible by the light proceeding from a *great eye* which shines in from the topmost corner of the apartment, by which eye the pious artist no doubt meant to designate Providence. On the other side of the mirror is a figure doing something, which puzzled me when a child, and continues to puzzle me now. The best I can make of it is, that it is a conspirator busy laying the train; but, then, why is he represented in the king's chamber? Conjecture upon so fantastical a design is vain; and I only notice the print as being one of the earliest graphic representations which woke my childhood into wonder, and doubtless combined, with the mummery before mentioned, to take off the edge of that horror which the naked historical mention of Guido's conspiracy could not have failed of exciting.

Now that so many years are past since that abominable machination was happily frustrated, it will not, I hope, be considered a profane sporting with the subject, if we take no very serious survey of the consequences that would have flowed from this plot if it had had a successful issue. The first thing that strikes us, in a selfish point of view, is the material change which it must have produced in the course of the nobility. All the ancient peerage being extinguished, as it was intended, at one blow, the *Red Book* must have been closed for ever, or a new race of peers must have been created to supply the deficiency. As the first part of this dilemma is a deal too shocking to think of, what a fund of mouthwatering reflections does this give rise to in the breast of us plebeians of A.D. 1823! Why, you or I, reader, might have been Duke of ——, or Earl of ——. I particularise no titles, to avoid the least suspicion of intention to usurp the dignities of the two noblemen whom I have in my eye; but a feeling more dignified than envy sometimes excites a sigh, when I think how the posterity of Guido's Legion of Honour (among whom you or I might have been) might have rolled down, "dulcified," as Burke expresses it, "by an exposure to the influence of heaven in a long flow of generations, from the hard, acidulous, metallic tincture of the spring." [1] What new orders of merit think you this English Napoleon would have chosen? Knights of the Barrel, or Lords of the Tub, Grand

Here, Moses the king:
'Tis a scandalous thing
That this Baskett should print for the Crown.

[1] Letter to a Noble Lord.

Almoners of the Cellar, or Ministers of Explosion? We should have given the train *couchant,* and the fire *rampant,* in our arms; we should have quartered the dozen white matches in our coats: the Shallows would have been nothing to us.

Turning away from these mortifying reflections, let us contemplate its effects upon the *other house;* for they were all to have gone together, —king, lords, commons.

To assist our imagination, let us take leave to suppose (and we do it in the harmless wantonness of fancy)—to suppose that the tremendous explosion had taken place in our days. We better know what a House of Commons is in our days, and can better estimate our loss. Let us imagine, then, to ourselves, the united members sitting in full conclave above; Faux just ready with his train and matches below,—in his hand a "reed tipp'd with fire." He applies the fatal engine.

To assist our notions still further, let us suppose some lucky dog of a reporter, who had escaped by miracle upon some plank of St. Stephen's benches, and came plump upon the roof of the adjacent Abbey; from whence descending, at some neighbouring coffee-house, first wiping his clothes and calling for a glass of lemonade, he sits down and reports what he had heard and seen (*quorum pars magna fuit*) for the Morning Post or the Courier. We can scarcely imagine him describing the event in any other words but some such as these:—

"A *motion* was put and carried, that this house do *adjourn;* that the Speaker do *quit the chair.* The house rose amid clamours for order."

In some such way the event might most technically have been conveyed to the public. But a poetical mind, not content with this dry method of narration, cannot help pursuing the effects of this tremendous blowing up, this adjournment in the air, *sine die.* It sees the benches mount,—the chair first, and then the benches; and first the treasury bench, hurried up in this nitrous explosion,—the members, as it were, pairing off; Whigs and Tories taking their friendly apotheosis together (as they did their sandwiches below in Bellamy's room). Fancy, in her flight, keeps pace with the aspiring legislators: she sees the awful seat of order mounting, till it becomes finally fixed, a constellation, next to Cassiopeia's chair,—the wig of him that sat in it taking its place near Berenice's curls. St. Peter, at heaven's wicket,—no, not St. Peter, —St. Stephen, with open arms, receives his own.

While Fancy beholds these celestial appropriations, Reason, no less pleased, discerns the mighty benefit which so complete a renovation must produce below. Let the most determined foe to corruption, the most thorough-paced redresser of abuses, try to conceive a more absolute purification of the house than this was calculated to produce. Why, Pride's Purge was nothing to it. The whole borough-mongering system would have been got rid of, fairly *exploded;* with it the senseless distinctions of Party must have disappeared, faction must have vanished, corruption have expired in air. From Hundred, Tything, and Wapentake, some new Alfred would have convened, in all its purity, the primitive Witenagemote,—fixed upon a basis of property or population, permanent as the poles.

From this dream of universal restitution, Reason and Fancy with difficulty awake to view the real state of things. But (blessed be Heaven!) St. Stephen's walls are yet standing, all her seats firmly secured; nay, some have doubted (since the Septennial Act) whether gunpowder itself, or anything short of a *committee above stairs,* would be able to shake any one member from his seat. That great and final improvement to the Abbey, which is all that seems wanting,—the removing of Westminster Hall and its appendages, and letting in the view of the Thames,—must not be expected in our days. Dismissing, therefore, all such speculations as mere tales of a tub, it is the duty of every honest Englishman to endeavour, by means more wholesome than Guido's, to ameliorate, without extinguishing, parliaments; to hold the *lantern* to the dark places of corruption; to apply the *match* to the rotten parts of the system only; and to wrap himself up, not in the muffling mantle of conspiracy, but in the warm, honest *cloak* of integrity and patriotic intention.

THE ILLUSTRIOUS DEFUNCT [1]

FROM THE "NEW MONTHLY MAGAZINE," 1825

> Nought but a blank remains, a dead void space,
> A step of life that promised such a race.—DRYDEN.

NAPOLEON has now sent us back from the grave sufficient echoes of his living renown: the twilight of posthumous fame has lingered long enough over the spot where the sun of his glory set; and his name must at length repose in the silence, if not in the darkness, of night. In this busy and evanescent scene, other spirits of the age are rapidly snatched away, claiming our undivided sympathies and regrets, until in turn they yield to some newer and more absorbing grief. Another name is now added to the list of the mighty departed,—a name whose influence upon the hopes and fears, the fates and fortunes, of our countrymen, has rivalled, and perhaps eclipsed, that of the defunct "child and champion of Jacobinism," while it is associated with all the sanctions of legitimate government, all the sacred authorities of social order and our most holy religion. We speak of one, indeed, under whose warrant heavy and incessant contributions were imposed upon our fellow-citizens, but who exacted nothing without the signet and the sign-manual of most devout

---

[1] Since writing this article, we have been informed that the object of our funeral oration is not definitively dead, but only moribund. So much the better: we shall have an opportunity of granting the request made to Walter by one of the children in the wood, and "kill him two times." The Abbé de Vertot having a siege to write, and not receiving the materials in time, composed the whole from his invention. Shortly after its completion, the expected documents arrived, when he threw them aside, exclaiming, "You are of no use to me now: I have carried the town."

Chancellors of the Exchequer. Not to dally longer with the sympathies of our readers, we think it right to premonish them that we are composing an epicedium upon no less distinguished a personage than the Lottery, whose last breath, after many penultimate puffs, has been sobbed forth by sorrowing contractors, as if the world itself were about to be converted into a blank. There is a fashion of eulogy, as well as of vituperation; and though the Lottery stood for some time in the latter predicament, we hesitate not to assert that *multis ille bonis flebilis occidit*. Never have we joined in the senseless clamour which condemned the only tax whereto we became voluntary contributors; the only resource which gave the stimulus without the danger or infatuation of gambling; the only alembic which in these plodding days sublimised our imaginations, and filled them with more delicious dreams than ever flitted athwart the sensorium of Alnaschar.

Never can the writer forget, when, as a child, he was hoisted upon a servant's shoulder in Guildhall, and looked down upon the installed and solemn pomp of the then drawing Lottery. The two awful cabinets of iron, upon whose massy and mysterious portals the royal initials were gorgeously emblazoned, as if, after having deposited the unfulfilled prophecies within, the king himself had turned the lock, and still retained the key in his pocket; the blue-coat boy, with his naked arm, first converting the invisible wheel, and then diving into the dark recess for a ticket; the grave and reverend faces of the commissioners eyeing the announced number; the scribes below calmly committing it to their huge books; the anxious countenances of the surrounding populace; while the giant figures of Gog and Magog, like presiding deities, looked down with a grim silence upon the whole proceeding,—constituted altogether a scene, which, combined with the sudden wealth supposed to be lavished from those inscrutable wheels, was well calculated to impress the imagination of a boy with reverence and amazement. Jupiter, seated between the two fatal urns of good and evil, the blind goddess with her cornucopia, the Parcæ wielding the distaff, the thread of life, and the abhorred shears, seemed but dim and shadowy abstractions of mythology, when I had gazed upon an assemblage exercising, as I dreamt, a not less eventful power, and all presented to me in palpable and living operation. Reason and experience, ever at their old spiteful work of catching and destroying the bubbles which youth delighted to follow, have indeed dissipated much of this illusion: but my mind so far retained the influence of that early impression, that I have ever since continued to deposit my humble offering at its shrine, whenever the ministers of the Lottery went forth with type and trumpet to announce its periodical dispensations; and though nothing has been doled out to me from its undiscerning coffers but blanks, or those more vexatious tantalisers of the spirit, denominated small prizes, yet do I hold myself largely indebted to this most generous diffuser of universal happiness. Ingrates that we are! are we to be thankful for no benefits that are not palpable to sense, to recognise no favours that are not of marketable value, to acknowledge no wealth unless it can be counted with the five fingers? If we admit the mind to be the sole depository of genuine joy, where is the bosom that has not been elevated into a temporary Elysium by the magic of the Lottery? Which of us has not converted his ticket, or even his sixteenth share of one, into a nest-egg of Hope, upon which he has sate brooding in the secret roosting-places of his heart, and hatched it into a thousand fantastical apparitions?

What a startling revelation of the passions if all the aspirations engendered by the Lottery could be made manifest! Many an impecuniary epicure has gloated over his locked-up warrant for future wealth, as a means of realising the dream of his namesake in the Alchemist:—

> My meat shall all come in in Indian shells,—
> Dishes of agate set in gold, and studded
> With emeralds, sapphires, hyacinths, and rubies;
> The tongues of carps, dormice, and camels' heels,
> Boil'd i' the spirit of Sol, and dissolved in pearl,
> (Apicius' diet 'gainst the epilepsy.)
> And I will eat these broths with spoons of amber,
> Headed with diamant and carbuncle.
> My footboy shall eat pheasants, calver'd salmons,
> Knots, gotwits, lampreys; I myself will have
> The beards of barbels served, instead of salads;
> Oiled mushrooms, and the swelling unctuous paps
> Of a fat pregnant sow, newly cut off,
> Dress'd with an exquisite and poignant sauce,
> For which I'll say unto my cook, "There's gold:
> Go forth, and be a knight."

Many a doting lover has kissed the scrap of paper whose promissory shower of gold was to give up to him his otherwise unattainable Danaë. Nimrods have transformed the same narrow symbol into a saddle, by which they have been enabled to bestride the backs of peerless hunters; while nymphs have metamorphosed its Protean form into—

> Rings, gauds, conceits,
> Knacks, trifles, nosegays, sweetmeats,

and all the braveries of dress, to say nothing of the obsequious husband, the two-footman'd carriage, and the opera-box. By the simple charm of this numbered and printed rag, gamesters have, for a time at least, recovered their losses; spendthrifts have cleared off mortgages from their estates; the imprisoned debtor has leaped over his lofty boundary of circumscription and restraint, and revelled in all the joys of liberty and fortune; the cottage walls have swelled out into more goodly proportion than those of Baucis and Philemon; poverty has tasted the luxuries of competence; labour has lolled at ease in a perpetual arm-chair of idleness; sickness has been bribed into banishment; life has been invested with new charms; and death deprived of its former terrors. Nor have the affections been less gratified than the wants, appetites, and ambition of mankind. By the conjurations of the same potent spell, kindred have lavished anticipated benefits upon one another, and charity upon all. Let it be termed a delusion,—a fool's paradise is better than the wise man's Tartarus; be it branded as an ignis-fatuus,—it was at least a benevolent one, which, instead of beguiling its followers into swamps, caverns, and pitfalls, allured them on with all the blandishments of enchantment to a garden of Eden,—an ever-blooming Elysium of delight. True, the pleasures which it bestowed were evanescent: but which of our joys are permanent? and who so inexperienced as not to know that anticipation is always of higher relish than reality, which strikes a balance both in our sufferings and enjoyments? "The fear of ill exceeds the ill we fear"; and fruition, in the same proportion, invariably falls short of hope. "Men are but children of a larger growth," who may amuse themselves for a long time in gazing at the reflection of the moon in the water; but, if they jump in to grasp it, they may grope for ever, and only get the farther from their object. He is the wisest who keeps feeding upon the future, and refrains as long as possible from undeceiving himself by converting his pleasant speculations into disagreeable certainties.

The true mental epicure always purchased his ticket early, and postponed inquiry into its fate to the last possible moment, during the whole of which intervening period he had an imaginary twenty thousand locked up in his desk; and was not this well worth all the money? Who would scruple to give twenty pounds interest for even the ideal enjoyment of as many thousands during two or three months? *Crede quod habes, et habes;* and the usufruct of such a capital is surely not dear at such a price. Some years ago, a gentleman in passing along Cheapside saw the figures 1,069, of which number he was the sole proprietor, flaming on the window of a lottery office as a capital prize. Somewhat flurried by this discovery, not less welcome than unexpected, he resolved to walk round St. Paul's that he might consider in what way to communicate the happy tidings to his wife and family; but, upon repassing the shop, he observed that the number was altered to 10,069, and, upon inquiry, had the mortification to learn that his ticket was a blank, and had only been stuck up in the window by mistake of the clerk. This effectually calmed his agitation; but he always speaks of himself as having once possessed twenty thousand pounds, and maintains that his ten minutes' walk round St. Paul's was worth ten times the purchase money of the ticket. A prize thus obtained has, moreover, this special advantage,—it is beyond the reach of fate; it cannot be squandered; bankruptcy cannot lay siege to it; friends cannot pull it down, nor enemies blow it up; it bears a charmed life, and none of woman born can break its integrity, even by the dissipation of a single fraction. Show me the property in these perilous times that is equally compact and impregnable. We can no longer become enriched for a quarter of an hour; we can no longer succeed in such splendid failures: all our chances of making such a miss have vanished with the last of the Lotteries.

Life will now become a flat, prosaic routine of matter-of-fact; and sleep itself, erst so prolific of numerical configurations and mysterious stimulants to lottery adventure, will be disfurnished of its figures and figments. People will cease to harp upon the one lucky number suggested in a dream, and which forms the exception, while they are scrupulously silent upon the ten thousand falsified dreams which constitute the rule. Morpheus will stifle Cocker with a handful of poppies, and our pillows will be no longer haunted by the book of numbers.

And who, too, shall maintain the art and mystery of puffing, in all its pristine glory, when the lottery professors shall have abandoned its cultivation? They were the first, as they will assuredly be the last, who fully developed the resources of that ingenious art; who cajoled and decoyed the most suspicious and wary reader into a perusal of their advertisements by devices of endless variety and cunning; who baited their lurking schemes with midnight murders, ghost stories, crim-cons, bon-mots, balloons, dreadful catastrophes, and every diversity of joy and sorrow, to catch newspaper gudgeons. Ought not such talents to be encouraged? Verily the abolitionists have much to answer for!

And now, having established the felicity of all those who gained imaginary prizes, let us proceed to show that the equally numerous class who were presented with real blanks have not less reason to consider themselves happy. Most of us have cause to be thankful for that which is bestowed; but we have all, probably, reason to be still more grateful for that which is withheld, and more especially for our being denied the sudden possession of riches. In the Litany, indeed, we call upon the Lord to deliver us "in all time of our wealth"; but how few of us are sincere in deprecating such a calamity! Massinger's Luke, and Ben Jonson's Sir Epicure Mammon, and Pope's Sir Balaam, and our own daily observation, might convince us that the Devil "now tempts by making rich, not making poor." We may read in the Guardian a circumstantial account of a man who was utterly ruined by gaining a capital prize; we may recollect what Dr. Johnson said to Garrick, when the latter was making a display of his wealth at Hampton Court,— "Ah, David, David! these are the things that make a death-bed terrible." We may recall the Scripture declaration, as to the difficulty a rich man finds in entering into the kingdom of Heaven; and, combining all these denunciations against opulence, let us heartily congratulate one another upon our lucky escape from the calamity of a twenty or thirty thousand pound prize! The fox in the fable, who accused the unattainable grapes of sourness, was more of a philosopher than we are generally willing to allow. He was an adept in that species of moral alchemy which turns everything to gold, and converts disappointment itself into a ground of resignation and content. Such we have shown to be the great lesson inculcated by the Lottery, when rightly contemplated; and, if we might parody M. de Chateaubriand's jingling expression,—"*le Roi est mort: vive le Roi!*"—we should be tempted to exclaim, "The Lottery is no more: long live the Lottery!"

THE RELIGION OF ACTORS

FROM THE "NEW MONTHLY MAGAZINE," 1826

THE world has hitherto so little troubled its head with the points of doctrine held by a community which contributes in other ways so largely to its amusement, that, before the late mischance of a celebrated tragic actor, it scarce condescended to look into the practice of any individual player, much less to inquire into the hidden and abscondite springs of his actions. Indeed, it is with some violence to the imagination that we conceive of an actor as belonging to the relations of private life, so closely do we identify these persons in our mind with the characters which they assume upon the stage. How oddly does it sound, when we are told that the late Miss Pope, for instance,—that is to say, in our notion of her Mrs. Candour,—was a good daughter, an affectionate sister, and exemplary in all the parts of domestic life! With still greater difficulty can we carry our notions to church, and conceive of Liston kneeling upon a hassock, or Munden uttering a pious ejaculation,— "making mouths at the invisible event." But the times are fast improving; and, if the process of sanctity begun under the happy auspices of the present licenser go on to its completion, it will be as necessary for a comedian to give an account of his faith as of his conduct. Fawcett must study the five points; and Dicky Suett, if he were alive, would have had to rub up his catechism. Already the effects of it begin to appear. A celebrated performer has thought fit to oblige the world with a confession of his faith,—or Br——'s *Religio Dramatici*. This gentleman, in his laudable attempt to shift from his person the obloquy of Judaism, with the forwardness of a new convert, in trying to prove too much, has, in the opinion of many, proved too little. A simple declaration of his Christianity was sufficient; but, strange to say, his apology has not a word about it. We are left to gather it from some expressions which imply that he is a Protestant; but we did not wish to inquire into the niceties of his orthodoxy. To his friends of the *old persuasion* the distinction was impertinent; for what cares Rabbi Ben Kimchi for the differences which have split our novelty? To the great body of Christians that hold the Pope's supremacy—that is to say, to the major part of the Christian world—his religion will appear as much to seek as ever. But perhaps he conceived that all Christians are Protestants, as children and the common people call all, that are not animals, Christians. The mistake was not very considerable in so young a proselyte, or he might think the general (as logicians speak) involved in the particular. All Protestants are Christians; but I am a Protestant; *ergo,* etc.: as if a marmoset, contending to be a man, over-leaping that term as too generic and vulgar, should at once roundly proclaim himself to be a gentleman. The argument would be, as we say, *ex abundanti.* From whichever cause this *excessus in terminis* proceeded, we can do no less than congratulate the general state of Christendom upon the accession of so extraordinary a convert. Who was the happy instrument of the conversion, we are yet to learn: it comes nearest to the attempt of the late pious Dr. Watts to Christianise the Psalms of the Old Testament. Something of the old Hebrew raciness is lost in the transfusion; but much of its asperity is softened and pared down in the adaptation.

The appearance of so singular a treatise at this conjuncture has set us upon an inquiry into the present state of religion upon the stage generally. By the favour of the Churchwardens of St. Martin's-in-the Fields, and St. Paul's, Covent Garden, who have very readily, and with great kindness, assisted our pursuit, we are enabled to lay before the public the following particulars. Strictly speaking, neither of the two great bodies is collectively a religious institution. We expected to find a chaplain among them, as at St. Stephen's and other Court establishments; and were the more surprised at the omission, as the last Mr. Bengough at the one house, and Mr. Powell at the other, from a gravity of speech and demeanour, and the habit of wearing black at their first appearances in the beginning of the *fifth* or the conclusion of *fourth* act, so eminently pointed out their qualifications for such office. These corporations, then, being not properly congregational, we must seek the solution of our question in the tastes, attainments, accidental breeding, and education of the individual members of them. As we were prepared to expect, a majority at both houses adhere to the religion of the Church Established,—only that at one of them a strong leaven of Roman Catholicism is suspected; which, considering the notorious education of the manager at a foreign seminary, is not so much to be wondered at. Some have gone so far as to report that Mr. T——y, in particular, belongs to an order lately restored on the Continent. We can contradict this: that gentleman is a member of the Kirk of Scotland; and his name is to be found, much to his honour, in the list of seceders from the congregation of Mr. Fletcher. While the generality, as we have said, are content to jog on in the safe trammels of national orthodoxy, symptoms of a sectarian spirit have broken out in quarters where we should least have looked for it. Some of the ladies at both houses are deep in controverted points. Miss F——e, we are credibly informed, is a *Sub-* and Madame V—— a *Supra*-Lapsarian. Mr. Pope is the last of the exploded sect of the Ranters. Mr. Sinclair has joined the Shakers. Mr. Grimaldi, sen., after being long a Jumper, has lately fallen into some whimsical theories respecting the fall of man; which he understands, not of an allegorical, but a *real tumble,* by which the whole body of humanity became, as it were, lame to the performance of good works. Pride he will have to be nothing but a stiff neck; irresolution, the nerves shaken; an inclination to sinister paths, crookedness of the joints; spiritual deadness, a paralysis; want of charity, a contraction in the fingers; despising of government, a broken head; the plaster, a sermon; the lint to bind it up, the text; the probers, the preachers; a pair of crutches, the old and new law; a bandage, religious obligation: a fanciful mode of illustration, derived from the accidents and habits of his past calling *spiritualised*, rather than from any accurate acquaintance with the Hebrew text, in which report speaks him but a raw scholar. Mr. Elliston, from all that we can learn, has his religion yet to choose; though some think him a Muggletonian.

THE ASS

FROM "HONE'S EVERY-DAY BOOK"

Mr. Collier, in his "Poetical Decameron" (Third Conversation) notices a tract printed in 1595, with the author's initials only, A. B., entitled "The Noblenesse of the Asse; a work rare, learned, and excellent." He has selected the following pretty passage from it: "He (the ass) refuseth no burden: he goes whither he is sent, without any contradiction. He lifts not his foote against any one; he bytes not; he is no fugitive, nor malicious affected. He doth all things in good sort, and to his liking that hath cause to employ him. If strokes be given him, he cares not for them; and, as our modern poet singeth,—

> "Thou wouldst (perhaps) he should become thy foe,
> And to that end dost beat him many times:
> He cares not for himself, much less thy blow." [1]

Certainly Nature foreseeing the cruel usage which this useful servant to man would receive at man's hand did prudently in furnishing him with a tegument impervious to ordinary stripes. The malice of a child or a weak hand can make only feeble impressions on him. His back offers no mark to a puny foeman. To a common whip or switch his hide presents an absolute insensibility. You might as well pretend to scourge a schoolboy with a tough pair of leather breeches on. His jerkin is well fortified; and therefore the costermongers, "between the years 1790 and 1800," did more politicly than piously in lifting up a part of his upper garment. I well remember that beastly and bloody custom. I have often longed to see one of those refiners in discipline himself at the cart's tail, with just such a convenient spot laid bare to the tender mercies of the whipster. But, since Nature has resumed her rights, it is to be hoped that this patient creature does not suffer to extremities; and that, to the savages who still belabour his poor carcass with their blows (considering the sort of anvil they are laid upon), he might in some sort, if he could speak, exclaim with the philosopher, "Lay on: you beat but upon the case of Anaxarchus." Contemplating this natural safeguard, this fortified exterior, it is with pain I view the sleek, foppish, combed, and curried person of this

---

[1] "Who this modern poet was," says Mr. Collier, "is a secret worth discovering." The wood-cut on the title of the pamphlet is—an ass, with a wreath of laurel round his neck.

animal as he is disnaturalised at watering-places, etc., where they affect
to make a palfrey of him. Fie on all such sophistications! It will never
do, master groom. Something of his honest, shaggy exterior will still
peep up in spite of you,—his good, rough, native, pine-apple coating.
You cannot "refine a scorpion into a fish, though you rinse it and scour
it with ever so cleanly cookery." [1]

The modern poet quoted by A. B. proceeds to celebrate a virtue for
which no one to this day had been aware that the ass was remarkable:—

> One other gift this beast hath as his owne,
> Wherewith the rest could not be furnishèd;
> On man himself the same was not bestowne:
> To wit, on him is ne'er engenderèd
> The hateful vermin that doth teare the skin,
> And to the bode [body] doth make his passage in.

And truly, when one thinks on the suit of impenetrable armour with
which Nature (like Vulcan to another Achilles) has provided him, these
subtle enemies to *our* repose would have shown some dexterity in getting into *his* quarters. As the bogs of Ireland by tradition expel toads
and reptiles, he may well defy these small deer in his fastnesses. It
seems the latter had not arrived at the exquisite policy adopted by the
human vermin "between 1790 and 1800."

But the most singular and delightful gift of the ass, according to the
writer of this pamphlet, is his *voice,* the "goodly, sweet, and continual
brayings" of which, "whereof they forme a melodious and proportionable kinde of musicke," seem to have affected him with no ordinary
pleasure. "Nor thinke I," he adds, "that any of our immoderate musi-
tians can deny but that their song is full of exceeding pleasure to be
heard; because therein is to be discerned both concord, discord, singing
in the meane, the beginning to sing in large compasse, then following
into rise and fall, the halfe note, whole note, musicke of five voices, firme
singing by four voices, three together, or one voice and a halfe. Then
their variable contrarieties amongst them, when one delivers forth a
long tenor or a short, the pausing for time, breathing in measure, breaking the minim or very least moment of time. Last of all, to heare the
musicke of five or six voices chaunged to so many of asses is amongst
them to heare a song of world without end."

There is no accounting for ears, or for that laudable enthusiasm with
which an author is tempted to invest a favourite subject with the most
incompatible perfections: I should otherwise, for my own taste, have
been inclined rather to have given a place to these extraordinary mu-
sicians at that banquet of nothing-less-than-sweet-sounds, imagined by
old Jeremy Collier (Essays, 1698, part ii. on Music), where, after describing the inspiriting effects of martial music in a battle, he hazards an
ingenious conjecture, whether a sort of *anti-music* might not be invented,
which should have quite the contrary effect of "sinking the spirits,

---

[1] Milton, *from memory.*

shaking the nerves, curdling the blood, and inspiring despair and cow-ardice and consternation." "'Tis probable," he says, "the roaring of lions, the warbling of cats and screech-owls, together with a mixture of the howling of dogs, judiciously imitated and compounded, might go a great way in this invention." The dose, we confess, is pretty potent, and skilfully enough prepared. But what shall we say to the Ass of Silenus, who, if we may trust to classic lore, by his own proper sounds, without thanks to cat or screech-owl, dismayed and put to rout a whole army of giants? Here was *anti-music* with a vengeance; a whole *Pan-Dis-Harmonicon* in a single lungs of leather.

But I keep you trifling too long on this asinine subject. I have al-ready passed the *Pons Asinorum,* and will desist, remembering the old pedantic pun of Jem Boyer, my schoolmaster:—

'Ass *in præsenti* seldom makes a WISE MAN *in futuro.*"

IN RE SQUIRRELS

FROM "HONE'S EVERY-DAY BOOK"

WHAT is gone with the cages with the climbing squirrel, and bells to them, which were formerly the indispensable appendage to the outside of a tin-man's shop, and were, in fact, the only live signs? One, we believe, still hangs out on Holborn; but they are fast vanishing with the good old modes of our ancestors. They seem to have been superseded by that still more ingenious refinement of modern humanity,—the tread-mill; in which *human* squirrels still perform a similar round of cease-less, improgressive clambering, which must be nuts to them.

We almost doubt the fact of the teeth of this creature being so purely orange-coloured as Mr. Urban's correspondent gives out. One of our old poets—and they were pretty sharp observers of Nature—describes them as brown. But perhaps the naturalist referred to meant "of the colour of a Maltese orange," which is rather more obfuscated than the fruit of Seville or St. Michael's, and may help to reconcile the difference. We cannot speak from observation; but we remember at school getting our fingers into the orangery of one of these little gentry (not having a due caution of the traps set there), and the result proved sourer than lemons. The author of the "Task" somewhere speaks of their anger as being "insignificantly fierce"; but we found the demonstration of it on this occasion quite as significant as we desired, and have not since been disposed to look any of these "gift horses" in the mouth. Maiden aunts keep these "small deer," as they do parrots, to bite people's fingers, on purpose to give them good advice "not to adventure so near the cage another time." As for their "six quavers divided into three quavers and a dotted crotchet," I suppose they may go into Jeremy Bentham's next budget of fallacies, along with the "melodious and pro-portionable kinde of musicke" recorded, in your last Number, of an-other highly gifted animal.

CHARLES LAMB'S AUTOBIOGRAPHY

CHARLES LAMB, born in the Inner Temple, 10th of February, 1775; educated in Christ's Hospital; afterwards a clerk in the Accountants' Office, East-India House; pensioned off from that service, 1825, after thirty-three years' service; is now a gentleman at large; can remember few specialities in his life worth noting, except that he once caught a swallow flying (*teste suâ manu*). Below the middle stature; cast of face slightly Jewish, with no Judaic tinge in his complexional religion; stammers abominably, and is therefore more apt to discharge his occasional conversation in a quaint aphorism, or a poor quibble, than in set and edifying speeches; has consequently been libelled as a person always aiming at wit; which, as he told a dull fellow that charged him with it, is at least as good as aiming at dulness. A small eater, but not drinker; confesses a partiality for the production of the juniper-berry; was a fierce smoker of tobacco, but may be resembled to a volcano burnt out, emitting only now and then a casual puff. Has been guilty of obtruding upon the public a tale, in prose, called "Rosamund Gray"; a dramatic sketch, named "John Woodvil"; a "Farewell Ode to Tobacco," with sundry other poems, and light prose matter, collected in two slight crown octavos, and pompously christened his works, though in fact they were his recreations. His true works may be found on the shelves of Leadenhall Street, filling some hundred folios. He is also the true Elia, whose Essays are extant in a little volume, published a year or two since, and rather better known from that name without a meaning than from anything he has done, or can hope to do, in his own name. He was also the first to draw the public attention to the old English dramatists, in a work called "Specimens of English Dramatic Writers who lived about the Time of Shakspeare," published about fifteen years since. In short, all his merits and demerits to set forth would take to the end of Mr. Upcott's book, and then not be told truly.

He died   18   , much lamented.

Witness his hand,

CHARLES LAMB.

18th April, 1827.

CAPTAIN STARKEY

TO THE EDITOR OF THE "EVERY-DAY BOOK":—

DEAR SIR—I read your account of this unfortunate being, and his forlorn piece of self-history,[1] with that smile of half-interest which the annals of insignificance excite, till I came to where he says, "I was

---

[1] "Memoirs of the Life of Benjamin Starkey, late of London, but now an inmate of the Freemen's Hospital in Newcastle. Written by himself. With a portrait of the author, and a fac-simile of his handwriting. Printed and sold by William Hall, Great Market, Newcastle." 1818. 12mo, pp. 14.

bound apprentice to Mr. William Bird, an eminent writer, and teacher
of languages and mathematics," etc.; when I started as one does in the
recognition of an old acquaintance in a supposed stranger. This, then,
was that Starkey of whom I have heard my sister relate so many pleasant
anecdotes; and whom, never having seen, I yet seem almost to remember. For nearly fifty years she had lost all sight of him; and, behold!
the gentle usher of her youth, grown into an aged beggar, dubbed with
an opprobrious title to which he had no pretensions; an object of a
May-game! To what base purposes may we not return! What may not
have been the meek creature's sufferings, what his wanderings, before
he finally settled down in the comparative comfort of an old hospitaller
of the almonry of Newcastle? And is poor Starkey dead?

I was a scholar of that "eminent writer" that he speaks of; but
Starkey had quitted the school about a year before I came to it. Still
the odour of his merits had left a fragrancy upon the recollection of the
elder pupils. The schoolroom stands where it did, looking into a discoloured, dingy garden in the passage leading from Fetter Lane into
Bartlett's Buildings. It is still a school, though the main prop, alas!
has fallen so ingloriously; and bears a Latin inscription over the entrance
in the lane, which was unknown in our humbler times. Heaven knows
what "languages" were taught in it then! I am sure that neither my
sister nor myself brought any out of it but a little of our native English. By "mathematics," reader, must be understood "ciphering." It
was, in fact, an humble day-school, at which reading and writing were
taught to us boys in the morning; and the same slender erudition was
communicated to the girls, our sisters, etc., in the evening. Now, Starkey
presided, under Bird, over both establishments. In my time, Mr. Cook,
now or lately a respectable singer and performer at Drury Lane Theatre,
and nephew to Mr. Bird, had succeeded to him. I well remember Bird.
He was a squat, corpulent, middle-sized man, with something of the
gentleman about him, and that peculiar mild tone—especially while he
was inflicting punishment—which is so much more terrible to children
than the angriest looks and gestures. Whippings were not frequent;
but, when they took place, the correction was performed in a private
room adjoining, whence we could only hear the plaints but saw nothing.
This heightened the decorum and the solemnity. But the ordinary
chastisement was the bastinado, a stroke or two on the palm with that
almost obsolete weapon now,—the ferule. A ferule was a sort of flat
ruler, widened, at the inflicting end, into a shape resembling a pear,—
but nothing like so sweet, with a delectable hole in the middle to raise
blisters, like a cupping-glass. I have an intense recollection of that
disused instrument of torture, and the malignancy, in proportion to the
apparent mildness, with which its strokes were applied. The idea of a
rod is accompanied with something ludicrous; but by no process can I
look back upon this blister-raiser with anything but unmingled horror.
To make him look more formidable,—if a pedagogue had need of these
heightenings,—Bird wore one of those flowered Indian gowns formerly

in use with schoolmasters, the strange figures upon which we used to interpret into hieroglyphics of pain and suffering. But, boyish fears apart, Bird, I believe, was, in the main, a humane and judicious master.

Oh, how I remember our legs wedged into those uncomfortable sloping desks, where we sat elbowing each other; and the injunctions to attain a free hand, unattainable in that position; the first copy I wrote after, with its moral lesson, "Art improves Nature"; the still earlier pot-hooks and the hangers, some traces of which I fear may yet be apparent in this manuscript; the truant looks side-long to the garden, which seemed a mockery of our imprisonment; the prize for best spelling which had almost turned my head, and which, to this day, I cannot reflect upon without a vanity, which I ought to be ashamed of; our little leaden ink-stands, not separately subsisting, but sunk into the desks; the bright, punctually-washed morning fingers, darkening gradually with another and another inkspot! What a world of little associated circumstances, pains, and pleasures, mingling their quotas of pleasure, arise at the reading of those few simple words,—"Mr. William Bird, an eminent writer, and teacher of languages and mathematics in Fetter Lane, Holborn!"

Poor Starkey, when young, had that peculiar stamp of old-fashioned-ness in his face which makes it impossible for a beholder to predicate any particular age in the object. You can scarce make a guess between seventeen and seven-and-thirty. This antique cast always seems to promise ill-luck and penury. Yet it seems he was not always the abject thing he came to. My sister, who well remembers him, can hardly forgive Mr. Thomas Ranson for making an etching so unlike her idea of him when he was a youthful teacher at Mr. Bird's school. Old age and poverty—a life-long poverty, she thinks—could at no time have so effaced the marks of native gentility which were once so visible in a face otherwise strikingly ugly, thin, and careworn. From her recollection of him, she thinks that he would have wanted bread before he would have begged or borrowed a halfpenny. "If any of the girls," she says, "who were my schoolfellows, should be reading, through their aged spectacles, tidings, from the dead, of their youthful friend Starkey, they will feel a pang, as I do, at having teased his gentle spirit." They were big girls, it seems, too old to attend his instruction with the silence necessary; and, however old age and a long state of beggary seem to have reduced his writing faculties to a state of imbecility, in those days his language occasionally rose to the bold and figurative: for, when he was in despair to stop their chattering, his ordinary phrase was, "Ladies, if you will not hold your peace, not all the powers in heaven can make you." Once he was missing for a day or two: he had run away. A little, old, unhappy-looking man brought him back, —it was his father,—and he did no business in the school that day, but sat moping in a corner, with his hands before his face; and the girls, his tormentors, in pity for his case, for the rest of that day forbore to annoy him. "I had been there but a few months," adds she, "when Starkey, who was the chief instructor of us girls, communicated to us a profound secret,—that the tragedy of Cato was shortly to be acted by the elder

boys, and that we were to be invited to the representation." That
Starkey lent a helping hand in fashioning the actors, she remembers;
and, but for his unfortunate person, he might have had some distinguished part in the scene to enact. As it was, he had the arduous task
of prompter assigned to him; and his feeble voice was heard clear and
distinct, repeating the text during the whole performance. She describes
her recollection of the cast of characters, even now, with a relish. Martia
by the handsome Edgar Hickman, who afterwards went to Africa, and
of whom she never afterwards heard tidings; Lucia, by Master Walker,
whose sister was her particular friend; Cato, by John Hunter, a masterly
declaimer, but a plain boy, and shorter by the head than his two sons
in the scene, etc. In conclusion, Starkey appears to have been one of
those mild spirits, which, not originally deficient in understanding, are
crushed by penury into dejection and feebleness. He might have proved
a useful adjunct, if not an ornament, to society, if Fortune had taken
him into a very little fostering; but, wanting that, he became a captain,—
a by-word,—and lived and died a broken bulrush.

A POPULAR FALLACY,
THAT A DEFORMED PERSON IS A LORD

FROM THE "NEW MONTHLY MAGAZINE," 1826

AFTER a careful perusal of the most approved works that treat of nobility,
and of its origin in these realms in particular, we are left very much in
the dark as to the original patent in which this branch of it is recognised.
Neither Camden, in his "Etymologie and Original of Barons" nor Dug-
dale, in his "Baronage of England," nor Selden (a more exact and laborious inquirer than either), in his "Titles of Honour," affords a glimpse
of satisfaction upon the subject. There is an heraldic term, indeed,
which seems to imply gentility, and the right to coat-armour (but nothing further), in persons thus qualified. But the *sinister bend* is more
probably interpreted, by the best writers on this science, of some irregularity of birth than of bodily conformation. Nobility is either hereditary, or by creation, commonly called a patent. Of the former kind,
the title in question cannot be, seeing that the notion of it is limited to
a personal distinction which does not necessarily follow in the blood.
Honours of this kind, as Mr. Anstey very well observes, descend, moreover, in a *right line*. It must be by patent, then, if anything. But who
can show it? How comes it to be dormant? Under what king's reign
is it patented? Among the grounds of nobility cited by the learned Mr.
Ashmole, after "Services in the Field or in the Council Chamber," he
judiciously sets down "Honours conferred by the Sovereign out of mere
benevolence, or as favouring one subject rather than another for some
likeness or conformity observed (or but supposed) in him to the royal
nature"; and he instances the graces showered upon Charles Brandon,
who, "in his goodly person being thought not a little to favour the port

and bearing of the king's own majesty, was by that sovereign, King Henry the Eighth, for some or one of these respects, highly promoted and preferred." Here, if anywhere, we thought we had discovered a clew to our researches. But after a painful investigation of the rolls and records under the reign of Richard the Third, or "Richard Crouchback," as he is more usually designated in the chronicles,—from a traditionary stoop or gibbosity in that part,—we do not find that that monarch conferred any such lordships as are here pretended, upon any subject or subjects, on a simple plea of "conformity" in that respect to the "royal nature." The posture of affairs, in those tumultuous times preceding the battle of Bosworth, possibly left him at no leisure to attend to such niceties. Further than his reign, we have not extended our inquiries; the kings of England who preceded or followed him being generally described by historians to have been of straight and clean limbs, the "natural derivative," says Daniel,[1] "of high blood, if not its primitive recommendation to such ennoblement, as denoting strength and martial prowess,—the qualities set most by in that fighting age." Another motive, which inclines us to scruple the validity of this claim, is the remarkable fact that not one of the persons in whom the right is supposed to be vested does ever insist upon it himself. There is no instance of any of them "suing his patent," as the law-books call it; much less of his having actually stepped up into his proper seat, as, so qualified, we might expect that some of them would have had the spirit to do, in the House of Lords. On the contrary, it seems to be a distinction thrust upon them. "Their title of 'lord,' " says one of their own body, speaking of the common people, "I never much valued, and now I entirely despise; and yet they will force it upon me as an honour which they have a right to bestow, and which I have none to refuse." [2] Upon a dispassionate review of the subject, we are disposed to believe that there is no right to the peerage incident to mere bodily configuration; that the title in dispute is merely honorary, and depending upon the breath of the common people, which in these realms is so far from the power of conferring nobility, that the ablest constitutionalists have agreed in nothing more unanimously than in the maxim, that "the king is the sole fountain of honour."

LETTER TO AN OLD GENTLEMAN WHOSE EDUCATION HAS BEEN NEGLECTED

FROM THE "LONDON MAGAZINE," 1825

TO THE EDITOR OF THE LONDON MAGAZINE:—

DEAR SIR—I send you a bantering "Epistle to an Old Gentleman whose Education is supposed to have been neglected." Of course, it was *suggested* by some letters of your admirable Opium-Eater, the discontinuance of which has caused so much regret to myself in common with most of your readers. You will do me injustice by supposing that, in the remotest degree, it was my intention to ridicule those papers. The

---

[1] History of England, "Temporibus Edwardi Primi et Sequentibus."
[2] Hay on Deformity.

ïact is, the most serious things may give rise to an innocent burlesque; and, the more serious they are, the fittel they become for that purpose. It is not to be supposed that Charles Cotton did not entertain a very high regard for Virgil, notwithstanding he travestied that poet. Yourself can testify the deep respect I have always held for the profound learning and penetrating genius of our friend. Nothing upon earth would give me greater pleasure than to find that he has not lost sight of his entertaining and instructive purpose.—I am, dear sir, yours and *his* sincerely, ELIA.

MY DEAR SIR—The question which you have done me the honour to propose to me, through the medium of our common friend, Mr. Grierson, I shall endeavour to answer with as much exactness as a limited observation and experience can warrant.

You ask,—or rather Mr. Grierson, in his own interesting language, asks for you,—"Whether a person at the age of sixty-three, with no more proficiency than a tolerable knowledge of most of the characters of the English alphabet at first sight amounts to, by dint of persevering application and good masters,—a docile and ingenuous disposition on the part of the pupil always presupposed,—may hope to arrive, within a presumable number of years, at that degree of attainments which shall entitle the possessor to the character, which you are on so many accounts justly desirous of acquiring, of a *learned man.*"

This is fairly and candidly stated,—only I could wish that on one point you had been a little more explicit. In the meantime, I will take it for granted, that by a "knowledge of the alphabetic characters" you confine your meaning to the single powers only, as you are silent on the subject of the diphthongs and harder combinations.

Why, truly, sir, when I consider the vast circle of sciences,—it is not here worth while to trouble you with the distinction between learning and science,—which a man must be understood to have made the tour of in these days, before the world will be willing to concede to him the title which you aspire to,—I am almost disposed to reply to your inquiry by a direct answer in the negative.

However, where all cannot be compassed, a great deal that is truly valuable may be accomplished. I am unwilling to throw out any remarks that should have a tendency to damp a hopeful genius; but I must not, in fairness, conceal from you that you have much to do. The consciousness of difficulty is sometimes a spur to exertion. Rome— or rather, my dear sir, to borrow an illustration from a place as yet more familiar to you, Rumford—Rumford was not built in a day.

Your mind as yet, give me leave to tell you, is in the state of a sheet of white paper. We must not blot or blur it over too hastily. Or, to use an opposite simile, it is like a piece of parchment all bescrawled and bescribbled over with characters of no sense or import, which we must carefully erase and remove before we can make way for the authentic characters or impresses which are to be substituted in their stead by the corrective hand of science.

Your mind, my dear sir, again, resembles that same parchment, which we will suppose a little hardened by time and disuse. We may apply the characters; but are we sure that the ink will sink?

You are in the condition of a traveller that has all his journey to begin. And, again, you are worse off than the traveller which I have supposed; for you have already lost your way.

You have much to learn, which you have never been taught; and more, I fear, to unlearn, which you have been taught erroneously. You have hitherto, I daresay, imagined that the sun moves round the earth. When you shall have mastered the true solar system, you will have quite a different theory upon that point, I assure you. I mention but this instance. Your own experience, as knowledge advances, will furnish you with many parallels.

I can scarcely approve of the intention, which Mr. Grierson informs me you had contemplated, of entering yourself at a common seminary, and working your way up from the lower to the higher forms with the children. I see more to admire in the modesty than in the expediency of such a resolution. I own I cannot reconcile myself to the spectacle of a gentleman at your time of life, seated, as must be your case at first, below a tyro of four or five; for at that early age the rudiments of education usually commence in this country. I doubt whether more might not be lost in the point of fitness than would be gained in the advantages which you propose to yourself by this scheme.

You say you stand in need of emulation; that this incitement is nowhere to be had but at a public school; that you should be more sensible of your progress by comparing it with the daily progress of those around you. But have you considered the nature of emulation, and how it is sustained at those tender years which you would have to come in competition with? I am afraid you are dreaming of academic prizes and distinctions. Alas! in the university for which you are preparing, the highest medal would be a silver penny; and you must graduate in nuts and oranges.

I know that Peter, the great Czar—or Emperor—of Muscovy, submitted himself to the discipline of a dockyard at Deptford, that he might learn and convey to his countrymen the noble art of shipbuilding. You are old enough to remember him, or at least the talk about him. I call to mind also other great princes, who, to instruct themselves in the theory and practice of war, and set an example of subordination to their subjects, have condescended to enroll themselves as private soldiers; and, passing through the successive ranks of corporal, quartermaster, and the rest, have served their way up to the station at which most princes are willing enough to set out,—of general and commander-in-chief over their own forces. But—besides that there is oftentimes great sham and pretence in their show of mock humility—the competition which they stooped to was with their coevals, however inferior to them in birth. Between ages so very disparate as those which you contemplate, no salutary emulation can, I fear, subsist.

Again: in the other alternative, could you submit to the ordinary reproofs and discipline of a day-school? Could you bear to be corrected for your faults? Or how would it look to see you put to stand, as must be the case sometimes, in a corner?

I am afraid the idea of a public school in your circumstances must be given up.

But is it impossible, my dear sir, to find some person of your own age,—if of the other sex, the more agreeable, perhaps,—whose information, like your own, has rather lagged behind his years, who should be willing to set out from the same point with yourself? to undergo the same tasks?—thus at once inciting and sweetening each other's labours in a sort of friendly rivalry. Such a one, I think, it would not be difficult to find in some of the western parts of this island,—about Dartmoor, for instance.

Or what if, from your own estate,—that estate, which, unexpectedly acquired so late in life, has inspired into you this generous thirst after knowledge,—you were to select some elderly peasant, that might best be spared from the land, to come and begin his education with you, that you might till, as it were, your minds together,—one whose heavier progress might invite, without a fear of discouraging, your emulation? We might then see—starting from an equal post—the difference of the clownish and the gentle blood.

A private education, then, or such a one as I have been describing, being determined on, we must in the next place look out for a preceptor; for it will be some time before either of you, left to yourselves, will be able to assist the other to any great purpose in his studies.

And now, my dear sir, if, in describing such a tutor as I have imagined for you, I use a style a little above the familiar one in which I have hitherto chosen to address you, the nature of the subject must be my apology. *Difficile est de scientiis inscienter loqui*; which is as much as to say, that, "in treating of scientific matters, it is difficult to avoid the use of scientific terms." But I shall endeavour to be as plain as possible. I am not going to present you with the *ideal* of a pedagogue as it may exist in my fancy, or has possibly been realised in the persons of Buchanan and Busby. Something less than perfection will serve our turn. The scheme which I propose in this first or introductory letter has reference to the first four or five years of your education only; and, in enumerating the qualifications of him that should undertake the direction of your studies, I shall rather point out the *minimum*, or *least*, that I shall require of him, than trouble you in the search of attainments neither common nor necessary to our immediate purpose.

He should be a man of deep and extensive knowledge. So much at least is indispensable. Something older than yourself, I could wish him, because years add reverence.

To his age and great learning, he should be blessed with a temper and a patience willing to accommodate itself to the imperfections of the slowest and meanest capacities. Such a one, in former days, Mr. Hartlib appears to have been; and such, in our days, I take Mr. Grierson to be: but our friend, you know, unhappily has other engagements. I do not demand a consummate grammarian; but he must be a thorough master of vernacular orthography, with an insight into the accentualities and punctualities of modern Saxon or English. He must be competently instructed (or how shall he instruct you?) in the tetralogy, or four first rules, upon which not only arithmetic, but geometry, and the pure mathematics themselves, are grounded. I do not require that he should have measured the globe with Cook or Ortelius; but it is desirable that he should have a general knowledge (I do not mean a very nice or pedantic one) of the great division of the earth into four parts, so as to teach you readily to name the quarters. He must have a genius capable in some degree of soaring to the upper element, to deduce from thence the not much dissimilar computation of the cardinal points, or hinges, upon which those invisible phenomena, which naturalists agree to term *winds,* do perpetually shift and turn. He must instruct you, in imitation of the old Orphic fragments (the mention of which has possibly escaped you), in numeric and harmonious responses, to deliver the number of solar revolutions within which each of the twelve periods of the *Annus Vulgaris,* or common year, is divided, and which doth usually complete and terminate itself. The intercalaries, and other subtle problems, he will do well to omit, till riper years, and course of study, shall have rendered you more capable thereof. He must be capable of embracing all history, so as, from the countless myriads of individual men who have peopled this globe of earth,—*for it is a globe,*—by comparison of their respective births, lives, deaths, fortunes, conduct, prowess, etc., to pronounce, and teach you to pronounce, dogmatically and catechetically, who was the richest, who was the strongest, who was the wisest, who was the meekest, man that ever lived; to the facilitation of which solution, you will readily conceive, a smattering of biography would in no inconsiderable degree conduce. Leaving the dialects of men (in one of which I shall take leave to suppose you by this time at least superficially instituted), you will learn to ascend with him to the contemplation of that unarticulated language which was before the written tongue; and, with the aid of the elder Phrygian or Æsopic key, to interpret the sounds by which the animal tribes communicate their minds, evolving moral instruction with delight from the dialogue of cocks, dogs, and foxes. Or, marrying theology with verse, from whose mixture a beautiful and healthy offspring may be expected, in your own native accents (but purified), you will keep time together to the profound harpings of the more modern or Wattsian hymnics.

Thus far I have ventured to conduct you to a "hillside, whence you may discern the right path of a virtuous and noble education; laborious indeed at the first ascent, but else so smooth, so green, so full of goodly prospects and melodious sounds on every side, that the harp of Orpheus was not more charming." [1]

With my best respects to Mr. Grierson, when you see him, I remain, dear sir, your obedient servant,   ELIA.

[1] Milton's Tractate on Education, addressed to Mr. Hartlib.

ON THE AMBIGUITIES ARISING FROM
PROPER NAMES

How oddly it happens that the same sound shall suggest to the minds of two persons hearing it ideas the most opposite! I was conversing, a few years since, with a young friend upon the subject of poetry, and particularly that species of it which is known by the name of the Epithalamium. I ventured to assert that the most perfect specimen of it in our language was the "Epithalamium" of Spenser upon his own marriage.

My young gentleman, who has a smattering of taste, and would not willingly be thought ignorant of anything remotely connected with the *belles-lettres,* expressed a degree of surprise, mixed with mortification, that he should never have heard of this poem; Spenser being an author with whose writings he thought himself peculiarly conversant.

I offered to show him the poem in the fine folio copy of the poet's works which I have at home. He seemed pleased with the offer, though the mention of the folio seemed again to puzzle him. But, presently after, assuming a grave look, he compassionately muttered to himself, "Poor Spencer!"

There was something in the tone with which he spoke these words that struck me not a little. It was more like the accent with which a man bemoans some recent calamity that has happened to a friend, than that tone of sober grief with which we lament the sorrows of a person, however excellent and however grievous his afflictions may have been, who has been dead more than two centuries. I had the curiosity to inquire into the reasons of so uncommon an ejaculation. My young gentleman, with a more solemn tone of pathos than before, repeated, "Poor Spencer!" and added, "He has lost his wife!"

My astonishment at this assertion rose to such a height, that I began to think the brain of my young friend must be cracked, or some unaccountable reverie had gotten possession of it. But upon further explanation, it appeared that the word "Spenser," which to you or me, reader, in a conversation upon poetry too, would naturally have called up the idea of an old poet in a ruff, one Edmund Spenser, that flourished in the days of Queen Elizabeth, and wrote a poem called "The Faëry Queen," with "The Shepherd's Calendar," and many more verses besides, did, in the mind of my young friend, excite a very different and quite modern idea; namely, that of the Honourable William Spencer, one of the living ornaments, if I am not misinformed, of this present poetical era, A.D. 1811.

ELIA ON "THE CONFESSIONS OF A DRUNKARD"

FROM THE "LONDON MAGAZINE," 1822

MANY are the sayings of Elia, painful and frequent his lucubrations, set forth for the most part (such his modesty!) without a name; scattered about in obscure periodicals and forgotten miscellanies. From the dust of some of these it is our intention occasionally to revive a tract or two that shall seem worthy of a better fate, especially at a time like the present, when the pen of our industrious contributor, engaged in a laborious digest of his recent Continental tour, may haply want the leisure to expatiate in more miscellaneous speculations. We have been induced, in the first instance, to reprint a thing which he put forth in a friend's volume some years since, entitled The Confessions of a Drunkard, seeing that Messieurs the Quarterly Reviewers have chosen to embellish their last dry pages with fruitful quotations therefrom; adding, from their peculiar brains, the gratuitous affirmation, that they have reason to believe that the describer (in his delineation of a drunkard, forsooth!) partly sat for his own picture. The truth is, that our friend had been reading among the essays of a contemporary, who has perversely been confounded with him, a paper in which Edax (or the Great Eater) humorously complaineth of an inordinate appetite; and it struck him that a better paper—of deeper interest and wider usefulness—might be made out of the imagined experiences of a Great Drinker. Accordingly he set to work, and, with that mock fervour and counterfeit earnestness with which he is too apt to over-realise his descriptions, has given us—a frightful picture indeed, but no more resembling the man Elia than the fictitious Edax may be supposed to identify itself with Mr. L. its author. It is, indeed, a compound extracted out of his long observations of the effects of drinking upon all the world about him; and this accumulated mass of misery he hath centred (as the custom is with judicious essayists) in a single figure. We deny not that a portion of his own experiences may have passed into the picture; (as who, that is not a washy fellow, but must at some times have felt the after-operation of a too-generous cup?) but then how heightened! how exaggerated! how little within the sense of the Review, where a part, in its slanderous usage, must be understood to stand for the whole! But it is useless to expostulate with this Quarterly slime, brood of Nilus, watery heads with hearts of jelly spawned under the sign of Aquarius, incapable of Bacchus, and therefore cold, washy, spiteful, bloodless. Elia shall string them up one day, and show their colours,—or, rather, how colourless and vapid the whole fry,—when he putteth forth his long-promised, but unaccountably hitherto delayed, Confessions of a Water-Drinker.

THE LAST PEACH

FROM THE "LONDON MAGAZINE," 1825

I AM the miserablest man living. Give me counsel, dear Editor. I was bred up in the strictest principles of honesty, and have passed my life in punctual adherence to them. Integrity might be said to be ingrained in our family. Yet I live in constant fear of one day coming to the gallows.

Till the latter end of last Autumn I never experienced these feelings of self-mistrust, which ever since have imbittered my existence. From the apprehension of that unfortunate man [1] whose story began to make so great an impression upon the public about that time, I date my horrors. I never can get it out of my head that I shall some time or other commit a forgery, or do some equally vile thing. To make matters worse, I am in a banking-house. I sit surrounded with a cluster of banknotes. These were formerly no more to me than meat to a butcher's dog. They are now as toads and aspics. I feel all day like one situated amidst gins and pitfalls. Sovereigns, which I once took such pleasure in counting out, and scraping up with my little tin shovel (at which I was the most expert in the banking-house), now scald my hands. When I go to sign my name, I set down that of another person, or write my own in a counterfeit character. I am beset with temptations without motive. I want no more wealth than I possess. A more contented being than myself, as to money matters, exists not. What should I fear?

When a child, I was once let loose, by favour of a nobleman's gardener, into his lordship's magnificent fruit garden, with full leave to pull the currants and the gooseberries; only I was interdicted from touching the wall fruit. Indeed, at that season (it was the end of Autumn), there was little left. Only on the south wall (can I forget the hot feel of the brickwork?) lingered the one last peach. Now, peaches are a fruit which I always had, and still have, an almost utter aversion to. There is something to my palate singularly harsh and repulsive in the flavour of them. I know not by what demon of contradiction inspired; but I was haunted with an irresistible desire to pluck it. Tear myself as often as I would from the spot, I found myself still recurring to it; till, maddening with desire (desire I cannot call it), with wilfulness rather,—without appetite,—against appetite, I may call it,—in an evil hour I reached out my hand, and plucked it. Some few raindrops just then fell; the sky (from a bright day) became overcast; and I was a type of our first parents, after the eating of that fatal fruit. I felt myself naked and ashamed, stripped of my virtue, spiritless. The downy fruit, the sight of which rather than its savour had tempted me, dropped from my hand, never to be tasted. All the commentators in the world cannot persuade me but that the Hebrew word, in the second chapter of Genesis, translated "apple," should be rendered "peach." Only this way can I reconcile that mysterious story.

Just such a child at thirty am I among the cash and valuables, longing to pluck, without an idea of enjoyment further. I cannot reason myself out of these fears: I dare not laugh at them. I was tenderly and lovingly brought up. What then? Who that in life's entrance had seen the babe F——, from the lap stretching out his little fond mouth to catch the maternal kiss, could have predicted, or as much as imagined, that

[1] Fauntleroy.

life's very different exit? The sight of my own fingers torments me;
they seem so admirably constructed for—pilfering. Then that jugular
vein, which I have in common ——; in an emphatic sense may I say
with David, I am "fearfully made." All my mirth is poisoned by these
unhappy suggestions. If, to dissipate reflection, I hum a tune, it changes
to the "Lamentations of a Sinner." My very dreams are tainted. I
awake with a shocking feeling of my hand in some pocket.

Advise me, dear Editor, on this painful heart-malady. Tell me, do
you feel anything allied to it in yourself? Do you never feel an itching,
as it were,— a *dactylomania*,—or am I alone? You have my honest confession. My next may appear from Bow Street.   SUSPENSURUS.

REFLECTIONS IN THE PILLORY

FROM THE "LONDON MAGAZINE," 1825

About the year 18—, one R——d, a respectable London merchant (since dead),
stood in the pillory for some alleged fraud upon the revenue. Among his papers were
found the following "Reflections," which we have obtained by favour of our friend
Elia, who knew him well, and had heard him describe the train of his feelings, upon
that trying occasion, almost in the words of the manuscript. Elia speaks of him as
a man (with the exception of the peccadillo aforesaid) of singular integrity in all his
private dealings, possessing great suavity of manner, with a certain turn for humour.
As our object is to present human nature under every possible circumstance, we do
not think that we shall sully our pages by inserting it.—EDITOR of the London Magazine.

SCENE,—*Opposite the Royal Exchange.*
TIME,—*Twelve to One, Noon.*

KETCH, my good fellow, you have a neat hand. Prithee, adjust this new
collar to my neck gingerly. I am not used to these wooden cravats.
There, softly, softly. That seems the exact point between ornament
and strangulation. A thought looser on this side. Now it will do. And
have a care in turning me, that I present my aspect due vertically. I
now face the Orient. In a quarter of an hour I shift Southward,—do
you mind?—and so on till I face the East again, travelling with the sun.
No half-points, I beseech you,—N.N. by W., or any such elaborate
niceties. They become the shipman's card, but not this mystery. Now
leave me a little to my own reflections.

Bless us, what a company is assembled in honour of me! How grand
I stand here! I never felt so sensibly before the effect of solitude in a
crowd. I muse in solemn silence upon that vast miscellaneous rabble
in the pit there. From my private box I contemplate, with mingled pity
and wonder, the gaping curiosity of those underlings. There are my
Whitechapel supporters. Rosemary Lane has emptied herself of the
very flower of her citizens to grace my show. Duke's place sits desolate.
What is there in my face, that strangers should come so far from the
East to gaze upon it? [*Here an egg narrowly misses him.*] That offering
was well meant, but not so cleanly executed. By the tricklings, it should

not be either myrrh or frankincense. Spare your presents, my friends: I
am noways mercenary. I desire no missive tokens of your approbation.
I am past those valentines. Bestow these coffins of untimely chickens
upon mouths that water for them. Comfort your addle spouses with them
at home, and stop the mouths of your brawling brats with such Olla
Podridas: they have need of them. [*A brick is let fly.*] Discase not, I
pray you, nor dismantle your rent and ragged tenements, to furnish me
with architectural decorations, which I can excuse. This fragment might
have stopped a flaw against snow comes. [*A coal flies.*] Cinders are dear,
gentlemen. This nubbling might have helped the pot boil, when your
dirty cuttings from the shambles at three-ha'pence a pound shall stand
at a cold simmer. Now, South about, Ketch! I would enjoy Australian
popularity.

What, my friends from over the water! Old benchers—flies of a
day—ephemeral Romans—welcome! Doth the sight of me draw souls
from limbo? can it dispeople purgatory?—Ha!

What am I, or what was my father's house, that I should thus be set
up a spectacle to gentlemen and others? Why are all faces, like Persians
at the sunrise, bent singly on mine alone? It was wont to be esteemed
an ordinary visnomy, a quotidian merely. Doubtless these assembled
myriads discern some traits of nobleness, gentility, breeding, which hitherto have escaped the common observation,—some intimations, as it
were, of wisdom, valour, piety, and so forth. My sight dazzles; and, if
I am not deceived by the too-familiar pressure of this strange neckcloth
that envelops it, my countenance gives out lambent glories. For some
painter now to take me in the lucky point of expression!—the posture
so convenient!—the head never shifting, but standing quiescent in a
sort of natural frame! But these artisans require a Westerly aspect.
Ketch, turn me.

Something of St. James's air in these my new friends. How my prospects shift and brighten! Now, if Sir Thomas Lawrence be anywhere
in that group, his fortune is made for ever. I think I see some one taking
out a crayon. I will compose my whole face to a smile, which yet shall
not so predominate but that gravity and gayety shall contend, as it were,
—you understand me? I will work up my thoughts to some mild rapture,—a gentle enthusiasm,—which the artist may transfer, in a manner, warm to the canvas. I will inwardly apostrophise my tabernacle.

Delectable mansion, hail! House not made of every wood! Lodging
that pays no rent; airy and commodious; which, owing no window tax,
art yet all casement, out of which men have such pleasure in peering and
overlooking, that they will sometimes stand an hour together to enjoy
thy prospects! Cell, recluse from the vulgar! Quiet retirement from
the great Babel, yet affording sufficient glimpses into it! Pulpit, that
instructs without note or sermon book; into which the preacher is
inducted without tenth or first fruit! Throne, unshared and single, that
disdainest a Brentford competitor! Honour without co-rival! Or hear-
est thou, rather, magnificent theatre, in which the spectator comes to

see and to be seen? From thy giddy heights I look down upon the common herd, who stand with eyes upturned, as if a winged messenger hovered over them; and mouths open, as if they expected manna. I feel, I feel the true episcopal yearnings. Behold in me, my flock, your true overseer! What though I cannot lay hands, because my own are laid; yet I can mutter benedictions. True *otium cum dignitate!* Proud Pisgah eminence! pinnacle sublime! O Pillory! 'tis thee I sing! Thou younger brother to the gallows, without his rough and Esau palms, that with ineffable contempt surveyest beneath thee the grovelling stocks, which claim presumptuously to be of thy great race! Let that low wood know that thou art far higher born. Let that domicile for groundling rogues and base earth-kissing varlets envy thy preferment, not seldom fated to be the wanton baiting-house, the temporary retreat, of poet and of patriot. Shades of Bastwick and of Prynne hover over thee. Defoe is there, and more greatly daring Shebbeare. From their (little more elevated) stations they look down with recognitions. Ketch, turn me!

I now veer to the North. Open thy widest gates, thou proud Exchange of London, that I may look in as proudly! Gresham's wonder, hail! I stand upon a level with all your kings. They and I, from equal heights, with equal superciliousness, o'erlook the plodding, money-hunting tribe below, who, busied in their sordid speculations, scarce elevate their eyes to notice your ancient, or my recent grandeur. The second Charles smiles on me from three pedestals![1] He closed the Exchequer: I cheated the Excise. Equal our darings; equal be our lot!

Are those the quarters? 'tis their fatal chime. That the ever-winged hours would but stand still! but I must descend,—descend from this dream of greatness. Stay, stay, a little while, importunate hour-hand! A moment or two, and I shall walk on foot with the undistinguished many. The clock speaks one. I return to common life. Ketch, let me out.

A CHARACTER OF THE LATE ELIA

BY A FRIEND

FROM THE "LONDON MAGAZINE," 1823

THIS gentleman, who for some months past had been in a declining way, hath at length paid his final tribute to Nature. He just lived long enough (it was what he wished) to see his papers collected into a volume. The pages of the London Magazine will henceforth know him no more.

Exactly at twelve, last night, his queer spirit departed; and the bells

---

[1] A statue of Charles II., by the elder Cibber, adorns the front of the Exchange. He stands also on high, in the train of his crowned ancestors, in his proper order, *within* that building; and the merchants of London, as a further proof of their loyalty, have, within a few years, caused to be erected another effigy of him on the ground in the centre of the interior.

of Saint Bride's rang him out with the old year. The mournful vibrations were caught in the dining-room of his friends T. and H.[1]; and the company, assembled there to welcome in another 1st of January, checked their carousals in mid-earth, and were silent. Janus wept. The gentle P——r,[2] in a whisper, signified his intention of devoting an elegy; and Allan C.,[3] nobly forgetful of his countrymen's wrongs, vowed a memoir to his *manes*, full and friendly, as a *Tale of Lyddalcross*.

To say truth, it is time he were gone. The humour of the thing, if there was ever much in it, was pretty well exhausted; and a two years and a half's existence has been a tolerable duration for a phantom.

I am now at liberty to confess, that much which I have heard objected to my late friend's writings was well founded. Crude they are, I grant you,—a sort of unlicked, incondite things,—villainously pranked in an affected array of antique modes and phrases. They had not been *his* if they had been other than such; and better it is that a writer should be natural in a self-pleasing quaintness, than to affect a naturalness (so called) that should be strange to him. Egotistical they have been pronounced by some who did not know that what he tells us as of himself was often true only (historically) of another; as in his Third Essay (to save many instances), where, under the *first person* (his favourite figure), he shadows forth the forlorn estate of a country boy placed at a London school, far from his friends and connections,—in direct opposition to his own early history. If it be egotism to imply and twine with his own identity the griefs and affections of another,—making himself many, or reducing many unto himself,—then is the skilful novelist, who all along brings in his hero or heroine, speaking of themselves, the greatest egotist of all; who yet has never, therefore, been accused of that narrowness. And how shall the intenser dramatist escape being faulty, who doubtless, under cover of passion uttered by another, oftentimes gives blameless vent to his most inward feelings, and expresses his own story modestly?

My late friend was in many respects a singular character. Those who did not like him hated him; and some, who once liked him, afterwards became his bitterest haters. The truth is, he gave himself too little concern about what he uttered, and in whose presence. He observed neither time nor place, and would ever out with what came uppermost. With the severe religionist he would pass for a free-thinker; while the other faction set him down for a bigot, or persuaded themselves that he belied his sentiments. Few understood him; and I am not certain that at all times he quite understood himself. He too much affected that dangerous figure,—irony. He sowed doubtful speeches, and reaped plain, unequivocal hatred. He would interrupt the gravest discussion with some light jest; and yet, perhaps, not quite irrelevant in ears that could understand it. Your long and much talkers hated him. The informal

---

[1] Taylor and Hessey, the publishers of the London Magazine.
[2] Procter, better known as Barry Cornwall.
[3] Cunningham.

habit of his mind, joined to an inveterate impediment of speech, forbade
him to be an orator; and he seemed determined that no one else should
play that part when he was present. He was *petit* and ordinary in his
person and appearance. I have seen him sometimes in what is called
good company, but, where he has been a stranger, sit silent, and be suspected for an odd fellow, till (some unlucky occasion provoking it) he
would stutter out some senseless pun (not altogether senseless perhaps,
if rightly taken), which has stamped his character for the evening. It
was hit or miss with him; but, nine times out of ten, he contrived by this
device to send away a whole company his enemies. His conceptions rose
kindlier than his utterance, and his happiest *impromptus* had the appearance of effort. He has been accused of trying to be witty, when in truth
he was but struggling to give his poor thoughts articulation. He chose
his companions for some individuality of character which they manifested. Hence not many persons of science, and few professed *literati*,
were of his councils. They were, for the most part, persons of an uncertain fortune; and as to such people, commonly, nothing is more obnoxious than a gentleman of settled (though moderate) income, he passed
with most of them for a great miser. To my knowledge, this was a mistake. His *intimados*, to confess a truth, were, in the world's eye, a ragged regiment. He found them floating on the surface of society; and
the colour, or something else, in the weed, pleased him. The burs stuck
to him; but they were good and loving burs for all that. He never
greatly cared for the society of what are called good people. If any of
these were scandalised (and offences were sure to arise), he could not
help it. When he has been remonstrated with for not making more concessions to the feelings of good people, he would retort by asking, What
one point did these good people ever concede to him? He was temperate
in his meals and diversions, but always kept a little on this side of
abstemiousness. Only in the use of the Indian weed he might be thought
a little excessive. He took it, he would say, as a solvent of speech.
Marry—as the friendly vapour ascended, how his prattle would curl
up sometimes with it! the ligaments, which tongue-tied him, were loosened, and the stammerer proceeded a statist!

I do not know whether I ought to bemoan or rejoice that my old
friend is departed. His jests were beginning to grow obsolete, and his
stories to be found out. He felt the approaches of age; and, while he
pretended to cling to life, you saw how slender were the ties left to bind
him. Discoursing with him latterly on this subject, he expressed himself with a pettishness which I though unworthy of him. In our walks
about his suburban retreat (as he called it) at Shacklewell, some children
belonging to a School of Industry met us, and bowed and courtesied, as
he thought, in an especial manner to *him*. "They take me for a visiting
governor," he muttered earnestly. He had a horror, which he carried to
a foible, of looking like anything important and parochial. He thought
that he approached nearer to that stamp daily. He had a general aversion from being treated like a grave or respectable character, and kept a

wary eye upon the advances of age that should so entitle him. He herded always, while it was possible, with people younger than himself. He did not conform to the march of time, but was dragged along in the procession. His manners lagged behind his years. He was too much of the boy-man. The *toga virilis* never sat gracefully on his shoulders. The impressions of infancy had burnt into him, and he resented the impertinence of manhood. These were weaknesses; but such as they were, they are a key to explicate some of his writings.

He left little property behind him. Of course, the little that is left (chiefly in India bonds) devolves upon his cousin Bridget. A few critical dissertations were found in his *escritoire*, which have been handed over to the editor of this magazine, in which it is to be hoped they will shortly appear, retaining his accustomed signature.

He has himself not obscurely hinted that his employment lay in a public office. The gentlemen in the export department of the East-India House will forgive me if I acknowledge the readiness with which they assisted me in the retrieval of his few manuscripts. They pointed out in a most obliging manner the desk at which he had been planted for forty years; showed me ponderous tomes of figures, in his own remarkably neat hand, which, more properly than his few printed tracts, might be called his "Works." They seemed affectionate to his memory, and universally commended his expertness in book-keeping. It seems he was the inventor of some ledger which should combine the precision and certainty of the Italian double entry (I think they called it) with the brevity and facility of some newer German system; but I am not able to appreciate the worth of the discovery. I have often heard him express a warm regard for his associates in office, and how fortunate he considered himself in having his lot thrown in amongst them. There is more sense, more discourse, more shrewdness, and even talent, among these clerks (he would say), than in twice the number of authors by profession that I have conversed with. He would brighten up sometimes upon the "old days of the India House," when he consorted with Woodroffe and Wissett, and Peter Corbet (a descendant and worthy representative, bating the point of sanctity, of old facetious Bishop Corbet); and Hoole, who translated Tasso; and Bartlemy Brown, whose father (God assoil him therefore!) modernised Walton; and sly, warmhearted old Jack Cole (King Cole they called him in those days), and Campe and Fombelle, and a world of choice spirits, more than I can remember to name, who associated in those days with Jack Burrell (the *bon vivant* of the South-Sea House); and little Eyton (said to be a *facsimile* of Pope,—he was a miniature of a gentleman), that was cashier under him; and Dan Voight of the Custom House, that left the famous library.

Well, Elia is gone,—for aught I know, to be reunited with them,— and these poor traces of his pen are all we have to show for it. How little survives of the wordiest authors! Of all they said or did in their lifetime, a few glittering words only! His Essays found some favourers, as they appeared separately. They shuffled their way in the crowd well enough singly: how they will *read*, now they are brought together, is a question for the publishers, who have thus ventured to draw out into one piece his "weaved-up follies." PHIL-ELIA.

LETTERS

UNDER ASSUMED SIGNATURES, PUBLISHED IN
"THE REFLECTOR"

THE LONDONER

TO THE EDITOR OF "THE REFLECTOR"

MR. REFLECTOR,—I was born under the shadow of St. Dunstan's steeple, just where the conflux of the eastern and western inhabitants of this twofold city meet and justle in friendly opposition at Temple Bar. The same day which gave me to the world, saw London happy in the celebration of her great annual feast. This I cannot help looking upon as a lively omen of the future great goodwill which I was destined to bear toward the city, resembling in kind that solicitude which every Chief Magistrate is supposed to feel for whatever concerns her interests and well-being. Indeed I consider myself in some sort a speculative Lord Mayor of London: for though circumstances unhappily preclude me from the hope of ever arriving at the dignity of a gold chain and Spital Sermon, yet thus much will I say of myself in truth, that Whittington with his Cat (just emblem of vigilance and a furred gown) never went beyond me in affection which I bear to the citizens.

I was born, as you have heard, in a crowd. This has begot in me an entire affection for that way of life, amounting to an almost insurmountable aversion from solitude and rural scenes. This aversion was never interrupted or suspended, except for a few years in the younger part of my life, during a period in which I had set my affections upon a charming young woman. Every man, while the passion is upon him, is for a time at least addicted to groves and meadows and purling streams. During this short period of my existence, I contracted just familiarity enough with rural objects to understand tolerably well ever after the *poets,* when they declaim in such passionate terms in favour of a country life.

For my own part, now the fit is past, I have no hesitation in declaring, that a mob of happy faces crowding up at the pit door of Drury Lane Theatre, just at the hour of six, gives me ten thousand sincerer pleasures, than I could ever receive from all the flocks of silly sheep that ever whitened the plains of Arcadia or Epsom Downs.

This passion for crowds is nowhere feasted so full as in London. The man must have a rare *recipe* for melancholy who can be dull in Fleet Street. I am naturally inclined to hypochondria, but in London it vanishes, like all other ills. Often, when I have felt a weariness or distaste at home, have I rushed out into her crowded Strand, and fed my humour, till tears have wetted my cheek for unutterable sympathies with the multitudinous moving picture, which she never fails to present at all hours, like the scenes of a shifting pantomime.

The very deformities of London, which give distaste to others, from habit do not displease me. The endless succession of shops where *Fancy miscalled Folly* is supplied with perpetual gauds and toys, excite in me no puritanical aversion. I gladly behold every appetite supplied with its proper food. The obliging customer, and the obliged tradesman— things which live by bowing, and things which exist but for homage— do not affect me with disgust; from habit I perceive nothing but urbanity, where other men, more refined, discover meanness: I love the very smoke of London, because it has been the medium most familiar to my vision. I see grand principles of honour at work in the dirty ring which encompasses two combatants with fists, and principles of no less eternal justice in the detection of a pickpocket. The salutary astonishment with which an execution is surveyed, convinces me more forcibly than a hundred volumes of abstract polity, that the universal instinct of man in all ages has leaned to order and good government.

Thus an art of extracting morality from the commonest incidents of a town life is attained by the same well-natured alchymy with which the Foresters of Arden, in a beautiful country,

> Found tongues in trees, books in the running brooks,
> Sermons in stones, and good in everything.

Where has spleen her food but in London! Humor, Interest, Curiosity, suck at her measureless breasts without a possibility of being satiated. Nursed amid her noise, her crowds, her beloved smoke, what have I been doing all my life, if I have not lent out my heart with usury to such scenes!—I am, Sir, your faithful servant,   A LONDONER.

ON BURIAL SOCIETIES; AND THE CHARACTER OF AN UNDERTAKER

TO THE EDITOR OF "THE REFLECTOR"

MR. REFLECTOR,—I was amused the other day with having the following notice thrust into my hand by a man who gives out bills at the corner of Fleet Market. Whether he saw any prognostics about me, that made him judge such notice seasonable, I cannot say; I might perhaps carry in a countenance (naturally not very florid) traces of a fever which had not long left me. Those fellows have a good instinctive way of guessing at the sort of people that are likeliest to pay attention to their papers.

"BURIAL SOCIETY"

"A favourable opportunity now offers to any person, of either sex, who would wish to be buried in a genteel manner, by paying one shilling entrance, and twopence per week for the benefit of the stock. Members to be free in six months. The money to be paid at Mr. Middleton's, at the sign of the *First* and the *Last*, Stonecutter's Street, Fleet Market. The deceased to be furnished as follows:—A strong elm coffin, covered with superfine black, and furnished with two rows, all round, close drove, best japanned nails, and adorned with ornamental drops, a handsome plate of inscription, Angel above, and Flower beneath, and four pair of handsome handles, with wrought gripes; the coffin to be well pitched, lined, and ruffled with fine crape; a handsome crape shroud, cap, and pillow. For use, a handsome velvet pall, three gentlemen's cloaks, three crape hat-bands, three hoods and scarfs, and six pair of gloves; two porters equipped to attend the funeral, a man to attend the same with band and gloves; also, the burial fees paid, if not exceeding one guinea."

"Man," says Sir Thomas Browne, "is a noble animal, splendid in ashes, and pompous in the grave." Whoever drew up this little advertisement certainly understood this appetite in the species, and has made abundant provision for it. It really almost induces a *tædium vitæ* upon one to read it. Methinks I could be willing to die, in death to be so attended. The two rows all round close-drove best black japanned nails, —how feelingly do they invite, and almost irresistibly persuade us to come and be fastened down! what aching head can resist the temptation to repose, which the crape shroud, the cap, and the pillow present; what sting is there in death, which the handles with wrought gripes are not calculated to pluck away? what victory in the grave, which the drops and the velvet pall do not render at least extremely disputable? but above all, the pretty emblematic plate with the Angel above and the Flower beneath, takes me mightily.

The notice goes on to inform us, that though the society has been established but a very few years, upwards of eleven hundred persons have put down their names. It is really an affecting consideration to think of so many poor people, of the industrious and hard-working class (for none but such would be possessed of such a generous forethought) clubbing their twopences to save the reproach of a parish funeral. Many a poor fellow, I dare swear, has that Angel and Flower kept from the *Angel* and *Punchbowl*, while, to provide himself a bier, he has curtailed himself of *beer*. Many a savoury morsel has the living body been deprived of, that the lifeless one might be served up in a richer state to the worms. And sure, if the body could understand the actions of the soul, and entertain generous notions of things, it would thank its provident partner, that she had been more solicitous to defend it from dishonours at its dissolution, than careful to pamper it with good things in the time of its union. If Cæsar were chiefly anxious at his death how he might die most decently, every Burial Society may be considered as a club of Cæsars.

Nothing tends to keep up, in the imaginations of the poorer sort of people, a generous horror of the workhouse more than the manner in which pauper funerals are conducted in this metropolis. The coffin nothing but a few naked planks coarsely put together,—the want of a pall (that decent and well-imagined veil, which, hiding the coffin that hides the body, keeps that which would shock us at two removes from us), the coloured coats of the men that are hired, at cheap rates, to carry the body,—altogether, give the notion of the deceased having been some person of an ill life and conversation, some one who may not claim the entire rites of Christian burial,—one by whom some parts of the sacred ceremony would be desecrated if they should be bestowed upon him. I meet these meagre processions sometimes in the street. They are sure to make me out of humour and melancholy all the day after. They have a harsh and ominous aspect.

If there is anything in the prospectus issued from Mr. Middleton's, Stonecutter's Street, which pleases me less than the rest, it is to find that the six pair of gloves are to be returned, that they are only lent, or, as the bill expresses it, for use, on the occasion. The hood, scarfs, and hat-bands, may properly enough be given up after the solemnity; the cloaks no gentlemen would think of keeping; but a pair of gloves, once fitted on, ought not in courtesy to be re-demanded. The wearer should certainly have the fee-simple of them. The cost would be but trifling, and they would be a proper memorial of the day. This part of the Proposal wants reconsidering. It is not conceived in the same liberal way of thinking as the rest. I am also a little doubtful whether the limit, within which the burial-fee is made payable, should not be extended to thirty shillings.

Some provision too ought undoubtedly to be made in favour of those well-intentioned persons and well-wishers to the fund, who, having all along paid their subscriptions regularly, are so unfortunate as to die before the six months, which would entitle them to their freedom, are quite completed. One can hardly imagine a more distressing case than that of a poor fellow lingering on in a consumption till the period of his freedom is almost in sight, and then finding himself going with a velocity which makes it doubtful whether he shall be entitled to his funeral honours: his quota to which he nevertheless squeezes out, to the diminution of the comforts which sickness demands. I think, in such cases, some of the contribution money ought to revert. With some such modifications, which might easily be introduced, I see nothing in these Proposals of Mr. Middleton which is not strictly fair and genteel; and heartily recommend them to all persons of moderate incomes, in either sex, who are willing that this perishable part of them should quit the scene of its mortal activities with as handsome circumstances as possible.

Before I quit the subject, I must guard my readers against a scandal, which they may be apt to take at the place whence these Proposals purport to be issued. From the sign of the *First* and the *Last*, they may conclude that Mr. Middleton is some publican, who, in assembling a club of this description at his house, may have a sinister end of his own, altogether foreign to the solemn purpose for which the club is pretended to be instituted. I must set them right by informing them that the issuer of these Proposals is no publican, though he hangs out a sign, but an honest superintendent of funerals, who, by the device of a Cradle and a Coffin, connecting both ends of human existence together, has most ingeniously contrived to insinuate, that the framers of these *first* and *last* receptacles of mankind divide this our life betwixt them, and that all that passes from the midwife to the undertaker may, in strict propriety, *go for nothing:* an awful and instructive lesson to human vanity.

Looking over some papers lately that fell into my hands by chance, and appear to have been written about the beginning of the last century, I stumbled, among the rest, upon the following short Essay, which the writer calls "The Character of an Undertaker." It is written with some stiffness and peculiarities of style, but some parts of it, I think, not unaptly characterise the profession to which Mr. Middleton has the honour to belong. The writer doubtless had in his mind the entertaining character of Sable, in Steele's excellent comedy of The Funeral.

CHARACTER OF AN UNDERTAKER

"He is master of the ceremonies at burials and mourning assemblies, grand marshal at funeral processions, the only true yeoman of the body, over which he exercises a dictatorial authority from the moment that the breath has taken leave to that of its final commitment to the earth. His ministry begins where the physician's, the lawyer's, and the divine's, end. Or if some part of the functions of the latter run parallel with his, it is only *in ordine ad spiritualia*. His temporalities remain unquestioned. He is arbitrator of all questions of honour which may concern the defunct; and upon slight inspection will pronounce how long he may remain in this upper world with credit to himself, and when it will be prudent for his reputation that he should retire. His determination in these points is peremptory and without appeal. Yet, with a modesty peculiar to his profession, he meddles not out of his own sphere. With the good or bad actions of the deceased in his lifetime he has nothing to do. He leaves the friends of the dead man to form their own conjectures as to the place to which the departed spirit is gone. His care is only about the exuviæ. He concerns not himself even about the body as it is a structure of parts internal, and a wonderful microcosm. He leaves such curious speculations to the anatomy professor. Or, if anything, he is averse to such wanton inquiries, as delighting rather that the parts which he has care of should be returned to their kindred dust in as handsome and unmutilated condition as possible; that the grave should have its full and unimpaired tribute,—a complete and just carcass. Nor is he only careful to provide for the body's entireness, but for its accommodation and ornament. He orders the fashion of its clothes, and designs the symmetry of its dwelling. Its vanity has an innocent survival in him. He is bed-maker to the dead. The pillows which he lays never rumple. The day of interment is the theatre in which he displays the mysteries of his art. It is hard to describe what he is, or rather to tell what he is not, on that day: for, being neither kinsman, servant, nor friend, he is all in turns; a transcendant, running through all those relations. His office is to supply the place of self-agency in the family, who are presumed incapable of it through grief. He is eyes, and ears, and hands, to the whole household. A draught of wine cannot go round to the mourners, but he must minister it. A chair may hardly be restored to its place by a less solemn hand than his. He takes upon himself all functions, and is a sort of ephemeral major-domo! He distributes his attentions among the company assembled according to the degree of affliction, which he calculates from the degree of kin to the deceased; and marshals them accordingly in the procession. He himself is of a sad and tristful countenance; yet such as (if well examined) is not without some show of patience and resignation at bottom; prefiguring, as it were, to the friends of the deceased, what their grief shall be when the hand of Time shall have softened and taken down the bitterness of their first anguish; so handsomely can he fore-shape and anticipate the work of Time. Lastly, with his wand, as with another divining rod, he calculates the depth of earth at which the bones of the dead man may rest, which he ordinarily contrives may be at such a distance from the surface of this earth, as may frustrate the profane attempts of such as would violate his repose, yet sufficiently on this side the centre to give his friends hopes of an easy and practicable resurrection. And here we leave him, casting in dust to dust, which is the last friendly office that he *undertakes* to do."

Begging your pardon for detaining you so long among "graves, and worms, and epitaphs," I am, Sir, your humble servant,   MORITURUS.

ON THE DANGER OF CONFOUNDING MORAL WITH PERSONAL DEFORMITY

WITH A HINT TO THOSE WHO HAVE THE FRAMING OF ADVERTISEMENTS FOR APPREHENDING OFFENDERS

TO THE EDITOR OF "THE REFLECTOR"

MR. REFLECTOR,—There is no science in their pretensions to which mankind are more apt to commit grievous mistakes, than in the supposed

very obvious one of physiognomy. I quarrel not with the principles of
this science, as they are laid down by learned professors; much less am
I disposed, with some people, to deny its existence altogether as any inlet
of knowledge that can be depended upon. I believe that there is, or may
be, an art to "read the mind's construction in the face." But, then, in
every species of *reading*, so much depends upon the eyes of the reader;
if they are blear, or apt to dazzle, or inattentive, or strained with too
much attention, the optic power will infallibly bring home false reports
of what it reads. How often do we say, upon a cursory glance at a
stranger, "What a fine open countenance he has!" who, upon second
inspection, proves to have the exact features of a knave? Nay, in much
more intimate acquaintances, how a delusion of this kind shall continue
for months, years, and then break up all at once.

Ask the married man, who has been so but for a short space of time,
if those blue eyes where, during so many years of anxious courtship,
truth, sweetness, serenity, seemed to be written in characters which
could not be misunderstood—ask him if the characters which they now
convey be exactly the same?—if for truth he does not *read* a dull virtue
(the mimic of constancy) which changes not, only because it wants the
judgment to make a preference?—if for sweetness he does not *read* a
stupid habit of looking pleased at everything?—if for serenity he does
not *read* animal tranquillity, the dead pool of the heart, which no breeze
of passion can stir into health? Alas! what is this book of the countenance good for, which when we have read so long, and thought that we
understood its contents, there comes a countless list of heart-breaking
errata at the end!

But these are the pitiable mistakes to which love alone is subject. I
have inadvertently wandered from my purpose, which was to expose
quite an opposite blunder, into which we are no less apt to fall, through
hate. How ugly a person looks upon whose reputation some awkward
aspersion hangs, and how suddenly his countenance clears up with his
character! I remember being persuaded of a man whom I had conceived an ill opinion of, that he had a very bad set of teeth; which, since
I have had better opportunities of being acquainted with his face and
facts, I find to have been the very reverse of the truth. That crooked
old woman, I once said, speaking of an ancient gentlewoman, whose
actions did not square altogether with my notions of the rule of right.
The unanimous surprise of the company before whom I uttered these
words soon convinced me that I had confounded mental with bodily
obliquity, and that there was nothing tortuous about the old lady but
her deeds.

This humour of mankind to deny personal comeliness to those with
whose moral attributes they are dissatisfied, is very strongly shown in
those advertisements which stare us in the face from the walls of every
street, and, with the tempting bait which they hang forth, stimulate at
once cupidity and an abstract love of justice in the breast of every passing peruser: I mean, the advertisements offering rewards for the appre-

hension of absconded culprits, strayed apprentices, bankrupts who have conveyed away their effects, debtors that have run away from their bail. I observe, that in exact proportion to the indignity with which the prosecutor, who is commonly the framer of the advertisement, conceives he has been treated, the personal pretensions of the fugitive are denied, and his defects exaggerated.

A fellow whose misdeeds have been directed against the public in general, and in whose delinquency no individual shall feel himself particularly interested, generally meets with fair usage. A coiner or a smuggler shall get off tolerably well. His beauty, if he has any, is not much underrated, his deformities are not much magnified. A runaway apprentice, who excites perhaps the next least degree of spleen in his prosecutor, generally escapes with a pair of bandy legs; if he has taken anything with him in his flight, a hitch in his gait is generally superadded. A bankrupt, who has been guilty of withdrawing his effects, if his case be not very atrocious, commonly meets with mild usage. But a debtor, who has left his bail in jeopardy, is sure to be described in characters of unmingled deformity. Here the personal feelings of the bail, which may be allowed to be somewhat poignant, are admitted to interfere; and, as wrath and revenge commonly strike in the dark, the colours are laid on with a grossness which I am convinced must often defeat its own purpose. The fish that casts an inky cloud about him that his enemies may not find him, cannot more obscure himself by that device than the blackening representations of these angry advertisers must inevitably serve to cloak and screen the persons of those who have injured them from detection. I have before me at this moment one of these bills, which runs thus:—

"FIFTY POUNDS REWARD"

"Run away from his bail, John Tomkins, formerly resident in Princes Street, Soho, but lately of Clerkenwell. Whoever shall apprehend, or cause to be apprehended and lodged in one of his Majesty's jails, the said John Tomkins, shall receive the above reward. He is a thickset, sturdy man, about five foot six inches high, halts in his left leg, with a stoop in his gait, with coarse red hair, nose short and cocked up, with little grey eyes (one of them bears the effect of a blow which he has lately received), with a pot belly; speaks with a thick and disagreeable voice; goes shabbily drest; had on when he went away a greasy shag great-coat with rusty yellow buttons."

Now although it is not out of the compass of possibility that John Tomkins aforesaid may comprehend in his agreeable person all the above-mentioned aggregate of charms; yet, from my observation of the manner in which these advertisements are usually drawn up, though I have not the pleasure of knowing the gentleman, yet would I lay a wager, that an advertisement to the following effect would have a much better chance of apprehending and laying by the heels this John Tomkins than the above description, although penned by one who, from the good services which he appears to have done for him, has not improbably been blessed with some years of previous intercourse with the said John. Taking, then, the above advertisement to be true, or nearly so, down to the words "left leg" inclusive (though I have some doubt if the blemish there implied amount to a positive lameness, or be perceivable by any but the nearest friends of John), I would proceed thus:—

—"Leans a little forward in his walk; his hair thick and inclining to auburn; his nose of the middle size, a little turned up at the end; lively hazel eyes (the contusion, as its effects are probably gone off by this time, I judge better omitted); inclines to be corpulent; his voice thick but pleasing, especially when he sings; had on a decent shag greatcoat with yellow buttons."

Now I would stake a considerable wager (though by no means a positive man) that some such mitigated description would lead the beagles of the law into a much surer track for finding this ungracious varlet, than to set them upon a false scent after fictitious ugliness and fictitious shabbiness; though, to do those gentlemen justice, I have no doubt their experience has taught them in all such cases to abate a great deal of the deformity which they are instructed to expect, and has discovered to them that the Devil's agents upon this earth, like their master, are far less ugly in reality than they are painted.

I am afraid, Mr. Reflector, that I shall be thought to have gone wide of my subject, which was to detect the practical errors of physiognomy, properly so called; whereas I have introduced physical defects, such as lameness, the effects of accidents upon a man's person, his wearing apparel, etc., as circumstances on which the eye of dislike, looking askance, may report erroneous conclusions to the understanding. But if we are liable, through a kind or an unkind passion, to mistake so grossly concerning things so exterior and palpable, how much more are we likely to err respecting those nicer and less perceptible hints of character in a face whose detection constitutes the triumph of the physiognomist?

To revert to those bestowers of unmerited deformity, the framers of advertisements for the apprehension of delinquents, a sincere desire of promoting the end of public justice induces me to address a word to them on the best means of attaining those ends. I will endeavour to lay down a few practical, or rather negative, rules for their use, for my ambition extends no further than to arm them with cautions against the self-defeating of their own purposes:—

1. Imprimis, then, Mr. Advertiser! If the culprit whom you are willing to recover be one to whom in times past you have shown kindness, and been disposed to think kindly of him yourself, but he has deceived your trust, and has run away, and left you with a load of debt to answer for him,—sit down calmly, and endeavour to behold him through the spectacles of memory rather than of present conceit. Image to yourself, before you pen a tittle of his description, the same plausible, good-looking man who took you in; and try to put away from your mind every intrusion of that deceitful spectre which perpetually obtrudes itself in

the room of your former friend's known visage. It will do you more credit to have been deceived by such a one; and depend upon it, the traitor will convey to the eyes of the world in general much more of that first idea which you formed (perhaps in part erroneous) of his physiognomy, than of that frightful substitute which you have suffered to creep in upon your mind and usurp upon it; a creature which has no archetype except in your own brain.

2. If you be a master that have to advertise a runaway apprentice, though the young dog's faults are known only to you, and no doubt his conduct has been aggravating enough, do not presently set him down as having crooked ankles. He may have a good pair of legs, and run away notwithstanding. Indeed, the latter does rather seem to imply the former.

3. If the unhappy person against whom your laudable vengeance is directed be a thief, think that a thief may have a good nose, good eyes, good ears. It is indispensable to his profession that he be possessed of sagacity, foresight, vigilance; it is more than probable, then, that he is endued with the bodily types or instruments of these qualities to some tolerable degree of perfectness.

4. If petty larceny be his offence, I exhort you, do not confound meanness of crime with diminutiveness of stature. These things have no connexion. I have known a tall man stoop to the basest action, a short man aspire to the height of crime, a fair man be guilty of the foulest actions, etc.

5. Perhaps the offender has been guilty of some atrocious and aggravated murder. Here is the most difficult case of all. It is above all requisite that such a daring violator of the peace and safety of society should meet with his reward, a violent and ignominious death. But how shall we get at him? Who is there among us that has known him before he committed the offence, that shall take upon him to say he can sit down coolly and pen a dispassionate description of a murderer? The tales of our nursery,—the reading of our youth,—the ill-looking man that was hired by the Uncle to despatch the Children in the Wood,—the grim ruffians who smothered the babes in the Tower,—the black and beetle-browed assassin of Mrs. Ratcliffe,—the shag-haired villain of Mr. Monk Lewis,—the Tarquin tread, and millstone dropping eyes, of Murder in Shakspeare,—the exaggerations of picture and of poetry,—what we have read and what we have dreamed of,—rise up and crowd in upon us such eye-scaring portraits of the man of blood, that our pen is absolutely forestalled; we commence poets when we should play the part of strictest historians, and the very blackness of horror which the deed calls up, serves as a cloud to screen the doer. The fiction is blameless, it is accordant with those wise prejudices with which nature has guarded our innocence, as with impassable barriers, against the commission of such appalling crimes; but, meantime, the criminal escapes; or if,—owing to that wise abatement in their expectation of deformity, which, as I hinted at before, the officers of pursuit never fail to make, and no doubt in

cases of this sort they make a more than ordinary allowance,—if, owing to this or any accident, the offender is caught and brought to his trial, who that has been led out of curiosity to witness such a scene has not with astonishment reflected on the difference between a real committer of a murder, and the idea of one which he has been collecting and heightening all his life out of books, dreams, etc. The fellow, perhaps, is a sleek, smug-looking man, with light hair and eyebrows,—the latter by no means jutting out or like a crag,—and with none of those marks which our fancy had pre-bestowed upon him.

I find I am getting unawares too serious; the best way on such occasions is to leave off, which I shall do by generally recommending to all prosecuting advertisers not to confound crimes with ugliness; or rather, to distinguish between that physiognomical deformity, which I am willing to grant always accompanies crime, and mere *physical ugliness,*—which signifies nothing, is the opponent of nothing, and may exist in a good or bad person indifferently.   CRITO.

ON THE INCONVENIENCES RESULTING FROM BEING HANGED

TO THE EDITOR OF "THE REFLECTOR"

SIR,—I am one of those unhappy persons whose misfortunes, it seems, do not entitle them to the benefit of pure pity. All that is bestowed upon me of that kindest alleviator of human miseries comes dashed with a double portion of contempt. My griefs have nothing in them that is felt as sacred by the bystanders. Yet is my affliction, in truth, of the deepest grain—the heaviest task that was ever given to mortal patience to sustain. Time, that wears out all other sorrows, can never modify or soften mine. Here they must continue to gnaw as long as that fatal mark——

Why was I ever born? Why was innocence in my person suffered to be branded with a stain which was appointed only for the blackest guilt? What had I done, or my parents, that a disgrace of mine should involve a whole posterity in infamy? I am almost tempted to believe, that, in some pre-existent state, crimes to which this sublunary life of mine hath been as much a stranger as the babe that is newly born into it, have drawn down upon me this vengeance, so disproportionate to my actions on this globe.

My brain sickens, and my bosom labours to be delivered of the weight that presses upon it, yet my conscious pen shrinks from the avowal. But out it must——

O, Mr. Reflector! guess at the wretch's misery who now writes this to you, when, with tears and burning blushes, he is obliged to confess that he has been—HANGED——

Methinks I hear an involuntary exclamation burst from you, as your imagination presents to you fearful images of your correspondent unknown—*hanged!*

Fear not, Mr. Editor. No disembodied spirit has the honour of addressing you. I am flesh and blood, an unfortunate system of bones, muscles, sinews, arteries, like yourself.

Then, I presume, you mean to be pleasant.—That expression of yours, Mr. Correspondent, must be taken somehow in a metaphorical sense——

In the plainest sense, without trope or figure—Yes, Mr. Editor! this neck of mine has felt the fatal noose,—these hands have tremblingly held up the corroborative prayer-book,—these lips have sucked the moisture of the last consolatory orange,—this tongue has chanted the doleful cantata which no performer was ever called upon to repeat,—this face has had the veiling night-cap drawn over it——

But for no crime of mine.—Far be it from me to arraign the justice of my country, which, though tardy, did at length recognize my innocence. It is not for me to reflect upon judge or jury, now that eleven years have elapsed since the erroneous sentence was pronounced. Men will always be fallible, and perhaps circumstances did appear at the time a little strong——

Suffice it to say, that after hanging four minutes (as the spectators were pleased to compute it,—a man that is being strangled, I know from experience, has altogether a different measure of time from his friends who are breathing leisurely about him,—I suppose the minutes lengthen as time approaches eternity, in the same manner as the miles get longer as you travel northward),—after hanging four minutes, according to the best calculation of the bystanders, a reprieve came, and I was cut DOWN——

Really I am ashamed of deforming your pages with these technical phrases—if I knew how to express my meaning shorter——

But to proceed.—My first care after I had been brought to myself by the usual methods (those methods that are so interesting to the operator and his assistants, who are pretty numerous on such occasions,—but which no patient was ever desirous of undergoing a second time for the benefit of science), my first care was to provide myself with an enormous stock or cravat to hide the place—you understand me;—my next care was to procure a residence as distant as possible from that part of the country where I had suffered. For that reason I chose the metropolis, as the place where wounded honour (I had been told) could lurk with the least danger of exciting inquiry, and stigmatised innocence had the best chance of hiding her disgrace in a crowd. I sought out a new circle of acquaintance, and my circumstances happily enabling me to pursue my fancy in that respect, I endeavoured, by mingling in all the pleasures which the town affords, to efface the memory of what I had undergone.

But, alas! such is the portentous and all-pervading chain of connexion which links together the head and members of this great community, my scheme of lying perdu was defeated almost at the outset. A countryman of mine, whom a foolish law-suit had brought to town, by chance met me, and the secret was soon blazoned about.

In a short time, I found myself deserted by most of those who had been my intimate friends. Not that any guilt was supposed to attach to my character. My officious countryman, to do him justice, had been candid enough to explain my perfect innocence. But, somehow or other, there is a want of strong virtue in mankind. We have plenty of the softer instincts, but the heroic character is gone. How else can I account for it, that of all my numerous acquaintance, among whom I had the honour of ranking sundry persons of education, talents, and worth, scarcely here and there one or two could be found who had the courage to associate with a man that had been hanged.

Those few who did not desert me altogether were persons of strong but coarse minds; and from the absence of all delicacy in them I suffered almost as much as from the superabundance of a false species of it in the others. Those who stuck by me were the jokers, who thought themselves entitled by the fidelity which they had shown towards me to use me with what familiarity they pleased. Many and unfeeling are the jests that I have suffered from these rude (because faithful) Achateses. As they passed me in the streets, one would nod significantly to his companion and say, pointing to me, Smoke his cravat, and ask me if I had got a wen, that I was so solicitous to cover my neck. Another would inquire, What news from * * * Assizes? (which you may guess, Mr. Editor, was the scene of my shame), and whether the sessions was like to prove a maiden one? A third would offer to insure me from drowning. A fourth would tease me with inquiries how I felt when I was swinging, whether I had not something like a blue flame dancing before my eyes? A fifth took a fancy never to call me anything but *Lazarus*. And an eminent bookseller and publisher,—who, in his zeal to present the public with new facts, had he lived in those days, I am confident, would not have scrupled waiting upon the person himself last mentioned, at the most critical period of his existence, to solicit a *few facts relative to resuscitation,*—had the modesty to offer me — guineas per sheet, if I would write, in his Magazine, a physiological account of my feelings upon coming to myself.

But these were evils which a moderate fortitude might have enabled me to struggle with. Alas! Mr. Editor, the women,—whose good graces I had always most assiduously cultivated, from whose softer minds I had hoped a more delicate and generous sympathy than I found in the men, —the women began to shun me—this was the unkindest blow of all.

But is it to be wondered at? How couldst thou imagine, wretchedest of beings, that that tender creature Seraphina would fling her pretty arms about that neck which previous circumstances had rendered infamous? That she would put up with the refuse of the rope, the leavings of the cord? Or that any analogy could subsist between the knot which binds true lovers, and the knot which ties malefactors?

I can forgive that pert baggage Flirtilla, who, when I complimented her one day on the execution which her eyes had done, replied, that, to be sure, Mr. * * was a judge of those things. But from thy more exalted mind, Celestina, I expected a more unprejudiced decision. The person whose true name I conceal under this appellation, of all the women that I was ever acquainted with, had the most manly turn of mind, which she had improved by reading and the best conversation. Her understanding was not more masculine than her manners and whole disposition were delicately and truly feminine. She was the daughter of an officer who had fallen in the service of his country, leaving his widow, and Celestina, an only child, with a fortune sufficient to set them above want, but not to enable them to live in splendour. I had the mother's permission to pay my addresses to the young lady, and Celestina seemed to approve of my suit.

Often and often have I poured out my overcharged soul in the presence of Celestina, complaining of the hard and unfeeling prejudices of the world; and the sweet maid has again and again declared, that no irrational prejudice should hinder her from esteeming every man according to his intrinsic worth. Often has she repeated the consolatory assurance, that she could never consider as essentially ignominious an *accident*, which was indeed to be deprecated, but which might have happened to the most innocent of mankind. Then would she set forth some illustrious example, which her reading easily furnished, of a Phocion or a Socrates unjustly condemned; of a Raleigh or a Sir Thomas More, to whom late posterity had done justice; and by soothing my fancy with some such agreeable parallel, she would make me almost to triumph in my disgrace, and convert my shame into glory.

In such entertaining and instructive conversations the time passed on, till I importunately urged the mistress of my affections to name the day for our union. To this she obligingly consented, and I thought myself the happiest of mankind. But how was I surprised one morning on the receipt of the following billet from my charmer:—

SIR,—You must not impute it to levity, or to a worse failing, ingratitude, if, with anguish of heart, I feel myself compelled by irresistible arguments to recall a vow which I fear I made with too little consideration. I never can be yours. The reasons of my decision, which is final, are in my own breast, and you must everlastingly remain a stranger to them. Assure yourself that I can never cease to esteem you as I ought.

CELESTINA.

At the sight of this paper, I ran in frantic haste to Celestina's lodgings, where I learned, to my infinite mortification, that the mother and daughter were set off on a journey to a distant part of the country, to visit a relation, and were not expected to return in less than four months.

Stunned by this blow, which left me without the courage to solicit an explanation by letter, even if I had known where they were (for the particular address was industriously concealed from me), I waited with impatience the termination of the period, in the vain hope that I might be permitted to have a chance of softening the harsh decision by a personal interview with Celestina after her return. But before three months were at an end, I learned from the newspapers that my beloved had— given her hand to another!

Heart-broken as I was, I was totally at a loss to account for the strange step which she had taken; and it was not till some years after that I learned the true reason from a female relation of hers, to whom it seems Celestina had confessed in confidence, that it was no demerit of mine that had caused her to break off the match so abruptly, nor any preference which she might feel for any other person, for she preferred me (she was pleased to say), to all mankind; but when she came to lay the matter closer to her heart, she found that she never should be able to bear the sight—(I give you her very words as they were detailed to me by her relation)—the sight of a man in a nightcap, who had appeared on a public platform—it would lead to such a disagreeable association of ideas! And to this punctilio I was sacrificed.

To pass over an infinite series of minor mortifications, to which this last and heaviest might well render me callous, behold me here, Mr. Editor! in the thirty-seventh year of my existence (the twelfth, reckoning from my re-animation), cut off from all respectable connexions; rejected by the fairer half of the community,—who in my case alone seem to have laid aside the characteristic pity of their sex; punished because I was once punished unjustly; suffering for no other reason than because I once had the misfortune to suffer without any cause at all. In no other country, I think, but this, could a man have been subject to such a life-long persecution, when once his innocence had been clearly established.

Had I crawled forth a rescued victim from the rack in the horrible dungeons of the Inquisition,—had I heaved myself up from a half bastinado in China, or been torn from the just-entering, ghastly impaling stake in Barbary,—had I dropt alive from the knout in Russia, or come off with a gashed neck from the half-mortal, scarce-in-time-retracted cimeter of an executioneering slave in Turkey,—I might have borne about the remnant of this frame (the mangled trophy of reprieved innocence) with credit to myself, in any of those barbarous countries. No scorn, at least, would have mingled with the pity (small as it might be) with which what was left of me would have been surveyed.

The singularity of my case has often led me to inquire into the reasons of the general levity with which the subject of hanging is treated as a topic in this country. I say, as a topic: for let the very persons who speak so lightly of the thing at a distance be brought to view the real scene,—let the platform be *bonâ fide* exhibited, and the trembling culprit brought forth,—the case is changed; but as a topic of conversation, I appeal to the vulgar jokes which pass current in every street. But why mention them, when the politest authors have agreed in making use of this subject as a source of the ridiculous? Swift, and Pope, and Prior, are fond of recurring to it. Gay has built an entire drama upon this single foundation. The whole interest of the Beggar's Opera may be said to hang upon it. To such writers as Fielding and Smollett it is a perfect *bonne-bouche*.—Hear the facetious Tom Brown, in his Comical View of London and Westminster, describe the *Order of the Show at one of the Tyburn Executions* in his time:—"Mr. Ordinary visits his melancholy flock in Newgate by eight. Doleful procession up Holborn Hill about eleven. Men handsome and proper that were never thought so before, which is some comfort however. Arrive at the fatal place by twelve. Burnt brandy, women, and Sabbath-breaking, repented of. Some few penitential drops fall under the gallows. Sheriff's men, parson, pickpockets, criminals, all very busy. The last concluding peremptory psalm struck up. Show over by one."—In this sportive strain does this misguided wit think proper to play with a subject so serious, which yet he would hardly have done if he had not known that there existed a predisposition in the habits of his unaccountable countrymen to consider the subject as a jest. But what shall we say to Shakspeare, who (not to mention the solution which the Grave-digger in Hamlet gives of his fellowworkman's problem), in that scene in Measure for Measure, where the Clown calls upon Master Barnardine to get up and be hanged, which he declines on the score of being sleepy, has actually gone out of his way to gratify this amiable propensity in his countrymen; for it is plain, from the use that was to be made of his head, and from Abhorson's asking, "Is the axe upon the block, sirrah?" that beheading, and not hanging, was the punishment to which Barnardine was destined. But Shakspeare knew that the axe and block were pregnant with no ludicrous images, and therefore falsified the historic truth of his own drama (if I may so speak), rather than he would leave out such excellent matter for a jest as the suspending of a fellow-creature in mid-air has been ever esteemed to be by Englishmen.

One reason why the ludicrous never fails to intrude itself into our contemplations upon this mode of death, I suppose to be, the absurd posture into which a man is thrown who is condemned to dance, as the vulgar delight to express it, upon nothing. To see him whisking and wavering in the air,

As the wind you know will wave a man [1] ;

to behold the vacant carcass, from which the life is newly dislodged, shifting between earth and heaven, the sport of every gust; like a weathercock, serving to show from which point the wind blows; like a maukin, fit only to scare away birds; like a nest left to swing upon a bough when the bird is flown: these are uses to which we cannot without a mixture of spleen and contempt behold the human carcass reduced. We string up dogs, foxes, bats, moles, weasels. Man surely deserves a steadier death.

Another reason why the ludicrous associates more forcibly with this than with any other mode of punishment, I cannot help thinking to be,

[1] Hieronimo in the Spanish Tragedy.

the senseless costume with which old prescription has thought fit to
clothe the exit of malefactors in this country. Let a man do what he will
to abstract from his imagination all idea of the whimsical, something of
it will come across him when he contemplates the figure of a fellow-
creature in the day-time (in however distressing a situation) in a night-
cap. Whether it be that this nocturnal addition has something discordant
with daylight, or that it is the dress which we are seen in at those times
when we are "seen," as the Angel in Milton expresses it, "least wise,"—
this, I am afraid, will always be the case; unless, indeed, as in my instance, some strong personal feeling overpower the ludicrous altogether.
To me, when I reflect upon the train of misfortunes which have pursued
men through life, owing to that accursed drapery, the cap presents as
purely frightful an object as the sleeveless yellow coat and devil-painted
mitre of the San Benitos.—An ancestor of mine, who suffered for his
loyalty in the time of the civil wars, was so sensible of the truth of what
I am here advancing, that on the morning of execution, no entreaties
could prevail upon him to submit to the odious dishabille, as he called it,
but he insisted upon wearing and actually suffered in, the identical, flowing periwig which he is painted in, in the gallery belonging to my uncle's
seat in ——shire.

Suffer me, Mr. Editor, before I quit the subject, to say a word or two
respecting the minister of justice in this country; in plain words, I mean
the hangman. It has always appeared to me that, in the mode of inflicting capital punishments with us, there is too much of the ministry of the
human hand. The guillotine, as performing its functions more of itself
and sparing human agency, though a cruel and disgusting exhibition, in
my mind has many ways the advantage over *our way.* In beheading, indeed, as it was formerly practised in England, and in whipping to death,
as is sometimes practised now, the hand of man is no doubt sufficiently
busy; but there is something less repugnant in these downright blows
than in the officious barber-like ministerings of *the other.* To have a
fellow with his hangman's hands fumbling about your collar, adjusting
the thing as your valet would regulate your cravat, valuing himself on
his menial dexterity——

I never shall forget meeting my rascal,—I mean the fellow who
officiated for me,—in London last winter. I think I see him now,—in a
waistcoat that had been mine,—smirking along as if he knew me——

In some parts of Germany, that fellow's office is by law declared infamous, and his posterity incapable of being ennobled. They have hereditary hangmen, or had at least, in the same manner as they had hereditary
other great officers of state; and the hangmen's families of two adjoining
parishes intermarried with each other, to keep the breed entire. I wish
something of the same kind were established in England.

But it is time to quit a subject which teems with disagreeable images——

Permit me to subscribe myself, Mr. Editor, your unfortunate friend,
                                                              PENSILIS.

ON THE MELANCHOLY OF TAILORS

Sedet, æternumque sedebit,
Infelix Theseus.   VIRGIL.

THAT there is a professional melancholy, if I may so express myself, incident to the occupation of a tailor, is a fact which I think very few will
venture to dispute. I may safely appeal to my readers, whether they
ever knew one of that faculty that was not of a temperament, to say the
least, far removed from mercurial or jovial.

Observe the suspicious gravity of their gait. The peacock is not more
tender, from a consciousness of his peculiar infirmity, than a gentleman
of this profession is of being known by the same infallible testimonies of
his occupation. "Walk, that I may know thee."

Do you ever see him go whistling along the footpath like a carman, or
brush through a crowd like a baker, or go smiling to himself like a lover?
Is he forward to thrust into mobs, or to make one at the ballad-singer's
audiences? Does he not rather slink by assemblies and meetings of the
people, as one that wisely declines popular observation?

How extremely rare is a noisy tailor! a mirthful and obstreperous
tailor!

"At my nativity," says Sir Thomas Browne, "my ascendant was the
earthly sign of Scorpius; I was born in the planetary hour of Saturn,
and I think I have a piece of that leaden planet in me." One would
think that he were anatomising a tailor! save that to the latter's occupation, methinks, a woollen planet would seem more consonant, and that
he should be born when the sun was in Aries.—He goes on: "I am no
way facetious, nor disposed for the mirth and galliardise of company."
How true a type of the whole trade! Eminently economical of his words,
you shall seldom hear a jest come from one of them. He sometimes furnishes subject for a repartee, but rarely (I think) contributes one *ore
proprio*.

Drink itself does not seem to elevate him, or at least to call out of him
any of the external indications of vanity. I cannot say that it never
causes his pride to swell, but it never breaks out. I am even fearful that
it may swell and rankle to an alarming degree inwardly. For pride is
near of kin to melancholy!—a hurtful obstruction from the ordinary
outlets of vanity being shut. It is this stoppage which engenders proud
humours. Therefore a tailor may be proud. I think he is never vain. The
display of his gaudy patterns, in that book of his which emulates the
rainbow, never raises any inflations of that emotion in him, corresponding to what the wig-maker (for instance) evinces, when he expatiates on
a curl or a bit of hair. He spreads them forth with a sullen incapacity
for pleasure, a real or affected indifference to grandeur. Cloth of gold
neither seems to elate, nor cloth of frieze to depress him—according to
the beautiful motto which formed the modest imprese of the shield worn

by Charles Brandon at his marriage with the king's sister. Nay, I doubt whether he would discover any vainglorious complacence in his colours, though "Iris" herself "dipt the woof."

In further corroboration of this argument—who ever saw the wedding of a tailor announced in the newspapers, or the birth of his eldest son?

When was a tailor known to give a dance, or to be himself a good dancer, or to perform exquisitely on the tight-rope, or to shine in any such light and airy pastimes? to sing, or play on the violin?

Do they much care for public rejoicings, lightings up, ringing of bells, firing of cannons, etc.?

Valiant I know they can be; but I appeal to those who were witnesses to the exploits of Eliot's famous troop, whether in their fiercest charges they betrayed anything of that thoughtless oblivion of death with which a Frenchman jigs into battle, or whether they did not show more of the melancholy valour of the Spaniard, upon whom they charged; that deliberate courage which contemplation and sedentary habits breathe?

Are they often great newsmongers?—I have known some few among them arrive at the dignity of speculative politicians; but that light and cheerful everyday interest in the affairs and goings on of the world, which makes the barber[1] such delightful company, I think is rarely observable in them.

This characteristic pensiveness in them being so notorious, I wonder none of those writers, who have expressly treated of melancholy, should have mentioned it. Burton, whose book is an excellent abstract of all the authors in that kind who preceded him, and who treats of every species of this malady, from the *hypochondriacal* or *windy* to the *heroical* or *love melancholy*, has strangely omitted it. Shakspeare himself has overlooked it. "I have neither the scholar's melancholy (saith Jaques), which is emulation; nor the courtier's, which is proud; nor the soldier's, which is politic; nor the lover's, which is all these": and then, when you might expect him to have brought in, "nor the tailor's, which is" so and so, he comes to an end of his enumeration, and falls to a defining of his own melancholy.

Milton likewise has omitted it, where he had so fair an opportunity of bringing it in, in his Penseroso.

But the partial omissions of historians proving nothing against the ex-

---

[1] Having inicidentally mentioned the barber in a comparison of professional temperaments, I hope no other trade will take offence, or look upon it as an incivility done to them, if I say, that in courtesy, humanity, and all the conversational and social graces which "gladden life," I esteem no profession comparable to his. Indeed, so great is the goodwill which I bear to this useful and agreeable body of men, that, residing in one of the Inns of Court (where the best specimens of them are to be found, except perhaps at the universities), there are seven of them to whom I am personally known, and who never pass me without the compliment of the hat on either side. My truly polite and urbane friend, Mr. A——m, of Flower-de-Luce Court, in Fleet Street, will forgive my mention of him in particular. I can truly say, that I never spent a quarter of an hour under his hands without deriving some profit from the agreeable discussions which are always going on there.

istence of any well-attested fact, I shall proceed and endeavour to ascertain the causes why this pensive turn should be so predominant in people of this profession above all others.

And first, may it not be, that the custom of wearing apparel being derived to us from the fall, and one of the most mortifying products of that unhappy event, a certain *seriousness* (to say no more of it) may in the order of things have been intended to be impressed upon the minds of that race of men to whom in all ages the care of contriving the human apparel has been entrusted, to keep up the memory of the first institution of clothes, and serve as a standing remonstrance against those vanities which the absurd conversion of a memorial of our shame into an ornament of our persons was destined to produce? Correspondent in some sort to this, it may be remarked, that the tailor sitting over a cave or hollow place, in the cabalistic language of his order is said to have *certain melancholy regions* always open under his feet.—But waiving further inquiry into final causes, where the best of us can only wander in the dark, let us try to discover the efficient causes of this melancholy.

I think, then, that they may be reduced to two, omitting some subordinate ones, viz.—

The sedentary habits of the tailor.—
Something peculiar in his diet.—

First, his *sedentary habits*.—In Doctor Norris's famous narrative of the frenzy of Mr. John Dennis, the patient, being questioned as to the occasion of the swelling in his legs, replies that it came "by criticism"; to which the learned doctor seeming to demur, as to a distemper which he had never read of, Dennis (who appears not to have been mad upon all subjects) rejoins, with some warmth, that it was no distemper, but a noble art; that he had sat fourteen hours a day at it; and that the other was a pretty doctor not to know that there was a communication between the brain and the legs!

When we consider that this sitting for fourteen hours continuously, which the critic probably practised only while he was writing his "remarks," is no more than what the tailor, in the ordinary pursuance of his art, submits to daily (Sundays excepted) throughout the year, shall we wonder to find the brain affected, and in a manner overclouded, from that indissoluble sympathy between the noble and less noble parts of the body which Dennis hints at? The unnatural and painful manner of his sitting must also greatly aggravate the evil, insomuch that I have sometimes ventured to liken tailors at their boards to so many envious Junos, *sitting cross-legged to hinder the birth of their own felicity*. The legs transversed thus ✕ crosswise, or decussated, was among the ancients the posture of malediction. The Turks, who practise it at this day, are noted to be a melancholy people.

Secondly, his *diet*.—To which purpose I find a most remarkable passage in Burton, in his chapter entitled "Bad diet a cause of melancholy." "Amongst herbs to be eaten (he says) I find gourds, cucumbers, melons, disallowed; but especially CABBAGE. It causeth troublesome dreams, and sends up black vapours to the brain. Galen, *Loc. Affect.* lib. iii. cap. 6, of all herbs condemns CABBAGE. And Isaack, lib. ii. cap. i, *animæ gravitatem facit*, it brings heaviness to the soul." I could not omit so flattering a testimony from an author who, having no theory of his own to serve, has so unconsciously contributed to the confirmation of mine. It is well known that this last-named vegetable has, from the earliest periods which we can discover, constituted almost the sole food of this extraordinary race of people.   BURTON, *Junior.*

HOSPITA ON THE IMMODERATE INDULGENCE OF THE PLEASURES OF THE PALATE

TO THE EDITOR OF "THE REFLECTOR"

MR. REFLECTOR,—My husband and I are fond of company, and being in easy circumstances, we are seldom without a party to dinner two or three days in a week. The utmost cordiality has hitherto prevailed at our meetings; but there is a young gentleman, a near relation of my husband's, that has lately come among us, whose preposterous behaviour bids fair, if not timely checked, to disturb our tranquillity. He is too great a favourite with my husband in other respects, for me to remonstrate with him in any other than this distant way. A letter printed in your publication may catch his eye; for he is a great reader, and makes a point of seeing all the new things that come out. Indeed, he is by no means deficient in understanding. My husband says that he has a good deal of wit; but for my part I cannot say I am any judge of that, having seldom observed him open his mouth except for purposes very foreign to conversation. In short, Sir, this young gentleman's failing is, an immoderate indulgence of his palate. The first time he dined with us, he thought it necessary to extenuate the length of time he kept the dinner on the table, by declaring that he had taken a very long walk in the morning, and came in fasting; but as that excuse could not serve above once or twice at most, he has latterly dropped the mask altogether, and chosen to appear in his own proper colours without reserve or apology.

You cannot imagine how unpleasant his conduct has become. His way of staring at the dishes as they are brought in, has absolutely something immodest in it: it is like the stare of an impudent man of fashion at a fine woman, when she first comes into a room. I am positively in pain for the dishes, and cannot help thinking they have consciousness, and will be put out of countenance, he treats them so like what they are not.

Then again he makes no scruple of keeping a joint of meat on the table, after the cheese and fruit are brought in, till he has what he calls *done with it.* Now how awkward this looks, where there are ladies, you may judge, Mr. Reflector,—how it disturbs the order and comfort of a meal. And yet I always make a point of helping him first, contrary to all good manners,—before any of my female friends are helped,—that he may avoid this very error. I wish he would eat before he comes out.

What makes his proceedings more particularly offensive at our house is, that my husband, though out of common politeness he is obliged to set dishes of animal food before his visitors, yet himself and his whole family (myself included), feed entirely on vegetables. We have a theory, that animal food is neither wholesome nor natural to man; and even vegetables we refuse to eat until they have undergone the operation of fire, in consideration of those numberless little living creatures which the glass helps us to detect in every fibre of the plant or root before it be dressed. On the same theory we boil our water, which is our only drink, before we suffer it to come to table. Our children are perfect little Pythagoreans: it would do you good to see them in their nursery, stuffing their dried fruits, figs, raisins, and *milk,* which is the only approach to animal food which is allowed. They have no notion how the substance of a creature that ever had life can become food for another creature. A beef-steak is an absurdity to them; a mutton-chop, a solecism in terms; a cutlet, a word absolutely without any meaning; a butcher is nonsense, except so far as it is taken for a man who delights in blood, or a hero. In this happy state of innocence we have kept their minds, not allowing them to go into the kitchen, or to hear of any preparations for the dressing of animal food, or even to know that such things are practised. But as a state of ignorance is incompatible with a certain age, and as my eldest girl, who is ten years old next Midsummer, must shortly be introduced into the world and sit at table with us, where she will see some things which will shock all her received notions, I have been endeavouring by little and little to break her mind, and prepare it for the disagreeable impressions which must be forced upon it. The first hint I gave her upon the subject, I could see her recoil from it with the same horror with which we listen to a tale of Anthropophagism; but she has gradually grown more reconciled to it, in some measure, from my telling her that it was the custom of the world,—to which, however senseless, we must submit, so far as we could do it with innocence, not to give offence; and she has shown so much strength of mind on other occasions, which I have no doubt is owing to the calmness and serenity superinduced by her diet, that I am in good hopes when the proper season for her *début* arrives, she may be brought to endure the sight of a roasted chicken or a dish of sweet-breads for the first time without fainting. Such being the nature of our little household, you may guess what inroads into the economy of it,—what revolutions and turnings of things upside down, the example of such a feeder as Mr. —— is calculated to produce.

I wonder, at a time like the present, when the scarcity of every kind of food is so painfully acknowledged, that *shame* has no effect upon him. Can he have read Mr. Malthus's Thoughts on the Ratio of Food to Population? Can he think it reasonable that one man should consume the sustenance of many?

The young gentleman has an agreeable air and person, such as are not unlikely to recommend him on the score of matrimony. But his fortune is not over large; and what prudent young woman would think of embarking hers with a man who would bring three or four mouths (or what is equivalent to them) into a family? She might as reasonably choose a widower in the same circumstances, with three or four children.

I cannot think who he takes after. His father and mother, by all accounts, were very moderate eaters; only I have heard that the latter swallowed her victuals very fast, and the former had a tedious custom of sitting long at his meals. Perhaps he takes after both.

I wish you would turn this in your thoughts, Mr. Reflector, and give us your ideas on the subject of excessive eating, and, particularly, of animal food.   HOSPITA.

EDAX ON APPETITE

TO THE EDITOR OF "THE REFLECTOR"

MR. REFLECTOR,—I am going to lay before you a case of the most iniquitous persecution that ever poor devil suffered.

You must know, then, that I have been visited with a calamity ever since my birth. How shall I mention it without offending delicacy? Yet out it must. My sufferings, then, have all arisen from a most inordinate appetite——

Not for wealth, not for vast possessions,—then might I have hoped to find a cure in some of those precepts of philosophers or poets,—those *verba et voces* which Horace speaks of:—

> quibus hunc lenire dolorem
> Possis, et magnam morbi deponere partem;

not for glory, not for fame, not for applause,—for against this disease, too, he tells us there are certain piacula, or, as Pope has chosen to render it,

> rhymes, which fresh and fresh applied,
> Will cure the arrant'st puppy of his pride;

nor yet for pleasure, properly so called: the strict and virtuous lessons which I received in early life from the best of parents,—a pious clergyman of the Church of England, now no more,—I trust have rendered me sufficiently secure on that side:——

No, Sir, for none of these things; but an appetite, in its coarsest and least metaphorical sense,—an appetite for *food*.

The exorbitances of my arrow-root and pappish days I cannot go back far enough to remember; only I have been told that my mother's constitution not admitting of my being nursed at home, the woman who had the care of me for that purpose used to make most extravagant demands for my pretended excesses in that kind; which my parents, rather than believe anything unpleasant of me, chose to impute to the known covetousness and mercenary disposition of that sort of people. This blindness continued on their part after I was sent for home, up to the period when it was thought proper, on account of my advanced age, that I should mix with other boys more unreservedly than I had hitherto done. I was accordingly sent to boarding-school.

Here the melancholy truth became too apparent to be disguised. The prying republic of which a great school consists soon found me out: there was no shifting the blame any longer upon other people's shoulders,—no good-natured maid to take upon herself the enormities of which I stood accused in the article of bread and butter, besides the crying sin of stolen ends of puddings, and cold pies strangely missing. The truth was but too manifest in my looks,—in the evident signs of inanition which I exhibited after the fullest meals, in spite of the double allowance which my master was privately instructed by my kind parents to give me. The sense of the ridiculous, which is but too much alive in grown persons, is tenfold more active and alert in boys. Once detected, I was the constant butt of their arrows,—the mark against which every puny leveller directed his little shaft of scorn. The very Graduses and Thesauruses were raked for phrases to pelt me with by the tiny pedants. *Ventri natus—Ventri deditus,—Vesana gula,—Escarum gurges,—Dapibus indulgens,—Non dans frœna gulœ,—Sectans lautœ fercula mensœ,* resounded wheresoever I passed. I led a weary life, suffering the penalties of guilt for that which was no crime, but only following the blameless dictates of nature. The remembrance of those childish reproaches haunts me yet oftentimes in my dreams. My school-days come again, and the horror I used to feel, when, in some silent corner, retired from the notice of my unfeeling playfellows, I have sat to mumble the solitary slice of ginger-bread allotted me by the bounty of considerate friends, and have ached at heart because I could not spare a portion of it, as I saw other boys do, to some favourite boy; for if I know my own heart, I was never selfish,—never possessed a luxury which I did not hasten to communicate to others; but my food, alas! was none; it was an indispensable necessary; I could as soon have spared the blood in my veins, as have parted that with my companions.

Well, no one stage of suffering lasts for ever: we should grow reconciled to it at length, I suppose, if it did. The miseries of my school-days had their end; I was once more restored to the paternal dwelling. The affectionate solicitude of my parents was directed to the good-natured purpose of concealing, even from myself, the infirmity which haunted me. I was continually told that I was growing, and the appetite I displayed was humanely represented as being nothing more than a symptom and an effect of that. I used even to be complimented upon it. But this temporary fiction could not endure above a year or two. I ceased to

grow, but, alas! I did not cease my demands for alimentary sustenance.
Those times are long since past, and with them have ceased to exist
the fond concealment—the indulgent blindness—the delicate overlooking—the compassionate fiction. I and my infirmity are left exposed and
bare to the broad, unwinking eye of the world, which nothing can elude.
My meals are scanned, my mouthfuls weighed in a balance; that which
appetite demands is set down to the account of gluttony,—a sin which
my whole soul abhors—nay, which Nature herself has put it out of my
power to commit. I am constitutionally disenabled from that vice; for
how can he be guilty of excess who never can get enough? Let them
cease, then, to watch my plate; and leave off their ungracious comparisons of it to the seven baskets of fragments, and the supernaturally-
replenished cup of old Baucis; and be thankful that their more phlegmatic stomachs, not their virtue, have saved them from the like reproaches. I do not see that any of them desist from eating till the holy
rage of hunger, as some one calls it, is supplied. Alas! I am doomed to
stop short of that continence.

What am I to do? I am by disposition inclined to conviviality and
the social meal. I am no gourmand: I require no dainties: I should
despise the board of Heliogabalus, except for its long sitting. Those vivacious, long-continued meals of the latter Romans, indeed, I justly
envy; but the kind of fare which the Curii and Dentati put up with, I
could be content with. Dentatus I have been called, among other un-
savoury jests. Doublemeal is another name which my acquaintance have
palmed upon me, for an innocent piece of policy which I put in practice
for some time without being found out; which was—going the round of
my friends, beginning with the most primitive feeders among them, who
take their dinner about one o'clock, and so successively dropping in upon
the next and the next, till by the time I got among my more fashionable
intimates, whose hour was six or seven, I have nearly made up the body
of a just and complete meal (as I reckon it), without taking more than
one dinner (as they account of dinners) at one person's house. Since I
have been found out, I endeavour to make up by a damper, as I call it,
at home, before I go out. But alas! with me, increase of appetite truly
grows by what it feeds on. What is peculiarly offensive to me at those
dinner-parties is, the senseless custom of cheese, and the dessert afterwards. I have a rational antipathy to the former; and for fruit, and
those other vain vegetable substitutes for meat (meat, the only legitimate
aliment for human creatures since the Flood, as I take it to be deduced
from that permission, or ordinance rather, given to Noah and his descendants), I hold them in perfect contempt. Hay for horses. I remember a pretty apologue, which Mandeville tells, very much to this purpose, in his Fable of the Bees:—He brings in a Lion arguing with a
Merchant, who had ventured to expostulate with this king of beasts upon
his violent methods of feeding. The Lion thus retorts:—"Savage I am;
but no creature can be called cruel but what either by malice or insensibility extinguishes his natural pity. The Lion was born without com-

passion; we follow the instinct of our nature; the gods have appointed us to live upon the waste and spoil of other animals, and as long as we can meet with dead ones, we never hunt after the living; 'tis only man, mischievous man, that can make death a sport. Nature taught your stomach to crave nothing but vegetables.—(Under favour of the Lion, if he meant to assert this universally of mankind, it is not true. However, what he says presently is very sensible.)—Your violent fondness to change, and greater eagerness after novelties, have prompted you to the destruction of animals without justice or necessity. The Lion has a ferment within him, that consumes the toughest skin and hardest bones, as well as the flesh of all animals, without exception. Your squeamish stomach, in which the digestive heat is weak and inconsiderable, won't so much as admit of the most tender parts of them, unless above half the concoction has been performed by artificial fire beforehand; and yet what animal have you spared, to satisfy the caprices of a languid appetite? Languid, I say; for what is man's hunger if compared with the Lion's? Yours, when it is at the worst, makes you faint; mine makes me mad: oft have I tried with roots and herbs to allay the violence of it, but in vain; nothing but large quantities of flesh can any ways appease it."—Allowing for the Lion not having a prophetic instinct to take in every *lusus naturæ* that was possible of the human appetite, he was, generally speaking, in the right; and the Merchant was so impressed with his argument that, we are told, he replied not, but fainted away. O, Mr. Reflector,—that I were not obliged to add, that the creature who thus argues was but a type of me! Miserable man! *I am that Lion!* "Oft have I tried with roots and herbs to allay that violence, but in vain; nothing but ————."

Those tales which are renewed as often as the editors of papers want to fill up a space in their unfeeling columns, of great eaters,—people that devour whole geese and legs of mutton *for wagers*,—are sometimes attempted to be drawn to a parallel with my case. This wilful confounding of motives and circumstances, which make all the difference of moral or immoral in actions, just suits the sort of talent which some of my acquaintance pride themselves upon. *Wagers!*—I thank Heaven, I was never mercenary, nor could consent to prostitute a gift (though but a left-handed one) of nature, to the enlarging of my worldly substance: prudent as the necessities, which that fatal gift have involved me in, might have made such a prostitution to appear in the eyes of an indelicate world.

Rather let me say, that to the satisfaction of that talent which was given me, I have been content to sacrifice no common expectation; for such I had from an old lady, a near relation of our family, in whose good graces I had the fortune to stand, till one fatal evening——. You have seen, Mr. Reflector, if you have ever passed your time much in country towns, the kind of suppers which elderly ladies in those places have lying *in petto* in an adjoining parlour, next to that where they are entertaining their periodically-invited coevals with cards and muffins. The cloth is usually spread some half-hour before the final rubber is decided, whence they adjourn to sup upon what may emphatically be called *nothing;*—a sliver of ham, purposely contrived to be transparent to show the china-dish through it, neighbouring a slip of invisible brawn, which abuts upon something they call a tartlet, as that is bravely supported by an atom of marmalade, flanked in its turn by a grain of potted beef, with a power of such dishlings, *minims of hospitality,* spread in defiance of human nature, or rather with an utter ignorance of what it demands. Being engaged at one of these card-parties, I was obliged to go a little before *supper-time* (as they facetiously called the point of time in which they are taking these shadowy refections), and the old lady, with a sort of fear shining through the smile of courteous hospitality that beamed in her countenance, begged me to step into the next room and take something before I went out in the cold,—a proposal which lay not in my nature to deny. Indignant at the airy prospect I saw before me, I set to, and in a trice despatched the whole meal intended for eleven persons,—fish, flesh, fowl, pastry,—to the sprigs of garnishing parsley, and the last fearful custard that quaked upon the board. I need not describe the consternation, when in due time the dowagers adjourned from their cards. Where was the supper?—and the servants' answer, Mr. —— had eat it all.—That freak, however, jested me out of a good three hundred pounds a year, which I afterwards was informed for a certainty the old lady meant to leave me. I mention it not in illustration of the unhappy faculty which I am possessed of; for any unlucky wag of a school boy, with a tolerable appetite, could have done as much without feeling any hurt after it,—only that you may judge whether I am a man likely to set my talent to sale, or to require the pitiful stimulus of a wager.

I have read in Pliny, or in some author of that stamp, of a reptile in Africa, whose venom is of that hot, destructive quality, that wheresoever it fastens its tooth, the whole substance of the animal that has been bitten in a few seconds is reduced to dust, crumbles away, and absolutely disappears: it is called, from this quality, the Annihilator. Why am I forced to seek, in all the most prodigious and portentous facts of Natural History, for creatures typical of myself? *I am that snake, that Annihilator:* "wherever I fasten, in a few seconds——."

O happy sick men, that are groaning under the want of that very thing, the excess of which is my torment! O fortunate, too fortunate, if you knew your happiness, invalids! What would I not give to exchange this fierce concoctive and digestive heat,—this rabid fury which vexes me, which tears and torments me,—for your quiet, mortified, hermit-like, subdued, and sanctified stomachs, your cool, chastened inclinations, and coy desires for food!

To what unhappy figuration of the parts intestine I owe this unnatural craving, I must leave to the anatomists and the physicians to determine: they, like the rest of the world, have doubtless their eye upon me; and as I have been cut up alive by the sarcasms of my friends, so I shudder when I contemplate the probability that this animal frame, when its restless appetites shall have ceased their importunity, may be cut up also (horrible suggestion!) to determine in what system of solids or fluids this original sin of my constitution lay lurking. What work will they make with their acids and alkalines, their serums and coagulums, effervescences, viscous matter, bile, chyle, and acrimonious juices, to explain that cause which Nature, who willed the effect to punish me for my sins, may no less have determined to keep in the dark from them, to punish them for their presumption!

You may ask, Mr. Reflector, to what purpose is my appeal to you; what can you do for me? Alas! I know too well that my case is out of the reach of advice,—out of the reach of consolation. But it is some relief to the wounded heart to impart its tale of misery; and some of my acquaintance, who may read my case in your pages under a borrowed name, may be induced to give it a more humane consideration than I could ever yet obtain from them under my own. Make them, if possible, to *reflect*, that an original peculiarity of constitution is no crime; that not that which goes into the mouth desecrates a man, but that which comes out of it,—such as sarcasm, bitter jests, mocks and taunts, and ill-natured observations; and let them consider, if there be such things (which we have all heard of) as Pious Treachery, Innocent Adultery, etc., whether there may not be also such a thing as Innocent Gluttony.—I shall only subscribe myself, your afflicted servant, EDAX.

MR. H——

A FARCE, IN TWO ACTS

AS IT WAS PERFORMED AT DRURY LANE THEATRE,
DECEMBER, 1806

"Mr. H——, thou wert DAMNED. Bright shone the morning on the play-bills that announced thy appearance, and the streets were filled with the buzz of persons asking one another if they would go to see Mr. H——, and answering that they would certainly; but before night the gaiety, not of the author, but of his friends and the town, was eclipsed, for thou wert DAMNED! Hadst thou been anonymous, thou haply mightst have lived. But thou didst come to an untimely end for thy tricks, and for want of a better name to pass them off——." Theatrical Examiner.

CHARACTERS

MR. H——	*Mr. Elliston.*
BELVIL	*Mr. Bartley.*
LANDLORD PRY	*Mr. Wewitzer.*
MELESINDA	*Miss Mellon.*
MAID TO MELESINDA	*Mrs. Harlowe.*

Gentlemen, Ladies, Waiters, Servants, etc.

(SCENE—*Bath.*)

PROLOGUE, SPOKEN BY MR. ELLISTON

IF we have sinn'd in paring down a name,
All civil, well-bred authors do the same.
Survey the columns of our daily writers—
You'll find that some Initials are great fighters.
How fierce the shock, how fatal is the jar,
When Ensign W. meets Lieutenant R.
With two stout seconds, just of their own gizzard,
Cross Captain X. and rough old General Izzard!
Letter to Letter spreads the dire alarms,
Till half the Alphabet is up in arms.
Nor with less lustre have Initials shone,
To grace the gentler annals of Crim. Con.
Where the dispensers of the public lash
Soft penance give; a letter and a dash—
Where Vice reduced in size shrinks to a failing,
And loses half her grossness by curtailing.
Faux pas are told in such a modest way,—
"The affair of Colonel B— with Mrs. A—"
You must forgive them—for what is there, say,
Which such a pliant Vowel must not grant
To such a very pressing Consonant?
Or who poetic justice dares dispute,
When, mildly melting at a lover's suit,
The wife's a Liquid, her good man a Mute?
Even in the homelier scenes of honest life,
The coarse-spun intercourse of man and wife,
Initials I am told have taken place
Of Deary, Spouse, and that old-fashion'd race;
And Cabbage, ask'd by brother Snip to tea,
Replies "I'll come—but it don't rest with me—
I always leaves them things to Mrs. C."
O should this mincing fashion ever spread
From names of living heroes to the dead,
How would Ambition sigh, and hang the head,
As each loved syllable should melt away—
Her Alexander turn'd into Great A—
A single C. her Cæsar to express—
Her Scipio shrunk into a Roman S—
And, nick'd and dock'd to these new modes of speech,
Great Hannibal himself a Mr. H——.

MR. H——

A FARCE, IN TWO ACTS

ACT I

(SCENE—*A Public Room in an Inn. Landlord, Waiters, Gentlemen, etc.*)

(*Enter* MR. H.)

MR. H. Landlord, has the man brought home my boots?

LANDLORD. Yes, Sir.

MR. H. You have paid him?

LANDLORD. There is the receipt, Sir, only not quite filled up, no name, only blank—"Blank, Dr. to Zekiel Spanish for one pair of best hessians." Now, Sir, he wishes to know what name he shall put in, who he shall say "Dr."

MR. H. Why, Mr. H. to be sure.

LANDLORD. So I told him, Sir; but Zekiel has some qualms about it. He says he thinks that Mr. H. only would not stand good in law.

MR. H. Rot his impertinence! Bid him put in Nebuchadnezzar, and not trouble me with his scruples.

LANDLORD. I shall, Sir.

(*Exit.*

(*Enter a Waiter.*)

WAITER. Sir, Squire Level's man is below, with a hare and a brace of pheasants for Mr. H.

MR. H. Give the man half a crown, and bid him return my best respects to his master. Presents, it seems, will find me out, with any name or no name.

(*Enter 2nd Waiter.*)

2ND WAITER. Sir, the man that makes up the Directory is at the door.

MR. H. Give him a shilling; that is what these fellows come for.

2ND WAITER. He has sent up to know by what name your Honour will please to be inserted.

MR. H. Zounds, fellow, I give him a shilling for leaving out my name, not for putting it in. This is one of the plaguy comforts of going anonymous.

(*Exit 2nd Waiter.*

(*Enter 3rd Waiter.*)

3RD WAITER. Two letters for Mr. H.

(*Exit.*

MR. H. From ladies (*opens them*). This from Melesinda, to remind me of the morning call I promised; the pretty creature positively languishes to be made Mrs. H. I believe I must indulge her (*affectedly*). This from her cousin, to bespeak me to some party, I suppose (*opening it*).—Oh, "this evening"—"Tea and cards"—(*surveying himself with complacency*). Dear H., thou art certainly a pretty fellow. I wonder what makes thee such a favourite among the ladies: I wish it may not be owing to the concealment of thy unfortunate——pshaw!

(*Enter 4th Waiter.*)

4TH WAITER. Sir, one Mr. Printagain is inquiring for you.

MR. H. Oh, I remember, the poet; he is publishing by subscription. Give him a guinea, and tell him he may put me down.

4TH WAITER. What name shall I tell him, Sir?

MR. H. Zounds, he is a poet; let him fancy a name.

(*Exit 4th Waiter.*

(*Enter 5th Waiter.*)

5TH WAITER. Sir, Bartlemy the lame beggar, that you sent a private donation to last Monday, has by some accident discovered his benefactor, and is at the door waiting to return thanks.

MR. H. Oh, poor fellow, who could put it into his head? Now I shall be teased by all his tribe, when once this is known. Well, tell him I am glad I could be of any service to him, and send him away.

5TH WAITER. I would have done so, Sir; but the object of his call now, he says, is only to know who he is obliged to.

MR. H. Why, me.

5TH WAITER. Yes, Sir.

MR. H. Me, me, me; who else, to be sure?

5TH WAITER. Yes, Sir; but he is anxious to know the name of his benefactor.

MR. H. Here is a pampered rogue of a beggar, that cannot be obliged to a gentleman in the way of his profession, but he must know the name, birth, parentage, and education of his benefactor! I warrant you, next he will require a certificate of one's good behaviour, and a magistrate's licence in one's pocket, lawfully empowering so and so to—give an alms. Anything more?

5TH WAITER. Yes, Sir; here has been Mr. Patriot, with the county petition to sign; and Mr. Failtime, that owes so much money, has sent to remind you of your promise to bail him.

MR. H. Neither of which I can do, while I have no name. Here is more of the plaguy comforts of going anonymous, that one can neither serve one's friend nor one's country. Damn it, a man had better be without a nose, than without a name. I will not live long in this mutilated, dismembered state; I will to Melesinda this instant, and try to forget these vexations. Melesinda! there is music in the name; but then, hang it! there is none in mine to answer to it.

(*Exit.*

(*While* MR. H. *has been speaking, two Gentlemen have been observing him curiously.*)

1ST GENT. Who the devil is this extraordinary personage?

2ND GENT. Who? Why 'tis Mr. H.

1ST GENT. Has he no more name?

2ND GENT. None that has yet transpired. No more! why that single letter has been enough to inflame the imaginations of all the ladies in Bath. He has been here but a fortnight, and is already received into all the first families.

1ST GENT. Wonderful! yet, nobody knows who he is, or where he comes from!

2ND GENT. He is vastly rich, gives away money as if he had infinity; dresses well, as you see; and for address, the mothers are all dying for fear the daughters should get him; and for the daughters, he may command them as absolutely as——. Melesinda, the rich heiress, 'tis thought, will carry him.

1ST GENT. And is it possible that a mere anonymous——

2ND GENT. Phoo! that is the charm.—Who is he? and what is he? and what is his name?——The man with the great nose on his face never excited more of the gaping passion of wonderment in the dames of Strasburg, than this new-comer, with the single letter to his name, has lighted up among the wives and maids of Bath: his simply having lodgings here, draws more visitors to the house than an election. Come with me to the Parade, and I will show you more of him.

(*Exeunt.*

(SCENE *in the Street.* MR. H. *walking,* BELVIL *meeting him.*)

BELVIL. My old Jamaica schoolfellow, that I have not seen for so many years? it must—it can be no other than Jack (*going up to him*). My dear Ho——

MR. H. (*Stopping his mouth*). Ho——! the devil, hush.

BELVIL. Why sure it is——

MR. H. It is, it is your old friend Jack, that shall be nameless.

BELVIL. My dear Ho——

MR. H. (*Stopping him*). Don't name it.

BELVIL. Name what?

MR. H. My curst unfortunate name. I have reasons to conceal it for a time.

BELVIL. I understand you—Creditors, Jack?

MR. H. No, I assure you.

BELVIL. Snapp'd up a ward, peradventure, and the whole Chancery at your heels?

MR. H. I don't use to travel with such cumbersome luggage.

BELVIL. You ha'n't taken a purse?

MR. H. To relieve you at once from all disgraceful conjecture, you must know, 'tis nothing but the sound of my name.

BELVIL. Ridiculous! 'tis true yours is none of the most romantic; but what can that signify in a man?

MR. H. You must understand that I am in some credit with the ladies.

BELVIL. With the ladies!

MR. H. And truly I think not without some pretensions. My fortune——

BELVIL. Sufficiently splendid, if I may judge from your appearance.

MR. H. My figure——

BELVIL. Airy, gay, and imposing.

MR. H. My parts——

BELVIL. Bright.

MR. H. My conversation——

BELVIL. Equally remote from flippancy and taciturnity.

MR. H. But then my name—damn my name!

BELVIL. Childish!

MR. H. Not so. Oh, Belvil, you are blest with one which sighing virgins may repeat without a blush, and for it change the paternal. But what virgin of any delicacy (and I require some in a wife) would endure to be called Mrs. ——?

BELVIL. Ha, ha, ha! most absurd. Did not Clementina Falconbridge, the romantic Clementina Falconbridge, fancy Tommy Potts? and Rosabella Sweetlips sacrifice her mellifluous appellative to Jack Deady? Matilda her cousin married a Gubbins, and her sister Amelia a Clutterbuck.

MR. H. Potts is tolerable, Deady is sufferable, Gubbins is bearable, and Clutterbuck is endurable, but Ho——

BELVIL. Hush, Jack, don't betray yourself. But you are really ashamed of the family name?

MR. H. Ay, and of my father that begot me, and my father's father, and all their forefathers that have borne it since the Conquest.

BELVIL. But how do you know the women are so squeamish?

MR. H. I have tried them. I tell you there is neither maiden of sixteen nor widow of sixty but would turn up their noses at it. I have been refused by nineteen virgins, twenty-nine relicts, and two old maids.

BELVIL. That was hard indeed, Jack.

MR. H. Parsons have stuck at publishing the banns, because they averred it was a heathenish name; parents have lingered their consent, because they suspected it was a fictitious name; and rivals have declined my challenges, because they pretended it was an ungentlemanly name.

BELVIL. Ha, ha, ha! but what course do you mean to pursue?

MR. H. To engage the affections of some generous girl, who will be content to take me as Mr. H.

BELVIL. Mr. H.

MR. H. Yes, that is the name I go by here; you know one likes to be as near the truth as possible.

BELVIL. Certainly. But what then? to get her to consent——

MR. H. To accompany me to the altar without a name——in short, to suspend her curiosity (that is all) till the moment the priest shall pronounce the irrevocable charm, which makes two names one.

BELVIL. And that name——and then she must be pleased, ha, Jack?

MR. H. Exactly such a girl it has been my fortune to meet with; hark'ee (*whispers*)——(*musing*). Yet, hang it! 'tis cruel to betray her confidence.

BELVIL. But the family name, Jack?

MR. H. As you say, the family name must be perpetuated.

BELVIL. Though it be but a homely one.

MR. H. True; but come, I will show you the house where dwells this credulous melting fair.

BELVIL. Ha, ha! my old friend dwindled down to one letter.

(*Exeunt.*

(SCENE.—*An Apartment in* MELESINDA'S *House.*
MELESINDA *sola, as if musing.*)

MELESINDA. H, H, H. Sure it must be something precious by its being concealed. It can't be Homer, that is a Heathen's name; nor Horatio, that is no surname; what if it be Hamlet? the Lord Hamlet—pretty, and I his poor distracted Ophelia! No, 'tis none of these; 'tis Harcourt or Hargrave, or some such sounding name, or Howard, highborn Howard, that would do; maybe it is Harley, methinks my H. resembles Harley, the feeling Harley. But I hear him! and from his own lips I will once for ever be resolved.

(*Enter* MR. H.)

MR. H. My dear Melesinda.

MELESINDA. My dear H., that is all you give me power to swear allegiance to,—to be enamoured of inarticulate sounds, and call with sighs upon an empty letter. But I will know.

MR. H. My dear Melesinda, press me no more for the disclosure of that, which in the face of day so soon must be revealed. Call it whim, humour, caprice, in me. Suppose I have sworn an oath, never, till the ceremony of our marriage is over, to disclose my true name.

MELESINDA. Oh! H, H, H. I cherish here a fire of restless curiosity which consumes me. 'Tis appetite, passion, call it whim, caprice, in me. Suppose I have sworn, I must and will know it this very night.

MR. H. Ungenerous Melesinda! I implore you to give me this one proof of your confidence. The holy vow once past, your H. shall not have a secret to withhold.

MELESINDA. My H. has overcome: his Melesinda shall pine away

and die, before she dare express a saucy inclination; but what shall I call
you till we are married?

MR. H. Call me? call me anything, call me Love, Love! ay Love: Love
will do very well.

MELESINDA. How many syllables is it, Love?

MR. H. How many? ud, that is coming to the question with a vengeance! One, two, three, four,—what does it signify how many syllables?

MELESINDA. How many syllables, Love?

MR. H. My Melesinda's mind, I had hoped, was superior to this childish curiosity.

MELESINDA. How many letters are there in it?

Exit MR. H. *followed by* MELESINDA, *repeating the question.*

(SCENE.—*A Room in the Inn. Two Waiters disputing.*)

1ST WAITER. Sir Harbottle Hammond, you may depend upon it.

2ND WAITER. Sir Harry Hardcastle, I tell you.

1ST WAITER. The Hammonds of Huntingdonshire.

2ND WAITER. The Hardcastles of Hertfordshire.

1ST WAITER. The Hammonds.

2ND WAITER. Don't tell me: does not Hardcastle begin with an H.?

1ST WAITER. So does Hammond for that matter.

2ND WAITER. Faith, so it does if you go to spell it. I did not think of
that. I begin to be of your opinion; he is certainly a Hammond.

1ST WAITER. Here comes Susan Chambermaid: maybe she can tell.

(*Enter* SUSAN.)

BOTH. Well, Susan, have you heard anything who the strange gentleman is?

SUSAN. Haven't you heard? it's all come out! Mrs. Guesswell, the
parson's widow, has been here about it. I overheard her talking in confidence to Mrs. Setter and Mrs. Pointer, and she says they were holding
a sort of a *cummitty* about it.

BOTH. What? What?

SUSAN. There can't be a doubt of it, she says, what from his *figger* and
the appearance he cuts, and his *sumpshous* way of living, and above all
from the remarkable circumstance that his surname should begin with
an H, that he must be———

BOTH. Well, well———

SUSAN. Neither more nor less than the Prince.

BOTH. Prince!

SUSAN. The Prince of Hessey-Cassel in disguise.

BOTH. Very likely, very likely.

SUSAN. Oh, there can't be a doubt on it. Mrs. Guesswell says she
knows it.

1ST WAITER. Now if we could be sure that the Prince of Hessey what-
do-you-call-him was in England on his travels.

2ND WAITER. Get a newspaper. Look in the newspapers.
SUSAN. Fiddle of the newspapers; who else can it be?
BOTH. That is very true (*gravely*).

(*Enter* LANDLORD.)

LANDLORD.—Here, Susan, James, Philip, where are you all? The London coach is come in, and there is Mr. Fillaside, the fat passenger, has been bawling for somebody to help him off with his boots.

(*The Chambermaid and Waiters slip out.*

(*Solus.*) The house is turned upside down since the strange gentleman came into it. Nothing but guessing and speculating, and speculating and guessing; waiters and chambermaids getting into corners and speculating; ostlers and stable-boys speculating in the yard; I believe the very horses in the stable are speculating too, for there they stand in a musing posture, nothing for them to eat, and not seeming to care whether they have anything or no; and after all what does it signify? I hate such curious —— odso, I must take this box up into his bedroom— he charged me to see to it myself;—I hate such inquisitive——I wonder what is in it—it feels heavy; (*reads*) "Leases, title-deeds, wills." Here now a man might satisfy his curiosity at once. Deeds must have names to them, so must leases and wills. But I wouldn't—no I wouldn't——it is a pretty box too—prettily dovetailed—I admire the fashion of it much. But I'd cut my fingers off, before I'd do such a dirty—what have I to do—curse the keys, how they rattle!—rattle in one's pockets—the keys and the halfpence (*takes out a bunch and plays with them*). I wonder if any of these would fit; one might just try them, but I wouldn't lift up the lid if they did. Oh no, what should I be the richer for knowing? (*All this time he tries the keys one by one.*) What's his name to me? a thousand names begin with an H. I hate people that are always prying, poking and prying into things,—thrusting their finger into one place—a mighty little hole this—and their keys into another. Oh Lord! little rusty fits it! but what is that to me? I wouldn't go to—no, no— but it is odd little rusty should just happen—(*While he is turning up the lid of the box,* MR. H. *enters behind him unperceived.*)

MR. H. What are you about, you dog?

LANDLORD. Oh, Lord, Sir! pardon; no thief, as I hope to be saved. Little Pry was always honest.

MR. H. What else could move you to open that box?

LANDLORD. Sir, don't kill me, and I will confess the whole truth. This box happened to be lying—that is, I happened to be carrying this box, and I happened to have my keys out, and so—little rusty happened to fit——

MR. H. So little rusty happened to fit!—and would not a rope fit that rogue's neck? I see the papers have not been moved: all is safe, but it was as well to frighten him a little (*aside*). Come, Landlord, as I think you honest, and suspect you only intended to gratify a little foolish curiosity——

LANDLORD. That was all, Sir, upon my veracity.

MR. H. For this time I will pass it over. Your name is Pry, I think?

LANDLORD. Yes, Sir, Jeremiah Pry, at your service.

MR. H. An apt name: you have a prying temper—I mean, some little curiosity—a sort of inquisitiveness about you.

LANDLORD. A natural thirst after knowledge you may call it, Sir. When a boy, I was never easy but when I was thrusting up the lids of some of my school-fellows' boxes,—not to steal anything, upon my honour, Sir,—only to see what was in them; have had pens stuck in my eyes for peeping through keyholes after knowledge; could never see a cold pie with the legs dangling out at top, but my fingers were for lifting up the crust,—just to try if it were pigeon or partridge,—for no other reason in the world. Surely I think my passion for nuts was owing to the pleasure of cracking the shell to get at something concealed, more than to any delight I took in eating the kernel. In short, Sir, this appetite has grown with my growth.

MR. H. You will certainly be hanged some day for peeping into some bureau or other, just to see what is in it.

LANDLORD. That is my fear, Sir. The thumps and kicks I have had for peering into parcels, and turning of letters inside out,—just for curiosity! The blankets I have been made to dance in for searching parish registers for old ladies' ages,—just for curiosity! Once I was dragged through a horse-pond, only for peeping into a closet that had glass doors to it, while my Lady Bluegarters was undressing,—just for curiosity!

MR. H. A very harmless piece of curiosity, truly; and now, Mr. Pry, first have the goodness to leave that box with me, and then do me the favour to carry your curiosity so far, as to inquire if my servants are within.

LANDLORD. I shall, Sir. Here, David, Jonathan,—I think I hear them coming,—shall make bold to leave you, Sir.

(*Exit.*

MR. H. Another tolerable specimen of the comforts of going anonymous!

(*Enter Two Footmen.*)

1ST FOOTMAN. You speak first.

2ND FOOTMAN. No, you had better speak.

1ST FOOTMAN. You promised to begin.

MR. H. They have something to say to me. The rascals want their wages raised, I suppose; there is always a favour to be asked when they come smiling. Well, poor rogues, service is but a hard bargain at the best. I think I must not be close with them. Well, David—well, Jonathan.

1ST FOOTMAN. We have served your honour faithfully——

2ND FOOTMAN. Hope your honour won't take offence——

MR. H. The old story, I suppose—wages?

1ST FOOTMAN. That's not it, your honour.

2ND FOOTMAN. You speak.

1ST FOOTMAN. But if your honour would just be pleased to——

2ND FOOTMAN. Only be pleased to——

MR. H. Be quick with what you have to say, for I am in haste.

1ST FOOTMAN. Just to——

2ND FOOTMAN. Let us know who it is——

1ST FOOTMAN. Who it is we have the honour to serve.

MR. H. Why me, me, me; you serve me.

2ND FOOTMAN. Yes, Sir; but we do not know who you are.

MR. H. Childish curiosity! do not you serve a rich master, a gay master, an indulgent master?

1ST FOOTMAN. Ah, Sir! the figure you make is to us, your poor servants, the principal mortification.

2ND FOOTMAN. When we get over a pot at the public-house, or in a gentleman's kitchen, or elsewhere, as poor servants must have their pleasures—when the question goes round, who is your master? and who do you serve? and one says, I serve Lord So-and-So, and another, I am Squire Such-a-one's footman——

1ST FOOTMAN. We have nothing to say for it, but that we serve Mr. H.

2ND FOOTMAN. Or Squire H.

MR. H. Really you are a couple of pretty modest, reasonable personages! but I hope you will take it as no offence, gentlemen, if, upon a dispassionate review of all that you have said, I think fit not to tell you any more of my name, than I have chosen for especial purposes to communicate to the rest of the world.

1ST FOOTMAN. Why, then, Sir, you may suit yourself.

2ND FOOTMAN. We tell you plainly, we cannot stay.

1ST FOOTMAN. We don't choose to serve Mr. H.

2ND FOOTMAN. Nor any Mr. or Squire in the alphabet——

1ST FOOTMAN. That lives in Chris-cross Row.

MR. H. Go, for a couple of ungrateful, inquisitive, senseless rascals! Go hang, starve, or drown!—Rogues, to speak thus irreverently of the alphabet—I shall live to see you glad to serve old Q—to curl the wig of great S—adjust the dot of little i—stand behind the chair of X, Y, Z —wear the livery of Etcætera—and ride behind the sulky of And-by-itself-and!

(Exit in a rage.

ACT II

(SCENE—*A handsome Apartment well lighted, Tea, Cards, etc.—A large party of Ladies and Gentlemen; among them* MELESINDA.)

1ST LADY. I wonder when the charming man will be here.

2ND LADY. He is a delightful creature! Such a polish——

3RD LADY. Such an air in all that he does or says——

4TH LADY. Yet gifted with a strong understanding——

5TH LADY. But has your ladyship the remotest idea of what his true name is?

1ST LADY. They say, his very servants do not know it. His French valet, that has lived with him these two years——

2ND LADY. There, Madam, I must beg leave to set you right: my coachman——

1ST LADY. I have it from the very best authority: my footman——

2ND LADY. Then, Madam, you have set your servants on——

1ST LADY. No, Madam, I would scorn any such little mean ways of coming at a secret. For my part, I don't think any secret of that consequence.

2ND LADY. That's just like me; I make a rule of troubling my head with nobody's business but my own.

MELESINDA. But then, she takes care to make everybody's business her own, and so to justify herself that way——

(Aside.)

1ST LADY. My dear Melesinda, you look thoughtful.

MELESINDA. Nothing.

2ND LADY. Give it a name.

MELESINDA. Perhaps it is nameless.

1ST LADY. As the object——Come, never blush, nor deny it, child. Bless me, what great ugly thing is that, that dangles at your bosom?

MELESINDA. This? it is a cross: how do you like it?

2ND LADY. A cross! Well, to me it looks for all the world like a great staring H.

(Here a general laugh.)

MELESINDA. Malicious creatures! Believe me it is a cross, and nothing but a cross.

1ST LADY. A cross, I believe, you would willingly hang at.

MELESINDA. Intolerable spite!

(MR. H. *is announced.*)

(*Enter* MR. H.)

1ST LADY. O, Mr. H., we are so glad——

2ND LADY. We have been so dull——

3RD LADY. So perfectly lifeless——You owe it to us, to be more than commonly entertaining.

MR. H. Ladies, this is so obliging——

4TH LADY. O, Mr. H., those ranunculas you said were dying, pretty things, they have got up——

5TH LADY. I have worked that sprig you commended—I want you to come——

MR. H. Ladies——

6TH LADY. I have sent for that piece of music from London.

MR. H. The Mozart—(*seeing* MELESINDA)—Melesinda!

SEVERAL LADIES AT ONCE. Nay, positively, Melesinda, you shan't engross him all to yourself.

> (*While the Ladies are pressing about* MR. H., *the gentlemen show signs of displeasure.*

1ST GENT. We shan't be able to edge in a word, now this coxcomb is come.

2ND GENT. Damn him, I will affront him.

1ST GENT. Sir, with your leave, I have a word to say to one of these ladies.

2ND GENT. If we could be heard——

> (*The Ladies pay no attention but to* MR. H.

MR. H. You see, gentlemen, how the matter stands. (*Hums an air.*) I am not my own master: positively I exist and breathe but to be agreeable to these——Did you speak?

1ST GENT. And affects absence of mind—Puppy!

MR. H. Who spoke of absence of mind; did you, Madam? How do you do, Lady Wearwell—how do? I did not see your ladyship before—what was I about to say—O—absence of mind. I am the most unhappy dog in that way, sometimes spurt out the strangest things—the most malapropos—without meaning to give the least offence, upon my honour—sheer absence of mind—things I would have given the world not to have said.

1ST GENT. Do you hear the coxcomb?

1ST LADY. Great wits, they say——

2ND LADY. Your fine geniuses are most given——

3RD LADY. Men of bright parts are commonly too vivacious——

MR. H. But you shall hear. I was to dine the other day at a great Nabob's that must be nameless, who, between ourselves, is strongly suspected of—being very rich, that's all. John, my valet, who knows my foible, cautioned me, while he was dressing me, as he usually does where he thinks there's a danger of my committing a *lapsus,* to take care in my conversation how I made any allusion direct or indirect to presents—you understand me? I set out double charged with my fellow's consideration and my own; and, to do myself justice, behaved with tolerable circumspection for the first half-hour or so—till at last a gentleman in company, who was indulging a free vein of raillery at the expense of the ladies, stumbled upon that expression of the poet, which calls them "fair defects."

1ST LADY. It is Pope, I believe, who says it.

MR. H. No, Madam; Milton. Where was I? Oh, "fair defects." This gave occasion to a critic in company, to deliver his opinion on the phrase —that led to an enumeration of all the various words which might have been used instead of "defect," as want, absence, poverty, deficiency, lack. This moment I, who had not been attending to the progress of the argument (as the denouement will show), starting suddenly up out of one of my reveries, by some unfortunate connexion of ideas, which the last fatal word had excited, the devil put it into my head to turn round to the Nabob, who was sitting next me, and in a very marked manner (as it seemed to the company) to put the question to him, Pray, Sir, what may be the exact value of a lack of rupees? You may guess the confusion which followed.

1ST LADY. What a distressing circumstance!

2ND LADY. To a delicate mind——

3RD LADY. How embarrassing——

4TH LADY. I declare, I quite pity you.

1ST GENT. Puppy!

MR. H. A Baronet at the table, seeing my dilemma, jogged my elbow; and a good-natured Duchess, who does everything with a grace peculiar to herself, trod on my toes at that instant: this brought me to myself, and—covered with blushes, and pitied by all the ladies—I withdrew.

1ST LADY. How charmingly he tells a story.

2ND LADY. But how distressing!

MR. H. Lord Squandercounsel, who is my particular friend, was pleased to rally me in his inimitable way upon it next day. I shall never forget a sensible thing he said on the occasion—speaking of absence of mind, my foible—says he, my dear Hogs——

SEVERAL LADIES. Hogs——what—ha——

MR. H. My dear Hogsflesh—my name—(*here a universal scream*)—O my cursed unfortunate tongue!—H. I mean—where was I?

1ST LADY. Filthy—abominable!

2ND LADY. Unutterable!

3RD LADY. Hogs—foh!

4TH LADY. Disgusting!

5TH LADY. Vile!

6TH LADY. Shocking!

1ST LADY. Odious!

2ND LADY. Hogs——pah!

3RD LADY. A smelling bottle—look to Miss Melesinda. Poor thing! it is no wonder. You had better keep off from her, Mr. Hogsflesh, and not be pressing about her in her circumstances.

1ST GENT. Good time of day to you, Mr. Hogsflesh.

2ND GENT. The compliments of the season to you, Mr. Hogsflesh.

MR. H. This is too much—flesh and blood cannot endure it.

1ST GENT. What flesh?—hog's-flesh?

2ND GENT. How he sets up his bristles!

MR. H. Bristles!

1ST GENT. He looks as fierce as a hog in armour.

MR. H. A hog!——Madam!——(*here he severally accosts the Ladies, who by turns repel him*).

1ST LADY. Extremely obliged to you for your attentions; but don't want a partner.

2ND LADY. Greatly flattered by your preference: but believe I shall remain single.

3RD LADY. Shall always acknowledge your politeness; but have no thoughts of altering my condition.

4TH LADY. Always be happy to respect you as a friend; but you must not look for anything further.

5TH LADY. No doubt of your ability to make any woman happy; but have no thoughts of changing my name.

6TH LADY. Must tell you, Sir, that if, by your insinuations, you think to prevail with me, you have got the wrong sow by the ear. Does he think any lady would go to pig with him?

OLD LADY. Must beg you to be less particular in your addresses to me. Does he take me for a Jew, to long after forbidden meats?

MR. H. I shall go mad!—to be refused by old Mother Damnable— she that's so old, nobody knows whether she was ever married or no, but passes for a maid by courtesy; her juvenile exploits being beyond the farthest stretch of tradition!—old Mother Damnable!

(Exeunt all, either pitying or seeming to avoid him.

(SCENE—*The street.* BELVIL *and another Gentleman.*)

BELVIL. Poor Jack, I am really sorry for him. The account which you give me of his mortifying change of reception at the assembly, would be highly diverting, if it gave me less pain to hear it. With all his amusing absurdities, and amongst them not the least, a predominant desire to be thought well of by the fair sex, he has an abundant share of good-nature, and is a man of honour. Notwithstanding all that has happened, Melesinda may do worse than take him yet. But did the women resent it so deeply as you say?

GENT. O, intolerably—they fled him as fearfully when 'twas once blown, as a man would be avoided, who was suddenly discovered to have marks of the plague, and as fast; when before they had been ready to devour the foolishest thing he could say.

BELVIL. Ha! ha! so frail is the tenure by which these women's favourites commonly hold their envied pre-eminence. Well, I must go find him out and comfort him. I suppose, I shall find him at the inn.

GENT. Either there or at Melesinda's—Adieu!

(Exeunt.

(SCENE—MR. H———'s *Apartment.*)

MR. H. (*solus.*) Was ever anything so mortifying? to be refused by old Mother Damnable!—with such parts and address,—and the little squeamish devils, to dislike me for a name, a sound.—Oh my cursed name! that it was something I could be revenged on! if it were alive, that I might tread upon it, or crush it, or pummel it, or kick it, or spit it out—for it sticks in my throat, and will choke me.

My plaguy ancestors! if they had left me but a Van, or a Mac, or an Irish O', it had been something to qualify it—Mynheer Van Hogsflesh,

—or Sawney Mac Hogsflesh,—or Sir Phelim O'Hogsflesh,—but down-right blunt———. If it had been any other name in the world, I could have borne it. If it had been the name of a beast, as Bull, Fox, Kid, Lamb, Wolf, Lion; or of a bird, as Sparrow, Hawk, Buzzard, Daw, Finch, Nightingale; or of a fish, as Sprat, Herring, Salmon; or the name of a thing, as Ginger, Hay, Wood; or of a colour, as Black, Grey, White, Green; or of a sound, as Bray; or the name of a month, as March, May; or of a place, as Barnet, Baldock, Hitchen; or the name of a coin, as Farthing, Penny, Twopenny; or of a profession, as Butcher, Baker, Carpenter, Piper, Fisher, Fletcher, Fowler, Glover; or a Jew's name, as Solomons, Isaacs, Jacobs; or a personal name, as Foot, Leg, Crookshanks, Heaviside, Sidebottom, Longbottom, Ramsbottom, Winterbottom; or a long name, as Blanchenhagen, or Blanchenhausen; or a short name, as Crib, Crisp, Crips, Tag, Trot, Tub, Phips, Padge, Papps, or Prig, or Wig, or Pip, or Trip; Trip had been something, but Ho———. (*Walks about in great agitation—recovering his calmness a little, sits down.*)

Farewell the most distant thoughts of marriage; the finger-circling ring, the purity-fingering glove, the envy-pining bridemaids, the wishing parson, and the simpering clerk. Farewell the ambiguous blush-raising joke, the titter-provoking pun, the morning-stirring drum.—No son of mine shall exist, to bear my ill-fated name. No nurse come chuckling, to tell me it is a boy. No midwife, leering at me from under the lids of professional gravity. I dreamed of caudle.—(*Sings in a melancholy tone.*) Lullaby, Lullaby,—hush-a-by-baby—how like its papa it is!— (*Makes motions as if he was nursing.*) And then, when grown up, "Is this your son, Sir?" "Yes, Sir, a poor copy of me, a sad young dog,—just what his father was at his age,—I have four more at home." Oh! oh! oh!

(*Enter* LANDLORD.)

MR. H. Landlord, I must pack up to-night; you will see all my things got ready.

LANDLORD. Hope your Honour does not intend to quit the Blue Boar, —sorry anything has happened.

MR. H. He has heard it all.

LANDLORD. Your Honour has had some mortification, to be sure, as a man may say; you have brought your pigs to a fine market.

MR. H. Pigs!

LANDLORD. What then? take old Pry's advice, and never mind it. Don't scorch your crackling for 'em, Sir.

MR. H. Scorch my crackling! a queer phrase; but I suppose he don't mean to affront me.

LANDLORD. What is done can't be undone; you can't make a silken purse out of a sow's ear.

MR. H. As you say, Landlord, thinking of a thing does but augment it.

LANDLORD. Does but *hogment* it, indeed, Sir.

MR. H. *Hogment* it! damn it, I said augment it.

LANDLORD. Lord, Sir, 'tis not everybody has such gift of fine phrases as your Honour, that can lard his discourse—

MR. H. Lard!

LANDLORD. Suppose they do smoke you—

MR. H. Smoke me!

LANDLORD. One of my phrases; never mind my words, Sir, my meaning is good. We all mean the same thing, only you express yourself one way, and I another, that's all. The meaning's the same; it is all pork.

MR. H. That's another of your phrases, I presume.

(Bell rings, and the Landlord called for.

LANDLORD. Anon, anon.

MR. H. Oh, I wish I were anonymous.

(Exeunt several ways.

(SCENE—*Melesinda's Apartment.* MELESINDA *and* Maid.)

MAID. Lord, Madam! before I'd take on as you do about a foolish—what signifies a name? Hogs—Hogs—what is it—is just as good as any other, for what I see.

MELESINDA. Ignorant creature! yet she is perhaps blest in the absence of those ideas, which, while they add a zest to the few pleasures which fall to the lot of superior natures to enjoy, doubly edge the——

MAID. Superior natures! a fig! If he's hog by name, he's not hog by nature, that don't follow—his name don't make him anything, does it? He don't grunt the more for it, nor squeak, that ever I hear; he likes his victuals out of a plate, as other Christians do; you never see him go to the trough——

MELESINDA. Unfeeling wretch! yet possibly her intentions——

MAID. For instance, Madam, my name is Finch—Betty Finch. I don't whistle the more for that, nor long after canary-seed while I can get good wholesome mutton—no, nor you can't catch me by throwing salt on my tail. If you come to that, hadn't I a young man used to come after me, they said courted me—his name was Lion, Francis Lion, a tailor; but though he was fond enough of me, for all that he never offered to eat me.

MELESINDA. How fortunate that the discovery has been made before it was too late! Had I listened to his deceits, and, as the perfidious man had almost persuaded me, precipitated myself into an inextricable engagement before——

MAID. No great harm if you had. You'd only have bought a pig in a poke—and what then? Oh, here he comes creeping——

(Enter MR. H. *abject.*)

Go to her, Mr. Hogs—Hogs—Hogsbristles, what's your name? Don't be afraid, man—don't give it up—she's not crying—only *summat* has made her eyes red—she has got a sty in her eye, I believe—(*going*).

MELESINDA. You are not going, Betty?

MAID. O, Madam, never mind me—I shall be back in the twinkling of a pig's whisker, as they say.

(*Exit.*

MR. H. Melesinda, you behold before you a wretch who would have betrayed your confidence—but it was love that prompted him; who would have trick'd you, by an unworthy concealment, into a participation of that disgrace which a superficial world has agreed to attach to a name—but with it you would have shared a fortune not contemptible, and a heart—but 'tis over now. That name he is content to bear alone —to go where the persecuted syllables shall be no more heard, or excite no meaning—some spot where his native tongue has never penetrated, nor any of his countrymen have landed, to plant their unfeeling satire, their brutal wit, and national ill manners—where no Englishmen— (*Here* MELESINDA, *who has been pouting during this speech, fetches a deep sigh*). Some yet undiscovered Otaheite, where witless, unapprehensive savages shall innocently pronounce the ill-fated sounds, and think them not inharmonious.

MELESINDA. Oh!

MR. H. Who knows but among the female natives might be found——

MELESINDA. Sir! (*raising her head*).

MR. H. One who would be more kind than—some Oberea—Queen Oberea.

MELESINDA. Oh!

MR. H. Or what if I were to seek for proofs of reciprocal esteem among unprejudiced African maids, in Monomotopa?

(*Enter Servant.*)

SERVANT. Mr. Belvil.

(*Exit.*

(*Enter* BELVIL.)

MR. H. Monomotopa (*musing*).

BELVIL. Heyday, Jack! what means this mortified face? nothing has happened, I hope, between this lady and you? I beg pardon, Madam, but understanding my friend was with you, I took the liberty of seeking him here. Some little difference possibly which a third person can adjust—not a word. Will you, Madam, as this gentleman's friend, suffer me to be the arbitrator—strange—hark'ee, Jack, nothing has come out, has there? you understand me. Oh, I guess how it is—somebody has got at your secret; you haven't blabbed it yourself, have you? ha! ha! ha! I could find in my heart—Jack, what would you give me if I should relieve you?

MR. H. No power of man can relieve me (*sighs*); but it must lie at the root, gnawing at the root—here it will lie.

BELVIL. No power of man? not a common man, I grant you: for instance, a subject—it's out of the power of any subject.

MR. H. Gnawing at the root—there it will lie.

BELVIL. Such a thing has been known as a name to be changed; but not by a subject—(*shows a Gazette*).

MR. H. Gnawing at the root—(*suddenly snatches the paper out of* BELVIL's *hand*)—ha! pish! nonsense! give it me—what! (*reads*) promotions, bankrupts—a great many bankrupts this week—there it will lie. (*Lays it down, takes it up again, and reads.*) "The King has been graciously pleased"—gnawing at the root—"graciously pleased to grant unto John Hogsflesh,"—the devil—"Hogsflesh, Esq., of Sty Hall, in the county of Hants, his royal licence and authority"—O Lord! O Lord!— "that he and his issue"—me and my issue—"may take and use the surname and arms of Bacon"—Bacon, the surname and arms of Bacon— "in pursuance of an injunction contained in the last will and testament of Nicholas Bacon, Esq., his late uncle, as well as out of grateful respect to his memory":—grateful respect! poor old soul——here's more— "and that such arms may be first duly exemplified"—they shall, I will take care of that—"according to the laws of arms, and recorded in the Herald's Office."

BELVIL. Come, Madam, give me leave to put my own interpretation upon your silence, and to plead for my friend, that now that only obstacle which seemed to stand in the way of your union is removed, you will suffer me to complete the happiness which my news seems to have brought him, by introducing him with a new claim to your favour, by the name of Mr. Bacon. (*Takes their hands and joins them, which* MELESINDA *seems to give consent to with a smile.*)

MR. H. Generous Melesinda! my dear friend—"he and his issue," me and my issue!—O Lord!——

BELVIL. I wish you joy, Jack, with all my heart.

MR. H. Bacon, Bacon, Bacon—how odd it sounds! I could never be tired of hearing it. There was Lord Chancellor Bacon. Methinks I have some of the Verulam blood in me already.—Methinks I could look through Nature—there was Friar Bacon, a conjurer,—I feel as if I could conjure too——

(*Enter a Servant.*)

SERVANT. Two young ladies and an old lady are at the door, inquiring if you see company, Madam.

MR. H. "Surname and arms"——

MELESINDA. Show them up,—My dear Mr. Bacon, moderate your joy.

(*Enter three Ladies, being part of those who were at the Assembly.*)

1ST LADY. My dear Melesinda, how do you do?

2ND LADY. How do you do? We have been so concerned for you——

OLD LADY. We have been so concerned—(*seeing him*)—Mr. Hogsflesh——

MR. H. There's no such person—nor there never was—nor 'tis not fit there should be—"surname and arms"——

BELVIL. It is true what my friend would express; we have been all in a mistake, ladies. Very true, the name of this gentleman was what you call it, but it is so no longer. The succession to the long-contested Bacon estate is at length decided, and with it my friend succeeds to the name of his deceased relative.

MR. H. "His Majesty has been graciously pleased"——

1ST LADY. I am sure we all join in hearty congratulation—(*sighs*).

2ND LADY. And wish you joy with all our hearts—(*heigh ho!*)

OLD LADY. And hope you will enjoy the name and estate for many years—(*cries*).

BELVIL. Ha! ha! ha! mortify them a little, Jack.

1ST LADY. Hope you intend to stay——

2ND LADY. With us some time——

OLD LADY. In these parts——

MR. H. Ladies, for your congratulations I thank you; for the favours you have lavished on me, and in particular for this lady's (*turning to the old Lady*) good opinion, I rest your debtor. As to any future favours—(*accosts them severally in the order in which he was refused by them at the assembly*)—Madam, shall always acknowledge your politeness; but at present, you see, I am engaged with a partner. Always be happy to respect you as a friend, but you must not look for anything further. Must beg of you to be less particular in your addresses to me. Ladies all, with this piece of advice, of Bath and you

Your ever grateful servant takes his leave.
Lay your plans surer when you plot to grieve;
See, while you kindly mean to mortify
Another, the wild arrow do not fly,
And gall yourself. For once you've been mistaken;
Your shafts have miss'd their aim—Hogsflesh has saved his Bacon.

JOHN WOODVIL

A TRAGEDY

CHARACTERS

SIR WALTER WOODVIL.

JOHN,
SIMON, } *his sons.*

LOVEL,
GRAY, } *pretended friends of John.*

SANDFORD. *Sir Walter's old steward.*
MARGARET. *Orphan ward of Sir Walter.*
FOUR GENTLEMEN. *John's riotous companions.*
SERVANTS.

SCENE—*for the most part Sir Walter's mansion in* DEVONSHIRE; *at other times in the Forest of* SHERWOOD.

TIME—*soon after the* RESTORATION.

JOHN WOODVIL

A TRAGEDY

ACT THE FIRST

(SCENE—*A Servants' Apartment in Woodvil Hall. Servants drinking.*
TIME—*the Morning.*)

(*A Song, by* DANIEL.)

"When the King enjoys his own again."

PETER. A delicate song. Where didst learn it, fellow?

DAN. Even there, where thou learnest thy oaths and thy politics—at our master's table.—Where else should a serving-man pick up his poor accomplishments?

MAR. Well spoken, Daniel. O rare Daniel! his oaths and his politics! excellent!

FRAN. And where didst pick up thy knavery, Daniel?

PETER. That came to him by inheritance. His family have supplied the shire of Devon, time out of mind, with good thieves and bad serving-men. All of his race have come into the world without their conscience.

MAR. Good thieves, and bad serving-men! Better and better. I marvel what Daniel hath got to say in reply.

DAN. I marvel more when thou wilt say anything to the purpose, thou shallow serving-men, whose swiftest conceit carries thee no higher than to apprehend with difficulty the stale jests of us thy compeers. When was't ever known to club thy own particular jest among us?

MAR. Most unkind Daniel, to speak such biting things of me!

FRAN. See—if he hath not brought tears into the poor fellow's eyes with the saltness of his rebuke.

DAN. No offence, brother Martin—I meant none. 'Tis true, Heaven gives gifts, and withholds them. It has been pleased to bestow upon me a nimble invention to the manufacture of a jest; and upon thee, Martin, an indifferent bad capacity to understand my meaning.

MAR. Is that all? I am content. Here's my hand.

FRAN. Well, I like a little innocent mirth myself, but never could endure bawdry.

DAN. *Quot homines tot sententiæ.*

MAR. And what is that?

DAN. 'Tis Greek, and argues difference of opinion.

427

MAR. I hope there is none between us.

DAN. Here's to thee, brother Martin. (*Drinks.*)

MAR. And to thee, Daniel. (*Drinks.*)

FRAN. And to thee, Peter. (*Drinks.*)

PETER. Thank you, Francis. And here's to thee. (*Drinks.*)

MAR. I shall be fuddled anon.

DAN. And drunkenness I hold to be a very despicable vice.

ALL. O! a shocking vice. (*They drink round.*)

PETER. Inasmuch as it taketh away the understanding.

DAN. And makes the eyes red.

PETER. And the tongue to stammer.

DAN. And to blab out secrets.

(*During this conversation they continue drinking.*

PETER. Some men do not know an enemy from a friend when they are drunk.

DAN. Certainly sobriety is the health of the soul.

MAR. Now I know I am going to be drunk.

DAN. How canst tell, dry-bones?

MAR. Because I begin to be melancholy. That's always a sign.

FRAN. Take care of Martin, he'll topple off his seat else.

(MARTIN *drops asleep.*

PETER. Times are greatly altered, since young master took upon himself the government of this household.

ALL. Greatly altered.

FRAN. I think everything be altered for the better since His Majesty's blessed restoration.

PETER. In Sir Walter's days there was no encouragement given to good housekeeping.

ALL. None.

DAN. For instance, no possibility of getting drunk before two in the afternoon.

PETER. Every man his allowance of ale at breakfast—his quart!

ALL. A quart!!   (*In derision.*)

DAN. Nothing left to our own sweet discretions.

PETER. Whereby it may appear, we were treated more like beasts than what we were—discreet and reasonable serving-men.

ALL. Like beasts.

MAR. (*opening his eyes*). Like beasts.

DAN. To sleep, wagtail!

FRAN. I marvel all this while where the old gentleman has found means to secrete himself. It seems no man has heard of him since the day of the King's return. Can any tell why our young master, being favoured by the court, should not have interest to procure his father's pardon?

DAN. Marry, I think 'tis the obstinacy of the old Knight, that will not be beholden to the court for his safety.

MAR. Now that is wilful.

FRAN. But can any tell me the place of his concealment?

PETER. That cannot I; but I have my conjectures.

DAN. Two hundred pounds, as I hear, to the man that shall apprehend him.

FRAN. Well, I have my suspicions.

PETER. And so have I.

MAR. And I can keep a secret.

FRAN. (*to* PETER). Warwickshire, you mean.   (*Aside.*

PETER. Perhaps not.

FRAN. Nearer, perhaps.

PETER. I say nothing.

DAN. I hope there is none in this company would be mean enough to betray him.

ALL. O Lord, surely not.

(They drink to SIR WALTER'S *safety.*

FRAN. I have often wondered how our master came to be excepted by name in the late Act of Oblivion.

DAN. Shall I tell the reason?

ALL. Ay, do.

DAN. 'Tis thought he is no great friend to the present happy establishment.

ALL. O! monstrous!

PETER. Fellow-servants, a thought strikes me.—Do we, or do we not, come under the penalties of the treason-act, by reason of our being privy to this man's concealment?

ALL. Truly a sad consideration.

(To them enters SANDFORD *suddenly.)*

SAND. You well-fed and unprofitable grooms,
Maintain'd for state, not use;
You lazy feasters at another's cost,
That eat like maggots into an estate,
And do as little work,
Being indeed but foul excrescences,
And no just parts in a well-order'd family;
You base and rascal imitators,
Who act up to the height your master's vices,
But cannot read his virtues in your bond:
Which of you, as I enter'd, spake of betraying?
Was it you, or you, or thin-face, was it you?

MAR. Whom does he call thin-face?

SAND. No prating, loon, but tell me who he was,
That I may brain the villain with my staff,
That seeks Sir Walter's life!
You miserable men,
With minds more slavish than your slave's estate
Have you that noble bounty so forgot,

Which took you from the looms, and from the ploughs,
Which better had ye follow'd, fed ye, clothed ye,
And entertain'd ye in a worthy service,
Where your best wages was the world's repute,
That thus ye seek his life, by whom ye live.
Have you forgot too,
How often in old times
Your drunken mirths have stunn'd day's sober ears,
Carousing full cups to Sir Walter's health?—
Whom now ye would betray, but that he lies
Out of the reach of your poor treacheries.
This learn from me,
Our master's secret sleeps with trustier tongues,
Than will unlock themselves to carls like you.
Go, get you gone, you knaves. Who stirs? this staff
Shall teach you better manners else.
    ALL. Well, we are going.
    SAND. And quickly too, ye had better, for I see
Young mistress Margaret coming this way.
                   (*Exeunt all but* SANDFORD.

    (*Enter* MARGARET, *as in a fright, pursued by a Gentleman, who, see-
ing* SANDFORD, *retires muttering a curse.*)

    SAND. Good-morrow to my fair mistress. 'Twas a chance
I saw you, lady, so intent was I
On chiding hence these graceless serving-men,
Who cannot break their fast at morning meals
Without debauch and mis-timed riotings.
This house hath been a scene of nothing else
But atheist riot and profane excess,
Since my old master quitted all his rights here.
    MARG. Each day I endure fresh insult from the scorn
Of Woodvil's friends, the uncivil jests
And free discourses of the dissolute men
That haunt this mansion, making me their mirth.
    SAND. Does my young master know of these affronts?
    MARG. I cannot tell. Perhaps he has not been told.
Perhaps he might have seen them if he would.
I have known him more quick-sighted. Let that pass.
All things seem changed, I think. I had a friend
(I can't but weep to think him alter'd too)—
These things are best forgotten; but I knew
A man, a young man, young, and full of honour,
That would have pick'd a quarrel for a straw,
And fought it out to the extremity,
E'en with the dearest friend he had alive,
On but a bare surmise, a possibility,

That Margaret had suffer'd an affront.
Some are too tame, that were too splenetic once.
SAND. 'Twere best he should be *told* of these affronts.
MARG. I am the daughter of his father's friend,
Sir Walter's orphan ward.
I am not his servant maid, that I should wait
The opportunity of a gracious hearing,
Enquire the times and seasons when to put
My peevish prayer up at young Woodvil's feet,
And sue to him for slow redress, who was
Himself a suitor late to Margaret.
I am somewhat proud: and Woodvil taught me pride.
I was his favourite once, his playfellow in infancy,
And joyful mistress of his youth.
None once so pleasant in his eyes as Margaret.
His conscience, his religion, Margaret was,
His dear heart's confessor, a heart within that heart,
And all dear things summ'd up in her alone.
As Margaret smil'd or frown'd John liv'd or died;
His dress, speech, gesture, studies, friendships, all
Being fashion'd to her liking.
His flatteries taught me first this self-esteem,
His flatteries and caresses, while he loved.
The world esteem'd her happy, who had won
His heart, who won all hearts;
And ladies envied me the love of Woodvil.
    SAND. He doth affect the courtier's life too much,
Whose art is to forget,
And that has wrought this seeming change in him,
That was by nature noble.
'Tis these court-plagues, that swarm about our house,
Have done the mischief, making his fancy giddy
With images of state, preferment, place,
Tainting his generous spirits with ambition.
    MARG. I know not how it is;
A cold protector is John grown to me.
The mistress, and presumptive wife, of Woodvil
Can never stoop so low to supplicate
A man, her equal, to redress those wrongs,
Which he was bound first to prevent;
But which his own neglects have sanction'd rather,
Both sanction'd and provok'd: a mark'd neglect,
And strangeness fastening bitter on his love,
His love, which long has been upon the wane.
For me, I am determined what to do:
To leave this house this night, and lukewarm John,
And trust for food to the earth and Providence.

SAND. O lady, have a care
Of these indefinite and spleen-bred resolves.
You know not half the dangers that attend
Upon a life of wand'ring, which your thoughts now,
Feeling the swellings of a lofty anger,
To your abused fancy, as 'tis likely,
Portray without its terrors, painting *lies*
And representments of fallacious liberty—
You know not what it is to leave the roof that shelters you.
    MARG. I have thought on every possible event,
The dangers and discouragements you speak of,
Even till my woman's heart hath ceased to fear them,
And cowardice grows enamour'd of rare accidents:
Nor am I so unfurnish'd, as you think,
Of practicable schemes.
    SAND. Now God forbid; think twice of this, dear lady.
    MARG. I pray you spare me, Mr. Sandford.
And once for all believe, nothing can shake my purpose.
    SAND. But what course have you thought on?
    MARG. To seek Sir Walter in the forest of Sherwood.
I have letters from young Simon,
Acquainting me with all the circumstances
Of their concealment, place, and manner of life,
And the merry hours they spend in the green haunts
Of Sherwood, nigh which place they have ta'en a house
In the town of Nottingham, and pass for foreigners,
Wearing the dress of Frenchmen.—
All which I have perused with so attent
And child-like longings, that to my doting ears
Two sounds now seem like one,
One meaning in two words, Sherwood and Liberty.
And, gentle Mr. Sandford,
'Tis you that must provide now
The means of my departure, which for safety
Must be in boy's apparel.
    SAND. Since you will have it so
(My careful age trembles at all may happen),
I will engage to furnish you.
I have the keys of the wardrobe, and can fit you
With garments to your size.
I know a suit
Of lively Lincoln green, that shall much grace you
In the wear, being glossy fresh, and worn but seldom.
Young Stephen Woodvil wore them while he lived.
I have the keys of all this house and passages,
And ere day-break will rise and let you forth.
What things soe'er you have need of I can furnish you;

And will provide a horse and trusty guide,
To bear you on your way to Nottingham.
MARG. That once this day and night were fairly past!
For then I'll bid this house and love farewell;
Farewell, sweet Devon; farewell, lukewarm John;
For with the morning's light will Margaret be gone.
Thanks, courteous Mr. Sandford.—

(Exeunt divers ways.

ACT THE SECOND

(SCENE—*An Apartment in Woodvil Hall.*)

JOHN WOODVIL—*alone. (Reading parts of a letter.*)

"When Love grows cold, and indifference has usurped upon old Esteem, it is no marvel if the world begin to account *that* dependence, which hitherto has been esteemed honourable shelter. The course I have taken (in leaving this house, not easily wrought thereunto), seemed to me best for the once-for-all releasing of yourself (who in times past have deserved well of me) from the now daily, and not-to-be-endured tribute of forced love, and ill-dissembled reluctance of affection.
"MARGARET."

Gone! gone! my girl? so hasty, Margaret!
And never a kiss at parting? shallow loves,
And likings of a ten days' growth, use courtesies,
And show red eyes at parting. Who bids "Farewell"
In the same tone he cries "God speed you, sir"?
Or tells of joyful victories at sea,
Where he hath ventures? does not rather muffle
His organs to emit a leaden sound,
To suit the melancholy dull "farewell,"
Which they in Heaven not use?—
So peevish, Margaret?
But 'tis the common error of your sex
When our idolatry slackens, or grows less,
(As who of woman born can keep his faculty
Of Admiration, being a decaying faculty,
For ever strain'd to the pitch? or can at pleasure
Make it renewable, as some appetites are,
As, namely, Hunger, Thirst?)—this being the case,
They tax us with neglect, and love grown cold,
Coin plainings of the perfidy of men,
Which into maxims pass, and apothegms

To be retail'd in ballads.—
                              I know them all.
They are jealous, when our larger hearts receive
More guests than one. (Love in a woman's heart
Being all in one.) For me, I am sure I have room here
For more disturbers of my sleep than one.
Love shall have part, but love shall not have all.
Ambition, Pleasure, Vanity, all by turns,
Shall lie in my bed, and keep me fresh and waking;
Yet Love not be excluded.—Foolish wench,
I could have loved her twenty years to come,
And still have kept my liking. But since 'tis so,
Why, fare thee well, old play-fellow! I'll try
To squeeze a tear for old acquaintance' sake.
I shall not grudge so much.——

(To him enters LOVEL.)

LOVEL. Bless us, Woodvil! what is the matter? I protest, man, I thought you had been weeping.

WOOD. Nothing is the matter; only the wench has forced some water into my eyes, which will quickly disband.

LOVEL. I cannot conceive you.

WOOD. Margaret is flown.

LOVEL. Upon what pretence?

WOOD. Neglect on my part: which it seems she has had the wit to discover, maugre all my pains to conceal it.

LOVEL. Then, you confess the charge?

WOOD. To say the truth, my love for her has of late stopped short on this side idolatry.

LOVEL. As all good Christians' should, I think.

WOOD. I am sure, I could have loved her still within the limits of warrantable love.

LOVEL. A kind of brotherly affection, I take it.

WOOD. We should have made excellent man and wife in time.

LOVEL. A good old couple, when the snows fell, to crowd about a sea-coal fire, and talk over old matters.

WOOD. While each should feel, what neither cared to acknowledge, that stories oft repeated may, at last, come to lose some of their grace by the repetition.

LOVEL. Which both of you may yet live long enough to discover. For, take my word for it, Margaret is a bird that will come back to you without a lure.

WOOD. Never, never, Lovel. Spite of my levity, with tears I confess it, she was a lady of most confirmed honour, of an unmatchable spirit, and determinate in all virtuous resolutions; not hasty to anticipate an affront, nor slow to feel, where just provocation was given.

LOVEL. What made you neglect her, then?

WOOD. Mere levity and youthfulness of blood, a malady incident to young men; physicians call it caprice. Nothing else. He that slighted her knew her value: and 'tis odds, but, for thy sake, Margaret, John will yet go to his grave a bachelor.

(A noise heard, as of one drunk and singing.

LOVEL. Here comes one, that will quickly dissipate these humours.

(Enter one drunk.)

DRUNKEN MAN. Good-morrow to you, gentlemen. Mr. Lovel, I am your humble servant. Honest Jack Woodvil, I will get drunk with you to morrow.

WOOD. And why to-morrow, honest Mr. Freeman?

DRUNKEN MAN. I scent a traitor in that question. A beastly question. Is it not His Majesty's birthday? the day of all days in the year, on which King Charles the Second was graciously pleased to be born. *(Sings.)* "Great pity 'tis such days as those should come but once a year."

LOVEL. Drunk in a morning; foh! how he stinks!

DRUNKEN MAN. And why not drunk in a morning? canst tell, bully?

WOOD. Because, being the sweet and tender infancy of the day, me-thinks, it should ill endure such early blightings.

DRUNKEN MAN. I grant you, 'tis in some sort the youth and tender nonage of the day. Youth is bashful, and I give it a cup to encourage it. *(Sings.)* "Ale that will make Grimalkin prate."—At noon I drink for thirst, at night for fellowship, but, above all, I love to usher in the bashful morning under the auspices of a freshening stoop of liquor. *(Sings.)* "Ale in a Saxon rumkin then, makes valour burgeon in tall men."—But, I crave pardon. I fear I keep that gentleman from serious thoughts. There be those that wait for me in the cellar.

WOOD. Who are they?

DRUNKEN MAN. Gentlemen, my good friends, Cleveland, Delaval, and Truby. I know by this time they are all clamorous for me.

(Exit singing.

WOOD. This keeping of open house acquaints a man with strange companions.

(Enter, at another door, Three calling for HARRY FREEMAN.*)*

Harry Freeman, Harry Freeman.

He is not here. Let us go look for him.

Where is Freeman?

Where is Harry?

(Exeunt the Three, calling for FREEMAN.*

WOOD. Did you ever see such gentry? *(laughing.)* These are they that fatten on ale and tobacco in a morning, drink burnt brandy at noon to promote digestion, and piously conclude with quart bumpers after supper, to prove their loyalty.

LOVEL. Come, shall we adjourn to the Tennis Court?

WOOD. No, you shall go with me into the gallery, where I will show you the Vandyke I have purchased: "The late King taking leave of his children."

LOVEL. I will but adjust my dress, and attend you.

(*Exit* LOVEL.

JOHN WOOD. (*alone*). Now Universal England getteth drunk
For joy, that Charles, her monarch, is restored:
And she, that sometime wore a saintly mask,
The stale-grown vizor from her face doth pluck,
And weareth now a suit of morris bells,
With which she jingling goes through all her towns and villages.
The baffled factions in their houses skulk;
The commonwealthsman, and state machinist,
The cropt fanatic, and fifth-monarchy-man,
Who heareth of these visionaries now?
They and their dreams have ended. Fools do sing,
Where good men yield God thanks; but politic spirits,
Who live by observation, note these changes
Of the popular mind, and thereby serve their ends.
Then why not I? What's Charles to me, or Oliver,
But as my own advancement hangs on one of them?
I to myself am chief.——I know,
Some shallow mouths cry out, that I am smit
With the gauds and show of state, the point of place,
And trick of precedence, the ducks, and nods
Which weak minds pay to rank. 'Tis not to sit
In place of worship at the royal masques,
Their pastimes, plays, and Whitehall banquetings,
For none of these,
Nor yet to be seen whispering with some great one,
Do I affect the favours of the court.
I would be great, for greatness hath great *power,*
And that's the fruit I reach at.—
Great spirits ask great play-room. Who could sit,
With these prophetic swellings in my breast,
That prick and goad me on, and never cease,
To the fortunes something tells me I was born to?
Who, with such monitors within to stir him,
Would sit him down, with lazy arms across,
A unit, a thing without a name in the state,
A something to be govern'd, not to govern,
A fishing, hawking, hunting, country gentleman?

(*Exit.*

(SCENE—*Sherwood Forest.*)

(SIR WALTER WOODVIL. SIMON WOODVIL. *Disguised as Frenchmen.*)

SIR W. How fares my boy, Simon, my youngest born.

My hope, my pride, young Woodvil, speak to me?
Some grief untold weighs heavy at thy heart:
I know it by thy alter'd cheer of late.
Thinkest thy brother plays thy father false?
It is a mad and thriftless prodigal,
Grown proud upon the favours of the court;
Court manners, and court fashions, he affects,
And in the heat and uncheck'd blood of youth,
Harbours a company of riotous men,
All hot, and young, court-seekers, like himself,
Most skilful to devour a patrimony;
And these have eat into my old estates,
And these have drain'd thy father's cellars dry;
But these so common faults of youth not named
(Things which themselves outgrow, left to themselves),
I know no quality that stains his honour.
My life upon his faith and noble mind,
Son John could never play thy father false.

SIMON. I never thought but nobly of my brother,
Touching his honour and fidelity.
Still I could wish him charier of his person,
And of his time more frugal, than to spend
In riotous living, graceless society,
And mirth unpalatable, hours better employ'd
(With those persuasive graces nature lent him)
In fervent pleadings for a father's life.

SIR W. I would not owe my life to a jealous court,
Whose shallow policy I know it is,
On some reluctant acts of prudent mercy,
(Not voluntary, but extorted by the times,
In the first tremblings of new-fixed power,
And recollection smarting from old wounds,)
On these to build a spurious popularity.
Unknowing what free grace or mercy mean,
They fear to punish, therefore do they pardon.
For this cause have I oft forbid my son,
By letters, overtures, open solicitings,
Or closet tamperings, by gold or fee,
To beg or bargain with the court for my life.

SIMON. And John has ta'en you, father, at your word,
True to the letter of his paternal charge.

SIR W. Well, my good cause, and my good conscience, boy,
Shall be for sons to me, if John prove false.
Men die but once, and the opportunity
Of a noble death is not an everyday fortune:
It is a gift which noble spirits pray for.

SIMON. I would not wrong my brother by surmise;

I know him generous, full of gentle qualities,
Incapable of base compliances,
No prodigal in his nature, but affecting
This show of bravery for ambitious ends.
He drinks, for 'tis the humour of the court,
And drink may one day wrest the secret from him,
And pluck you from your hiding-place in the sequel.

 SIR W. Fair death shall be my doom, and foul life his.
Till when, we'll live as free in this green forest,
As yonder deer, who roam unfearing treason:
Who seem the aborigines of this place,
Or Sherwood theirs by tenure.

 SIMON. 'Tis said, that Robert Earl of Huntingdon,
Men call'd him Robin Hood, an outlaw bold,
With a merry crew of hunters here did haunt,
Not sparing the king's venison. May one believe
The antique tale?

 SIR W.   There is much likelihood,
Such bandits did in England erst abound,
When polity was young. I have read of the pranks
Of that mad archer, and of the tax he levied
On travellers, whatever their degree,
Baron, or knight, whoever pass'd these woods,
Layman, or priest, not sparing the bishop's mitre
For spiritual regards; nay, once, 'tis said,
He robb'd the king himself.

 SIMON.   A perilous man (*smiling*).

 SIR W. How quietly we live here,
Unread in the world's business,
And take no note of all its slippery changes.
'Twere best we make a world among ourselves,
A little world,
Without the ills and falsehoods of the greater;
We too being all the inhabitants of ours,
And kings and subjects both in one.

 SIMON. Only the dangerous errors, fond conceits,
Which make the business of that greater world,
Must have no place in ours:
As, namely, riches, honours, birth, place, courtesy,
Good fame and bad, rumours and popular noises,
Books, creeds, opinions, prejudices national,
Humours particular,
Soul-killing lies, and truths that work small good,
Feuds, factions, enmities, relationships,
Loves, hatreds, sympathies, antipathies,
And all the intricate stuff quarrels are made of.

(MARGARET *enters in boy's apparel.*)

SIR W. What pretty boy have we here?

MARG. *Bon jour, messieurs.* Ye have handsome English faces,
I should have ta'en ye else for other two,
I came to seek in the forest.

SIR W.   Who are they?

MARG. A gallant brace of Frenchmen, curl'd monsieurs,
That, men say, haunt these woods, affecting privacy,
More than the manner of their countrymen.

SIMON. We have here a wonder.
The face is Margaret's face.

SIR W. The face is Margaret's, but the dress the same
My Stephen sometime wore.

(*To* MARGARET.

Suppose us them; whom do men say we are?
Or know you what you seek?

MARG. A worthy pair of exiles,
Two whom the politics of state revenge,
In final issue of long civil broils,
Have houseless driven from your native France,
To wander idle in these English woods,
Where now ye live; most part
Thinking on home, and all the joys of France,
Where grows the purple vine.

SIR W. These woods, young stranger,
And grassy pastures, which the slim deer loves,
Are they less beauteous than the land of France,
Where grows the purple vine?

MARG.   I cannot tell.
To an indifferent eye both show alike.
'Tis not the scene,
But all familiar objects in the scene,
Which now ye miss, that constitute a difference.
Ye had a country, exiles, ye have none now;
Friends had ye, and much wealth, ye now have nothing;
Our manners, laws, our customs, all are foreign to you,
I know ye loathe them, cannot learn them readily;
And there is reason, exiles, ye should love
Our English earth less than your land of France,
Where grows the purple vine; where all delights grow
Old custom has made pleasant.

SIR W.   You, that are read
So deeply in our story, what are you?

MARG. A bare adventurer; in brief a woman,
That put strange garments on, and came thus far
To seek an ancient friend:

And having spent her stock of idle words,
And feeling some tears coming,
Hastes now to clasp Sir Walter Woodvil's knees,
And beg a boon for Margaret; his poor ward.

(Kneeling.

SIR W. Not at my feet, Margaret; not at my feet.
MARG. Yes, till her suit is answered.
SIR W. Name it.
MARG. A little boon, and yet so great a grace,
She fears to ask it.
SIR W.   Some riddle, Margaret?
MARG. No riddle, but a plain request.
SIR W. Name it.
MARG.   Free liberty of Sherwood,
And leave to take her lot with you in the forest.
SIR W. A scant petition, Margaret; but take it,
Seal'd with an old man's tears.—
Rise, daughter of Sir Rowland.

(Addressing them both.
O you most worthy,
You constant followers of a man proscribed,
Following poor misery in the throat of danger;
Fast servitors to crazed and penniless poverty,
Serving poor poverty without hope of gain;
Kind children of a sire unfortunate;
Green clinging tendrils round a trunk decay'd,
Which needs must bring on you timeless decay;
Fair living forms to a dead carcass join'd;—
What shall I say?
Better the dead were gather'd to the dead,
Than death and life in disproportion meet.—
Go, seek your fortunes, children.—
SIMON. Why, whither should we go?
SIR W. *You* to the Court, where now your brother John
Commits a rape on Fortune.
SIMON.   Luck to John!
A light-heel'd strumpet, when the sport is done.
SIR W. *You* to the sweet society of your equals,
Where the world's fashion smiles on youth and beauty.
MARG. Where young men's flatteries cozen young maids' beauty.
There pride oft gets the vantage hand of duty,
There sweet humility withers.
SIMON.   Mistress Margaret,
How fared my brother John, when you left Devon?
MARG. John was well, sir.
SIMON.   'Tis now nine months almost,
Since I saw home. What new friends has John made?

Or keeps he his first love?—I did suspect
Some foul disloyalty. Now do I know,
John has proved false to her, for Margaret weeps.
It is a scurvy brother.
    SIR W.   Fie upon it.
All men are false, I think. The date of love
Is out, expired; its stories all grown stale,
O'erpast, forgotten, like an antique tale
Of Hero and Leander.
    SIMON. I have known some men that are too general-contemplative for the narrow passion. I am in some sort a *general* lover.
    MARG. In the name of the boy God, who plays at hoodman blind with the Muses, and cares not whom he catches: what is it *you* love?
    SIMON. Simply, all things that live,
From the crook'd worm to man's imperial form,
And God-resembling likeness. The poor fly,
That makes short holiday in the sunbeam,
And dies by some child's hand. The feeble bird
With little wings, yet greatly venturous
In the upper sky.   The fish in th' other element,
That knows no touch of eloquence. What else?
Yon tall and elegant stag,
Who paints a dancing shadow of his horns
In the water, where he drinks.
    MARG. I myself love all these things, yet so as with a difference:—for example, some animals better than others, some men rather than other men; the nightingale before the cuckoo, the swift and graceful palfrey before the slow and asinine mule.   Your humour goes to confound all qualities. What sports do you use in the forest?—
    SIMON. Not many; some few, as thus:—
To see the sun to bed, and to arise,
Like some hot amourist with glowing eyes,
Bursting the lazy bands of sleep that bound him,
With all his fires and travelling glories round him.
Sometimes the moon on soft night clouds to rest,
Like beauty nestling in a young man's breast,
And all the winking stars, her handmaids, keep
Admiring silence, while those lovers sleep.
Sometimes outstretcht, in very idleness,
Nought doing, saying little, thinking less,
To view the leaves, thin dancers upon air,
Go eddying round; and small birds, how they fare,
When mother Autumn fills their beaks with corn,
Filch'd from the careless Amalthea's horn;
And how the woods berries and worms provide
Without their pains, when earth has nought beside
To answer their small wants.

To view the graceful deer come tripping by,
Then stop, and gaze, then turn, they know not why,
Like bashful younkers in society.
To mark the structure of a plant or tree,
And all fair things of earth, how fair they be.
    MARG. (*smiling*). And, afterwards, them paint in simile.
    SIR W. Mistress Margaret will have need of some refreshment. Please
you, we have some poor viands within.
    MARG. Indeed I stand in need of them.
    SIR W. Under the shade of a thick-spreading tree,
Upon the grass, no better carpeting,
We'll eat our noon-tide meal; and, dinner done,
One of us shall repair to Nottingham,
To seek some safe night-lodging in the town,
Where you may sleep, while here with us you dwell,
By day, in the forest, expecting better times,
And gentler habitations, noble Margaret.
    SIMON. *Allons,* young Frenchman——
    MARG. *Allons,* Sir Englishman. The time has been
I've studied love-lays in the English tongue,
And been enamour'd of rare poesy:
Which now I must unlearn. Henceforth,
Sweet mother-tongue, old English speech, adieu;
For Margaret has got new name and language new.
                                        (*Exeunt.*

ACT THE THIRD

(SCENE—*An Apartment of State in Woodvil Hall. Cavaliers drinking.*)

(JOHN WOODVIL, LOVEL, GRAY, *and four more.*)

    JOHN. More mirth, I beseech you, gentlemen—Mr. Gray, you are
not merry——
    GRAY. More wine, say I, and mirth shall ensue in course. What! we
have not yet above three half pints a man to answer for. Brevity is the
soul of drinking, as of wit. Despatch, I say. More wine. (*Fills.*)
    1ST GENT. I entreat you, let there be some order, some method, in our
drinkings. I love to lose my reason with my eyes open, to commit the
deed of drunkenness with forethought and deliberation. I love to feel the
fumes of the liquor gathering here, like clouds.
    2ND GENT. And I am for plunging into madness at once. Damn order,
and method and steps, and degrees, that he speaks of. Let confusion
have her legitimate work.
    LOVEL. I marvel why the poets, who, of all men, methinks, should

possess the hottest livers, and most empyreal fancies, should affect to see such virtues in cold water.

GRAY. Virtue in cold water! ha! ha! ha!——

JOHN. Because your poet-born hath an internal wine, richer than lippara or canaries, yet uncrushed from any grapes of earth, unpressed in mortal winepresses.

3RD GENT. What may be the name of this wine?

JOHN. It hath as many names as qualities. It is denominated indifferently, wit, conceit, invention, inspiration, but its most royal and comprehensive name is *fancy*.

3RD GENT. And where keeps he this sovereign liquor?

JOHN. Its cellars are in the brain, whence your true poet deriveth intoxication at will; while his animal spirits, catching a pride from the quality and neighbourhood of their noble relative, the brain, refuse to be sustained by wines and fermentations of earth.

3RD GENT. But is your poet-born always tipsy with this liquor?

JOHN. He hath his stoopings and reposes; but his proper element is the sky, and in the suburbs of the empyrean.

3RD GENT. Is your wine-intellectual so exquisite? Henceforth, I, a man of plain conceit, will, in all humility, content my mind with canaries.

4TH GENT. I am for a song or a catch. When will the catches come on, the sweet wicked catches?

JOHN. They cannot be introduced with propriety before midnight. Every man must commit his twenty bumpers first. We are not yet well roused. Frank Lovel, the glass stands with you.

LOVEL. Gentlemen, the Duke. (*Fills.*)

ALL. The Duke. (*They drink.*)

GRAY. Can any tell, why his Grace, being a Papist——

JOHN. Pshaw! we will have no questions of state now. Is not this His Majesty's birthday?

GRAY. What follows?

JOHN. That every man should sing, and be joyful, and ask no questions.

2ND GENT. Damn politics, they spoil drinking.

3RD GENT. For certain, 'tis a blessed monarchy.

2ND GENT. The cursed fanatic days we have seen! The times have been when swearing was out of fashion.

3RD GENT. And drinking.

1ST GENT. And wenching.

GRAY. The cursed yeas and forsooths, which we have heard uttered, when a man could not rap out an innocent oath, but straight the air was thought to be infected.

LOVEL. 'Twas a pleasant trick of the saint, which that trim puritan *Swear-not-at-all Smooth-speech* used, when his spouse chid him with an oath for committing with his servant-maid, to cause his house to be fumigated with burnt brandy, and ends of scripture, to disperse the devil's breath, as he termed it.

ALL. Ha! ha! ha!

GRAY. But 'twas pleasanter, when the other saint *Resist-the-devil-and-he-will-flee-from-thee Pure-man* was overtaken in the act, to plead an *illusio visûs*, and maintain his sanctity upon a supposed power in the adversary to counterfeit the shapes of things.

ALL. Ha! ha! ha!

JOHN. Another round, and then let every man devise what trick he can in his fancy, for the better manifesting our loyalty this day.

GRAY. Shall we hang a puritan?

JOHN. No, that has been done already in Coleman Street.

2ND GENT. Or fire a conventicle?

JOHN. That is stale too.

3RD GENT. Or burn the Assembly's catechism?

4TH GENT. Or drink the king's health, every man standing upon his head naked?

JOHN (*to* LOVEL). We have here some pleasant madness.

3RD GENT. Who shall pledge me in a pint bumper, while we drink to the king upon our knees?

LOVEL. Why on our knees, Cavalier?

JOHN (*smiling*). For more devotion, to be sure. (*To a servant*) Sirrah, fetch the gilt goblets.

(*The goblets are brought. They drink the King's health, kneeling. A shout of general approbation following the first appearance of the goblets.*

JOHN. We have here the unchecked virtues of the grape. How the vapours curl upwards! It were a life of gods to dwell in such an element: to see, and hear, and talk brave things. Now fie upon these casual potations. That a man's most exalted reason should depend upon the ignoble fermenting of a fruit, which sparrows pluck at as well as we!

GRAY (*aside to* LOVEL). Observe how he is ravished.

LOVEL. Vanity and gay thoughts of wine do meet in him and engender madness.

(*While the rest are engaged in a wild kind of talk,* JOHN *advances to the front of the stage, and soliloquises.*

JOHN. My spirits turn to fire, they mount so fast.
My joys are turbulent, my hopes show like fruition.
These high and gusty relishes of life, sure,
Have no allayings of mortality in them.
I am too hot now, and o'ercapable,
For the tedious processes, and creeping wisdom,
Of human acts, and enterprises of a man.
I want some seasonings of adversity,
Some strokes of the old mortifier Calamity,
To take these swellings down, divines call vanity.

1ST GENT. Mr. Woodvil, Mr. Woodvil.

2ND GENT. Where is Woodvil?

GRAY. Let him alone. I have seen him in these lunes before. His abstractions must not taint the good mirth.

JOHN (*continuing to soliloquise*). O for some friend now,
To conceal nothing from, to have no secrets.
How fine and noble a thing is confidence,
How reasonable too, and almost godlike!
Fast cement of fast friends, band of society,
Old natural go-between in the world's business,
Where civil life and order, wanting this cement,
Would presently rush back
Into the pristine state of singularity,
And each man stand alone.

(*A Servant enters.*)

SERVANT. Gentlemen, the fireworks are ready.

1ST GENT. What be they?

LOVEL. The work of London artists which our host has provided in honour of this day.

2ND GENT. 'Sdeath, who would part with his wine for a rocket?

LOVEL. Why truly, gentlemen, as our kind host has been at the pains to provide this spectacle, we can do no less than be present at it. It will not take up much time. Every man may return fresh and thirsting to his liquor.

3RD GENT. There's reason in what he says.

2ND GENT. Charge on then, bottle in hand. There's husbandry in that.

(*They go out, singing. Only* LOVEL *remains, who observes* WOODVIL.

JOHN (*still talking to himself*). This Lovel here's of a tough honesty,
Would put the rack to the proof. He is not of that sort
Which haunt my house, snorting the liquors,
And when their wisdoms are afloat with wine,
Spend vows as fast as vapours, which go off
Even with the fumes, their fathers. He is one,
Whose sober morning actions
Shame not his o'ernight's promises;
Talks little, flatters less, and makes no promises;
Why this is he, whom the dark-wisdom'd fate
Might trust her counsels of predestination with,
And the world be no loser,
Why should I fear this man?

· (*Seeing* LOVEL.

Where is the company gone?

LOVEL. To see the fireworks, where you will be expected to follow. But I perceive you are better engaged.

JOHN. I have been meditating this half hour
On all the properties of a brave friendship,
The mysteries that are in it, the noble uses,

Its limits withal, and its nice boundaries.
Exempli gratiâ, how far a man
May lawfully forswear himself for his friend;
What quantity of lies, some of them brave ones,
He may lawfully incur in a friend's behalf;
What oaths, blood-crimes, hereditary quarrels,
Night brawls, fierce words, and duels in the morning,
He need not stick at, to maintain his friend's honour, or his cause.

    LOVEL. I think many men would die for their friends.

    JOHN. Death! why 'tis nothing. We go to it for sport,
To gain a name, or purse, or please a sullen humour,
When one has worn his fortune's livery threadbare,
Or his spleen'd mistress frowns. Husbands will venture on it,
To cure the hot fits and cold shakings of jealousy.
A friend, sir, must do more.

    LOVEL. Can he do more than die?

    JOHN. To serve a friend this he may do. Pray mark me.
Having a law within (great spirits feel one)
He cannot, ought not, to be bound by any
Positive laws or ord'nances extern,
But may reject all these: by the law of friendship
He may do so much, be they, indifferently,
Penn'd statutes, or the land's unwritten usages,
As public fame, civil compliances,
Misnamed honour, trust in matter of secrets,
All vows and promises, the feeble mind's religion
(Binding our morning knowledge to approve
What last night's ignorance spake);
The ties of blood withal, and prejudice of kin.
Sir, these weak terrors
Must never shake me. I know what belongs
To a worthy friendship. Come, you shall have my confidence.

    LOVEL. I hope you think me worthy.

    JOHN. You will smile to hear now—
Sir Walter never has been out of the island.

    LOVEL. You amaze me.

    JOHN. That same report of his escape to France
Was a fine tale, forged by myself——
Ha! ha!
I knew it would stagger him.

    LOVEL.   Pray, give me leave.
Where has he dwelt, how lived, how lain conceal'd?
Sure I may ask so much.

    JOHN. From place to place, dwelling in no place long
My brother Simon still hath borne him company
('Tis a brave youth, I envy him all his virtues).
Disguised in foreign garb, they pass for Frenchmen,

Two Protestant exiles from the Limousin
Newly arrived. Their dwelling's now at Nottingham,
Where no soul knows them.

LOVEL. Can you assign any reason, why a gentleman of Sir Walter's
known prudence should expose his person so lightly?

JOHN. I believe, a certain fondness,
A child-like cleaving to the land that gave him birth,
Chains him like fate.

LOVEL. I have known some exiles thus
To linger out the term of the law's indulgence.
To the hazard of being known.

JOHN. You may suppose sometimes
They use the neighb'ring Sherwood for their sport,
Their exercise and freer recreation.—
I see you smile. Pray now, be careful.

LOVEL. I am no babbler, sir; you need not fear me.

JOHN. But some men have been known to talk in their sleep.
And tell fine tales that way.

LOVEL. I have heard so much. But, to say truth, I mostly sleep alone.

JOHN. Or drink, sir? do you never drink too freely?
Some men will drink, and tell you all their secrets.

LOVEL. Why do you question me, who know my habits?

JOHN. I think you are no sot,
No tavern-troubler, worshipper of the grape;
But all men drink sometimes,
And veriest saints at festivals relax,
The marriage of a friend, or a wife's birth-day.

LOVEL. How much, sir, may a man with safety drink?

(*Smiling.*

JOHN. Sir, three half pints a day is reasonable;
I care not if you never exceed that quantity.

LOVEL. I shall observe it;
On holidays two quarts.

JOHN. Or stay; you keep no wench?

LOVEL. Ha!

JOHN. No painted mistress for your private hours?
You keep no whore, sir?

LOVEL. What does he mean?

JOHN. Who for a close embrace, a toy of sin,
And amorous praising of your worship's breath,
In rosy junction of four melting lips,
Can kiss out secrets from you?

LOVEL. How strange this passionate behaviour shows in you!
Sure you think me some weak one.

JOHN. Pray pardon me some fears.
You have now the pledge of a dear father's life.
I am a son—would fain be thought a loving one;

You may allow me some fears: do not despise me,
If, in a posture foreign to my spirit,
And by our well-knit friendship I conjure you,
Touch not Sir Walter's life.

(Kneels.

You see these tears. My father's an old man.
Pray let him live.

    LOVEL. I must be bold to tell you, these new freedoms
Show most unhandsome in you.

    JOHN (rising).   Ha! do you say so?
Sure, you are not grown proud upon my secret!
Ah! now I see it plain. He would be babbling.
No doubt a garrulous and hard-faced traitor—
But I'll not give you leave.

(Draws.

    LOVEL. What does this madman mean?

    JOHN. Come, sir; here is no subterfuge;
You must kill me, or I kill you.

    LOVEL (drawing). Then self-defence plead my excuse.
Have at you, sir.

(They fight.

    JOHN.   Stay, sir.
I hope you have made your will.
If not, 'tis no great matter.
A broken cavalier has seldom much
He can bequeath: an old worn peruke,
A snuff-box with a picture of Prince Rupert,
A rusty sword he'll swear was used at Naseby,
Though it ne'er came within ten miles of the place;
And, if he's very rich,
A cheap edition of the Icon Basilike,
Is mostly all the wealth he dies possest of.
You say few prayers, I fancy;—
So to it again.

(They fight again. LOVEL is disarmed.

    LOVEL. You had best now take my life. I guess you mean it.

    JOHN (musing). No:—Men will say I fear'd him, if I kill'd him.
Live still, and be a traitor in thy wish,
But never act thy thought, being a coward.
That vengeance, which thy soul shall nightly thirst for,
And this disgrace I've done you cry aloud for,
Still have the will without the power to execute.
So now I leave you,
Feeling a sweet security. No doubt
My secret shall remain a virgin for you!—

(Goes out smiling, in scorn.

    LOVEL (rising). For once you are mistaken in your man.

The deed you wot of shall forthwith be done.
A bird let loose, a secret out of hand,
Returns not back. Why, then 'tis baby policy
To menace him who hath it in his keeping.
I will go look for Gray;
Then, northward ho! such tricks as we shall play
Have not been seen, I think, in merry Sherwood,
Since the days of Robin Hood, that archer good.

ACT THE FOURTH

(SCENE—*An Apartment in Woodvil Hall.*)

JOHN WOODVIL. (*Alone.*)

A weight of wine lies heavy on my head,
The unconcocted follies of last night.
Now all those jovial fancies, and bright hopes,
Children of wine, go off like dreams.
This sick vertigo here
Preacheth of temperance, no sermon better.
These black thoughts, and dull melancholy,
That stick like burrs to the brain, will they ne'er leave me?
Some men are full of choler, when they are drunk;
Some brawl of matter foreign to themselves;
And some, the most resolved fools of all,
Have told their dearest secrets in their cups.

(SCENE—*The Forest.*)

(SIR WALTER. SIMON. LOVEL. GRAY.)

LOVEL. Sir, we are sorry we cannot return your *French* salutation.

GRAY. Nor otherwise consider this garb you trust to than as a poor disguise.

LOVEL. Nor use much ceremony with a traitor.

GRAY. Therefore, without much induction of superfluous words, I attach you, Sir Walter Woodvil, of High Treason, in the King's name.

LOVEL. And of taking part in the great Rebellion against our late lawful Sovereign, Charles the First.

SIMON. John has betrayed us, father.

LOVEL. Come, sir, you had best surrender fairly. We know you, sir.

SIMON. Hang ye, villains, ye are two better known than trusted. I have seen those faces before. Are ye not two beggarly retainers, trencher-parasites, to John? I think ye rank among his footmen. A sort of bed and board worms—locusts that infest our house; a leprosy that long has hung upon its walls and princely apartments, reaching to fill all the corners of my brother's once noble heart.

GRAY. We are his friends.

SIMON. Fie, sir, do not weep. How these rogues will triumph! Shall I whip off their heads, father?   (*Draws.*

LOVEL. Come, sir, though this show handsome in you, being his son, yet the law must have its course.

SIMON. And if I tell ye the law shall not have its course, cannot ye be content? Courage, father; shall such things as these apprehend a man? Which of ye will venture upon me?—Will you, Mr. Constable self-elect? or you, sir, with a pimple on your nose, got at Oxford by hard drinking, your only badge of loyalty?

GRAY. 'Tis a brave youth—I cannot strike at him.

SIMON. Father, why do you cover your face with your hands? Why do you fetch your breath so hard? See, villains, his heart is burst! O villains, he cannot speak. One of you run for some water; quickly, ye knaves; will ye have your throats cut?

                                                  (*They both slink off.*

How is it with you, Sir Walter? Look up, sir, the villains are gone. He hears me not, and this deep disgrace of treachery in his son hath touched him even to the death. O most distuned and distempered world, where sons talk their aged fathers into their graves! Garrulous and diseased world, and still empty, rotten and hollow *talking* world, where good men decay, states turn round in an endless mutability, and still for the worse; nothing is at a stay, nothing abides but vanity, chaotic vanity.—Brother, adieu!

There lies the parent stock which gave us life,
Which I will see consign'd with tears to earth.
Leave thou the solemn funeral rites to me,
Grief and a true remorse abide with thee.

                                            (*Bears in the body.*

(SCENE—*Another Part of the Forest.*)

MARG. (*alone*). It was an error merely, and no crime,
An unsuspecting openness in youth,
That from his lips the fatal secret drew,
Which should have slept like one of nature's mysteries,
Unveil'd by any man.
Well, he is dead!
And what should Margaret do in the forest?
O ill-starr'd John!
O Woodvil, man enfeoff'd to despair!
Take thy farewell of peace.
O never look again to see good days,
Or close thy lids in comfortable nights,

Or ever think a happy thought again,
If what I have heard be true.—
Forsaken of the world must Woodvil live,
If he did tell these men.
No tongue must speak to him, no tongue of man
Salute him, when he wakes up in a morning;
Or bid "good-night" to John. Who seeks to live
In amity with thee, must for thy sake
Abide the world's reproach. What then?
Shall Margaret join the clamours of the world
Against her friend? O undiscerning world,
That cannot from misfortune separate guilt,
No, not in thought! O never, never, John.
Prepared to share the fortunes of her friend
For better or for worse thy Margaret comes,
To pour into thy wounds a healing love,
And wake the memory of an ancient friendship.
And pardon me, thou spirit of Sir Walter,
Who, in compassion to the wretched living,
Have but few tears to waste upon the dead.

(Scene—*Woodvil Hall.*)

(Sandford. Margaret. *As from a Journey.*)

SAND. The violence of the sudden mischance hath so wrought in him, who by nature is allied to nothing *less* than a self-debasing humour of dejection, that I have never seen anything more changed and spirit-broken. He hath, with a peremptory resolution, dismissed the partners of his riots and late hours, denied his house and person to their most earnest solicitings, and will be seen by none. He keeps ever alone, and his grief (which is solitary) does not so much seem to possess and govern in him, as it is by him, with a wilfulness of most manifest affection, entertained and cherished.

MARG. How bears he up against the common rumour?

SAND. With a strange indifference, which whosoever dives not into the niceness of his sorrow might mistake for obdurate and insensate. Yet are the wings of his pride for ever clipt; and yet a virtuous predominance of filial grief is so ever uppermost, that you may discover his thoughts less troubled with conjecturing what living opinions will say, and judge of his deeds, than absorbed and buried with the dead, whom his indiscretion made so.

MARG. I knew a greatness ever to be resident in him, to which the admiring eyes of men should look up even in the declining and bankrupt state of his pride. Fain would I see him, fain talk with him; but that a sense of respect, which is violated, when without deliberation we press

into the society of the unhappy, checks and holds me back. How, think
you, he would bear my presence?

SAND. As of an assured friend, whom in the forgetfulness of his fortunes he past by. See him you must; but not to-night. The newness of
the sight shall move the bitterest compunction and the truest remorse;
but afterwards, trust me, dear lady, the happiest effects of a returning
peace, and a gracious comfort, to him, to you, and all of us.

MARG. I think he would not deny me. He hath ere this received farewell letters from his brother, who hath taken a resolution to estrange
himself, for a time, from country, friends, and kindred, and to seek occupation for his sad thoughts in travelling in foreign places, where sights
remote and extern to himself may draw from him kindly and not painful ruminations.

SAND. I was present at the receipt of the letter. The contents seemed
to affect him, for a moment, with a more lively passion of grief than he
has at any time outwardly shown. He wept with many tears (which I
had not before noted in him), and appeared to be touched with the
sense as of some unkindness; but the cause of their sad separation and
divorce quickly recurring, he presently returned to his former inward-
ness of suffering.

MARG. The reproach of his brother's presence at this hour would have
been a weight more than could be sustained by his already oppressed and
sinking spirit.—Meditating upon these intricate and widespread sorrows, hath brought a heaviness upon me, as of sleep. How goes the
night?

SAND. An hour past sunset. You shall first refresh your limbs (tired
with travel) with meats and some cordial wine, and then betake your no
less wearied mind to repose.

MARG. A good rest to us all.

SAND. Thanks, lady.

ACT THE FIFTH

(JOHN WOODVIL *dressing.*)

JOHN. How beautiful (*handling his mourning*)
And comely do these mourning garments show!
Sure Grief hath set his sacred impress here,
To claim the world's respect! they note so feelingly
By outward types the serious man within.—
Alas! what part or portion can I claim
In all the decencies of virtuous sorrow,
Which other mourners use? as namely,
This black attire, abstraction from society,
Good thoughts, and frequent sighs, and seldom smiles,

A cleaving sadness native to the brow,
All sweet condolements of like-grieved friends
(That steal away the sense of loss almost),
Men's pity, and good offices
Which enemies themselves do for us then,
Putting their hostile disposition off,
As we put off our high thoughts and proud looks.
                   (Pauses, and observes the pictures.
These pictures must be taken down:
The portraitures of our most ancient family
For nigh three hundred years! How have I listen'd,
To hear Sir Walter, with an old man's pride,
Holding me in his arms, a prating boy,
And pointing to the pictures where they hung,
Repeat by course their worthy histories
(As Hugh de Widville, Walter, first of the name,
And Anne the handsome, Stephen, and famous John:
Telling me, I must be his famous John).
But that was in old times.
Now, no more
Must I grow proud upon our house's pride.
I rather, I, by most unheard-of crimes,
Have backward tainted all their noble blood,
Rased out the memory of an ancient family,
And quite reversed the honors of our house.
Who now shall sit and tell us anecdotes?
The secret history of his own times,
And fàshions of the world when he was young:
How England slept out three-and-twenty years,
While Carr and Villiers ruled the baby king:
The costly fancies of the pedant's reign,
Balls, feastings, huntings, shows in allegory,
And Beauties of the court of James the First.

              (Margaret *enters.*)

    john. Comes Margaret here to witness my disgrace?
O lady, I have suffer'd loss,
And diminution of my honour's brightness.
You bring some images of old times, Margaret,
That should be now forgotton.
    marg. Old times should never be forgotten, John.
I came to talk about them with my friend.
    john. I did refuse you, Margaret, in my pride.
    marg. If John rejected Margaret in his pride
(As who does not, being splenetic, refuse
Sometimes old playfellows), the spleen being gone,

The offence no longer lives.
O Woodvil, those were happy days,
When we two first began to love. When first,
Under pretence of visiting my father
(Being then a stripling nigh upon my age),
You came a-wooing to his daughter, John.
Do you remember,
With what a coy reserve and seldom speech
(Young maidens must be chary of their speech),
I kept the honours of my maiden pride?
I was your favorite then.

    JOHN. O Margaret, Margaret!
These your submissions to my low estate,
And cleavings to the fates of sunken Woodvil,
Write bitter things 'gainst my unworthiness.
Thou perfect pattern of thy slander'd sex.
Whom miseries of mine could never alienate,
Nor change of fortune shake; whom injuries,
And slights (the worst of injuries) which moved
Thy nature to return scorn with like scorn,
Then when you left in virtuous pride this house,
Could not so separate, but now in this
My day of shame, when all the world forsake me,
You only visit me, love, and forgive me.

    MARG. Dost yet remember the green arbor, John,
In the south gardens of my father's house,
Where we have seen the summer sun go down,
Exchanging true love's vows without restraint?
And that old wood, you call'd your wilderness,
And vow'd in sport to build a chapel in it,
There dwell

> Like hermit poor
> In pensive place obscure,

And tell your Ave Maries by the curls
(Dropping like golden beads) of Margaret's hair;
And make confession seven times a day
Of every thought that stray'd from love and Margaret;
And I your saint the penance should appoint—
Believe me, sir, I will not now be laid
Aside, like an old fashion.

    JOHN. O lady, poor and abject are my thoughts;
My pride is cured, my hopes are under clouds,
I have no part in any good man's love,
In all earth's pleasures portion have I none,
I fade and wither in my own esteem,
This earth holds not alive so poor a thing as I am.

I was not always thus.   (*Weeps.*

MARG.   Thou noble nature,
Which lion-like didst awe the inferior creatures,
Now trampled on by beasts of basest quality,
My dear heart's lord, life's pride, soul-honour'd John!
Upon her knees (regard her poor request)
Your favourite, once beloved Margaret, kneels.

JOHN. What would'st thou, lady, ever honour'd Margaret?

MARG. That John would think more nobly of himself,
More worthily of high Heaven;
And not for one misfortune, child of chance,
No crime, but unforeseen, and sent to punish
The less offence with image of the greater,
Thereby to work the soul's humility
(Which end hath happily not been frustrate quite),
O not for one offence mistrust Heaven's mercy,
Nor quit thy hope of happy days to come—
John yet has many happy days to live;
To live and make atonement.

JOHN.   Excellent lady,
Whose suit hath drawn this softness from my eyes,
Not the world's scorn, nor falling off of friends,
Could ever do. Will you go with me, Margaret?

MARG. (*rising*). Go whither, John?

JOHN.   Go in with me,
And pray for the peace of our unquiet minds?

MARG. That I will, John.

                                        (*Exeunt.*

(SCENE—*An inner Apartment.*)

(JOHN *is discovered kneeling.*—MARGARET *standing over him.*)

JOHN (*rises*). I cannot bear
To see you waste that youth and excellent beauty
('Tis now the golden time of the day with you),
In tending such a broken wretch as I am.

MARG. John will break Margaret's heart, if he speak so.
O sir, sir, sir, you are too melancholy,
And I must call it caprice. I am somewhat bold
Perhaps in this. But you are now my patient
(You know you gave me leave to call you so),
And I must chide these pestilent humours from you.

JOHN. They are gone.—
Mark, love, how cheerfully I speak!
I can smile too, and I almost begin
To understand what kind of creature Hope is.

MARG. Now this is better, this mirth becomes you, John.
JOHN. Yet tell me, if I over-act my mirth
(Being but a novice, I may fall into that error).
That were a sad indecency, you know.
MARG. Nay, never fear.
I will be mistress of your humours,
And you shall frown or smile by the book.
And herein I shall be most peremptory,
Cry, "This shows well, but that inclines to levity;
This frown has too much of the Woodvil in it,
But that fine sunshine has redeem'd it quite."
JOHN. How sweetly Margaret robs me of myself!
MARG. To give you in your stead a better self!
Such as you were, when these eyes first beheld
You mounted on your sprightly steed, White Margery,
Sir Rowland my father's gift,
And all my maidens gave my heart for lost.
I was a young thing then, being newly come
Home from my convent education, where
Seven years I had wasted in the bosom of France:
Returning home true Protestant, you call'd me
Your little heretic nun. How timid-bashful
Did John salute his love, being newly seen!
Sir Rowland term'd it a rare modesty,
And praised it in a youth.
JOHN. Now Margaret weeps herself.

(A noise of bells heard.)

MARG. Hark the bells, John.
JOHN. Those are the church bells of St. Mary Ottery.
MARG. I know it.
JOHN. St. Mary Ottery, my native village
In the sweet shire of Devon.
Those are the bells.
MARG.   Wilt go to church, John?
JOHN. I have been there already.
MARG. How canst say thou hast been there already? The bells are only
now ringing for morning service, and hast thou been at church already?
JOHN. I left my bed betimes, I could not sleep,
And when I rose, I look'd (as my custom is)
From my chamber window, where I can see the sunrise;
And the first object I discern'd
Was the glistering spire of St. Mary Ottery.
MARG. Well, John.
JOHN. Then I remember'd 'twas the Sabbath-day.
Immediately a wish arose in my mind,

To go to church and pray with Christian people.
And then I check'd myself, and said to myself,
"Thou hast been a heathen, John, these two years past
(Not having been at church in all that time),
And is it fit, that now for the first time
Thou should'st offend the eyes of Christian people
With a murderer's presence in the house of prayer?
Thou would'st but discompose their pious thoughts,
And do thyself no good: for how could'st thou pray,
With unwash'd hands, and lips unused to the offices?"
And then I at my own presumption smiled;
And then I wept that I should smile at all,
Having such cause of grief! I wept outright;
Tears like a river flooded all my face,
And I began to pray, and found I could pray;
And still I yearn'd to say my prayers in the church.
"Doubtless (said I) one might find comfort in it."
So stealing down the stairs, like one that fear'd detection,
Or was about to act unlawful business
At that dead time of dawn,
I flew to the church, and found the doors wide open
(Whether by negligence I knew not,
Or some peculiar grace to me vouchsafed,
For all things felt like mystery).
    MARG. Yes.
    JOHN. So entering in, not without fear,
I past into the family pew,
And covering up my eyes for shame,
And deep perception of unworthiness,
Upon the little hassock knelt me down,
Where I so oft had kneel'd,
A docile infant by Sir Walter's side;
And, thinking so, I wept a second flood
More poignant than the first;
But afterwards was greatly comforted.
It seem'd, the guilt of blood was passing from me
Even in the act and agony of tears,
And all my sins forgiven.

THE WIFE'S TRIAL;

OR,

THE INTRUDING WIDOW

A Dramatic Poem

FOUNDED ON MR. CRABBE'S TALE OF "THE CONFIDANT"

CHARACTERS

MR. SELBY, *A Wiltshire Gentleman.*
KATHERINE, *Wife to Selby.*
LUCY, *Sister to Selby.*
MRS. FRAMPTON, *A Widow.*
SERVANTS.

SCENE—*at Mr. Selby's House, or in the grounds adjacent.*

THE WIFE'S TRIAL;

OR,

THE INTRUDING WIDOW

(SCENE—*A Library.*)

MR. SELBY. KATHERINE.

SELBY. Do not far mistake me, gentlest wife;
I meant to chide your virtues, not yourself,
And those too with allowance. I have not
Been blest by thy fair side with five white years
Of smooth and even wedlock, now to touch
With any strain of harshness on a string
Hath yielded me such music. 'Twas the quality
Of a too grateful nature in my Katherine,
That to the lame performance of some vows,
And common courtesies of man to wife,
Attributing too much, hath sometimes seem'd
To esteem as favours, what in that blest union
Are but reciprocal and trivial dues,
As fairly yours as mine: 'twas this I thought
Gently to reprehend.
            KATH.   In friendship's barter
The riches we exchange should hold some level,
And corresponding worth. Jewels for toys
Demand some thanks thrown in. You took me, sir,
To that blest haven of my peace, your bosom,
An orphan founder'd in the world's black storm.
Poor, you have made me rich; from lonely maiden,
Your cherish'd and your full-accompanied wife.
            SELBY. But to divert the subject: Kate too fond,
I would not wrest your meanings; else that word
Accompanied, and full-accompanied too,
Might raise a doubt in some men, that their wives
Haply did think their company too long;
And over-company, we know by proof,
Is worse than no attendance.
            KATH.   I must guess,
You speak this of the widow—

461

SELBY.   'Twas a bolt
At random shot; but if it hit, believe me,
I am most sorry to have wounded you
Through a friend's side. I know not how we have swerved
From our first talk. I was to caution you
Against this fault of a too grateful nature:
Which, for some girlish obligations past,
In that relenting season of the heart,
When slightest favours pass for benefits
Of endless binding, would entail upon you
An iron slavery of obsequious duty
To the proud will of an imperious woman.
    KATH. The favours are not slight to her I owe.
    SELBY. Slight or not slight, the tribute she exacts
Cancels all dues—
                              (*A voice within.*

               Even now I hear her call you
In such a tone, as lordliest mistresses
Expect a slave's attendance. Prithee, Kate,
Let her expect a brace of minutes or so.
Say you are busy. Use her by degrees
To some less hard exactions.
    KATH.   I conjure you,
Detain me not. I will return—
    SELBY.   Sweet wife,
Use thy own pleasure—
                          (*Exit* KATHERINE.

               but it troubles me.
A visit of three days, as was pretended,
Spun to ten tedious weeks, and no hint given
When she will go! I would this buxom Widow
Were a thought handsomer! I'd fairly try
My Katherine's constancy; make desperate love
In seeming earnest; and raise up such broils,
That she, not I, should be the first to warn
The insidious guest depart.

          (*Re-enter* KATHERINE.)
                 So soon return'd!
What was our Widow's will?
    KATH.   A trifle, sir.
    SELBY. Some toilet service—to adjust her head,
Or help to stick a pin in the right place—
    KATH. Indeed 'twas none of these.
    SELBY.   Or new vamp up
The tarnish'd cloak she came in. I have seen her
Demand such service from thee, as her maid,

Twice told to do it, would blush angry-red,
And pack her few clothes up. Poor fool! fond slave!
And yet my dearest Kate!—This day at least
(It is our wedding-day) we spend in freedom,
And will forget our Widow.—Philip, our coach—
Why weeps my wife? You know, I promised you
An airing o'er the pleasant Hampshire downs
To the blest cottage on the green hillside,
Where first I told my love. I wonder much,
If the crimson parlor hath exchanged its hue
For colours not so welcome. Faded though it be,
It will not show less lovely than the tinge
Of this faint red, contending with the pale,
Where once the full-flush'd health gave to this cheek
An apt resemblance to the fruit's warm side,
That bears my Katherine's name.—
                              Our carriage, Philip.

                    (*Enter a Servant.*)

Now, Robin, what make you here?
          SERVANT.   May it please you,
The coachman has driven out with Mrs. Frampton.
          SELBY. He had no orders—
          SERVANT.   None, sir, that I know of,
But from the lady, who expects some letter
At the next Post Town.
          SELBY.   Go, Robin.

                                   (*Exit Servant.*
                    How is this?
          KATH. I came to tell you so, but fear'd your anger—
          SELBY. It was ill done though of this Mistress Frampton,
This forward Widow. But a ride's poor loss
Imports not much. In to your chamber, love,
Where you with music may beguile the hour,
While I am tossing over dusty tomes,
Till our most reasonable friend returns.
          KATH. I am all obedience.

                                   (*Exit* KATHERINE.
          SELBY.   Too obedient, Kate,
And to too many masters. I can hardly
On such a day as this refrain to speak
My sense of this injurious friend, this pest,
This household evil, this close-clinging fiend,
In rough terms to my wife. 'Death, my own servants
Controll'd above me! orders countermanded!
What next?

                    (*Servant enters and announces the Sister.*

(*Enter* LUCY.)

Sister! I know you are come to welcome
This day's return. 'Twas well done.
　　　LUCY.　　　　　　　　You seem ruffled.
In years gone by this day was used to be
The smoothest of the year. Your honey turn'd
So soon to gall?
　　　SELBY.　　　　　　Gall'd am I, and with cause,
And rid to death, yet cannot get a riddance,
Nay, scarce a ride, by this proud Widow's leave.
　　　LUCY. Something you wrote me of a Mistress Frampton.
　　　SELBY. She came at first a meek admitted guest,
Pretending a short stay; her whole deportment
Seem'd as of one obliged. A slender trunk,
The wardrobe of her scant and ancient clothing,
Bespoke no more. But in few days her dress,
Her looks, were proudly changed. And now she flaunts it
In jewels stolen or borrow'd from my wife;
Who owes her some strange service, of what nature
I must be kept in ignorance. Katherine's meek
And gentle spirit cowers beneath her eye,
As spell-bound by some witch.
　　　LUCY.　　　　　　　Some mystery hangs on it.
How bears she in her carriage towards yourself?
　　　SELBY. As one who fears, and yet not greatly cares
For my displeasure. Sometimes I have thought,
A secret glance would tell me she could love,
If I but gave encouragement. Before me
She keeps some moderation; but is never
Closeted with my wife, but in the end
I find my Katherine in briny tears.
From the small chamber, where she first was lodged,
The gradual fiend by specious wriggling arts
Has now ensconced herself in the best part
Of this large mansion; calls the left wing her own;
Commands my servants, equipage.—I hear
Her hated tread. What makes she back so soon?

(*Enter* MRS. FRAMPTON.)

　　　MRS. F. O, I am jolter'd, bruis'd, and shook to death
With your vile Wiltshire roads. The villain Philip
Chose, on my conscience, the perversest tracks,
And stoniest hard lanes in all the county,
Till I was fain get out, and so walk back,
My errand unperform'd at Andover.
　　　LUCY. And I shall love the knave for ever after.
　　　　　　　　　　　　　　　　　　　　　(*Aside.*

MRS. F. A friend with you!

SELBY.   My eldest sister, Lucy,
Come to congratulate this returning morn.—
Sister, my wife's friend, Mistress Frampton.

MRS. F.   Pray,
Be seated, for your brother's sake, you are welcome.
I had thought this day to have been spent in homely fashion.
With the good couple, to whose hospitality
I stand so far indebted. But your coming
Makes it a feast.

LUCY.   She does the honours naturally—

(Aside.

SELBY. As if she were the mistress of the house—

(Aside.

MRS. F. I love to be at home with loving friends.
To stand on ceremony with obligations,
Is to restrain the obliger. That old coach, though,
Of yours jumbles one strangely.

SELBY.   I shall order
An equipage soon, more easy to you, madam—

LUCY. To drive her and her pride to Lucifer,
I hope he means.

(Aside.

MRS. F. I must go trim myself; this humble garb
Would shame a wedding-feast. I have your leave
For a short absence?—and your Katherine—

SELBY. You'll find her in her closet—

MRS. F.   Fare you well, then.

(Exit.

SELBY. How like you her assurance?

LUCY.   Even so well,
That if this Widow were my guest, not yours,
She should have coach enough, and scope to ride.
My merry groom should in a trice convey her
To Sarum Plain, and set her down at Stonehenge,
To pick her path through those antiques at leisure;
She should take sample of our Wiltshire flints.
O, be not lightly jealous! nor surmise,
That to a wanton bold-faced thing like this
Your modest shrinking Katherine could impart
Secrets of any worth, especially
Secrets that touch'd your peace. If there be aught,
My life upon't, 'tis but some girlish story
Of a First Love; which even the boldest wife
Might modestly deny to a husband's ear,
Much more your timid and too sensitive Katherine.

SELBY. I think it is no more; and will dismiss

My further fears, if ever I have had such.

LUCY. Shall we go walk? I'd see your gardens, brother;
And how the new trees thrive, I recommended.
Your Katherine is engaged now—

    SELBY.   I'll attend you.

                                            (*Exeunt.*

(SCENE—*Servant's Hall.*)

(HOUSEKEEPER, PHILIP, *and others, laughing.*)

HOUSEKEEPER. Our Lady's guest, since her short ride, seems ruffled,
And somewhat in disorder. Philip, Philip,
I do suspect some roguery. Your mad tricks
Will some day cost you a good place, I warrant.

PHILIP. Good Mistress Jane, our serious housekeeper,
And sage Duenna to the maids and scullions,
We must have leave to laugh; our brains are younger,
And undisturb'd with care of keys and pantries.
We are wild things.

    BUTLER.   Good Philip, tell us all.

ALL. Ay, as you live, tell, tell—

PHILIP. Mad fellows, you shall have it.
The Widow's bell rang lustily and loud—

BUTLER. I think that no one can mistake her ringing.

WAITING-MAID. Our Lady's ring is soft sweet music to it,
More of entreaty hath it than command.

PHILIP. I lose my story, if you interrupt me thus.
The bell, I say, rang fiercely; and a voice
More shrill than bell, call'd out for "Coachman Philip!"
I straight obey'd, as 'tis my name and office.
"Drive me," quoth she, "to the next market town,
Where I have hope of letters." I made haste;
Put to the horses, saw her safely coach'd,
And drove her—

WAITING-MAID. By the straight high road to Andover,
I guess—

PHILIP. Pray, warrant things within your knowledge,
Good Mistress Abigail; look to your dressings,
And leave the skill in horses to the coachmen.

BUTLER. He'll have his humour; best not interrupt him.

PHILIP. 'Tis market-day, thought I; and the poor beasts,
Meeting such droves of cattle and of people,
May take a fright; so down the lane I trundled,
Where Goodman Dobson's crazy mare was founder'd,
And where the flints were biggest, and ruts widest,
By ups and downs, and such bone-cracking motions
We flounder'd on a furlong, till my madam,

In policy, to save the few joints left her,
Betook her to her feet, and there we parted.
ALL. Ha! ha! ha!
BUTLER. Hang her, 'tis pity such as she should ride.
WAITING-MAID. I think she is a witch; I have tired myself out
With sticking pins in her pillow; still she 'scapes them—
BUTLER. And I with helping her to mum for claret,
But never yet could cheat her dainty palate.
HOUSEKEEPER. Well, well, she is the guest of our good Mistress,
And so should be respected. Though, I think,
Our Master cares not for her company,
He would ill brook we should express so much
By rude discourtesies, and short attendance,
Being but servants. (*A Bell rings furiously.*)
              'Tis her bell speaks now;
Good, good, bestir yourselves: who knows who's wanted?
BUTLER. But 'twas a merry trick of Philip coachman.
                                     (*Exeunt.*)

(SCENE—*Mrs. Selby's Chamber.*)

(MRS. FRAMPTON, KATHERINE, *working.*)

MRS. F. I am thinking, child, how contrary our fates
Have traced our lots through life.—Another needle,
This works untowardly.—An heiress born
To splendid prospects, at our common school
I was as one above you all, not of you;
Had my distinct prerogatives; my freedoms,
Denied to you. Pray, listen—
KATH.   I must hear,
What you are pleased to speak—how my heart sinks here!
                                     (*Aside.*)

MRS. F. My chamber to myself, my separate maid,
My coach, and so forth.—Not that needle, simple one,
With the great staring eye fit for a Cyclops!
Mine own are not so blinded with their griefs,
But I could make a shift to thread a smaller.
A cable or a camel might go through this,
And never strain for the passage.
KATH.   I will fit you.—
Intolerable tyranny!
                                     (*Aside.*)

MRS. F.   Quick, quick;
You were not once so slack.—As I was saying,
Not a young thing among ye, but observed me
Above the mistress. Who but I was sought to
In all your dangers, all your little difficulties,

Your girlish scrapes? I was the scape-goat still,
To fetch you off; kept all your secrets, some,
Perhaps, since then—
  KATH.   No more of that, for mercy,
If you'd not have me, sinking at your feet,
Cleave the cold earth for comfort.

                 (Kneels.

  MRS. F.   This to me?
This posture to your friend had better suited
The orphan Katherine in her humble school-days
To the *then* rich heiress, than the wife of Selby,
Of wealthy Mr. Selby,
To the poor widow Frampton, sunk as she is.
Come, come,
'Twas something, or 'twas nothing, that I said;
I did not mean to fright you, sweetest bed-fellow!
You once were so, but Selby now engrosses you.
I'll make him give you up a night or so;
In faith I will: that we may lie, and talk
Old tricks of school-days over.
  KATH.   Hear me, madam—
  MRS. F. Not by that name. Your friend—
  KATH.   My truest friend,
And saviour of my honour!
  MRS. F.   This sounds better;
You still shall find me such.
  KATH.   That you have graced
Our poor house with your presence hitherto,
Has been my greatest comfort, the sole solace
Of my forlorn and hardly guess'd estate.
You have been pleased
To accept some trivial hospitalities,
In part of payment of a long arrear
I owe to you, no less than for my life.
  MRS. F. You speak my services too large.
  KATH.   Nay, less;
For what an abject thing were life to me
Without your silence on my dreadful secret!
And I would wish the league we have renew'd
Might be perpetual—
  MRS. F.   Have a care, fine madam!

                (Aside.

  KATH. That one house still might hold us. But my husband
Has shown himself of late—
  MRS. F.   How, Mistress Selby?
  KATH. Not, not impatient. You misconstrue him.
He honours, and he loves, nay, he must love

The friend of his wife's youth. But there are moods,
In which—
    MRS. F. I understand you;—in which husbands,
And wives that love, may wish to be alone,
To nurse the tender fits of new-born dalliance,
After a five years' wedlock.
    KATH.   Was that well,
Or charitably put? do these pale cheeks
Proclaim a wanton blood? This wasting form
Seem a fit theatre for Levity
To play his love-tricks on; and act such follies,
As even in Affection's first bland Moon
Have less of grace than pardon in best wedlocks?
I was about to say, that there are times,
When the most frank and sociable man
May surfeit on most loved society,
Preferring loneness rather—
    MRS. F.   To my company—
    KATH. Ay, yours, or mine, or any one's. Nay, take
Not this unto yourself. Even in the newness
Of our first married loves 'twas sometimes so.
For solitude, I have heard my Selby say,
Is to the mind as rest to the corporal functions;
And he would call it oft, the *day's soft sleep.*
    MRS. F. What is your drift? and whereto tends this speech,
Rhetorically labour'd?
    KATH.   That you would
Abstain but from our house a month, a week;
I make request but for a single day.
    MRS. F. A month, a week, a day! A single hour
Is every week, and month, and the long year,
And all the years to come! My footing here,
Slipt once, recovers never. From the state
Of gilded roofs, attendance, luxuries,
Parks, gardens, sauntering walks, or wholesome rides,
To the bare cottage on the withering moor,
Where I myself am servant to myself,
Or only waited on by blackest thoughts—
I sink, if this be so. No; here I sit.
    KATH. Then I am lost for ever!
                 (*Sinks at her feet—curtain drops.*

(SCENE—*An Apartment contiguous to the last.* SELBY, *as if listening.*)

    SELBY. The sounds have died away. What am I changed to?
What do I here, list'ning like to an abject
Or heartless wittol, that must hear no good,

If he hear aught? "This shall to the ear of your husband."
It was the Widow's word. I guess'd some mystery,
And the solution with a vengeance comes.
What can my wife have left untold to me,
That must be told by proxy? I begin
To call in doubt the course of her life past
Under my very eyes. She hath not been good,
Not virtuous, not discreet; she hath not outrun
My wishes still with prompt and meek observance.
Perhaps she is not fair, sweet-voiced; her eyes
Not like the dove's; all this as well may be,
As that she should entreasure up a secret
In the peculiar closet of her breast,
And grudge it to my ear. It is my right
To claim the halves in any truth she owns,
As much as in the babe I have by her;
Upon whose face henceforth I fear to look,
Lest I should fancy in its innocent brow
Some strange shame written.

(Enter LUCY.)

      Sister, an anxious word with you.
From out the chamber, where my wife but now
Held talk with her encroaching friend, I heard
(Not of set purpose heark'ning, but by chance)
A voice of chiding, answer'd by a tone
Of replication, such as the meek dove
Makes, when the kite has clutch'd her. The high Widow
Was loud and stormy. I distinctly heard
One threat pronounced—"Your husband shall know all."
I am no listener, sister; and I hold
A secret, got by such unmanly shift,
The pitiful'st of thefts; but what mine ear,
I not intending it, receives perforce,
I count my lawful prize. Some subtle meaning
Lurks in this fiend's behaviour; which, by force,
Or fraud, I must make mine.
  LUCY.   The gentlest means
Are still the wisest. What, if you should press
Your wife to a disclosure?
  SELBY.   I have tried
All gentler means; thrown out low hints, which though
Merely suggestions still, have never fail'd
To blanch her cheek with fears. Roughlier to insist,
Would be to kill, where I but meant to heal.
  LUCY. Your own description gave that Widow out
As one not much precise, nor over coy,

And nice to listen to a suit of love.
What if you feign'd a courtship, putting on
(To work the secret from her easy faith).
For honest ends, a most dishonest seeming?
    SELBY. I see your drift, and partly meet your counsel
But must it not in me appear prodigious,
To say the least, unnatural, and suspicious,
To move hot love, where I have shown cool scorn,
And undissembled looks of blank aversion?
    LUCY. Vain woman is the dupe of her own charms,
And easily credits the resistless power,
That in besieging beauty lies, to cast down
The slight-built fortress of a casual hate.
    SELBY. I am resolved—
    LUCY.   Success attend your wooing!
    SELBY. And I'll about it roundly, my wise sister.

                                          (*Exeunt.*

    (SCENE—*The Library.* MR. SELBY. MRS. FRAMPTON.)

    SELBY. A fortunate encounter, Mistress Frampton.
My purpose was, if you could spare so much
From your sweet leisure, a few words in private.
    MRS. F. What mean his alter'd tones? These looks to me,
Whose glances yet he has repell'd with coolness?
Is the wind changed? I'll veer about with it,
And meet him in all fashions.

                                          (*Aside.*

                    All my leisure,
Feebly bestow'd upon my kind friends here,
Would not express a tithe of the obligements
I every hour incur.
    SELBY.   No more of that.
I know not why, my wife hath lost of late
Much of her cheerful spirits.
    MRS. F.   It was my topic
To-day; and every day, and all day long,
I still am chiding with her. "Child," I said,
And said it pretty roundly—it may be
I was too peremptory—we elder school-fellows,
Presuming on the advantage of a year
Or two, which, in that tender time, seem'd much,
In after years, much like to elder sisters,
Are prone to keep the authoritative style,
When time has made the difference most ridiculous—
    SELBY. The observation's shrewd.
    MRS. F.   "Child," I was saying,

"If some wives had obtain'd a lot like yours,"
And then perhaps I sigh'd, "they would not sit
In corners moping, like to sullen moppets,
That want their will, but dry their eyes, and look
Their cheerful husbands in the face," perhaps
I said, their Selbys, "with proportion'd looks
Of honest joy."

SELBY.   You do suspect no jealousy?
MRS. F. What is his import? Whereto tends his speech?

(Aside.

Of whom, or what, should she be jealous, sir?
SELBY. I do not know, but women have their fancies;
And underneath a cold indifference,
Or show of some distaste, husbands have mask'd
A growing fondness for a female friend,
Which the wife's eye was sharp enough to see,
Before the friend had wit to find it out.
You do not quit us soon?
MRS. F.   'Tis as I find;
Your Katherine profits by my lessons, sir.—
Means this man honest? Is there no deceit?

(Aside.

SELBY. She cannot choose.—Well, well, I have been thinking,
And if the matter were to do again—
MRS. F. What matter, sir?
SELBY.   This idle bond of wedlock;
These sour-sweet briars, fetters of harsh silk;
I might have made, I do not say a better,
But a more fit choice in a wife.
MRS. F.   The parch'd ground,
In hottest Julys, drinks not in the showers
More greedily than I his words!

(Aside.

SELBY.   My humour
Is to be frank and jovial; and that man
Affects me best, who most reflects me in
My most free temper.
MRS. F.   Were you free to choose,
As jestingly I'll put the supposition,
Without a thought reflecting on your Katherine,
What sort of Woman would you make your choice?
SELBY. I like your humour and will meet your jest.
She should be one about my Katherine's age;
But not so old, by some ten years, in gravity,
One that would meet my mirth, sometimes outrun it;
No puling, pining moppet, as you said,
Nor moping maid that I must still be teaching

The freedoms of a wife all her life after:
But one that, having worn the chain before
(And worn it lightly, as report gave out),
Enfranchised from it by her poor fool's death,
Took it not so to heart that I need dread
To die myself, for fear a second time
To wet a widow's eye.

MRS. F.   Some widows, sir,
Hearing you talk so wildly, would be apt
To put strange misconstruction on your words,
As aiming at a Turkish liberty,
Where the free husband hath his several mates,
His Penseroso, his Allegro wife,
To suit his sober or his frolic fit.

SELBY. How judge you of that latitude?

MRS. F.   As one,
In European customs bred, must judge. Had I
Been born a native of the liberal East,
I might have thought as they do. Yet I knew
A married man that took a second wife,
And (the man's circumstances duly weigh'd,
With all their bearings) the considerate world
Nor much approved, nor much condemn'd the deed.

SELBY. You move my wonder strangely. Pray, proceed.

MRS. F. An eye of wanton liking he had placed
Upon a Widow, who liked him again,
But stood on terms of honourable love,
And scrupled wronging his most virtuous wife—
When to their ears a lucky rumour ran,
That this demure and saintly-seeming wife
Had a first husband living; with the which
Being question'd, she but faintly could deny.
"A priest indeed there was; some words had pass'd,
But scarce amounting to a marriage rite.
Her friend was absent; she supposed him dead;
And, seven years parted, both were free to choose."

SELBY. What did the indignant husband? Did he not
With violent handlings stigmatise the cheek
Of the deceiving wife, who had entail'd
Shame on their innocent babe?

MRS. F.   He neither tore
His wife's locks nor his own; but wisely weighing
His own offence with hers in equal poise,
And woman's weakness 'gainst the strength of man,
Came to a calm and witty compromise.
He coolly took his gay-faced widow home,
Made her his second wife; and still the first

Lost few or none of her prerogatives.
The servants call'd her mistress still; she kept
The keys, and had the total ordering
Of the house affairs; and, some slight toys excepted,
Was all a moderate wife would wish to be.

SELBY. A tale full of dramatic incident!—
And if a man should put it in a play,
How should he name the parties?

MRS. F.   The man's name
Through time I have forgot—the widow's too;—
But his first wife's name, her maiden one,
Was—not unlike to *that* your Katherine bore,
Before she took the honour'd style of Selby.

SELBY. A dangerous meaning in your riddle lurks.
One knot is yet unsolved; that told, this strange
And most mysterious drama ends. The name
Of that first husband—

(Enter LUCY.*)*

MRS. F.   Sir, your pardon—
The allegory fits your private ear.
Some half-hour hence, in the garden's secret walk,
We shall have leisure.

                                        (Exit.

SELBY.   Sister, whence come you?
LUCY. From your poor Katherine's chamber, where she droops
In sad presageful thoughts, and sighs, and weeps,
And seems to pray by turns. At times she looks
As she would pour her secret in my bosom—
Then starts, as I have seen her, at the mention
Of some immodest act. At her request
I left her on her knees.

SELBY.   The fittest posture;
For great has been her fault to Heaven and me.
She married me with a first husband living,
Or not known not to be so, which, in the judgment
Of any but indifferent honesty,
Must be esteem'd the same. The shallow Widow,
Caught by my art, under a riddling veil
Too thin to hide her meaning, hath confess'd all.
Your coming in broke off the conference,
When she was ripe to tell the fatal *name*
That seals my wedded doom.

LUCY.   Was she so forward
To pour her hateful meanings in your ear
At the first hint?

SELBY.   Her newly flatter'd hopes

Array'd themselves at first in forms of doubt;
And with a female caution she stood off
Awhile, to read the meaning of my suit,
Which with such honest seeming I enforced,
That her cold scruples soon gave way; and now
She rests prepared, as mistress, or as wife,
To seize the place of her betrayèd friend—
My much offending, but more suffering, Katherine.

    LUCY. Into what labyrinth of fearful shapes
My simple project has conducted you—
Were but my wit as skilful to invent
A clue to lead you forth!—I call to mind
A letter, which your wife received from the Cape,
Soon after you were married, with some circumstances
Of mystery too.

    SELBY.   I well remember it.
That letter did confirm the truth (she said)
Of a friend's death, which she had long fear'd true,
But knew not for a fact. A youth of promise
She gave him out—a hot adventurous spirit—
That had set sail in quest of golden dreams,
And cities in the heart of Central Afric;
But named no names, nor did I care to press
My question further, in the passionate grief
She show'd at the receipt. Might this be he?

    LUCY. Tears were not all. When that first shower was past,
With clasp'd hands she raised her eyes to Heav'n,
As if in thankfulness for some escape,
Or strange deliverance, in the news implied,
Which sweeten'd that sad news.

    SELBY.   Something of that
I noted also—

    LUCY.   In her closet once,
Seeking some other trifle, I espied
A ring, in mournful characters deciphering
The death of "Robert Halford, aged two
And twenty." Brother, I am not given
To the confident use of wagers, which I hold
Unseemly in a woman's argument;
But I am strangely tempted now to risk
A thousand pounds out of my patrimony
(And let my future husband look to it,
If it be lost), that this immodest Widow
Shall name the name that tallies with that ring.

    SELBY. That wager lost, I should be rich indeed—
Rich in my rescued Kate—rich in my honour,
Which now was bankrupt. Sister, I accept

Your merry wager, with an aching heart
For very fear of winning. 'Tis the hour
That I should meet my Widow in the walk,
The south side of the garden. On some pretence
Lure forth my Wife that way, that she may witness
Our seeming courtship. Keep us still in sight,
Yourselves unseen; and by some sign I'll give
(A finger held up, or a kerchief waved),
You'll know your wager won—then break upon us,
As if by chance.

    LUCY.   I apprehend your meaning—

    SELBY. And may you prove a true Cassandra here,
Though my poor acres smart for't, wagering sister!

                                    (*Exeunt.*

(SCENE—*Mrs. Selby's Chamber.* MRS. FRAMPTON. KATHERINE.)

    MRS. F. Did I express myself in terms so strong?

    KATH. As nothing could have more affrighted me.

    MRS. F. Think it a hurt friend's jest, in retribution
Of a suspected cooling hospitality.
And, for my staying here, or going hence
(Now I remember something of our argument),
Selby and I can settle that between us.
You look amazed. What if your husband, child,
Himself has courted me to stay?

    KATH.   You move
My wonder and my pleasure equally.

    MRS. F. Yes, courted me to stay, waived all objections,
Made it a favour to yourselves; not me,
His troublesome guest, as you surmised. Child, child,
When I recall his flattering welcome, I
Begin to think the burden of my presence
Was—

    KATH. What, for Heaven—

    MRS. F.   A little, little spice
Of jealousy—that's all—an honest pretext,
No wife need blush for. Say that you should see
(As oftentimes we widows take such freedoms,
Yet still on this side virtue), in a jest
Your husband pat me on the cheek, or steal
A kiss, while you were by,—not else, for virtue's sake.

    KATH. I could endure all this, thinking my husband
Meant it in sport—

    MRS. F.   But if in downright earnest
(Putting myself out of the question here)
Your Selby, as I partly do suspect,

Own'd a divided heart—
 KATH.   My own would break—
MRS. F. Why, what a blind and witless fool it is,
That will not see its gains, its infinite gains—
 KATH. Gain in a loss.
       Or mirth in utter desolation!
MRS. F. He doating on a face—suppose it mine,
Or any other's tolerably fair—
What need you care about a senseless secret?
 KATH. Perplex'd and fearful woman! I in part
Fathom your dangerous meaning. You have broke
The worse than iron band, fretting the soul,
By which you held me captive. Whether my husband
Is what you gave him out, or your fool'd fancy
But dreams he is so, either way I am free.
 MRS. F. It talks it bravely blazons out its shame;
A very heroine while on its knees;
Rowe's Penitent, an absolute Calista?
 KATH. Not to thy wretched self these tears are falling;
But to my husband, and offended Heaven,
Some drops are due—and then I sleep in peace,
Relieved from frightful dreams, my dreams though sad.

                (*Exit*

 MRS. F. I have gone too far. Who knows but in this mood
She may forestall my story, win on Selby
By a frank confession?—and the time draws on
For our appointed meeting. The game's desperate,
For which I play. A moment's difference
May make it hers or mine. I fly to meet him.

                (*Exit*

   (SCENE—*A Garden.* MR. SELBY. MRS. FRAMPTON.)

 SELBY. I am not so ill a guesser, Mrs. Frampton,
Not to conjecture, that some passages
In your unfinish'd story, rightly interpreted,
Glanced at my bosom's peace;
        You knew my wife?
 MRS. F. Even from her earliest school-days—What of that?
Or how is she concern'd in my fine riddles,
Framed for the hour's amusement?
 SELBY.   By my *hopes*
Of my new interest conceived in you,
And by the honest passion of my heart,
Which not obliquely I to you did hint;
Come from the clouds of misty allegory,
And in plain language let me hear the worst.

Stand I disgraced, or no?

MRS. F.   Then, by *my* hopes
Of my new interest conceived in you,
And by the kindling passion in *my* breast,
Which through my riddles you had almost read,
Adjured so strongly, I will tell you all.
In her school years, then bordering on fifteen,
Or haply not much past, she loved a youth—

SELBY. My most ingenuous Widow—

MRS. F.   Met him oft
By stealth, where I still of the party was—

SELBY. Prime confidant to all the school, I warrant,
And general go-between—

                                                      (*Aside.*

MRS. F.   One morn he came
In breathless haste. "The ship was under sail,
Or in few hours would be, that must convey
Him and his destinies to barbarous shores,
Where, should he perish by inglorious hands,
It would be consolation in his death
To have call'd his Katherine *his*."

SELBY.   Thus far the story
Tallies with what I hoped.

                                                      (*Aside.*

MRS. F.   Wavering between
The doubt of doing wrong, and losing him;
And my dissuasions not o'er hotly urged,
Whom he had flatter'd with the bride-maid's part;—

SELBY. I owe my subtle Widow, then, for this.

                                                      (*Aside.*

MRS. F. Briefly, we went to church. The ceremony
Scarcely was huddled over, and the ring
Yet cold upon her finger, when they parted—
He to his ship; and we to school got back,
Scarce miss'd, before the dinner-bell could ring.

SELBY. And from that hour—

MRS. F.   Nor sight, nor news of him,
For aught that I could hear, she e'er obtain'd.

SELBY. Like to a man that hovers in suspense
Over a letter just received, on which
The black seal hath impress'd its ominous token,
Whether to open it or no, so I
Suspended stand, whether to press my fate
Further, or check ill curiosity,
That tempts me to more loss.—The name, the name
Of this fine youth?

MRS. F. What boots it, if 'twere told?

SELBY.   Now, by our loves,

And by my hopes of happier wedlocks, some day
To be accomplish'd, give me his name!
   MRS. F. 'Tis no such serious matter. It was—Huntingdon.
   SELBY. How have three little syllables pluck'd from me
A world of countless hopes!—

                                    (*Aside.*

                  Evasive Widow.
   MRS. F. How, sir!—I like not this.

                                      (*Aside.*

   SELBY.   No, no, I meant
Nothing but good to thee. That other woman,
How shall I call her but evasive, false,
And treacherous?—by the trust I place in thee,
Tell me, and tell me truly, was the name
As you pronounced it?
   MRS. F.   Huntingdon—the name,
Which his paternal grandfather assumed,
Together with the estates of a remote
Kinsman: but our high-spirited youth—
   SELBY.   Yes—
   MRS. F.   Disdaining
For sordid pelf to truck the family honours,
At risk of the lost estates, resumed the old style,
And answer'd only to the name of—
   SELBY.   What—
   MRS. F. Of Halford—
   SELBY. A Huntingdon to Halford changed so soon!
Why, then I see, a witch hath her good spells,
As well as bad, and can by a backward charm
Unruffle the foul storm she has just been raising.
                      (*Aside. He makes the signal.*
My frank, fair-spoken Widow! let this kiss,
Which yet aspires no higher, speak my thanks,
Till I can think on greater.

            (*Enter* LUCY *and* KATHERINE.)
   MRS. F.   Interrupted!
   SELBY. My sister here! and see, where with her comes
My serpent gliding in an angel's form,
To taint the new-born Eden of our joys.
Why should we fear them? We'll not stir a foot,
Nor coy it for their pleasures.

                     (*He courts the Widow.*
   LUCY (*to* KATHERINE).   This your free,
And sweet ingenuous confession, binds me
For ever to you; and it shall go hard,
But it shall fetch you back your husband's heart,
That now seems blindly straying; or, at worst,

In me you have still a sister.—Some wives, brother,
Would think it strange to catch their husbands thus
Alone with a trim widow; but your Katherine
Is arm'd, I think, with patience.
    KATH.   I am fortified
With knowledge of self-faults to endure worse wrongs,
If they be wrongs, than he can lay upon me;
Even to look on, and see him sue in earnest,
As now I think he does it but in seeming,
To that ill woman.
    SELBY.   Good words, gentle Kate,
And not a thought irreverent of our Widow.
Why 'twere unmannerly at any time,
But most uncourteous on our wedding day,
When we should show most hospitable.—Some wine!
                                      (Wine is brought.

I am for sports. And now I do remember,
The old Egyptians at their banquets placed
A charnel sight of dead men's skulls before them,
With images of cold mortality,
To temper their fierce joys when they grew rampant.
I like the custom well: and ere we crown   •
With freer mirth the day, I shall propose,
In calmest recollection of our spirits,
We drink the solemn "Memory of the Dead"—
    MRS. F. Or the supposed dead—
                                      (Aside to him.

    SELBY.   Pledge me, good wife—
                                          (She fills.

Nay, higher yet, till the brimm'd cup swell o'er.
    KATH. I catch the awful import of your words;
And, though I could accuse you of unkindness,
Yet as your lawful and obedient wife,
While that name last (as I perceive it fading,
Nor I much longer may have leave to use it)
I calmly take the office you impose;
And on my knees, imploring their forgiveness,
Whom I in heaven or earth may have offended.   •
Exempt from starting tears, and woman's weakness,
I pledge you, sir—the Memory of the Dead!
                                  (She drinks kneeling.

    SELBY. 'Tis gently and discreetly said, and like
My former loving Kate.
    MRS. F.   Does he relent?
                                        (Aside.

    SELBY. That ceremony past, we give the day
To unabated sport. And, in requital
Of certain stories and quaint allegories,

Which my rare Widow hath been telling to me
To raise my morning mirth, if she will lend
Her patient hearing, I will here recite
A Parable; and, the more to suit her taste,
The scene is laid in the East.
 MRS. F.   I long to hear it.
Some tale, to fit his wife.

                (*Aside.*

 KATH.   Now, comes my TRIAL.
 LUCY. The hour of your deliverance is at hand,
If I presage right. Bear up, gentlest sister.
 SELBY. "The Sultan Haroun"—Stay—O now I have it—
"The Caliph Haroun in his orchards had
A fruit-tree, bearing such delicious fruits,
That he reserved them for his proper gust;
And through the Palace it was Death proclaim'd
To any one that should purloin the same."
 MRS. F. A heavy penance for so light a fault—
 SELBY. Pray you, be silent, else you put me out.
"A crafty page, that for advantage watch'd,
Detected in the act a brother page,
Of his own years, that was his bosom friend;
And thenceforth he became that other's lord,
And like a tyrant he demean'd himself,
Laid forced exactions on his fellow's purse;
And when that poor means fail'd, held o'er his head
Threats of impending death in hideous forms;
Till the small culprit on his nightly couch
Dream'd of strange pains, and felt his body writhe
In tortuous pangs around the impaling stake."
 MRS. F. I like not this beginning—
 SELBY.   Pray you, attend.
"The Secret, like a night-hag, rid his sleeps,
And took the youthful pleasures from his days,
And chased the youthful smoothness from his brow,
That from a rose-cheek'd boy he waned and waned
To a pale skeleton of what he was;
And would have died, but for one lucky chance."
 KATH. Oh!
 MRS. F. Your wife—she faints—some cordial—smell to this.
 SELBY. Stand off. My sister best will do that office.
 MRS. F. Are all his tempting speeches come to this?

                (*Aside.*

 SELBY. What ail'd my wife?
 KATH.   A warning faintness, sir,
Seized on my spirits, when you came to where
You said "a lucky chance." I am better now:
Please you go on.

SELBY.   The sequel shall be brief.

KATH. But, brief or long, I feel my fate hangs on it.

(Aside.

SELBY. "One morn the Caliph, in a covert hid,
Close by an arbour where the two boys talk'd
(As oft, we read, that Eastern sovereigns
Would play the eavesdropper, to learn the truth,
Imperfectly received from mouths of slaves),
O'erheard their dialogue; and heard enough
To judge aright the cause, and know his cue.
The following day a Cadi was despatch'd
To summon both before the judgment-seat;
The lickerish culprit, almost dead with fear,
And the informing friend, who readily,
Fired with fair promises of large reward,
And Caliph's love, the hateful truth disclosed."

MRS. F. What did the Caliph to the offending boy,
That had so grossly err'd?

SELBY.   His sceptred hand
He forth in token of forgiveness stretch'd,
And clapp'd his cheeks, and courted him with gifts,
And he became once more his favourite page.

MRS. F. But for that other—

SELBY.   He dismiss'd him straight,
From dreams of grandeur, and of Caliph's love,
To the bare cottage on the withering moor,
Where friends, turn'd fiends, and hollow confidants,
And widows, hide, who in a husband's ear
Pour baneful truths, but tell not all the truth;
And told him not that Robin Halford died
Some moons before *his* marriage-bells were rung.
Too near dishonour hast thou trod, dear wife,
And on a dangerous cast our fates were set;
But Heav'n, that will'd our wedlock to be blest,
Hath interposed to save it gracious too.
Your penance is—to dress your cheek in smiles,
And to be once again my merry Kate.—
Sister, your hand.
Your wager won makes me a happy man,
Though poorer, Heav'n knows, by a thousand pounds.
The sky clears up after a dubious day.
Widow, your hand. I read a penitence
In this dejected brow; and in this shame
Your fault is buried. You shall in with us,
And, if it please you, taste our nuptial fare:
For, till this moment, I can joyful say,
Was never truly Selby's Wedding Day.

THE

PAWNBROKER'S DAUGHTER

A FARCE

CHARACTERS

FLINT, *a Pawnbroker.*
DAVENPORT, *in love with Marian.*
PENDULOUS, *a Reprieved Gentleman.*
CUTLET, *a Sentimental Butcher.*
GOLDING, *a Magistrate.*
WILLIAM, *Apprentice to Flint.*
BEN, *Cutlet's Boy.*
MISS FLYN.
BETTY, *her Maid.*
MARIAN, *Daughter to Flint.*
LUCY, *her Maid.*

THE

PAWNBROKER'S DAUGHTER

A FARCE

ACT I

(SCENE—*An Apartment at* FLINT'S *House.* FLINT. WILLIAM.)

FLINT. Carry those umbrellas, cottons, and wearing apparel, upstairs. You may send that chest of tools to Robins's.

WILLIAM. That which you lent six pounds upon to the journeyman carpenter that had the sick wife?

FLINT. The same.

WILLIAM. The man says, if you can give him till Thursday—

FLINT. Not a minute longer. His time was out yesterday. These improvident fools!

WILLIAM. The finical gentleman has been here about that seal that was his grandfather's.

FLINT. He cannot have it. Truly, our trade would be brought to a fine pass if we were bound to humour the fancies of our customers. This man would be taking a liking to a snuff-box that he had inherited, and that gentlewoman might conceit a favourite chemise that had descended to her.

WILLIAM. The lady in the carriage has been here crying about those jewels. She says, if you cannot let her have them at the advance she offers, her husband will come to know that she has pledged them.

FLINT. I have use for those jewels. Send Marian to me. (*Exit* WILLIAM.) I know no other trade that is expected to depart from its fair advantages but ours. I do not see the baker, the butcher, the shoemaker, or, to go higher, the lawyer, the physician, the divine, give up any of their legitimate gains, even when the pretences of their art had failed; yet *we* are to be branded with an odious name, stigmatised, discountenanced even by the administrators of those laws which acknowledge us,—scowled at by lower sort of people, whose needs we serve!

(*Enter* MARIAN.)

Come hither, Marian. Come, kiss your father. The report runs that he is full of spotted crime. What is your belief, child?

MARIAN. That never good report went with our calling, father. I have

485

heard you say, the poor look only to the advantages which we derive from them, and overlook the accommodations which they receive from us. But the poor *are* the poor, father, and have little leisure to make distinctions. I wish we could give up this business.

FLINT. You have not seen that idle fellow, Davenport?

MARIAN. No, indeed, father, since your injunction.

FLINT. I take but my lawful profit. The law is not over-favourable to us.

MARIAN. Marian is no judge of these things.

FLINT. They call me oppressive, grinding—I know not what—

MARIAN. Alas!

FLINT. Usurer, extortioner. Am I these things?

MARIAN. You are Marian's kind and careful father. That is enough for a child to know.

FLINT. Here, girl, is a little box of jewels, which the necessities of a foolish woman of quality have transferred into our true and lawful possession. Go, place them with the trinkets that were your mother's. They are all yours, Marian, if you do not cross me in your marriage. No gentry shall match into this house to flout their wife hereafter with her parentage. I will hold this business with convulsive grasp to my dying day. I will plague these *poor*, whom you speak so tenderly of.

MARIAN. You frighten me, father. Do not frighten Marian.

FLINT. I have heard them say, "There goes Flint! Flint, the cruel pawnbroker!"

MARIAN. Stay at home with Marian. You shall hear no ugly words to vex you.

FLINT. You shall ride in a gilded chariot upon the necks of these *poor*, Marian. Their tears shall drop pearls for my girl. Their sighs shall be good wind for us. They shall blow good for my girl. Put up the jewels, Marian.

(*Exit.*

(*Enter* LUCY.)

LUCY. Miss, miss, your father has taken his hat, and stepped out; and Mr. Davenport is on the stairs; and I come to tell you—

MARIAN. Alas! who let him in?

(*Enter* DAVENPORT.)

DAV. My dearest girl—

MARIAN. My father will kill me if he finds you have been here!

DAV. There is no time for explanations. I have positive information that your father means, in less than a week, to dispose of you to that ugly Saunders. The wretch has bragged of it to his acquaintance, and already calls you *his*.

MARIAN. O Heavens!

DAV. Your resolution must be summary, as the time which calls for it. Mine or his you must be, without delay. There is no safety for you under this roof.

MARIAN. My father—

DAV. Is no father, if he would sacrifice you.

MARIAN. But he is unhappy. Do not speak hard words of my father.

DAV. Marian must exert her good sense.

LUCY (*as if watching at the window*). Oh miss, your father has suddenly returned! I see him with Mr. Saunders coming down the street! Mr. Saunders, ma'am!

MARIAN. Begone, begone, if you love me, Davenport!

DAV. You must go with me, then, else here I am fixed.

LUCY. Ay, miss, you must go, as Mr. Davenport says. Here is your cloak, miss, and your hat, and your gloves. Your father, ma'am!—

MARIAN. Oh where? where? Whither do you hurry me, Davenport?

DAV. Quickly, quickly, Marian! At the back-door.

(*Exit* MARIAN, *with* DAVENPORT, *reluctantly; in her flight still holding the jewels.*)

LUCY. Away!—away! What a lucky thought of mine to say her father was coming! he would never have got her off else. Lord, Lord, I do love to help lovers!

(*Exit, following them.*

(SCENE—*A Butcher's Shop.* CUTLET. BEN.)

CUTLET. Reach me down that book off the shelf where the shoulder of veal hangs.

BEN. Is this it?

CUTLET. No,—this is "Flowers of Sentiment": the other,—ay, this is a good book: "An Argument against the Use of Animal Food. By J. R." *That* means Joseph Ritson. I will open it anywhere, and read, just as it happens. One cannot dip amiss into such a book as this. The motto, I see, is from Pope; I daresay, very much to the purpose. (*Reads:*)—

> "The lamb thy riot dooms to bleed to-day;
> Had he thy reason, would he skip and play?
> Pleased to the last he crops the flowery food,
> And licks the hand"—

Bless us! is that saddle of mutton gone home to Mrs. Simpson's? It should have gone an hour ago.

BEN. I was just going with it.

CUTLET. Well, go. Where was I? Oh!—

> "And licks the hand just raised to shed its blood."

What an affecting picture! (*Turns over the leaves and reads:*)—

> "It is probable that the long lives which are recorded of the people before the Flood were owing to their being confined to vegetable diet."

BEN. The young gentleman in Pullen's Row, Islington, that has got the consumption, has sent to know if you can let him have a sweetbread.

CUTLET. Take two,—take all that are in shop. What a disagreeable interruption! (*Reads again:*)—

"Those fierce and angry passions, which impel man to wage destructive war with man, may be traced to the ferment in the blood, produced by animal diet."

BEN. The two pounds of rump-steaks must go home to Mr. Molyneux's. He is in training to fight Cribb.

CUTLET. Well, take them: go along, and do not trouble me with your disgusting details.

CUTLET (*throwing down the book*). Why was I bred to this detestable business? Was it not plain that this trembling sensibility, which has marked my character from earliest infancy, must disqualify me for a profession which—what do ye want?—what do ye buy? Oh! it is only somebody going past. I thought it had been a customer—Why was not I bred a glover, like my cousin Langston? To see him poke his two little sticks into a delicate pair of real Woodstock,—"A very little stretching, ma'am, and they will fit exactly."—Or a haberdasher, like my next-door neighbour,—"Not a better bit of lace in all town, my lady: Mrs. Break-stock took the last of it last Friday; all but this bit, which I can afford to let your ladyship have at a bargain. Reach down that drawer on your left hand, Miss Fisher."

(*Enter in haste* DAVENPORT, MARIAN, *and* LUCY.)

LUCY. This is the house I saw a bill up at, ma'am; and a droll creature the landlord is.

DAV. We have no time for nicety.

CUTLET. What do ye want? what do ye buy? Oh! it is only Mrs. Lucy.

(LUCY *whispers* CUTLET.)

CUTLET. I have a set of apartments at the end of my garden. They are quite detached from the shop. A single lady at present occupies the ground floor.

MARIAN. Ay, ay, anywhere.

DAV. In, in—

CUTLET. Pretty lamb!—she seems agitated.

(DAVENPORT *and* MARIAN *go in with* CUTLET.)

LUCY. I am mistaken if my young lady does not find an agreeable companion in these apartments. Almost a namesake. Only the difference of Flyn and Flint. I have some errands to do, or I would stop and have some fun with this droll butcher.

(CUTLET *returns*.)

CUTLET. Why, how odd this is! *Your* young lady knows *my* young lady. They are as thick as flies.

LUCY. You may thank me for your new lodger, Mr. Cutlet. But, bless me, you do not look well!

CUTLET. To tell you the truth, I am rather heavy about the eyes. Want of sleep, I believe.

LUCY. Late hours, perhaps. Raking last night?

CUTLET. No: that is not it, Mrs. Lucy. My repose was disturbed by a very different cause from what you may imagine. It proceeded from too much thinking.

LUCY. The deuce it did! And what, if I may be so bold, might be the subject of your Night Thoughts?

CUTLET. The distress of my fellow-creatures. I never lay my head down on my pillow but I fall a-thinking, how many at this very instant are perishing!—some with cold—

LUCY. What! in the midst of Summer?

CUTLET. Ay. Not here; but in countries abroad, where the climate is different from ours. Our Summers are their Winters, and *vice versâ,* you know. Some with cold—

LUCY. What a canting rogue it is! I should like to trump up some fine story to plague him.

(Aside.

CUTLET. Others with hunger; some a prey to the rage of wild beasts—

LUCY. He has got this by rote, out of some book.

CUTLET. Some drowning, crossing crazy bridges in the dark; some by violence of the devouring flame—

LUCY. I have it. For that matter, you need not send your humanity a-travelling, Mr. Cutlet. For instance, last night—

CUTLET. Some by fevers, some by gunshot-wounds—

LUCY. Only two streets off—

CUTLET. Some in drunken quarrels—

LUCY *(aloud).* The butcher's shop at the corner.

CUTLET. What were you saying about poor Cleaver?

LUCY. He has found his ears at last. *(Aside.)* That he has had his house burnt down.

CUTLET. Bless me!

LUCY. I saw four small children taken in at the greengrocer's.

CUTLET. Do you know if he is insured?

LUCY. Some say he is, but not to the full amount.

CUTLET. Not to the full amount?—how shocking! He killed more meat than any of the trade between here and Carnaby Market; and the poor babes,—four of them, you say,—what a melting sight! He served some good customers about Marybone— I always think more of the children, in these cases, than of the fathers and mothers— Lady Love-brown liked his veal better than any man's in the market— I wonder whether her ladyship is engaged— I must go and comfort poor Cleaver, however.

(Exit.

LUCY. Now is this pretender to humanity gone to avail himself of a neighbour's supposed ruin to inveigle his customers from him. Fine feelings!—pshaw!

(Exit.

(*Re-enter* CUTLET.)

CUTLET. What a deceitful young hussy! there is not a word of truth in her. There has been no fire. How can people play with one's feelings so? (*Sings:*)—

"For tenderness form'd"—

No: I'll try the air I made upon myself. The words may compose me. (*Sings:*)—

"A weeping Londoner I am;
A washer-woman was my dam;
She bred me up in a cock-loft,
And fed my mind with sorrows soft.

"For when she wrung, with elbows stout,
From linen wet the water out,
The drops so like the tears did drip,
They gave my infant nerves the hyp.

"Scarce three clean muckingers a week
Would dry the brine that dew'd my cheek;
So, while I gave my sorrow scope,
I almost ruin'd her in soap.

"My parish learning I did win
In ward of Farringdon-Within;
Where, after school, I did pursue
My sports, as little boys will do.

"Cockchafers—none like me was found
To set them spinning round and round.
Oh, how my tender heart would melt
To think what those poor varmin felt!

"I never tied tin-kettle, clog,
Or salt-box, at the tail of dog,
Without a pang more keen at heart
Than he felt at his outward part.

"And when the poor thing clatter'd off,
To all the unfeeling mob a scoff,
Thought I, 'What that dumb creature feels,
With half the parish at his heels!'

"Arrived, you see, to man's estate,
The butcher's calling is my fate;
Yet still I keep my feeling ways,
And leave the town on slaughtering-days.

"At Kentish Town, or Highgate Hill,
I sit, retired, beside some rill;
And tears bedew my glistening eye,
To think my playful lambs must die.

"But, when they're dead, I sell their meat
On shambles kept both clean and neat:
Sweetbreads also I guard full well,
And keep them from the blue-bottle.

"Envy, with breath sharp as my steel,
Has ne'er yet blown upon my veal;
And mouths of dames, and daintiest fops,
Do water at my nice lamb-chops."

(Exit, half laughing, half crying.

(SCENE—*A Street.* DAVENPORT, *solus.*)

DAV. Thus far have I secured my charming prize. I can appreciate, while I lament, the delicacy which makes her refuse the protection of my sister's roof. But who comes here?

(Enter PENDULOUS, *agitated.*)

It must be. That fretful animal-motion,—that face working up and down with uneasy sensibility, like new yeast,—Jack—Jack Pendulous!

PEN. It is your old friend, and very miserable.

DAV. Vapours, Jack. I have not known you fifteen years to have to guess at your complaint. Why, they troubled you at school. Do you remember when you had to speak the speech of Buckingham, when he is going to execution?

PEN. Execution!—he has certainly heard it.

(Aside.

DAV. What a pucker you were in over-night!

PEN. May be so, may be so, Mr. Davenport. That was an imaginary scene. I have had real troubles since.

DAV. Pshaw! so you call every common accident.

PEN. Do you call my case so common, then?

DAV. What case?

PEN. You have not heard, then?

DAV. Positively, not a word.

PEN. You must know I have been—(*whispers*)—tried for a felony since then.

DAV. Nonsense!

PEN. No subject for mirth, Mr. Davenport. A confounded short-sighted fellow swore that I stopped him and robbed him on the York race-ground, at nine on a fine moonlight evening, when I was two hundred miles off in Dorsetshire. These hands have been held up at a common bar.

DAV. Ridiculous!—it could not have gone so far.

PEN. A great deal farther, I assure you, Mr. Davenport. I am ashamed to say how far it went. You must know, that, in the first shock and surprise of the accusation, shame—you know I was always susceptible—shame put me upon disguising my *name,* that, at all events, it might bring no disgrace upon my family. I called myself *James Thompson.*

DAV. For Heaven's sake, compose yourself.

PEN. I will. An old family ours, Mr. Davenport,—never had a blot upon it till now,—a family famous for the jealousy of its honour for many generations,—think of that, Mr. Davenport,—that felt a stain like a wound—

DAV. Be calm, my dear friend.

PEN. This served the purpose of a temporary concealment well enough; but, when it came to the—*alibi*, I think they call it,—excuse these technical terms, they are hardly fit for the mouth of a gentleman,— the *witnesses*—that is another term—that I had sent for up from Melcombe Regis, and relied upon for clearing up my character, by disclosing my real name, *John Pendulous*, so discredited the cause which they came to serve, that it had quite a contrary effect to what was intended. In short, the usual forms passed, and you behold me here the miserablest of mankind.

DAV. (*aside*). He must be light-headed.

PEN. Not at all, Mr. Davenport. I hear what you say; though you speak it all one side, as they do at the play-house.

DAV. The sentence could never have been carried into—pshaw!—you are joking: the truth must have come out at last.

PEN. So it did, Mr. Davenport,—just two minutes and a second too late, by the sheriff's stop-watch. Time enough to save my life,—my wretched life,—but an age too late for my honour. Pray, change the subject: the detail must be as offensive to you.

DAV. With all my heart, to a more pleasing theme. The lively Maria Flyn—are you friends in that quarter still? Have the old folks relented?

PEN. They are dead, and have left her mistress of her inclinations. But it requires great strength of mind to—

DAV. To what?

PEN. To stand up against the sneers of the world. It is not every young lady that feels herself confident against the shafts of ridicule, though aimed by the hand of prejudice. Not but in her heart, I believe, she prefers me to all mankind. But think, what would the world say, if, in defiance of the opinions of all mankind, she should take to her arms a— reprieved man!

DAV. Whims! You might turn the laugh of the world upon itself in a fortnight. These things are but nine-days' wonders.

PEN. Do you think so, Mr. Davenport?

DAV. Where does she live?

PEN. She has lodgings in the next street, in a sort of garden-house, that belongs to one Cutlet. I have not seen her since the affair. I was going there at her request.

DAV. Ha, ha, ha!

PEN. Why do you laugh?

DAV. The oddest fellow! I will tell you— But here he comes.

(*Enter* CUTLET.)

CUTLET (*to* DAVENPORT). Sir, the young lady at my house is desirous you should return immediately. She has heard something from home.

PEN. What do I hear?

DAV. 'Tis her fears, I daresay. My dear Pendulous, you will excuse me— I must not tell him our situation at present, though it cost him a fit of jealousy. We shall have fifty opportunities for explanation.

(*Exit.*

PEN. Does that gentleman visit the lady at your lodgings?

CUTLET. He is quite familiar there, I assure you. He is all in all with her, as they say.

PEN. It is but too plain. Fool that I have been, not to suspect, that, while she pretended scruples, some rival was at the root of her infidelity!

CUTLET. You seem distressed, sir. Bless me!

PEN. I am, friend, above the reach of comfort.

CUTLET. Consolation, then, can be to no purpose?

PEN. None.

CUTLET. I am so happy to have met with him!

PEN. Wretch, wretch, wretch!

CUTLET. There he goes! How he walks about biting his nails! I would not exchange this luxury of unavailing pity for worlds.

PEN. Stigmatised by the world—

CUTLET. My case exactly. Let us compare notes.

PEN. For an accident which—

CUTLET. For a profession which—

PEN. In the eye of reason, has nothing in it—

CUTLET. Absolutely nothing in it—

PEN. Brought up at a public bar—

CUTLET. Brought up to an odious trade—

PEN. With nerves like mine—

CUTLET. With nerves like mine—

PEN. Arraigned, condemned—

CUTLET. By a foolish world—

PEN. By a judge and jury—

CUTLET. By an invidious exclusion, disqualified for sitting upon a jury at all—

PEN. Tried, cast, and—

CUTLET. What?

PEN. HANGED, sir; HANGED by the neck till I was—

CUTLET. Bless me!

PEN. Why should not I publish it to the whole world, since she, whose prejudice alone I wished to overcome, deserts me?

CUTLET. Lord have mercy upon us! Not so bad as that comes to, I hope?

PEN. When she joins in the judgment of an illiberal world against me—

CUTLET. You said HANGED, sir; that is, I mean—perhaps I mistook you. How ghostly he looks!

PEN. Fear me not, my friend: I am no ghost, though I heartily wish I were one.

CUTLET. Why, then, ten to one you were—

PEN. *Cut down.* The odious words shall out, though it choke me.

CUTLET. Your case must have some things in it very curious. I daresay you kept a journal of your sensations!

PEN. Sensations!

CUTLET. Ay: while you were being—you know what I mean. They say, persons in your situation have lights dancing before their eyes,— bluish. But, then, the worst of all is coming to one's self again.

PEN. Plagues, furies, tormentors! I shall go mad!

(*Exit.*

CUTLET. There, he says he shall go mad! Well, my head has not been very right of late: it goes with a whirl and a buzz, somehow. I believe I must not think so deeply. Common people, that don't reason, know nothing of these aberrations.

> "Great wits go mad, and small ones only dull;
> Distracting cares vex not the empty skull:
> They seize on heads that think, and hearts that feel,
> As flies attack the better sort of veal."

ACT II

(SCENE *at* FLINT'S. FLINT. WILLIAM.)

FLINT. I have over-walked myself, and am quite exhausted. Tell Marian to come and play to me.

WILLIAM. I will, sir.

FLINT. I have been troubled with an evil spirit of late; I think, an evil spirit. It goes and comes, as my daughter is with or from me. It cannot stand before her gentle look, when, to please her father, she takes down her music-book.

(*Enter* WILLIAM.)

WILLIAM. Miss Marian went out soon after you, and is not returned.

FLINT. That is a pity,—that is a pity! Where can the foolish girl be gadding?

WILLIAM. The shopmen say she went out with Mr. Davenport.

FLINT. Davenport? Impossible!

WILLIAM. They say they are sure it was he, by the same token that they saw her slip into his hand, when she was past the door, the casket which you gave her.

FLINT. Gave her, William? I only intrusted it to her. She has robbed me! Marian is a thief! You must go to the justice, William, and get out a warrant against her immediately. Do you help them in the description. Put in "Marian Flint," in plain words,—no remonstrances, William —"daughter of Reuben Flint,"—no remonstrances; but do it—

WILLIAM. Nay, sir—

FLINT. I am rock, absolute rock, to all that you can say,—a piece of solid rock. What is it that makes my legs to fail, and my whole frame to totter, thus? It is my over-walking. I am very faint: support me in, William.

(*Exeunt.*

(SCENE—*The Apartment of* MISS FLYN. MISS FLYN. BETTY.)

MISS F. 'Tis past eleven. Every minute I expect Mr. Pendulous here. What a meeting do I anticipate!

BETTY. Anticipate, truly! What other than a joyful meeting can it be between two agreed lovers, who have been parted for these four months?

MISS F. But, in that cruel space, what accidents have happened!—(*aside*)—As yet, I perceive she is ignorant of this unfortunate affair.

BETTY. Lord, madam! what accidents? He has not had a fall or a tumble, has he? He is not coming upon crutches?

MISS F. Not exactly a fall—(*aside*)—I wish I had courage to admit her to my confidence.

BETTY. If his neck is whole, his heart is so too, I warrant it.

MISS F. His neck!—(*aside*)—She certainly mistrusts something. He writes me word that this must be his last interview.

BETTY. Then I guess the whole business. The wretch is unfaithful. Some creature or other has got him into a noose.

MISS F. A noose!

BETTY. And I shall never more see him hang—

MISS F. Hang! did you say, Betty?

BETTY. About that dear, fond neck, I was going to add, madam; but you interrupted me.

MISS F. I can no longer labour with a secret which oppresses me thus. Can you be trusty?

BETTY. Who? I, madam?—(*aside*)—Lord, I am so glad! Now I shall know all!

MISS F. This letter discloses the reasons of his unaccountable long absence from me. Peruse it, and say if we have not reason to be unhappy.

(BETTY *retires to the window to read the letter.* MR. PENDULOUS *enters.*

MISS F. My dear Pendulous!

PEN. Maria!—Nay, shun the embrace of a disgraced man, who comes but to tell you that you must renounce his society for ever.

MISS F. Nay, Pendulous, avoid me not.

PEN. (*aside*). That was tender. I may be mistaken. Whilst I stood on honourable terms, Maria might have met my caresses without a blush.

(BETTY, *who has not attended to the entrance of* PENDULOUS, *through her eagerness to read the letter, comes forward.*

BETTY. Ha, ha, ha! What a funny story, madam! And is this all you make such a fuss about? I would not care if twenty of my lovers had been—(*seeing* PENDULOUS)—Lord! sir, I ask pardon.

PEN. Are we not alone, then?

MISS F. 'Tis only Betty, my old servant. You remember Betty?

PEN. What letter is that?

MISS F. Oh! something from her sweetheart, I suppose.

BETTY. Yes, ma'am; that is all. I shall die of laughing.

PEN. You have not surely been showing her—

MISS F. I must be ingenuous. You must know, then, I was just giving Betty a hint, as you came in.

PEN. A hint?

MISS F. Yes, of our unfortunate embarrassment.

PEN. My letter!

MISS F. I thought it as well that she should know it at first.

PEN. 'Tis mighty well, madam!—'tis as it should be. I was ordained to be a wretched laughing-stock to all the world; and it is fit that our drabs and servant wenches should have their share of the amusement.

BETTY. Marry, come up! Drabs and servant wenches! and this from a person in his circumstances!

(BETTY *flings herself out of the room, muttering.*

MISS F. I understand not this language. I was prepared to give my Pendulous a tender meeting; to assure him, that, however in the eyes of the superficial and the censorious he may have incurred a partial degradation, in the esteem of one, at least, he stood as high as ever; that it was not in the power of a ridiculous *accident*—involving no guilt, no shadow of imputation—to separate two hearts cemented by holiest vows, as ours have been. This untimely repulse to my affections may awaken scruples in me, which hitherto, in tenderness to you, I have suppressed.

PEN. I very well understand what you call tenderness, madam; but, in some situations, pity—pity—is the greatest insult.

MISS F. I can endure no longer. When you are in a calmer mood, you will be sorry that you have wrung my heart so.

(*Exit.*

PEN. Maria! She is gone—in tears; yet, it seems, she has had her scruples. She said she had tried to smother them. Her maid Betty intimated as much.

(*Re-enter* BETTY.)

BETTY. Never mind Betty, sir: depend upon it, she will never peach.

PEN. Peach!

BETTY. Lord, sir, these scruples will blow over. Go to her again when she is in a better humour. You know, we must stand off a little at first, to save appearances.

PEN. Appearances! *we!*

BETTY. It will be decent to let some time elapse.

PEN. Time elapse!

> "Lost, wretched Pendulous! to scorn betray'd,—
> The scoff alike of mistress and of maid!
> What now remains for thee, forsaken man,
> But to complete thy fate's abortive plan,
> And finish what the feeble law began?"

(*Exeunt.*

(*Re-enter* MISS FLYN, *with* MARIAN.)

MISS F. Now both our lovers are gone, I hope my friend will have less reserve. You must consider this apartment as yours while you stay here. 'Tis larger and more commodious than your own.

MARIAN. You are kind, Maria. My sad story I have troubled you with. I have some jewels here, which I unintentionally brought away. I have only to beg you will take the trouble to restore them to my father; and, without disclosing my present situation, to tell him that my next step—with or without the concurrence of Mr. Davenport—shall be to throw myself at his feet to be forgiven. I dare not see him till you have explored the way for me. I am convinced that I was tricked into this elopement.

MISS F. Your commands shall be obeyed implicitly.

MARIAN. You are good. (*Agitated.*)

MISS F. Moderate your apprehensions, my sweet friend. I, too, have known my sorrows—(*smiling*)—You have heard of the ridiculous affair?

MARIAN. Between Mr. Pendulous and you? Davenport informed me of it; and we both took the liberty of blaming the over-niceness of your scruples.

MISS F. You mistake me. The refinement is entirely on the part of my lover. He thinks me not nice enough. I am obliged to feign a little reluctance, that he may not take quite a distaste to me. Will you believe it, that he turns my very constancy into a reproach; and declares that a woman must be devoid of all delicacy, that, after a thing of that sort, could endure the sight of her husband in—

MARIAN. In what?

MISS F. The sight of a man at all in—

MARIAN. I comprehend you not.

MISS F. In—in a—(*whispers*)—night-cap, my dear; and now the mischief is out.

MARIAN. Is there no way to cure him?

MISS F. None; unless I were to try the experiment, by placing myself in the hands of justice for a little while, how far an equality in misfortune might breed a sympathy in sentiment. Our reputations would be both upon a level then, you know. What think you of a little innocent shop-lifting, in sport?

MARIAN. And, by that contrivance, to be taken before a magistrate? The project sounds oddly.

MISS F. And yet I am more than half-persuaded it is feasible.

(*Enter* BETTY.)

BETTY. Mr. Davenport is below, ma'am, and desires to speak with you.

MARIAN. You will excuse me. (*Going—turning back.*) You will remember the casket?

(*Exit.*

MISS F. Depend on me.

BETTY. And a strange man desires to see you, ma'am. I do not half like his looks.

MISS F. Show him in.

(*Exit* BETTY, *and returns with a Police Officer.* BETTY *goes out.*

OFFICER. Your servant, ma'am. Your name is—

MISS F. Flyn, sir. Your business with me?

OFFICER (*alternately surveying the lady and his paper of instructions*). Marian Flint?

MISS F. Maria Flyn.

OFFICER. Ay, ay: Flyn or Flint. 'Tis all one. Some write plain Mary, and some put Ann after it. I come about a casket.

MISS F. I guess the whole business. He takes me for my friend. Something may come out of this. I will humour him.

OFFICER (*aside*). Answers to the description to a tittle. "Soft, gray eyes; pale complexion"—

MISS F. Yet I have been told by flatterers that my eyes were blue— (*takes out a pocket-glass*). I hope I look pretty tolerable to-day.

OFFICER. "Blue!"—they are a sort of bluish-gray, now I look better; and as for colour, that comes and goes. Blushing is often a sign of a hardened offender. Do you know anything of a casket?

MISS F. Here is one which a friend has just delivered to my keeping.

OFFICER. And which I must beg leave to secure, together with your ladyship's person. "Garnets, pearls, diamond-bracelet,"—here they are, sure enough.

MISS F. Indeed I am innocent.

OFFICER. Every man is presumed so till he is found otherwise.

MISS F. Police wit! Have you a warrant?

OFFICER. Tolerably cool, that. Here it is, signed by Justice Golding, at the requisition of Reuben Flint, who deposes that you have robbed him.

MISS F. How lucky this turns out!—(*aside*)—can I be indulged with a coach?

OFFICER. To Marlborough Street? certainly—an old offender—(*aside*) —The thing shall be conducted with as much delicacy as is consistent with security.

MISS F. Police manners! I will trust myself to your protection, then.

(*Exeunt.*

(SCENE—*Police Office.*)

(JUSTICE, FLINT, OFFICERS, ETC.)

JUSTICE. Before we proceed to extremities, Mr. Flint, let me entreat you to consider the consequences. What will the world say to your exposing your own child?

FLINT. The world is not my friend. I belong to a profession which has long brought me acquainted with its injustice. I return scorn for scorn, and desire its censure above its plaudits.

JUSTICE. But, in this case, delicacy must make you pause.

FLINT. Delicacy! ha, ha!—pawnbroker!—fitly these words suit. Delicate pawnbroker!—delicate devil!—let the law take its course.

JUSTICE. Consider, the jewels are found.

FLINT. 'Tis not the silly baubles I regard. Are you a man? are you a father? and think you I could stoop so low, vile as I stand here, as to make money—filthy money—of the stuff which a daughter's touch has desecrated? Deep in some pit first I would bury them.

JUSTICE. Yet pause a little. Consider. An only child.

FLINT. Only, only;—there, it is that which stings me,—makes me mad. She was the only thing I had to love me,—to bear me up against the nipping injuries of the world. I prate when I should act. Bring in your prisoner.

(*The* JUSTICE *makes a sign to the* OFFICER, *who goes out, and returns with* MISS FLYN.

FLINT. What a mockery of my sight is here! This is no daughter.

OFFICER. Daughter or no daughter, she has confessed to this casket.

FLINT (*handling it*). The very same. Was it in the power of these pale splendours to dazzle the sight of honesty,—to put out the regardful eye of piety and daughter-love? Why, a poor glow-worm shows more brightly. Bear witness how I valued them!—(*tramples on them*). Fair lady, know you aught of my child?

MISS F. I shall here answer no questions.

JUSTICE. You must explain how you came by these jewels, madam.

MISS F. (*aside*). Now, confidence assist me! A gentleman in the neighbourhood will answer for me.

JUSTICE. His name?

MISS F. Pendulous.

JUSTICE. That lives in the next street?

MISS F. The same. Now I have him, sure.

JUSTICE. Let him be sent for: I believe the gentleman to be respectable, and will accept his security.

FLINT. Why do I waste my time where I have no business? None,—I have none any more in the world,—none.

(*Enter* PENDULOUS.)

PEN. What is the meaning of this extraordinary summons?—Maria here!

FLINT. Know you anything of my daughter, sir?

PEN. Sir, I neither know her nor yourself, nor why I am brought hither; but for this lady, if you have anything against her, I will answer with my life and fortune.

JUSTICE. Make out the bail-bond.

OFFICER (*surveying* PENDULOUS). Please your worship, before you take that gentleman's bond, may I have leave to put in a word.

PEN. (*agitated*). I guess what is coming.

OFFICER. I have seen that gentleman hold up his hand at a criminal bar.

JUSTICE. Ha!

MISS F. (*aside*). Better and better.

OFFICER. My eyes cannot deceive me. His lips quivered about, while he was being tried, just as they do now. His name is not Pendulous.

MISS F. Excellent.

OFFICER. He pleaded to the name of Thompson at York Assizes.

JUSTICE. Can this be true?

MISS F. I could kiss the fellow!

OFFICER. He was had up for a foot-pad.

MISS F. A dainty fellow!

PEN. My iniquitous fate pursues me everywhere.

JUSTICE. You confess, then?

PEN. I am steeped in infamy.

MISS F. I am as deep in the mire as yourself.

PEN. My reproach can never be washed out.

MISS F. Nor mine.

PEN. I am doomed to everlasting shame.

MISS F. We are both in a predicament.

JUSTICE. I am in a maze where all this will end.

(*Enter* MARIAN *and* DAVENPORT.)

MARIAN (*kneeling*). My dear father!

FLINT. Do I dream?

MARIAN. I am your Marian.

JUSTICE. Wonders thicken.

FLINT. The casket—

MISS F. Let me clear up the rest.

FLINT. The casket—

MISS F. Was inadvertently in your daughter's hand, when, by an artifice of her maid Lucy, set on, as she confesses, by this gentleman here—

DAV. I plead guilty.

MISS F. She was persuaded that you were, in a hurry, going to marry her to an object of her dislike; nay, that he was actually in the house for the purpose. The speed of her flight admitted not of her depositing the jewels; but to me, who have been her inseparable companion since she quitted your roof, she intrusted the return of them, which the precipitate measures of this gentleman (*pointing to the* OFFICER) alone prevented. Mr. Cutlet, whom I see coming, can witness this to be true.

(*Enter* CUTLET, *in haste*.)

CUTLET. Ay, poor lamb! poor lamb! I can witness. I have run in such haste, hearing how affairs stood, that I have left my shambles without a protector. If your worship had seen how she cried (*pointing to*

MARIAN) and trembled, and insisted upon being brought to her father! Mr. Davenport here could not stay her.

FLINT. I can forbear no longer. Marian, will you play once again, to please your old father?

MARIAN. I have a good mind to make you buy me a new grand piano for your naughty suspicions of me.

DAV. What is to become of me?

FLINT. I will do more than that: the poor lady shall have her jewels again.

MARIAN. Shall she?

FLINT. Upon reasonable terms (*smiling*). And now, I suppose, the court may adjourn.

DAV. Marian!

FLINT. I guess what is passing in your mind, Mr. Davenport: but you have behaved, upon the whole, so like a man of honour, that it will give me pleasure, if you will visit at my house for the future; but—(*smiling*) —not clandestinely, Marian.

MARIAN. Hush, father!

FLINT. I own I had prejudices against gentry; but I have met with so much candour and kindness among my betters this day,—from this gentleman in particular (*turning to the* JUSTICE),—that I begin to think of leaving off business, and setting up for a gentleman myself.

JUSTICE. You have the feelings of one.

FLINT. Marian will not object to it.

JUSTICE. But—(*turning to* MISS FLYN)—what motive could induce this lady to take so much disgrace upon herself, when a word's explanation might have relieved her?

MISS F. This gentleman—(*turning to* PENDULOUS)—can explain.

PEN. The devil!

MISS F. This gentleman, I repeat it, whose backwardness in concluding a long and honourable suit, from a mistaken delicacy—

PEN. How?

MISS F. Drove me upon the expedient of involving myself in the same disagreeable embarrassments with himself, in the hope that a more perfect sympathy might subsist between us for the future.

PEN. I see it—I see it all!

JUSTICE (*to* PENDULOUS). You were then tried at York?

PEN. I was—CAST—

JUSTICE. Condemned.

PEN. EXECUTED.

JUSTICE. IIow!

PEN. CUT DOWN, and CAME TO LIFE AGAIN! False delicacy, adieu! The true sort—which this lady has manifested, by an expedient, which, at first sight, might seem a little unpromising—has cured me of the other. We are now on even terms.

MISS F. And may—

PEN. Marry,—I know it was your word.

MISS F. And make a very quiet—

PEN. Exemplary—

MISS F. Agreeing pair of—

PEN. ACQUITTED FELONS.

FLINT. And let the prejudiced against our profession acknowledge that a money-lender may have the heart of a father; and that, in the casket, the loss of which grieved him so sorely, he valued nothing so dear as— (*turning to* MARIAN)—one poor domestic jewel.

THE WITCH

A DRAMATIC SKETCH OF THE SEVEN-
TEENTH CENTURY

THE WITCH

A DRAMATIC SKETCH OF THE SEVEN-
TEENTH CENTURY

CHARACTERS

(OLD SERVANT *in the Family of* SIR FRANCIS FAIRFORD, STRANGER.)

SERVANT. One summer night Sir Francis, as it chanced,
Was pacing to and fro in the avenue
That westward fronts our house,
Among those aged oaks, said to have been planted
Three hundred years ago,
By a neighb'ring prior of the Fairford name.
Being o'ertask'd in thought, he heeded not
The importunate suit of one who stood by the gate,
And begg'd an alms.
Some say he shoved her rudely from the gate
With angry chiding; but I can never think
(Our master's nature hath a sweetness in it)
That he could use a woman, an old woman,
With such discourtesy; but he refused her—
And better had he met a lion in his path
Than that old woman that night;
For she was one who practised the black arts,
And served the devil, being since burnt for witchcraft.
She look'd at him as one that meant to blast him,
And with a frightful noise
('Twas partly like a woman's voice,
And partly like the hissing of a snake),
She nothing said but this
(Sir Francis told the words):—

> A mischief, mischief, mischief,
> And a nine-times killing curse,
> By day and by night, to the caitiff wight,
> Who shakes the poor like snakes from his door,
> And shuts up the womb of his purse.

And still she cried—

> A mischief,
> And a nine-fold withering curse:
> For that shall come to thee that will undo thee,
> Both all that thou fearest and worse.

So saying, she departed,
Leaving Sir Francis like a man, beneath
Whose feet a scaffolding was suddenly falling;
So he described it.

    STRANGER. A terrible curse! What follow'd?

    SERVANT. Nothing immediate, but some two months after,
Young Philip Fairford suddenly fell sick,
And none could tell what ail'd him; for he lay,
And pined, and pined, till all his hair fell off,
And he, that was full-flesh'd, became as thin
As a two-months' babe that has been starved in the nursing.
And sure I think
He bore his death-wound like a little child;
With such rare sweetness of dumb melancholy
He strove to clothe his agony in smiles,
Which he would force up in his poor pale cheeks,
Like ill-timed guests that had no proper dwelling there;
And, when they ask'd him his complaint, he laid
His hand upon his heart to show the place,
Where Susan came to him a-nights, he said,
And prick'd him with a pin.—
And thereupon Sir Francis call'd to mind
The beggar-witch that stood by the gateway
And begg'd an alms.

    STRANGER.   But did the witch confess?

    SERVANT. All this and more at her death.

    STRANGER. I do not love to credit tales of magic.
Heaven's music, which is Order, seems unstrung,
And this brave world
(The mystery of God) unbeautified,
Disorder'd, marr'd, where such strange things are acted.

POEMS

DEDICATION[1]

TO S. T. COLERIDGE, Esq.

My dear Coleridge—You will smile to see the slender labours of your friend designated by the title of *Works;* but such was the wish of the gentlemen who have kindly undertaken the trouble of collecting them, and from their judgment could be no appeal.

It would be a kind of disloyalty to offer to any one but yourself a volume containing the *early pieces,* which were first published among your poems, and were fairly derivatives from you and them. My friend Lloyd and myself came into our first battle (authorship is a sort of warfare) under cover of the greater Ajax. How this association, which shall always be a dear and proud recollection to me, came to be broken,—who snapped the threefold cord,—whether yourself (but I know that was not the case) grew ashamed of your former companions,—or whether (which is by much the more probable) some ungracious bookseller was author of the separation,—I cannot tell;—but wanting the support of your friendly elm (I speak for myself), my vine has, since that time, put forth few or no fruits; the sap (if ever it had any) has become, in a manner, dried up and extinct; and you will find your old associate, in his second volume, dwindled into prose and *criticism.*

Am I right in assuming this as the cause? or is it that, as years come upon us (except with some more healthy-happy spirits), Life itself loses much of its Poetry for us? we transcribe but what we read in the great volume of Nature; and, as the characters grow dim, we turn off, and look another way. You yourself write no Christabels, nor Ancient Mariners, now.

Some of the Sonnets, which shall be carelessly turned over by the general reader, may happily awaken in you remembrances, which I should be sorry should be ever totally extinct—the memory

Of summer days and of delightful years—

even so far back as to those old suppers at our old * * * * * * * * * * Inn,—when life was fresh, and topics exhaustless,—and you first kindled in me, if not the power, yet the love of poetry, and beauty, and kindliness.—

What words have I heard
Spoke at the Mermaid!

The world has given you many a shrewd nip and gird since that time, but either my eyes are grown dimmer, or my old friend is the *same* who stood before me three-and-twenty years ago—his hair a little confessing the hand of Time, but still shrouding the same capacious brain,—his heart not altered, scarcely where it "alteration finds."

One piece, Coleridge, I have ventured to publish in its original form, though I have heard you complain of a certain over-imitation of the antique in the style.

[1] Prefixed to the Author's works published in 1818.

509

If I could see any way of getting rid of the objection, without re-writing it entirely, I would make some sacrifices. But when I wrote John Woodvil,[1] I never proposed to myself any distinct deviation from common English. I had been newly initiated in the writings of our elder dramatists: Beaumont and Fletcher, and Massinger, were then a *first love;* and from what I was so freshly conversant in, what wonder if my language imperceptibly took a tinge? The very *time* which I had chosen for my story, that which immediately followed the Restoration, seemed to require, in an English play, that the English should be of rather an older cast than that of the precise year in which it happened to be written. I wish it had not some faults, which I can less vindicate than the language.—I remain, my dear Coleridge, yours, with unabated esteem,

C. LAMB.

[1] Page 425 of the present edition.

POEMS

HESTER

WHEN maidens such as Hester die,
Their place ye may not well supply,
Though ye among a thousand try,
    With vain endeavour.

A month or more hath she been dead,
Yet cannot I by force be led
To think upon the wormy bed,
    And her together.

A springy motion in her gait,
A rising step, did indicate
Of pride and joy no common rate,
    That flush'd her spirit.

I know not by what name beside
I shall it call:—if 'twas not pride,
It was a joy to that allied,
    She did inherit.

Her parents held the Quaker rule,
Which doth the human feeling cool,
But she was train'd in Nature's school,
    Nature had blest her.

A waking eye, a prying mind,
A heart that stirs, is hard to bind,
A hawk's keen sight ye cannot blind,
    Ye could not Hester.

My sprightly neighbour! gone before
To that unknown and silent shore,
Shall we not meet, as heretofore,
    Some summer morning,

When from thy cheerful eyes a ray
Hath struck a bliss upon the day,
A bliss that would not go away,
    A sweet fore-warning?

TO CHARLES LLOYD

AN UNEXPECTED VISITOR

ALONE, obscure, without a friend,
   A cheerless, solitary thing,
Why seeks my Lloyd the stranger out?
   What offering can the stranger bring

Of social scenes, home-bred delights,
   That him in aught compensate may
For Stowey's pleasant winter nights,
   For loves and friendships far away?

In brief oblivion to forego
   Friends, such as thine, so justly dear,
And be awhile with me content
   To stay, a kindly loiterer, here:

For this a gleam of random joy
   Hath flush'd my unaccustom'd cheek;
And, with an o'ercharged bursting heart,
   I feel the thanks I cannot speak.

Oh! sweet are all the Muses' lays,
   And sweet the charm of matin bird;
'Twas long since these estrangèd ears
   The sweeter voice of friend had heard.

The voice hath spoke: the pleasant sounds
   In memory's ear in after time
Shall live, to sometimes rouse a tear,
   And sometimes prompt an honest rhyme.

For, when the transient charm is fled,
   And when the little week is o'er,
To cheerless, friendless, solitude
   When I return, as heretofore,

Long, long, within my aching heart
   The grateful sense shall cherish'd be;
I'll think less meanly of myself,
   That Lloyd will sometimes think on me.

THE THREE FRIENDS

THREE young maids in friendship met;
Mary, Martha, Margaret.
Margaret was tall and fair,
Martha shorter by a hair;
If the first excell'd in feature,
Th' other's grace and ease were greater;
Mary, though to rival loth,
In their best gifts equall'd both.
They a due proportion kept;
Martha mourn'd if Margaret wept;
Margaret joy'd when any good
She of Martha understood;
And in sympathy for either
Mary was outdone by neither.
Thus far, for a happy space,
All three ran an equal race,
A most constant friendship proving,
Equally beloved and loving;
All their wishes, joys, the same;
Sisters only not in name.

Fortune upon each one smiled,
As upon a fav'rite child;
Well to do and well to see
Were the parents of all three;
Till on Martha's father crosses
Brought a flood of worldly losses,
And his fortunes rich and great
Changed at once to low estate;
Under which o'erwhelming blow
Martha's mother was laid low;
She a hapless orphan left,
Of maternal care bereft,
Trouble following trouble fast,
Lay in a sick bed at last.

In the depth of her affliction
Martha now received conviction,
That a true and faithful friend
Can the surest comfort lend.
Night and day, with friendship tried,
Ever constant by her side
Was her gentle Mary found,
With a love that knew no bound;

And the solace she imparted
Saved her dying broken-hearted.

In this scene of earthly things
Not one good unmixèd springs.
That which had to Martha proved
A sweet consolation, moved
Different feelings of regret
In the mind of Margaret.
She, whose love was not less dear,
Nor affection less sincere
To her friend, was, by occasion
Of more distant habitation,
Fewer visits forced to pay her;
When no other cause did stay her;
And her Mary living nearer,
Margaret began to fear her,
Lest her visits day by day
Martha's heart should steal away.
That whole heart she ill could spare her,
Where till now she'd been a sharer.
From this cause with grief she pined,
Till at length her health declined.
All her cheerful spirits flew,
Fast as Martha's gather'd new;
And her sickness waxèd sore,
Just when Martha felt no more.

Mary, who had quick suspicion
Of her alter'd friend's condition,
Seeing Martha's convalescence
Less demanded now her presence,
With a goodness, built on reason,
Changed her measures with the season;
Turn'd her steps from Martha's door,
Went where she was wanted more;
All her care and thoughts were set
Now to tend on Margaret.
Mary living 'twixt the two,
From her home could oft'ner go,
Either of her friends to see,
Than they could together be.

Truth explain'd is to suspicion
Evermore the best physician.
Soon her visits had the effect;
All that Margaret did suspect,

From her fancy vanish'd clean;
She was soon what she had been,
And the colour she did lack
To her faded cheek came back.
Wounds which love had made her feel,
Love alone had power to heal.

Martha, who the frequent visit
Now had lost, and sore did miss it,
With impatience waxèd cross,
Counted Margaret's gain her loss:
All that Mary did confer
On her friend, thought due to her.
In her girlish bosom rise
Little foolish jealousies,
Which into such rancour wrought,
She one day for Margaret sought;
Finding her by chance alone,
She began, with reasons shown,
To insinuate a fear
Whether Mary was sincere;
Wish'd that Margaret would take heed
Whence her actions did proceed.
For herself, she'd long been minded
Not with outsides to be blinded;
All that pity and compassion,
She believed was affectation;
In her heart she doubted whether
Mary cared a pin for either.
She could keep whole weeks at distance,
And not know of their existence,
While all things remain'd the same;
But, when some misfortune came,
Then she made a great parade
Of her sympathy and aid,—
Not that she did really grieve,
It was only *make-believe*,
And she cared for nothing, so
She might her fine feelings show,
And get credit, on her part,
For a soft and tender heart.

With such speeches, smoothly made,
She found methods to persuade
Margaret (who, being sore
From the doubts she'd felt before,
Was preparèd for mistrust)

To believe her reasons just;
Quite destroy'd that comfort glad,
Which in Mary late she had;
Made her, in experience' spite,
Think her friend a hypocrite,
And resolve, with cruel scoff,
To renounce and cast her off.

See how good turns are rewarded!
She of both is now discarded,
Who to both had been so late
Their support in low estate,
All their comfort, and their stay—
Now of both is cast away.
But the league her presence cherish'd,
Losing its best prop, soon perish'd;
She, that was a link to either,
To keep them and it together,
Being gone, the two (no wonder)
That were left, soon fell asunder;—
Some civilities were kept,
But the heart of friendship slept;
Love with hollow forms was fed,
But the life of love lay dead:—
A cold intercourse they held,
After Mary was expell'd.

Two long years did intervene
Since they'd either of them seen,
Or, by letter, any word
Of their old companion heard,—
When, upon a day once walking,
Of indifferent matters talking,
They a female figure met;
Martha said to Margaret,
"That young maid in face does carry
A resemblance strong of Mary."
Margaret, at nearer sight,
Own'd her observation right;
But they did not far proceed
Ere they knew 'twas she indeed.
She—but, ah! how changed they view her
From that person which they knew her!
Her fine face disease had scarr'd,
And its matchless beauty marr'd:—
But enough was left to trace
Mary's sweetness—Mary's grace.

When her eye did first behold them,
How they blush'd!—but, when she told them,
How on a sick bed she lay
Months, while they had kept away,
And had no inquiries made
If she were alive or dead;—
How, for want of a true friend,
She was brought near to her end,
And was like so to have died,
With no friend at her bed-side;—
How the constant irritation,
Caused by fruitless expectation
Of their coming, had extended
The illness, when she might have mended,—
Then, O then, how did reflection
Come on them with recollection!
All that she had done for them,
How it did their fault condemn!

But sweet Mary, still the same,
Kindly eased them of their shame;
Spoke to them with accents bland,
Took them friendly by the hand;
Bound them both with promise fast,
Not to speak of troubles past;
Made them on the spot declare
A new league of friendship there;
Which, without a word of strife,
Lasted thenceforth long as life.
Martha now and Margaret
Strove who most should pay the debt
Which they owed her, nor did vary
Ever after from their Mary.

TO A RIVER IN WHICH A CHILD WAS DROWNED

SMILING river, smiling river,
  On thy bosom sun-beams play;
Though they're fleeting, and retreating,
  Thou hast more deceit than they.

In thy channel, in thy channel,
  Choked with ooze and grav'lly stones,
Deep immersèd, and unhearsèd,
  Lies young Edward's corse: his bones

Ever whitening, ever whitening,
　　As thy waves against them dash;
What thy torrent, in the current,
　　Swallow'd, now it helps to wash.

As if senseless, as if senseless
　　Things had feeling in this case;
What so blindly, and unkindly,
　　It destroy'd, it now does grace.

THE OLD FAMILIAR FACES

I HAVE had playmates, I have had companions,
In my days of childhood, in my joyful school-days—
All, all are gone, the old familiar faces.

I have been laughing, I have been carousing,
Drinking late, sitting late, with my bosom cronies—
All, all are gone, the old familiar faces.

I loved a love once, fairest among women;
Closed are her doors on me, I must not see her—
All, all are gone, the old familiar faces.

I have a friend, a kinder friend has no man;
Like an ingrate, I left my friend abruptly;
Left him, to muse on the old familiar faces.

Ghost-like I paced round the haunts of my childhood.
Earth seem'd a desert I was bound to traverse,
Seeking to find the old familiar faces.

Friend of my bosom, thou more than a brother,
Why wert not thou born in my father's dwelling?
So might we talk of the old familiar faces—

How some they have died, and some they have left me,
And some are taken from me; all are departed;
All, all are gone, the old familiar faces.

HELEN

HIGH-BORN Helen, round your dwelling
　　These twenty years I've paced in vain:
Haughty beauty, thy lover's duty
　　Hath been to glory in his pain.

High-born Helen, proudly telling
　　Stories of thy cold disdain;
I starve, I die, now you comply,
　　And I no longer can complain.

These twenty years I've lived on tears,
　　Dwelling for ever on a frown;
On sighs I've fed, your scorn my bread;
　　I perish now you kind are grown.

Can I, who loved my beloved
　　But for the scorn "was in her eye,"
Can I be moved for my beloved,
　　When she "returns me sigh for sigh"?

In stately pride, by my bed-side,
　　High-born Helen's portrait's hung;
Deaf to my praise, my mournful lays
　　Are nightly to the portrait sung.

To that I weep, nor ever sleep,
　　Complaining all night long to her—
Helen, grown old, no longer cold,
　　Said, "You to all men I prefer."

A VISION OF REPENTANCE

I SAW a famous fountain, in my dream,
　　Where shady pathways to a valley led;
A weeping willow lay upon that stream,
　　And all around the fountain brink were spread
Wide-branching trees, with dark green leaf rich clad,
Forming a doubtful twilight—desolate and sad.

The place was such, that whoso enter'd in,
　　Disrobèd was of every earthly thought,
And straight became as one that knew not sin,
　　Or to the world's first innocence was brought;
Enseem'd it now, he stood on holy ground,
In sweet and tender melancholy wrapt around.

A most strange calm stole o'er my soothèd sprite;
　　Long time I stood, and longer had I stayed,
When lo! I saw, saw by the sweet moon-light,

Which came in silence o'er that silent shade,
Where, near the fountain, SOMETHING like DESPAIR
Made, of that weeping willow, garlands for her hair.

And eke with painful fingers she inwove
    Many an uncouth stem of savage thorn—
"The willow garland, *that* was for her love,
    And *these* her bleeding temples would adorn."
With sighs her heart nigh burst, salt tears fast fell,
As mournfully she bended o'er that sacred well.

To whom when I addrest myself to speak,
    She lifted up her eyes, and nothing said;
The delicate red came mantling o'er her cheek,
    And, gath'ring up her loose attire, she fled
To the dark covert of that woody shade,
And in her goings seem'd a timid gentle maid.

Revolving in my mind what this should mean,
    And why that lovely lady plainèd so;
Perplex'd in thought at that mysterious scene,
    And doubting if 'twere best to stay or go,
I cast mine eyes in wistful gaze around,
When from the shades came slow a small and plaintive sound.

"PSYCHE am I, who love to dwell
    In these brown shades, this woody dell
Where never busy mortal came,
Till now, to pry upon my shame.

"At thy feet what thou dost see
    The waters of repentance be,
Which, night and day, I must augment
With tears, like a true penitent,

"If haply so my day of grace
    Be not yet past; and this lone place,
O'er-shadowy dark, excludeth hence
All thoughts but grief and penitence."

"*Why dost thou weep, thou gentle maid!*
And wherefore in this barren shade
Thy hidden thoughts with sorrow feed?
Can thing so fair repentance need?"

"O! I have done a deed of shame,
And tainted is my virgin fame,
And stain'd the beauteous maiden white
In which my bridal robes were dight."

*"And who the promised spouse? declare:
And what those bridal garments were."*

"Severe and saintly righteousness
Composed the clear white bridal dress;
JESUS, the Son of Heaven's high King,
Bought with His blood the marriage ring.

"A wretched sinful creature, I
Deem'd lightly of that sacred tie,
Gave to a treacherous WORLD my heart,
And play'd the foolish wanton's part.
Soon to these murky shades I came,
To hide from the sun's light my shame.
And still I haunt this woody dell,
And bathe me in that healing well,
Whose waters clear have influence
From sin's foul stains the soul to cleanse;
And, night and day, I them augment,
With tears, like a true penitent,
Until, due expiation made,
And fit atonement fully paid,
The Lord and Bridegroom me present,
Where in sweet strains of high consent,
God's throne before, the Seraphim
Shall chant the ecstatic marriage hymn."

"Now Christ restore thee soon"—I said,
And thenceforth all my dream was fled.

DIALOGUE BETWEEN A MOTHER AND CHILD

CHILD

"O LADY, lay your costly robes aside,
No longer may you glory in your pride."

MOTHER

Wherefore to-day art singing in mine ear
Sad songs were made so long ago, my dear?

This day I am to be a bride, you know,
Why sing sad songs, were made so long ago?

CHILD

O mother, lay your costly robes aside,
For you may never be another's bride.
That line I learn'd not in the old sad song.

MOTHER

I pray thee, pretty one, now hold thy tongue,
Play with the bride-maids; and be glad, my boy,
For thou shalt be a second father's joy.

CHILD

One father fondled me upon his knee.
One father is enough, alone, for me.

QUEEN ORIANA'S DREAM

ON a bank with roses shaded,
Whose sweet scent the violets aided,
Violets whose breath alone
Yields but feeble smell or none
(Sweeter bed Jove ne'er reposed on
When his eyes Olympus closed on),
While o'erhead six slaves did hold
Canopy of cloth o' gold,
And two more did music keep,
Which might Juno lull to sleep,
Oriana, who was queen
To the mighty Tamerlane,
That was lord of all the land
Between Thrace and Samarchand,
While the noontide fervour beam'd,
Mused herself to sleep, and *dream'd*.

Thus far, in magnific strain,
A young poet soothed his vein,
But he had nor prose nor numbers
To express a princess' slumbers.—
Youthful Richard had strange fancies,
Was deep versed in old romances,
And could talk whole hours upon
The Great Cham and Prester John,—

Tell the field in which the Sophi
From the Tartar won a trophy—
What he read with such delight of,
Thought he could as eas'ly write of—
But his over-young invention
Kept not pace with brave intention.
Twenty suns did rise and set,
And he could no further get;
But, unable to proceed,
Made a virtue out of need,
And, his labours wiselier deem'd of,
Did omit *what the queen dream'd of.*

A BALLAD

NOTING THE DIFFERENCE OF RICH AND POOR, IN THE WAYS
OF A RICH NOBLE'S PALACE AND A POOR WORKHOUSE

To the Tune of the "Old and Young Courtier."

IN a costly palace Youth goes clad in gold;
In a wretched workhouse Age's limbs are cold:
There they sit, the old men by a shivering fire,
Still close and closer cowering, warmth is their desire.

In a costly palace, when the brave gallants dine,
They have store of good venison, with old canary wine,
With singing and music to heighten the cheer;
Coarse bits, with grudging, are the pauper's best fare.

In a costly palace Youth is still carest
By a train of attendants which laugh at my young Lord's jest;
In a wretched workhouse the contrary prevails:
Does Age begin to prattle?—no man heark'neth to his tales.

In a costly palace if the child with a pin
Do but chance to prick a finger, straight the doctor is called in;
In a wretched workhouse men are left to perish
For want of proper cordials, which their old age might cherish.

In a costly palace Youth enjoys his lust;
In a wretched workhouse Age, in corners thrust,
Thinks upon the former days, when he was well to do,
Had children to stand by him, both friends and kinsmen too.

In a costly palace Youth his temples hides
With a new-devised peruke that reaches to his sides;

In a wretched workhouse Age's crown is bare,
With a few thin locks just to fence out the cold air.

In peace, as in war, 'tis our young gallants' pride,
To walk, each one i' the streets, with a rapier by his side,
That none to do them injury may have pretence;
Wretched Age, in poverty, must brook offence.

HYPOCHONDRIACUS

By myself walking,
To myself talking,
When as I ruminate
On my untoward fate,
Scarcely seem I
Alone sufficiently,
Black thoughts continually
Crowding my privacy;
They come unbidden,
Like foes at a wedding,
Thrusting their faces
In better guests' places,
Peevish and malecontent,
Clownish, impertinent,
Dashing the merriment:
So in like fashions
Dim cogitations
Follow and haunt me,
Striving to daunt me,
In my heart festering,
In my ears whispering,
"Thy friends are treacherous,
Thy foes are dangerous,
Thy dreams ominous."

Fierce Anthropophagi,
Spectra, Diaboli,
What scared St. Anthony,
Hobgoblins, Lemures,
Dreams of Antipodes,
Night-riding Incubi
Troubling the fantasy,
All dire illusions
Causing confusions;
Figments heretical,
Scruples fantastical,

Doubts diabolical;
Abaddon vexeth me,
Mahu perplexeth me,
Lucifer teareth me——

Jesu! Maria! liberate nos ab his diris tentationibus Inimici.

A FAREWELL TO TOBACCO

MAY the Babylonish curse
Straight confound my stammering verse,
If I can a passage see
In this word-perplexity,
Or a fit expression find,
Or a language to my mind
(Still the phrase is wide or scant)
To take leave of thee, GREAT PLANT!
Or in any terms relate
Half my love, or half my hate:
For I hate, yet love, thee so,
That, whichever thing I show,
The plain truth will seem to be
A constrain'd hyperbole,
And the passion to proceed
More from a mistress than a weed.

Sooty retainer to the vine,
Bacchus' black servant, negro fine;
Sorcerer, that mak'st us dote upon
Thy begrimed complexion,
And, for thy pernicious sake,
More and greater oaths to break
Than reclaimèd lovers take
'Gainst women: thou thy siege dost lay
Much too in the female way,
While thou suck'st the lab'ring breath
Faster than kisses or than death.

Thou in such a cloud dost bind us,
That our worst foes cannot find us,
And ill fortune, that would thwart us,
Shoots at rovers, shooting at us;
While each man, through thy height'ning steam,
Does like a smoking Etna seem,
And all about us does express
(Fancy and wit in richest dress)
A Sicilian fruitfulness.

Thou through such a mist dost show us,
That our best friends do not know us,
And, for those allowèd features,
Due to reasonable creatures,   /
Liken'st us to fell Chimeras,
Monsters that, who see us, fear us;
Worse than Cerberus or Geryon,
Or, who first loved a cloud, Ixion.

Bacchus we know, and we allow
His tipsy rites. But what art thou,
That but by reflex canst show
What his deity can do,
As the false Egyptian spell
Aped the true Hebrew miracle?
Some few vapours thou may'st raise,
The weak brain may serve to amaze,
But to the reins and nobler heart
Canst nor life nor heat impart.

Brother of Bacchus, later born,
The old world was sure forlorn
Wanting thee, that aidest more
The god's victories than before
All his panthers, and the brawls
Of his piping Bacchanals.
These, as stale, we disallow,
Or judge of *thee* meant: only thou
His true Indian conquest art;
And, for ivy round his dart,
The reformèd god now weaves
A finer thyrsus of thy leaves.

Scent to match thy rich perfume
Chemic art did ne'er presume
Through her quaint alembic strain,
None so sov'reign to the brain.
Nature, that did in thee excel,
Framed again no second smell.
Roses, violets, but toys
For the smaller sort of boys,
Or for greener damsels meant;
Thou art the only manly scent.

Stinking'st of the stinking kind,
Filth of the mouth and fog of the mind,
Africa, that brags her foison,

Breeds no such prodigious poison,
Henbane, nightshade, both together,
Hemlock, aconite——

          Nay, rather
Plant divine, of rarest virtue;
Blisters on the tongue would hurt you.
'Twas but in a sort I blamed thee;
None e'er prosper'd who defamed thee;
Irony all, and feign'd abuse,
Such as perplex'd lovers use,
At a need, when, in despair
To paint forth their fairest fair,
Or in part but to express
That exceeding comeliness
Which their fancies doth so strike,
They borrow language of dislike;
And, instead of Dearest Miss,
Jewel, Honey, Sweetheart, Bliss,
And those forms of old admiring,
Call her Cockatrice and Siren,
Basilisk, and all that's evil,
Witch, Hyena, Mermaid, Devil,
Ethiop, Wench, and Blackamoor,
Monkey, Ape, and twenty more;
Friendly Trait'ress, loving Foe,—
Not that she is truly so,
But no other way they know
A contentment to express,
Borders so upon excess,
That they do not rightly wot
Whether it be pain or not.

Or, as men, constrain'd to part
With what's nearest to their heart,
While their sorrow's at the height,
Lose discrimination quite,
And their hasty wrath let fall,
To appease their frantic gall,
On the darling thing whatever,
Whence they feel it death to sever,
Though it be, as they, perforce,
Guiltless of the sad divorce.

For I must (nor let it grieve thee,
Friendliest of plants, that I must) leave thee.
For thy sake, TOBACCO, I

Would do anything but die,
And but seek to extend my days
Long enough to sing thy praise.
But, as she, who once hath been
A king's consort, is a queen
Ever after, nor will bate
Any tittle of her state,
Though a widow, or divorced,
So I, from my converse forced,
The old name and style retain,
A right Katherine of Spain;
And a seat, too, 'mongst the joys
Of the blest Tobacco Boys;
Where, though I, by sour physician,
Am debarr'd the full fruition
Of thy favours, I may catch
Some collateral sweets, and snatch
Sidelong odours, that give life
Like glances from a neighbour's wife;
And still live in the by-places
And the suburbs of thy graces;
And in thy borders take delight,
And unconquer'd Canaanite.

TO T. L. H.

A CHILD

MODEL of thy parent dear,
Serious infant worth a fear:
In thy unfaltering visage well
Picturing forth the son of TELL,
When on his forehead, firm and good,
Motionless mark, the apple stood;
Guileless traitor, rebel mild,
Convict unconscious, culprit child!
Gates that close with iron roar
Have been to thee thy nursery door;
Chains that chink in cheerless cells
Have been thy rattles and thy bells;
Walls contrived for giant sin
Have hemm'd thy faultless weakness in;
Near thy sinless bed black Guilt
Her discordant house hath built,
And fill'd it with her monstrous brood—
Sights, by thee not understood—

Sights of fear, and of distress,
That pass a harmless infant's guess!

But the clouds, that overcast
Thy young morning, may not last;
Soon shall arrive the rescuing hour
That yields thee up to Nature's power:
Nature, that so late doth greet thee,
Shall in o'erflowing measure meet thee.
She shall recompense with cost
For every lesson thou hast lost.
Then wandering up thy sire's loved hill,[1]
Thou shalt take thy airy fill
Of health and pastime. *Birds shall sing
For thy delight each May morning.*
'Mid new-yean'd lambkins thou shalt play,
Hardly less a lamb than they.
Then thy prison's lengthen'd bound
Shall be the horizon skirting round:
And, while thou fillest thy lap with flowers,
To make amends for wintry hours,
The breeze, the sunshine, and the place,
Shall from thy tender brow efface
Each vestige of untimely care,
That sour restraint had graven there;
And on thy every look impress
A more excelling childishness.

So shall be thy days beguiled,
THORNTON HUNT, my favourite child.

BALLAD

FROM THE GERMAN

THE clouds are blackening, the storms threatening,
    And ever the forest maketh a moan:
Billows are breaking, the damsel's heart aching,
    Thus by herself she singeth alone,
        Weeping right plenteously.

"The world is empty, the heart is dead surely,
    In this world plainly all seemeth amiss:
To thy breast, holy one, take now thy little one,
    I have had earnest of all earth's bliss,
        Living right lovingly."

[1] Hampstead.

DAVID IN THE CAVE OF ADULLAM

DAVID and his three captains bold
Kept ambush once within a hold.
It was in Adullam's cave,
Nigh which no water they could have,
Nor spring, nor running brook was near
To quench the thirst that parch'd them there.
Then David, king of Israël,
Straight bethought him of a well,
Which stood beside the city gate,
At Bethlem; where, before his state
Of kingly dignity, he had
Oft drunk his fill, a shepherd lad;
But now his fierce Philistine foe
Encamp'd before it he does know.
Yet ne'er the less, with heat opprest,
Those three bold captains he addrest;
And wish'd that one to him would bring
Some water from his native spring.
His valiant captains instantly
To execute his will did fly.
The mighty Three the ranks broke through
Of armèd foes, and water drew
For David, their beloved king,
At his own sweet native spring.
Back through their arm'd foes they haste,
With the hard-earn'd treasure graced.
But when the good king David found
What they had done, he on the ground
The water pour'd. "Because," said he,
"That it was at the jeopardy
Of your three lives this thing ye did,
That I should drink it, God forbid."

SALOME

ONCE on a charger there was laid,
And brought before a royal maid,
As price of attitude and grace,
A guiltless head, a holy face.

It was on Herod's natal day,
Who o'er Judea's land held sway.
He married his own brother's wife,
Wicked Herodias. She the life

Of John the Baptist long had sought,
Because he openly had taught
That she a life unlawful led,
Having her husband's brother wed.

This was he, that saintly John,
Who in the wilderness alone
Abiding, did for clothing wear
A garment made of camel's hair;
Honey and locusts were his food,
And he was most severely good.
He preachèd penitence and tears,
And waking first the sinner's fears,
Prepared a path, made smooth a way,
For his diviner Master's day.

Herod kept in princely state
His birthday. On his throne he sate,
After the feast, beholding her
Who danced with grace peculiar;
Fair Salome, who did excel
All in that land for dancing well.
The feastful monarch's heart was fired,
And whatsoe'er thing she desired,
Though half his kingdom it should be,
He in his pleasure swore that he
Would give the graceful Salome.
The damsel was Herodias' daughter:
She to the queen hastes, and besought her
To teach her what great gift to name.
Instructed by Herodias, came
The damsel back: to Herod said,
"Give me John the Baptist's head;
And in a charger let it be
Hither straightway brought to me."
Herod her suit would fain deny,
But for his oath's sake must comply.

When painters would by art express
Beauty in unloveliness,
Thee, Herodias' daughter, thee,
They fittest subject take to be.
They give thy form and features grace;
But ever in thy beauteous face
They show a steadfast cruel gaze,
An eye unpitying; and amaze

In all beholders deep they mark,
That thou betrayest not one spark
Of feeling for the ruthless deed,
That did thy praiseful dance succeed.
For on the head they make you look,
As if a sullen joy you took,
A cruel triumph, wicked pride,
That for your sport a saint had died.

LINES

SUGGESTED BY A PICTURE OF TWO FEMALES BY LEONARDO DA VINCI

THE lady Blanch, regardless of all her lover's fears,
To the Urs'line convent hastens, and long the Abbess hears,
"O Blanch, my child, repent ye of the courtly life ye lead."
Blanch look'd on a rose-bud and little seem'd to heed.
She look'd on the rose-bud, she look'd round, and thought
On all her heart had whisper'd, and all the Nun had taught.
"I am worshipp'd by lovers, and brightly shines my fame,
All Christendom resoundeth the noble Blanch's name.
Nor shall I quickly wither like the rose-bud from the tree,
My queen-like graces shining when my beauty's gone from me.
But when the sculptured marble is rais'd o'er my head,
And the matchless Blanch lies lifeless among the noble dead,
This saintly lady Abbess hath made me justly fear,
It nothing will avail me that I were worshipp'd here."

LINES

ON THE SAME PICTURE BEING REMOVED TO MAKE PLACE FOR A PORTRAIT
OF A LADY BY TITIAN

WHO are thou, fair one, who usurp'st the place
Of Blanch, the lady of the matchless grace?
Come, fair and pretty, tell to me,
Who, in thy lifetime, thou might'st be.
Thou pretty art and fair,
But with the lady Blanch thou never must compare.
No need for Blanch her history to tell;
Whoever saw her face, they there did read it well.
But when I look on thee, I only know
There lived a pretty maid some hundred years ago.

LINES

ON THE CELEBRATED PICTURE BY LEONARDO DA VINCI, CALLED THE VIRGIN OF THE ROCKS

WHILE young John runs to greet
The greater Infant's feet,
The Mother standing by, with trembling passion
Of devout admiration,
Beholds the engaging mystic play, and pretty adoration;
Nor knows as yet the full event
Of those so low beginnings,
From whence we date our winnings,
But wonders at the intent
Of those new rites, and what that strange child-worship meant.
But at her side
An angel doth abide,
With such a perfect joy
As no dim doubts alloy,
An intuition,
A glory, an amenity,
Passing the dark condition
Of blind humanity,
As if he surely knew
All the blest wonder should ensue,
Or he had lately left the upper sphere,
And had read all the sovran schemes and divine riddles there.

ON THE SAME

MATERNAL lady with the virgin grace,
Heaven-born thy Jesus seemeth sure,
And thou a virgin pure.
Lady most perfect, when thy sinless face
Men look upon, they wish to be
A Catholic, Madonna fair, to worship thee.

ANGEL HELP [1]

THIS rare tablet doth include
Poverty with Sanctitude.
Past midnight this poor maid hath spun,

[1] Suggested by a drawing in the possession of Charles Aders, Esq., in which is represented the legend of a poor female Saint, who, having spun past midnight, to maintain a bed-rid mother, has fallen asleep from fatigue, and Angels are finishing her work. In another part of the chamber, an angel is tending a lily, the emblem of purity.

And yet the work is not half done,
Which must supply from earnings scant
A feeble bed-rid parent's want.
Her sleep-charged eyes exemption ask
And Holy hands take up the task;
Unseen the rock and spindle ply,
And do her earthly drudgery.
Sleep, saintly poor one! sleep, sleep on;
And, waking, find thy labours done.
Perchance she knows it by her dreams;
Her eye hath caught the golden gleams,
Angelic presence testifying,
That round her everywhere are flying;
Ostents from which she may presume,
That much of heaven is in the room.
Skirting her own bright hair they run,
And to the sunny add more sun:
Now on that aged face they fix,
Streaming from the Crucifix;
The flesh-clogg'd spirit disabusing,
Death-disarming sleeps infusing,
Prelibations, foretastes high,
And equal thoughts to live or die.
Gardener bright from Eden's bower,
Tend with care that lily flower;
To its leaves and root infuse
Heaven's sunshine, Heaven's dews.
'Tis a type, and 'tis a pledge,
Of a crowning privilege.
Careful as that lily flower,
This Maid must keep her precious dower;
Live a sainted Maid, or die
Martyr to virginity.

ON AN INFANT DYING AS SOON AS BORN

I SAW where in the shroud did lurk
A curious frame of Nature's work.
A flow'ret crushed in the bud,
A nameless piece of Babyhood,
Was in her cradle-coffin lying;
Extinct, with scarce the sense of dying:
So soon to exchange the imprisoning womb
For darker closets of the tomb!
She did but ope an eye, and put
A clear beam forth, then straight up shut

For the long dark: ne'er more to see
Through glasses of mortality.
Riddle of destiny, who can show
What thy short visit meant, or know
What thy errand here below?
Shall we say, that Nature blind
Check'd her hand, and changed her mind,
Just when she had exactly wrought
A finish'd pattern without fault?
Could she flag, or could she tire,
Or lack'd she the Promethean fire
(With her nine moons' long workings sicken'd)
That should thy little limbs have quicken'd?
Limbs so firm, they seem'd to assure
Life of health and days mature:
Woman's self in miniature!
Limbs so fair, they might supply
(Themselves now but cold imagery)
The sculptor to make Beauty by.
Or did the stern-eyed Fate descry,
That babe, or mother, one must die;
So in mercy left the stock,
And cut the branch; to save the shock
Of young years widow'd; and the pain,
When Single State comes back again
To the lone man who, 'reft of wife,
Thenceforward drags a maimed life?
The economy of Heaven is dark;
And wisest clerks have miss'd the mark,
Why Human Buds, like this, should fall,
More brief than fly ephemeral,
That has his day; while shrivell'd crones
Stiffen with age to stocks and stones;
And crabbed use the conscience sears
In sinners of an hundred years.
Mother's prattle, mother's kiss,
Baby fond, thou ne'er wilt miss.
Rites, which custom does impose,
Silver bells and baby clothes;
Coral redder than those lips,
Which pale death did late eclipse;
Music framed for infants' glee,
Whistle never tuned for thee;
Though thou want'st not, thou shalt have them,
Loving hearts were they which gave them.
Let not one be missing; nurse,
See them laid upon the hearse

Of infant slain by doom perverse.
Why should kings and nobles have
Pictured trophies to their grave;
And we, churls, to thee deny
Thy pretty toys with thee to lie,
A more harmless vanity?

THE CHRISTENING

ARRAY'D—a half-angelic sight—
In vests of pure Baptismal white,
The Mother to the Font doth bring
The little helpless nameless thing,
With hushes soft and mild caressing,
At once to get—a name and blessing.
Close by the babe the Priest doth stand,
The Cleansing Water at his hand,
Which must assoil the soul within
From every stain of Adam's sin.
The Infant eyes the mystic scenes,
Nor knows what all this wonder means;
And now he smiles, as if to say
"I am a Christian made this day";
Now frighted clings to Nurse's hold,
Shrinking from the water cold,
Whose virtues, rightly understood,
Are, as Bethesda's waters, good.
Strange words—The World, The Flesh, The Devil—
Poor Babe, what can it know of Evil?
But we must silently adore
Mysterious truths, and not explore.
Enough for him, in after-times,
When he shall read these artless rhymes,
If, looking back upon this day
With quiet conscience, he can say—
"I have in part redeem'd the pledge
Of my Baptismal privilege;
And more and more will strive to flee
All which my Sponsors kind did then renounce for me."

THE YOUNG CATECHIST [1]

WHILE this tawny Ethiop prayeth,
Painter, who is she that stayeth
By, with skin of whitest lustre,

[1] A picture by Henry Meyer, Esq.

Sunny locks, a shining cluster,
Saint-like seeming to direct him
To the Power that must protect him?
Is she of the Heaven-born Three,
Meek Hope, strong Faith, sweet Charity;
Or some Cherub?—

               They you mention
Far transcend my weak invention.
'Tis a simple Christian child,
Missionary young and mild,
From her stock of Scriptural knowledge,
Bible-taught without a college,
Which by reading she could gather,
Teaches him to say OUR FATHER
To the common Parent, who
Colour not respects, nor hue.
White and black in Him have part,
Who looks not to the skin, but heart.

TO A YOUNG FRIEND,

ON HER TWENTY-FIRST BIRTHDAY

CROWN me a cheerful goblet, while I pray
A blessing on thy years, young Isola;
Young, but no more a child. How swift have flown
To me thy girlish times, a woman grown
Beneath my heedless eyes! in vain I rack
My fancy to believe the almanac,
That speaks thee Twenty-One. Thou shouldst have still
Remain'd a child, and at thy sovereign will
Gambol'd about our house, as in times past.
Ungrateful Emma, to grow up so fast,
Hastening to leave thy friends!—for which intent,
Fond Runagate, be this thy punishment:
After some thirty years, spent in such bliss
As this earth can afford, where still we miss
Something of joy entire, may'st thou grow old
As we whom thou hast left! That wish was cold.
O far more aged and wrinkled, till folks say,
Looking upon thee reverend in decay,
"This Dame, for length of days, and virtues rare,
With her respected Grandsire may compare."
Grandchild of that respected Isola,
Thou shouldst have had about thee on this day
Kind looks of Parents, to congratulate

Their Pride grown up to woman's grave estate.
But they have died, and left thee, to advance
Thy fortunes how thou may'st, and owe to chance
The friends which nature grudged. And thou wilt find,
Or make such, Emma, if I am not blind
To thee and thy deservings. That last strain
Had too much sorrow in it. Fill again
Another cheerful goblet, while I say
"Health, and twice health, to our lost Isola."

SHE IS GOING

For their elder Sister's hair
Martha does a wreath prepare
Of bridal rose, ornate and gay:
To-morrow is the wedding day.
              She is going.

Mary, youngest of the three,
Laughing idler, full of glee,
Arm in arm does fondly chain her,
Thinking, poor trifler, to detain her—
              But she's going.

Vex not, maidens, nor regret
Thus to part with Margaret.
Charms like yours can never stay
Long within doors: and one day
              You'll be going.

CHILDHOOD

In my poor mind it is most sweet to muse
Upon the days gone by; to act in thought
Past seasons o'er, and be again a child;
To sit in fancy on the turf-clad slope,
Down which the child would roll; to pluck gay flowers,
Make posies in the sun, which the child's hand
(Childhood offended soon, soon reconciled),
Would throw away, and straight take up again,
Then fling them to the winds, and o'er the lawn
Bound with so playful and so light a foot,
That the press'd daisy scarce declined her head.

THE GRANDAME

On the green hill top,
Hard by the house of prayer, a modest roof,
And not distinguish'd from its neighbour-barn,
Save by a slender-tapering length of spire,
The Grandame sleeps. A plain stone barely tells
The name and date to the chance passenger.
For lowly born was she, and long had eat,
Well-earn'd, the bread of service:—hers was else
A mountain spirit, one that entertain'd
Scorn of base action, deed dishonourable,
Or aught unseemly. I remember well
Her reverend image; I remember, too,
With what a zeal she served her master's house;
And how the prattling tongue of garrulous age
Delighted to recount the oft-told tale
Or anecdote domestic. Wise she was,
And wondrous skill'd in genealogies,
And could in apt and voluble terms discourse
Of births, of titles, and alliances;
Of marriages, and intermarriages;
Relationship remote, or near of kin;
Of friends offended, family disgraced—
Maiden high-born, but wayward, disobeying
Parental strict injunction, and regardless
Of unmix'd blood, and ancestry remote,
Stooping to wed with one of low degree.
But these are not thy praises; and I wrong
Thy honour'd memory, recording chiefly
Things light or trivial. Better 'twere to tell,
How with a nobler zeal, and warmer love,
She served her *heavenly Master*. I have seen
That reverend form bent down with age and pain,
And rankling malady. Yet not for this
Ceased she to praise her Maker, or withdrew
Her trust in Him, her faith, an humble hope—
So meekly had she learn'd to bear her cross—
For she had studied patience in the school
Of Christ; much comfort she had thence derived,
And was a follower of the Nazarene.

THE SABBATH BELLS

The cheerful Sabbath bells, wherever heard,
Strike pleasant on the sense, most like the voice

Of one, who from the far-off hills proclaims
Tidings of good to Zion: chiefly when
Their piercing tones fall *sudden* on the ear
Of the contemplant, solitary man,
Whom thoughts abstruse or high have chanced to lure
Forth from the walks of men, revolving oft,
And oft again, hard matter, which eludes
And baffles his pursuit—thought-sick and tired
Of controversy, where no end appears,
No clue to his research, the lonely man
Half wishes for society again.
Him, thus engaged, the Sabbath bells salute
Sudden! his heart awakes, his ears drink in
The cheering music; his relenting soul
Yearns after all the joys of social life,
And softens with the love of human kind.

FANCY EMPLOYED ON DIVINE SUBJECTS

THE truant Fancy was a wanderer ever,
A lone enthusiast maid. She loves to walk
In the bright visions of empyreal light,
By the green pastures, and the fragrant meads,
Where the perpetual flowers of Eden blow;
By crystal streams, and by the living waters,
Along whose margin grows the wondrous tree
Whose leaves shall heal the nations; underneath
Whose holy shade a refuge shall be found
From pain and want, and all the ills that wait
On mortal life, from sin and death for ever.

COMPOSED AT MIDNIGHT

FROM broken visions of perturbèd rest
I wake, and start, and fear to sleep again.
How total a privation of all sounds,
Sights, and familiar objects, man, bird, beast,
Herb, tree, or flower, and prodigal light of heaven.
'Twere some relief to catch the drowsy cry
Of the mechanic watchman, or the noise
Of revel reeling home from midnight cups.
Those are the moanings of the dying man,
Who lies in the upper chamber; restless moans.
And interrupted only by a cough
Consumptive, torturing the wasted lungs.

So in the bitterness of death he lies,
And waits in anguish for the morning's light.
What can that do for him, or what restore?
Short taste, faint sense, affecting notices,
And little images of pleasures past,
Of health, and active life—health not yet slain,
Nor the other grace of life, a good name, sold
For sin's black wages. On his tedious bed
He writhes, and turns him from the accusing light,
And finds no comfort in the sun, but says
"When night comes I shall get a little rest."
Some few groans more, death comes, and there an end.
'Tis darkness and conjecture all beyond;
Weak Nature fears, though Charity must hope,
And Fancy, most licentious on such themes
Where decent reverence well had kept her mute,
Hath o'er-stock'd hell with devils, and brought down,
By her enormous fablings and mad lies,
Discredit on the gospel's serious truths
And salutary fears. The man of parts,
Poet, or prose declaimer, on his couch
Lolling, like one indifferent, fabricates
A heaven of gold, where he, and such as he,
Their heads encompassèd with crowns, their heels
With fine wings garlanded, shall tread the stars
Beneath their feet, heaven's pavement, far removed
From damnèd spirits, and the torturing cries
Of men, his brethren, fashion'd of the earth,
As he was, nourish'd with the self-same bread,
Belike his kindred or companions once—
Through everlasting ages now divorced,
In chains and savage torments to repent
Short years of folly on earth. Their groans unheard
In heav'n, the saint nor pity feels, nor care,
For those thus sentenced—pity might disturb
The delicate sense and most divine repose
Of spirits angelical. Blessed be God,
The measure of His judgments is not fix'd
By man's erroneous standard. He discerns
No such inordinate difference and vast
Betwixt the sinner and the saint, to doom
Such disproportion'd fates. Compared with Him,
No man on earth is holy call'd: they best
Stand in His sight approved, who at His feet
Their little crowns of virtue cast, and yield
To Him of His own works the praise, His due.

PINDARIC ODE TO THE TREAD-MILL

I.

INSPIRE my spirit, Spirit of De Foe,
That sang the Pillory,
In loftier strains to show
A more sublime Machine
Than that, where thou wert seen,
With neck out-stretcht and shoulders ill awry,
Courting coarse plaudits from vile crowds below—
A most unseemly show!

II.

In such a place
Who could expose thy face,
Historiographer of deathless Crusoe!
That paint'st the strife
And all the naked ills of savage life,
Far above Rousseau?
Rather myself had stood
In that ignoble wood,
Bare to the mob, on holyday or high day.
If nought else could atone
For waggish libel,
I swear on Bible,
I would have spared him for thy sake alone,
Man Friday!

III.

Our ancestors were sour days,
Great Master of Romance!
A milder doom had fallen to thy chance
In our days:
Thy sole assignment
Some solitary confinement
(Not worth thy care a carrot),
Where in world-hidden cell
Thou thy own Crusoe might have acted well,
Only without the parrot;
By sure experience taught to know,
Whether the qualms thou mak'st him feel were truly such or no.

IV.

But stay! methinks in statelier measure—
A more companionable pleasure—
I see thy steps the mighty Tread-Mill trace
(The subject of my song,
Delay'd however long),
And some of thine own race,
To keep thee company, thou bring'st with thee along.
There with thee go,
Link'd in like sentence,
With regulated pace and footing slow,
Each old acquaintance,
Rogue—harlot—thief—that live to future ages;
Through many a labour'd tome,
Rankly embalm'd in thy too natural pages.
Faith, friend De Foe, thou art quite at home!
Not one of thy great offspring thou dost lack,
From pirate Singleton to pilfering Jack.
Here Flandrian Moll her brazen incest brags;
Vice-stript Roxana, penitent in rags,
There points to Amy, treading equal chimes,
The faithful handmaid to her faithless crimes.

v.

Incompetent my song to raise
To its just height thy praise,
Great Mill!
That by thy motion proper
(No thanks to wind, or sail, or working rill),
Grinding that stubborn corn, the Human will,
Turn'st out men's consciences,
That were begrimed before, as clean and sweet
As flour from purest wheat,
Into thy hopper.
All reformation short of thee but nonsense is,
Or human, or divine.

VI.

Compared with thee,
What are the labours of that Jumping Sect,
Which feeble laws connive at rather than respect?
Thou dost not bump,
Or jump,
But *walk* men into virtue; betwixt crime

And slow repentance giving breathing time,
And leisure to be good;
Instructing with discretion demi-reps
How to direct their steps.

VII.

Thou best Philosopher made out of wood!
Not that which framed the tub,
Where sate the Cynic cub,
With nothing in his bosom sympathetic;
But from those groves derived, I deem,
Where Plato nursed his dream
Of immortality;
Seeing that clearly
Thy system all is merely
Peripatetic.
Thou to thy pupils dost such lessons give
Of how to live
With temperance, sobriety, morality
(A new art),
That from thy school, by force of virtuous deeds,
Each Tyro now proceeds
A "Walking Stewart!"

GOING OR GONE

I.

FINE merry franions,
Wanton companions,
My days are ev'n banyans
    With thinking upon ye!
How Death, that last stinger,
Finis-writer, end-bringer,
Has laid his chill finger,
    Or is laying on ye.

II.

There's rich Kitty Wheatley,
With footing it featly
That took me completely,
    She sleeps in the Kirk House;
And poor Polly Perkin,
Whose Dad was still firking
The jolly ale firkin,
    She's gone to the Workhouse;

III.

Fine Gard'ner, Ben Carter
(In ten counties no smarter)
Has ta'en his departure
    For Proserpine's orchards:
And Lily, postilion,
With cheeks of vermilion,
Is one of a million
    That fill up the churchyards;

IV.

And, lusty as Dido,
Fat Clemitson's widow
Flits now a small shadow
    By Stygian hid ford;
And good Master Clapton
Has thirty years napt on,
The ground he last hapt on,
    Intomb'd by fair Widford;

V.

And gallant Tom Dockwra,
Of Nature's finest crockery,
Now but thin air and mockery,
    Lurks by Avernus,
Whose honest grasp of hand
Still, while his life did stand,
At friend's or foe's command,
    Almost did burn us.

VI.

Roger de Coverley
Not more good man than he;
Yet has he equally
    Push'd for Cocytus,
With drivelling Worral,
And wicked old Dorrell,
'Gainst whom I've a quarrel,
    Whose end might affright us!—

VII.

Kindly hearts have I known;
Kindly hearts, they are flown;

Here and there if but one
    Linger yet uneffaced,
Imbecile tottering elves,
Soon to be wreck'd on shelves,
These scarce are half themselves,
    With age and care crazed.

VIII.

But this day Fanny Hutton
Her last dress has put on;
Her fine lessons forgotten,
    She died, as the dunce died;
And prim Betsy Chambers,
Decay'd in her members,
No longer remembers
    Things as she once did;

IX.

And prudent Miss Wither
Not in jest now doth *wither,*
And soon must go—whither
    Nor I well, nor you know;
And flaunting Miss Waller,
That soon must befall her,
Whence none can recall her,
    Though proud once as Juno!

FREE THOUGHTS ON SEVERAL EMINENT COMPOSERS

Some cry up Haydn, some Mozart,
Just as the whim bites; for my part,
I do not care a farthing candle
For either of them, or for Handel.—
Cannot a man live free and easy,
Without admiring Pergolesi?
Or through the world with comfort go,
That never heard of Doctor Blow?
So help me heaven, I hardly have;
And yet I eat, and drink, and shave,
Like other people, if you watch it,
And know no more of stave or crotchet
Than did the primitive Peruvians;
Or those old ante-queer-diluvians
That lived in the unwash'd world with Jubal,
Before that dirty blacksmith Tubal

By stroke on anvil, or by summ'at,
Found out, to his great surprise, the gamut.
I care no more for Cimarosa
Than he did for Salvator Rosa,
Being no painter; and bad luck
Be mine, if I can bear that Gluck!
Old Tycho Brahe, and modern Herschel,
Had something in them; but who's Purcel?
The devil, with his foot so cloven,
For aught I care, may take Beethoven;
And, if the bargain does not suit,
I'll throw him Weber in to boot.
There's not the splitting of a splinter
To choose 'twixt him last named, and Winter.
Of Doctor Pepusch old Queen Dido
Knew just as much, God knows, as I do.
I would not go four miles to visit
Sebastian Bach; (or Batch, which is it?)
No more I would for Bononcini.
As for Novello, or Rossini,
I shall not say a word to grieve 'em,
Because they're living; so I leave 'em.

ALBUM AND COMMENDATORY VERSES

IN THE AUTOGRAPH BOOK OF
MRS. SERJEANT W——

HAD I a power, Lady, to my will,
You should not want Hand Writings. I would fill
Your leaves with Autographs—resplendent names
Of Knights and Squires of old, and courtly Dames,
Kings, Emperors, Popes. Next under these should stand
The hands of famous Lawyers—a grave band—
Who in their Courts of Law or Equity
Have best upheld Freedom and Property.
These should moot cases in your book, and vie
To show their reading and their Serjeantry.
But I have none of these; nor can I send
The notes by Bullen to her Tyrant penn'd
In her authentic hand; nor in soft hours
Lines writ by Rosamund in Clifford's bowers.
The lack of curious Signatures I moan,
And want the courage to subscribe my own.

TO DORA W——,

ON BEING ASKED BY HER FATHER TO WRITE IN HER ALBUM

An Album is a Banquet: from the store,
In his intelligential Orchard growing,
Your Sire might heap your board to overflowing:
One shaking of the Tree—'twould ask no more
To set a Salad forth, more rich than that
Which Evelyn [1] in his princely cookery fancied:
Or that more rare, by Eve's neat hands enhanced,
Where, a pleaséd guest, the Angelic Virtue sat.
But like the all-grasping Founder of the Feast,
Whom Nathan to the sinning king did tax,
From his less wealthy neighbours he exacts;
Spares his own flocks, and takes the poor man's beast.
Obedient to his bidding, lo, I am,
A zealous, meek, *contributory*   LAMB.

IN THE ALBUM OF A CLERGYMAN'S LADY

An Album is a Garden, not for show
Planted, but use; where wholesome herbs should grow.
A Cabinet of curious porcelain, where
No fancy enters, but what's rich or rare.
A Chapel, where mere ornamental things
Are pure as crowns of saints, or angels' wings.
A List of living friends; a holier Room
For names of some since mouldering in the tomb,
Whose blooming memories life's cold laws survive;
And, dead elsewhere, they here yet speak and live.
Such, and so tender, should an Album be;
And, Lady, such I wish this book to thee.

IN THE ALBUM OF EDITH S——

In Christian world MARY the garland wears!
REBECCA sweetens on a Hebrew's ear;
Quakers for pure PRISCILLA are more clear;
And the light Gaul by amorous NINON swears.
Among the lesser lights how LUCY shines!
What air of fragrance ROSAMOND throws round!
How like a hymn doth sweet CECILIA sound!
Of MARTHAS, and of ABIGAILS, few lines

---

[1] Acetaria, a Discourse of Sallets, by J. E., 1706.

Have bragg'd in verse.   Of coarsest household stuff
Should homely JOAN be fashion'd.   But can
You BARBARA resist, or MARIAN?
And is not CLARE for love excuse enough?
Yet, by my faith in numbers, I profess,
These all, than Saxon EDITH, please me less.

IN THE ALBUM OF ROTHA Q——

A PASSING glance was all I caught of thee,
In my own Enfield haunts at random roving.
Old friends of ours were with thee, faces loving;
Time short: the salutations cursory,
Though deep, and hearty. The familiar Name
Of you, yet unfamiliar, raised in me
Thoughts—what the daughter of that Man should be,
Who call'd our Wordsworth friend. My thoughts did frame
A growing Maiden, who, from day to day
Advancing still in stature, and in grace,
Would all her lonely Father's griefs efface,
And his paternal cares with usury pay.
I still retain the phantom, as I can;
And call the gentle image—Quillinan.

IN THE ALBUM OF CATHERINE ORKNEY

CANADIA! boast no more the toils
Of hunters for the furry spoils;
Your whitest ermines are but foils
       To brighter Catherine Orkney.

That such a flower should ever burst
From climes with rigorous winter curst!—
We bless you, that so kindly nurst
       This flower, this Catherine Orkney.

We envy not your proud display
Of lake—wood—vast Niagara;
Your greatest pride we've borne away.
       How spared you Catherine Orkney?

That Wolfe on Heights of Abraham fell,
To your reproach no more we tell:
Canadia, you repaid us well
       With rearing Catherine Orkney.

O Britain, guard with tenderest care
The charge allotted to your share:
You've scarce a native maid so fair,
   So good, as Catherine Orkney.

IN THE ALBUM OF LUCY BARTON

LITTLE Book, surnamed of *white*,
Clean as yet, and fair to sight,
Keep thy attribution right.

Never disproportion'd scrawl;
Ugly blot, that's worse than all;
On thy maiden clearness fall!

In each letter, here design'd,
Let the reader emblem'd find
Neatness of the owner's mind.
Gilded margins count a sin,
Let thy leaves attraction win
By the golden rules within;

Sayings fetch'd from sages old;
Laws which Holy Writ unfold,
Worthy to be graved in gold:

Lighter fancies not excluding;
Blameless wit, with nothing rude in,
Sometimes mildly interluding

Amid strains of graver measure:
Virtue's self hath oft her pleasure
In sweet Muses' groves of leisure.

Riddles dark, perplexing sense;
Darker meanings of offence;
What but *shades*—be banish'd hence.

Whitest thoughts in whitest dress,
Candid meanings, best express
Mind of quiet Quakeress.

IN THE ALBUM OF MRS. JANE TOWERS

LADY Unknown, who crav'st from me Unknown
The trifle of a verse these leaves to grace,

How shall I find fit matter? with what face
Address a face that ne'er to me was shown?
Thy looks, tones, gesture, manners, and what not,
Conjecturing, I wander in the dark.
I know thee only Sister to Charles Clarke!
But at that name my cold muse waxes hot,
And swears that thou art such a one as he,
Warm, laughter-loving, with a touch of madness,
Wild, glee-provoking, pouring oil of gladness
From frank heart without guile. And, if thou be
The pure reverse of this, and I mistake—
Demure one, I will like thee for his sake.

IN THE ALBUM OF MISS ——

I.

Such goodness in your face doth shine,
With modest look, without design,
That I despair, poor pen of mine
    Can e'er express it.
To give it words I feebly try;
My spirits fail me to supply
Befitting language for 't, and I
    Can only bless it!

II.

But stop, rash verse! and don't abuse
A bashful Maiden's ear with news
Of her own virtues. She'll refuse
    Praise sung so loudly.
Of that same goodness you admire,
The best part is, she don't aspire
To praise—nor of herself desire
    To think too proudly.

IN MY OWN ALBUM

Fresh clad from heaven in robes of white,
A young probationer of light,
Thou wert, my soul, an album bright,

A spotless leaf; but thought, and care,
And friend and foe, in foul or fair,
Have "written strange defeatures" there;

And Time with heaviest hand of all,
Like that fierce writing on the wall,
Hath stamp'd sad dates—he can't recall;

And error gilding worst designs—
Like speckled snake that strays and shines—
Betrays his path by crooked lines;

And vice hath left his ugly blot;
And good resolves, a moment hot,
Fairly began—but finish'd not;

And fruitless, late remorse doth trace—
Like Hebrew lore a backward pace—
Her irrecoverable race.

Disjointed numbers; sense unknit;
Huge reams of folly, shreds of wit;
Compose the mingled mass of it.

My scalded eyes no longer brook
Upon this ink-blurr'd thing to look—
Go, shut the leaves, and clasp the book.

TO MARTIN CHARLES BURNEY, ESQ.

FORGIVE me, BURNEY, if to thee these late
And hasty products of a critic pen,
Thyself no common judge of books and men,
In feeling of thy worth I dedicate.
My *verse* was offered to an older friend;
The humbler *prose* has fallen to thy share:
Nor could I miss the occasion to declare,
What spoken in thy presence must offend—
That, set aside some few caprices wild,
Those humorous clouds that flit o'er brightest days,
In all my threadings of this worldly maze
(And I have watched thee almost from a child),
Free from self-seeking, envy, low design,
I have not found a whiter soul than thine.

TO J. S. KNOWLES, ESQ.

ON HIS TRAGEDY OF VIRGINIUS

TWELVE years ago I knew thee, Knowles, and then
Esteemed you a perfect specimen

Of those fine spirits warm-soul'd Ireland sends,
To teach us colder English how a friend's
Quick pulse should beat. I knew you brave, and plain,
Strong-sensed, rough-witted, above fear or gain;
But nothing further had the gift to espy.
Sudden you reappear. With wonder I
Hear my old friend (turn'd Shakspeare) read a scene
Only to *his* inferior in the clean
Passes of pathos: with such fence-like art—
Ere we can see the steel, 'tis in our heart.
Almost without the aid language affords,
Your piece seems wrought. That huffing medium, *words*
(Which in the modern Tamburlaines quite sway
Our shamed souls from their bias) in your play
We scarce attend to. Hastier passion draws
Our tears on credit: and we find the cause
Some two hours after, spelling o'er again
Those strange few words at ease, that wrought the pain.
Proceed, old friend; and, as the year returns,
Still snatch some new old story from the urns
Of long-dead virtue. We, that knew before
Your worth, may admire, we cannot love you more.

TO THE AUTHOR OF POEMS,

PUBLISHED UNDER THE NAME OF BARRY CORNWALL

LET hate, or grosser heats, their foulness mask
Under the vizor of a borrow'd name;
Let things eschew the light deserving blame:
No cause hast thou to blush for thy sweet task.
"Marcian Colonna" is a dainty book;
And thy "Sicilian Tale" may boldly pass;
Thy "Dream" 'bove all, in which, as in a glass,
On the great world's antique glories we may look.
No longer than, as "lowly substitute,
Factor, or PROCTER, for another's gains,"
Suffer the admiring world to be deceived;
Lest thou thyself, by self of fame bereaved,
Lament too late the lost prize of thy pains,
And heavenly tunes piped through an alien flute.

TO THE EDITOR OF THE "EVERY-DAY BOOK"

I LIKE you, and your book, ingenious Hone!
In whose capacious all-embracing leaves
The very marrow of tradition's shown;
And all that history—much that fiction—weaves.

By every sort of taste your work is graced.
    Vast stores of modern anecdote we find,
With good old story quaintly interlaced—
    The theme as various as the reader's mind.

Rome's lie-fraught legends you so truly paint—
    Yet kindly,—that the half-turn'd Catholic
Scarcely forbears to smile at his own saint,
    And cannot curse the candid heretic.

Rags, relics, witches, ghosts, fiends, crowd your page;
    Our fathers' mummeries we well-pleased behold,
And, proudly conscious of a purer age,
    Forgive some fopperies in the times of old.

Verse-honouring Phœbus, Father of bright *Days,*
    Must needs bestow on you both good and many,
Who, building trophies of his Children's praise,
    Run their rich Zodiac through, not missing any.

Dan Phœbus loves your book—trust me, friend Hone—
    The title only errs, he bids me say:
For while such art, wit, reading, there are shown,
    He swears, 'tis not a work of *every day.*

TO T. STOTHARD, ESQ.

ON HIS ILLUSTRATIONS OF THE POEMS OF MR. ROGERS

Consummate Artist, whose undying name
With classic Rogers shall go down to fame,
Be this thy crowning work! In my young days
How often have I, with a child's fond gaze,
Pored on the pictur'd wonders[1] thou hadst done:
Clarissa mournful, and prim Grandison!
All Fielding's, Smollett's heroes, rose to view;
I saw, and I believed the phantoms true.
But, above all, that most romantic tale[2]
Did o'er my raw credulity prevail,
Where Glums and Gawries wear mysterious things,

---

[1] Illustrations of the British Novelists.
[2] Peter Wilkins.

That serve at once for jackets and for wings.
Age, that enfeebles other men's designs,
But heightens thine, and thy free draught refines.
In several ways distinct you make us feel—
Graceful as Raphael, as Watteau *genteel*.
Your lights and shades, as Titianesque, we praise;
And warmly wish you Titian's length of days.

TO A FRIEND ON HIS MARRIAGE

WHAT makes a happy wedlock? What has fate
Not given to thee in thy well-chosen mate?
Good sense—good humour;—these are trivial things,
Dear M——, that each trite encomiast sings.
But she hath these, and more. A mind exempt
From every low-bred passion, where contempt,
Nor envy, nor detraction, ever found
A harbour yet; an understanding sound;
Just views of right and wrong; perception full
Of the deform'd, and of the beautiful,
In life and manners; wit above her sex,
Which, as a gem, her sprightly converse decks;
Exuberant fancies, prodigal of mirth,
To gladden woodland walk, or winter hearth;
A noble nature, conqueror in the strife
Of conflict with a hard discouraging life,
Strengthening the veins of virtue, past the power
Of those whose days have been one silken hour,
Spoil'd fortune's pamper'd offspring; a keen sense
Alike of benefit, and of offence.
With reconcilement quick, that instant springs
From the charged heart with nimble angel wings;
While grateful feelings, like a signet sign'd
By a strong hand, seem burn'd into her mind.
If these, dear friend, a dowry can confer
Richer than land, thou hast them all in her;
And beauty, which some hold the chiefest boon,
Is in thy bargain for a make-weight thrown.

[In a leaf of a quarto edition of the "Lives of the Saints, written in Spanish by the learned and reverend father, Alfonso Villegas, Divine, of the Order of St. Dominick, set forth in English by John Heigham, Anno 1630," bought at a Catholic book-shop in Duke Street, Lincoln's Inn Fields, I found, carefully inserted, a painted flower, seemingly coeval with the book itself; and did not, for some time, discover that it opened in the middle, and was the cover to a very humble draught of a St. Anne, with the Virgin and Child; doubtless the performance of some poor but pious Catholic, whose meditations it assisted.]

C LIFT with reverent hand that tarnish'd flower,
That shrines beneath her modest canopy
Memorials dear to Romish piety;
Dim specks, rude shapes, of Saints! in fervent hour
The work perchance of some meek devotee,
Who, poor in worldly treasures to set forth
The sanctities she worshipp'd to their worth,
In this imperfect tracery might see
Hints, that all Heaven did to her sense reveal.
Cheap gifts best fit poor givers. We are told
Of the lone mite, the cup of water cold,
That in their way approved the offerer's zeal.
True love shows costliest, where the means are scant;
And, in their reckoning, they *abound*, who *want*.

THE SELF-ENCHANTED

I HAD a sense in dreams of a beauty rare,
Whom Fate had spell-bound, and rooted there,
Stooping, like some enchanted theme,
Over the marge of that crystal stream,
Where the blooming Greek, to Echo blind,
With Self-love fond, had to waters pined.
Ages had waked, and ages slept,
And that bending posture still she kept:
For her eyes she may not turn away,
'Till a fairer object shall pass that way——
'Till an image more beauteous this world can show,
Than her own which she sees in the mirror below.
Pore on, fair Creature! for ever pore,
Nor dream to be disenchanted more:
For vain is expectance, and wish is vain,
'Till a new Narcissus can come again.

TO LOUISA M——,

WHOM I USED TO CALL "MONKEY"

LOUISA, serious grown and mild,
I knew you once a romping child,

Obstreperous much and very wild.
Then you would clamber up my knees,
And strive with every art to tease,
When every art of yours could please.
Those things would scarce be proper now,
But they are gone, I know not how,
And woman's written on your brow.
Time draws his finger o'er the scene;
But I cannot forget between
The Thing to me you once have been;
Each sportive sally, wild escape,—
The scoff, the banter, and the jape,—
And antics of my gamesome Ape.

SONNETS

I.

TO MISS KELLY

You are not, Kelly, of the common strain,
That stoop their pride and female honour down
To please that many-headed beast *the town*,
And vend their lavish smiles and tricks for gain;
By fortune thrown amid the actors' train,
You keep your native dignity of thought;
The plaudits that attend you come unsought,
As tributes due unto your natural vein.
Your tears have passion in them, and a grace
Of genuine freshness, which our hearts avow;
Your smiles are winds whose ways we cannot trace,
That vanish and return we know not how—
And please the better from a pensive face,
A thoughtful eye, and a reflecting brow.

II.

ON THE SIGHT OF SWANS IN KENSINGTON GARDEN

Queen-bird that sittest on thy shining nest,
And thy young cygnets without sorrow hatchest,
And thou, thou other royal bird, that watchest
Lest the white mother wandering feet molest:
Shrined are your offspring in a crystal cradle,
Brighter than Helen's ere she yet had burst
Her shelly prison. They shall be born at first
Strong, active, graceful, perfect, swan-like able
To tread the land or waters with security.
Unlike poor human births, conceived in sin,
In grief brought forth, both outwardly and in
Confessing weakness, error, and impurity.
Did heavenly creatures own succession's line,
The births of heaven like to yours would shine.

III.

Was it some sweet device of Faery
That mock'd my steps with many a lonely glade,
And fancied wanderings with a fair-hair'd maid?
Have these things been? or what rare witchery,
Impregning with delights the charmèd air,
Enlighted up the semblance of a smile
In those fine eyes? methought they spake the while
Soft soothing things, which might enforce despair
To drop the murdering knife, and let go by
His foul resolve.   And does the lonely glade
Still court the footsteps of the fair-hair'd maid?
Still in her locks the gales of summer sigh?
While I forlorn do wander, reckless where,
And 'mid my wanderings meet no Anna there.

IV.

Methinks how dainty sweet it were, reclined
Beneath the vast out-stretching branches high
Of some old wood, in careless sort to lie,
Nor of the busier scenes we left behind
Aught envying.   And, O Anna! mild-eyed maid!
Beloved! I were well content to play
With thy free tresses all a summer's day,
Losing the time beneath the greenwood shade.
Or we might sit and tell some tender tale
Of faithful vows repaid by cruel scorn,
A tale of true love, or of friend forgot;
And I would teach thee, lady, how to rail
In gentle sort, on those who practice not
Or love or pity, though of woman born.

V.

When last I roved these winding wood-walks green,
Green winding walks, and shady pathways sweet,
Oft-times would Anna seek the silent scene,
Shrouding her beauties in the lone retreat.
No more I hear her footsteps in the shade:
Her image only in these pleasant ways
Meets me self-wandering, where in happier days
I held free converse with the fair-hair'd maid.
I pass'd the little cottage which she loved,
The cottage which did once my all contain;
It spake of days which ne'er must come again,

Spake to my heart, and much my heart was moved.
"Now fair befall thee, gentle maid!" said I,
And from the cottage turn'd me with a sigh.

VI.

THE FAMILY NAME

WHAT reason first imposed thee, gentle name,
Name that my father bore, and his sire's sire,
Without reproach? we trace our stream no higher;
And I, a childless man, may end the same.
Perchance some shepherd on Lincolnian plains,
In manners guileless as his own sweet flocks,
Received thee first amid the merry mocks
And arch allusions of his fellow swains.
Perchance from Salem's holier fields return'd,
With glory gotten on the heads abhorr'd
Of faithless Saracens, some martial lord
Took HIS meek title, in whose zeal he burn'd.
Whate'er the fount whence thy beginnings came,
No deed of mine shall shame thee, gentle name.

VII.

IF from my lips some angry accents fell,
Peevish complaint, or harsh reproof unkind,
'Twas but the error of a sickly mind
And troubled thoughts, clouding the purer well,
And waters clear, of Reason; and for me
Let this my verse the poor atonement be—
My verse, which thou to praise wert ever inclined
Too highly, and with a partial eye to see
No blemish. Thou to me didst ever show
Kindest affection; and would oft-times lend
An ear to the desponding love-sick lay,
Weeping my sorrows with me, who repay
But ill the mighty debt of love I owe,
Mary, to thee, my sister and my friend.

VIII.

A TIMID grace sits trembling in her eye,
As loath to meet the rudeness of men's sight,
Yet shedding a delicious lunar light,
That steeps in kind oblivious ecstasy
The care-crazed mind, like some still melody:
Speaking most plain the thoughts which do possess
Her gentle sprite: peace, and meek quietness,

And innocent loves, and maiden purity:
A look whereof might heal the cruel smart
Of changèd friends, or fortune's wrongs unkind;
Might to sweet deeds of mercy move the heart
Of him who hates his brethren of mankind.
Turn'd are those lights from me, who fondly yet
Past joys, vain loves, and buried hopes regret.

IX.

TO JOHN LAMB, ESQ., OF THE SOUTH-SEA HOUSE

JOHN, you were figuring in the gay career
Of blooming manhood with a young man's joy,
When I was yet a little peevish boy—
Though time has made the difference disappear
Betwixt our ages, which *then* seem'd so great—
And still by rightful custom you retain
Much of the old authoritative strain,
And keep the elder brother up in state.
O! you do well in this. 'Tis man's worst deed
To let the "things that have been" run to waste,
And in the unmeaning present sink the past:
In whose dim glass even now I faintly read
Old buried forms, and faces long ago,
Which you, and I, and one more, only know.

X.

O! I COULD laugh to hear the midnight wind,
That, rushing on its way with careless sweep,
Scatters the ocean waves. And I could weep
Like to a child. For now to my raised mind
On wings of winds comes wild-eyed Phantasy,
And her rude visions give severe delight.
O wingèd bark! how swift along the night
Pass'd thy proud keel! nor shall I let go by
Lightly of that drear hour the memory,
When wet and chilly on thy deck I stood,
Unbonneted, and gazed upon the flood,
Even till it seem'd a pleasant thing to die,—
To be resolv'd into th' elemental wave,
Or take my portion with the winds that rave.

XI.

WE were two pretty babes, the youngest she,
The youngest, and the loveliest far, I ween,

And INNOCENCE her name. The time has been,
We two did love each other's company;
Time was, we two had wept to have been apart.
But when by show of seeming good beguiled,
I left the garb and manners of a child,
And my first love for man's society,
Defiling with the world my virgin heart—
My loved companion dropp'd a tear, and fled,
And hid in deepest shades her awful head.
Beloved, who shall tell me where thou art—
In what delicious Eden to be found—
That I may seek thee the wide world around?

HARMONY IN UNLIKENESS

By Enfield lanes, and Winchmore's verdant hill,
Two lovely damsels cheer my lonely walk:
The fair Maria, as a vestal, still;
And Emma brown, exuberant in talk.
With soft and Lady speech the first applies
The mild correctives that to grace belong
To her redundant friend, who her defies
With jest, and mad discourse, and bursts of song.
O differing Pair, yet sweetly thus agreeing,
What music from your happy discord rises,
While your companion hearing each, and seeing,
Nor this, nor that, but both together, prizes;
This lesson teaching, which our souls may strike,
That harmonies may be in things unlike!

WRITTEN AT CAMBRIDGE

I WAS not train'd in Academic bowers,
And to those learned streams I nothing owe
Which copious from those twin fair founts do flow;
Mine have been anything but studious hours.
Yet can I fancy, wandering mid thy towers,
Myself a nursling, Granta, of thy lap;
My brow seems tightening with the Doctor's cap,
And I walk *gowned;* feel unusual powers.
Strange forms of logic clothe my admiring speech,
Old Ramus' ghost is busy at my brain;
And my skull teems with notions infinite.
Be still, ye reeds of Camus, while I teach
Truths which transcend the searching School-men's vein,
And half had stagger'd that stout Stagirite!

TO A CELEBRATED FEMALE PERFORMER IN THE "BLIND BOY"

RARE artist! who with half thy tools, or none,
Canst execute with ease thy curious art,
And press thy powerful'st meanings on the heart,
Unaided by the eye, expression's throne!
While each blind sense, intelligential grown
Beyond its sphere, performs the effect of sight:
Those orbs alone, wanting their proper might,
All motionless and silent seem to moan
The unseemly negligence of nature's hand,
That left them so forlorn. What praise is thine,
O mistress of the passions; artist fine!
Who dost our souls against our sense command,
Plucking the horror from a sightless face,
Lending to blank deformity a grace.

WORK

WHO first invented work, and bound the free
And holyday-rejoicing spirit down
To the ever-haunting importunity
Of business in the green fields, and the town—
To plough, loom, anvil, spade—and oh! most sad
To that dry drudgery at the desk's dead wood?
Who but the Being unblest, alien from good,
Sabbathless Satan! he who his unglad
Task ever plies 'mid rotatory burnings,
That round and round incalculably reel—
For wrath divine hath made him like a wheel—
In that red realm from which are no returnings:
Where toiling, and turmoiling, ever and aye
He, and his thoughts, keep pensive working-day.

LEISURE

THEY talk of time, and of time's galling yoke,
That like a millstone on man's mind doth press,
Which only works and business can redress:
Of divine Leisure such foul lies are spoke,
Wounding her fair gifts with calumnious stroke.
But might I, fed with silent meditation,
Assoiled live from that fiend Occupation—
Improbus Labor, which my spirits hath broke—
I'd drink of time's rich cup, and never surfeit:

Fling in more days than went to make the gem
That crown'd the white top of Methusalem:
Yea on my weak neck take, and never forfeit,
Like Atlas bearing up the dainty sky,
The heaven-sweet burthen of eternity.

DEUS NOBIS HÆC OTIA FECIT.

TO SAMUEL ROGERS, ESQ.

ROGERS, of all the men that I have known
But slightly, who have died, your Brother's loss
Touch'd me most sensibly. There came across
My mind an image of the cordial tone
Of your fraternal meetings, where a guest
I more than once have sat; and grieve to think,
That of that threefold cord one precious link
By Death's rude hand is sever'd from the rest.
Of our old gentry he appear'd a stem—
A Magistrate who, while the evil-doer
He kept in terror, could respect the Poor,
And not for every trifle harass them,
As some, divine and laic, too oft do.
This man's a private loss, and public too.

THE GIPSY'S MALISON

"SUCK, baby, suck! mother's love grows by giving;
Drain the sweet founts that only thrive by wasting;
Black manhood comes, when riotous guilty living
Hands thee the cup that shall be death in tasting.

"Kiss, baby, kiss! mother's lips shine by kisses;
Choke the warm breath that else would fall in blessings;
Black manhood comes, when turbulent guilty blisses
Tend thee the kiss that poisons 'mid caressings.

"Hang, baby, hang! mother's love loves such forces,
Strain the fond neck that bends still to thy clinging;
Black manhood comes, when violent lawless courses
Leave thee a spectacle in rude air swinging."

So sang a wither'd Beldam energetical,
And bann'd the ungiving door with lips prophetical.

TRANSLATIONS
FROM THE LATIN OF VINCENT BOURNE

I.

THE BALLAD SINGERS

WHERE seven fair Streets to one tall Column [1] draw,
Two Nymphs have ta'en their stand, in hats of straw;
Their yellower necks huge beads of amber grace,
And by their trade they're of the Sirens' race:
With cloak loose-pinn'd on each, that has been red,
But long with dust and dirt discoloured
Belies its hue; in mud behind, before,
From heel to middle leg becrusted o'er.
One a small infant at the breast does bear;
And one in her right hand her tuneful ware,
Which she would vend. Their station scarce is taken,
When youths and maids flock round. His stall forsaken,
Forth comes a Son of Crispin, leathern-capt,
Prepared to buy a ballad, if one apt
To move his fancy offers. Crispin's sons
Have, from uncounted time, with ale and buns,
Cherish'd the gift of *Song,* which sorrow quells;
And, working single in their low-rooft cells,
Oft cheat the tedium of a winter's night
With anthems warbled in the Muses' spight.—
Who now hath caught the alarm? the Servant Maid
Hath heard a buzz at distance; and, afraid
To miss a note, with elbows red comes out.
Leaving his forge to cool, Pyracmon stout
Thrusts in his unwash'd visage. *He* stands by,
Who the hard trade of Porterage does ply
With stooping shoulders. What cares he? he sees
The assembled ring, nor heeds his tottering knees,
But pricks his ears up with the hopes of song.
So, while the Bard of Rhodope his wrong
Bewail'd to Proserpine on Thracian strings,
The tasks of gloomy Orcus lost their stings,

[1] Seven Dials.

And stone-vext Sysiphus forgets his load.
Hither and thither from the sevenfold road
Some cart or waggon crosses, which divides
The close-wedged audience; but, as when the tides
To ploughing ships give way, the ship being past,
They re-unite, so these unite as fast.
The older Songstress hitherto hath spent
Her elocution in the argument
Of their great song in *prose;* to wit, the woes
Which Maiden true to faithless Sailor owes—
Ah! *"Wandering He!"*—which now in loftier *verse*
Pathetic they alternately rehearse.
All gaping wait the event. This Critic opes
His right ear to the strain. The other hopes
To catch it better with his left. Long trade
It were to tell, how the deluded Maid
A victim fell. And now right greedily
All hands are stretching forth the songs to buy,
That are so tragical; which She, and She,
Deals out, and *sings the while;* nor can there be
A breast so obdurate here, that will hold back
His contribution from the gentle rack
Of Music's pleasing torture. Irus' self,
The staff-propt Beggar, his thin gotten pelf
Brings out from pouch, where squalid farthings rest,
And boldly claims his ballad with the best.
An old Dame only lingers. To her purse
The penny sticks. At length, with harmless curse,
"Give me," she cries. "I'll paste it on my wall,
While the wall lasts, to show what ills befall
Fond hearts, seduced from Innocency's way;
How Maidens fall, and Mariners betray."

II.

TO DAVID COOK,

OF THE PARISH OF ST. MARGARET'S, WESTMINSTER, WATCHMAN

FOR much good-natured verse received from thee,
A loving verse take in return from me.
"Good morrow to my masters," is your cry;
And to our David "twice as good," say I.
Not Peter's monitor, shrill Chanticleer,
Crows the approach of dawn in notes more clear,
Or tells the hours more faithfully. While night
Fills half the world with shadows of affright,
You with your lantern, partner of your round,

Traverse the paths of Margaret's hallow'd bound.
The tales of ghosts which old wives' ears drink up,
The drunkard reeling home from tavern cup,
Nor prowling robber, your firm soul appal;
Arm'd with thy faithful staff, thou slight'st them all.
But if the market gard'ner chance to pass,
Bringing to town his fruit, or early grass,
The gentle salesman you with candour greet,
And with reit'rated "good mornings" meet.
Announcing your approach by formal bell,
Of nightly weather you the changes tell;
Whether the Moon shines, or her head doth steep
In rain-portending clouds. When mortals sleep
In downy rest, you brave the snows and sleet
Of winter; and in alley, or in street,
Relieve your midnight progress with a verse.
What though fastidious Phœbus frown averse
On your didactic strain—indulgent Night
With caution hath seal'd up both ears of Spite,
And critics sleep while you in staves do sound
The praise of long-dead Saints, whose Days abound
In wintry months; but Crispin chief proclaim:
Who stirs not at that Prince of Cobblers' name?
Profuse in loyalty some couplets shine,
And wish long days to all the Brunswick line!
To youths and virgins they chaste lessons read;
Teach wives and husbands how their lives to lead;
Maids to be cleanly, footmen free from vice;
How death at last all ranks doth equalise;
And, in conclusion, pray good years befall,
With store of wealth, your "worthy masters all."
For this and other tokens of goodwill,
On boxing-day may store of shillings fill
Your Christmas purse; no householder give less,
When at each door your blameless suit you press:
And what you wish to us (it is but reason)
Receive in turn—the compliments o' th' season?

III.

ON A SEPULCHRAL STATUE OF AN
INFANT SLEEPING

BEAUTIFUL Infant, who dost keep
Thy posture here, and sleep'st a marble sleep,
May the repose unbroken be,
Which the fine Artist's hand hath lent to thee,

While thou enjoy'st long with it
That which no art, or craft, could ever hit,
Or counterfeit to mortal sense,
The heaven-infusèd sleep of Innocence!

IV.

EPITAPH ON A DOG

POOR Irus' faithful wolf-dog here I lie,
That wont to tend my old blind master's steps,
His guide and guard; nor, while my service lasted,
Had he occasion for that staff, with which
He now goes picking out his path in fear
Over the highways and crossings, but would plant,
Safe in the conduct of my friendly string,
A firm foot forward still, till he had reach'd
His poor seat on some stone, nigh where the tide
Of passers-by in thickest confluence flow'd:
To whom with loud and passionate laments
From morn to eve his dark estate he wail'd.
Nor wail'd to all in vain: some here and there,
The well-disposed and good, their pennies gave.
I meantime at his feet obsequious slept;
Not all-asleep in sleep, but heart and ear
Prick'd up at his least motion, to receive
At his kind hand my customary crumbs,
And common portion in his feast of scraps;
Or when night warn'd us homeward, tired and spent
With our long day and tedious beggary.
These were my manners, this my way of life,
Till age and slow disease me overtook,
And sever'd from my sightless master's side.
But lest the grace of so good deeds should die,
Through tract of years in mute oblivion lost,
This slender tomb of turf hath Irus rear'd,
Cheap monument of no ungrudging hand,
And with short verse inscribed it, to attest,
In long and lasting union to attest,
The virtues of the Beggar and his Dog.

V.

THE RIVAL BELLS

A TUNEFUL challenge rings from either side
Of Thames' fair banks. Thy twice six Bells, St. Bride,

Peal swift and shrill; to which more slow reply
The deep-toned eight of Mary Overy.
Such harmony from the contention flows,
That the divided ear no preference knows;
Betwixt them both disparting Music's State,
While one exceeds in number, one in weight.

VI.

NEWTON'S PRINCIPIA

GREAT Newton's self, to whom the world's in debt.
Owed to School Mistress sage his Alphabet;
But quickly wiser than his Teacher grown,
Discover'd properties to her unknown;
Of A *plus* B, or *minus,* learn'd the use,
Known Quantities from unknown to educe;
And made—no doubt to that old dame's surprise—
The Christ-Cross-Row his Ladder to the skies.
Yet, whatsoe'er Geometricians say,
Her lessons were his true PRINCIPIA!

VII.

THE HOUSEKEEPER

THE frugal snail, with forecast of repose,
Carries his house with him, where'er he goes;
Peeps out—and if there comes a shower of rain,
Retreats to his small domicile amain.
Touch but a tip of him, a horn—'tis well—
He curls up in his sanctuary shell.
He's his own landlord, his own tenant; stay
Long as he will, he dreads no Quarter Day.
Himself he boards and lodges; both invites,
And feasts, himself; sleeps with himself o'nights.
He spares the upholsterer trouble to procure
Chattels; himself is his own furniture,
And his sole riches.   Wheresoe'er he roam—
Knock when you will—he's sure to be at home.

VIII.

ON A DEAF AND DUMB ARTIST [1]

AND hath thy blameless life become
A prey to the devouring tomb?
A more mute silence hast thou known,

[1] Benjamin Ferrers—died A.D. 1732.

A deafness deeper than thine own,
While Time was? and no friendly Muse,
That mark'd thy life, and knows thy dues,
Repair with quickening verse the breach,
And write thee into light and speech?
The Power, that made the Tongue, restrain'd
Thy lips from lies, and speeches feign'd;
Who made the Hearing, without wrong
Did rescue thine from Siren's song.
He let thee *see* the ways of men,
Which thou with pencil, not with pen,
Careful Beholder, down didst note,
And all their motley actions quote,
Thyself unstain'd the while. From look
Or gesture reading, more than *book,*
In letter'd pride thou took'st no part,
Contented with the Silent Art,
Thyself as silent. Might I be
As speechless, deaf, and good, as He!

IX.

THE FEMALE ORATORS

NIGH London's famous Bridge, a Gate more famed
Stands, or once stood, from old Belinus named,
So judged Antiquity; and therein wrongs
A name, allusive strictly to *two Tongues.*[1]
Her School hard by the Goddess Rhetoric opes,
And *gratis* deals to Oyster-wives her Tropes.
With Nereid green, green Nereid disputes,
Replies, rejoins, confutes, and still confutes.
One her coarse sense by metaphors expounds,
And one in literalities abounds;
In mood and figure these keep up the din:
Words multiply, and every word tells in.
Her hundred throats here bawling Slander strains;
And unclothed Venus to her tongue gives reins
In terms, which Demosthenic force outgo,
And baldest jests of foul-mouth'd Cicero.
Right in the midst great Atè keeps her stand,
And from her sovereign station taints the land.
Hence Pulpits rail; grave Senates learn to jar;
Quacks scold; and Billingsgate infects the Bar.

[1] *Bilinguis* in the Latin.

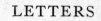

LETTERS

CHAPTER I

1796-1800

LETTERS TO COLERIDGE, SOUTHEY, ROBERT LLOYD, AND MANNING

To SAMUEL TAYLOR COLERIDGE.

LETTER I.]   *May 27, 1796.*

Dear Coleridge—Make yourself perfectly easy about May. I paid his bill when I sent your clothes. I was flush of money, and am so still to all the purposes of a single life; so give yourself no further concern about it. The money would be superfluous to me if I had it.

When Southey becomes as modest as his predecessor, Milton, and publishes his Epics in duodecimo, I will read 'em; a guinea a book is somewhat exorbitant, nor have I the opportunity of borrowing the work. The extracts from it in the *Monthly Review,* and the short passages in your *Watchman,* seem to me much superior to any thing in his partnership account with Lovell. Your poems I shall procure forthwith. There were noble lines in what you inserted in one of your Numbers from *Religious Musings;* but I thought them elaborate. I am somewhat glad you have given up that paper: it must have been dry, unprofitable, and of "dissonant mood" to your disposition. I wish you success in all your undertakings, and am glad to hear you are employed about the *Evidences of Religion.* There is need of multiplying such books a hundredfold in this philosophical age, to *prevent* converts to atheism, for they seem too tough disputants to meddle with afterwards.

Le Grice is gone to make puns in Cornwall. He has got a tutorship to a young boy living with his mother, a widow lady. He will, of course, initiate him quickly in "whatsoever things are honest, lovely, and of good report." He has cut Miss Hunt completely: the poor girl is very ill on the occasion; but he laughs at it, and justifies himself by saying, "she does not see me laugh." Coleridge, I know not what suffering scenes you have gone through at Bristol. My life has been somewhat diversified of late. The six weeks that finished last year and began this, your very humble servant spent very agreeably in a madhouse, at Hoxton. I am got somewhat rational now, and don't bite any one. But mad I was; and many a vagary my imagination played with me, enough to make a volume, if all were told. My Sonnets I have extended to the number of nine since I saw you, and will some day communicate to you. I am beginning

573

a poem in blank verse, which, if I finish, I publish. White is on the eve of publishing (he took the hint from *Vortigern*) "Original letters of Falstaff, Shallow," etc.; a copy you shall have when it comes out. They are without exception the best imitations I ever saw. Coleridge, it may convince you of my regards for you when I tell you my head ran on you in my madness, as much almost as on another person, who I am inclined to think was the more immediate cause of my temporary frenzy.

The Sonnet I send you has small merit as poetry; but you will be curious to read it when I tell you it was written in my prison-house in one of my lucid intervals.

TO MY SISTER.

If from my lips some angry accents fell,
Peevish complaint, or harsh reproof unkind,
'Twas but the error of a sickly mind
And troubled thoughts, clouding the purer well
And waters clear of Reason; and for me,
Let this my verse the poor atonement be—
My verse, which thou to praise wert e'er inclined
Too highly, and with a partial eye to see
No blemish. Thou to me didst ever show
Kindest affection; and would'st oft-times lend
An ear to the desponding love-sick lay,
Weeping my sorrows with me, who repay
But ill the mighty debt of love I owe,
Mary, to thee, my sister and my friend.

With these lines, and with that sister's kindest remembrances to C——, I conclude.

Yours sincerely,   LAMB.

Your *Conciones ad Populum* are the most eloquent politics that ever came in my way.

Write when convenient—not as a task, 'for there is nothing in this letter to answer.

We cannot send our remembrances to Mrs. C., not having seen her, but believe me our best good wishes attend you both.

My civic and poetic compliments to Southey if at Bristol. Why, he is a very Leviathan of Bards!—the small minnow, I!

LETTER II.]   *June* 1796.

I am in such violent pain with the headache, that I am fit for nothing but transcribing, scarce for that. When I get your poems, and the *Joan of Arc,* I will exercise my presumption in giving you my opinion of 'em. The mail does not come in before to-morrow (Wednesday) morning. The following Sonnet was composed during a walk down into Hertfordshire early in last Summer:—

The Lord of Light shakes off his drowsyhed.
　　Fresh from his couch up springs the lusty sun,
　　And girds himself his mighty race to run;
Meantime, by truant love of rambling led,
I turn my back on thy detested walls,
　　Proud City, and thy sons I leave behind,
　　A selfish, sordid, money-getting kind,
Who shut their ears when holy Freedom calls.
I pass not thee so lightly, humble spire,
　　That mindest me of many a pleasure gone,
　　Of merriest days, of Love and Islington,
Kindling anew the flames of past desire;
　　And I shall muse on thee, slow journeying on,
To the green plains of pleasant Hertfordshire.

The last line is a copy of Bowles's, "To the green Hamlet in the peaceful Plain." Your ears are not so very fastidious; many people would not like words so prosaic and familiar in a Sonnet as Islington and Hertfordshire. The next was written within a day or two of the last, on revisiting a spot where the scene was laid of my first Sonnet that "mock'd my step with many a lonely glade."

When last I roved these winding wood-walks green,
　　Green winding walks, and shady pathways sweet,
Oft-times would Anna seek the silent scene,
　　Shrouding her beauties in the lone retreat.
No more I hear her footsteps in the shade;
　　Her image only in these pleasant ways
　　Meets me, self-wandering, where in happier days
I held free converse with my fair-hair'd maid.
　　I pass'd the little cottage which she loved,
The cottage which did once my all contain:
It spake of days that ne'er must come again;
　　Spake to my heart, and much my heart was moved.
Now "Fair befall thee, gentle maid," said I;
And from the cottage turn'd me with a sigh.

The next retains a few lines from a Sonnet of mine which you once remarked had no "body of thought" in it. I agree with you, but have preserved a part of it, and it runs thus. I flatter myself you will like it:—

A timid grace sits trembling in her eye,
　　As loth to meet the rudeness of men's sight
　　Yet shedding a delicious lunar light,
That steeps in kind oblivious ecstasy
The care-crazed mind, like some still melody:
　　Speaking most plain the thoughts which do possess
　　Her gentle sprite, peace and meek quietness,
And innocent loves, and maiden purity:
　　A look whereof might heal the cruel smart
Of changed friends, or Fortune's wrongs unkind;
　　Might to sweet deeds of mercy move the heart
Of him who hates his brethren of mankind.
　　Turn'd are those beams from me, who fondly yet
　　Past joys, vain loves, and buried hopes regret.

The next and last I value most of all. 'Twas composed close upon the heels of the last, in that very wood I had in mind when I wrote "Methinks how dainty sweet."

> We were two pretty babes, the youngest she,
> The youngest, and the loveliest far, I ween,
> And Innocence her name. The time has been
> We two did love each other's company;
> Time was, we two had wept to have been apart:
> But when, with show of seeming good beguiled,
> I left the garb and manners of a child,
> And my first love for man's society,
> Defiling with the world my virgin heart,
> My loved companion dropp'd a tear and fled,
> And hid in deepest shades her awful head.
> Beloved! who can tell me where thou art—
> In what delicious Eden to be found—
> That I may seek thee the wide world around?

Since writing it, I have found in a poem by Hamilton of Bangor, these two lines to "Happiness:"—

> "Nun, sober and devout, where art thou fled
> To hide in shades thy meek, contented head?"

Lines eminently beautiful; but I do not remember having read them previously, for the credit of my tenth and eleventh lines. Parnell has two lines (which probably suggested the above) to "Contentment:"

> "Whither, ah! whither art thou fled,
> To hide thy meek, contented head?"

Cowley's exquisite "Elegy on the death of his friend Harvey," suggested the phrase of "we two."

> "Was there a tree that did not know
> The love betwixt us two?"

So much for acknowledged plagiarisms, the confession of which I know not whether it has more of vanity or modesty in it. As to my blank verse, I am so dismally slow and sterile of ideas (I speak from my heart) that I much question if it will ever come to any issue. I have hitherto only hammered out a few independent, unconnected snatches, not in a capacity to be sent. I am very ill, and will rest till I have read your poems, for which I am very thankful. I have one more favour to beg of you, that you never mention Mr. May's affair in any sort, much less *think* of repaying. Are we not flocci-nauci-what-d'ye-call-'em-ists? We have just learned that my poor brother has had a sad accident: a large stone, blown down by yesterday's high wind, has bruised his leg in a most shocking manner; he is under the care of Cruikshanks. Coleridge! there are 10,000 objections against my paying you a visit at Bristol; it cannot be else; but in this world 'tis better not to think too much of pleasant possibles, that we may not be out of humour with present insipids. Should anything bring you to London, you will recollect No. 7, Little Queen Street, Holborn.

I shall be too ill to call on Wordsworth myself, but will take care to transmit him his poem, when I have read it. I saw Le Grice the day before his departure, and mentioned incidentally his "teaching the young idea how to shoot." Knowing him and the probability there is of people having a propensity to pun in his company, you will not wonder that we both stumbled on the same pun at once, he eagerly anticipating me,—"he would teach him to shoot!" Poor Le Grice! if wit alone could entitle a man to respect, etc., he has written a very witty little pamphlet lately, satirical, upon college declamations. When I send White's book, I will add that. I am sorry there should be any difference between you and Southey. "Between you two there should be peace," tho' I must say I have borne him no good will since he spirited you away from among us. What is become of Moschus? You sported some of his sublimities, I see, in your *Watchman*. Very decent things. So much for to-night from your afflicted, headachey, sorethroaty, humble servant,   C. LAMB.

Tuesday Night.—Of your *Watchmen,* the Review of Burke was the best prose. I augured great things from the first Number. There is some exquisite poetry interspersed. I have re-read the extract from the *Religious Musings,* and retract whatever invidious there was in my censure of it as elaborate. There are times when one is not in a disposition thoroughly to relish good writing. I have re-read it in a more favourable moment, and hesitate not to pronounce it sublime. If there be any thing in it approaching to tumidity (which I meant not to infer, by *elaborate* I meant simply laboured), it is the gigantic hyperbole by which you describe the evils of existing society: "snakes, lions, hyenas, and behemoths," is carrying your resentment beyond bounds. The pictures of "The Simoom," of "Frenzy and Ruin," of "The Whore of Babylon," and "The Cry of the Foul Spirits disherited of Earth," and "the strange beatitude" which the good man shall recognise in heaven, as well as the particularising of the children of wretchedness (I have unconsciously included every part of it), from a variety of uniform excellence. I hunger and thirst to read the poem complete. That is a capital line in your sixth Number:

"This dark, frieze-coated, hoarse, teeth-chattering month."

They are exactly such epithets as Burns would have stumbled on, whose poem on the ploughed-up daisy you seem to have had in mind. Your complaint that of your readers some thought there was too much, some too little original matter in your Numbers, reminds me of poor dead Parsons in the *Critic.* "Too little incident! Give me leave to tell you, sir, there is too much incident." I had like to have forgot thanking you for that exquisite little morsel, the first Sclavonian Song. The expression in the second,—"more happy to be unhappy in hell:" is it not very quaint? Accept my thanks, in common with those of all who love good poetry, for "The Braes of Yarrow." I congratulate you on the enemies you must have made by your splendid invective against the barterers in human flesh and sinews. Coleridge, you will rejoice to hear that Cowper is recovered from his lunacy, and is employed on his translation of the Italian, etc., poems of Milton for an edition where Fuseli presides as designer. Coleridge, to an idler like myself, to write and receive letters are both very pleasant; but I wish not to break in upon your valuable time by expecting to hear very frequently from you. Reserve that obligation for your moments of lassitude, when you have nothing else to do; for your loco-restive and all your idle propensities, of course, have given way to the duties of providing for a family. The mail is come in, but no parcel; yet this is Tuesday. Farewell, then, till to-morrow; for a niche and a nook I must leave for criticisms. By the way, I hope you do not send your only copy of *Joan of Arc:* I will in that case return it immediately.

Your parcel *is* come: you have been *lavish* of your presents. Wordsworth's poem I have hurried through, not without delight. Poor Lovell! my heart almost accuses me for the light manner I lately spoke of him, not dreaming of his death. My heart bleeds for your accumulated troubles: God send you through 'em with patience. I conjure you, dream not that I will ever think of being repaid; the very word is galling to the ears. I have read all your *Religious Musings* with uninterrupted feelings of profound admiration. You may safely rest your fame on it. The best remaining things are what I have before read, and they lose nothing by my recollection of your manner of reciting 'em, for I too bear in mind "the voice, the look" of absent friends, and can occasionally mimic their manner for the amusement of those who have seen 'em. Your impassioned manner of recitation I can recall at any time to mine own heart and to the ears of the bystanders. I rather wish you had left the monody on Chatterton concluding, as it did, abruptly. It had more of unity. The conclusion of your *Religious Musings,* I fear, will entitle you to the reproof of your beloved woman, who wisely will not suffer your fancy to run riot, but bids you walk humbly with your God. The last words.

> "I discipline my young and novice thought
> In ministries of heart-stirring song,"

though not now new to me, cannot be enough admired. To speak politely, they are a well-turned compliment to Poetry. I hasten to read *Joan of Arc,* etc. I have read your lines at the beginning of the second book: they are worthy of Milton; but in my mind yield to your *Religious Musings.* I shall read the whole carefully, and in some future letter take the liberty to particularise my opinions of it. Of what is new to me among your poems next to the "Musings," that beginning "My Pensive Sara" gave me most pleasure: the lines in it I just alluded to are most exquisite; they made my sister and self smile, as conveying a pleasing picture of Mrs. C. checking your wild wanderings, which we were so fond of hearing you indulge when among us. It has endeared us more than any thing to your good lady; and your own self-reproof that follows, delighted us. 'Tis a charming poem throughout. (You have well remarked that *charming, admirable, exquisite* are the words expressive of feelings more than conveying of ideas; else I might plead very well want of room in my paper as excuse of generalising.) I want room to tell you how we are charmed with your verses in the manner of Spenser, etc., etc., etc., etc., etc. I am glad you resume the *Watchman*. Change the name: leave out all articles of news, and whatever things are peculiar to newspapers, and confine yourself to ethics, verse, criticism; or, rather do not confine yourself. Let your plan be as diffuse as the *Spectator*, and I'll answer for it the work prospers. If I am vain enough to think I can be a contributor, rely on my inclinations. Coleridge, in reading your *Religious Musings* I felt a transient superiority over you. I *have* seen Priestley. I love to see his name repeated in your writings. I love and honour him, almost profanely. You would be charmed with his *Sermons*, if you never read 'em. You have doubtless read his books illustrative of the doctrine of Necessity. Prefixed to a late work of his, in answer to Paine, there is a Preface, giving an account of the man, and his services to men, written by Lindsey, his dearest friend, well worth your reading.

Tuesday Eve.—Forgive my prolixity, which is yet too brief for all I could wish to say. God give you comfort, and all that are of your household! Our loves and best good wishes to Mrs. C. C. LAMB.

LETTER III.] *June* 10, 1796.

With *Joan of Arc* I have been delighted, amazed. I had not presumed to expect any thing of such excellence from Southey. Why, the poem is alone sufficient to redeem the character of the age we live in from the imputation of degenerating in Poetry, were there no such beings extant as Burns, and Bowles, Cowper, and ——: fill up the blank how you please; I say nothing. The subject is well chosen. It opens well. To become more particular, I will notice in their order a few passages that chiefly struck me on perusal. Page 26, "Fierce and terrible Benevolence!" is a phrase full of grandeur and originality. The whole context made me feel *possessed*, even like Joan herself. Page 28, "It is most horrible with the keen sword to gore the finely-fibred human frame," and what follows, pleased me mightily. In the 2nd Book, the first forty lines in particular are majestic and high-sounding. Indeed the whole vision of the Palace of Ambition and what follows are supremely excellent. Your simile of the Laplander,

> . . . . . . "by Niemi lake
> Or Balda Zhiok, or the mossy stone
> Of Solfar-kapper,"

will bear comparison with any in Milton for fulness of circumstance and lofty pacedness of versification. Southey's similes, though many of 'em are capital, are all inferior. In one of his books, the simile of the oak in the storm occurs, I think, four times. To return: the light in which you view the heathen deities is accurate and beautiful. Southey's personifications in this book are so many fine and faultless pictures. I was much pleased with your manner of accounting for the reason why monarchs take delight in war. At the 447th line you have placed Prophets and Enthusiasts cheek by jowl, on too intimate a footing for the dignity of the former. Necessarian-like-speaking, it is correct. Page 98, "Dead is the Douglas! cold thy warrior frame, illustrious Buchan," etc., are of kindred excellence with Gray's "Cold is Cadwallo's tongue," etc. How famously the Maid baffles the Doctors, Seraphic and Irrefragable, "with all their trumpery!" Page 126, the procession, the appearances of the Maid, of the Bastard Son of Orleans and of Tremouille, are full of fire and fancy, and exquisite melody of versification. The personifications from line 303 to 309, in the heat of the battle, had better been omitted; they are not very striking, and only encumber. The converse which Joan and Conrade hold on the banks of the Loire is altogether beautiful. Page 313, the conjecture that in dreams "all things are that seem," is one of those conceits which the Poet delights to admit into his creed; a creed, by the way, more marvellous and mystic than ever Athanasius dreamed of. Page 315, I need only *mention* those lines ending with "She saw a serpent gnawing at her heart!" They are good imitative lines, "he toiled and toiled, of toil to reap no end, but endless toil and never-ending woe." Page 347, Cruelty is such as Hogarth might have painted her. Page 361, all the passage about Love (where he seems to confound conjugal love with creating and preserving love) is very confused, and sickens me with a load of useless personifications; else that ninth Book is the finest in the volume—an exquisite combination of the ludicrous and the terrible: I have never read either, even in translation, but such as I conceive to be the manner of Dante or Ariosto. The tenth Book is the most languid. On the whole, considering the celerity wherewith the poem was finished, I was astonished at the infrequency of weak lines. I had expected to find it verbose. Joan, I think, does too little in battle; Dunois perhaps the same; Conrade too much. The anecdotes interspersed among the battles refresh the mind very agreeably, and I am delighted with the very many passages of simple pathos abounding throughout the poem; passages which the author of "Crazy Kate" might have written. Has not Master Southey spoke very slightly, in his Preface, and disparagingly of Cowper's Homer? What makes him reluctant to give Cowper his fame? And does not Southey use too often the expletives "did," and "does?" They have a good effect at times, but are too inconsiderable, or rather become blemishes, when they mark a style. On the whole, I expect Southey one day to rival Milton:·I already deem him equal to Cowper, and superior to all living poets besides. What says Coleridge? The "Monody on Henderson" is *immensely good:* the rest of that little volume is *readable, and above mediocrity.* I proceed to a more pleasant task; pleasant because the poems are yours; pleasant because you impose the task on me; and pleasant, let me add, because it will confer a whimsical importance on me to sit in judgment upon your rhymes. First, though, let me thank you again and again, in my own and my sister's name, for your invitations. Nothing could give us more pleasure than to come, but (were there no other reasons) while my brother's leg is so bad it is out of the question. Poor fellow! he is very feverish and light-headed; but Cruikshanks has pronounced the symptoms favourable, and gives us every hope that there will be no need of amputation: God send, not! We are necessarily confined with him all the afternoon and evening till very late, so that I am stealing a few minutes to write to you.

Thank you for your frequent letters: you are the only correspondent, and I might add, the only friend I have in the world. I go nowhere, and have no acquaintance. Slow of speech, and reserved of manners, no one seeks or cares for my society; and I am left alone. Allen calls very occasionally, as though it were a duty rather, and seldom stays ten minutes. Then judge how thankful I am for your letters! Do not, however, burthen yourself with the correspondence. I trouble you again so soon, only in obedience to your injunctions. Complaints apart, proceed we to our task. I am called away to tea; thence must wait upon my brother; so must delay till tomorrow. Farewell!—*Wednesday*.

Thursday.—I will first notice what is new to me. Thirteenth page: "The thrilling tones that concentrate the soul" is a nervous line; and the first six lines of page 14 are very pretty; the twenty-first effusion is a perfect thing. That in the manner of Spenser is very sweet, particularly at the close: the thirty-fifth effusion is most exquisite; that line in particular, "And, tranquil, muse upon tranquillity." It is the very reflex pleasure that distinguishes the tranquillity of a thinking being from that of a shepherd, a modern one I would be understood to mean, a Damœtas, one that keeps other people's sheep. Certainly, Coleridge, your letter from Shurton Bars has less merit than most things in your volume; personally, it may chime in best with your own feelings, and therefore you love it best. It has, however, great merit. In your fourth epistle, *that* is an exquisite paragraph, and fancy-full, of "A stream there is which rolls in lazy flow," etc., etc. "Murmurs sweet undersong 'mid jasmine bowers" is a sweet line; and so are the three next. The concluding simile is far-fetched—"tempest-honoured" is a quaintish phrase. Of the Monody on Henderson I will here only notice these lines, as superlatively excellent. That energetic one, "Shall I not praise thee, scholar, Christian, friend," like to that beautiful climax of Shakspeare's "King, Hamlet, Royal Dane, Father;" "yet memory turns from little men to thee," "And sported careless round their fellow child." The whole, I repeat it, is immensely good.

Yours is a poetical family. I was much surprised and pleased to see the signature of Sara to that elegant composition, the fifth epistle. I dare not *criticise* the *Religious Musings:* I like not to select any part, where all is excellent. I can only admire, and thank you for it in the name of a Christian, as well as a lover of good poetry: only let me ask, Is not that thought and those words in Young, "stands in the sun,"—or is it only such as Young, in one of his *better moments,* might have writ?—

> "Believe thou, O my soul,
> Life is a vision, shadowy of Truth;
> And vice, and anguish, and the wormy grave,
> Shapes of a dream!"

I thank you for these lines in the name of a necessarian, and for what follows in the next paragraph, in the name of a child fancy. After all, you cannot, nor ever will, write any thing with which I shall be so delighted as what I have heard yourself repeat. You came to town, and I saw you at a time when your heart was yet bleeding with recent wounds. Like yourself, I was sore galled with disappointed hope. You had

> .   .   .   "many an holy lay
> That, mourning, soothed the mourner on his way."

I had ears of sympathy to drink them in, and they yet vibrate pleasant on the sense. When I read in your little volume, your nineteenth effusion, or the twenty-eighth or twenty-ninth, or what you call the "Sigh," I think I hear *you* again. I image to myself the little smoky room at the *Salutation and Cat,* where we have sat together through the winter nights, beguiling the cares of life with Poesy. When you left London I felt a dismal void in my heart. I found myself cut off, at one and the same time, from two most dear to me. "How blest with ye the path could I have trod of quiet life!" In your conversation you had blended so many pleasant fancies that they cheated me of my grief. But in your absence the tide of melancholy rushed in again, and did its worst mischief by overwhelming my reason. I have recovered, but feel a stupor that makes me indifferent to the hopes and fears of this life. I sometimes wish to introduce a religious turn of mind; but habits are strong things, and my religious fervours are confined, alas! to some fleeting moments of occasional solitary devotion. A correspondence, opening with you, has roused me a little from my lethargy, and made me conscious of existence. Indulge me in it: I will not be very troublesome. At some future time I will amuse you with an account, as full as my memory will permit, of the strange turn my frenzy took. I look back upon it at times with a gloomy kind of envy; for, while it lasted, I had many, many hours of pure happiness. Dream not, Coleridge, of having tasted all the grandeur and wildness of fancy till you have gone mad! All now seems to me vapid, comparatively so. Excuse this selfish digression. Your "Monody" is so superlatively excellent, that I can only wish it perfect, which I can't help feeling it is not quite. Indulge me in a few conjectures. What I am going to propose would make it more compressed, and, I think, more energetic, though I am sensible at the expense of many beautiful lines. Let it begin "Is this the land of song-ennobled line?" and proceed to "Otway's famish'd form;" then, "Thee, Chatterton," to "blaze of Seraphim;" then, "clad in Nature's rich array," to "orient day;" then, "but soon the scathing lightning," to "blighted land;" then, "sublime of thought," to "his bosom glows;" then

> "But soon upon his poor unshelter'd head
> Did Penury her sickly mildew shed:
> Ah! where are fled the charms of vernal Grace,
> And Joy's wild gleams that lighten'd o'er his face?"

Then "youth of tumultuous soul" to "sigh," as before. The rest may all stand down to "gaze upon the waves below." What follows now may come next as detached verses, suggested by the Monody, rather than a part of it. They are indeed, in themselves, very sweet:

> "And we, at sober eve, would round thee throng
> Hanging, enraptured, on thy stately song,"

in particular, perhaps. If I am obscure, you may understand me by counting lines. I have proposed omitting twenty-four lines. I feel that thus compressed it would gain energy, but think it most likely you will not agree with me; for who shall go to bring opinions to the bed of Procrustes, and introduce among the sons of men a monotony of identical feelings? I only propose with diffidence. Reject, if you please, with as little remorse as you would the colour of a coat or the pattern of a buckle, where our fancies differed. The lines "Friend to the Friendless," etc., which you may think rudely disbranched from the Chatterton, will patch in with the Man of Ross, where they were at once at home, with two more which I recollect,

> "And o'er the dowried virgin's snowy cheek
> Bade bridal Love suffuse his blushes meek,"

very beautiful.

The "Pixies" is a perfect thing; and so are the "Lines on the Spring," page 28. The "Epitaph on an Infant," like a Jack-o'-lantern, has danced about (or like Dr. Forster's scholars) out of the *Morning Chronicle* into the *Watchman,* and thence back into your Collection. It is very pretty, and you seem to think so; but, may be, o'erlooked its chief merit, that of filling up a whole page. I had once deemed Sonnets of unrivalled use that way; but your Epitaphs, I find, are the more diffuse. "Edmund" still holds its place among your best verses. "Ah! fair delights" to "roses round," in your Poem called "Absence," recall (none more forcibly) to my mind the tones in which *you recite it.* I will not notice, in this tedious (to you) manner, verses which have been so long delightful to me, and which you already know my opinion of. Of this kind are Bowles, Priestley, and that most exquisite and most Bowles-like of all, the nineteenth effusion. It would have better ended with "agony of care:" the last two lines are obvious and unnecessary, and you need not now make fourteen lines of it: now it is rechristened from a Sonnet to an Effusion. Schiller might have written the twentieth Effusion: 'tis worthy of him in any sense. I was glad to meet with those lines you sent me, when my sister was so ill: I had lost the copy, and I felt not a little proud at seeing my name in your verse. The "Complaint of Ninathoma" (first stanza in particular) is the best, or only good imitation, of Ossian I ever saw, your "Restless Gale" excepted. "To an Infant" is most sweet. Is not "foodful," though, very harsh? Would not "dulcet" fruit be less harsh, or some other friendly bi-syllable? In "Edmund," "Frenzy, fierce-eyed child," is not so well as "frantic," though that is an epithet adding nothing to the meaning. Slander *couching* was better than "squatting." In the "Man of Ross" it *was* a better line thus:

"If 'neath this roof thy wine-cheer'd moments pass,"

than as it stands now. Time nor nothing can reconcile me to the concluding five lines of "Kosciusko:" call it anything you will but sublime. In my twelfth effusion I had rather have seen what I wrote myself, though they bear no comparison with your exquisite lines—

"On rose-leaf'd beds, amid your faery bowers," etc.

I love my Sonnets because they are reflected images of my own feelings at different times. To instance, in the thirteenth—

"How reason reel'd," etc.,

are good lines, but must spoil the whole with me, who know it is only a fiction of yours, and that the "rude dashings" did in fact not "rock me to repose." I grant the same objection applies not to the former Sonnet; but still I love my own feelings: they are dear to memory, though they now and then wake a sigh or a tear. "Thinking on divers things foredone," I charge you, Coleridge, spare my ewe lambs; and though a gentleman may borrow six lines in an epic poem (I should have no objection to borrow five hundred, and without acknowledging), still, in a sonnet, a personal poem, I do not "ask my friend the aiding verse." I would not wrong your feelings by proposing any improvements (did I think myself capable of suggesting 'em) in such personal poems as "Thou bleedest, my poor heart!"—'od so,—I am caught—I have already done it; but that simile I propose abridging, would not change the feeling or introduce any alien ones. Do you understand me? In the twenty-eighth, however, and in the "Sigh," and that composed at Clevedon, things that come from the heart direct, not by the medium of the fancy, I would not suggest an alteration. When my blank verse is finished, or any long fancy-poems, *propino tibi alterandum, cut-up-andum, abridgandum,* just what you will with it; but spare my ewe lambs! That to "Mrs. Siddons," now, you were welcome to improve, if it had been worth it; but I say unto you again, Coleridge, spare my ewe lambs! I must confess were they mine, I should omit, *in editione secundâ,* Effusions two and three, because satiric, and below the dignity of the poet of *Religious Musings,* fifth, seventh, half of the eighth, that "Written in early youth," as far as "thousand eyes,"—though I part not unreluctantly with that lively line—

"Chaste joyance dancing in her bright blue eyes,"

and one or two more just thereabouts. But I would substitute for it that sweet poem called "Recollection," in the fifth Number of the *Watchman;* better, I think, than the remainder of this poem, though not differing materially: as the poem now stands it looks altogether confused. And do not omit those lines upon the "Early Blossom," in your sixth Number of the *Watchman:* and I would omit the tenth Effusion or, what would do better, alter and improve the last four lines. In fact, I suppose, if they were mine, I should *not* omit 'em. But your verse is, for the most part, so exquisite, that I like not to see aught of meaner matter mixed with it. Forgive my petulance, and often, I fear, ill-founded criticisms; and forgive me that I have, by this time, made your eyes and head ache with my long letter; but I cannot forego hastily the pleasure and pride of thus conversing with you. You did not tell me whether I was to include the *Conciones ad Populum* in my remarks on your poems. They are not unfrequently sublime; and I think you could not do better than to turn 'em into verse, if you have nothing else to do. Allen, I am sorry to say, is a *confirmed* Atheist. Stoddart, a cold-hearted, well-bred, conceited disciple of Godwin, does him no good. His wife has several daughters (one of 'em as old as himself). Surely there is something unnatural in such a marriage.

How I sympathise with you on the dull duty of a reviewer, and heartily damn with you Ned Evans and the Prosodist. I shall, however, wait impatiently for the articles in the *Critical Review,* next month, because they are *yours.* Young Evans (W. Evans, a branch of a family you were once so intimate with) is come into our office, and sends his love to you! Coleridge, I devoutly wish that Fortune, who has made sport with you so long, may play one freak more,—throw you into London, or some spot near it, and there snug-ify you for life. 'Tis a selfish, but natural wish for me, cast as I am "on life's wide plain, friendless." Are you acquainted with Bowles? I see, by his last Elegy (written at Bath), you are near neighbours.—*Thursday.*

"And I can think I can see the groves again—was it the voice of thee—turns not the voice of thee, my buried friend—who dries with her dark locks the tender tear," are touches as true to Nature as any in his other Elegy, written at the Hot Wells, about poor Russell, etc. You are doubtless acquainted with it.

I do not know that I entirely agree with you in your stricture upon my Sonnet "To Innocence." To men whose hearts are not quite deadened by their commerce with the world, innocence (no longer familiar) becomes an awful idea. So I felt when I wrote it. Your other censures (qualified and sweetened, though, with praises somewhat extravagant) I perfectly coincide with; yet I choose to retain the word "lunar." Indulge a "lunatic" in his loyalty to his mistress the Moon. I have just been reading a most pathetic copy of verses on Sophia Pringle, who was hanged and burnt for coining. One of the strokes of pathos (which are very many, all somewhat obscure), is "She lifted up her guilty forger to heaven." A note explains, by "forger," her right hand, with which she forged or coined the base metal. For "pathos" read *bathos*. You have put me out of conceit with my blank verse by your *Religious Musings*. I think it will come to nothing. I do not like 'em enough to send 'em. I have just been reading a book which I may be too partial to, as it was the delight of my childhood; but I will recommend it to you: it is Izaak Walton's *Complete Angler*. All the scientific part you may omit in reading. The dialogue is very simple, full of pastoral beauties, and will charm you. Many pretty old verses are interspersed. This letter, which would be a week's work reading only, I do not wish you to answer it in less than a month. I shall be richly content with a letter from you some day early in July; though, if you get anyhow *settled* before then, pray let me know it immediately; 'twould give me so much satisfaction. Concerning the Unitarian chapel, the salary is the only scruple that the most rigid moralist would admit as valid. Concerning the tutorage, is not the salary low, and absence from your family unavoidable? London is the only fostering soil for genius. Nothing more occurs just now; so I will leave you, in mercy, one small white spot empty below, to repose your eyes upon, fatigued as they must be with the wilderness of words they have by this time painfully travelled through. God love you, Coleridge, and prosper you through life; though mine will be loss if your lot is to be cast at Bristol, or at Nottingham, or anywhere but London. Our loves to Mrs. C——.   C. L.

Friday, 10*th June* 1796.

LETTER IV.]   *Monday Night, June* 13, 1796.

Unfurnished at present with any sheet-filling subject, I shall continue my letter gradually and journal-wise. My second thoughts entirely coincide with your comments on *Joan of Arc*, and I can only wonder at my childish judgment which overlooked the 1st book, and could prefer the 9th: not that I was insensible to the soberer beauties of the former; but the latter caught me with its glare of magic: the former, however, left a more pleasing general recollection in my mind. Let me add, the 1st book was the favourite of my sister; and *I* now, with Joan, often "think on Domremi and the fields of Arc." I must not pass over without acknowledging my obligations to your full and satisfactory account of personifications. I have read it again and again, and it will be a guide to my future taste. Perhaps I had estimated Southey's merits too much by number, weight, and measure. I now agree completely and entirely in your opinion of the genius of Southey. Your own image of Melancholy is illustrative of what you teach, and in itself masterly. I conjecture it is "disbranched" from one of your embryo "hymns." When they are mature of birth (were I you) I should print 'em, in one separate volume, with *Religious Musings* and your part of the *Joan of Arc*. Birds of the same soaring wing should hold on their flight in company. Once for all (and by renewing the subject you will only renew in me the condemnation of Tantalus), I hope to be able to pay you a visit (if you are then at Bristol) some time in the latter end of August or beginning of September, for a week or fortnight: before that time office business puts an absolute veto on my coming.

> "And if a sigh that speaks regret of happier times appear,
> A glimpse of joy that we have met shall shine and dry the tear."

Of the blank verse I spoke of, the following lines are the only tolerably complete ones I have writ out of not more than one hundred and fifty. That I get on so slowly you may fairly impute to want of practice in composition, when I declare to you that (the few verses which you have seen excepted) I have not writ fifty lines since I left school. It may not be amiss to remark that my grandmother (on whom the verses are written) lived housekeeper in a family the fifty or sixty last years of her life—that she was a woman of exemplary piety and goodness—and for many years before her death was terribly afflicted with a cancer in her breast, which she bore with true Christian patience. You may think that I have not kept enough apart the ideas of her heavenly and her earthly master; but recollect I have designedly given in to her own way of feeling; and if she had a failing 'twas that she respected her master's family too much, not reverenced her Maker too little. The lines begin imperfectly, as I may probably connect 'em if I finish at all: and if I do, Biggs shall print 'em (in a more economical way than you yours), for, Sonnets and all, they won't make a thousand lines as I propose completing 'em, and the substance must be wire-drawn.

LETTER V.]   *Tuesday Evening, June 14, 1796.*

I am not quite satisfied now with the Chatterton, and, with your leave, will try my hand at it again. A master joiner, you know, may leave a cabinet to be finished by his journeyman, when his own hands are full.

To your list of illustrative personifications, into which a fine imagination enters, I will take leave to add the following from Beaumont and Fletcher's *Wife for a Month;* 'tis the conclusion of a description of a sea fight:—"The game of *death* was never played so nobly: the meagre thief grew wanton in his mischiefs; and his shrunk, hollow eyes smiled on his ruins." There is fancy in these of a lower order, from *Bonduca;*—"Then did I see these valiant men of Britain, like boding owls creep into tods of ivy, and hoot their fears to one another nightly." Not that it is a personification; only it just caught my eye in a little extract book I keep, which is full of quotations from Beaumont and Fletcher in particular, in which authors I can't help thinking there is a greater richness of poetical fancy than in any one, Shakspeare excepted. Are you acquainted with Massinger? At a hazard I will trouble you with a passage from a play of his called *A Very Woman.* The lines are spoken by a lover (disguised) to his faithless mistress. You will remark the fine effect of the double endings. You will by your ear distinguish the lines, for I write 'em as prose. "Not far from where my father lives, *a lady,* a neighbour by, blest with as great a *beauty* as Nature durst bestow without *undoing,* dwelt, and most happily, as I thought then, and blest the house a thousand times she *dwelt* in. This beauty, in the blossom of my youth, when my first fire knew no adulterate *incense,* nor I no way to flatter but my *fondness;* in all the bravery my friends could *show me,* in all the faith my innocence could *give me,* in the best language my true tongue could *tell me,* and all the broken sighs my sick heart *lend me,* I sued and served. Long did I serve this *lady,* long was my travail, long my trade to *win her:* with all the duty of my soul I SERVED HER." "Then she must love." "She did, but never me: she could not *love me;* she would not love, she hated,— more, she *scorn'd me;* and in so poor and base a way *abused me* for all my services, for all my *bounties,* so bold neglects flung on me." "What out of love, and worthy love, I *gave her* (shame to her most unworthy mind!), to fools, to girls, to fiddlers, and her boys she flung, all in disdain of me." One more passage strikes my eye from Beaumont and Fletcher's *Palamon and Arcite.* One of 'em complains in prison:

> "This is all our world:
> We shall know nothing here but one another;
> Hear nothing but the clock that tells our woes.
> The vine shall grow, but we shall never see it."

Is not the last circumstance exquisite? I mean not to lay myself open by saying they exceed Milton, and perhaps Collins, in sublimity. But don't you conceive all poets, after Shakspeare, yield to 'em in variety of genius? Massinger treads close on their heels; but you are most probably as well acquainted with his writings as your humble servant. My quotations, in that case, will only serve to show my barrenness of matter. Southey, in simplicity and tenderness, is excelled decidedly only, I think, by Beaumont and Fletcher—in his "Maid's Tragedy" and some parts of "Philaster" in particular, and elsewhere occasionally; and perhaps by Cowper in his "Crazy Kate," and in parts of his translation, such as the speeches of Hecuba and Andromache. I long to know your opinion of that translation. The Odyssey especially is surely very Homeric. What nobler than the appearance of Phœbus at the beginning of the Iliad—the lines ending with "Dread sounding, bounding on the silver bow!"

I beg you will give me your opinion of the translation; it afforded me high pleasure. As curious a specimen of translation as ever fell into my hands is a young man's in our office, of a French novel. What in the original was literally "amiable delusions of the fancy," he proposed to render "the fair frauds of the imagination!" I had much trouble in licking the book into any meaning at all. Yet did the knave clear fifty or sixty pounds by subscription and selling the copyright: the book itself not a week's work! To-day's portion of my journalising epistle has been very dull and poverty-stricken. I will here end.

Tuesday Night.—I have been drinking egg-hot and smoking Oronooko (associated circumstances, which ever forcibly recall to my mind our evenings and nights at the *Salutation*). My eyes and brain are heavy and asleep, but my heart is awake; and if words came as ready as ideas, and ideas as feelings, I could say ten hundred kind things. Coleridge, you know not my supreme happiness at having one on earth (though counties separate us) whom I can call a friend. Remember you those tender lines of Logan's?—

> "Our broken friendships we deplore,
> And loves of youth that are no more;
> No after-friendships e'er can raise
> Th' endearments of our early days,
> And ne'er the heart such fondness prove
> As when we first began to love."

I am writing at random, and half-tipsy, what you may not *equally* understand, as you will be sober when you read it; but *my* sober and *my* half-tipsy hours you are alike a sharer in. Good-night.

> "Then up rose our bard, like a prophet in drink,
> Craigdoroch, thou'lt soar when creation shall sink."
>
> BURNS.

Thursday.—I am now in high hopes to be able to visit you, if perfectly convenient on your part, by the end of next month—perhaps the last week or fortnight in July. A change of scene and a change of faces would do me good, even if that scene were not to be Bristol, and those faces Coleridge's and his friends. In the words of Terence, a little altered, *Tædet me hujus quotidiani mundi,* I am heartily sick of the every-day scenes of life. I shall half wish you unmarried (don't show this to Mrs. C.) for one evening only, to have the pleasure of smoking with you and drinking egg-hot in some little smoky room in a pot-house, for I know not yet how I shall like you in a decent room and looking quite happy. My best love and respects to Sara notwithstanding.

Yours sincerely,
CHARLES LAMB.

LETTER VI.]   *July* 1, 1796.

The first moment I can come I will; but my hopes of coming yet a while yet hang on a ticklish thread. The coach I come by is immaterial, as I shall so easily, by your direction, find ye out. My mother is grown so entirely helpless (not having any use of her limbs) that Mary is necessarily confined from ever sleeping out, she being her bed-fellow. She thanks you though, and will accompany me in spirit. Most exquisite are the lines from Withers. Your own lines, introductory to your poem on "Self," run smoothly and pleasurably, and I exhort you to continue 'em. What shall I say to your "Dactyls"? They are what you would call good *per se;* but a parody on some of 'em is just now suggesting itself, and you shall have it rough and unlicked. I mark with figures the lines parodied:—

> 4.—Sorely your Dactyls do drag along limp-footed.
> 5.—Sad is the measure that hangs a clod round 'em so.
> 6.—Meagre and languid, proclaiming its wretchedness.
> 1.—Weary, unsatisfied, not little sick of 'em.
> 11.—Cold is my tired heart, I have no charity.
> 2.—Painfully travelling thus over the rugged road.
> 7.—O begone, measure, half Latin, half English, then.
> 12.—Dismal your Dactyls are, God help ye, rhyming ones!

I possibly may not come this fortnight; therefore all thou hast to do is not to look for me any particular day, only to write word immediately, if at any time you quit Bristol, lest I come and Taffy be not at home. I *hope* I can come in a day or two; but young Savory, of my office, is suddenly taken ill in this very nick of time, and I must officiate for him till he can come to work again. Had the knave gone sick, and died, and putrefied, at any other time, philosophy might have afforded one comfort; but just now I have no patience with him. Quarles I am as great a stranger to as I was to Withers. I wish you would try and do something to bring our elder bards into more general fame. I writhe with indignation when, in books of criticism, where commonplace quotation is heaped upon quotation, I find no mention of such men as Massinger, or Beaumont and Fletcher,—men with whom succeeding dramatic writers (Otway alone excepted) can bear no manner of comparison. Stupid Knox hath noticed none of 'em among his extracts.

Thursday.—Mrs. C—— can scarce guess how she has gratified me by her very kind letter and sweet little poem. I feel that I *should* thank her in rhyme; but she must take my acknowledgment, at present, in plain honest prose. The uncertainty in which I yet stand, whether I can come or no, damps my spirits, reduces me a degree below prosaical, and keeps me in a suspense that fluctuates between hope and fear. Hope is a charming, lively, blue-eyed wench, and I am always glad of her company, but could dispense with the visitor she brings with her—her younger sister, Fear,—a white-livered, lily-cheeked, bashful, palpitating, awkward hussy, that hangs, like a green girl, at her sister's apron-strings, and will go with her whithersoever *she* goes. For the life and soul of me I could not improve those lines in your poem on the Prince and Princess; so I changed them to what you bid me, and left 'em at Perry's. I think 'em altogether good, and do not see why you were solicitous about *any* alteration. I have not yet seen, but will make it my business to see, to-day's *Chronicle,* for your verses on Horne Tooke. Dyer stanza'd him in one of the papers t'other day; but, I think, unsuccessfully. Tooke's friends' meeting was, I suppose, a dinner of condolence. I am not sorry to find you (for all Sara) immersed in clouds of smoke and metaphysics. You know I had a sneaking kindness for this last noble science, and you taught me some smattering of it. I look to become no mean proficient under your tuition. Coleridge, what do you mean by saying you wrote to me about Plutarch and Porphyry? I received no such letter, nor remember a syllable of the matter, yet am not apt to forget any part of your epistles, least of all, an injunction like that. I will cast about for 'em, tho' I am a sad hand to know what books are worth, and both worthy gentlemen are alike out of my line. To-morrow I shall be less suspensive, and in better cue to write; so good-bye at present.

Friday Evening.—That execrable aristocrat and knave, Richardson, has given me an absolute refusal of leave. The *poor man* cannot guess at my disappointment. Is it not hard, "this dread dependence on the low-bred mind?" Continue to write to me tho', and I must be content. Our loves and best good wishes attend upon you both.   LAMB.

Savory did return, but there are two or three more ill and absent, which was the plea for refusing me. I will never commit my peace of mind by depending on such a wretch for a favour in future, so I shall never have heart to ask for holidays again. The man next him in office, Cartwright, furnished him with the objections.

C. LAMB.

LETTER VII.]   *July* 5, 1796.

Let us prose.

What can I do till you send word what priced and placed house you should like? Islington, possibly, you would not like; to me 'tis classical ground. Knightsbridge is a desirable situation for the air of the parks. St. George's Fields is convenient for its contiguity to the Bench. Choose! But are you really coming to town? The hope of it has entirely disarmed my petty disappointment of its nettles; yet I rejoice so much on my own account, that I fear I do not feel enough pure satisfaction on yours. Why, surely, the joint editorship of the [*Morning*] *Chronicle* must be a very comfortable and secure living for a man. But should not you read French, or do you? and can you write with sufficient moderation, as 'tis called, when one suppresses the one half of what one feels or could say on a subject, to chime in the better with popular lukewarmness? White's "Letters" are near publication. Could you review 'em, or get 'em reviewed? Are you not connected with the *Critical Review?* His frontispiece is a good conceit: Sir John learning to dance to please Madame Page, in dress of doublet, etc., from the upper half; and modern pantaloons, with shoes, etc., of the eighteenth century, from the lower half; and the whole work is full of goodly quips and rare fancies, "all deftly masqued like hoar antiquity"—much superior to Dr. Kenrick's *Falstaff's Wedding,* which you may have seen. Allen sometimes laughs at superstition, and religion, and the like. A living fell vacant lately in the gift of the Hospital: White informed him that he stood a fair chance for it. He scrupled and scrupled about it, and at last, to use his own words, "tampered" with Godwin to know whether the thing was honest or not.

Godwin said nay to it, and Allen rejected the living! Could the blindest poor papist have bowed more servilely to his priest or casuist? Why sleep the *Watchman's* answers to that Godwin? I beg you will not delay to alter, if you mean to keep, those last lines I sent you. Do that, and read these for your pains:—

TO THE POET COWPER.

Cowper, I thank my God that thou art heal'd!
Thine was the sorest malady of all;
And I am sad to think that it should light
Upon the worthy head! But thou art heal'd,
And thou art yet, we trust, the destined man,
Born to reanimate the lyre, whose chords
Have slumber'd, and have idle lain so long;
To the immortal sounding of whose strings
Did Milton frame the stately-pacèd verse;
Among whose wires with light finger playing,
Our elder bard, Spenser, a gentle name,
The lady Muses' dearest darling child,
Elicited the deftest tunes yet heard
In hall or bower, taking the delicate ear
Of Sidney and his peerless Maiden Queen.

Thou, then, take up the mighty epic strain,
Cowper, of England's Bards, the wisest and the best.

1796.

I have read your climax of praises in those three Reviews. These mighty spouters out of panegyric waters have, two of 'em, scattered their spray even upon me, and the waters are cooling and refreshing. Prosaically, the *Monthly* reviewers have made indeed a large article of it, and done you justice. The *Critical* have, in their wisdom, selected not the very best specimens, and notice not, except as one name on the muster-roll, the *Religious Musings*. I suspect Master Dyer to have been the writer of that article, as the substance of it was the very remarks and the very language he used to me one day. I fear you will not accord entirely with my sentiments of Cowper, as *expressed* above (perhaps scarcely just), but the poor gentleman has just recovered from his lunacies, and that begets pity, and pity love, and love admiration; and then it goes hard with people, but they lie! Have you read the Ballad called "Leonora," in the second Number of the *Monthly Magazine?* If you have ! ! ! ! There is another fine song, from the same author (Burger), in the third Number, of scarce inferior merit; and (vastly below these) there are some happy specimens of English hexameters, in an imitation of Ossian, in the fifth Number. For your Dactyls—I am sorry you are so sore about 'em—a very Sir Fretful! In good troth, the Dactyls are good Dactyls, but their measure is naught. Be not yourself "half anger, half agony," if I pronounce your darling lines not to be the best you ever wrote—you have written much.

Have a care, good Master poet, of the Statute *de Contumeliâ.* What do you mean by calling Madame Mara "harlot" and other naughty things? The goodness of the verse would not save you in a Court of Justice. But are you really coming to town? Coleridge, a gentleman called in London lately from Bristol, and inquired whether there were any of the family of a Mr. Chambers living: this Mr. Chambers, he said, had been the making of a friend's fortune, who wished to make some return for it. He went away without seeing her. Now, a Mrs. Reynolds, a very intimate friend of ours, whom you have seen at our house, is the only daughter, and all that survives, of Mr. Chambers; and a very little supply would be of service to her, for she married very unfortunately, and has parted with her husband. Pray find out this Mr. Pember (for that was the gentleman's friend's name); he is an attorney, and lives at Bristol. Find him out, and acquaint him with the circumstances of the case, and offer to be the medium of supply to Mrs. Reynolds, if he chooses to make her a present. She is in very distressed circumstances. Mr. Pember, attorney, Bristol. Mr. Chambers lived in the Temple; Mrs. Reynolds, his daughter, was my schoolmistress, and is in the room at this present writing. This last circumstance induced me to write so soon again. I have not further to add. Our loves to Sara.   C. LAMB.

Thursday.

LETTER VIII.]   *September 27, 1796.*

My dearest Friend—White, or some of my friends, or the public papers, by this time may have informed you of the terrible calamities that have fallen on our family. I will only give you the outlines:—My poor dear, dearest sister, in a fit of insanity, has been the death of her own mother. I was at hand only time enough to snatch the knife out of her grasp. She is at present in a madhouse, from whence I fear she must be moved to an hospital. God has preserved to me my senses: I eat, and drink, and sleep, and have my judgment, I believe, very sound. My poor father was slightly wounded, and I am left to take care of him and my aunt. Mr. Norris, of the Bluecoat School, has been very very kind to us, and we have no other friend; but, thank God, I am very calm and composed, and able to do the best that remains to do. Write as religious a letter as possible, but no mention of what is gone and done with. With me "the former things are passed away," and I have something more to do than to feel.

God Almighty have us all in His keeping!   C. LAMB.

Mention nothing of poetry. I have destroyed every vestige of past vanities of that kind. Do as you please, but if you publish, publish mine (I give free leave) without name or initial, and never send me a book, I charge you.

Your own judgment will convince you not to take any notice of this yet to your dear wife. You look after your family; I have my reason and strength left to take care of mine. I charge you, don't think of coming to see me. Write. I will not see you if you come. God Almighty love you and all of us!   C. LAMB.

October 3, 1796.

My dearest Friend—Your letter was an inestimable treasure to me. It will be a comfort to you, I know, to know that our prospects are somewhat brighter. My poor dear, dearest sister, the unhappy and unconscious instrument of the Almighty's judgments on our house, is restored to her senses,—to a dreadful sense and recollection of what has past, awful to her mind, and impressive (as it must be to the end of life), but tempered with religious resignation and the reasonings of a sound judgment, which, in this early stage, knows how to distinguish between a deed committed in a transient fit of frenzy and the terrible guilt of a mother's murder. I have seen her. I found her, this morning, calm and serene; far, very very far from an indecent forgetful serenity: she has a most affectionate and tender concern for what has happened. Indeed, from the beginning—frightful and hopeless as her disorder seemed—I had confidence enough in her strength of mind and religious principle, to look forward to a time when *even she* might recover tranquillity. God be praised, Coleridge! wonderful as it is to tell, I have never once been otherwise than collected and calm; even on the dreadful day, and in the midst of the terrible scene, I preserved a tranquillity which bystanders may have construed into indifference—a tranquillity not of despair. Is it folly or sin in me to say that it was a religious principle that *most* supported me? I allow much to other favourable circumstances. I felt that I had something else to do than to regret. On that first evening my aunt was lying insensible—to all appearance like one dying; my father, with his poor forehead plaistered over from a wound he had received from a daughter, dearly loved by him, and who loved him no less dearly; my mother a dead and murdered corpse in the next room; yet was I wonderfully supported. I closed not my eyes in sleep that night, but lay without terrors and without despair. I have lost no sleep since. I had been long used not to rest in things of sense,—had endeavoured after a comprehension of mind, unsatisfied with the "ignorant present time;" and *this* kept me up. I had the whole weight of the family thrown on me; for my brother, little disposed (I speak not without tenderness for him) at any time to take care of old age and infirmities, had now, with his bad leg, an exemption from such duties, and I was now left alone. One little incident may serve to make you understand my way of managing my mind: Within a day or two after the fatal one, we dressed for dinner a tongue, which we had had salted for some weeks in the house. As I sat down, a feeling like remorse struck me: this tongue poor Mary got for me; and can I partake of it now, when she is far away? A thought occurred and relieved me:—if I give into this way of feeling, there is not a chair, a room, an object in our rooms, that will not awaken the keenest griefs. I must rise above such weaknesses. I hope this was not want of true feeling. I did not let this carry me, though, too far. On the very second day (I date from the day of horrors), as is usual in such cases, there were a matter of twenty people, I do think, supping in our room: they prevailed on me to eat *with them* (for to eat I never refused). They were all making merry in the room! Some had come from friendship, some from busy curiosity, and some from interest. I was going to partake with them, when my recollection came that my poor dead mother was lying in the next room—the very next room;—a mother who, through life, wished nothing but her children's welfare. Indignation, the rage of grief, something like remorse, rushed upon my mind. In an agony of emotion I found my way mechanically to the adjoining room, and fell on my knees by the side of her coffin, asking forgiveness of Heaven, and sometimes of her, for forgetting her so soon. Tranquillity returned, and it was the only violent emotion that mastered me. I think it did me good.

I mention these things because I hate concealment, and love to give a faithful journal of what passes within me. Our friends have been very good. Sam Le Grice, who was then in town, was with me the first three or four days, and was as a brother to me; gave up every hour of his time, to the very hurting of his health and spirits, in constant attendance and humouring my poor father; talked with him, read to him, played at cribbage with him (for so short is the old man's recollection, that he was playing at cards, as though nothing had happened, while the coroner's inquest was sitting over the way!). Samuel wept tenderly when he went away, for his mother wrote him a very severe letter on his loitering so long in town, and he was forced to go. Mr. Norris, of Christ's Hospital, has been as a father to me—Mrs. Norris as a mother; though we had few claims on them. A gentleman, brother to my godmother, from whom we never had right or reason to expect any such assistance, sent my father twenty pounds; and to crown all these God's blessings to our family at such a time, an old lady, a cousin of my father and aunt's, a gentlewoman of fortune, is to take my aunt and make her comfortable, for the short remainder of her days. My aunt is recovered, and as well as ever, and highly pleased at thoughts of going—and has generously given up the interest of her little money (which was formerly paid my father for her board) wholely and solely to my sister's use. Reckoning this, we have, Daddy and I, for our two selves and an old maid-servant to look after him, when I am out, which will be necessary, £170 (or £180 rather) a-year, out of which we can spare £50 or £60 at least for Mary, while she stays at Islington, where she must and shall stay during her father's life, for his and her comfort. I know John will make speeches about it but she shall not go into an hospital. The good lady of the madhouse, and her daughter, an elegant, sweet-behaved young lady, love her, and are taken with her amazingly; and I know from her own mouth she loves them, and longs to be with them as much. Poor thing, they say she was but the other morning saying she knew she must go to Bedlam for life; that one of her brothers would have it so, but the other would wish it not, but be obliged to go with the stream; that she had often as she passed Bedlam thought it likely, "here it may be my fate to end my days," conscious of a certain flightiness in her poor head oftentimes, and mindful of more than one severe illness of that nature before. A legacy of £100, which my father will have at Christmas, and this £20 I mentioned before, with what is in the house, will much more than set us clear. If my father, an old servant-maid, and I, can't live, and live comfortably, on £130 or £120 a-year, we ought to burn by slow fires; and I almost would, that Mary might not go into an hospital. Let me not leave one unfavourable impression on your mind respecting my brother. Since this has happened, he has been very kind and brotherly; but I fear for his mind: he has taken his ease in the world, and is not fit himself to struggle with difficulties, nor has much accustomed himself to throw himself into their way; and I know his language is already, "Charles, you must take care of yourself; you must not abridge yourself of a single pleasure you have been used to," etc. etc., and in that style of talking. But you, a Necessarian, can respect a difference of mind, and love what *is amiable* in a character not perfect. He has been very good; but I fear for his mind. Thank God, I can unconnect myself with him, and shall manage all my father's moneys in future myself, if I take charge of Daddy, which poor John has not even hinted a wish, at any future time even, to share with me. The lady at this madhouse assures me that I may dismiss immediately both doctor and apothecary, retaining occasionally a composing draught or so for a while; and there is a less expensive establishment in her house, where she will only not have a room and nurse to herself, for £50 or guineas a-year—the outside would be £60. You know, by economy, how much more even I shall be able to spare for her comforts. She will I fancy, if she stays, make one of the family, rather than of the patients; and the old and young ladies I like exceedingly, and she loves dearly; and they, as the saying is, take to her very extraordinarily, if it is extraordinary that people who see my sister should love her. Of all the people I ever saw in the world, my poor sister was most and thoroughly devoid of the least tincture of selfishness. I will enlarge upon her qualities, poor dear, dearest soul, in a future letter, for my own comfort, for I understand her thoroughly; and, if I mistake not, in the most trying situation that a human being can be found in, she will be found—(I speak not with sufficient humility, I fear), but humanly and foolishly speaking, she will be found, I trust, uniformly great and amiable. God keep her in her present mind!—to whom be thanks and praise for all His dispensations to mankind.   C. LAMB.

These mentioned good fortunes and change of prospects had almost brought my mind over to the extreme, the very opposite to despair. I was in danger of making myself too happy. Your letter brought me back to a view of things which I had entertained from the beginning. I hope (for Mary I can answer)—but I hope that *I* shall through life never have less recollection nor a fainter impression of what has happened than I have now. 'Tis not a light thing, nor meant by the Almighty to be received lightly. I must be serious, circumspect, and deeply religious through life; and by such means may *both* of us escape madness in future, if it so please the Almighty.

Send me word how it fares with Sara. I repeat it, your letter was, and will be, an inestimable treasure to me. You have a view of what my situation demands of me, like my own view, and I trust a just one.

Coleridge, continue to write; but do not for ever offend me by talking of sending me cash. Sincerely, and on my soul, we do not want it. God love you both!

I will write again very soon. Do you write directly.

LETTER X.]   *October* 17, 1796.

My dearest Friend—I grieve from my very soul to observe you, in your plans of life, veering about from this hope to the other, and settling nowhere. Is it an untoward fatality (speaking humanly) that does this for you—a stubborn, irresistible concurrence of events? or lies the fault, as I fear it does, in your own mind? You seem to be taking up splendid schemes of fortune only to lay them down again; and your fortunes are an *ignis fatuus* that has been conducting you, in thought, from Lancaster Court, Strand, to somewhere near Matlock; then jumping across to Dr. Somebody's, whose son's tutor you were likely to be; and would to God the dancing demon *may* conduct you at last, in peace and comfort, to the "life and labours of a cottager." You see, from the above awkward playfulness of fancy, that my spirits are not quite depressed. I should ill deserve God's blessings, which, since the late terrible event, have come down in mercy upon us, if I indulged regret or querulousness. Mary continues serene and cheerful. I have not by me a little letter she wrote to me; for, though I see her almost every day, yet we delight to write to one another, for we can scarce see each other but in company with some of the people of the house.

I have not the letter by me, but will quote from memory what she wrote in it: "I have no bad terrifying dreams. At midnight, when I happen to awake, the nurse sleeping by the side of me, with the noise of the poor mad people around me, I have no fear. The spirit of my mother seems to descend and smile upon me, and bid me live to enjoy the life and reason which the Almighty has given me. I shall see her again in heaven: she will then understand me better. My grandmother, too, will understand me better, and will then say no more, as she used to do, 'Polly, what are those poor crazy moythered brains of yours thinking of always?' " Poor Mary! my mother indeed *never understood* her right. She loved her, as she loved us all, with a mother's love; but in opinion, in feeling, and sentiment, and disposition, bore so distant a resemblance to her daughter, that she never understood her right; never could believe how much *she* loved her; but met her caresses, her protestations of filial affection, too frequently with coldness and repulse. Still she was a good mother. God forbid I should think of her but *most* respectfully, *most* affectionately. Yet she would always love my brother above Mary, who was not worthy of one-tenth of that affection which Mary had a right to claim. But it is my sister's gratifying recollection that every act of duty and of love she could pay, every kindness (and I speak true, when I say to the hurting of her health, and, most probably, in great part to the derangement of her senses), through a long course of infirmities and sickness, she could show her, she ever did. I will, some day, as I promised, enlarge to you upon my sister's excellences: 'twill seem like exaggeration; but I will do it. At present, short letters suit my state of mind best. So take my kindest wishes for your comfort and establishment in life, and for Sara's welfare and comforts with you. God love you! God love us all! C. Lamb.

Letter XI.]   *October* 24, 1796.

Coleridge, I feel myself much your debtor for that spirit of confidence and friendship which dictated your last letter. May your soul find peace at last in your cottage life! I only wish you were but settled. Do continue to write to me. I read your letters with my sister, and they give us both abundance of delight. Especially they please us when you talk in a religious strain: not but we are offended occasionally with a certain freedom of expression, a certain air of mysticism, more consonant to the conceits of pagan philosophy than consistent with the humility of genuine piety. To instance now, in your last letter you say, "It is by the press that God hath given finite spirits, both evil and good (I suppose you mean *simply* bad men and good men), a portion as it were of His Omnipresence!" Now, high as the human intellect comparatively will soar, and wide as its influence, malign or salutary, can extend, is there not, Coleridge, a distance between the Divine Mind and it, which makes such language blasphemy? Again, in your first fine consolatory epistle, you say, "you are a temporary sharer in human misery, that you may be an eternal partaker of the Divine Nature." What more than this do those men say who are for exalting the man Christ Jesus into the second person of an unknown Trinity?—men whom you or I scruple not to call idolaters. Man, full of imperfections at best, and subject to wants which momentarily remind him of dependence; man, a weak and ignorant being, "servile" from his birth "to all the skiey influences," with eyes sometimes open to discern the right path, but a head generally too dizzy to pursue it; man, in the pride of speculation, forgetting his nature, and hailing in himself the future God, must make the angels laugh. Be not angry with me Coleridge: I wish not to cavil; I know I cannot instruct you; I only wish to remind you of that humility which best becometh the Christian character. God, in the New Testament (*our best guide*), is represented to us in the kind, condescending, amiable, familiar light of a *parent;* and in my poor mind 'tis best for us so to consider him, as our *heavenly* father, and our *best friend*, without indulging too bold conceptions of his nature. Let us learn to think humbly of ourselves, and rejoice in the appellation of "dear children," "brethren," and "co-heirs with Christ of the promises," seeking to know no further.

I am not insensible, indeed I am not, of the value of that first letter of yours, and I shall find reason to thank you for it again and again, long after that blemish in it is forgotten. It will be a fine lesson of comfort to us, whenever we read it; and read it we often shall, Mary and I.

Accept our loves and best kind wishes for the welfare of yourself and wife and little one. Nor let me forgot to wish you joy on your birthday, so lately past; I thought you had been older. My kind thanks and remembrances to Lloyd.

God love us all!—and may He continue to be the father and the friend of the whole human race! C. LAMB.

Sunday Evening.

LETTER XII.] *October* 28, 1796.

My dear Friend—I am not ignorant that to be "a partaker of the Divine Nature" is a phrase to be met with in Scripture: I am only apprehensive, lest we in these latter days, tinctured (some of us perhaps pretty deeply) with mystical notions and the pride of metaphysics, might be apt to affix to such phrases a meaning, which the primitive users of them, the simple fishermen of Galilee for instance, never intended to convey. With that other part of your apology I am not quite so well satisfied. You seem to me to have been straining your comparing faculties to bring together things infinitely distant and unlike,—the feeble narrow-sphered operations of the human intellect and the everywhere diffused mind of Deity, the peerless wisdom of Jehovah. Even the expression appears to me inaccurate—"portion of Omnipresence." Omnipresence is an attribute the very essence of which is unlimitedness. How can Omnipresence be affirmed of anything in part? But enough of this spirit of disputatiousness. Let us attend to the proper business of human life, and talk a little together respecting our domestic concerns. Do you continue to make me acquainted with what you are doing, and how soon you are likely to be settled, once for all.

I have satisfaction in being able to bid you rejoice with me in my sister's continued reason, and composedness of mind. Let us both be thankful for it. I continue to visit her very frequently, and the people of the house are vastly indulgent to her. She is likely to be as comfortably situated in all respects as those who pay twice or thrice the sum. They love her, and she loves them, and makes herself very useful to them. Benevolence sets out on her journey with a good heart, and puts a good face on it, but is apt to limp and grow feeble, unless she calls in the aid of self-interest, by way of crutch. In Mary's case, as far as respects those she is with, 'tis well that these principles are so likely to co-operate. I am rather at a loss sometimes for books for her: our reading is somewhat confined, and we have nearly exhausted our London library. She has her hands too full of work to read much; but a little she must read, for reading was her daily bread.

Have you seen Bowles's new poem on "Hope?" What character does it bear? Has he exhausted his stores of tender plaintiveness? or is he the same in this last as in all his former pieces? The duties of the day call me off from this pleasant intercourse with my friend: so for the present adieu. Now for the truant borrowing of a few minutes from business. Have you met with a new poem called the *Pursuits of Literature?* From the extracts in the *British Review* I judge it to be a very humorous thing. In particular, I remember what I thought a very happy character of Dr. Darwin's poetry. Among all your quaint readings did your ever light upon Walton's *Complete Angler?* I asked you the question once before: it breathes the very spirit of innocence, purity, and simplicity of heart. There are many choice old verses interspersed in it. It would sweeten a man's temper at any time to read it; it would Christianise every discordant angry passion. Pray make yourself acquainted with it. Have you made it up with Southey yet? Surely one of you two must have been a very silly fellow, and the other not much better, to fall out like boarding-school misses. Kiss, shake hands, and make it up.

When will he be delivered of his new epic? *Madoc,* I think, is to be the name of it; though that is a name not familiar to my ears. What progress do you make in your hymns? What Review are you connected with? If with any, why do you delay to notice White's book? You are justly offended at its profaneness; but surely you have undervalued its *wit,* or you would have been more loud in its praises. Do not you think that in *Slender's* death and madness there is most exquisite humour, mingled with tenderness, that is irresistible, truly Shakspearian? Be more full in your mention of it. Poor fellow, he has (very undeservedly) lost by it; nor do I see that it is likely ever to reimburse him the charge of printing, etc. Give it a lift, if you can. I suppose you know that Allen's wife is dead, and he, just situated as he was, never the better, as the worldly people say, for her death, her money with her children being taken off his hands. I am just now wondering whether you will ever come to town again, Coleridge; 'tis among the things I dare not hope, but can't help wishing. For myself, I can live in the midst of town luxury and superfluity, and not long for them, and I can't see why your children might not hereafter do the same. Remember, you are not in Arcadia when you are in the west of England, and they may catch infection from the world without visiting the metropolis. But you seem to have set your heart upon this same cottage plan; and God prosper you in the experiment! I am at a loss for more to write about; so 'tis as well that I am arrived at the bottom of my paper.

God love you, Coleridge!—Our best loves and tenderest wishes await on you, your Sara, and your little one.   C. L.

LETTER XIII.]   *November* 8, 1796.

My brother, my friend,—I am distress'd for you, believe me I am; not so much for your painful, troublesome complaint, which, I trust, is only for a time, as for those anxieties which brought it on, and perhaps even now may be nursing its malignity. Tell me, dearest of my friends, is your mind at peace? or has anything, yet unknown to me, happened to give you fresh disquiet, and steal from you all the pleasant dreams of future rest? Are you still (I fear you are) far from being comfortably settled? Would to God it were in my power to contribute towards the bringing of you into the haven where you would be! But you are too well skilled in the philosophy of consolation to need my humble tribute of advice. In pain, and in sickness, and in all manner of disappointments, I trust you have that within you which shall speak peace to your mind. Make it, I entreat you, one of your puny comforts, that I feel for you, and share all your griefs with you. I feel as if I were troubling you about *little* things, now I am going to resume the subject of our last two letters; but it may divert us both from unpleasanter feelings to make such matters, in a manner, of importance. Without further apology, then, it was not that I did not relish, that I did not in my heart thank you for those little pictures of your feelings which you lately sent me, if I neglected to mention them. You may remember you had said much the same things before to me on the same subject in a former letter, and I considered those last verses as only the identical thoughts better clothed; either way (in prose or verse) such poetry must be welcome to me. I love them as I love the Confessions of Rousseau, and for the same reason: the same frankness, the same openness of heart, the same disclosure of all the most hidden and delicate affections of the mind. They make me proud to be thus esteemed worthy of the place of friend-confessor, brother-confessor, to a man like Coleridge. This last is, I acknowledge, language too high for friendship; but it is also, I declare, too sincere for flattery. Now, to put on stilts, and talk magnificently about trifles,—I condescend, then, to your counsel, Coleridge, and allow my first Sonnet (sick to death am I to make mention of my Sonnets, and I blush to be so taken up with them, indeed I do); I allow it to run thus: *Fairy Land*, etc. etc., as I last wrote it.

The Fragments I now send you, I want printed to get rid of 'em; for, while they stick burr-like to my memory, they tempt me to go on with the idle trade of versifying, which I long (most sincerely I speak it) I long to leave off, for it is unprofitable to my soul; I feel it is; and these questions about words, and debates about alterations, take me off, I am conscious, from the properer business of my life. Take my Sonnets, once for all; and do not propose any reamendments, or mention them again in any shape to me, I charge you. I blush that my mind can consider them as things of any worth. And, pray, admit or reject these fragments as you like or dislike them, without ceremony. Call 'em Sketches, Fragments, or what you will; but do not entitle any of my *things* Love Sonnets, as I told you to call 'em; 'twill only make me look little in my own eyes; for it is a passion of which I retain nothing. 'Twas a weakness, concerning which I may say, in the words of Petrarch (whose Life is now open before me), "if it drew me out of some vices, it also prevented the growth of many virtues, filling me with the love of the creature rather than the Creator, which is the death of the soul." Thank God, the folly has left me for ever. Not even a review of my love verses renews one wayward wish in me; and if I am at all solicitous to trim 'em out in their best apparel, it is because they are to make their appearance in good company. Now to my fragments. Lest you have lost my "Grandame," she shall be one. 'Tis among the few verses I ever wrote, that to Mary is another, which profit me in the recollection. God love her!—and may we two never love each other less!

These, Coleridge, are the few sketches I have thought worth preserving. How will they relish thus detached? Will you reject all or any of them? They are thine: do whatsoever thou listest with them. My eyes ache with writing long and late, and I wax wondrous sleepy. God bless you and yours, me and mine! Good-night.   C. LAMB.

I will keep my eyes open reluctantly a minute longer to tell you that I love you for those simple, tender, heart-flowing lines which you conclude your last, and in my eyes best, "Sonnet" (so you call 'em)—

> "So, for the mother's sake, the child was dear;
> And dearer was the mother for the child."

Cultivate simplicity, Coleridge; or rather, I should say, banish elaborateness; for simplicity springs spontaneous from the heart, and carries into daylight its own modest buds, and genuine, sweet, and clear flowers of expression. I allow no hot-beds in the gardens of Parnassus. I am unwilling to go to bed and leave my sheet unfilled (a good piece of nightwork for an idle body like me), so will finish with begging you to send me the earliest account of your complaint, its progress, or (as I hope to God you will be able to send me) the tale of your recovery, or at least amendment. My tenderest remembrances to your Sara——
Once more, Good-night.

LETTER XIV.]   *November 14,* 1796.

Coleridge, I love you for dedicating your poetry to Bowles. Genius of the sacred fountain of tears, it was he who led you gently by the hand through all this valley of weeping; showed you the dark green yew trees, and the willow shades, where, by the fall of waters, you might indulge an uncomplaining melancholy, a delicious regret for the past, or weave fine visions of that awful future,

> "When all the vanities of life's brief day
> Oblivion's hurrying hand hath swept away,
> And all its sorrows, at the awful blast
> Of the archangel's trump, are but as shadows past."

I have another sort of dedication in my head for my few things, which I want to know if you approve of, and can insert. I mean to inscribe them to my sister. It will be unexpected, and it will give her pleasure; or do you think it will look whimsical at all? As I have not spoke to her about it I can easily reject the idea. But there is a monotony in the affections, which people living together, or, as we do now, very frequently seeing each other, are apt to give in to; a sort of indifference in the expression of kindness for each other, which demands that we should sometimes call to our aid the trickery of surprise. Do you publish with Lloyd, or without him? In either case my little portion may come last; and after the fashion of orders to a country correspondent, I will give directions how I should like to have 'em done. The title-page to stand thus:—

POEMS

BY

CHARLES LAMB, OF THE INDIA HOUSE.

Under this title the following motto, which, for want of room, I put over leaf, and desire you to insert, whether you like it or no. May not a gentleman choose what arms, mottoes, or armorial bearings the Herald will give him leave, without consulting his republican friend, who might advise none? May not a publican put up the sign of the *Saracen's Head*, even though his undiscerning neighbour should prefer, as more genteel, the *Cat and Gridiron?*

[MOTTO.]

"This beauty, in the blossom of my youth,
When my first fire knew no adulterate incense,
Nor I no way to flatter but my fondness,
In the best language my true tongue could tell me,
And all the broken sighs my sick heart lend me,
I sued and served. Long did I love this lady."

MASSINGER.

THE DEDICATION.

THE FEW FOLLOWING POEMS,
CREATURES OF THE FANCY AND THE FEELING
IN LIFE'S MORE VACANT HOURS,
PRODUCED, FOR THE MOST PART, BY
LOVE IN IDLENESS,
ARE,
WITH ALL A BROTHER'S FONDNESS,
INSCRIBED TO

MARY ANNE LAMB,

THE AUTHOR'S BEST FRIEND AND SISTER.

This is the pomp and paraphernalia of parting, with which I take my leave of a passion which has reigned so royally (so long) within me; thus with its trappings of laureatship, I fling it off, pleased and satisfied with myself that the weakness troubles me no longer. I am wedded, Coleridge, to the fortunes of my sister and my poor old father. Oh, my friend! I think sometimes, could I recall the days that are past, which among them should I choose? not those "merrier days," not the "pleasant days of hope," not "those wanderings with a fair-hair'd maid," which I have so often and so feelingly regretted, but the days, Coleridge, of a *mother's* fondness for her *school-boy*. What would I give to call her back to earth for *one* day!—on my knees to ask her pardon for all those little asperities of temper which, from time to time, have given her gentle spirit pain!— and the day, my friend, I trust, will come. There will be "time enough" for kind offices of love, if "Heaven's eternal year" be ours. Hereafter, her meek spirit shall not reproach me. Oh, my friend, cultivate the filial feelings! and let no man think himself released from the kind "charities" of relationship: these shall give him peace at the last; these are the best foundation for every species of benevolence. I rejoice to hear, by certain channels, that you, my friend, are reconciled with all your relations. 'Tis the most kindly and natural species of love, and we have all the associated train of early feelings to secure its strength and perpetuity. Send me an account of your health: *indeed* I am solicitous about you. God love you and yours.   C. LAMB.

LETTER XV.]   *December 2, 1796.*

I have delayed writing thus long, not having by me my copy of your poems, which I had lent. I am not satisfied with all your intended omissions. Why omit 40, 63, 84? Above all, let me protest strongly against your rejecting the "Complaint of Ninathoma," 86. The words, I acknowledge, are Ossian's, but you have added to them the "music of Caril." If a vicarious substitute be wanting, sacrifice (and 'twill be a piece of self-denial too), the "Epitaph on an Infant," of which its author seems so proud, so tenacious. Or, if your heart be set on *perpetuating* the four-line wonder, I'll tell you what to do; sell the copyright of it at once to a country statuary. Commence in this manner Death's prime poet-laureate; and let your verses be adopted in every village round, instead of those hitherto famous ones:—

> "Afflictions sore long time I bore;
> Physicians were in vain."

I have seen your last very beautiful poem in the *Monthly Magazine:* write thus, and you most generally have written thus, and I shall never quarrel with you about simplicity. With regard to my lines—

> "Laugh all that weep," etc.,

I would willingly sacrifice them; but my portion of the volume is so ridiculously little, that, in honest truth, I can't spare 'em. As things are, I have very slight pretensions to participate in the title-page. White's book is at length reviewed in the *Monthly;* was it your doing, or Dyer's, to whom I sent him?—or, rather, do you not write in the *Critical?*—for I observed, in an article of this month's, a line quoted out of that Sonnet on Mrs. Siddons,

"With eager wondering, and perturb'd delight."

And a line from *that* Sonnet would not readily have occurred to a stranger. That sonnet, Coleridge, brings afresh to my mind the time when you wrote those on Bowles, Priestley, Burke;—'twas two Christmases ago, and in that nice little smoky room at the *Salutation*, which is even now continually presenting itself to my recollection, with all its associated train of pipes, tobacco, egg-hot, welsh-rabbit, metaphysics, and poetry.—Are we *never* to meet again? How differently I am circumstanced now! I have never met with anyone—never shall meet with anyone—who could or can compensate me for the loss of your society. I have no one to talk all these matters about to; I lack friends. I lack books to supply their absence; but these complaints ill become me. Let me compare my present situation, prospects, and state of mind, with what they were but two months back—but two months! O my friend, I am in danger of forgetting the awful lessons then presented to me! Remind me of them; remind me of my duty! Talk seriously with me when you do write! I thank you, from my heart I thank you, for your solicitude about my sister. She is quite well, but must not, I fear, come to live with us yet a good while. In the first place, because, at present, it would hurt her, and hurt my father, for them to be together; secondly, from a regard to the world's good report; for, I fear, tongues will be busy whenever that event takes place. Some have hinted, one man has pressed it on me, that she should be in perpetual confinement: what she hath done to deserve, or the necessity of such an hardship, I see not; do you? I am starving at the India House,—near seven o'clock without my dinner; and so it has been, and will be, almost all the week. I get home at night o'erwearied, quite faint, and then to cards with my father, who will not let me enjoy a meal in peace; but I must conform to my situation; and I hope I am, for the most part, not unthankful.

I am got home at last, and, after repeated games at cribbage, have got my father's leave to write awhile; with difficulty got it, for when I expostulated about playing any more, he very aptly replied, "If you won't play with me, you might as well not come home at all." The argument was unanswerable, and I set to afresh. I told you I do not approve of your omissions; neither do I quite coincide with you in your arrangements. I have not time to point out a better, and I suppose some self-associations of your own have determined their place as they now stand. Your beginning, indeed, with the *Joan of Arc* lines, I coincide entirely with. I love a splendid outset—a magnificent portico; and the diapason is grand. When I read the *Religious Musings*, I think how poor, how unelevated, unoriginal, my blank verse is—"Laugh all that weep," especially, where the subject demanded a grandeur of conception; and I ask what business they have among yours? but friendship covereth a multitude of defects. I want some loppings made in the "Chatterton:" it wants but a little to make it rank among the finest irregular lyrics I ever read. Have you time and inclination to go to work upon it?—or is it too late?—or do you think it needs none? Don't reject those verses in your *Watchman*, "Dear native brook," etc.; nor I think those last lines you sent me, in which "all effort-less" is without doubt to be preferred to "inactive." If I am writing more than ordinarily dully, 'tis that I am stupefied with a tooth-ache. Hang it! do not omit 48, 52, and 53: what you do retain, though, call Sonnets, for heaven's sake, and not Effusions. Spite of your ingenious anticipation of ridicule in your Preface, the last five lines of 50 are too good to be lost; the rest are not much worth. My tooth becomes importunate: I must finish. Pray, pray, write to me: if you knew with what an anxiety of joy I open such a long packet as you last sent me, you would not grudge giv-ing a few minutes now and then to this intercourse (the only intercourse I fear we two shall ever have)—this conversation with your friend: such I boast to be called. God love you and yours! Write to me when you move, lest I should direct wrong. Has Sara no poems to publish? Those lines, 129, are probably too light for the volume where the *Religious Musings* are; but I remember some very beautiful lines, addressed by somebody at Bristol to somebody in London. God bless you once more. *Thursday Night.*   C. LAMB.

LETTER XVI.]   [Fragment.]   *December* 5, 1796.

At length I have done with verse-making; not that I relish other peo-ple's poetry less: theirs comes from 'em without effort; mine is the difficult operation of a brain scanty of ideas, made more difficult by disuse. I have been reading "The Task" with fresh delight. I am glad you love Cowper. I could forgive a man for not enjoying Milton; but I would not call that man my friend who should be offended with the "divine chit-chat of Cow-per." Write to me, God love you and yours!   C. L.

LETTER XVII.]   *December* 10, 1796.

I had put my letter into the post rather hastily, not expecting to have to acknowledge another from you so soon. This morning's present has made me alive again. My last night's epistle was childishly querulous: but you have put a little life into me, and I will thank you for your re-membrance of me, while my sense of it is yet warm; for if I linger a day or two I may use the same phrase of acknowledgment, or similar, but the feeling that dictates it now will be gone. I shall send you a *caput mor-tuum*, not a *cor vivens*. Thy *Watchman's*, thy bellman's verses, I do re-tort upon thee, thou libellous varlet! Why you cried the hours yourself, and who made you so proud! But I submit, to show my humility most implicitly to your dogmas. I reject entirely the copy of verses you reject. With regard to my leaving off versifying, you have said so many pretty things, so many fine compliments, ingeniously decked out in the garb of sincerity, and undoubtedly springing from a present feeling somewhat like sincerity, that you might melt the most un-muse-ical soul—did you not (now for a Rowland compliment for your profusion of Olivers!) did you not in your very epistle, by the many pretty fancies and profusion of heart displayed in it, dissuade and discourage me from attempting anything after you? At present I have not leisure to make verses, nor anything approaching to a fondness for the exercise. In the ignorant present time, who can answer for the future man? "At lovers' perjuries Jove laughs;" and poets have sometimes a disingenuous way of forswearing their occupation. This though is not my case. The tender cast of soul, sombred with melancholy and subsiding recollections, is favourable to the Sonnet or the Elegy; but from

> "The sainted growing woof
> The teasing troubles keep aloof."

The music of poesy may charm for a while the importunate teasing cares of life; but the teased and troubled man is not in a disposition to make that music.

You sent me some very sweet lines relative to Burns, but it was at a time when in my highly agitated and perhaps somewhat distorted state of mind I thought it a duty to read 'em hastily and burn 'em. I burned all my own verses; all my book of extracts from Beaumont and Fletcher and a thousand sources; I burned a little journal of my foolish passion which I had a long time kept—

> "Noting ere they past away
> The little lines of yesterday."

I almost burned all your letters,—I did as bad, I lent 'em to a friend to keep out of my brother's sight, should he come and make inquisition into our papers; for, much as he dwelt upon your conversation while you were among us, and delighted to be with you, it has been his fashion ever since to depreciate and cry you down: you were the cause of my madness—you and your "damned foolish sensibility and melancholy;" and he lamented, with a true brotherly feeling, that we ever met; even as the sober citizen, when his son went astray upon the mountains of Parnassus, is said to have "cursed Wit and Poetry and Pope." I quote wrong, but no matter. These letters I lent to a friend to be out of the way for a season; but I have claimed 'em in vain, and shall not cease to regret their loss. Your packets, posterior to the date of my misfortunes, commencing with that valuable consolatory epistle, are every day accumulating: they are sacred things with me.

Publish your Burns when and how you like, it will be new to me: my memory of it is very confused, and tainted with unpleasant associations. Burns was the god of my idolatry, as Bowles is of yours. I am jealous of your fraternising with Bowles, when I think you relish him more than Burns, or my old favourite, Cowper. But you conciliate matters when you talk of the "divine chit-chat" of the latter: by that expression I see you thoroughly relish him. I love Mrs. Coleridge for her excuses an hundredfold more dearly than if she heaped "line upon line," out-Hannah-ing

Hannah More; and would rather hear you sing "Did a very little baby," by your family fire-side, than listen to you when you were repeating one of Bowles's sweetest sonnets, in your sweet manner, while we two were indulging sympathy, a solitary luxury, by the fire-side at the *Salutation*. Yet have I no higher ideas of heaven. Your company was one "cordial in this melancholy vale:" the remembrance of it is a blessing partly, and partly a curse. When I can abstract myself from things present, I can enjoy it with a freshness of relish; but it more constantly operates to an unfavourable comparison with the uninteresting converse I always and *only* can partake in. Not a soul loves Bowles here; scarce one has heard of Burns; few but laugh at me for reading my Testament. They talk a language I understand not. I conceal sentiments that would be a puzzle to them. I can only converse with you by letter, and with the dead in their books. My sister, indeed, is all I can wish in a companion; but our spirits are alike poorly, our reading and knowledge from the self-same sources; our communication with the scenes of the world alike narrow. Never having kept separate company, or any "company" *"together"*— never having read separate books, and few books *together*—what knowledge have we to convey to each other? In our little range of duties and connections, how few sentiments can take place, without friends, with few books, with a taste for religion, rather than a strong religious habit! We need some support, some leading-strings to cheer and direct us. You talk very wisely; and be not sparing of *your advice*. Continue to remember us, and to show us you do remember us: we will take as lively an interest in what concerns you and yours. All I can add to your happiness will be sympathy: you can add to mine *more;* you can teach me wisdom. I am indeed an unreasonable correspondent; but I was unwilling to let my last night's letter go off without this qualifier: you will perceive by this my mind is easier, and you will rejoice. I do not expect or wish you to write till you are moved; and, of course, shall not, till you announce to me that event, think of writing myself. Love to Mrs. Coleridge and David Hartley, and my kind remembrance to Lloyd, if he is with you.

C. LAMB.

I will get *Nature and Art:* have not seen it yet, nor any of Jeremy Taylor's works.

LETTER XVIII.]　　　　　　　　　　　　*December* 10, 1796.

I am sorry I cannot now relish your poetical present so thoroughly as I feel it deserves; but I do not the less thank Lloyd and you for it.

In truth, Coleridge, I am perplexed, and at times almost cast down. I am beset with perplexities. The old hag of a wealthy relation who took my aunt off our hands in the beginning of trouble, has found out that she is "indolent and mulish"—I quote her own words, and that her attachment to us is so strong that she can never be happy apart. The lady, with delicate irony, remarks, that if I am not an hypocrite I shall rejoice to receive her again; and that it will be a means of making me more fond of

home to have so dear a friend to come home to! The fact is, she is jealous
of my aunt's bestowing any kind recollections on us while she enjoys the
patronage of her roof. She says she finds it inconsistent with her own
"ease and tranquillity," to keep her any longer; and, in fine, summons me
to fetch her home. Now, much as I should rejoice to transplant the poor
old creature from the chilling air of such patronage, yet I know how
straitened we are already, how unable already to answer any demand
which sickness or any extraordinary expense may make. I know this;
and all unused as I am to struggle with perplexities, I am somewhat non-
plussed, to say no worse. This prevents me from a thorough relish of
what Lloyd's kindness and yours have furnished me with. I thank you
though from my heart, and feel myself not quite alone in the earth.

Before I offer, what alone I have to offer, a few obvious remarks on the
poems you sent me, I can but notice the odd coincidence of two young
men, in one age, carolling their grandmothers. Love, what L. calls the
"feverish and romantic tie," hath too long domineered over all the charities of home: the dear domestic ties of father, brother, husband. The
amiable and benevolent Cowper has a beautiful passage in his "Task,"—
some natural and painful reflections on his deceased parents: and Hay-
ley's sweet lines to his mother are notoriously the best things he ever
wrote. Cowper's lines, some of them are—

> "How gladly would the man recall to life
> The boy's neglected sire! a Mother, too,
> That softer friend, perhaps more gladly still,
> Might he demand them at the gates of death."

I cannot but smile to see my granny so gaily decked forth: though, I
think, whoever altered "thy" praises to "her" praises—"thy" honoured
memory to "her" honoured memory, did wrong; they best expressed my
feelings. There is a pensive state of recollection in which the mind is disposed to apostrophise the departed objects of its attachment; and, breaking loose from grammatical precision, changes from the first to the third,
and from the third to the first person, just as the random fancy or the
feeling directs. Among Lloyd's sonnets, the 6th, 7th, 8th, 9th, and 11th
are eminently beautiful. I think him too lavish of his expletives: the *do's*
and *did's,* when they occur too often, bring a quaintness with them along
with their simplicity, or rather air of antiquity, which the patrons of them
seem desirous of conveying.

Another time, I may notice more particularly Lloyd's, Southey's, Der-
mody's Sonnets. I shrink from them now: my teasing lot makes me too
confused for a clear judgment of things, too selfish for sympathy; and
these ill-digested, meaningless remarks, I have imposed on myself as a
task, to lull reflection, as well as to show you I did not neglect reading
your valuable present. Return my acknowledgments to Lloyd; you two
seem to be about realising an Elysium upon earth, and, no doubt, I shall
be happier. Take my best wishes. Remember me most affectionately to
Mrs. C.——, and give little David Hartley (God bless its little heart!) a

kiss for me. Bring him up to know the meaning of his Christian name, and what that name (imposed upon him) will demand of him.

God love you!　　　　　　　　　　　　　　　　C. Lamb.

I write, for one thing, to say that I shall write no more till you send me word where you are, for you are so soon to move.

My sister is pretty well, thank God. We think of you very often. God bless you: continue to be my correspondent, and I will strive to fancy that this world is *not* "all barrenness."

Letter XIX.]　　　　　　　　　　　　　　　*January* 2, 1797.

If the fraternal sentiment conveyed in the following lines will atone for the total want of anything like merit or genius in it, I desire you will print it next after my other Sonnet to my Sister.

> Friend of my earliest years and childish days,
> My joys, my sorrows, thou with me hast shared,
> Companion dear; etc.

This has been a sad long letter of business, with no room in it for what honest Bunyan terms heart-work. I have just room left to congratulate you on your removal to Stowey; to wish success to all your projects; to "bid fair peace" be to that house; to send my love and best wishes, breathed warmly, after your dear Sara, and her little David Hartley. If Lloyd be with you, bid him write to me: I feel to whom I am obliged primarily for two very friendly letters I have received already from him. A dainty sweet book that *Nature and Art* is. I am at present re-re-reading Priestley's Examination of the Scotch Doctors: how the rogue strings 'em up! three together! You have no doubt read that clear, strong, humorous, most entertaining piece of reasoning. If not, procure it, and be exquisitely amused. I wish I could get more of Priestley's works. Can you recommend me to any more books, easy of access, such as circulating shops afford? God bless you and yours.

Monday Morning, at Office.

Poor Mary is very unwell with a sore throat and a slight species of scarlet fever. God bless her too.

Letter XX.]　　　　　　　　　　　　　　　*January* 5, 1797.

Sunday Morning.—You cannot surely mean to degrade the Joan of Arc into a pot-girl. You are not going, I hope, to annex to that most splendid ornament of Southey's poem all this cock-and-a-bull story of Joan, the publican's daughter of Neufchatel, with the lamentable episode of a waggoner, his wife, and six children. The texture will be most lamentably disproportionate. The first forty or fifty lines of these addenda are, no doubt, in their way, admirable, too; but many would prefer the Joan of Southey.

"On mightiest deeds to brood
Of shadowy vastness, such as made my heart
Throb fast; anon I paused, and in a state
Of half expectance listen'd to the wind;"

"They wonder'd at me, who had known me once
A cheerful careless damsel;"

"The eye,
That of the circling throng and of the visible world
Unseeing, saw the shapes of holy phantasy;"

I see nothing in your description of the Maid equal to these. There is a fine originality certainly in those lines—

"For she had lived in this bad world
As in a place of tombs,
And touch'd not the pollutions of the dead;"

but your "fierce vivacity" is a faint copy of the "fierce and terrible benevolence" of Southey; added to this, that it will look like rivalship in you, and extort a comparison with Southey,—I think to your disadvantage. And the lines, considered in themselves as an addition to what you had before written (strains of a far higher mood), are but such as Madame Fancy loves in some of her more familiar moods, at such times as she has met Noll Goldsmith, and walked and talked with him, calling him "old acquaintance." Southey certainly has no pretensions to vie with you in the sublime of poetry; but he tells a plain tale better than you. I will enumerate some woful blemishes, some of 'em sad deviations from that simplicity which was your aim. "Hail'd who might be near" (the "canvas-coverture moving," by the by, is laughable); "a woman and six children" (by the way,—why not nine children? It would have been just half as pathetic again): "statues of sleep they seem'd:" "frost-mangled wretch:" "green putridity:" "hail'd him immortal" (rather ludicrous again): "voic'd a sad and simple tale" (abominable!): "unprovender'd:" "such his tale:" "Ah! suffering to the height of what was suffer'd" (a most *insufferable line*): "amazements of affright:" "the hot sore brain attributes its own hues of ghastliness and torture" (what shocking confusion of ideas!).

In these delineations of common and natural feelings, in the familiar walks of poetry, you seem to resemble Montauban dancing with Roubigné's tenants, *"much of his native loftiness remained in the execution."*

I was reading your *Religious Musings* the other day, and sincerely I think it the noblest poem in the language, next after the *Paradise Lost;* and even that was not made the vehicle of such grand truths. "There is one mind," etc., down to "Almighty's throne," are without a rival in the whole compass of my poetical reading.

"Stands in the sun, and with no partial gaze
Views all creation."

I wish I could have written those lines. I rejoice that I am able to relish them. The loftier walks of Pindus are your proper region. There you have no compeer in modern times. Leave the lowlands, unenvied, in possession of such men as Cowper and Southey. Thus am I pouring balsam into the wounds I may have been inflicting on my poor friend's vanity.

In your notice of Southey's new volume you omit to mention the most pleasing of all, the "Miniature"—

> "There were
> Who form'd high hopes and flattering ones of thee,
> Young Robert,
> Spirit of Spenser!—was the wanderer wrong?"

Fairfax I have been in quest of a long time. Johnson, in his "Life of Waller," gives a most delicious specimen of him, and adds, in the true manner of that delicate critic, as well as amiable man, "It may be presumed that this old version will not be much read after the elegant translation of my friend, Mr. Hoole." I endeavoured—I wished to gain some idea of Tasso from this Mr. Hoole, the great boast and ornament of the India House, but soon desisted. I found him more vapid than smallest small beer "sun-vinegared." Your "Dream," down to that exquisite line—

> "I can't tell half his adventures,"

is a most happy resemblance of Chaucer. The remainder is so so. The best line, I think, is, "He belong'd, I believe, to the witch Melancholy." By the way, when will our volume come out? Don't delay it till you have written a new Joan of Arc. Send what letters you please by me, and in any way you choose, single or double. The India Company is better adapted to answer the cost than the generality of my friend's correspondents,—such poor and honest dogs as John Thelwall, particularly. I cannot say I know Colson, at least intimately. I once supped with him and Allen: I think his manners very pleasing. I will not tell you what I think of Lloyd, for he may by chance come to see this letter, and that thought puts a restraint on me. I cannot think what subject would suit your epic genius; some philosophical subject, I conjecture, in which shall be blended the sublime of poetry and of science. Your proposed "Hymns" will be a fit preparatory study wherewith "to discipline your young noviciate soul." I grow dull; I'll go walk myself out of my dulness.

Sunday Night.—You and Sara are very good to think so kindly and so favourably of poor Mary; I would to God all did so too. But I very much fear she must not think of coming home in my father's lifetime. It is very hard upon her; but our circumstances are peculiar, and we must submit to them. God be praised she is so well as she is. She bears her situation as one who has no right to complain. My poor old aunt, whom you have seen, the kindest, goodest creature to me when I was at school; who used to toddle there to bring me good things, when I, school-boy like, only despised her for it, and used to be ashamed to see her come and sit herself down on the old coal-hole steps as you went into the old grammar-school, and open her apron, and bring out her bason, with some nice things she had caused to be saved for me; the good old creature is now lying on her death-bed. I cannot bear to think on her deplorable state. To the shock she received on that our evil day, from which she never completely recovered, I impute her illness. She says, poor thing, she is glad she is come home to die with me. I was always her favourite:

"No after friendship e'er can raise
The endearments of our early days,
Nor e'er the heart such fondness prove,
As when it first began to love."

Lloyd has kindly left me, for a keep-sake, *John Woolman*. You have read it, he says, and like it. Will you excuse one short extract? I think it could not have escaped you:—"Small treasure to a resigned mind is sufficient. How happy is it to be content with a little, to live in humility, and feel *that* in us, which breathes out this language—Abba! Father!"

——I am almost ashamed to patch up a letter in this miscellaneous sort; but I please myself in the thought, that anything from me will be acceptable to you. I am rather impatient, childishly so, to see our names affixed to the same common volume. Send me two, when it does come out; two will be enough—or indeed one—but two better. I have a dim recollection that, when in town, you were talking of the Origin of Evil as a most prolific subject for a long poem. Why not adopt it, Coleridge?— there would be room for imagination. Or the description (from a Vision or Dream, suppose) of an Utopia in one of the planets (the Moon, for instance). Or a Five Days' Dream, which shall illustrate, in sensible imagery, Hartley's five Motives to Conduct:—1. Sensation; 2. Imagination; 3. Ambition; 4. Sympathy; 5. Theopathy:—*First*. Banquets, music, etc., effeminacy,—and their insufficiency. *Second*. "Beds of hyacinth and roses, where young Adonis oft reposes;" "Fortunate Isles;" "The pagan Elysium," etc.; poetical pictures; antiquity as pleasing to the fancy;—their emptiness, madness, etc. *Third*. Warriors, Poets; some famous yet more forgotten; their fame or oblivion now alike indifferent; pride, vanity, etc. *Fourth*. All manner of pitiable stories, in Spenser-like verse; love; friendship, relationship, etc. *Fifth*. Hermits; Christ and his apostles; martyrs; heaven, etc. An imagination like yours, from these scanty hints, may expand into a thousand great ideas, if indeed you at all comprehend my scheme, which I scarce do myself.

Monday Morn.—"A London letter—Ninepence half-penny!" Look you, master poet, I have remorse as well as another man, and my bowels can sound upon occasion. But I must put you to this charge, for I cannot keep back my protest, however ineffectual, against the annexing your latter lines to those former—this putting of new wine into old bottles. This my duty done, I will cease from writing till you invent some more reasonable mode of conveyance. Well may the "ragged followers of the Nine" set up for flocci-nauci-what-do-you-call-'em-ists! and I do not wonder that in their splendid visions of Utopias in America they protest against the admission of those *yellow*-complexioned, *copper*-coloured, *white*-livered gentlemen, who never proved themselves their friends. Don't you think your verses on a "Young Ass" too trivial a companion for the

"Religious Musings"?—"Scoundrel monarch," alter that; and the "Man of Ross" is scarce admissible, as it now stands, curtailed of its fairer half: reclaim its property from the "Chatterton," which it does but encumber, and it will be a rich little poem. I hope you expunge great part of the old notes in the new edition: that, in particular, most barefaced, unfounded, impudent assertion, that Mr. Rogers is indebted for his story to *Loch Lomond,* a poem by Bruce! I have read the latter. I scarce think you have. Scarce anything is common to them both. The poor author of the *Pleasures of Memory* was sorely hurt, Dyer says, by the accusation of unoriginality. He never saw the poem. I long to read your poem on Burns; I retain so indistinct a memory of it. In what shape and how does it come into public? As you leave off writing poetry till you finish your Hymns, I suppose you print, now, all you have got by you. You have scarce enough unprinted to make a second volume with Lloyd. Tell me all about it. What is become of Cowper? Lloyd told me of some verses on his mother. If you have them by you, pray send 'em me. I do so love him! Never mind their merit. May be *I* may like 'em, as your taste and mine do not always exactly *identify.* Yours,

C. LAMB.

LETTER XXI.]   *January* 10, 1797.

I need not repeat my wishes to have my little sonnets printed *verbatim* my last way. In particular, I fear lest you should prefer printing my first sonnet, as you have done more than once, "Did the wand of Merlin wave?" It looks so like *Mr.* Merlin, the ingenious successor of the immortal Merlin, now living in good health and spirits, and flourishing in magical reputation in Oxford Street; and, on my life, one half who read it would understand it so. Do put 'em forth, finally, as I have in various letters settled it; for first a man's self is to be pleased, and then his friends; and, of course, the greater number of his friends, if they differ *inter se.* Thus taste may safely be put to the vote. I do long to see our names together; not for vanity's sake, and naughty pride of heart altogether, for not a living soul I know, or am intimate with, will scarce read the book: so I shall gain nothing, *quoad famam;* and yet there is a little vanity mixes in it, I cannot help denying. I am aware of the unpoetical cast of the six last lines of my last sonnet, and think myself unwarranted in smuggling so tame a thing into the book; only the sentiments of those six lines are thoroughly congenial to me in my state of mind, and I wish to accumulate perpetuating tokens of my affection to poor Mary. That it has no originality in its cast, nor anything in the feelings but what is common and natural to thousands, nor ought properly to be called poetry, I see; still it will tend to keep present to my mind a view of things which I ought to indulge. These six lines, too, have not, to a reader, a connectedness with the foregoing.—Omit it, if you like. —What a treasure it is to my poor, indolent, and unemployed mind, thus to lay hold on a subject to talk about, though 'tis but a sonnet, and that of the lowest order! How mournfully inactive I am!—'Tis night: Goodnight.

My sister, I thank God, is nigh recovered: she was seriously ill. Do, in your next letter, and that right soon, give me some satisfaction respecting your present situation at Stowey. Is it a farm you have got? And what does your worship know about farming?

Coleridge, I want you to write an epic poem. Nothing short of it can satisfy the vast capacity of true poetic genius. Having one great end to direct all your poetical faculties to, and on which to lay out your hopes, your ambition will show you to what you are equal. By the sacred energies of Milton! by the dainty, sweet, and soothing phantasies of honey-tongued Spenser! I adjure you to attempt the epic, or do something more ample than writing an occasional brief ode or sonnet; something, "to make yourself for ever known,—to make the age to come your own." But I prate; doubtless you meditate something. When you are exalted among the lords of epic fame, I shall recall with pleasure, and exultingly, the days of your humility, when you disdained not to put forth, in the same volume with mine, your *Religious Musings* and that other poem from the *Joan of Arc*, those promising first-fruits of high renown to come. You have learning, you have fancy, you have enthusiasm, you have strength, and amplitude of wing enow for flights like those I recommend. In the vast and unexplored regions of fairy-land there is ground enough unfound and uncultivated: search there, and realise your favourite Susquehannah scheme. In all our comparisons of taste, I do not know whether I have ever heard your opinion of a poet, very dear to me,—the now-out-of-fashion Cowley. Favour me with your judgment of him, and tell me if his prose essays, in particular, as well as no inconsiderable part of his verse, be not delicious. I prefer the graceful rambling of his essays, even to the courtly elegance and ease of Addison; abstracting from this the latter's exquisite humour.

When the little volume is printed, send me three or four, at all events not more than six copies, and tell me if I put you to any additional expense, by printing with you. I have no thought of the kind, and in that case must reimburse you.

Priestley, whom I sin in almost adoring, speaks of "such a choice of company as tends to keep up that right bent and firmness of mind which a necessary intercourse with the world would otherwise warp and relax." "Such fellowship is the true balsam of life; its cement is infinitely more durable than that of the friendships of the world; and it looks for its proper fruit and complete gratification to the life beyond the grave." Is there a possible chance for such an one as I to realise in this world such friendships? Where am I to look for 'em? What testimonials shall I bring of my being worthy of such friendship? Alas! the great and good go together in separate herds, and leave such as I to lag far, far behind in all intellectual, and, far more grievous to say, in all moral accomplishments. Coleridge, I have not one truly elevated character among my acquaintance: not one Christian: not one but undervalues Christianity. Singly, what am I to do? Wesley (have you read his life?) was *he* not an elevated character? Wesley has said, "Religion is not a solitary thing." Alas! it necessarily is so with me, or next to solitary. 'Tis true you write to me; but correspondence by letter, and personal intimacy, are very widely different. Do, do write to me, and do some good to my mind, already how much "warped and relaxed" by the world! 'Tis the conclusion of another evening. Good night. God have us all in his keeping!

If you are sufficiently at leisure, oblige me with an account of your plan of life at Stowey—your literary occupations and prospects; in short, make me acquainted with every circumstance which, as relating to you, can be interesting to me. Are you yet a Berkleyan? Make me one. I rejoice in being, speculatively, a Necessarian. Would to God, I were habitually a practical one! Confirm me in the faith of that great and glorious doctrine, and keep me steady in the contemplation of it. You some time since expressed an intention you had of finishing some extensive work on the Evidences of Natural and Revealed Religion. Have you let that intention go? Or are you doing anything towards it? Make to yourself other ten talents. My letter is full of nothingness. I talk of nothing. But I must talk. I love to write to you. I take a pride in it. It makes me think less meanly of myself. It makes me think myself not totally disconnected from the better part of mankind. I know I am too dissatisfied with the beings around me; but I cannot help occasionally exclaiming, "Woe is me, that I am constrained to dwell with Meshech, and to have my habitation among the tents of Kedar!" I know I am noways better in practice than my neighbours, but I have a taste for religion, an occasional earnest aspiration after perfection, which they have not. I gain nothing by being with such as myself: we encourage one another in mediocrity. I am always longing to be with men more excellent than myself. All this must sound odd to you; but these are my predominant feelings when I sit down to write to you, and I should put force upon my mind were I to reject them. Yet I rejoice, and feel my privilege with gratitude, when I have been reading some wise book, such as I have just been reading, *Priestley on Philosophical Necessity,* in the thought that I enjoy a kind of communion, a kind of friendship even, with the great and good. Books are to me instead of friends. I wish they did not resemble the latter in their scarceness.

And how does little David Hartley? *"Ecquid in antiquam virtutem?"* Does his mighty name work wonders yet upon his little frame and opening mind? I did not distinctly understand you: you don't mean to make an actual ploughman of him! Is Lloyd with you yet? Are you intimate with Southey? What poems is he about to publish? He hath a most prolific brain, and is indeed a most sweet poet. But how can you answer all the various mass of interrogation I have put to you in the course of this sheet? Write back just what you like, only write something, however brief. I have now nigh finished my page, and got to the end of another evening (Monday evening), and my eyes are heavy and sleepy, and my brain unsuggestive. I have just heart enough awake to say good-night

once more, and God love you, my dear friend; God love us all! Mary
bears an affectionate remembrance of you.   CHARLES LAMB.

LETTER XXII.]   *January* 16, 1797.
Dear C——,—You have learned by this time, with surprise, no doubt,
that Lloyd is with me in town. The emotions I felt on his coming so unlooked for, are not ill expressed in what follows, and what (if you do not
object to them as too personal, and to the world obscure, or otherwise
wanting in worth) I should wish to make a part of our little volume. I
shall be sorry if that volume comes out, as it necessarily must do, unless
you print those very schoolboy-ish verses I sent you on not getting leave
to come down to Bristol last Summer. I say I shall be sorry that I have
addressed you in nothing which can appear in our joint volume; so frequently, so habitually, as you dwell in my thoughts, 'tis some wonder
those thoughts came never yet in contact with a poetical mood. But you
dwell in my heart of hearts, and I love you in all the naked honesty of
prose. God bless you, and all your little domestic circle! My tenderest
remembrances to your beloved Sara, and a smile and a kiss from me to
your dear dear little David Hartley. The verses I refer to above, slightly
amended, I have sent (forgetting to ask your leave, tho' indeed I gave
them only your initials) to the *Monthly Magazine,* where they may possibly appear next month, and where I hope to recognise your poem on
Burns.

TO CHARLES LLOYD, AN UNEXPECTED VISITOR.

Alone, obscure, without a friend,
  A cheerless, solitary thing,
Why seeks my Lloyd the stranger out?
  What offering can the stranger bring

Of social scenes, home-bred delights,
  That him in aught compensate may
For Stowey's pleasant winter nights,
  For loves and friendships far away,

In brief oblivion to forego
  Friends, such as thine, so justly dear,
And be awhile with me content
  To stay, a kindly loiterer, here?

For this a gleam of random joy
  Hath flush'd my unaccustomed cheek;
And, with an o'er-charged bursting heart,
  I feel the thanks I cannot speak.

O! sweet are all the Muse's lays,
  And sweet the charm of matin bird—
'Twas long, since these estranged ears
  The sweeter voice of friend had heard.

The voice hath spoke: the pleasant sounds,
  In memory's ear, in after time
Shall live, to sometimes rouse a tear,
  And sometimes prompt an honest rhyme

For when the transient charm is fled,
  And when the little week is o'er,
To cheerless, friendless solitude
  When I return, as heretofore—

Long, long, within my aching heart
  The grateful sense shall cherished be;
I'll think less meanly of myself,
  That Lloyd will sometimes think on me.

O Coleridge, would to God you were in London with us, or we two at Stowey with you all! Lloyd takes up his abode at the *Bull and Mouth;* the *Cat and Salutation* would have had a charm more forcible for me. *O noctes cœnæque Deûm!* Anglice—Welsh rabbit, punch, and poesy. Should you be induced to publish those very schoolboy-ish verses, print 'em as they will occur, if at all, in the *Monthly Magazine;* yet I should feel ashamed that to you I wrote nothing better: but they are too personal, and almost trifling and obscure withal. Some lines of mine to Cowper were in the last *Monthly Magazine:* they have not body of thought enough to plead for the retaining of 'em. My sister's kind love to you all.

                                                                C. LAMB.

LETTER XXIII.]   *February* 13, 1797.

Your poem is altogether admirable: parts of it are even exquisite; in particular, your personal account of the Maid far surpasses anything of the sort in Southey. I perceived all its excellences, on a first reading, as readily as now you have been removing a supposed film from my eyes. I was only struck with a certain faulty disproportion in the matter and the *style*, which I still think I perceive, between these lines and the former ones. I had an end in view: I wished to make you reject the poem only as being discordant with the other; and, in subservience to that end, it was politically done in me to overpass and make no mention of merit, which, could you think me capable of *overlooking*, might reasonably damn for ever in your judgment all pretensions, in me, to be critical. There—I will be judged by Lloyd, whether I have not made a very handsome recantation. I was in the case of a man whose friend has asked him his opinion of à certain young lady. The deluded wight gives judgment against her *in toto*—doesn't like her face, her walk, her manners; finds fault with her eyebrows; can see no wit in her. His friend looks blank; he begins to smell a rat; wind veers about; he acknowledges her good sense, her judgment in dress, a certain simplicity of manners and honesty of heart, something too in her manners which gains upon you after a short acquaintance; and then her accurate pronunciation of the French language, and a pretty uncultivated taste in drawing. The reconciled gentleman smiles applause, squeezes him by the hand, and hopes he will do him the honour of taking a bit of dinner with Mrs. —— and him,—a plain family dinner—some day next week; "for, I suppose, you never heard we were married. I'm glad to see you like my wife, however; you'll come and see her, ha?" Now am I too proud to retract entirely? Yet I do perceive I am in some sort straitened. You are manifestly wedded to this poem; and what fancy has joined let no man separate. I turn me to the *Joan of Arc*, second book.

The solemn openings of it are with sounds which, Lloyd would say, "are silence to the mind." The deep preluding strains are fitted to initiate the mind, with a pleasing awe, into the sublimest mysteries of theory concerning man's nature, and his noblest destination—the philosophy of a first cause—of subordinate agents in creation superior to man—the subserviency of pagan worship and pagan faith to the introduction of a purer and more perfect religion, which you so elegantly describe as winning, with gradual steps, her difficult way northward from Bethabara. After all this cometh Joan, a *publican's* daughter, sitting on an ale-house *bench*, and marking the *swingings* of the *signboard*, finding a poor man, his wife, and six children, starved to death with cold, and thence roused into a state of mind proper to receive visions, emblematical of equality; which, what the devil Joan had to with, I don't know, or indeed with the French and American revolutions; though that needs no pardon, it is executed so nobly. After all, if you perceive no disproportion, all argument is vain: I do not so much object to parts. Again, when you talk of building your fame on these lines in preference to the *Religious Musings*, I cannot help conceiving of you, and of the author of that, as two different persons, and I think you a very vain man.

I have been re-reading your letter. Much of it I *could* dispute; but with the latter part of it, in which you compare the two Joans with respect to their predispositions for fanaticism, I, *toto corde*, coincide; only I think that Southey's strength rather lies in the description of the emotions of the Maid under the weight of inspiration. These (I see no mighty difference between *her* describing them or *your* describing them), these if you only equal, the previous admirers of his poem, as is natural, will prefer his. If you surpass, prejudice will scarcely allow it, and I scarce think you will surpass, though your specimen at the conclusion (I am in earnest) I think very nigh equals them. And in an account of a fanatic or of a prophet, the description of her *emotions* is expected to be most highly finished. By the way, I spoke far too disparagingly of your lines, and I am ashamed to say, purposely. I should like you to specify or particularise. The story of the "Tottering Eld," of "his eventful years all come and gone," is too general. Why not make him a soldier, or some character, however, in which he has been witness to frequency of "cruel wrong and strange distress!" I think I should. When I laughed at the "miserable man crawling from beneath the coverture," I wonder I did not perceive that it was a laugh of horror—such as I have laughed at Dante's picture of the famished Ugolino. Without falsehood, I perceive an hundred beauties in your narrative. Yet I wonder you do not perceive something out-of-the-way, something unsimple and artificial in the expression, "voiced a sad tale." I hate made-dishes at the muses' banquet. I believe I was wrong in most of my other objections. But surely "hailed him immortal," adds nothing to the terror of the man's death, which it was your business to heighten, not diminish by a phrase which takes away all terror from it. I like that line, "They closed their eyes in sleep, nor knew 'twas death." Indeed there is scarce a line I do not like. *"Turbid* ecstasy," is surely not so good as what you *had* written, "troublous." Turbid rather suits the muddy kind of inspiration which London porter confers. The versification is, throughout, to my ears unexceptionable, with no disparagement to the measure of the *Religious Musings,* which is exactly fitted to the thoughts.

You were building your house on a rock when you rested your fame on that poem. I can scarce bring myself to believe that I am admitted to a familiar correspondence, and all the licence of friendship, with a man who writes blank verse like Milton. Now, this is delicate flattery, *indirect* flattery. Go on with your *Maid of Orleans,* and be content to be second to yourself. I shall become a convert to it when 'tis finished.

This afternoon I attend the funeral of my poor old aunt, who died on Thursday. I own I am thankful that the good creature has ended all her days of suffering and infirmity. She was to me the "cherisher of infancy," and one must fall on those occasions into reflections, which it would be commonplace to enumerate, concerning death, "of chance and change, and fate in human life." Good God, who could have foreseen all this but four months back! I had reckoned, in particular, on my aunt's living many years; she was a very hearty old woman. But she was a mere skeleton before she died, looked more like a corpse that had lain weeks in the grave, than one fresh dead. "Truly the light is sweet, and a pleasant thing it is for the eyes to behold the sun; but if a man live many years and rejoice in them all, yet let him remember the days of darkness, for they shall be many." Coleridge, why are we to live on after all the strength and beauty of existence is gone, when all the life of life is fled, as poor Burns expresses it? Tell Lloyd I have had thoughts of turning Quaker, and have been reading, or am rather just beginning to read, a most capital book, good thoughts in good language, William Penn's *No Cross, no Crown.* I like it immensely. Unluckily I went to one of his meetings, tell him, in St. John Street, yesterday, and saw a man under all the agitations and workings of a fanatic, who believed himself under the influence of some "inevitable presence." This cured me of Quakerism. I love it in the books of Penn and Woolman; but I detest the vanity of a man thinking he speaks by the Spirit, when what he says an ordinary man might say without all that quaking and trembling. In the midst of his inspiration (and the effects of it were most noisy) was handed into the midst of the meeting a most terrible blackguard Wapping sailor. The poor man, I believe, had rather have been in the hottest part of an engagement, for the congregation of broad-brims, together with the ravings of the prophet, were too much for his gravity, though I saw even he had delicacy enough not to laugh out. And the inspired gentleman, though his manner was so supernatural, yet neither talked nor professed to talk anything more than

good sober sense, common morality, with now and then a declaration of
not speaking from himself. Among other things, looking back to his childhood and early youth, he told the meeting what a graceless young dog he
had been; that in his youth he had a good share of wit. Reader, if thou
hadst seen the gentleman, thou wouldst have sworn that it must indeed
have been many years ago, for his rueful physiognomy would have scared
away the playful goddess from the meeting, where he presided, for ever.
A wit! a wit! what could he mean? Lloyd, it minded me of *Falkland* in
the *Rivals*, "Am I full of wit and humour? No, indeed you are not. Am
I the life and soul of every company I come into? No, it cannot be said
you are." That hard-faced gentleman, a wit! Why, Nature wrote on his
fanatic forehead fifty years ago, "Wit never comes, that comes to all." I
should be as scandalised at a *bon mot* issuing from his oracle-looking
mouth, as to see Cato go down a country dance. God love you all! You
are very good to submit to be pleased with reading my nothings. 'Tis the
privilege of friendship to talk nonsense, and to have her nonsense respected.—Yours ever,   C. LAMB.

LETTER XXIV.]   *April* 7, 1797.

Your last letter was dated the 10th of February; in it you promised to
write again the next day. At least, I did not expect so long, so unfriend-
like a silence. There was a time, Col., when a remissness of this sort in a
dear friend would have lain very heavy on my mind; but latterly I have
been too familiar with neglect to feel much from the semblance of it. Yet,
to suspect one's self overlooked, and in the way to oblivion, is a feeling
rather humbling; perhaps, as tending to self-mortification, not unfavourable to the spiritual state. Still, as you meant to confer no benefit on the
soul of your friend, you do not stand quite clear from the imputation of
unkindliness (a word, by which I mean the diminutive of unkindness).

Lloyd tells me he has been very ill, and was on the point of leaving you.
I addressed a letter to him at Birmingham: perhaps he got it not, and is
still with you. I hope his ill-health has not prevented his attending to a
request I made in it, that he would write again very soon to let me know
how he was. I hope to God poor Lloyd is not very bad, or in a very bad
way. Pray satisfy me about these things.

And then David Hartley was unwell; and how is the small philosopher,
the minute philosopher? and David's mother? Coleridge, I am not
trifling; nor are these matter-of-fact questions only. You are all very dear
and precious to me. Do what you will, Coleridge, you may hurt me and
vex me by your silence, but you cannot estrange my heart from you all.
I cannot scatter friendships like chuck-farthings, nor let them drop from
mine hand like hour-glass sand. I have but two or three people in the
world to whom I am more than indifferent, and I can't afford to whistle
them off to the winds.

By the way, Lloyd may have told you about my sister. I told him. If
not, I have taken her out of her confinement, and taken a room for her at
Hackney, and spend my Sundays, holidays, etc., with her. She boards

herself. In a little half-year's illness, and in such an illness, of such a nature, and of such consequences, to get her out into the world again, with a prospect of her never being so ill again,—this is to be ranked not among the common blessings of Providence. May that merciful God make tender my heart, and make me as thankful, as in my distress I was earnest, in my prayers. Congratulate me on an ever-present and never-alienable friend like her. And do, do insert, if you have not *lost*, my Dedication. It will have lost half its value by coming so late. If you really are going on with that volume, I shall be enabled in a day or two to send you a short poem to insert. Now, do answer this. Friendship, and acts of friendship, should be reciprocal, and free as the air. A friend should never be reduced to beg an alms of his fellow; yet I will beg an alms: I entreat you to write, and tell me all about poor Lloyd, and all of you. God love and preserve you all!   C. LAMB.

LETTER XXV.]   *April* 15, 1797.

The above you will please to print immediately before the blank verse fragments. Tell me if you like it. I fear the latter half is unequal to the former, in parts of which I think you will discover a delicacy of pencilling not quite un-Spenser-like. The latter half aims at the *measure*, but has failed to attain the *poetry* of Milton in his *Comus*, and Fletcher in that exquisite thing ycleped the *Faithful Shepherdess*, where they both use eight-syllable lines. But this latter half was finished in great haste, and as a task, not from that impulse which affects the name of inspiration.

By the way, I have lit upon Fairfax's *Godfrey of Bullen*, for half-a-crown. Rejoice with me.

Poor dear Lloyd! I had a letter from him yesterday; his state of mind is truly alarming. He has, by his own confession, kept a letter of mine unopened three weeks; afraid, he says, to open it, lest I should speak upbraidingly to him; and yet this very letter of mine was in answer to one, wherein he informed me that an alarming illness had alone prevented him from writing. You will pray with me, I know, for his recovery; for surely, Coleridge, an exquisiteness of feeling like this must border on derangement. But I love him more and more, and will not give up the hope of his speedy recovery, as he tells me he is under Dr. Darwin's regimen.

God bless us all, and shield us from insanity, which is "the sorest malady of all."

My kind love to your wife and child.   C. LAMB.
Pray write now.

LETTER XXVI.]   *June* 13, 1797.

I stared with wild wonderment to see thy well-known hand again. It revived many a pleasing recollection of an epistolary intercourse, of late strangely suspended, once the pride of my life. Before I even opened thy letter I figured to myself a sort of complacency which my little hoard at home would feel at receiving the newcomer into the little drawer where I keep my treasures of this kind. You have done well in writing to me. The little room (was it not a little one?) at the *Salutation* was already in the way of becoming a fading idea! It had begun to be classed in my memory with those "wanderings with a fair-hair'd maid," in the recollection of which I feel I have no property. You press me, very kindly do you press me, to come to Stowey. Obstacles, strong as death, prevent me at present; maybe I may be able to come before the year is out. Believe me, I will come as soon as I can; but I dread naming a probable time. It depends on fifty things, besides the expense, which is not nothing. Lloyd wants me to come to see him; but, besides that you have a prior claim on me, I should not feel myself so much at home with him, till he gets a house of his own. As to Richardson, caprice may grant what caprice only refused; and it is no more hardship, rightly considered, to be dependent on him for pleasure, than to lie at the mercy of the rain and sunshine for the enjoyment of a holiday: in either case we are not to look for a suspension of the laws of Nature. "Gryll will be Gryll." Vide Spenser.

I could not but smile at the compromise you make with me for printing Lloyd's poems first; but there is in nature, I fear, too many tendencies to envy and jealousy not to justify you in your apology. Yet, if any one is welcome to pre-eminence from me, it is Lloyd, for he would be the last to desire it. So pray, let his name *uniformly* precede mine, for it would be treating me like a child to suppose it could give me pain. Yet, alas! I am not insusceptible of the bad passions. Thank God, I have the ingenuousness to be ashamed of them. I am dearly fond of Charles Lloyd; he is all goodness; and I have too much of the world in my composition to feel myself thoroughly deserving of his friendship.

Lloyd tells me that Sheridan put you upon writing your tragedy. I hope you are only Coleridgeising when you talk of finishing it in a few days. Shakspeare was a more modest man; but you best know your own power.

Of my last poem you speak slightingly. Surely the longer stanzas were pretty tolerable: at least there was one good line in it,

"Thick-shaded trees, with dark green leaf rich clad."

To adopt your own expression, I call this a "rich" line, a fine full line. And some others I thought even beautiful. Believe me, my little gentleman will feel some repugnance at riding behind in the basket; though, I confess, in pretty good company. Your picture of idiocy, with the sugarloaf head, is exquisite; but are you not too severe upon our more favoured brethren in fatuity? Lloyd tells me how ill your wife and child have been. I rejoice that they are better. My kindest remembrances, and those of my sister. I send you a trifling letter; but you have only to think that I have been skimming the superficies of my mind, and found it only froth.

Now, do write again! You cannot believe how I long and love always to hear about you. Yours most affectionately,

CHARLES LAMB.

Monday Night.

LETTER XXVII.]   *June* 24, 1797.

Did you seize the grand opportunity of seeing Kosciusko while he was at Bristol? I never saw a hero; I wonder how they look. I have been reading a most curious romance-like work, called the *Life of John Buncle, Esq.* 'Tis very interesting, and an extraordinary compound of all manner of subjects, from the depth of the ludicrous to the heights of sublime religious truth. There is much abstruse science in it above my cut, and an infinite fund of pleasantry. John Buncle is a famous fine man, formed in Nature's most eccentric hour. I am ashamed of what I write; but I have no topic to talk of. I see nobody. I sit and read, or walk alone, and hear nothing. I am quite lost to conversation from disuse; and out of the sphere of my little family (who, I am thankful, are dearer and dearer to me every day) I see no face that brightens up at my approach. My friends are at a distance. Worldly hopes are at a low ebb with me, and unworldly thoughts are familiarised to me, though I occasionally indulge in them. Still I feel a calm not unlike content. I fear it is sometimes more akin to physical stupidity than to a heaven-flowing serenity and peace. What right have I to obtrude all this upon you? and what is such a letter to you? and if I come to Stowey, what conversation can I furnish to compensate my friend for those stores of knowledge and of fancy; those delightful treasures of wisdom which I know he will open to me? But it is better to give than to receive; and I was a very patient hearer and docile scholar, in our winter evening meetings at Mr. May's; was I not, Col.? What I have owed to thee, my heart can ne'er forget.

God love you and yours!   C. L.

Saturday.

LETTER XXVIII.]   *July* 1797.

I discern a possibility of my paying you a visit next week. May I, can I, shall I come so soon? Have you *room* for me, *leisure* for me? and are you pretty well? Tell me all this honestly—immediately. And by what *day* coach could I come soonest and nearest to Stowey? A few months hence may suit you better; certainly me, as well. If so, say so. I long, I yearn, with all the longings of a child do I desire to see you, to come among you—to see the young philosopher, to thank Sara for her last year's invitation in person—to read your tragedy—to read over together our little book—to breathe fresh air—to revive in me vivid images of *"Salutation* scenery." There is a sort of sacrilege in my letting such ideas slip out of my mind and memory. Still that Richardson remaineth—a thorn in the side of Hope, when she would lean towards Stowey. Here I will leave off, for I dislike to fill up this paper (which involves a question so connected with my heart and soul) with meaner matter, or subjects to me less interesting. I can talk, as I can think, nothing else.

Thursday. C. LAMB.

LETTER XXIX.] (*Late in*) *July* 1797.

I am scarcely yet so reconciled to the loss of you, or so subsided into my wonted uniformity of feeling, as to sit calmly down to think of you and write to you. But I reason myself into the belief that those few and pleasant holidays shall not have been spent in vain. I feel improvement in the recollection of many a casual conversation. The names of Tom Poole, of Wordsworth and his good sister, with thine and Sara's, are become "familiar in my mouth as household words." You would make me very happy if you think W. has no objection, by transcribing for me that Inscription of his. I have some scattered sentences ever floating in my memory, teasing me that I cannot remember more of it. You may believe I will make no improper use of it. Believe me I can think now of many subjects on which I had planned gaining information from you; but I forgot my "treasure's worth" while I possessed it. Your leg is now become to me a matter of much more importance; and many a little thing, which when I was present with you seemed scarce to *indent* my notice, now presses painfully on my remembrance. Is the Patriot come? Are Wordsworth and his sister gone yet? I was looking out for John Thelwall all the way from Bridgewater; and had I met him, I think it would have moved almost me to tears. You will oblige me, too, by sending me my great-coat, which I left behind in the oblivious state the mind is thrown into at parting. Is it not ridiculous that I sometimes envy that great-coat lingering so cunningly behind! At present I have none: so send it to me by a Stowey waggon, if there be such a thing, directing for C. L., No. 45, Chapel Street, Pentonville, near London. But above all, *that Inscription!* It will recall to me the tones of all your voices, and with them many a remembered kindness to one who could and can repay you all only by the silence of a grateful heart. I could not talk much while I was with you; but my silence was not sullenness, nor I hope from any bad motive; but, in truth, disuse has made me awkward at it. I know I behaved myself, particularly at Tom Poole's, and at Cruikshank's, most like a sulky child; but company and converse are strange to me. It was kind in you all to endure me as you did.

Are you and your dear Sara—to me also very dear, because very kind —agreed yet about the management of little Hartley? And how go on the little rogue's teeth! I will see White to-morrow and he shall send you information on that matter; but as perhaps I can do it as well, after talking with him, I will keep this letter open.

My love and thanks to you and all of you. C. L.

Wednesday Evening.

LETTER XXX.]   *September* 1797.

WRITTEN A TWELVEMONTH AFTER THE EVENTS.

[*Friday next, Coleridge, is the day on which my Mother died.*]

Alas! how I am changed! Where be the tears
The sobs, and forced suspensions of the breath
And all the dull desertions of the heart
With which I hung o'er my dear mother's corse?
Where be the blest subsidings of the storm
Within; the sweet resignedness of hope
Drawn heavenward, and strength of filial love,
In which I bow'd me to my Father's will?
My God and my Redeemer, keep not thou
My heart in brute and sensual thanklessness
Seal'd up, oblivious ever of that dear grace,
And health restor'd to my long-loved friend,
Long-lov'd, and worthy known! Thou didst not leave
Her soul in death. O leave not now, my Lord,
Thy servants in far worse—in spiritual death
And darkness—blacker than those feared shadows
O' the valley all must tread. Lend us thy balms,
Thou dear Physician of the sin-sick soul,
And heal our cleansed bosoms of the wounds
With which the world hath pierc'd us thro' and thro'!
Give us new flesh, new birth; Elect of heaven
May we become, in thine election sure
Contain'd, and to one purpose steadfast drawn—
Our souls' salvation.
             Thou and I, dear friend,
With filial recognition sweet, shall know
One day the face of our dear mother in heaven,
And her remember'd looks of love shall greet
With answering looks of love, her placid smiles
Meet with a smile as placid, and her hand
With drops of fondness wet, nor fear repulse.

Be witness for me, Lord, I do not ask
Those days of vanity to return again
(Nor fitting me to ask, nor thee to give),
Vain loves, and "wanderings with a fair-hair'd maid;"
(Child of the dust as I am), who so long
My foolish heart steep'd in idolatry,
And creature-loves. Forgive it, O my Maker!
If in a mood of grief, I sin almost
In sometimes brooding on the days long past,
(And from the grave of time wishing them back),
Days of a mother's fondness to her child—
Her little one! Oh, where be now those sports
And infant play-games? Where the joyous troops
Of children, and the haunts I did so love?
O my companions! O ye loved names
Of friend, or playmate dear, gone are ye now.
Gone divers ways; to honour and credit some;
And some, I fear, to ignominy and shame!
I only am left, with unavailing grief

One parent dead to mourn, and see one live
Of all life's joys bereft, and desolate:
Am left, with a few friends, and one above
The rest, found faithful in a length of years,
Contented as I may, to bear me on,
T' the not unpeaceful evening of a day
Made black by morning storms.

The following I wrote when I had returned from Charles Lloyd, leaving him behind at Burton, with Southey. To understand some of it you must remember that at that time he was very much perplexed in mind.

A stranger, and alone, I pass'd those scenes
We pass'd so late together; and my heart
Felt something like desertion, as I look'd
Around me, and the pleasant voice of friend
Was absent, and the cordial look was there
No more, to smile on me. I thought on Lloyd—
All he had been to me! And now I go
Again to mingle with a world impure;
With men who make a mock of holy things,
Mistaken, and of man's best hope think scorn.
The world does much to warp the heart of man;
And I may sometimes join its idiot laugh:
Of this I now complain not. Deal with me,
Omniscient Father, as thou judgest best,
And in *thy* season soften thou my heart.
I pray not for myself: I pray for him
Whose soul is sore perplexed. Shine thou on him,
Father of lights! and in the difficult paths
Make plain his way before him: his own thoughts
May he not think—his own ends not pursue—
So shall he best perform thy will on earth.
Greatest and Best, Thy will be ever ours!

The former of these poems I wrote with unusual celerity t'other morning at office. I expect you to like it better than anything of mine; Lloyd does, and I do myself.

You use Lloyd very ill, never writing to him. I tell you again that his is not a mind with which you should play tricks. He deserves more tenderness from you.

For myself, I must spoil a little passage of Beaumont and Fletcher's to adapt it to my feelings:—

"I am prouder
That I was once your friend, tho' now forgot,
Than to have had another true to me."

If you don't write to me now, as I told Lloyd, I shall get angry, and call you hard names—Manchineel, and I don't know what else. I wish you would send me my great-coat. The snow and the rain season is at hand, and I have but a wretched old coat, once my father's, to keep 'em off, and that is transitory.

"When time drives flocks from field to fold,
When ways grow foul and blood gets cold,"

I shall remember where I left my coat. Meet emblem wilt thou be, old
Winter, of a friend's neglect—cold, cold, cold!   C. LAMB.

LETTER XXXI.]   *January* 28, 1798.

You have writ me many kind letters, and I have answered none of
them. I don't deserve your attentions. An unnatural indifference has
been creeping on me since my last misfortunes, or I should have seized
the first opening of a correspondence with *you*. To you I owe much, under
God. In my brief acquaintance with you in London, your conversations
won me to the better cause, and rescued me from the polluting spirit of
the world. I might have been a worthless character without you; as it is,
I do possess a certain improvable portion of devotional feelings, tho'
when I view myself in the light of divine truth, and not according to the
common measures of human judgment, I am altogether corrupt and sinful. This is no cant. I am very sincere.

These last afflictions, Coleridge, have failed to soften and bend my
will. They found me unprepared. My former calamities produced in me
a spirit of humility and a spirit of prayer. I thought they had sufficiently
disciplined me; but the event ought to humble me. If God's judgment now
fail to take away from me the heart of stone, what more grievous trials
ought I not to expect? I have been very querulous, impatient under the
rod—full of little jealousies and heart-burnings. I had well-nigh quarrelled with Charles Lloyd; and for no other reason, I believe, than that
the good creature did all he could to make me happy. The truth is, I
thought he tried to force my mind from its natural and proper bent. He
continually wished me to be from home; he was drawing me *from* the consideration of my poor dear Mary's situation, rather than assisting me to
gain a proper view of it with religious consolations. I wanted to be left to
the tendency of my own mind, in a solitary state, which in times past, I
knew had led to quietness and a patient bearing of the yoke. He was hurt
that I was not more constantly with him; but he was living with White,
a man to whom I had never been accustomed to impart my *dearest feelings*, tho' from long habits of friendliness, and many a social and good
quality, I loved him very much. I met company there sometimes—indiscriminate company. Any society almost, when I am in affliction, is
sorely painful to me. I seem to breathe more freely, to think more col-
lectedly, to feel more properly and calmly, when alone. All these things
the good creature did with the kindest intentions in the world, but they
produced in me nothing but soreness and discontent. I became, as he
complained, "jaundiced" towards him . . . but he has forgiven me; and
his smile, I hope, will draw all such humours from me. I am recovering,
God be praised for it, a healthiness of mind, something like calmness;
but I want more religion. I am jealous of human helps and leaning-places.
I rejoice in your good fortunes. May God at the last settle you!—You
have had many and painful trials; humanly speaking they are going to
end; but we should rather pray that discipline may attend us thro' the
whole of our lives. . . . A careless and a dissolute spirit has advanced upon

me with large strides. Pray God that my present afflictions may be sanctified to me! Mary is recovering; but I see no opening yet of a situation for her. Your invitation went to my very heart; but you have a power of exciting interest, of leading all hearts captive, too forcible to admit of Mary's being with you. I consider her as perpetually on the brink of madness. I think you would almost make her dance within an inch of the precipice; she must be with duller fancies, and cooler intellects. I know a young man of this description, who has suited her these twenty years, and may live to do so still, if we are one day restored to each other. In answer to your suggestions of occupation for me, I must say that I do not think my capacity altogether suited for disquisitions of that kind. . . . I have read little, I have a very weak memory, and retain little of what I read; am unused to compositions in which any methodising is required; but I thank you sincerely for the hint, and shall receive it as far as I am able; that is, endeavour to engage my mind in some constant and inno-cent pursuit. I know my capacities better than you do.

Accept my kindest love, and believe me yours, as ever.

C. L.

S. T. Coleridge,
at the Reverend A. Rowe's,
Shrewsbury.

To ROBERT SOUTHEY.

LETTER XXXII.] *July 28, 1798.*

Dear Southey—I am ashamed that I have not thanked you before this for the *Joan of Arc,* but I did not know your address, and it did not occur to me to write through Cottle. The poem delighted me, and the notes amused me; but methinks she of Neufchatel, in the print, holds her sword too "like a dancer." I sent your *notice* to Phillips, particularly requesting an immediate insertion, but I suppose it came too late. I am sometimes curious to know what progress you make in that same "Calendar": whether you insert the nine worthies and Whittington? what you do or how you can manage when two Saints meet and quarrel for precedency? Martlemas, and Candlemas, and Christmas, are glorious themes for a writer like you, antiquity-bitten, smit with the love of boars' heads and rosemary; but how you can ennoble the 1st of April I know not. By the way, I had a thing to say, but a certain false modesty has hitherto prevented me: perhaps I can best communicate my wish by a hint. My birthday is on the 10th of February, New Style; but if it interferes with any remarkable event, why rather than my country should lose her fame, I care not if I put my nativity back eleven days. Fine family patronage for your "Calendar," if that old lady of prolific memory were living, who lies (or lyes) in some church in London (saints forgive me, but I have forgot *what* church), attesting that enormous legend of as many children as days in the year. I marvel her impudence did not grasp at a leap-year. Three hundred and sixty-five dedications, and all in a family! You might spit, in spirit, on the oneness of Mæcenas's patronage!

Samuel Taylor Coleridge, to the eternal regret of his native Devonshire, emigrates to Westphalia: "Poor Lamb" (these were his last words), "if he wants any *knowledge*, he may apply to me." In ordinary cases I thanked him. I have an "Encyclopædia" at hand; but on such an occasion as going over to a German university, I could not refrain from sending him the following propositions, to be by him defended or oppugned (or both) at Leipsic or Göttingen.

THESES QUÆDAM THEOLOGICÆ.

I.

"Whether God loves a lying angel better than a true man?"

II.

"Whether the archangel Uriel *could* knowingly affirm an untruth, and whether, if he *could,* he *would?*"

III.

"Whether honesty be an angelic virtue, or not rather belonging to that class of qualities which the schoolmen term 'virtutes minus splendidæ, et hominis et terræ nimis participes'?"

IV.

"Whether the seraphim ardentes do not manifest their goodness by the way of vision and theory? and whether practice be not a sub-celestial, and merely human virtue?"

V.

"Whether the higher order of seraphim illuminati ever *sneer?*"

VI.

"Whether pure intelligences can *love*, or whether they can love anything besides pure intellect?"

VII.

"Whether the beatific vision be anything more or less than a perpetual representment to each individual angel of his own present attainments, and future capabilities, something in the manner of mortal looking-glasses?"

VIII.

"Whether an 'immortal and amenable soul' may not come *to be damned at last, and the man never suspect it beforehand?*"

Samuel Taylor Coleridge hath not deigned an answer. Was it impertinent of me to avail myself of that offered source of knowledge?
Wishing *Madoc* may be born into the world with as splendid promise

as the second birth, or purification, of the Maid of Neufchatel,—I remain
yours sincerely,   C. LAMB.

I hope Edith is better; my kindest remembrances to her. You have a
good deal of trifling to forgive in this letter.
"Love and remembrances to Cottle."

LETTER XXXIII.]   *October* 18, 1798.

Dear Southey—I have at last been so fortunate as to pick up Wither's
Emblems for you, that "old book and quaint," as the brief author of
Rosamund Gray hath it; it is in a most detestable state of preservation,
and the cuts are of a fainter impression than I have seen. Some child, the
curse of antiquaries and bane of bibliopical rarities, hath been dabbling
in some of them with its paint and dirty fingers; and, in particular, hath
a little sullied the author's own portraiture, which I think valuable, as
the poem that accompanies it is no common one; this last excepted, the
the Emblems are far inferior to old Quarles. I once told you otherwise,
but I had not then read old Quarles with attention. I have picked up, too,
another copy of Quarles for ninepence!!! O tempora! O lectores! so
that if you have lost or parted with your own copy, say so, and I can
furnish you, for you prize these things more than I do. You will be
amused, I think, with honest Wither's "Supersedeas to all them whose
custom it is, without any deserving, to importune authors to give unto
them their books." I am sorry 'tis imperfect, as the lottery board annexed to it also is. Methinks you might modernise and elegantise this
Supersedeas, and place it in front of your *Joan of Arc*, as a gentle hint to
Messrs. Parke, etc. One of the happiest emblems, and comicalest cuts,
is the owl and little chirpers, page 63.
Wishing you all amusement, which your true emblem-fancier can
scarce fail to find in even bad emblems, I remain your caterer to command,   C. LAMB.

Love and respects to Edith. I hope she is well. How does your Calendar prosper?

LETTER XXXIV.]   *October* 29, 1798.

Dear Southey—I thank you heartily for the Eclogue; it pleases me
mightily, being so full of picture work and circumstances. I find no fault
in it, unless perhaps that Joanna's ruin is a catastrophe too trite; and
this is not the first or second time you have clothed your indignation, in
verse, in a tale of ruined innocence. The old lady, spinning in the sun, I
hope would not disdain to claim some kindred with old Margaret. I could
almost wish you to vary some circumstances in the conclusion. A gentleman seducer has so often been described in prose and verse. What if you
had accomplished Joanna's ruin by the clumsy arts and rustic gifts of
some country-fellow? I am thinking, I believe, of the song—

"An old woman clothed in gray,
 Whose daughter was charming and young,
  And she was deluded away
  By Roger's false flattering tongue."

A Roger-Lothario would be a novel character; I think you might paint him very well. You may think this is a very silly suggestion, and so indeed it is; but, in good truth, nothing else but the first words of that foolish ballad put me upon scribbling my *Rosamund*. But I thank you heartily for the poem. Not having anything of my own to send you in return (though, to tell truth, I am at work upon something, which, if I were to cut away and garble, perhaps I might send you an extract or two that might not displease you; but I will not do that; and whether it will come to anything I know not, for I am as slow as a Fleming painter, when I compose anything) I will crave leave to put down a few lines of old Christopher Marlow's; I take them from his tragedy, *Jew of Malta*. The Jew is a famous character, quite out of nature; but, when we consider the terrible idea our simple ancestors had of a Jew, not more to be discommended for a certain discolouring (I think Addison calls it) than the witches and fairies of Marlow's mighty successor. The scene is betwixt *Barabbas*, the Jew, and *Ithamore*, a Turkish captive, exposed to sale for a slave.

BARABBAS.

(*A precious rascal.*)

"As for myself, I walk abroad a-nights,
 And kill sick people groaning under walls;
 Sometimes I go about, and poison wells;
 And now and then, to cherish Christian thieves,
 I am content to lose some of my crowns,
 That I may, walking in my gallery,
 See 'm go pinion'd along by my door.
 Being young, I studied physic, and began
 To practise first upon the Italian:
 There I enrich'd the priests with burials,
 And always kept the sexton's arms in use
 With digging graves, and ringing dead men's knells
 And after that was I an engineer,
 And in the wars 'twixt France and Germany,
 Under pretence of serving Charles the Fifth,
 Slew friends and enemy with my stratagems.
 Then after that was I an usurer,
 And with extorting, cozening, forfeiting,
 And tricks belong unto brokery,
 I fill'd the jails with bankrupts in a year,
 And with young orphans planted hospitals,
 And every moon made some or other mad,
 And now and then one hang himself for grief,
 Pinning upon his breast a long great scroll,
 How I with interest had tormented him."

(Now hear Ithamore, the other gentle nature.)

ITHAMORE.

(A comical dog.)

"Faith, master, and I have spent my time
In setting Christian villages on fire,
Chaining of eunuchs, binding galley slaves.
One time I was an hostler at an inn,
And in the night time secretly would I steal
To travellers' chambers, and there cut their throats.
Once at Jerusalem, where the pilgrims kneel'd,
I strew'd powder on the marble stones,
And therewithal their knees would rankle so,
That I have laugh'd a good to see the cripples
Go limping home to Christendom on stilts."

BARABBAS.

"Why, this is something."

There is a mixture of the ludicrous and the terrible in these lines, brimful of genius and antique invention, that at first reminded me of your old description of cruelty in hell, which was in the true Hogarthian style. I need not tell *you* that Marlow was author of that pretty madrigal, "Come live with me and be my Love," and of the tragedy of Edward II., in which are certain *lines* unequalled in our English tongue. Honest Walton mentions the said madrigal under the denomination of "certain smooth verses made long since by Kit Marlow."

I am glad you have put me on the scent after old Quarles. If I do not put up those eclogues, and that shortly, say I am no true-nosed hound. I have had a letter from Lloyd; the young metaphysician of Caius is well, and is busy recanting the new heresy, metaphysics, for the old dogma, Greek. My sister, I thank you, is quite well. She had a slight attack the other day, which frightened me a good deal, but it went off unaccountably. Love and respects to Edith.

Yours sincerely,   C. LAMB.

To ROBERT LLOYD

LETTER XXXV.]   *October* 1798.

My dear Robert—I am a good deal occupied with a calamity near home, but not so much as to prevent my thinking about you with the warmest affection—you are among my very dearest friends. I know you will feel deeply when you hear that my poor sister is unwell again; one of her old disorders, but I trust it will hold no longer than her former illnesses have done. Do not imagine, Robert, that I sink under this misfortune; I have been season'd to such events, and think I could bear anything tolerably well. My own health is left me, and my good spirits, and I have some duties to perform—these duties shall be *my object.* I wish, Robert, *you* could find an object. I know the painfulness of vacuity, all its achings and inexplicable longings. I wish to God I could recommend any plan to you. Stock your mind well with religious knowledge; discipline it to wait with patience for duties that may be your lot in life; prepare yourself not to expect too much out of yourself; *read* and *think*. This is all commonplace advice, I know. I know, too, that it is easy to give advice which in like circumstances we might not follow ourselves. You must depend upon yourself—there will come a time when you will wonder you were not more content. I know you will excuse my saying any more.

Be assured of my kindest, warmest affection.

C. LAMB.

LETTER XXXVI.]   *October (later)* 1798.

My dear Robert—Mary is better, and I trust that she will yet be restored to me. I am in good spirits, so do not be anxious about me. I hope you get reconciled to your situation. The worst in it is that you have no *friend* to talk to—but wait in patience, and you will in good time make friends. The having a friend is not indispensably necessary to virtue or happiness. Religion removes those barriers of sentiment which partition us from the disinterested love of our brethren—we are commanded to love our enemies, to do good to those that hate us; how much more is it our duty then to cultivate a forbearance and complacence towards those who only differ from us in dispositions and ways of thinking? There is always, without very unusual care there must always be, something of Self in friendship; we love our friend because he is like ourselves; can consequences altogether unmix'd and pure be reasonably expected from such a source—do not even the publicans and sinners the same? Say, that you love a friend for his moral qualities, is it not rather because those qualities resemble what you fancy your own? This, then, is not without danger. The only true cement of a valuable friendship, the only thing that even makes it not sinful, is when two friends propose to become mutually of benefit to each other in a moral or religious way. But even this friendship is perpetually liable to the mixture of something not pure; we love our friend, because he is *ours*—so we do our money, our wit, our knowledge, our virtue; and wherever this sense of APPROPRIATION and PROPERTY enters, so much is to be subtracted from the value of that friendship or that virtue. Our duties are to do good, expecting nothing again; to bear with contrary dispositions; to be candid and forgiving, not to crave and long after a communication of sentiment and feeling, but rather to avoid dwelling upon those feelings, however good, because they are our own. A man may be intemperate and selfish who indulges in *good feelings* for the mere pleasure they give him. I do not wish to deter you from making a friend, a true friend, and such a friendship, where the parties are not blind to each other's faults, is very useful and valuable. I perceive a tendency in you to this error, Robert. I know you have chosen to take up an high opinion of my moral worth, but I say it before God, and I do not lie, you are mistaken in me. I could not bear to lay open all my failings to you, for the sentiment of shame would be too pungent. Let this be as an example to you. Robert, friends fall off, friends mistake us, they change, they grow unlike us, they go away, they die; but God is everlasting and incapable of change, and to Him we may look with cheerful, unpresumptuous hope, while we discharge the duties of life in situations more untowardly than yours. You complain of the impossibility of improving yourself, but be assured that the opportunity of improvement lies more in the mind than the situation. Humble yourself before God, cast out the selfish principle, wait in patience, do good in every way you can to all sorts of people, never be easy to neglect a duty tho' a small one, praise God for all, and see His hand in all things, and He will in time raise you up *many friends*—or be Himself instead an unchanging friend. God bless you. C. LAMB.

LETTER XXXVII.] *October (later)* 1798.

My dear Robert—I acknowledge I have been sadly remiss of late. If I descend to any excuse (and all excuses that come short of a direct denial of a charge are poor creatures at best), it must be taken from my state of mind for some time past, which has been stupid rather, and unfilled with any object, than occupied, as you may imagine, with any favourite idea to the exclusion of friend Robert. You, who are subject to all the varieties of the mind, will give me credit in this.

I am sadly sorry that you are relapsing into your old complaining strain. I wish I could adapt my consolations to your disease, but, alas! I have none to offer which your own mind, and the suggestions of books, cannot better supply. Are you the first whose situation hath not been exactly squar'd to his ideas? or rather, will you find me that man who does not complain of the one thing wanting? That thing obtained, another wish will start up. While this eternal craving of the mind keeps up its eternal hunger, no feast that my palate knows of will satisfy that hunger till we come to drink the new wine (whatever it be) in the Kingdom of the Father. See what trifles disquiet us.—You are Unhappy because your Parents expect you to attend meetings. I don't know much of Quakers' meetings, but I believe I may moderately reckon them to take up the space of six hours in the week. Six hours to please your parents—and that time not absolutely lost. Your mind remains, you may think, and plan, remember, and foresee, and do all human acts of mind sitting as well as walking. You are quiet at meeting: one likes to be so sometimes; you may advantageously crowd your day's devotions into that space. Nothing you see or hear there can be unfavourable to it—you are for that time at least exempt from the counting-house, and your parents cannot chide you there; surely at so small expense you cannot grudge to observe the Fifth Commandment. I decidedly consider your refusal as a breach of that God-descended precept—Honour and observe thy parents in all lawful things. Silent worship cannot be *Un*lawful; there is no Idolatry, no invocation of saints, no bowing before the consecrated wafer in all this, nothing which a wise man would refuse, or a good man fear to do. What is it? Sitting a few hours in a week with certain good people who call *that* worship. You subscribe to no articles—if your mind wanders, it is no crime in you who do not give credit to these infusions of the spirit. They sit in a temple, you sit as in a room adjoining, only do not disturb their pious work with gabbling, nor your own necessary peace with heart-burnings at your not ill-meaning parents, nor a silly contempt of the work which is going on before you. I know that if my parents were to live again, I would do more things to please them than merely sitting still six hours in a week. Perhaps I enlarge too much on this affair, but indeed your objection seems to me ridiculous, and involving in it a principle of frivolous and vexatious resistance.

You have often borne with my freedoms, bear with me once more in this. If I did not love you, I should not trouble myself whether you went to meeting or not—whether you conform'd or not to the will of your father.

I am now called off to dinner before one o'clock; being a holyday we dine early, for Mary and me to have a long walk afterwards. My kindest remembrance to Charles.

God give him all joy and quiet.

Mary sends her LOVE. C. L.

To ROBERT SOUTHEY.

LETTER XXXVIII.]   *November* 3, 1798.

I have read your Eclogue repeatedly, and cannot call it bald, or without interest; the cast of it and the design are completely original, and may set people upon thinking. It is as poetical as the subject requires, which asks no poetry; but it is defective in pathos. The woman's own story is the tamest part of it; I should like you to remould that: it too much resembles the young maid's history; both had been in service. Even the omission would not injure the poem: after the words "growing wants," you might, not unconnectedly, introduce "look at that little chub" down to "welcome one." And, decidedly, I would have you end it somehow thus,—

> "Give them at least this evening a good meal.
>   [*Gives her money.*
> Now, fare thee well; hereafter you have taught me
> To give sad meaning to the village bells," etc.,

which would leave a stronger impression (as well as more pleasingly recall the beginning of the Eclogue) than the present commonplace reference to a better world, which the woman "must have heard at church." I should like you too a good deal to enlarge the most striking part, as it might have been, of the poem—"Is it idleness?" etc.: that affords a good field for dwelling on sickness, and inabilities, and old age. And you might also a good deal enrich the piece with a picture of a country wedding. The

woman might very well, in a transient fit of oblivion, dwell upon the ceremony and circumstances of her own nuptials six years ago, the smugness
of the bridegroom, the feastings, the cheap merriment, the welcomings,
and the secret envyings of the maidens; then dropping all this, recur to
her present lot. I do not know that I can suggest anything else, or that
I have suggested anything new or material. I do not much prefer this
Eclogue to the last. Both are inferior to the former.

> "And when he came to shake me by the hand,
> And spake as kindly to me as he used,
> I hardly knew his voice—"

is the only passage that affected me. When servants speak, their language
ought to be plain, and not much raised above the common, else I should
find fault with the pathos of this passage,—

> "And when I heard the bell strike out,
> I thought (what?) that I had never heard it toll
> So dismally before."

I like the destruction of the martins' old nests hugely, having just such
a circumstance in my memory. I shall be very glad to see your remaining
Eclogue, if not too much trouble, as you give me reason to expect it will
be the second best. I shall be very glad to see some more poetry; though,
I fear, your trouble in transcribing will be greater than the service my remarks may do them.

Yours affectionately,   C. LAMB.

I cut my letter short because I am called off to business.

LETTER XXXIX.]   *November* 8, 1798.

I perfectly accord with your opinion of old Wither; Quarles is a wittier
writer, but Wither lays more hold of the heart. Quarles thinks of his audience when he lectures; Wither soliloquizes in company from a full heart.
What wretched stuff are the "Divine Fancies" of Quarles! Religion appears to him no longer valuable than it furnishes matter for quibbles and
riddles; he turns God's grace into wantonness. Wither is like an old
friend, whose warm-heartedness and estimable qualities make us wish he
possessed more genius, but at the same time make us willing to dispense
with that want. I always love Wither, and sometimes admire Quarles.
Still that portrait poem is a fine one; and the extract from "Shepherds'
Hunting" places him in a starry height far above Quarles. If you wrote
that review in the *Critical Review*, I am sorry you are so sparing of praise
to the *Ancient Marinere*. So far from calling it as you do, with some wit,
but more severity, a "Dutch Attempt," etc., I call it a right English attempt, and a successful one, to dethrone German sublimity. You have
selected a passage fertile in unmeaning miracles, but have passed by fifty
passages as miraculous as the miracles they celebrate. I never so deeply
felt the pathetic as in that part,

> "A spring of love gush'd from my heart,
> And I bless'd them unaware."

It stung me into high pleasure through sufferings. Lloyd does not like it; his head is too metaphysical, and your taste too correct; at least I must allege something against you both, to excuse my own dotage—

> "So lonely 'twas, that God himself
> Scarce seem'd there to be!"—etc. etc.

But you allow some elaborate beauties: you should have extracted 'em. The *Ancient Marinere* plays more tricks with the mind than that last poem, which is yet one of the finest written. But I am getting too dogmatical; and before I degenerate into abuse, I will conclude with assuring you that I am

Sincerely yours,

C. Lamb.

I am going to meet Lloyd at Ware on Saturday, to return on Sunday. Have you any commands or commendations to the metaphysician? I shall be very happy if you will dine or spend any time with me in your way through the great ugly city; but I know you have other ties upon you in these parts.

Love and respects to Edith, and friendly remembrances to Cottle.

To ROBERT LLOYD.

Letter XL.]   *November* 13, 1798.

Now 'tis Robert's turn.

My dear Robert—One passage in your Letter a little displeas'd me. The rest was nothing but kindness, which Robert's letters are ever brimful of. You say that "this World to you seems drain'd of all its sweets!" At first I had hoped you only meant to insinuate the high price of Sugar! but I am afraid you meant more. O Robert, I don't know what you call sweet. Honey and the honeycomb, roses and violets, are yet in the earth. The sun and moon yet reign in Heaven, and the lesser lights keep up their pretty twinklings. Meats and drinks, sweet sights and sweet smells, a country walk, spring and autumn, follies and repentance, quarrels and reconcilements, have all a sweetness by turns. Good humour and good nature, friends at home that love you, and friends abroad that miss you, you possess all these things, and more innumerable, and these are all sweet things. . . . You may extract honey from everything; do not go a gathering after gall. The Bees are wiser in their generation than the race of sonnet writers and complainers, Bowles's and Charlotte Smiths, and all that tribe, who can see no joys but what are past, and fill people's heads with notions of the unsatisfying nature of Earthly comforts. I assure you I find this world a very pretty place. My kind love to all your Sisters and to Thomas—he never writes to me—and tell Susanna I forgive her.

C. Lamb.

London, the 13*th November* 1798.

LETTER XLI.]   *November 20, 1798.*

As the little copy of verses I sent gave Priscilla and Robert some pleasure, I now send them another little tale, which is all I can send, for my stock will be exhausted. . . . 'Tis a tale of witchcraft, told by an old Steward in the family to Margaret, the ward of Sir Walter Woodvil. *Who* Sir Walter is you may come to know bye and bye, when I have finish'd a Poem, from which this and the other are extracts, and all the extracts I can make without mutilating:

> OLD STEWARD.   One summer night Sir Walter, as it chanc'd,
> Was pacing to and fro in the avenue
> That westward fronts our house,
> Among those aged oaks said to have been planted
> Three hundred years ago
> By a neighb'ring Prior of the Woodvil name;
> But so it was,
> Being o'er task'd in thought he heeded not
> The importune suit of one who stood by the gate,
> And begg'd an alms.
> Some say, he shov'd her rudely from the gate
> With angry chiding; but I can never think,
> (Sir Walter's nature hath a sweetness in it,)
> That he could treat a woman, an old woman
> With such discourtesy,
> For old she was who begg'd an alms of him.
> Well, he refus'd her.
> (Whether for importunity I know not,
> Or that she came between his meditations,)
> But better had he met a Lion in the Streets,
> Than this old woman that night,
> For she was one who practis'd the black arts,
> And serv'd the Devil, being since burnt for witchcraft.
> She look'd at him like one that meant to blast him,
> And with a frightful noise,
> ('Twas partly like a woman's voice,
> And partly like the hissing of a snake,)
> She nothing spake but this: Sir Walter told the words
>
> "A mischief, mischief, mischief,
>   And a nine times killing curse,
> By day and by night, to the caitive wight,
> Who shakes the poor, like snakes, from his door,
>   And shuts up the womb of his purse:
>   And a mischief, mischief, mischief,
>   And a ninefold with'ring curse—
> For that shall come to thee, that will undo thee,
> Both all that thou fear'st and worst."
>
> These words four times repeated, she departed
> Leaving Sir Walter like a man, beneath
> Whose feet a scaffolding had suddenly fall'n.
> MARGARET.   A terrible curse!
> OLD STEWARD.   O Lady! such bad things are said of that
>   old woman,
> You would be loth to hear them!
> As, namely, that the milk she gave was sour,

And the babe, who suck'd her, shrivell'd like a mandrake*
And things besides, with a bigger horror in them
Almost, I think, unlawful to be told!
MARGARET. Then I must never hear them. But proceed
And say what follow'd on the witch's curse.
OLD STEWARD. Nothing immediate; but some nine months
    after
Young Stephen Woodvil suddenly fell sick,
And none could tell what ail'd him; for he lay,
And pin'd, and pin'd, till all his hair came off,
And he, that was full flesh'd, became as thin
As a two months' babe that has been starv'd in the nursing.
And sure, I think,
He bore his illness like a little child;
With such rare sweetness, and dumb melancholy,
He strove to clothe his agony in smiles,
Which he would force up in his poor pale cheeks,
Like ill-tim'd guests that had no proper dwelling there.
And, when they ask'd him his complaint, he laid
His hand upon his heart to show the place
Where Susan came to him a nights, he said,
And prick'd him with a pin.
And thereupon Sir Walter call'd to mind
The beggar witch who stood in the gateway,
And begg'd an alms.
MARGARET. And so he died?
OLD STEWARD. 'Tis thought so.
MARGARET. But did the witch confess?
OLD STEWARD. All this and more at her death.
MARGARET. I do not love to credit tales of magic.
Heav'n's music, which is order, seems unstrung,
And this brave world,
Creation's beauteous workmanship, unbeautify'd,
Disorder'd, marr'd, where such strange things are acted.

* A *mandrake* is a root resembling the human form, as sometimes a carrot does, and the old superstition is, that when the mandrake is torn out
of the earth a dreadful shriek is heard, which makes all who hear it go
mad. 'Tis a fatal poison besides.

I will here conclude my tiny portion of Prose with hoping you may like
the story, and my kind remembrances to all.   C. LAMB.

Write soon, Robert.

To ROBERT SOUTHEY.

LETTER XLII.| *November* 28, 1798.

I can have no objection to your printing "Mystery of God" with my
name, and all due acknowledgments for the honour and favour of the
communication; indeed, 'tis a poem that can dishonour no name. Now,
that is in the true strain of modern modestovanitas. . . . But for the sonnet, I heartily wish it, as I thought it was, dead and forgotten. If the exact circumstances under which I wrote could be known or told, it would
be an interesting sonnet; but to an indifferent and stranger reader it

must appear a very bald thing, certainly inadmissible in a compilation. I wish you could affix a different name to the volume. There is a contemptible book, a wretched assortment of vapid feelings, entitled *Pratt's Gleanings,* which hath damned and impropriated the title for ever. Pray think of some other. The gentleman is better known (better had he remained unknown) by an Ode to Benevolence, written and spoken for and at the annual dinner of the Humane Society, who walk in procession once a year, with all the objects of their charity before them, to return God thanks for giving them such benevolent hearts.

I like "Bishop Bruno," but not so abundantly as your "Witch Ballad," which is an exquisite thing of its kind.

I showed my "Witch" and "Dying Lover" to Dyer last night; but George could not comprehend how *that* could be poetry which did not go upon ten feet, as George and his predecessor had taught it to do; so George read me some lectures on the distinguishing qualities of the Ode, the Epigram, and the Epic, and went home to illustrate his doctrine, by correcting a proof sheet of his own Lyrics. George writes odes where the rhymes, like fashionable man and wife, keep a comfortable distance of six or eight lines apart, and calls that "observing the laws of verse!" George tells you, before he recites, that you must listen with great attention, or you'll miss the rhymes. I did so, and found them pretty exact. George, speaking of the dead Ossian, exclaimeth, "Dark are the poet's eyes!" I humbly represented to him that his own eyes were dark, and many a living bard's besides, and recommended "Closed are the poet's eyes." But that would not do. I found there was an antithesis between the darkness of his eyes and the splendour of his genius; and I acquiesced.

Your recipe for a Turk's poison is invaluable, and truly Marlowish. . . . Lloyd objects to "shutting up the womb of his purse" in my curse (which, for a Christian witch in a Christian country, is not too mild, I hope). Do you object? I think there is a strangeness in the idea, as well as "shaking the poor like snakes from his door," which suits the speaker. Witches illustrate, as fine ladies do, from their own familiar objects, and snakes and the shutting up of wombs are in their way. I don't know that this last charge has been before brought against 'em nor either the sour milk or the mandrake babe; but I affirm these be things a witch would do if she could.

My Tragedy will be a medley (as I intend it to be a medley) of laughter and tears, prose and verse, and in some places rhyme, songs, wit, pathos, humour, and, if possible, sublimity; at least it is not a fault in my intention if it does not comprehend most of these discordant atoms. Heaven send they dance not the "Dance of Death!" I hear that the Two Noble Englishmen have parted no sooner than they set foot on German earth; but I have not heard the reason. Possibly to give moralists an handle to exclaim, "Ah me! what things are perfect?" I think I shall adopt your emendation in the "Dying Lover," though I do not myself feel the objection against "Silent Prayer."

My tailor has brought me home a new coat lapelled, with a velvet collar. He assures me everybody wears velvet collars now. Some are born fashionable, some achieve fashion, and others, like your humble servant, have fashion thrust upon them. The rogue has been making inroads hitherto by modest degrees, foisting upon me an additional button, recommending gaiters; but to come upon me thus, in a full tide of luxury, neither becomes him as a tailor nor the ninth of a man. My meek gentleman was robbed the other day, coming with his wife and family in a one-horse shay from Hampstead. The villains rifled him of four guineas, some shillings and half-pence, and a bundle of customers' measures, which they swore were bank notes. They did not shoot him, and when they rode off he addrest them with profound gratitude, making a congee: "Gentlemen, I wish you good-night, and we are very much obliged to you that you have not used us ill!" And this is the cuckoo that has had the audacity to foist upon me ten buttons on a side, and a black velvet collar! A cursed ninth of a scoundrel!

When you write to Lloyd, he wishes his Jacobin correspondents to address him as *Mr.* C. L. Love and respects to Edith. I hope she is well.

Yours sincerely, C. LAMB.

LETTER XLIII.] *December 27, 1798.*

Dear Southey—Your friend John May has formerly made kind offers to Lloyd of serving me in the India House, by the interest of his friend Sir Francis Baring. It is not likely that I shall ever put his goodness to the test on my own account, for my prospects are very comfortable; but I know a man, a young man, whom he could serve through the same channel, and, I think, would be disposed to serve if he were acquainted with his case. This poor fellow (whom I know just enough of to vouch for his strict integrity and worth) has lost two or three employments from illness, which he cannot regain; he was once insane, and, from the distressful uncertainty of his livelihood, has reason to apprehend a return of that malady. He has been for some time dependent on a woman whose lodger he formerly was, but who can ill afford to maintain him; and I know that on Christmas night last he actually walked about the streets all night, rather than accept of her bed, which she offered him, and offered herself to sleep in the kitchen; and that, in consequence of that severe cold, he is labouring under a bilious disorder, besides a depression of spirits, which incapacitates him from exertion when he most needs it. For God's sake, Southey, if it does not go against you to ask favours, do it now; ask it as for me: but do not do a violence to your feelings, because he does not know of this application, and will suffer no disappointment. What I meant to say was this,—there are in the India House, what are called *extra clerks,* not on the establishment, like me, but employed in extra business, by-jobs; these get about £50 a year, or rather more, but never rise. A director can put in at any time a young man in this office, and it is by no means considered so great a favour as making an established clerk. He would think himself as rich as an emperor if he could get such a certain situation, and be relieved from those disquietudes which, I do fear, may one day bring back his distemper.

You know John May better than I do, but I know enough to believe that he is a good man. He did make me that offer I have mentioned, but you will perceive that such an offer cannot authorise me in applying for another person.

But I cannot help writing to you on the subject, for the young man is perpetually before my eyes, and I shall feel it a crime not to strain all my petty interest to do him service, though I put my own delicacy to the question by so doing. I have made one other unsuccessful attempt already. At all events I will thank you to write, for I am tormented with anxiety.   C. Lamb.

Letter XLIV.]   *January* 21, 1799.

I am requested by Lloyd to excuse his not replying to a kind letter received from you. He is at present situated in most distressful family perplexities, which I am not at liberty to explain, but they are such as to demand all the strength of his mind, and quite exclude any attention to foreign objects. His brother Robert (the flower of his family) hath eloped from the persecutions of his father, and has taken shelter with me. What the issue of his adventure will be, I know not. He hath the sweetness of an angel in his heart, combined with admirable firmness of purpose; an uncultivated, but very original, and I think superior, genius. But this step of his is but a small part of their family troubles.

I am to blame for not writing to you before on *my own account;* but I know you can dispense with the expressions of gratitude, or I should have thanked you before for all May's kindness. He has liberally supplied the person I spoke to you of with money, and had procured him a situation just after himself had lighted upon a similar one, and engaged too far to recede. But May's kindness was the same, and my thanks to you and him are the same. May went about on this business as if it had been his own. But you knew John May before this, so I will be silent.

I shall be very glad to hear from you when convenient. I do not know how your Calendar and other affairs thrive; but above all, I have not heard a great while of your "Madoc"—the *opus magnum.* I would willingly send you something to give a value to this letter; but I have only one slight passage to send you, scarce worth the sending, which I want to edge in somewhere into my play, which, by the way, hath not received the addition of ten lines, besides, since I saw you. A father, old Walter Woodvil (the witch's *protégé*), relates this of his son John, who "fought in adverse armies," being a royalist, and his father a parliamentary man:—

> "I saw him in the day of Worcester fight,
> Whither he came at twice seven years,
> Under the discipline of the Lord Falkland
> (His uncle by the mother's side,
> Who gave his youthful politics a bent

Quite *from* the principles of his father's house) ;
There did I see this valiant Lamb of Mars,
This sprig of honour, this unbearded John,
This veteran in green years, this sprout, this Woodvil
(With dreadless ease guiding a fire-hot steed,
Which seem'd to scorn the manage of a boy),
Prick forth with such a *mirth* into the field,
To mingle rivalship and acts of war
Even with the sinewy masters of the art.
You would have thought the work of blood had been
A play-game merely, and the rabid Mars
Had put his harmful hostile nature off
To instruct raw youth in images of war,
And practice of the unedged players' foils.
The rough fanatic and blood-practised soldiery
Seeing such hope and virtue in the boy,
Disclosed their ranks to let him pass unhurt,
Checking their swords' uncivil injuries,
As loth to mar that curious workmanship
Of Valour's beauty portray'd in his face."

Lloyd objects to "portray'd in his face," do you? I like the line.
I shall clap this in somewhere. I think there is a spirit through the
lines; perhaps the 7th, 8th, and 9th owe their origin to Shakspeare,
though no image is borrowed.
He says in *Henry the Fourth*—

"This infant Hotspur,
Mars in swathing clothes."

But pray did Lord Falkland die before Worcester fight? In that case I
must make bold to unclify some other nobleman.
Kind love and respects to Edith.   C. LAMB.

LETTER XLV.]   *March* 15, 1799.

Dear Southey—I have received your little volume, for which I thank
you, though I do not entirely approve of this sort of intercourse, where
the presents are all one side. I have read the last Eclogue again with great
pleasure. It hath gained considerably by abridgment, and now I think it
wants nothing but enlargement. You will call this one of tyrant Procrustes's criticisms, to cut and pull so to his own standard; but the old lady is
so great a favourite with me, I want to hear more of her; and of "Joanna"
you have given us still less. But the picture of the rustics leaning over the
bridge, and the old lady travelling abroad on summer evening to see her
garden watered, are images so new and true, that I decidedly prefer this
"Ruin'd Cottage" to any poem in the book. Indeed I think it the only one
that will bear comparison with your "Hymn to the Penates," in a former
volume.
I compare dissimilar things, as one would a rose and a star, for the
pleasure they give us, or as a child soon learns to choose between a cake
and a rattle; for dissimilars have mostly some points of comparison.
The next best poem, I think, is the first Eclogue; 'tis very complete,

and abounding in little pictures and realities. The remainder Eclogues, excepting only the "Funeral," I do not greatly admire. I miss *one*, which had at least as good a title to publication as the "Witch," or the "Sailor's Mother." You call'd it the "Last of the Family." The "Old Woman of Berkeley" comes next; in some humours I would give it the preference above any. But who the devil is Matthew of Westminster? You are as familiar with these antiquated monastics, as Swedenborg, or, as his followers affect to call him, the Baron, with his invisibles. But you have raised a very comic effect out of the true narrative of Matthew of Westminster. 'Tis surprising with how little addition you have been able to convert, with so little alteration, his incidents, meant for terror, into circumstances and food for the spleen. The Parody is *not* so successful; it has one famous line, indeed, which conveys the finest death-bed image I ever met with:—

"The doctor whisper'd the nurse, and the surgeon knew what he said."

But the offering the bribe three times bears not the slightest analogy or proportion to the fiendish noises three times heard! In "Jaspar," the circumstance of the great light is very affecting. But I had heard you mention it before. The "Rose" is the only insipid piece in the volume; it hath neither thorns nor sweetness; and, besides, sets all chronology and probability at defiance.

"Cousin Margaret," you know, I like. The allusions to the *Pilgrim's Progress* are particularly happy, and harmonise tacitly and delicately with old cousins and aunts. To familiar faces we do associate familiar scenes and accustomed objects: but what hath Apollidon and his sea-nymphs to do in these affairs? Apollyon I could have borne, though he stands for the devil; but who is Apollidon? I think you are too apt to conclude faintly, with some cold moral, as in the end of the poem called "The Victory"—

"Be thou her comforter, who art the widow's friend;"

a single commonplace line of comfort, which bears no proportion in weight or number to the many lines which describe suffering. This is to convert religion into mediocre feelings, which should burn, and glow, and tremble. A moral should be wrought into the body and soul, the matter and tendency of a poem, not tagged to the end, like a "God send the good ship into harbour," at the conclusion of our bills of lading. The finishing of the "Sailor" is also imperfect. Any dissenting minister may say and do as much.

These remarks, I know, are crude and unwrought, but I do not lay much claim to accurate thinking. I never judge system-wise of things, but fasten upon particulars. After all, there is a great deal in the book that I must, for time, leave *unmentioned*, to deserve my thanks for its own sake, as well as for the friendly remembrances implied in the gift. I again return you my thanks.

Pray present my love to Edith.   C. L.

LETTER XLVI.]   *March* 20, 1799.

I am hugely pleased with your "Spider," "your old freemason," as you call him. The first three stanzas are delicious; they seem to me a compound of Burns and Old Quarles, the kind of home-strokes, where more is felt than strikes the ear; a terseness, a jocular pathos, which makes one feel in laughter. The measure, too, is novel and pleasing. I could almost wonder Robert Burns in his lifetime never stumbled upon it. The fourth stanza is less striking, as being less original. The fifth falls off. It has no felicity of phrase, no old-fashioned phrase or feeling.

"Young hopes, and love's delightful dreams,"

savour neither of Burns nor Quarles; they seem more like shreds of many a modern sentimental sonnet. The last stanza hath nothing striking in it, if I except the two concluding lines, which are Burns all over. I wish, if you concur with me, these things could be looked to. I am sure this is a kind of writing, which comes tenfold better recommended to the heart, comes there more like a neighbour or familiar, than thousands of Hamnels, and Zillahs, and Madelons. I beg you will send me the "Holly Tree," if it at all resemble this, for it must please me. I have never seen it. I love this sort of poems, that open a new intercourse with the most despised of the animal and insect race. I think this vein may be further opened. Peter Pindar hath very prettily apostrophised a fly; Burns hath his mouse and his louse; Coleridge less successfully hath made overtures of intimacy to a jackass, therein only following, at unresembling distance, Sterne, and greater Cervantes. Besides these, I know of no other examples of breaking down the partition between us and our "poor earth-born companions." It is sometimes revolting to be put in a track of feeling by other people, not one's own immediate thoughts, else I would persuade you, if I could (I am in earnest), to commence a series of these animals' poems, which might have a tendency to rescue some poor creatures from the antipathy of mankind. Some thoughts came across me: for instance—to a rat, to a toad, to a cockchafer, to a mole. People bake moles alive by a slow oven fire to cure consumption. Rats are, indeed, the most despised and contemptible parts of God's earth. I killed a rat the other day by punching him to pieces, and feel a weight of blood upon me to this hour. Toads you know are made to fly, and tumble down and crush all to pieces. Cockchafers are old sport. Then again to a worm, with an apostrophe to anglers, those patient tyrants, meek inflictors of pangs intolerable, cool devils; to an owl; to all snakes, with an apology for their poison; to a cat in boots or bladders. Your own fancy, if it takes a fancy to these hints, will suggest many more. A series of such poems, suppose them accompanied with plates descriptive of animal torments, cooks roasting lobsters, fishmongers crimping skates, etc. etc., would take excessively. I will willingly enter into a partnership in the plan with you: I think my heart and soul would go with it too—at least, give it a thought. My plan is but this minute come into my head; but it strikes me instantaneously as something new, good, and useful, full of pleasure, and full of moral. If old Quarles and Wither could live again, we would invite them into our firm. Burns hath done his part.

Poor Sam Le Grice! I am afraid the world, and the camp, and the university, have spoilt him among them. 'Tis certain he had at one time a strong capacity of turning out something better. I knew him, and that not long since, when he had a most warm heart. I am ashamed of the indifference I have sometimes felt towards him. I think the devil is in one's heart. I am under obligations to that man for the warmest friendship, and heartiest sympathy exprest both by word and deed and tears for me, when I was in my greatest distress. But I have forgot that! as, I fear, he has nigh forgot the awful scenes which were before his eyes when he served the office of a comforter to me. No service was too mean or troublesome for him to perform. I can't think what but the devil, "that old spider," could have suck'd my heart so dry of its sense of all gratitude. If he does come in your way, Southey, fail not to tell him that I retain a most affectionate remembrance of his old friendliness, and an earnest wish to resume our intercourse. In this I am serious. I cannot recommend him to your society, because I am afraid whether he be quite worthy of it; but I have no right to dismiss him from *my* regard. He was at one time, and in the worst of times, my own familiar friend, and great comfort to me then. I have known him to play at cards with my father, meal-times excepted, literally all day long, in long days too, to save me from being teased by the old man, when I was not able to bear it.

God bless him for it, and God bless you, Southey. C. L.

LETTER XLVII.] *April 20, 1799.*

The following is a second extract from my tragedy—*that is to be.* 'Tis narrated by an old Steward to Margaret, orphan ward of Sir Walter Woodvil. . . . This and the Dying Lover I gave you are the only extracts I can give without mutilation. . . . I expect you to like the old woman's curse:—

> *Old Steward.*—One summer night, Sir Walter, as it chanced,
> Was pacing to and fro in the avenue
> That westward fronts our house,
> Among those aged oaks, said to have been planted
> Three hundred years ago
> By a neighbouring Prior of the Woodvil name, etc.

This is the extract I bragged of as superior to that I sent you from Marlow: perhaps you will smile. But I should like your remarks on the above, as you are deeper witch-read than I.

Yours ever, C. LAMB.

Rob. Southey, Esq.,
    Mr. Cottle's, Bookseller,
        High Street, Bristol.

LETTER XLVIII.]   *May* 20, 1799.

Dear Southey—I thank you heartily for your intended presents, but do by no means see the necessity you are under of burthening yourself thereby. You have read old Wither's Supersedeas to small purpose. You object to my pauses being at the end of my lines; I do not know any great difficulty I should find in diversifying or changing my blank verse; but I go upon the model of Shakspeare in my Play, and endeavour after a colloquial ease and spirit, something like him. I could as easily imitate Milton's versification, but my ear and feeling would reject it, or any approaches to it, in the *drama*. I do not know whether to be glad or sorry that witches have been detected aforetimes in the shutting up of wombs. I certainly invented that conceit, and its coincidence with fact is accidental, for I never heard it. I have not seen those verses on Colonel Despard: I do not read any newspapers. Are they short to copy without much trouble? I should like to see them.

I just send you a few rhymes from my play, the only rhymes in it. A forest liver gives an account of his amusements:—

> What sports have you in the forest?
> Not many,—some few,—as thus,
> To see the sun to bed, to see him rise,
> Like some hot amourist with glowing eyes,
> Bursting the lazy bands of sleep that bound him;
> With all his fires and travelling glories round him; etc.

I love to anticipate charges of unoriginality: the first line is almost Shakspeare's:—

> "To have my love to bed and to arise."
>   *A Midsummer Night's Dream.*

I think there is a sweetness in the versification not unlike some rhymes in that exquisite play, and the last line but three is yours:

> "An eye
> That met the gaze, or turn'd it knew not why."
>   *Rosamund's Epistle.*

I shall anticipate all my play, and have nothing to show you. An idea for Leviathan: Commentators on Job have been puzzled to find out a meaning for Leviathan. 'Tis a whale, say some; a crocodile, say others. In my simple conjecture, Leviathan is neither more nor less than the Lord Mayor of London for the time being.

Rosamund sells well in London, malgré the non-reviewal of it. I sincerely wish you better health, and better health to Edith. Kind remembrances to her.   C. LAMB.

My sister Mary was never in better health or spirits than now.

To ROBERT LLOYD.

LETTER XLIX.] *September* 1799.

My dear Robert—I suppose by this time you have returned from Worcester with Uncle Nehemiah. You neglected to inform me whether Charles is yet at Birm. I have heard here that he is returned to Cambridge. Give him a gentle tap on the shoulder to remind him how truly acceptable a letter from him would be. I have nothing to write about.

Thomson remains with me. He is perpetually getting into mental vagaries. He is in LOVE! and tosses and tumbles about in his bed like a man in a barrel of spikes. He is more sociable, but I am heartily sick of him domesticating with me; he wants so many sympathies of mine, and I want his, that we are daily declining into *civility*. I shall be truly glad when he is gone. I find 'tis a dangerous experiment to grow too familiar. Some natures cannot bear it without converting into indifference. I know but one Being that I could ever consent to live perpetually with, and that is Robert. But Robert must go whither prudence and paternal regulations indicate a way. I shall not soon forget you—do not fear that—nor grow cool towards Robert. My not writing is no proof of these disloyalties. Perhaps I am unwell, or vexed, or spleen'd, or something, when I should otherwise write.

Assure Charles of my unalterable affection, and present my warmest wishes for his and Sophia's happiness. How goes on Priscilla? I am much pleased with his Poems in the Anthology—One in Particular. The other is a kind and no doubt just tribute to Robert and Olivia, but I incline to opinion that these domestic addresses should not always be made public. I have, I know, more than once exposed my own secretest feelings of that nature, but I am sorry that I did. Nine out of ten readers laugh at them. When a man dies leaving the name of a great author behind him, any unpublished relicks which let one into his domestic retirements are greedily gathered up, which in his lifetime, and before his fame had ripened, would by many be considered as impertinent. But if Robert and his sister were gratify'd with seeing their brother's heart in Print, let the rest of the world go hang. They may prefer the remaining trumpery of the Anthology. All I mean to say is, I think I perceive an indelicacy in thus exposing one's virtuous feelings to criticism. But of delicacy Charles is at least as true a judge as myself.

Pray request him to let me somehow have a sight of his novel. I declined offering it here for sale, for good reasons as I thought—being unknown to Booksellers, and not made for making bargains; but for that reason I am not to be punished with not seeing the book.

I shall count it a kindness if Chas. will send me the manuscript, which shall certainly be returned.

[The remainder of this letter has been torn off.]

To ROBERT SOUTHEY.

LETTER L.]   *October* 31, 1799.

Dear Southey—I have but just got your letter, being returned from Herts, where I have passed a few red-letter days with much pleasure. I would describe the county to you, as you have done by Devonshire; but alas! I am a poor pen at that same. I could tell you of an old house with a tapestry bedroom, the "Judgment of Solomon" composing one panel, and "Actæon spying Diana naked" the other. I could tell of an old marble hall, with Hogarth's prints, and the Roman Cæsars in marble hung round. I could tell of a *wilderness,* and of a village church, and where the bones of my honoured grandam lie; but there are feelings which refuse to be translated, sulky aborigines, which will not be naturalised in another soil. Of this nature are old family faces, and scenes of infancy.

I have given your address, and the books you want, to the Arches; they will send them as soon as they can get them, but they do not seem quite familiar to their names. I have seen Gebor! Gebor aptly so denominated from Geborish, *quasi* Gibberish. But Gebor hath some lucid intervals. I remember darkly one beautiful simile veiled in uncouth phrases about the youngest daughter of the Ark. I shall have nothing to communicate, I fear, to the Anthology. You shall have some fragments of my play, if you desire them; but I think I would rather print it whole. Have you seen it, or shall I lend you a copy? I want your opinion of it.

I must get to business; so farewell. My kind remembrances to Edith.

C. LAMB.

To THOMAS MANNING.

LETTER LI.]   *December* 28, 1799.

Dear Manning—Having suspended my correspondence a decent interval, as knowing that even good things may be taken to satiety, a wish cannot but recur to learn whether you be still well and happy. Do all things continue in the state I left them in Cambridge?

Do your night parties still flourish? and do you continue to bewilder your company with your thousand faces, running down through all the keys of idiotism (like Lloyd over his perpetual harpsichord), from the smile and the glimmer of half-sense and quarter-sense, to the grin and hanging lip of Betty Foy's own Johnny? And does the face-dissolving curfew sound at twelve? How unlike the great originals were your petty terrors in the postscript! not fearful enough to make a fairy shudder, or a Lilliputian fine lady, eight months full of child, miscarry. Yet one of them, which had more beast than the rest, I thought faintly resembled *one* of your brutifications. But, seriously, I long to see your own honest Manning-face again. I did not mean a pun,—your *man's* face, you will be apt to say, I know your wicked will to pun. I cannot now write to Lloyd and you too; so you must convey as much interesting intelligence as this may contain, or be thought to contain, to him and Sophia, with my dearest love and remembrances.

By the by, I think you and Sophia both incorrect with regard to the *title* of the *play*. Allowing your objection (which is not necessary, as pride may be, and is in real life often, cured by misfortunes not directly originating from its own acts, as Jeremy Taylor will tell you a naughty desire is sometimes sent to cure it; I know you read these *practical divines*)—but allowing your objection, does not the betraying of his father's secret directly spring from pride?—from the pride of wine, and a full heart, and a proud over-stepping of the ordinary rules of morality, and contempt of the prejudices of mankind, which are not to bind superior souls—"as *trust* in *the matter* of *secrets* all *ties* of *blood*, etc. etc., keeping of *promises*, the feeble mind's religion, binding our *morning knowledge* to the performance of what *last night's ignorance* spake"—does he not prate, that *"Great Spirits"* must do more than die for their friend? Does not the pride of wine incite him to display some evidence of friendship, which its own irregularity shall make great? This I know, that I meant his punishment not alone to be a cure for his daily and habitual *pride*, but the direct consequence and appropriate punishment of a particular act of pride.

If you do not understand it so, it is my fault in not explaining my meaning.

I have not seen Coleridge since, and scarcely expect to see him,—perhaps he has been at Cambridge.

Need I turn over to blot a fresh clean half-sheet, merely to say, what I hope you are sure of without my repeating it, that I would have you consider me, dear Manning, Your sincere friend,

C. LAMB.

LETTER LII.] *December* 1799.

Dear Manning—The particular kindness, even up to a degree of attachment, which I have experienced from you, seems to claim some distinct acknowledgment on my part. I could not content myself with a bare remembrance to you, conveyed in some letter to Lloyd.

Will it be agreeable to you, if I occasionally recruit your memory of me, which must else soon fade, if you consider the brief intercourse we have had. I am not likely to prove a troublesome correspondent. My scribbling days are past. I shall have no sentiments to communicate, but as they spring up from some living and worthy occasion.

I look forward with great pleasure to the performance of your promise, that we should meet in London early in the ensuing year. The century must needs commence auspiciously for me, that brings with it Manning's friendship, as an earnest of its after gifts.

I should have written before, but for a troublesome inflammation in one of my eyes, brought on by night travelling with the coach windows sometimes up.

What more I have to say shall be reserved for a letter to Lloyd. I must not prove tedious to you in my first outset, lest I should affright you by my ill-judged loquacity.

I am, yours most sincerely,   C. LAMB.

CHAPTER II

1800–1809

To SAMUEL TAYLOR COLERIDGE.

LETTER LIII.] *January 2, 1800.*

Dear Coleridge—Now I write, I cannot miss this opportunity of acknowledging the obligations myself, and the readers in general of that luminous paper, the *Morning Post,* are under to you for the very novel and exquisite manner in which you combined political with grammatical science in your yesterday's dissertation on Mr. Wyndham's unhappy composition. It must have been the death-blow to that ministry. I expect Pitt and Grenville to resign. More especially the delicate and Cottrellian grace with which you officiated, with a ferula for a white wand, as gentleman usher to the word "also," which it seems did not know its place.

I expect Manning of Cambridge in town to-night. Will you fulfil your promise of meeting him at my house? He is a man of a thousand. Give me a line to say what day, whether Saturday, Sunday, Monday, etc., and if Sara and the Philosopher can come. I am afraid if I did not at intervals call upon you, I should *never see you.* But I forget, the affairs of the nation engross your time and your mind.

Farewell. C. L.

To THOMAS MANNING.

LETTER LIV.] *February 13, 1800.*

Dear Manning—Olivia is a good girl, and if you turn to my letter you will find that this very plea you set up to vindicate Lloyd, I had made use of as a reason why he should never have employed Olivia to make a copy of such a letter!—a letter I could not have sent to my Enemy's B——, if she had thought proper to seek me in the way of marriage. But you see it in one view, I in another. Rest you merry in your opinion! Opinion is a species of property; and though I am always desirous to share with my friend to a certain extent, I shall ever like to keep some tenets, and some property, properly my own. Some day, Manning, when we meet, substituting Corydon and fair Amaryllis for Charles Lloyd and Mary Hayes, we will discuss together this question of moral feeling, "In what cases, and how far, sincerity is a virtue?" I do not mean Truth, a good Olivia-like creature, God bless her, who, meaning no offence, is always ready to give an answer when she is asked why she did so and so; but a certain forward-talking half-brother of hers, Sincerity, that amphibious gentleman, who is so ready to perk up his obnoxious sentiments unasked into your notice, as Midas would his ears into your face, uncalled for. But I despair of doing anything by a letter in the way of explaining or coming to explanations. A good wish, or a pun, or a piece of secret history, may be well enough that way conveyed; nay, it has been known, that intelligence of a turkey hath been conveyed by that medium, without much ambiguity. Godwin I am a good deal pleased with. He is a very well-behaved, decent man; nothing very brilliant about him or imposing, as you may suppose; quite another guess sort of gentleman from what your anti-jacobin Christians imagine him. I was well pleased to find he has neither horns nor claws; quite a tame creature, I assure you: a middle-sized man, both in stature and in understanding; whereas, from his noisy fame, you would expect to find a Briareus Centimanus, or a Tityus tall enough to pull Jupiter from his heavens.

I begin to think you atheists not quite so tall a species! Coleridge inquires after you pretty often. I wish to be the Pandar to bring you together again once before I die. When we die, you and I must part; the sheep, you know, take the right-hand sign-post, and the goats the left. Stript of its allegory, you must know the sheep are—I, the Apostles, and the martyrs, and the Popes, and Bishop Taylor, and Bishop Horsley, and Coleridge, etc., etc. The goats are the atheists, and adulterers, and fornicators, and dumb dogs, and Godwin, and M——g, and that Thyestæan crew! Egad, how my saintship sickens at the idea! You shall have my play and the Falstaff's Letters in a day or two. I will write to Ll[oyd] by this day's Post.

Pray, is it a part of your sincerity to show my letters to Lloyd? for, really, gentlemen ought to explain their virtues upon a first acquaintance, to prevent mistakes.

God bless you, Manning. Take my trifling *as trifling;* and believe me, seriously and deeply,

Your well-wisher and friend,　　　　C. L.

LETTER LV.]　　　　　　　　　　　　　　　　　　*March* 1, 1800.

I hope by this time you are prepared to say, the "Falstaff's letters" are a bundle of the sharpest, queerest, profoundest humours, of any these juice-drained latter times have spawned. I should have advertised you, that the meaning is frequently hard to be got at; and so are the future guineas, that now lie ripening and aurifying in the womb of some undiscovered Potosi; but dig, dig, dig, dig, Manning! I set to, with an unconquerable propulsion to write, with a lamentable want of what to write. My private goings on are orderly as the movements of the spheres, and stale as their music to angels' ears. Public affairs—except as they touch upon me, and so turn into private,—I cannot whip up my mind to feel any interest in. I grieve, indeed, that War, and Nature, and Mr. Pitt, that hangs up in Lloyd's best parlour, should have conspired to call up three necessaries, simple commoners as our fathers knew them, into the upper house of luxuries; bread, and beer, and coals, Manning. But as to France and Frenchmen, and the Abbé Sièyes and his constitutions, I cannot make these present times present to me. I read histories of the past, and I live in them; although, to abstract senses, they are far less momentous than the noises which keep Europe awake. I am reading *Burnet's History of his own Times.* Did you ever read that garrulous, pleasant history? He tells his story like an old man past political service, bragging to his sons on winter evenings of the part he took in public transactions, when his "old cap was new." Full of scandal, which all true history is. No palliatives; but all the stark wickedness, that actually gives the *momentum* to national actors. Quite the prattle of age, and out-lived importance. Truth and sincerity staring out upon you perpetually in *alto relievo.* Himself a party man—he makes you a party man. None of the cursed philosophical Humcian indifference, so cold, and unnatural, and inhuman! None of the cursed Gibbonian fine writing, so fine and composite! None of Dr. Robertson's periods with three members. None of Mr. Roscoe's sage remarks, all so apposite, and coming in so clever, lest the reader should have had the trouble of drawing an inference. Burnet's good old prattle I can bring present to my mind: I can make the revolution present to me: the French revolution, by a converse perversity in my nature, I fling as far *from* me. To quit this tiresome subject, and to relieve you from two or three dismal yawns, which I hear in spirit, I here conclude my more than commonly obtuse letter; dull, up to the dulness of a Dutch commentator on Shakspeare.

My love to Lloyd and to Sophia.   C. L.

LETTER LVI.]   *March* 17, 1800.

Dear Manning—I am living in a continuous feast. Coleridge has been with me now for nigh three weeks, and the more I see of him in the quotidian undress and relaxation of his mind, the more cause I see to love him, and believe him a *very good man,* and all those foolish impressions to the contrary fly off like morning slumbers. He is engaged in translations, which I hope will keep him this month to come. He is uncommonly kind and friendly to me. He ferrets me day and night to *do something.* He tends me, amidst all his own worrying and heart-oppressing occupations, as a gardener tends his young *tulip.* Marry come up; what a pretty similitude, and how like your humble servant! He has lugged me to the brink of engaging to a newspaper, and has suggested to me, for a first plan, the forgery of a supposed manuscript of Burton, the anatomist of melancholy. I have even written the introductory letter; and if I can pick up a few guineas this way, I feel they will be most *refreshing,* bread being so dear. If I go on with it, I will apprise you of it, as you may like to see my things! and the *tulip,* of all flowers, loves to be admired most.

Pray pardon me, if my letters do not come very thick. I am so taken up with one thing or other, that I cannot pick out (I will not say time, but) fitting times to write to you. My dear love to Lloyd and Sophia, and pray split this thin letter into three parts, and present them with the *two biggest* in my name.

They are my oldest friends; but, ever the new friend driveth out the old, as the ballad sings! God bless you all three! I would hear from Lloyd if I could.

Flour has just fallen nine shillings a sack: we shall be all too rich.

Tell Charles I have seen his mamma, and have almost fallen in love with *her*, since I mayn't with Olivia. She is so fine and graceful, a complete matron-lady-quaker. She has given me two little books. Olivia grows a charming girl—full of feeling, and thinner than she was; but I have not time to fall in love.

Mary presents her *general compliments*. She keeps in fine health.

Huzza boys! and down with the Atheists!

To SAMUEL TAYLOR COLERIDGE.

LETTER LVII.]   *May* 12, 1800.

My dear Coleridge—I don't know why I write, except from the propensity which misery has to tell her griefs. Hetty died on Friday night, about eleven o'clock, after eight days' illness. Mary, in consequence of fatigue and anxiety, is fallen ill again, and I was obliged to remove her yesterday. I am left alone in a house with nothing but Hetty's dead body to keep me company. To-morrow I bury her, and then I shall be quite alone, with nothing but a cat, to remind me that the house has been full of living beings like myself. My heart is quite sunk, and I don't know where to look for relief. Mary will get better again, but her constantly being liable to such relapses is dreadful; nor is it the least of our evils that her case and all our story is so well known around us. We are in a manner *marked*. Excuse my troubling you, but I have nobody by me to speak to me. I slept out last night, not being able to endure the change and the stillness; but I did not sleep well, and I must come back to my own bed. I am going to try and get a friend to come and be with me to-morrow. I am completely shipwrecked. My head is quite bad. I almost wish that Mary were dead. God bless you! Love to Sara and Hartley.

C. LAMB.

Monday.

To THOMAS MANNING.

LETTER LVIII.]   *May* 17, 1800.

Dear Manning—I am quite out of spirits, and feel as if I should never recover them. But why should not this pass away? I am foolish, but judge of me by my situation. Our servant is dead, and my sister is ill— so ill as to make a removal to a place of confinement absolutely necessary.

I have been left *alone* in a house where but ten days since living beings were, and noises of life were heard. I have made the experiment and find I cannot bear it any longer. Last night I went to sleep at White's, with whom I am to be until I can find a settlement. I have given up my house, and must look out for lodgings. I expect Mary will get better before many weeks are gone,—but at present I feel my daily and hourly prop has fallen from me. I totter and stagger with weakness, for nobody can supply her place to me. White has *all kindness,* but not *sympathy.* R. Lloyd, my only correspondent, you except, is a good Being, but a weak one. I know not where to look but to you. If you will suffer me to weary your shoulders with part of my Burthen, I shall write again to let you know how I go on. Meantime a letter from you would be a considerable relief to me.—Believe me, yours most sincerely, C. L.

LETTER LIX.] [*Before June*] 1800.

Dear Manning—I feel myself unable to thank you sufficiently for your kind letter. It was doubly acceptable to me, both for the choice poetry and the kind honest prose which it contained. It was just such a letter as I should have expected from Manning.

I am in much better spirits than when I wrote last. I have had a very eligible offer to lodge with a friend in town. He will have rooms to let at Midsummer; by which time I hope my sister will be well enough to join me. It is a great object to me to live in town, where we shall be much more *private,* and to quit a house and a neighbourhood where poor Mary's disorder, so frequently recurring, has made us a sort of marked people. We can be nowhere private except in the midst of London. We shall be in a family where we visit very frequently; only my landlord and I have not yet come to a conclusion. He has a partner to consult. I am still on the tremble, for I do not know where we could go into lodgings that would not be, in many respects, highly exceptionable. Only God send Mary well again, and I hope all will be well! The prospect, such as it is, has made me quite happy. I have just time to tell you of it, as I know it will give you pleasure.—Farewell. C. LAMB.

To SAMUEL TAYLOR COLERIDGE.

LETTER LX.] *June* 22, 1800.

By some fatality, unusual with me, I have mislaid the list of books which you want. Can you, from memory, easily supply me with another?

I confess to Statius and I detained him wilfully, out of a reverent regard to your style. Statius, they tell me, is turgid. As to that other Latin book, since you know neither its name nor subject, your wants (I crave leave to apprehend) cannot be very urgent. Meanwhile, dream that it is one of the lost Decades of Livy.

Your partiality to me has led you to form an erroneous opinion as to the measure of delight you suppose me to take in obliging. Pray be careful that it spread no further. 'Tis one of those heresies that is very pregnant. Pray rest more satisfied with the portion of learning which you have got, and disturb my peaceful ignorance as little as possible with such sort of commissions.

Did you never observe an appearance well known by the name of the man in the moon? Some scandalous old maids have set on foot a report that it is Endymion.

Your theory about the first awkward step a man makes being the consequence of learning to dance, is not universal. We have known many youths bred up at Christ's, who never learned to dance, yet the world imputes to them no very graceful motions. I remember there was little Hudson, the immortal precentor of St. Paul's, to teach us our quavers; but, to the best of my recollection, there was no master of motions when we were at Christ's.—Farewell, in haste.   C. L.

To ROBERT LLOYD.

LETTER LXI.]   *July* 2, 1800.

Dear Robert—My mind has been so barren and idle of late, that I have done nothing. I have received many a summons from you, and have repeatedly sat down to write, and broke off from despair of sending you anything worthy your acceptance. I have had such a deadness about me. Man delights not me nor woman neither. I impute it in part, or altogether, to the stupefying effect which continued fine weather has upon me. I want some rains, or even snow and intense cold winter nights, to bind me to my habitation, and make me value it as a home—a sacred character which it has not attained with me hitherto. I cannot read or write when the sun shines: I can only walk.

I must tell you that, since I wrote last I have been two days at Oxford, on a visit (long put off) to Gutch's family (my landlord). I was much gratified with the Colleges and Libraries and what else of Oxford I could see in so short a time. In the All Souls' Library is a fine head of Bishop Taylor, which was one great inducement to my Oxford visit. In the Bodleian are many Portraits of illustrious Dead, the only species of painting I value at a farthing. But an indubitable good Portrait of a great man is worth a pilgrimage to go and see. Gutch's family is a very fine one, consisting of well-grown sons and daughters, and all likely and well-favour'd. What is called a Happy family—that is, according to my interpretation, a numerous assemblage of young men and women, all fond of each other to a certain degree, and all happy together, but where the very number forbids any two of them to get close enough to each other to share secrets and *be friends*. That close intercourse can only exist (commonly, I think,) in a family of two or three. I do not envy large families. The fraternal affection by diffusion and multi-participation is ordinarily thin and weak. They don't get near enough to each other.

I expected to have had an account of Sophia's being brought to bed before this time; but I remain in confidence that you will send me the earliest news. I hope it will be happy.

Coleridge is settled at Keswick, so that the probability is that he will be once again united with your Brother. Such men as he and Wordsworth would exclude solitude in the Hebrides or Thule.

Pray have you seen the New Edition of Burns, including his posthumous works? I want very much to get a sight of it, but cannot afford to buy it, my Oxford Journey, though very moderate, having pared away all superfluities.

Will you accept of this short letter, accompanied with professions of deepest regard for you?—Yours unalterably,   C. LAMB.

To SAMUEL TAYLOR COLERIDGE.

LETTER LXII.]   *August* 6, 1800.

Dear Coleridge—I have taken to-day, and delivered to L. and Co., *Imprimis:* your books, viz., three ponderous German dictionaries, one volume (I can find no more) of German and French ditto, sundry other German books unbound, as you left them, *Percy's Ancient Poetry,* and one volume of *Anderson's Poets.* I specify them, that you may not lose any. *Secundo:* a dressing-gown (value, fivepence) in which you used to sit and look like a conjurer, when you were translating *Wallenstein.* A case of two razors, and a shaving-box and strap. This it has cost me a severe struggle to part with. They are in a brown-paper parcel, which also contains sundry papers and poems, sermons, *some few Epic* Poems,—one about Cain and Abel, which came from Poole, etc. etc., and also your tragedy; with one or two small German books, and that drama in which Got-fader performs. *Tertio:* a small oblong box containing *all your letters,* collected from all your waste papers, and which fill the said little box. All other waste papers, which I judged worth sending, are in the paper parcel aforesaid. But you will find *all* your letters in the box by themselves. Thus have I discharged my conscience and my lumber-room of all your property, save and except a folio entitled *Tyrrell's Bibliotheca Politica,* which you used to learn your politics out of when you wrote for the *Post, mutatis mutandis, i.e.,* applying past inferences to modern *data.* I retain that, because I am sensible I am very deficient in the politics myself; and I have torn up (don't be angry, waste paper has risen forty per cent., and I can't afford to buy it) all *Buonaparte's Letters, Arthur Young's Treatise on Corn,* and one or two more light-armed infantry, which I thought better suited the flippancy of London discussion than the dignity of Keswick thinking. Mary says you will be in a passion about them, when you come to miss them; but you must study philosophy. Read *Albertus Magnus de Chartis Amissis* five times over after phlebotomising,—'tis Burton's recipe,—and then be angry with an absent friend if you can.

Sara is obscure. Am I to understand by her letter, that she sends a *kiss* to Eliza Buckingham? Pray tell your wife that a note of interrogation on the superscription of a letter is highly ungrammatical: she proposes writing my name *Lambe?* Lamb is quite enough. I have had the Anthology, and like only one thing in it, *Lewti;* but of that the last stanza is detestable, the rest most exquisite: the epithet *enviable* would dash the finest poem. For God's sake (I never was more serious) don't make me ridiculous any more by terming me gentle-hearted in print, or do it in better verses. It did well enough five years ago when I came to see you, and was moral coxcomb enough at the time you wrote the lines, to feed upon such epithets; but, besides that, the meaning of "gentle" is equivocal at best, and almost always means poor-spirited; the very quality of gentleness is abhorrent to such vile trumpetings. My *sentiment* is long since vanished. I hope my *virtues* have done *sucking*. I can scarce think but you meant it in joke. I hope you did, for I should be ashamed to believe that you could think to gratify me by such praise, fit only to be a cordial to some green-sick sonneteer.

I have hit off the following in imitation of old English poetry, which, I imagine, I am a dab at. The measure is unmeasurable; but it most resembles that beautiful ballad, the "Old and Young Courtier;" and in its feature of taking the extremes of two situations for just parallel, it resembles the old poetry certainly. If I could but stretch out the circumstances to twelve more verses, *i.e.*, if I had as much genius as the writer of that old song, I think it would be excellent. It was to follow an imitation of Burton in prose, which you have not seen. But fate "and wisest Stewart" say No.

I can send you 200 pens and six quires of paper *immediately,* if they will answer the carriage by coach. It would be foolish to pack 'em up *cum multis libris et cæteris;* they would all spoil. I only wait your commands to coach them. I would pay five-and-forty thousand carriages to read W.'s tragedy, of which I have heard so much and seen so little—only what I saw at Stowey. Pray give me an order in writing on Longman for *Lyrical Ballads.* I have the first volume, and, truth to tell, six shillings is a broad shot. I cram all I can in, to save a multiplying of letters,—those pretty comets with swinging tails.

I'll just crowd in, God bless you!   C. Lamb.
Wednesday night.

To THOMAS MANNING.

Letter LXIII.]   *August* 1800.

Dear Manning—I am going to ask a favour of you, and am at a loss how to do it in the most delicate manner. For this purpose I have been looking into Pliny's Letters, who is noted to have had the best grace in begging of all the ancients (I read him in the elegant translation of Mr. Melmoth), but not finding any case there exactly similar with mine, I am constrained to beg in my own barbarian way. To come to the point then, and hasten into the middle of things: have you a copy of your Algebra to give away? I do not ask it for myself; I have too much reverence for the Black Arts ever to approach thy circle, illustrious Trismegist! But that worthy man, and excellent poet, George Dyer, made me a visit yesternight, on purpose to borrow one; supposing, rationally enough, I must

~ay, that you had made me a present of one before this; the omission of
/hich I take to have proceeded only from negligence; but it is a fault. I
could lend him no assistance. You must know he is just now diverted from
the pursuit of the BELL LETTERS by a paradox, which he has heard his
friend Frend (that learned mathematician) maintain, that the negative
quantities of mathematicians were *meræ nugæ*, things scarcely *in rerum
naturâ*, and smacking too much of mystery for gentlemen of Mr. Frend's
clear Unitarian capacity. However, the dispute once set a-going, has
seized violently on George's pericranick; and it is necessary for his health
that he should speedily come to a resolution of his doubts. He goes about
teasing his friends with his new mathematics: he even frantically talks of
purchasing Manning's Algebra, which shows him far gone; for, to my
knowledge, he has not been master of seven shillings a good time. George's
pockets and ———'s brain are two things in nature which do not abhor a
vacuum. . . . Now, if you could step in, in this trembling suspense of his
reason, and he should find on Saturday morning, lying for him at the Porter's Lodge, Clifford's Inn (his safest address), Manning's Algebra, with a
neat manuscription in the blank leaf, running thus "FROM THE AUTHOR,"
it might save his wits, and restore the unhappy author to those studies of
poetry and criticism which are at present suspended, to the infinite regret
of the whole literary world. *N.B.*—Dirty backs, smeared leaves, and dogs'
ears, will be rather a recommendation than otherwise. *N.B.*—He must
have the book as soon as possible, or nothing can withhold him from
madly purchasing the book on tick. . . . Then shall we see him sweetly
restored to the chair of Longinus—to dictate in smooth and modest phrase
the laws of verse; to prove that Theocritus first introduced the Pastoral,
and Virgil and Pope brought it to its perfection; that Gray and Mason
(who always hunt in couples in George's brain) have shown a great
deal of poetical fire in their lyric poetry; that Aristotle's rules are not to
be servilely followed, which George has shown to have imposed great
shackles upon modern genius. His poems, I find, are to consist of two
vols.—reasonable octavo; and a third book will exclusively contain criticisms, in which he asserts he has gone *pretty deeply* into the laws of blank
verse and rhyme—epic poetry, dramatic and pastoral ditto—all which is
to come out before Christmas. But, above all, he has *touched* most *deeply*
upon the Drama, comparing the English with the modern German stage,
their merits and defects. Apprehending that his *studies* (not to mention
his *turn*, which I take to be chiefly towards the lyrical poetry) hardly qualified him for these disquisitions, I modestly inquired what plays he had
read? I found by George's reply that he *had* read Shakspeare, but that
was a good while since: he calls him a great but irregular genius, which I
think to be an original and just remark. Beaumont and Fletcher, Massinger, Ben Jonson, Shirley, Marlowe, Ford, and the worthies of Dodsley's
Collection—he confessed he had read none of them, but professed his *intention* of looking through them all, so as to be able to *touch* upon them in
his book. So Shakspeare, Otway, and I believe Rowe, to whom he was
naturally directed by Johnson's Lives, and these not read lately, are to

stand him in stead of a general knowledge of the subject. God bless his dear absurd head!

By the by, did I not write you a letter with something about an invitation in it? But let this pass; I suppose it is not agreeable.

N.B.—It would not be amiss if you were to accompany your *present* with a dissertation on negative quantities. C. L.

LETTER LXIV.] 1800.

George Dyer is an Archimedes, and an Archimagus, and a Tycho Brahe, and a Copernicus; and thou art the darling of the Nine, and midwife to their wandering babe also! We take tea with that learned poet and critic on Tuesday night, at half-past five, in his neat library. The repast will be light and Attic, with criticism. If thou couldst contrive to wheel up thy dear carcass on the Monday, and after dining with us on tripe, calves' kidneys, or whatever else the Cornucopia of St. Clare may be willing to pour out on the occasion, might we not adjourn together to the Heathen's —thou with thy Black Back, and I with some innocent volume of the Bell Letters, Shenstone, or the like: it would make him wash his old flannel gown (that has not been washed to my knowledge since it has been *his*— Oh the long time!) with tears of joy. Thou shouldst settle his scruples and unravel his cobwebs, and sponge off the sad stuff that weighs upon his dear wounded pia mater. Thou shouldst restore light to his eyes, and him to his friends and the public. Parnassus should shower her civic crowns upon thee for saving the wits of a citizen! I thought I saw a lucid interval in George the other night; he broke in upon my studies just at tea-time, and brought with him Dr. Anderson, an old gentleman who ties his breeches' knees with packthread, and boasts that he has been disappointed by ministers. The Doctor wanted to see *me;* for I being a Poet, he thought I might furnish him with a copy of verses to suit his *Agricultural Magazine.* The Doctor, in the course of the conversation, mentioned a poem called the "Epigoniad," by one Wilkie, an epic poem, in which there is not one tolerable good line all through, but every incident and speech borrowed from Homer. George had been sitting inattentive, seemingly, to what was going on—hatching of negative quantities— when, suddenly, the name of his old friend Homer stung his pericranicks, and, jumping up, he begged to know where he could meet with Wilkie's works. It was a curious fact, he said, that there should be such an epic poem and he not know of it; and he *must* get a copy of it, as he was going to touch pretty deeply upon the subject of the Epic—and he was sure there must be some things good in a poem of 8000 lines! I was pleased with this transient return of his reason and recurrence to his old ways of thinking: it gave me great hopes of a recovery, which nothing but your book can completely insure. Pray come on Monday, if you *can,* and stay your own time. I have a good large room with two beds in it, in the handsomest of which thou shalt repose a-nights, and dream of Spheroides. I hope you will understand by the nonsense of this letter that I am *not* melancholy at the thoughts of thy coming: I thought it necessary to add this, because you love *precision*. Take notice that our stay at Dyer's will not exceed eight o'clock; after which our pursuits will be our own. But indeed I think a little recreation among the Bell Letters and poetry will do you some service in the interval of severer studies. I hope we shall fully discuss with George Dyer what I have never yet heard done to my satisfaction, the reason of Dr. Johnson's malevolent strictures on the higher species of the Ode.

LETTER LXV.]   [*August* 9, 1800.]

Dear Manning—I suppose you have heard of Sophia Lloyd's good fortune, and paid the customary compliments to the parents. Heaven keep the new-born infant from star blasting and moon blasting, from epilepsy, marasmus, and the devil! May he live to see many days, and they good ones; some friends, and they *pretty regular correspondents!* with as much wit and wisdom as will eat their bread and cheese together under a poor roof without quarreling! as much goodness as will earn heaven. Here I must leave off, my benedictory powers failing me.

And now, when shall I catch a glimpse of your honest face-to-face countenance again?—your fine *dogmatical sceptical* face by punch-light? Oh! one glimpse of the human face, and shake of the human hand, is better than whole reams of this cold, thin correspondence; year, of more worth than all the letters that have sweated the fingers of sensibility, from Madame Sévigné and Balzac to Sterne and Shenstone.

Coleridge is settled with his wife and the young philosopher at Keswick, with the Wordsworths. They have contrived to spawn a new volume of lyrical ballads, which is to see the light in about a month, and causes no little excitement in the *literary world*. George Dyer too, that good-natured heathen, is more than nine months gone with his twin volumes of ode, pastoral, sonnet, elegy, Spenserian, Horatian, Akensidish, and Masonic verse. Clio prosper the birth! it will be twelve shillings out of somebody's pocket. I find he means to exclude "personal satire," so it appears by his truly original advertisement. Well, God put it into the hearts of the English gentry to come in shoals and subscribe to his poems, for He never put a kinder heart into flesh of man than George Dyer's!

Now farewell, for dinner is at hand.   C. L.

LETTER LXVI.]   *August* 11, 1800.

My dear fellow (*N.B.* mighty familiar of late!) for me to come to Cambridge now is one of heaven's impossibilities. Metaphysicians tell us, even it can work nothing which implies a contradiction. I can explain this by telling you that I am engaged to do double duty (this hot weather!) for a man who has taken advantage of this very weather to go and cool himself in "green retreats" all the month of August.

But for you to come to London instead!—muse upon it, revolve it, cast it about in your mind. I have a bed at your command. You shall drink rum, brandy, gin, aqua-vitæ, usquebaugh, or whiskey a' nights; and for the after-dinner trick, I have eight bottles of genuine port, which, mathematically divided, gives 1 1/7 for every day you stay, provided you stay a week. Hear John Milton sing,

> "Let Euclid rest and Archimedes pause."
> *Twenty-first Sonnet.*

And elsewhere,—

> "What neat repast shall feast us, light [1] and choice,
> Of Attic taste, with wine,[2] whence we may rise
> To hear the lute well touch'd, or artful voice
> Warble immortal notes and Tuscan air?"

Indeed the poets are full of this pleasing morality,—

> "Veni cito, Domine Manning!"

Think upon it. Excuse the paper; it is all I have.

C. LAMB.

To SAMUEL TAYLOR COLERIDGE.

LETTER LXVII.]   *August* 14, 1800.

My head is playing all the tunes in the world, ringing such peals! It has just finished the "Merry Christ Church Bells," and absolutely is beginning "Turn again, Whittington," Buz, buz, buz, bum, bum, bum, wheeze, wheeze, wheeze, fen, fen, fen, tinky, tinky, tinky, *cr'annch*. I shall certainly come to be condemned at last. I have been drinking too much for two days running. I find my moral sense in the last stage of a consumption, and my religion getting faint. This is disheartening; but I trust the devil will not overpower me. In the midst of this infernal larum, Conscience is barking and yelping as loud as any of them. I have sat down to read over again your satire upon me in the *Anthology*, and I think I do begin to spy out something like beauty and design in it. I perfectly accede to all your alterations, and only desire that you had cut deeper, when your hand was in.

In sober truth, I cannot see any great truth in the little dialogue called "Blenheim." It is rather novel and pretty, but the thought is very obvious and is but poor prattle, a thing of easy imitation. *Pauper vult videri et est.*

In the next edition of the *Anthology* (which Phœbus avert, and those nine other wandering maids also!) please to blot out "gentle-hearted,"

---

[1] We poets generally give *light* dinners.
[2] No doubt the poet here alludes to port wine at 38s. the dozen.

and substitute drunken dog, ragged head, seld-shaven, odd-eyed, stuttering, or any other epithet which truly and properly belongs to the gentlemen in question. And for Charles read Tom, or Bob, or Richard for mere delicacy. Hang you, I was beginning to forgive you, and believe in earnest that the lugging in of my proper name was purely unintentional on your part, when looking back for further conviction, stares me in the face, "Charles Lamb of the *India House.*" *Now* I am convinced it was all done in malice, heaped sack-upon-sack, congregated, studied malice. You dog! your 141st page shall not save you. I own I was just ready to acknowledge that there is a something not unlike good poetry in that page, if you had not run into the unintelligible abstraction-fit about the matter of the Deity's making spirits perceive his presence. God, nor created thing alive can receive any honour from such thin show-box attributes. By the by, where did you pick up that scandalous piece of private history about the angel and the Duchess of Devonshire? If it is a fiction of your own, why truly it was a very modest one *for you.* Now I do affirm, that "Lewti" is a very beautiful poem. I *was* in earnest when I praised it. It describes a silly species of one not the wisest of passions. *Therefore* it cannot deeply affect a disenthralled mind. But such imagery, such novelty, such delicacy, and such versification never got into an *Anthology* before. I am only sorry that the cause of all the passionate complaint is not greater than the trifling circumstance of Lewti being out of temper one day. "Gaulberto" certainly has considerable originality, but sadly wants finishing. It is, as it is, one of the very best in the book. Next to "Lewti" I like the "Raven," which has a good deal of humour. I was pleased to see it again, for you once sent it me, and I have lost the letter which contained it. Now I am on the subject of Anthologies, I must say I am sorry the old pastoral way has fallen into disrepute. The gentry which now indite sonnets are certainly the legitimate descendants of the ancient shepherds. The same simpering face of description, the old family face, is visibly continued in the line. Some of their ancestors' labours are yet to be found in Allan Ramsay's and Jacob Tonson's Miscellanies. But miscellanies decaying, and the old pastoral way dying of mere want, their successors (driven from their paternal acres) now-a-days settle and lie upon Magazines and Anthologies. This race of men are uncommonly addicted to superstition. Some of them are idolators, and worship the moon. Others deify qualities, as Love, Friendship, Sensibility; or bare accidents, as Solitude. Grief and Melancholy have their respective altars and temples among them, as the heathens builded theirs to Mors, Febris, Pallor, etc. They all agree in ascribing a peculiar sanctity to the number 14. One of their own legislators affirmeth, that whatever exceeds that number "encroacheth upon the province of the elegy"—*vice versa*, whatever "cometh short of that number abutteth upon the premises of the epigram." I have been able to discover but few *images* in their temples, which, like the caves of Delphos of old, are famous for giving *echoes*. They impute a religious importance to the letter O, whether because by its roundness it is thought to typify the moon, their principal goddess, or for its analogies to their own labours, all ending where they began, or for whatever other high and mystical reference, I have never been able to discover, but I observe they never begin their invocations to their gods without it, except indeed one insignificant sect among them, who use the Doric A, pronounced like Ah! broad, instead. These boast to have restored the old Dorian mood.

Now I am on the subject of poetry, I must announce to you, who doubtless in your remote part of the island have not heard tidings of so great a blessing, that George Dyer hath prepared two ponderous volumes full of poetry and criticism. They impend over the town, and are threatened to fall in the Winter. The first volume contains every sort of poetry, except personal satire, which George, in his truly original prospectus, renounceth for ever, whimsically foisting the intention in between the price of his book and the proposed number of subscribers. (If I can, I will get you a copy of his *handbill*.) He has tried his *vein* in every species besides—the Spenserian, Thomsonian, Masonic, and Akensidish more especially. The second volume is all criticism; wherein he demonstrates to the entire satisfaction of the literary world, in a way that must silence all reply for ever, that the Pastoral was introduced by Theocritus, and polished by Virgil and Pope; that Gray and Mason (who always hunt in couples in George's brain) have a good deal of poetical fire and true lyric genius; that Cowley was ruined by excess of wit (a warning to all moderns); that Charles Lloyd, Charles Lamb, and William Wordsworth, in later days, have struck the true chords of poesy. O George, George! with a head uniformly wrong, and a heart uniformly right, that I had power and might equal to my wishes: then I would call the gentry of thy native island, and they should come in troops, flocking at the sound of thy prospectus trumpet, and crowding who shall be first to stand in thy list of subscribers! I can only put twelve shillings into thy pocket (which, I will answer for them, will not stick there long), out of a pocket almost as bare as thine. Is it not a pity so much fine writing should be erased? But, to tell the truth, I began to scent that I was getting into that sort of style which Longinus and Dionysius Halicarnassus aptly call "the affected."   C. L.

To THOMAS MANNING.

LETTER LXVIII.]   *August* 22, 1800.

Dear Manning—You needed not imagine any apology necessary. Your fine hare and fine birds (which are just now dangling by our kitchen blaze) discourse most eloquent music in your justification. You just nicked my palate. For with all due decorum and leave may it be spoken, my worship hath taken physic to-day, and being low and puling, requireth to be pampered. Foh! how beautiful and strong those buttered onions come to my nose! For you know we extract a divine spirit of gravy from those materials, which, duly compounded with a consistence of bread and cream (y'clept bread-sauce), each to each giving double grace, do mutually illustrate and set off (as skilful gold foils to rare jewels) your partridge, pheasant, woodcock, snipe, teal, widgeon and the other lesser daughters of the ark. My friendship, struggling with my carnal and fleshly prudence (which suggests that a bird a man is the proper allotment in such cases), yearneth sometimes to have thee here to pick a wing or so. I question if your Norfolk sauces match our London culinaric.

George Dyer has introduced me to the table of an agreeable old gentleman, Dr. Anderson, who gives hot legs of mutton and grape pies at his sylvan lodge at Isleworth; where, in the middle of a street, he has shot up a wall most preposterously before his small dwelling, which, with the circumstance of his taking several panes of glass out of bedroom windows (for air), causeth his neighbours to speculate strangely on the state of the good man's pericranicks. Plainly, he lives under the reputation of being deranged. George does not mind this circumstance; he rather likes him the better for it. The Doctor, in his pursuits, joins agricultural to poetical science, and has set George's brains mad about the old Scotch writers, Barbour, Douglas's Æneid, Blind Harry, etc. We returned home in a return postchaise (having dined with the Doctor), and George kept wondering and wondering, for eight or nine turnpike miles, what was the name, and striving to recollect the name, of a poet anterior to Barbour. I begged to know what was remaining of his works. "There is nothing *extant* of his works, Sir; but by all accounts he seems to have been a fine genius!" This fine genius, without anything to show for it, or any title beyond George's courtesy, without even a name; and Barbour, and Douglas, and Blind Harry now are the predominant sounds in George's pia mater, and their buzzings exclude politics, criticism, and algebra—the late lords of that illustrious lumber-room. Mark, he has never read any of these books, but is impatient till he reads them *all* at the Doctor's suggestion. Poor Dyer! his friends should be careful what sparks they let fall into such inflammable matter.

Could I have my will of the heathen, I would lock him up from all access of new ideas; I would exclude all critics that would not swear me first (upon their Virgil) that they would feed him with nothing but the old, safe, familiar notions and sounds (the rightful aborigines of his brain)—Gray, Akenside, and Mason. In these sounds, reiterated as often as possible, there could be nothing painful, nothing distracting.

God bless me, here are the birds, smoking hot! All that is gross and unspiritual in me rises at the sight!

Avaunt friendship, and all memory of absent friends!   C. LAMB.

To SAMUEL TAYLOR COLERIDGE.

LETTER LXIX.]   [Early in *August*] 1800.

Dear Coleridge—Soon after I wrote to you last, an offer was made me by Gutch (you must remember him, at Christ's; you saw him, slightly, one day with Thomson at our house), to come and lodge with him, at his house in Southampton Buildings, Chancery Lane. This was a very comfortable offer to me, the rooms being at a reasonable rent, and including the use of an old servant, besides being infinitely preferable to ordinary lodgings *in our case*, as you must perceive. As Gutch knew all our story and the perpetual liability to a recurrence in my sister's disorder, probably to the end of her life, I certainly think the offer very generous and very friendly. I have got three rooms (including servant) under £34 a year. Here I soon found myself at home; and here, in six weeks after, Mary was well enough to join me. So we are once more settled. I am afraid we are not placed out of the reach of future interruptions. But I am determined to take what snatches of pleasure we can between the acts of our distressful drama. . . . I have passed two days at Oxford, on a visit which I have long put off, to Gutch's family. The sight of the Bodleian Library, and, above all, a fine bust of Bishop Taylor, at All Souls', were particularly gratifying to me. Unluckily, it was not a family where I could take Mary with me, and I am afraid there is something of dishonesty in any pleasures I take without *her*. She never goes anywhere. I do not know what I can add to this letter. I hope you are better by this time; and I desire to be affectionately remembered to Sara and Hartley.

I expected before this to have had tidings of another little philosopher. Lloyd's wife is on the point of favouring the world.

Have you seen the new edition of Burns? his posthumous works and letters? I have only been able to procure the first volume, which contains his life—very confusedly and badly written, and interspersed with dull pathological and *medical* discussion. It is written by a Dr. Currie. Do you know the well-meaning doctor? Alas, *ne sutor ultra crepidam!*

I hope to hear again from you very soon. Godwin is gone to Ireland on a visit to Grattan. Before he went I passed much time with him, and he has showed me particular attentions: N.B. A thing I much like. Your books are all safe: only I have not thought it necessary to fetch away your last batch, which I understand are at Johnson's, the bookseller, who has got quite as much room, and will take as much care of them as myself; and you can send for them immediately from him.

I wish you would advert to a letter I sent you at Grassmere about *Christabel*, and comply with my request contained therein.

Love to all friends round Skiddaw.   C. LAMB.

To J. M. GUTCH.

LETTER LXX.]   [Probably Autumn of 1800.]

Dear Gutch—Anderson is not come home, and I am almost afraid to tell you what has happened, lest it should seem to have happened by my fault in not writing for you home sooner. This morning Henry, the eldest lad, was missing: we supposed he was only gone out on a morning's stroll, and that he would return; but he did not return, and we discovered that he had opened your desk before he went, and I suppose taken all the money he could find, for on diligent search I could find none, and on opening your letter to Anderson, which I thought necessary to get at the key, I learn that you had a good deal of money there. Several people have been here after you to-day, and the boys seem quite frightened and do not know what to do. In particular one gentleman wants to have some writings finished by Tuesday. For God's sake, set out by the first coach! Mary has been crying all day about it, and I am now just going to some law-stationer in the neighbourhood that the eldest boy has recommended, to get him to come and be in the house for a day or two to manage. I cannot think what detains Anderson. His sister is quite frightened about him. I am very sorry I did not write yesterday, but Henry persuaded me to wait till he could ascertain when some job must be done for Mr. Foulkes, and as nothing had occurred besides, I did not like to disturb your pleasures. I now see my error, and shall be heartily ashamed to see your— (*At this point the reader of the letter turns over the leaf, and finds*)

A BITE ! ! !

Anderson is come home, and the wheels of thy business are going on as ever!

The boy is honest, and I am thy friend! And how does the coach-maker's daughter? Thou art her Phæton, her Gig, and her Sociable. Commend me to Rob   C. LAMB.
Saturday.

To SAMUEL TAYLOR COLERIDGE.

LETTER LXXI.]   *August 26, 1800.*

How do you like this little epigram? It is not my writing, nor had I any finger in it. If you concur with me in thinking it very elegant and very original, I shall be tempted to name the author to you. I will just hint that it is almost or quite a first attempt.

HELEN.

HIGH-BORN Helen, round your dwelling
  These twenty years I've paced in vain:
Haughty beauty, thy lover's duty
  Hath been to glory in his pain.

High-born Helen, proudly telling
 Stories of thy cold disdain;
I starve, I die, now you comply,
 And I no longer can complain.

These twenty years I've lived on tears,
 Dwelling for ever on a frown;
On sighs I've fed, your scorn my bread;
 I perish now you kind are grown.

Can I, who loved my beloved
 But for the scorn "was in her eye,"
Can I be moved for my beloved,
 When she "returns me sigh for sigh?"

In stately pride, by my bed-side,
 High-born Helen's portrait's hung;
Deaf to my praise, my mournful lays
 Are nightly to the portrait sung.

To that I weep, nor ever sleep,
 Complaining all night long to her,
Helen, grown old, no longer cold,
 Said, "You to all men I prefer."

By the by, I have a sort of recollection that somebody, I think *you,* promised me a sight of Wordsworth's Tragedy. I should be very glad of it just now; for I have got Manning with me, and should like to read it *with him.* But this, I confess, is a refinement. Under any circumstances, alone, in Cold-Bath prison, or in the desert island, just when Prospero and his crew had set off, with Caliban in a cage, to Milan, it would be a treat to me to read that play. Manning has read it, so has Lloyd, and all Lloyd's family; but I could not get him to betray his trust by giving *me* a sight of it. Lloyd is sadly deficient in some of those virtuous vices. I have just lit upon a most beautiful fiction of Hell punishments by the author of *Hurlothrumbo,* a mad farce. The inventor imagines that in Hell there is a great caldron of hot water, in which a man can scarce hold his finger, and an immense sieve over it, into which the probationary souls are put—

"And all the little souls
 Pop thro' the riddle holes!"

George Dyer is the only literary character I am happily acquainted with. The oftener I see him, the more deeply I admire him. He is goodness itself. If I could but calculate the precise date of his death, I would write a novel on purpose to make George the hero. I could hit him off to a hair.

George brought a Dr. Anderson to see me. The doctor is a very pleasant old man, a great genius for agriculture, one that ties his breeches-knees with pack thread, and boasts of having had disappointments from ministers. The Doctor happened to mention an epic poem by one Wilkie, called the *Epigoniad,* in which he assured us there is not one tolerable line from beginning to end, but that all the characters, incidents, etc., are verbally copied from *Homer.* George, who had been sitting quite inattentive to the Doctor's criticism, no sooner heard the sound of *Homer* strike his pericranicks, than up he gets, and declares he must see that poem immediately: where was it to be had? An epic poem of 8000 lines, and *he* not hear of it! There must be some good things in it, and it was necessary he should see it, for he had touched pretty deeply upon that subject in his criticisms on the Epic. George has touched pretty deeply upon the Lyric, I find; he has also prepared a dissertation on the Drama and the comparison of the English and German theatres. As I rather doubted his competency to do the latter, knowing that his peculiar *turn* lies in the lyric species of composition, I questioned George what English plays he had read. I found that he *had* read Shakspeare (whom he calls an original, but irregular, genius); but it was a good while ago; and he has dipped into Rowe and Otway, I suppose having found their names in *Johnson's Lives* at full length; and upon this slender ground he has undertaken the task. He never seemed even to have heard of Fletcher, Ford, Marlowe, Massinger, and the worthies of Dodsley's collection; but he is to read all these, to prepare him for bringing out his "Parallel" in the Winter. I find he is also determined to vindicate poetry from the shackles which Aristotle and some others have imposed upon it, which is very good-natured of him, and very necessary just now. Now I am *touching* so *deeply* upon poetry, can I forget that I have just received from Cottle a magnificent copy of his Guinea *Alfred.* Four-and-twenty books to read in the dog-days! I got as far as the Mad Monk the first day, and fainted. Mr. Cottle's genius strongly points him to the *Pastoral,* but his inclinations divert him perpetually from his calling. He imitates Southey, as Rowe did Shakspeare, with his "Good morrow to ye; good master Lieutenant." Instead of *a* man, *a* woman, *a* daughter, he constantly writes, one a man, one a woman, one his daughter. Instead of *the* king, *the* hero, he constantly writes, he the king, he the hero; two flowers of rhetoric, palpably from the "Joan." But Mr. Cottle soars a higher pitch: and when he *is* original, it is in a most original way indeed. His terrific scenes are indefatigable. Serpents, asps, spiders, ghosts, dead bodies, staircases made of nothing, with adders' tongues for bannisters. What a brain he must have! He puts as many plums in his pudding as my grandmother used to do;—and then his emerging from Hell's horrors into light, and treading on pure flats of this earth—for twenty-three books together! C. L.

To THOMAS MANNING.

October 5, 1800.

C. L.'s moral sense presents her compliments to Doctor Manning, is very thankful for his medical advice, but is happy to add that her disorder has died of itself.

Dr. Manning, Coleridge has left us, to go into the North, on a visit to Wordsworth. With him have flown all my splendid prospects of engagement with the *Morning Post,* all my visionary guineas, the deceitful wages of unborn scandal. In truth, I wonder you took it up so seriously. All my intention was but to make a little sport with such public and fair game as Mr. Pitt, Mr. Wilberforce, Mrs. Fitzherbert, the Devil, etc.— gentry dipped in Styx all over, whom no paper-javclinlings can touch. To have made free with these cattle, where was the harm? 'twould have been but giving a polish to lamp-black, not nigrifying a negro primarily. After all, I cannot but regret my involuntary virtue. Damn virtue that's thrust upon us; it behaves itself with such constraint, till conscience opens the window and lets out the goose. I had struck off two imitations of Burton, quite abstracted from any modern allusions, which it was my intent only to lug in from time to time to make 'em popular.

Stuart has got these, with an introductory letter; but, not hearing from him, I have ceased from my labours, but I write to him to-day to get a final answer. I am afraid they won't do for a paper. Burton is a scarce gentleman, not much known, else I had done 'em pretty well.

I have also hit off a few lines in the name of Burton, being a "Conceit of Diabolic Possession." Burton was a man often assailed by deepest melancholy, and at other times much given to laughing and jesting, as is the way with melancholy men. I will send them to you: they were almost extempore, and no great things; but you will indulge them. Robert Lloyd is come to town. Priscilla meditates going to see *Pizarro* at Drury Lane to-night (from her uncle's), under cover of coming to dine with me . . . *heu tempora! heu mores!*—I have barely time to finish, as I expect her and Robin every minute.—Yours as usual.   C. L.

To SAMUEL TAYLOR COLERIDGE.

LETTER LXXIII.]   *October* 9, 1800.

I suppose you have heard of the death of Amos Cottle. I paid a solemn visit of condolence to his brother, accompanied by George Dyer, of burlesque memory. I went trembling to see poor Cottle so immediately upon the event. He was in black; and his younger brother was also in black. Everything wore an aspect suitable to the respect due to the freshly dead. For some time after our entrance, nobody spake till George modestly put in a question, whether *Alfred* was likely to sell. This was Lethe to Cottle, and his poor face, wet with tears, and his kind eye brightened up in a moment. Now I felt it was my cue to speak. I had to thank him for a present of a magnificent copy, and had promised to send him my remarks,—the least thing I could do; so I ventured to suggest, that I perceived a considerable improvement he had made in his first book since the state in which he first read it to me. Joseph, who till now had sat with his knees cowering in by the fireplace, wheeled about, and with great difficulty of body shifted the same round to the corner of a table where I was sitting, and first stationing one thigh over the other, which is his sedentary mood, and placidly fixing his benevolent face right against mine, waited my observations. At that moment it came strongly into my mind, that I had got Uncle Toby before me, he looked so kind and so good. I could not say an unkind thing of *Alfred*. So I set my memory to work to recollect what was the name of Alfred's Queen, and with some adroitness recalled the well-known sound to Cottle's ears of Alswitha. At that moment I could perceive that Cottle had forgot his brother was so lately become a blessed spirit. In the language of mathematicians the author was as 9, the brother as 1. I felt my cue, and strong pity working at the root, I went to work, and beslabber'd *Alfred* with most unqualified praise, or only qualifying my praise by the occasional politic interposition of an exception taken against trivial faults, slips, and human imperfections, which, by removing the appearance of insincerity, did but in truth heighten the relish. Perhaps I might have spared that refinement, for Joseph was in a humour to hope and believe *all things*. What I said was beautifully supported, corroborated, and confirmed by the stupidity of his brother on my left hand, and by George on my right, who has an utter incapacity of comprehending that there can be anything bad in poetry. All poems are *good* poems to George; all men are *fine geniuses*. So what with my actual memory, of which I made the most, and Cottle's own helping me out, for I *really* had forgotten a good deal of *Alfred,* I made shift to discuss the most essential parts entirely to the satisfaction of its author, who repeatedly declared that he loved nothing better than *candid* criticism. Was I a candid grayhound now for all this? or did I do right? I believe I did. The effect was luscious to my conscience. For all the rest of the evening Amos was no more heard of, till George revived the subject by inquiring whether some account should not be drawn up by the friends of the deceased to be inserted in Phillips's Monthly Obituary; adding, that Amos was estimable both for his head and heart, and would have made a fine poet if he had lived. To the expediency of this measure Cottle fully assented, but could not help adding that he always thought that the qualities of his brother's heart exceeded those of his head. I believe his brother, when living, had formed precisely the same idea of him; and I apprehend the world will assent to both judgments. I rather guess that the Brothers were poetical rivals. I judged so when I saw them together. Poor Cottle, I must leave him after his short dream, to muse again upon his poor brother, for whom I am sure in secret he will yet shed many a tear. Now send me in return some Greta news.   C. L.

To WORDSWORTH

LETTER LXXIV.]   *October* 13, 1800.

Dear Wordsworth—I have not forgot your commissions. But the truth is (and why should I not confess it?) I am not plethorically abounding in cash at this present. Merit, God knows, is very little rewarded; but it does not become me to speak of myself. My motto is "contented with little, yet wishing for more." Now, the books you wish for would require some pounds, which, I am sorry to say, I have not by me; so I will say at once, if you will give me a draft upon your town banker for any sum you propose to lay out, I will dispose of it to the very best of my skill in choice old books, such as my own soul loveth. In fact, I have been waiting for the liquidation of a debt to enable myself to set about your commission handsomely; for it is a scurvy thing to cry, "Give me the money first," and I am the first of the family of the Lambs that have done it for many centuries; but the debt remains as it was, and my old friend that I accommodated has generously forgot it! The books which you want, I calculate at about £8. Ben Jonson is a guinea book. Beaumont and Fletcher, in folio, the right folio, not now to be met with; the octavos are about £3. As to any other dramatists, I do not know where to find them, except what are in Dodsley's Old Plays, which are about £3 also. Massinger I never saw but at one shop, and it is now gone; but one of the editions of Dodsley contains about a fourth (the best) of his plays. Congreve, and the rest of King Charles's moralists, are cheap and accessible. The works on Ireland I will inquire after; but I fear Spenser's is not to be had apart from his poems; I never saw it. But you may depend upon my sparing no pains to furnish you as complete a library of old poets and dramatists as will be prudent to buy; for, I suppose you do not include the £20 edition of *Hamlet,* single play, which Kemble has. Marlowe's plays and poems are totally vanished; only one edition of Dodsley retains one, and the other two of his plays: but John Ford is the man after Shakspeare. Let me know your will and pleasure soon, for I have observed, next to the pleasure of buying a bargain for one's self, is the pleasure of persuading a friend to buy it. It tickles one with the image of an imprudency, without the penalty usually annexed.

C. LAMB.

To THOMAS MANNING.

LETTER LXXV.] *October* 16, 1800.

Dear Manning—Had you written one week before you did, I certainly should have obeyed your injunction; you should have seen me before my letter. I will explain to you my situation. There are six of us in one department. Two of us (within these four days) are confined with severe fevers; and two more, who belong to the Tower Militia, expect to have marching orders on Friday. Now six are absolutely necessary. I have already asked and obtained two young hands to supply the loss of the *feverites.* And, with the other prospect before me, you may believe I cannot decently ask leave of absence for myself. All I can promise (and I do promise, with the sincerity of St. Peter, and the contrition of sinner Peter if I fail) is that I will come *the very first spare week,* and go nowhere till I have been at Cambridge. No matter if you are in a state of pupilage when I come; for I can employ myself in Cambridge very pleasantly in the mornings. Are there not libraries, halls, colleges, books, pictures, statues? I wish you had made London in your way. There is an exhibition quite uncommon in Europe, which could not have escaped *your genius,*—a live rattlesnake, ten feet in length, and the thickness of a big leg. I went to see it last night by candlelight. We were ushered into a room very little bigger than ours at Pentonville. A man and woman and four boys live in this room, joint tenants with nine snakes, most of them such as no remedy has been discovered for their bite. We walked into the middle, which is formed by a half moon of wired boxes, all mansions of *snakes*—whip-snakes, thunder-snakes, pignose-snakes, American vipers, and *this monster.* He lies curled up in folds. Immediately a stranger entered (for he is used to the family, and sees them play at cards), he set up a rattle like a watchman's in London, or near as loud, and reared up a head, from the midst of these folds, like a toad, and shook his head, and showed every sign a snake can show of irritation. I had the foolish curiosity to strike the wires with my finger, and the devil flew at me with his toad-mouth wide open; the inside of his mouth is quite white. I had got my finger away, nor could he well have bit me with his big mouth, which would have been certain death in five minutes. But it frightened me so much, that I did not recover my voice for a minute's space. I forgot, in my fear, that he was secured. You would have forgot too, for 'tis incredible how such a monster can be confined in small gauzy-looking wires. I dreamed of snakes in the night. I wish to heaven you could see it. He absolutely swelled with passion to the bigness of a large thigh. I could not retreat without infringing on another box; and just behind, a little devil not an inch from my back had got his nose out, with some difficulty and pain, quite through the bars! He was soon taught better manners. All the snakes were curious, and objects of terror: but this monster, like Aaron's serpent, swallowed up the impression of the rest. He opened his cursed mouth, when he made at me, as wide as his head was broad. I hallooed out quite loud, and felt pains all over my body with the fright.

I have had the felicity of hearing George Dyer read out one book of the *Farmer's Boy.* I thought it rather childish. No doubt, there is originality in it (which, in your self-taught geniuses, is a most rare quality, they generally getting hold of some bad models, in a scarcity of books, and forming their taste on them), but no *selection. All* is described.

Mind, I have only heard read one book.—Yours sincerely, Philo-Snake,   C. L.

November 3, 1800.

Ecquid meditatur Archimedes? What is Euclid doing? What hath happened to learned Trismegist? Doth he take it in ill part, that his humble friend did not comply with his courteous invitation? Let it suffice, I could not come. Are impossibilities nothing?—be they abstractions of the intellect?—or not (rather) most sharp and mortifying realities? nuts in the Will's mouth too hard for her to crack? brick and stone walls in her way, which she can by no means eat through? sore lets, *impedimenta viarum* no thoroughfares? *racemi nimium alte pendentes?* Is the phrase classic? I allude to the grapes in Æsop, which cost the fox a strain, and gained the world an aphorism. Observe the superscription of this letter. In adapting the size of the letters, which constitute *your* name and Mr. *Crisp's* name respectively, I had an eye to your different stations in life. 'Tis truly curious and must be soothing to an *aristocrat.* I wonder it has never been hit on before my time. I have made an acquisition latterly of a *pleasant hand,* one Rickman, to whom I was introduced by George Dyer, not the most flattering auspices under which one man can be introduced to another. George brings all sorts of people together, setting up a sort of agrarian law, or common property, in matter of society; but for once he has done me a great pleasure, while he was only pursuing a principle, as *ignes fatui may* light you home. This Rickman lives in our Buildings, immediately opposite our house; the finest fellow to drop in a' nights, about nine or ten o'clock—cold bread and cheese time—just in the *wishing* time of the night, when you *wish* for somebody to come in, without a distinct idea of a probable anybody. Just in the nick, neither too early to be tedious, nor too late to sit a reasonable time. He is a most pleasant hand; a fine rattling fellow, has gone through life laughing at solemn apes;—himself hugely literate, oppressively full of information in all stuff of conversation, from matter of fact to Xenophon and Plato—can talk Greek with Porson, politics with Thelwall, conjecture with George Dyer, nonsense with me, and anything with anybody; a great farmer, somewhat concerned in an agricultural magazine; reads no poetry but Shakspeare; very intimate with Southey, but never reads his poetry; relishes George Dyer; thoroughly penetrates into the ridiculous wherever found; understands the *first time* (a great desideratum in common minds)—you need never twice speak to him; does not want explanations, translations, limitations, as Professor Godwin does when you make an assertion; *up* to anything; *down* to everything; whatever *sapit hominem.* A perfect *man.* All this farrago, which must perplex you to read, and has put me to a little trouble to *select,* only proves how impossible it is to describe a *pleasant hand.* You must see Rickman to know him, for he is a species in one; a new class; an exotic; any slip of which I am proud to put in my garden-pot; the clearest headed fellow; fullest of matter, with least verbosity. If there be any alloy in my fortune to have met with such a man, it is that he commonly divides his time between town and country, having some foolish family ties at Christchurch, by which means he can only gladden our London hemisphere with returns of light. He is now going for six weeks.

At last I have written to Kemble, to know the event of my play, which was presented last Christmas. As I suspected, came an answer back that the copy was lost, and could not be found—no hint that anybody had to this day ever looked into it—with a courteous (reasonable!) request of another copy (if I had one by me), and a promise of a definite answer in a week. I could not resist so facile and moderate a demand; so scrib bled out another, omitting sundry things, such as the witch story, about half of the forest scene (which is too leisurely for story), and transposing that soliloquy about England getting drunk, which, like its reciter, stupidly stood alone, nothing prevenient or antevenient; and cleared away a good deal besides; and sent this copy, written *all out* (with alterations, etc., *requiring judgment*) in one day and a half! I sent it last night, and am in weekly expectation of the tolling bell and death-warrant.

This is all my London news. Send me some from the *banks of Cam,* as the poets delight to speak, especially George Dyer, who has no other name nor idea nor definition of Cambridge. Its being a market town, sending members to Parliament, never entered into his definition. It was and is simply the banks of the Cam, or the fair Cam, as Oxford is the banks of the Isis, or the fair Isis. Yours in all humility, most illustrious Trismegist, C. LAMB.

(Read on; there's more at the bottom.)

You ask me about the *Farmer's Boy.* Don't you think the fellow who wrote it (who is a shoemaker) has a poor mind? Don't you find he is always silly about *poor Giles,* and those abject kind of phrases, which mark a man that looks up to wealth? None of Burns's poet dignity. What do you think? I have just opened him; but he makes me sick.

Dyer knows the shoemaker, a damn'd stupid hound in company; but George promises to introduce him indiscriminately to all friends.

LETTER LXXVII.] *November 28, 1800.*

Dear Manning—I have received a very kind invitation from Lloyd and Sophia, to go and spend a month with them at the Lakes. Now it fortunately happens (which is so seldom the case) that I have spare cash by me, enough to answer the expenses of so long a journey; and I am determined to get away from the office by some means. The purpose of this letter is to request of you (my dear friend), that you will not take it unkind if I decline my proposed visit to Cambridge *for the present.* Perhaps I shall be able to take Cambridge *in my way,* going or coming. I need not describe to you the expectations which such an one as myself, pent up all my life in a dirty city, have formed of a tour to the Lakes. Consider Grasmere! Ambleside! Wordsworth! Coleridge! I hope you will. Hills, woods, lakes, and mountains, to the devil. I will eat snipes with thee, Thomas Manning. Only confess, confess, a *bite.*

P.S.—I think you named the 16th; but was it not modest of Lloyd to send such an invitation! It shows his knowledge of *money* and *time.* I should be loth to think he meant

"Ironic satire sidelong sklented
On my poor pursie."—BURNS.

For my part, with reference to my friends northward, I must confess that I am not romance-bit about *Nature*. The earth, the sea, and sky (when all is said), is but as a house to dwell in. If the inmates be courteous, and good liquors flow like the conduits at an old coronation, if they can talk sensibly, and feel properly, I have no need to stand staring upon the gilded looking-glass (that strained my friend's purse-strings in the purchase) nor his five-shilling print, over the mantelpiece, of old Nabbs the carrier (which only betrays his false taste). Just as important to me (in a sense) is all the furniture of my world; eye-pampering, but satisfies no heart. Streets, streets, streets, markets, theatres, churches, Covent Gardens, shops sparkling with pretty faces of industrious milliners, neat sempstresses, ladies cheapening, gentlemen behind counters lying, authors in the street with spectacles, George Dyers (you may know them by their gait), lamps lit at night, pastrycooks' and silversmiths' shops, beautiful Quakers of Pentonville, noise of coaches, drowsy cry of mechanic watchmen at night, with bucks reeling home drunk; if you happen to wake at midnight, cries of "Fire!" and "Stop thief!"; inns of court, with their learned air, and halls, and butteries, just like Cambridge colleges; old book-stalls, "Jeremy Taylors," "Burtons on Melancholy," and "Religio Medicis," on every stall. These are thy pleasures, O London! with thy many sins. O city, abounding in w . . ., for these may Keswick and her giant brood go hang!   C. L.

To WILLIAM GODWIN.

Thursday Morning,
LETTER LXXVIII.]   *December* 4, 1800.

Dear Sir—I send this speedily after the heels of Cooper (O! the dainty expression) to say that Mary is obliged to stay at home on Sunday to receive a female friend, from whom I am equally glad to escape. So that we shall be by ourselves. I write, because it may make *some* difference in your marketing, etc.   C. L.

I am sorry to put you to the expense of twopence postage. But I calculate thus: if Mary comes she will—

eat Beef 2 plates, ...	4d.
Batter Pudding 1 do.	2d.
Beer, a pint, ...	2d.
Wine, 3 glasses, ...	11d. I drink no wine!
Chestnuts, after dinner, . . .	2d.
Tea and supper at moderate calculation, .	9d.

2s. 6d.
From which deduct   2d. postage.

2s. 4d.

You are a clear gainer by her not coming.

Wednesday Morning,

LETTER LXXIX.]   *December* 11, 1800.

Dear Sir—I expected a good deal of pleasure from your company to-morrow, but I am sorry I must beg of you to excuse me. I have been confined ever since I saw you with one of the severest colds I ever experienced, occasioned by being in the night air on Sunday and on the following day very foolishly. I am neither in health nor spirits to meet company. I hope and trust I shall get out on Saturday night. You will add to your many favours by transmitting to me as early as possible as many tickets as conveniently you can spare,—Yours truly,   C. L.

I have been plotting how to abridge the Epilogue. But I cannot see that any lines can be spared, retaining the connection, except these two, which are better out.

> "Why should I instance, etc.,
> The sick man's purpose, etc.,"

and then the following line must run thus,

> "The truth by an example best is shown."

Excuse this *important* postscript.

To THOMAS MANNING

LETTER LXXX.]   *December* 13, 1800.

I have received your letter *this moment,* not having been at the office. I have just time to scribble down the epilogue. To your epistle I will just reply, that I will certainly come to Cambridge before January is out; I'll come *when I can.* You shall have an amended copy of my play early next week. Mary thanks you; but her handwriting is too feminine to be exposed to a Cambridge gentleman, though I endeavour to persuade her that you understand algebra, and must understand her hand. The play is the man's you wot of; but for Heaven's sake do not mention it: it is to come out in a feigned name, as one Tobin's. I will omit the introductory lines which connect it with the play, and give you the concluding tale, which is the mass and bulk of the epilogue. The name is *Jack Incident.* It is all about promise-breaking: you will see it all, if you read the *papers.*

> "Jack, of dramatic genius justly vain,
> Purchased a renter's share at Drury Lane;
> A prudent man in every other matter,
> Known at his club-room for an honest hatter;
> Humane and courteous, led a civil life,
> And has been seldom known to beat his wife;
> But Jack is now grown quite another man,
> Frequents the green-room, knows the plot and plan
>   Of each new piece,

And has been seen to talk with Sheridan!
In at the play-house just at six he pops,
And never quits it till the curtain drops,
Is never absent on the *author's night,*
Knows actresses and actors too——by sight;
So humble, that with Suett he'll confer,
Or take a pipe with plain Jack Bannister;
Nay, with an author has been known so free,
He once suggested a catastrophe—
In short, John dabbled till his head was turn'd;
His wife remonstrated, his neighbours mourn'd,
His customers were dropping off apace,
And Jack's affairs began to wear a piteous face.
  One night his wife began a curtain lecture;
'My dearest Johnny, husband, spouse, protector,
Take pity on your helpless babes and me,
Save us from ruin, you from bankruptcy—
Look to your business, leave these cursed plays,
And try again your old industrious ways.'
  Jack who was always scared at the Gazette,
And had some bits of scull uninjured yet,
Promised amendment, vow'd his wife spake reason,
'He would not see another play that season—'
  Three stubborn fortnights Jack his promise kept,
Was late and early in his shop, eat, slept,
And walk'd and talk'd, like ordinary men;
No *wit,* but John the hatter once again—
Visits his club: when lo! one *fatal night*
His wife with horror view'd the well-known sight—
John's *hat, wig, snuff-box*—well she knew his tricks—
And Jack decamping at the hour of six;
Just at the counter's edge a playbill lay,
Announcing that 'Pizarro' was the play—
'O Johnny, Johnny, this is your old doing.'
Quoth Jack, 'Why what the devil storm's a-brewing?
About a harmless play why all this fright?
I'll go and see it if it's but for spite—
Zounds, woman! Nelson's to be there to-night.' "

N.B.—This was intended for Jack Bannister to speak; but the sage managers have chosen Miss *Heard,* except Miss Tidswell the worst actress ever seen or *heard.* Now I remember I have promised the loan of my play. I will lend it *instantly,* and you shall get it ('pon honour!) by this day week.

I must go and dress for the boxes! First night! Finding I have time, I transcribe the rest. Observe, you must read the last first; it begins thus:—(The names I took from a little outline G. gave me. I have not read the play.)

"Ladies, ye've seen how Guzman's consort died,
Poor victim of a Spaniard brother's pride,
When Spanish honour through the world was blown,
And Spanish beauty for the best was known.
In that romantic, unenlighten'd time,
A *breach of promise* was a sort of crime—
Which of you handsome English ladies here,
But deems the penance bloody and severe?

A whimsical old Saragossa fashion,
That a dead father's dying inclination,
Should *live* to thwart a living daughter's passion:
Unjustly on the sex *we* men exclaim,
Rail at *your* vices,—and commit the same;—
Man is a promise-breaker from the womb,
And goes a promise-breaker to the tomb—
What need we instance here the lover's vow,
The sick man's purpose, or the great man's bow?
The truth by few examples best is shown—
Instead of many which are better known,
Take poor Jack Incident, that's dead and gone.
Jack," etc. etc. etc.

Now you have it all—how do you like it? I am going to hear it recited ! ! !   C. L.

To WILLIAM GODWIN.

LETTER LXXXI.]   *Late o' Sunday, December* 14, 1800.

Dear Sir—I have performed my office in a slovenly way, but judge for
me. I sat down at six o'clock, and never left reading (and I read out to
Mary) your play till 10. In this sitting I noted down lines as they occurred, exactly as you will read my rough paper. Do not be frightened
at the bulk of my remarks, for they are almost all upon single lines,
which, put together, do not amount to a hundred, and many of them
merely verbal. I had but one object in view, abridgment for compression
sake. I have used a dogmatical language (which is truly ludicrous when
the trivial nature of my remarks is considered); and, remember, my
office was to hunt out faults. You may fairly abridge one half of them,
as a fair deduction for the infirmities of Error and a single reading,
which leaves only fifty objections, most of them merely against words,
on no short play. Remember, you constituted me Executioner, and a
hangman has been seldom seen to be ashamed of his profession before
Master Sheriff. We'll talk of the Beauties (of which I am more than
ever sure) when we meet.—Yours truly,   C. L.

I will barely add, as you are on the very point of printing, that in my
opinion neither prologue nor epilogue should accompany the play. It can
only serve to remind your readers of its fate. *Both* suppose an audience,
and, that jest being gone, must convert into burlesque. Nor would I (but
therein custom and decorum must be a law) print the actors' names.
Some things must be kept out of sight.

I have done, and I have but a few square inches of paper to fill up. I
am emboldened by a little jorum of punch (vastly good) to say that next
to *one man,* I am the most hurt at our ill success. The breast of Hecuba,
where she did suckle Hector, looked not to be more lovely than Marshal's
forehead when it spit forth sweat, at Critic-swords contending. I remem-

ber two honest lines by Marvel (whose poems by the way I am just going
to possess).

> "Where every Mower's wholesome heat
> Smells like an Alexander's sweat."

To THOMAS MANNING.

Letter LXXXII.]   *December* 16, 1800.

We are damn'd!—Not the facetious epilogue itself could save us; for,
as the editor of the *Morning Post* (quick-sighted gentleman!) hath this
morning truly observed (I beg pardon if I falsify his *words;* their profound *sense* I am sure I retain;) both prologue and epilogue were worthy
of accompanying such a piece; and indeed (mark the profundity, Mr.
Manning!) were received with proper indignation by such of the audience only as thought either worth attending to. Professor, thy glories
wax dim! Again, the incomparable author of the *True Briton* declareth
in *his* paper (bearing same date) that the epilogue was an indifferent attempt at humour and character, and failed in both. I forbear to mention
the other papers, because I have not read them. O Professor, how different thy feelings now (*quantum mutatus ab illo professore, qui in agris
philosophiæ tantas victorias acquisivisti*),—how different thy proud
feelings but one little week ago—thy anticipations of thy nine nights—
those visionary claps, which have soothed thy soul by day and thy
dreams by night! Calling in accidentally on the Professor while he was
out, I was ushered into the study; and my nose quickly (most sagacious
always) pointed me to four tokens lying loose upon thy table, Professor,
which indicated thy violent and satanical pride of heart. *Imprimis,*
there caught mine eye a list of six persons, thy friends, whom thou didst
meditate inviting to a sumptuous dinner on the Thursday, anticipating
the profits of thy Saturday's play to answer charges: I was in the honoured file! Next (a stronger evidence of thy violent and almost satanical
pride) lay a list of all the morning papers (from the *Morning Chronicle*
downwards to the *Porcupine*), with the places of their respective offices,
where thou wast meditating to insert, and didst insert, an elaborate
sketch of the story of thy play; stones in thy enemy's hand to bruise thee
with, and severely wast thou bruised, O Professor! nor do I know what
oil to pour into thy wounds. Next (which convinced me to a dead conviction of thy pride, violent and almost satanical pride!) lay a list of
books which thy un-tragedy-favoured pocket could never answer; Dodsley's Old Plays, Malone's Shakspeare (still harping upon thy play, thy
philosophy abandoned meanwhile to Christians and superstitious
minds); nay, I believe (if I can believe my memory) that the ambitious
Encyclopædia itself was part of thy meditated acquisitions; but many
a playbook was there. All these visions are *damned;* and

thou, Professor, must read Shakspeare in future out of a common edition; and, hark ye! pray read him to a little better purpose. Last and strongest against thee (in colours manifest as the hand upon Belshazzar's wall) lay a volume of poems by C. Lloyd and C. Lamb. Thy heart misgave thee, that thy assistant might possibly not have talent enough to furnish thee an epilogue! Manning, all these things came over my mind; all the gratulations that would have thickened upon him, and even some have glanced aside upon his humble friend; the vanity, and the fame, and the profits (the Professor is £500 ideal money out of pocket by this failure, besides £200 he would have got for the copyright, and the Professor is never much beforehand with the world; what he gets is all by the sweat of his brow and dint of brain, for the Professor, though a sure man, is also a slow); and now to muse upon thy altered physiognomy, thy pale and squalid appearance (a kind of *blue sickness* about the eyelids), and thy crest fallen, and thy proud demand of £200 from thy bookseller changed to an uncertainty of his taking it at all, or giving the full £50. The Professor has won my heart by this *his* mournful catastrophe. You remember Marshall, who dined with him at my house; I met him in the lobby immediately after the damnation of the Professor's play, and he looked to me like an angel; his face was lengthened, and all over perspiration. I never saw such a care-fraught visage; I could have hugged him, I loved him so intensely. "From every pore of him a perfume fell." I have seen that man in many situations, and, from my soul, I think that a more god-like honest soul exists not in this world. The Professor's poor nerves trembling with the recent shock, he hurried him away to my house to supper, and there we comforted him as well as we could. He came to consult me about a change of catastrophe; but alas! the piece was condemned long before that crisis. I at first humoured him with a specious proposition, but have since joined his true friends in advising him to give it up. He did it with a pang, and is to print it as *his*.   L.

LETTER LXXXIII.]   *December* 27, 1800.

At length George Dyer's phrenitis has come to a crisis; he is raging and furiously mad. I waited upon the heathen, Thursday was a se'nnight. The first symptom which struck my eye, and gave me incontrovertible proof of the fatal truth, was a pair of nankeen pantaloons four times too big for him, which the said Heathen did pertinaciously affirm to be new.

They were absolutely ingrained with the accumulated dirt of ages; but he affirmed them to be clean. He was going to visit a lady that was nice about those things, and that's the reason he wore nankeen that day. And then he danced, and capered, and fidgeted, and pulled up his pantaloons, and hugged his intolerable flannel vestment closer about his poetic loins. Anon he gave it loose to the zephyrs which plentifully insinuate their tiny bodies through every crevice, door, window, or wainscot, expressly formed for the exclusion of such impertinents. Then he caught at a proof sheet, and catched up a laundress's bill instead—made a dart at Bloomfield's Poems, and threw them in agony aside. I could not bring him to one direct reply; he could not maintain his jumping mind in a right line for the tithe of a moment by Clifford's Inn clock. He must go to the printer's immediately: (the most unlucky accident!) he had struck off five hundred impressions of his Poems, which were ready for delivery to subscribers, and the Preface must all be expunged. There were eighty pages of Preface, and not till that morning had he discovered that in the very first page of said Preface he had set out with a principle of Criticism fundamentally wrong, which vitiated all his following reasoning. The Preface must be expunged, although it cost him £30, the lowest calculation, taking in paper and printing! In vain have his real friends remonstrated against this Midsummer madness. George is as obstinate as a Primitive Christian, and wards and parries off all our thrusts with one unanswerable fence:—"Sir, 'tis of great consequence that the *world* is not *misled!*"

As for the other Professor, he has actually begun to dive into Tavernier and Chardin's *Persian* Travels for a story, to form a new drama for the sweet tooth of this fastidious age. Hath not Bethlehem College a fair action for non-residence against such professors? Are poets so *few* in *this age,* that He must write poetry? *Is morals* a subject so exhausted, that he must quit that line? Is the metaphysic well (without a bottom) drained dry?

If I can guess at the wicked pride of the Professor's heart, I would take a shrewd wager that he disdains ever again to dip his pen in *Prose.* Adieu, ye splendid theories! Farewell, dreams of political justice! Lawsuits, where I was council for Archbishop Fenelon *versus* my own mother, in the famous fire cause!

Vanish from my mind, professors, one and all! I have metal more attractive on foot.

Man of many snipes,—I will sup with thee (Deo volente, et diabolo nolente,) on Monday night, the 5th of January, in the new year, and crush a cup to the infant century.

A word or two of my progress: Embark at six o'clock in the morning, with a fresh gale, on a Cambridge one-decker; very cold till eight at night; land at St. Mary's lighthouse, muffins and coffee upon table (or any other curious production of Turkey, or both Indies), snipes exactly at nine, punch to commence at ten, with *argument;* difference of opinion is expected to take place about eleven; perfect unanimity, with some haziness and dimness, before twelve. *N.B.*—My single affection is not so singly wedded to snipes; but the curious and epicurean eye would also take a pleasure in beholding a delicate and well-chosen assortment of teals, ortolans, the unctuous and palate-soothing flesh of geese, wild and tame, nightingales' brains, the sensorium of a young sucking pig, or any other Christmas dish, which I leave to the judgment of you and the cook of Gonville.   C. LAMB.

To SAMUEL TAYLOR COLERIDGE.

LETTER LXXXIV.] [No date—end of 1800.]

I send you, in this parcel, my play, which I beg you to present in my name, with my respect and love, to Wordsworth, and his sister. You blame us for giving your direction to Miss Wesley. The woman has been ten times after us about it, and we gave it her at last, under the idea that no further harm would ensue; but she would *once* write to you, and you would bite your lips and forget to answer it, and so it would end. You read us a dismal homily upon "Realities." We know, quite as well as you do, what are shadows and what are realities. You, for instance, when you are over your fourth or fifth jorum, chirping about old school occurrences, are the best of realities. Shadows are cold, thin things, that have no warmth or grasp in them. Miss Wesley and her friend, and a tribe of authoresses that come after you here daily, and, in defect of you, hive and cluster upon us, are the shadows. You encouraged that mopsey, Miss Wesley, to dance after you, in the hope of having her nonsense put into a nonsensical Anthology. We have pretty well shaken her off by that simple expedient of referring her to you; but there are more burs in the wind. I came home t' other day from business, hungry as a hunter, to dinner, with nothing, I am sure, of the author but *hunger* about me; and whom found I closeted with Mary but a friend of this Miss Wesley, one Miss Benjay or Benje; I don't know how she spells her name. I just came in time enough, I believe, luckily to prevent them from exchanging vows of eternal friendship. It seems she is one of your authoresses, that you first foster, and then upbraid us with. But I forgive you. "The rogue has given me potions to make me love him." Well; go she would not, nor step a step over our threshold, till we had promised to come and drink tea with her next night. I had never seen her before, and could not tell who the devil it was that was so familiar. We went, however, not to be impolite. Her lodgings are up two pair of stairs in East Street. Tea and coffee, and macaroons—a kind of cake I much love. We sat down. Presently Miss Benjay broke the silence, by declaring herself quite of a different opinion from *D'Israeli,* who supposes the differences of human intellect to be the mere effect of organisation. She begged to know my opinion. I attempted to carry it off with a pun upon organ, but that went off very flat. She immediately conceived a very low opinion of my metaphysics; and, turning round to Mary, put some question to her in French, —possibly having heard that neither Mary nor I understood French. The explanation that took place occasioned some embarrassment and much wondering. She then fell into an insulting conversation about the comparative genius and merits of all modern languages, and concluded with asserting that the Saxon was esteemed the purest dialect in Germany. From thence she passed into the subject of poetry; where I, who had hitherto sat mute, and a hearer only, humbly hoped I might now put in a word to some advantage, seeing that it was my own trade in a manner. But I was stopped by a round assertion, that no good poetry had appeared since Dr. Johnson's time. It seems the Doctor has suppressed many hopeful geniuses that way, by the severity of his critical strictures in his *Lives of the Poets*. I here ventured to question the fact, and was beginning to appeal to names, but I was assured "it was certainly the case." Then we discussed Miss More's book on education, which I had never read. It seems Dr. Gregory, another of Miss Benjay's friends, has found fault with one of Miss More's metaphors. Miss More has been at some pains to vindicate herself,—in the opinion of Miss Benjay not without success. It seems the Doctor is invariably against the use of broken or mixed metaphor, which he reprobates, against the authority of Shakspeare himself. We next discussed the question, whether Pope was a poet? I find Dr. Gregory is of opinion he was not, though Miss Seward does not at all concur with him in this. We then sat upon the comparative merits of the ten translations of *Pizarro,* and Miss Benjay or Benje advised Mary to take two of them home (she thought it might afford her some pleasure to compare them *verbatim*); which we declined. It being now nine o'clock, wine and macaroons were again served round, and we parted, with a promise to go again next week, and meet the Miss Porters, who, it seems, have heard much of Mr. Coleridge, and wish to meet *us,* because we are *his* friends. I have been preparing for the occasion. I crowd cotton in my ears. I read all the reviews and magazines of the past month against the dreadful meeting, and I hope by these means to cut a tolerable second-rate figure.

Pray let us have no more complaints about shadows. We are in a fair way, *through you,* to surfeit sick upon them.

Our loves and respects to your host and hostess. Our dearest love to Coleridge.

Take no thought about your proof sheets; they shall be done as if Woodfall himself did them. Pray send us word of Mrs. Coleridge and little David Hartley, your little reality.

Farewell, dear Substance. Take no umbrage at anything I have written.   C. LAMB, *Umbra.*

Land of Shadows,
Shadow Month the 16th or 17th, 1800.

Coleridge, I find loose among your papers a copy of *Christabel.* It wants about thirty lines; you will very much oblige me by sending me the beginning as far as that line,—

"And the spring comes slowly up this way;"

and the intermediate lines between—

"The lady leaps up suddenly,
The lovely Lady Christabel;"

and the lines,—

"She folded her arms beneath her cloak,
And stole to the other side of the oak."

The trouble to you *will be small,* and the benefit to us *very great.* A pretty antithesis! A figure in speech I much applaud.

Godwin has called upon us. He spent one evening here: was very friendly: kept us up till midnight, drank punch, and talked about you. He seems above all men mortified at your going away. Suppose you were to write to that good-natured heathen: "Or is he a *shadow?*"

If I do not *write,* impute it to the long postage, of which you have so much cause to complain. I have scribbled over a *queer letter,* as I find by perusal, but it means no mischief.

I am, and will be, yours ever, in sober sadness,   C. L.

Write your *German* as plain as sunshine, for that must correct itself. You know I am *homo unius linguæ:* in English—illiterate, a dunce, a ninny.

To WILLIAM WORDSWORTII.

LETTER LXXXV.]   *January* 30, 1801.

I ought before this to have replied to your very kind invitation into Cumberland. With you and your sister I could gang anywhere; but I am afraid whether I shall ever be able to afford so desperate a journey. Separate from the pleasure of your company, I don't much care if I never see a mountain in my life. I have passed all my days in London, until I have formed as many and intense local attachments as any of you mountaineers can have done with dead Nature. The lighted shops of the Strand and Fleet Street; the innumerable trades, tradesmen, and customers, coaches, waggons, playhouses; all the bustle and wickedness round about Covent Garden; the very women of the Town; the watchmen, drunken scenes, rattles; life awake, if you awake, at all hours of the night; the impossibility of being dull in Fleet Street; the crowds, the very dirt and mud, the sun shining upon houses and pavements, the print shops, the old bookstalls, parsons cheapening books, coffee-houses, steams of soups from kitchens, the pantomimes—London itself a pantomime and a masquerade—all these things work themselves into my mind, and feed me, without a power of satiating me. The wonder of these sights impels me into night-walks about her crowded streets, and I often shed tears in the motley Strand from fulness of joy at so much life. All these emotions must be strange to you; so are your rural emotions to me. But consider, what must I have been doing all my life, not to have lent great portions of my heart with usury to such scenes?

My attachments are all local, purely local. I have no passion (or have had none since I was in love, and then it was the spurious engendering of poetry and books) for groves and valleys. The rooms where I was born, the furniture which has been before my eyes all my life, a book-case which has followed me about like a faithful dog (only exceeding him in knowledge), wherever I have moved, old chairs, old tables, streets, squares, where I have sunned myself, my old school,—these are my mistresses. Have I not enough, without your mountains? I do not envy you. I should pity you, did I not know that the mind will make friends of anything. Your sun, and moon, and skies, and hills, and lakes, affect me no more, or scarcely come to me in more venerable characters, than as a gilded room with tapestry and tapers, where I might live with handsome visible objects. I consider the clouds above me but as a roof beautifully painted, but unable to satisfy the mind: and at last, like the pictures of the apartment of a connoisseur, unable to afford him any longer a pleasure. So fading upon me, from disuse, have been the beauties of Nature, as they have been confinedly called; so ever fresh, and green, and warm are all the inventions of men, and assemblies of men in this great city. I should certainly have laughed with dear Joanna.

Give my kindest love, and my sister's, to D. and yourself; and a kiss from me to little Barbara Lewthwaite. Thank you for liking my play.

C. L.

LETTER LXXXVI.]　　　　　　　　　　　*January* 1801.

Thanks for your letter and present. I had already borrowed your second volume. What most pleases me is, "The Song of Lucy." *Simon's sickly daughter,* in "The Sexton," made me *cry.* Next to these are the description of these continuous echoes in the story of "Joanna's Laugh," where the mountains and all the scenery absolutely seem alive; and that fine Shakspearian character of the "happy man," in the "Brothers,"

> ————"that creeps about the fields,
> Following his fancies by the hour, to bring
> Tears down his cheek, or solitary smiles
> Into his face, until the setting sun
> Write Fool upon his forehead!"

I will mention one more—the delicate and curious feeling in the wish for the "Cumberland Beggar," that he may have about him the melody of birds, although he hear them not. Here the mind knowingly passes a fiction upon herself, first substituting her own feeling for the Beggar's, and in the same breath detecting the fallacy, will not part with the wish. The "Poet's Epitaph" is disfigured, to my taste, by the common satire upon parsons and lawyers in the beginning, and the coarse epithet of "pin-point," in the sixth stanza. All the rest is eminently good, and your own. I will just add that it appears to me a fault in the "Beggar," that the instructions conveyed in it are too direct, and like a lecture: they don't slide into the mind of the reader while he is imagining no such matter. An intelligent reader finds a sort of insult in being told, "I will teach you how to think upon this subject." This fault, if I am right, is in a ten-thousandth worse degree to be found in Sterne, and in many novelists and modern poets, who continually put a sign-post up to show where you are to feel. They set out with assuming their readers to be stupid; very different from *Robinson Crusoe*, the *Vicar of Wakefield, Roderick Random*, and other beautiful, bare narratives. There is implied an unwritten compact between author and reader; "I will tell you a story, and I suppose you will understand it." Modern novels, *St. Leons* and the like, are full of such flowers as these—"Let not my reader suppose," "Imagine, if you can, modest!" etc. I will here have done with praise and blame. I have written so much, only that you may not think I have passed over your book without observation. . . . I am sorry that Coleridge has christened his *Ancient Marinere*, a *Poet's Reverie;* it is as bad as Bottom the Weaver's declaration that he is not a lion, but only the scenical representation of a lion. What new idea is gained by this title but one subversive of all credit—which the tale should force upon us—of its truth!

For me, I was never so affected with any human tale. After first reading it, I was totally possessed with it for many days. I dislike all the miraculous part of it; but the feelings of the man under the operation of such scenery, dragged me along like Tom Pipe's magic whistle. I totally differ from your idea that the *Marinere* should have had a character and profession. This is a beauty in *Gulliver's Travels,* where the mind is kept in a placid state of little wonderments; but the *Ancient Marinere* undergoes such trials as overwhelm and bury all individuality or memory of what he was—like the state of a man in a bad dream, one terrible peculiarity of which is, that all consciousness of personality is gone. Your other observation is, I think as well, a little unfounded: the "Marinere," from being conversant in supernatural events, *has* acquired a supernatural and strange cast of phrase, eye, appearance, etc., which frighten the "wedding guest." You will excuse my remarks, because I am hurt and vexed that you should think it necessary, with a prose apology, to open the eyes of dead men that cannot see.

To sum up a general opinion of the second volume, I do not feel any one poem in it so forcibly as the *Ancient Marinere,* and the "Mad Mother," and the "Lines at Tintern Abbey" in the first.

To ROBERT LLOYD.

LETTER LXXXVII.]   *February* 7, 1801.

Dear Robert—I shall expect you to bring me a brimful account of the pleasure which Walton has given you, when you come to town. It must square with your mind. The delightful innocence and healthfulness of the Angler's mind will have blown upon yours like a Zephyr. Don't you already feel your spirit *filled* with the scenes?—the banks of rivers—the cowslip beds—the pastoral scenes—the neat alehouses—and hostesses and milkmaids, as far exceeding Virgil and Pope, as the *Holy Living* is beyond Thomas à Kempis. Are not the eating and drinking joys painted to the Life? Do they not inspire you with an immortal hunger? Are not you ambitious of being made an Angler? What edition have you got? is it Hawkins's, with plates of Piscator, etc.? That sells very dear. I have only been able to purchase the last edition without the old Plates which pleased my childhood; the plates being worn out, and the old Edition difficult and expensive to procure. The *Complete Angler* is the only Treatise written in Dialogues that is worth a halfpenny. Many elegant dialogues have been written (such as Bishop Berkeley's *Minute Philosopher*), but in all of them the Interlocutors are merely abstract arguments personify'd; not living dramatic characters, as in Walton, where *every thing* is *alive;* the fishes are absolutely *charactered;* and birds and animals are as interesting as men and women.

I need not be at much pains to get the *Holy Livings.* We can procure them in ten minutes' search at any stall or shop in London. By your engaging one for Priscilla, it should seem *she* will be in Town—is that the case? I thought she was fix'd at the Lakes.

I perfectly understand the nature of your solitariness at Birm., and wish I could divide myself, "like a bribed haunch," between London and it. But courage! you will soon be emancipated, and (it may be) have a frequent power of visiting this great place. Let them talk of lakes and mountains and romantic dales—all that fantastic stuff; give me a ramble by night, in the winter nights in London—the Lamps lit—the pavements of the motley Strand crowded with to and fro passengers—the shops all brilliant, and stuffed with obliging customers and obliged tradesmen— give me the old book-stalls of London—a walk in the bright Piazzas of Covent Garden. I defy a man to be dull in such places—perfect Ma-hometan paradises upon earth! I have lent out my heart with usury to such scenes from my childhood up, and have cried with fulness of joy at the multitudinous scenes of Life in the crowded streets of ever dear London. I wish you could fix here. I don't know if you quite comprehend my low Urban Taste; but depend upon it that a man of any feeling will have given his heart and his love in childhood and in boyhood to any scenes where he has been bred, as well to dirty streets (and smoky walls as they are called) as to green lanes, "where live nibbling sheep," and to the everlasting hills and the Lakes and ocean. A mob of men is better than a flock of sheep, and a crowd of happy faces justling into the play-house at the hour of six is a more beautiful spectacle to man than the shepherd driving his "silly" sheep to fold. Come to London and learn to sympathise with my unrural notions.

Wordsworth has published a second vol.—*Lyrical Ballads.* Most of them very good, but not so good as first vol. What more can I tell you? I believe I told you I have been to see Manning. He is a dainty chiel.— A man of great Power—an enchanter almost.—Far beyond Coleridge or any man in power of impressing—when he gets you alone, he can act the wonders of Egypt. Only he is lazy, and does not always put forth all his strength; if he did, I know no man of genius at all comparable to him.

Yours as ever,   C. L.

To THOMAS MANNING.

LETTER LXXXVIII.]   *February* 15, 1801.

I had need be cautious henceforward what opinion I give of the *Lyrical Ballads*. All the North of England are in a turmoil. Cumberland and Westmoreland have already declared a state of war. I lately received from Wordsworth a copy of the second volume, accompanied by an acknowledgment of having received from me many months since a copy of a certain Tragedy, with excuses for not having made any acknowledgment sooner, it being owing to an "almost insurmountable aversion from Letter-writing." This letter I answered in due form and time, and enumerated several of the passages which had most affected me, adding, unfortunately, that no single piece had moved me so forcibly as the "Ancient Mariner," "The Mad Mother," or the "Lines at Tintern Abbey." The Post did not sleep a moment. I received almost instantaneously a long letter of four sweating pages from my Reluctant Letter-Writer, the purport of which was, that he was sorry his 2nd vol. had not given me more pleasure (Devil a hint did I give that it had *not pleased me*), and "was compelled to wish that my range of sensibility was more extended, being obliged to believe that I should receive large influxes of happiness and happy Thoughts" (I suppose from the L. B.)—with a deal of stuff about a certain Union of Tenderness and Imagination, which in the sense he used Imagination was not the characteristic of Shakspeare, but which Milton possessed in a degree far exceeding other Poets: which Union, as the highest species of Poetry, and chiefly deserving that name, "He was most proud to aspire to;" then illustrating the said Union by two quotations from his own 2nd vol. (which I had been so unfortunate as to miss). 1st Specimen—a father addresses his son:—

> "When thou
> First camest into the World, as it befalls
> To new-born Infants, thou didst sleep away
> Two days: and *Blessings from thy father's Tongue
> Then fell upon thee.*"

The lines were thus undermarked, and then followed "This Passage, as combining in an extraordinary degree that Union of Imagination and Tenderness which I am speaking of, I consider as one of the Best I ever wrote!"

2nd Specimen.—A youth, after years of absence, revisits his native place, and thinks (as most people do) that there has been strange alteration in his absence:—

> "And that the rocks
> And everlasting Hills themselves were changed."

You see both these are good Poetry: but after one has been reading Shakspeare twenty of the best years of one's life, to have a fellow start up, and prate about some unknown quality which Shakspeare possessed in a degree inferior to Milton and *somebody else! !* This was not to be *all* my castigation. Coleridge, who had not written to me some months before, starts up from his bed of sickness to reprove me for my hardy presumption: four long pages, equally sweaty and more tedious, came from him; assuring me that, when the works of a man of true genius such as W. undoubtedly was, do not please me at first sight, I should suspect the fault to lie "in me and not in them," etc. etc. etc. etc. etc. What am I to do with such people? I certainly shall write them a very merry Letter. Writing to *you*, I may say that the 2nd vol. has no such pieces as the three I enumerated. It is full of original thinking and an observing mind, but it does not often make you laugh or cry.—It too artfully aims at simplicity of expression. And you sometimes doubt if Simplicity be not a cover for Poverty. The best Piece in it I will send you, being *short*. I have grievously offended my friends in the North by declaring my undue preference; but I need not fear you:—

> "She dwelt among the untrodden ways
>   Beside the Springs of Dove,
> A maid whom there were few (*sic*) to praise
>   And very few to love.
>
> A violet, by a mossy stone,
>   Half hidden from the eye.
> Fair as a star when only one
>   Is shining in the sky.
>
> She lived unknown; and few could know
>   When Lucy ceased to be.
> But she is in the grave, and oh!
>   The difference to me."

This is choice and genuine, and so are many, many more. But one does not like to have 'em rammed down one's throat. "Pray, take it—it's very good—let me help you—eat faster."

At length George Dyer's first vol. is come to a birth. One volume of three—Subscribers being *allowed* by the Prospectus to pay for all at once (tho' it's very doubtful if the rest ever come to anything, this having been already some years getting out). I paid two guineas for you and myself, which entitle us to the whole. I will send you your copy, if you are in a *great hurry*. Meantime you owe me a guinea. George skipped about like a scorched pea at the receipt of so much cash. To give you a specimen of the beautiful absurdity of the Notes, which defy imitation, take one: "Discrimination is not the *aim* of the present volume. It will be more strictly attended to in the next." One of the sonnets purports to have been written in Bedlam! This for a man to own! The rest are addressed to Science, Genius, Melancholy—etc. etc.—two, to the River Cam—an Ode to the Nightingale. Another to Howard, beginning "Spirit of meek Philanthropy!" One is entitled *The Madman—* "being collected by the author from several Madhouses." It begins "Yes,

yes—'tis He!" A long poetical satire is addressed to "John Disney, D.D.—his wife and daughter ! ! ! "

Now to my own affairs. I have not taken that thing to Colman, but I have proceeded one step in the business. I have inquired his address, and am promised it in a few days. Meantime three acts and a half are finished galloping, of a Play on a Persian Story which I must father in April. But far, very far, from *Antonio* in composition. O Jephtha, Judge of Israel, what a fool I was! C. LAMB.

LETTER LXXXIX.] [*February* or *March*] 1801.

You masters of logic ought to know (logic is nothing more than a knowledge of *words,* as the Greek etymon implies) that all words are no more to be taken in a literal sense at all times than a promise given to a tailor. When I exprest an apprehension that you were mortally offended, I meant no more than by the application of a certain formula of efficacious sounds, which had *done* in similar cases before, to rouse a sense of decency in you, and a remembrance of what was due to me! You masters of logic should advert to this phenomenon in human speech, before you arraign the usage of us dramatic geniuses. Imagination is a good blood mare, and goes well: but the misfortune is, she has too many paths before her. 'Tis true I might have imagined to myself that you had trundled your frail carcass to Norfolk. I might also, and did imagine, that you had not, but that you were lazy, or inventing new properties in a triangle, and for that purpose moulding and squeezing Landlord Crisp's three-cornered beaver into fantastic experimental forms; or, that Archimedes was meditating to repulse the French, in case of a Cambridge invasion, by a geometric hurling of folios on their red caps; or, peradventure, that you were in extremities, in great wants, and just set out for Trinity Bogs when my letters came. In short, my genius (which is a short word, nowadays, for what-a-great-man-am-I)! was absolutely stifled and over-laid with its own riches. Truth is one and poor, like the cruse of Elijah's widow. Imagination is the bold face that multiplies its oil; and thou, the old cracked pipkin, that could not believe it could be put to such purposes. Dull pipkin, to have Elijah for thy cook! Imbecile recipient of so fat a miracle! I send you George Dyer's Poems, the richest production of the lyrical muse *this century* can justly boast: for Wordsworth's L. B. were published, or at least written, before Christmas.

Please to advert to pages 291 to 296 for the most astonishing account of where Shakspeare's muse has been all this while. I thought she had been dead, and buried in Stratford Church, with the young man *that kept her company,*—

> "But it seems, like the Devil,
> Buried in Cole Harbour,
> Some say she's risen again,
> 'Gone prentice to a barber."

N.B.—I don't charge anything for the additional manuscript notes, which are the joint productions of myself and a learned translator of Schiller, John Stoddart, Esq.

N.B. the 2nd.—I should not have blotted your book, but I had sent my own out to be bound, as I was in duty bound. A liberal criticism upon the several pieces, lyrical, heroical, amatory, and satirical, would be acceptable. So, you don't think there's a Word's—worth of good poetry in the great L. B.! I daren't put the dreaded syllables at their just length, for my back tingles from the northern castigation. I send you the three letters, which I beg you to return along with those former letters (which I hope you are not going to print, by your detention). But don't be in a hurry to send them. When you come to town will do. Apropos of coming to town: Last Sunday was a fortnight, as I was *coming to town* from the Professor's inspired with new rum, I tumbled down and broke my nose. I drink nothing stronger than malt liquors.

I am going to change my lodgings, having received a hint that it would be agreeable, at our Lady's next feast. I have partly fixed upon most delectable rooms, which look out (when you stand a tip-toe) over the Thames and Surrey Hills; at the upper end of King's Bench Walks, in the Temple. There I shall have all the privacy of a house without the encumbrance, and shall be able to lock my friends out as often as I desire to hold free converse with my immortal mind; for my present lodgings resemble a minister's levee, I have so increased my acquaintance (as they call 'em) since I have resided in town. Like the country mouse, that had tasted a little of urbane manners, I long to be nibbling my own cheese by my dear self, without mouse-traps and time-traps. By my new plan, I shall be as airy, up four pair of stairs, as in the country; and in a garden, in the midst of enchanting (more than Mahometan paradise) London, whose dirtiest drab-frequented alley, and her lowest bowing tradesman, I would not exchange for Skiddaw, Helvellyn, James, Walter, and the parson into the bargain. O her lamps of a night! her rich gold-smiths, print-shops, toy-shops, mercers, hardwaremen, pastry-cooks, St. Paul's Churchyard, the Strand, Exeter Change, Charing Cross, with the man *upon* a black horse! These are thy gods, O London! A'nt you mightily moped on the banks of the Cam? Had you not better come and set up here? You can't think what a difference. All the streets and pavements are pure gold, I warrant you. At least, I know an alchemy that turns her mud into that metal,—a mind that loves to be at home in crowds.

'Tis half-past twelve o'clock, and all sober people ought to be a-bed. Between you and me the L. Ballads are but drowsy performances.

C. Lamb (as you may guess).

To ROBERT LLOYD.

Letter XC.] *April 6, 1801.*

Fletcher's *Purple Island* is a tedious Allegory of the Parts of the Human body. I would not advise you to lay out six *pence* upon it. It is not the work of Fletcher, the Coadjutor of Beaumont, but one Phineas, a kinsman of his.

If by the work of Bishop Taylor, whose Title you have not given correctly, you mean his CONTEMPLATIONS on the State of Man in this Life and that which is to come, I dare hope you will join with me in believing it to be spurious. The suspicious circumstance of its being a posthumous work, with the total dissimilarity in style to the genuine works, I think evince that it never was the work of DOCTOR JEREMY TAYLOR, Late Lord Bishop of Down and Connor in Ireland, and Administrator of the See of Dromore; such are the titles which his sounding title-pages give him, and I love the man, and I love his paraphernalia, and I like to name him with all his attributions and additions. If you are yet but lightly acquainted with his real manner, take up and read the whole first chapter of the Holy DYING; in particular turn to the first paragraph of the second section of that chapter for a simile of a rose, or more truly many similes within simile; for such were the riches of his fancy, that when a beauteous image offered, before he could stay to expand it into all its capacities, throngs of new coming images came up, and justled out the first, or blended in disorder with it, which imitates the order of every rapid mind. But read all the first chapter by my advice; and I know I need not advise you, when you have read it, to read the second.

Or for another specimen (where so many beauties crowd, the judgment has yet vanity enough to think it can discern a handsomest, till a second judgment and a third *ad infinitum* start up to disallow their elder brother's pretensions) turn to the story of the Ephesian Matron in the second section of the 5th chapter of the same Holy DYING (I still refer to the *Dying* part, because it contains better matter than the "Holy Living," which deals more in rules than illustrations—I mean in comparison with the other only, else it has more and more beautiful illustrations— than any prose book besides)—read it yourself and show it to Plumstead (with my LOVE, and bid him write to me), and ask him if WILLY himself has ever told a story with more circumstances of FANCY and HUMOUR.

The paragraph begins, "But that which is to be faulted," and the story not long after follows. Make these references while P. is with you, that you may stir him up to the Love of Jeremy Taylor, and make a convertite of him. Coleridge was the man who first solemnly exhorted me to "study" the works of Dr. Jeremy Taylor, and I have had reason to bless the hour in which he did it. Read as many of his works as you can get. I will assist you in getting them when we go a stall hunting together in London, and it's odds if we don't get a good Beaumt. and Fletcher cheap.

Bp. Taylor has more and more beautiful imagery, and (what is more to a Lover of Willy) more knowledge and description of human life and manners than any prose book in the language: he has more delicacy and sweetness than any mortal, the "gentle" Shakspeare hardly excepted,— his similes and allusions are taken, as the bees take honey, from all the youngest, greenest, exquisitest parts of nature, from plants, and flowers, and fruit, young boys and virgins, from little children perpetually, from sucking infants, babies' smiles, roses, gardens,—his imagination was a spacious Garden, where no vile insects could crawl in; his apprehension a "COURT" where no foul thoughts kept "leets and holy-days."

> "Snail and worm, give no offence,
> Newt nor blind worm be not seen,
> Come not near our fairy queen."

You must read Bishop Taylor with allowances for the subjects on which he wrote, and the age *in* which. You may skip or patiently endure his tedious discourses on rites and ceremonies, Baptism, and the Eucharist, the Clerical function, and the antiquity of Episcopacy, a good deal of which are inserted in works not purely controversial; his polemical works you may skip altogether, unless you have a taste for the exertions of vigorous reason and subtle distinguishing on uninteresting topics. Such of his works as you should begin with, to get a taste for him (after which your Love will lead you to his Polemical and drier works, as Love led Leander "over boots" knee-deep thro' the Hellespont), but read first the *Holy Living and Dying,* and his *Life of Christ* and *Sermons,* both in folio. And, above all, try to get a beautiful little tract on the "Measures and offices of Friendship," printed with his *opuscula* duodecimo, and also at the end of his Polemical Discourses in folio. Another thing you will observe in Bp. Taylor, without which consideration you will do him injustice. He wrote to different classes of people. His *Holy Living and Dying* and *Life of Christ* were designed and have been used as popular books of family Devotion, and have been thumbed by old women, and laid about in the window seats of old houses in great families, like the Bible, and the "Queene-like-Closet or rare boke of Recipes in medicine and cookery, fitted to all capacities."

Accordingly in these *the fancy* is perpetually applied to; any slight conceit, allusion, or analogy, any "prettiness," a story true or false, serves for an argument adapted to women and young persons, and "incompetent judgments;" whereas the *Liberty of Prophecy* (a book in your father's bookcase) is a series of severe and masterly reasoning, fitted to great Clerks and learned Fathers, with no more of Fancy than is subordinate and ornamental.—Such various powers had the Bishop of Down and Connor, Administrator of the See of Dromore!

My theme and my story!—Farewell.   C. LAMB.

To THOMAS MANNING.

LETTER XCI.]   *April* 1801.

I was not aware that you owed me anything beside that guinea; but I daresay you are right. I live at No. 16 Mitre Court Buildings, a pistol-shot off Baron Maseres'. You must introduce me to the Baron. I think we should suit one another mainly. He lives on the ground floor, for convenience of the gout; I prefer the attic story, for the air. He keeps three footmen and two maids; I have neither maid nor laundress, not caring to be troubled with them. His forte, I understand, is the higher mathematics; my turn, I confess, is more to poetry and the belles lettres. The very antithesis of our characters would make up a harmony. You must bring the Baron and me together. *N.B.*—When you come to see me, mount up to the top of the stairs—I hope you are not asthmatical— and come in flannel, for 'tis pure airy up there. And bring your glass, and I will show you the Surrey Hills. My bed faces the river, so as by perking up upon my haunches, and supporting my carcass with my elbows, without much wrying my neck, I can see the white sails glide by the bottom of the King's Bench Walks as I lie in my bed. An excellent tiptoe prospect in the best room:—casement windows, with small panes, to look more like a cottage. Mind, I have got no bed for you, that's flat; sold it to pay expenses of moving,—the very bed on which Manning lay; the friendly, the mathematical Manning! How forcibly does it remind me of the interesting Otway! "The very bed which on thy marriage night gave thee into the arms of Belvidera, by the coarse hands of ruffians " (upholsterers' men), etc. My tears will not give me leave to go on. But a bed I will get you, Manning, on condition you will be my day-guest.

I have been ill more than a month, with a bad cold, which comes upon me (like a murderer's conscience) about midnight, and vexes me for many hours. I have successively been drugged with Spanish licorice, opium, ipecacuanha, paregoric, and tincture of foxglove (tinctura purpuræ digitalis of the ancients). I am afraid I must leave off drinking.

To ROBERT LLOYD.

LETTER XCII.]   *April* 1891.

I am not dead nor asleep. But Manning is in town, and Coleridge is in town, and I am making a thorough alteration in the structure of my play for Publication. My brain is overwrought with variety of worldly-intercourse. I have neither time nor mind for scribbling. Who shall deliver me from the body of this Death?

Only continue to write and to believe that when the Hour comes I shall strike like Jack of the Clock, *id est,* I shall once more become a regular correspondent of Robert and Plumstead. How is the benevolent, loud-talking, Shakspeare-loving Brewer?

To your inquiry respecting a selection from Bp. Taylor I answer—it cannot be done, and if it could, it would not *take* with John Bull. It cannot be done, for who can disentangle and unthread the rich texture of Nature and Poetry, sewn so thick into a stout coat of theology, without spoiling both *lace* and *coat?* How beggarly and how bald do even Shakspeare's Princely Pieces look when thus violently divorced from *connection* and *circumstance!* When we meet with "To be or not to be," or Jacques' moralisings upon the Deer, or Brutus and Cassius' quarrel and reconciliation—in an Enfield Speaker, or in Elegant Extracts,—how we stare, and will scarcely acknowledge to ourselves (what we are conscious we feel) that they are flat and have no power. Something exactly like this have I experienced when I have picked out similes and stars from "Holy Dying" and shown them *per se,* as you'd show specimens of minerals or pieces of rock. Compare the grand effect of the star-paved firmament, and imagine a boy capable of picking out those pretty twinklers one by one and playing at chuck-farthing with them. Everything in heaven and earth, in man and in story, in books and in fancy, acts by Confederacy, by juxtaposition, by circumstance and place. Consider a fine family (if I were not writing to you I might instance your own) of sons and daughters, with a respectable father and a handsome mother at their heads, all met in one house, and happy round one table. Earth cannot show a more lovely and venerable sight, such as the Angels in heaven might lament that in their country there is no marrying or giving in marriage. Take and split this Body into individuals—show the separate caprices, vagaries, etc., of Charles, Rob, or Plum, one a Quaker, another a Churchman. The eldest daughter seeking a husband out of the pale of parental faith—another warping, perhaps—the father a prudent, circumspective, do-me-good sort of a man *blest* with children whom no ordinary rules can circumscribe. I have not room for all particulars—but just as this happy and venerable Body of a family loses by splitting and considering individuals too nicely, so it is when we pick out Best Bits out of a great writer. 'Tis the *sum* total of his mind which affects us.

C. L.

To WILLIAM GODWIN.

LETTER XCIII.]   *June 29, 1801.*

Dear Sir—Dr. Christy's Brother and Sister are come to town and have shown me great civilities. I in return wish to requite them, having, *by God's grace,* principles of generosity *implanted* (as the moralists say) in my nature, which have been duly cultivated and watered by good and religious friends, and a pious education. They have picked up in the northern parts of the island an astonishing admiration of the great author of the New Philosophy in England, and I have ventured to promise their taste an evening's gratification by seeing Mr. Godwin *face* to *face* ! ! ! ! ! Will you do them, and me *in* them, the pleasure of drinking tea and supping with me at the *old* number 16 on Friday or Saturday next? An early nomination of the day will very much oblige yours sincerely,

CH. LAMB.

To ROBERT LLOYD.

LETTER XCIV.]   *July 26, 1801.*

Cooke in "Richard the Third" is a perfect caricature. He gives you the *monster* Richard, but not the *man* Richard. Shakspeare's bloody character impresses you with awe and deep admiration of his witty parts, his consummate hypocrisy, and indefatigable prosecution of purpose. You despise, detest, and loathe the cunning, vulgar, low and fierce Richard, which Cooke substitutes in his place. He gives you no other idea than of a vulgar villain, rejoicing in his being able to overreach, and not possessing that joy in *silent* consciousness, but betraying it, like a *poor* villain, in sneers and distortions of the face, like a droll at a country fair: not to add that cunning so self-betraying and manner so vulgar could never have deceived the politic Buckingham nor the soft Lady Anne: *both* bred in courts, would have turned with disgust from such a fellow. Not but Cooke has *powers;* but not of discrimination. His manner is strong, coarse, and vigorous, and well adapted to some characters. But the lofty imagery and high sentiments and high passions of *Poetry* come black and prose-smoked from his prose Lips. I have not seen him in Overreach, but from what I remember of the character, I think he could not have chosen one more fit. I thought the play a highly finished one when I read it some time back. I *remember* a most noble image. Sir Giles drawing his sword in the last scene, says:

> "Some undone widow sits upon mine arm,
> And takes away the use on't."

This is horribly fine, and I am not sure that it did not suggest to me my conclusion of "Pride's Cure"; but my imitation is miserably inferior:

> This arm was busy in the day of Naseby:
> 'Tis paralytic now, and knows no use of weapons.

Pierre and Jaffier are the best things in Otway. Belvidera is a poor Creature, and has had more than her due fame. Monimia is a little better, but she *whines*. I like Calista in the "Fair Penitent" better than either of Otway's women. Lee's "Massacre of Paris" is a noble play, very chastely and finely written. His Alexander is full of that madness "which rightly should possess a poet's brain." "Œdipus" is also a fine play, but less so than these two. It is a joint production of Lee and Dryden. "All For Love" begins with uncommon Spirit, but soon flags, and is of no worth upon the whole. The last scene of "Young's Revenge" is sublime: the rest of it not worth 1d.

I want to have your opinion and Plumstead's on Cooke's "Richard the Third." I am possessed with an admiration of the genuine Richard, his genius, and his mounting spirit, which no consideration of his cruelties can depress. Shakspeare has not made Richard so black a Monster as is supposed. Wherever he is monstrous, it was to conform to vulgar opinion. But he is generally a Man. Read his most exquisite address to the Widowed Queen to court her daughter for him—the topics of maternal feeling, of a deep knowledge of the heart, are such as no monster could have supplied. Richard must have *felt* before he could feign so well; tho' ambition choked the good seed. I think it the most finished piece of Eloquence in the world; of *persuasive* oratory far above Demosthenes,

Burke, or any man, far exceeding the courtship of Lady Anne. *Her* relenting is barely natural, after all; the more perhaps S.'s merit to make *impossible appear probable*, but the *Queen's consent*) taking in all the circumstances and topics, *private* and *public*, with his angelic address, able to draw the host of [piece cut out of letter] Lucifer) is *probable;* and [piece cut out of letter] resisted it. This observation applies to many other parts. All the inconsistency is, that Shakspeare's better genius was forced to struggle against the prejudices which made a monster of Richard. He set out to paint a *monster*, but his human sympathies produced a *man*.

Are you not tired with all this *ingenious* criticism? I am.

Richard itself is totally metamorphosed in the wretched *acting play* of that name, which you will see, altered by *Cibber*.

God bless you.   C. LAMB.

To MR. WALTER WILSON.

LETTER XCV.]   *August* 14, 1801.

Dear Wilson—I am extremely sorry that any serious differences should subsist between us, on account of some foolish behaviour of mine at Richmond; you knew me well enough before, that a very little liquor will cause a considerable alteration in me.

I beg you to impute my conduct solely to that, and not to any deliberate intention of offending you, from whom I have received so many friendly attentions. I know that you think a very important difference in opinion with respect to some more serious subjects between us makes me a dangerous companion; but do not rashly infer, from some slight and light expressions which I may have made use of in a moment of levity, in your presence, without sufficient regard to your feelings—do not conclude that I am an inveterate enemy to all religion. I have had a time of seriousness, and I have known the importance and reality of a religious belief. Latterly, I acknowledge, much of my seriousness has gone off, whether from new company, or some other new associations; but I still retain at bottom a conviction of the truth, and a certainty of the usefulness of religion. I will not pretend to more gravity or feeling than I at present possess; my intention is not to persuade you that any great alteration is probable in me; sudden converts are superficial and transitory; I only want you to believe that I have *stamina* of seriousness within me, and that I desire nothing more than a return of that friendly intercourse which used to subsist between us, but which my folly has suspended.

Believe me, very affectionately yours,   C. LAMB.

To THOMAS MANNING.

LETTER XCVI.]   [*August*] 1801.

Dear Manning—I have forborne writing so long (and so have you for the matter of that), until I am almost ashamed either to write or to forbear any longer. But as your silence may proceed from some worse cause than neglect—from illness, or some mishap which may have befallen you, I begin to be anxious. You may have been burnt out, or you may have married, or you may have broken a limb, or turned country parson: any of these would be excuse sufficient for not coming to my supper. I am not so unforgiving as the nobleman in Saint Mark. For me, nothing new has happened to me, unless that the poor *Albion* died last Saturday of the world's neglect, and with it the fountain of my puns is choked up for ever.

All the Lloyds wonder that you do not write to them. They apply to me for the cause. Relieve me from this weight of ignorance, and enable me to give a truly oracular response.

I have been confined some days with swelled cheek and rheumatism: they divide and govern me with a viceroy-headache in the middle. I can neither write nor read without great pain. It must be something like obstinacy that I choose this time to write to you in after many months' interruption.

I will close my letter of simple inquiry with an epigram on Mackintosh, the *Vindiciæ Gallicæ* man—who has got a place at last—one of the last I *did* for the Albion:—

> "Though thou'rt like Judas, an apostate black,
> In the resemblance one thing thou dost lack:
> When he had gotten his ill-purchased pelf,
> He went away, and wisely hang'd himself:
> This thou may'st do at last; yet much I doubt,
> If thou hast any *bowels* to gush out!"

Yours, as ever,   C. Lamb.

Letter XCVII.]   *August* 31, 1801.

I heard that you were going to China, with a commission from the Wedgwoods to collect hints for their pottery, and to teach the Chinese *perspective;* but I did not know that London lay in your way to Pekin. I am seriously glad of it, for I shall trouble you with a small present for the Emperor of Usbeck Tartary, as you go by his territories: it is a fragment of a "Dissertation on the state of political parties in England at the end of the eighteenth century," which will no doubt be very interesting to his Imperial Majesty. It was written originally in English for the use of the *two* and *twenty readers* of the *Albion* (this *calculation* includes a printer, four pressmen, and a devil); but becoming of no use when the *Albion* stopped, I got it translated into Usbeck Tartar by my good friend Tibet Kulm, who is to come to London with a *civil* invitation from the Cham to the English nation to go over to the worship of the Lama.

The *Albion* is dead—dead as nail in door—and my revenues have died with it; but I am not as a man without hope. I have got a sort of opening to the *Morning Chronicle,* by means of that common dispenser of benevolence, Mister Dyer. I have not seen Perry, the editor, yet: but I am preparing a specimen. I shall have a difficult job to manage, for you must know that Mr. Perry, in common with the great body of the Whigs, thinks the *Albion* very low. I find I must rise a peg or so, be a little more decent, and less abusive; for, to confess the truth, I had arrived to an abominable pitch; I spared neither age nor sex when my cue was given me. *N'importe* (as they say in French), any climate will suit me. So you are about to bring your old face-making face to London. You could not come in a better time for my purposes; for I have just lost Rickman, a faint idea of whose character I sent you. He has gone to Ireland for a year or two to make his fortune; and I have lost by his going what seems to me I can never recover—*a finished man.* His memory will be to me as the brazen serpent to the Israelites,—I shall look up to it, to keep me upright and honest. But he may yet bring back his honest face to England one day. I wish your affairs with the Emperor of China had not been *so urgent,* that you might have stayed in Great Britain a year or two longer, to have seen him; for, judging from *my own* experience, I almost dare pronounce you never saw his equal. I never saw a man that could be at all a second or substitute for him in any sort.

Imagine that what is here erased was an apology and explanation, perfectly satisfactory you may be sure for rating this man so highly at the expense of ——, and ——, and ——, and M——, and ——, and ——, and ——. But Mr. Burke has explained this phenomenon of our nature very prettily in his letter to a Member of the National Assembly, or else in Appeal to the old Whigs, I forget which. Do you remember an instance from Homer (who understood these matters tolerably well), of Priam driving away his other sons with expressions of wrath and bitter reproach, when Hector was just dead?

I live where I did, in a *private* manner, because I don't like *state.* Nothing is so disagreeable to me as the clamours and applauses of the mob. For this reason I live in an *obscure* situation in one of the courts of the Temple.   C. L.

I send you all of Coleridge's letters to me, which I have preserved: some of them are upon the subject of my play. I also send you Kemble's two letters, and the prompter's courteous epistle, with a curious critique on "Pride's Cure," by a young physician from EDINBRO', who modestly suggests quite another kind of a plot. These are monuments of my disappointment which I like to preserve.

In Coleridge's letters you will find a good deal of amusement, to see genuine talent struggling against a pompous display of it. I also send you the Professor's letter to me (careful Professor! to conceal his *name* even from his correspondent), ere yet the Professor's pride was cured. Oh monstrous and almost satanical pride!

You will carefully keep all (except the Scotch Doctor's, *which burn*) *in statu quo,* till I come to claim mine own.   C. LAMB.

To WILLIAM GODWIN.

LETTER XCVIII.]   [*Margate?*] *September* 9, 1801.

Dear Sir—Nothing runs in my head when I think of your story, but that you should make it as like the life of Savage as possible. That is a known and familiar tale, and its effect on the public mind has been very great. Many of the incidents in the true history are readily made dramatical. For instance, Savage used to walk backwards and forwards o' nights to his mother's window, to catch a glimpse of her, as she passed with a candle. With some such situation the play might happily open. I would plunge my Hero, exactly like Savage, into difficulties and embarrassments, the consequences of an unsettled mind: out of which he may be extricated by the unknown interference of his mother. He should be attended from the beginning by a Friend, who should stand in much the same relation towards him as Horatio to Altamont in the play of the "Fair Penitent." A character of this sort seems indispensable. This Friend might gain interviews with the mother, when the son was refused sight of her. Like Horatio with Calista, he might wring her soul. Like Horatio, he might learn the secret *first*. He might be exactly in the same perplexing situation, when he had learned it, whether to tell it or conceal it from the Son (I have still Savage in my head), who might *kill* a man (as he did) in an affray—he should receive a pardon, as Savage did— and the mother might interfere to have him *banished*. This should provoke the friend to demand an interview with her husband, and disclose the whole secret. The husband, refusing to believe anything to her dishonour, should fight with him. The husband repents before he dies. The mother explains and confesses everything in his presence. The son is admitted to an interview with his now acknowledged mother. Instead of embraces, she resolves to abstract herself from all pleasure, even from his sight, in a voluntary penance all her days after. This is crude indeed! ! but I am totally unable to suggest a better. I am the worst hand in the world at a plot. But I understand enough of passion to predict that your story, with some of Savage's, which has no repugnance, but a natural alliance with it, cannot fail. The mystery of the suspected relationship—the suspicion, generated from slight and forgotten circumstances, coming at last to act as Instinct, and so to be mistaken for Instinct—the son's unceasing pursuit and throwing of himself in his mother's way, something like Falkland's eternal persecution of Williams —the high and intricate passion in the mother, the being obliged to shun and keep at a distance the thing nearest to her heart—to be cruel, where her heart yearns to be kind, without a possibility of explanation. You have the power of life and death and the hearts of your auditors in your hands—still Harris will want a skeleton, and he must have it. I can only put in some sorry hints. The discovery to the son's friend may take place not before the third act—in some such way as this. The mother may cross the street—he may point her out to some gay companion of his as the Beauty of Leghorn—the pattern for wives, etc. etc. His companion, who is an Englishman, laughs at his mistake, and knows her to have been the famous Nancy Dawson, or any one else, who captivated the English king. Some such way seems dramatic, and speaks to the Eye. The audience will enter into the Friend's surprise and into the perplexity of his situation. These Ocular Scenes are so many great landmarks, rememberable headlands and lighthouses in the voyage. Macbeth's witch has a good advice to a tragic writer, what to do with his spectator.

> "*Show* his *eyes*, and grieve his heart."

The most difficult thing seems to be, What to do with the husband? You will not make him jealous of his own son? that is a stale and an unpleasant trick in Douglas, etc. Can't you keep him out of the way till you want him, as the husband of Isabella is conveniently sent off till his cue comes? There will be story enough without him, and he will only puzzle all. Catastrophes are worst of all. Mine is most stupid. I only propose it to fulfil my engagement, not in hopes to convert you.

It is always difficult to get rid of a woman at the end of a tragedy. *Men* may fight and die. A woman must either take poison, *which is a nasty trick*, or go mad, which is not fit to be shown—or retire, which is poor: only retiring is most reputable.

I am sorry I can furnish you no better: but I find it extremely difficult to settle my thoughts upon anything but the scene before me, when I am from home: I am from home so seldom. If any the least hint crosses me, I will write again, and I very much wish to read your plan, if you could abridge and send it. In this little scrawl you must take the will for the deed, for I most sincerely wish success to your play.—Farewell,

C. L.

To JOHN RICKMAN, Esq.

Letter XCIX.] [*September* 16, 1801.]

Dear Rickman—Your Letter has found me at Margate, where I am come with Mary to drink sea water and pick up shells. I am glad to hear that your new dignities sit so easy upon you. ' No doubt you are one of those easy "well dressed" gentlemen, that we may know at first sight to belong to the "Castle," when we meet them in the Park. Your Letter contains a very fair offer about my Play, which I must first dispatch. I seriously feel very much obliged to you *and all that,* but I have a scheme in my head to print it about Xmas time, when the Town is fuller! ! about that time I expect the repayment of a Loan, which was bigger than I ought to have trusted, but I hope not bigger than my borrowing friend will then be able to repay. If he should disappoint me, I may throw myself upon you: meantime I am too proud ever to etc. . . . I do not write in *any* paper. George Dyer, that common Lyar of Benevolence, has taken some pains to introduce me to the *Morning Chronicle,* and I did something for them, but I soon found that it was a different thing writing for the Lordly Editor of the great Whig Paper to what it was scribbling for the poor *Albion*. More than three-fourths of what I did was superciliously rejected; whereas in the old *Albion* the seal of my well-known handwriting was enough to drive any nonsense current. I believe I shall give up this way of writing, and turn honest, scramble on as well as I can for a year, and make a Book, for why should every creature make books but I?

G. Burnett had just finished his Essay when I came away. Mushrooms scramble up in a night; but diamonds, you know, lie a long while ripening in the bed. The purport of it is to persuade the world that opinions tending to the subversion of Established Religion and Governments, systems of medicine, etc., should not be rashly vented in every company: a good orthodox doctrine which has been preached up with the "holy text of Pike and Gun" with you in Ireland, and is pretty familiar in England, but it is novel to George; at least he never wrote an Essay upon the subject before. Critics should think of this, before they loosely cry out, This is commonplace, what is there new in it? it may be all new to the Author, *he* may never have thought of it before, and it may have cost him as much brain-sweat as a piece of the most inveterate originality. However George is in pretty good keeping, while the merits of his essay lie under consideration. He has got into joint rooms with a young Surgeon, whose Uncle is an eminent wine merchant, and gives his nephew long tick, so they drink two sorts of wine, and live happy. George was turned out of his White Friars Lodging because he wanted too much attendance. He used to call up the girl, and send her down again, because he had forgot what he wanted; and then call her again, when his thought came back, to ask what a Clock it was. Fenwick has been urgent with me to write to you about his plan, and I gave him a drunken promise that I would, but you have saved me a disagreeable topic, for I know you have enough to do, and must serve him at your leisure. The Welfare of Ireland, perhaps of the whole world, must not stand still, while the interests of a newspaper are debating! ! He is very sanguine, and if he tells true, he has had very important encouragement; but he always said and thought, that the *Albion* had very sufficient patronage. Some people can *see anything* but their own interest, and they chuse to look at that through glasses. Dr. Christie has transported his solemn physiognomy to Portsmouth in his way to India. He departed without calling upon me, tho' he never could have called upon a more welcome occasion; consequently he did not get your letter, but I imparted its contents to his brother. I know no more news from here except that the Professor (Godwin) is COURTING. The Lady is a Widow [1] with green spectacles and one child, and the Professor is grown quite juvenile. He bows when he is spoke to, and smiles without occasion, and wriggles as fantastically as Malvolio, and has more affectation than a canary bird pluming his

---

[1] A very disgusting woman.

feathers when he thinks somebody looks at him. He lays down his spectacles, as if in scorn, and takes 'em up again from necessity, and winks that she mayn't see he gets sleepy about eleven o'Clock. You never saw such a philosophic coxcomb, nor any one play the Romeo so unnaturally. His second play, my god-son, is flatly rejected by Harris, because it is a Persian story about Shaw Abbas and the valiant Sefi his son: but Harris has offered to pay him at all events, if he will take a domestic plain story, not heroic nor foreign; so, after many indignant declarations that he could not bear such a *creeping way* (his expression) his proud heart has come down to Harris's proposals; so he is filching a tale out of one of Defoe's novels, and has made me write him hints. Floreat Tertia!——

Margate, Wednesday, *September* 16,
    where I stay a week longer.

And now farewell, Master Secretary!—and if your Diplomatic Majesty has any commissions for tape or bone lace, etc. in London, depend upon a faithful performance of the same. I could find matter for a longer Letter, and will another day, if you will find time to read it. Meantime believe me, yours sincerely. Mary sends her kindest remembrances. No hurry for the Pork.   C. LAMB.

John Rickman, Esq.,
    Dublin Castle.

To WILLIAM GODWIN.

LETTER C.]   *Margate, September* 17, 1801.

[*Fragment*.]

I shall be glad to come home and talk these matters over with you. I have read your scheme very attentively. That Arabella has been mistress to King Charles is sufficient to all the purposes of the story. It can only diminish that respect we feel for her to make her turn whore to one of the Lords of his Bedchamber. Her son must not know that she has been a whore: it matters not that she has been whore to a *King:* equally in both cases, it is against decorum and against the delicacy of a son's respect that he should be privy to it. No doubt, many sons might feel a wayward pleasure in the honourable guilt of their mothers; but is it a true feeling? Is it the best sort of feeling? Is it a feeling to be exposed on theatres to mothers and daughters? Your conclusion (or rather Defoe's) comes far short of the tragic ending, which is always expected; and it is not safe to disappoint. A tragic auditory wants *blood*. They care but little about a man and his wife parting. Besides, what will you do with the son, after all his pursuits and adventures? Even quietly leave him to take guinea-and-a-half lodgings with mamma in Leghorn! O impotent and pacific measures! . . . I am certain that you must mix up some strong ingredients of distress to give a savour to your pottage.

I still think that you may, and must, graft the story of Savage upon Defoe. Your hero must *kill* a *man* or *do something*. Can't you bring him to the gallows or some great mischief, out of which she *must* have recourse to an explanation with her husband to save him. Think on this. The husband, for instance, has great friends in Court at Leghorn. The son is condemned to death. She cannot tease him for a stranger. She must tell the whole truth. Or she *may* tease him, as for a stranger, till (like Othello in Cassio's case) he begins to suspect her for her importunity. Or, being pardoned, can she not tease her husband to get him banished? Something of this I suggested before. *Both* is best. The murder and the pardon will make business for the fourth act, and the banishment and explanation (by means of the *Friend* I want you to draw) the fifth. You must not open any of the truth to Dawley by means of a letter. A letter is a feeble messenger on the stage. Somebody, the son or his friend, must, as a *coup de main*, be exasperated, and obliged to tell the husband. Damn the husband and his "gentleman-like qualities." Keep him out of sight, or he will trouble all. Let him be in England on trade, and come home as Biron does in *Isabella*, in the fourth act, when he is wanted. I am for introducing situations, sort of counterparts to situations which have been tried in other plays—*like*, but not the *same*. On this principle I recommended a friend like Horatio in the "Fair Penitent," and on this principle I recommend a situation like Othello, with relation to Desdemona's intercession for Cassio. Byescenes may likewise receive hints. The son may see his mother at a mask or Feast, as Romeo, Juliet. The festivity of the company contrasts with the strong perturbations of the individuals. Dawley may be told his wife's past unchastity at a mask by some witch-character, as Macbeth upon the heath, in dark sentences. This may stir his brain, and be forgot, but come in aid of stronger proof hereafter. From this what you will perhaps call whimsical way of counterparting, this honest stealing, and original mode of plagiarism, much yet, I think, remains to be sucked. Excuse these abortions. I thought you would want the draught soon again, and I would not send it empty away.—Yours truly,

WILLIAM GODWIN! ! !

Somers Town, September 17, 1801.

To JOHN RICKMAN, Esq.

LETTER CI.]   *October* 9, 1801.

I called lately upon our common friend G. Dyer of Cliffords Inn. I found him inconsolable and very dirty. It seems that Gilbert Wakefield is dead, and George had not got his tribute ready for Mr. Phillips's magazine this month, and Dr. Aikin had sent a little tribute, and Miss Aikin had also sent a *tribute,* and the world would expect a tribute from his pen. At first I imagined that George was touched with some sense of kindred mortality, such as Methusaleh himself must have felt, when he was qualmish; but no, all that disturbed George was, that he had not got a *tribute. George* the *second,* George Burnett, supt with me last night. He is not got quite well of the metaphyz, but I hope and trust that last night's paroxysm will be the last, and that his disorder has come to its crisis. He maintained that if a highwayman, who is going to kill you, *spares* your *life* on your expressly promising to *spare his,* that is, not to prosecute, you are under no obligation to keep your word, because you were in a state of violence, when the promise was made, and the Good of the Whole, which may be partially endangered by suffering that man to live, is to be preferred to any such promise in such circumstances made. If I ever turn freebooter, and light upon George Burnett in my travels, I shall remember what I have to trust to. But saving his metaphyz (which goes off after the first heats of youth like the green sickness) George the 2nd has good parts. He only wants fortune. He as ill becomes adversity, as George the first would do prosperity, if any one should leave him a rich legacy. Another of fortune's *humble servants* is a visitor of mine, who in the language of antiquity would have been nominated Simonds-with-the-slit-lip. I cannot say his linen was of Tarsus, nor quite so ro-bust as Russian, but it certainly craved bleaching, but saving his dirty shirt, and his physiognomy and his 'bacco box, together with a certain kiddy air in his walk, a man would have gone near to have mistaken him for a gentleman. He has a sort of ambition to be so misunderstood. It seems the Treasury does not pay with that weekly promptitude, and ac-commodating periodicalness, it was wont; and some constitutions *cannot wait.* He craved the loan of a half guinea; could I refuse a GENTLEMAN who seemed in distress? He dropt some words, as if he were desirous of trying what effect the Irish air would have upon a *poor* constitution. Couldn't you make him a door-keeper, or a game-keeper, or find some post for him, not altogether so brilliant as useful? Some situation under the *mint-master?*—I leave him to your mercy and ability. There is no hurry, for what you have given him will keep him in *work* some time, and for *pay,* why 'tis just as his Majesty's ministers shall please. So, Cottle's Psalms are come out hot press'd for six shillings. Of course I shall send you a copy. "Poetry is never more delightfully employed than when in the service of its Creator." *Vide* Preface to the Translation (if he had writ one, but he has not).

Quid majus!—the Professor is not married, the *Plough* is yet *in posse* —peace is all the cry here—fireworks, lights, etc., abound—White sta-tioned himself at Temple Bar among the boys, and threw squibs; burned one man's cravat.—This is the cream of London intelligence—you shall have the earliest tidings of all new movements.   C. L.

   John Rickman, Esq.,
     Dublin Castle.

LETTER CII.]   *Tuesday, November 24,* 1801.

   Dr Rickman—I have just put my finishing hand to my play to alter it for publishing. I have made a thorough change in the structure of the latter part, omitting all those scenes which shew'd John under the first impression of his father's death. I have done this, because I had made him too weak, and to expose himself before his servants, which was an indecorum; and from a theory that poetry has nothing to do to give *pain;* the imbecilities, and deformities, the dotages of human nature, are not fit objects to be shewn. Instead of these rejected scenes I have told his feelings in a *narrative* of the old servant to Margaret, which is a relief to the oppression of John so often talking in his own person.—I have cut out all the interview of John and Simon, and they do not meet at all, and I have expunged Simon's bloody resolution, which offended you so much from him. I have sent him to *improve* himself by travel, and it is explained that his presence (who is the *good son* in my *parable*) would have been too much of a reproach and a pain to *my prodigal* in the first hour of his grief.—The whole ends with Margaret's Consolation, where it *should* end, without any pert incident of surprise and trick to make a catastrophe. Moreover, I have excluded the two tales of the Witch and the Gentleman who died for love, having since discovered by searching the parish register of St. Mary Ottery, that his disorder was a stranguary, tho' some rimes upon his grave-stone did a little lean to my hypothesis.—Moreover, I have gone through and cut out all the Ahs! and Ohs! and sundry weak parts, which I thought so fine three or four years ago. When it comes out you must let me know in what manner I can transmit you a copy or two. I have been so particular, because you have shewn more liking to my Margaret than most people, and my alterations were *in part* the offspring of your suggestions; not wholly, for I have long smelt a jumble. I hope you will find it now nearly all of a piece. I am to christen it "John Woodvil" simply—not "Pride's Cure."—As Dyer says, "I am no enemy to candid and ingenuous criticism, I only deprecate the arrows of calumny": *vide* most of the prefaces of G. Dyer. Dyer regularly dines with me when he does not go a visiting and brings his shilling. He has pick'd up amazingly. I never saw him happier. He has had his doors listed and his casements puttied, and bought a handsome *screen* of the last century. Only his poems do not get finished. One volume is printing, but the second wants a good deal doing to it. I do not expect that he will make much progress with his Life and Opinions, till his detestable Lyric Poetry is delivered to subscribers. I shall make him not deliver one vol. till both are ready, else he would infallibly have made two troubles and two expences of it. He talks of marrying, but this *en passant* (as he says) and *entre nous,* for God's sake don't mention it to him, for he has not forgiven me for betraying to you his purpose of writing his own Life. He says, that if it once spreads, so many people will expect and wish to have a place in it, that he is sure he shall disoblige all his friends.——

G. Burnett shewed me your rouzing Letter. If I had not known your theory and design, I must have called it a very cruel Letter, and sure as I was that your general idea of the treatment, which is best for Burnetts and George the Seconds, was right, I could not help thinking you had gone too far, even so far that he could not put up with it or you ever after, without doing a moral injury to himself. But you must pursue your own course, which nine times out of ten will be more judicious than mine. The less of interference in these cases, the better. I was principally (if not only) sorry, that you assured him of Southey's opinion of the mediocrity of his understanding perfectly agreeing with your own. Southey was the last plank of the scaffold which propt up George in his opinion of himself. But I dare not affirm you did wrong. I am not a teacher in Israel. Yours truly,   C. LAMB.

   John Rickman, Esq.,
     Dublin Castle.
LETTER CIII.]

   For John Rickman, Esq.,
     Dublin Castle.   [1801.]

I was the moon-struck man, that was inspired to write on the pacquet "for John Rickman," and must hasten to clear Burnett of that part of his *Indictment*. He brought to me his Letter and his Essay, or rather two Essays, and desired me to write myself and put up all together in a parcel. I had no leisure to write then, but I did up his things, and when I had done so the enormous bulk staggered me, and I preferred that obnoxious indorsement to enlarging it with another cover. I was guided by the usages of the India House, where I have often received superscriptions similar, and escaped shot-free. I will never practise upon your pocket in the like manner again, but Burnett stands acquitted. None but the Bishop could have composed that illustrious specimen of ignorance which you extract, and he alone, in all England, would not understand the absurdity of it, if it were to be pointed out. Still I wish something could be done for him, even if he waited six weeks, *or a day over*, for it. Methinks! (as the Poets say) I see Preferment waiting at the door, *afraid to come in,* 'till his Worship has finished his Introduction, that she may not deprive the World of his matchless labours.

   I have nothing to communicate, but my thanks. I do assure you that I retain a very lively memory of our old Smoking Evenings in Southampton Buildings. G. Dyer, our illustrious Co-Puffer, has emigrated to Enfield, where some rich man, that has got two Country Houses, allows him the use of a very large one, with a library, where he is getting the final vol. of his Poems ready, and then I shall set him about his Life: by *use* in a sentence back, I mean dirting and littering.

   Southey is not arrived.
   Yours sincerely,   C. LAMB.

   I forgot to notice an anachronism in your 1st Letter, which I am glad to see you correct in a subsequent—you accost me my dear SIR. By what twist of association in your unlucky Pericranium have you connected that Honour with my cognomen?

   Mary thanks you, but she prefers *Rum*.

I have literally *this moment* rec^d your packet for Southey. I mean Burnett's History of his own times. And your letter. For your kind mention of Slit-lips take my warmest thanks. He will have no objection to wait six weeks or *a day over,* tho' it may be damnably more inconvenient for him to *wait,* than for the Bishop. The fact of the "strange flesh" which he is reported to have eaten, astounds me, but I can believe and tremble.—Never mind the ceremony of franking to me. John Company pays.

LETTER CIV.]   [No date or post-mark, 1801.]

I sincerely thank you for your repeated offer, but I have just received as much as £50, an old debt which I told you of, and that will a good deal and more than cover the expences of printing. I expect to be able to send you some copies in a few weeks. I have not had a proof sheet yet. I have nothing to claim upon Dyer's account. He paid me from the beginning as near as I can calculate, and I solemnly protest it, to a penny for all the expences he put me to, and whenever he dines with us he regularly brings his shilling, which is a fair average for what his gluttony devours. To be sure he has occasionally an eleemosynary whiff of tobacco, for which I cannot sconce the Poet. I am afraid he sometimes does not come when he has not got a shilling. I cannot force him, for now his health is come back, he is the most unmanageable of God's creatures. He goes about fetching and carrying for Ladies, and always thinking he *must* call upon this Lady and t'other Gentleman. His first vol. is nearly printed, but he is projecting new odes and impertinences for the 2d, and I cannot foresee a period. Still he seems by fits bent upon writing his Life, and will do it if the Prototype is not overtaken with death. I quite give up any hope of reducing him to common sense and human conduct. All that can be done is to bolster up his carcase by a daily habit of Dining, until he finishes his mortal pilgrimage. Poor G. Burnett is very ill and reduced. You would deposit your fierce anger if you saw the metaphysician. He has brought his Introduction to a finish at last, but he is not in a capacity to go on. Coleridge has recommended him to the Editor of the *Morning Post,* who has promised to employ him. But a Lion is in his foot-path, and he cannot *begin yet.* I suppose he will write to you, and it will be needless to say more of him here. The goul has a gouless and two, if not three young gouls. The goul has not paid me the pittance, for 'twas not much, he borrowed of me, but I have reason to believe his circumstances are so squalid, that it would be more to expect of him than can be expected from man or goul, to divert his Comings in from the service of genuine hunger and thirst.—Fenwick's *Plough* (how one idea of Poverty introduces another!) is degenerated already from a daily to a weekly paper. I wish it may not vanish into thin air, or come out the same day as Burnett's Historia Romana issues from the press. I meantime have made some overtures to the Editor of the Morning Post thro' Coleridge, who writes for that paper, and hope I am on the point of being engaged.—I have seen Southey several times. His wife is considerably improved, and will talk if she is talked to, but she bitterly complains that when literary men get together, they never speak to the women. Mrs. Lovel is also in town and Southey's mother, who is DYING:—"So am not I, said the foolish fat scullion." Do you remember our unfeeling behaviour at the funeral of that dear young Lady, who was withered in her bloom by the untimely stroke of Death, and lies in what-d'ye-call-'em Church yard? The tear is falling while I remember—don't you perceive the Ink is rather *brackish?* as G. Burnett asked in a company at my brother's the other day, whether the Thames Water at Blackfriars Bridge was not a little Brackish.—The Professor has not yet thrown himself away. I am sorry to find he is about to commit a folly, for I hear that She has no fortune and has one child, and they propose that she shall ease the burden of the family expences by translating from the French.— Fell, the inevitable shadow of everything which Godwin does, is absolutely writing a Play. It is a Comedy. It is just finished, and I go this evening in the hope to see it. It will have one trait in it. There can be no mirth in it. An Owl making a Pun would be no bad emblem of the unnatural attempt. To your enquiry whether Mary swallows certain mixed Liquors, she answers that I unfortunately misunderstood that advice, as if it had been addrest to me, and have almost killed myself by the Blunder. But she will profit by the correction. She desires her love and remembrance. White often enquires after you, and as often desires to be mentioned to you, which I as regularly forget. Stoddart is going to begin the study of Civil Law at the Commons.

Farewell, old Comrade and new Secretary,
Thine,   C. L.

You must send up your St. Helena letter *immediately,* and I will drop it in our Box. I can't frank it, John Company never franks *outwards.* A ship, the *Marquis of Ely,* goes at Xmas. The *Armston* goes next Wednesday.

Since I wrote last Leaf, I have read Fell's Comedy, and am surprized to find it contain, if not sterling wit or character, a liveliness and knowledge of the present popular taste, which has astonish'd me. The serious parts are damn'd flat. But I should not at all wonder, he having a pretty good introduction, even if it should please highly. He has been a minute observer of what *takes* in Reynolds's plays, and has had real actors continually in his view.—Who knows, but Owls *do* make Puns, when they hoot by moonshine? I shall hear from the *Morning Post* this day, and shall endeavour to get the Theatrical Reports, not *all,* but Kemble's chief characters, and Cooke's, etc.

John Rickman, Esq.,
    Dublin Castle.

LETTER CV.]   *January* 9, 1802.

Please to send me *one* Letter with the *Broad Seal,* for a friend who is
curious in impressions.

I am to be sure much gratified with your use of Margaret as a kind of
rack to extract confession from women.   But don't give me out as your
Rack-maker, lest the women retort upon me the fate of Perillus, which
you may read in your Ainsworth under the article Phalaris; or you may
find the story more at large by perusing the Controversy between Bentley
and Boyle.   I have delayed to write (I believe I am telling a Lye) until I
should get a book ready to send (but I believe this has been all along a
pretext recurred to, a kind of after-motive, when the resolution was taken
a priori, rather than the true cause, which was mixed up of busy days and
riotous nights, doing the Company's business in a morning, straining for
Jokes in the afternoon, and retailing them (not being yet published) over
punch at night.   The Lungs of Stentor could not long sustain the Life
I have led.   I get into parties, or treat them with Pope Joan four times
in a week.   You have dropt in ere now when Norris was courting at such
a party, and you know the game.   I stick to it like any *Papist.*   'Tis better than Poetry, Mechanics, Politics, or Metaphysics.   That's a stop—
there's pope—you did not take your ace—what a magic charm in sounds.
. . . I begin not to wonder at the bloodshed which dyed Christian Europe
concerning Omousia and Omoiousia.—A party of people's *faces* about a
fire grinning over cards and forgetting that they have got to go home is
the supreme felicity, the Maximum Bonum.   White has or is about to
write you at my suggestion.   We desire nothing so vigorously as to see
Master Secretary in these parts.   There are Liquors and fumes extant,
which have power to detain a Bachelor from his cold Bed till cock crow.

Fenwick gives routs and balls and suppers (not balls) but splendid
entertainments out of the first fruits of the *Plow*—he had some hundreds
of pounds from unthinking Nobility.   It is no breach of charity to suppose that part is expended—his wife and daughter have got magnificent
Hats, which Mary waggishly has christen'd Northumberland Hats, from
his great Patron at Charing Cross.

Dyer has at last met with a madman more mad than himself—the
Earl of Buchan, brother to the Erskines and eccentric biographer of
Fletcher of Saltoun.   This old man of near eighty is come to London in
his way to France, and George and he go about everywhere.   George
brought the mad Lord up to see me—I wan't at home but Mary was
washing—a pretty pickle to receive an Earl in!   Lord have mercy upon
us! a Lord in my garret!   My utmost ambition was some time or other
to receive a Secretary!   Well, I am to breakfast with this mad Lord on
Sunday.   I am studying manners.   George and my Lord of Buchan went
on Thursday last to Richmond in the Long Coach to pay their devotions
to the shrine of Thomson!   The coldest day in the year.   Enough to cool
a Jerusalem-Padder.   George is as proud as a Turkey Cock and can talk
of nothing else; always taking care to hedge in at the end that he don't
value Lords, and that the Earl has nothing of the Lord about him.   O hu-

man nature! human Nature! for my part I have told every Body, how I had an Earl come to see me. . . . George describes the Earl as a very worthy man, who has his hobby horses; for instance, George says, he will stop you in the street, when you are walking with him, and hold you by the button, and talk so loud, that all the Passers by look at you. So you may guess *why* he cleaves to George the first. If you have read the *Post*, you may have seen a dissertation on Cooke's Richard the 3d. which is the best thing I have done. It was in last Monday; stray Jokes I will not *mark*, hoping you will always take the good ones to be mine, and the bad ones to be done by John a Nokes, etc.

In haste. Happy New Year to Master Secretary.   C. L.

I had, before your injunction came, given a hint to the Goul, that you were disposed to serve him; this to rear him from the dreary state of despair he was in. But now, *mum*. I wish to God you may do any thing: for all the Elements have fought against him.

My play will most likely accompany my *next*. Fell's goes on slow and sure, like his own long stories. It is *much, much*, better than I could believe. Some of it is very *good farce*, which is all a modern play need be.

To John Rickman, Esq.,
    Dublin Castle.

LETTER CVI.]   *January* 14, 1802.

You may suspect as much as you please (suspicion ever haunts the guilty mind) that I did not do that thing about Richard, but I tell you I did, and I also made the Lord Mayor's Bed, which you are welcome to rumple as much as you please. I plead guilty to certain "felicities of phrase"—*Noviciate* used as an adjective I myself suspected, but did not know that *novice* was any other than a substantive. But what the devil's all this coil for about delightful artifices and elastic minds? and how should a man at Bantry Bay know anything about good English? the fact is, that it was but an unfinished affair at first, and by the *intelligent artifice* of the Editor it was made more chaotic still. As it stands, it is more than half *introduction:* half of which was to be *note*. But it is most probably the last theatrical morceau I shall do: for they want 'em done the same night, and I tried it once, and found myself non compos. I can't *do* a thing against time. If I use "do" and "did" to excess, 'tis because I know 'em to be good English, that you can't deny. My Editor uniformly rejects all that I do considerable in length. I shall only do paragraphs, with now and then a slight poem such as "Dick Strype," if you read it, which was but a long Epigram. So I beg you not to read with much expectation, for my poor paragraphs do only get in, when there are none of any body's else. Most of them are rejected; all, almost, that are *personal*, where my forte lies. And I cannot get at once out of the delightful regions of scurrility, the "Delectable Mountains" of *Albion* where whilom I fed my sheep, into the kickshaws of fashionable tittle-tattle, which I *must learn.* I cannot have the conscience to order a Paper for Xt Church, on the hypothesis that it is on my account (which is modest) for no paragraphs can be worth eight guineas a year. However I will try and see, if I can get it at an under price as you proposed.—I sent 'em Mottoes for 12th Day at their own desire—how did they serve me? the first day they put in mottoes by another (most stupid) hand, and the next day mottoes by ditto with some of mine tacked to 'em. They rejected a pretty good one on Dr. Solomon.

> My namesake, sprung from Jewish Breeder,
> Knew *from* the Hyssop *to* the Cedar,
> But I, unlike the Jewish Leader,
> Scarce know the Hyssop *from* the Cedar.

Another of the rejected ones, on Count Rumford—

> I deal in Aliments fictitious,
> And teaze the Poor with soups nutritious;
> Of bones and flint I make dilution,
> And belong to the National Institution.

Maybe you didn't see what were *in* of mine. The Best was

> ADDINGTON
>
> I put my night cap on my head,
> And went as usual to my bed,
> And most surprizing to relate!
> I woke a Minister of State!

Another

> FRERE AND CANNING
>
> At Eton School brought up with dull boys,
> We shone like *men* among the *school boys;*
> But since we in the world have been
> We are but *schoolboys* among men.

Your advice about getting a share of the *Post as fast as I can !!* I shall certainly follow. I wish I may hold my two guinea matter.

My scrawl costs you nothing; and me only so much Ink. Mary's Love. We are just setting out on a night expedition freezing (the glass at 23 as I *hear,* for I don't know a thermometer from a barometer) to Pentonville to see Mister Comedy Fell and his pretty spouse.

Yours etc.   C. L.

To John Rickman, Esq.,
      Dublin Castle.

LETTER CVII.]   *January* 18, 1802.

George the 2nd has just arrived, has stayed over his time!! and written to Ld. Stanhope without telling his Ld.ship where to find him, accordingly must write again.

Dear Rickman—I have not been able to find a chapman, who will pay half thy father's newspapers. I already read the *Post* upon nearly a similar Plan; 7 or 8 of us subscribe. One keeps it and pays 1/2. But to avert thy wrath and indignation which I know will burn most furiously if I omit thy commission, I have ordered one at full cost, and there will go the first with the same Post which carries this. As Mary seldom sees a Paper she will thank your father for the liberty of reading it first, and take care only to send it by the same day's Post. She will pay such proportion as a Jury before Lord Kenyon shall award.

Dinner is smoking.

Yours truly, C. LAMB.

To John Rickman, Esq.,
    Dublin Castle.

LETTER CVIII.]   *February* 1, 1802.

Dear Rickman—Not having known the sweet girl deceased, your humble servant cannot endite with true passion a suitable Epitaph. Here is a kind of substitute for feeling—but your own Prose, or nakedly the Letter which you sent me, which was in some sort an Epitaph, and the best one, would do better on her grave stone than the cold Lines of a Stranger.

> A Heart which felt Unkindness, yet complain'd not;
> A Tongue which spake the simple Truth, and feign'd not;
> A Soul as white as the pure marble Skin
> (The beauteous Mansion it was lodgèd in)
> Which, unrespected, could itself respect:
>   On Earth was all the Portion of a Maid,
>   Who in this common Sanctuary laid
> Sleeps unoffended by the World's Neglect.

I have not seen Southey to talk with him about it, but I conclude you addrest a Letter to that import to him, as *his* came along with mine.—If you stay a little, perhaps he or I may hit upon a Better, for I suspect it sadly of common place.

I had hoped ere this to send you a Book, but the Boarders are shockingly dilatory, and seem never to have heard of the fabulous stories of the Anxiety of Authors and Parents.

You will see almost as soon as the Receipt of this a first Number of a Paper in the *Morning Post,* which I have undertaken solus, to be called the *Londoner;* I think you will like the First Number, as it jumps with your Notions about a Country Life, etc. . . . I have done no more, so I have all the world before me where to chuse. I think you could give me hints. I have seen light Papers in the Agricult. Mag. which would suit the *Londoner* to a tittle. G. Burnett surprized us with a visit yesterday. His Two young Lords have run away—George deposes, that he was Teaching them their Lesson, when he was called down by Ld. Stanhope to be introduced to his Lordship's Mother; when he returned his Pupils were flown. They had gone out of Window with their best Coats and Linen.—The

Eldest Son of Ld. S. served him exactly the same Trick, and his Lordship sets it down, that these striplings as well as the former (who never came back) were spirited away by the Pitt and Grenville Party, to whom he is allied by marriage. He says, that Pitt will make them Villains. Ministers have already bought off his Son and his Son-in-Law: and he meant to bring up these young ones (the eldest 16) to mechanics or manufactures. It is very probable what he says—for the P's and G's (writing to a Secretary I dare not be more explicit) would go some steps to stop the growth of Democratic Peers.—George declares that he is only sorry on Ld. Stan-hope's account, who is much agitated, but on his own he don't care at all: nay I have no doubt he is ready to leap at his heart, for Lord S. desires he will stay in his house, and he will try to get him something. So George has got his old desirable prospect of food and clothing with no Duty to perform for it. I could fill vols. with a History of his absurdities since the date of my Last. . . . Take one or 2.—Imprimis, he overstay'd his 3 weeks—then he wrote to Lord S. from town to write to him, but forgot to mention his own address—then he was forced to write again to say he forgot, and begg'd his Lordship to tell him the Exact situation where his Lordship's House stood, that he might have no trouble in finding it!!! to write to a Peer of the Realm to tell the number of his house! Then he determines to set off for Chevening next morning, and writes that he will come down by the 3 o'clock stage—then he comes to us the night before at 11 and complains bitterly of the difficulty of getting up so early—then he goes away, and White and I lay wagers that he won't go at all. Next morning 11 o'clock—enter Geo. the 2nd in a dirty neckcloth—he could not go because he had no Linen, and he had not time to go to Southey and borrow it, and inadvertently slips out that to be sure there was a Coach went at ½ past 10. Then my Tutor gapes, and stares, and borrows a neckcloth and sets off with all proper humility to My Lord's in a Post Chaise—drives up to the Door in Style—and there I leave him bowing and gaping to see the fine Pictures.

Yours truly,   C. LAMB.

Mary's grateful thanks for your indulgence by which she reads my works.

To John Rickman, Esq.,
    Dublin Castle.

LETTER CIX.]   *February* 4, 1802.

Dear Rickman—I send you three Copies. Keep one yourself, and distribute the others. Perhaps you will send one to her, "whom you in sport do call your Margaret," but this is mere conjecture.

G. Dyer is sitting by me, he begs to be kindly remembered. He has brought news, that a Mr. Wainewright, with a Mr. Frend the Pamphleteer, and Mr. Perry the Chronicleer, have set up as a Committee to procure him an annuity by subscription. Ld. Stanhope has sent £50.

Talking of money, you owe me £22—which I paid in advance for your father's Papers.

Yours truly, C. L.

To John Rickman, Esq.
Dublin Castle.

LETTER CX.] *February* 14, 1802.

"I take thy groat in earnest of Revenge." One-and-twenty Margarets fall to the disposal of your dainty Cousin. I sup with him at Southey's on Tuesday, God willing.—Your guineas (which, let me tell you, are too much, but you shall have your way) are not absolutely mal-a-pros, for by a cruel reverse of Fortune, that Dame who is painted with a wheel to signify to you, that she is changes, and rollings, and mutabilities, I am no longer Paragraph spinner. The fact is, that Stuart was wonderfully polite and civil at first, I suppose because Coleridge recommended me, from whose assistance in the Paper he expected great things, but Coleridge from ill health and unsettlement having hung back, I gradually got out of favor, and Stuart has at last twice told me that I must take more pains about my paragraphs, for he has not been able to draw above one in five from what I have sent him. This in connection with his altered behaviour was hint quite enough for me, who do not require hints as big as St. Paul's Church to make me understand a coldness, excited my magnanimous spirit to endite a valorous Letter of Resignation, which I did with some qualms, when I remembered what I gave up: but to tell truth, all the little I have done has been very irksome, and rendered ten times more so from a sense of my employer not being fully satisfied: and that little has subtracted from my pleasure of walking, reading, idling, etc., which are as necessary to me as the "golden vapour" of Life itself. My health (silly as it seems to relate) has suffered bitterly. My Spirits absolutely require freedom and leisure, and I think I shall never engage to do task work any more, for I am sick. —I must cut closer. I am almost ashamed at my capriciousness, as must seem to you, but upon a serious review I do approve of what I've done. I've foolishly involved you (I fear) in an expense of 8 guineas a year, which I *think* was on my acct. but as it is for *whom* it is, I must not call it foolish. A Paper in a Country Town is a kind of London. But I would gladly purchase your acquiescence by paying half, which I know you won't accept. I have given this up only two days, and I feel myself at elbow room, free and happy. I can scribble now at my heart's Leisure, if I have an impulse, and tho' I know I speak as a fool, I am sure I can write better gratis. Say no more about it. I have weighed my loss and my gain, and I write *Profit.*

I may yet do the *Londoners* at my Leisure.

This Letter is short for I have got a bad headache. Mr. Abbot's elevation, you may be sure, surprized me. I take it for granted you will not be a Loser. I am sure I shall be a gainer, if an Easterly wind wafts you to England.

Frend was here yesterday. He desires me to set down every day Dyer dines with me, and the Committee will pay me, as George is to have no money of his own. George contrives constantly to dine here, when he says he shan't over night, which is very *convenient*, and vice versa. It is the damned Vanity of being supposed to be always engaged. Now he is got well, he is as freakish as King David at Gath. Nothing can be done with him; save that the Committee will preserve him from felo de se, that he shan't starve himself.

George the 2nd discharges his important Trust, of doing *nothing* for Ld. S. with fidelity and diligence. His Lordship sends him to town upon any fiddle-faddle errand, and George fancies himself essential to his Lordship's comfort. He looks more important than Mr. Dressin, King's messenger.

Mary always desires to be most kindly remembered by you. She bids me *not* tell you that an Epigram called *Helen,* in my little Book, is of her writing. But it is, every tittle of it. I hope you do not dislike it. We remain yours truly, C. L., M. L.

To John Rickman, Esq.,
Dublin Castle.

To THOMAS MANNING.

LETTER CXI.] *February* 15, 1802.

Apropos, I think you wrong about my play. All the omissions are right. And the supplementary scene, in which Sandford narrates the manner in which his master is affected, is the best in the book. It stands where a hodge-podge of German puerilities used to stand. I insist upon it that you like that scene. Love me, love that scene. I will now transcribe the "Londoner" (No. 1), and wind up all with affection and humble servant at the end.

[Here was transcribed the essay called "The Londoner," see Page 375.]

"What is all this about?" said Mrs. Shandy. "A story of a cock and a bull," said Yorick: and so it is; but Manning will take good-naturedly what *God will send him* across the water: only I hope he won't *shut* his *eyes,* and *open* his *mouth,* as the children say, for that is the way to *gape,* and not to *read.* Manning, continue your laudable purpose of making me your register. I will render you back all your remarks; and *I, not you,* shall have received usury by having read them. In the meantime, may the great Spirit have you in his keeping, and preserve our Englishman from the inoculation of frivolity and sin upon French earth.

Allons—or what is it you say, instead of *good-bye?*

Mary sends her kind remembrance, and covets the remarks equally with me. C. LAMB.

Not a sentence, not a syllable of Trismegistus shall be lost through my
neglect. I am his word-banker, his storekeeper of puns and syllogisms.
You cannot conceive (and if Trismegistus cannot, no man can) the
strange joy which I felt at the receipt of a letter from Paris. It seemed to
give me a learned importance, which placed me above all who had not Pa-
risian correspondents. Believe that I shall carefully husband every scrap,
which will save you the trouble of memory, when you come back. You
cannot write things so trifling, let them only be about Paris, which I shall
not treasure. In particular, I must have parallels of actors and actresses.
I must be told if any building in Paris is at all comparable to St. Paul's,
which, contrary to the usual mode of that part of our nature called admiration, I have looked up to with unfading wonder, every morning at ten
o'clock, ever since it has lain in my way to business. At noon I casually
glance upon it, being hungry; and hunger has not much taste for the fine
arts. Is any night-walk comparable to a walk from St. Paul's to Charing
Cross, for lighting and paving, crowds going and coming without respite,
the rattle of coaches, and the cheerfulness of shops? Have you seen a man
guillotined yet? Is it as good as hanging? Are the women *all* painted, and
the men *all* monkeys? or are there not a *few* that look like *rational* of *both
sexes?* Are you and the first consul *thick?* All this expense of ink I may
fairly put you to, as your letters will not be solely for my proper pleasure;
but are to serve as memoranda and notices, helps for short memory, a
kind of Rumfordising recollection, for yourself on your return. Your letter was just what a letter should be, crammed, and very funny. Every
part of it pleased me till you came to Paris; then your philosophical indolence, or indifference, stung me. You cannot stir from your rooms till you
know the language! What the devil!—are men nothing but word-trum-
pets? Are men all tongue and ear? Have these creatures, that you and I
profess to know *something about,* no faces, gestures, gabble, no folly, no
absurdity, no induction of French education upon the abstract idea of
men and women, no similitude nor dissimilitude to English! Why, thou
cursed Smellfungus! your account of your landing and reception, and
Bullen, (I forget how you spell it, it was spelt my way in Harry the
Eighth's time), was exactly in that minute style which strong impressions
INSPIRE (writing to a Frenchman, I write as a Frenchman would). It appears to me as if I should die with joy at the first landing in a foreign
country. It is the nearest pleasure which a grown man can substitute for
that unknown one, which he can never know, the pleasure of the first entrance into life from the womb. I dare say, in a short time, my habits
would come back like a "stronger man" armed, and drive out that new
pleasure; and I should soon sicken for known objects. Nothing has transpired here that seems to me of sufficient importance to send dry-shod over
the water: but I suppose you will want to be told some news. The best
and the worst to me is, that I have given up two guineas a week at the
Post, and regained my health and spirits, which were upon the wane. I

grew sick, and Stuart unsatisfied. *Ludisti satis, tempus abire est;* I must cut closer, that's all. Mister Fell, or as you, with your usual facetiousness and drollery, call him, Mr. F+ll, has stopped short in the middle of his play. Some *friend* has told him that it has not the least merit in it. Oh that I had the rectifying of the Litany! I would put in a *libera nos* (*Scriptores videlicet*) *ab amicis!* That's all the news. *Apropos:* is it pedantry, writing to a Frenchman, to express myself sometimes by a French word, when an English one would not do as well? Methinks my thoughts fall naturally into it.

In all this time I have done but one thing, which I reckon tolerable, and that I will transcribe, because it may give you pleasure, being a picture of *my* humours. You will find it in my last page. It absurdly is a first Number of a series, thus strangled in embryo.

More news! The Professor's Rib has come out to be a disagreeable woman, so much so as to drive me and some more old cronies from his house. He must not wonder if people are shy of coming to see him because of the "snakes." C. L.

To Mr. RICKMAN.

LETTER CXIII.] *April* 10, 1802.

Dear Rickman—The enclosed letter explains itself. It will save me the danger of a corporal interview with the man-eater, who, if very sharp set, may take a fancy to me, if you will give me a short note, declaratory of probabilities. These from him who hopes to see you once or twice more before he goes hence, to be no more seen: for there is no tipple nor tobacco in the grave, whereunto he hasteneth. C. LAMB.

16, Mitre Court Buildings,
Inner Temple.

How clearly the Ghoul writes, and like a gentleman!

To SAMUEL TAYLOR COLERIDGE.

LETTER CXIV.] *September* 8, 1802.

Dear Coleridge—I thought of not writing till we had performed some of our commissions; but we have been hindered from setting about them, which yet shall be done to a tittle. We got home very pleasantly on Sunday. Mary is a good deal fatigued, and finds the difference of going *to* a place, and coming *from* it. I feel that I shall remember your mountains to the last day I live. They haunt me perpetually. I am like a man who has been falling in love unknown to himself, which he finds out when he leaves the lady. I do not remember any very strong impression while they were present; but, being gone, their mementos are shelved in my brain. We passed a very pleasant little time with the Clarksons. The Wordsworths are at Montagu's rooms, near neighbours to us. They dined with us yesterday, and I was their guide to Bartlemy Fair!

To Mrs. GODWIN.

LETTER CXV.]   [Early in *September* 1802?]

Dear Mrs. G.—Having observed with some concern that Mr. Godwin is a little fastidious in what he eats for supper, I herewith beg to present his palate with a piece of dried salmon. I am assured it is the best that swims in Trent. If you do not know how to dress it, allow me to add, that it should be cut in thin slices and broiled in paper *previously prepared in butter*. Wishing it exquisite, I remain,—Much as before, yours sincerely,

                                                     C. LAMB.

Some add *mashed potatoes*.

To THOMAS MANNING.

LETTER CXVI.]   *London, September* 24, 1802.

My dear Manning—Since the date of my last letter I have been a traveller. A strong desire seized me of visiting remote regions. My first impulse was to go and see Paris. It was a trivial objection to my aspiring mind, that I did not understand a word of the language, since I certainly intend some time in my life to see Paris, and equally certainly intend never to learn the language; therefore that could be no objection. However, I am very glad I did not go, because you had left Paris (I see) before I could have set out. I believe, Stoddart promising to go with me another year prevented that plan. My next scheme (for to my restless, ambitious mind London was become a bed of thorns) was to visit the far-famed peak in Derbyshire, where the Devil sits, they say, without breeches. *This* my purer mind rejected as indelicate. And my final resolve was, a tour to the Lakes. I set out with Mary to Keswick, without giving Coleridge any notice, for my time, being precious, did not admit of it. He received us with all the hospitality in the world, and gave up his time to show us all the wonders of the country. He dwells upon a small hill by the side of Keswick, in a comfortable house, quite enveloped on all sides by a net of mountains: great floundering bears and monsters they seemed, all couchant and asleep. We got in in the evening, travelling in a post-chaise from Penrith, in the midst of a gorgeous sunshine, which transmuted all the mountains into colours, purple, etc. etc. We thought we had got into fairyland. But that went off (as it never came again; while we stayed we had no more fine sunsets), and we entered Coleridge's comfortable study just in the dusk, when the mountains were all dark with clouds upon their heads. Such an impression I never received from objects of sight before, nor do I suppose I can ever again. Glorious creatures, fine old fellows, Skiddaw, etc. I never shall forget ye, how ye lay about that night, like an intrenchment; gone to bed, as it seemed for the night, but promising that ye were to be seen in the morning. Coleridge had got a blazing fire in his study; which is a large antique, ill-shaped room, with an old-fashioned organ, never played upon, big enough for a church, shelves of scattered folios, an Æolian harp, and an old sofa, half bed, etc. And all looking out upon the last fading view of Skiddaw, and his broad-breasted brethren: what a night! Here we stayed three full weeks, in which time I visited Wordsworth's cottage, where we stayed a day or two with the Clarksons (good people, and most hospitable, at whose house we tarried one day and night), and saw Lloyd. The Wordsworths were gone to Calais. They have since been in London, and past much time with us: he is now gone into Yorkshire to be married. So we have seen Keswick, Grasmere, Ambleside, Ulswater (where the Clarksons live), and a place at the other end of Ulswater; I forget the name; to which we travelled on a very sultry day, over the middle of Helvellyn. We have clambered up to the top of Skiddaw, and I have waded up the bed of Lodore. In fine, I have satisfied myself that there is such a thing as that which tourists call *romantic*, which I very much suspected before: they make such a spluttering about it, and toss their splendid epithets around them, till they give as dim a light as at four o'clock next morning the lamps do after an illumination. Mary was excessively tired when she got about half-way up Skiddaw, but we came to a cold rill (than which nothing can be imagined more cold, running over cold stones), and with the reinforcement of a draught of cold water she surmounted it most manfully. Oh, its fine black head, and the bleak air atop of it, with a prospect of mountains all about and about, making you giddy; and then Scotland afar off, and the border countries so famous in song and ballad! It was a day that will stand out, like a mountain, I am sure, in my life. But I am returned (I have now been come home near three weeks; I was a month out), and you cannot conceive the degradation I felt at first, from being accustomed to wander free as air among mountains, and bathe in rivers without being controlled by any one, to come home and *work*. I felt very *little*. I had been dreaming I was a very great man. But that is going off, and I find I shall conform in time to that state of life to which it has pleased God to call me. Besides, after all, Fleet Street and the Strand are better places to live in for good and all than amidst Skiddaw. Still, I turn back to those great places where I wandered about, participating in their greatness. After all, I could not *live* in Skiddaw. I could spend a year, two, three years among them, but I must have a prospect of seeing Fleet Street at the end of that time, or I should mope and pine away, I know. Still, Skiddaw is a fine creature. My habits are changing, I think, *i.e.* from drunk to sober. Whether I shall be happier or not remains to be proved. I shall certainly be more happy in a morning; but whether I shall not sacrifice the fat, and the marrow, and the kidneys, *i.e.* the night, glorious care-drowning night, that heals all our wrongs, pours wine into our mortifications, changes the scene from indifferent and flat to bright and brilliant! O Manning, if I should have formed a diabolical resolution, by the time you come to England, of not admitting any spirituous liquors into my house, will you be my guest on such shameworthy terms? Is life, with such limitations, worth trying? The truth is, that my liquors bring a nest of friendly harpies about my house, who consume me. This is a pitiful tale to be read at St. Gothard, but it is just now nearest my heart. Fenwick is a ruined man. He is hiding himself from his creditors, and has sent his wife and children into the country. Fell, my other drunken companion (that has been: *nam hic cæstus artemque repono*), is turned editor of a Naval Chronicle. Godwin continues a steady friend, though the same facility does not remain of visiting him often. That . . . has detached Marshall from his house; Marshall, the man who went to sleep when the "Ancient Mariner" was reading; the old, steady, unalterable friend of the Professor. Holcroft is not yet come to town. I expect to see him, and will deliver your message. Things come crowding in to say, and no room for 'em. Some things are too little to be told, *i.e.* to have a preference; some are too big and circumstantial. Thanks for yours, which was most delicious. Would I had been with you, benighted, etc.! I fear my head is turned with wandering. I shall never be the same acquiescent being. Farewell. Write again quickly, for I shall not like to hazard a letter, not knowing where the fates have carried you. Farewell, my dear fellow. C. LAMB.

To SAMUEL TAYLOR COLERIDGE.

LETTER CXVII.] *October* 9, 1802.

CAROLUS AGNUS COLERIDGIO SUO S.

Carissime—Scribis, ut nummos scilicet epistolarios solvam et postremo in Tartara abeam: immo tu potius Tartaricum (ut aiunt) deprehendisti, qui me vernaculâ meâ linguâ pro scribâ conductitio per tot annos satis eleganter usum ad Latinè impure et canino fere ore latrandum per tuasmet epistolas benè compositas et concinnatas percellere studueris. Conabor tamen: Attamen vereor, ut Ædes istas nostri Christi, inter quas tantâ diligentiâ magistri improbâ bonis literulis, quasi per clysterem quendam injectis, infrà supràque olim penitùs imbutus fui, Barnesii et Marklandii doctissimorum virorum nominibus adhuc guadentes, barbarismis meis peregrinis et aliunde quæsitis valde dehonestavero. Sed pergere quocunque placet. Adeste igitur, quotquot estis, conjugationum declinationumve turmæ, terribilia spectra, et tu imprimis ades, Umbra et Imago maxima obsoletæ (Diis gratiæ) Virgæ, quâ novissime in mentem receptâ, horrescunt subito natales, et parum deest quo minùs braccas meas ultro usque ad crura demittam, et ipse puer pueriliter ejulem.

Ista tua Carmina Chamouniana satis grandia esse mihi constat; sed hoc mihi nonnihil displicet, quòd in iis illæ montium Grisosonum inter se responsiones totidem reboant anglicè, *God, God,* haud aliter atque temet audivi tuas montes Cumbrianas resonare docentem, *Dodd, Dodd,* nempe Doctorem infelicem: vocem certe haud Deum Sonantem. Pro cæteris plaudo.

Itidem comparationes istas tuas satis callidas et lepidas certè novi: sed quid hoc ad verum? cum illi Consulari viro et *mentem irritabilem* istum Julianum: et etiam *astutias frigidulas* quasdam Augusto propriores, nequaquam congruenter uno afflatu comparationis causâ insedisse affirmaveris: necnon nescio quid similitudinis etiam cum Tiberio tertio in loco solicite produxeris. Quid tibi equidem cum uno vel altero Cæsare, cùm universi Duodecim ad comparationes tuas se ultro tulerint? Præterea, vetustati adnutans, comparationes iniquas odi.

Istas Wordsworthianas nuptias (vel potius cujusdam *Edmundii* tui) te retulisse mirificum gaudeo. Valeas, Maria, fortunata nimium, et antiquæ illæ Mariæ Virgini (comparatione plusquam Cæsareanâ) forsitan comparanda, quoniam "beata inter mulieres:" et etiam fortasse Wordsworthium ipsum tuum maritum Angelo Salutatori æquare fas erit, quoniam e Cœlo (ut ille) descendunt et Musæ et ipsi Musicolæ: at Wordsworthium Musarum observantissimum semper novi. Necnon te quoque affinitate hâc novâ, Dorothea, gratulor: et tu certe alterum *donum Dei*.

Istum Ludum, quem tu, Coleridgi, Americanum garris, a Ludo (ut Ludi sunt) maximè abhorrentem prætereo: nempe quid ad Ludum attinet, totius illæ gentis Columbianæ, a nostrâ gente, eadem stirpe ortâ, ludi singuli causa voluntatem perperam alienare? Quæso ego materiam ludi: tu Bella ingeris.

Denique valeas, et quid de Latinitate meâ putes, dicas: facias ut opossum illum nostrum volantem vel (ut tu malis) quendam Piscem errabundum, a me salvum et pulcherrimum esse jubeas. Valeant uxor tua cum Hartleiio nostro. Soror mea salva est et ego: vos et ipsa salvere jubet. Ulterius progrediri non liquet: homo sum æratus.

P.S.—Pene mihi exciderat, apud me esse Librorum a Johanno Miltono Latinè scriptorum volumina duo, quæ (Deo volente) cum cæteris tuis libris ocyùs citiùs per Mariam ad te missura curabo; sed me in hoc tali genere rerum nullo modo *festinantem* novisti: habes confitentem reum. Hoc solum dici restat, prædicta volumina pulchra esse et omnia opera Latina J. M. in se continere. Circa defensionem istam Pro Pop°. Ang°. acerrimam in præsens ipse præclaro gaudio moror.

Jussa tua Stuartina faciam ut diligenter colam.

Iterum iterumque valeas:

Et facias memor sis nostri.

LETTER CXVIII.] *October* 11, 1802.

Dear Coleridge—Your offer about the German poems is exceedingly kind: but I do not think it a wise speculation, because the time it would take you to put them into prose would be nearly as great as if you versified them. Indeed I am sure you could do the one nearly as soon as the other; so that instead of a division of labour, it would be only a multiplication. But I will think of your offer in another light. I daresay I could find many things, of a light nature, to suit that paper, which you would not object to pass upon Stuart as your own, and I should come in for some light profits, and Stuart think the more highly of your assiduity. "Bishop Hall's Characters" I know nothing about, having never seen them. I will reconsider your offer, which is very plausible; but as to the drudgery of going every day to an editor with my scraps, like a pedler, for him to pick out and tumble about my ribbons and posies, and to wait in his lobby, etc., no money could make up for the degradation. You are in too high request with him to have anything unpleasant of that sort to submit to.

It was quite a slip of my pen, in my Latin letter, when I told you I had Milton's Latin Works. I ought to have said his Prose Works, in two volumes, Birch's edition, containing all, both Latin and English, a fuller and better edition than Lloyd's of Toland. It is completely at your service, and you must accept it from me; at the same time I shall be much obliged to you for your Latin Milton, which you think you have at Howitt's; it will leave me nothing to wish for but the *History of England,* which I shall soon pick up for a trifle. But you must write me word whether the Miltons are worth paying carriage for. You have a Milton; but it is pleasanter to eat one's own pease out of one's own garden, than to buy them by the peck at Covent Garden; and a book reads the better, which is our own, and has been so long known to us, that we know the topography of its blots and dog's-ears, and can trace the dirt in it to having read it at tea with buttered muffins, or over a pipe, which I think is the maximum. But, Coleridge, you must accept these little things, and not think of returning money for them, for I do not set up for a factor or general agent. As for the fantastic debt of £15, I'll think you were dreaming, and not trouble myself seriously to attend to you. My bad Latin you properly correct; but *natales* for *nates* was an inadvertency: I knew better. *Progrediri,* or *progredi,* I thought indifferent, my authority being Ainsworth. However, as I have got a fit of Latin, you will now and then indulge me with an *epistola.* I pay the postage of this, and propose doing it by turns. In that case I can now and then write to you without remorse; not that you would mind the money, but you have not always ready cash to answer small demands, the *epistolarii nummi.*

Your "Epigram on the Sun and Moon in Germany" is admirable. Take 'em all together, they are as good as Harrington's. I will muster up all the conceits I can, and you shall have a packet some day. You and I together can answer all demands surely: you, mounted on a terrible charger (like Homer, in the Battle of the Books), at the head of the cavalry: I will lead the light horse. I have just heard from Stoddart. Allen and he intend taking Keswick in their way home. Allen wished particularly to have it a secret that he is in Scotland, and wrote to me accordingly very urgently. As luck was, I had told not above three or four; but Mary had told Mrs. Green, of Christ's Hospital! For the present, farewell: never forgetting love to Pipos and his friends.   C. LAMB.

LETTER CXIX.]   *October* 23, 1802.

I read daily your political essays. I was particularly pleased with "Once a Jacobin:" though the argument is obvious enough, the style was less swelling than your things sometimes are, and it was plausible *ad populum*. A vessel has just arrived from Jamaica with the news of poor Sam Le Grice's death. He died at Jamaica of the yellow fever. His course was rapid, and he had been very foolish; but I believe there was more of kindness and warmth in him than in almost any other of our schoolfellows. The annual meeting of the Blues is to-morrow, at the London Tavern, where poor Sammy dined with them two years ago, and attracted the notice of all by the singular foppishness of his dress. When men go off the stage so early, it scarce seems a noticeable thing in their epitaphs, whether they had been wise or silly in their lifetime.

I am glad the snuff and Pi-pos's books please. "Goody Two Shoes" is almost out of print. Mrs. Barbauld's stuff has banished all the old classics of the nursery; and the shopman at Newberry's hardly deigned to reach them off an old exploded corner of a shelf, when Mary asked for them. Mrs. Barbauld's and Mrs. Trimmer's nonsense lay in piles about. Knowledge insignificant and vapid as Mrs. Barbauld's books convey, it seems, must come to a child in the *shape of knowledge;* and his empty noddle must be turned with conceit of his own powers when he has learnt that a horse is an animal, and Billy is better than a horse, and such like; instead of that beautiful interest in wild tales, which made the child a man, while all the time he suspected himself to be no bigger than a child. Science has succeeded to poetry no less in the little walks of children than with men. Is there no possibility of averting this sore evil? Think what you would have been now, if, instead of being fed with tales and old wives' fables in childhood, you had been crammed with geography and natural history!

Hang them!—I mean the cursed Barbauld crew, those blights and blasts of all that is human in man and child.

As to the translations, let me do two or three hundred lines, and then do you try the nostrums upon Stuart in any way you please. If they go down I will bray more. In fact, if I got or could but get £50 a year only, in addition to what I have, I should live in affluence.

Have you anticipated it, or could you not give a parallel of Buonaparte with Cromwell, particularly as to the contrast in their deeds affecting *foreign* States? Cromwell's interference for the Albigenses, Buonaparte's against the Swiss. Then religion would come in; and Milton and you could rant about our countrymen of that period. This is a hasty suggestion, the more hasty because I want my supper. I have just finished Chapman's Homer. Did you ever read it? it has the continuous power of interesting you all along, like a rapid original, more than any; and in the uncommon excellence of the more finished parts goes beyond Fairfax or any of 'em. The metre is fourteen syllables, and capable of all sweetness and grandeur. Cowper's blank verse detains you every step with some heavy Miltonism; Chapman gallops off with you his own free pace. Take a simile for example. The council breaks up—

> "Being abroad, the earth was overlaid
> With flockers to them, that came forth; as when of frequent bees
> Swarms rise out of a hollow rock, repairing the degrees

Of their egression endlessly, with ever rising new
From forth their sweet nest; as their store, still as it faded, grew,
And never would cease sending forth her clusters to the spring,
They still crowd out so; this flock here, that there, belabouring
The loaded flowers. So," etc. etc.

What *endless egression of phrases* the dog commands!

Take another, Agamemnon wounded, bearing his wound heroically for
the sake of the army (look below), to a woman in labour.

"He, with his lance, sword, mighty stones, pour'd his heroic wreak
On other squadrons of the foe, whiles yet warm blood did break
Thro' his cleft veins; but when the wound was quite exhaust and crude,
The eager anguish did approve his princely fortitude.
As when most sharp and bitter pangs distract a labouring dame,
Which the divine Ilithiæ, that rule the painful frame
Of human childbirth, pour on her; the Ilithiæ that are
The daughters of Saturnia; with whose extreme repair
The woman in her travail strives, to take the worst it gives;
With thought, it *must be, 'tis love's fruit, the end for which she lives;*
The mean to make herself new born, what comforts will redound:
So," etc.

I will tell you more about Chapman and his peculiarities in my next. I
am much interested in him.

Yours ever affectionately, and Pi-Pos's.   C. L.

LETTER CXX.]   *November* 4, 1802.

Observe, there comes to you, by the Kendal waggon to-morrow, the
illustrious 5th of November, a box, containing the Miltons, the strange
American Bible, with White's brief note, to which you will attend; *Baxter's Holy Commonwealth,* for which you stand indebted to me 3s. 6d.;
an odd volume of Montaigne, being of no use to me, I having the whole;
certain books belonging to Wordsworth, as do also the strange thick-
hoofed shoes, which are very much admired in London. All these sundries
I commend to your most strenuous looking after. If you find the Miltons
in certain parts dirtied and soiled with a crumb of right Gloucester,
blacked in the candle (my usual supper), or peradventure a stray ash of
tobacco wafted into the crevices, look to that passage more especially;
depend upon it, it contains good matter. I have got your little Milton,
which, as it contains "Salmasius," and I make a rule of never hearing but
one side of the question (why should I distract myself?), I shall return to
you when I pick up the *Latina opera.* The first Defence is the greatest
work among them, because it is uniformly great, and such as is befitting
the very mouth of a great nation, speaking for itself. But the second Defence, which is but a succession of splendid episodes, slightly tied together, has one passage, which, if you have not read, I conjure you to lose no
time, but read it: it is his consolations in his blindness, which had been
made a reproach to him. It begins whimsically, with poetical flourishes
about Tiresias and other blind worthies (which still are mainly interest-

ing as displaying his singular mind, and in what degree poetry entered into his daily soul, not by fits and impulses, but engrained and innate), but the concluding page, *i.e.* of *this passage* (not of the *Defensio*), which you will easily find, divested of all brags and flourishes, gives so rational, so true an enumeration of his comforts, so human, that it cannot be read without the deepest interest. Take one touch of the religious part:—"Et sane haud ultima Dei cura cæci—*we blind folks,* I understand it (not *nos* for *ego;*)—su:nus; qui nos, quominus quicquam aliud præter ipsum cernere valemus, eo clementius atque benignius respicere dignatur. Væ qui illudit nos, væ qui lædit, execratione publica devovendo; nos ab injuriis hominum non modo incolumes, sed pene sacros, divina lex reddidit, divinus favor: nec tam *oculorum hebetudine* quam *cœlestium alarum umbrâ* has nobis fecisse tenebras videtur, factas illustrare rursus interiore ac longe præstabiliore lumine haud raro solet. Huc refero, quod et amici officiosius nunc etiam quam solebant, colunt, observant, adsunt, quod et nonnulli sunt, quibuscum Pyladeas atque Theseas alternare voces verorum amicorum liceat.

> "Vade gubernaculum mei pedis.
> Da manum ministro amico
> Da collo manum tuam, ductor autem viæ ero tibi ego."

All this, and much more, is highly pleasing to know. But you may easily find it; and I don't know why I put down so many words about it but for the pleasure of writing to you, and the want of another topic.

Yours ever, C. LAMB.

To-morrow I expect with anxiety S. T. C.'s letter to Mr. Fox.

To THOMAS MANNING.

LETTER CXXI.] *November* 1802.

My dear Manning—I must positively write, or I shall miss you at Toulouse. I sit here like a decayed minute hand; (I lie: *that* does not *sit;*) and being myself the exponent of no time, take no heed how the clocks about me are going. You possibly by this time may have explored all Italy, and toppled, unawares, into Etna, while you went too near those rotten-jawed, gap-toothed, old worn-out chaps of hell,—while I am meditating a quiescent letter to the honest post-master of Toulouse. But in case you should not have been *felo de se,* this is to tell you, that your letter was quite to my palate: in particular your just remarks upon Industry, cursed Industry (though indeed you left me to explore the reason), were highly relishing. I have often wished I had lived in the golden age, when shepherds lay stretched upon flowers, and roused themselves at their leisure,—the genius there is in a man's natural idle face, that has not learned his multiplication table! before doubt, and propositions, and corollaries, got into the world!

Now, as Joseph Cottle, a Bard of Nature, sings, going up Malvern Hills,

> "How steep! how painful the ascent!
> It needs the evidence of *close deduction*
> To know that ever I shall gain the top."

You must know that Joe is lame, so that he had some reason for so singing. These two lines, I assure you, are taken *totidem literis* from a very *popular* poem. Joe is also an Epic Poet as well as a Descriptive, and has written a tragedy, though both his drama and epopoiea are strictly *descriptive*, and chiefly of the *Beauties of Nature*, for Joe thinks *man* with all his passions and frailties not a proper subject of the *Drama*. Joe's tragedy hath the following surpassing speech in it. Some king is told that his enemy has engaged twelve archers to come over in a boat from an enemy's country and waylay him; he thereupon pathetically exclaims—

> "*Twelve*, dost thou say? Curse on those dozen villains!"

Cottle read two or three acts out to us, very gravely on both sides till he came to this heroic touch,—and then he asked what we laughed at? I had no more muscles that day. A poet that chooses to read out his own verses has but a limited power over you. There is a bound where his authority ceases. *Apropos*, if you should go to Florence or to Rome, inquire what works are extant in gold, silver, bronze, or marble, of Benvenuto Cellini, a Florentine artist, whose life, doubtless, you have read, or if not, without controversy you must read—so haste ye, send for it immediately from Lane's circulating Library. It is always put among the Romances, but you have read it I suppose. In particular, inquire at Florence for his colossal bronze statue (in the Grand Square, or somewhere) of Perseus. You may read the story in Tooke's *Pantheon*. Nothing material has transpired in these parts. Coleridge has indited a violent Philippic against Mr. Fox in the *Morning Post*, which is a compound of expressions of humility, gentleman-ushering-in most arrogant charges. It will do Mr. Fox no real injury among those that know him.

LETTER CXXII.]   *February* 19, 1803.

My dear Manning—The general scope of your letter afforded no indications of insanity, but some particular points raised a scruple. For God's sake don't think any more of "Independent Tartary." What are you to do among such Ethiopians? Is there no *lineal descendant* of Prester John? Is the chair empty? Is the sword unswayed? Depend upon it they'll never make you their king, as long as any branch of that great stock is remaining. I tremble for your Christianity. They will certainly circumcise you. Read Sir John Mandeville's travels to cure you, or come over to England. There is a Tartar-man now exhibiting at Exeter Change. Come and talk with him, and hear what he says first. Indeed he is no very favourable specimen of his countrymen! But perhaps the best thing you can do is to *try* to get the idea out of your head. For this purpose repeat to yourself every night, after you have said your prayers, the words Independent

Tartary, Independent Tartary, two or three times, and associate with them the *idea* of *oblivion* ('tis Hartley's method with obstinate memories), or say, Independent, Independent, have I not already got an *independence?* That was a clever way of the old puritans, pun-divinity. My dear friend, think what a sad pity it would be to bury such *parts* in heathen countries, among nasty, unconversable, horse-belching, Tartar-people! Some say, they are Cannibals; and then, conceive a Tartar-fellow *eating* my friend, and adding the *cool malignity* of mustard and vinegar! I am afraid 'tis the reading of Chaucer has misled you; his foolish stories about Cambuscan, and the ring, and the horse of brass. Believe me, there are no such things, 'tis all the poet's *invention;* but if there were such darling things as old Chaucer sings, I would *up* behind you on the horse of brass, and frisk off for Prester John's country. But these are all tales; a horse of brass never flew, and a king's daughter never talked with birds! The Tartars, really, are a cold, insipid, smouchy set. You'll be sadly moped (if you are not eaten) among them. Pray *try* and cure yourself. Take hellebore (the counsel is Horace's, 'twas none of my thought *originally*). Shave yourself oftener. Eat no saffron, for saffron-eaters contract a terrible Tartar-like yellow. Pray, to avoid the fiend. Eat nothing that gives the heart-burn. *Shave the upper lip.* Go about like an European. Read no books of voyages (they are nothing but lies), only now and then a romance, to keep the fancy *under.* Above all, don't go to any sights of *wild beasts. That has been your ruin.* Accustom yourself to write familiar letters, on common subjects, to your friends in England, such as are of a moderate understanding. And think about common things more. There's your friend Holcroft, now, has written a Play. You used to be fond of the drama. Nobody went to see it. Notwithstanding this, with an audacity perfectly original, he faces the town down in a preface that they *did* like it very much. I have heard a waspish punster say, "Sir, why did you not laugh at my jest?" But for a man boldly to face one out with "Sir, I maintain it, you *did* laugh at my jest," is a little too much. I have seen H. but once. He spoke of you to me in honourable terms. H. seems to me to be drearily dull. G———— is dull, then he has a dash of affectation, which smacks of the coxcomb, and your coxcombs are always agreeable. I supped last night with Rickman, and met a merry *natural* captain, who pleases himself vastly with once having made a pun at Otaheite in the O. language. 'Tis the same man who said Shakspeare he liked, because he was *so much of the gentleman.* Rickman is a man "absolute in all numbers." I think I may one day bring you acquainted, if you do not go to Tartary first; for you'll never come back. Have a care, my dear friend, of Anthropophagi! their stomachs are always craving. 'Tis terrible to be weighed out at fivepence a-pound; to sit at table (the reverse of fishes in Holland) not as a guest, but as a meat.

God bless you: do come to England. Air and exercise may do great things. Talk with some minister. Why not your father?

God dispose all for the best. I have discharged my duty.

Your sincere friend,

C. LAMB.

Letter CXXIII.] *March* 1803.

Dear Manning—I send you some verses I have made on the death of a young Quaker you may have heard me speak of as being in love with for some years while I lived at Pentonville, though I had never spoken to her in my life. She died about a month since. If you have interest with the Abbé de Lisle, you may get 'em translated; he has done as much for the Georgics.

To SAMUEL TAYLOR COLERIDGE.

Letter CXXIV.] *March* 20, 1803.

Mary sends love from home.

Dear Coleridge—I do confess that I have not sent your books as I ought to have done; but you know how the human free will is tethered, and that we perform promises to ourselves no better than to our friends. A watch is come for you. Do you want it soon, or shall I wait till some one travels your way? You, like me, I suppose, reckon the lapse of time from the waste thereof, as boys let a cock run to waste; too idle to stop it, and rather amused with seeing it dribble. Your poems have begun printing; Longman sent to me to arrange them, the old and the new together. It seems you have left it to him; so I classed them, as nearly as I could, according to dates. First, after the Dedication (which must march first), and which I have transplanted from before the Preface (which stood like a dead wall of prose between), to be the first poem; then comes "The Pixies," and the things most juvenile; then on "To Chatterton," etc.,— on, lastly, to the "Ode on the Departing Year," and "Musings,"—which finish. Longman wanted the Ode first, but the arrangement I have made is precisely that marked out in the Dedication, following the order of time. I told Longman I was sure that you would omit a good portion of the first edition. I instanced several sonnets, etc.; but that was not his plan, and, as you have done nothing in it, all I could do was to arrange 'em on the supposition that all were to be retained. A few I positively rejected; such as that of "The Thimble," and that of "Flicker and Flicker's Wife," and that *not* in the manner of Spenser, which you yourself had stigmatised—and the "Man of Ross,"—I doubt whether I should this last. It is not too late to save it. The first proof is only just come. I have been forced to call that Cupid's Elixir, "Kisses." It stands in your first volume, as an Effusion, so that, instead of prefixing "The Kiss" to that of "One Kiss, dear Maid," etc., I have ventured to entitle it "To Sara." I am aware of the nicety of changing even so mere a trifle as a title to so short a piece, and subverting old associations; but two called "Kisses" would have been absolutely ludicrous, and "Effusion" is no name, and these poems come close together. I promise you not to alter one word in any poem whatever, but to take your last text, where two are. Can you send any wishes about the book? Longman, I think, should have settled with you; but it seems you have left it to him. Write as soon as you possibly can; for, without making myself responsible, I feel myself, in some sort, accessory to the selection, which I am to proof-correct; but I decidedly said to Biggs that I was sure you would omit more. Those I have positively rubbed off, I can swear to *individually* (except the "Man of Ross," which is too familiar in Pope), but no others—you have your cue. For my part, I would rather all the *Juvenilia* were kept—*memoriæ causâ*.

Robert Lloyd has written me a masterly letter, containing a character of his father. See how different from Charles he views the old man! (*Literatim*): "My father smokes, repeats Homer in Greek, and Virgil, and is learning, when from business, with all the vigour of a young man, Italian. He is, really, a wonderful man. He mixes public and private business, the intricacies of disordering life, with his religion and devotion. No one more rationally enjoys the romantic scenes of Nature, and the chit-chat and little vagaries of his children; and, though surrounded with an ocean of affairs, the very neatness of his most obscure cupboard in the house passes not unnoticed. I never knew any one view with such clearness, nor so well satisfied with things as they are, and make such allowance for things which must appear perfect Syriac to him." By the last he means the Lloydisms of the younger branches. His portrait of Charles (exact as far as he has had opportunities of noting him) is most exquisite:—"Charles is become steady as a church, and as straightforward as a Roman road. It would distract him to mention anything that was not as plain as sense; he seems to have run the whole scenery of life, and now rests as the formal precisian of non-existence." Here is genius, I think, and 'tis seldom a young man, a Lloyd, looks at a father (so differing) with such good-nature while he is alive. Write—

I am in post-haste,   C. LAMB.

Love, etc., to Sara, P., and H.

LETTER CXXV.]   *April* 13, 1803.

My dear Coleridge—Things have gone on better with me since you left me. I expect to have my old housekeeper home again in a week or two. She has mended most rapidly. My health too has been better since you took away that Montero cap. I have left off cayenned eggs and such bolsters to discomfort. There was death in that cap. I mischievously wished that by some inauspicious jolt the whole contents might be shaken, and the coach set on fire; for you said they had that property. How the old gentleman, who joined you at Grantham, would have clapp'd his hands to his knees, and not knowing but it was an immediate visitation of God that burnt him, how pious it would have made him!—him, I mean, that brought the Influenza with him, and only took places for one—an old sinner; he must have known what he had got with him! However, I wish the cap no harm for the sake of the *head it fits,* and could be content to see it disfigure my healthy sideboard again.

What do you think of smoking? I want your sober, *average, noon opinion* of it. I generally am eating my dinner about the time I should determine it.

Morning is a girl, and can't smoke—she's no evidence one way or the other; and Night is so evidently *bought over*, that he can't be a very upright judge. May be the truth is, that *one* pipe is wholesome, *two* pipes toothsome, *three* pipes noisome, *four* pipes fulsome, *five* pipes quarrelsome, and that's the *sum* on't. But that is deciding rather upon rhyme than reason. . . . After all, our instincts *may* be best. Wine, I am sure—good mellow, generous Port—can hurt nobody, unless those who take it to excess, which they may easily avoid if they observe the rules of temperance.

Bless you, old sophist, who next to human nature taught me all the corruption I was capable of knowing! And bless your Montero cap, and your trail (which shall come after you whenever you appoint), and your wife and children—Pipos especially.

When shall we two smoke again? Last night I had been in a sad quandary of spirits, in what they call the evening; but a pipe, and some generous Port, and *King Lear* (being alone), had their effects as solacers. I went to bed pot-valiant. By the way, may not the Ogles of Somersetshire be remotely descended from King Lear? C. L.

To THOMAS MANNING.

LETTER CXXVI.] *April 23, 1803.*

My dear Manning—Although something of the latest, and after two months' waiting, your letter was highly gratifying. Some parts want a little explication; for example, "the god-like face of the first consul." *What god* does he most resemble, Mars, Bacchus, or Apollo? or the god Serapis, who, flying (as Egyptian chronicles deliver) from the fury of the dog Anubis (the hieroglyph of an English mastiff), lighted upon Monomotapa (or the land of apes), by some thought to be Old France, and there set up a tyranny, etc. Our London prints of him represent him gloomy and sulky, like an angry Jupiter. I hear that he is very small, even less than me. I envy you your access to this great man, much more than your séances and conversaziones, which I have a shrewd suspicion must be something dull. What you assert concerning the actors of Paris, that they exceed our comedians, bad as ours are, is *impossible*. In one sense it may be true, that their fine gentlemen, in what is called genteel comedy, may possibly be more brisk and *dégagé* than Mr. Caulfield, or Mr. Whitfield; but have any of them the power to move *laughter in excess?* or can a Frenchman *laugh?* Can they batter at your judicious ribs till they *shake*, nothing loth to be so shaken? This is John Bull's criterion, and it shall be mine. Your are Frenchified. Both your tastes and morals are corrupt and perverted. By and by you will come to assert that Buonaparte is as great a general as the old Duke of Cumberland, and deny that one Englishman can beat three Frenchmen. Read *Henry the Fifth* to restore your orthodoxy.

All things continue at a stay-till in London. I cannot repay your new novelties with my stale reminiscences. Like the prodigal, I have spent my patrimony, and feed upon the superannuated chaff and dry husks of repentance; yet sometimes I remember with pleasure the hounds and horses, which I kept in the days of my prodigality. I find nothing new, nor anything that has so much of the gloss and dazzle of novelty as may rebound in narrative, and cast a reflective glimmer across the channel. Something I will say about people that you and I know. Fenwick is still in debt, and the Professor has not done making love to his new spouse. I think he never looks into an almanack, or he would have found by the calendar that the honeymoon was extinct a moon ago. Southey is Secretary to the Chancellor of the Irish Exchequer; £400 a year. Stoddart is turned Doctor of Civil Law, and dwells in Doctors' Commons. I fear *his* commons are short, as they say. Did I send you an epitaph I scribbled upon a poor girl who died at nineteen?—a good girl, and a pretty girl, and a clever girl, but strangely neglected by all her friends and kin.

> "Under this cold marble stone
> Sleep the sad remains of one
> Who, when alive, by few or none
> Was loved, as loved she might have been,
> If she prosperous days had seen,
> Or had thriving been, I ween.
> Only this cold funeral stone
> Tells she was beloved by one,
> Who on the marble graves his moan."

Brief, and pretty, and tender, is it not? I send you this, being the only piece of poetry I have *done* since the Muses all went with T. M. to Paris. I have neither stuff in my brain, nor paper in my drawer, to write you a longer letter. Liquor and company and wicked tobacco, a'nights, have quite dispericraniated me, as one may say; but you, who spiritualise upon Champagne, may continue to write long letters, and stuff 'em with amusement to the end. Too long they cannot be, any more than a codicil to a will, which leaves me sundry parks and manors not specified in the deed. But don't be *two months* before you write again. These from merry old England, on the day of her valiant patron St. George.

C. LAMB.

To SAMUEL TAYLOR COLERIDGE.

LETTER CXXVII.]   *May 27, 1803.*

My dear Coleridge—The date of my last was one day prior to the receipt of your letter, full of foul omens. I explain this lest you should have thought mine too light a reply to such sad matter. I seriously hope by this time you have given up all thoughts of journeying to the green Islands of the Bless'd—(voyages in time of war are very precarious)— or at least, that you will take them in your way to the Azores. Pray be careful of this letter till it has done its duty, for it is to inform you that I have booked off your watch (laid in cotton like an untimely fruit), and with it Condillac, and all other books of yours which were left here. These will set out on Monday next, the 29th May, by Kendal waggon, from White Horse, Cripplegate. You will make seasonable inquiries, for a watch mayn't come your way again in a hurry. I have been repeatedly after Tobin, and now hear that he is in the country, not to return till the middle of June. I will take care and see him with the earliest. But cannot you write pathetically to him, enforcing a speeding mission of your books for literary purposes? He is too good a retainer to Literature to let her interests suffer through his default. And why, in the name of Beelzebub, are your books to travel from Barnard's Inn to the Temple, and thence circuitously to Cripplegate, when their business is to take a short cut down Holborn Hill, up Snow ditto, on to Wood Street, etc.? The former mode seems a sad superstitious sub-division of labour. Well! the "Man of Ross" is to stand; Longman begs for it; the printer stands with a wet sheet in one hand, and a useless Pica in the other, in tears, pleading for it; I relent. Besides, it was a *Salutation* poem, and has the mark of the beast "Tobacco" upon it. Thus much I have done; I have swept off the lines about *widows* and *orphans* in second edition, which (if you remember) you most awkwardly and illogically caused to be inserted between two *Ifs*, to the great breach and disunion of said *Ifs*, which now meet again (as in first edition), like two clever lawyers arguing a case. Another reason for subtracting the pathos was, that the "Man of Ross" is too familiar to need telling what he did, especially in worse lines than Pope told it, and it now stands simply as "Reflections at an Inn about a known Character," and sucking an old story into an accommodation with present feelings. Here is no breaking spears with Pope, but a new, independent, and really a very pretty poem. In fact 'tis as I used to admire it in the first volume, and I have even dared to restore

> "If neath this roof thy *wine cheer'd* moments pass,"

for

> "Beneath this roof if thy cheer'd moments pass."

"Cheer'd" is a sad general word, *"wine-cheer'd"* I'm sure you'd give me, if I had a speaking-trumpet to sound to you 300 miles. But I am your *factotum;* and that (save in this instance, which is a single case, and I can't get at you) shall be next to a *fac-nihil*—at most a *fac-simile*. I have ordered "Imitation of Spenser" to be restored on Wordsworth's authority; and now, all that you will miss will be "Flicker and Flicker's Wife," "The Thimble," "Breathe *dear harmonist,"* and *I believe,* "The Child that was fed with Manna." Another volume will clear off all your Anthologic Morning-Postian Epistolary Miscellanies; but pray don't put "Christabel" therein; don't let that sweet maid come forth attended with Lady Holland's mob at her heels. Let there be a separate volume of Tales, Choice Tales, "Ancient Mariners," etc. A word of your health will be richly acceptable.   C. LAMB.

To MR. RICKMAN.

LETTER CXXVIII.]   *Saturday Morning, July 16, 1803.*

Dear Rickman—I enclose you a wonder, a letter from the shades. A dead body wants to return, and be inrolled *inter vivos.* 'Tis a gentle ghost, and in this Galvanic age it may have a chance.

Mary and I are setting out for the Isle of Wight. We make but a short stay, and shall pass the time betwixt that place and Portsmouth, where Fenwick is. I sadly wanted to explore the Peak this Summer; but Mary is against steering without card or compass, and we should be at large in Darbyshire.

We shall be at home this night and to-morrow, if you can come and take a farewell pipe.

I regularly transmitted your Notices to the *Morning Post,* but they have not been duly honoured. The fault lay not in me.—Yours truly,

C. LAMB.

To RICKMAN.

LETTER CXXIX.]   *July 27, 1803.*

(The earlier part of this letter is by Captain Burney, and is in his handwriting.)

Dear Rickman—We are at Cowes the whole flock, Sheep and Lambs —and in good pasturage—for notwithstanding that I joined, or rather acquiesced, in your dispraise of Cowes, in a dry summer like this it is a very pleasant place. We were much harassed by hot travelling and uncertainties till we fixed at this haven; and now I could feel myself thoroughly well disposed to indulge in a week of compleat idleness, if my senses were not invaded by the din of preparation, and the account which every day's paper brings of the universal bustle that prevails everywhere.

We purpose however to stay here one week longer reckoning from this date, and then to return to the defence of the Capital after so well having guarded the sea coast. We have visited Newport and Carisbrook Castle where we saw a deep well and a cross old woman. We went by water, and friend Lamb (to give a specimen of his Seamanship) very ingeniously and unconsciously cast loose the fastenings of the mast, so that mast, sprit, sails, and all the rest tumbled overboard with a crash, and not less to his surprise than to the surprise of every other person in the boat. I doubt whether any of us will muster up sufficient activity to go to the South part of the Island. We do everything that is idle, such as reading books from a circulating library, sauntering, hunting little crabs among the rocks, reading Church yard poetry which is as bad at Cowes as any Church yard in the Kingdom can produce. Miss Lamb is the only person among us who is not idle. All the cares she takes into her keeping. At night however we do a little business in the smoking line, and Martin endeavours to make Conundrums, but alas! he is not equal to the achievement. Such is the edifying life we lead at the Isle of Wight. Let us know how you take care of the Capital. An old sea saying is, "Give a sprat to catch a Mackarel," so pray send us your Mackarel and accept this sprat.

[Lamb's part begins here.]

I testify that this is a pretty good outline of our doings, but the filling it up requires the hand of a Master. A volume might be made of Martin's blunders which parental tenderness omits. Such as his letting the packet-boat's boat go without him from the quay at Southampton, while he stood hiatusing, smit with the love of a Naiad; his tumbling back over a stone twice the height of himself, and daubing himself; his getting up to bathe at six o'clock, and forgetting it, and in consequence staying in his room in a process of annihilation, etc., etc., then the time expended in *Martin being scolded* would serve as great a sinner as Judas to repent in. In short nothing in this house goes right till after supper, then a gentle circumambience of the weed serves to shut out Isle of Wight impertinent scenery and brings us back in fancy to Mutton Lane and the romantic alleys ever green of nether-Holborn, green that owes nothing to grass, but the simple effect of cabbage-water, tripe-cauls, etc. The fact of my setting the mast upside down is partly true. Indeed it was never properly nailed down, or the accident could not have happened.—Capt. Burney does nothing but teach his children bad habits. He surfeits them with cherries and black currants till they can eat no supper and then claps down the fruit expended to the common stock, and deducts what the surfeit saves from his part. There's a little girl he's brought with him that has cost I don't know what in codlings.—No ordinary orchard would be a jointure for her.—To add to our difficulties Martin has brought down a Terence, which he renders out loud into canine Latin at Breakfast and other meals, till the eyes of the infatuated Parent let slip water for joy, and the ears of every body beside shed their wax for being tired. More I could add but it is unsafe.

From the White Isle (date unknown)   C. L.

To John Rickman, Esq.,
    Dublin Castle.

To WILLIAM GODWIN.

LETTER CXXX.]   *November 8, 1803.*

My dear Sir—I have been sitting down for three or four days successively to the review, which I so much wished to do well, and to your satisfaction. But I can produce nothing but absolute flatness and nonsense. My health and spirits are so bad, and my nerves so irritable, that I am sure, if I persist, I shall tease myself into a fever. You do not know how sore and weak a brain I have, or you would allow for many things in me which you set down for whims. I solemnly assure you that I never more wished to prove to you the value which I have for you than at this moment; but although so seemingly trifling a service, I cannot get through with it: I pray to impute it to this one sole cause, ill health. I hope I am above subterfuge, and that you will do me this justice to think so.

You will give me great satisfaction by sealing my pardon and oblivion in a line or two, before I come to see you, or I shall be ashamed to come. —Your, with great truth,   C. LAMB.

LETTER CXXXI.]   *November* 10, 1803.

Dear Godwin—You never made a more unlucky and perverse mistake than to suppose that the reason of my not writing that cursed thing was to be found in your book. I assure you most sincerely that I have been greatly delighted with "Chaucer." I may be wrong, but I think there is one considerable error runs through it, which is a conjecturing spirit, a fondness for filling out the picture by supposing what Chaucer did and how he felt, where the materials are scanty. So far from meaning to withhold from you (out of mistaken tenderness) this opinion of mine, I plainly told Mrs. Godwin that I did find a *fault,* which I should reserve naming until I should see you and talk it over. This she may very well remember, and also that I declined naming this fault until she drew it from me by asking me if there was not too much fancy in the work. I then confessed generally what I felt, but refused to go into particulars until I had seen you. I am never very fond of saying things before third persons, because in the relation (such is human nature) something is sure to be dropped. If Mrs. Godwin has been the cause of your misconstruction, I am very angry, tell her; yet it is not an anger unto death. I remember also telling Mrs. G. (which she may have *dropt*) that I was by turns considerably more delighted than I expected. But I wished to reserve all this until I saw you. I even had conceived an expression to meet you with, which was thanking you for some of the most exquisite pieces of criticism I had ever read in my life. In particular, I should have brought forward that on "Troilus and Cressida" and Shakspeare which, it is little to say, delighted me, and instructed me (if not absolutely *instructed* me, yet put into *full-grown sense* many conceptions which had arisen in me before in my most discriminating moods). All these things I was preparing to say, and bottling them up till I came, thinking to please my friend and host the author, when lo! this deadly blight intervened.

I certainly ought to make great allowances for your misunderstanding me. You, by long habits of composition and a greater command gained over your own powers, cannot conceive of the desultory and uncertain way in which I (an author by fits) sometimes cannot put the thoughts of a common letter into sane prose. Any work which I take upon myself as an engagement will act upon me to torment, *e.g.* when I have undertaken, as three or four times I have, a schoolboy copy of verses for Merchant Taylors' boys, at a guinea a copy, I have fretted over them in perfect inability to do them, and have made my sister wretched with my wretchedness for a week together. The same, till by habit I have acquired a mechanical command, I have felt in making paragraphs. As to reviewing, in particular, my head is so whimsical a head, that I cannot, after reading another man's book, let it have been never so pleasing, give any account of it in any methodical way. I cannot follow his train. Something like this you must have perceived of me in conversation. Ten thousand times I have confessed to you, talking of my talents, my utter inability to remember in any comprehensive way what I read. I can vehemently applaud, or perversely stickle, at *parts;* but I cannot grasp at a whole. This infirmity (which is nothing to brag of) may be seen in my two little compositions, the tale and my play, in both which no reader, however partial, can find any story. I wrote such stuff about Chaucer, and got into such disgressions, quite irreducible into $1 \ 1/5$ column of a paper, that I was perfectly ashamed to show it you. However, it is become a serious matter that I should convince you I neither slunk from the task through a wilful deserting neglect, or through any (most imaginery on your part) distaste of "Chaucer"; and I will try my hand again, I hope with better luck. My health is bad and my time taken up; but all I can spare between this and Sunday shall be employed for you, since you desire it: and if I bring you a crude, wretched paper on Sunday, you must burn it, and forgive me; if it proves anything better than I predict, may it be a peace-offering of sweet incense between us.

C. LAMB.

To ROBERT LLOYD.

LETTER CXXXII.]　　　　　　　　　　　　　　*March* 13, 1804.

Dear Robert—I receive your notes safe, and thank you for them. It seems you are about to be married. Joy to you and uninterrupted satisfaction in that state. But who is the Lady? It is the character of your letters that you omit facts, dates, names, and matter, and describe nothing but feelings, in which, as I cannot always partake, as being more intense in degree or different in kind from my own tranquil ones, I cannot always well tell how to reply. Your dishes are too much sauced and spiced and flavoured for me to suppose that you can relish my plain meats and vulgar aliment. Still, Robert, if I cannot always send you of the same, they have a smack and a novelty, a Robert-ism about them, that makes them a dainty stimulus to my palate at times. I have little to tell you of. You are mistaken, I am disengaged from all newspaper connections, and breathe a freer air in consequence. I was bound, like Gulliver, in a multitude of little chains, which, by quotidian leasing swelled to a rack and a gibbet in the year's account. I am poorer but happier. Your three pounds came seasonably, but I doubt whether I am fairly entitled to them as a debt.

I am obliged to break off here, and would not send this unfinished, but that you might otherwise be uneasy about the moneys.

Am I ever to see you? for it is like letters to the dead, or for a friend to write to his friend in the Fortunate Isles, or the Moon, or at the Antipodes, to address a line to ONE in Warwickshire that I am never to see in London. I shall lose the very face of Robert by disuse, and I question, if I were a painter, if I could now paint it from memory.

I could tell you many things, but you are so spiritual and abstracted, that I fear to insult you with tidings of this world. But may your approaching husband-hood humanise you. I think I see a dawn. I am sure joy is rising upon you, and I stand a tiptoe to see the sun ascending till it gets up and up, and "while a man tells the story," shows at last a fair face and a full light.

God bless you, Robt.   C. L.

LETTER CXXXIII.]   *September* 13, 1804.

Dear Robert—I was startled in a very pleasant manner by the contents of your letter. It was like your good self to take so handsome an opportunity of renewing an old friendship. I thank you kindly for your offers to bring me acquainted with Mrs. Ll. I cannot come now, but assuredly I will some time or other, to see how this new relation sits upon you. I am naturally shy of new faces; but the Lady who has chosen my old friend Robert cannot have a repelling one. Assure her of my sincere congratulations and friendly feelings. Mary joins in both with me, and considers herself as only left out of your kind invitation by some LAPSUS STYLI. We have already had all the holydays we can have this year. We have been spending our usual summer month at Richmond, from which place we traced the banks of the old Thames for ten and twenty miles, in daily walks or rides, and found beauties which may compare with Ulswater and Windermere. We visited Windsor, Hampton, etc. etc.—but this is a deviation from the subject with which I began my letter.

Some day I certainly shall come and see you in your new light; no longer the restless (but good) [? single] Robert; but now the staid, sober (and not less good) married Robert. And how does Plumstead, the impetuous, take your getting the start of him? When will he subside into matrimony? Priscilla has taken a long time indeed to think about it. I will suppose that her first choice is now her final; though you do not expressly say that she is to be a Wordsworth. I wish her, and dare promise her, all happiness.

All these new nuptials do not make me unquiet in the perpetual prospect of celibacy. There is a quiet dignity in old bachelorhood, a leisure from cares, noise, etc., an enthronisation upon the armed-chair of a man's feeling that he may sit, walk, read, unmolested, to none accountable—but hush! or I shall be torn in pieces like a churlish Orpheus by young married women and bridemaids of Birmingham. The close is this, to every man that way of life, which in his election is best. Be as happy in yours as I am determined to be in mine, and we shall strive lovingly who shall sing best the praises of matrimony, and the praises of singleness.

Adieu, my old friend in a new character, and believe me that no "wounds" have pierced our friendship; only a long want of seeing each other has disfurnished us of topics on which to talk. Is not your new fortunes a topic which may hold us for some months (the honey months at least)? C. LAMB.

To ROBERT SOUTHEY.

LETTER CXXXIV.]   *November 7, 1804.*

Dear Southey—You were the last person from whom we heard of Dyer, and if you know where to forward to him the news I now send I shall be obliged to you to lose no time. Dyer's sister-in-law, who lives in St. Dunstan's Court, wrote to him about three weeks ago to the Hoop Inn, Cambridge, to inform him that Squire Houlbert, or some such name, of Denmark Hill, has died, and left her husband a thousand pounds, and two or three hundred to Dyer. Her letter got no answer, and she does not know where to direct to him; so she came to me, who am equally in the dark. Her story is, that Dyer's immediately coming to town now, and signing some papers, will save him a considerable sum of money; how, I don't understand; but it is very right he should hear of this. She has left me barely time for the post; so I conclude with love to all at Keswick.

Dyer's brother, who by his wife's account has got £1000 left him, is father of the little dirty girl, Dyer's niece and factotum.—In haste,

Yours truly,   C. LAMB.

If you send George this, cut off the last paragraph.

D.'s laundress had a letter a few days since; but George never dates.

To THOMAS MANNING.

LETTER CXXXV.]   16, *Mitre Court Buildings,*
                         Saturday, February 24, 1805.

Dear Manning—I have been very unwell since I saw you: a sad depression of spirits, a most unaccountable nervousness; from which I have been partially relieved by an odd accident. You knew Dick Hopkins, the swearing scullion of Caius? This fellow, by industry and agility, has thrust himself into the important situations (no sinecures, believe me) of cook to Trinity Hall and Caius College: and the generous creature has contrived, with the greatest delicacy imaginable, to send me a present of Cambridge brawn. What makes it the more extraordinary is, that the man never saw me in his life that I know of. I suppose he has *heard* of me. I did not immediately recognise the donor; but one of Richard's cards, which had accidentally fallen into the straw, detected him in a moment. Dick, you know, was always remarkable for flourishing. His card imports, that "orders (to wit, for brawn) from any part of England, Scotland, or Ireland, will be duly executed," etc. At first, I thought of declining the present; but Richard knew my blind side when he pitched upon brawn. 'Tis of all my hobbies the supreme in the eating way. He might have sent sops from the pan, skimmings, crumpets, chips, hog's lard, the tender brown judiciously scalped from a fillet of veal (dexterously replaced by a salamander), the tops of asparagus, fugitive livers, runaway gizzards of fowls, the eyes of martyred pigs, tender effusions of laxative woodcocks, the red spawn of lobsters, leverets' ears, and such pretty filchings common to cooks; but these had been ordinary presents, the everyday courtesies of dish-washers to their sweethearts. Brawn was a noble thought. It is not every common gullet-fancier that can properly esteem it. It is like a picture of one of the choice old Italian masters. Its gusto is of that hidden sort. As Wordsworth sings of a modest poet,— "you must love him, ere to you he will seem worthy of your love;" so brawn, you must taste it ere to you it will seem to have any taste at all. But 'tis nuts to the adept: those that will send out their tongue and feelers to find it out. It will be wooed, and not unsought be won. Now, ham-essence, lobsters, turtle, such popular minions, absolutely *court you,* lay themselves out to strike you at first smack, like one of David's pictures (they call him *Darveed*) compared with the plain russet-coated wealth of a Titian or a Correggio, as I illustrated above. Such are the obvious glaring heathen virtues of a corporation dinner, compared with the reserved collegiate worth of brawn. Do me the favour to leave off the business which you may be at present upon, and go immediately to the kitchens of Trinity and Caius, and make my most respectful compliments to Mr. Richard Hopkins, and assure him that his brawn is most excellent; and that I am moreover obliged to him for his innuendo about salt water and bran, which I shall not fail to improve. I leave it to you whether you shall choose to pay him the civility of asking him to dinner while you stay in Cambridge, or in whatever other way you may best like to show your gratitude to *my friend*. Richard Hopkins, considered in many points of view, is a very extraordinary character. Adieu. I hope to see you to supper in London soon, where we will taste Richard's brawn, and drink his health in a cheerful but moderate cup. We have not many such men in any rank of life as Mr. R. Hopkins. Crisp, the barber, of St. Mary's, was just such another. I wonder *he* never sent me any little token, some chestnuts, or a puff, or two pound of hair: just to remember him by. Gifts are like nails. *Præsens ut absens;* that is, your *present* makes amends for your absence.

Yours,   C. LAMB.

To Miss WORDSWORTH.

LETTER CXXXVI.]   *June* 14, 1805.

My dear Miss Wordsworth—Your long kind letter has not been thrown away (for it has given me great pleasure to find you are all resuming your old occupations, and are better); but poor Mary, to whom it is addressed, cannot yet relish it. She has been attacked by one of her severe illnesses, and is at present *from home*. Last Monday week was the day she left me, and I hope I may calculate upon having her again in a month or little more. I am rather afraid late hours have in this case contributed to her indisposition. But when she discovers symptoms of approaching illness, it is not easy to say what is best to do. Being by ourselves is bad, and going out is bad. I get so irritable and wretched with fear, that I constantly hasten on the disorder. You cannot conceive the misery of such a foresight. I am sure that, for the week before she left me, I was little better than light-headed. I now am calm, but sadly taken down and flat. I have every reason to suppose that this illness, like all her former ones, will be but temporary; but I cannot always feel so. Meantime she is dead to me, and I miss a prop. All my strength is gone, and I am like a fool, bereft of her co-operation. I dare not think, lest I should think wrong; so used am I to look up to her in the least and the biggest perplexity. To say all that I know of her would be more than I think anybody could believe, or even understand; and when I hope to have her well again with me, it would be sinning against her feelings to go about to praise her; for I can conceal nothing that I do from her. She is older and wiser and better than I, and all my wretched imperfections I cover to myself by resolutely thinking on her goodness. She would share life and death, heaven and hell, with me. She lives but for me; and I know I have been wasting and teasing her life for five years past incessantly with my cursed drinking and ways of going on. But even in this upbraiding of myself I am offending against her, for I know that she has cleaved to me for better, for worse; and if the balance has been against her hitherto, it was a noble trade. I am stupid, and lose myself in what I write. I write rather what answers to my feelings (which are sometimes sharp enough) than express my present ones, for I am only flat and stupid. I am sure you will excuse my writing any more, I am so very poorly.

I cannot resist transcribing three or four lines which poor Mary made upon a picture (a Holy Family) which we saw at an auction only one week before she left home. She was then beginning to show signs of ill boding. They are sweet lines and upon a sweet picture; but I send them only as the latest memorial of her.

"VIRGIN AND CHILD, L. DA VINCI.

"Maternal Lady, with thy virgin grace,
Heaven-born, thy Jesus seemeth sure,
And thou a virgin pure.

> Lady most perfect, when thy angel face
> Men look upon, they wish to be
> A Catholic, Madonna fair, to worship thee."

You had her lines about the "Lady Blanch." You have not had some which she wrote upon a copy of a girl from Titian, which I had hung up where that print of Blanch and the Abbess (as she beautifully interpreted two female figures from L. da Vinci) had hung in our room. 'Tis light and pretty:—

> "Who art thou, fair one, who usurp'st the place
> Of Blanch, the lady of the matchless grace?
> Come, fair and pretty, tell to me
> Who in thy lifetime thou mightst be?
> Thou pretty art and fair,
> But with the Lady Blanch thou never must compare.
> No need for Blanch her history to tell,
> Whoever saw her face, they there did read it well;
> But when I look on thee, I only know
> There lived a pretty maid some hundred years ago."

This is a little unfair, to tell so much about ourselves, and to advert so little to your letter, so full of comfortable tidings of you all. But my own cares press pretty close upon me, and you can make allowance. That you may go on gathering strength and peace is my next wish to Mary's recovery.

I had almost forgot your repeated invitation. Supposing that Mary will be well and able, there is another *ability* which you may guess at, which I cannot promise myself. In prudence we ought not to come. This illness will make it still more prudential to wait. It is not a balance of this way of spending our money against another way, but an absolute question of whether we shall stop now, or go on wasting away the little we have got beforehand, which my wise conduct has already encroach'd upon one half. My best love, however, to you all; and to that most friendly creature, Mrs. Clarkson, and better health to her, when you see or write to her. CHARLES LAMB.

To THOMAS MANNING.

LETTER CXXXVII.]   [*July* 27, 1805.]

Dear Archimedes—Things have gone on badly with thy ungeometrical friend; but they are on the turn. My old housekeeper has shown signs of convalescence, and will shortly resume the power of the keys, so I shan't be cheated of my tea and liquors. Wind in the West, which promotes tranquillity. Have leisure now to anticipate seeing thee again. Have been taking leave of tobacco in a rhyming address. Had thought *that vein* had long since closed up. Find I can rhyme and reason too. Think of studying mathematics, to restrain the fire of my genius, which G. D. recommends. Have frequent bleedings at the nose, which shows plethoric. Maybe shall try the sea myself, that great scene of wonders. Got incredibly sober and regular; shave oftener, and hum a tune, to signify cheerfulness and gallantry.

Suddenly disposed to sleep, having taken a quart of pease with bacon and stout. Will not refuse Nature, who has done such things for me! Nurse! don't call me unless Mr. Manning comes.—What! the gentleman in spectacles?—Yes.

Dormit.   C. L.

Saturday,
    Hot Noon.

To WILLIAM WORDSWORTH.

LETTER CXXXVIII.]   *September* 28, 1805.

My dear Wordsworth (or Dorothy rather, for to you appertains the biggest part of this answer by right)—I will not again deserve reproach by so long a silence. I have kept deluding myself with the idea that Mary would write to you, but she is so lazy (or, which I believe is the true state of the case, so diffident), that it must revert to me as usual. Though she writes a pretty good style, and has some notion of the force of words, she is not always so certain of the true orthography of them; and that, and a poor handwriting (in this age of female calligraphy), often deters her, where no other reason does.

We have neither of us been very well for some weeks past. I am very nervous, and she most so at those times when I am; so that a merry friend, adverting to the noble consolation we were able to afford each other, denominated us, not unaptly, Gum-boil and Tooth-Ache, for they used to say that a gum-boil is a great relief to a tooth-ache.

We have been two tiny excursions this Summer, for three or four days each, to a place near Harrow, and to Egham, where Cooper's Hill is: and that is the total history of our rustications this year. Alas! how poor a round to Skiddaw and Halvellyn, and Borrowdale, and the magnificent sesquipedalia of the year 1802! Poor old Molly! to have lost her pride, that "last infirmity of noble minds," and her cow. Fate need not have set her wits to such an old Molly. I am heartily sorry for her. Remember us lovingly to her; and in particular remember us to Mrs. Clarkson in the most kind manner.

I hope, by "southwards," you mean that she will be at or near London, for she is a great favourite of both of us, and we feel for her health as much as possible for any one to do. She is one of the friendliest, comfortablest women we know, and made our little stay at your cottage one of the pleasantest times we ever past. We were quite strangers to her. Mr. C. is with you too; our kindest separate remembrances to him. As to our special affairs, I am looking about me. I have done nothing since the beginning of last year, when I lost my newspaper job; and having had a long idleness, I must do something, or we shall get very poor. Sometimes I think of a farce, but hitherto all schemes have gone off; an idle brag or two of an evening, vapouring out of a pipe, and going off in the morning; but now I have bid farewell to my "sweet enemy," Tobacco, I shall perhaps set nobly to work. Hang work!

I wish that all the year were holiday; I am sure that indolence—indefeasible indolence—is the true state of man, and business the invention of the old Teazer, whose interference doomed Adam to an apron and set him a hoeing. Pen and ink, and clerks and desks, were the refinements of this old torturer some thousand years after, under pretence of "Commerce allying distant shores, promoting and diffusing knowledge, good," etc. etc.

I wish you may think this a handsome farewell to my "Friendly Traitress." Tobacco has been my evening comfort and my morning curse for these five years; and you know how difficult it is from refraining to pick one's lips even, when it has become a habit. This poem is the only one which I have finished since so long as when I wrote "Hester Savory." I have had it in my head to do it these two years, but tobacco stood in its own light when it gave me headaches that prevented my singing its praises. Now you have got it, you have got all my store, for I have absolutely not another line. No more has Mary. We have nobody about us that cares for poetry; and who will rear grapes when he shall be the sole eater? Perhaps if you encourage us to show you what we may write, we may do something now and then before we absolutely forget the quantity of an English line for want of practice. The "Tobacco," being a little in the way of Wither (whom Southey so much likes), perhaps you will somehow convey it to him with my kind remembrances. Then, everybody will have seen it that I wish to see it, I having sent it to Malta.

I remain, dear W. and D., yours truly. C. LAMB.

To WILLIAM HAZLITT.

LETTER CXXXIX.] *November* 10, 1805.

Dear Hazlitt—I was very glad to hear from you, and that your journey was so *picturesque*. We miss you, as we foretold we should. One or two things have happened, which are beneath the dignity of epistolary communication, but which, seated about our fireside at night (the winter hands of pork have begun), gesture and emphasis might have talked into some importance. Something about Rickman's wife; for instance, how tall she is, and that she visits pranked up like a Queen of the May, with green streamers: a good-natured woman though, which is as much as you can expect from a friend's wife, whom you got acquainted with a bachelor. Some things too about Monkey, which can't so well be written: how it set up for a fine lady, and thought it had got lovers, and was obliged to be convinced of its age from the parish register, where it was proved to be only twelve; and an edict issued, that it should not give itself airs yet these four years; and how it got leave to be called Miss, by grace; these, and such like hows, were in my head to tell you; but who can write? Also how Manning is come to town in spectacles, and studies physic; is melancholy, and seems to have something in his head, which he don't impart. Then, how I am going to leave off smoking. O la! your Leonardos of Oxford made my mouth water. I was hurried through the gallery, and they escaped me. What do I say? I was a Goth then, and should not have noticed them. I had not settled my notions of beauty: I have now for ever!—the small head, the long eye,—that sort of peering curve,—the wicked Italian mischief; the stick-at-nothing, Herodias's daughter kind of grace. You understand me? But you disappoint me in passing over in absolute silence the Blenheim Leonardo. Didn't you see it? Excuse a lover's curiosity. I have seen no pictures of note since, except Mr. Dawe's gallery. It is curious to see how differently two great men treat the same subject, yet both excellent in their way. For instance, Milton and Mr. Dawe. Mr. D. has chosen to illustrate the story of Samson exactly in the point of view in which Milton has been most happy: the interview between the Jewish hero, blind and captive, and Delilah. Milton has imagined his locks grown again, strong as horse-hair or porcupine's bris-tles; doubtless shaggy and black, as being hairs "which, of a nation armed, contained the strength." I don't remember he *says* black; but could Milton imagine them to be yellow? Do you? Mr. Dawe, with striking originality of conception, has crowned him with a thin yellow wig, in colour precisely like Dyson's; in curl and quantity, resembling Mrs. Professor's; his limbs rather stout,—about such a man as my broth-er or Rickman,—but no Atlas nor Hercules, nor yet so long as Dubois, the clown of Sadler's Wells. This was judicious, taking the spirit of the story rather than the fact; for doubtless God could communicate na-tional salvation to the trust of flax and tow as well as hemp and cordage, and could draw down a temple with a golden tress as soon as with all the cables of the British navy.

Wasn't you sorry for Lord Nelson? I have followed him in fancy ever since I saw him walking in Pall Mall (I was prejudiced against him be-fore), looking just as a hero should look; and I have been very much cut about it indeed. He was the only pretence of a great man we had. No-body is left of any name at all. His secretary died by his side. I imagined him a Mr. Scott, to be the man you met at Hume's; but I learnt from Mrs. Hume that it is not the same. I met Mrs. H. one day, and agreed to go on the Sunday to tea, but the rain prevented us, and the distance. I have been to apologise, and we are to dine there the first fine Sunday. Strange perverseness! I never went while you stayed here; and now I *go to find you!* What other news is there, Mary? What puns have I made in the last fortnight? You never remember them. You have no relish for the comic. "Oh! tell Hazlitt not to forget to send the *American Farmer.* I daresay it is not so good as he fancies; but a book's a book." I have not heard from Wordsworth or from Malta since. Charles Kemble, it seems, enters into possession to-morrow. We sup at 109 Russell Street, this evening. I wish your brother would not drink. 'Tis a blemish in the greatest characters. You send me a modern quotation poetical. How do you like this in an old play? Vittoria Corombona, a spunky Italian lady, a Leonardo one, nicknamed the White Devil, being on her trial for murder, etc.—and questioned about seducing a duke from his wife and the state, makes answer:—

> "Condemn you me for that the Duke did love me?
> So may you blame some fair and crystal river,
> For that some melancholic distracted man
> Hath drown'd himself in it."

N.B.—I shall expect a line from you, if but a bare line, whenever you write to Russell Street, and a letter often when you do not. I pay no postage; but I will have consideration for you until Parliament time and franks. Luck to Ned Search, and the new art of colouring. Monkey sends her love; and Mary especially.

Yours truly,   C. LAMB.

To THOMAS MANNING

LETTER CXL.]   [*November* 15, 1805.]

Dear Manning—Certainly you could not have called at all hours from two till ten, for we have been only out of an evening Monday and Tuesday in this week. But if you think you have, your thought shall go for the deed. We did pray for you on Wednesday night. Oysters unusually luscious; pearls of extraordinary magnitude found in them. I have made bracelets of them; given them in clusters to ladies. Last night we went out in despite, because you were not come at your hour.

This night we shall be at home; so shall we certainly, both, on Sunday, Monday, Tuesday, and Wednesday. Take your choice, mind I don't say of one: but choose which evening you will not come, and come the other four. Doors open at five o'clock. Shells forced about nine. Every gentleman smokes or not as he pleases.   C. L.

To WILLIAM HAZLITT.

LETTER CXLI.]   *January* 15, 1806.

Dear Hazlitt—Godwin went to Johnson's yesterday about your business. Johnson would not come down, or give any answer, but has promised to open the manuscript, and to give you an answer in one month. Godwin will punctually go again (Wednesday is Johnson's open day) yesterday four weeks next: *i.e.* in one lunar month from this time; till when, Johnson positively declines giving any answer. I wish you joy on ending your Search. Mrs. H. was naming something about a "Life of Fawcett," to be by you undertaken: the great Fawcett, as she explained to Manning, when he asked, *"What Fawcett?"* He innocently thought *Fawcett the Player*. But Fawcett the divine is known to many people, albeit unknown to the Chinese inquirer. I should think, if you liked it, and Johnson declined it, that Phillips is the man. He is perpetually bringing out biographies,—Richardson, Wilks, Foot, Lee Lewis,—without number: little trim things in two easy volumes, price 12s. the two, made up of letters to and from, scraps, posthumous trifles, anecdotes, and about forty pages of hard biography. You might dish up a Fawcettiad in three months, and ask £60 or £80 for it. I should dare say that Phillips would catch at it. I wrote to you the other day in a great hurry. Did you get it? This is merely a letter of business at Godwin's request. Lord Nelson is quiet at last. His ghost only keeps a slight fluttering in odes and elegies in newspapers, and impromptus, which could not be got ready before the funeral.

As for news, Fenwick is coming to town on Monday (if no kind angel intervene) to surrender himself to prison. He hopes to get the rules of the Fleet. On the same, or nearly the same day, Fell, my other quondam co-friend and drinker, will go to Newgate, and his wife and four children, I suppose, to the parish. Plenty of reflection and motives of gratitude to the wise Disposer of all things in *us*, whose prudent conduct has hitherto ensured us a warm fire and snug roof over our heads. *Nullum numen abest si sit Prudentia.* Alas! Prudentia is in the last quarter of her tutelary shining over me. A little time and I——; but maybe I may, at last, hit upon some mode of collecting some of the vast superfluities of this money-voiding town. Much is to be got, and I do not want much. All I ask is time and leisure; and I am cruelly off for them. When you have the inclination, I shall be very glad to have a letter from you. Your brother and Mrs. H., I am afraid, think hardly of us for not coming oftener to see them; but we are distracted beyond what they can conceive with visitors and visitings. I never have an hour for my head to work quietly its own workings; which you know is as necessary to the human system as sleep. Sleep, too, I can't get for these winds of a night: and without sleep and rest what should ensue? Lunacy. But I trust it won't.

Yours, dear H.,   C. LAMB.

To MR. RICKMAN.

LETTER CXLII.]   *January* 25, 1806.

Dear Rickman—You do not happen to have any place at your disposal which would suit a decayed Literatus? I do not much expect that you have, or that you will go much out of the way to serve the object, when you hear it is Fell. But the case is, by a *mistaking* of his *turn*, as they call it, he is reduced, I am afraid, to extremities, and would be extremely glad of a place in an office. Now it does sometimes happen, that just as a man wants a place, a place wants him; and though this is a lottery to which none but G. Burnett would choose to trust his all, there is no harm just to call in at Despair's office for a friend, and see if *his* number is come up (Burnett's further case I enclose by way of episode). Now, if you should happen, or anybody you know, to want a *hand*, here is a young man of solid but not brilliant genius, who would turn his hand to the making out of dockets, penning a manifesto, or scoring a tally, not the worse (I hope) for knowing Latin and Greek, and having in youth conversed with the philosophers. But from these follies I believe he is thoroughly awakened, and would bind himself by a terrible oath never to imagine himself an extraordinary genius again.

Yours, etc.,   C. LAMB.

To WILLIAM HAZLITT.

LETTER CXLIII.]   *February* 19, 1806.

Dear H.—Godwin has just been here in his way from Johnson's. Johnson has had a fire in his house; this happened about five weeks ago; it was in the daytime, so it did not burn the house down, but it did so much damage that the house must come down, to be repaired. His nephew that we met on Hampstead Hill put it out. Well, this fire has put him so back, that he craves one more month before he gives you an answer. I will certainly goad Godwin (if necessary) to go again this very day four weeks; but I am confident he will want no goading. Three or four most capital auctions of pictures are advertised: in May, *Wellbore Ellis Agar's*, the first private collection in England, so Holcroft says; in March, Sir George Young's in Stratford Place (where Cosway lives), and a Mr. Hulse's at Blackheath, both very capital collections, and have been announced for some months. Also the Marquis of Lansdowne's pictures in March; and though inferior to mention, lastly, the Tructhsessian Gallery. Don't your mouth water to be here? T'other night Loftus called, whom we have not seen since you went before. We meditate a stroll next Wednesday, fast-day. He happened to light upon Mr. Holcroft, wife, and daughter, their first visit at our house. Your brother called last night. We keep up our intimacy. He is going to begin a large Madonna and child from Mrs. H. and baby. I fear he goes astray after *ignes fatui*. He is a clever man. By the by, I saw a miniature of his as far excelling any in his show cupboard (that of your sister not excepted) as that show cupboard excels the show things you see in windows—an old woman (damn her name!), but most superlative; he has it to clean—I'll ask him the name—but the best miniature I ever saw. But for oil pictures!— what has he to do with Madonnas? If the Virgin Mary were alive and visitable, he would not hazard himself in a Covent Garden pit-door crowd to see her. It isn't his style of beauty, is it? But he will go on painting things he ought not to paint, and not painting things he ought to paint. Manning is not gone to China, but talks of going this Spring. God forbid! Coleridge not heard of. I am going to leave off smoke. In the meantime I am so smoky with last night's ten pipes, that I must leave off. Mary begs her kind remembrances. Pray write to us. This is no letter; but I supposed you grew anxious about Johnson.

N.B.—Have taken a room at three shillings a week, to be in between five and eight at night, to avoid my *nocturnal*, alias *knock-eternal*, visitors. The first-fruits of my retirement has been a farce, which goes to manager to-morrow. *Wish my ticket luck.* God bless you; and do write. —Yours, *fumosissimus,*   C. LAMB.

To MR. RICKMAN.

LETTER CXLIV.]   *March* 1806.

Dear Rickman—I send you some papers about a salt water soap, for which the inventor is desirous of getting a parliamentary reward, like Dr. Jenner. Whether such a project be feasible, I mainly doubt, taking for granted the equal utility. I should suppose the usual way of paying such projectors is by patent and contracts. The patent, you see, he has got. A contract he is about with the Navy Board. Meantime, the projector is hungry. Will you answer me two questions, and return them with the papers as soon as you can? Imprimis, is there any chance of success in application to Parliament for a reward? Did you ever hear of the invention? You see its benefits and saving to the nation (always the first motive with a true projector) are feelingly set forth: the last paragraph but one of the estimate, in enumerating the shifts poor seamen are put to, even approaches to the pathetic. But, agreeing to all he says, is there the remotest chance of Parliament giving the projector anything? And *when* should application be made, now, or after a report (if he can get it) from the Navy Board? Secondly, let the infeasibility be as great as you will, you will oblige me by telling me the way of introducing such an application in Parliament, without buying over a majority of members, which is totally out of projector's power. I vouch nothing for the soap myself; for I always wash in *fresh water,* and find it answers tolerably well for all purposes of cleanliness; nor do I know the projector; but a relation of mine has put me on writing to you, for whose parliamentary knowledge he has great veneration.

P.S.—The Capt. and Mrs. Burney and Phillips take their chance at cribbage here on Wednesday. Will you and Mrs. R. join the party? Mary desires her compliments to Mrs. R., and joins in the invitation.

Yours truly,   C. LAMB.

To WILLIAM HAZLITT.

LETTER CXLV.]   *March* 15, 1806.

Dear H.—I am a little surprised at no letter from you. This day week, to wit, Saturday, the 8th of March, 1806, I booked off by the Wem coach, Bull and Mouth Inn, directed to *you,* at the Rev. Mr. Hazlitt's, Wem, Shropshire, a parcel containing, besides a book, etc., a rare print, which I take to be a Titian; begging the said W. H. to acknowledge the receipt thereof; which he not having done, I conclude the said parcel to be lying at the inn, and may be lost; for which reason, lest you may be a Wales-hunting at this instant, I have authorised any of your family, whosoever first gets this, to open it, that so precious a parcel may not moulder away for want of looking after.

What do you in Shropshire when so many fine pictures are a-going every day in London? Monday I visit the Marquis of Lansdowne's, in Berkeley Square. Catalogue 2s. 6d. Leonardos in plenty. Some other day this week I go to see Sir Wm. Young's, in Stratford Place. Hulse's, of Blackheath, are also to be sold this month; and in May, the first private collection in Europe, Welbore Ellis Agar's. And there are you, perverting Nature in lying landscapes, filched from old rusty Titians, such as I can scrape up here to send you, with an additament from Shropshire Nature thrown in to make the whole look unnatural. I am afraid of your mouth watering when I tell you that Manning and I got into Angerstein's on Wednesday. *Mon Dieu!* Such Claudes! Four Claudes bought for more than £10,000; (those who talk of Wilson being equal to Claude are either mainly ignorant or stupid) one of these was perfectly miraculous. What colours short of *bonâ fide* sunbeams it could be painted in, I am not earthly colourman enough to say; but I did not think it had been in the possibility of things. Then, a music piece by Titian, a thousand-pound picture, five figures standing behind a piano, the sixth playing—none of the heads, as M. observed, indicating great men, or affecting it, but so sweetly disposed—all leaning separate ways, but so easy—like a flock of some divine shepherd; the colouring, like the economy of the picture, so sweet and harmonious—as good as Shakspeare's *Twelfth Night,—almost,* that is. It will give you a love of order, and cure you of restless, fidgety passions for a week after—more musical than the music which it would, but cannot, yet in a manner *does,* show. I have no room for the rest. Let me say, Angerstein sits in a room—his study (only that and the library are shown), when he writes a common letter, as I am doing, surrounded with twenty pictures worth £60,000. What a luxury! Apicius and Heliogabalus, hide your diminished heads!

Yours, my dear painter,   C. LAMB.

Mr. Wm. Hazlitt,
   Wem, Shropshire.
In his absence, to be opened immediately.

To THOMAS MANNING.

LETTER CXLVI.]   *May* 10, 1806.

My dear Manning—I didn't know what your going was till I shook a last fist with you, and then 'twas just like having shaken hands with a wretch on the fatal scaffold, for when you are down the ladder you can never stretch out to him again. Mary says you are dead, and there's nothing to do but to leave it to time to do for us in the end what it always does for those who mourn for people in such a case. But she'll see by your letter you are not quite dead. A little kicking and agony, and then ———. Martin Burney *took me out* a walking that evening, and we talked of Manning; and then I came home and smoked for you; and at twelve o'clock came home Mary and Monkey Louisa from the play, and there was more talk and more smoking, and they all seemed first-rate characters, because they knew a certain person. But what's the use of talking about 'em? By the time you'll have made your escape from the Kalmuks, you'll have stayed so long I shall never be able to bring to your mind who Mary was, who will have died about a year before, nor who the Holcrofts were! Me perhaps you will mistake for Phillips, or confound me with Mr. Dawe, because you saw us together. Mary (whom you seem to remember yet) is not quite easy that she had not a formal parting from you. I wish it had so happened. But you must bring her a token, a shawl or something, and remember a sprightly little mandarin for our mantelpiece, as a companion to the child I am going to purchase at the museum. She says you saw her writings about the other day, and she wishes you should know what they are. She is doing for Godwin's bookseller twenty of Shakspeare's plays, to be made into children's tales. Six are already done by her; to wit, the *Tempest*, the *Winter's Tale, Midsummer Night's Dream, Much Ado about Nothing*, the *Two Gentlemen of Verona*, and *Cymbeline*. The *Merchant of Venice* is in forwardness. I have done *Othello* and *Macbeth*, and mean to do all the tragedies. I think it will be popular among the little people, besides money. It is to bring in sixty guineas. Mary has done them capitally, I think you'd think. These are the humble amusements we propose, while you are gone to plant the cross of Christ among barbarous pagan anthropophagi. Quam homo homini præstat! but then, perhaps, you'll get murdered, and we shall die in our beds with a fair literary reputation. Be sure, if you see any of those people whose heads do grow beneath their shoulders, that you make a draught of them. It will be very curious. Oh Manning, I am serious to sinking almost, when I think that all those evenings which you have made so pleasant, are gone perhaps for ever. Four years, you talk of, may be ten, and you may come back and find such alterations! Some circumstances may grow up to you or to me, that may be a bar to the return of any such intimacy. I daresay all this is hum! and that all will come back; but indeed we die many deaths before we die, and I am almost sick when I think that such a hold as I had of you is gone. I have friends, but some of 'em are changed. Marriage, or some circumstance, rises up to make them not the same. But I felt sure of you. And that last token you gave me of expressing a wish to have my name joined with yours, you know not how it affected me: like a legacy.

God bless you in every way you can form a wish. May He give you health, and safety, and the accomplishment of all your objects, and return you again to us, to gladden some fireside or other (I suppose we shall be moved from the Temple). I will nurse the remembrance of your steadiness and quiet, which used to infuse something like itself into our nervous minds. Mary called you our ventilator. Farewell, and take her best wishes and mine.

Good-bye.   C. L.

To WILLIAM WORDSWORTH.

LETTER CXLVII.]   *June* 26, 1806.

Mary is just stuck fast in "All's Well that Ends Well." She complains of having to set forth so many female characters in boys' clothes. She begins to think Shakspeare must have wanted—imagination! I, to encourage her (for she often faints in the prosecution of her great work), flatter her with telling her how well such a play and such a play is done. But she is stuck fast, and I have been obliged to promise to assist her. To do this it will be necessary to leave off tobacco. But I had some thoughts of doing that before, for I sometimes think it does not agree with me. Wm. Hazlitt is in town. I took him to see a very pretty girl, professedly, where there were two young girls (the very head and sum of the girlery was two young girls); they neither laughed, nor sneered, nor giggled, nor whispered—but they were young girls—and he sat and frowned blacker and blacker, indignant that there should be such a thing as youth and beauty, till he tore me away before supper, in perfect misery, and owned he could not bear young girls; they drove him mad. So I took him home to my old nurse, where he recovered perfect tranquillity. Independent of this, and as I am not a young girl myself, he is a great acquisition to us. He is, rather imprudently I think, printing a political pamphlet on his own account, and will have to pay for the paper, etc. The first duty of an author, I take it, is never to pay anything. But *non cuivis contigit adire Corinthum.* The managers, I thank my stars, have settled that question for me.

Yours truly,   C. LAMB.

LETTER CXLVIII.]   *June* 1806.

Dear Wordsworth—We are pleased, you may be sure, with the good news of Mrs. W——. Hope all is well over by this time. "A fine boy. Have you any more?—one more and a girl—poor copies of me!" vide *Mr. H.,* a farce which the proprietors have done me the honour——; but I will set down Mr. Wroughton's own words. *N.B.*—The ensuing letter was sent in answer to one which I wrote, begging to know if my piece had any chance, as I might make alterations, etc. I writing on Monday, there comes this letter on the Wednesday. Attend!

[Copy of a Letter from Mr. R. Wroughton.]

"Sir—Your piece of *Mr. H.,* I am desired to say, is accepted at Drury Lane Theatre, by the proprietors, and, if agreeable to you, will be brought forwards when the proper opportunity serves. The piece shall be sent to you, for your alterations, in the course of a few days, as the same is not in my hands, but with the proprietors.

"I am, sir, your obedient servant,

"RICHARD WROUGHTON.

[Dated]
"66, Gower Street,
"Wednesday, June 11, 1806."

On the following Sunday Mr. Tobin comes. The scent of a manager's letter brought him. He would have gone further any day on such a business. I read the letter to him. He deems it authentic and peremptory. Our conversation naturally fell upon pieces, different sorts of pieces; what is the best way of offering a piece, how far the caprice of managers is an obstacle in the way of a piece, how to judge of the merits of a piece, how long a piece may remain in the hands of the managers before it is acted; and my piece, and your piece, and my poor brother's piece—my poor brother was all his life endeavouring to get a piece accepted. I am not sure that, when my poor brother bequeathed the care of his pieces to Mr. Tobin, he did not therein convey a legacy which in some measure mollified the otherwise first stupefactions of grief. It cannot be expected that the present Earl Nelson passes all his time in watering the laurels of the admiral with Right-Reverend tears. Certainly he steals a fine day now and then to plot how to lay out the grounds and mansion at Burnham most suitable to the late Earl's taste, if he had lived, and how to spend the hundred thousand pounds which Parliament has given him in erecting some little neat monument to his memory.

I wrote that in mere wantonness of triumph. Have nothing more to say about it. The managers, I thank my stars, have decided its merits for ever. They are the best judges of pieces, and it would be insensible in me to affect a false modesty after the very flattering letter which I have received.

> ADMIT
> TO
> BOXES.
> MR. H.
> *Ninth Night.*
> CHARLES LAMB.

I think this will be as good a pattern for orders as I can think on. A little thin flowery border, round, neat, not gaudy, and the Drury Lane Apollo, with the harp at the top. Or shall I have no Apollo?—simply nothing? Or perhaps the comic muse?

The same form, only I think without the Apollo, will serve for the pit and galleries. I think it will be best to write my name at full length; but then if I give away a great many, that will be tedious. Perhaps *Ch. Lamb* will do.

BOXES, now I think on it, I'll have in capitals. The rest, in a neat Italian hand. Or better, perhaps 𝔅𝔬𝔵𝔢𝔰, in old English characters, like "Madoc" or "Thalaba?"

A-propos of Spenser (you will find him mentioned a page or two before, near enough for an *a-propos*), I was discoursing on poetry (as one's apt to deceive one's self, and when a person is willing to *talk* of what one likes, to believe that he also likes the same, as lovers do) with a young gentleman of my office, who is deep read in Anacreon Moore, Lord Strangford, and the principal modern poets, and I happened to mention Epithalamiums, and that I could show him a very fine one of Spenser's. At the mention of this, my gentleman, who is a very fine gentleman, and is brother to the Miss Evans whom Coleridge so narrowly escaped marrying, pricked up his ears and expressed great pleasure, and begged that I would give him leave to copy it: he did not care how long it was (for I objected the length), he should be very happy to see *anything by him.* Then pausing, and looking sad, he ejaculated "POOR SPENCER!" I begged to know the reason of his ejaculation, thinking that time had by this time softened down any calamities which the bard might have endured. "Why, poor fellow," said he, "he has lost his wife!" "Lost his wife!" said I, "whom are you talking of?" "Why, Spencer," said he; "I've read the *Monody* he wrote on the occasion, and *a very pretty thing it is.*" This led to an explanation (it could be delayed no longer) that the sound *Spenser*, which, when poetry is talked of, generally excites an image of an old bard in a ruff, and sometimes with it dim notions of Sir P. Sydney, and perhaps Lord Burleigh, had raised in my gentleman a quite contrary image of the Honourable William Spencer, who has translated some things from the German very prettily, which are published with Lady Di. Beauclerk's designs. Nothing like defining of terms when we talk. What blunders might I have fallen into of quite inapplicable criticism, but for this timely explanation!

N.B.—At the beginning of *Edm.* Spenser (to prevent mistakes), I have copied from my own copy, and primarily from a book of Chalmers's on Shakspeare, a sonnet of Spenser's never printed among his poems. It is curious, as being manly, and rather Miltonic, and as a sonnet of Spenser's with nothing in it about love or knighthood. I have no room for remembrances; but I hope our doing your commission will prove we do not quite forget you. C. L.

To THOMAS MANNING.

LETTER CXLIX.] *December* 5, 1806.

Manning, your letter dated Hottentots, August (the what-was-it?) came to hand. I can scarce hope that mine will have the same luck. China! Canton! Bless us—how it strains the imagination and makes it ache! I write under another uncertainty, whether it can go tomorrow by a ship which I have just learned is going off direct to your part of the world, or whether the despatches may not be sealed up and this have to wait, for if it is detained here, it will grow staler in a fortnight than in a five months' voyage coming to you. It will be a point of conscience to send you none but bran-new news (the latest edition), which, like oranges, will but grow the better for a sea voyage. Oh that you should be so many hemispheres off!—if I speak incorrectly you can correct me—why the simplest death or marriage that takes place here must be important to you as news in the old Bastile. There's your friend Tuthill has got away from France; you remember France?—and Tuthill—ten to one but he writes by this post, if he don't get my note in time, apprising him of the vessel's sailing. Know then that he has found means to obtain leave from Buonaparte (without making use of any *incredible romantic pretences* as some have done, who never meant to fulfil them) to come home, and I have seen him here and at Holcroft's. Aren't you glad about Tuthill? Now then, be sorry for Holcroft, whose new play, called the *Vindictive Man*, was damned about a fortnight since. It died in part of its own weakness, and in part for being choked up with bad actors. The two principal parts were destined to Mrs. Jordan and Mr. Bannister, but Mrs. J. has not come to terms with the managers; they have had some squabble; and Bannister shot some of his fingers off by the going off of a gun. So Miss Duncan had her part, and Mr. de Camp took his. His part, the principal comic hope of the play, was most unluckily *Goldfinch*, taken out of the *Road to Ruin*, not only the same character, but the identical *Goldfinch*—the same as *Falstaff* is in two plays of Shakspeare's. As the devil of ill-luck would have it, half the audience did not know that Holcroft had written it, but were displeased at his stealing from the *Road to Ruin;* and those who might have borne a gentlemanly coxcomb with his "That's your sort," "Go it"—such as Lewis is—did not relish the intolerable vulgarity and inanity of the idea stript of his manner. De Camp was hooted, more than hist, hooted and bellowed off the stage before the second act was finished; so that the remainder of his part was forced to be, with some violence to the play, omitted. In addition to this, a whore was another principal character—a most unfortunate choice in this moral day. The audience were as scandalised as if you were to introduce such a personage to their private tea tables. Besides, her action in the play was gross—wheedling an old man into marriage. But the mortal blunder of the play was that which, oddly enough, Holcroft took pride in, and exultingly told me of the night before it came out, that there were no less than eleven principal characters in it, and I believe he meant of the men only, for the play-bill expressed as much, not reckoning one woman, and one whore; and true it was, for Mr. Powell, Mr. Raymond, Mr. Bartlett, Mr. H. Siddons, Mr. Barrymore, etc. etc., to the number of eleven, had all parts equally prominent, and there was as much of them in quantity and rank as of the hero and heroine—and most of them gentlemen who seldom appear but as the hero's friend in a farce, for a minute or two; and here they all had their ten-minute speeches, and one of them gave the audience a serious account of how he was now a lawyer but had been a poet, and then a long enumeration of the inconveniences of authorship, rascally booksellers, reviewers, etc.; which first set the audience a-gaping; but I have said enough. You will be so sorry, that you will not think the best of me for my detail; but news is news at Canton. Poor Holcroft I fear will feel the disappointment very seriously in a pecuniary light. From what I can learn he has saved nothing. You and I were hoping one day that he had, but I fear he has nothing but his pictures and books, and a no very flourishing business, and to be obliged to part with his long-necked Guido that hangs opposite as you enter, and the game-piece that hangs in the back drawing-room, and all those Vandykes, etc.! God should temper the wind to the shorn connoisseur. I hope I need not say to you, that I feel for the weather-beaten author, and for all his household. I assure you his fate has soured a good deal the pleasure I should have otherwise taken in my own little farce being accepted, and I hope about to be acted: it is in rehearsal actually, and I expect it to come out next week. It is kept a sort of secret, and the rehearsals have gone on privately, lest by many folks knowing it, the story should come out, which would infallibly damn it. You remember I had sent it before you went. Wroughton read it, and was much pleased with it. I speedily got an answer. I took it to make alterations, and lazily kept it some months, then took courage and furbished it up in a day or two and took it. In less than a fortnight I heard the principal part was given to Elliston, who liked it and only wanted a prologue, which I have since done and sent, and I had a note the day before yesterday from the manager, Wroughton (bless his fat face! he is not a bad actor in some things), to say that I should be summoned to the rehearsal after the next, which next was to be yesterday. I had no idea it was so forward. I have had no trouble, attended no reading or rehearsal, made no interest. What a contrast to the usual parade of authors. But it is peculiar to modesty to do all things without noise or pomp. I have some suspicion it will appear in public on Wednesday next, for Wroughton says in his note, it is so forward that if wanted it may come out next week, and a new melodrame is announced for every day till then; and "a new farce is in rehearsal," is put up in the bills. Now you'd like to know the subject. The title is *Mr. H.*, no more. How simple, how taking! A great H. sprawling over the play-bill and attracting eyes at every corner. The story is a coxcomb appearing at Bath, vastly rich—all the ladies dying for him—all bursting to know who he is; but he goes by no other name than Mr. H.—a curiosity like that of the dames of Strasburg about the man with the great nose. But I won't tell you any more about it. Yes, I will; but I can't give you an idea how I have done it. I'll just tell you that after much vehement admiration, when his true name comes out, "Hogsflesh," all the women shun him, avoid him, and not one can be found to change their name for him. That's the idea. How flat it is here—but how whimsical in the farce! And only think how hard upon me it is that the ship is despatched to-morrow, and my triumph cannot be ascertained till the Wednesday after; but all China will ring of it by and by. *N.B.* (But this is a secret). The Professor has got a tragedy coming out, with the young Roscius in it, in January next, as we say— January last it will be with you—and though it is a profound secret now, as all his affairs are, it cannot be much of one by the time you read this.

However, don't let it go any further. I understand there are dramatic exhibitions in China. One would not like to be forestalled. Do you find in all this stuff I have written anything like those feelings which one should send my old adventuring friend, that is gone to wander among Tartars and may never come again? I don't; but your going away, and all about you, is a threadbare topic. I have worn it out with thinking: it has come to me when I have been dull with anything, till my sadness has seemed more to have come from it than to have introduced it. I want you, you don't know how much; but if I had you here in my European garret, we should but talk over such stuff as I have written—so. Those *Tales from Shakspeare* are near coming out, and Mary has begun a new work. Mr. Dawe is turned author; he has been in such a way lately—Dawe, the painter, I mean—he sits and stands about at Holcroft's and says nothing; then sighs and leans his head on his hand. I took him to be in love; but it seems he was only meditating a work,—"The Life of Morland." The young man is not used to composition. Rickman and Captain Burney are well; they assemble at my house pretty regularly of a Wednesday—a new institution. Like other great men I have a public day, cribbage and pipes, with Phillips and noisy Martin.

Good God! what a bit only I've got left! How shall I squeeze all I know into this morsel! Coleridge is come home, and is going to turn lecturer on Taste at the Royal Institution. I shall get £200 from the theatre if *Mr. H.* has a good run, and I hope £100 for the copyright. Nothing if it fails; and there never was a more ticklish thing. The whole depends on the manner in which the name is brought out, which I value myself on, as a *chef-d'œuvre*. How the paper grows less and less! In less than two minutes I shall cease to talk to you, and you may rave to the great wall of China. *N.B.* Is there such a wall? Is it as big as old London Wall, by Bedlam? Have you met with a friend of mine, named Ball, at Canton! If you are acquainted, remember me kindly to him. May be you'll think I have not said enough of Tuthill and the Holcrofts. Tuthill is a noble fellow, as far as I can judge. The H.'s bear their disappointment pretty well, but indeed they are sadly mortified. Mrs. H. is cast down. It was well, if it were but on this account, that T. is come home. *N.B.* If my little thing don't succeed I shall easily survive, having, as it were, compared to H.'s venture, but a sixteenth in the lottery. Mary and I are to sit next the orchestra in the pit, next the tweedledees. She remembers you. You are more to us than five hundred farces, clappings, etc.

Come back one day.   C. LAMB.

To MISS STODDART.

LETTER CL.]   *December* 11, 1806.

Don't mind this being a queer letter. I am in haste, and taken up by visitors, condolers, etc.

God bless you.

Dear Sarah—Mary is a little cut at the ill success of *Mr. H.*, which came out last night and *failed*. I know you'll be sorry, but never mind. We are determined not to be cast down. I am going to leave off tobacco, and then we must thrive. A smoking man must write smoky farces.

Mary is pretty well, but I persuaded her to let me write. We did not apprise you of the coming out of *Mr. H.* for fear of ill luck. You were much better out of the house. If it had taken, your partaking of our good luck would have been one of our greatest joys. As it is, we shall expect you at the time you mentioned. But whenever you come you shall be most welcome.

God bless you, dear Sarah,

Yours most truly, C. L.

Mary is by no means unwell, but I made her let me write.

To WILLIAM WORDSWORTH.

LETTER CLI.] *December* 11, 1806.

Mary's love to all of you—I wouldn't let her write.

Dear Wordsworth—*Mr. H.* came out last night, and failed. I had many fears; the subject was not substantial enough. John Bull must have solider fare than a *letter*. We are pretty stout about it; have had plenty of condoling friends; but, after all, we had rather it should have succeeded. You will see the prologue in most of the morning papers. It was received with such shouts as I never witnessed to a prologue. It was attempted to be encored. How hard!—a thing I did merely as a task, because it was wanted, and set no great store by; and *Mr. H. ! !* The number of friends we had in the house—my brother and I being in public offices, etc.—was astonishing, but they yielded at length to a few hisses. A hundred hisses! (Damn the word, I write it like kisses—how different!)—a hundred hisses outweigh a thousand claps. The former come more directly from the heart. Well, 'tis withdrawn, and there is an end.

Better luck to us. C. LAMB.

[Turn over]

P.S.—Pray, when any of you write to the Clarksons, give our kind loves, and say we shall not be able to come and see them at Christmas, as I shall have but a day or two, and tell them we bear our mortification pretty well.

To WILLIAM GODWIN.

LETTER CLII.] 1806.

I repent. Can that God whom thy votaries say that thou hast demolished expect more? I did indite a splenetic letter, but did the black

Hypocondria never gripe *thy* heart, till thou hast taken a friend for an enemy? The foul fiend Flibbertigibbet leads me over four-inched bridges, to course my own shadow for a traitor. There are certain positions of the moon, under which I counsel thee not to take anything written from this domicile as serious.

I rank thee with Alves,—*Latinè*, Helvetius, or any of his accursed crew? Thou art my friend, and henceforth my philosoper. Thou shalt teach Distinction to the junior branches of my household and Deception to the gray-haired Janitress at my door.

What! Are these atonements? Can Arcadias be brought upon knees, creeping and crouching?

Come, as Macbeth's drunken porter says, knock, knock, knock, knock, knock, knock, knock—seven times a day shalt thou batter at my peace, and if I shut aught against thee, save the Temple of Janus, may Briareus, with his hundred hands, in each a brass knocker, lead me such a life.

C. LAMB.

To WILLIAM WORDSWORTH.

LETTER CLIII.]   *Thursday, January 29, 1807.*

Dear Wordsworth—We have book'd off from Swan and Two Necks, Lad Lane, this day (per Coach) the Tales from Shakspeare. You will forgive the plates, when I tell you they were left to the direction of Godwin, who left the choice of subjects to the bad baby, who from mischief (I suppose) has chosen one from damn'd beastly vulgarity (vide *Merch. Venice*) where no atom of authority was in the tale to justify it; to another has given a name which exists not in the tale, Nic Bottom, and which she thought would be funny, though in this I suspect *his* hand, for I guess her reading does not reach far enough to know Bottom's Christian name; and one of Hamlet and grave-digging, a scene which is not hinted at in the story, and you might as well have put King Canute the Great reproving his courtiers. The rest are giants and giantesses. Suffice it, to save our taste and damn our folly, that we left it all to a friend. W. G., who in the first place cheated me into putting a name to them, which I did not mean, but do not repent, and then wrote a puff about their *simplicity*, etc., to go with the advertisement as in my name! Enough of this egregious dupery. I will try to abstract the load of teasing circumstances from the stories and tell you that I am answerable for *Lear, Macbeth, Timon, Romeo, Hamlet, Othello*, for occasionally a tailpiece or correction of grammar, for none of the cuts and all of the spelling. The rest is my Sister's.——We think Pericles of hers the best, and Othello of mine; but I hope all have some good. *As you like It*, we like least. So much, only begging you to tear out the cuts and give them to Johnny, as "Mrs. Godwin's fancy"! !—   C. L.

Our love to all.

I had almost forgot, My part of the Preface begins in the middle of a sentence, in last but one page, after a colon, thus—

:—*which if they be happily so done, etc.*

the former part hath a more feminine turn and does hold me up something as an instructor to young ladies: but upon my modesty's honour I wrote it not.

Godwin told my Sister that the Baby chose the subjects: a fact in taste.

To REV. W. HAZLITT.

LETTER CLIV.]   *Temple, February* 18, 1808.

Sir—I am truly concerned that any mistake of mine should have caused you uneasiness, but I hope we have got a clue to William's absence, which may clear up all apprehensions. The people where he lodges in town have received direction from him to forward some linen to a place called Winterslow, in the county of Wilts (not far from Salisbury), where the lady lives, whose cottage, pictured upon a card, if you opened my letter you have doubtless seen; and though we have had no explanation of the mystery since, we shrewdly suspect that at the time of writing that letter which has given you all this trouble, a certain son of yours (who is both painter and author) was at her elbow, and did assist in framing that very cartoon which was sent to amuse and mislead us in town, as to the real place of his destination. And some words at the back of the said cartoon, which we had not marked so narrowly before, by the similarity of the handwriting to William's, do very much confirm the suspicion. If our theory be right, they have had the pleasure of their jest, and I am afraid you have paid for it in anxiety. But I hope your uneasiness will now be removed, and you will pardon a suspense occasioned by LOVE, who does so many worse mischiefs every day.

The letter to the people where William lodges says, moreover, that he shall be in town in a fortnight.

My sister joins in respects to you and Mrs. Hazlitt, and in our kindest remembrances and wishes for the restoration of Peggy's health.

I am, Sir, your humble servant,   CH. LAMB.

Rev. W. Hazlitt, Wem, Shropshire.

To THOMAS MANNING.

LETTER CLV.]   *February* 26, 1808.

Dear Missionary—Your letters from the farthest ends of the world have arrived safe. Mary is very thankful for your remembrance of her; and with the less suspicion of mercenariness, as the silk, the *symbolum materiale* of your friendship, has not yet appeared. I think Horace says somewhere, *nox longa*. I would not impute negligence or unhandsome delays to a person whom you have honoured with your confidence, but

I have not heard of the silk, or of Mr. Knox, save by your letter. Maybe he expects the first advances! or it may be that he has not succeeded in getting the article on shore, for it is among the *res prohibiæ et non nisis smuggle-ationis viâ fruendæ*. But so it is, in the friendships between *wicked men* the very expressions of their goodwill cannot but be sinful. I suppose you know my farce was damned. The noise still rings in my ears. Were you ever in the pillory? —being damned is something like that. A treaty of marriage is on foot between William Hazlitt and Miss Stoddart. Something about settlements only retards it. She has somewhere about £80 a year, to be £120 when her mother dies. He has no settlement except what he can claim from the Parish. *Pauper est Cinna, sed amat*. The thing is therefore in abeyance. But there is love a-both sides. Little Fenwick (you don't see the connection of ideas here; how the devil should you?) is in the rules of the Fleet. Cruel creditors! operation of iniquitous laws. Is Magna Charta then a mockery? Why, in general (here I suppose you to ask a question) my spirits are pretty good; but I have my depressions, black as a smith's beard, Vulcanic, Stygian. At such times I have recourse to a pipe, which is like not being at home to a dun: he comes again with tenfold bitterness the next day.— (Mind, I am not in debt; I only borrow a similitude from others; it shows imagination.) I have done two books since the failure of my farce; they will both be out this Summer. The one is a juvenile book—the *Adventures of Ulysses*, intended to be an introduction to the reading of *Telemachus!* It is done out of the *Odyssey*, not from the Greek (I would not mislead you), nor yet from Pope's *Odyssey*, but from an older translation of one Chapman. The *Shakspeare Tales* suggested the doing of it. Godwin is in both those cases my bookseller. The other is done for Longman, and is *Specimens of English Dramatic Poets contemporary with Shakspeare*. Specimens are becoming fashionable. We have "Specimens of Ancient English Poets," "Specimens of Modern English Poets," "Specimens of Ancient English Prose Writers," without end. They used to be called "Beauties." You have seen "Beauties of Shakspeare"? so have many people that never saw any beauties in Shakspeare. Longman is to print it, and be at all the expense and risk, and I am to share the profits after all deductions; *i.e.* a year or two hence I must pocket what they please to tell me is due to me. But the book is such as I am glad there should be. It is done out of old plays at the Museum, and out of Dodsley's collection, etc. It is to have notes. So I go creeping on since I was lamed with that cursed fall from off the top of Drury Lane Theatre into the pit, something more than a year ago. However, I have been free of the house ever since, and the house was pretty free with me upon that occasion. Damn 'em, how they hissed! It was not a hiss neither, but a sort of a frantic yell, like a congregation of mad geese, with roaring sometimes, like bears, mows and mops like apes, sometimes snakes, that hiss'd me into madness. 'Twas like St. Anthony's temptations. Mercy on us, that God should give his favourite children, men, mouths to speak with, to discourse rationally, to promise smoothly, to flatter agreeably, to encourage warmly, to counsel wisely, to sing with, to drink with, and to hiss with, and that they should turn them into mouths of adders, bears, wolves, hyenas, and whistle like tempests, and emit breath through them like distillations of aspic poison, to asperse and vilify the innocent labours of their fellow-creatures who are desirous to please them! Heaven be pleased to make the breath stink and teeth rot out of them all therefore: make them a reproach, and all that pass by them to loll out their tongue at them! Blind mouths! as Milton somewhere calls them. Do you like Braham's singing? The little Jew has bewitched me. I follow him like as the boys followed Tom the Piper. He cures me of melancholy as David cured Saul: but I don't throw stones at him as Saul did at David in payment. I was insensible to music till he gave me a new sense. Oh that you could go to the new opera of *Kais* to-night! 'Tis all about Eastern manners; it would just suit you. It describes the wild Arabs, wandering Egyptians, lying dervises, and all that sort of people, to a hair. You needn't ha' gone so far to see what you see, if you saw it as I do every night at Drury Lane Theatre. Braham's singing, when it is impassioned, is finer than Mrs. Siddons's or Mr. Kemble's acting! and when it is not impassioned, it is as good as hearing a person of fine sense talking. The brave little Jew! Old Sergeant Hill is dead. Mrs. Rickman is in the family way. It is thought that Hazlitt will have children if he marries Miss Stoddart. I made a pun the other day, and palmed it upon Holcroft, who grinned like a Cheshire cat. (Why do cats grin in Cheshire?—Because it was once a county palatine, and the cats cannot help laughing whenever they think of it, though I see no great joke in it.) I said that Holcroft, on being asked who were the best dramatic writers of the day, replied, "HOOK AND I." Mr. Hook is author of several pieces, *Tekeli*, etc. You know what *hooks and eyes* are, don't you? They are what little boys do up their breeches with. Your letter had many things in it hard to be understood: the puns were ready and Swift-like; but don't you begin to be melancholy in the midst of Eastern customs? "The mind does not easily conform to foreign usages, even in trifles: it requires something that it has been familiar with." That begins one of Dr. Hawkesworth's papers in the *Adventurer*, and is, I think, as sensible a remark as ever fell from the Doctor's mouth. White is at Christ's Hospital, a wit of the first magnitude, but would rather be thought a gentleman, like Congreve. You know Congreve's repulse which he gave to Voltaire, when he came to visit him as a *literary man*, that he wished to be considered only in the light of a private gentleman. I think the impertinent Frenchman was properly answered. I should just serve any member of the French Institute in the same manner, that wished to be introduced to me. Buonaparte has voted 5000 livres to Davy, the great young English Chemist! but it has not arrived. Coleridge has delivered two lectures at the Royal Institution; two more were attended, but he did not come. It is thought he has gone sick upon them. He isn't well, that's certain. Wordsworth is coming to see him. He sits up in a two pair of stairs room at the *Courier* Office, and receives visitors. . . .

Does any one read at Canton? Lord Moira is President of the Westminster Library. I suppose you might have interest with Sir Joseph
Banks to get to be president of any similar institution that should be set
up at Canton. I think public reading-rooms the best mode of educating
young men. Solitary reading is apt to give the headache. Besides, who
knows that you *do* read? There are ten thousand institutions similar to
the Royal Institution which have sprung up from it. There is the London
Institution, the Southwark Institution, the Russell Square Rooms Institution, etc.—*College quasi Conlege,* a place where people read together.
Wordsworth, the great poet, is coming to town; he is to have apartments
in the Mansion House. He says he does not see much difficulty in writing
like Shakspeare, if he had a mind to try it. It is clear, then, nothing is
wanting but the mind. Even Coleridge a little checked at this hardihood
of assertion. Dyer came to me the other evening at 11 o'clock, when there
was a large room full of company, which I usually get together on a
Wednesday evening (all great men have public days), to propose to me to
have my face done by a Miss Beetham (or Betham), a miniature painter,
some relation to Mrs. Beetham the Profilist or Pattern Mangle woman
opposite St. Dunstan's, to put before my book of Extracts. I declined
it.

Well, my dear Manning, talking cannot be infinite. I have said all I
have to say; the rest is but remembrances of you, which we shall bear in
our heads while we have heads. Here is a packet of trifles nothing worth;
but it is a trifling part of the world where I live: emptiness abounds. But
in fulness of affection, we remain yours,　　　　　　　　　　　C. L.

To WILLIAM GODWIN.

Letter CLVI.]　　　　　　　　　　　　　　　　　*March* 11, 1808.

Dear Godwin—The giant's vomit was perfectly nauseous, and I am
glad you pointed it out. I have removed the objection. To the other
passages I can find no other objection but what you may bring to numberless passages besides, such as of Scylla snatching up the six men, etc.,
—that is to say, they are lively images of *shocking* things. If you want
a book, which is not occasionally to *shock,* you should not have thought
of a tale which was so full of anthropophagi and wonders. I cannot alter
these things without enervating the Book, and I will not alter them if
the penalty should be that you and all the London booksellers should
refuse it. But speaking as author to author, I must say that I think *the
terrible* in those two passages seems to me so much to preponderate over
the nauseous, as to make them rather fine than disgusting. Who is to
read them, I don't know: who is it that reads "Tales of Terror" and
"Mysteries of Udolpho"? Such things sell. I only say that I will not
consent to alter such passages, which I know to be some of the best in the
book. As an author, I say to you, an author: touch not my work. As to
a bookseller I say, Take the work such as it is, or refuse it. You are as

free to refuse it as when we first talked of it. As to a friend I say, Don't plague yourself and me with nonsensical objections. I assure you I will not alter one more word.

To GEORGE DYER.

From my desk in Leadenhall Street,
                                  December 5, 1808.

Dear Dyer—Coleridge is not so bad as your fears have represented him: it is true he is Bury'd, although he is not dead; to understand this quibble you must know that he is at Bury St. Edmonds, relaxing after the fatigues of lecturing and Londonising. The little Rickmaness whom you inquire after so kindly, thrives and grows apace; she is already a prattler, and 'tis thought that on some future day she may be a speaker. We hold our weekly meetings still at No. 16, where although we are not so high as the top of Malvern we are involved in almost as much mist. Miss B.'s merit "in every point of view" I am not disposed to question, although I have not been indulged with any view of that lady, back, side or front— fie, Dyer, to praise a female in such common market phrases—you who are so courtly and so attentive. My book is not yet out, that is, not my *Extracts;* my *Ulysses* is, and waits your acceptance. When you shall come to town, I hope to present you both together, never thinking of your buying the *Extracts*—half a guinea books were never calculated for my friends. More poets have started up since your departure; William Hazlitt, your friend and mine, is putting to press a collection of verses, chiefly amatory, some of them pretty enough. How these painters encroach on our province! There's Hopner, Shee, Westall, and I don't know who beside, and Tresham. It seems, on confession, that they are not at the top of their own art, when they seek to eke out their fame with the assistance of another's; no large tea-dealer sells cheeses, and no great silversmith deals in razor-straps; it is only your petty dealers who mix commodities. If Nero had been a great emperor he would never have played the violoncello. Who ever caught you, Dyer, designing a landscape or taking a likeness? I have no more to add, who am a friend of virtue, poetry, and painting, therefore, in an especial manner, unalterably thine,   C. LAMB.

To G. Dyer, Esq.,
    Jas. Martin's Wood,
        Overbury, Worcestershire.

To MRS. HAZLITT.

Saturday, December 10, 1808.

There came this morning a printed Prospectus from "S. T. Coleridge, Grasmere," of a Weekly Paper, to be called *The Friend;* a flaming Prospectus. I have no time to give the heads of it. To commence the first Saturday in January. There came also notice of a turkey from Mr. Clarkson, which I am more sanguine in expecting the accomplishment of than I am of Coleridge's prophecy. C. LAMB.

Mrs. Hazlitt, Winterslow,
near Sarum, Wilts.

CHAPTER III

1809-1816

LETTERS TO MANNING, COLERIDGE, WORDSWORTH, AND OTHERS

To ROBERT LLOYD.

LETTER CLIX.]   *Saturday, February 25, 1809.*

Dear Robert—A great gap has been filled up since our intercourse was broken off. We shall at least have some things to talk over when we meet. That you should never have been in London since I saw you last is a fact which I cannot account for on the principles of my own mental formation. You are worthy to be mentioned with Claudian's "Old Man of Verona." I forbear to ask you any questions concerning your family: *who* are dead, and *who* married; I will not anticipate our meeting. I have been in total darkness respecting you all these years. I am just up; and have heard, without being able to confirm the fact, that Drury Lane Theatre is burnt to the ground. Of Walton's *Angler* a new edition is just published with the original plates revived. I think of buying it. The old editions are two guineas, and two guineas and a half. I have not forgotten our ride from Saffron Walden, and the madness of young parson Thomson of Cambridge, that I took your brother to see. He is gone as a missionary to the East.

I live at present at No. 16 Mitre Court Buildings, Inner Temple. I shall move at Lady Day, or a little later: if you don't find me in M.C.B., I shall be at No. 2 *or* 4 Inner Temple Lane, at either of which places I shall be happy to shake my old friend Robert by the hand.   C. L.

To THOMAS MANNING.

LETTER CLX.]   34 *Southampton Buildings,*
March 28, 1809.

Dear Manning—I sent you a long letter by the ships which sailed the beginning of last month, accompanied with books, etc. Since I last wrote Holcroft is dead. He died on Thursday last. So there is one of your friends whom you will never see again! Perhaps the next fleet may bring you a letter from Martin Burney, to say that he writes by desire of Miss Lamb, who is not well enough to write herself, to inform you that her brother died on Thursday last, 14th June, etc. But I hope *not*. I should be sorry to give occasion to open a correspondence between Martin and you. This letter must be short, for I have driven it off to the very moment of doing up the packets; and besides, that which I refer to above is a very long one; and if you have received my books, you will have enough to do to read them. While I think on it, let me tell you, we are moved. Don't come any more to Mitre Court Buildings. We are at 34, Southampton Buildings, Chancery Lane, and shall be here till about the end of May; then we remove to No. 4, Inner Temple Lane, where I mean to live and die; for I have such horror of moving, that I would not take a benefice from the King if I was not indulged with non-residence. What a dislocation of comfort is comprised in that word "moving"! Such a heap of little nasty things, after you think all is got into the cart: old dredging-boxes, worn-out brushes, gallipots, vials, things that it is impossible the most necessitous person can ever want, but which the women, who preside on these occasions, will not leave behind if it was to save your soul. They'd keep the cart ten minutes to stow in dirty pipes and broken matches, to show their economy. Then you can find nothing you want for many days after you get into your new lodgings. You must comb your hair with your fingers, wash your hands without soap, go about in dirty gaiters. Were I Diogenes, I would not move out of a kilderkin into a hogshead, though the first had had nothing but small beer in it, and the second reeked claret. Our place of final destination—I don't mean the grave, but No. 4, Inner Temple Lane—looks out upon a gloomy churchyard-like court, called Hare Court, with three trees and a pump in it. Do you know it? I was born near it, and used to drink at that pump when I was a Rechabite of six years old. If you see newspapers you will read about Mrs. Clarke. The sensation in London about this nonsensical business is marvellous. I remember nothing in my life like it: thousands of ballads, caricatures, lives of Mrs. Clarke, in every blind alley. Yet in the midst of this stir, a sublime abstracted dancing-master, who attends a family we know at Kensington, being asked a question about the progress of the examinations in the House, inquired who Mrs. Clarke was? He had heard nothing of it. He had evaded this omnipresence by utter insignificancy! The Duke should make that man his confidential valet. I proposed locking him up, barring him the use of his fiddle and red pumps, until he had minutely perused and committed to memory the whole body of the examinations, which employed the House of Commons a fortnight, to teach him to be more attentive to what concerns the public. I think I told you of Godwin's little book and of Coleridge's prospectus, in my last; if I did not, remind me of it, and I will send you them, or an account of them, next fleet. I have no conveniency of doing it by this. Mrs. Godwin grows every day in disfavour with me. I will be buried with this inscription over me:— "Here lies C. L., the woman-hater:" I mean that hated one woman: for the rest, God bless them! How do you like the Mandarinesses? Are you on some little footing with any of them? This is Wednesday. On Wednesdays is my levee. The Captain, Martin, Phillips (not the Sheriff),

Rickman, and some more, are constant attendants, besides stray visitors. We play at whist, eat cold meat and hot potatoes, and any gentleman that chooses smokes. Why do you never drop in? You'll come some day, won't you?   C. LAMB, etc.

To SAMUEL TAYLOR COLERIDGE.

LETTER CLXI.]   *June* 7, 1809.

Dear Coleridge—I congratulate you on the appearance of the *Friend*. Your first Number promises well, and I have no doubt the succeeding Numbers will fulfil the promise. I had a kind letter from you some time since, which I have left unanswered. I am also obliged to you, I believe, for a review in the Annual, am I not? The *Monthly Review* sneers at me, and asks "if *Comus* is not *good enough* for Mr. Lamb?" because I have said no good serious dramas have been written since the death of Charles the First, except *Samson Agonistes*. So because they do not know, or won't remember, that *Comus* was written long before, I am to be set down as an undervaluer of Milton! O Coleridge, do kill those reviews, or they will kill us; kill all we like. Be a friend to all else, but their foe. I have been turned out of my chambers in the Temple by a landlord who wanted them for himself, but I have got other at No. 4, Inner Temple Lane, far more commodious and roomy. I have two rooms on the third floor and five rooms above, with an inner staircase to myself, and all new painted, etc., and all for £30 a year! I came into them on Saturday week; and on Monday following Mary was taken ill with the fatigue of moving; and affected, I believe, by the novelty of the home she could not sleep, and I am left alone with a maid quite a stranger to me, and she has a month or two's sad distraction to go through. What sad large pieces it cuts out of life!—out of *her* life, who is getting rather old; and we may not have many years to live together. I am weaker, and bear it worse than I ever did. But I hope we shall be comfortable by and by. The rooms are delicious, and the best look backwards into Hare Court, where there is a pump always going. Just now it is dry. Hare Court trees come in at the window, so that 'tis like living in a garden. I try to persuade myself it is much pleasanter than Mitre Court; but, alas! the household gods are slow to come in a new mansion. They are in their infancy to me; I do not feel them yet; no hearth has blazed to them yet. How I hate and dread new places!

I was very glad to see Wordsworth's book advertised: I am to have it to-morrow lent me, and if Wordsworth don't send me an order for one upon Longman, I will buy it. It is greatly extolled and liked by all who have seen it. Let me hear from some of you, for I am desolate. I shall have to send you, in a week or two, two volumes of Juvenile Poetry, done by Mary and me within the last six months, and that tale in prose which Wordsworth so much liked, which was published at Christmas, with nine others, by us, and has reached a second edition. There's for you. We have almost worked ourselves out of child's work, and I don't know what to do. Sometimes I think of a drama, but I have no head for play-making; I can do the dialogue, and that's all. I am quite aground for a plan; but I must do something for money. Not that I have immediate wants, but I have prospective ones. O money, money, how blindly thou hast been worshipped, and how stupidly abused! Thou art health and liberty and strength; and he that has thee may rattle his pockets at the Devil.

Nevertheless, do not understand by this that I have not quite enough for my occasions for a year or two to come. While I think on it, Cole-ridge, I fetch'd away my books which you had at the *Courier* Office, and found all but a third volume of the old plays, containing the *White Devil*, Green's *Tu Quoque*, and the *Honest Whore*, perhaps the most valuable volume of them all—*that* I could not find. Pray, if you can, remember what you did with it, or where you took it out with you a walking per-haps; send me word, for, to use the old plea, it spoils a set. I found two other volumes (you had three), the *Arcadia*, and *Daniel*, enriched with manuscript notes. I wish every book I have were so noted. They have thoroughly converted me to relish *Daniel*, or to say I relish him, for after all, I believe I did relish him. You well call him sober-minded. Your notes are excellent. Perhaps you've forgot them. I have read a review in the *Quarterly*, by Southey, on the Missionaries, which is most masterly. I only grudge its being there. It is quite beautiful. Do remember my Dodsley; and, pray, do write, or let some of you write. Clarkson tells me you are in a smoky house. Have you cured it? It is hard to cure any-thing of smoking. Our little poems are but humble, but they have no name. You must read them, remembering they were task work; and perhaps you will admire the number of subjects, all of children, picked out by an old Bachelor and an old Maid. Many parents would not have found so many. Have you read *Cœlebs?* It has reached eight editions in so many weeks, yet literally it is one of the very poorest sort of com-mon novels, with the draw-back of dull religion in it. Had the religion been high and flavoured, it would have been something. I borrowed this *Cœlebs in Search of a Wife*, of a very careful, neat lady, and returned it with this stuff written in the beginning:—

> "If ever I marry a wife
>   I'll marry a landlord's daughter,
> For then I may sit in the bar,
>   And drink cold brandy and water."

I don't expect you can find time from your *Friend* to write to me much; but write something, for there has been a long silence. You know Hol-croft is dead. Godwin is well. He has written a very pretty, absurd book about sepulchres. He was affronted because I told him it was bet-ter than Hervey, but not so good as Sir T. Browne. This letter is all about books; but my head aches, and I hardly know what I write, but I could not let the *Friend* pass without a congratulatory epistle. I won't criticise till it comes to a volume. Tell me how I shall send my packet to you?—by what conveyance?—by Longman, Short-man, or how? Give my kindest remembrances to Wordsworth. Tell him he must give me a book. My kind love to Mrs. W. and to Dorothy separately and conjointly. I wish you could all come and see me in my new rooms. God bless you all. C. L.

To CHARLES LLOYD, THE ELDER.

LETTER CLXII.] *July 31, 1809.*

Dear Sir—The general impression made by your Translation on the mind of my friend who kept your MS. so unreasonably long, as well as on another friend who read over a good part of it with me, was that it gave a great deal more of the sense of Homer than either of his two great modern Translators have done. In several expressions which they at first objected to, on turning to the Greek they found it completely warranted you in the use of them; and they were even surprised that you could combine so much fidelity with so much of the turn of the best modern improvements in the Couplet versification. I think of the two, I rather prefer the Book of the Iliad which you sent me, for the sound of the verse; but the difference of subject almost involuntarily modifies verse. I find Cowper is a favourite with nobody. His injudicious use of the stately slow Miltonic verse in a subject so very different, has given a distaste. Nothing can be more unlike to my fancy than Homer and Milton. Homer is perfect prattle, tho' exquisite prattle, compared to the deep oracular voice of Milton. In Milton you love to stop, and saturate your mind with every great image or sentiment; in Homer you want to go on, to have more of his agreeable narrative. Cowper delays you as much, walking over a Bowling Green, as the other does, travelling over steep Alpine heights, where the labour enters into and makes a part of the pleasure. From what I have seen, I would certainly be glad to hear that you continued your employment quite through the Poem: that is, for an agreeable and honourable recreation to yourself; though I should scarce think that (Pope having got the ground) a translation in Pope's Couplet versification would ever supersede his to the public, however faithfuller or in some respects better. Pitt's Virgil is not much read, I believe, though nearer to the Original than Dryden's. Perhaps it is, that people do not like two Homers or Virgils—there is a sort of confusion in it to an English reader, who has not a centre of reference in the Original: when Tate and Brady's Psalms came out in our Churches, many pious people would not substitute them in the room of David's, as they call'd Sternhold and Hopkins's. But if you write for a relaxation from other sort of occupations I can only congratulate you, Sir, on the noble choice, as it seems to me, which you have made, and express my wonder at the facility which you suddenly have arrived at, if (as I suspect) these are indeed the first specimens of this sort which you have produced. But I cannot help thinking that you betray a more practised gait than a late beginner could so soon acquire. Perhaps you have only resumed what you had formerly laid aside as interrupting more necessary avocations.

I need not add how happy I shall be to see at any time what you may please to send me. In particular, I should be glad to see that you had taken up Horace, which I think you enter into as much as any man that was not born in his days, and in the *Via Longa* or *Flaminia,* or near the *Forum.*

With many apologies for keeping your MS. so long, which my friend's engagements in business must excuse,—I remain, Dear Sir, yours truly,

C. L.

My kind respects to Mrs. Ll., and my remembrances to Robert, etc. etc.

To SAMUEL TAYLOR COLERIDGE.

LETTER CLXIII.] *Monday, October* 30, 1809.

Dear Coleridge—I have but this moment received your letter, dated the 9th instant, having just come off a journey from Wiltshire, where I have been with Mary on a visit to Hazlitt. The journey has been of infinite service to her. We have had nothing but sunshiny days, and daily walks from eight to twenty miles a day; have seen Wilton, Salisbury, Stonehenge, etc. Her illness lasted but six weeks; it left her weak, but the country has made us whole. We came back to our Hogarth Room. I have made several acquisitions since you saw them,—and found Nos. 8, 9, 10 of the *Friend.* The account of Luther in the Warteburg is as fine as anything I ever read. God forbid that a man who has such things to say should be silenced for want of £100. This Custom-and-Duty Age would have made the Preacher on the Mount take out a licence, and St. Paul's Epistles would not have been missible without a stamp. O that you may find means to go on! But alas! where is Sir G. Beaumont?—Sotheby? What has become of the rich Auditors in Albemarle Street? Your letter has saddened me.

I am so tired with my journey, being up all night, that I have neither things nor words in my power. I believe I expressed my admiration of the pamphlet. Its power over me was like that which Milton's pamphlets must have had on his contemporaries, who were tuned to them. What a piece of prose! Do you hear if it is read at all? I am out of the world of readers. I hate all that do read, for they read nothing but reviews and new books. I gather myself up unto the old things.

I have put up shelves. You never saw a book-case in more true harmony with the contents than what I've nailed up in a room, which, though new, has more aptitudes for growing old than you shall often see —as one sometimes gets a friend in the middle of life, who becomes an old friend in a short time. My rooms are luxurious; one is for prints and one for books; a Summer and a Winter parlour. When shall I ever see you in them?   C. L.

To ROBERT LLOYD.

Letter CLXIV.] *January 1, 1810.*

Dear Robert—In great haste I write. The Turkey is down at the fire, and some pleasant friends are come in to partake of it. The-Sender's Health shall not be forgot. What you tell me of your Father's perseverance in his honourable task gives me great pleasure. Seven Books are a serious earnest of the whole, which I hope to see finish'd.

We had a delightful month in Wiltshire, four weeks of uniform fine weather, the only fine days which had been all the summer. Saw Salisbury Cathedral, Stonehenge, Wilton, etc. etc. Mary is in excellent health, and sends her Love. Accept of mine, with my kind respects to Mrs. Ll—— and to your father and mother.

Coleridge's *Friend* is occasionally sublime. What do you think of that Description of Luther in his Study in one of the earlier numbers? The worst is, he is always promising something which never comes; it is now 18th Number, and continues introductory; the 17th (that stupid long letter) was nothing better than a Prospectus, and ought to have preceded the 1st Number. But I rejoice that it lives.

When you come to London, you will find us at No. 4, Inner Temple Lane, with a few old Books, a few old Hogarths round the room, and the Household Gods at last establish'd. The feeling of Home, which has been slow to come, has come at last. May I never move again, but may my next Lodging be my Coffin.

Yours truly,   C. Lamb.

To THOMAS MANNING.

Letter CLXV.] *January 2, 1810.*

Dear Manning—When I last wrote to you I was in lodgings. I am now in chambers, No. 4, Inner Temple Lane, where I should be happy to see you any evening. Bring any of your friends, the Mandarins, with you. I have two sitting-rooms: I call them so *par excellence,* for you may stand, or loll, or lean, or try any posture in them, but they are best for sitting; not squatting down Japanese fashion, but the more decorous use of the haunches which European usage has consecrated. I have two of these rooms on the third floor, and five sleeping, cooking, etc., rooms, on the fourth floor. In my best room is a choice collection of the works of Hogarth, an English painter of some humour. In my next best are shelves containing a small but well-chosen library. My best room commands a court, in which there are trees and a pump, the water of which is excellent cold, with brandy, and not very insipid without. Here I hope to set up my rest, and not quit till Mr. Powell, the undertaker, gives me notice that I may have possession of my last lodging. He lets lodgings for single gentlemen. I sent you a parcel of books by my last, to give you some idea of the state of European literature. There comes with this two volumes, done up as letters, of minor poetry, a sequel to "Mrs. Leicester"; the best you may suppose mine; the next best are my coadjutor's. You may amuse yourself in guessing them out; but I must tell you mine are but one-third in quantity of the whole. So much for a very delicate subject. It is hard to speak of one's self, etc. Holcroft had finished his life when I wrote to you, and Hazlitt has since finished his life; I do not mean his own life, but he has finished a life of Holcroft, which is going to press. Tuthill is Dr. Tuthill. I continue Mr. Lamb. I have published a little book for children on titles of honour; and to give them some idea of the difference of rank and gradual rising, I have made a little scale, supposing myself to receive the following various accessions of dignity from the king, who is the fountain of honour—As at first, 1, Mr. C. Lamb; 2, C. Lamb, Esq.; 3, Sir C. Lamb, Bart.; 4, Baron Lamb, of Stamford; 5, Viscount Lamb; 6, Earl Lamb; 7, Marquis Lamb; 8, Duke Lamb. It would look like quibbling to carry it on further, and especially as it is not necessary for children to go beyond the ordinary titles of sub-regal dignity in our own country; otherwise I have sometimes in my dreams imagined myself still advancing, as 9th, King Lamb; 10th, Emperor Lamb; 11th, Pope Innocent; higher than which is nothing upon earth. Puns I have not made many (nor punch much) since the date of my last; one I cannot help relating. A constable in Salisbury Cathedral was telling me that eight people dined at the top of the spire of the cathedral; upon which I remarked, that they must be very sharp set. But in general I cultivate the reasoning part of my mind more than the imaginative. I am stuffed out so with eating turkey for dinner, and another turkey for supper yesterday (Turkey in Europe and Turkey in Asia), that I can't jog on. It is New Year here; that is, it was New Year half a year back, when I was writing this. Nothing puzzles me more than time and space; and yet nothing puzzles me less, for I never think about them. The Persian ambassador is the principal thing talked of now. I sent some people to see him worship the sun on Primrose Hill, at half-past six in the morning, 28th November; but he did not come, which makes me think the old fire-worshippers are a sect almost extinct in Persia. The Persian ambassador's name is Shaw Ali Mirza. The common people call him Shaw Nonsense. While I think of it, I have put three letters, besides my own three, into the India Post for you, from your brother, sister, and some gentleman whose name I forget. Will they, have they, did they come safe? The distance you are at, cuts up tenses by the root. I think you said you did not know Kate * * * * * * * * *. I express her by nine stars, though she is but one. You must have seen her at her father's. Try and remember her. Coleridge is bringing out a paper in weekly Numbers, called the *Friend*, which I would send if I could; but the difficulty I had in getting the packets of books out to you before, deters me; and you'll want something new to read when you come home. It is chiefly intended to puff off Wordsworth's poetry; but there are some noble things in it by the by. Except Kate, I have had no vision of excellence this year, and she passed by like the Queen on her coronation day; you don't know whether you saw her or not. Kate is fifteen: I go about moping, and sing the old pathetic ballad I used to like in my youth—

> "She's sweet fifteen,
> I'm *one year more*."

Mrs. Bland sang it in boy's clothes the first time I heard it. I sometimes think the lower notes in my voice are like Mrs. Bland's. That glorious singer, Braham, one of my lights, is fled. He was for a season. He was a rare composition of the Jew, the gentleman, and the angel; yet all these elements mixed up so kindly in him, that you could not tell which preponderated; but he is gone, and one Phillips is engaged instead. Kate is vanished, but Miss B— — is always to be met with!

> "Queens drop away, while blue-legg'd Maukin thrives;
> And courtly Mildred dies while country Madge survives."

That is not my poetry, but Quarles's; but haven't you observed that the rarest things are the least obvious? Don't show anybody the names in this letter. I write confidentially, and wish this letter to be considered as *private*. Hazlitt has written a *grammar* for Godwin. Godwin sells it bound up with a treatise of his own on language; but the *gray mare is the better horse*. I don't allude to Mrs. Godwin, but to the word *grammar*, which comes near to *gray mare*, if you observe, in sound. That figure is called paronomasia in Greek. I am sometimes happy in it. An old woman begged of me for charity. "Ah! sir," said she, "I have seen better days." "So have I, good woman," I replied; but I meant, literally, days not so rainy and overcast as that on which she begged: she meant more prosperous days. Mr. Dawe is made associate of the Royal Academy. By what law of association I can't guess. Mrs. Holcroft, Miss Holcroft, Mr. and Mrs. Godwin, Mr. and Mrs. Hazlitt, Mrs. Martin and Louisa, Mrs. Lum, Capt. Burney, Mrs. Burney, Martin Burney, Mr. Rickman, Mrs. Rickman, Dr. Stoddart, William Dollin, Mr. Thompson, Mr. and Mrs. Norris, Mr. Fenwick, Mrs. Fenwick, Miss Fenwick, a man that saw you at our house one day, and a lady that heard me speak of you; Mrs. Buffam that heard Hazlitt mention you, Dr. Tuthill, Mrs. Tuthill, Colonel Harwood, Mrs. Harwood, Mr. Collier, Mrs. Collier, Mr. Sutton, Nurse, Mr. Fell, Mrs. Fell, Mr. Marshall, are very well, and occasionally inquire after you.

I remain yours ever, Ch. Lamb.

To CHARLES LLOYD, THE ELDER.

Letter CLXVI.] *March* 10, 1810. *E. I. Ho.*

My dear Sir—The above are all the faults I, who profess myself to be a mere English Reader, could find after a scrupulous perusal twice over of your neat little Book. I assure you it gave me great pleasure in the perusal, much more in this shape than in the Manuscript, and I should be very sorry you should give up the finishing of it on so poor pretence as your *Age* [sixty-two], which is not so much by ten years as Dryden's when he wrote his fables, which are his best works allowed, and not more than Milton's when he had scarce entered upon his original Epic Poem. You have done nearly a third; persevere and let us see the whole. I am sure I should prize it for its Homeric plainness and truth above the confederate jumble of Pope, Broome and Fenton which goes under Pope's name, and is far inferior to his ILIAD. I have picked out what I think blemishes, but they are but a score of words (I am a mere word-pecker) in six times as many pages. The rest all gave me pleasure, and most of all the Book [the Sixth] in which Ulysses and Nausicaa meet. You have infused a kind of biblical patriarchal manner into it, it reads like some story of Jacob and Rachel, or some of those primitive manners. I am ashamed to carp at words, but I did it in obedience to your desires, and the plain reason why I did not acknowledge your kind present *sooner* was that I had no criticisms of value to make. I shall certainly beg the opinion of my friend who read the two first Books on this enlarged Performance. But he is so very much engaged that I cannot at present get at him, and besides him I have no acquaintance that takes much interest in Poetry, Greek or English. But I hope and adjure you to go on, and do not make excuses of Age till you have completed the Odyssey, and done a great part of Horace besides. Then you will be entitled to hang up your Harp.

I am, Dear Sir, with Love to all your family, your hble. Serv.,

C. LAMB.

To JOHN MATHEW GUTCH.

LETTER CLXVII.]   *April* 9, 1810.

Dear Gutch—I did not see your brother, who brought me Wither; but he understood, he said, you were daily expecting to come to town: this has prevented my writing. The books have pleased me excessively: I should think you could not have made a better selection. I never saw *Philarete* before—judge of my pleasure. I could not forbear scribbling certain critiques in pencil on the blank leaves. Shall I send them, or may I expect to see you in town? Some of them are remarks on the character of Wither and of his writings. Do you mean to have anything of that kind? What I have said on *Philarete* is poor, but I think some of the rest not so bad: perhaps I have exceeded my commission in scrawling over the copies; but my delight therein must excuse me, and pencilmarks will rub out. Where is the Life? Write, for I am quite in the dark.

Yours, with many thanks,   C. LAMB.

Perhaps I could digest the few critiques prefixed to the Satires, Shepherds Hunting, etc., into a short abstract of Wither's character and works, at the end of his Life. But, may be, you don't want anything, and have said all you wish in the Life.

To BASIL MONTAGU.

LETTER CLXVIII.]

Winterslow, near Sarum,
July 12, 1810.

Dear Montagu—I have turned and twisted the MSS. in my head, and can make nothing of them. I knew when I took them that I could not, but I do not like to do an act of ungracious necessity at once; so I am ever committing myself by half engagements, and total failures. I cannot make anybody understand why I can't do such things; it is a defect in my occiput. I cannot put other people's thoughts together; I forget every paragraph as fast as I read it; and my head has received such a shock by an all-night journey on the top of the coach, that I shall have enough to do to nurse it into its natural pace before I go home. I must devote myself to imbecility; I must be gloriously useless while I stay here. How is Mrs. M.? will she pardon my inefficiency? The city of Salisbury is full of weeping and wailing. The bank has stopped payment; and everybody in the town kept money at it, or has got some of its notes. Some have lost all they had in the world. It is the next thing to seeing a city with the plague within its walls. The Wilton people are all undone; all the manufacturers there kept cash at the Salisbury bank; and I do suppose it to be the unhappiest county in England this, where I am making holiday. We propose setting out for Oxford Tuesday fortnight, and coming thereby home. But no more night travelling. My head is sore (understand it of the inside) with that deduction from my natural rest which I suffered coming down. Neither Mary nor I can spare a morsel of our rest: it is incumbent on us to be misers of it. Travelling is not good for us, we travel so seldom. If the sun be hell, it is not for the fire, but for the sempiternal motion of that miserable body of light. How much more dignified leisure hath a mussel glued to his unpassable rocky limit two inch square! He hears the tide roll over him, backwards and forwards twice a day (as the Salisbury long coach goes and returns in eight-and-forty hours), but knows better than to take an outside night place a top on't. He is the owl of the sea—Minerva's fish—the fish of wisdom.

Our kindest remembrances to Mrs. M.

Yours truly,   C. LAMB.

To WILLIAM HAZLITT.

LETTER CLXIX.]   *Thursday* [*August* 9, 1810].

Dear H.—Epistemon is not well. Our pleasant excursion has ended sadly for one of us. You will guess I mean my sister. She got home very well (I was very ill on the journey) and continued so till Monday night, when her complaint came on, and she is now absent from home.

I am glad to hear you are all well. I think I shall be mad if I take any more journeys, with two experiences against it. I found all well here. Kind remembrances to Sarah,—have just got her letter.

H. Robinson has been to Blenheim. He says you will be sorry to hear that we should not have asked for the Titian Gallery there. One of his friends knew of it, and asked to see it. It is never shown but to those who inquire for it.

The pictures are all Titians, Jupiter and Ledas, Mars and Venuses, etc., all naked pictures, which may be a reason they don't show them to females. But he says they are very fine; and perhaps they are shown separately to put another fee into the shower's pocket. Well, I shall never see it.

I have lost all wish for sights. God bless you. I shall be glad to see you in London.

Yours truly,   C. LAMB.

Mr. Hazlitt, Winterslow,
     near Salisbury.

To MISS WORDSWORTH.

LETTER CLXX.]   [Autumn 1810.]

Mary has left a little space for me to fill up with nonsense, as the geographers used to cram monsters in the voids of the maps, and call it Terra Incognita. She has told you how she has taken to water like a hungry otter. I too limp after her in lame imitation, but it goes against me a little at first. I have been acquaintance with it now for full four days, and it seems a moon. I am full of cramps and rheumatisms, and cold internally, so that fire won't warm me; yet I bear all for virtue's sake. Must I then leave you, gin, rum, brandy, aqua-vitæ, pleasant jolly fellows? Damn temperance and he that first invented it!—some Anti-Noahite. Coleridge has powdered his head, and looks like Bacchus, Bacchus ever sleek and young. He is going to turn sober, but his clock has not struck yet; meantime he pours down goblet after goblet, the second to see where the first is gone, the third to see no harm happens to the second, a fourth to say there is another coming, and a fifth to say he is not sure he is the last.

To WILLIAM WORDSWORTH.

LETTER CLXXI.]   *Friday, October* 19, 1810. *E. I. Ho.*

Dear W.—Mary has been very ill, which you have heard, I suppose, from the Montagus. She is very weak and low-spirited now. I was much pleased with your continuation of the Essay on Epitaphs. It is the only sensible thing which has been written on that subject, and it goes to the bottom. In particular I was pleased with your translation of that turgid epitaph into the plain feeling under it. It is perfectly a test. But what is the reason we have no good epitaphs after all?

A very striking instance of your position might be found in the churchyard of Ditton-upon-Thames, if you know such a place. Ditton-upon-Thames has been blessed by the residence of a poet, who for love or money —I do not well know which—has dignified every gravestone, for the last few years, with bran-new verses, all different, and all ingenious, with the author's name at the bottom of each. This sweet Swan of Thames has so artfully diversified his strains and his rhymes, that the same thought never occurs twice; more justly, perhaps, as no thought ever occurs at all, there was a physical impossibility that the same thought should recur. It is long since I saw and read these inscriptions, but I remember the impression was of a smug usher at his desk in the intervals of instruction, levelling his pen. Of death, as it consists of dust and worms, and mourners and uncertainty, he had never thought; but the word "death" he had often seen separate and conjunct with other words, till he had learned to speak of all its attributes as glibly as Unitarian Belsham will discuss you the attributes of the word "God" in a pulpit; and will talk of infinity with a tongue that dangles from a skull that never reached in thought and thorough imagination two inches, or further than from his hand to his mouth, or from the vestry to the sounding-board of the pulpit.

But the epitaphs were trim, and sprag, and patent, and pleased the survivors of Thames-Ditton above the old mumpsimus of "Afflictions Sore." . . . To do justice though, it must be owned that even the excellent feeling which dictated this dirge when new must have suffered something in passing through so many thousand applications, many of them no doubt quite misplaced, as I have seen in Islington churchyard (I think) an Epitaph to an infant who died "*Ætatis* four months," with this seasonable inscription appended, "Honour thy father and thy mother, that thy days may be long in the land," etc. Sincerely wishing your children long life to honour, etc.

I remain,   C. LAMB.

To MISS WORDSWORTH.

LETTER CLXXII.]   *November 23, 1810.*

We are in a pickle. Mary, from her affectation of physiognomy, has hired a stupid big country wench, who looked honest, as she thought, and has been doing her work some days, but without eating—eats no butter, nor meat, but prefers cheese with her tea for breakfast; and now it comes out that she was ill when she came, with lifting her mother about (who is now with God) when she was dying, and with riding up from Norfolk, four days and nights in the waggon. She got advice yesterday, and took something which has made her bring up a quart of blood, and she now lies in her bed, a dead weight upon our humanity, incapable of getting up, refusing to go into an hospital, having nobody in town but a poor asthmatic uncle whose son lately married a drab who fills his house, and there is nowhere she can go, and she seems to have made up her mind to take her flight to heaven from our bed. Oh for the little wheel-barrow which trundled the hunchback from door to door to try the various charities of different professions of mankind! Here's her uncle just crawled up. He is far liker Death than she. Oh the Parish, the Parish, the hospital, the infirmary, the charnel-house!—these are places meet for such guests, not our quiet mansion, where nothing but affluent plenty and literary ease should abound.—Howard's House, Howard's House, or where the Paralytic descended through the skylight (what a God's gift!) to get at our Saviour. In this perplexity such topics as Spanish papers and Monkhouses sink into comparative insignificance. What shall we do? If she died, it were something: gladly would I pay the coffin-maker, and the bell-man and searchers.   C. L.

To Miss Wordsworth, Grasmere,
   near Kendal, Westmoreland.

To WILLIAM HAZLITT.

Letter CLXXIII.]   *Wednesday, November 28, 1810.*

Dear Hazlitt—I sent you on Saturday a Cobbett, containing your reply to the *Edinburgh Review,* which I thought you would be glad to receive as an example of attention on the part of Mr. Cobbett to insert it so speedily. Did you get it? We have received your pig, and return you thanks; it will be dressed in due form, with appropriate sauce, this day. Mary has been very ill indeed since you saw her; that is, as ill as she can be to remain at home. But she is a good deal better now, owing to a very careful regimen. She drinks nothing but water, and never goes out; she does not even go to the Captain's. Her indisposition has been ever since that night you left town; the night Miss W[ordsworth] came. Her coming, and that d——d Mrs. Godwin coming and staying so late that night, so overset her that she lay broad awake all that night, and it was by a miracle that she escaped a very bad illness, which I thoroughly expected. I have made up my mind that she shall never have any one in the house again with her, and that no one shall sleep with her, not even for a night; for it is a very serious thing to be always living with a kind of fever upon her; and therefore I am sure you will take it in good part if I say that if Mrs. Hazlitt comes to town at any time, however glad we shall be to see her in the daytime, I cannot ask her to spend a night under our roof. Some decision we must come to, for the harassing fever that we have both been in, owing to Miss Wordsworth's coming, is not to be borne; and I would rather be dead than so alive. However, at present, owing to a regimen and medicines which Tuthill has given her, who very kindly volunteer'd the care of her, she is a great deal quieter, though too much harassed by company, who cannot or will not see how late hours and society teaze her.

Poor Phillips had the cup dash'd out of his lips as it were. He had every prospect of the situation, when about ten days since one of the council of the R—— Society started for the place himself, being a rich merchant who lately failed, and he will certainly be elected on Friday next. P. is very sore and miserable about it.

Coleridge is in town, or at least at Hammersmith. He is writing or going to write in the *Courier* against Cobbett, and in favour of paper money. No news. Remember me kindly to Sarah. I write from the office.

Yours ever,   C. LAMB.

I just open'd it to say the pig, upon proof, hath turned out as good as I predicted. My fauces yet retain the sweet porcine odour. I find you have received the Cobbett. I think your paper complete.

Mrs. Reynolds, who is a sage woman, approves of the pig.

Mr. Hazlitt, Winterslow,
    near Salisbury, Wilts.

To HENRY CRABB ROBINSON.

LETTER CLXXIV.]   [1810.]

Dear R.—My brother, whom you have met at my rooms (a plump, good-looking man of seven-and-forty) has written a book about humanity, which I transmit to you herewith. Wilson, the publisher, has put it into his head that you can get it reviewed for him. I dare say it is not in the scope of your review; but if you could put it in any likely train, he would rejoice. For alas! our boasted humanity partakes of vanity. As it is, he teazes me to death with choosing to suppose that I could get it into all the reviews at a moment's notice. I!! who have been set up as a mark for them to throw at, and would willingly consign them all to Megæra's snaky locks.

But here's the book, and don't show it to Mrs. Collier, for I remember she makes excellent *eel* soup, and the leading points of the book are directed against that very process.

Yours truly,   C. LAMB.

To WILLIAM HAZLITT.

LETTER CLXXV.]   *October* 2, 1811.

Dear Hazlitt—I cannot help accompanying my sister's congratulations to Sarah with some of my own to you on this happy occasion of a man child being born.

Delighted fancy already sees him some future rich alderman or opulent merchant, painting perhaps a little in his leisure hours, for amusement, like the late H. Bunbury, Esq.

Pray, are the Winterslow estates entailed? I am afraid lest the young dog when he grows up should cut down the woods, and leave no groves for widows to take their lonesome solace in. The Wem estate of course can only devolve on him in case of your brother's leaving no male issue.

Well, my blessing and heaven's be upon him, and make him like his father, with something a better temper, and a smoother head of hair; and then all the men and women must love him.

Martin and the card-boys join in congratulations. Love to Sarah. Sorry we are not within caudle-shot.   C. LAMB.

If the widow be assistant on this notable occasion, give our due respects and kind remembrances to her.

Mr. Hazlitt, Winterslow,
    near Sarum, Wilts.

To WILLIAM GODWIN.

"Bis dat qui dat cito."

LETTER CLXXVI.]   [1811].

I hate the pedantry of expressing that in another language which we have sufficient terms for in our own. So in plain English I very much wish you to give your vote to-morrow at Clerkenwell, instead of Saturday. It would clear up the brows of my favourite candidate, and stagger the hands of the opposite party. It commences at nine. How easy, as you come from Kensington (à propos, how is your excellent family?) to turn down Bloomsbury, through Leather Lane (avoiding Lay Stall St. for the disagreeableness of the name)! Why, it brings you in four minutes and a half to the spot renowned on northern milestones, "where Hicks' Hall formerly stood." There will be good cheer ready for every independent freeholder; where you see a green flag hang out, go boldly in, call for ham, or beef, or what you please, and a mug of Meux's best. How much more gentleman-like to come in the front of the battle, openly avowing one's sentiments, than to lag in on the last day, when the adversary is dejected, spiritless, laid low! Have the first cut at them. By Saturday you'll cut into the mutton. I'd go cheerfully myself, but I am no freeholder; (Fuimus Troes, fuit Ilium), but I sold it for £50. If they'd accept a copyholder, we clerks are naturally copy-holders.

By the way, get Mrs. Hume, or that agreeable Amelia or Caroline, to stick a bit of green in your hat. Nothing daunts the adversary more than to wear the colours of your party. Stick it in cockade-like. It has a martial and by no means disagreeable effect.

Go, my dear freeholder, and if any chance calls you out of this transitory scene earlier than expected, the coroner shall sit lightly on your corpse. He shall not too anxiously inquire into the circumstances of blood found upon your razor. That might happen to any gentleman in shaving. Nor into your having been heard to express a contempt of life, or for scolding Louisa for what Julia did, and other trifling incoherencies.

Yours sincerely, C. LAMB.

To SAMUEL TAYLOR COLERIDGE.

LETTER CLXXVII.]   *August* 13, 1814.

Dear Resuscitate—There comes to you by the vehicle from Lad Lane this day a volume of German; what it is I cannot justly say, the characters of those northern nations having been always singularly harsh and unpleasant to me. It is a contribution of Dr. Southey's towards your wants, and you would have had it sooner but for an odd accident. I wrote for it three days ago, and the Doctor, as he thought, sent it me. A book of like exterior he did send, but being disclosed, how far unlike! It was the *Well-bred Scholar*,—a book with which it seems the Doctor laudably fills up those hours which he can steal from his medical avocations. Chesterfield, Blair, Beattie, portions from the *Life of Savage*, make up a prettyish system of morality and the belles-lettres, which Mr. Mylius, a schoolmaster, has properly brought together, and calls the collection by the denomination above mentioned. The Doctor had no sooner discovered his error than he dispatched man and horse to rectify the mistake, and with a pretty kind of ingenuous modesty in his note, seemeth to deny any knowledge of the *Well-bred Scholar;* false modesty surely, and a blush misplaced: for what more pleasing than the consideration of professional austerity thus relaxing, thus improving! But so, when a child, I remember blushing, being caught on my knees to my Maker, or doing otherwise some pious and praiseworthy action: *now* I rather love such things to be seen. Henry Crabb Robinson is out upon his circuit, and his books are inaccessible without his leave and key. He is attending the Norfolk Circuit,—a short term, but to him, as to many young lawyers, a long vacation, sufficiently dreary. I thought I could do no better than transmit to him, not extracts, but your very letter itself, than which I think I never read anything more moving, more pathetic, or more conducive to the purpose of persuasion. The Crab is a sour Crab if it does not sweeten him. I think it would draw another third volume of Dodsley out of me; but you say you don't want any English books. Perhaps, after all, that's as well; one's romantic credulity is for ever misleading one into misplaced acts of foolery. Crab might have answered by this time: his juices take a long time supplying, but they'll run at last—I know they will—pure golden pippin. A fearful rumour has since reached me that the Crab is on the eve of setting out for France. If he is in England your letter will reach him, and I flatter myself a touch of the persuasive of my own, which accompanies it, will not be thrown away; if it be, he is a sloe, and no true-hearted Crab, and there's an end. For that life of the German conjuror which you speak of, *Colerus de Vitâ Doctoris vix-Intelligibilis*, I perfectly remember the last

evening we spent with Mrs. Morgan and Miss Brent, in London Street,—
(by that token we had raw rabbits for supper, and Miss B. prevailed upon
me to take a glass of brandy and water, which is not my habit),—I perfectly remember reading portions of that life in their parlour, and I think
it must be among their packages. It was the very last evening we were at
that house. What is gone of that frank-hearted circle, Morgan, and his
cos-lettuces? He ate walnuts better than any man I ever knew. Friendships in these parts stagnate.

.   .   .   .   .

I am going to eat turbot, turtle, venison, marrow pudding,—cold punch,
claret, Madeira,—at our annual feast, at half-past four this day. They
keep bothering me (I'm at office), and my ideas are confused. Let me
know if I can be of any service as to books. God forbid the Architectoni-
can should be sacrificed to a foolish scruple of some book proprietor, as if
books did not belong with the highest propriety to those that understand
'em best.   C. LAMB.

To WILLIAM WORDSWORTH.

LETTER CLXXVIII.]   *August* 14, 1814.

Dear Wordsworth—I cannot tell you how pleased I was at the receipt
of the great armful of poetry which you have sent me; and to get it before
the rest of the world too! I have gone quite through with it, and was
thinking to have accomplished that pleasure a second time before I wrote
to thank you, but M. Burney came in the night (while we were out) and
made holy theft of it, but we expect restitution in a day or two. It is the
noblest conversational poem I ever read—a day in Heaven. The part (or
rather main body) which has left the sweetest odour on my memory (a
bad term for the remains of an impression so recent) is the Tales of the
Churchyard; the only girl among seven brethren, born out of due time,
and not duly taken away again,—the deaf man and the blind man;—the
Jacobite and the Hanoverian, whom antipathies reconcile; the Scarron-
entry of the rusticating parson upon his solitude;—these were all new to
me too. My having known the story of Margaret (at the beginning), a
very old acquaintance, even as long back as when I saw you first at Stowey, did not make her reappearance less fresh. I don't know what to pick
out of this best of books upon the best subjects for partial naming. That
gorgeous sunset is famous; I think it must have been the identical one we
saw on Salisbury Plain five years ago, that drew Phillips from the card-
table, where he had sat from rise of that luminary to its unequalled set;
but neither he nor I had gifted eyes to see those symbols of common things
glorified, such as the prophets saw them in that sunset—the wheel, the
potters' clay, the wash-pot, the wine-press, the almond-tree rod, the basket
of figs, the fourfold visaged head, the throne, and Him that sat thereon.
One feeling I was particularly struck with, as what I recognised so very
lately at Harrow Church on entering in it after a hot and secular day's

pleasure, the instantaneous coolness and calming, almost transforming, properties of a country church just entered; a certain fragrance which it has, either from its holiness, or being kept shut all the week, or the air that is let in being pure country, exactly what you have reduced into words; but I am feeling that which I cannot express. Reading your lines about it fixed me for a time, a monument in Harrow Church. Do you know it? with its fine long spire, white as washed marble, to be seen, by vantage of its high site, as far as Salisbury spire itself almost.

I shall select a day or two, very shortly, when I am coolest in brain, to have a steady second reading, which I feel will lead to many more, for it will be a stock book with me while eyes or spectacles shall be lent me. There is a great deal of noble matter about mountain scenery, yet not so much as to overpower and discountenance a poor Londoner or south-countryman entirely, though Mary seems to have felt it occasionally a little too powerfully, for it was her remark during reading it, that by your system it was doubtful whether a liver in towns had a soul to be saved. She almost trembled for that invisible part of us in her.

Save for a late excursion to Harrow, and a day or two on the banks of the Thames this Summer, rural images were fast fading from my mind, and by the wise provision of the Regent, all that was country-fy'd in the Parks is all but obliterated. The very colour of green is vanished; the whole surface of Hyde Park is dry crumbling sand (*Arabia Arenosa*), not a vestige or hint of grass ever having grown there. Booths and drinking-places go all round it for a mile and half, I am confident—I might say two miles in circuit. The stench of liquors, *bad* tobacco, dirty people and provisions, conquers the air, and we are stifled and suffocated in Hyde Park.

Order after order has been issued by Lord Sidmouth in the name of the Regent (acting in behalf of his Royal father) for the dispersion of the varlets, but in vain. The *vis unita* of all the publicans in London, West-minster, Marylebone, and miles round, is too powerful a force to put down. The Regent has raised a phantom which he cannot lay. There they'll stay probably for ever. The whole beauty of the place is gone—that lake-look of the Serpentine—it has got foolish ships upon it; but something whispers to have confidence in Nature and its revival—

> At the coming of the *milder day,*
> These monuments shall all be overgrown.

Meantime I confess to have smoked one delicious pipe in one of the clean-liest and goodliest of the booths; a tent rather—

> "Oh call it not a booth!"

erected by the public spirit of Watson, who keeps the Adam and Eve at Pancras (the ale-houses have all emigrated, with their train of bottles, mugs, corkscrews, waiters, into Hyde Park—whole ale-houses, with all their ale!), in company with some of the Guards that had been in France, and a fine French girl, habited like a princess of banditti, which one of the dogs had transported from the Garonne to the Serpentine. The unusual scene in Hyde Park, by candle-light, in open air,—good tobacco, bottled stout,—made it look like an interval in a campaign, a repose after battle. I almost fancied scars smarting, and was ready to club a story with my comrades of some of my lying deeds. After all, the fireworks were splendid; the rockets in clusters, in trees and all shapes, spreading about like young stars in the making, floundering about in space (like unbroke horses), till some of Newton's calculations should fix them; but then they went out. Any one who could see 'em, and the still finer showers of gloomy rain-fire that fell sulkily and angrily from 'em, and could go to bed without dreaming of the last day, must be as hardened an atheist as . . .

The conclusion of this epistle getting gloomy, I have chosen this part to desire *our* kindest loves to Mrs. Wordsworth and to Dorothea. Will none of you ever be in London again?

Again let me thank you for your present, and assure you that fireworks and triumphs have not distracted me from receiving a calm and noble enjoyment from it (which I trust I shall often), and I sincerely congratulate you on its appearance.

With kindest remembrances to you and your household, we remain, yours sincerely,   C. LAMB and Sister.

To SAMUEL TAYLOR COLERIDGE.

LETTER CLXXIX.]   *August* 26, 1814.

Let the hungry soul rejoice, there is corn in Egypt. Whatever thou hast been told to the contrary by designing friends, who perhaps inquired carelessly, or did not inquire at all, in hope of saving their money, there is a stock of "Remorse" on hand—enough, as Pople conjectures, for seven years' consumption; judging from experience of the last two years. Methinks it makes for the benefit of sound literature, that the best books do not always go off best. Inquire in seven years' time for the *Rokebys* and the *Laras,* and where shall they be found?—fluttering fragmentally in some thread-paper; whereas thy *Wallenstein* and thy *Remorse* are safe on Longman's or Pople's shelves, as in some Bodleian; there they shall remain; no need of a chain to hold them fast—perhaps for ages—tall copies —and people shan't run about hunting for them as in old Ezra's shrievalty they did for a Bible, almost without effect till the great-great-grand-niece (by the mother's side) of Jeremiah or Ezekiel (which was it?) remembered something of a book, with odd reading in it, that used to lie in the green closet in her aunt Judith's bedchamber.

Thy caterer, Price, was at Hamburgh when last Pople heard of him, laying up for thee like some miserly old father for his generous-hearted son to squander.

Mr. Charles Aders, whose books also pant for that free circulation which thy custody is sure to give them, is to be heard of at his kinsmen, Messrs. Jameson and Aders, No. 7, Laurence Pountney Lane, London, according to the information which Crabius with his parting breath left me. Crabius is gone to Paris. I prophesy he and the Parisians will part with mutual contempt. His head has a twist Allemagne, like thine, dear mystic. I have been reading Madame Stael on Germany: an impudent clever woman. But if *Faust* be no better than in her abstract of it, I counsel thee to let it alone. How canst thou translate the language of cat-monkeys? Fie on such fantasies! But I will not forget to look for *Proclus*. It is a kind of book which, when we meet with it, we shut up faster than we opened it. Yet I have some bastard kind of recollection that somewhere, some time ago, upon some stall or other, I saw it. It was either that or *Plotinus*, or Saint Augustine's *City of God*. So little do some folks value, what to others, *sc.* to you, "well used," had been the "Pledge of Immortality." Bishop Bruno I never touched upon. Stuffing too good for the brains of such a "Hare" as thou describest. May it burst his pericranium, as the gobbets of fat and turpentine (a nasty thought of the seer) did that old dragon in the Apocrypha! May he go mad in trying to understand his author! May he lend the third volume of him before he has quite translated the second, to a friend who shall lose it, and so spoil the publication, and may his friend find it and send it him just as thou or some such less dilatory spirit shall have announced the whole for the press. So I think I have answered all thy questions except about Morgan's coslettuce. The first personal peculiarity I ever observed of him (all worthy souls are subject to 'em) was a particular kind of rabbit-like delight in munching salads with oil without vinegar after dinner—a steady contemplative browsing on them—didst never take note of it? Canst think of any other queries in the solution of which I can give thee satisfaction? Do you want any books that I can procure for you? Old Jimmy Boyer is dead at last. Trollope has got his living, worth £1000 a year net. See, thou sluggard, thou heretic-sluggard, what mightest thou not have arrived at! Lay thy animosity against Jimmy in the grave. Do not *entail* it on thy posterity. CHARLES LAMB.

To WILLIAM WORDSWORTH.

LETTER CLXXX.] *August 29, 1814.*

My dear W.—I have scarce time or quiet to explain my present situation, how unquiet and distracted it is, owing to the absence of some of my compeers, and to the deficient state of payments at E. I. H., owing to bad peace speculations in the calico market. (I write this to W. W., Esq., Collector of Stamp Duties for the Conjoint Northern Counties, not to W. W., Poet.) I go back, and have for many days past, to evening work, generally at the rate of nine hours a day. The nature of my work, too, puzzling and hurrying, has so shaken my spirits, that my sleep is nothing but a succession of dreams of business I cannot do, of assistants that give me no assistance, of terrible responsibilities. I reclaimed your book, which Hazlitt has uncivilly kept, only two days ago, and have made shift to read it again with shattered brain. It does not lose—rather some parts have come out with a prominence I did not perceive before—but such was my aching head yesterday (Sunday), that the book was like a mountain landscape to one that should walk on the edge of a precipice; I perceive beauty dizzily. Now, what I would say is, that I see no prospect of a quiet half-day, or hour even, till this week and the next are past. I then hope to get four weeks' absence, and if *then* is time enough to begin, I will most gladly do what is required, though I feel my inability, for my brain is always desultory, and snatches off hints from things, but can seldom follow a "work" methodically. But that shall be no excuse. What I beg you to do is, to let me know from Southey, if that will be time enough for the *Quarterly, i.e.* suppose it done in three weeks from this date (19th Sept.): if not, it is my bounded duty to express my regret, and decline it. Mary thanks you, and feels highly grateful for your "Patent of Nobility," and acknowledges the author of the *Excursion* as the legitimate Fountain of Honour. We both agree that, to our feeling, Ellen is best as she is. To us there would have been something repugnant in her challenging her Penance as a Dowry: the fact is explicable; but how few are those to whom it would have been rendered explicit! The unlucky reason of the detention of the *Excursion* was Hazlitt and we having a misunderstanding. He blowed us up about six months ago, since which the union hath snapt; but M. Burney borrowed it for him, and after reiterated messages I only got it on Friday. His remarks had some vigour in them; particularly something about an old ruin being *too modern for your Primeval Nature* and about *a lichen*. I forget the passage, but the whole wore a slovenly air of despatch. That objection which M. Burney had imbibed from him about Voltaire I explained to M. B. (or tried) exactly on your principle of its being a characteristic speech. That it was no settled comparative estimate of Voltaire with any of his own tribe of buffoons—no injustice, even if *you* spoke it, for I dared say you never could relish *Candide.* I know I tried to get through it about a twelvemonth since, and couldn't for the dulness. Now I think I have a wider range in buffoonery than you. Too much toleration perhaps.

I finish this after a raw ill-baked dinner fast gobbled up to set me off to office again, after working there till near four. Oh how I wish I were a rich man! even though I were squeezed camel-fashion at getting through that needle's eye that is spoken of in the *Written Word.* Apropos; are you a Christian? or is it the Pedler and the Priest that are?

I find I miscalled that celestial splendour of the mist going off, a *sunset.* That only shows my inaccuracy of head.

Do, pray, indulge me by writing an answer to the point of time mentioned above, or *let Southey.* I am ashamed to go bargaining in this way, but indeed I have no time I can reckon on till the first week in October. God send I may not be disappointed in that! Coleridge swore in a letter to me he would review the *Excursion* in the *Quarterly.* Therefore, though *that* shall not stop me, yet if I can do anything *when* done, I must know of him if he has anything ready, or I shall fill the world with loud exclaims.

I keep writing on, knowing the postage is no more for much writing, else so fagged and dispirited I am with cursed India House work, I scarce know what I do. My left arm reposes on the *Excursion.* I feel what it would be in quiet. It is now a sealed book. C. LAMB.

LETTER CLXXXI.] 1814.

Dear W.—Your experience about tailors seems to be in point blank opposition to Burton, as much as the author of the *Excursion* does, *toto cœlo*, differ in his notion of a country life from the picture which W. H. has exhibited of the same. But, with a little explanation, you and B. may be reconciled. It is evident that he confined his observations to the genuine native London tailor. What freaks tailor-nature may take in the country is not for him to give account of. And certainly some of the freaks recorded do give an idea of the persons in question being beside themselves, rather than in harmony with the common, moderate, self-enjoyment of the rest of mankind. A flying tailor, I venture to say, is no more *in rerum naturâ* than a flying horse or a gryphon. His wheeling his airy flight from the precipice you mention had a parallel in the melancholy Jew who toppled from the monument. Were his limbs ever found? Then, the man who cures diseases by words is evidently an inspired tailor. Burton never affirmed that the art of sewing disqualified the practiser of it from being a fit organ for supernatural revelation. He never enters into such subjects. 'Tis the common, uninspired tailor which he speaks of. Again, the person who makes his smiles to be *heard* is evidently a man under possession—a demoniac tailor. A greater hell than his own must have a hand in this. I am not certain that the cause which you advocate has much reason for triumph. You seem to me to substitute light-headedness for light-heartedness by a trick, or not to know the difference. I confess, a grinning tailor would shock me. Enough of tailors!

The " 'scapes" of the great god Pan, who appeared among your mountains some dozen years since, and his narrow chance of being submerged by the swains, afforded me much pleasure. I can conceive the water-nymphs pulling for him. He would have been another Hylas—W. Hylas. In a mad letter which Capel Lofft wrote to M [*onthly*] M [*agazine*] Philips (now Sir Richard), I remember his noticing a metaphysical article on Pan, signed H., and adding, "I take your correspondent to be the same with Hylas." Hylas had put forth a pastoral just before. How near the unfounded conjecture of the certainly inspired Lofft (unfounded as we thought it) was to being realised! I can conceive him being "good to all that wander in that perilous flood." One J. Scott (I know no more) is editor of the *Champion*. Where is Coleridge?

That Review you speak of, I am only sorry it did not appear last month. The circumstances of haste and peculiar bad spirits under which it was written would have excused its slightness and inadequacy, the full load of which I shall suffer from its lying by so long, as it will seem to have done, from its postponement. I write with great difficulty, and can scarce command my own resolution to sit at writing an hour together. I am a poor creature, but I am leaving off gin. I hope you will see good-will in the thing. I had a difficulty to perform not to make it all panegyric; I have attempted to personate a mere stranger to you; perhaps with too much strangeness. But you must bear that in mind when you read it, and not think that I am, in mind, distant from you or your poem, but that both are close to me, among the nearest of persons and things. I do but act the stranger in the Review. Then, I was puzzled about extracts, and determined upon not giving one that had been in the *Examiner;* for extracts repeated give an idea that there is a meagre allowance of good things. By this way, I deprived myself of *Sir Alfred Irthing,* and the reflections that conclude his story, which are the flower of the poem. Hazlitt had given the reflections before me. *Then* it is the first review I ever did, and I did not know how long I might make it. But it must speak for itself, if Gifford and his crew do not put words in its mouth, which I expect. Farewell. Love to all. Mary keeps very bad.   C. LAMB.

LETTER CLXXXII.]   1814.

Dear Wordsworth—I told you my Review was a very imperfect one. But what you will see in the *Quarterly* is a spurious one, which Mr. Baviad Gifford has palmed upon it for mine. I never felt more vexed in my life than when I read it. I cannot give you an idea of what he has done to it, out of spite at me, because he once suffered me to be called a lunatic in his Review. The *language* he has altered throughout. Whatever inadequateness it had to its subject, it was, in point of composition, the prettiest piece of prose I ever writ: and so my sister (to whom alone I read the MS.) said. That charm, if it had any, is all gone: more than a third of the substance is cut away, and that not all from one place, but *passim,* so as to make utter nonsense. Every warm expression is changed for a nasty cold one.

I have not the cursed alteration by me; I shall never look at it again; but for a specimen, I remember I had said the poet of the *Excursion* "walks through common forests as through some Dodona or enchanted wood, and every casual bird that flits upon the boughs, like that miraculous one in Tasso, but in language more piercing than any articulate sounds, reveals to him far higher love-lays." It is now (besides half-a-dozen alterations in the same half-dozen lines) "but in language more *intelligent* reveals to him;"—that is one I remember.

But that would have been little, putting his damn'd shoemaker phraseology (for he was a shoemaker) instead of mine, which has been tinctured with better authors than his ignorance can comprehend;—for I reckon myself a dab at *prose;*—verse I leave to my betters: God help them, if they are to be so reviewed by friend and foe as you have been this quarter! I have read "It won't do." But worse than altering words; he has kept a few members only of the part I had done best, which was to explain all I could of your "Scheme of Harmonies," as I had ventured to call it, between the external universe and what within us answers to it. To do this I had accumulated a good many short passages, rising in length to the end, weaving in the extracts as if they came in as a part of the text naturally, not intruding them as specimens. Of this part a little is left, but so as, without conjuration, no man could tell what I was driving at. A proof of it you may see (though not judge of the whole of the injustice) by these words. I had spoken something about "natural methodism;" and after follows, "and *therefore* the tale of Margaret should have been postponed" (I forget my words, or his words); now the reasons for postponing it are as deducible from what goes before as they are from the 104th Psalm. The passage whence I deduced it has vanished, but clapping a colon before a *therefore* is always reason enough for Mr. Baviad Gifford to allow to a reviewer that is not himself. I assure you my complaints are well founded. I know how sore a word altered makes one; but, indeed, of this review the whole complexion is gone. I regret only that I did not keep a copy. I am sure you would have been pleased with it, because I have been feeding my fancy for some months with the notion of pleasing you. Its imperfection or inadequateness in size and method I knew; but for the *writing part* of it I was fully satisfied; I hoped it would make more than atonement. Ten or twelve distinct passages come to my mind, which are gone; and what is left is, of course, the worse for their having been there; the eyes are pulled out, and the bleeding sockets are left.

I read it at Arch's shop with my face burning with vexation secretly, with just such a feeling as if it had been a review written against myself, making false quotations from me. But I am ashamed to say so much about a short piece. How are *you* served! and the labours of years turned into contempt by scoundrels!

But I could not but protest against your taking that thing as mine. Every *pretty* expression (I know there were many), every warm expression (there was nothing else), is vulgarised and frozen. But if they catch me in their camps again, let them spitchcock me! They had a right to do it, as no name appears to it; and Mr. Shoemaker Gifford, I suppose, never waived a right he had since he commenced author. God confound him and all caitiffs! C. L.

LETTER CLXXXIII.] [1815].

Dear Wordsworth—You have made me very proud with your successive book presents. I have been carefully through the two volumes, to see that nothing was omitted which used to be there. I think I miss nothing but a character in the antithetic manner, which I do not know why you left out,—the moral to the boys building the giant, the omission whereof leaves it, in my mind, less complete,—and one admirable line gone (or something come instead of it), "the stone-chat, and the glancing sandpiper," which was a line quite alive. I demand these at your hand. I am glad that you have not sacrificed a verse to those scoundrels. I would not have had you offer up the poorest rag that lingered upon the stript shoulders of little Alice Fell, to have atoned all their malice; I would not have given 'em a red cloak to save their souls. I am afraid lest that substitution of a shell (a flat falsification of the history) for the household implement, as it stood at first, was a kind of tub thrown out to the beast, or rather thrown out for him. The tub was a good honest tub in its place, and nothing could fairly be said against it. You say you made the alteration for the "friendly reader," but the "malicious" will take it to himself. Damn 'em, if you give 'em an inch, etc. The Preface is noble, and such as you should write. I wish I could set my name to it, *Imprimatur*,—but you have set it there yourself, and I thank you. I would rather be a doorkeeper in your margin, than have their proudest text swelling with my eulogies. The poems in the volumes which are new to me are so much in the old tone that I hardly received them as novelties. Of those of which I had no previous knowledge, the "Four Yew Trees," and the mysterious company which you have assembled there, most struck me—"Death the Skeleton and Time the Shadow." It is a sight not for every youthful poet to dream of; it is one of the last results he must have gone thinking on for years for. "Laodamia" is a very original poem; I mean original with reference to your own manner. You have nothing like it. I should have seen it in a strange place, and greatly admired it, but not suspected its derivation.

Let me in this place, for I have writ you several letters naming it, mention that my brother, who is a picture-collector, has picked up an undoubtable picture of Milton. He gave a few shillings for it, and could get no history with it, but that some old lady had had it for a great many years. Its age is ascertainable from the state of the canvas, and you need only see it to be sure that it is the original of the heads in the Tonson editions, with which we are all so well familiar. Since I saw you I have had a treat in the reading way, which comes not every day, the Latin Poems of V. Bourne, which were quite new to me. What a heart that man had! all laid out upon town schemes, a proper counterpoise to *some people's* rural extravaganzas. Why I mention him is, that your "Power of Music" reminded me of his poem of "The Ballad Singer in the Seven Dials." Do you remember his epigram on the old woman who taught Newton the A B C? which, after all, he says, he hesitates not to call Newton's "Principia." I was lately fatiguing myself with going through a volume of fine words by Lord Thurlow; excellent words; and if the heart could live by words alone, it could desire no better regales; but what an aching vacuum of matter! I don't stick at the madness of it, for that is only a consequence of shutting his eyes and thinking he is in the age of the old Elizabeth poets. From thence I turned to Bourne. What a sweet, unpretending, pretty-mannered, *matter-ful* creature! sucking from every flower, making a flower of everything, his diction all Latin, and his thoughts all English. Bless him! Latin wasn't good enough for him. Why wasn't he content with the language which Gay and Prior wrote in?

I am almost sorry that you printed extracts from those first poems, or that you did not print them at length. They do not read to me as they do altogether. Besides, they have diminished the value of the original, which I possess as a curiosity. I have hitherto kept them distinct in my mind as referring to a particular period of your life. All the rest of your poems are so much of a piece, they might have been written in the same week; these decidedly speak of an earlier period. They tell more of what you had been reading. We were glad to see the poems "by a female friend." The one on the Wind is masterly, but not new to us. Being only three, perhaps you might have clapt a D. at the corner, and let it have past as a printer's mark to the uninitiated, as a delightful hint to the better instructed. As it is, expect a formal criticism on the poems of your female friend, and she must expect it. I should have written before, but I am cruelly engaged, and like to be. On Friday I was at office from ten in the morning (two hours dinner except) to eleven at night; last night till nine. My business and office business in general have increased so; I don't mean I am there every night, but I must expect a great deal of it. I never leave till four, and do not keep a holiday now once in ten times, where I used to kep all red-letter days, and some five days besides, which I used to dub Nature's holidays. I have had my day. I had formerly little to do. So of the little that is left of life, I may reckon two-thirds as dead, for time that a man may call his own is his life; and hard work and thinking about it taints even the leisure hours,—stains Sunday with work-day contemplations. This is Sunday: and the headache I have is part late hours at work the two preceding nights, and part later hours over a consoling pipe afterwards. But I find stupid acquiescence coming over me. I bend to the yoke, and it is almost with me and my household as with the man and his consort—

"To them each evening had its glittering star,
And every Sabbath Day its golden sun"—

to such straits am I driven for the life of life, Time! O that from that superfluity of holiday leisure my youth wasted, "Age might but take some hours youth wanted not!" N.B.—I have left off spirituous liquors for four or more months, with a moral certainty of its lasting. Farewell, dear Wordsworth!

O happy Paris, seat of idleness and pleasure! from some returned English I hear that not such a thing as a counting-house is to be seen in her streets,—scarce a desk. Earthquakes swallow up this mercantile city and its "gripple merchants," as Drayton hath it—"born to be the curse of this brave isle!" I invoke this, not on account of any parsimonious habits the mercantile interest may have, but, to confess truth, because I am not fit for an office.

Farewell, in haste, from a head that is too ill to methodise, a stomach too weak to digest, and all out of tune. Better harmonies await you!

C. LAMB.

LETTER CLXXXIV.]

Excuse this maddish letter: I am too tired to write *in formâ*.

1815.

Dear Wordsworth—The more I read of your last two volumes, the more I feel it necessary to make my acknowledgments for them in more than one short letter. The "Night Piece," to which you refer me, I meant fully to have noticed; but, the fact is, I come so fluttering and languid from business, tired with thoughts of it, frightened with the fears of it, that when I get a few minutes to sit down to scribble (an action of the hand now seldom natural to me—I mean voluntary pen-work) I lose all presential memory of what I had intended to say, and say what I can, talk about Vincent Bourne, or any casual image, instead of that which I had meditated (by the way, I must look out V. B. for you). So I meant to mention "Yarrow Visited," with that stanza, "But thou that didst appear so fair;" than which I think no lovelier stanza can be found in the wide world of poetry;—yet the poem, on the whole, seems condemned to leave behind it a melancholy of imperfect satisfaction, as if you had wronged the feeling with which, in what preceded it, you had resolved never to visit it, and as if the Muse had determined, in the most delicate manner, to make you, and *scarce make you*, feel it. Else, it is far superior to the other, which has but one exquisite verse in it, the last but one, or the last two: this is all fine, except perhaps that *that* of "studious ease and generous cares" has a little tinge of the *less romantic* about it. "The Farmer of Tilsbury Vale" is a charming counterpart to "Poor Susan," with the addition of that delicacy towards aberrations from the strict path, which is so fine in the "Old Thief and the Boy by his side," which always brings water into my eyes. Perhaps it is the worse for being a repetition; "Susan" stood for the representative of poor *Rus in Urbe*. There was quite enough to stamp the moral of the thing never to be forgotten; "bright volumes of vapour," etc. The last verse of Susan was to be got rid of, at all events. It threw a kind of dubiety upon Susan's moral conduct. Susan is a servant maid. I see her trundling her mop, and contemplating the whirling phenomenon through blurred optics; but to term her "a poor outcast" seems as much as to say that poor Susan was no better than she should be, which I trust was not what you meant to express. Robin Goodfellow supports himself without that *stick* of a moral which you have thrown away; but how I can be brought in *felo de omittendo* for that ending to the Boy-builders is a mystery. I can't say positively now,—I only know that no line oftener or readier occurs than that "Light-hearted boys, I will build up a Giant with you." It comes naturally, with a warm holiday, and the freshness of the blood. It is a perfect summer amulet, that I tie round my legs to quicken their motion when I go out a maying. (*N.B.*) I don't often go out a *may*ing;—*must* is the tense with me now. Do you take the pun? Young Romilly is divine; the reasons of his mother's grief being remediless. I never saw parental love carried up so high, towering above the other loves. Shakspeare had done something for the filial, in Cordelia, and, by implication, for the fatherly too, in Lear's resentment; he left it for you to explore the depths of the maternal heart. I get stupid, and flat, and flattering. What's the use of telling you what good things you have written, or—I hope I may add—that I know them to be good? Apropos— when I first opened upon the just mentioned poem, in a careless tone, I said to Mary, as if putting a riddle, *"What is good for a bootless bene?"* To which, with infinite presence of mind (as the jest-book has it), she answered, "a shoeless pea." It was the first joke she ever made. Joke the second I make. You distinguish well, in your old preface, between the verses of Dr. Johnson, of the "Man in the Strand," and those from "The

Babes in the Wood." I was thinking, whether taking your own glorious lines—

"And from the love which was in her soul
For her youthful Romilly,"

which, by the love I bear my own soul, I think have no parallel in any of the best old ballads, and just altering them to—

"And from the great respect she felt
For Sir Samuel Romilly,"

would not have explained the boundaries of prose expression, and poetic feeling, nearly as well. Excuse my levity on such an occasion. I never felt deeply in my life if that poem did not make me feel, both lately and when I read it in MS. No alderman ever longed after a haunch of buck venison more than I for a spiritual taste of that "White Doe" you promise. I am sure it is superlative, or will be when *drest, i.e.* printed. All things read raw to me in MS.; to compare *magna parvis,* I cannot endure my own writings in that state. The only one which I think would not very much win upon me in print is "Peter Bell." But I am not certain. You ask me about your preface. I like both that and the supplement, without an exception. The account of what you mean by imagination is very valuable to me. It will help me to like some things in poetry better, which is a little humiliating in me to confess. I thought I could not be instructed in that science (I mean the critical), as I once heard old obscene, beastly Peter Pindar, in a dispute on Milton, say he thought that if he had reason to value himself upon one thing more than another, it was in knowing what good verse was. Who looked over your proof sheets and left *ordebo* in that line of Virgil?

My brother's picture of Milton is very finely painted; that is, it might have been done by a hand next to Vandyke's. It is the genuine Milton, and an object of quiet gaze for the half-hour at a time. Yet though I am confident there is no better one of him, the face does not quite answer to Milton. There is a tinge of *petit* (or *petite,* how do you spell it?) querulousness about it; yet, hang it! now I remember better, there is not; it is calm, melancholy, and poetical. *One* of the copies of the poems you sent has precisely the same pleasant blending of a sheet of second volume with a sheet of first. I think it was page 245; but I sent it and had it rectified. It gave me in the first impetus of cutting the leaves, just such a cold squelch as going down a plausible turning and suddenly reading "No thoroughfare!" Robinson's is entire: I wish you would write more criticism about Spenser, etc. I think I could say something about him myself; but, Lord bless me! these "merchants and their spicy drugs," which are so harmonious to sing of, they lime-twig up my poor soul and body, till I shall forget I ever thought myself a bit of a genius! I can't even put a few thoughts on paper for a newspaper. I "engross" when I should "pen" a paragraph. Confusion blast all mercantile transactions, all traffic, exchange of commodities, intercourse between nations, all the consequent civilisation, and wealth, and amity, and link of society, and getting rid of prejudices, and getting a knowledge of the face of the globe; and rotting the very firs of the forest, that look so romantic alive, and die into desks! *Vale.*

Yours, dear W., and all yours,   C. LAMB.

To ROBERT SOUTHEY.

LETTER CLXXXV.]   *London, May 6, 1815.*

Dear Southey—I have received from Longman a copy of *Roderick*, with the Author's Compliments, for which I much thank you. I don't know where I shall put all the noble presents I have lately received in that way: the *Excursion*, Wordsworth's two last vols., and now *Roderick*, have come pouring in upon me like some irruption from Helicon. The story of the brave Maccabee was already, you may be sure, familiar to me in all its parts. I have, since the receipt of your present, read it quite through again, and with no diminished pleasure. I don't know whether I ought to say that it has given me more pleasure than any of your long poems. *Kehama* is doubtless more powerful, but I don't feel that firm footing in it that I do in *Roderick:* my imagination goes sinking and floundering in the vast spaces of unopened-before systems and faiths; I am put out of the pale of my old sympathies; my moral sense is almost outraged; I can't believe, or with horror am made to believe, such desperate chances against Omnipotence, such disturbances of faith to the centre; the more potent the more painful the spell. Jove, and his brotherhood of gods, tottering with the giant assailings, I can bear, for the soul's hopes are not struck at in such contests; but your Oriental almighties are too much types of the intangible prototype to be meddled with without shuddering. One never connects what are called the attributes with Jupiter.—I mention only what diminishes my delight at the wonder-workings of *Kehama*, not what impeaches its power, which I confess with trembling; but *Roderick* is a comfortable poem. It reminds me of the delight I took in the first reading of the *Joan of Arc*. It is maturer and better than *that*, though not better to me now than that was then. It suits me better than *Madoc*. I am at home in Spain and Christendom. I have a timid imagination, I am afraid. I do not willingly admit of strange beliefs, or out-of-the-way creeds or places. I never read books of travels, at least not farther than Paris or Rome. I can just endure Moors, because of their connection as foes with Christians; but Abyssinians, Ethiops, Esquimaux, Dervises, and all that tribe, I hate. I believe I fear them in some manner. A Mahometan turban on the stage, though enveloping some well-known face (Mr. Cook or Mr. Maddox, whom I see another day good Christian and English waiters, innkeepers, etc.), does not give me pleasure unalloyed. I am a Christian, Englishman, Londoner, *Templar.* God help me when I come to put off these snug relations, and to get abroad into the world to come! I shall be like *the crow on the sand,* as Wordsworth has it; but I won't think on it: no need, I hope, yet.

The parts I have been most pleased with, both on first and second readings, perhaps, are Florinda's palliation of Roderick's crime, confessed to him in his disguise—the retreat of the Palayos family first discovered—his being made king—"For acclamation one form must serve *more solemn for the breach* of *old observances.*" Roderick's vow is extremely fine, and his blessing on the vow of Alphonso:

> "Towards the troop he spread his arms,
> As if the expanded soul diffused itself,
> And carried to all spirits *with the act*
> Its affluent inspiration."

It struck me forcibly that the feeling of these last lines might have been suggested to you by the Cartoon of Paul at Athens. Certain it is that a better motto or guide to that famous attitude can nowhere be found. I shall adopt it as explanatory of that violent but dignified motion. I must read again Landor's *Julian.* I have not read it some time. I think he must have failed in Roderick, for I remember nothing of him, nor of any distinct character as a character—only fine-sounding passages. I remember thinking also he had chosen a point of time after the event, as it were, for Roderick survives to no use; but my memory is weak, and I will not wrong a fine poem by trusting to it.

The notes to your poem I have not read again: but it will be a take-downable book on my shelf, and they will serve sometimes at breakfast, or times too light for the text to be duly appreciated. Though some of 'em —one of the serpent penance—is serious enough, now I think on't. Of Coleridge I hear nothing, nor of the Morgans. I hope to have him like a reappearing star, standing up before me some time when least expected in London, as has been the case whilere.

I am *doing* nothing (as the phrase is) but reading presents, and walk away what of the day hours I can get from hard occupation. Pray accept once more my hearty thanks, and expression of pleasure for your remembrance of me. My sister desires her kind respects to Mrs. S. and to all at Keswick.

Yours truly, C. Lamb.

The next present I look for is the *White Doe.*

Have you seen Mat. Betham's *Lay of Marie?* I think it very delicately pretty as to sentiment, etc.

R. Southey, Esq.,
 Keswick, near Penrith,
  Cumberland.

Letter CLXXXVI.] *August 9, 1815.*

Dear Southey—Robinson is not on the circuit, as I erroneously stated in a letter to W. W., which travels with this, but is gone to Brussels, Ostend, Ghent, etc. But his friends, the Colliers, whom I consulted respecting your friend's fate, remember to have heard him say Father Pardo had effected his escape (the cunning greasy rogue!), and to the best of their belief is at present in Paris. To my thinking, it is a small matter whether there be one fat friar more or less in the world. I have rather a taste for clerical executions, imbibed from early recollections of the fate of the excellent Dodd. I hear Buonaparte has sued his habeas corpus, and the twelve judges are now sitting upon it at the Rolls.

Your boute-feu (bonfire) must be excellent of its kind. Poet Settle presided at the last great thing of the kind in London, when the pope was burnt in form. Do you provide any verses on this occasion? Your fear for Hartley's intellectuals is just and rational. Could not the Chancellor be petitioned to remove him? His lordship took Mr. Betty from under the paternal wing. I think at least he should go through a course of matter-of-fact with some sober man after the mysteries. Could not he spend a week at Poole's before he goes back to Oxford? Tobin is dead. But there is a man in my office, a Mr. Hedges, who proses it away from morning to night, and never gets beyond corporal and material verities. He'd get these crack-brain metaphysics out of the young gentleman's head as soon as any one I know. When I can't sleep o' nights, I imagine a dialogue with Mr. Hedges, upon any given subject, and go prosing on in fancy with him, till I either laugh or fall asleep. I have literally found it answer. I am going to stand godfather; I don't like the business; I cannot muster up decorum for these occasions; I shall certainly disgrace the font. I was at Hazlitt's marriage, and had like to have been turned out several times during the ceremony. Anything awful makes me laugh. I misbehaved once at a funeral. Yet I can read about those ceremonies with pious and proper feelings. The realities of life only seem the mockeries. I fear I must get cured along with Hartley, if not too inveterate. Don't you think Louis the Desirable is in a sort of quandary?

After all, Buonaparte is a fine fellow, as my barber says, and I should not mind standing bareheaded at his table to do him service in his fall. They should have given him Hampton Court or Kensington, with a tether extending forty miles round London. Qu. Would not the people have ejected the Brunswicks some day in his favour? Well, we shall see.

C. Lamb.

To WILLIAM WORDSWORTH.

Letter CLXXXVII.]   *August* 9, 1815.

Dear Wordsworth—We acknowledge with pride the receipt of both your handwritings, and desire to be ever had in kindly remembrance by you both and by Dorothy. Alsager, whom you call Alsinger (and indeed he is rather *singer* than *sager*, no reflection upon his naturals neither), is well, and in harmony with himself and the world. I don't know how he, and those of his constitution, keep their nerves so nicely balanced as they do. Or, have they any? Or, are they made of packthread? He is proof against weather, ingratitude, meat underdone, every weapon of fate. I have just now a jagged end of a tooth pricking against my tongue, which meets it half way, in a wantonness of provocation; and there they go at it, the tongue pricking itself, like the viper against the file, and the tooth galling all the gum inside and out to torture; tongue and tooth, tooth and tongue, hard at it; and I to pay the reckoning, till all my mouth is as hot as brimstone; and I'd venture the roof of my mouth, that at this moment, at which I conjecture my full-happiness'd friend is picking his crackers, not one of the double rows of ivory in his privileged mouth has as much as a flaw in it, but all perform their functions, and, having performed them, expect to be picked (luxurious steeds!), and rubbed down. I don't think he could be robbed, or have the house set on fire, or ever want money. I have heard him express a similar opinion of his own impassibility. I keep acting here Heautontimorumenos.

Mr. Burney has been to Calais, and has come a travelled Monsieur. He speaks nothing but the Gallic Idiom. Field is on circuit. So now I believe I have given account of most that you saw at our Cabin.

Have you seen a curious letter in the *Morning Chronicle*, by C. L. [Capell Lofft,] the genius of absurdity, respecting Buonaparte's suing out his Habeas Corpus? That man is his own moon. He has no need of ascending into that gentle planet for mild influences.

Mary and I felt quite queer after your taking leave (you W. W.) of us in St. Giles's. We wish we had seen more of you, but felt we had scarce been sufficiently acknowledging for the share we had enjoyed of your company. We felt as if we had been not enough *expressive* of our pleasure. But our manners *both* are a little too much on this side of too-much-cordiality. We want presence of mind and presence of heart. What we feel comes too late, like an afterthought impromptu. But perhaps you observed nothing of that which we have been painfully conscious of, and are every day in our intercourse with those we stand affected to through all the degrees of love. Robinson is on the circuit. Our panegyrist I thought had forgotten one of the objects of his youthful admiration, but I was agreeably removed from that scruple by the laundress knocking at my door this morning, almost before I was up, with a present of fruit from my young friend, etc. There is something inexpressibly pleasant to me in these *presents,* be it fruit, or fowl, or brawn, or *what not.* Books are a legitimate cause of acceptance. If presents be not the soul of friendship, undoubtedly they are the most spiritual part of the body of that intercourse. There is too much narrowness of thinking in this point. The punctilio of acceptance, methinks, is too confined and strait-laced. I could be content to receive money, or clothes, or a joint of meat from a friend. Why should he not send me a dinner as well as a dessert? I would taste him in the beasts of the field, and through all creation. Therefore did the basket of fruit of the juvenile Talfourd not displease me; not that I have any thoughts of bartering or reciprocating these things. To send him anything in return, would be to reflect suspicion of mercenariness upon what I know he meant a freewill offering. Let him overcome me in bounty. In this strife a generous nature loves to be overcome. You wish me some of your leisure. I have a glimmering aspect, a chink-light of liberty before me, which I pray God may prove not fallacious. My remonstrances have stirred up others to remonstrate, and altogether, there is a plan for separating certain parts of business from our department; which, if it take place, will produce me more time, *i.e.* my evenings free. It may be a means of placing me in a more conspicuous situation, which will knock at my nerves another way, but I wait the issue in submission. If I can but begin my own day at four o'clock in the afternoon, I shall think myself to have Eden days of peace and liberty to what I have had. As you say, how a man can fill three volumes up with an essay on the drama is wonderful; I am sure a very few sheets would hold all I had to say on the subject.

Did you ever read "Charron on Wisdom"? or "Patrick's Pilgrim"? If neither, you have two great pleasures to come. I mean some day to attack Caryl on Job, six folios. What any man can write, surely I may read. If I do but get rid of auditing warehousekeepers' accounts and get no worse-harassing task in the place of it, what a lord of liberty I shall be! I shall dance and skip, and make mouths at the invisible event, and pick the thorns out of my pillow, and throw 'em at rich men's night-caps, and talk blank verse, hoity-toity, and sing—"A clerk I was in London gay," "Ban, ban, Ca-Caliban," like the emancipated monster, and go where I like, up this street or down that alley. Adieu, and pray that it may be my luck.

Good-bye to you all.   C. LAMB.

To MISS HUTCHINSON.

LETTER CLXXXVIII.]   *Thursday, October* 19, 1815.

Dear Miss H.—I am forced to be the replier to your letter, for Mary has been ill, and gone from home these five weeks yesterday. She has left me very lonely and very miserable. I stroll about, but there is no rest but at one's own fireside, and there is no rest for me there now. I look forward to the worse half being past, and keep up as well as I can. She has begun to show some favourable symptoms. The return of her disorder has been frightfully soon this time, with scarce a six months' interval. I am almost afraid my worry of spirits about the E. I. House was partly the cause of her illness, but one always imputes it to the cause next at hand; more probably it comes from some cause we have no control over or conjecture of. It cuts sad great slices out of the time, the little time, we shall have to live together. I don't know but the recurrence of these illnesses might help me to sustain her death better than if we had had no partial separations. But I won't talk of death. I will imagine us immortal, or forget that we are otherwise. By God's blessing, in a few weeks we may be making our meal together, or sitting in the front row of the Pit at Drury Lane, or taking our evening walk past the theatres, to look at the outside of them, at least, if not to be tempted in. Then we forget we are assailable; we are strong for the time as rocks;—"the wind is tempered to the shorn Lambs." Poor C. Lloyd, and poor Priscilla! I feel I hardly feel enough for him; my own calamities press about me, and involve me in a thick integument not to be reached at by other folks' misfortunes. But I feel all I can—all the kindness I can, towards you all —God bless you! I hear nothing from Coleridge.

Yours truly, C. Lamb.

To THOMAS MANNING.

Letter CLXXXIX.] *December 25, 1815.*

Dear old Friend and absentee—This is Christmas Day 1815 with us; what it may be with you I don't know, the 12th of June next year perhaps; and if it should be the consecrated season with you, I don't see how you can keep it. You have no turkeys; you would not desecrate the festival by offering up a withered Chinese bantam, instead of the savoury grand Norfolcian holocaust, that smokes all around my nostrils at this moment from a thousand firesides. Then what puddings have you? Where will you get holly to stick in your churches, or churches to stick your dried tea-leaves (that must be the substitute) in? What memorials you can have of the holy time, I see not. A chopped missionary or two may keep up the thin idea of Lent and the wilderness; but what standing evidence have you of the Nativity? 'Tis our rosy-cheeked, homestalled divines, whose faces shine to the tune of "Unto us a child was born," faces fragrant with the mince-pies of half a century, that alone can authenticate the cheerful mystery. I feel my bowels refreshed with the holy tide; my zeal is great against the unedified heathen. Down with the Pagodas —down with the idols—Ching-chong-fo—and his foolish priesthood! Come out of Babylon, O my friend! for her time is come; and the child that is native, and the Proselyte of her gates, shall kindle and smoke together! And in sober sense what makes you so long from among us, Manning? You must not expect to see the same England again which you left.

Empires have been overturned, crowns trodden into dust, the face of the western world quite changed. Your friends have all got old—those you left blooming; myself (who am one of the few that remember you), those golden hairs which you recollect my taking a pride in, turned to silvery and gray. Mary has been dead and buried many years: she desired to be buried in the silk gown you sent her. Rickman, that you remember active and strong, now walks out supported by a servant maid and a stick. Martin Burney is a very old man. The other day an aged woman knocked at my door, and pretended to my acquaintance. It was long before I had the most distant cognition of her; but at last, together, we made her out to be Louisa, the daughter of Mrs. Topham, formerly Mrs. Morton, who had been Mrs. Reynolds, formerly Mrs. Kenney, whose first husband was Holcroft, the dramatic writer of the last century. St. Paul's Church is a heap of ruins; the Monument isn't half so high as you knew it, divers parts being successively taken down which the ravages of time had rendered dangerous; the horse at Charing Cross is gone, no one knows whither; and all this has taken place while you have been settling whether Ho-hing-tong should be spelt with a ——, or a ——. For aught I see you might almost as well remain where you are, and not come like a Struldbrug into a world were few were born when you went away. Scarce here and there one will be able to make out your face. All your opinions will be out of date, your jokes obsolete, your puns rejected with fastidiousness as wit of the last age. Your way of mathematics has already given way to a new method, which after all is I believe the old doctrine of Maclaurin, new-vamped up with what he borrowed of the negative quantity of fluxions from Euler.

Poor Godwin! I was passing his tomb the other day in Cripplegate churchyard. There are some verses upon it written by Miss ——, which if I thought good enough I would send you. He was one of those who would have hailed your return, not with boisterous shouts and clamours, but with the complacent gratulations of a philosopher anxious to promote knowledge as leading to happiness; but his systems and his theories are ten feet deep in Cripplegate mould. Coleridge is just dead, having lived just long enough to close the eyes of Wordsworth, who paid the debt to Nature but a week or two before. Poor Col., but two days before he died he wrote to a bookseller, proposing an epic poem on the "Wanderings of Cain," in twenty-four books. It is said he has left behind him more than forty thousand treatises in criticism, metaphysics, and divinity, but few of them in a state of completion. They are now destined, perhaps, to wrap up spices. You see what mutations the busy hand of Time has produced, while you have consumed in foolish voluntary exile that time which might have gladdened your friends—benefited your country; but reproaches are useless. Gather up the wretched reliques, my friends, as fast as you can, and come to your old home. I will rub my eyes and try to recognise you. We will shake withered hands together, and talk of old things—of St. Mary's Church and the barber's opposite, where the young students in mathematics used to assemble. Poor Crips, that kept it afterwards, set up a fruiterer's shop in Trumpington Street, and for aught I know resides there still, for I saw the name up in the last journey I took there with my sister just before she died. I suppose you heard that I had left the India House, and gone into the Fishmongers' Almshouses over the bridge. I have a little cabin there, small and homely, but you shall be welcome to it. You like oysters, and to open them yourself; I'll get you some if you come in oyster time. Marshall, Godwin's old friend, is still alive, and talks of the faces you used to make.

Come as soon as you can.   C. LAMB.

LETTER CXC.]   *December* 26, 1815.

Dear Manning—Following your brother's example, I have just ventured one letter to Canton, and am now hazarding another (not exactly a duplicate) to St. Helena. The first was full of unprobable romantic fictions, fitting the remoteness of the mission it goes upon; in the present I mean to confine myself nearer to truth as you come nearer home. A correspondence with the uttermost parts of the earth necessarily involves in it some heat of fancy; it sets the brain agoing, but I can think on the half-way house tranquilly. Your friends then are not all dead or grown forgetful of you through old age, as that lying letter asserted, anticipating rather what must happen if you kept tarrying on for ever on the skirts of creation, as there seemed a danger of your doing; but they are all tolerably well and in full and perfect comprehension of what is meant by Manning's coming home again. Mrs. Kenney never lets her tongue run riot more than in remembrances of you. Fanny expends herself in phrases that can only be justified by her romantic nature. Mary reserves a portion of your silk, not to be buried in (as the false nuncio asserts), but to make up spick and span into a bran-new gown to wear when you come. I am the same as when you knew me, almost to a surfeiting identity. This very night I am going to *leave off tobacco!* Surely there must be some other world in which this unconquerable purpose shall be realised. The soul hath not her generous aspirings implanted in her in vain. One that you knew, and I think the only one of those friends we knew much of in common, has died in earnest. Poor Priscilla! Her brother Robert is also dead, and several of the grown-up brothers and sisters, in the compass of a very few years. Death has not otherwise meddled much in families that I know. Not but he has his eye upon us, and is whetting his feathered dart every instant, as you see him truly pictured in that impressive moral picture, "The good man at the hour of death." I have in trust to put in the post four letters from Diss, and one from Lynn, to St. Helena, which I hope will accompany this safe, and one from Lynn, and the one before spoken of from me, to Canton. But we all hope that these letters may be waste paper. I don't know why I have forborne writing so long; but it is such a forlorn hope to send a scrap of paper straggling over wide oceans! And yet I know, when you come home, I shall have you sitting before me at our fireside just as if you had never been away. In such an instant does the return of a person dissipate all the weight of imaginary perplexity from distance of time and space! I'll promise you good oysters. Corry is dead that kept the shop opposite St. Dunstan's; but the tougher materials of the shop survive the perishing frame of its keeper. Oysters continue to flourish there under as good auspices. Poor Corry! but if you will absent yourself twenty years together, you must not expect numerically the same population to congratulate your return which wetted the sea-beach with their tears when you went away. Have you recovered the breathless stone-staring astonishment into which you must have been thrown upon learning at landing that an Emperor of France was living in St. Helena? What an event in the solitude of the seas! like finding a fish's bone at the top of Plinlimmon; but these things are nothing in our western world. Novelties cease to affect. Come and try what your presence can.

God bless you.—Your old friend,   C. LAMB.

To WILLIAM WORDSWORTH.

LETTER CXCI.]   *April* 9, 1816.

Dear Wordsworth—Thanks for the books you have given me and for all the books you mean to give me. I will bind up the Political Sonnets and Ode according to your suggestion. I have not bound the poems yet. I wait till people have done borrowing them. I think I shall get a chain and chain them to my shelves, *more Bodleiano*, and people may come and read them at chain's length. For of those who borrow, some read slow; some mean to read but don't read; and some neither read nor meant to read, but borrow to leave you an opinion of their sagacity. I must do my money-borrowing friends the justice to say that there is nothing of this caprice or wantonness of alienation in them. When they borrow my money they never fail to make use of it. Coleridge has been here about a fortnight. His health is tolerable at present, though beset with temptations. In the first place, the Covent Garden Manager has declined accepting his Tragedy, though (having read it) I see no reason upon earth why it might not have run a very fair chance, thought it certainly wants a prominent part for a Miss O'Neil or a Mr. Kean. However, he is going to-day to write to Lord Byron to get it to Drury. Should you see Mrs. C., who has just written to C. a letter, which I have given him, it will be as well to say nothing about its fate, till some answer is shaped from Drury. He has two volumes printing together at Bristol, both finished as far as the composition goes; the latter containing his fugitive poems, the former his Literary Life. Nature, who conducts every creature, by instinct, to its best end, has skilfully directed C. to take up his abode at a Chemist's Laboratory in Norfolk Street. She might as well have sent a *Helluo Librorum* for cure to the Vatican. God keep him inviolate among the traps and pitfalls! He has done pretty well as yet.

Tell Miss H[utchinson] my sister is every day wishing to be quietly sitting down to answer her very kind letter, but while C. stays she can hardly find a quiet time; God bless him!

Tell Mrs. W. her postscripts are always agreeable. They are so legible too. Your manual-graphy is terrible, dark as Lycophron. "Likelihood," for instance, is thus typified . . . . I should not wonder if the constant making out of such paragraphs is the cause of that weakness in Mrs. W.'s eyes, as she is tenderly pleased to express it. Dorothy, I hear, has mounted spectacles; so you have deoculated two of your dearest relations in life. Well, God bless you, and continue to give you power to write with a finger of power upon our hearts what you fail to impress in corresponding lucidness, upon our outward eye-sight!

Mary's love to all; she is quite well.

I am called off to do the deposits on Cotton Wool; but why do I relate this to you, who want faculties to comprehend the great mystery of deposits, of interests, of warehouse rent, and contingent fund? Adieu!

                                                    C. LAMB.

A longer letter when C. is gone back into the country, relating his success, etc.—*my* judgment of *your* new books, etc. etc.—I am scarce quiet enough while he stays.

Yours again,   C. L.

LETTER CXCII.]   *Accountant's Office, April* 26, 1816.

Dear W.—I have just finished the pleasing task of correcting the revise of the poems and letter. I hope they will come out faultless. One blunder I saw and shuddered at. The hallucinating rascal had printed *battered* for *battened,* this last not conveying any distinct sense to his gaping soul. The Reader (as they call 'em) had discovered it, and given it the marginal brand, but the substitutory *n* had not yet appeared. I accompanied his notice with a most pathetic address to the printer not to neglect the correction. I know how such a blunder would "batter at your peace." With regard to the works, the Letter I read with unabated satisfaction. Such a thing was wanted—called for. The parallel of Cotton with Burns I heartily approve. Izaak Walton hallows any page in which his reverend name appears. "Duty archly bending to purposes of general benevolence" is exquisite. The poems I endeavoured not to understand, but to read them with my eye alone, and I think I succeeded. (Some people will do that when they come out, you'll say.) As if I were to luxuriate to-morrow at some picture gallery I was never at before, and going by to-day by chance, found the door open, and had but five minutes to look about me, peeped in; just such a *chastised* peep I took with my mind at the lines my luxuriating eye was coursing over unrestrained, not to anticipate another day's fuller satisfaction. Coleridge is printing "Christabel," by Lord Byron's recommendation to Murray, with what he calls a vision, "Kubla Khan," which said vision he repeats so enchantingly that it irradiates and brings heaven and elysian bowers into my parlour while he sings or says it; but there is an observation, "Never tell thy dreams," and I am almost afraid that "Kubla Khan" is an owl that won't bear daylight. I fear lest it should be discovered by the lantern of typography and clear reducting to letters no better than nonsense or no sense. When I was young I used to chant with ecstasy "MILD ARCADIANS EVER BLOOMING," till somebody told me it was meant to be nonsense. Even yet I have a lingering attachment to it, and I think it better than "Windsor Forest," "Dying Christian's Address," etc. Coleridge has sent his tragedy to D[rury] L[ane] T[heatre]. It cannot be acted this season; and by their manner of receiving, I hope he will be able to alter it to make them accept it for next. He is, at present, under the medical care of a Mr. Gillman (Killman?) a Highgate apothecary, where he plays at leaving off laud—m. I think his essentials not touched: he is very bad; but then he wonderfully picks up another day, and his face, when he repeats his verses, hath its ancient glory; an archangel a little damaged. Will Miss H. pardon our not replying at length to her kind letter? We are not quiet enough; Morgan is with us every day, going betwixt Highgate and the Temple. Coleridge is absent but four miles, and the neighbourhood of such a man is as exciting as the presence of fifty ordinary persons. 'Tis enough to be within the whiff and wind of his genius for us not to possess our souls in quiet. If I lived with him or the Author of the *Excursion*, I should, in a very little time, lose my own identity, and be dragged along in the current of other people's thoughts, hampered in a net. How cool I sit in this office, with no possible interruption further than what I may term *material!* There is not as much metaphysics in thirty-six of the people here as there is in the first page of Locke's "Treatise on the Human Understanding," or as much poetry as in any ten lines of the "Pleasures of Hope," or more natural "Beggar's Petition." I never entangle myself in any of their speculations. Interruptions, if I try to write a letter even, I have dreadful. Just now, within four lines, I was called off for ten minutes to consult dusty old books for the settlement of obsolete errors. I hold you a guinea you don't find the chasm where I left off, so excellently the wounded sense closed again and was healed.

N.B.—Nothing said above to the contrary, but that I hold the personal presence of the two mentioned potent spirits at a rate as high as any; but I pay dearer. What amuses others robs me of myself: my mind is positively discharged into their greater currents, but flows with a willing violence. As to your question about work, it is far less oppressive to me than it was, from circumstances. It takes all the golden part of the day away, a solid lump, from ten to four; but it does not kill my peace as before. Some day or other I shall be in a taking again. My head aches, and you have had enough. God bless you!   C. Lamb.

To Miss MATILDA BETHAM.

Letter CXCIII.]   *East India House, June 1, 1816.*

Dear Miss Betham—All this while I have been tormenting myself with the thought of having been ungracious to you, and you have been all the while accusing yourself. Let us absolve one another, and be quiet. My head is in such a state from incapacity for business that I certainly know it to be my duty not to undertake the veriest trifle in addition. I hardly know how I can go on. I have tried to get some redress by explaining my health, but with no great success. No one can tell how ill I am because it does not come out to the exterior of my face, but lies in my skull, deep and invisible. I wish I was leprous, and black jaundiced skin over, and that all was as well within as my cursed looks. You must not think me worse than I am. I am determined not to be overset, but to give up business rather, and get 'em to allow me a trifle for services past. Oh! that I had been a shoemaker, or a baker, or a man of large independent fortune! Oh! darling laziness! heaven of Epicurus! Saint's Everlasting Rest! that I could drink vast potations of thee thro' unmeasured Eternity—Otium *cum,* vel *sine* dignitate. Scandalous, dishonourable—any kind of *repose.* I stand not upon the dignified sort. Accursed, damned desks, trade, commerce, business! Inventions of the old original busy-body, brain-working Satan—Sabbathless, restless Satan! A curse relieves: do you ever try it?

A strange letter to write to a lady; but more honeyed sentences will not distil. I dare not ask who revises in my stead. I have drawn you into a scrape and am ashamed; but I know no remedy. My unwellness must be my apology. God bless you (tho' He curse the India House, and fire it *to the ground*), and may no unkind error creep into "Marie"! May all its readers like it as well as I do, and everybody about you like its kind author no worse! Why the devil am I never to have a chance of scribbling my own free thoughts, verse or prose, again? Why must I write of tea and drugs, and price goods and the bales of indigo? Farewell.

C. LAMB.

Mary goes to her place on Sunday—I mean your maid, foolish Mary; she wants a very little brains only to be an excellent servant; she is excellently calculated for the country, where nobody has brains.

Have you seen "Christabel" since its publication?

To H. DODWELL.

LETTER CXCIV.]   *July* 1816.

My dear fellow—I have been in a lethargy this long while, and forgotten London, Westminster, Marybone, Paddington—they all went clean out of my head, till happening to go to a neighbor's in this good borough of Calne, for want of whist players, we fell upon *Commerce:* the word awoke me to a remembrance of my professional avocations and the long-continued strife which I have been these 24 years endeavoring to compose between those grand Irreconcileables Cash and Commerce; I instantly called for an almanack, which with some difficulty was procured at a fortuneteller's in the vicinity (for the happy holyday people here having nothing to do, keep no account of time), and found that by dint of duty I must attend in Leadenhall on Wednesy. morning next, and shall attend accordingly. Does Master Hannah give macaroons still, and does he fetch the Cobbetts from my Attic? Perhaps it wouldn't be too much trouble for him to drop the inclosed up at my aforesaid Chamber, and any letters, etc., with it; but the inclosed should go without delay. *N.B.*—He isn't to fetch Monday's Cobbett, but it is to wait my reading when I come back. Heigh Ho! Lord have mercy upon me, how many does two and two make? I am afraid I shall make a poor clerk in future, I am spoiled with rambling among haycocks and cows and pigs. Bless me! I had like to have forgot (the air is so temperate and oblivious here) to say I have seen your brother, and hope he is doing well in the finest spot of the world. More of these things when I return. Remember me to the gentlemen,—I forget names. Shall I find all my letters at my rooms on Tuesday? If you forgot to send 'em never mind, for I don't much care for reading and writing now; I shall come back again by degrees, I suppose, into my former habits. How is Bruce de Ponthieu, and Porcher and Co.?—the tears come into my eyes when I think how long I have neglected ——.

Adieu! ye fields, ye shepherds and—herdesses, and dairies and creampots, and fairies and dances upon the green.

I come, I come. Don't drag me so hard by the hair of my head, Genius of British India! I know my hour is come, Faustus must give up his soul, O Lucifer, O Mephistopheles! Can you make out what all this letter is about? I am afraid to look it over.　　　　　　　　　Ch. Lamb.

　　Calne, Wilts, Friday,
July something, old style, 1816.

No new style here, all the styles are old, and some of the gates too for that matter.

[Addressed] H. Dodwell, Esq.,
　　　　　　India House, London.
In his absence may be opened by Mr. Chambers.

To JOHN RICKMAN.

Letter CXCV.]　　　　　　　　　　　December 30, 1816.

Dear R.—Your goose found her way into our Larder with infinite discretion. Judging by her Giblets which we have sacrificed first, she is a most sensible Bird. Mary bids me say, first, that she thanks you for your remembrance, next that Mr. Norris and his family are no less indebted to you as the cause of his reverend and amiable visage being perpetuated when his Soul is flown. Finding nothing like a Subscription going on for the unhappy Lady, and not knowing how to press an actual Sum upon her, she hit upon the expedient of making believe that Mr. N. wanted his miniature (which his chops did seem to water after, I must confess, when 'twas first proposed, though with a *Nolo Pingier* for modesty), and the likeness being completed, your £5 is to go as from him. This I must confess is robbing Peter, or like the equitable distribution in Alexander's Feast, "Love was crowned" though somebody else "won the cause." And Love himself, smiling Love, he might have sat for, so complacent he sat as he used to sit when in his days of Courtship he ogled thro' his Spectacles. I have a shrewd suspicion he has an Eye upon his Spouse's picture after this, and probably some collateral branches may follow of the Norris or Faint Stock, so that your forerunner may prove a notable Decoy duck. The Colliers are going to sit. Item, her knightly Brother in Ireland is soon coming over, apprized of her difficulties, and I confidently hope an emergence for her. But G. Dyer Executor to a Nobleman! G. D. Residuary Legatee! What whirligig of Fortune is this? *Valet ima Summis.* Strange world, strange kings, strange composition!—I can't enjoy it sufficiently till I get a more active belief in it. You've seen the will of

Ld. Stanhope. Conceive his old floor strew'd with *disjecta membra Poeseōs*, now loaden with codicils, deeds of Trust, Letters of attorney, Bonds, obligations, Forfeitures, Exchequer Bills, Noverint Universis. "Mr. Serjeant Best, pray take my arm-chair. My Lord Holland sit here, Lord Grantly will your Lordship take the other? Mr. Jekyll excuse my offering you the window seat—We'll now have that clause read over again."

B. and Fletcher describe a little French Lawyer spoilt by an acciden· tal duel he got thrust into, from a Notable Counsellor turned into a Bravo. Here is G. D. more contra-naturally metamorphosed. My life on it, henceforth he explodes his old Hobby Horses. No more poring into Cambridge records—here are other Title deeds to be looked into—now can he make any Joan a Lady. And if he don't get too proud to marry, that long unsolved Problem of G. D. is in danger of being quickly melted. They can't choose but come and make offer of their coy wares. I see Miss H. prim up her chin, Miss B-n-j-o cock her nose.

He throws his dirty glove. G. D., *Iratis Veneribus*, marries, for my life on't.

And 'tis odds in that case but he leaves off making Love and Verses.

Indeed I look upon our friend as dead, dead to all his desperate fancies, pleasures,—he has lost the dignity of verse, the dignity of poverty, the dignity of digging on in desperation through mines of Literature that yielded nothing. Adieu! the wrinkled brow, the chin half shaved, the Ruined arm-chair, the wind-admitting and expelling screen, the fluttering Pamphlets, the lost Letters, the documents never to be found when wanting, the unserviceable comfortable Landress.

> G. D.'s occupation's o'er!
> Demptus per vim mentis gratissimus Error!

Hæc pauca de amico nostro antiquo accipe pro næniis, exequiis et ejusdem generis aliis. Vale noster G. D.

From yours as he was, unchanged by Fortune.

C. L.

John Rickman, Esq.,
  New Palace Yard,
  Westminster.

CHAPTER IV.

1817–1823.

To WILLIAM AYRTON, Esq.

LETTER CXCVI.]   *May* 17, 1817.

My dear friend,
Before I end,
Have you any
More orders for Don Giovanni,
To give
Him that doth live
Your faithful Zany?

Without raillery,
I mean Gallery
Ones:
For I am a person that shuns
All ostentation
And being at the top of the fashion;
And seldom go to operas
But *in formâ pauperis!*

I go to the play
In a very economical sort of a way,
Rather to see
Than be seen;
Though I'm no ill sight
Neither,
By candle-light
And in some kinds of weather.
You might pit me
For height
Against Kean;
But in a grand tragic scene
I'm nothing:

It would create a kind of loathing
To see me act Hamlet;
There'd be many a damn let
Fly
At my presumption,
If I should try,
Being a fellow of no gumption.

By the way, tell me candidly how you relish
This, which they call
The lapidary style?
Opinions vary.
The late Mr. Mellish
Could never abide it;
He thought it vile,
And coxcombical.
My friend the poet laureat,
Who is a great lawyer at
Anything comical,
Was the first who tried it;
But Mellish could never abide it;
But it signifies very little what Mellish said,
Because he is dead.

For who can confute
A body that's mute?
Or who would fight
With a senseless sprite?
Or think of troubling
An inpenetrable old goblin,
That's dead and gone,
And stiff as stone,
To convince him with arguments pro and con,
As if some live logician,
Bred up at Merton,—
Or Mr. Hazlitt, the metaphysician;—
Hey, Mr. Ayrton!
With all your rare tone.

For tell how should an apparition
List to your call,
Though you talk'd for ever,
Ever so clever:
When his ear itself,
By which he must hear, or not hear at all,
Is laid on the shelf?
Or put the case

(For more grace),
It were a female spectre—
Now could you expect her
To take much gust
In long speeches,
With her tongue as dry as dust,
In a sandy place,
Where no peaches,
Nor lemons, nor limes, nor oranges hang,
To drop on the drought of an arid harangue,
Or quench,
With their sweet drench,
The fiery pangs which the worms inflict,
With their endless nibblings,
Like quibblings,
Which the corpse may dislike, but can ne'er contradict?
Hey, Mr. Ayrton!
With all your rare tone.

I am,

C. LAMB.

To MR. BARRON FIELD.

LETTER CXCVII.]   *August* 31, 1817.

My dear Barron—The bearer of this letter so far across the seas is Mr. Lawrey, who comes out to you as a missionary, and whom I have been strongly importuned to recommend to you as a most worthy creature by Mr. Fenwick, a very old, honest friend of mine; of whom, if my memory does not deceive me, you have had some knowledge heretofore as editor of the *Statesman;* a man of talent, and patriotic. If you can show him any facilities in his arduous undertaking, you will oblige us much. Well, and how does the land of thieves use you? and how do you pass your time, in your extra-judicial intervals? Going about the streets with a lantern, like Diogenes, looking for an honest man? You may look long enough, I fancy. Do give me some notion of the manners of the inhabitants where you are. They don't thieve all day long, do they? No human property could stand such continuous battery. And what do they do when they an't stealing?

Have you got a theatre? What pieces are performed? Shakspeare's, I suppose; not so much for the poetry, as for his having once been in danger of leaving his country on account of certain "small deer."

Have you poets among you? Damn'd plagiarists, I fancy, if you have any. I would not trust an idea, or a pocket-handkerchief of mine, among 'em. You are almost competent to answer Lord Bacon's problem, whether a nation of atheists can subsist together. You are practically in one:—

"So thievish 'tis, that the eighth commandment itself
Scarce seemeth there to be."

Our old honest world goes on with little perceptible variation. Of course you have heard of poor Mitchell's death, and that G. Dyer is one of Lord Stanhope's residuaries. I am afraid he has not touched much of the residue yet. He is positively as lean as Cassius. Barnes is going to Demerara, or Essequibo, I am not quite certain which. Alsager is turned actor. He came out in genteel comedy at Cheltenham this season, and has hopes of a London engagement.

For my own history, I am just in the same spot, doing the same thing (videlicet, little or nothing) as when you left me; only I have positive hopes that I shall be able to conquer that inveterate habit of smoking which you may remember I indulged in. I think of making a beginning this evening, viz. Sunday, 31st Aug. 1817, not Wednesday, 2nd Feb. 1818, as it will be perhaps when you read this for the first time. There is the difficulty of writing from one end of the globe (hemispheres, I call 'em) to another! Why, half the truths I have sent you in this letter will become lies before they reach you, and some of the lies (which I have mixed for variety's sake, and to exercise your judgment in the finding of them out) may be turned into sad realities before you shall be called upon to detect them. Such are the defects of going by different chronologies. Your "now" is not my "now"; and again, your "then" is not my "then"; but my "now" may be your "then," and vice versâ. Whose head is competent to these things?

How does Mrs. Field get on in her geography? Does she know where she is by this time? I am not sure sometimes you are not in another planet; but then I don't like to ask Capt. Burney, or any of those that know anything about it, for fear of exposing my ignorance.

Our kindest remembrances, however, to Mrs. F., if she will accept of reminiscences from another planet, or at least another hemisphere.

C. L.

MARY LAMB to Miss WORDSWORTH.

LETTER CXCVIII.] *November 21, 1817.*

My dear Miss Wordsworth—Your kind letter has given us very great pleasure; the sight of your handwriting was a most welcome surprise to us. We have heard good tidings of you by all our friends who were so fortunate as to visit you this Summer, and rejoice to see it confirmed by yourself. You have quite the advantage, in volunteering a letter; there is no merit in replying to so welcome a stranger.

We have left the Temple. I think you will be sorry to hear this. I know I have never been so well satisfied with thinking of you at Rydal Mount, as when I could connect the idea of you with your own Grasmere Cottage. Our rooms were dirty and out of repair, and the inconveniences of living in chambers became every year more irksome, and so, at last, we mustered up resolution enough to leave the good old place, that so long had sheltered us, and here we are, living at a brazier's shop, No. 20, in Russell Street, Covent Garden, a place all alive with noise and bustle; Drury Lane Theatre in sight from our front, and Covent Garden from our back windows. The hubbub of the carriages returning from the play does not annoy me in the least; strange that it does not, for it is quite tremendous. I quite enjoy looking out of the window, and listening to the calling up of the carriages, and the squabbles of the coachmen and linkboys. It is the oddest scene to look down upon; I am sure you would be amused with it. It is well I am in a cheerful place, or I should have many misgivings about leaving the Temple. I look forward with great pleasure to the prospect of seeing my good friend, Miss Hutchinson. I wish Rydal Mount, with all its inhabitants enclosed, were to be transplanted with her, and to remain stationary in the midst of Covent Garden.

I passed through the street lately where Mr. and Mrs. Wordsworth lodged; several fine new houses, which were then just rising out of the ground, are quite finished, and a noble entrance made that way into Portland Place. I am very sorry for Mr. De Quincey. What a blunder the poor man made when he took up his dwelling among the mountains! I long to see my friend Pypos. Coleridge is still at Little Hampton with Mrs. Gillman; he has been so ill as to be confined to his room almost the whole time he has been there.

Charles has had all his Hogarths bound in a book; they were sent home yesterday, and now that I have them altogether, and perceive the advantage of peeping close at them through my spectacles, I am reconciled to the loss of them hanging round the room, which has been a great mortification to me—in vain I tried to console myself with looking at our new chairs and carpets, for we have got new chairs, and carpets covering all over our two sitting-rooms; I missed my old friends and could not be comforted—then I would resolve to learn to look out of the window, a habit I never could attain in my life, and I have given it up as a thing quite impracticable—yet when I was at Brighton, last Summer, the first week I never took my eyes off from the sea, not even to look in a book: I had not seen the sea for sixteen years. Mrs. Morgan, who was with us, kept her liking, and continued her seat in the window till the very last, while Charles and I played truants, and wandered among the hills, which we magnified into little mountains, and *almost as good as* Westmoreland scenery: certainly we made discoveries of many pleasant walks, which few of the Brighton visitors have ever dreamed of—for, like as is the case in the neighbourhood of London, after the first two or three miles we were sure to find ourselves in a perfect solitude. I hope we shall meet before the walking faculties of either of us fail; you say you can walk fifteen miles with ease; that is exactly my stint, and more fatigues me; four or five miles every third or fourth day, keeping very quiet between, was all Mrs. Morgan could accomplish.

God bless you and yours. Love to all and each one.

I am ever yours most affectionately,   M. LAMB.

To Miss WORDSWORTH.

LETTER CXCIX.]   *November* 21, 1817.

Dear Miss Wordsworth—Here we are, transplanted from our native soil. I thought we never could have been torn up from the Temple. Indeed it was an ugly wrench, but like a tooth, now 'tis out, and I am easy. We never can strike root so deep in any other ground. This, where we are, is a light bit of gardener's mould, and if they take us up from it, it will cost no blood and groans, like mandrakes pulled up. We are in the individual spot I like best, in all this great city. The theatres, with all their noises. Covent Garden, dearer to me than any gardens of Alcinous, where we are morally sure of the earliest peas and 'sparagus. Bow Street, where the thieves are examined, within a few yards of us. Mary had not been here four-and-twenty hours before she saw a thief. She sits at the window working; and casually throwing out her eyes, she sees a concourse of people coming this way, with a constable to conduct the solemnity. These little incidents agreeably diversify a female life.

Mary has brought her part of this letter to an orthodox and loving conclusion, which is very well, for I have no room for pansies and remembrances. What a nice holyday I got on Wednesday by favour of a princess dying!   C. L.

To J. PAYNE COLLIER.

The Garden of England,
LETTER CC.]   *December* 10, 1817.

Dear J. P. C.—I know how zealously you feel for our friend S. T. Coleridge; and I know that you and your family attended his lectures four or five years ago. He is in bad health, and worse mind: and unless something is done to lighten his mind he will soon be reduced to his extremities; and even these are not in the best condition. I am sure that you will do for him what you can; but at present he seems in a mood to do for himself. He projects a new course, not of physic, nor of metaphysic, nor a new course of life, but a new course of lectures on Shakspeare and Poetry. There is no man better qualified (always excepting number one); but I am pre-engaged for a series of dissertations on India and Indiapendence, to be completed, at the expense of the Company, in I know not (yet) how many volumes foolscap folio. I am busy getting up my Hindoo mythology; and, for the purpose, I am once more enduring Southey's curse. To be serious, Coleridge's state and affairs make me so; and there are particular reasons just now, and have been any time for the last twenty years, why he should succeed. He will do so with a little encouragement. I have not seen him lately; and he does not know that I am writing.

Yours (for Coleridge's sake) in haste,   C. LAMB.

To BENJAMIN ROBERT HAYDON.

LETTER CCI.]   *December* 1817.

My dear Haydon—I will come with pleasure to 22, Lisson Grove, North, at Rosse's, half-way up, right-hand side, if I can find it.
Yours,   C. LAMB.

20, Russell Court,
 Covent Garden, East.
  Half-way up, next the corner.
   Left-hand side.

To MRS. WORDSWORTH.

          East India House,
LETTER CCII.]   *February* 18, 1818.

My dear Mrs. Wordsworth—I have repeatedly taken pen in hand to answer your kind letter. My sister should more properly have done it, but she having failed, I consider myself answerable for her debts. I am now trying to do it in the midst of commercial noises, and with a quill which seems more ready to glide into arithmetical figures and names of gourds, cassia, cardamoms, aloes, ginger, or tea, than into kindly responses and friendly recollections. The reason why I cannot write letters at home is, that I am never alone. Plato's—(I write to W. W. now)—Plato's double-animal parted never longed more to be reciprocally re-united in the system of its first creation than I sometimes do to be but for a moment single and separate. Except my morning's walk to the office, which is like treading on sands of gold for that reason, I am never so. I cannot walk home from office but some officious friend offers his unwelcome courtesies to accompany me. All the morning I am pestered. I could sit and gravely cast up sums in great books, or compare sum with sum, and write "paid" against this, and "unpaid" against t'other, and yet reserve in some corner of my mind "some darling thoughts all my own,"—faint memory of some passage in a book, or the tone of an absent friend's voice—a snatch of Miss Burrell's singing, or a gleam of Fanny Kelly's divine plain face. The two operations might be going on at the same time without thwarting, as the sun's two motions (earth's, I mean), or as I sometimes turn round till I am giddy, in my back parlour, while my sister is walking longitudinally in the front; or as the shoulder of veal twists round with the spit, while the smoke wreathes up the chimney. But there are a set of amateurs of the Belles Lettres—the gay science—who come to me as a sort of rendezvous, putting questions of criticism, of British Institutions, Lalla Rookhs, etc.—what Coleridge said at the lecture last night— who have the form of reading men, but, for any possible use reading can

be to them, but to talk of, might as well have been Ante-Cadmeans born,
or have lain sucking out the sense of an Egyptian hieroglyph as long as
the pyramids will last, before they should find it. These pests worrit me at
business, and in all its intervals, perplexing my accounts, poisoning my
little salutary warming-time at the fire, puzzling my paragraphs if I take
a newspaper, cramming in between my own free thoughts and a column
of figures, which had come to an amicable compromise but for them.
Their noise ended, one of them, as I said, accompanies me home, lest I
should be solitary for a moment; he at length takes his welcome leave at
the door; up I go, mutton on table, hungry as hunter, hope to forget my
cares, and bury them in the agreeable abstraction of mastication; knock
at the door, in comes Mr. Hazlitt, or Mr. Martin Burney, or Morgan
Demigorgon, or my brother, or somebody, to prevent my eating alone—
a process absolutely necessary to my poor wretched digestion. O the
pleasure of eating alone!—eating my dinner alone! let me think of it.
But in they come, and make it absolutely necessary that I should open a
bottle of orange; for my meat turns into stone when any one dines with
me, if I have not wine. Wine can mollify stones; then *that* wine turns
into acidity, acerbity, misanthropy, a hatred of my interrupters— (God
bless 'em! I love some of 'em dearly), and with the hatred, a still greater
aversion to their going away. Bad is the dead sea they bring upon me,
choking and deadening, but worse is the deader dry sand they leave me
on, if they go before bed-time. Come never, I would say to these spoilers
of my dinner; but if you come, never go! The fact is, this interruption
does not happen very often; but every time it comes by surprise, that
present bane of my life, orange wine, with all its dreary stifling consequences, follows. Evening company I should always like had I any mornings, but I am saturated with human faces (*divine* forsooth!) and voices
all the golden morning; and five evenings in a week would be as much as
I should covet to be in company; but I assure you that is a wonderful
week in which I can get two, or one to myself. I am never C. L., but always C. L. and Co. He who thought it not good for man to be alone,
preserve me from the more prodigious monstrosity of being never by myself! I forget bed-time, but even there these sociable frogs clamber up
to annoy me. Once a week, generally some singular evening that, being
alone, I go to bed at the hour I ought always to be a-bed; just close to my
bedroom window is the club-room of a public-house, where a set of singers, I take them to be chorus-singers of the two theatres (it must be *both
of them*), begin their orgies. They are a set of fellows (as I conceive)
who, being limited by their talents to the burthen of the song at the playhouses, in revenge have got the common popular airs by Bishop, or some
cheap composer, arranged for choruses; that is, to be sung all in chorus.
At least I never can catch any of the text of the plain song, nothing but
the Babylonish choral howl at the tail on't. "That fury being quenched"
—the howl, I mean—a burden succeeds of shouts and clapping, and
knocking of the table. At length overtasked nature drops under it, and

escapes for a few hours into the society of the sweet silent creatures of dreams, which go away with mocks and mows at cockcrow. And then I think of the words Christabel's father used (bless me, I have dipt in the wrong ink!) to say every morning by way of variety when he awoke:

> "Every knell, the Baron saith,
> Wakes us up to a world of death".—

or something like it. All I mean by this senseless interrupted tale, is, that by my central situation I am a little over-companied. Not that I have any animosity against the good creatures that are so anxious to drive away the happy solitude from me. I like 'em, and cards, and a cheerful glass; but I mean merely to give you an idea, between office confinement and after-office society, how little time I can call my own. I mean only to draw a picture, not to make an inference. I would not that I know of have it otherwise. I only wish sometimes I could exchange some of my faces and voices for the faces and voices which a late visitation brought most welcome, and carried away, leaving regret, but more pleasure, even a kind of gratitude, at being so often favoured with that kind northern visitation. My London faces and noises don't hear me— I mean no disrespect, or I should explain myself, that instead of their return 220 times a year, and the return of W. W., etc., seven times in 104 weeks, some more equal distribution might be found. I have scarce room to put in Mary's kind love, and my poor name,   C. LAMB.

W. H. goes on lecturing against W. W. and making copious use of quotations from said W. W. to give a zest to said lectures. S. T. C. is lecturing with success. I have not heard either him or H., but I dined with S. T. C. at Gillman's a Sunday or two since, and he was well and in good spirits. I mean to hear some of the course; but lectures are not much to my taste, whatever the lecturer may be. If *read,* they are dismal flat, and you can't think why you are brought together to hear a man read his works, which you could read so much better at leisure yourself. If delivered extempore, I am always in pain lest the gift of utterance should suddenly fail the orator in the middle, as it did me at the dinner given in honour of me at the London tavern. "Gentlemen," said I, and there I stopped; the rest my feelings were under the necessity of supplying. Mrs. Wordsworth *will* go on, kindly haunting us with visions of seeing the lakes once more, which never can be realised. Between us there is a great gulf, not of inexplicable moral antipathies and distances, I hope, as there seemed to be between me and that gentleman concerned in the Stamp Office, that I so strangely recoiled from at Haydon's. I think I had an instinct that he was the head of an office. I hate all such people—accountants' deputy accountants. The dear abstract notion of the East India Company, as long as she is unseen, is pretty, rather poetical; but as she makes herself manifest by the persons of such beasts, I loathe and detest her as the scarlet what-do-you-call-her of Babylon. I thought, after abridging us of all our red-letter days, they had done their worst; but I was deceived in the length to which the heads of offices, those true liberty-haters, can go. They are the tyrants; not Ferdinand, nor Nero. By a decree passed this week, they have abridged us of the immemorially-observed custom of going at one o'clock of a Saturday, the little shadow of a holiday left us. Dear W. W., be thankful for liberty.

To Messrs. OLLIER.

LETTER CCIII.]   *June* 18, 1818.

Dear Sir (whichever opens it)—I am going off to Birmingh^m. I find my books, whatever faculty of selling they may have (I wish they had more for ${your \atop my}$ sake), are admirably adapted for giving away. You have been bounteous. Six more, and I shall have satisfied all just claims. Am I taking too great a liberty in begging you to send 4 as follows, and reserve 2 for me when I come home? That will make 31. Thirty-one times 12 is 372 shillings—eighteen pounds twelve shillings! ! ! But here are my friends, to whom, if you *could* transmit them, as I shall be away a month, you will greatly

Oblige the obliged,

C. LAMB.

Mr. Ayrton, James Street, Buckingham Gate;
Mr. Alsager, Suffolk Street East, Southwark, by Horsemonger Lane;
And in one parcel,
directed to R. Southey, Esq., Keswick, Cumberland:
One for R. S.;
And one for W^m. Wordsworth, Esq.
If you will be kind enough simply to write "From the Author" in all 4, you will still further, etc.
Either Longman or Murray is in the frequent habit of sending books to Southey, and will take charge of the parcel. It will be as well to write in at the beginning thus:
"R. Southey, Esq. From the Author."
"W. Wordsworth, Esq. From the Author."
Then, if I can find the remaining 2 left for me at Russell St. when I return, rather than encroach any more on the heap, I will engage to make no more new friends *ad infinitum*, yourselves being the last.
Yours truly,   C. L.

I think Southey will give us a lift in that damn'd *Quarterly*. I meditate an attack upon that Cobbler Gifford, which shall appear immediately after any favourable mention which S. may make in the *Quarterly*. It can't, in decent *gratitude*, appear *before*.

To ROBERT SOUTHEY.

LETTER CCIV.] *Monday, October 26, 1818.*

Dear Southey—I am pleased with your friendly remembrances of my little things. I do not know whether I have done a silly thing or a wise one, but it is of no great consequence. I run no risk, and care for no censures. My bread and cheese is stable as the foundations of Leadenhall Street, and if it hold out as long as the "foundations of our Empire in the East," I shall do pretty well. You and W. W. should have had your presentation copies more ceremoniously sent, but I had no copies when I was leaving town for my holidays, and rather than delay, commissioned my bookseller to send them thus nakedly. By not hearing from W. W. or you, I began to be afraid Murray had not sent them. I do not see S. T. C. so often as I could wish. He never comes to me; and though his host and hostess are very friendly, it puts me out of my way to go see one person at another person's house. It was the same when he resided at Morgan's. Not but they also were more than civil; but, after all, one feels so welcome at one's own house. Have you seen poor Miss Betham's "Vignettes"? Some of them, the second particularly, "To Lucy," are sweet and good as herself, while she was herself. She is in some measure abroad again. I am *better than I deserve* to be. The hot weather has been such a treat! Mary joins in this little corner in kindest remembrances to you all. C. L.

To SAMUEL TAYLOR COLERIDGE.

LETTER CCV.] *December 24, 1818.*

My dear Coleridge—I have been in a state of incessant hurry ever since the receipt of your ticket. It found me incapable of attending you, it being the night of Kenney's new comedy, which has utterly failed. You know my local aptitudes at such a time; I have been a thorough rendezvous for all consultations. My head begins to clear up a little, but it has had bells in it. Thank you kindly for your ticket, though the mournful prognostic which accompanies it certainly renders its permanent pretensions less marketable; but I trust to hear many a course yet. You excepted Christmas week, by which I understood *next week;* I thought Christmas week was that which Christmas Sunday ushered in. We are sorry it never lies in your way to come to us; but, dear Mahomet, we will come to you. Will it be convenient to all the good people of Highgate, if we take a stage up, *not next Sunday,* but the following, viz., 3rd January, 1819? Shall we be too late to catch a skirt of the old out-goer? How the years crumble from under us! We shall hope to see you before then; but, if not, let us know if *then* will be convenient. Can we secure a coach home?

Believe me ever yours, C. LAMB.

I have but one holiday, which is Christmas Day itself nakedly: no pretty garnish and fringes of St. John's Day, Holy Innocents, etc., that used to bestud it all around in the calendar. *Improbe labor!* I write six hours every day in this candle-light fog-den at Leadenhall.

To JOHN CHAMBERS.

LETTER CCVI.]   [1818.]

Dear C.—I steal a few minutes from a painful and laborious avocation, aggravated by the absence of some that should assist me, to say how extremely happy we should be to see you return clean as the cripple out of the pool of Bethesda. That damn'd scorbutic—how came you by it? . . . You are now fairly a damaged lot; as Venn would say, One Scratched. You might play Scrub in the *Beaux' Stratagem*. The best post your friends could promote you to would be a scrubbing post. "Aye, there's the rub." I generally get tired after the third rubber. But you, I suppose, tire twice the number every day. First, there's your mother, she begins after breakfast; then your little sister takes it up about Nuncheon time, till her bones crack, and some kind neighbour comes in to lend a hand, scrub, scrub, scrub, and nothing will get the intolerable itch (for I am persuaded it is the itch) out of your penance-doing bones. A cursed thing just at this time, when everybody wants to get out of town as well as yourself. Of course, I don't mean to reproach you. You can't help it, the whoreson tingling in your blood. I dare say you would if you could. But don't you think you could do a little work, if you came? as much as D—— does before 12 o'Clock. Hang him, there he sits at that cursed *Times*—and latterly he has had the *Berkshire Chronicle* sent him every Tuesday and Friday to get at the County news. Why, that letter which you favored him with, appears to me to be very well and clearly written. The man that wrote that might make out warrants, or write Committees. There was as much in quantity written as would have filled four volumes of the Indigo appendix; and when we are so busy as we are, every little helps. But I throw out these observations merely as innuendos. By the way there's a Doctor Lamert in Leadenhall Street, who sells a mixture to purify the blood. No. 114 Leadenhall Street, near the market. But it is necessary that his Patients should be on the spot, that he may see them every day. There's a sale of Indigo advertised for July, forty thousand lots—10,000 chests only, but they sell them in quarter chests which makes 40,000. By the bye a droll accident happened here on Thursday, Wadd and Plumley got quarrelling about a kneebuckle of Hyde's which the latter affirmed not to be standard; Wadd was nettled at this, and said something reflecting on tradesmen and shopkeepers, and Plumley struck him. . . . Friend is married; he has married a Roman Catholic, which has offended his family, but they have come to an agreement, that the boys (if they have children) shall be bred up in the father's religion, and the girls in the mother's, which I think equitable enough. . . . I am determined my children shall be brought up in their father's religion, if they can find out what it is. Bye is about publishing a volume of poems which he means to dedicate to Matthie. Methinks he might have found a better Mecænas. They are chiefly amatory, others of them stupid, the greater part very far below mediocrity; but they discover much tender feeling; they are most like Petrarch of any foreign Poet, or what we might have supposed Petrarch would have written if Petrarch had been born a fool! Grinwallows is made master of the ceremonies at Dandelion, near Margate; of course he gives up the office. "My Harry" makes so many faces that it is impossible to sit opposite him without smiling. Dowley danced a Quadrille at Court on the Queen's birthday with Lady Thynne, Lady Desbrow, and Lady Louisa Manners. It is said his performance was graceful and airy. Cabel has taken an unaccountable fancy into his head that he is Fuller, member for Sussex. He imitates his blunt way of speaking. I remain much the same as you remember, very universally beloved and esteemed, possessing everybody's good-will, and trying at least to deserve it; the same steady adherence to principle, and correct regard for truth, which always marked my conduct, marks it still. If I am singular in anything it is in too great a squeamishness to anything that remotely looks like a falsehood. I am call'd Old Honesty; sometimes Upright Telltruth, Esq., and I own it tickles my vanity a little. The Committee have formally abolish'd all holydays whatsoever—for which may the Devil, who keeps no holydays, have them in his eternal burning workshop. When I say holydays, I mean Calendar holydays, for a Medley's instigation they have agreed to a sort of scale by which the Chief has power to give leave of absence, viz.:—

Those who have been 50 years and upwards to be absent 4 days in the year, but not without leave of the Chief.
> 35 years and upward, 3 days,
> 25 years and upward, 2 days,
> 18 years and upward, 1 day,

which I think very Liberal. We are also to sign our name when we *go* as well as when we *come,* and every quarter of an hour we sign, to show that we are here. Mins and Gardner take it in turn to bring round the book —O here *is* Mins with the Book—no, it's Gardner—"What's that, G.?" "The appearance book, Sir" (with a gentle inclination of his head, and smiling). "What the devil, is the quarter come again?" It annoys Dodwell amazingly; he sometimes has to sign six or seven times while he is reading the Newspaper—

> [*Unfinished.*]

To WILLIAM WORDSWORTH.

LETTER CCVII.]   *May* 1819.

Dear Wordsworth—I received a copy of "Peter Bell" a week ago, and I hope the author will not be offended if I say I do not much relish it.

The humour, if it is meant for humour, is forced; and then the price!—sixpence would have been dear for it. Mind, I do not mean *your* "Peter Bell," but *a* "Peter Bell" which preceded it about a week, and is in every bookseller's shop window in London, the type and paper nothing differing from the true one, the preface signed W. W., and the supplementary preface quoting as the author's words an extract from the supplementary preface to the "Lyrical Ballads." Is there no law against these rascals? I would have this Lambert Simnel whipt at the cart's tail. Then there is Rogers! He has been re-writing your Poem of the Strid, and publishing it at the end of his "Human Life." Tie him up to the cart, hangman, while you are about it. Who started the spurious "P. B." I have not heard. I should guess, one of the sneering brothers, the vile Smiths; but I have heard no name mentioned. "Peter Bell" (not the mock one) is excellent; for its matter, I mean. I cannot say that the style of it quite satisfies me. It is too lyrical. The auditors to whom it is feigned to be told, do not *arride* me. I would rather it had been told me, the reader, at once. "Heartleap Well" is the tale for me; in matter as good as this; in manner infinitely before it, in my poor judgment. Why did you not add "The Waggoner"?—Have I thanked you though, yet, for "Peter Bell"? I would not *not have it* for a good deal of money. C—— is very foolish to scribble about books. Neither his tongue nor fingers are very retentive. But I shall not say anything to him about it. He would only begin a very long story, with a very long face; and I see him far too seldom to teaze him with affairs of business or conscience when I do see him. He never comes near our house; and when we go to see him he is generally writing, or thinking. He is writing in his study till the dinner comes, and that is scarce over before the stage summons us away. The mock "P. B." had only this effect on me, that after twice reading it over in hopes to find something diverting in it, I reached your two books off the shelf, and set into a steady reading of them, till I had nearly finished both before I went to bed: the two of your last edition, of course, I mean: and in the morning I awoke determining to take down the *Excursion.* I wish the scoundrel imitator could know this. But why waste a wish on him? I do not believe that paddling about with a stick in a pond, and fishing up a dead author, whom *his* intolerable wrongs had driven to that deed of desperation, would turn the heart of one of these obtuse literary BELLS. There is no Cock for such Peters;—damn 'em! I am glad this aspiration came upon the red ink line. It is more of a bloody curse. I have delivered over your other presents to Alsager and G. D. A., I am sure, will value it, and be proud of the hand from which it came. To G. D. a poem is a poem. His own as good as anybody's, and (God bless him!) anybody's as good as his own; for I do not think he has the most distant guess of the possibility of one poem being better than another. The gods, by denying him the very faculty itself of discrimination, have effectually cut off every seed of envy in his bosom. But with envy, they excited curiosity also; and if you wish the copy again, which you destined for him, I think I shall be able to find it again for you, on his third shelf, where he stuffs his presentation copies, uncut, in shape and matter resembling a lump of dry dust; but on carefully removing that stratum, a thing like a pamphlet will emerge. I have tried this with fifty different poetical works that have been given G. D. in return for as many of his own performances; and I confess I never had any scruple in taking *my own* again, wherever I found it, shaking the adherences off; and by this means one copy of "my works" served for G. D., and, with a little dusting, was made over to my good friend Dr. G——, who little thought whose leavings he was taking when he made that graceful bow. By the way, the Doctor is the only one of my acquaintance who bows gracefully; my town acquaintance, I mean. How do you like my way of writing with two inks? I think it is pretty and motley. Suppose Mrs. W. adopts it, the next time she holds the pen for you. My dinner waits. I have no time to indulge any longer in these laborious curiosities. God bless you, and cause to thrive and burgeon whatsoever you write, and fear no inks of miserable poetasters.

Yours truly,   CHARLES LAMB.
Mary's love.

To THOMAS MANNING.

LETTER CCVIII.]   *May* 28, 1819.

My dear M.—I want to know how your brother is, if you have heard lately. I want to know about you. I wish you were nearer. How are my cousins, the Gladmans of Wheathamstead, and farmer Bruton? Mrs. Bruton is a glorious woman.

"Hail, Mackery End"—

This is a fragment of a blank verse poem which I once meditated, but got no further. The E. I. H. has been thrown into a quandary by the strange phenomenon of poor Tommy Bye, whom I have known man and madman twenty-seven years, he being elder here than myself by nine years and more. He was always a pleasant, gossiping, half-headed, muzzy, dozing, dreaming, walk-about, inoffensive chap; a little too fond of the creature—(who isn't at times?); but Tommy had not brains to work off an over-night's surfeit by ten o'clock next morning; and unfortunately, in he wandered the other morning drunk with last night, and with a superfœtation of drink taken in since he set out from bed. He came staggering under his double burthen, like trees in Java, bearing at once blossom, fruit, and falling fruit, as I have heard you or some other traveller tell, with his face literally as blue as the bluest firmament; some wretched calico, that he had mopped his poor oozy front with, had rendered up its native dye; and the devil a bit would he consent to wash it, but swore it was characteristic, for he was going to the sale of indigo, and set up a laugh which I did not think the lungs of mortal man were competent to.

It was like a thousand people laughing, or the Goblin Page. He imagined afterwards that the whole office had been laughing at him, so strange did his own sounds strike upon his *non*sensorium! But Tommy has laughed his last laugh, and awoke the next day to find himself reduced from an abused income of £600 per annum to one-sixth of the sum, after thirty-six years' tolerably good service. The quality of mercy was not strained in his behalf: the gentle dews dropt not on him from heaven. It just came across me that I was writing to Canton. Will you drop in to-morrow night? Fanny Kelly is coming, if she does not cheat us. Mrs. *Gold* is well, but proves "uncoined," as the lovers about Wheathamstead would say.

I have not had such a quiet half hour to sit down to a quiet letter for many years. I have not been interrupted above four times. I wrote a letter the other day, in alternate lines, black ink and red, and you cannot think how it chilled the flow of ideas. Next Monday is Whit-Monday. What a reflection! Twelve years ago, and I should have kept that and the following holidays in the fields a-Maying. All of those pretty pastoral delights are over. This dead, everlasting dead desk,—how it weighs the spirit of a gentleman down! This dead wood of the desk, instead of your living trees! But then again, I hate the Joskins, *a name for Hertford-shire bumpkins*. Each state of life has its inconvenience; but then again, mine has more than one. Not that I repine, or grudge, or murmur at my destiny. I have meat and drink, and decent apparel; I shall, at least, when I get a new hat.

A red-haired man has just interrupted me. He has broke the current of my thoughts. I haven't a word to add. I don't know why I send this letter, but I have had a hankering to hear about you some days. Perhaps it will go off before your reply comes. If it don't, I assure you no letter was ever welcomer from you, from Paris or Macao.   C. LAMB.

To WILLIAM WORDSWORTH.

LETTER CCIX.]   *June* 7, 1819.

My dear Wordsworth—You cannot imagine how proud we are here of the dedication. We read it twice for once that we do the poem. I mean all through; yet "Benjamin" is no common favourite; there is a spirit of beautiful tolerance in it. It is as good as it was in 1806; and it will be as good in 1829, if our dim eyes shall be awake to peruse it. Methinks there is a kind of shadowing affinity between the subject of the narrative and the subject of the dedication; but I will not enter into personal themes; else, substituting * * * * * * for Ben, and the Hon-ourable United Company of Merchants trading to the East Indies, for the master of the misused team, it might seem, by no far-fetched analogy, to point its dim warnings hitherward; but I reject the omen, especially as its import seems to have been diverted to another victim.

I will never write another letter with alternate inks. You cannot imagine how it cramps the flow of the style. I can conceive Pindar (I do not mean to compare myself to *him*), by the command of Hiero, the Sicilian tyrant (was not he the tyrant of some place? fie on my neglect of history!)—I can conceive him by command of Hiero or Perillus set down to pen an Isthmian or Nemean panegyric in lines, alternate red and black. I maintain he couldn't have done it; it would have been a strait-laced torture to his muse; he would have call'd for the bull for a relief. Neither could Lycidas, nor the Chorics (how do you like the word?) of Samson Agonistes, have been written with two inks. Your couplets, with points, epilogues to Mr. H.'s, etc., might be even benefited by the twyfount, where one line (the second) is for point, and the first for rhyme. I think the alternation would assist, like a mould. I maintain it, you could not have written your stanzas on pre-existence with two inks. Try another; and Rogers, with his silver standish, having one ink only, I will bet my "Ode on Tobacco," against the "Pleasures of Memory,"— and "Hope," too, shall put more fervour of enthusiasm into the same subject than you can with your two; he shall do it *stans pede in uno,* as it were.

The "Waggoner" is very ill put up in boards; at least it seems to me always to open at the dedication; but that is a mechanical fault. I re-read the "White Doe of Rylstone;" the title should be always written at length, as Mary Sabilla Novello, a very nice woman of our acquaintance, always signs hers at the bottom of the shortest note. Mary told her, if her name had been Mary Ann, she would have signed M. A. Novello, or M. only, dropping the A.; which makes me think, with some other trifles, that she understands something of human nature. My pen goes galloping on most rhapsodically, glad to have escaped the bondage of two inks.

Manning had just sent it home, and it came as fresh to me as the immortal creature it speaks of. M. sent it home with a note, having this passage in it: "I cannot help writing to you while I am reading Wordsworth's poem. I am got into the third canto, and say that it raises my opinion of him very much indeed. 'Tis broad, noble, poetical, with a masterly scanning of human actions, absolutely above common readers. What a manly (implied) interpretation of (bad) party-actions, as trampling the Bible, etc.!" and so he goes on.

I do not know which I like best,—the prologue (the latter part especially) to "P. Bell," or the epilogue to "Benjamin." Yes, I tell stories; I do know I like the last best; and the "Waggoner" altogether is a pleasanter remembrance to me than the "Itinerant." If it were not, the page before the first page would and ought to make it so. The sonnets are not all new to me; of those which are new, the ninth I like best. Thank you for that to Walton. I take it as a favour done to me, that, being so old a darling of mine, you should bear testimony to his worth in a book containing a dedic——: I cannot write the vain word at full length any longer.

If, as you say, the "Waggoner," in some sort, came at my call, oh for a potent voice to call forth the "Recluse" from his profound dormitory, where he sleeps forgetful of his foolish charge—the world! Had I three inks, I would invoke him! Talfourd has written a most kind review of J. Woodvil, etc., in the *Champion*. He is your most zealous admirer, in solitude and in crowds. H. Crabb Robinson gives me any dear prints that I happen to admire; and I love him for it and for other things. Alsager shall have his copy; but at present I have lent it *for a day only*, not choosing to part with my own. Mary's love. How do you all do, amanuenses both—marital and sororal?   C. LAMB.

To JOSEPH COTTLE.

LETTER CCX.]   *Nov.* 5, 1819.

Dear Sir—It is so long since I have seen or heard from you, that I fear that you will consider a request I have to make as impertinent. About three years since when I was one day in Bristol, I made an effort to see you; but you were from home. The request I have to make is, that you would very much oblige me, if you have any small portrait of yourself, by allowing me to have it copied, to accompany a selection of "Likenesses of Living Bards" which a most particular friend of mine is making. If you have no objections, and could oblige me by transmitting such portrait to me at No. 44 Russell Street, Covent Garden, I will answer for taking the greatest care of it, and returning it safely the instant the copier has done with it. I hope you will pardon the liberty from an old friend and well-wisher,   CHARLES LAMB.

LETTER CCXI.]   [*November* or *December*] 1819.

Dear Sir—My friend, whom you have obliged by the loan of your picture, has had it very exactly copied (and a very spirited drawing it is; so every one thinks who has seen it). The copy is not much inferior, done by a daughter of Joseph's R.A. He purposes sending you back the original, which I must accompany with my warm thanks, both for that, and your better favour, the Messiah, which I assure you I have read through with great pleasure; the verses have great sweetness, and a New Testament-plainness about them which affected me very much. I could just wish that in page 63 you had omitted the lines 71 and 72, and had ended the period with—

> "The willowy brook was there, but that sweet sound—
> *When* to be heard again on Earthly ground?"

Two very sweet lines, and the sense perfect.
And in page 154, line 68,—"I come ordained a world to save"—these words are hardly borne out by the story, and seem scarce accordant with

the modesty with which our Lord came to take his common portion among the baptismal candidates. They also anticipate the beauty of John's recognition of the Messiah, and the subsequent confirmation from the voice and Dove.

You will excuse the remarks of an old brother bard, whose career, though long since pretty well stopped, was coeval in its beginning with your own, and who is sorry his lot has been always to be so distant from you. It is not likely that C. L. will see Bristol again; but, if J. C. should ever visit London, he will be a most welcome visitor to C. L. My sister joins in cordial remembrances. . . .

Dear Sir, yours truly, CHARLES LAMB.

LETTER CCXII.] *London, India House,*
[Close of year] 1819.

My dear Sir—I am quite ashamed of not having acknowledged your kind present earlier; but that unknown something, which was never yet discovered, though so often speculated upon, which stands in the way of lazy folks answering letters, has presented its usual obstacle. It is not forgetfulness nor disrespect nor incivility, but terribly like all these bad things.

I have been in my time a great epistolary scribbler: but the passion, and with it the facility, at length wears out; and it must be pumped up again by the heavy machinery of duty or gratitude, when it should run free. I have read your "Fall of Cambria" with as much pleasure as I did your "Messiah." Your Cambrian Poem I shall be tempted to repeat oftenest, as human poems take me in a mood more frequently congenial than divine. The character of Llewellyn pleases me more than anything else, perhaps; and then some of the lyrical pieces are fine varieties.

It was quite a mistake that I could dislike anything you should write against Lord Byron; for I have a thorough aversion to his character, and a very moderate admiration of his genius: he is great in so little a way. To be a Poet is to be the Man, not a petty portion of occasional low passion worked up in a permanent form of humanity. Shakspeare has thrust such rubbishly feelings into a corner—the dark dusky heart of Don John, in the *Much Ado about Nothing.* The fact is, I have not seen your "Expostulatory Epistle" to him. I was not aware, till your question, that it was out. I shall inquire, and get it forthwith.

Southey is in town, whom I have seen slightly; Wordsworth expected, whom I hope to see much of. I write with accelerated motion; for I have two or three bothering clerks and brokers about me, who always press in proportion as you seem to be doing something that is not business. I could exclaim a little profanely; but I think you do not like swearing.

I conclude, begging you to consider that I feel myself much obliged by your kindness; and shall be most happy at any and at all times to hear from you.

Dear Sir, yours truly, CHARLES LAMB.

To SAMUEL TAYLOR COLERIDGE.

LETTER CCXIII.]   *November* 1819.

Dear Coleridge—Your sonnet is capital. The paper is ingenious, only that it split into four parts (besides a side splinter) in the carriage. I have transferred it to the common English paper *manufactured of rags*, for better preservation. I never knew before how the *Iliad* and *Odyssey* were written. 'Tis strikingly corroborated by observations on Cats. These domestic animals, put 'em on a rug before the fire, wink their eyes up, and listen to the kettle, and then purr, which is *their* poetry.

On Sunday week we kiss your hands (if they are clean). This next Sunday I have been engaged for some time.

With remembrances to your good host and hostess,

Yours ever,   C. LAMB.

To MISS WORDSWORTH.

LETTER CCXIV.]   *November* 25, 1819.

Dear Miss Wordsworth—You will think me negligent: but I wanted to see more of Willy before I ventured to express a prediction. Till yesterday I had barely seen him—*Virgilium tantum vidi*—but yesterday he gave us his small company to a bullock's heart, and I can pronounce him a lad of promise. He is no pedant, nor bookworm; so far I can answer. Perhaps he has hitherto paid too little attention to other men's inventions, preferring, like Lord Foppington, the "natural sprouts of his own." But he has observation, and seems thoroughly awake. I am ill at remembering other people's *bon mots*, but the following are a few:—Being taken over Waterloo Bridge, he remarked, that if we had no mountains, we had a fine river at least; which was a touch of the comparative: but then he added, in a strain which augured less for his future abilities as a political economist, that he supposed they must take at least a pound a week toll. Like a curious naturalist he inquired if the tide did not come up a little salty. This being satisfactorily answered, he put another question, as to the flux and reflux; which being rather cunningly evaded than artfully solved by that she-Aristotle, Mary,—who muttered something about its getting up an hour sooner and sooner every day,—he sagely replied, "Then it must come to the same thing at last;" which was a speech worthy of an infant Halley! The lion in the 'Change by no means came up to his ideal standard; so impossible is it for Nature, in any of her works, to come up to the standard of a child's imagination! The whelps (lionets) he was sorry to find were dead; and on particular inquiry, his old friend the ourang-outang had gone the way of all flesh also. The grand tiger was also sick, and expected in no short time to exchange this transitory world for another, or none. But again, there was a golden eagle (I do not mean that of Charing) which did much arride and console him. William's genius, I take it, leans a little to the figurative; for, being at play at tricktrack (a kind of minor billiard-table which we keep for smaller wights, and sometimes refresh our own mature fatigues with taking a hand at), not being able to hit a ball he had iterate aimed at, he cried out, "I cannot hit that beast!" Now the balls are usually called men, but he felicitously hit upon a middle term; a term of approximation and imaginative reconciliation; a something where the two ends of the brute matter (ivory), and their human and rather violent personification into men, might meet, as I take it—illustrative of that excellent remark, in a certain preface about imagination, explaining "Like a sea-beast that had crawled forth to sun himself!" Not that I accuse William Minor of hereditary plagiary, or conceive the image to have come *ex traduce*. Rather he seemeth to keep aloof from any source of imitation, and purposely to remain ignorant of what mighty poets have done in this kind before him; for, being asked if his father had ever been on Westminster Bridge, he answered that he did not know!

It is hard to discern the oak in the acorn, or a temple like St. Paul's in the first stone which is laid; nor can I quite prefigure what destination the genius of William Minor hath to take. Some few hints I have set down, to guide my future observations. He hath the power of calculation, in no ordinary degree for a chit. He combineth figures, after the first boggle, rapidly; as in the tricktrack board, where the hits are figured. At first he did not perceive that 15 and 7 made 22; but by a little use he could combine 8 with 25, and 33 again with 16, which approacheth something in kind (far let me be from flattering him by saying in degree) to that of the famous American boy. I am sometimes inclined to think I perceive the future satirist in him, for he hath a subsardonic smile which bursteth out upon occasion; as when he was asked if London were as big as Ambleside; and indeed no other answer was given, or proper to be given, to so ensnaring and provoking a question. In the contour of the skull, certainly I discern something paternal. But whether in all respects the future man shall transcend his father's fame, Time, the trier of Geniuses, must decide. Be it pronounced peremptorily at present, that Willy is a well-mannered child, and though no great student, hath yet a lively eye for things that lie before him.

Given in haste from my desk at Leadenhall.

Yours, and yours most sincerely,   C. LAMB.

To SAMUEL TAYLOR COLERIDGE.

LETTER CCXV.]   *January* 10, 1820.

Dear Coleridge—A letter written in the blood of your poor friend would indeed be of a nature to startle you; but this is nought but harmless red ink, or, as the witty mercantile phrase hath it, clerk's blood. Hang 'em! my brain, skin, flesh, bone, carcase, soul, time is all theirs. The Royal Exchange, Gresham's Folly, hath me body and spirit. I admire some of Lloyd's lines on you, and I admire your postponing reading them. He is a sad tattler; but this is under the rose. Twenty years ago he estranged one friend from me quite, whom I have been regretting, but never could regain since. He almost alienated you also from me, or me from you, I don't know which; but that breach is closed. The "dreary sea" is filled up. He has lately been at work "telling again," as they call it, a most gratuitous piece of mischief, and has caused a coolness betwixt me and (not a friend exactly, but) an intimate acquaintance. I suspect also he saps Manning's faith in me, who am to Manning more than an acquaintance. Still I like his writing verses about you. Will your kind host and hostess give us a dinner next Sunday; and, better still, *not expect us* if the weather is very bad? Why you should refuse twenty guineas per sheet for Blackwood's, or any other magazine, passes my poor comprehension. But, as Strap says, "you know best." I have no quarrel with you about præprandial avocations; so don't imagine one. That Manchester sonnet I think very likely is Capel Lofft's. Another sonnet appeared with the same initials in the same paper, which turned out to be Procter's. What do the rascals mean? Am I to have the fathering of what idle rhymes every beggarly poetaster pours forth? Who put your marine sonnet, and about Browne, into *Blackwood?*—I did not. So no more, till we meet.

Ever yours, C. L.

To Miss WORDSWORTH.

LETTER CCXVI.] [*Thursday, May* 25, 1820.]

Dear Miss W.—I have volunteered to reply to your note because of a mistake I am desirous of rectifying on the spot. There can be none to whom the last volume of W. W. has come more welcome than to me. I have traced the Duddon in thought and with repetition along the banks (alas!) of the Lea—(unpoetical name): it is always flowing and murmuring in my ears. The story of Dion is divine—the genius of Plato falling on him like moonlight—the finest thing ever expressed.

Then there is *Elidure* and *Kirkstone Pass*—the last not new to me—and let me add one of the sweetest of all to me, *The Longest Day.* Loving all these as much as I can love Poetry, new to me, what could I wish or desire or extravagantly desiderate in a new volume? That I did not write to W. W. was simply that he was to come so soon, and that flattens letters.

I admired your averted looks on Saturday. You did not observe M. Burney's averted look also? You might have been supposed two Antipathies, or quarrelled lovers. The fact was, M. B. had a black eye he was desirous of concealing—an artificial one I mean, not of nature's making, but of art's reflecting, for nobody quarrels with the black eyes the former gives —but it was curious to see you both ashamed of such Panegyrical objects as black eyes and white teeth have always been considered. . . . Mary is not here to see the stuff I write, else she would snatch the pen out of my hand and conclude with some sober kind messages.

We sincerely wish your brother better.

Yours, both of us kindly,   C. L. and M. L.

To THOMAS ALLSOP.

LETTER CCXVII.]   *March* 30, 1821.

My dear Sir—If you can come next Sunday we shall be equally glad to see you, but do not trust to any of Martin's appointments, except on business, in future. He is notoriously faithless in that point, and we did wrong not to have warned you. Leg of Lamb, as before, hot at 4. And the heart of Lamb ever.

Yours truly,   C. L.

To SAMUEL TAYLOR COLERIDGE.

LETTER CCXVIII.]   *May* 1, 1821.

Dr. C.—I will not fail you on Friday by six, and Mary, perhaps, earlier. I very much wish to meet Master Mathew, and am very much obliged to the Gillmans for the opportunity. Our kind respects to them always,

ELIA.

To MR. GILLMAN.

LETTER CCXIX.]   *Wednesday, May* 2, '21.

Dear Sir—You dine so late on Friday, it will be impossible for us to go home by the eight o'clock stage. Will you oblige me by securing us beds in some house from which a stage goes to the Bank in the morning? I would write to Coleridge, but cannot think of troubling a dying man with such a request.

Yours truly,   C. LAMB.

If the beds in the town are all engaged, in consequence of Mr. Mathews's appearance, a hackney coach will serve.

We shall neither of us come much before the time.

To JOHN PAYNE COLLIER.

LETTER CCXX.]
[Kingsland Row, Dalston],
May 16, 1821.

Dear J. P. C.—Many thanks for the "Decameron": I have not such a gentleman's book in my collection: it was a great treat to me, and I got it just as I was wanting something of the sort. I take less pleasure in books than heretofore, but I like books about books. In the second volume, in particular, are treasures—your discoveries about "Twelfth Night," etc. What a Shakspearian essence that speech of Osrades for food!—Shakspeare is coarse to it—beginning "Forbear and eat no more." Osrades warms up to that, but does not set out ruffian-swaggerer. The character of the Ass with those three lines, worthy to be set in gilt vellum, and worn in frontlets by the noble beasts for ever—

> "Thou would, perhaps, he should become thy foe,
> And to that end dost beat him many times:
> He cares not for himself, much less thy blow."

Cervantes, Sterne, and Coleridge, have said positively nothing for asses compared with this.

I write in haste; but p. 24, vol. i., the line you cannot appropriate is Gray's sonnet, specimenifyed by Wordsworth in first preface to L. B., as mixed of bad and good style: p. 143, 2nd vol., you will find last poem but one of the collection on Sidney's death in Spenser, the line,

> "Scipio, Cæsar, Petrarch of our time."

This fixes it to be Raleigh's: I had guess'd it to be Daniel's. The last after it, "Silence augmenteth rage," I will be crucified if it be not Lord Brooke's. Hang you, and all meddling researchers, hereafter, that by raking into learned dust may find me out wrong in my conjecture!

Dear J. P. C., I shall take the first opportunity of personally thanking you for my entertainment. We are at Dalston for the most part, but I fully hope for an evening soon with you in Russell or Bouverie Street, to talk over old times and books. Remember *us* kindly to Mrs. J. P. C.

Yours very kindly,   CHARLES LAMB.
I write in misery.

N.B.—The best pen I could borrow at our butcher's; the ink, I verily believe, came out of the kennel.

To J. TAYLOR.

LETTER CCXXI.]   *July* 30, 1821.

Dear Sir—You will do me injustice if you do not convey to the writer of the beautiful lines, which I now return you, my sense of the extreme kindness which dictated them. Poor Elia (call him *Ellia*) does not pretend to so very clear revelations of a future state of being as Olen seems gifted with. He stumbles about dark mountains at best; but he knows at least how to be thankful for this life, and is too thankful indeed for certain relationships lent him here, not to tremble for a possible resumption of the gift. He is too apt to express himself lightly, and cannot be sorry for the present occasion, as it has called forth a reproof so Christian-like. His *animus* at least (whatever become of it in the female termination) hath always been *cum Christianis*.

Pray make my gratefullest respects to the Poet (do I flatter myself when I hope it may be Montgomery?) and say how happy I should feel myself in an acquaintance with him. I will just mention that in the middle of the second column, where I have affixed a cross, the line

"One in a skeleton's ribb'd hollow cooped,"

is undoubtedly wrong. Should it not be—

"A skeleton's rib or ribs?"

or,

"In a skeleton ribb'd, hollow-coop'd?"

I perfectly remember the plate in Quarles. In the first page esoteric is pronounced esóteric. It should be (if that is the word) esotéric. The false accent may be corrected by omitting the word *old*. Pray, for certain reasons, give me to the 18th *at furthest extremity* for my next.

Poor ELIA, the real (for I am but a counterfeit), is dead. The fact is, a person of that name, an Italian, was a fellow-clerk of mine at the South Sea House, thirty (not forty) years ago, when the characters I described there existed, but had left it like myself many years; and I having a brother now there, and doubting how he might relish certain descriptions in it, I clapt down the name of Elia to it, which passed off pretty well, for Elia himself added the function of an author to that of a scrivener, like myself.

I went the other day (not having seen him for a year) to laugh over with him at my usurpation of his name, and found him, alas! no more than a name, for he died of consumption eleven months ago, and I knew not of it.

So the name has fairly devolved to me, I think; and 'tis all he has left me.

Dear sir, yours truly,   C. LAMB.

Messrs. Taylor & Hessey, Fleet Street,
    for J. Taylor, Esq.

To C. COWDEN CLARKE.

LETTER CCXXII.]   [1821].

My dear Sir—Your letter has lain in a drawer of my desk, upbraiding me every time I open the said drawer, but it is almost impossible to answer such a letter in such a place, and I am out of the habit of replying to epistles otherwhere than at office. You express yourself concerning Hunt like a true friend, and have made me feel that I have somehow neglected him, but without knowing very well how to rectify it. I live so remote from him —by Hackney—that he is almost out of the pale of visitation at Hampstead. And I come but seldom to Covt. Gardn. this summer time, and when I do, am sure to pay for the late hours and pleasant Novello suppers which I incur. I also am an invalid. But I will hit upon some way, that you shall not have cause for your reproof in future. But do not think I take the hint unkindly. When I shall be brought low by any sickness or untoward circumstance, write just such a letter to some tardy friend of mine—or come up yourself with your friendly Henshaw face—and that will be better. I shall not forget in haste our casual day at Margate. May we have many such there or elsewhere! God bless you for your kindness to H., which I will remember. But do not show Novello this, for the flouting infidel doth mock when Christians cry God bless us. Yours and *his*, *too*, and all our little circle's most affect^e. C. LAMB.

Mary's love included.

To JOHN RICKMAN.

LETTER CCXXIII.]

E. I. House,
November 20, 1821.

Dear Rickman—The Poor Admiral's death would have been a greater shock to me, but that I have been used to death lately. Poor Jim White's departure last year first broke the spell. I had been so fortunate as to have lost no friend in that way for many long years, and began to think people did not die. But they have since gone off thickly. My brother's death happened when my sister was incapable of feeling it, but the knowledge of it was communicated to her at the time, and she had not to receive it as a shock when she came back to reason. I have reason to think this circumstance a great alleviation. She is now perfectly recovered after a very long illness, and pretty well resigned. We come to town this day and shall be glad to receive a visit from you or to pay you one.

M. C. B. I have neither seen nor heard from for these two months. I hope your hopes will be justified in him. I am, dear R., yours faithfully,
C. LAMB.

To SAMUEL TAYLOR COLERIDGE.

LETTER CCXXIV.]

March 9, 1822.

Dear Coleridge—It gives me great satisfaction to hear that the pig turned out so well: they are interesting creatures at a certain age. What a pity such buds should blow out into the maturity of rank bacon! You had all some of the crackling and brain sauce. Did you remember to rub it with butter, and gently dredge it a little, just before the crisis? Did the eyes come away kindly with no Œdipean avulsion? Was the crackling the colour of the ripe pomegranate? Had you no complement of boiled neck of mutton before it, to blunt the edge of delicate desire? Did you flesh maiden teeth in it? Not that *I* sent the pig, or can form the remotest guess what part Owen could play in the business. I never knew him give anything away in my life. He would not begin with strangers. I suspect the pig, after all, was meant for me; but at the unlucky juncture of time being absent, the present somehow went round to Highgate. To confess an honest truth, a pig is one of those things which I could never think of sending away. Teal, widgeon, snipes, barn-door fowls, ducks, geese—your tame villatic things—Welsh mutton, collars of brawn, sturgeon, fresh or pickled, your potted char, Swiss cheeses, French pies, early grapes, muscadines, I impart as freely unto my friends as to myself. They are but self-extended; but pardon me if I stop somewhere. Where the fine feeling of benevolence giveth a higher smack than the sensual rarity, there my friends (or any good man) may command me; but pigs are pigs, and I myself therein am nearest to myself. Nay, I should think it an affront, an undervaluing done to Nature who bestowed such a boon upon me, if in a churlish mood I parted with the precious gift. One of the bitterest pangs of remorse I ever felt was when a child—when my kind old aunt had strained her pocket-strings to bestow a sixpenny whole plum-cake upon me. In my way home through the Borough I met a venerable old man, not a mendicant, but thereabouts; a look-beggar, not a verbal petitionist; and in the coxcombry of taught charity I gave away the cake to him. I walked on a little in all the pride of an Evangelical peacock, when of a sudden my old aunt's kindness crossed me; the sum it was to her; the pleasure she had a right to expect that I—not the old impostor—should take in eating her cake; the ingratitude by which, under the colour of a Christian virtue, I had frustrated her cherished purpose. I sobbed, wept, and took it to heart so grievously, that I think I never suffered the like; and I was right. It was a piece of unfeeling hypocrisy, and it proved a lesson to me ever after. The cake has long been masticated, consigned to the dunghill with the ashes of that unseasonable pauper.

But when Providence, who is better to us all than our aunts, gives me a pig, remembering my temptation and my fall, I shall endeavour to act towards it more in the spirit of the donor's purpose.

Yours (short of pig) to command in everything.   C. L.

To WILLIAM WORDSWORTH.

LETTER CCXXV.]   *March* 20, 1822.

My dear Wordsworth—A letter from you is very grateful; I have not seen a Kendal postmark so long! We are pretty well, save colds and rheumatics, and a certain deadness to everything, which I think I may date from poor John's loss, and another accident or two at the same time, that have made me almost bury myself at Dalston, where yet I see more faces than I could wish. Deaths overset one, and put one out long after the recent grief. Two or three have died within the last two twelve-months, and so many parts of me have been numbed. One sees a picture, reads an anecdote, starts a casual fancy, and thinks to tell of it to this person in preference to every other: the person is gone whom it would have peculiarly suited. It won't do for another. Every departure destroys a class of sympathies. There's Captain Burney gone! What fun has whist now? What matters it what you lead, if you can no longer fancy him looking over you? One never hears anything, but the image of the particular person occurs with whom alone almost you would care to share the intelligence. Thus one distributes oneself about; and now for so many parts of me I have lost the market. Common natures do not suffice me. Good people, as they are called, won't serve. I want individuals. I am made up of queer points, and I want so many answering needles. The going away of friends does not make the remainder more precious. It takes so much from them as there was a common link. A. B. and C. make a party. A. dies. B. not only loses A.; but all A.'s part in C. C. loses A.'s part in B., and so the alphabet sickens by subtraction of interchangeables. I express myself muddily, *capite dolent*. I have a dulling cold. My theory is to enjoy life, but my practice is against it. I grow ominously tired of official confinement. Thirty years have I served the Philistines, and my neck is not subdued to the yoke. You don't know how wearisome it is to breathe the air of four pent walls without relief, day after day, all the golden hours of the day between ten and four, without ease or interposition. *Tædet me harum quotidianarum formarum*, these pestilential clerk-faces always in one's dish. Oh for a few years between the grave and the desk!—they are the same, save that at the latter you are the outside machine. The foul enchanter——("letters four do form his name"—Busirane is his name in hell), that has curtailed you of some domestic comforts, hath laid a heavier hand on me, not in present infliction, but in taking away the hope of enfranchisement. I dare not whisper to myself a pension on this side of absolute incapacitation and infirmity, till years have sucked me dry;— *Otium cum indignitate*. I had thought in a green old age (Oh green thought!) to have retired to Ponder's End (emblematic name, how beautiful!), in the Ware Road, there to have made up my accounts with Heaven and the company, toddling about between it and Cheshunt; anon stretching, on some fine Izaak Walton morning, to Hoddesdon or Amwell, careless as a beggar; but walking, walking ever till I fairly walked myself off my legs, dying walking! The hope is gone. I sit like Philomel all day (but not singing), with my breast against this thorn of a desk, with the only hope that some pulmonary affliction may relieve me. *Vide* Lord Palmerston's report of the clerks in the War Office (Debates in this morning's *Times*), by which it appears, in twenty years as many clerks have been coughed and catarrhed out of it into their freer graves. Thank you for asking about the pictures. Milton hangs over my fire-side in Covent Garden (when I am there), the rest have been sold for an old song, wanting the eloquent tongue that should have set them off! You have gratified me with liking my meeting with Dodd. For the Malvolio story—the thing is become in verity a sad task, and I eke it out with anything. If I could slip out of it I should be happy, but our chief-reputed assistants have forsaken us. The Opium-Eater crossed us once with a dazzling path, and hath as suddenly left us darkling; and, in short, I shall go on from dull to worse, because I cannot resist the booksellers' importunity—the old plea you know of authors, but I believe on my part sincere. Hartley I do not so often see; but I never see him in unwelcome hour. I thoroughly love and honour him. I send you a frozen epistle, but it is Winter and dead time of the year with me. May heaven keep something like Spring and Summer up with you, strengthen your eyes, and make mine a little lighter to encounter with them, as I hope they shall yet and again, before all are closed.

Yours, with every kind remembrance. C. L.

I had almost forgot to say, I think you thoroughly right about presentation copies. I should like to see you print a book I should grudge to purchase for its size. Hang me, but I would have it, though!

To WILLIAM GODWIN.

LETTER CCXXVI.]   *India House, April* 13, 1822.

Dear Godwin—I cannot imagine how you, who never in your writings have expressed yourself disrespectfully of any one but your Maker, can have given offence to Rickman.

I have written to the Numberer of the People to ask when it will be convenient to him to be at home to Mr. Booth. I think it probable he may be out of town in the Parliamentary recess, but doubt not of a speedy answer. Pray return my recognition to Mr. Booth, from whose excellent Tables of Interest I daily receive inexpressible official facilities.

Yours ever,   C. LAMB.

LETTER CCXXVII.]   *May* 16, 1822.

Dear Godwin—I sincerely feel for all your trouble. Pray use the enclosed £50, and pay me when you can. I shall make it my business to see you very shortly.

Yours truly,   C. LAMB.

To JOHN CLARE.

LETTER CCXXVIII.]   *India House, August* 31, 1822.

Dear Clare—I thank you heartily for your present. I am an inveterate old Londoner, but while I am among your choice collections I seem to be native to them and free of the country. The quality of your observation has astonished me. What have most pleased me have been "Recollections after a Ramble," and those "Grongar Hill" kind of pieces in eight syllable lines, my favourite measure, such as "Cooper Hill" and "Solitude." In some of your story-telling Ballads the provincial phrases sometimes startle me. I think you are too profuse with them. In poetry *slang* of every kind is to be avoided. There is a rustic Cockneyism, as little pleasing as ours of London. Transplant Arcadia to Helpstone. The true rustic style I think is to be found in Shenstone. Would his "Schoolmistress," the prettiest of poems, have been better if he had used quite the Goody's own language? Now and then a home rusticism is fresh and startling; but when nothing is gained in expression, it is out of tenor. It may make folks smile and stare; but the ungenial coalition of barbarous with refined phrases will prevent you in the end from being so generally tasted, as you desire to be. Excuse my freedom, and take the same liberty with my *puns*.

I send you two little volumes of my spare hours. They are of all sorts: there is a Methodist hymn for Sundays and a farce for Saturday night. Pray give them a place on your shelf. Pray accept a little volume, of which I have a duplicate, that I may return in equal number to your welcome presents. I think I am indebted to you for a sonnet in the *London* for August?

Since I saw you I have been in France, and have eaten frogs. The nicest little rabbity things you ever tasted. Do look about for them. Make Mrs. Clare pick off the hind quarters, boil them plain, with parsley and butter. The fore quarters are not so good. She may let them hop off by themselves.

Yours sincerely, CHAS. LAMB.

To BERNARD BARTON.

LETTER CCXXIX.]

India House,
September 11, 1822.

Dear Sir—You have misapprehended me sadly, if you suppose that I meant to impute any inconsistency in your writing poetry with your religious profession. I do not remember what I said, but it was spoken sportively, I am sure—one of my levities, which you are not so used to as my older friends. I probably was thinking of the light in which your so indulging yourself would appear to Quakers, and put their objection in my own foolish mouth. I would eat my words (provided they should be written on not very coarse paper) rather than I would throw cold water upon your, and my once, harmless occupation.

I have read "Napoleon" and the rest with delight. I like them for what they are, and for what they are not. I have sickened on the modern rhodomontade and Byronism, and your plain Quakerish beauty has captivated me. It is all wholesome cates; ay, and toothsome too; and withal Quakerish. If I were George Fox, and George Fox licenser of the press, they should have my absolute *imprimatur*. I hope I have removed the impression.

I am, like you, a prisoner to the desk. I have been chained to that galley thirty years,—a long shot. I have almost grown to the wood. If no imaginative poet, I am sure I am a figurative one. Do "Friends" allow puns? *verbal* equivocations? They are unjustly accused of it; and I did my little best in the "Imperfect Sympathies" to vindicate them. I am very tired of clerking it, but have no remedy. Did you see a Sonnet to this purpose in the *Examiner?*—

> "*Who* first invented work, and bound the free
> And holy-day rejoicing spirit down
> To the ever-haunting importunity
> Of business, in the green fields and the town,
> To plough, loom, anvil, spade; and oh, most sad,
> To that dry drudgery at the desk's dead wood?
> Who but the being unblest, alien from good,
> Sabbathless Satan! he who his unglad
> Task ever plies, 'mid rotatory burnings,
> That round and round incalculably reel;
> For wrath Divine hath made him like a wheel
> In that red realm from which are no returnings;
> Where, toiling and turmoiling, ever and aye,
> He and his thoughts keep pensive worky-day."

I fancy the sentiment exprest above will be nearly your own. The expression of it probably would not so well suit with a follower of John Woolman. But I do not know whether diabolism is a part of your creed, or where indeed to find exposition of your creed at all. In feelings and matters not dogmatical, I hope I am half a Quaker. Believe me, with great respect, yours, C. LAMB.

I shall always be happy to see or hear from you.

To MRS. KENNEY.

LETTER CCXXX.]   *London, September* 11, 1822.

Dear Mrs. K.—Mary got home safe on Friday night. She has suffered only a common fatigue, but as she is weakly, begs me to thank you in both our names for all the trouble she has been to you. She did not succeed in saving Robinson's fine waistcoat. They could not comprehend how a waistcoat, marked Henry Robinson, could be a part of Miss Lamb's wearing apparel. So they seized it for the king, who will probably appear in it at the next levee. Next to yourself, our best thanks to H. Payne. I was disappointed he came not with her. Tell Kenney the Cow has got out, by composition, paying so much in the pound. The canary bird continues her sleep-persuading strains. Pray say to Ellen that I think the verses very pretty which she slipt into my pocket on the last day of my being at Versailles. The stanzas on Ambition are fine, allowing for the age of the writer. The thought that the present King of Spain whom I suppose she means by the "brown monarch," sitting in state among his grandees, is like

"A sparrow lonely on the house's top,"

is perhaps a little forced. The next line is better,

"Too high to stoop, though not afraid to drop."

Pray deliver what follows to my dear wife Sophy.

My dear Sophy—The few short days of connubial felicity which I passed with you among the pears and apricots of Versailles were some of the happiest of my life. But they are flown! And your other half—your dear co-twin—that she-you—that almost equal sharer of my affections: you and she are my better half, a quarter a-piece. She and you are my pretty sixpence—you the head, and she the tail. Sure, Heaven that made you so alike must pardon the error of an inconsiderate moment, should I for love of you, love her too well. Do you think laws were made for lovers? I think not.

Adieu, amiable Pair, Yours and yours   C. LAMB.

P.S.—I enclose half a dear kiss a-piece for you.

TO MR. BARRON FIELD.

LETTER CCXXXI.]   *September 22, 1822.*

My dear F.—I scribble hastily at office. Frank wants my letter presently. I and sister are just returned from Paris!! We have eaten frogs. It has been such a treat! You know our monotonous tenor. Frogs are the nicest little delicate things—rabbity-flavoured. Imagine a Lilliputian rabbit! They fricassee them; but in my mind, drest seethed, plain, with parsley and butter, would have been the decision of Apicius. Paris is a glorious picturesque old city. London looks mean and new to it, as the town of Washington would, seem after it. But they have no St. Paul's, or Westminster Abbey. The Seine, so much despised by Cockneys, is exactly the size to run through a magnificent street; palaces a mile long on one side, lofty Edinbro' stone (O the glorious antiques!) houses on the other. The Thames disunites London and Southwark. I had Talma to supper with me. He has picked up, as I believe, an authentic portrait of Shakspeare. He paid a broker about £40 English for it. It is painted on the one half of a pair of bellows,—a lovely picture, corresponding with the folio head. The bellows has old carved *wings* round it, and round the visnomy is inscribed, as near as I remember, not divided into rhyme—I found out the rhyme—

"Whom have we here,
Stuck on the bellows,
But the Prince of good fellows,
Willy Shakspeare?"

At top—

> "O base and coward luck
> To be here stuck!"—POINS.

At bottom—

> "Nay! rather a glorious lot is to him assign'd,
> Who, like the Almighty, rides upon the *wind.*"
>
> PISTOL.

This is all in old carved wooden letters. The countenance smiling, sweet, and intellectual beyond measure, even as he was immeasurable. It may be a forgery. They laugh at me and tell me Ireland is in Paris, and has been putting off a portrait of the Black Prince. How far old wood may be imitated I cannot say. Ireland was not found out by his parchments, but by his poetry. I am confident no painter on either side the Channel could have painted anything near like the face I saw. Again, would such a painter and forger have taken £40 for a thing, if authentic, worth £4000? Talma is not in the secret, for he had not even found out the rhymes in the first inscription. He is coming over with it, and, my life to Southey's Thalaba, it will gain universal faith.

The letter is wanted, and I am wanted. Imagine the blank filled up with all kind things.

Our joint hearty remembrances to both of you.

Yours, as ever,   C. LAMB.

To BERNARD BARTON.

East India House,
LETTER CCXXXII.]   *October* 9, 1822.

Dear Sir—I am ashamed not sooner to have acknowledged your letter and poem. I think the latter very temperate, very serious, and very seasonable. I do not think it will convert the club at Pisa, neither do I think it will satisfy the bigots on our side the water. Something like a parody on the song of Ariel would please them better:—

> "Full fathom five the Atheist lies,
> Of his bones are hell-dice made."

I want time, or fancy, to fill up the rest. I sincerely sympathise with you on your doleful confinement. Of time, health, and riches, the first in order is not last in excellence. Riches are chiefly good because they give us Time. What a weight of wearisome prison hours have I to look back and forward to, as quite cut out of life! and the sting of the thing is, that for six hours every day I have no business which I could not contract into two, if they would let me work task-work. I shall be glad to hear that your grievance is mitigated. Shelley I saw once. His voice was the most obnoxious squeak I ever was tormented with, ten thousand times worse than the Laureate's, whose voice is the worst part about him, except his

Laureateship. Lord Byron opens upon him on Monday in a parody (I suppose) of the *Vision of Judgment*, in which latter the Poet I think did not much show *his*. To award his Heaven and his Hell in the presumptuous manner he has done, was a piece of immodesty as bad as Shelleyism.

I am returning a poor letter. I was formerly a great scribbler in that way, but my hand is out of order. If I said my head too, I should not be very much out, but I will tell no tales of myself; I will therefore end (after my best thanks, with a hope to see you again some time in London), begging you to accept this letteret for a letter—a leveret makes a better present than a grown hare, and short troubles (as the old excuse goes) are best.

I hear that Lloyd is well, and has returned to his family. I think this will give you pleasure to hear.

I remain, dear sir, yours truly,   C. LAMB.

To B. R. HAYDON.

LETTER CCXXXIII.]   *India House, October* 19, 1822.

Dear Haydon—Poor Godwin has been turned out of his house and business in Skinner Street, and if he does not pay two years' arrears of rent, he will have the whole stock, furniture, etc., of his new house (in the Strand) seized when term begins. We are trying to raise a subscription for him. My object in writing this is simply to ask you, if this is a kind of case which would be likely to interest Mrs. Coutts in his behalf, and *who*, in your opinion, is the best person to speak with her on his behalf. Without the aid of from £300 to £400 by that time, early in November, he will be ruined. You are the only person I can think of, of his acquaintance, and can perhaps, if not yourself, recommend the person most likely to influence her. Shelley had engaged to clear him of all demands, and he has gone down to the deep insolvent.

Yours truly,   C. LAMB.

Is Sir Walter to be applied to, and by what channel?

LETTER CCXXXIV.]   *Tuesday* [*October* 29, 1822].

Dear H.—I have written a very respectful letter to Sir W. S. Godwin did not write, because he leaves all to his Committee, as I will explain to you. If this rascally weather holds you will see but one of us on that day.

Yours, with many thanks,   CHARLES LAMB.

To JOHN HOWARD PAYNE.

LETTER CCXXXV.]   *Thursday, November* 1822.

"Ali Pacha" will do. I sent my sister the first night, not having been able to go myself, and her report of its effect was most favourable. I saw it last night—the third night—and it was most satisfactorily received. I have been sadly disappointed in Talfourd, who does the critiques in the "Times," and who promised his strenuous services; but by some damn'd arrangement he was sent to the wrong house, and a most iniquitous account of "Ali" substituted for his, which I am sure would have been a kind one. The "Morning Herald" did it ample justice, without appearing to puff it. It is an abominable misrepresentation of the "Times," that Farren played Ali like Lord Ogilby. He acted infirmity of body, but not of voice or purpose. His manner was even grand. A grand old gentleman. His falling to the earth when his son's death was announced was fine as anything I ever saw. It was as`if he had been blasted. Miss Foote looked helpless and beautiful, and greatly helped the piece. It is going on steadily, I am sure, for *many nights*. Marry, I was a little disappointed with Hassan, who tells us he subsists by cracking court jests before Hali; but he made none. In all the rest, scenery and machinery, it was faultless. I hope it will bring you here. I should be most glad of that. I have a room for you, and you shall order your own dinner three days in the week. I must retain my own authority for the rest. As far as magazines go, I can answer for Talfourd in the "New Monthly." He cannot be put out there. But it is established as a favourite, and can do without these expletives. I long to talk over with you the Shakspeare Picture. My doubts of its being a forgery mainly rest upon the goodness of the picture. The bellows might be trumped up, but where did the painter spring from? Is Ireland a consummate artist—or any of Ireland's accomplices?—but we shall confer upon it, I hope. The "New Times," I understand was favourable to "Ali," but I have not seen it. I am sensible of the want of method in this letter, but I have been deprived of the connecting organ by a practice I have fallen into since I left Paris, of taking too much strong spirits of a night. I must return to the Hotel de l'Europe and Macon.

How is Kenney? Have you seen my friend White? What is Poole about, etc.? Do not write, but come and answer me.

The weather is charming, and there is a mermaid to be seen in London. You may not have the opportunity of inspecting such a *Poissarde* once again in ten centuries.

My sister joins me in the hope of seeing you.

Yours truly,　　　　　　　　　　　　　　　　　　C. LAMB.

LETTER CCXXXVI.]　　　　　　　　*Wednesday, November* 13, '22.

Dear P.—Owing to the inconvenience of having two lodgings, I did not get your letter quite so soon as I should. The India House is my proper address, where I am sure for the fore part of every day. The instant I got it, I addressed a letter, for Kemble to see, to my friend Henry Robertson, the Treasurer of Covent Garden Theatre. He had a conference with Kemble, and the result is, that Robertson, in the name of the management, recognised to me the full ratifying of your bargain: £250 for Ali, the "Slaves," and another piece which they had not received. He assures me the whole will be paid you, or the proportion for the two former, as soon as ever the Treasury will permit it. He offered to write the same to you, if I pleased. He thinks in a month or so they will be able to liquidate it. He is positive no trick could be meant you, as Mr. Planché's alterations, which were trifling, were not at all considered as affecting your bargain. With respect to the copyright of "Ali," he was of opinion no money would be given for it, as "Ali" is quite laid aside. This explanation being given, you would not think of printing the two copies together by way of recrimination. He told me the secret of the two "Galley Slaves" at Drury Lane. Elliston, if he is informed right, engaged Poole to translate it, but before Poole's translation arrived, finding it coming out at Cov. Gar., he procured copies of two several translations of it in London. So you see here are four translations, reckoning yours. I fear no copyright would be got for it, for anybody may print it and anybody has. Yours has run seven nights, and R. is of opinion it will not exceed in number of nights the nights of "Ali"—about thirteen. But your full right to your bargain with the management is in the fullest manner recognised by him officially. He gave me every hope the money will be spared as soon as they can spare it. He said *a month or two*, but seemed to me to mean about *a month*. A new lady is coming out in Juliet, to whom they look very confidently for replenishing their treasury. Robertson is a very good fellow and I can rely upon his statement. Should you have any more pieces, and want to get a copyright for them, I am the worst person to negotiate with any bookseller, having been cheated by all I have had to do with (except Taylor and Hessey,—but they do not publish theatrical pieces), and I know not how to go about it, or who to apply to. But if you had no better negotiator, I should know the minimum you expect, for I should not like to make a bargain out of my own head, being (after the Duke of Wellington) the worst of all negotiators. I find from Robertson you have written to Bishop on the subject. Have you named anything of the copyright of the "Slaves"? R. thinks no publisher would pay for it, and you would not risk it on your own account. This is a mere business letter, so I will just send my love to my little wife at Versailles, to her dear mother, etc.

Believe me, yours truly,   C. L.

To J. TAYLOR.

LETTER CCXXXVII.]   *December* 7, 1822.

Dear Sir—I should like the enclosed Dedication to be printed, unless you dislike it. I like it. It is in the olden style. But if you object to it, put forth the book as it is; only pray don't let the printer mistake the word *curt* for *curst*.   C. L.

DEDICATION.

TO THE FRIENDLY AND JUDICIOUS READER,

who will take these Papers, as they were meant; not understanding every-thing perversely in its absolute and literal sense, but giving fair construc-tion, as to an after-dinner conversation; allowing for the rashness and necessary incompleteness of first thoughts; and not remembering, for the purpose of an after taunt, words spoken peradventure after the fourth glass, the Author wishes (what he would will for himself) plenty of good friends to stand by him, good books to solace him, prosperous events to all his honest undertakings, and a candid interpretation to his most hasty words and actions. The other sort (and he hopes many of them will pur-chase his book too) he greets with the curt invitation of Timon, "Uncover, dogs, and lap:" or he dismisses them with the confident security of the philosopher,—"you beat but on the case of Elia." On better considera-tion, pray omit that Dedication. The Essays want no Preface: they are *all Preface.* A Preface is nothing but a talk with the reader; and they do nothing else. Pray omit it.

There will be a sort of Preface in the next Magazine, which may act as an advertisement, but not proper for the volume.

Let ELIA come forth bare as he was born.   C. L.

Messrs. Taylor and Hessey,
        Booksellers, Fleet Street.

No Preface.

To Mr. WALTER WILSON.

LETTER CCXXXVIII.]   *E. I. H., December* 16, 1822.

Dear Wilson—*Lightning* I was going to call you. You must have thought me negligent in not answering your letter sooner. But I have a habit of never writing letters but at the office; 'tis so much time cribbed out of the Company; and I am just got out of the thick of a tea-sale, in which most of the entry of notes, deposits, etc., usually falls to my share.

I have nothing of De Foe's but two or three novels and the "Plague History." I can give you no information about him. As a slight general character of what I remember of them (for I have not looked into them latterly), I would say that in the appearance of *truth,* in all the incidents and conversations that occur in them, they exceed any works of fiction I am acquainted with. It is perfect illusion. The *author* never appears in these self-narratives (for so they ought to be called, or rather autobiogra-phies), but the *narrator* chains us down to an implicit belief in everything he says. There is all the minute detail of a log-book in it. Dates are pain-fully pressed upon the memory. Facts are repeated over and over in varying phases, till you cannot choose but believe them. It is like reading evidence given in a court of justice. So anxious the story-teller seems that the truth should be clearly comprehended, that when he has told us a matter of fact or a motive, in a line or two farther down he *repeats* it, with his favourite figure of speech, "I say," so and so, though he had made it abundantly plain before. This is in imitation of the common people's way of speaking, or rather of the way in which they are addressed by a master or mistress, who wishes to impress something upon their memories, and has a wonderful effect upon matter-of-fact readers. Indeed it is to such principally that he writes. His style is everywhere beautiful, but plain and *homely*. Robinson Crusoe is delightful to all ranks and classes, but it is easy to see that it is written in phraseology peculiarly adapted to the lower conditions of readers; hence it is an especial favourite with seafaring men, poor boys, servant-maids, etc. His novels are capital kitchen-reading, while they are worthy, from their deep interest, to find a shelf in the libraries of the wealthiest and the most learned. His passion for *matter-of-fact narrative* sometimes betrayed him into a long relation of common incidents, which might happen to any man, and have no interest but the intense appearance of truth in them, to recommend them. The whole latter half or two-thirds of "Colonel Jack" is of this description. The beginning of "Colonel Jack" is the most affecting natural picture of a young thief that was ever drawn. His losing the stolen money in the hollow of a tree, and finding it again when he was in despair, and then being in equal distress at not knowing how to dispose of it, and several similar touches in the early history of the Colonel, evince a deep knowledge of human nature; and putting out of question the superior *romantic* interest of the latter, in my mind very much exceed Crusoe. "Roxana" (first edition) is the next in interest, though he left out the best part of it in subsequent editions from a foolish hypercriticism of his friend Southerne. But "Moll Flanders," the "Account of the Plague," etc., are all of one family, and have the same stamp of character.

Believe me, with friendly recollections, *Brother* (as I used to call you), yours, C. LAMB.

To BERNARD BARTON.

LETTER CCXXXIX.] *December 23, 1822.*

Dear Sir—I have been so distracted with business and one thing or other, I have not had a quiet quarter of an hour for epistolary purposes. Christmas, too, is come, which always puts a rattle into my morning skull. It is a visiting, unquiet, unquakerish season. I get more and more in love with solitude, and proportionately hampered with company. I hope you have some holidays at this period. I have one day—Christmas Day; alas! too few to commemorate the season. All work and no play dulls me. Company is not play, but many times hard work. To play, is for a man to do what he pleases, or to do nothing—to go about soothing his particular fancies. I have lived to a time of life to have outlived the good hours, the nine o'clock suppers, with a bright hour or two to clear up in afterwards. Now you cannot get tea before that hour, and then sit gaping, music-bothered perhaps, till half-past twelve brings up the tray; and what you steal of convivial enjoyment after, is heavily paid for in the disquiet of to-morrow's head.

I am pleased with your liking *John Woodvil*, and amused with your knowledge of our drama being confined to Shakspeare and Miss Baillie. What a world of fine territory between Land's End and Johnny Groat's have you missed traversing! I could almost envy you to have so much to read. I feel as if I had read all the books I want to read. O to forget Fielding, Steele, etc., and read 'em new!

Can you tell me a likely place where I could pick up, cheap, Fox's journal? There are no Quaker circulating libraries? Elwood, too, I must have. I rather grudge that Southey has taken up the history of your people: I am afraid he will put in some levity. I am afraid I am not quite exempt from that fault in certain magazine articles, where I have introduced mention of them. Were they to do again, I would reform them. Why should not you write a poetical account of your old worthies, deducing them from Fox to Woolman? But I remember you did talk of something in that kind, as a counterpart to the "Ecclesiastical Sketches." But would not a poem be more consecutive than a string of sonnets? You have no martyrs *quite to the fire*, I think, among you; but plenty of heroic confessors, spirit-martyrs, lamb-lions. Think of it; it would be better than a series of sonnets on "Eminent Bankers." I like a hit at our way of life, though it does well for me, better than anything short of *all one's time to one's self;* for which alone I rankle with envy at the rich. Books are good, and pictures are good, and money to buy them therefore good; but to buy *time!* in other words, life!

The "compliments of the time" to you should end my letter; to a Friend, I suppose, I must say the "sincerity of the season"; I hope they both mean the same. With excuses for this hastily-penned note, believe me, with great respect,   C. LAMB.

To MISS WORDSWORTH.

LETTER CCXL.]

Mary perfectly approves of the appropriation of the *feathers,* and wishes them peacock's for your fair niece's sake.

Christmas 1822.

Dear Miss Wordsworth—I had just written the above endearing words when Monkhouse tapped me on the shoulder with an invitation to cold goose pie, which I was not bird of that sort enough to decline. Mrs. M——, I am most happy to say, is better. Mary has been tormented with rheumatism, which is leaving her. I am suffering from the festivities of the season. I wonder how my misused carcass holds it out. I have played the experimental philosopher on it, that's certain. Willy shall be welcome to a mince-pie, and a bout at commerce whenever he comes. He was in our eye. I am glad you liked my new year's speculations: everybody likes them, except the author of the *Pleasures of Hope*. Disappointment attend him! How I like to be liked, and *what I do* to be liked! They flatter me in magazines, newspapers, and all the minor reviews; the Quarterlies hold aloof. But they must come into it in time, or their leaves be waste paper. Salute Trinity Library in my name. Two special things are worth seeing at Cambridge, a portrait of Cromwell, at Sydney, and a better of Dr. Harvey (who found out that blood was red), at Dr. Davy's; you should see them. Coleridge is pretty well. I have not seen him, but hear often of him from Allsop, who sends me hares and pheasants twice a week; I can hardly take so fast as he gives. I have almost forgotten butcher's meat, as plebeian. Are you not glad the cold is gone? I find Winters not so agreeable as they used to be "when Winter bleak had charms for me." I cannot conjure up a kind similitude for those snowy flakes. Let them keep to twelfth cakes!

Mrs. Paris, our Cambridge friend, has been in town. You do not know the Watfords in Trumpington Street. They are capital people. Ask anybody you meet who is the biggest woman in Cambridge, and I'll hold you a wager they'll say Mrs. Smith. She broke down two benches in Trinity gardens, one on the confines of St. John's, which occasioned a litigation between the Societies as to repairing it. In warm weather she retires into an ice-cellar (literally!) and dates the returns of the years from a hot Thursday some twenty years back. She sits in a room with opposite doors and windows, to let in a thorough draught, which gives her slenderer friends tooth-aches. She is to be seen in the market every morning, at ten, cheapening fowls, which I observe the Cambridge poulterers are not sufficiently careful to stump.

Having now answered most of the points contained in your letter, let me end with assuring you of our very best kindness, and excuse Mary from not handling the pen on this occasion, especially as it has fallen into so much better hands! Will Dr. W. accept of my respects at the end of a foolish letter? C. L.

To —— DIBDIN, Esq.

LETTER CCXLI.] 1822.

It is hard when a gentleman cannot remain concealed, who affecteth obscurity with greater avidity than most do seek to have their good deeds brought to light—to have a prying inquisitive finger (to the danger of its own scorching) busied in removing the little peck measure (scripturally a bushel) under which one had hoped to bury his small candle. The receipt of fern-seed, I think, in this curious age, would scarce help a man to walk invisible.

Well, I am discovered—and thou thyself, who thoughtest to shelter under the pease-cod of initiality (a stale and shallow device), art no less dragged to light. Thy slender anatomy—thy skeletonian D—— fleshed and sinewed out to the plump expansion of six characters—thy tuneful genealogy deduced.

By the way, what a name is Timothy! Lay it down, I beseech thee, and in its place take up the properer sound of Timotheus.

Then mayst thou with unblushing fingers handle the lyre "familiar to the D——n name."

With much difficulty have I traced thee to thy lurking-place. Many a goodly name did I run over, bewildered between Dorrien, and Doxat, and Dover, and Dakin, and Daintry—a wilderness of D's—till at last I thought I had hit it—my conjectures wandering upon a melancholy Jew —you wot the Israelite upon 'Change—Master Daniels, a contemplative Hebrew, to the which guess I was the rather led by the consideration that most of his nation are great readers.

Nothing is so common as to see them in the Jews' Walk, with a bundle of scrip in one hand and the *Man of Feeling* or a volume of Sterne in the other.

I am a rogue if I can collect what manner of face thou carriest, though thou seemest so familiar with mine. If I remember thou didst not dimly resemble the man Daniels, whom at first I took thee for—a careworn, mortified, economical, commercio-political countenance, with an agreeable limp in thy gait, if Elia mistake thee not. I think I should shake hands with thee, if I met thee.

To Mr. AND Mrs. BRUTON.

LETTER CCXLII.]   *January* 6, 1823.

The pig was above my feeble praise. It was a dear pigmy. There was some contention as to who should have the ears; but, in spite of his obstinacy (deaf as these little creatures are to advice), I contrived to get at one of them.

It came in boots too, which I took as a favour. Generally these pretty toes, pretty toes! are missing; but I suppose he wore them to look taller.

He must have been the least of his race. His little foots would have gone into the silver slipper. I take him to have been a Chinese and a female.

If Evelyn could have seen him, he would never have farrowed two such prodigious volumes; seeing how much good can be contained in—how small a compass!

He crackled delicately.

I left a blank at the top of my letter, not being determined which to address it to: so farmer and farmer's wife will please to divide our thanks. May your granaries be full, and your rats empty, and your chickens plump, and your envious neighbours lean, and your labourers busy, and you as idle and as happy as the day is long!

VIVE L'AGRICULTURE!

How do you make your pigs so little?
They are vastly engaging at the age:
    I was so myself.
Now I am a disagreeable old hog,
A middle-aged gentleman-and-a-half,
My faculties (thank God!) are not much impaired.

I have my sight, hearing, taste, pretty perfect; and can read the Lord's Prayer in common type, by the help of a candle, without making many mistakes.

Believe me, that while my faculties last, I shall ever cherish a proper appreciation of your many kindnesses in this way, and that the last lingering relish of past favours upon my dying memory will be the smack of that little ear. It was the left ear, which is lucky. Many happy returns, not of the pig, but of the New Year, to both! Mary, for her share of the pig and the memoirs, desires to send the same.

Yours truly,   C. LAMB.

To BERNARD BARTON.

LETTER CCXLIII.]   *January* 9, 1823.

"Throw yourself on the world without any rational plan of support, beyond what the chance employ of booksellers would afford you!!!"

Throw yourself rather, my dear sir, from the steep Tarpeian rock, slap-dash headlong upon iron spikes. If you had but five consolatory minutes between the desk and the bed, make much of them, and live a century in them, rather than turn slave to the booksellers. They are Turks and Tartars when they have poor authors at their beck. Hitherto you have been at arm's length from them. Come not within their grasp. I have known many authors for bread, some repining, others envying the blessed security of a counting-house, all agreeing they would rather have been tailors, weavers,—what not, rather than the things they were. I have known some starved, some to go mad, one dear friend literally dying in a workhouse. You know not what a rapacious, dishonest set these booksellers are. Ask even Southey, who (a single case almost) has made a fortune by book drudgery, what he has found them. Oh, you know not (may you never know!) the miseries of subsisting by authorship. 'Tis a pretty appendage to a situation like yours or mine; but a slavery, worse than all slavery, to be a bookseller's dependant, to drudge your brains for pots of ale and breasts of mutton, to change your free thoughts and voluntary numbers for ungracious task-work. Those fellows hate *us*. The reason I take to be, that contrary to other trades, in which the master gets all the credit (a jeweller or silversmith for instance), and the journeyman, who really does the fine work, is in the background,—in *our* work the world gives all the credit to us, whom *they* consider as *their* journeymen, and therefore do they hate us, and cheat us, and oppress us, and would wring the blood of us out, to put another sixpence in their mechanic pouches! I contend that a bookseller has a *relative honesty* towards authors, not like his honesty to the rest of the world. B., who first engaged me as "Elia," has not paid me up yet (nor any of us without repeated mortifying appeals), yet how the knave fawned when I was of service to him! Yet I dare say the fellow is punctual in settling his milk-score, etc.

Keep to your bank, and the bank will keep you. Trust not to the public; you may hang, starve, drown yourself, for anything that worthy *personage* cares. I bless every star that Providence, not seeing good to make me independent, has seen it next good to settle me upon the stable foundation of Leadenhall. Sit down, good B. B., in the banking-office. What! is there not from six to eleven *p.m.* six days in the week, and is there not all Sunday? Fie, what a superfluity of man's time, if you could think so!—enough for relaxation, mirth, converse, poetry, good thoughts, quiet thoughts. Oh the corroding, torturing, tormenting thoughts, that disturb the brain of the unlucky wight who must draw upon it for daily sustenance! Henceforth I retract all my fond complaints of mercantile employment; look upon them as lovers' quarrels. I was but half in earnest. Welcome dead timber of a desk, that makes me live. A little grumbling is a wholesome medicine for the spleen; but in my inner heart do I approve and embrace this our close but unharassing way of life. I am quite serious. If you can send me Fox, I will not keep it *six weeks,* and will return it, with warm thanks to yourself and friend, without blot or dog's ear. You will much oblige me by this kindness.

Yours truly, C. LAMB.

To J. HOWARD PAYNE.

LETTER CCXLIV.] *January* 23, '23.

Dear Payne—I have no mornings (my day begins at 5 P.M.) to transact business in, or talents for it, so I employ Mary, who has seen Robertson, who says that the Piece which is to be Operafied was sent to you six weeks since by a Mr. Hunter, whose journey has been delayed, but he supposes you have it by this time. On receiving it back properly done, the rest of your dues will be forthcoming. You have received £30 from Harwood, I hope? Bishop was at the theatre when Mary called, and he has put your other piece into C. Kemble's hands (the piece you talk of offering Elliston) and C. K. sent down word that he had not yet had time to read it. So stand your affairs at present. Glossop has got the

"Murderer." Will you address him on the subject, or shall I—that is, Mary? She says you must write more *showable* letters about these matters, for, with all our trouble of crossing out this word, and giving a cleaner turn to th' other, and folding down at this part, and squeezing an obnoxious epithet into a corner, she can hardly communicate their contents without offence. What, man, put less gall in your ink, or write me a biting tragedy!   C. LAMB.

To BERNARD BARTON.

LETTER CCXLV.]   *February* 17, 1823.

My dear Sir—I have read quite through the ponderous folio of George Fox. I think Sewell has been judicious in omitting certain parts, as for instance where G. F. *has* revealed to him the natures of all the creatures in their names, as Adam had. He luckily turns aside from that compendious study of natural history, which might have superseded Buffon, to his proper spiritual pursuits, only just hinting what a philosopher he might have been. The ominous passage is near the beginning of the book. It is clear he means a physical knowledge, without trope or figure. Also, pretences to miraculous healing, and the like, are more frequent than I should have suspected from the epitome in Sewell. He is nevertheless a great spiritual man, and I feel very much obliged by your procuring me the loan of it. How I like the Quaker phrases!—though I think they were hardly completed till Woolman. A pretty little manual of Quaker language (with an endeavour to explain them) might be gathered out of his book. Could not you do it? I have read through G. F. without finding any explanation of the term *first volume* in the title-page. It takes in all, both his life and his death. Are there more last words of him? Pray how may I return it to Mr. Sewell at Ipswich? I fear to send such a treasure by a stage-coach; not that I am afraid of the coachman or the guard's *reading it;* but it might be lost. Can you put me in a way of sending it in safety? The kind-hearted owner trusted it to me for six months; I think I was about as many days in getting through it, and I do not think that I skipped a word of it. I have quoted G. F. in my "Quaker's Meeting," as having said he was "lifted up in spirit" (which I felt at the time to be not a Quaker phrase), "and the judge and jury were as dead men under his feet." I find no such words in his journal, and I did not get them from Sewell, and the latter sentence I am sure I did not mean to invent: I must have put some other Quaker's words into his mouth. Is it a fatality in me, that everything I touch turns into "a lie"? I once quoted two lines from a translation of Dante, which Hazlitt very greatly admired, and quoted in a book as proof of the stupendous power of that poet; but no such lines are to be found in the translation, which has been searched for the purpose. I must have dreamed them, for I am quite certain I did not forge them knowingly. What a misfortune to have a lying memory! Yes,

I have seen Miss Coleridge, and wish I had just such a—daughter. God love her! To think she should have had to toil through five octavos of that cursed (I forget I write to a Quaker) Abbeypony History, and then to abridge them to three, and all for £113!—at her years to be doing stupid Jesuits' Latin into English, when she should be reading or writing romances! Heaven send her uncle do not breed her up a Quarterly Reviewer! which reminds me that he has spoken very respectfully of you in the last Number, which is the next thing to having a Review all to one's self. Your description of Mr. Mitford's place makes me long for a pippin and some caraways, and a cup of sack in his orchard, when the sweets of the night come in.

Farewell,   C. Lamb.

To J. HOWARD PAYNE.

Letter CCXLVI.]   *February* 1823.

My dear Miss Lamb—I have enclosed for you Mr. Payne's piece called "Grandpapa," which I regret to say is not thought to be of the nature that will suit this theatre; but as there appears to be much merit in it, Mr. Kemble strongly recommends that you should send it to the English Opera House, for which it seems to be excellently adapted. As you have already been kind enough to be our medium of communication with Mr. Payne, I have imposed this trouble upon you; but if you do not like to act for Mr. Payne in the business, and have no means of disposing of the piece, I will forward it to Paris or elsewhere as you think he may prefer.

Very truly yours,   Henry Robertson.

T. R. C. G., Feb. 8, 1823.

Dear P—— We have just received the above, and want your instructions. It strikes me as a very merry little piece, that should be played by *very young actors*. It strikes me that Miss Clara Fisher would play the *boy* exactly. She is just such a forward chit. No young *man* would do it without its appearing absurd, but in a girl's hands it would have just all the reality that a short drama of an act requires. Then for the sister, if Miss Stevenson that was were Miss Stevenson and younger, they two would carry it off. I do not know who they have got in that young line, besides Miss C. F., at Drury, nor how you would like Elliston to have it —has he not had it? I am thick with Arnold, but I have always heard that the very slender profits of the English Opera House do not admit of his giving above a trifle, or next to none, for a piece of this kind. Write me what I should do, what you would ask, etc. The music (printed) is returned with the piece, and the French original. Tell Mr. Grattan I thank him for his book, which as far as I have read it is a very *companionable one*. I have but just received it. It came the same hour with your packet from Cov. Gar., *i.e.* yester-night late, to my summer residence, where, tell Kenney, the cow is quiet. Love to all at Versailles. Write quickly. C. L.

I have no acquaintance with Kemble at all, having only met him once or twice; but any information, etc., I can get from R., who is a good fellow, you may command. I am sorry the rogues are so dilatory, but I distinctly believe they mean to fulfil their engagement. I am sorry you are not here to see to these things. I am a poor man of business, but command me to the short extent of my tether. My sister's kind remembrance ever. C. L.

To WALTER WILSON.

LETTER CCXLVII.] *February* 24, 1823.

Dear W.—I write that you may not think me neglectful, not that I have anything to say. In answer to your questions, it was at your house I saw an edition of "Roxana," the preface to which stated that the author had left out that part of it which related to Roxana's daughter persisting in imagining herself to be so, in spite of the mother's denial, from certain hints she had picked up, and throwing herself continually in her mother's way (as Savage is said to have done in his, prying in at windows to get a glimpse of her), and that it was by advice of Southern, who objected to the circumstances as being untrue, when the rest of the story was founded on fact; which shows S. to have been a stupid-ish fellow. The incidents so resemble Savage's story, that I taxed Godwin with taking Falkner from his life by Dr. Johnson. You should have the edition (if you have not parted with it), for I saw it never but at your place at the Mews' Gate, nor did I then read it to compare it with my own; only I know the daughter's curiosity is the best part of *my* "Roxana." The prologue you speak of was mine, and so named, but not worth much. You ask me for two or three pages of verse. I have not written so much since you knew me. I am altogether prosaic. May be I may touch off a sonnet in time. I do not prefer "Colonel Jack" to either "Robinson Crusoe" or "Roxana." I only spoke of the beginning of it, his childish history. The rest is poor. I do not know anywhere any good character of De Foe besides what you mention. I do not know that Swift mentions him; Pope does. I forget if D'Israeli has. Dunlop I think has nothing of him. He is quite new ground, and scarce known beyond "Crusoe." I do not know who wrote "Quarl." I never thought of "Quarl" as having an author. It is a poor imitation; the monkey is the best in it, and his pretty dishes made of shells. Do you know the paper in the *Englishman* by Sir Richard Steele, giving an account of Selkirk? It is admirable, and has all the germs of "Crusoe." You must quote it entire. Captain G. Carleton wrote his own Memoirs; they are about Lord Peterborough's campaign in Spain, and a good book. "Puzzelli" puzzles me, and I am in a cloud about "Donald M'Leod." I never heard of them; so you see, my dear Wilson, what poor assistances I can give in the way of information. I wish your book out, for I shall like to see anything about De Foe or from you.

Your old friend, C. LAMB.

From my and your old compound.

To BERNARD BARTON.

LETTER CCXLVIII.] *March* 5, 1823.

Dear Sir—You must think me ill-mannered not to have replied to your first letter sooner, but I have an ugly habit of aversion from letter writing, which makes me an unworthy correspondent. I have had no spring, or cordial call to the occupation of late. I have been not well lately, which must be my lame excuse. Your Poem, which I consider very affecting, found me engaged about a humorous Paper for the *London*, which I had called "A Letter to an *Old Gentleman* whose education had been neglected"—and when it was done Taylor and Hessey would not print it, and it discouraged me from doing anything else; so I took up Scott, where I had scribbled some petulant remarks, and for a make-shift father'd them on Ritson. It is obvious I could not make your Poem a part of them; and as I did not know whether I should ever be able to do to my mind what you suggested, I thought it not fair to keep back the verses for the chance. Mr. Mitford's Sonnet I like very well; but as I also have my reasons against interfering at all with the Editorial arrangement of the *London*, I transmitted it (not in my own handwriting) to them, who I doubt not will be glad to insert it. What eventual benefit it can be to you (otherwise than that a kind man's wish is a benefit) I cannot conjecture. Your Society are eminently men of business, and will probably regard you as an idle fellow, possibly disown you; that is to say, if you had put your own name to a Sonnet of that sort; but they cannot excommunicate Mr. Mitford; therefore I thoroughly approve of printing the said verses. When I see any Quaker names to the Concert of Ancient Music, or as Directors of the British Institution, or bequeathing medals to Oxford for the best classical themes, etc., then I shall begin to hope they will emancipate you. But what as a Society can they do for you? You would not accept a commission in the army, nor they be likely to procure it. Posts in Church or State have they none in their giving; and then, if they disown you,—think—you must live "a man forbid."

I wished for you yesterday. I dined in Parnassus, with Wordsworth, Coleridge, Rogers, and Tom Moore,—half the poetry of England constellated and clustered in Gloucester Place! It was a delightful evening. Coleridge was in his finest vein of talk—had all the talk; and let 'em talk as evilly as they do of the envy of poets, I am sure not one there but was content to be nothing but a listener. The Muses were dumb while Apollo lectured on his and their fine art. It is a lie that poets are envious. I have known the best of them, and can speak to it, that they give each other their merits, and are the kindest critics as well as best authors. I am scribbling a muddy epistle with an aching head, for we did not quaff Hippocrene last night; marry, it was Hippocrass rather. Pray accept this as a letter in the meantime, and do me the favour to mention my respects to Mr. Mitford, who is so good as to entertain good thoughts of Elia, but don't show this almost impertinent scrawl. I will write more respectfully next time, for believe me, if not in words, in feelings yours most so,   C. L.

LETTER CCXLIX.]   *March* 11, 1823.

Dear Sir—The approbation of my little book by your sister is very pleasing to me. The Quaker incident did not happen to me, but to Carlisle the surgeon, from whose mouth I have twice heard it, at an interval of ten or twelve years, with little or no variation, and have given it as exactly as I could remember it. The gloss which your sister or you have put upon it does not strike me as correct. Carlisle drew no inference from it against the honesty of the Quakers, but only in favour of their surpassing coolness; that they should be capable of committing a good joke, with an utter insensibility to its being any jest at all. I have reason to believe in the truth of it, because, as I have said, I heard him repeat it without variation at such an interval. The story loses sadly in print, for Carlisle is the best story-teller I ever heard. The idea of the discovery of roasting pigs I also borrowed, from my friend Manning, and am willing to confess both my plagiarisms. Should fate ever so order it that you shall be in town with your sister, mine bids me say, that she shall have great pleasure in being introduced to her. I think I must give up the cause of the Bank; from 9 to 9 is galley slavery, but I hope it is but temporary. Your endeavour at explaining Fox's insight into the natures of animals must fail, as I shall transcribe the passage. It appears to me that he stopt short in time, and was on the brink of falling with his friend Naylor, my favourite. The book shall be forthcoming whenever your friend can make convenient to call for it.

They have dragged me again into the Magazine, but I feel the spirit of the thing in my own mind quite gone. "Some brains" (I think Ben Jonson says it) "will endure but one skimming." We are about to have an inundation of poetry from the Lakes: Wordsworth and Southey are coming up strong from the North. The She Coleridges have taken flight, to my regret. With Sara's own-made acquisitions, her unaffectedness and no-pretensions are beautiful. You might pass an age with her without suspecting that she knew anything but her mother's tongue. I don't mean any reflections on Mrs. Coleridge here. I had better have said her vernacular idiom. Poor C., I wish he had a home to receive his daughter in; but he is but as a stranger or a visitor in this world.

How did you like Hartley's sonnets? The first, at least, is vastly fine. I am ashamed of the shabby letters I send, but I am by nature anything but neat. Therein my mother bore me no Quaker. I never could seal a letter without dropping the wax on one side, besides scalding my fingers. I never had a seal, too, of my own. Writing to a great man lately, who is moreover very heraldic, I borrowed a seal of a friend, who by the female side quarters the Protectorial arms of Cromwell. How they must have puzzled my correspondent! My letters are generally charged as double at the Post Office, from their inveterate clumsiness of foldure; so you must not take it disrespectful to yourself if I send you such ungainly scraps. I think I lose £100 a year at the India House, owing solely to my want of neatness in making up accounts. How I puzzle 'em out at last is the wonder. I have to do with millions!!

It is time to have done my incoherences.

Believe me, yours truly, C. LAMB.

To J. HOWARD PAYNE.

LETTER CCL.] 1823.

Dear Payne—Your little books are most acceptable. 'Tis a delicate edition. They are gone to the binder's. When they come home I shall have two—the "Camp" and "Patrick's Day"—to read for the first time. I may say three, for I never read the "School for Scandal." "*Seen* it I have, and in its happier days." With the books Harwood left a truncheon or mathematical instrument, of which we have not yet ascertained the use. It is like a telescope, but unglazed. Or a ruler, but not smooth enough. It opens like a fan, and discovers a frame such as they weave lace upon at Lyons and Chambery. Possibly it is from those parts. I do not value the present the less for not being quite able to detect its purport. When I can find any one coming your way I have a volume for you, my Elias collected. Tell Poole, his Cockney in the Lon. Mag. tickled me exceedingly. Harwood is to be with us this evening with Fanny, who comes to introduce a literary lady, who wants to see me,—and whose portentous name is *Plura*, in English, "many things." Now, of all God's creatures, I detest letters-affecting, authors-hunting ladies. But Fanny "will have it so." So Miss Many-Things and I are to have a conference, of which you shall have the result. I dare say she does not play at whist. Treasurer Robertson, whose coffers are absolutely swelling with pantomimic receipts, called on me yesterday to say he is going to write to you, but if I were also, I might as well say that your last bill is at the Banker's, and will be honoured on the instant receipt of the third Piece, which you have stipulated for. If you have any such in readiness, strike while the iron is hot, before the Clown cools. Tell Mrs. Kenney, that the Miss F. H. (or H. F.) Kelly, who has begun so splendidly in Juliet, is the identical little Fanny Kelly, who used to play on their green before their great Lying-Inn Lodgings at Bayswater. Her career has stopt short by the injudicious bringing her out in a vile new Tragedy, and for a third character in a stupid old one,—the "Earl of Essex." This is Macready's doing, who taught her. Her recitation, etc. (*not her voice or person*), is masculine. It is so clever, it seemed a male *Debût*. But cleverness is the bane of Female Tragedy especially. Passions uttered logically, etc. It is bad enough in men-actors. Could you do nothing for little Clara Fisher? Are there no French Pieces with a Child in them? By Pieces I mean here dramas, to prevent male-constructions. Did not the Blue Girl remind you of some of Congreve's women? Angelica or Millamant? To me she was a vision of Genteel Comedy realised. Those kind of people never come to see one. *N'import*—haven't I Miss Many-Things coming? Will you ask Horace Smith to——[*The remainder of this letter has been lost.*]

LETTER CCLI.] 1823.

Dear Payne—A friend and fellow-clerk of mine, Mr. White (a good fellow) coming to your parts, I would fain have accompanied him, but am forced instead to send a part of me, verse and prose, most of it from 20 to 30 years old, such as I then was, and I am not much altered.

Paris, which I hardly knew whether I liked when I was in it, is an object of no small magnitude with me now. I want to be going to the Jardin des Plantes (is that right, Louisa?) with you—to Pere la Chaise, La Morgue, and all the sentimentalities. How is Talma, and his (my) dear Shakspeare?

N.B.—My friend White knows Paris thoroughly, and does not want a guide. We did, and had one. We both join in thanks. Do you remember a Blue-Silk Girl (English) at the Luxembourg, that did not much seem to attend to the Pictures, who fell in love with you, and whom I fell in love with—an inquisitive, prying, curious Beauty—where is she?

Votre Très Humble Serviteur,

CHARLOIS AGNEAU,

alias C. LAMB.

Guichy is well, and much as usual. He seems blind to all the distinctions of life, except to those of sex. Remembrance to Kenney and Poole.

To B. W. PROCTER.

LETTER CCLII.] *April* 13, 1823.

Dear Lad—You must think me a brute beast, a rhinoceros, never to have acknowledged the receipt of your precious present. But indeed I am none of those shocking things, but have arrived at that indisposition to letter-writing which would make it a hard exertion to write three lines to a king to spare a friend's life: whether it is that the Magazine paying me so much a page I am loath to throw away composition. How much a sheet do you give your correspondents? I have hung up Pope, and a gem it is, in my town room; I hope for your approval. Though it accompanies the *Essay on Man*, I think that was not the poem he is here meditating. He would have looked up, somehow affectedly, if he were just conceiving "Awake, my St. John." Neither is he in the *Rape of the Lock* mood exactly. I think he has just made out the last lines of the "Epistle to Jervis," between gay and tender,

"And other beauties envy Worsley's eyes."

I'll be d . . .'d if that isn't the line. He is brooding over it, with a dreamy phantom of Lady Mary floating before him. He is thinking which is the earliest possible day and hour that she will first see it. What a miniature piece of gentility it is! Why did you give it me? I do not like you enough to give you anything so good.

I have dined with T. Moore and breakfasted with Rogers, since I saw you; have much to say about them when we meet, which I trust will be in a week or two. I have been over-watched and over-poeted since Wordsworth has been in town. I was obliged for health's sake to wish him gone, but now he is gone I feel a great loss. I am going to Dalston to recruit, and have serious thoughts of altering my condition, that is, of taking to sobriety. What do you advise me?

Rogers spake very kindly of you, as everybody does, and none with so much reason as your   C. L.

To Miss HUTCHINSON.

LETTER CCLIII.]   *April* 25, 1823.

Dear Miss H.—Mary has such an invincible reluctance to any epistolary exertion, that I am sparing her a mortification by taking the pen from her. The plain truth is, she writes such a pimping, mean, detestable hand, that she is ashamed of the formation of her letters. There is an essential poverty and abjectness in the frame of them. They look like begging letters. And then she is sure to omit a most substantial word in the second draught (for she never ventures an epistle without a foul copy first), which is obliged to be interlined; which spoils the neatest epistle, you know. Her figures, 1, 2, 3, 4, etc., where she has occasion to express numerals, as in the date (25th April 1823), are not figures, but figurantes; and the combined posse go staggering up and down shameless, as drunkards in the day-time. It is no better when she rules her paper. Her lines "are not less erring" than her words. A sort of unnatural parallel lines, that are perpetually threatening to meet; which, you know, is quite contrary to Euclid. Her very blots are not bold like this [*here a large blot is inserted*], but poor smears, half left in and half scratched out, with another smear left in their place. I like a clear letter; a bold free hand, and a fearless flourish. Then she has always to go through them (a second operation) to dot her *i*'s and cross her *t*'s. I don't think she can make a corkscrew if she tried, which has such a fine effect at the end or middle of an epistle, and fills up.

There is a corkscrew!—one of the best I ever drew. By the way, what incomparable whisky that was of Monkhouse's! But if I am to write a letter, let me begin, and not stand flourishing, like a fencer at a fair.

April 25, 1823.

Dear Miss H.—It gives me great pleasure (the letter now begins) to hear that you got down so smoothly, and that Mrs. Monkhouse's spirits are so good and enterprising. It shows, whatever her posture may be, that her mind at least is not supine. I hope the excursion will enable the former to keep pace with its outstripping neighbour. Pray present our kindest wishes to her and all (that sentence should properly have come into the Postscript, but we airy mercurial spirits, there is no keeping us in). "Time" (as was said of one of us) "toils after us in vain." I am afraid our co-visit with Coleridge was a dream. I shall not get away before the end (or middle) of June, and then you will be frog-hopping at Boulogne; and besides, I think the Gillmans would scarce trust him with us; I have a malicious knack at cutting of apron-strings. The Saints' days you speak of have long since fled to heaven, with Astræa, and the cold piety of the age lacks fervour to recall them; only Peter left his key—the iron one of the two that "shuts amain"—and that is the reason I am locked up. Meanwhile of afternoons we pick up primroses at Dalston, and Mary corrects me when I call 'em cow-slips. God bless you all; and pray remember me euphoniously to Mr. Gruvellegan. That Lee Priory must be a dainty bower. Is it built of flints?—and does it stand at Kingsgate?

To BERNARD BARTON.

LETTER CCLIV.]   *May 3, 1823.*

Dear Sir—I am vexed to be two letters in your debt, but I have been quite out of the vein lately. A philosophical treatise is wanting, of the causes of the backwardness with which persons after a certain time of life set about writing a letter. I always feel as if I had nothing to say, and the performance generally justifies the presentiment. Taylor and Hessey did foolishly in not admitting the sonnet. Surely it might have followed the B. B. I agree with you in thinking Bowring's paper better than the former. I will inquire about my letter to the old gentleman, but I expect it to *go in.* after those to the young gentleman are completed.

I do not exactly see why the goose and little goslings should emblematise *a Quaker poet that has no children*. But, after all, perhaps it is a pelican. The "Mene, Mene, Tekel, Upharsin" around it I cannot decipher. The songster of the night pouring out her effusions amid a silent meeting of madge-owlets, would be at least intelligible. A full pause here comes upon me, as if I had not a word more left. I will shake my brain, Once! Twice!—nothing comes up. George Fox recommends waiting on these occasions. I wait. Nothing comes. G. Fox—that sets me off again. I have finished the "Journal," and 400 more pages of the *"Doctrinals,"* which I picked up for 7s. 6d. If I get on at this rate, the society will be in danger of having two Quaker poets to patronise. I am at Dalston now; but if when I go back to Covent Garden I find thy friend has not called for the "Journal," thee must put me in the way of sending it; and if it should happen the lender of it, knowing that volume, has not the other, I shall be most happy in his accepting the *"Doctrinals,"* which I shall read but once certainly. It is not a splendid copy, but perfect, save a leaf of Index.

I cannot but think that the *London* drags heavily. I miss Janus. And oh how it misses Hazlitt! Procter too is affronted.

Believe me cordially yours,   C. LAMB.

To J. B. DIBDIN.

LETTER CCLV.]   *May* 6, 1823.

Dear Sir—Your verses were very pleasant, and I shall like to see more of them—I do not mean *addressed to me*.

I do not know whether you live in town or country, but if it suits your convenience I shall be glad to see you some evening—say Thursday—at 20 Great Russell Street, Covent Garden. If you can come do not trouble yourself to write. We are old-fashioned people who *drink tea* at six, or not much later, and give cold mutton and pickle at nine, the good old hour. I assure you (if it suit you) we shall be glad to see you.

Yours, etc.   C. LAMB.

My love to Mr. Railton, the same to Mr. Rankin, to the whole Firm indeed.

E.I.H., Tuesday,
        Some day of May 1823.
                Not official.

To WILLIAM HONE.

LETTER CCLVI.]   *E. I. H., May* 19, '23.

Dear Sir—I have been very agreeably entertained with your present, which I found very curious and amusing. What wiseacres our forefathers appear to have been! It should make *us* thankful, who are grown so rational and polite. I should call to thank you for the book, but go home to Dalston at present. I shall beg your acceptance (when I see you) of my little book. I have Ray's *Collections of English Words not generally Used,* 1691; and in page 60 ("North Country words") occurs *"Rynt ye"* —"by your leave," "stand handsomely." As, "Rynt you, witch," quoth Besse Locket to her mother; Proverb, Cheshire.—Doubtless this is the "Aroint" of Shakspeare.

In the same collection I find several Shakspearisms. "Rooky" wood: a Northern word for "reeky," "misty," etc. "Shandy," a north country word for "wild." Sterne was York.

Yours obliged,   C. LAMB.

I am at 14, Kingsland Row, Dalston. Will you take a walk over on Sunday? We dine exactly at 4, and shall be most glad to see you. If I don't hear from you (by note to E. I. Ho.) I will expect you.

Mr. Hone, 45, Ludgate Hill.

To CHARLES LLOYD.

LETTER CCLVII.]   1823.

Your lines are not to be understood reading on one leg. They are sinuous, and to be won with wrestling. I do assure you in sincerity that nothing you have done has given me greater satisfaction. Your obscurity, where you are dark, which is seldom, is that of too much meaning, not the painful obscurity which no toil of the reader can dissipate; not the dead vacuum and floundering place in which imagination finds no footing: it is not the dimness of positive darkness, but of distance; and he that reads and not discerns must get a better pair of spectacles. I admire every piece in the collection. I cannot say the first is best: when I do so, the last read rises up in judgment. To your Mother, to your Sister (is Mary dead?), they are all weighty with thought and tender with sentiment. Your poetry is like no other. Those cursed dryads and pagan trumperies of modern verse have put me out of conceit of the very name of poetry. Your verses are as good and as wholesome as prose, and I have made a sad blunder if I do not leave you with an impression that your present is rarely valued.   CHARLES LAMB.

To BERNARD BARTON.

LETTER CCLVIII.]   *July* 10, 1823.

Dear Sir—I shall be happy to read the MS. and to forward it; but T[aylor] and H[essey] must judge for themselves of publication. If it prove interesting (as I doubt not) I shall not spare to say so, you may depend upon it. Suppose you direct it to Accountant's Office, India House. I am glad you have met with some sweetening circumstances to your unpalatable draught. I have just returned from Hastings, where are exquisite views and walks, and where I have given up my soul to walking, and I am now suffering sedentary contrasts. I am a long time reconciling to town after one of these excursions. Home is become strange, and will remain so yet a while; home is the most unforgiving of friends, and always resents absence; I know its old cordial looks will return, but they are slow in clearing up. That is one of the features of this *our* galley slavery; that peregrination ended makes things worse. I felt out of water (with all the sea about me) at Hastings; and just as I had learned to domiciliate there, I must come back to find a home which is no home. I abused Hastings, but learned its value. There are spots, inland bays, etc., which realise the notions of Juan Fernandez. The best thing I lit upon by accident was a small country church (by whom or when built unknown), standing bare and single in the midst of a grove, with no house or appearance of habitation within a quarter of a mile, only passages diverging from it through beautiful woods to so many farmhouses. There it stands like the first idea of a church, before parishioners were thought of, nothing but birds for its congregation; or like a hermit's oratory (the hermit dead), or a mausoleum; its effect singularly impressive, like a church found in a desert isle to startle Crusoe with a home image. You must make out a vicar and a congregation from fancy, for surely none come there; yet it wants not its pulpit, and its font, and all the seemly additaments of *our* worship.

Southey has attacked "Elia" on the score of infidelity, in the *Quarterly* article, "Progress of Infidelity." I had not, nor have seen the *Monthly.* He might have spared an old friend such a construction of a few careless flights, that meant no harm to religion. If all *his* unguarded expressions on the subject were to be collected——! But I love and respect Southey, and will not retort. I hate his review, and his being a reviewer. The hint he has dropped will knock the sale of the book on the head, which was almost at a stop before. Let it stop,—there is corn in Egypt, while there is cash at Leadenhall. You and I are something besides being writers, thank God!

Yours truly,   C. L.

To THOMAS ALLSOP.

LETTER CCLIX.]   *E. I. House, August* 9, 1823.

My dear A.—I am going to ask you to do me the greatest favour which a man can do for another. I want to make my will, and to leave my property in trust for my Sister. *N.B.*—I am not therefore going to die.— Would it be unpleasant for you to be named for one? The other two I shall beg the same favour of are Talfourd and Procter. If you feel reluctant, tell me, and it shan't abate one jot of my friendly feeling toward you.

Yours ever, C. LAMB.

To BERNARD BARTON.

LETTER CCLX.]   *September 2, 1823.*

Dear B. B.—What will you say to my not writing! You cannot say I do not write now. Hessey has not used your kind sonnet, nor have I seen it. Pray send me a copy. Neither have I heard any more of your friend's MS., which I will reclaim whenever you please. When you come London-ward you will find me no longer in Covent Garden. I have a cottage in Colebrook Row, Islington; a cottage, for it is detached; a white house, with six good rooms; the New River (rather elderly by this time) runs (if a moderate walking pace may be so termed) close to the foot of the house; and behind is a spacious garden with vines (I assure you), pears, strawberries, parsnips, leeks, carrots, cabbages, to delight the heart of old Alcinous. You enter without passage into a cheerful dining-room, all studded over and rough with old books: and above is a lightsome drawing-room, three windows, full of choice prints. I feel like a great lord, never having had a house before.

The *London,* I fear, falls off. I linger among its creaking rafters, like the last rat; it will topple down if they don't get some buttresses. They have pulled down three: Hazlitt, Procter, and their best stay, kind, light-hearted Wainwright, their Janus. The best is, neither of our fortunes is concerned in it.

I heard of you from Mr. Pulham this morning, and that gave a fillip to my laziness, which has been intolerable; but I am so taken up with pruning and gardening, quite a new sort of occupation to me. I have gathered my jargonels, but my Windsor pears are backward. The former were of exquisite raciness. I do now sit under my own vine, and contemplate the growth of vegetable nature. I can now understand in what sense they speak of father Adam. I recognise the paternity while I watch my tulips. I almost fell with him, for the first day I turned a drunken gardener (as he let in the serpent) into my Eden, and he laid about him, lopping off some choice boughs, etc., which hung over from a neighbour's garden, and in his blind zeal laid waste a shade, which had sheltered their window from the gaze of passers-by. The old gentlewoman (fury made her not handsome) could scarcely be reconciled by all my fine words. There was no buttering her parsnips. She talked of the law. What a lapse to commit on the first day of my happy "garden-state!"

I hope you transmitted the Fox-Journal to its owner, with suitable thanks. Mr. Cary, the Dante-man, dines with me to-day. He is a model of a country parson, lean (as a curate ought to be), modest, sensible, no obtruder of church dogmas, quite a different man from Southey. You would like him. Pray accept this for a letter, and believe me, with sincere regards,

Yours,   C. L.

To THOMAS HOOD.

LETTER CCLXI.]   [Late in 1823.]

And what dost thou at the Priory? *Cucullus non facit Monachum.* English me that, and challenge old Lignum Janua to make a better.

My old New River has presented no extraordinary novelties lately; but there Hope sits every day, speculating upon traditionary gudgeons. I think she has taken the fisheries. I now know the reason why our fore-fathers were denominated East and West Angles. Yet is there no lack of spawn; for I wash my hands in fishets that come through the pump every morning thick as motelings,—little things that perish untimely, and never taste the brook. You do not tell me of those romantic land bays that be as thou goest to Lover's Seat: neither of that little churchling in the midst of a wood (in the opposite direction, nine furlongs from the town), that seems dropped by the Angel that was tired of carrying two packages; marry, with the other he made shift to pick his flight to Loretto. Inquire out, and see my little Protestant Loretto. It stands apart from trace of human habitation; yet hath it pulpit, reading-desk, and trim font of mas-siest marble, as if Robinson Crusoe had reared it to soothe himself with old church-going images. I forget its Christian name, and what she-saint was its gossip.

You should also go to No. 13, Standgate Street,—a baker, who has the finest collection of marine monsters in ten sea counties,—sea dragons, polypi, mer-people, most fantastic. You have only to name the old gen-tleman in black (not the Devil) that lodged with him a week (he'll re-member) last July, and he will show courtesy. He is by far the foremost of the savants. His wife is the funniest thwarting little animal! They are decidedly the Lions of green Hastings. Well, I have made an end of my say. My epistolary time is gone by when I could have scribbled as long (I will not say as agreeable) as thine was to both of us. I am dwindled to notes and letterets. But, in good earnest, I shall be most happy to hail thy return to the waters of Old Sir Hugh. There is nothing like inland mur-murs, fresh ripples, and our native minnows.

> "He sang in meads how sweet the brooklets ran,
> To the rough ocean and red restless sands."

I design to give up smoking; but I have not yet fixed upon the equivalent vice. I must have *quid pro quo;* or *quo pro quid,* as Tom Woodgate would correct me. My service to him.   C. L.

To THOMAS ALLSOP.

LETTER CCLXII.]   *September* 10, 1823.

My dear A.—Your kindness in accepting my request no words of mine
can repay. It has made you overflow into some romance which I should
have check'd at another time, I hope it may be in the scheme of Providence that my sister may go first (if ever so little a precedence), myself
next, and my good Executors survive to remember us with kindness many
years. God bless you.

I will set Procter about the will forthwith.   C. LAMB.

To BERNARD BARTON.

LETTER CCLXIII.]   *September* 17, 1823.

Dear Sir—I have again been reading your "Stanzas on Bloomfield,"
which are the most appropriate that can be imagined,—sweet with Doric
delicacy. I like that,—

> "Our own more chaste Theocritus"—

just hinting at the fault of the Grecian. I love that stanza ending with,

> "Words, phrases, fashions, pass away;
> But truth and nature live through all."

But I shall omit in my own copy the one stanza which alludes to Lord B.
I suppose. It spoils the sweetness and oneness of the feeling. Cannot we
think of Burns, or Thomson, without sullying the thought with a reflection out of place upon Lord Rochester? These verses might have been inscribed upon a tomb; are in fact an epitaph; satire does not look pretty
upon a tombstone. Besides, there is a quotation in it, always bad in verse,
seldom advisable in prose. I doubt if their having been in a paper will not
prevent T. and H. from insertion; but I shall have a thing to send in a day
or two, and shall try them. Omitting that stanza, a very little alteration is
wanting in the beginning of the next. You see, I use freedom. How happily (I flatter not) you have brought in his subjects; and (I suppose) his
favourite measure, though I am not acquainted with any of his writings
but the *Farmer's Boy*. He dined with me once, and his manners took me
exceedingly.

I rejoice that you forgive my long silence. I continue to estimate my
own-roof comforts highly. How could I remain all my life a lodger! My
garden thrives (I am told), though I have yet reaped nothing but some
tiny salad and withered carrots. But a garden's a garden anywhere, and
twice a garden in London.

Somehow I cannot relish that word "Horkey." Cannot you supply it by circumlocution, and direct the reader by a note to explain that it means the Horkey. But Horkey chokes me in the text. It raises crowds of mean associations, hawking and sp——g, gawky, stalky, mawkin! The sound is everything, in such dulcet modulations 'specially. I like

"Gilbert Meldrum's sterner tones,"

without knowing who Gilbert Meldrum is. You have slipt in your rhymes as if they grew there, so natural-artificially, or artificial-naturally. There's a vile phrase!

Do you go on with your "Quaker Sonnets"? Have 'em ready with Southey's "Book of the Church." I meditate a letter to S. in the *London,* which perhaps will meet the fate of the Sonnet.

Excuse my brevity, for I write painfully at office, liable to a hundred callings off; and I can never sit down to an epistle elsewhere. I read or walk. If you return this letter to the Post Office, I think they will return fourpence, seeing it is but half a one. Believe me, though,

Entirely yours,   C. L.

To THOMAS ALLSOP.

LETTER CCLXIV.]   1823.

Dear A.—Your Cheese is the best I ever tasted; Mary will tell you so hereafter. She is at home, but has disappointed me. She has gone back rather than improved. However, she has sense enough to value the present; for she is greatly fond of Stilton. Yours is the delicatest, rainbow-hued, melting piece I ever flavoured. Believe me, I took it the more kindly, following so great a kindness.

Depend upon't, yours shall be one of the first houses we shall present ourselves at, when we have got our Bill of Health.

Being both yours and Mrs. Allsop's truly,   C. L. and M. L.

To Rev. H. F. CARY.

LETTER CCLXV.]   *India Office, October* 14, 1823.

Dear Sir—If convenient, will you give us house room on Saturday next? I can sleep anywhere. If another Sunday suit you better, pray let me know. We were talking of Roast *Shoulder* of Mutton with onion sauce; but I scorn to prescribe to the hospitalities of mine host.

With respects to Mrs. C., yours truly,   C. LAMB.

To J. B. DIBDIN.

LETTER CCLXVI.]   *October* 28, 1823.

My dear Sir—Your Pig was a *picture* of a pig, and your Picture a pig of a picture. The former was delicious but evanescent, like a hearty fit of mirth, or the crackling of thorns under a pot; but the latter is an *idea,* and abideth. I never before saw swine upon satin. And then that pretty strawy canopy about him! he seems to purr (rather than grunt) his satisfaction. Such a gentlemanlike porker too! Morland's are absolutely clowns to it. Who the deuce painted it? I have ordered a little gilt shrine for it, and mean to wear it for a locket—a shirt-pig.

I admire the pretty toes shrouded in a veil of something, not *mud* but that warm soft consistency which the dust takes in Elysium after a spring shower—it perfectly engloves him.

I cannot enough thank you and your country friend for the delicate double present—the *utile et decorum.*

(Three times have I attempted to write this sentence and failed, which shows that I am not cut out for a pedant.)

Sir!—as I say to Southey—Will you come and see us at our poor cottage of Colebrook to tea to-morrow evening, as early as six? I have some friends coming at that hour.

The panoply which covered your material pig shall be forthcoming. The pig pictorial with its trappings domesticate with me.

Your greatly obliged   ELIA.

J. B. Dibdin, Esq.,
    Messrs. Rankings,
        113 Cheapside.

To ROBERT SOUTHEY.

LETTER CCLXVII.]   *E. I. H., November* 21, 1823.

Dear Southey—The kindness of your note has melted away the mist which was upon me. I have been fighting against a shadow. That accursed *Q. R.* had vexed me by a gratuitous speaking, of its own knowledge, that the *Confessions of a D——d* was a genuine description of the state of the writer. Little things, that are not ill-meant, may produce much ill. *That* might have injured me alive and dead. I am in a public office, and my life is insured. I was prepared for anger, and I thought I saw, in a few obnoxious words, a hard case of repetition directed against me. I wished both magazine and review at the bottom of the sea. I shall be ashamed to see you, and my sister (though innocent) will be still more so; for the folly was done without her knowledge, and has made her uneasy ever since. My guardian angel was absent at that time.

I will muster up courage to see you, however, any day next week (Wednesday excepted). We shall hope that you will bring Edith with you. That will be a second mortification. She will hate to see us; but come and heap embers. We deserve it; I for what I've done, and she for being my sister.

Do come early in the day, by sun-light, that you may see my *Milton.*

I am at Colebrook Cottage, Colebrook Row, Islington: a detached whitish house, close to the New River end of Colebrook Terrace, left hand from Sadler's Wells.

Will you let me know the day before?

Your penitent,   C. Lamb.

P. S.—I do not think your handwriting at all like ****'s. I do not think many things I did think.

To BERNARD BARTON.

Letter CCLXVIII.]   *November 22, 1823.*

Dear B. B.—I am ashamed at not acknowledging your kind little poem, which I must needs like much; but I protest I thought I had done it at the moment. Is it possible a letter has miscarried? Did you get one in which I sent you an extract from the poems of Lord Stirling? I should wonder if you did, for I sent you none such. There was an incipient lie strangled in the birth. Some people's conscience is so tender! But, in plain truth, I thank you very much for the verses. I have a very kind letter from the Laureate, with a self-invitation to come and shake hands with me. This is truly handsome and noble. 'Tis worthy of my old idea of Southey. Shall not I, think you, be covered with a red suffusion?

You are too much apprehensive of your complaint: I know many that are always ailing of it, and live on to a good old age. I know a merry fellow (you partly know him) who, when his medical adviser told him he had drunk away all *that part*, congratulated himself (now his liver was gone) that he should be the longest liver of the two.

The best way in these cases is to keep yourself as ignorant as you can, as ignorant as the world was before Galen, of the entire inner construction of the animal man; not to be conscious of a midriff; to hold kidneys (save of sheep and swine) to be an agreeable fiction; not to know whereabout the gall grows; to account the circulation of the blood an idle whimsey of Harvey's; to acknowledge no mechanism not visible. For, once fix the seat of your disorder, and your fancies flux into it like bad humours. Those medical gentries choose each his favourite part; one takes the lungs, another the aforesaid liver, and refer to that whatever in the animal economy is amiss. Above all, use exercise, take a little more spirituous liquors, learn to smoke, continue to keep a good conscience, and avoid tampering with hard terms of art—viscosity, scirrhosity, and those bugbears by which simple patients are scared into their graves. Believe the general sense of the mercantile world, which holds that desks are not deadly. It is the mind, good B. B., and not the limbs, that taints by long sitting. Think of the patience of tailors! Think how long the Lord Chancellor sits! Think of the brooding hen! I protest I cannot answer thy sister's kind inquiry;

but I judge, I shall put forth no second volume. More praise than buy; and T. and H. are not particularly disposed for martyrs. Thou wilt see a funny passage, and yet a true history, of George Dyer's aquatic incursion in the next *London*. Beware his fate, when thou comest to see me at my Colebrook Cottage. I have filled my little space with my little thoughts. I wish thee ease on thy sofa; but not too much indulgence on it. From my poor desk, thy fellow-sufferer, this bright November, C. L.

To MRS. HAZLITT.

LETTER CCLXIX.] [*November* 1823.]

Dear Mrs. H.—Sitting down to write a letter is such a painful operation to Mary, that you must accept me as her proxy. You have seen our house. What I now tell you is literally true. Yesterday week George Dyer called upon us, at one o'clock (*bright noonday*), on his way to dine with Mrs. Barbauld at Newington. He sat with Mary about half an hour, and took leave. The maid saw him go out, from her kitchen window, but suddenly losing sight of him, ran up in a fright to Mary. G. D., instead of keeping the slip that leads to the gate, had deliberately, staff in hand, in broad open day, marched into the New River. He had not his spectacles on, and you know his absence. Who helped him out they can hardly tell, but between 'em they got him out, drenched thro' and thro'. A mob collected by that time, and accompanied him in. "Send for the Doctor," they said: and a one-eyed fellow, dirty and drunk, was fetched from the public-house at the end, where it seems he lurks, for the sake of picking up water practice; having formerly had a medal from the Humane Society for some rescue. By his advice the patient was put between blankets; and when I came home at 4 to dinner, I found G. D. a-bed, and raving, light-headed, with the brandy and water which the doctor had administered. He sang, laughed, whimpered, screamed, babbled of guardian angels, would get up and go home; but we kept him there by force; and by next morning he departed sober, and seems to have received no injury. All my friends are open-mouth'd about having paling before the river; but I cannot see, that because a lunatic chooses to walk into a river with his eyes open at midday, I am any the more likely to be drowned in it, coming home at midnight.

I had the honour of dining at the Mansion House on Thursday last by special card from the Lord Mayor, who never saw my face, nor I his; and all from being a writer in a magazine. The dinner costly, served on massy plate; champagne, pines, etc.; 47 present, among whom the Chairman and two other directors of the India Company.

There's for you! and got away pretty sober. Quite saved my credit.

We continue to like our house prodigiously.

Does Mary Hazlitt go on with her novel? or has she begun another? I would not discourage her, though we continue to think it (so far) in its present state not saleable. Our kind remembrances to her and hers, and you and yours.

Yours truly,   C. LAMB.

I am pleased that H. liked my letter to the Laureate.

Mrs. Hazlitt,
    Alphington, near Exeter.

To Mr. AINSWORTH.

LETTER CCLXX.]   *India House, December* 9, 1823.

Dear Sir—I should have thanked you for your books and compliments sooner, but have been waiting for a revise to be sent, which does not come, though I returned the proof on the receipt of your letter. I have read Warner with great pleasure. What an elaborate piece of alliteration and antithesis! why it must have been a labour far above the most difficult versification. There is a fine simile or picture of Semiramis arming to repel a siege. I do not mean to keep the book, for I suspect you are forming a curious collection, and I do not pretend to anything of the kind. I have not a black-letter book among mine, old Chaucer excepted, and am not bibliomanist enough to like black-letter. It is painful to read; therefore I must insist on returning it at opportunity, not from contumacy and reluctance to be obliged, but because it must suit you better than me. The loss of a present *from* should never exceed the gain of a present *to*. I hold this maxim infallible in the accepting line. I read your magazines with satisfaction. I thoroughly agree with you as to "The German Faust," as far as I can do justice to it from an English translation. 'Tis a disagreeable canting tale of seduction, which has nothing to do with the spirit of Faustus— Curiosity. Was the dark secret to be explored to end in the seducing of a weak girl, which might have been accomplished by earthly agency? When Marlow gives *his* Faustus a mistress, he flies him at Helen, flower of Greece, to be sure, and not at Miss Betsy, or Miss Sally Thoughtless.

> "Cut is the branch that bore the goodly fruit,
>   And wither'd is Apollo's laurel tree:
>   Faustus is dead."

What a noble natural transition from metaphor to plain speaking! as if the figurative had flagged in description of such a loss, and was reduced to tell the fact simply.

I must now thank you for your very kind invitation. It is not out of prospect that I may see Manchester some day, and then I will avail myself of your kindness. But holidays are scarce things with me, and the laws of attendance are getting stronger and stronger at Leadenhall. But I shall bear it in mind. Meantime something may (more probably) bring you to town, where I shall be happy to see you. I am always to be found (alas!) at my desk in the fore part of the day.

I wonder why they do not send the revise. I leave late at office, and my abode lies out of the way, or I should have seen about it. If you are impatient, perhaps a line to the printer, directing him to send it me, at Accountant's Office, may answer. You will see by the scrawl that I only snatch a few minutes from intermitting business.

Your obliged servant,   C. LAMB.

(If I had time I would go over this letter again, and dot all my *i*'s.)

LETTER CCLXXI.]   *I. H., December* 29, 1823.

My dear Sir—You talk of months at a time, and I know not what inducements to visit Manchester, Heaven knows how gratifying! but I have had my little month of 1823 already. It is all over; and without incurring a disagreeable favour I cannot so much as get a single holiday till the season returns with the next year. Even our half-hour's absences from office are set down in a book! Next year, if I can spare a day or two of it, I will come to Manchester; but I have reasons at home against longer absences.

I am so ill just at present (an illness of my own procuring last night; who is perfect?) that nothing but your very great kindness could make me write. I will bear in mind the letter to W. W., and you shall have it quite in time, before the 12th.

My aching and confused head warns me to leave off. With a muddled sense of gratefulness, which I shall apprehend more clearly to-morrow, I remain, your friend unseen,   C. L.

Will your occasions or inclination bring you to London? It will give me great pleasure to show you everything that Islington can boast, if you know the meaning of that very Cockney sound. We have the New River! I am ashamed of this scrawl; but I beg you to accept it for the present. I am full of qualms.

"A fool at fifty is a fool indeed."

CHAPTER V.

1824–1827.

To BERNARD BARTON.

LETTER CCLXXII.] *January* 9, 1824.

Dear B. B.—Do you know what it is to succumb under an unsurmount-able day-mare,—"a whoreson lethargy," Falstaff calls it,—an indisposi-tion to do anything, or to be anything,—a total deadness and distaste, a suspension of vitality,—an indifference to locality,—a numb, soporifical, good-for-nothingness,—an ossification all over,—an oyster-like insensibil-ity to the passing events,—a mind-stupor,—a brawny defiance to the needles of a thrusting-in conscience? Did you ever have a very bad cold, with a total irresolution to submit to water-gruel processes? This has been for many weeks my lot and my excuse. My fingers drag heavily over this paper, and to my thinking it is three-and-twenty furlongs from here to the end of this demi-sheet. I have not a thing to say; nothing is of more im-portance than another; I am flatter than a denial or a pancake; emptier than Judge Park's wig when the head is in it; duller than a country stage when the actors are off it; a cipher, an o! I acknowledge life at all, only by an occasional convulsional cough, and a permanent phlegmatic pain in the chest. I am weary of the world; life is weary of me. My day is gone into twilight, and I don't think it worth the expense of candles. My wick hath a thief in it, but I can't muster courage to snuff it. I inhale suffoca-tion; I can't distinguish veal from mutton; nothing interests me. 'Tis twelve o'clock, and Thurtell is just now coming out upon the New Drop, Jack Ketch alertly tucking up his greasy sleeves to do the last office of mortality; yet cannot I elicit a groan or a moral reflection. If you told me the world will be at an end to-morrow, I should just say, "Will it?" I have not volition enough to dot my *i*'s, much less to comb my eyebrows; my eyes are set in my head; my brains are gone out to see a poor relation in Moorfields, and they did not say when they'd come back again; my skull is a Grub Street attic, to let—not so much as a joint-stool or a crack'd jordan left in it; my hand writes, not I, from habit, as chickens run about a little when their heads are off. O 'for a vigorous fit of gout, cholic, tooth-ache,—an earwig in my auditory, a fly in my visual organs! Pain is life—the sharper, the more evidence of life; but this apathy, this death! Did

876

you ever have an obstinate cold,—a six or seven weeks' unintermitting chill and suspension of hope, fear, conscience, and everything? Yet do I try all I can to cure it; I try wine, and spirits, and smoking, and snuff in unsparing quantities; but they all only seem to make me worse, instead of better. I sleep in a damp room, but it does me no good; I come home late o' nights, but do not find any visible amendment! Who shall deliver me from the body of this death?

It is just fifteen minutes after twelve. Thurtell is by this time a good way on his journey, baiting at Scorpion perhaps; Ketch is bargaining for his cast coat and waistcoat. The Jew demurs at first at three half-crowns; but, on consideration that he may get somewhat by showing 'em in the town, finally closes.   C. L.

LETTER CCLXXIII.]   *January 23, 1824.*

My dear Sir—That peevish letter of mine, which was meant to convey an apology for my incapacity to write, seems to have been taken by you in too serious a light; it was only my way of telling you I had a severe cold. The fact is, I have been insuperably dull and lethargic for many weeks, and cannot rise to the vigour of a letter, much less an essay. The *London* must do without me for a time, for I have lost all interest about it; and whether I shall recover it again I know not. I will bridle my pen another time, and not teaze and puzzle you with my aridities. I shall begin to feel a little more alive with the Spring. Winter is to me (mild or harsh) always a great trial of the spirits. I am ashamed not to have noticed your tribute to Woolman, whom we love so much. It is done in your good manner. Your friend Taylor called upon me some time since, and seems a very amiable man. His last story is painfully fine. His book I like; it is only too stuffed with Scripture, too parsonish. The best thing in it is the boy's own story. When I say it is too full of Scripture, I mean it is too full of direct quotations. No book can have too much of silent Scripture in it; but the natural power of a story is diminished when the uppermost purpose in the writer seems to be to recommend something else, viz. Religion. You know what Horace says of the *Deus intersit*. I am not able to explain myself,—you must do it for me. My sister's part in the "Leicester School" (about two-thirds) was purely her own; as it was (to the same quantity) in the "Shakspeare Tales" which bear my name. I wrote only the "Witch Aunt"; the "First Going to Church"; and the final story, about "A little Indian Girl" in a ship. Your account of my black-balling amused me. *I think, as Quakers, they did right.* There are some things hard to be understood. The more I think, the more I am vexed at having puzzled you with that letter; but I have been so out of letter-writing of late years, that it is a sore effort to sit down to it; and I felt in your debt, and sat down waywardly to pay you in bad money. Never mind my dulness; I am used to long intervals of it. The heavens seem brass to me; then again comes the refreshing shower—

"I have been merry once or twice ere now."

You said something about Mr. Mitford in a late letter, which I believe I did not advert to. I shall be happy to show him my Milton (it is all the show things I have) at any time he will take the trouble of a jaunt to Islington. I do also hope to see Mr. Taylor there some day. Pray say so to both. Coleridge's book is in good part printed, but sticks a little for *more copy*. It bears an unsaleable title, "Extracts from Bishop Leighton"; but I am confident there will be plenty of good notes in it, more of Bishop Coleridge than Leighton, I hope; for what is Leighton? Do you trouble yourself about libel cases? The decision against Hunt for the "Vision of Judgment" made me sick. What is to become of the good old talk about our good old King?—his personal virtues saving us from a revolution, etc. etc.! Why, none that think can utter it now. It must stink. And the "vision" is really, as to him-ward, such a tolerant, good-humoured thing. What a wretched thing a Lord Chief Justice is, always was, and will be!

Keep your good spirits up, dear B. B.; mine will return; they are at present in abeyance; but I am rather lethargic than miserable. I don't know but a good horsewhip would be more beneficial to me than physic. My head, without aching, will teach yours to ache. It is well I am getting to the conclusion. I will send a better letter when I am a better man. Let me thank you for your kind concern for me (which I trust will have reason soon to be dissipated), and assure you that it gives me pleasure to hear from you.

Yours truly,   C. L.

To CHARLES OLLIER.

LETTER CCLXXIV.]   [*January* 27, 1824.]

Dear Ollier—Many thanks from both of us for *Inesilla*. I wished myself younger, that I might have more enjoyed the terror of that desolate city, and the damned palace. I think it as fine as anything in its way, and wish you joy of success, etc.

With better weather, I shall hope to see you at Islington.

Meantime, believe me, yours truly,   C. LAMB.

Scribbled midst official flurry.

To BERNARD BARTON.

LETTER CCLXXV.]   *February* 25, 1824.

My dear Sir—Your title of "Poetic Vigils" arrides me much more than a volume of verse, which is no meaning. The motto says nothing, but I cannot suggest a better. I do not like mottoes but where they are singularly felicitous; there is foppery in them. They are unplain, un-Quakerish. They are good only where they flow from the title, and are a kind of justification of it. There is nothing about watchings or lucubrations in the one you suggest; no commentary on vigils. By the way, a wag would recommend you to the line of Pope,

"Sleepless himself—to give his readers sleep."

I by no means wish it; but it may explain what I mean,—that a neat motto is child of the title. I think "Poetic Vigils" as short and sweet as can be desired; only have an eye on the proof, that the printer do not substitute Virgils, which would ill accord with your modesty or meaning. Your suggested motto is antique enough in spelling, and modern enough in phrases,—a good modern antique; but the matter of it is germane to the purpose, only supposing the title proposed a vindication of yourself from the presumption of authorship. The first title was liable to this objection—that if you were disposed to enlarge it, and the bookseller insisted on its appearance in two tomes, how oddly it would sound, "A Volume of Verse in Two Volumes, Second Edition," etc. You see through my wicked intention of curtailing this epistolet by the above device of large margin. But in truth the idea of letterising has been oppressive to me of late above your candour to give me credit for. There is Southey, whom I ought to have thanked a fortnight ago for a present of the "Church Book": I have never had courage to buckle myself in earnest even to acknowledge it by six words; and yet I am accounted by some people a good man! How cheap that character is acquired! Pay your debts, don't borrow money, nor twist your kitten's neck off, nor disturb a congregation, etc., your business is done. I know things (thoughts or things, thoughts *are* things) of myself, which would make every friend I have fly me as a plague patient. I once * * *, and set a dog upon a crab's leg that was shoved out under a mass of sea-weeds,—a pretty little feeler. Oh pah! how sick I am of that! and a lie, a mean one, I once told!—I stink in the midst of respect. I am much hypt. The fact is, my head is heavy, but there is hope; or if not, I am better than a poor shell-fish; not morally, when I set the whelp upon it, but have more blood and spirits. Things may turn up, and I may creep again into a decent opinion of myself. Vanity will return with sunshine. Till then, pardon my neglects, and impute it to the wintry solstice. C. LAMB.

LETTER CCLXXVI.] *March* 24, 1824.

Dear B. B.—I hasten to say that if my opinion can strengthen you in your choice, it is decisive for your acceptance of what has been so handsomely offered. I can see nothing injurious to your most honourable sense. Think that you are called to a poetical Ministry—nothing worse: the Minister is worthy of the hire. The only objection I feel is founded on a fear that the acceptance may be a temptation to you to let fall the bone (hard as it is) which is in your mouth, and must afford tolerable pickings,

for the shadow of independence. You cannot propose to become independent on what the low state of interest could afford you from such a
principal as you mention; and the most graceful excuse for the acceptance
would be, that it left you free to your voluntary functions. That is the less
light part of the scruple. It has no darker shade. I put in *darker* because
of the ambiguity of the word "light," which Donne, in his admirable poem
on the Metempsychosis, has so ingeniously illustrated in his invocation—

1   2   1   2

"Make my *dark heavy* poem, *light* and *light,*"

where the two senses of *light* are opposed to different opposites. A trifling
criticism. I can see no reason for any scruple then but what arises from
your own interest; which is in your own power, of course, to solve. If you
still have doubts, read over Sanderson's *Cases of Conscience,* and Jeremy
Taylor's *Ductor Dubitantium;* the first a moderate octavo, the latter a
folio of 900 close pages; and when you have thoroughly digested the admirable reasons *pro* and *con* which they give for every possible case, you
will be—— just as wise as when you began. Every man is his own best
casuist; and after all, as Ephraim Smooth, in the pleasant comedy of *Wild
Oats,* has it, "there is no harm in a Guinea." *A fortiori* there is less in
2000.

I therefore most sincerely congratulate with you, excepting so far as excepted above. If you have fair prospects of adding to the principal, cut
the Bank; but in either case do not refuse an honest service. Your heart
tells you it is not offered to bribe you *from* any duty, but *to* a duty which
you feel to be your vocation. Farewell heartily.   C. L.

LETTER CCLXXVII.]   *April* 1824.

Dear B. B.—I am sure I cannot fill a letter, though I should disfurnish
the skull to fill it; but you expect something, and shall have a notelet. Is
Sunday, not divinely speaking, but humanly and holidaysically, a blessing? Without its institution, would our rugged taskmasters have given us
a leisure day, so often, think you, as once in a month? or, if it had not
been instituted, might they not have given us every sixth day? Solve me
this problem. If we are to go three times a-day to church, why has Sunday
slipped into the notion of *holli*day? A HoLyday I grant it. The Puritans,
I have read in Southey's book, knew the distinction. They made people
observe Sunday rigorously, would not let a nursery-maid walk out in the
fields with children for recreation on that day. But *then*—they gave the
people a holiday from all sorts of work every second Tuesday. This was
giving to the two Cæsars that which was *his* respective. Wise, beautiful,
thoughtful, generous legislators! Would Wilberforce give us our Tuesdays? No: (d—n him!)—he would turn the six days into sevenths,

"And those three smiling seasons of the year
Into a Russian Winter."—OLD PLAY.

I am sitting opposite a person who is making strange distortions with the gout, which is not unpleasant—to me at least. What is the reason we do not sympathise with pain, short of some terrible surgical operation! Hazlitt, who boldly says all he feels, avows that not only he does not pity sick people, but he hates them. I obscurely recognise his meaning. Pain is probably too selfish a consideration, too simply a consideration of self-attention. We pity poverty, loss of friends, etc.—more complex things, in which the sufferer's feelings are associated with others. This is a rough thought suggested by the presence of gout; I want head to extricate it and plane it. What is all this to your letter? I felt it to be a good one, but my turn, when I write at all, is perversely to travel out of the record, so that my letters are anything but answers. So you still want a motto! You must not take my ironical one, because your book, I take it, is too serious for it. Bickerstaff might have used it for *his* lucubrations. What do you think of (for a title) *Religio Tremuli?* or *Tremebundi?* There is *Religio-Medici* and *Laici*. But perhaps the volume is not quite Quakerish enough, or exclusively so, for it. Your own "Vigils" is perhaps the best. While I have space, let me congratulate with you the return of Spring: what a summery Spring too! all those qualms about the dog and cray-fish melt before it. I am going to be happy and *vain* again.

A hasty farewell,   C. LAMB.

LETTER CCLXXVIII.]   *May* 15, 1824.

Dear B. B.—I am oppressed with business all day, and Company all night. But I will snatch a quarter of an hour. Your recent acquisitions of the Picture and the Letter are greatly to be congratulated. I too have a picture of my father and the copy of his first love verses; but they have been mine long. Blake is a real name, I assure you, and a most extraordinary man, if he be still living. He is the Robert Blake, whose wild designs accompany a splendid folio edition of the "Night Thoughts," which you may have seen, in one of which he pictures the parting of soul and body by a solid mass of human form floating off, God knows how, from a lumpish mass (fac Simile to itself) left behind on the dying bed. He paints in water colours marvellous strange pictures, visions of his brain, which he asserts that he has seen. They have great merit. He has *seen* the old Welsh bards on Snowdon—he has seen the Beautifullest, the strongest, and the Ugliest Man, left alone from the Massacre of the Britons by the Romans, and has painted them from memory (I have seen his paintings), and asserts them to be as good as the figures of Raphael and Angelo, but not better, as they had precisely the same retro-visions and prophetic visions with themself [himself]. The painters in oil (which he will have it that neither of them practised) he affirms to have been the ruin of art, and affirms that all the while he was engaged in his Water paintings, Titian was disturbing him, Titian the Ill Genius of Oil Painting. His Pictures—one in particular, the Canterbury Pilgrims (far above Stothard's)—have great merit, but hard, dry, yet with grace. He has written a Catalogue of them with a most spirited criticism on Chaucer, but mystical and full of Vision. His poems have been sold hitherto only in Manuscript. I never read them; but a friend at my desire procured the "Sweep Song." There is one to a tiger, which I have heard recited, beginning—

> "Tiger, Tiger, burning bright,
> Thro' the desarts of the night,"

which is glorious, but, alas! I have not the books; for the man is flown, whither I know not—to Hades or a Mad House. But I must look on him as one of the most extraordinary persons of the age. Montgomery's book I have not much hope from. The Society, with the affected name, has been labouring at it for these 20 years, and made few converts. I think it was injudicious to mix stories avowedly colour'd by fiction with the sad true statements from the parliamentary records, etc., but I wish the little Negroes all the good that can come from it. I batter'd my brains (not butter'd them—but it is a bad *a*) for a few verses for them, but I could make nothing of it. You have been luckier. But Blake's are the flower of the set, you will, I am sure, agree, tho' some of Montgomery's at the end are pretty; but the Dream awkwardly paraphras'd from B.

With the exception of an Epilogue for a Private Theatrical, I have written nothing now for near 6 months. It is in vain to spur me on. I must wait. I cannot write without a genial impulse, and I have none. 'Tis barren all and dearth. No matter; life is something without scribbling. I have got rid of my bad spirits, and hold up pretty well this rain-damn'd May.

So we have lost another Poet. I never much relished his Lordship's mind, and shall be sorry if the Greeks have cause to miss him. He was to me offensive, and I never can make out his great *power*, which his admirers talk of. Why, a line of Wordsworth's is a lever to lift the immortal spirit! Byron can only move the Spleen. He was at best a Satyrist,—in any other way, he was mean enough. I daresay I do him injustice; but I cannot love him, nor squeeze a tear to his memory. He did not like the world, and he has left it, as Alderman Curtis advised the Radicals, "If they don't like their Country, damn 'em, let 'em leave it," they possessing no rood of ground in England, and he 10,000 acres. Byron was better than many Curtises.

Farewell, and accept this apology for a letter from one who owes you so much in that kind.

Yours ever truly,   C. L.

B. Barton, Esq., Woodbridge, Suffolk.

LETTER CCLXXIX.]   *July* 7, 1824.

Dear B. B.—I have been suffering under a severe inflammation of the eyes, notwithstanding which I resolutely went through your very pretty volume at once, which I dare pronounce in no ways inferior to former lucubrations. *"Abroad"* and *"lord"* are vile rhymes notwithstanding, and if you count you will wonder how many times you have repeated the word *unearthly;* thrice in one poem. It is become a slang word with the bards; avoid it in future lustily. "Time" is fine; but there are better a good deal, I think. The volume does not lie by me; and after a long day's smarting fatigue, which has almost put out my eyes (not blind however to your merits), I dare not trust myself with long writing. The verses to Bloomfield are the sweetest in the collection. Religion is sometimes lugged in, as if it did not come naturally. I will go over carefully when I get my seeing, and exemplify. You have also too much of singing metre, such as requires no deep ear to make; lilting measure, in which you have done Woolman injustice. Strike at less superficial melodies. The piece on Nayler is more to my fancy.

My eye runs waters. But I will give you a fuller account some day. The book is a very pretty one in more than one sense. The decorative harp, perhaps, too ostentatious; a simple pipe preferable.

Farewell, and many thanks. C. LAMB.

To JOHN B. DIBDIN.

LETTER CCLXXX.] *July 28, 1824.*

My dear Sir—I must appear negligent in not having thanked you for the very pleasant books you sent me. *Arthur,* and the Novel, we have both of us read with unmixed satisfaction. They are full of quaint conceits, and running over with good-humour and good-nature. I naturally take little interest in story, but in these the manner and not the end is the interest; it is such pleasant travelling one scarce cares whither it leads us. Pray express our pleasure to your father with my best thanks.

I am involved in a routine of visiting among the family of Barron Field, just returned from Botany Bay. I shall hardly have an open evening before *Tuesday* next. Will you come to us then?

Yours truly, C. LAMB.

To THE REV. H. F. CARY.

LETTER CCLXXXI.] *East India House, August 19, 1824.*

Dear Sir—I shall have much pleasure in dining with you on Wednesday next, with much shame that I have not noticed your kind present of the *Birds,* which I found very chirping and whimsical. I believe at the time I was daily thinking of paying you a visit, and put it off—till I should come. Somehow it slipt, and I must crave your pardon.

Yours truly, C. LAMB.

To BERNARD BARTON.

LETTER CCLXXXII.]   *August* 1824.

Dear B. B.—I congratulate you on getting a house over your head. I find the comfort of it I am sure. At my town lodgings the mistress was always quarrelling with our maid, and at my place of rustication the whole family were always beating one another, brothers beating sisters (one, a most beautiful girl, lamed for life), father beating sons and daughters, and son again beating his father, knocking him fairly down, a scene I never before witnessed, but was called out of bed by the unnatural blows, the parricidal colour of which, though my morals could not but condemn, yet my reason did heartily approve, and in the issue the house was quieter for a day or so than I had ever known. I am now all harmony and quiet, even to the sometimes wishing back again some of the old rufflings. There is something stirring in these civil broils.

The album shall be attended to. If I can light upon a few appropriate rhymes (but rhymes come with difficulty from me now) I shall beg a place in the neat margin of your young housekeeper.

The "Prometheus," *unbound*, is a capital story. The literal rogue! What if you had ordered "Elfrida" in *sheets!* she'd have been sent up I warrant you. Or bid him clasp his Bible (*i.e.* to his bosom), he'd have clapt on a brass clasp, no doubt.

I can no more understand Shelley than you can. His poetry is "thin sown with profit or delight." Yet I must point to your notice a sonnet conceived and expressed with a witty delicacy. It is that addressed to one who hated him, but who could not persuade him to hate *him* again. His coyness to the other's passion—(for hate demands a return as much as love, and starves without it)—is most arch and pleasant. Pray, like it very much. For his theories and nostrums, they are oracular enough; but I either comprehend 'em not, or there is "miching malice" and mischief in 'em, but, for the most part, ringing with their own emptiness. Hazlitt said well of 'em—"Many are the wiser and better for reading Shakspeare, but nobody was ever wiser or better for reading Shelley." I wonder you will sow your correspondence on so barren a ground as I am, that make such poor returns. But my head aches at the bare thought of letter-writing. I wish all the ink in the ocean dried up, and would listen to the quills shivering up in the candle flame, like parching martyrs. The same indisposition to write has stopped my "Elias"; but you will see a futile effort in the next Number, "wrung from me with slow pain." The fact is, my head is seldom cool enough. I am dreadfully indolent. To have to do anything —to order me a new coat, for instance, though my old buttons are shelled like beans—is an effort. My pen stammers like my tongue. What cool craniums those old inditers of folios must have had!—what a mortified pulse! Well; once more I throw myself on your mercy. Wishing peace in thy new dwelling,   C. LAMB.

Little book, surnamed of *white*,
Clean as yet, and fair to sight,
Keep thy attribution right.

Never disproportion'd scrawl,
Ugly blot (that's worse than all)
On thy maiden clearness fall!

In each letter here design'd,
Let the reader emblem'd find
Neatness of the owner's mind.

Gilded margins count a sin;
Let thy leaves attraction win
By the golden rules within;

Sayings fetch'd from sages old;
Laws which Holy Writ unfold,
Worthy to be graved in gold:

Lighter fancies not excluding;
Blameless wit, with nothing rude in,
Sometimes mildly interluding

Amid strains of graver measure:
Virtue's self hath oft her pleasure
In sweet Muses' groves of leisure.

Riddles dark, perplexing sense;
Darker meanings of offence;
What but *shades*—be banish'd hence!

Whitest thoughts, in whitest dress,
Candid meanings, best express
Mind of quiet Quakeress.

Dear B. B.—"I am ill at these numbers"; but if the above be not too mean to have a place in thy daughter's sanctum, take them with pleasure. I assume that her name is Hannah, because it is a pretty scriptural cognomen.

I began on another sheet of paper, and just as I had penned the second line of stanza two, an ugly blot fell, to illustrate my counsel. I am sadly given to blot, and modern blotting-paper gives no redress; it only smears, and makes it worse. The only remedy is scratching out, which gives it a clerkish look. The most innocent blots are made with red ink, and are rather ornamental. Marry, they are not always to be distinguished from the effusions of a cut finger. Well, I hope and trust thy tick-doleru, or however you spell it, is vanished, for I have frightful impressions of that tick, and do altogether hate it, as an unpaid score, or the tick of a death-watch. I take it to be a species of Vitus's dance. (I omit the sanctity, writing to "one of the men called friends.") I knew a young lady who could dance no other; she danced it through life, and very queer and fantastic were her steps.

Heaven bless thee from such measures, and keep thee from the foul fiend, who delights to lead after false fires in the night, Flibbertigibbet, that gives the web and the pin, and I forget what else.

From my den, as Bunyan has it, 30th Sep. 1824.   C. L.

To Mrs. COLLIER.

LETTER CCLXXXIV.]   *November* 2, 1824.

Dear Mrs. Collier—We receive so much pig from your kindness, that I really have not phrase enough to vary successive acknowledgments.

I think I shall get a printed form to serve on all occasions.

To say it was young, crisp, short, luscious, dainty-toed, is but to say what all its predecessors have been. It was eaten on Sunday and Monday, and doubts only exist as to which temperature it eat best, hot or cold. I incline to the latter. The Petty-feet made a pretty surprising prægustation for supper on Saturday night, just as I was loathingly in expectation of brencheese. I spell as I speak.

I do not know what news to send you. You will have heard of Alsager's death, and your son John's success in the Lottery. I say he is a wise man if he leaves off while he is well. The weather is wet to weariness; but Mary goes puddling about a-shopping after a gown for the winter. She wants it good and cheap. Now I hold that no good things are cheap, pig-presents always excepted. In this mournful weather I sit moping, where I now write, in an office dark as Erebus, jammed in between four walls, and writing by Candle-Light, most melancholy. Never see the light of the sun six hours in the day; and am surprised to find how pretty it shines on Sundays. I wish I were a Caravan driver, or a Penny postman, to earn my bread in air and sunshine. Such a pedestrian as I am, to be tied by the legs, like a Fauntleroy, without the pleasure of his Exactions! I am interrupted here with an official question which will take me up till it's time to go to dinner. So with repeated thanks and both our kindest remembrances to Mr. Collier and yourself, I conclude in haste,

Yours and his sincerely,   C. LAMB.

On further inquiry Alsager is not dead; but Mrs. A. is bro^t to bed.

From my Den in Leadenhall.

To B. W. PROCTER.

LETTER CCLXXXV.]   *Leadenhall, November* 11, '24.

My dear Procter—I do agnise a shame in not having been to pay my congratulations to Mrs. Procter and your happy self, but on Sunday (my only morning) I was engaged to a country walk; and in virtue of the hypostatical union between us, when Mary calls, it is understood that I call too, we being univocal.

But indeed I am ill at these ceremonious inductions. I fancy I was not born with a call on my head, though I have brought one down upon it with a vengeance. I love not to pluck that sort of fruit crude, but to stay its ripening into visits. In probability Mary will be at Southampton Row this morning, and something of that kind be matured between you, but in any case not many hours shall elapse before I shake you by the hand.

Meantime give my kindest felicitations to Mrs. Procter, and assure her I look forward with the greatest delight to our acquaintance. By the way, the deuce a bit of cake has come to hand, which hath an inauspicious look at first, but I comfort myself that that Mysterious Service hath the property of Sacramental Bread, which mice cannot nibble, nor time moulder.

I am married myself to a severe step-wife, who keeps me, not at bed and board, but at desk and board, and is jealous of my morning aberrations. I cannot slip out to congratulate kinder unions. It is well she leaves me alone o'nights,—the d——d Day-hag *Business.* She is even now peeping over me to see I am writing no love letters. I come, my dear—Where is the Indigo Sale Book?

Twenty adieus, my dear friends, till we meet.

Yours most truly,   C. LAMB.

To MISS HUTCHINSON.

LETTER CCLXXXVI.]   *Desk, November* 11, 1824.

My dear Miss Hutchinson—Mary bids me thank you for your kind letter. We are a little puzzled about your whereabouts. Miss Wordsworth writes Torkay, and you have queerly made it Torquay. Now Tokay we have heard of, and Torbay, which we take to be the true *male* spelling of the place; but somewhere we fancy it to be on "Devon's leafy shores," where we heartily wish the kindly breezes may restore all that is invalid among you. Robinson is returned, and speaks much of you all. We shall be most glad to hear good news from you from time to time. The best is, Procter is at last married. We have made sundry attempts to see the bride, but have accidentally failed, she being gone out a-gadding. We had promised our dear friends the Monkhouses—promised ourselves rather— a visit to them at Ramsgate; but I thought it best, and Mary seemed to have it at heart too, not to go far from home these last holydays. It is connected with a sense of unsettlement, and secretly I know she hoped that such abstinence would be friendly to her health. She certainly has escaped her sad yearly visitation, whether in consequence of it, or of faith in it, and we have to be thankful for a good 1824. To get such a notion into our heads may go a great way another year. Not that we quite confined ourselves; but assuming Islington to be headquarters, we made timid flights to Ware, Watford, etc., to try how the trouts tasted, for a night out or so, not long enough to make the sense of change oppressive, but sufficient to scour the rust of home. Coleridge is not returned from the sea. As a little scandal may divert you recluses, we were in the Summer dining at a clergyman of Southey's "Church of England," at Hertford, the same who officiated to Thurtell's last moments, and indeed an old contemporary Blue of C.'s and mine at school. After dinner we talked of C.; and F., who is a mighty good fellow in the main, but hath his cassock prejudices, inveighed against the moral character of C. I endeavoured to enlighten him on the subject, till having driven him out of some of his holds, he stopped my mouth at once by appealing to me whether it was not very well known that C. "at that very moment was living in a state of open adultery with Mrs. * * * * * * at Highgate?" Nothing I could say, serious or bantering, after that, could remove the deep inrooted conviction of the whole company assembled that such was the case! Of course you will keep this quite close, for I would not involve my poor blundering friend, who I daresay believed it all thoroughly. My interference of course was imputed to the goodness of my heart, that could imagine nothing wrong, etc. Such it is if ladies will go gadding about with other people's husbands at watering-places. How careful we should be to avoid the appearance of evil!

I thought this anecdote might amuse you. It is not worth resenting seriously; only I give it as a specimen of orthodox candour. O Southey, Southey, how long would it be before you would find one of us Unitarians propagating such unwarrantable scandal! Providence keep you all from the foul fiend, scandal, and send you back well and happy to dear Gloster Place!   C. L.

Miss Hutchinson,
    T. Monkhouse, Esq.,
        Strand, Torkay, Torbay, Devon.

To BERNARD BARTON.

LETTER CCLXXXVII.]   *December* 1, 1824.

Dear B. B.—If Mr. Mitford will send me a full and circumstantial description of his desired vases, I will transmit the same to a gentleman resident at Canton, whom I think I have interest enough in to take the proper care for their execution. But Mr. M. must have patience. China is a great way off, further perhaps than he thinks; and his next year's roses must be content to wither in a Wedgwood pot. He will please to say whether he should like his Arms upon them, etc. I send herewith some patterns which suggest themselves to me at the first blush of the subject, but he will probably consult his own taste after all.

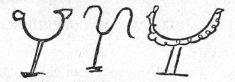

The last pattern is obviously fitted for ranunculuses only. The two former may indifferently hold daisies, marjoram, sweet-williams, and that sort. My friend in Canton is Inspector of Teas; his name is Ball; and I can think of no better tunnel. I shall expect Mr. M.'s decision.

Taylor and Hessey finding their magazine goes off very heavily at 2s. 6d. are prudently going to raise their price another shilling; and having already more authors than they want, intend to increase the number of them. If they set up against the *New Monthly* they must change their present hands. It is not tying the dead carcase of a Review to a half-dead Magazine will do their business. It is like George Dyer multiplying his volumes to make 'em sell better. When he finds one will not go off, he publishes two; two stick, he tries three; three hang fire, he is confident that four will have a better chance.

And now, my dear sir, trifling apart, the gloomy catastrophe of yesterday morning prompts a sadder vein. The fate of the unfortunate Fauntleroy makes me, whether I will or not, to cast reflecting eyes around on such of my friends as, by a parity of situation, are exposed to a similarity of temptation. My very style seems to myself to become more impressive than usual, with the change of theme. Who that standeth, knoweth but he may yet fall? Your hands as yet, I am most willing to believe, have never deviated into other's property. You think it impossible that you could ever commit so heinous an offence; but so thought Fauntleroy once; so have thought many besides him, who at last have expiated as he hath done. You are as yet upright; but you are a banker, at least the next thing to it. I feel the delicacy of the subject; but cash must pass through your hands, sometimes to a great amount. If in an unguarded hour—— but I will hope better. Consider the scandal it will bring upon those of your persuasion. Thousands would go to see a Quaker hanged, that would be indifferent to the fate of a Presbyterian or an Anabaptist. Think of the effect it would have on the sale of your poems alone, not to mention higher considerations! I tremble, I am sure, at myself, when I think that so many poor victims of the law, at one time of their life, made as sure of never being hanged, as I in my presumption am too ready to do myself. What are we better than they? Do we come into the world with different necks? Is there any distinctive mark under our left ears? Are we unstrangulable, I ask you? Think of these things. I am shocked sometimes at the shape of my own fingers, not for their resemblance to the ape tribe (which is something), but for the exquisite adaptation of them to the purposes of picking, fingering, etc. No one that is so framed, I maintain it, but should tremble. C. L.

To SAMUEL TAYLOR COLERIDGE.

LETTER CCLXXXVIII.] 1824.

Dear Coleridge—Why will you make your visits, which should give pleasure, matter of regret to your friends? You never come but you take away some folio, that is part of my existence. With a great deal of difficulty I was made to comprehend the extent of my loss. My maid, Becky, brought me a dirty bit of paper, which contained her description of some book which Mr. Coleridge had taken away. It was "Luster's Tables," which, for some time, I could not make out. "What! has he carried away any of the *tables,* Becky?" "No, it wasn't any tables, but it was a book that he called Luster's Tables." I was obliged to search personally among my shelves, and a huge fissure suddenly disclosed to me the true nature of the damage I had sustained. That book, Coleridge, you should not have taken away, for it is not mine; it is the property of a friend, who does not know its value, nor indeed have I been very sedulous in explaining to him the estimate of it; but was rather contented in giving a sort of corroboration to a hint that he let fall, as to its being suspected to be not genuine, so that in all probability it would have fallen to me as a deodand; not but I am as sure it is Luther's as I am sure that Jack Bunyan wrote the *Pilgrim's Progress;* but it was not for me to pronounce upon the validity of testimony that had been disputed by learneder clerks than I; so I quietly let it occupy the place it had usurped upon my shelves, and should never have thought of issuing an ejectment against it; for why should I be so bigoted as to allow rites of hospitality to none but my own books, children, etc.?—a species of egotism I abhor from my heart. No; let 'em all snug together, Hebrews and Proselytes of the gate; no selfish partiality of mine shall make distinction between them. I charge no warehouse room for my friends' commodities; they are welcome to come and stay as long as they like, without paying rent. I have several such strangers that I treat with more than Arabian courtesy. There's a copy of More's fine poem, which is none of mine, but I cherish it as my own. I am none of those churlish landlords that advertise the goods to be taken away in ten days' time, or then to be sold to pay expenses. So you see I had no right to lend you that book. I may lend you my own books, because it is at my own hazard; but it is not honest to hazard a friend's property; I always make that distinction. I hope you will bring it with you, or send it by Hartley; or he can bring that, and you the *Polemical Discourses,* and come and eat some atoning mutton with us one of these days shortly. We are engaged two or three Sundays deep, but always dine at home on weekdays at half-past four. So come all four—men and books I mean. My third shelf (northern compartment) from the top has two devilish gaps, where you have knocked out its two eye-teeth.

Your wronged friend,   C. LAMB.

To LEIGH HUNT.

LETTER CCLXXXIX.]   [End of 1824.]

ILLUSTREZZIMO SIGNOR—I have obeyed your mandate to a tittle. I accompany this with a volume; but what have you done with the first I sent you? Have you swapped it with some lazzaroni for macaroni, or pledged it with a gondolierer for a passage? Peradventuri the Cardinal Gonsalvi took a fancy to it: his Eminence has done my Nearness an honour. 'Tis but a step to the Vatican. As you judge, my works do not enrich the workman; but I get *vat I can* for 'em. They keep dragging me on, a poor, worn mill-horse, in the eternal round of the damned magazine; but 'tis they are blind, not I. Colburn (where I recognise with delight the gay W. Honeycomb renovated) hath the ascendency. I was with the Novellos last week. They have a large, cheap house and garden, with a dainty library (magnificent) without books; but what will make you bless yourself (I am too old for wonder), something has touched the right organ in Vincentio at last. He attends a Wesleyan chapel on Kingsland Green. He at first tried to laugh it off; he only went for the singing; but the cloven foot—I retract—the lamb's trotters are at length apparent. Mary Isabella attributes it to a lightness induced by his headaches; but I think I see in it a less accidental influence. Mr. Clark is at perfect staggers! the whole fabric of his infidelity is shaken. He has no one to join him in his horse-insults and indecent obstreperousnesses against Christianity; for Holmes (the bonny Holmes) is gone to Salisbury to be organist, and Isabella and the Clark make but a feeble quorum. The children have all neat little clasped pray-books; and I have laid out seven shillings and eight-pence in Watts's Hymns for Christmas presents for them. The eldest girl alone holds out. She has been at Boulogne, skirting upon the vast focus of Atheism, and imported bad principles in patois French. But the strong-holds are crumbling. N. appears as yet to have but a confused notion of the Atonement. It makes him giddy, he says, to think much about it; but such giddiness is spiritual sobriety. Well, Byron is gone; and —— is now the best poet in England. Fill up the gap to your fancy. Barry Cornwall has at last carried the pretty A[nne] S[kepper]. They are just in the treacle-moon. Hope it won't clog his wing (gaum, we used to say at school). Mary, my sister, has worn me out with eight weeks' cold and toothache, her average complement in the Winter; and it will not go away. She is otherwise well, and reads novels all day long. She has had an exempt year, a good year; for which, forgetting the minor calamity, she and I are most thankful. Alsager is in a flourishing house, with wife and children about him, in Mecklenburg Square,—almost too fine to visit. Barron Field is come home from Sydney; but as yet I can hear no tidings of a pension. He is plump and friendly; his wife, really a very superior woman. He resumes the bar. I have got acquainted with Mr. Irving, the Scotch preacher, whose fame must have reached you. He is an humble disciple at the foot of Gamaliel S. T. C. Judge how his own sectarists must stare, when I tell you he has dedicated a book to S. T. C., acknowledging to have learnt more of the nature of faith, Christianity, and Christian Church, from him than from all the men he ever conversed with! He is a most amiable, sincere, modest man in a room, this Boanerges in the temple. Mrs. Montague told him the dedication would do him no good. "That shall be a reason for doing it," was his answer. Judge, now, whether this man be a quack. Dear H., take this imperfect notelet for a letter: it looks so much the more like conversing on nearer terms. Love to all the Hunts, old friend Thornton, and all.

Yours ever, C. LAMB.

To THOMAS ALLSOP.

LETTER CCXC.]

Colebrook Cottage, Islington,
January 7, 1825.

Dear Allsop—I acknowledge with thanks the receipt of a draft on Messrs. Wms. for £81:11:3 which I haste to cash in the present alarming state of the money market. Hurst and Robinson gone. I have imagined a Chorus of ill-used Authors singing on the Occasion:

What should we when Booksellers break?
We should rejoice.
Da capo.

We regret exceedingly Mrs. Allsop's being unwell. Mary or both will come and see her soon. The frost is cruel, and we have both colds. I take Pills again, which battle with your Wine; and Victory hovers doubtful. By the by, tho' not disinclined to presents, I remember our bargain to take a dozen at sale price, and must demur.

With once again thanks and best loves to Mrs. A.

Turn over—Yours, C. LAMB.

To JOHN B. DIBDIN.

LETTER CCXCI.] *E. I. H., January 11, 1825.*

My Dear Sir—Pray return my best thanks to your father for his little volume. It is like all of his I have seen—spirited, good-humoured, and redolent of the wit and humour of a century ago. He should have lived with Gay and his set. The *Chessiad* is so clever that I relished it in spite of my total ignorance of the game. I have it not before me, but I remember a capital simile of the Charwoman letting in her Watchman husband, which is better than Butler's Lobster turned to Red. Hazard is a grand character—Jove in his Chair. When you are disposed to leave your one room for my six, Colebrooke is where it was; and my sister begs me to add that as she is disappointed of meeting your sister *your way,* we shall be most happy to see her *our way,* when you have an evening to spare. Do not stand on ceremonies and introductions, but come at once. I need not say that if you can induce your father to join the party it will be so much the pleasanter. Can you name an evening *next week?* I give you long credit.

Meantime am, as usual, yours truly,   C. L.

When I saw the *Chessiad* advertised by C. D. the younger, I hoped it might be yours. What title is left for you?

Charles Dibdin the younger, *junior.*

O no, you are Timothy!

To Miss HUTCHINSON.

LETTER CCXCII.]

The brevity of this is owing to scratching it off at my desk amid expected interruptions. By habit, I can write letters only at office.

January 20, 1825.

Dear Miss H.—Thank you for a noble goose, which wanted only the massive incrustation that we used to pick-axe open, about this season, in Old Gloucester Place. When shall we eat another goose pie together? The pheasant, too, must not be forgotten; twice as big, and half as good as a Partridge. You ask about the editor of the *London;* I know of none. This first specimen is flat and pert enough to justify subscribers who grudge t'other shilling. De Quincey's "Parody" was submitted to him before printed, and had his *Probatum.* The "Horns" is in a poor taste, resembling the most laboured papers in the *Spectator.* I had signed it "Jack Horner"; but Taylor and Hessey said it would be thought an offensive article unless I put my known signature to it, and wrung from me my slow consent. But did you read the "Memoir of Liston"?—and did you guess whose it was? Of all the lies I ever put off, I value this most. It is from top to toe, every paragraph, Pure Invention, and has passed for gospel; has been republished in newspapers, and in the penny play-bills of the night, as an authentic account. I shall certainly go to the naughty man some day for my fibbings. In the next Number I figure as a Theologian! and have attacked my late brethren, the Unitarians. What Jack-Pudding tricks I shall play next, I know not; I am almost at the end of my tether. Coleridge is quite blooming, but his book has not budded yet. I hope I have spelt Torquay right now, and that this will find you all mending, and looking forward to a London flight with the Spring. Winter, *we* have had none, but plenty of foul weather. I have lately picked up an epigram which pleased me—

"Two noble earls, whom if I quote,
　Some folks might call me sinner,
The one invented half a coat,
　The other half a dinner.

"The plan was good, as some will say;
　And fitted to console one;
Because, in this poor starving day
　Few can afford a whole one."

I have made the lame one still lamer by imperfect memory; but spite of bald diction, a little done to it might improve it into a good one. You have nothing else to do at Torquay. Suppose you try it. Well, God bless you all, as wishes Mary most sincerely, with many thanks for letter, etc.

ELIA.

To VINCENT NOVELLO.

Colebrook, Tuesday,

LETTER CCXCIII.]　　　　　　　　　　　　　　　Jan. 25, 1825.

Dear Novello—My sister's cold is as obstinate as an old Handelian, whom a modern amateur is trying to convert to Mozart-ism. As company must, and always does, injure it, Emma and I propose to come to you in the evening of to-morrow, *instead of meeting here.* An early bread-and-cheese supper at half-past eight will oblige us. Loves to the bearer of many children.　　　　　　　　　　　　　　　　　　　C. LAMB.

I sign with a black seal, that you may [begin] to think her cold has killed Mary; which will be an agreeable unsurprise when you read the note.

V. Novello, Esq., Green, Shacklewell.

To BERNARD BARTON.

LETTER CCXCIV.]　　　　　　　　　　　　　　*February* 10, 1825.

Dear B. B.—I am vexed that ugly paper should have offended. I kept it as clear from objectionable phrases as possible, and it was Hessey's fault, and my weakness, that it did not appear anonymous. No more of it, for God's sake. The "Spirit of the Age" is by Hazlitt. The characters of Coleridge, etc., he had done better in former publications, the praise and the abuse much stronger, etc.; but the new ones are capitally done. Horne Tooke is a matchless portrait. My advice is, to borrow it rather than buy it. I have it. He has laid too many colours on my likeness; but I have had so much injustice done me in my own name, that I make a rule of accepting as much over-measure to Elia as gentlemen think proper to bestow. Lay it on and spare not. Your gentleman brother sets my mouth a-watering after liberty. Oh that I were kicked out of Leadenhall with every mark of indignity, and a competence in my fob! The birds of the air would not be so free as I should. How I would prance and curvet it, and pick up cowslips, and ramble about purposeless, as an idiot! The Authormometer is a good fancy. I have caused great speculation in the dramatic (not *thy*) world by a lying "Life of Liston," all pure invention. The town has swallowed it, and it is copied into newspapers, play-bills, etc., as authentic. You do not know the Droll, and possibly missed reading the article (in our first Number, new series). A life more improbable for him to have lived would not be easily invented. But your rebuke, coupled with "Dream on J. Bunyan," checks me. I'd rather do more in my favourite way, but feel dry. I must laugh sometimes. I am poor Hypochondriacus, and *not* Liston. The second Number is all trash. What are T. and H. about? Why did poor Scott die? There was comfort in writing with such associates as were his little band of scribblers; some gone away, some affronted away, and I am left as the solitary widow looking for water-cresses. The only clever hand they have is Darley, who has written on the Dramatists under the name of John Lacy. But his function seems suspended.

I have been harassed more than usually at office, which has stopt my correspondence lately. I write with a confused aching head, and you must accept this apology for a letter.

I will do something soon, if I can, as a peace-offering to the queen of the East Angles—something she shan't scold about. For the present farewell.

Thine,   C. L.

I am fifty years old this day. Drink my health.

To THOMAS MANNING.

LETTER CCXCV.]   [Early in 1825.]

My dear M.—You might have come inopportunely a week since, when we had an inmate. At present and for as long as *ever* you like, our castle is at your service. I saw T[uthill] yesternight, who has done for me what may

> "To all my nights and days to come,
> Give solely sovran sway and masterdom."

But I dare not hope, for fear of disappointment. I cannot be more explicit at present. But I have it under his own hand, that I am *non*-capacitated (I cannot write it *in*-) for business. O joyous imbecility! Not a susurration of this to *anybody!*

Mary's love.   C. LAMB.

To BERNARD BARTON.

LETTER CCXCVI.]   *March* 23, 1825.

Dear B. B.—I have had no impulse to write, or attend to any single object but myself for weeks past—my single self, I—by myself—I. I am sick of hope deferred. The grand wheel is in agitation, that is to turn up my Fortune; but round it rolls, and will turn up nothing. I have a glimpse of freedom, of becoming a Gentleman at large; but I am put off from day to day. I have offered my resignation, and it is neither accepted nor rejected. Eight weeks am I kept in this fearful suspense. Guess what an absorbing stake I feel it. I am not conscious of the existence of friends present or absent. The East India Directors alone can be that thing to me or not. I have just learned that nothing will be decided this week. Why the next? Why any week? It has fretted me into an itch of the fingers; I rub 'em against paper, and write to you, rather than not allay this scorbuta.

While I can write, let me abjure you to have no doubts of IRVING. Let Mr. Mitford drop his disrespect. Irving has prefixed a dedication (of a missionary subject, first part) to Coleridge, the most beautiful, cordial, and sincere. He there acknowledges his obligation to S. T. C. for his knowledge of Gospel truths, the nature of a Christian Church, etc., to the talk of Samuel Taylor Coleridge (at whose Gamaliel feet he sits weekly), rather than to that of all the men living. This from him, the great dandled and petted sectarian—to a religious character so equivocal in the world's eyes as that of S. T. C., so foreign to the Kirk's estimate—can this man be a quack? The language is as affecting as the spirit of the dedication. Some friend told him, "This dedication will do you no good," *i.e.* not in the world's repute, or with your own people. "That is a reason for doing it," quoth Irving.

I am thoroughly pleased with him. He is firm, out-speaking, intrepid, and docile as a pupil of Pythagoras. You must like him.

Yours, in tremors of painful hope,   C. LAMB.

To WILLIAM WORDSWORTH.

LETTER CCXCVII.]   *Colebrook Cottage, April* 6, 1825.

Dear Wordsworth—I have been several times meditating a letter to you concerning the good thing which has befallen me, but the thought of poor Monkhouse came across me. He was one that I had exulted in the prospect of congratulating me. He and you were to have been the first participators, for indeed it has been ten weeks since the first motion of it. Here am I then, after thirty-three years' slavery, sitting in my own room at eleven o'clock this finest of all April mornings, a freed man, with £441 a year for the remainder of my life, live I as long as John Dennis, who outlived his annuity and starved at ninety; £441, *i.e.* £450, with a deduction of £9 for a provision secured to my sister, she being survivor, the pension guaranteed by Act Georgii Tertii, etc.

I came home FOR EVER on Tuesday in last week. The incomprehensibleness of my condition overwhelmed me. It was like passing from life into eternity. Every year to be as long as three, *i.e.* to have three times as much real time (time that is my own) in it! I wandered about thinking that I was happy, but feeling I was not. But that tumultuousness is passing off, and I begin to understand the nature of the gift. Holydays, even the annual month, were always uneasy joys; their conscious fugitiveness; the craving after making the most of them. Now, when all is holyday, there are no holydays. I can sit at home, in rain or shine, without a restless impulse for walkings. I am daily steadying, and shall soon find it as natural to me to be my own master, as it has been irksome to have had a master. Mary wakes every morning with an obscure feeling that some good has happened to us.

Leigh Hunt and Montgomery, after their releasements, describe the shock of their emancipation much as I feel mine. But it hurt their frames. I eat, drink, and sleep as sound as ever. I lay no anxious schemes for going hither and thither, but take things as they occur. Yesterday I excursioned twenty miles; to-day I write a few letters. Pleasuring was for fugitive play-days; mine are fugitive only in the sense that life is fugitive. Freedom and life co-existent!

At the foot of such a call upon you for gratulation, I am ashamed to advert to that melancholy event. Monkhouse was a character I learned to love slowly, but it grew upon me, yearly, monthly, daily. What a chasm has it made in our pleasant parties! His noble friendly face was always coming before me, till this hurrying event in my life came, and for the time has absorbed all interest; in fact it has shaken me a little. My old desk companions, with whom I have had such merry hours, seem to reproach me for removing my lot from among them. They were pleasant creatures; but to the anxieties of business, and a weight of possible worse ever impending, I was not equal. Tuthill and Gillman gave me my certificates. I laughed at the friendly lie implied in them; but my sister shook her head, and said it was all true. Indeed, this last Winter I was jaded out: Winters were always worse than other parts of the year, because the spirits are worse, and I had no daylight. In Summer I had daylight evenings. The relief was hinted to me from a superior Power, when I, poor slave, had not a hope but that I must wait another seven years with Jacob: and lo! the Rachel which I coveted is brought to me!

Have you read the noble dedication of Irving's "Missionary Orations" to S. T. C.? Who shall call this man a quack hereafter? What the Kirk will think of it neither I nor Irving care. When somebody suggested to him that it would not be likely to do him good, videlicet, among his own people, "That is a reason for doing it," was his noble answer. That Irving thinks he has profited mainly by S. T. C., I have no doubt. The very style of the Dedication shows it.

Communicate my news to Southey, and beg his pardon for my being so long acknowledging his kind present of the "Church," which circumstances, having no reference to himself, prevented at the time. Assure him of my deep respect and friendliest feelings.

Divide the same, or rather each take the whole to you—I mean you and all yours. To Miss Hutchinson I must write separate.

Farewell! and end at last, long selfish letter. C. LAMB.

To BERNARD BARTON.

LETTER CCXCVIII.]   *April* 6, 1825.

Dear B. B.—My spirits are so tumultuary with the novelty of my recent emancipation, that I have scarce steadiness of hand, much more
mind, to compose a letter. I am free, B. B.—free as air!

> "The little bird that wings the sky
> Knows no such liberty."

I was set free on Tuesday in last week at four o'clock. I came home for
ever!

I have been describing my feelings as well as I can to Wordsworth in a
long letter, and don't care to repeat. Take it briefly, that for a few days
I was painfully oppressed by so mighty a change, but it is becoming daily
more natural to me. I went and sat among 'em all at my old thirty-three
years' desk yester morning; and, deuce take me, if I had not yearnings
at leaving all my old pen-and-ink fellows, merry, sociable lads, at leaving
them in the lurch, fag, fag, fag!—The comparison of my own superior
felicity gave me anything but pleasure.

B. B., I would not serve another seven years for seven hundred thousand pounds! I have got £441 net for life, sanctioned by Act of Parliament, with a provision for Mary if she survives me. I will live another
fifty years; or, if I live but ten, they will be thirty, reckoning the quantity of real time in them, *i.e.* the time that is a man's own. Tell me how
you like "Barbara S." Will it be received in atonement for the foolish
"Vision"?—I mean by the lady. *A-propos*, I never saw Mrs. Crawford
in my life; nevertheless 'tis all true of somebody.

Address me, in future, Colebrook Cottage, Islington. I am really nervous (but that will wear off), so take this brief announcement.

Yours truly,   C. L.

To MISS HUTCHINSON.

LETTER CCXCIX.]   *April* 18, 1825.

Dear Miss Hutchinson—You want to know all about by gaol delivery.
Take it then. About twelve weeks since I had a sort of intimation that a
resignation might be well accepted from me. This was a kind bird's whisper. On that hint I spake. Gillman and Tuthill furnished me with certificates of wasted health and sore spirits—not much more than the truth,
I promise you—and for nine weeks I was kept in a fright. I had gone
too far to recede, and they might take advantage, and dismiss me with a
much less sum than I had reckoned on. However, liberty came at last,
with a liberal provision. I have given up what I could have lived on in
the country; but have enough to live here, by management and scribbling

occasionally. I would not go back to my prison for seven years longer for £10,000 a year; seven years after one is fifty, is no trifle to give up. Still I am a young *pensioner,* and have served but thirty-three years; very few, I assure you, retire before forty, forty-five, or fifty years' service.

You will ask how I bear my freedom? Faith, for some days I was staggered; could not comprehend the magnitude of my deliverance; was confused, giddy; knew not whether I was on my head or my heel, as they say. But those giddy feelings have gone away, and my weather-glass stands at a degree or two above

CONTENT.

I go about quiet, and have none of that restless hunting after recreation which made holydays formerly uneasy joys. All being holydays, I feel as if I had none, as they do in heaven, where 'tis all red-letter days. I have a kind letter from the Wordsworths, *congratulatory* not a little. It is a damp, I do assure you, amid all my prospects, that I can receive *none* from a quarter upon which I had calculated, almost more than from any, upon receiving congratulations. I had grown to like poor Monkhouse more and more. I do not esteem a soul living or not living more warmly than I had grown to esteem and value him. But words are vain. We have none of us to count upon many years. That is the only cure for sad thoughts. If only some died, and the rest were permanent on earth, what a thing a friend's death would be then!

I must take leave, having put off answering a load of letters to this morning; and this, alas! is the first. Our kindest remembrances to Mrs. Monkhouse,

And believe us yours most truly, C. LAMB.

To WILLIAM WORDSWORTH.

LETTER CCC.] [Middle of *May* 1825.]

Dear W.—I write post-haste to ensure a frank. Thanks for your hearty congratulations. I may now date from the sixth week of my "Hegira, or Flight from Leadenhall." I have lived so much in it, that a Summer seems already past; and 'tis but early May yet with you and other people. How I look down on the slaves and drudges of the world! Its inhabitants are a vast cotton-web of spin-spin-spinners! O the carking cares! O the money-grubbers! Sempiternal muckworms!

Your Virgil I have lost sight of, but suspect it is in the hands of Sir G. Beaumont; I think that circumstances made me shy of procuring it before. Will you write to him about it?—and your commands shall be obeyed to a tittle.

Coleridge has just finished his prize Essay by which, if it get the prize, he'll touch an additional £100 I fancy. His book, too ("Commentary on Bishop Leighton"), is quite finished, and *penes* Taylor and Hessey.

In the *London Magazine,* which is just out (1st of May), are two papers entitled the "Superannuated Man," which I wish you to see; and also, 1st of April, a little thing called "Barbara S——," a story gleaned from Miss Kelly. The *London Magazine,* if you can get it, will save my enlargement upon the topic of my manumission.

I must scribble to make up my *hiatus crumenæ;* for there are so many ways, pious and profligate, of getting rid of money in this vast city and suburbs, that I shall miss my THIRDS. But *couragio!* I despair not. Your kind hint of the cottage was well thrown out; an anchorage for *age* and school of economy, when necessity comes; but without this latter, I have an unconquerable terror of changing place. It does not agree with us. I say it from conviction; else I do sometimes ruralise in fancy.

Some d—d people are come in, and I must finish abruptly. By d—d, I only mean deuced. 'Tis these suitors of Penelope that makes it necessary to *authorise* a little for gin and mutton, and such trifles.

Excuse my abortive scribble.

Yours, not in more haste than heart,   C. L.

Love and recollects to all the Wms., Doras, Marys, round your Wrekin.

Mary is capitally well. Do write to Sir G. B., for I am shyish of applying to him.

To BERNARD BARTON.

LETTER CCCI.]   *July 2, 1825.*

My dear B. B.—My nervous attack has so unfitted me that I have not courage to sit down to a letter. My poor pittance in the *London* you will see is drawn from my sickness. Your book is very acceptable to me, because most of it is new to me; but your book itself we cannot thank you for more sincerely than for the introduction you favoured us with to Anne Knight. Now cannot I write *Mrs.* Anne Knight for the life of me. She is a very pleas——, but I won't write all we have said of her so often to ourselves, because I suspect you would read it to her. Only give my sister's and my kindest *remembrances* to her, and how glad we are we can say that word. If ever she come to Southwark again, I count upon another pleasant Bridge walk with her. Tell her, I got home, time for a rubber; but poor Tryphena will not understand that phrase of the worldling.

I am hardly able to appreciate your volume now: but I liked the dedication much, and the apology for your bald burying grounds. To Shelley; but *that* is not new. To the young Vesper-singer, Great Bealings, Playford, and what not.

If there be a cavil, it is that the topics of religious consolation, however beautiful, are repeated till a sort of triteness attends them. It seems as if you were for ever losing friends' children by death, and reminding their parents of the Resurrection. Do children die so often, and so good, in your parts? The topic taken from the consideration that they are snatched away from *possible vanities,* seems hardly sound; for to an Omniscient eye their conditional failings must be one with their actual; but I am too unwell for theology.

Such as I am,

I am yours and A[nne] K[night's] truly,   C. LAMB.

To SAMUEL TAYLOR COLERIDGE.

LETTER CCCII.]   *Islington,* July 2, 1825.

Dear C.—We are going off to Enfield, to Allsop's, for a day or two, with some intention of succeeding them in their lodging for a time, for this damned nervous fever (vide *London Magazine* for July) indisposes me for seeing any friends, and never any poor devil was so befriended as I am. Do you know any poor solitary human that wants that cordial to life, a true friend? I can spare him twenty: he shall have 'em good cheap. I have gallipots of 'em—genuine balm of cares—a going, a going, a going! Little plagues plague me a thousand times more than ever. I am like a disembodied soul in this, my eternity. I feel everything entirely, all in all, and all in, etc. This price I pay for liberty, but am richly content to pay it. The Odes are four-fifths done by Hood, a silentish young man you met at Islington one day, an invalid. The rest are Reynolds's, whose sister H. has recently married. I have not had a broken finger in them.

They are hearty, good-natured things, and I would put my name to 'em cheerfully, if I could as honestly. I complimented 'em in a newspaper, with an abatement for those puns you laud so. They are generally an excess. A Pun is a thing of too much consequence to be thrown in as a make-weight. You shall read one of the "Addresses" over and miss the puns, and it shall be quite as good, and better, than when you discover 'em. A Pun is a noble thing *per se:* O never lug it in as an accessory. A Pun is a sole object for Reflection (*vide my* "Aids" to that recessment from a savage state)—it is entire, it fills the mind; it is perfect as a sonnet, better. It limps ashamed in the train and retinue of Humour: it knows it should have an establishment of its own. The one, for instance, I made the other day,—I forget what it was.

Hood will be gratified, as much as I am, by your mistake. I liked "Grimaldi" the best; it is true painting of abstract clownery, and that precious concrete of a clown: and the rich succession of images, and words almost such, in the first half of the "Magnum Ignotum." . . . Hood has just come in; his sick eyes sparked into health when he read your approbation. They had meditated a copy for you, but postponed it till a neater second edition which is at hand. We are walking out to Enfield after our Beans and Bacon which are just smoking. Kindest remembrances to the G.'s ever. From Islington, 1st Day, 3rd month of my Hegira, or Flight from Leadenhall.   C. L., *Olim Clericus.*

To BERNARD BARTON.

LETTER CCCIII.]   *August* 10, 1825.

We shall be soon again at Colebrook.

Dear B. B.—You must excuse my not writing before, when I tell you we are on a visit at Enfield, where I do not feel it natural to sit down to a letter. It is at all times an exertion. I would rather talk with you and Anne Knight quietly at Colebrook Lodge, over the matter of your last. You mistake me when you express misgivings about my relishing a series of scriptural poems. I wrote confusedly. What I meant to say was, that one or two consolatory poems on deaths would have had a more condensed effect than many. Scriptural, devotional topics admit of infinite variety. So far from poetry tiring me because religious, I can read, and I say it seriously, the homely old version of the Psalms in our Prayer Books for an hour or two together sometimes without sense of weariness.

I did not express myself clearly about what I think a false topic insisted on so frequently in consolatory addresses on the death of infants. I know something like it is in Scripture, but I think humanly spoken. It is a natural thought, a sweet fallacy to the survivors, but still a fallacy. If it stands on the doctrine of this being a probationary state, it is liable to this dilemma. Omniscience, to whom possibility must be clear as act, must know of the child, what it would hereafter turn out: if good, then the topic is false to say it is secured from falling into future wilfulness, vice, etc. If bad, I do not see how its exemption from certain future overt acts, by being snatched away, at all tells in its favour. You stop the arm of a murderer, or arrest the finger of a pickpurse; but is not the guilt incurred as much by the intent as if never so much acted? Why children are hurried off, and old reprobates of a hundred left, whose trial humanly we may think was complete at fifty, is among the obscurities of Providence. The very notion of a state of probation has darkness in it. The All-knower has no need of satisfying His eyes by seeing what we will do, when He knows before what we will do. Methinks we might be condemned before commission. In these things we grope and flounder, and if we can pick up a little human comfort that the child taken is snatched from vice (no great compliment to it, by the by), let us take it. And as to where an untried child goes, whether to join the assembly of its elders who have borne the heat of the day—fire-purified martyrs, and torment-sifted confessors—what know we! We promise heaven, methinks, too cheaply and assign large revenues to minors, incompetent to manage them. Epitaphs run upon this topic of consolation, till the very frequency induces a cheapness. Tickets for admission into Paradise are sculptured out at a penny a letter, twopence a syllable, etc. It is all a mystery; and the more I try to express my meaning (having none that is clear), the more I flounder. Finally, write what your own conscience, which to you is the unerring judge, seems best, and be careless about the whimsies of such a half-baked notionist as I am. We are here in a most pleasant country, full of walks, and idle to our hearts' desire. Taylor has dropt the *London*. It was indeed a dead weight. It has got in the Slough of Despond. I shuffle off my part of the pack, and stand like Christian with light and merry shoulders. It had got silly, indecorous, pert, and everything that is bad. Both our kind *remembrances* to Mrs. K. and yourself, and strangers'-greeting to Lucy (is it Lucy or Ruth?) that gathers wise sayings in a Book. C. LAMB.

To ROBERT SOUTHEY.

LETTER CCCIV.] *August* 19, 1825.

Dear Southey—You'll know who this letter comes from by opening slap-dash upon the text, as in the good old times. I never could come into the custom of envelopes; 'tis a modern foppery; the Plinian correspondence gives no hint of such. In singleness of sheet and meaning, then, I thank you for your little book. I am ashamed to add a codicil of thanks for your "Book of the Church." I scarce feel competent to give an opinion of the latter; I have not reading enough of that kind to venture at it. I can only say the fact, that I have read it with attention and interest. Being, as you know, not quite a Churchman, I felt a jealousy at the Church taking to herself the whole deserts of Christianity, Catholic and Protestant, from Druid extirpation downwards. I call all good Christians the Church, Capillarians and all. But I am in too light a humour to touch these matters. May all our churches flourish! Two things staggered me in the poem (and one of them staggered both of us). I cannot away with a beautiful series of verses, as I protest they are, commencing "Jenner." 'Tis like a choice banquet opened with a pill or an electuary—physic stuff. T'other is, we cannot make out how Edith should be no more than ten years old. By'r Lady, we had taken her to be some sixteen or upwards. We suppose you have only chosen the round number for the metre. Or poem and dedication may be both older than they pretend to; but then some hint might have been given; for, as it stands, it may only serve some day to puzzle the parish reckoning. But without inquiring further (for 'tis ungracious to look into a lady's years), the dedication is eminently pleasing and tender, and we wish Edith May Southey joy of it. Something, too, struck us as if we had heard of the death of John May. A John May's death was a few years since in the papers. We think the tale one of the quietest, prettiest things we have seen. You have been temperate in the use of localities, which generally spoil poems laid in exotic regions. You mostly cannot stir out (in such things) for humming-birds and fire-flies. A tree is a Magnolia, etc.—Can I but like the truly Catholic spirit? "Blame as thou mayest the Papist's erring creed"—which, and other passages, brought me back to the old Anthology days, and the admonitory lesson to "Dear George" on the "The Vesper Bell," a little poem which retains its first hold upon me strangely.

The compliment to the translatress is daintily conceived. Nothing is choicer in that sort of writing than to bring in some remote, impossible parallel,—as between a great empress and the inobtrusive quiet soul who digged her noiseless way so perseveringly through that rugged Paraguay mine. How she Dobrizhoffered it all out, it puzzles my slender Latinity to conjecture. Why do you seem to sanction Landor's unfeeling allegorising away of honest Quixote! He may as well say Strap is meant to symbolise the Scottish nation before the Union, and Random since that act of dubious issue; or that Partridge means the Mystical Man, and Lady Bellaston typifies the Woman upon Many Waters. Gebir, indeed, may mean the state of the hop markets last month, for anything I know to the contrary. That all Spain overflowed with romancical books (as Madge Newcastle calls them) was no reason that Cervantes should not smile at the matter of them; nor even a reason that, in another mood, he might not multiply them, deeply as he was tinctured with the essence of them. Quixote is the father of gentle ridicule, and at the same time the very depository and treasury of chivalry and highest notions. Marry, when somebody persuaded Cervantes that he meant only fun, and put him upon writing that unfortunate Second Part with the confederacies of that unworthy duke and most contemptible duchess, Cervantes sacrificed his instinct to his understanding.

We got your little book but last night, being at Enfield, to which place we came about a month since, and are having quiet holydays. Mary walks her twelve miles a day some days, and I my twenty on others. 'Tis all holyday with me now, you know. The change works admirably.

For literary news, in my poor way, I have a one-act farce going to be acted at the Haymarket; but when? is the question. 'Tis an extravaganza, and like enough to follow *Mr. H.* The *London Magazine* has shifted its publishers once more, and I shall shift myself out of it. It is fallen. My ambition is not at present higher than to write nonsense for the playhouses, to eke out a somewhat contracted income. *Tempus erat.* There was a time, my dear Cornwallis, when the Muse, etc. But I am now in Mac Fleckno's predicament,—

"Promised a play, and dwindled to a farce."

Coleridge is better (was, at least, a few weeks since) than he has been for years. His accomplishing his book at last has been a source of vigour to him. We are on a half visit to his friend Allsop, at a Mrs. Leishman's, Enfield, but expect to be at Colebrook Cottage in a week or so, where, or anywhere, I shall be always most happy to receive tidings from you. G. Dyer is in the height of an uxorious paradise. His honeymoon will not wane till he wax cold. Never was a more happy pair since Acme and Sentimius, and longer. Farewell, with many thanks, dear S. Our loves to all round your Wrekin.

Your old friend, C. LAMB.

To WILLIAM HONE.

LETTER CCCV.]   *September* 30, 1825.

Dear H.—I came home in a week from Enfield, worse than I went. My sufferings have been intense, but are abating. I begin to know what a little sleep is. My sister has sunk under her anxieties about me. She is laid up, deprived of reason for many weeks to come, I fear. She is in the same house, but we do not meet. It makes both worse. I can just hobble down as far as the "Angel" once a day; further kills me. When I can stretch to Copenh[agen] Street I will. If you come this way any morning, I can only just shake you by the hand. This gloomy house does not admit of making my friends welcome. You have come off triumphant with Bartholomew Fair.

Yours (writ with difficulty),   C. LAMB.

Mr. Hone,
    Ludgate Hill.

To THOMAS MANNING.

LETTER CCCVI.]   *December* 10, 1825.

My dear M.—We have had sad ups and downs since you saw us, but we are at present *in* untroubled waters though not *by* them, for our old New River has taken a jaundice of the muds and rains, and looks as yellow as Miss ——.

Your red trunk (not *hose*, tho' a flame-coloured pair was once esteemed a luxury) is safe deposited at the Peacock, who by the by is worth your seeing. She has had her tail brushed up, and looks as pert as *A-goose* with a hundred eyes in *My*-thology: I don't know what *yours* says of it. Your gown will be at the Bell, Totteridge, by the Telegraph on Monday; time enough, I hope, to go out to the curate's to an early Tea in it. We have a corner at *double dumbee* for you, whenever you are disposed to change your Inn.

Believe us, yours as ever,

CHARLES AND MARY LAMB.

From Colebrook, this Saturday, the 10th of December 1825.

To CHARLES OLLIER.

LETTER CCCVII.]
Colebrook Cottage, Colebrook Row,
Tuesday [*January* 1826.]

Dear Ollier—I send you two more proverbs, which will be the last of this batch, unless I send you one more by the post on THURSDAY; none will come after that day; so do not leave any open room in that case.

Hood sups with me to-night. Can you come and eat grouse? 'Tis not often I offer at delicacies.
Yours most kindly,   C. LAMB.

LETTER CCCVIII.]   *January* 1826.

Dear O.—We lamented your absence last night. The grouse were piquant: the backs incomparable. You must come in to cold mutton and oysters some evening. Name your evening; though I have qualms at the distance. Do you never leave early? My head is very queerish, and indisposed for much company; but we will get Hood, that half Hogarth, to meet you. The scrap I send should come in AFTER the "Rising with the Lark."
Yours truly.

Colburn, I take it, pays postages.

To BERNARD BARTON.

LETTER CCCIX.]   *February* 7, 1826.

Dear B. B.—I got your book not more than five days ago, so am not so negligent as I must have appeared to you with a fortnight's sin upon my shoulders. I tell you with sincerity, that I think you have completely succeeded in what you intended to do. What is poetry may be disputed. These are poetry, to me at least. They are concise, pithy, and moving. Uniform as they are, and untristorify'd, I read them through at two sittings, without one sensation approaching to tedium. I do not know that among your many kind presents of this nature, this is not my favourite volume. The language is never lax, and there is a unity of design and feeling. You wrote them *with love*—to avoid the cox*combical* phrase, *con amore*. I am particularly pleased with the "Spiritual Law," pages 34 and 35. It reminded me of Quarles, and "holy Mr. Herbert," as Izaak Walton calls him; the two best, if not only, of our devotional poets, though some prefer Watts, and some *Tom Moore*. I am far from well, or in my right spirits, and shudder at pen-and-ink work. I poke out a monthly crudity for Colburn in his magazine, which I call "Popular Fallacies," and periodically crush a proverb or two, setting up my folly against the wisdom of nations. Do you see the *New Monthly?*
One word I must object to in your little book, and it recurs more than once—*fadeless* is no genuine compound; loveless is, because love is a noun as well as verb; but what is a fade? And I do not quite like whipping the Greek drama upon the back of "Genesis," page 8. I do not like praise handed in by disparagement; as I objected to a side censure on Byron, etc., in the "Lines on Bloomfield." With these poor cavils excepted, your verses are without a flaw.   C. LAMB.

Dear B. B.—You may know my letters by the paper and the folding. For the former, I live on scraps obtained in charity from an old friend, whose stationery is a permanent perquisite; for folding, I shall do it neatly when I learn to tie my neckcloths. I surprise most of my friends by writing to them on ruled paper, as if I had not got past pot-hooks and hangers. Sealing-wax, I have none on my establishment; wafers of the coarsest bran supply its place. When my epistles come to be weighed with Pliny's, however superior to the Roman in delicate irony, judicious reflections, etc., his gilt post will bribe over the judges to him. All the time I was at the E. I. H. I never mended a pen; I now cut 'em to the stumps, marring rather than mending the primitive goose-quill. I cannot bear to pay for articles I used to get for nothing. When Adam laid out his first penny upon nonpareils at some stall in Mesopotamos, I think it went hard with him, reflecting upon his old goodly orchard, where he had so many for nothing. When I write to a great man at the Court end, he opens with surprise upon a naked note, such as Whitechapel people interchange, with no sweet degrees of envelope. I never enclosed one bit of paper in another, nor understood the rationale of it. Once only I sealed with borrowed wax, to set Walter Scott a wondering, signed with the imperial quartered arms of England, which my friend Field gives in compliment to his descent, in the female line, from Oliver Cromwell. It must have set his antiquarian curiosity upon watering. To your questions upon the currency, I refer you to Mr. Robinson's last speech, where, if you can find a solution, I can not. I think this, though, the best ministry we ever stumbled upon;—gin reduced four shillings in the gallon, wine two shillings in the quart! This comes home to men's minds and bosoms. My tirade against visitors was not meant *particularly* at you or A. K——. I scarce know what I meant, for I do not just now feel the grievance. I wanted to make an *article*. So in another thing I talked of somebody's *insipid wife*, without a correspondent object in my head: and a good lady, a friend's wife, whom I really *love* (don't startle, I mean in a licit way), has looked shyly on me ever since. The blunders of personal application are ludicrous. I send out a character every now and then, on purpose to exercise the ingenuity of my friends. "Popular Fallacies" will go on; that word "concluded" is an erratum, I suppose, for "continued." I do not know how it got stuffed in there. A little thing without name will also be printed on the Religion of the Actors, but it is out of your way, so I recommend you, with true author's hypocrisy, to skip it. We are about to sit down to roast beef, at which we could wish A. K., B. B., and B. B.'s pleasant daughter to be humble partakers. So much for my hint at visitors, which was scarcely calculated for droppers-in from Woodbridge; the sky does not drop such larks every day. My very kindest wishes to you all three, with my sister's best love.   C. LAMB.

To SAMUEL TAYLOR COLERIDGE.

LETTER CCCXI.]   *March* 22, 1826.

Dear Coleridge—We will with great pleasure be with you on Thursday in the next week early. May we venture to bring Emma with us? Your finding out my style in your nephew's pleasant book is surprising to me. I want eyes to descry it. You are a little too hard upon his morality, though I confess he has more of Sterne about him than of Sternhold. But he saddens into excellent sense before the conclusion. Your query shall be submitted to Miss Kelly, though it is obvious that the pantomime, when done, will be more easy to decide upon than in proposal. I say, do it by all means. I have Decker's play by me, if you can filch anything out of it. Miss Gray, with her kitten eyes, is an actress, though she shows it not at all; and pupil to the former, whose gestures she mimics in comedy to the disparagement of her own natural manner, which is agreeable. It is funny to see her bridling up her neck, which is native to F. K.; but there is no setting the manners of others upon one's shoulders any more than their head. I am glad you esteem Manning, though you see but his husk or shrine. He discloses not, save to select worshippers, and will leave the world without any one hardly but me knowing how stupendous a creature he is. I am perfecting myself in the "Ode to Eton College" against Thursday, that I may not appear unclassic. I have just discovered that it is much better than the "Elegy."

In haste,   C. L.

P.S.—I do not know what to say to your *latest* theory about Nero being the Messiah, thought by all accounts he was a 'nointed one.

To THE REV. H. F. CARY.

LETTER CCCXII.]   *April* 3, 1826.

Dear Sir—It is whispered me that you will not be unwilling to look into our doleful hermitage. Without more preface, you will gladden our cell by accompanying our old chums of the *London,* Darley and A[llan] C[unningham], to Enfield on Wednesday. You shall have hermit's fare, with talk as seraphical as the novelty of the divine life will permit, with an innocent retrospect to the world which we have left, when I will thank you for your hospitable offer at Chiswick, and with plain hermit reasons evince the necessity of abiding here.

Without hearing from you, then, you shall give us leave to expect you. I have long had it on my conscience to invite you, but spirits have been low; and I am indebted to chance for this awkward but most sincere invitation.

Yours, with best loves to Mrs. Cary,   C. LAMB.

D. knows all about the coaches. Oh for a Museum in the wilderness!

To VINCENT NOVELLO.

LETTER CCCXIII.]   *May* 9, 1826.

Dear N.—You will not expect us to-morrow, I am sure, while these damn'd North-Easters continue. We must wait the Zephyrs' pleasure. By the bye, I was at Highgate on Wednesday, the only one of the party.
Yours truly,   C. LAMB.

Summer, as my friend Coleridge waggishly writes, has set in with its usual severity.
Kind remembces. to Mrs. Novello, etc.

To BERNARD BARTON.

LETTER CCCXIV.]   *May* 16, 1826.

Dear B. B.—I have had no spirits lately to begin a letter to you, though I am under obligations to you (how many!) for your neat little poem. 'Tis just what it professes to be, a simple tribute, in chaste verse, serious and sincere.

I do not know how friends will relish it, but we outlyers, honorary friends, like it very well. I have had my head and ears stuffed up with the East winds: a continual ringing in my brain of bells jangled, or the spheres touched by some raw angel. Is it not George the Third trying the Hundredth Psalm? I gct my music for nothing. But the weather seems to be softening, and will thaw my stunnings. Coleridge, writing to me a week or two since, begins his note—"Summer has set in with its usual severity." A cold Summer is all I know of disagreeable in cold. I do not mind the utmost rigour of real Winter, but these smiling hypocrites of Mays wither me to death. My head has been a ringing chaos, like the day the winds were made, before they submitted to the discipline of a weathercock, before the quarters were made. In the street, with the blended noises of life about me, I hear, and my head is lightened; but in a room the hubbub comes back, and I am deaf as a sinner. Did I tell you of a pleasant sketch Hood has done, which he calls—*"Very deaf indeed"*? It is of a good-natured stupid-looking old gentleman, whom a footpad has stopped, but for his extreme deafness cannot make him understand what he wants. The unconscious old gentleman is extending his ear-trumpet very complacently, and the fellow is firing a pistol into it to make him hear, but the ball will pierce his skull sooner than the report will reach his sensorium. I choose a very little bit of paper, for my ear hisses when I bend down to write. I can hardly read a book, for I miss that small soft voice which the idea of articulated words raises (almost imperceptibly to you) in a silent reader. I seem too deaf to see what I read. But with a touch or two of returning zephyr my head will melt. What lies you poets tell about the May! It is the most ungenial part of the year. Cold crocuses, cold primroses, you take your blossoms in ice—a painted sun.

> "Unmeaning joy around appears,
> And Nature smiles as if she sneers."

It is ill with me when I begin to look which way the wind sets. Ten years ago, I literally did not know the point from the broad end of the vane, which it was that indicated the quarter. I hope these ill winds have blown *over* you as they do through me.

Kindest remembrances to you and yours.   C. L.

To SAMUEL TAYLOR COLERIDGE.

LETTER CCCXV.]   *June* 1, 1826.

Dear Coleridge—If I know myself, nobody more detests the display of personal vanity, which is implied in the act of sitting for one's picture, than myself. But the fact is, that the likeness which accompanies this letter was stolen from my person at one of my unguarded moments by some too partial artist, and my friends are pleased to think that he has not much flattered me. Whatever its merits may be, you, who have so great an interest in the original, will have a satisfaction in tracing the features of one that has so long esteemed you. There are times when in a friend's absence these graphic representations of him almost seem to bring back the man himself. The painter, whoever he was, seems to have taken me in one of those disengaged moments, if I may so term them, when the native character is so much more honestly displayed than can be possible in the restraints of an enforced sitting attitude. Perhaps it rather describes me as a thinking man, than a man in the act of thought. Whatever its pretensions, I know it will be dear to you, towards whom I should wish my thoughts to flow in a sort of an undress rather than in the more studied graces of diction.

I am, dear Coleridge, yours sincerely,   C. LAMB.

To J. B. DIBDIN.

LETTER CCCXVI.]   *Friday, some day in June,* 1826.

Dear D.—My first impulse upon opening your letter was pleasure at seeing your old neat hand, nine parts gentlemanly with a modest dash of the clerical: my second, a Thought, natural enough this hot weather—am I to answer all this? Why 'tis as long as those to the Ephesians and Galatians put together, I have counted the words for curiosity. . . . I never knew an enemy to puns who was not an ill-natured man. Your fair critic in the coach reminds me of a Scotchman who assured me he did not see much in Shakspeare. I replied, I dare say *not*. He felt the equivoke, looked awkward and reddish, but soon returned to the attack by saying that he thought Burns was as good as Shakspeare. I said that I had no doubt he was—to a *Scotchman*. We exchanged no more words that day. Your account of the fierce faces in the Hangings, with the presumed interlocution of the Eagle and the Tiger, amused us greatly. You cannot be so very bad while you can pick mirth off from rotten walls. But let me hear you have escaped out of your oven. . . . Your business, I take it, is bathing, not baking.

Let me hear that you have clambered up to Lover's Seat: it is as fine in that neighbourhood as Juan Fernandez—as lonely, too, when the Fishing-boats are not out; I have sat for hours, staring upon a shipless sea. The salt sea is never so grand as when it is left to itself. One cockboat spoils it—a sea-mew or two improves it. And go to the little church which is a very Protestant Loretto, and seems dropt by some angel for the use of a hermit who was at once parishioner and a whole parish. It is not too big. Go in the night; bring it away in your portmanteau, and I will plant it in my garden. It must have been erected in the very infancy of British Christianity, for the two or three first converts; yet with it all the appertances of a church of the first magnitude—its pulpit, its pews, its baptismal font; a cathedral in a nut-shell. Seven people would crowd it like a Caledonian Chapel. The minister that divides the Word there must give lumping pennyworths. It is built to the text of "two or three assembled in my name." It reminds me of the grain of mustard seed. If the glebe-land is proportionate it may yield two potatoes. Tithes out of it could be no more split than a hair. Its First fruits must be its Last, for 'twould never produce a couple. It is truly the strait and narrow way, and few there be (of London visitants) that find it. The still small voice is surely to be found there, if anywhere. A sounding-board is merely there for ceremony. It is secure from earthquakes, not more from sanctity than size, for 'twould feel a mountain thrown upon it no more than a taper-worm would. *Go and see, but not without your spectacles.* By the way, there's a capital farm-house two-thirds of the way to the Lover's Seat, with incomparable plum cake, ginger-beer, etc. Mary bids me warn you not to read the *Anatomy of Melancholy* in your present *low way*. You'll fancy yourself a pipkin or a headless bear, as Burton speaks of. You'll be lost in a maze of remedies for a labyrinth of diseasements—a plethora of cures. Read Fletcher; above all the *Spanish Curate*, the *Thief, or Little Night Walker*, the *Wit Without Money*, and the *Lover's Pilgrimage*. Laugh and come home fat. Neither do we think Sir T. Browne quite the thing for you just at present. Fletcher is as light as soda-water. Browne and Burton are too strong potions for an Invalid. And don't thumb and dirt the books. Take care of the bindings. Lay a leaf of silver paper under 'em as you read them. And don't smoke tobacco over 'em—the leaves will fall in and burn or dirty their namesakes. If you find any dusty atoms of the Indian Weed crumbled up in the Beaumont and Fletcher, they are *mine*. But then, you know, so is the Folio also. A pipe and a comedy of Fletcher's the last thing of a night is the best recipe for light dreams, and to scatter away Nightmares. *Probatum est*. But do as you like about the former. Only, cut the Baker's. You will come home else all crust; Rankings must chip you before you can appear in his counting-house. And, my dear Peter Fin Junr., do contrive to see the sea at least once before you return. You'll be asked about it in the Old Jewry. It will appear singular not to have seen it. And rub up your Muse— the family Muse—and send us a rhyme or so. Don't waste your wit upon that damned Dry Salter. I never knew but one Dry Salter who could relish those mellow effusions, and he broke. You knew Tommy Hill, the wittiest of Dry Salters. Dry Salters! what a word for this thirsty weather! I must drink after it. Here's to thee, my dear Dibdin, and to our having you again snug and well at Colebrooke. But our nearest hopes are to hear again from you shortly. An epistle only a quarter as agreeable as your last would be a treat.

Yours most truly,   C. LAMB.

Timothy B. Dibdin, Esq.,
     No. 9, Blucher Row,
          Priory, Hastings.

To LOUISA HOLCROFT.

LETTER CCCXVII.]   *Enfield, June* 17, 1826.

Dear Louisa—I think I know the House you have in view. It is a Capital old Manor House lately in possession of Lord Cadogan. But whether it be that or another, we shall have in the meantime a small room and bed to let, pretty cheap, only Two Smiles a week, and find your own washing. If you are not already on the road, set out from the Bell, Holborn, at ½ past 4, and ask to be set down at Mr. Lamb's on the Chase. Mary joins in the hope of seeing you very speedily, and in love to you all.

Yours truly,   C. LAMB.

Mary has left off writing letters, I do all.

To J. B. DIBDIN.

LETTER CCCXVIII.]   *July* 14, 1826.

BECAUSE you boast poetic grandsire,
And rhyming kin, both uncle *and* sire,
Dost think that none but *their* descendings
Can tickle folks with double endings?
I had a Dad that would for half a bet

Have put down thine thro' half the alphabet.
Thou who would be Dan Prior the Second,
For Dan Posterior must be reckoned.
In faith, dear Tim, your rhymes are slovenly,
As a man may say, dough-baked and ovenly;
Tedious and long as two Long Acres,
And smell most vilely of the Baker's.
(I have been cursing every limb o' thee,
Because I could not hitch in *Timothy*.
Jack, Will, Tom, Dick's a serious evil,
But Tim, plain Tim's the very Devil.)
Thou most incorrigible scribbler,
Right Watering Place and Cockney Dribbler,
What *child*, that barely understands *A
B C*, would ever dream that stanza
Would tinkle into rhyme with "Plan, Sir"?
Go, go—you are not worth an answer.
I had a sire, that at plain Crambo
Had hit you o'er the head a damn'd blow.
How now? may I die game, and you die brass,
But I had stol'n a quip from Hudibras!
'Twas thinking on that fine old suttler,
That was in faith a second Butler;
Had as queer rhymes as he, and subtler.
He would have put you to 't this weather
For rattling syllables together.
Rhymed you to death, like "rats in Ireland,"
Except that he was born in High'r Land.
His chimes, not cramped like thine, and rung ill,
Had made Job split his sides on dunghill.
There was no limit to his merryings
At christ'nings, weddings, nay at buryings.
No undertaker would live near him,
Those grave practitioners did fear him;
Mutes, at his merry mops, turned "vocal,"
And fellows, hired for silence, "spoke all."
No *body* could be laid in cavity
Long as he lived, with proper gravity.
His mirth-fraught eye had but to glitter,
And every mourner round must titter.
The Parson, prating of Mount Hermon,
Stood still to laugh in midst of sermon.
The final sexton (smile he *must* for him)
Could hardly get to "dust to dust" for him.
He lost three pall-bearers their livelihood,
Only with simpering at his lively mood:

Provided that they fresh and neat came,
All jests were fish that to his net came.
He'd banter Apostolic castings
As you jeer fishermen at Hastings.
When the fly bit, *like me,* he leapt o'er all,
And stood not much on what was Scriptural.
P.S. I had forgot, at Small Bohemia *
(Enquire the way of your maid, Euphemia)
Are sojourning, of all good fellows
The prince and princess, the *Novellos.*
Pray seek 'em out, and give my love to 'em;
You'll find you'll soon be hand and glove to 'em.

C. L.

* In prose, Little Bohemia, about a mile from Hastings in the Hollington Road, when you can get as far. This letter will introduce you, if 'tis agreeable. Take a donkey—'tis Novello the Composer and his wife, our very good friends. Dear Dib, I find relief in a word or two of prose. In truth my rhymes come slow. You have "routh of 'em." It gives us pleasure to find you keep your good spirits. Your letter did us good. Pray Heaven you are got out at last. Write quickly.

For Tim Dibdin,
  At No. 4 Meadow Cottages,
    Hastings.

To WILLIAM HONE.

LETTER CCCXIX.]   [*Enfield, July* 25, 1826.]

Dear H.—The Quotidian came in as pleasantly as it was looked for at breakfast time yesterday. You have repaid my poor stanzas with interest. This last interlineation is one of those instances of affectation rightly applied. Read the sentence without it, how bald it is! Your idea of "worsted in the dog-days" was capital.

We are here so comfortable that I am confident we shall stay one month, from this date, most probably longer; so if you please, you can cut your out-of-town room for that time. I have sent up my petit farce altered; and Harley is at the theatre now. It cannot come out for some weeks. When it does, we think not of leaving her, but to borrow a bed of you for the night.

I write principally to say that the 4th of August is coming,—Dogget's Coat and Badge Day on the water. You will find a good deal about him in *Cibber's Apology,* octavo, facing the window; and something haply in a thin blackish quarto among the plays, facing the fireside.

You have done with mad dogs; else there is a print of Rowlandson's, or somebody's, of people in pursuit of one in a village, which might have come in: also Goldsmith's verses.

Mary's kind remembrance.   C. LAMB.

Mr. Hone,
    Colebrook Cottage,
        Islington.

To J. B. DIBDIN.

LETTER CCCXX.]   *Saturday, September* 9, 1826.

An answer is requested.

Dear D.—I have observed that a Letter is never more acceptable than when received upon a rainy day, especially a rainy Sunday; which moves me to send you somewhat, however short. This will find you sitting after Breakfast, which you will have prolonged as far as you can with consistency to the poor handmaid that has the reversion of the Tea Leaves; making two nibbles of your last morsel of *stale* roll (you cannot have hot new ones on the Sabbath), and reluctantly coming to an end, because when that is done, what can you do till dinner? You cannot go to the Beach, for the rain is drowning the sea, turning rank Thetis fresh, taking the brine out of Neptune's pickles, while mermaids sit upon rocks with umbrellas, their ivory combs sheathed for spoiling in the wet of waters foreign to them. You cannot go to the Library, for it's shut. You are not religious enough to go to Church. O it is worth while to cultivate piety to the gods, to have something to fill the heart up on a wet Sunday. You cannot cast accounts, for your Ledger is being eaten up with moths in the Ancient Jewry. You cannot play at Draughts, for there is none to play with you, and besides there is not a draught-board in the house. You cannot go to market, for it closed last light. You cannot look into the shops, their backs are shut upon you. You cannot while away an hour with a friend, for you have no friend round that Wrekin. You cannot divert yourself with a stray acquaintance, for you have picked none up. You cannot bear the chiming of Bells, for they invite you to a banquet where you are no visitant. You cannot cheer yourself with the prospect of tomorrow's letter, for none come on Mondays. You cannot count those endless vials on the mantelpiece with any hope of making a variation in their numbers. You have counted your spiders: your Bastile is exhausted. You sit and deliberately curse your hard exile from all familiar sights and sounds. Old Ranking poking in his head unexpectedly would just now be as good to you as Grimaldi. Anything to deliver you from this intolerable weight of ennui. You are too ill to shake it off: not ill enough to submit to it, and to lie down as a Lamb under it. The Tyranny of sickness is nothing to the cruelty of Convalescence: 'tis to have Thirty Tyrants for one. That pattering rain drops on your brain. You'll be worse after dinner, for you must dine at one to-day that Betty may go to afternoon service. She insists upon having her chopped hay. And then when she goes out, who *was* something to you, something to speak to—what an interminable afternoon you'll have to go thro'. You can't break yourself from your locality: you cannot say, "to-morrow morning I set off for Banstead," for you are booked for Wednesday. Foreseeing this, I thought a *cheerful letter* would come in opportunely. If any of the little topics for mirth I have thought upon should serve you in this utter extinguishment of sunshine, to make you a little merry, I shall have had my ends. I love to make things comfortable. . . . That which is scratched out was the most material thing I had to say, but on maturer thoughts I defer it.

P.S.—We are just sitting down to dinner with a pleasant party—Coleridge, Reynolds the dramatist, and Sam Bloxam: to-morrow (that is, *to-day*), Liston and Wyat of the Wells, dine with us. May this find you as jolly and freakish as we mean to be.　　　　　　　　　C. LAMB.

Addressed—
　　T. Dibdin, Esq.,
　　　　4 Meadow Cottages,
　　　　　　Hastings.

To BERNARD BARTON.

LETTER CCCXXI.]　　　　　　　　　　*September* 26, 1826.

Dear B. B.—I don't know why I have delayed so long writing. 'Twas a fault. The under-current of excuse to my mind was that I had heard of the vessel in which Mitford's jars were to come; that it had been obliged to put into Batavia to refit (which accounts for its delay), but was daily expected. Days are past, and it comes not, and the mermaids may be drinking their tea out of his china for aught I know; but let's hope not. In the meantime I have paid £28, etc., for the freight and prime cost, which I a little expected he would have settled in London. But do not mention it. I was enabled to do it by a receipt of £30 from Colburn, with whom, however, I have done. I should else have run short; for I only just make ends meet. We will wait the arrival of the trinkets, and to ascertain their full expense, and then bring in the bill. Don't mention it, for I daresay 'twas mere thoughtlessness. I am sorry you and yours have any plagues about dross matters. I have been sadly puzzled at the defalcation of more than one-third of my income, out of which when entire I saved nothing. But cropping off wine, old books, etc. etc., in short, all that can be called pocket-money, I hope to be able to go on at the cottage. Remember, I beg of you not to say anything to Mitford, for if he be honest it will vex him: if not, which I as little expect as that you should be, I have a hank still upon the jars.

Colburn had something of mine in last month, which he has had in hand these seven months, and had lost, or couldn't find room for: I was used to different treatment in the *London,* and have forsworn periodicals. I am going thro' a course of reading at the Museum: the Garrick plays, out of part of which I formed my specimens. I have two thousand to go thro'; and in a few weeks have despatched the tythe of 'em. It is a sort of office to me; hours, ten to four, the same. It does me good. Man must have regular occupation, that has been used to it.

So A. K. keeps a school; she teaches nothing wrong, I'll answer for't. I have a Dutch print of a schoolmistress; little old-fashioned Fleming-lings, with only one face among them. She a princess of a schoolmistress, wielding a rod for form more than use; the scene, an old monastic chapel, with a Madonna over her head, looking just as serious, as thoughtful, as pure, as gentle as herself. 'Tis a type of thy friend.

Will you pardon my neglect? Mind, again I say, don't show this to M.; let me wait a little longer to know the event of his luxuries. I am sure he is a good fellow, tho' I made a serious Yorkshire lad stare when I said he was a clergyman. He is a pleasant layman spoiled. Heaven send him his jars uncrack'd, and me my——

Yours, with kindest wishes to your daughter and friend, in which Mary joins,

C. L.

LETTER CCCXXII.] [End of 1826.]

Dear B. B. (the *Busy Bee,* as Hood after Dr. Watts apostrophises thee, and well dost thou deserve it for thy labours in the Muses' gardens, wandering over parterres of Think-on-mes and Forget-me-nots, to a total impossibility of forgetting thee), thy letter was acceptable, thy scruples may be dismissed, thou art *rectus in curiâ,* not a word more to be said, *verbum sapienti,* and so forth, the matter is decided with a white stone, classically, mark me, and the apparitions vanish'd which haunted me, only the cramp, Caliban's distemper, clawing me in the calvish part of my nature, makes me ever and anon roar bullishly, squeak cowardishly, and limp cripple-ishly. Do I write quakerly and simply, 'tis my most Master Mathews's like intention to do it. See Ben Jonson.—I think you told me your acquaintance with the Drama was confin'd to Shakspeare and Miss Baillie: some read only Milton and Croly. The gap is as from an ananas to a turnip. I have fighting in my head the plots, characters, situations, and sentiments of 400 old plays (bran new to me) which I have been digesting at the Museum, and my appetite sharpens to twice as many more, which I mean to course over this Winter. I can scarce avoid dialogue fashion in this letter. I soliloquise my meditations, and habitually speak dramatic blank verse without meaning it. Do you see Mitford? He will tell you something of my labours. Tell him I am sorry to have missed seeing him, to have talked over those old Treasures. I am still more sorry for his missing Pots. But I shall be sure of the earliest intelligence of the Lost Tribes. His Sacred Specimens are a thankful addition to my shelves. Marry, I could wish he had been more careful of corrigenda. I have discover'd certain which have slipt his errata. I put 'em in the next page, as perhaps thou canst transmit them to him; for what purpose but to grieve him (which yet I should be sorry to do), but then it shows my learning, and the excuse is complimentary, as it implies their correction in a future edition. His own things in the book are magnificent, and as an old Christ's Hospitaller I was particularly refresh'd with his eulogy on our Edward. Many of the choice excerpta were new to me. Old Christmas is a-coming, to the confusion of Puritans, Muggletonians, Anabaptists, Quakers, and that unwassailing crew. He cometh not with his wonted gait; he is shrunk nine inches in his girth, but is yet a lusty fellow. Hood's book is mighty clever, and went off 600 copies the first day. Sion's Songs do not disperse so quickly. The next leaf is for Rev. J. M. In this adieu, thine briefly, in a tall friendship,

C. LAMB.

To MR. H. C. ROBINSON.

LETTER CCCXXIII.]

Colebrooke Row, Islington,
Saturday, January 20, 1827.

Dear Robinson—I called upon you this morning, and found that you were gone to visit a dying friend. I had been upon a like errand. Poor Norris has been lying dying for now almost a week, such is the penalty we pay for having enjoyed a strong constitution. Whether he knew me or not, I know not; or whether he saw me through his poor glazed eyes; but the group I saw about him I shall not forget. Upon the bed, or about it, were assembled his wife and two daughters, and poor deaf Richard, his son, looking doubly stupefied. There they were, and seemed to have been sitting all the week. I could only reach out a hand to Mrs. Norris. Speaking was impossible in that mute chamber. By this time I hope it is all over with him. In him I have a loss the world cannot make up. He was my friend and my father's friend all the life I can remember. I seem to have made foolish friendships ever since. Those are friendships which outlive a second generation. Old as I am waxing, in his eyes I was still the child he first knew me. To the last he called me Charley. I have none to call me Charley now. He was the last link that bound me to the Temple. You are but of yesterday. In him seem to have died the old plainness of manners and singleness of heart. Letters he knew nothing of, nor did his reading extend beyond the pages of the *Gentleman's Magazine.* Yet there was a pride of literature about him from being amongst books (he was librarian), and from some scraps of doubtful Latin which he had picked up in his office of entering students, that gave him very diverting airs of pedantry. Can I forget the erudite look with which, when he had been in vain trying to make out a black-letter text of Chaucer in the Temple Library, he laid it down and told me that—"in those old books, Charley, there is sometimes a deal of very indifferent spelling;" and seemed to console himself in the reflection! His jokes, for he had his jokes, are now ended; but they were old trusty perennials, staples that pleased after *decies repetita,* and were always as good as new. One song he had, which was reserved for the night of Christmas Day, which we always spent in the Temple. It was an old thing, and spoke of the flat bottoms of our foes, and the possibility of their coming over in darkness, and alluded to threats of an invasion many years blown over; and when he came to the part—

> "We'll still make 'em run, and we'll still make 'em sweat,
> In spite of the Devil and *Brussels Gazette,*"

his eyes would sparkle as with the freshness of an impending event. And what is the *Brussels Gazette* now? I cry while I enumerate these trifles. "How shall we tell them in a stranger's ear?" His poor good girls will now have to receive their afflicted mother in an unsuccessful hovel in an obscure village in Herts, where they have been long struggling to make a school without effect; and poor deaf Richard, and the more helpless for being so, is thrown on the wide world.

My first motive in writing, and indeed in calling on you, was to ask if you were enough acquainted with any of the Benchers to lay a plain statement before them of the circumstances of the family. I almost fear not, for you are of another hall. But if you can oblige me and my poor friend, who is now insensible to any favours, pray exert yourself. You cannot say too much good of poor Norris and his poor wife.

Yours ever,   CHARLES LAMB.

To THOMAS ALLSOP.

LETTER CCCXXIV.]   *January* 25, 1827.

My dear Allsop—I cannot forbear thanking you for your kind interference with Taylor, whom I do not expect to see in haste at Islington.

It is hardly weather to ask a dog up here, but I need hardly say how happy we shall be to see you. I cannot be out of evenings till John Frost be routed. We came home from Newman St. the other night late, and I was crampt all night.

Love to Mrs. Allsop.

Yours truly,   C. L.

To WILLIAM HONE.

LETTER CCCXXV.]   *January* 27, 1827.

Dear Sir—It is not unknown to you, that about sixteen years since I published "Specimens of English Dramatic Poets who lived about the time of Shakspeare." For the scarcer plays, I had recourse to the collection bequeathed to the British Museum by Mr. Garrick. But my time was but short; and my subsequent leisure has discovered in it a treasure rich and exhaustless beyond what I then imagined. In it is to be found almost every production, in the shape of a play, that has appeared in print since the time of the old mysteries and moralities to the days of Crown and D'Urfey. Imagine the luxury to one like me,—who, above every other form of poetry, have ever preferred the dramatic,—of sitting in the princely apartments, for such they are, of poor, condemned Montagu House,—which, I predict, will not soon be followed by a handsomer, —and culling at will the flowers of some thousand dramas! It is like having the range of a nobleman's library, with the librarian to your friend. Nothing can exceed the courteousness and attentions of the gentleman who has the chief direction of the reading-rooms here; and you have scarce to ask for a volume before it is laid before you. If the occasional extracts which I have been tempted to bring away may find an appropriate place in your "Table Book," some of them are weekly at your service. By those who remember the "Specimens," these must be considered as mere after-gleanings, supplementary to that work, only comprising a longer period. You must be content with sometimes a scene, sometimes a song, a speech, a passage, or a poetical image, as they happen to strike me. I read without order of time; I am a poor hand at dates; and, for any biography of the dramatists, I must refer to writers who are more skilful in such matters. My business is with their poetry only.

Your well-wisher,   C. LAMB.

LETTER CCCXXVI.]   [*February* 5, 1827.]

For God's sake be more sparing of your poetry: your this week's Number has an excess of it.

In haste,   C. L.

Mr. Hone,
  22, Belvidere Place,
    near Suffolk Street,
      Borough.

LETTER CCCXXVII.]   [*March* 20, 1827.]

Damnable *erratum* (can't you notice it?) in the last line but two of the last *Extract* in *No.* 9, *Garrick Plays*—

> "Blushing forth golden hair and glorious red:"

A sun-bright line spoiled by *Blush* for *Blushing*.

N.B.—The general Number was excellent. Also a few lines higher—

> "Restrained Liberty attain'd is sweet"

should have a full stop. 'Tis the end of the old man's speech. These little blemishes kill such delicate things: prose feeds on grosser punctualities.

You have now 3 Numbers in hand; one I sent you yesterday. Of course I send no more till Sunday week.

P.S.—Omitted above—"Dear Hone." C. L.

Mr. Hone,
    No. 22, Belvidere Place,
        Southwark.

To B. R. HAYDON.

LETTER CCCXXVIII.] *March* 1827.

Dear Raffaele Haydon—Did the maid tell you I came to see your picture, not on Sunday but the day before? I think the face and bearing of the Bucephalus tamer very noble, his flesh too effeminate or painty. The skin of the female's back kneeling is much more carnous. I had small time to pick out praise or blame, for two lord-like Bucks came in, upon whose strictures my presence seemed to impose restraint; I plebeian'd off therefore.

I think I have hit on a subject for you, but can't swear it was never executed—I never heard of its being—"Chaucer beating a Franciscan Friar in Fleet Street." Think of the old dresses, houses, etc. "It seemeth that both these learned men (Gower and Chaucer) were of the Inner Temple; for not many years since Master Buckley did see a record in the same house where Geoffry Chaucer was fined two shillings for beating a Franciscan Friar in Fleet Street."

Yours in haste (salt fish waiting), C. LAMB.

To VINCENT NOVELLO.

LETTER CCCXXIX.] *April* 1827.

Dear Sir—I conjure you, in the name of all the Sylvan Deities, and of the Muses, whom you honour, and they reciprocally love and honour you, rescue this old and passionate *Ditty*—the very flower of an old, forgotten *Pastoral,* which had it been in all parts equal, the *Faithful Shepherdess* of Fletcher had been but a second name in this sort of Writing—rescue it from the profane hands of every Common Composer; and in one of your tranquillest moods, when you have most leisure from those sad thoughts which sometimes unworthily beset you—yet a mood in itself not unallied to the better sort of melancholy—laying by, for once, the lofty Organ, with which you shake the Temples, attune, as to the Pipe of Paris himself, to some milder and love-according instrument, this pretty Courtship between Paris and his (then-not-as-yet-forsaken) Œnone. Oblige me, and all more knowing Judges of Music and of Poesy, by the adaptation of fit musical numbers, which it only wants, to be the rarest Love Dialogue in our Language.

Your Implorer C. L.

To WILLIAM HONE.

LETTER CCCXXX.]   [*May* 1827.]

Sir—A correspondent in your last number rather hastily asserts that there is no other authority than Davenport's Tragedy for the poisoning of Matilda by King John. It oddly enough happens, that in the same number appears an extract from a play of Heywood's, of an older date, in two parts, in which play the fact of such poisoning, as well as her identity with Maid Marian, are equally established. Michael Drayton, also, hath a legend confirmatory (so far as poetical authority can go) of the violent manner of her death. But neither he nor Davenport confounds her with Robin's mistress. Besides the named authorities, old Fuller, I think, somewhere relates, as matter of chronicle-history, that old Fitzwater (he is called Fitzwater both in Heywood and in Davenport), being banished after his daughter's murder,—some years subsequently, King John, at a tournament in France, being delighted with the valiant bearing of a combatant in the lists, and enquiring his name, was told it was his old servant, the banished Fitzwater, who desired nothing more heartily than to be reconciled to his liege; and an affecting reconciliation followed. In the common collection, called "Robin Hood's Garland" (I have not seen Ritson's), no mention is made, if I remember, of the nobility of Marian. Is she not the daughter of old Squire Gamwell, of Gamwell Hall? Sorry that I cannot gratify the curiosity of your "disembodied spirit" (who, as such is, methinks, sufficiently "veiled" from our notice) with more authentic testimonies, I rest,

Your humble Abstractor,   C. L.

To BERNARD BARTON.

LETTER CCCXXXI.]   *Enfield, and for some weeks to come,*
June 11, 1827.

Dear B. B.—One word more of the picture verses, and that for good and all; pray with a neat pen alter one line

"His learning seems to lay small stress on"

to

"His learning lays no mighty stress on"

to avoid the unseemly recurrence (ungrammatical also) of "seems" in the next line, besides the nonsense of "but" there, as it now stands. And I request you, as a personal favour to me, to erase the last line of all, which I should never have written from myself. The fact is, it was a silly joke of Hood's, who gave me the frame (you judged rightly it was not its own) with the remark that you would like it because it was b—d b—d; and I lugged it in: but I shall be quite hurt if it stands, because tho' you and yours have too good sense to object to it, I would not have a sentence of mine seen that to any foolish ear might seem unrespectful to thee. Let it end at "appalling": the joke is coarse and useless, and hurts the tone of the rest. Take your best "ivory-handled" and scrape it forth.

Your specimen of what you might have written is hardly fair. Had it been a present to me, I should have taken a more sentimental tone: but of a trifle from me it was my cue to speak in an underish tone of commendation. Prudent *givers* (what word for such a nothing) disparage their gifts; 'tis an art we have. So you see you wouldn't have been so wrong taking a higher tone. But enough of nothing. By the by, I suspected M. of being the disparager of the frame: hence a *certain line.*

For the frame, 'tis as the room is where it hangs. It hung up fronting my old cobwebby folios and battered furniture (the fruit piece has resumed its place), and was much better than a spick and span one. But if your room be very neat and your *other pictures* bright with gilt, it should be so too. I can't judge, not having seen, but my dingy study it suited.

Martin's "Belshazzar" (the picture) I have seen. Its architectural effect is stupendous; but the human figures, the squalling contorted little antics that are playing at being frightened, like children at a sham ghost, who half know it to be a mask, are detestable. Then the *letters* are nothing more than a transparency lighted up, such as a Lord might order to be lit up on a sudden at a Christmas gambol, to scare the ladies. The *type* is as plain as Baskerville's: they should have been dim, full of mystery, letters to the mind rather than the eye.

Rembrandt has painted only Belshazzar and a courtier or two (taking a part of the banquet for the whole), not fribbled out a mob of fine folks. Then everything is so distinct, to the very necklaces, and that foolish little prophet. What *one* point is there of interest? The ideal of such a subject is, that you the spectator should see nothing but what at the time you would have seen,—the *hand,* and the *King,*—not to be at leisure to make tailor-remarks on the dresses, or, Dr. Kitchener-like, to examine the good things at table.

Just such a confused piece is his "Joshua," frittered into a thousand fragments, little armies here, little armies there—you should see only the *Sun* and *Joshua.* If I remember, he has not left out that luminary entirely; but for Joshua, I was ten minutes a finding him out. Still he is showy in all that is not the human figure or the preternatural interest: but the first are below a drawing-school girl's attainment, and the last is a phantasmagoric trick,—"Now you shall see what you shall see, dare is Balshazar and dare is Daniel."

You have my thoughts of M., and so adieu! C. LAMB.

To WILLIAM HONE.

LETTER CCCXXXII.] [*June* 1827.]

Dear Sir—Somebody has fairly play'd a *hoax* on you (I suspect that pleasant rogue *Moxon*) in sending you the sonnet in my name inserted in your last number. True it is that I must own to the verses being mine, but not written on the occasion there pretended; for I have not yet had the pleasure of seeing the lady in the part of Emmeline; and I have understood that the force of her acting in it is rather in the expression of new-born sight, than of the previous want of it. The lines were really written upon her performance in the "Blind Boy," and appeared in the "Morning Chronicle" some years back. I suppose our facetious friend thought they would serve again, like an old coat new-turned.

Yours (and his, nevertheless),　　　　　　　　　　C. Lamb.

To Mr. PATMORE.

Letter CCCXXXIII.]　　　　　　　　　*Londres, Julie* 19, 1827.

Dear P.—I am so poorly. I have been to a funeral, where I made a pun, to the consternation of the rest of the mourners. And we had wine. I can't describe to you the howl which the widow set up at proper intervals. Dash could, for it was not unlike what he makes.

The letter I sent you was one directed to the care of E. W.——, India House, for Mrs. H[azlitt]. *Which* Mrs. H—— I don't yet know; but A—— has taken it to France on speculation. Really it is embarrassing. There is Mrs. present H., Mrs. late H., and Mrs. John H., and to which of the three Mrs. Wigginses it appertains, I know not. I wanted to open it, but 'tis transportation.

I am sorry you are plagued about your book. I would strongly recommend you to take for one story Massinger's "Old Law." It is exquisite. I can think of no other.

Dash is frightful this morning. He whines and stands up on his hind legs. He misses Becky, who is gone to town. I took him to Barnet the other day, and he couldn't eat his vittles after it. Pray God his intellectuals be not slipping.

Mary is gone out for some soles. I suppose 'tis no use to ask you to come and partake of 'em; else there is a steam vessel.

I am doing a tragi-comedy in two acts, and have got on tolerably; but it will be refused, or worse. I never had luck with anything my name was put to.

O, I am so poorly! I *waked* it at my cousin's the bookbinder, who is now with God; or, if he is not, 'tis no fault of mine.

We hope the Frank wines do not disagree with Mrs. P——. By the way, I like her.

Did you ever taste frogs? Get them if you can. They are like little Lilliput rabbits, only a thought nicer.

How sick I am!—not of the world, but of the widow's shrub. She's sworn under £6000, but I think she perjured herself. She howls in E *la,* and I comfort her in B flat. You understand music?

If you hav'n't got Massinger, you have nothing to do but go to the first Bibliothèque you can light upon at Boulogne, and ask for it (Gifford's edition); and if they hav'n't got it you can have "Athalie" par Monsieur Racine, and make the best of it. But that "Old Law" is delicious.

"No shrimps!" (that's in answer to Mary's question about how the soles are to be done).

I am uncertain where this wandering letter may reach you. What you mean by Poste Restante, God knows. Do you mean I must pay the postage? So I do, to Dover.

We had a merry passage with the widow at the Commons. She was howling—part howling and part giving directions to the proctor—when crash! down went my sister through a crazy chair, and made the clerks grin, and I grinned, and the widow tittered, and then I knew that she was not inconsolable. Mary was more frightened than hurt.

She'd make a good match for anybody (by she, I mean the widow).

> "If he bring but a *relict* away,
> He is happy, nor heard to complain."
> SHENSTONE.

Procter has got a wen growing out at the nape of his neck, which his wife wants him to have cut off; but I think it is rather an agreeable excrescence: like his poetry, redundant. Hone has hanged himself for debt. Godwin was taken up for picking pockets. Moxon has fallen in love with Emma, our nut-brown maid. Becky takes to bad courses. Her father was blown up in a steam machine. The coroner found it "insanity." I should not like him to sit on my letter.

Do you observe my direction. Is it Gallic—classical? Do try and get some frogs. You must ask for "grenouilles" (green eels). They don't understand "frogs," though 'tis a common phrase with us.

If you go through Bulloign (Boulogne), inquire if old Godfrey is living, and how he got home from the crusades. He must be a very old man.

If there is anything new in politics or literature in France, keep it till I see you again, for I'm in no hurry. Chatty Briant is well I hope.

I think I have no more news; only give both our loves (all three, says Dash), to Mrs. P——, and bid her get quite well, as I am at present, bating qualms, and the grief incident to losing a valuable relation.

                                                        C. L.

To MRS. SHELLEY.

LETTER CCCXXXIV.]   *Enfield, July* 26, 1827.

Dear Mrs. Shelley—At the risk of throwing away some fine thoughts, I must write to say how pleased we were with your very kind remembering of us (who have unkindly run away from all our friends) before you go. Perhaps you are gone, and then my tropes are wasted. If any piece of better fortune has lighted upon you than you expected, but less than we wish you, we are rejoiced. We are here trying to like solitude, but have scarce enough to justify the experiment. We get some, however. The six days are our Sabbath; the seventh—why, Cockneys will come for a little fresh air, and so—

But by *your month,* or October at furthest, we hope to see Islington; I, like a giant refreshed with the leaving off of wine; and Mary, pining for Mr. Moxon's books and Mr. Moxon's society. Then we shall meet.

I am busy with a farce in two acts; the incidents tragi-comic. I can do the dialogue *commey for:* but the damned plot—I believe I must omit it altogether. The scenes come after one another like geese, not marshalling like cranes or a Hyde Park review. The story is as simple as G[eorge] D[yer], and the language plain as his spouse. The characters are three women to one man; which is one more than laid hold on him in the "Evangely." I think that prophecy squinted towards my drama.

I want some Howard Paine to sketch a skeleton of artfully succeeding scenes through a whole play, as the courses are arranged in a cookery book: I to find wit, passion, sentiment, character, and the like trifles: to lay in the dead colours,—I'd Titianesque 'em up: to mark the channel in a cheek (smooth or furrowed, yours or mine), and where tears should course I'd draw the waters down: to say where a joke should come in or a pun be left out: to bring my *personæ* on and off like a Beau Nash; and I'd Frankenstein them there: to bring three together on the stage at once; they are so shy with me, that I can get no more than two; and there they stand till it is the time, without being the season, to withdraw them.

I am teaching Emma Latin to qualify her for a superior governess-ship; which we see no prospect of her getting. 'Tis like feeding a child with chopped hay from a spoon. Sisyphus his labours were as nothing to it.

Actives and passives jostle in her nonsense, till a deponent enters, like Chaos, more to embroil the fray. Her prepositions are suppositions; her conjunctions copulative have no connection in them; her concords disagree; her interjections are purely English "Ah!" and "Oh!" with a yawn and a gape in the same tongue; and she herself is a lazy, blockheadly supine. As I say to her, ass *in præsenti* rarely makes a wise man *in futuro.*

But I daresay it was so with you when you began Latin, and a good while after.

Good-by! Mary's love.

Yours truly,   C. LAMB.

To SIR JOHN STODDART.

LETTER CCCXXXV.]   [*August* 9, 1827.]

Dear Knight—Old Acquaintance—'Tis with a violence to the *pure imagination* (*vide* the "Excursion" *passim*) that I can bring myself to believe I am writing to Dr. Stoddart once again, at Malta. But the deductions of severe reason warrant the proceeding. I write from Enfield, where we are seriously weighing the advantages of dulness over the over-excitement of too much company, but have not yet come to a conclusion. What is the news? for we see no paper here; perhaps you can send us an old one from Malta. Only, I heard a butcher in the market-place whisper something about a change of ministry. I don't know who's in or out, or care, only as it might affect *you*. For domestic doings, I have only to tell, with extreme regret, that poor Elisa Fenwick (that was)—Mrs. Rutherford—is dead; and that we have received a most heart-broken letter from her mother—left with four grandchildren, orphans of a living scoundrel lurking about the pothouses of Little Russell Street, London: they and she—God help 'em!—at New York. I have just received Godwin's third volume of the *Republic,* which only reaches to the commencement of the Protectorate. I think he means to spin it out to his life's thread. Have you seen Fearn's *Anti-Tooke?* I am no judge of such things—you are; but I think it very clever indeed. If I knew your bookseller, I'd order it for you at a venture: 'tis two octavos, Longman and Co. Or do you read now? Tell it not in the Admiralty Court, but my head aches *hesterno vino.* I can scarce pump up words, much less ideas, congruous to be sent so far. But your son must have this by to-night's post. . . . Manning is gone to Rome, Naples, etc., probably to touch at Sicily, Malta, Guernsey, etc.; but I don't know the map. Hazlitt is resident at Paris, whence he pours his lampoons in safety at his friends in England. He has his boy with him. I am teaching Emma Latin. By the time you can answer this, she will be qualified to instruct young ladies: she is a capital English reader: and S. T. C. acknowledges that a part of a passage in Milton she read better than he, and part he read best, her part being the shorter. But, seriously, if Lady St——— (oblivious pen, that was about to write *Mrs.!*) could hear of such a young person wanted (she smatters of French, some Italian, music of course), we'd send our loves by her. My congratulations and assurances of old esteem.   C. L.

To BERNARD BARTON.

LETTER CCCXXXVI.]   *August* 10, 1827.

Dear B. B.—I have not been able to answer you, for we have had and are having (I just snatch a moment) our poor quiet retreat, to which we fled from society, full of company—some staying with us; and this moment, as I write, almost, a heavy importation of two old ladies has come in. Whither can I take wing from the oppression of human faces? Would I were in a wilderness of apes, tossing cocoa-nuts about, grinning and grinned at!

Mitford was hoaxing you, surely, about my engraving; 'tis a little sixpenny thing, too like by half, in which the draughtsman has done his best to avoid flattery. There have been two editions of it, which I think are all gone, as they have vanished from the window where they hung—a print-shop, corner of Great and Little Queen Streets, Lincoln's Inn Fields, where any London friend of yours may inquire for it; for I am (though you *won't understand it*) at Enfield Chase (Mrs. Leishman's). We have been here near three months, and shall stay two more, if people will let us alone; but they persecute us from village to village. So, don't direct to

Islington again, till further notice. I am trying my hand at a drama, in two acts, founded on Crabbe's "Confidant," *mutatis mutandis.* You like the Odyssey. Did you ever read my "Adventures of Ulysses," founded on Chapman's old translation of it? For children or men. Chapman is divine, and my abridgment has not quite emptied him of his divinity. When you come to town I'll show it to you. You have well described your old-fashioned grand paternal hall. Is it not odd that every one's earliest recollections are of some such place! I had my Blakesware (Blakesmoor in the *London*). Nothing fills a child's mind like a large old mansion; better if un—or partially—occupied; peopled with the spirits of deceased members of the county and Justices of the Quorum. Would I were buried in the peopled solitude of one, with my feelings at seven years old! Those marble busts of the Emperors, they seemed as if they were to stand for ever, as they had stood from the living days of Rome, in that old marble hall, and I to partake of their permanency. Eternity was, while I thought not of Time. But he thought of me, and they are toppled down, and corn covers the spot of the noble old dwelling and its princely gardens. I feel like a grasshopper that, chirping about the grounds, escaped his scythe only by my littleness. Even now he is whetting one of his smallest razors to clean wipe me out, perhaps. Well!

To WILLIAM HONE.

LETTER CCCXXXVII.]   [*August* 10, 1827.]

My dear Hone—We are both excessively grieved at dear Matilda's illness, whom we have ever regarded with the greatest respect. Pray God, your next news, which we shall expect most anxiously, shall give hopes of her recovery.

Mary keeps her health very well, and joins in kind remembrances and best wishes.

A few more Numbers (about 7) will empty my Extract Book; then we will consult about the "Specimens." By then, I hope you will be able to talk about business. How you continue your book at all, and so well, in trying circumstances, I know not. But don't let it stop. Would to God I could help you!—but we have the house full of company, which we came to avoid.

God bless you.   C. L.

Mr. Hone,
  22, Belvidere Place,
    Southwark.

To BERNARD BARTON.

LETTER CCCXXXVIII.]   *August* 28, 1827.

Dear B. B.—I am thankful to you for your ready compliance with my wishes. Emma is delighted with your verses, to which I have appended this notice, "The sixth line refers to the child of a dear friend of the author's, named Emma," without which it must be obscure, and have sent it with four album poems of my own (your daughter's with your heading, requesting it a place next mine), to a Mr. Fraser, who is to be editor of a more superb pocket-book than has yet appeared, by far! the property of some wealthy booksellers; but whom, or what its name, I forgot to ask. It is actually to have in it schoolboy exercises by his present Majesty and the late Duke of York. So Lucy will come to Court; how she will be stared at! Wordsworth is named as a contributor. Fraser, whom I have slightly seen, is editor of a forthcome or coming Review of foreign books, and is intimately connected with Lockhart, etc. So I take it that this is a concern of Murray's. Walter Scott also contributes mainly. I have stood off a long time from these annuals, which are ostentatious trumpery, but could not withstand the request of Jameson, a particular friend of mine and Coleridge.

I shall hate myself in frippery, strutting along, and vying finery with beaux and belles, with "future Lord Byrons and sweet L. E. L.'s." Your taste, I see, is less simple than mine, which the difference of our persuasions has doubtless effected. In fact, of late you have so Frenchified your style, larding it with *hors de combats,* and *au desopoirs,* that o' my conscience the Foxian blood is quite dried out of you, and the skipping Monsieur spirit has been infused. Doth Lucy go to balls? I must remodel my lines, which I wrote for her. I hope A. K. keeps to her primitives.

If you have anything you'd like to send further, I daresay an honourable place would be given to it; but I have not heard from Fraser since I sent mine, nor shall probably again, and therefore I do not solicit it as from him. Yesterday I sent off my tragi-comedy to Mr. Kemble. Wish it luck. I made it all ('tis blank verse, and I think of the true old dramatic cut) or most of it in the green lanes about Enfield, where I am, and mean to remain, in spite of your peremptory doubts on that head. Your refusal to lend your poetical sanction to my "Icon," and your reasons to Evans, are most sensible. Maybe I may hit on a line or two of my own jocular; maybe not. Do you never Londonise again? I should like to talk over old poetry with you of which I have much, and you, I think, little. Do your Drummonds allow no holidays? I would willingly come and work for you a three weeks or so, to let you loose. Would I could sell or give you some of my leisure! Positively, the best thing a man can have to do is nothing, and next to that perhaps—good works. I am but poorlyish, and feel myself writing a dull letter; poorlyish from company; not generally, for I never was better, nor took more walks, fourteen miles a day on an average, with a sporting dog, Dash. You would not know the plain poet, any more than he doth recognise James Nayler trick'd out *au deserpoy* (how do you spell it?) *En passant, J'aime entendre de mon bon homme sur surveillance de croix, ma pas l'homme figuratif.* Do you understand me?

C. LAMB.

To WILLIAM HONE.

LETTER CCCXXXIX.]   *Sunday, September 2* [1827].

Dear Hone—By the verses in yesterday's *Table Book*, sign'd *, I judge you are going on better; but *I want to be resolv'd*. Allsop promised to call on you, and let me know, but has not. Pray attend to this; and send me the number before the present (pages 225 to 256), which my newsman has neglect'd. Your book improves every week. I have written here a thing in 2 acts, and sent it to Cov^t Gard.

Yours,   C. LAMB.

To J. B. DIBDIN.

LETTER CCCXL.]   *September* 5, 1827.

Dear Dib.—Emma Isola, who is with us, has opened an *album:* bring some verses with you for it on Saturday evening. Any *fun* will do. I am teaching her Latin; you may make something of that. Don't be modest. For in it you *shall* appear, if I rummage out some of your old pleasant letters for rhymes. But an original is better.

Has your Pa * any scrap?   C. L.

We shall be *most* glad to see your sister or *sisters* with you. Can't you contrive it? Write in that case.

                    * The infantile word for father.

T. Dibdin, Esq.,
    Messrs. Railtons',
        Old Jewry, London.

LETTER CCCXLI.]   *September* 13, 1827.

Dear *John*—Your verses are very pleasant, and have been adopted into the splendid Emmatic constellation, where they are not of the least magnitude. She is delighted with their merit and readiness. They are just the thing. The 14th line is found. We advertised it. "Hell is cooling for want of company." We shall make it up, along with our kitchen fire to roast you into our new House where I hope you will find us in a few Sundays. We have actually taken it, and a compact thing it will be.

Kemble does not return till the month's end.

My heart sometimes is good, sometimes bad about it, as the day turns out wet or walky.

Emma has just died, choked with a Gerund-in-dum. On opening her, we found a Participle-in-rus in the pericardium. The King never dies, which may be the reason that it always *reigns* here.

We join in loves.   C. L. his orthograph.

What a pen!

Mr. John B. Dibdin,
        Messrs. Rankings,
            Old Jewry.

To THOMAS HOOD.

LETTER CCCXLII.]   *Tuesday [September* 18, 1827].

Dear Hood—If I have anything in my head, I will send it to Mr. Watts. Strictly speaking, he should have had my album-verses, but a very intimate friend importun'd me for the trifles, and I believe I forgot Mr. Watts, or lost sight at the time of his similar *souvenir*. Jamieson conveyed the farce from me to Mrs. C. Kemble; *he* will not be in town before the 27th. Give our kind loves to all at Highgate, and tell them that we have finally torn ourselves outright away from Colebrook, where I had *no* health, and are about to domicilate for good at Enfield, where I have experienced *good*.

> "Lord, what good hours do we keep!
> How quietly we sleep!"

See the rest in the *Complete Angler*.

We have got our books into our new house. I am a dray-horse, if I was not asham'd of the undigested, dirty lumber, as I toppled 'em out of the cart, and blest Becky that came with 'em for her having an unstuff'd brain with such rubbish. We shall get in by Michael's Mass. 'Twas with some pain we were evuls'd from Colebrook. You may find some of our flesh sticking to the door-posts. To change habitations is to die to them; and in my time I have died seven deaths. But I don't know whether every such change does not bring with it a rejuvenescence. 'Tis an enterprise; and shoves back the sense of death's approximating, which, tho' not terrible to me, is at all times particularly distasteful. My house-deaths have generally been periodical, recurring after seven years; but this last is premature by half that time. Cut off in the flower of Colebrook! The Middletonian stream, and all its echoes, mourn. Even minnows dwindle. *A parvis fiunt minimi!* I fear to invite Mrs. Hood to our new mansion, lest she envy it, and hate us. But when we are fairly in, I hope she will come and try it. I heard she and you were made uncomfortable by some unworthy-to-be-cared-for attacks, and have tried to set up a feeble counter-action thro' the *Table Book* of last Saturday. Has it not reach'd you, that you are silent about it? Our new domicile is no manor-house; but new, and externally not inviting, but furnish'd within with every convenience: capital new locks to every door, capital grates in every room; with nothing to pay for incoming; and the rent £10 less than the Islington one. It was built, a few years since, at £1100 expense, they tell me—and I perfectly believe it. And I get it for £35, exclusive of moderate taxes. We think ourselves most lucky.

It is not our intention to abandon Regent Street, and West-End perambulations (monastic and terrible thought!), but occasionally to breathe the fresher air of the metropolis. We shall put up a bedroom or two (all we want) for occasional ex-rustication, where we shall visit—not be visited. Plays, too, we'll see—perhaps our own; Urbani Sylvani and Sylvan

Urbanuses in turn; courtiers for a sport, then philosophers; old, homely tell-truths and learn-truths in the virtuous shades of Enfield, liars again and mocking gibers in the coffee-houses and resorts of London. What can a mortal desire more for his bi-parted nature?

O, the curds-and-cream you shall eat with us here!
O, the turtle-soup and lobster-salads we shall devour with you there!
O, the old books we shall peruse here!
O, the new nonsense we shall trifle over there!
O, Sir T. Browne, here!
O, Mr. Hood and Mr. Jerdan, there!
Thine,
      C. (URBANUS) L. (SYLVANUS)—(ELIA ambo)——

Inclos'd are verses which Emma sat down to write (her first) on the eve after your departure. Of course, they are only for Mrs. H.'s perusal. They will shew, at least, that one of our party is not willing to cut old friends. What to call 'em I don't know. Blank verse they are not, because of the rhymes; rhymes they are not, because of the blank verse; heroics they are not, because they are lyric; lyric they are not, because of the heroic measure. They must be call'd Emmaics.

The Hoods, 2, Robert Street,
    Adelphi, London.

To J. B. DIBDIN.

LETTER CCCXLIII.]   *September* 18, 1827.

My dear, and now more so, *John*—How that name smacks! What an honest, full, English, and yet withal holy and apostolic sound it bears, above the methodistical priggish Bishoppy name of Timothy, under which I had obscured your merits!

What I think of the paternal verses you shall read within, which I assure you is not pen praise but heart praise.

It is the gem of the Dibdin Muses. I have got all my books into my new house, and their readers in a fortnight will follow, to whose joint converse nobody shall be more welcome than you, and *any of yours*.

The house is perfection to our use and comfort. Milton is come. I wish Wordsworth were here to met him. The next importation is of pots and saucepans, window curtains, crockery, and such base ware.

The pleasure of moving, when Becky moves for you. O the moving Becky! I hope you will come and *warm* the house with the first.

From my temporary domicile, Enfield.

            Elia, that "is to go."

Mr. John Dibdin,
    Messrs. Rankings,
        Old Jewry.

To HENRY COLBURN.

Enfield Chase Side,
September 25, 1827.

Dear Sir—I beg leave in the warmest manner to recommend to your notice Mr. Moxon, the bearer of this, if by any chance yourself should want a steady hand in your business, or know of any Publisher that may want such a one. He is at present in the house of Messrs. Longman and Co., where he has been established for more than six years, and has the conduct of one of the four departments of the Country Line. A difference respecting salary, which he expected to be a little raised on his last promotion, makes him wish to try to better himself. I believe him to be a young man of the highest integrity and a thorough man of business, and should not have taken the liberty of recommending him, if I had not thought him capable of being highly useful.

I am, Sir, with great respect, your h'ble servant,   CHARLES LAMB.

To P. G. PATMORE.

Mrs. Leishman's, Chase, Enfield,
September 1827.

Dear P.—Excuse my anxiety, but how is Dash? I should have asked if Mrs. Patmore kept her rules, and was improving; but Dash came uppermost. The order of our thoughts should be the order of our writing. Goes he muzzled, or *aperto ore?* Are his intellects sound, or does he wander a little in *his* conversation? You cannot be too careful to watch the first symptoms of incoherence. The first illogical snarl he makes, to St. Luke's with him! All the dogs here are going mad, if you believe the overseers; but I protest they seem to me very rational and collected. But nothing is so deceitful as mad people, to those who are not used to them. Try him with hot water: if he won't lick it up it is a sign he does not like it. Does his tail wag horizontally, or perpendicularly? That has decided the fate of many dogs in Enfield. Is his general deportment cheerful? I mean when he is pleased—for otherwise there is no judging. You can't be too careful. Has he bit any of the children yet? If he has, have them shot, and keep *him* for curiosity, to see if it was the hydrophobia. They say all our army in India had it at one time; but that was in *Hyder*-Ally's time. Do you get paunch for him? Take care the sheep was sane. You might pull out his teeth (if he would let you), and then you need not mind if he were as mad as a Bedlamite. It would be rather fun to see his odd ways. It might amuse Mrs. P—— and the children. They'd have more sense than he. He'd be like a fool kept in a family, to keep the household in good humour with their own understanding. You might teach him the mad dance, set to the mad howl. *Madge Owlet* would be nothing to him. "My! how he capers!" [*In the margin is written, "One of the children speaks this."*] . . . What I scratch out is a German quotation, from Lessing, on the bite of rabid animals; but I remember you don't read German. But Mrs. P—— may, so I wish I had let it stand. The meaning in English is—"Avoid to approach an animal suspected of madness, as you would avoid fire or a precipice," which I think is a sensible observation. The Germans are certainly profounder than we. If the slightest suspicion arises in your breast that all is not right with him, muzzle him and lead him in a string (common pack-thread will do—he don't care for twist) to Mr. Hood's, his quondam master, and he'll take him in at any time. You may mention your suspicion, or not, as you like, or as you think it may wound or not Mr. H.'s feelings. Hood, I know, will wink at a few follies in Dash, in consideration of his former sense. Besides, Hood is deaf, and if you hinted anything, ten to one he would not hear you. Besides, you will have discharged your conscience, and laid the child at the right door, as they say.

We are dawdling our time away very idly and pleasantly at a Mrs. Leishman's, Chase, Enfield, where, if you come a-hunting, we can give you cold meat and a tankard. Her husband is a tailor; but that, you know, does not make her one. I knew a jailor (which rhymes), but his wife was a fine lady.

Let us hear from you respecting Mrs. P——'s regimen. I send my love in a —— to Dash.   C. LAMB.

[What follows was written on the *outside* of the letter:—]
Seriously, I wish you would call upon Hood when you are that way. He's a capital fellow. I've sent him two poems, one ordered by his wife, and written to order; and 'tis a week since, and I've not heard from him. I fear something is the matter.
Our kindest remembrance to Mrs. P.

To H. CRABB ROBINSON.

LETTER CCCXLVI.]   *Chase Side, October 1, 1827.*

Dear R.—I am settled for life I hope at Enfield. I have taken the prettiest, compactest house I ever saw, near to Antony Robinson's! but, alas! at the expense of poor Mary, who was taken ill of her old complaint the night before we got into it. So I must suspend the pleasure I expected in the surprise you would have had in coming down, and finding us householders. Farewell, till we can all meet comfortable. Pray apprise Martin Burney. Him I longed to have seen with you; but our house is too small to meet either of you without *her* knowledge.
God bless you.

To J. B. DIBDIN.

LETTER CCCXLVII.] *October 2, 1827.*

My dear Dibdin—It gives me great pain to have to say that I cannot have the pleasure of seeing you for some time. We are in our house, but Mary has been seized with one of her periodical disorders—a temporary derangement—which commonly lasts for two months. You shall have the first notice of her convalescence. Can you not send your manuscript by the coach? directed to Chase Side, next to Mr. Westwood's Insurance Office. I will take great care of it.

Yours most truly, C. LAMB.

To BARRON FIELD.

LETTER CCCXLVIII.] *October 4, 1827.*

I am not in humour to return a fit reply to your pleasant letter. We are fairly housed at Enfield, and an angel shall not persuade me to wicked London again. We have now six Sabbath-days in a week for—*none!* The change has worked on my sister's mind to make her ill; and I must wait a tedious time before we can hope to enjoy this place in unison. Enjoy it, when she recovers, I know we shall. I see no shadow, but in her illness, for repenting the step! For Mathews—I know my own utter unfitness for such a task. I am no hand at describing costumes, a great requisite in an account of mannered pictures. I have not the slightest acquaintance with pictorial language even. An imitator of me, or rather pretender to be *me,* in his "Rejected Articles," has made me minutely describe the dresses of the poissardes at Calais!—I could as soon resolve Euclid. I have no eye for forms and fashions. I substitute analysis, and get rid of the phenomenon by slurring in for it its impression. I am sure you must have observed this defect, or peculiarity, in my writings; else the delight would be incalculable in doing such a thing for Mathews—whom I greatly like —and Mrs. Mathews, whom I almost greatlier like. What a feast 'twould be to be sitting at the pictures painting 'em into words; but I could almost as soon make words into pictures. I speak this deliberately, and not out of modesty. I pretty well know what I can't do.

My sister's verses are homely, but just what they should be; I send them, not for the poetry, but the good sense and good will of them. I was beginning to transcribe; but Emma is sadly jealous of its getting into more hands, and I won't spoil it in her eyes by divulging it. Come to Enfield, and *read it.* As my poor cousin, the bookbinder, now with God, told me most sentimentally, that having purchased a picture of fish at a dead man's sale, his heart ached to see how the widow grieved to part with it, being her dear husband's favourite; and he almost apologised for his generosity by saying he could not help telling the widow she was "welcome to come and look at it"—*e.g.* at *his house*—"as often as she pleased." There was the germ of generosity in an uneducated mind. He had just *reading* enough from the backs of books for the "nec sinit esse feros"; had he read inside, the same impulse would have led him to give back the two-guinea thing—with a request to see it, now and then, at *her* house. We are parroted into delicacy.—Thus you have a tale for a Sonnet.

Adieu! with (imagine both) our loves.   C. L.

To H. DODWELL.

LETTER CCCXLIX.]   *October* 7, 1827.

Let us meet if possible when you hobble to *town*. *Enfield Chase,* nearly opposite to the 1st chapel; or better to define it, east side opposite a white House in which *a* Mrs. Vaughan (in ill health) still resides.

My dear Dodwell—Your little pig found his way to Enfield this morning without his feet, or rather his little feet came first, and as I guessed the rest of him soon followed. He is quite a beauty. It was a pity to kill him, or *rather*, as Rice would say, it would have been a pity not to kill him in his state of innocence. He might have lived to be corrupted by the ways of the world, and for all his delicate promise have turned out, like an old Tea Broker you and I remember, a lump of fat rusty Bacon. Bacon was a Beast, my friend at Calne, Marsh, used to say—or was it Bendry? A rasher of the latter still hangs up in Leadenhall. Your kind letter has left a relish upon my taste; it read warm and short as to-morrow's crackling.

I am not quite so comfortable *at home* yet as I should be else in the neatest compactest house I ever got—a perfect God-send; but for some weeks I must enjoy it alone. *She* always comes round again. It is a house of a few years' standing, built (for its size with every convenience) by an old humourist for himself, which he tired of as soon as he got warm in it. Grates, locks, a pump, convenience indescribable, and cheap as if it had been old and craved repairs. For me, who always take the first thing that offers, how lucky that the best should first offer itself! My books, my prints are up, and I seem (so like this room I write in is to a room there) to have come here transported in the night, like Gulliver in his flying house; and to add to the deception, the New River has come down from Islington with me. 'Twas what I wished—to move my *house,* and I have realised it. Only instead of company seven nights in the week, I see my friends on the First Day of it, and enjoy six real Sabbaths. The Museum is a loss, but I am not so far but I can visit it occasionally: and I have exhausted the Plays there.

"Indisputably I shall allow no sage and onion to be cramm'd into the throat of so tender a suckling.

"Bread and milk with some odoriferous mint, and the liveret minced.

"Come and tell me when he cries, that I may catch his little eyes.

"And do it nice and *crips*." (That's the Cook's word.) You'll excuse me, I have been only speaking to Becky about the dinner to-morrow. After it, a glass of seldom-drunk wine to my friend Dodwell, and, if he will give a stranger leave, to Mrs. Dodwell: then to the memory of the last, and of the last but one, learned Dodwell, of whom, but not whom, I have read so much. The next to the "Outward and Homeward bound ships"—and, if the bottle lasts, to the Chairman, Deputy-Chairman, the Court of Directors, the Secretary, the Treasurer, and Accomptant-General, of the East India Company, with a blunt bumper at parting to P——. All I can do, I cannot make P—— look like a G——n, yet he is portly, majestic, hath his nods, his condescensions, his variety of behaviour to suit your Director, your Upper Clerk, your Ryles, and your Winfields; he tempers mirth with gravity, gives no affront, and expects to receive none, is honourable, mannered, of good bearing, looks like a man who, accustomed to respect others, silently extorts respect from them, has it as a sort of *in course;* without claiming it, finds it. What do I miss in him, then, of the essentials of gentlemanhood? He is right sterling—but then, somehow, he always has that d——d large Goldsmith's Hall mark staring upon him. Possibly he is too fat for a gentleman—then I think of Charles Fox in the Dropsy: and the burly old Duke of Norfolk, a nobleman, every stun of him!

I am afraid now you and —— are gone, there's scarce an officer in the Civil Service quite comes up to my notion of a gentleman. D—— certainly does *not*, nor his friend B——.

C—— bobs. K—— *curtsies.* W—— bows like the son of a citizen; F—— like a village apothecary; C—— like the Squire's younger Brother; R—— like a crocodile on his hind legs; H—— never bows at all—at least to me. S—— spulters and stutters. W—— halters and smatters. R—— is a coal-heaver. Wolf wants my clothing. C—— simmers, but never boils over. D—— is a Butterfirkin, salt butter. C——, a pepper-box, cayenne. For A——, E——, and O——, I can answer that they have not the slightest pretensions to anything but rusticity. Marry, the remaining vowels had something of civility about them. Can you make top or tail of this nonsense, or tell where it begins? I will page it. How an error in the outset infects to the end of life, or of a sheet of paper! Cordially adieu.   C. LAMB.

H. Dodwell, Esq.
Maidenhead,
Berks.

To WILLIAM HONE.

LETTER CCCL.]   [*October* 1827.]

Dear Hone—I was most sensibly gratified by receiving the T. B. on Friday evening at Enfield!!
Thank you. In haste,   C. L.

Don't spare the Extracts. They'll eke out till Christmas.
How is your daughter?

Mr. Hone,
    22, Belvidere Place,
        Southwark.

To BERNARD BARTON.

Chase Side, Enfield,
LETTER CCCLI.]   *November* 1827.

My dear B. B.—You will understand my silence when I tell you that
my sister, on the very eve of entering into a new house we have taken at
Enfield, was surprised with an attack of one of her sad long illnesses,
which deprive me of her society, though not of her domestication, for
eight or nine weeks together. I see her, but it does her no good. But for
this, we have the snuggest, most comfortable house, with everything most
compact and desirable. Colebrook is a wilderness. The books, prints, etc.,
are come here, and the New River came down with us. The familiar
prints, the bust, the Milton, seem scarce to have changed their rooms.
One of her last observations was "How frightfully like this room is to our
room in Islington!"—our up-stairs room, she meant. How I hope you
will come some better day, and judge of it! We have tried quiet here for
four months, and I will answer for the comfort of it enduring.

On emptying my bookshelves I found an Ulysses, which I will send to
A. K. when I go to town, for her acceptance—unless the book be out of
print. One likes to have one copy of everything one does. I neglected to
keep one of "Poetry for Children," the joint production of Mary and me,
and it is not to be had for love or money. It had in the title-page "by
the Author of Mrs. Lester's School." Know you any one that has it, and
would exchange it?

Strolling to Waltham Cross the other day, I hit off these lines. It is
one of the crosses which Edward I. caused to be built for his wife at every
town where her corpse rested between Northamptonshire and London:—

> A stately cross each sad spot doth attest,
> Whereat the corpse of Eleanor did rest,
> From Harby fetch'd—her spouse so honour'd her—
> To sleep with royal dust at Westminster.
> And, if less pompous obsequies were thine,
> Duke Brunswick's daughter, princely Caroline,
> Grudge not, great ghost, nor count thy funeral losses:
> Thou in thy life-time had'st thy share of crosses.

My dear B.—My head aches with this little excursion. Pray accept
two sides for three for once, and believe me yours sadly,   C. L.

LETTER CCCLII.]   *December* 4, 1827.

My dear B. B.—I have scarce spirits to write, yet am harassed with not writing. Nine weeks are completed, and Mary does not get any better. It is perfectly exhausting. Enfield, and everything, is very gloomy. But for long experience I should fear her ever getting well. I feel most thankful for the spinsterly attentions of your sister. Thank the kind "knitter in the sun!" What nonsense seems verse, when one is seriously out of hope and spirits! I mean, that at this time I have some nonsense to write, under pain of incivility. Would to the fifth heaven no coxcombess had invented Albums!

I have not had a Bijoux, nor the slightest notice from Pickering about omitting four out of five of my things. The best thing is never to hear of such a thing as a bookseller again, or to think there are publishers. Second-hand stationers and old book-stalls for me. Authorship should be an idea of the past. Old kings, old bishops, are venerable; all present is hollow. I cannot make a letter. I have no straw, not a pennyworth of chaff, only this may stop your kind importunity to know about us. Here is a comfortable house, but no tenants. *One* does not make a household. Do not think I am quite in despair; but, in addition to hope protracted, I have a stupefying cold and obstructing headache, and the sun is dead.

I will not fail to apprise you of the revival of a beam. Meantime accept this, rather than think I have forgotten you all. Best remembrances.

Yours and theirs truly,   C. LAMB.

To LEIGH HUNT.

LETTER CCCLIII.]   [*December*] 1827.

Dear H.—I am here almost in the eleventh week of the longest illness my sister ever had, and no symptoms of amendment. Some had begun, but relapsed with a change of nurse. If she ever gets well, you will like my house, and I shall be happy to show you Enfield country.

As to my head, it is perfectly at your or any one's service; either Myers' or Hazlitt's,—which last (done fifteen or twenty years since) White, of the Accountant's Office, India House, has; he lives in Kentish Town—I forget where; but is to be found in Leadenhall daily. Take your choice. I should be proud to hang up as an alehouse-sign even; or, rather, I care not about my head or anything, but how we are to get well again, for I am tired out.

God bless you and yours from the worst calamity.

Yours truly,   C. L.

Kindest remembrances to Mrs. Hunt. H.'s is in a queer dress. M.'s would be preferable *ad populum*.

To THOMAS ALLSOP.

LETTER CCCLIV.] *December 20, 1827.*

My dear Allsop—I have writ to say to you that I hope to have a comfortable X-mas-day with Mary, and I cannot bring myself to go from home at present. Your kind offer, and the kind consent of the young Lady to come, we feel as we should do; pray accept all of you our kindest thanks: at present I think a Visitor (good and excellent as we remember her to be) might a little put us out of our way. Emma is with us, and our small house just holds us, without obliging Mary to sleep with Becky, etc.

We are going on extremely comfortable, and shall soon be in capacity of seeing our friends. Much weakness is left still. With thanks and old remembrances,

Yours,   C. L.

To BERNARD BARTON.

LETTER CCCLV.] *[December]* 1827.

My dear B.—We are all pretty well again and comfortable, and I take a first opportunity of sending the "Adventures of Ulysses," hoping that among us—Homer, Chapman, and Co.—we shall afford you some pleasure. I fear it is out of print; if not, A. K. will accept it, with wishes it were bigger; if another copy is not to be had, it reverts to me and my heirs *for ever*. With it I send a trumpery book; to which, without my knowledge, the editor of the Bijoux has contributed Lucy's verses; I am ashamed to ask her acceptance of the trash accompanying it. Adieu to Albums—for a great while—I said when I came here, and had not been fixed for two days; but my landlord's daughter (not at the Pothouse) requested me to write in her female friends' and in her own. If I go to —— thou art there also, O all pervading Album! All over the Leeward Islands, in Newfoundland, and the Back Settlements, I understand there is no other reading. They haunt me. I die of Albophobia!   C. L.

LETTER CCCLVI.] *[December]* 1827.

My dear B. B.—A gentleman I never saw before brought me your welcome present. Imagine a scraping, fiddling, fidgeting, petit-maître of a dancing school advancing into my plain parlour with a toupée and a sideling bow, and presenting the book as if he had been handing a glass of lemonade to a young miss: imagine this, and contrast it with the serious nature of the book presented! Then task your imagination, reversing this picture, to conceive of quite an opposite messenger, a lean, straitlocked, whey-faced Methodist, for such was he in reality who brought it, the Genius (it seems) of the Wesleyan Magazine. Certes, friend B., thy

Widow's Tale is too horrible, spite of the lenitives of Religion, to embody
in verse, I hold prose to be the appropriate expositor of such atrocities!
No offence, but it is a cordial that makes the heart sick. Still thy skill
in compounding it I do not deny. I turn to what gave me less mingled
pleasure. I find mark'd with pencil these pages in thy pretty book, and
fear I have been penurious:—

Page 52, 53—Capital.
„   59—6th stanza, exquisite simile.
„   61—11th stanza, equally good.
„   108—3rd stanza, I long to see Van Balen.
„   111—A downright good sonnet. *Dixi.*
„   153—Lines at the bottom.

So you see, I read, hear, and *mark,* if I don't learn. In short, this little
volume is no discredit to any of your former, and betrays none of the
senility you fear about. *Apropos* of Van Balen, an artist who painted me
lately had painted a blackamoor praying, and not filling his canvas,
stuffed in his little girl aside of Blackey, gaping at him unmeaningly;
and then didn't know what to call it. Now for a picture to be promoted
to the Exhibition (Suffolk Street) as *Historical,* a subject is requisite.
What does me? I but christened it the "Young Catechist" and furbish'd
it with dialogue following, which dubb'd it an Historical Painting. Nothing to a friend at need.

> "While this tawny Ethiop prayeth,
> Painter, who is she that stayeth
> By, with skin of whitest lustre;
> Sunny locks, a shining cluster;
> Saint-like seeming to direct him
> To the Power that must protect him?
> Is she of the heav'n born Three,
> Meek Hope, strong Faith, sweet Charity?
> Or some Cherub?
>   "They you mention
> Far transcend my weak invention.
> 'Tis a simple Christian child,
> Missionary young and mild,
> From her store of script'ral knowledge
> (Bible-taught without a college),
> Which by reading she could gather,
> Teaches him to say Our Father
> To the common Parent, who
> Colour not respects, nor hue.
> White and black in Him have part,
> Who looks not to the skin, but heart."

When I'd done it, the artist (who had clapt in Miss merely as a fill-
space) swore I exprest his full meaning, and the damosel bridled up into
a missionary's vanity. I like verses to explain pictures; seldom pictures
to illustrate poems. Your woodcut is a rueful lignum mortis. By the by,
is the widow likely to marry again?

I am giving the fruit of my old play reading at the Museum to Hone, who sets forth a portion weekly in the *Table Book*. Do you see it? How is Mitford?—I'll just hint that the pitcher, the chord, and the bowl are a little too often repeated (passim) in your book, and that in page 17, last line but 4, *him* is put for *he;* but the poor widow I take it had small leisure for grammatical niceties. Don't you see there's *he, myself,* and *him;* why not both *him?* likewise *imperviously* is cruelly spelt *imperiously.* These are trifles, and I honestly like your book, and you for giving it, though I really am ashamed of so many presents. I can think of no news; therefore I will end with mine and Mary's kindest remembrances to you and yours.   C. L.

CHAPTER VI.

1828–1834.

To THOMAS ALLSOP.

LETTER CCCLVII.]   *January 2, 1828.*

Dear Allsop—I have been very poorly and nervous lately, but am recovering sleep, etc. I do not write or make engagements for particular days: but I need not say how pleasant your dropping in any Sunday morning would be. Perhaps Jameson would accompany you. Pray beg him to keep an accurate record of the warning I sent him to old Pau., for I dread lest he should at the 12 months' end deny the warning. The house is his daughter's, but we took it through him, and have paid the rent to his receipts for his daughter's. Consult J. if he thinks the warning sufficient. I am very nervous, or have been, about the house; lost my sleep, and expected to be ill; but slumbered gloriously last night, golden slumbers. I shall not relapse; you fright me with your inserted slips in the most welcome Atlas. They begin to charge double for it, and call it two sheets. How can I confute them by opening it, when a note of yours might slip out, and we get in a hobble? When you write, write real letters. Mary's best love and mine to Mrs. A.

Yours ever,   C. LAMB.

To C. COWDEN CLARKE.

LETTER CCCLVIII.]   *Enfield, February 25 [1828].*

My dear Clarke—You have been accumulating on me such a heap of pleasant obligations, that I feel uneasy in writing as to a Benefactor. Your smaller contributions, the little weekly rills, are refreshments in the Desart; but your large books were feasts. I hope Mrs. Hazlitt, to whom I encharged it, has taken Hunt's *Lord B.* to the Novellos. His picture of Literary Lordship is as pleasant as a disagreeable subject can be made; his own poor man's Education at dear Christ's is as good and hearty as the subject. Hazlitt's speculative episodes are capital; I skip the Battles. But how did I deserve to have the book? The "Companion"

943

has too much of Madame Pasta. Theatricals have ceased to be popular attractions. His walk home after the play is as good as the best of the old "Indicators." The watchmen are emboxed in a niche of fame, save the skaiting one that must be still fugitive. I wish I could send a scrap for goodwill. But I have been most seriously unwell and nervous a long, long time. I have scarce mustered courage to begin this short note, but conscience duns me.

I had a pleasant letter from your sister, greatly overacknowledging my poor sonnet. I think I should have replied to it, but tell her I think so. Alas! for sonneting, 'tis as the nerves are; all the summer I was dawdling among green lanes, and verses came as thick as fancies. I am sunk winterly below prose and zero.

But I trust the vital principle is only as under snow. That I shall yet laugh again.

I suppose the great change of place affects me; but I could not have lived in Town; I could not bear company.

I see Novello flourishes in the Del Capo line, and dedications are not forgotten. I read the *Atlas*. When I pitched on the Dedication, I looked for the Broom of *"Cowden* knows" to be harmonised, but 'twas summat of Rossini's.

I want to hear about Hone. Does he stand above water? how is his son? I have delay'd writing to him till it seems impossible. Break the ice for me.

The wet ground here is intolerable, the sky above clear and delusive; but under foot quagmires from night showers, and I am cold-footed and moisture-abhorring as a cat; nevertheless I yesterday tramped to Waltham Cross; perhaps the poor bit of exertion necessary to scribble this was owing to that unusual bracing.

If I get out, I shall get stout, and then something will out—I mean for the "Companion"—you see I rhyme insensibly.

Traditions are rife here of one Clarke a schoolmaster and a run-away pickle named Holmes; but much obscurity hangs over it. Is it possible they can be any relations?

'Tis worth the research, when you can find a sunny day, with ground firm, etc. Master Sexton is intelligent, and for half-a-crown he'll pick up a Father.

In truth, we shall be glad to see any of the Novellian circle, middle of the week such as can come, or Sunday, as can't. But Spring will burgeon out quickly, and then we'll talk more.

You'd like to see the improvements on the Chase, the new cross in the market-place, the Chandler's shop from whence the rods were fetch'd. They are raised a farthing since the spread of Education. But perhaps you don't care to be reminded of the Holofernes' days, and nothing remains of the old laudable profession but the clear, firm impossible-to-be-mistaken schoolmaster text hand with which is subscribed the ever-welcome name of Chas. Cowden C. Let me crowd in both our loves to all.

C. L.

[*Added on the fold-down of the letter:*] Let me never be forgotten to include in my remembᶜᵉˢ my good friend and whilom correspondent, Master Stephen.

How, especially, is Victoria?

I try to remember all I used to meet at Shacklewell. The little household, cake-producing, wine-bringing out, Emma—the old servant, that didn't stay, and ought to have stayed, and was always very dirty and friendly; and Miss H., the counter-tenor with a fine voice, whose sister married Thurtell. They all live in my mind's eye, and Mr. N.'s and Holmes's walks with us half back after supper. Troja fuit!

To Mr. MOXON.

Letter CCCLIX.]   *March* 18, 1828.

My dear M.—It is my firm determination to have nothing to do with "Forget-me-Nots"; pray excuse me as civilly as you can to Mr. Hurst. I will take care to refuse any other applications. The things which Pickering has, if to be had again, I have promised absolutely, you know, to poor Hood, from whom I had a melancholy epistle yesterday; besides that Emma has decided objections to her own and her friend's album verses being published; but if she gets over that, they are decidedly Hood's.

Till we meet, farewell. Loves to Dash.   C. L.

To Rev. E. IRVING.

Letter CCCLX.]   *Enfield Chase, April* 3, 1828.

Dear Sir—I take advantage from the kindness which I have experienced from you in a slight acquaintance to introduce to you my very respected friend Mr. Hone, who is of opinion that your interference in a point which he will mention to you may prove of essential benefit to him in some present difficulties. I should not take this liberty if I did not feel that you are a person not to be prejudiced by an obnoxious name. All that I know of him obliges me to respect him, and to request your kindness for him, if you can serve him.

With feelings of kindest respect, I am, dear Sir, yours truly.

Chas. Lamb.

To BERNARD BARTON.

Letter CCCLXI.]   *April* 21, 1828.

Dear B. B.—You must excuse my silence. I have been in very poor health and spirits, and cannot write letters. I only write to assure you, as you wish'd, of my existence. All that which Mitford tells you of H.'s book is rhodomontade, only H. has written unguardedly about me, and nothing makes a man more foolish than his own foolish panegyric. But I am pretty well cased to flattery, and its contrary. Neither affect me a turnip's worth. Do you see the author of "May you like it"? Do you write to him? Will you give my present plea to him of ill health for not acknowledging a pretty book with a pretty frontispiece he sent me. He is most esteemed by me. As for subscribing to books, in plain truth I am a man of reduced income, and don't allow myself 12 shillings a-year to buy old books with; which must be my excuse. I am truly sorry for Murray's demur; but I wash my hands of all booksellers, and hope to know them no more. I am sick and poorly, and must leave off with our joint kind remembrances to your daughter and friend A. K.

C. L.

To WILLIAM HONE.

LETTER CCCLXII.]

Enfield, Wednesday,
May 2, 1828.

Dear H.—Valter Vilson dines with us to-morrow. Vell! How I should like to see Hone!

C. LAMB.

Mr. Hone,
22, Belvidere Place,
near the Obelisk, Southwark.

To MR. MOXON.

LETTER CCCLXIII.]

Enfield, May 3, 1828.

Dear M.—My friend Patmore, author of the *Months,* a very pretty publication,—of sundry Essays in the *London, New Monthly,* etc., wants to dispose of a volume or two of "Tales." Perhaps they might chance to suit Hurst; but be that as it may, he will call upon you *under favour of my recommendation;* and as he is returning to France, where he lives, if you can do anything for him in the Treaty line, to save him dancing over the Channel every week, I am sure you will. I said I'd never trouble you again; but how vain are the resolves of mortal man! P. is a very hearty, friendly fellow, and was poor John Scott's Second, as I will be yours when you want one. May you never be mine!
Yours truly,

C. L.

Mr. Moxon,
Messrs. Hurst and Co.,
Booksellers,
St. Paul's Churchyard.

To Rev. H. F. CARY.

LETTER CCCLXIV.]   *June* 10, 1828.

Dear Sir—I long to see Wordsworth once more before he goes hence, but it would be at the expense of health and comfort my infirmities cannot afford. Once only I have been at a dinner party, to meet him, for a whole year past, and I do not know that I am not the worse for it now. There is a necessity for my drinking too much (don't show this to the Bishop of ——, your friend) at and after dinner; then I require spirits at night to allay the crudity of the weaker Bacchus; and in the morning I cool my parched stomach with a fiery libation. Then I am aground in town, and call upon my London friends, and get new wets of ale, porter, etc.; then ride home, drinking where the coach stops, as duly as Edward set up his Waltham Crosses. This, or near it, was the process of my experiment of dining at Talfourd's to meet Wordsworth, and I am not well now. Now let me beg that we may meet here with assured safety to both sides. Darley and Procter come here on Sunday morning; pray arrange to come along with them. Here I can be tolerably moderate. In town, the very air of town turns my head and is intoxication enough, if intoxication knew a limit. I am a poor country mouse, and your cates disturb me. Tell me you will come. We have a bed, and a half or three quarters bed, at all your services; and the adjoining inn has many. If engaged on Sunday, tell me when you will come; a Saturday will suit as well. I would that Wordsworth would come too. Pray believe that 'tis my health only, which brought me here, that frightens me from the wicked town. Mary joins in kind remembrances to Mrs. Cary and yourself.

Yours truly,   C. LAMB.

To Mrs. BASIL MONTAGU.

LETTER CCCLXV.]   [Summer 1828.]

Dear Madam—I return your list with my name. I should be sorry that any respect should be going on towards Clarkson, and I be left out of the conspiracy. Otherwise I frankly own that to pillarise a man's good feelings in his lifetime is not to my taste. Monuments to goodness, even after death, are equivocal. I turn away from Howard's, I scarce know why. Goodness blows no trumpet, nor desires to have it blown. *We should be modest for a modest man*—as he is for himself. The vanities of life—art, poetry, skill military—are subjects for trophies; not the silent thoughts arising in a good man's mind in lonely places. Was I Clarkson, I should never be able to walk or ride near the spot again. Instead of bread, we are giving him a stone. Instead of the locality recalling the noblest moment of his existence, it is a place at which his friends (that is, himself) blow to the world, "What a good man is he!" I sat down upon a hillock at Forty Hill yesternight,—a fine contemplative evening,—with a thousand good speculations about mankind. How I yearned with cheap benevolence! I shall go and inquire of the stone-cutter, that cuts the tombstones here, what a stone with a short inscription will cost; just to say, "Here C. Lamb loved his brethren of mankind." Everybody will come there to love. As I can't well put my own name, I shall put about a subscription:

		£	s	d
Mrs. ——	. .	£0	5	0
Procter	. .	0	2	6
G. Dyer	. .	0	1	0
Mr. Godwin	.	0	0	0
Mrs. Godwin	.	0	0	0
Mr. Irving	. .		a watch-chain.	
Mr. ——	. . {	the proceeds of —— first edition.		

£0　8　6

I scribble in haste from here, where we shall be some time. Pray request Mr. Montagu to advance the guinea for me, which shall faithfully be forthcoming, and pardon me that I don't see the proposal in quite the light that he may. The kindness of his motives, and his power of appreciating the noble passage, I thoroughly agree in.

With most kind regards to him, I conclude, dear madam, yours truly,

C. LAMB.

From Mrs. Leishman's, Chase, Enfield.

To B. R. HAYDON.

LETTER CCCLXVI.]　　　　　　　　　　　　*August* 1828.

Dear Haydon—I have been tardy in telling you that your Chairing the Member gave me great pleasure—'tis true broad Hogarthian fun, the High Sheriff capital. Considering, too, that you had the materials imposed upon you, and that you did not select them from the rude world as H. did, I hope to see many more such from your hand. If the former picture went beyond this I have had a loss, and the King a bargain. I longed to rub the back of my hand across the hearty canvas that two senses might be gratified. Perhaps the subject is a little discordantly placed opposite to another act of Chairing, where the huzzas were Hosannahs! but I was pleased to see so many of my old acquaintances brought together notwithstanding.

Believe me, yours truly,　　　　　　　　　　　　　　C. LAMB.

To JOHN RICKMAN, Esq.

LETTER CCCLXVII.] *September 11, 1828.*

Dear Rickman—We are just come home from a London visit and are mortified to learn that we missed you on Saturday.—The same absence cannot recur before the 29th, or feast of St. Michael, on which day I pay my quarterly respects to the India Directors. If you can make another day between, you are sure of finding us.

The Nuts are very acceptable, Mary being a grievous offender that way; but to think of bringing *apples* to the Proprietor of a whole Tree, almost an Orchard, and who actually has an apple chamber redolent, was a solecism.

Yours ever.   C. LAMB.

Do you ever light upon G. D. now?—Could you bring him?

To LOUISA HOLCROFT.

LETTER CCCLXVIII.] *October 2, 1828.*

Mary Lamb has written her last letter in this world. Do not imagine that her individual substance has perished! 'Tis extant yet and sleek, but her epistolary part is dead before her, and has left me *writing legatee*. Could not you have slipt down for a day or two this Michaelmas vacation? 'Twould have been worth while to have seen the difference in our green. On the 28th 'twas whitened over with those pretty birds that look like snow in summer, and cackle like ice breaking up: the fatal 29th arrove (is that English?), and their place knew them no more. Here and there a solitary duck survives to remind one of the superior race which had been extinguished—swans to *them*.

You remember I asked a large party of them into our grounds to meet *you*. Of all that pleasant party, your dear self excepted, not one remains with a whole throat.

You send loves to Mrs. Morgan—who or what is she, or what dream was it that any such person is here? You add, too, that she is grown plump—is that a reason why love should be sent her? I understand neither the logic nor affection implied in that passage.

I have nearly lost my arithmetic since you went, but *count* upon renewing it some day with you. Enfield is dull, but London is turbulent. We have disqualified ourselves for a town life by migrating here, but cannot (for our Cockney souls) get up a rural taste, so we hang suburbian.

I could not bring myself to face Mr. Kenny in Brunswick Square (time and next occasion may take off the terror). I thought it would look so like coming to be *repaid* for any little hospitalities which I might have had in my power to show him while he staid at Enfield, which were no more than one gentleman ought to do to another—marry, 'tis well if he thought 'em so much.

And how are all the little orphans committed to your trust? Mind their morals first. I would not give two-pence for all the learning you can put into them in comparison with that. Do they lay three in a bed? Do you see them properly lain and tidy before you go to bed yourself of a night—I mean before you lie yourself down to sleep?

Mary tells me to say that Mrs. Collier knows we shall be happy to see her any day without ceremony.

And to have you again when you have vacation, for you were not very troublesome—indeed, we are more hospitable by nature than some folks would guess from our practice. With best loves to Mrs. Kenny, twins and no twins, yours truly, C. and M. LAMB.

Miss Holcroft,
  Monsr. Kenny's,
    12 Brunswick Square.

To JOHN RICKMAN, ESQ.

LETTER CCCLXIX.] *October* 4, 1828.

Meditanti mihi rescribere ad te Latinam aliquam epistolam pro tuâ ipsius expolitissima occurrerunt obstacula non nulla quotidiana, et inter prima amicus noster inconditus Martinus Burneius, qui commoratus erat apud nos aliquandiu, et per dies singulos Notitias Legales, et nihil nisi Legales, balbutiens, incusserat mihi metum, ne Latine cupiens scribere, loquendi formulas barbaras et forensicas, potius quam Ciceronianas, edidissem. Nam universus est in Legi-studiis; edit, bibit, ludit (scilicet cum pictis chartis) nil omnino nisi Legem; *Ignoramum* in Fabulâ agens ita pertinaciter, ut jarares habitare in medullis istius capitis intimis (num anatomice loquor?) septem—non Diabolos, sicut in Parabola—sed Leguleios, qui sensus ipsius (et amicorum) cum strepitu et multiloquentia penitus confundant. Librum secum, suppellectile solum, huc apportaverat, cui titulus "Fearne on Contingent Remainders," qui nimium perlectus, et nimis tenuiter intellectus, pene denuo effecerat, ut cerebro legentis vix quæque *remanentia,* quæ contigerint, superfuerint. Dimisso M. B. cum suppellectile suo, ad debitum meum erga te revertor. Iter tibi reverso cum commentariis non sine voluptate maxima iterum atque iterum relego, utpote qui ex usitatis rebus semper aliquid novi referas. Quod mones me de milliaribus nostris, nempe erroribus scatentibus, exponam brevibus quare instructionibus tuis minus audiens fiam. Si de rebus istiusmodi cum primoribus conferrem, "Heus Tu," exclamaret aliquis vel ex Viarum Curatoribus, vel Parochiæ Supervisoribus, "quid hæ res

ad te? Tu ex Domiciliatore vis fieri Domi-magister?" Licet scias, me
Domum proprium in agro Enfeldio, sororis nominibus, per fictionem
naturalem et domesticam, conduxerim, laborum atque ærumnarum, cum
comitialium (Vestry meetings) tum parochialium, istiusmodi vitanda-
rum causa, et ni ipse supervisor, vel saltem aliquis vir magnus, evasissem.
Quale respondissem? Otium cum dignitate quam minimâ assecutus sum.
Et, ut vera confitear, arrident mihi haud leviter, et mentem gratissime
tangunt, hæ anomaliæ prædictæ quas perstringis. Absoluto prorsus a
negotiis mundanis omnigeneris (quorsus aliter superannuatus fierem?)
errores hi viatici non multum mihi displicent, utpote habenti mundum
(quod aiunt) præ oculos, et a distinctionibus, cum spatii tum temporis,
nimis accuratis penitus submoto. Hac ratione quasi immortalis prodeo;
in cœlorum etenim supernorum infinitis spatiis (quæ tenuitate meorum
locorum imitari aveo quantum possum) quid opus esset milliarium? Ad
negotia humana attinent differentiæ locales. Ipse ambulo otiosus, et
quasi incircumscriptus. Quocirca Horologia etiam nostra Enfeldiensia
haud parum laudo, quorum pars plurima horas indicant nequaquam ser-
viliter, ad nutum solis mundani, et subter empyreum positi, sed quæque
diverse pro arbitriis suis dulcibus feriantia, et resonantia ad libitum—
one, two, three—ut evenerit—mihi ipsi, sicut feliciori cuidam Whitting-
tonio, prædicantia festive, quod, quoad me saltem, extinctum fuerit
Tempus. Hæ sunt rationes quare expostulationibus tuis, hominis nego-
tiosi et sub-solaris, in hac re minus obtemporatus sim. Alioquin, cum ad
milliare quoddam accedo, distantias computans ab Aula Hickesiana
(The Middx. Sessions House) quæ extat, dignitatem Aulicam in præsenti agnosco; et, si furcifer essem, pertremiscerem. Accedens ad alterum
quod computaverit a Situ quo Aula predicta olim steterat, de lapsis mole
et magnitudine meditationes volvo, et mecum reputo, quam caduca sit
splendidissimarum structionum humanarum conditio, et cogitationibus
hujusmodi omnem fastum et arrogantiam depono. Hisce meditationibus
cor indies melius fit. Alicui (mei consimili) iter facienti, quæ a milliaribus apte dispositis eveniant commoda, arctiùs et concinniùs me docuit V.
Bournius, carmine cui titulus hic ipse "Milliaria," ita concluso—(me-
ministine, vel totum transcribam?)

> Ignotæ tantum præstat Distantia nota;
> Millia quæ reddit plura, minusque viæ.
> How well the Milestones' use doth this express,
> Which make the Miles more, and the way seem less!

Quid vult in epistola tua "Utor manu et stylo nostri juvenis," nempe
filii? Oculis nostris antiquis diligenter inspicientibus apparet, immo
prælucet, stylus ipsius tuus, manus ipsissima. Aut Rickmanni aut Diaboli. Solutionem differo ad congressionem nostram proximam, quæ ne ad
longinquum tempus differatur, precor.
Deficiente mihi Latinitate, quod suprà a limationibus conjectare possis,

quid restat nisi hoc? Valeto et facito, ut Domina Rickmanna tecum vivat
haud immemor nostri   C. LAMB.

Enfield Chase Side,
   October 4, 1828.

I can't put this properly into Latin. Dabam, what is it?

To John Rickman, Esq.,
   Portsmouth, Hants.

To BERNARD BARTON.

LETTER CCCLXX.]   *October* 11, 1828.

A splendid edition of "Bunyan's Pilgrim"! Why, the thought is enough
to turn one's moral stomach. His cockle-hat and staff transformed to a
smart cock'd beaver and a jemmy cane; his amice gray, to the last Regent
Street cut; and his painful palmer's pace to the modern swagger. Stop
thy friend's sacrilegious hand. Nothing can be done for B. but to reprint
the old cuts in as homely but good a style as possible. The Vanity Fair,
and the Pilgrims there—the silly-soothness in his setting-out countenance
—the Christian Idiocy (in a good sense) of his admiration of the shepherds on the Delectable Mountains; the lions, so truly allegorical, and
remote from any similitude to Pidcock's; the great head (the author's),
capacious of dreams and similitudes, dreaming in the dungeon. Perhaps
you don't know my edition, what I had when a child. If you do, can you
bear new designs from Martin, enamelled into copper or silver plate by
Heath, accompanied with verses from Mrs. Hemans's pen, O how unlike
his own!

> "Wouldst thou divert thyself from melancholy?
> Wouldst thou be pleasant, yet be far from folly?
> Wouldst thou read riddles, and their explanation?
> Or else be drownèd in thy contemplation?
> Dost thou love picking meat? or wouldst thou see
> A man in the clouds, and hear him speak to thee?
> Wouldst thou be in a dream, and yet not sleep?
> Or wouldst thou in a moment laugh and weep?
> Or wouldst thou lose thyself, and catch no harm,
> And find thyself again without a charm?
> Wouldst read *thyself*, and read thou knowest not what,
> And yet know whether thou art blest or not
> By reading the same lines? O then come hither,
> And lay my book, thy head, and heart together.
>   "JOHN BUNYAN."

Show me such poetry in any of the fifteen forthcoming combinations of
show and emptiness, yclept "Annuals." So there's verses for thy verses;

and now let me tell you, that the sight of your hand gladdened me. I have been daily trying to write to you, but paralysed. You have spurred me on this tiny effort, and at intervals I hope to hear from and talk to you. But my spirits have been an opprest way for a long long time, and they are things which must be to you of faith, for who can explain depression? Yes, I am hooked into the "Gem," but only for some lines written on a dead infant of the Editor's, which being, as it were, his property, I could not refuse their appearing; but I hate the paper, the type, the gloss, the dandy plates, the names of contributors poked up into your eyes in first page, and whistled through all the covers of magazines, the barefaced sort of emulation, the immodest candidateship, brought into so little space—in those old "Londons" a signature was lost in the wood of matter, the paper coarse (till latterly, which spoiled them); in short, I detest to appear in an Annual. What a fertile genius (and a quiet good soul withal) is Hood! He has fifty things in hand: farces to supply the Adelphi for the season; a comedy for one of the great theatres, just ready; a whole entertainment, by himself, for Mathews and Yates to figure in; a meditated Comic Annual for next year, to be nearly done by himself. You'd like him very much.

Wordsworth, I see, has a good many pieces announced in one of 'em, not our *Gem*. W. Scott has distributed himself like a bribe haunch among 'em. Of all the poets, Cary has had the good sense to keep quite clear of 'em, with clergy-gentlemanly right notions. Don't think I set up for being proud on this point; I like a bit of flattery, tickling my vanity, as well as any one. But these pompous masquerades without masks (naked names or faces) I hate. So there's a bit of my mind. Besides, they infallibly cheat you; I mean the booksellers. If I get but a copy, I only expect it from Hood's being my friend. Coleridge has lately been here. He too is deep among the prophets, the year-servers,—the mob of gentlemen annuals. But they'll cheat him, I know. And now, dear B. B., the sun shining out merrily, and the dirty clouds we had yesterday having washed their own faces clean with their own rain, tempts me to wander up Winchmore Hill, or into some of the delightful vicinages of Enfield, which I hope to show you at some time when you can get a few days up to the great town. Believe me, it would give both of us great pleasure to show you all three (we can lodge you) our pleasant farms and villages.

We both join in kindest loves to you and yours.

C. LAMB.
C. LAMB, *redivivus*.

To THOMAS HOOD.

LETTER CCCLXXI.] *Enfield* [*October* 1828].

Dear Lamb—You are an impudent varlet; but I will keep your secret. We dine at Ayrton's on Thursday, and shall try to find Sarah and her two spare beds for that night only. Miss M. and her tragedy may be dished: so may *not* you and your rib. Health attend you.

     Yours,   T. Hood, Esq.

Miss Bridget Hood sends love.

To C. COWDEN CLARKE.

LETTER CCCLXXII.]   [*Enfield, October* 1828.]

Dear Clarke—We did expect to see you with Victoria and the Novellos before this, and do not quite understand why we have not. Mrs. N. and V. [Vincent] promised us after the York expedition; a day being named before, which fail'd. 'Tis not too late. The autumn leaves drop gold, and Enfield is beautifuller—to a common eye—than when you lurked at the Greyhound. Benedicks are close; but how I so totally missed you at that time, going for my morning cup of ale duly, is a mystery. 'Twas stealing a match before one's face in earnest. But certainly we had not a dream of your appropinquity. I instantly prepared an Epithalamium, in the form of a Sonata—which I was sending to Novello to compose; but Mary forbid it me as too light for the occasion—as if the subject required anything heavy: so in a tiff with her I sent no congratulation at all. Tho' I promise you the wedding was very pleasant news to me indeed. Let your reply name a day this next week, when you will come as many as a coach will hold; such a day as we had at Dulwich. My very kindest love and Mary's to Victoria and the Novellos. The enclosed is from a friend nameless, but highish in office, and a man whose accuracy of statement may be relied on with implicit confidence. He wants the *exposé* to appear in a newspaper as the "greatest piece of legal and Parliamentary villainy he ever remember'd," and he had experience of both; and thinks it would answer afterwards in a cheap pamphlet printed at Lambeth in 8vo sheet, as 16,000 families in that parish are interested. I know not whether the present "Examiner" keeps up the character of exposing abuses, for I scarce see a paper now. If so, you may ascertain Mr. Hunt of the strictest truth of the statement, at the peril of my head. But if this won't do, transmit it me back, I beg, per coach—or better, bring it with you.

     Yours unaltered,   C. Lamb.

To VINCENT NOVELLO.

LETTER CCCLXXIII.]   [*Enfield, November* 6, 1828.]

My dear Novello—I am afraid I shall appear rather tardy in offering my congratulations, however sincere, upon your daughter's marriage. The truth is I had put together a little Serenata upon the occasion, but was prevented from sending it by my sister, to whose judgment I am apt to defer too much in these kind of things; so that, now I have her consent, the offering, I am afraid, will have lost the grace of seasonableness. Such as it is, I send it. She thinks it a little too old-fashioned in the manner, too much like what they wrote a century back. But I cannot write in the modern style, if I try ever so hard. I have attended to the proper divisions for the music, and you will have little difficulty in composing it. If I may advise, make Pepusch your model, or Blow. It will be necessary to have a good second voice, as the stress of the melody lies there:—

SERENATA, FOR TWO VOICES,

On the Marriage of Charles Cowden Clarke, Esqre., to Victoria, eldest daughter of Vincent Novello, Esqre.

DUETTO.

Wake th' harmonious voice and string,
Love and Hymen's triumph sing,
Sounds with secret charms combining,
In melodious union joining,
Best the wondrous joys can tell,
That in hearts united dwell.

RECITATIVE.

First Voice.

To young Victoria's happy fame
  Well may the Arts a trophy raise,
  Music grows sweeter in her praise,
And, own'd by her, with rapture speaks her name.
To touch the brave Cowdenio's heart,
  The Graces all in her conspire;
Love arms her with his surest dart,
  Apollo with his lyre.

AIR.

The list'ning Muses all around her,
  Think 'tis Phœbus' strain they hear;
And Cupid, drawing near to wound her,
  Drops his bow, and stands to hear.

RECITATIVE.

Second Voice.

While crowds of rivals with despair
Silent admire, or vainly court the Fair,
Behold the happy conquest of her eyes,
A Hero is the glorious prize!
In courts, in camps, thro' distant realms renown'd,
  Cowdenio comes!—Victoria, see,
He comes with British honour crown'd.
  Love leads his eager steps to thee.

AIR.

In tender sighs he silence breaks,
  The Fair his flame approves,
Consenting blushes warm her cheeks,
  She smiles, she yields, she loves.

RECITATIVE.

First Voice.

Now Hymen at the altar stands,
And while he joins their faithful hands,
Behold! by ardent vows brought down,
Immortal Concord, heavenly bright,
Array'd in robes of purest light,
Descends, th' auspicious rites to crown.
Her golden harp the goddess brings;
Its magic sound
Commands a sudden silence all around,
And strains prophetic thus attune the strings.

DUETTO.

First Voice.

The Swain his Nymph possessing,

Second Voice.

The Nymph her Swain caressing,

First and Second.

Shall still improve the blessing,
For ever kind and true.

Both.

While rolling years are flying,
Love, Hymen's lamp supplying,
With fuel never dying,
Shall still the flame renew.

To so great a master as yourself I have no need to suggest that the
peculiar tone of the composition requires sprightliness, occasionally
checked by tenderness, as in the second air,—

She smiles,—she yields,—she loves.

Again, you need not be told that each fifth line of the two first recitatives
requires a crescendo.

And your exquisite taste will prevent your falling into the error of Pur-
cell, who at a passage similar to *that* in my first air,

Drops his bow, and stands to hear,

directed the first violin thus:—

Here the first violin must drop his *bow.*

But, besides the absurdity of disarming his principal performer of so
necessary an adjunct to his instrument, in such an emphatic part of the
composition too, which must have had a droll effect at the time, all such
minutiæ of adaptation are at this time of day very properly exploded,
and Jackson of Exeter very fairly ranks them under the head of puns.

Should you succeed in the setting of it, we propose having it performed (we have one very tolerable second voice here, and Mr. Holmes, I dare say, would supply the minor parts) at the Greyhound. But it must be a secret to the young couple till we can get the band in readiness.

Believe me, dear Novello, yours truly, C. LAMB.

To LAMAN BLANCHARD.

LETTER CCCLXXIV.] *Enfield, November* 9, 1828.

Sir—I beg to return my acknowledgments for the present of your elegant volume, which I should have esteemed, without the bribe of the name prefixed to it. I have been much pleased with it throughout, but am most taken with the peculiar delicacy of some of the sonnets. I shall put them up among my poetical treasures.

Your obliged Servant, C. LAMB.

To BERNARD BARTON.

LETTER CCCLXXV.] *December* 5, 1828.

Dear B. B.—I am ashamed to receive so many nice books from you, and to have none to send you in return. You are always sending me some fruits or wholesome potherbs, and mine is the garden of the Sluggard, nothing but weeds, or scarce they. Nevertheless, if I knew how to transmit it, I would send you Blackwood's of this month, which contains a little drama, to have your opinion of it, and how far I have improved, or otherwise, upon its prototype. Thank you for your kind sonnet. It does me good to see the Dedication to a Christian Bishop. I am for a comprehension, as divines call it; but so as that the Church shall go a good deal more than half way over to the silent Meeting-house. I have ever said that the Quakers are the only *professors* of Christianity as I read it in the Evangiles. I say *professors:* marry, as to practice, with their gaudy hot types and poetical vanities, they are much at one with the sinful. Martin's Frontispiece is a very fine thing, let *C. L.* say what he pleases to the contrary. Of the Poems, I like them as a volume, better than any one of the preceding; particularly, "Power and Gentleness"—"The Present"—"Lady Russell"; with the exception that I do not like the noble act of Curtius, true or false—one of the grand foundations of old Roman patriotism—to be sacrificed to Lady R.'s taking notes on her husband's trial. If a thing is good, why invidiously bring it into light with something better? There are too few heroic things in this world, to admit of our marshalling them in anxious etiquettes of precedence. Would you make a poem on the story of Ruth (pretty story!), and then say—Ay, but how much better is the story of Joseph and his brethren! To go on, the stanzas to "Chalon" want the *name* of Clarkson in the body of them; it is left to inference. The "Battle of Gibeon" is spirited, again; but you sacrifice it in the last stanza to the song at Bethlehem. Is it quite ortho-dox to do so? The first was good, you suppose, for that dispensation. Why set the Word against the Word? It puzzles a weak Christian. So Watts's Psalms are an implied censure on David's. But as long as the Bi-ble is supposed to be an equally divine emanation with the Testament, so long it will stagger weaklings to have them set in opposition. "Godiva" is delicately touched. I have always thought it a beautiful story, charac-teristic of the old English times. But I could not help amusing myself with the thought—if Martin had chosen this subject for a frontispiece— there would have been in some dark corner a white lady, white as the walker on the waves, riding upon some mystical quadruped; and high above would have risen "tower above tower a massy structure high"— the Tenterden steeples of Coventry, till the poor cross would scarce have known itself among the clouds; and far above them all the distant Clint Hills peering over chimney-pots, piled up, Ossa-on-Olympus fashion, till the admiring spectator (admirer of a noble deed) might have gone look for the lady, as you must hunt for the other in the lobster. But M[artin] should be made royal architect. What palaces he would pile! But then, what parliamentary grants to make them good! Nevertheless, I like the frontispiece. "The Elephant" is pleasant; and I am glad you are getting into a wider scope of subjects. There may be too much, not religion, but too many *good words* in a book, till it becomes, as Sh—— says of Re-ligion, a rhapsody of words. I will just name, that you have brought in the "Song to the Shepherds" in four or five, if not six places. Now this is not good economy. The "Enoch" is fine; and here I can sacrifice "Eli-jah" to it, because 'tis illustrative only, and not disparaging of the latter prophet's departure. I like this best in the book. Lastly, I much like the "Heron"; 'tis exquisite. Know you Lord Thurlow's Sonnet to a bird of that sort on Lacken water? If not, 'tis indispensable I send it you, with my Blackwood, if you tell me how best to send them. "Fludyer" is pleas-ant,—you are getting gay and Hoodish. What is the enigma? Money? If not, I fairly confess I am foiled, and sphynx must . . . *eat me.* Four times I've tried to write "eat me," and the blotting pen turns it into *cat me.* And now I will take my leave with saying, I esteem thy verses, like thy present, honour thy frontispiecer, and right reverence thy patron and dedicatee, and am, dear B. B.,

Yours heartily,   C. LAMB.

Our joint kindest loves to A. K. and your daughter.

To LOUISA HOLCROFT.

LETTER CCCLXXVI.]   *December* 5, 1828.

Dear Miss H.—Mary, who never writes, bids me thank you for the handkerchief. I do not understand such work, but if I apprehend her rightly, she would have preferred blonde to white sarcenet for the trim-ming; but she did not wish me to tell you so. I only hint it for the next.

We are sorry for the mess of illness you are involved in. Are you stout enough to be the general nurse? Who told you we should not be glad to see you on Sundays and all? Tho' we devote that day to its proper duties, as you know, yet you are come of a religious stock, and to you it is not irksome to join in our simple forms, where the heart is all. Your little protégée is well, and as yet honest, but she has no one to give her caps now.

Thus far I had written last night. You will see by my altered scrawl that I am not so well this morning. I got up with a fevered skin, and spots are come out all over me. Pray God it is not the measles. You did not let any of the children touch the seal with their little measly hands, did you? You should be careful when contagion is in the house. Pray God, your letter may not have conveyed the disorder. Our poor Postman looks flushed since. What a thing it would be to introduce a disease into a whole village! Yet so simple a thing as a letter has been known to convey a malady. I look at your note. I see it is wafered, not sealed. That makes it more likely. Wafers are flour, and I've known a serious illness to be communicated in a piece of plum cake. I never had the measles. How my head throbs! You cannot be too cautious, dear Louisa, what you do under such circum——

I am a little better than when I broke off at the last word. Your good sense will point out to you that the deficient syllables should be "stances." Circumstances. If I am incoherent, impute it to alarm. I will walk in the air——

I am not much refreshed. The air seemed hot and muggy. Somehow I feel quite irritable—there is no word in English—à la variole—we have no phrase to answer it—smallpoxical comes the nearest. Maybe 'twas worse than the measles what Charles has. I will send for Mr. Asbury.

I have seen the apothecary. He pronounces my complaint to be, as I feared, of the variola kind, but gives me hopes I shall not be much marked. I hope we shall get well together. But at my time of life it is attended with more hazards. Whatever becomes of me, I shall leave the world without a harsh thought of you. It was only a girlish imprudence. I am quite faint. Two pimples more came out within this last minute. Mary is crying. She looks red. So does Becky. I must go to bed.

Yours in constant Pain,   C. L.

You will see by my Will, if it comes to that—I bear you no ill w——. Oh!

Miss Holcroft,
   Mr. Kenny's,
    12 Brunswick Square.

To C. COWDEN CLARKE.

LETTER CCCLXXVII.]   [*December* 1828.]

My dear three C.'s—The way from Southgate to Colney Hatch thro' the unfrequentedest Blackberry paths that ever concealed their coy bunches from a truant Citizen, we have accidentally fallen upon—the giant Tree by Chestnut we have missed, but keep your chart to go by, unless you will be our conduct. At present I am disabled from further flights than just to skirt round Clay Hill, with a peep at the fine back-woods, by strained tendons, got by skipping a skipping rope at 53—*hei mihi non sum qualis;* but do you know, now you come to talk of walks, a ramble of four hours or so—there and back to the willow and laven-der plantations at the south corner of Northaw Church by a well dedi-cated to Saint Claridge, with the clumps of finest moss rising hillock fash-ion, which I counted to the number of two hundred and sixty, and are called "Claridge's covers," the tradition being that that saint entertained so many angels or hermits there, upon occasion of blessing the waters? The legends have set down the fruits spread upon that occasion, and in the "Black Book of St. Albans," some are named which are not supposed to have been introduced into this island until a century later. But waiv-ing the miracle, a sweeter spot is not in ten counties round; you are knee-deep in clover, that is to say, if you are not above a middling man's height; from this paradise, making a day of it, you go to see the ruins of an old convent at March Hall, where some of the painted glass is yet whole and fresh.

If you do not know this, you do not know the capabilities of this coun-try; you may be said to be a stranger to Enfield. I found it out one morning in October, and so delighted was I that I did not get home before dark, well a-paid.

I shall long to show you the Clump Meadows, as they are called—we might do that without reaching March Hall; when the days are longer we might take both, and come home by Forest Cross, so skirt over Penn-ington and the cheerful little village of Churchley to Forty Hill.

But these are dreams till summer; meanwhile we should be most glad to see you for a lesser excursion—say Sunday next, you and *another*, or if more, best on a week-day with a notice, but o' Sundays, as far as a leg of mutton goes, most welcome.

We can squeeze out a bed. Edmonton coaches run every hour, and my pen has run out its quarter. Heartily farewell.

To B. W. PROCTER.

LETTER CCCLXXVIII.]   *January* 19, 1829.

My dear Procter—I am ashamed not to have taken the drift of your pleasant letter, which I find to have been pure invention; but jokes are not suspected in Bœotian Enfield. We are plain people, and our talk is of corn and cattle and Waltham markets. Besides, I was a little out of sorts when I received it. The fact is, I am involved in a case which has fretted me to death, and I have no reliance except on you to extricate me. I am sure you will give me your best legal advice, having no professional friend besides but Robinson and Talfourd, with neither of whom, at present, I am on the best of terms. My brother's widow left a will, made during the lifetime of my brother, in which I am named sole executor, by which she bequeaths forty acres of arable property, which it seems she held under covert baron, unknown to my brother, to the heirs of the body of Elizabeth Dowden, her married daughter by a first husband, in fee simple, recoverable by fine; invested property, mind, for there is the difficulty; subject to leet and quit-rent; in short, worded in the most guarded terms, to shut out the property from Isaac Dowden, the husband. Intelligence has just come of the death of this person in India, where he made a will, entailing this property (which seemed entangled enough already) to the heirs of his body that should not be born of his wife; for it seems by the law in India, natural children can recover. They have put the cause into Exchequer process here, removed by *certiorari* from the native courts; and the question is, whether I should, as executor, try the cause here, or again re-remove it to the Supreme Sessions at Bangalore, which I understand I can, or plead a hearing before the Privy Council here. As it involves all the little property of Elizabeth Dowden, I am anxious to take the fittest steps, and what may be least expensive. For God's sake assist me, for the case is so embarrassed that it deprives me of sleep and appetite. M. Burney thinks there is a case like it in chap. 170, sec. 5, in "Fearn's Contingent Remainders." Pray read it over with him dispassionately, and let me have the result. The complexity lies in the questionable power of the husband to alienate *in usum* enfeoffments whereof he was only collaterally seized, etc.

I had another favour to beg, which is the beggarliest of beggings: a few lines of verse for a young friend's album (six will be enough). M. Burney will tell you who she is I want 'em for. A girl of gold. Six lines—make 'em eight—signed Barry C——. They need not be very good, as I chiefly want 'em as a foil to mine. But I shall be seriously obliged by any refuse scrap. We are in the last ages of the world, when St. Paul prophesied that women should be "headstrong, lovers of their own wills, having albums." I fled hither to escape the albumean persecution, and had not been in my new house twenty-four hours when the daughter of the next house came in with a friend's album to beg a contribution, and the following day intimated she had one of her own. Two more have sprung up since. "If I take the wings of the morning" and fly unto the uttermost parts of the earth, there will albums be. New Holland has albums. But the age is to be complied with. M. B. will tell you the sort of girl I request the ten lines for. Somewhat of a pensive cast, what you admire. The lines may come before the law question, as that cannot be determined before Hilary Term, and I wish your deliberate judgment on that. The other may be flimsy and superficial. And if you have not burnt your returned letter, pray resend it me, as a monumental token of my stupidity. 'Twas a little unthinking of you to touch upon a sore subject. Why, by dabbling in those accursed Annuals I have become a byword of infamy all over the kingdom. I have sicken'd decent women for asking me to write in albums. There be dark "jests" abroad, Master Cornwall, and some riddles may live to be cleared up. And 'tisn't every saddle is put on the right steed. And forgeries and false Gospels are not peculiar to the age following the Apostles. And some tubs don't stand on their right bottom, which is all I wish to say in these ticklish times; and so your servant.   CH. LAMB.

LETTER CCCLXXIX.]   *January 22, 1829.*

Don't trouble yourself about the verses. Take 'em coolly as they come. Any day between this and Midsummer will do. Ten lines the extreme. There is no mystery in my incognita. She has often seen you, though you may not have observed a silent brown girl, who for the last twelve years has rambled about our house in her Christmas holidays. She is Italian by name and extraction. Ten lines about the blue sky of her country will do, as 'tis her foible to be proud of it.—Item: I have made her a tolerable Latinist. She is called Emma Isola. I approve heartily of your turning your four vols. into a lesser compass. 'Twill Sybillise the gold left. I shall, I think, be in town in a few weeks, when I will assuredly see you. I will put in here Loves to Mrs. Procter and the anti-Capulets, because Mary tells me I omitted them in my last. I like to see my friends here. I have put my lawsuit into the hands of an Enfield practitioner, a plain man, who seems perfectly to understand it, and gives me hopes of a favourable result.

Rumour tells us that Miss Holcroft is married. Who is Badman, or Bed'em? Have I seen him at Montacute's? I hear he is a great chymist. I am sometimes chymical myself. A thought strikes me with horror. Pray heaven he may not have done it for the sake of trying chymical experiments upon her,—young female subjects are so scarce. Louisa would make a capital shot. Aren't you glad about Burke's case? We may set off the Scotch murders against the Scotch novels: Hare, the Great Un-hanged!

M. B. is richly worth your knowing. He is on the top scale of my friendship ladder, on which an angel or two is still climbing, and some, alas! descending. I am out of the literary world at present. Pray, is there anything new from the admired pen of the author of the *Pleasures of Hope?* Has Mrs. He-mans (double masculine) done anything pretty lately? Why sleeps the lyre of Hervey, and of Alaric Watts? Is the muse of L. E. L. silent? Did you see a sonnet of mine in Blackwood's last? Curious construction! Elaborata facilitas! And now I'll tell. 'Twas written for the *Gem,* but the editors declined it, on the plea that it would *shock all mothers;* so they published the "Widow," instead. I am born out of time. I have no conjecture about what the present world calls delicacy. I thought *Rosamund Gray* was a pretty modest thing.

Hessey assures me that the world would not bear it. I have lived to grow into an indecent character. When my sonnet was rejected, I exclaimed, "Damn the age! I will write for Antiquity."

Erratum in Sonnet:—Last line but something, for "tender," read *tend*. The Scotch do not know our law terms; but I find some remains of honest, plain, old writing lurking there still. They were not so mealy-mouthed to refuse my verses. Maybe 'tis their oatmeal.

Blackwood sent me £20 for the drama. Somebody cheated me out of it next day; and my new pair of breeches, just sent home, cracking at first putting on, I exclaimed in my wrath, "All tailors are cheats, and all men are tailors." Then I was better.   C. L.

LETTER CCCLXXX.]   *January* 29, 1829.

When Miss Ouldcroft (who is now Mrs. Beddome, and Bed—dom'd to her) was at Enfield, which she was in Summer time, and owed her health to its suns and genial influences, she visited (with young ladylike impertinence) a poor man's cottage that had a pretty baby (O the yearnling!) gave it fine caps and sweetmeats. On a day, broke into the parlour our two maids uproarious. "O ma'am, who do you think Miss Ouldcroft (they pronounce it Holcroft) has been working a cap for?" "A child," answered Mary, in true Shandean female simplicity. " 'Tis the man's child as was taken up for sheep-stealing." Miss Ouldcroft was staggered, and would have cut the connexion, but by main force I made her go and take her leave of her protégée. I thought, if she went no more, the Abactor or the Abactor's wife (vide Ainsworth) would suppose she had heard something, and I have delicacy for a sheep-stealer. The overseers actually overhauled a mutton pie at the Baker's (his first, last, and only hope of mutton pie,) which he never came to eat, and thence inferred his guilt. Per occasionem cujus, I framed the sonnet; observe its elaborate construction. I was four days about it.

THE GYPSY'S MALISON.

"Suck, baby, suck! mother's love grows by giving,
  Drain the sweet founts that only thrive by wasting;
Black manhood comes, when riotous guilty living
Hands thee the cup that shall be death in tasting.
Kiss, baby, kiss! Mother's lips shine by kisses,
  Choke the warm breath that else would fall in blessings;
Black Manhood comes, when turbulent guilty blisses
Tend thee the kiss that poisons 'mid caressings.
Hang, baby, hang! mother's love loves such forces,
  Strain the fond neck that bends still to thy clinging;
Black manhood comes, when violent lawless courses
Leave thee a spectacle in rude air swinging."
  So sang a wither'd Sybil energetical,
  And bann'd the ungiving door with lips prophetical.

Barry, study that sonnet. It is curiously and perversely elaborate. 'Tis a choking subject, and therefore the reader is directed to the structure of it. See you? and was this a fourteener to be rejected by a trumpery annual? Forsooth, 'twould shock all mothers; and may all mothers, who would so be shocked, bed-domd! as if mothers were such sort of logicians as to infer the future hanging of *their* child from the theoretical hangibility (or capacity of being hanged, if the judge pleases) of every infant born with a neck on. Oh B. C.! my whole heart is faint, and my whole head is sick (how is it?) at this damn'd canting unmasculine age!

LETTER CCCLXXXI.]　　　　　　　　　　　　　　[1829.]

The comings in of an incipient conveyancer are not adequate to the receipt of three twopenny post nonpaids in a week. Therefore, after this, I condemn my stub to long and deep silence, or shall awaken it to write to Lords. Lest those raptures in this honeymoon of my correspondence, which you avow for the gentle person of my Nuncio, after passing through certain natural grades, as Love, Love and Water, Love with the chill off, then subsiding to that point which the Heroic Suitor of his wedded dame, the noble-spirited Lord Randolph in the Play, declares to be the ambition of his passion, a reciprocation of "complacent kindness,"—should suddenly plump down (scarce staying to bait at the mid point of indifference, so hungry it is for distaste) to a loathing and blank aversion, to the rendering probable such counter expressions as this,—"Damn that infernal twopenny postman" (words which make the not yet glutted inamorato "lift up his hands and wonder who can use them.") While, then, you are not ruined, let me assure thee, O thou above the Painter, and next only under Giraldus Cambrensis, the most immortal and worthy to be immortal Barry, thy most ingenious and golden cadences do take my fancy mightily. They are at this identical moment under the snip and the paste of the fairest hands (bating chilblains) in Cambridge, soon to be transplanted to Suffolk, to the envy of half of the young ladies in Bury. But tell me, and tell me truly, gentle Swain, is that Isola Bella a true spot in geographical denomination, or a floating Delos in thy brain? Lurks that fair island in verity in the bosom of Lake Maggiore, or some other with less poetic name, which thou hast Cornwallised for the occasion? And what if Maggiore itself be but a coinage of adaptation? Of this, pray resolve me immediately, for my Albumess will be catechised on this subject; and how can I prompt her? Lake Leman, I know, and Lemon Lake (in a Punch Bowl) I have swum in, though those Lymphs be long since dry. But Maggiore may be in the moon. Unsphinx this riddle for me, for my shelves have no Gazetteer. And mayest thou never murder thy father-in-law in the Trivia of Lincoln's Inn New Square Passage, nor afterwards make absurd proposals to the Widow M[ontagu]. But I know you abhor any such notions. Nevertheless so did O-Edipus (as Admiral Burney used to call him, splitting the diphthong in spite or ignorance) for that matter.　　　　　　　　　　　　　　　　　C. L.

LETTER CCCLXXXII.] *February* 2, 1829.

Facundissime Poeta! quanquam istiusmodi epitheta oratoribus potiùs quam poetis attinere facilè scio—tamen, facundissime!

Commoratur nobiscum jamdiu, in agro Enfeldiense, scilicet, leguleius futurus, illustrissimus Martinus Burneius otium agens, negotia nominalia, et officinam clientum vacuam, paululum fugiens. Orat, implorat te—nempe, Martinus—ut si (quôd Dii faciant) fortè fortunâ, absente ipso, advenerit tardus cliens, eum certiorem feceris per literas hûc missas. Intelligisne? an me Anglicè et barbarice ad te hominem perdoctum scribere oportet? C. Agnus.

Sit status de franco tenemento datur avo, et in eodem facto si mediate vel immediate datur *hæredibus vel hæredibus corporis dicti avi,* postrema hæc verba sunt Limitationis non Perquisitionis.

Dixi. CARLAGNULUS.

To COWDEN CLARKE.

LETTER CCCLXXXIII.] *Edmonton, February* 2, 1829.

Dear Cowden—Your books are as the gushing of streams in a desert. By the way, you have sent no autobiographies. Your letter seems to imply you had. Nor do I want any. Cowden, they are of the books which I give away. What damn'd Unitarian skewer-soul'd things the general biographies turn out! "Rank and Talent" you shall have when Mrs. May has done with 'em. Mary likes Mrs. Bedinfield much. For me, I read nothing but *Astrea*—it has turn'd my brain—I go about with a switch turn'd up at the end for a crook; and Lambs being too old, the butcher tells me, my cat follows me in a green ribband. Becky and her cousin are getting pastoral dresses, and then we shall all four go about Arcadising. O cruel Shepherdess! Inconstant, yet fair, and more inconstant for being fair! Her gold ringlets fell in a disorder superior to order! Come and join us.

I am called the Black Shepherd—you shall be Cowden with the Tuft.

Prosaically, we shall be glad to have you both—or any two of you—drop in by surprise some Saturday night.

This must go off.

Loves to Vittoria. C. L.

To H. C. ROBINSON.

LETTER CCCLXXXIV.] *Enfield, February* 27, 1829.

Dear R.—Expectation was alert on the receipt of your strange-shaped present, while yet undisclosed from its fusc envelope. Some said, 'tis a *viol da Gamba,* others pronounced it a fiddle; I, myself, hoped it a liqueur case, pregnant with *eau-de-vie* and such odd nectar. When midwife into daylight, the gossips were at a loss to pronounce upon its species. Most took it for a marrow spoon, an apple scoop, a banker's guinea shovel; at length its true scope appeared, its drift, to save the backbone of my sister stooping to scuttles: a philanthropic intent; borrowed, no doubt, from some of the Colliers. You save people's backs one way, and break 'em again by loads of obligation. The spectacles are delicate and Vulcanian. No lighter texture than their steel did the cuckoldy blacksmith frame to catch Mrs. Vulcan and the Captain in. For ungalled forehead, as for back unbursten, you have Mary's thanks. Marry, for my own peculium of obligation, 'twas supererogatory. A second part of Pamela was enough in conscience. Two Pamelas in a house are too much, without two Mr. B's to reward 'em.

Mary, who is handselling her new aerial perspectives upon a pair of old worsted stockings trod out in Cheshunt lanes, sends her love: I, great good-liking. Bid us a personal farewell before you see the Vatican.

CHARLES LAMB.

To BERNARD BARTON.

LETTER CCCLXXXV.] *March* 25, 1829.

Dear B. B.—I send you by desire Darley's very poetical poem. You will like, I think, the novel headings of each scene. Scenical directions in verse are novelties. With it I send a few *duplicates*, which are *therefore* of no value to me; and may amuse an idle hour. Read "Christmas": 'tis the production of a young author, who reads all your writings. A good word from you about his little book would be as balm to him. It has no pretensions, and makes none. But parts are pretty. In Field's Appendix turn to a poem called the Kangaroo. It is in the best way of our old poets, if I mistake not. I have just come from town, where I have been to get my bit of quarterly pension; and have brought home, from stalls in Barbican, the old "Pilgrim's Progress" with the prints— Vanity Fair, etc.—now scarce. Four shillings. Cheap. And also one of whom I have oft heard and had dreams, but never saw in the flesh— that is in sheepskin—"The whole theologic works of

THOMAS AQUINAS."

My arms ached with lugging it a mile to the stage; but the burden was a pleasure, such as old Anchises was to the shoulders of Æneas, or the Lady to the Lover in old romance, who having to carry her to the top of a high mountain (the price of obtaining her,) clambered with her to the top, and fell dead with fatigue.

"Oh the glorious old Schoolmen !"

There must be something in him. Such great names imply greatness. Who hath seen Michael Angelo's things—of us that never pilgrimaged to Rome—and yet which of us disbelieves his greatness? How I will revel in his cobwebs and subtleties, till my brain spins!

N.B. I have writ in the old Hamlet: offer it to Mitford in my name, if he have not seen it. 'Tis woefully below our editions of it. But keep it, if you like. (What is M. to me?)

I do not mean this to go for a letter, only to apprise you that the parcel is booked for you this 25th March, 1829, from the Four Swans, Bishopsgate. With both our loves to Lucy and A. K. Yours ever, C. L.

To H. C. ROBINSON.

LETTER CCCLXXXVI.] *April* 10, 1829.

Dear Robinson—We are afraid you will slip from us from England without again seeing us. It would be charity to come and see me. I have these three days been laid up with strong rheumatic pains, in loins, back, shoulders. I shriek sometimes from the violence of them. I get scarce any sleep, and the consequence is, I am restless, and want to change sides as I lie, and I cannot turn without resting on my hands, and so turning all my body all at once, like a log with a lever. While this rainy weather lasts, I have no hope of alleviation. I have tried flannels and embrocation in vain. Just at the hip joint the pangs sometimes are so excruciating, that I cry out. It is as violent as the cramp, and far more continuous. I am ashamed to whine about these complaints to you, who can ill enter into them; but indeed they are sharp. You go about, in rain or fine, at all hours, without discommodity. I envy you your immunity at a time of life not much removed from my own. But you owe your exemption to temperance, which it is too late for me to pursue. I, in my lifetime, have had my good things. Hence my frame is brittle—yours strong as brass. I never knew any ailment you had. You can go out at night in all weathers, sit up all hours. Well, I don't want to moralise; I only wish to say that if you are inclined to a game at doubledumby, I would try and bolster myself in a chair for a rubber or so. My days are tedious, but less so, and less painful than my nights. May you never know the pain and difficulty I have in writing so much! Mary, who is most kind, joins in the wish. C. LAMB.

LETTER CCCLXXXVII.] *April* 17, 1829.

I do confess to mischief. It was the subtlest diabolical piece of malice heart of man has contrived. I have no more rheumatism than that poker. Never was freer from all pains and aches. Every joint sound, to the tip of the ear from the extremity of the lesser toe. The report of thy torments was blown circuitously here from Bury. I could not resist the jeer. I conceived you writhing when you should just receive my congratulations. How mad you'd be! Well, it is not in my method to inflict pangs. I leave that to Heaven: but in the existing pangs of a friend I have a share. His disquietude crowns my exemptions. I imagine you howling, and pace across the room, shooting out my free arms, legs, etc., this way and that way, with an assurance of not kindling a spark of pain from them. I deny that Nature meant us to sympathise with agonies. Those face-contortions, retortions, distortions have the merriness of antics. Nature meant them for farce—not so pleasant to the actor, indeed; but Grimaldi cries when we laugh, and 'tis but one that suffers to make thousands rejoice.

You say that shampooing is ineffectual; but, *per se*, it is good, to show the introvolutions, extravolutions, of which the animal frame is capable—to show what the creature is receptible of, short of dissolution.

You are worst of nights, an't you? You never was rack'd, was you? I should like an authentic map of those feelings.

You seem to have the flying gout. You can scarcely screw a smile out of your face, can you? I sit at immunity and sneer *ad libitum*. 'Tis now the time for you to make good resolutions. I may go on breaking 'em for anything the worse I find myself. Your doctor seems to keep you on the long cure. Precipitate healings are never good. Don't come while you are so bad; I shan't be able to attend to your throes and the dumby at once. I should like to know how slowly the pain goes off. But don't write, unless the motion will be likely to make your sensibility more exquisite.

Your affectionate and truly healthy friend,   C. LAMB.

Mary thought a letter from me might amuse you in your torment.

To GEORGE DYER.

LETTER CCCLXXXVIII.]   *Enfield, April 29, 1829.*

Dear Dyer—As well as a bad pen can do it, I must thank you for your friendly attention to the wishes of our young friend Emma, who was packing up for Bury when your sonnet arrived, and was too hurried to express her sense of its merits. I know she will treasure up that and your second communication among her choicest rarities, as from her *grandfather's* friend, whom not having seen, she loves to hear talked of. The second letter shall be sent after her, with our first parcel to Suffolk, where she is, to us, alas dead and Bury'd; we sorely miss her. Should you at any hour think of four or six lines, to send her, addressed to herself simply, naming her grandsire, and to wish she may pass through life as much respected, with your own G. Dyer at the end, she would feel rich indeed, for the nature of an Album asks for verses that have not been in print before; but this quite at your convenience: and to be less trouble to yourself, four lines would be sufficient. Enfield has come out in summer beauty. Come when you will and we will give you a bed.

Emma has left hers, you know. I remain, my dear Dyer, your affectionate friend, CHARLES LAMB.

To WALTER WILSON.

LETTER CCCLXXXIX.] *May* 28, 1829.

Dear W.—Introduce this, or omit it, as you like. I think I wrote better about it in a letter to you from India H. If you have that, perhaps out of the two I could patch up a better thing, if you'd return both. But I am very poorly, and have been harassed with an illness of my sister's.

The Ode was printed in the *New Times* nearly the end of 1825, and I have only omitted some silly lines, call it a corrected copy.

Yours ever, C. LAMB.

Put my name to either, or both, as you like.

Walter Wilson, Esq.,
   Burnett House,
     Near Bath, Somersetshire.

To THOMAS ALLSOP.

LETTER CCCXC.] [Summer 1829.]

At midsummer, or soon after (I will let you know the previous day), I will take a day with you in the purlieus of my old haunts. No offence has been taken, any more than meant. My house is full at present, but empty of its chief pride. She is dead to me for many months. But when I see you, then I will say, Come and see me. With undiminished friendship to you both.

Your faithful, but queer, C. L.

How you frighted me! Never write again, "Coleridge is dead," at the end of a line, and tamely come in with, "to his friends" at the beginning of another. Love is quicker, and fear from love, than the transition ocular from line to line.

To BERNARD BARTON.

LETTER CCCXCI.] *July* 3, 1829.

Dear B. B.—I am very much grieved indeed for the indisposition of poor Lucy. Your letter found me in domestic troubles. My sister is again taken ill, and I am obliged to remove her out of the house for many weeks, I fear, before I can hope to have her again. I have been very desolate indeed. My loneliness is a little abated by our young friend Emma having just come here for her holidays, and a schoolfellow of hers that was, with her. Still the house is not the same, though she is the same. Mary had been pleasing herself with the prospect of seeing her at this time; and with all their company, the house feels at times a frightful solitude. May you and I in no very long time have a more cheerful theme to write about, and congratulate upon a daughter's and a sister's perfect recovery. Do not be long without telling me how Lucy goes on. I have a right to call her by her quaker-name, you know. Emma knows that I am writing to you, and begs to be remembered to you with thankfulness for your ready contribution. Her album is filling apace. But of her contributors, one, almost the flower of it, a most amiable young man and late acquaintance of mine, has been carried off by consumption, on return from one of the Azores islands, to which he went with hopes of mastering the disease, came back improved, went back to a most close and confined counting-house, and relapsed. His name was Dibdin, grandson of the songster.

To get out of home themes, have you seen Southey's Dialogues? His lake descriptions, and the account of his library at Keswick, are very fine. But he needed not have called up the ghost of More to hold the conversations with; which might as well have passed between A and B, or Caius and Lucius. It is making too free with a defunct Chancellor and Martyr.

I feel as if I had nothing farther to write about. O I forget the prettiest letter I ever read, that I have received from "Pleasures of Memory" Rogers, in acknowledgment of a sonnet I sent him on the loss of his brother.

It is too long to transcribe, but I hope to show it you some day, as I hope some time again to see you, when all of us are well. Only it ends thus: "We were nearly of an age; he was the elder. He was the only person in the world in whose eyes I always appeared young." I will now take my leave with assuring you that I am most interested in hoping to hear favourable accounts from you. With kindest regards to A. K. and you, yours truly,
                                                            C. L.

LETTER CCCXCII.]

Enfield Chase Side, Saturday,
25th of July, A.D. 1829, 11 A.M.

There!—a fuller, plumper, juicier date never dropt from Idumean palm. Am I in the *date*-ive case now? If not, a fig for dates, which is more than a date is worth. I never stood much affected to these limitary specialties; least of all, since the date of my superannuation.

> "What have I with time to do?
> Slaves of desks, 'twas meant for you."

Dear B. B.—Your handwriting has conveyed much pleasure to me in report of Lucy's restoration. Would I could send you as good news of my poor Lucy. But some wearisome weeks I must remain lonely yet. I have had the loneliest time, near ten weeks, broken by a short apparition of Emma for her holidays, whose departure only deepened the returning solitude, and by ten days I have passed in town. But town, with all my native hankering after it, is not what it was. The streets, the shops are left; but all old friends are gone! And in London I was frightfully convinced of this as I passed houses and places, empty caskets now. I have ceased to care almost about anybody. The bodies I cared for are in graves, or dispersed. My old clubs, that lived so long and flourished so steadily, are crumbled away. When I took leave of our adopted young friend at Charing Cross, 'twas heavy unfeeling rain, and I had nowhere to go. Home have I none, and not a sympathising house to turn to in the great city. Never did the waters of heaven pour down on a forlorner head. Yet I tried ten days at a sort of friend's house, but it was large and straggling,—one of the individuals of my old long knot of friends, card-players, pleasant companions, that have tumbled to pieces, into dust and other things; and I got home on Thursday, convinced that I was better to get home to my hole at Enfield, and hide like a sick cat in my corner. Less than a month I hope will bring home Mary. She is at Fulham, looking better in her health than ever, but sadly rambling, and scarce showing any pleasure in seeing me, or curiosity when I should come again. But the old feelings will come back again, and we shall drown old sorrows over a game of picquet again. But 'tis a tedious cut out of a life of 64, to lose 12 or 13 weeks every year or two. And to make me more alone, our ill-tempered maid is gone, who, with all her airs, was yet a home-piece of furniture, a record of better days. The young thing that has succeeded her is good and attentive, but she is nothing. And I have no one here to talk over old matters with. Scolding and quarrelling have something of familiarity, and a community of interest; they imply acquaintance; they are of resentment, which is of the family of dearness.

I can neither scold nor quarrel at this insignificant implement of household services: she is less than a cat, and just better than a deal dresser. What I can do, and do over-do, is to walk; but deadly long are the days, these Summer all-day days, with but a half-hour's candlelight, and no fire-light. I do not write, tell your kind inquisitive Eliza, and can hardly read. In the ensuing *Blackwood* will be an old rejected farce of mine, which may be new to you, if you see that same medley. What things are all the magazines now! I contrive studiously not to see them. The popular *New Monthly* is perfect trash. Poor Hessey, I suppose you see, has failed; Hunt and Clarke too. Your "Vulgar Truths" will be a good name; and I think your prose must please—me at least. But 'tis useless to write poetry with no purchasers. 'Tis cold work authorship, without something to puff one into fashion. Could you not write something on Quakerism, for Quakers to read, but nominally addressed to Non-Quakers, explaining your dogmas—waiting on the Spirit —by the analogy of human calmness and patient waiting on the judgment? I scarcely know what I mean, but to make Non-Quakers reconciled to your doctrines, by showing something like them in mere human operations; but I hardly understand myself; so let it pass for nothing. I pity you for over-work; but I assure you, no work is worse. The mind preys on itself, the most unwholesome food. I bragged formerly that I could not have too much time. I have a surfeit. With few years to come, the days are wearisome. But weariness is not eternal. Something will shine out to take the load off that flags me, which is at present intolerable. I have killed an hour or two in this poor scrawl. I am a sanguinary murderer of time, and would kill him inch-meal just now. But the snake is vital. Well: I shall write merrier anon. 'Tis the present copy of my countenance I send, and to complain is a little to alleviate. May you enjoy yourself as far as the wicked wood will let you, and think that you are not quite alone as I am! Health to Lucia, and to Anna, and kind remembrances.

Your forlorn,   C. L.

To SAMUEL TAYLOR COLERIDGE.

LETTER CCCXCIII.]   *Tuesday*, 1829.

My dear Coleridge—With pain and grief, I must entreat you to excuse us on Thursday. My head, though externally correct, has had a severe concussion in my long illness, and the very idea of an engagement hanging over for a day or two, forbids my rest, and I get up miserable. I am not well enough for company. I do assure you, no other thing prevents my coming. I expect Field and his brothers this or to-morrow evening, and it worries me to death that I am not ostensibly ill enough to put 'em off. I will get better, when I shall hope to see your nephew. He will come again. Mary joins in best love to the Gillmans. Do, I earnestly entreat you, excuse me. I assure you, again, that I am not fit to go out yet.

Yours (though shattered),   C. LAMB.

To C. A. ELTON.

India House
(*to which place all letters addressed
to C. L. commonly come*),

LETTER CCCXCIV.]   *August* 12, 1829.

My dear Sir—You have overwhelmed me with your favours. I have received positively a little library from Baldwyn's. I do not know how I have deserved such a bounty.

We have been up to the ear in classics ever since it came. I have been greatly pleased, but most, I think, with the Hesiod,—the Titan battle quite amazed me. Gad, it was no child's play—and then the homely aphorisms at the end of the works—how adroitly you have turned them! Can he be the same Hesiod who did the Titans? the latter is—

"——wine
Which to madness does incline."

But to read the *Days and Weeks* is like eating nice brown bread, homely sweet and nutritive. Apollonius was new to me: I had confounded him with the conjuror of that name. Medea is glorious; but I must give up Dido. She positively is the only Fine Lady of Antiquity: her courtesy to the Trojans is altogether queen-like. Eneas is a most disagreeable person: Ascanius a pretty young master. Mezentius for my money—his dying speech shames Turpin—not the Archbishop, but the roadster of that name, I mean.

I have been ashamed to find how many names of classics (and more than their names) you have introduced me to that before I was ignorant of.

Your commendation of Master Chapman arrideth me. Can any one read the pert, modern, Frenchified notes, etc., in Pope's translation, and contrast them with solemn weighty prefaces of Chapman, writing in full faith, as he evidently does, of the plenary inspiration of his author—worshipping his meanest scraps and relics as divine—without one sceptical misgiving of their authenticity, and doubt which was the properest to expound Homer to his countrymen? Reverend Chapman! you have read his hymn to Pan (the Homeric)—why, it is Milton's blank verse clothed with rhyme! *Paradise Lost* could scarce lose, could it be so accoutred.

I shall die in the belief that he has improved upon Homer, in the *Odyssey* in particular—the disclosure of Ulysses of himself to Alcinous—his previous behaviour at the song of the stern strife arising between Achilles and himself (how it raises him above the *Iliad* Ulysses!)—but you know all these things quite as well as I do. But what a deaf ear old C. would have turned to the doubters in Homer's real personality! He apparently believed all the fables of Homer's birth, etc. etc.

Those notes of Bryant have caused the greatest disorder in my brain-pan. Well, I will not flatter when I say that we have had two or three long evenings' *good reading* out of your kind present.

I will say nothing of the tenderest parts in your own little volume, at the end of such slatternly scribble as this, but indeed they cost us some tears. I scrawl on because of interruptions every moment. You guess how it is in a busy office—papers thrust into your hand when your hand is busiest—and every anti-classical disavocation.

C. A. Elton, Esq.,
    Clifton, Bristol.

To Mr. SERJEANT TALFOURD.

Letter CCCXCV.]   [1829.]

Dear Talfourd—You could not have told me of a more friendly thing than you have been doing. I am proud of my namesake. I shall take care never to do any dirty action, pick pockets, or anyhow get myself hanged, for fear of reflecting ignominy upon your young Chrisom. I have now a motive to be good. I shall not *omnis moriar;*—my name borne down the black gulf of oblivion.

I shall survive in eleven letters, five more than Cæsar. Possibly I shall come to be knighted, or more! Sir C. L. Talfourd, Bart.!

Yet hath it an authorish twang with it, which will wear out my name for poetry. Give him a smile from me till I see him. If you do not drop down before, some day in the *week after next* I will come and take one night's lodging with you, if convenient, before you go hence. You shall name it. We are in town to-morrow *speciali gratiâ*, but by no arrangement can get up near you.

Believe us both, with greatest regards, yours and Mrs. Talfourd's.

CHARLES LAMB-PHILO-TALFOURD.

I come as near it as I can.

To MR. GILLMAN.

LETTER CCCXCVI.] *Chase Side, Enfield, October* 26, 1829.

Dear Gillman—Allsop brought me your kind message yesterday. How can I account for having not visited Highgate this long time? Change of place seemed to have changed me. How grieved I was to hear in what indifferent health Coleridge has been, and I not to know of it! A little school divinity, well applied, may be healing. I send him honest Tom of Aquin; that was always an obscure great idea to me: I never thought or dreamed to see him in the flesh, but t'other day I rescued him from a stall in Barbican and brought him off in triumph. He comes to greet Coleridge's acceptance, for his shoe-latchets I am unworthy to unloose. Yet there are pretty pro's and con's, and such unsatisfactory learning in him. Commend me to the question of etiquette—*"utrum annunciatio debuerit fieri per angelum"*—*Quæst.* 30, *Articulus* 2. I protest, till now I had thought Gabriel a fellow of some mark and livelihood, not a simple esquire, as I find him. Well, do not break your lay brains, nor I neither, with these curious nothings. They are nuts to our dear friend, whom hoping to see at your first friendly hint that it will be convenient, I end with begging our very kindest loves to Mrs. Gillman. We have had a sorry house of it here. Our spirits have been reduced till we were at hope's end what to do. Obliged to quit this house, and afraid to engage another, till in extremity, I took the desperate resolve of kicking house and all down, like Bunyan's pack; and here we are in a new life at board and lodging with an honest couple our neighbours. We have ridded ourselves of the cares of dirty acres; and the change, though of less than a week, has had the most beneficial effects on Mary already. She looks two years and a half younger for it. But we have had sore trials.

God send us one happy meeting!—Yours faithfully, C. LAMB.

To VINCENT NOVELLO.

LETTER CCCXCVII.]   [*October* 1829.]

Dear Fugueist,
   or hear'st thou rather
   Contrapuntist?—

We expect you four (as many as the table will hold without squeezing)
at Mrs. Westwood's Table d'Hôte on Thursday. You will find the White
House shut up, and us moved under the wing of the Phœnix, which gives
us friendly refuge. Beds for guests, marry, we have none, but cleanly
accommodings at the Crown and Horse-Shoe.

Yours harmonically,   C. L.

Vincentio (what, ho!) Novello, a Squire,
   66, Great Queen Street, Lincoln's Inn Fields.

To WALTER WILSON.

LETTER CCCXCVIII.]   *Enfield, November* 15, 1829.

My dear Wilson—I have not opened a packet of unknown contents
for many years that gave me so much pleasure as when I disclosed your
three volumes. I have given them a careful perusal, and they have taken
their degree of classical books upon my shelves. De Foe was always my
darling; but what darkness was I in as to far the larger part of his
writings! I have now an epitome of them all. I think the way in which
you have done the "Life" the most judicious you could have pitched
upon. You have made him tell his own story, and your comments are in
keeping with the tale. Why, I never heard of such a work as the *Review*.
Strange that in my stall-hunting days I never so much as lit upon an odd
volume of it. This circumstance looks as if they were never of any great
circulation. But I may have met with 'em, and not knowing the prize,
overpast 'em. I was almost a stranger to the whole history of Dissenters
in those reigns, and picked my way through that strange book the "Con-
solidator" at random. How affecting are some of his personal appeals!
What a machine of projects he set on foot! and following writers have
picked his pocket of the patents. I do not understand whereabouts in
"Roxana" he himself left off. I always thought the complete-tourist-
sort of description of the town she passes through on her last embarkation
miserably unseasonable and out of place. I knew not they were spurious. Enlighten me as to where the apocryphal matter commences. I, by
accident, can correct one A. D., "Family Instructor," vol. ii. 1718; you
say his first volume had then reached the fourth edition; now I have
a fifth, printed from Eman Matthews, 1717. So have I plucked one rotten date, or rather picked it up where it had inadvertently fallen, from
your flourishing date tree, the Palm of Engaddi. I may take it for my

pains. I think yours a book which every public library must have, and every English scholar should have. I am sure it has enriched my meagre stock of the author's works. I seem to be twice as opulent. Mary is by my side, just finishing the second volume. It must have interest to divert her away so long from her modern novels. Colburn will be quite jealous. I was a little disappointed at my "Ode to the Treadmill" not finding a place, but it came out of time. The two papers of mine will puzzle the reader, being so akin. Odd, that never keeping a scrap of my own letters, with some fifteen years' interval I should nearly have said the same things. But I shall always feel happy in having my name go down anyhow with De Foe's, and that of his historiographer. I promise myself, if not immortality, yet diuternity of being read in consequence. We have both had much illness this year; and feeling infirmities and fretfulness grow upon us, we have cast off the cares of housekeeping, sold off our goods, and commenced boarding and lodging with a very comfortable old couple next door to where you found us. We use a sort of common table. Nevertheless, we have reserved a private one for an old friend; and when Mrs. Wilson and you revisit Babylon, we shall pray you to make it yours for a season. Our very kindest remembrances to you both.

From your old friend and *fellow-journalist*, now in *two instances*,

C. LAMB.

Hazlitt is going to make your book a basis for a review of De Foe's Novels in the "Edinbro'." I wish I had health and spirits to do it. Hone I have not seen, but I doubt not he will be much pleased with your performance. I very much hope you will give us an account of Dunton, etc. But what I should more like to see would be a Life and Times of Bunyan. Wishing health to you, and long life to your healthy book, again I subscribe me,

Yours in verity,   C. L.

To MR. GILLMAN.

LETTER CCCXCIX.]   *November 30, 1829.*

Dear G.—The excursionists reached home, and the good town of Enfield, a little after four, without slip or dislocation. Little has transpired concerning the events of the back-journey, save that on passing the house of 'Squire Mellish, situate a stone-bow's cast from the hamlet, Father Westwood, with a good-natured wonderment, exclaimed, "I cannot think what is gone of Mr. Mellish's rooks. I fancy they have taken flight somewhere, but I have missed them two or three years past." All this while, according to his fellow-traveller's report, the rookery was darkening the air above with undiminished population, and deafening all ears but his with their cawings. But Nature has been gently withdrawing such phenomena from the notice of two of Thomas Westwood's senses, from the time he began to miss the rooks. T. Westwood has passed a retired life in this hamlet, of thirty or forty years, living upon the minimum which is consistent with gentility, yet a star among the minor gentry, receiving the bows of the tradespeople, and courtesies of the alms-women, daily. Children venerate him not less for his external show of gentry, than they wonder at him for a gentle rising endorsation of the person, not amounting to a hump, or if a hump, innocuous as the hump of the buffalo, and coronative of as mild qualities. 'Tis a throne on which patience seems to sit,—the proud perch of a self-respecting humility, stooping with condescension. Thereupon the cares of life have sate, and rid him easily. For he has thrid the *angustiæ domûs* with dexterity. Life opened upon him with comparative brilliancy. He set out as a rider or traveller for a wholesale house, in which capacity he tells of many hair-breadth escapes that befell him; one especially, how he rode a mad horse into the town of Devizes; how horse and rider arrived in a foam, to the utter consternation of the expostulating hostlers, inn-keepers, etc. It seems it was sultry weather, piping hot; the steed tormented into frenzy with gad-flies, long past being road-worthy; but safety and the interest of the house he rode for were incompatible things; a fall in serge cloth was expected, and a mad entrance they made of it. Whether the exploit was purely voluntary, or partially; or whether a certain personal defiguration in the man part of this extraordinary centaur (non-assistive to partition of natures) might not enforce the conjunction, I stand not to inquire. I look not with 'skew eyes into the deeds of heroes. The hosier that was burnt with his shop, in Field Lane, on Tuesday night, shall have past to heaven for me like a Marian Martyr, provided always that he consecrated the fortuitous incremation with a short ejaculation in the exit, as much as if he had taken his state degrees of martyrdom *informâ* in the market vicinage. There is adoptive as well as acquisitive sacrifice. Be the animus what it might, the fact is indisputable, that this composition was seen flying all abroad, and mine host of Daintry may yet remember its passing through his town, if his scores are not more faithful than his memory. After this exploit (enough for one man), Thomas Westwood seems to have subsided into a less hazardous occupation: and in the twenty-fifth year of his age we find him a haberdasher in Bow Lane: yet still retentive of his early riding (though leaving it to rawer stomachs), and Christmasly at night sithence to this last, and shall to his latest Christmas, hath he, doth he, and shall he, tell after supper the story of the insane steed and the desperate rider. Save for Bedlam or Luke's no eye could have guessed that melting day what house he rid for. But he reposes on his bridles, and after the ups and downs (metaphoric only) of a life behind the counter—hard riding sometimes, I fear, for poor T. W. —with the scrapings together of the shop, and *one anecdote*, he hath finally settled at Enfield; by hard economising, gardening, building for himself, hath reared a mansion; married a daughter; qualified a son for a counting-house; gotten the respect of high and low; served for self or substitute the greater parish offices; hath a special voice at vestries; and, domiciliating us, hath reflected a portion of his house-keeping respectability upon your humble servants. We are greater, being his lodgers, than when we were substantial renters. His name is a passport to take off the sneers of the native Enfielders against obnoxious foreigners. We are endenizened. Thus much of T. Westwood have I thought fit to acquaint you, that you may see the exemplary reliance upon Providence with which I entrusted so dear a charge as my own sister to the guidance of a man that rode the mad horse into Devizes. To come from his heroic character, all the amiable qualities of domestic life concentre in this tamed Bellerophon. He is excellent over a glass of grog; just as pleasant without it; laughs when he hears a joke, and when (which is much oftener) he hears it not; sings glorious old sea-songs on festival nights; and but upon a slight acquaintance of two years, Coleridge, is as dear a deaf old man to us as old Norris (rest his soul!) was after fifty. To him and his scanty literature (what there is of it, *sound*) have we flown from the metropolis and its damn'd annualists, reviewers, authors, and the whole muddy ink press of that stagnant pool.

Now, Gillman again, you do not know the treasure of the Fullers. I calculate on having massy reading till Christmas. All I want here is books of the true sort, not those things in boards that moderns mistake for books, what they club for at book-clubs.

I did not mean to cheat you with a blank side, but my eye smarts, for which I am taking medicine, and abstain, this day at least, from any aliments but milk porridge, the innocent taste of which I am anxious to renew after a half-century's disacquaintance. If a blot fall here like a tear, it is not pathos, but an angry eye.

Farewell, while my *specilla* are sound.

Yours and yours,   C. LAMB.

LETTER CCCC.]   [*December*] 1829.

Pray trust me with the "Church History," as well as the "Worthies." A moon shall restore both. Also give me back "Him of Aquinum." In return you have the *light of my countenance*. Adieu.

P.S.—A sister also of mine comes with it. A son of Nimshi drives her. Their driving will have been furious, impassioned. Pray God they have not toppled over the tunnel! I promise you I fear their steed, bred out of the wind without father, semi-Melchisedecish, hot, phaetontic. From my country lodgings at Enfield.   C. L.

LETTER CCCCI.]   [*December*] 1829.

Dear Gillman—Pray do you, or S. T. C., immediately write to say you have received back the golden works of the dear, fine, silly old angel, which I part from, bleeding, and to say how the Winter has used you all.

It is our intention soon, weather permitting, to come over for a day at Highgate; for beds we will trust to the Gate-House, should you be full; tell me if we may come casually, for in this change of climate there is no naming a day for walking. With best loves to Mrs. Gillman, etc.

Yours, mopish, but in health, C. LAMB.

I shall be uneasy till I hear of Fuller's safe arrival.

To BERNARD BARTON.

LETTER CCCCII.] *December 8, 1829.*

My dear B. B.—You are very good to have been uneasy about us, and I have the satisfaction to tell you that we are both in better health and spirits than we have been for a year or two past; I may say than we have been since we have been at Enfield. The cause may not appear quite adequate, when I tell you that a course of ill-health and spirits brought us to the determination of giving up our house here, and we are boarding and lodging with a worthy old couple, long inhabitants of Enfield, where everything is done for us without our trouble, further than a reasonable weekly payment. We should have done so before, but it is not easy to flesh and blood to give up an ancient establishment, to discard old Penates, and from house keepers to turn house sharers. (*N.B.* We are not in the workhouse.) Diocletian, in his garden, found more repose than on the imperial seat of Rome; and the nob of Charles the Fifth ached seldomer under a monk's cowl than under the diadem. With such shadows of assimilation we countenance our degradation. With such a load of dignified cares just removed from our shoulders, we can the more understand and pity the accession to yours, by the advancement to an assigneeship. I will tell you honestly, B. B., that it has been long my deliberate judgment that all bankrupts, of whatsoever denomination, civil or religious, ought to be hanged. The pity of mankind has for ages run in a wrong channel, and has been diverted from poor creditors—(how many I have known sufferers! Hazlitt has just been defrauded of £100 by his bookseller-friends breaking)—to scoundrel debtors. I know all the topics—that distress may come upon an honest man without his fault; that the failure of one that he trusted was his calamity, etc. Then let *both* be hanged. O how careful it would make traders! These are my deliberate thoughts, after many years' experience in matters of trade. What a world of trouble it would have saved you, if Friend * * * * had been immediately hanged, without benefit of clergy, which (being a Quaker I presume) he could not reasonably insist upon. Why, after slaving twelve months in your assign-business, you will be enabled to declare 7d. in the pound in all human probability. B. B., he should be *hanged*. Trade will never re-flourish in this land till such a law is established. I write big, not to save ink but eyes, mine having been troubled with reading through three folios of old Fuller in almost as few days, and I went to bed last night in agony, and am writing with a vial of eye-water before me, alternately dipping in vial and inkstand. This may inflame my zeal against bankrupts, but it was my speculation when I could see better. Half the world's misery (Eden else) is owing to want of money, and all that want is owing to bankrupts. I declare I would, if the state wanted practitioners, turn hangman myself, and should have great pleasure in hanging the first bankrupt after my salutary law should be established. I have seen no Annuals, and wish to see none. I like your fun upon them, and was quite pleased with Bowles's sonnet. Hood is, or was, at Brighton; but a note (prose or rhyme) to him, Robert Street, Adelphi, I am sure, would extract a copy of *his*, which also I have not seen. Wishing you and yours all health, I conclude while these frail glasses are to me—eyes.   C. L.

To WILLIAM WORDSWORTH.

LETTER CCCCIII.]   *January* 22, 1830.

And is it a year since we parted from you at the steps of Edmonton stage? There are not now the years that there used to be. The tale of the dwindled age of men, reported of successional mankind, is true of the same man only. We do not live a year in a year now. 'Tis a *punctum stans*. The seasons pass us with indifference. Spring cheers not, nor Winter heightens our gloom; Autumn hath foregone its moralities,—they are "hey-pass repass," as in a show-box. Yet, as far as last year occurs back, —for they scarce show a reflex now, they make no memory as heretofore,—'twas sufficiently gloomy. Let the sullen nothing pass. Suffice it, that after sad spirits, prolonged through many of its months, as it called them, we have cast our skins; have taken a farewell of the pompous, troublesome trifle, called housekeeping, and are settled down into poor boarders and lodgers at next door with an old couple, the Baucis and Baucida of dull Enfield. Here we have nothing to do with our victuals but to eat them; with the garden but to see it grow; with the tax-gatherer but to hear him knock; with the maid but to hear her scolded. Scot and lot, butcher, baker, are things unknown to us, save as spectators of the pageant. We are fed we know not how; quietists—confiding ravens. We have *otium pro dignitate*, a respectable insignificance. Yet in the self-condemned obliviousness, in the stagnation, some molesting yearnings of life, not quite killed, rise, prompting me that there was a London, and that I was of that old Jerusalem. In dreams I am in Fleet Market, but I wake and cry to sleep again. I die hard, a stubborn Eloisa in this detestable Paraclete. What have I gained by health? Intolerable dulness. What by early hours and moderate meals? A total blank. O never let the lying poets be believed, who 'tice men from the cheerful haunts of streets, or think they mean it not of a country village. In the ruins of Palmyra

I could gird myself up to solitude, or muse to the snorings of the Seven Sleepers; but to have a little teazing image of a town about one; country folks that do not look like country folks; shops two yards square, half-a-dozen apples, and two penn'orth of overlooked ginger-bread, for the lofty fruiterers of Oxford Street; and, for the immortal book and print stalls, a circulating library that stands still, where the show-picture is a last year's Valentine, and whither the fame of the last ten Scotch novels has not yet travelled,—(marry, they just begin to be conscious of the *Redgauntlet*:) —to have a new plastered flat church, and to be wishing that it was but a cathedral! The very blackguards here are degenerate; the topping gentry, stockbrokers; the passengers too many to insure your quiet, or let you go about whistling or gaping, too few to be the fine indifferent pageants of Fleet Street. Confining, roomkeeping, thickest Winter, is yet more bearable here than the gaudy months. Among one's books at one's fire by candle, one is soothed into an oblivion that one is not in the country; but with the light the green fields return, till I gaze, and in a calenture can plunge myself into St. Giles's. O let no native Londoner imagine that health, and rest, and innocent occupation, interchange of converse sweet, and recreative study, can make the country anything better than altogether odious and detestable! A garden was the primitive prison, till man, with Promethean felicity and boldness, luckily sinned himself out of it. Thence followed Babylon, Nineveh, Venice, London, haberdashers, goldsmiths, taverns, playhouses, satires, epigrams, puns,—these all came in on the town part, and the thither side of innocence. Man found out inventions. From my den I return you condolence for your decaying sight; not for anything there is to see in the country, but for the miss of the pleasure of reading a London newspaper. The poets are as well to listen to; anything high may, nay must, be read out; you read it to yourself with an imaginary auditor; but the light paragraphs must be glid over by the proper eye; mouthing mumbles their gossamery substance. 'Tis these trifles I should mourn in fading sight. A newspaper is the single gleam of comfort I receive here; it comes from rich Cathay with tidings of mankind. Yet I could not attend to it, read out by the most beloved voice. But your eyes do not get worse, I gather. O for the collyrium of Tobias inclosed in a whiting's liver, to send you with no apocryphal good wishes! The last long time I heard from you, you had knocked your head against something. Do not do so; for your head (I do not flatter) is not a knob, or the top of a brass rail, or the end of a nine pin,—unless a Vulcanian hammer could fairly batter a "Recluse" out of it; then would I bid the smirched god knock and knock lustily, the two-handed skinker. Mary must squeeze out a line *propriâ manu*, but indeed her fingers have been incorrigibly nervous to letter writing for a long interval. 'Twill please you all to hear, that though I fret like a lion in a net, her present health and spirits are better than they have been for some time past. She is absolutely three years and a half younger, as I tell her, since we have adopted this boarding plan.

Our providers are an honest pair, Dame W[estwood] and her husband.

He, when the light of prosperity shined on them, a moderately thriving haberdasher, within Bow bells, retired since with something under a competence; writes himself parcel gentleman; hath borne parish offices; sings fine old sea songs at threescore and ten; sighs only now and then when he thinks that he has a son on his hands, about fifteen, whom he finds a difficulty in getting out into the world, and then checks a sigh with muttering, as I once heard him prettily, not meaning to be heard, "I have married my daughter, however;" takes the weather as it comes; outsides it to town in severest season; and o'winter nights tells old stories not tending to literature (how comfortable to author-rid folks!), and has *one anecdote*, upon which and about forty pounds a year he seems to have retired in green old age. It was how he was a rider in his youth, travelling for shops, and once (not to balk his employer's bargain) on a sweltering day in August, rode foaming into Dunstable upon a mad horse, to the dismay and expostulatory wonderment of innkeepers, ostlers, etc., who declared they would not have bestrid the beast to win the Derby. Understand, the creature galled to death and desperation by gad-flies, cormorant-winged, worse than beset Inachus's daughter. This he tells, this he brindles and burnishes on a Winter's eve; 'tis his star of set glory, his rejuvenescence, to descant upon. Far from me be it (*dii avertant*) to look a gift story in the mouth, or cruelly to surmise (as those who doubt the plunge of Curtius) that the inseparate conjuncture of man and beast, the centaur-phenomenon that staggered all Dunstable, might have been the effect of unromantic necessity; that the horse-part carried the reasoning, willy nilly; that needs must when such a devil drove; that certain spiral configurations in the frame of T[homas] W[estwood] unfriendly to alighting, made the alliance more forcible than voluntary. Let him enjoy his fame for me, nor let me hint a whisper that shall dismount Bellerophon. But in case he was an involuntary martyr, yet if in the fiery conflict he buckled the soul of a constant haberdasher to him, and adopted his flames, let accident and him share the glory. You would all like Thomas Westwood. How weak is painting to describe a man! Say that he stands four feet and a nail high by his own yard measure, which, like the sceptre of Agamemnon, shall never sprout again, still you have no adequate idea; nor when I tell you that his dear hump, which I have favoured in the picture, seems to me of the buffalo—indicative and repository of mild qualities, a budget of kindnesses—still you have not the man. Knew you old Norris of the Temple? sixty years ours and our father's friend? He was not more natural to us than this old W., the acquaintance of scarce more weeks. Under his roof now ought I to take my rest, but that back-looking ambition tells me I might yet be a Londoner! Well, if we ever do move, we have incumbrances the less to impede us; all our furniture has faded under the auctioneer's hammer, going for nothing, like the tarnished frippery of the prodigal, and we have only a spoon or two left to bless us. Clothed we came into Enfield, and naked we must go out of it. I would live in London, shirtless, bookless. Henry Crabb is at Rome; advices to that effect have reached Bury. But by solemn legacy he bequeathed at parting (whether he should live or die) a turkey of Suffolk to be sent every succeeding Christmas to us and divers other friends. What a genuine old bachelor's action! I fear he will find the air of Italy too classic. His station is in the Harz forest; his soul is be-Goethed. Miss Kelly we never see; Talfourd not this half-year: the latter flourishes, but the exact number of his children (God forgive me!) I have utterly forgotten. We single people are often out in our count there. Shall I say two? We see scarce anybody. Can I cram loves enough to you all in this little O? Excuse particularising.   C. L.

To BERNARD BARTON.

LETTER CCCCIV.]   *February* 25, 1830.

Dear B. B.—To reply to you by return of post, I must gobble up my dinner and despatch this *in propriâ personâ* to the office, to be in time. So take it from me hastily, that you are perfectly welcome to furnish A C. with the scrap, which I had almost forgotten writing. The more my character comes to be known, the less my veracity will come to be suspected. Time every day clears up some suspected narrative of Herodotus, Bruce, and others of us great travellers. Why, that Joseph Paice was as real a person as Joseph Hume, and a great deal pleasanter. A careful observer of life, Bernard, has no need to invent. Nature romances it for him. Dinner plates rattle, and I positively shall incur indigestion by carrying it half concocted to the post-house. Let me congratulate you on the Spring coming in, and do you in return condole with me on the Winter going out. When the old one goes, seldom comes a better. I dread the prospect of Summer, with his all-day-long days. No need of his assistance to make country places dull. With fire of candle-light I can dream myself in Holborn. With lightsome skies shining in to bed-time I can not. This Mesech, and these tents of Kedar—I would dwell in the skirts of Jericho rather, and think every blast of the coming-in mail a ram's horn. Give me old London at fire and plague times, rather than these tepid gales, healthy country air, and purposeless exercise.

Leg of mutton absolutely on the table.

Take our hasty loves and short farewell.   C. L.

To MRS. HAZLITT.

LETTER CCCCV.]   *March* 4, 1830.

Dear Sarah—I was meditating to come and see you, but I am unable for the walk. We are both very unwell, and under affliction for poor Emma, who has had a very dangerous brain fever, and is lying very ill at Bury, from whence I expect a summons to fetch her. We are very sorry for your confinement. Any books I have are at your service. I am almost, I may say *quite* sure, that letters to India pay no postage, and may go by the regular Post Office, now in St. Martin's le Grand. I think any receiving house would take them. I wish I could confirm your hopes about Dick Norris. But it is quite a dream. Some old Bencher of his surname is made *Treasurer* for the year, I suppose, which is an annual office. Norris was Sub-Treasurer, quite a different thing. They were pretty well in the Summer; since when we have heard nothing of them.

Mrs. Reynolds is better than she has been for years. She is with a disagreeable woman that she has taken a mighty fancy to, out of spite to a rival woman she used to live and quarrel with. She grows quite *fat,* they tell me, and may live as long as I do, to be a tormenting rent-charge to my diminished income. We go on pretty comfortably in our new place. I will come and have a talk with you when poor Emma's affair is settled, and will bring books. At present I am weak, and could hardly bring my legs home yesterday after a much shorter stroll than to Northaw. Mary has got her bonnet on for a short expedition. May you get better, as the Spring comes on. She sends her best love.

With mine.   C. L.

Mrs. Hazlitt,
 Mrs. Tomlinson's,
 Northaw, near Potter's Bar, Herts.

To Rev. JAMES GILLMAN.

LETTER CCCCVI.]   *March* 8, 1830.

My dear G.—Your friend Battin (for I knew him immediately by the smooth satinity of his style) must excuse me for advocating the cause of his friends in Spitalfields. The fact is, I am retained by the Norwich people, and have already appeared in their paper under the signatures of "Lucius Sergius," "Bluff," "Broad-Cloth," "No-trade-to-the-Woollen-Trade," "Anti-plush," etc., in defence of druggets and long camblets. And without this pre-engagement, I feel I should naturally have chosen a side opposite to ——, for in the silken seemingness of his nature there is that which offends me. My flesh tingles at such caterpillars. He shall not crawl me over. Let him and his workmen sing the old burthen,

"Heigh ho, ye weavers!"

for any aid I shall offer them in this emergency. I was over St. Luke's the other day with my friend Tuthill, and mightily pleased with one of his contrivances for the comfort and amelioration of the students. They have double cells, in which a pair may lie feet to feet horizontally, and chat the time away as rationally as they can. It must certainly be more sociable for them these warm raving nights. The right-hand truckle in one of these friendly recesses, at present vacant, was preparing, I understood, for Mr. Irving. Poor fellow! it is time he removed from Pentonville. I followed him as far as to Highbury the other day, with a mob at his heels, calling out upon Ermigiddon, who I suppose is some Scotch moderator. He squinted out his favourite eye last Friday, in the fury of possession, upon a poor woman's shoulders that was crying matches, and has not missed it. The companion truck, as far as I could measure it with my eye, would conveniently fit a person about the length of Coleridge, allowing for a reasonable drawing up of the feet, not at all painful. Does he talk of moving this quarter? You and I have too much sense to trouble ourselves with revelations; marry, to the same in Greek you may have something professionally to say. Tell C. that he was to come and see us some fine day. Let it be before he moves, for in his new quarters he will necessarily be confined in his conversation to his brother prophet. Conceive the two Rabbis foot to foot, for there are no Gamaliels there to affect an humbler posture! All are masters in that Patmos, where the law is perfect equality; Latmos I should rather say, for they will be Luna's twin darlings; her affection will be ever at the full. Well; keep *your* brains moist with gooseberry this mad March, for the devil of exposition seeketh dry places.   C. L.

To WILLIAM AYRTON.

Letter CCCCVII.]   *Mr. Westwood's, Chase Side, Enfield,*
March 14, 1830.

My dear Ayrton—Your letter, which was only not so pleasant as your appearance would have been, has revived some old images,—Phillips (not the Colonel), with his few hairs bristling up at the charge of a revoke, which he declares impossible; the old Captain's significant nod over the right shoulder (was it not?); Mrs. B——'s determined questioning of the score, after the game was absolutely gone to the d—l; the plain but hospitable cold boiled-beef suppers at sideboard: all which fancies, red-olent of middle age and strengthful spirits, come across us ever and anon in this vale of deliberate senectitude, ycleped Enfield.

You imagine a deep gulf between you and us; and there is a pitiable hiatus in *kind* between St. James's Park and this extremity of Middlesex. But the mere distance in turnpike roads is a trifle. The roof of a coach swings you down in an hour or two. We have a sure hot joint on a Sunday; and when had we better? I suppose you know that ill health has obliged us to give up housekeeping; but we have an asylum at the very next door (only twenty-four inches further from town, which is not material in a country expedition), where a *table d'hôte* is kept for us, without trouble on our parts, and we adjourn after dinner, when one of the old world (old friends) drops casually down among us. Come and find us out; and seal our judicious change with your approbation, whenever the whim bites, or the sun prompts. No need of announcement, for we are sure to be at home.

I keep putting off the subject of my answer. In truth I am not in spirits at present to see Mr. Murray on such a business; but pray offer him my acknowledgments, and an assurance that I should like at least one of his propositions, as I have so much additional matter for the SPECIMENS as might make two volumes in all; or ONE (new edition), omitting such better-known authors as Beaumont and Fletcher, Jonson, etc.

But we are both in trouble at present. A very dear young friend of ours, who passed her Christmas holidays here, has been taken dangerously ill with a fever, from which she is very precariously recovering, and I expect a summons to fetch her when she is well enough to bear the journey from Bury. It is Emma Isola, with whom we got acquainted at our first visit to your sister at Cambridge, and she has been an occasional inmate with us (and of late years much more frequently) ever since. While she is in this danger, and till she is out of it, and here in a probable way to recovery, I feel that I have no spirits for an engagement of any kind. It has been a terrible shock to us; therefore I beg that you will make my handsomest excuses to Mr. Murray.

Our very kindest loves to Mrs. A. and the younger A.'s.

Your unforgotten,   C. LAMB.

To MRS. WILLIAMS.

LETTER CCCCVIII.]   *Enfield, April* 2, 1830.

Dear Madam—I have great pleasure in letting you know Miss Isola has suffered very little from fatigue on her long journey. I am ashamed to say that I came home rather the more tired of the two; but I am a very unpractised traveller. We found my sister very well in health, only a little impatient to see her; and after a few hysterical tears for gladness, all was comfortable again. We arrived here from Epping between five and six.

The incidents of our journey were trifling, but you bade us tell them. We had then in the coach a rather talkative gentleman, but very civil all the way; and took up a servant maid at Stortford going to a sick mistress. To the latter a participation in the hospitalities of your nice rusks and sandwiches proved agreeable, as it did to my companion, who took merely a sip of the weakest wine and water with them. The former engaged me in a discourse for full twenty miles, on the probable advantages of steam carriages, which, being merely problematical, I bore my part in with some credit, in spite of my totally un-engineer-like faculties. But when, somewhere about Stanstead, he put an unfortunate question to me, as to "the probability of its turning out a good turnip season," and when I, who am still less of an agriculturist than a steam philosopher, not knowing a turnip from a potato ground, innocently made answer, "I believe it depends very much upon boiled legs of mutton," my unlucky reply set Miss Isola a laughing to a degree that disturbed her tranquillity for the only moment in our journey. I am afraid my credit sank very low with my other fellow-traveller, who had thought he had met with a *well-informed passenger*, which is an accident so desirable in a stage coach. We were rather less communicative, but still friendly, the rest of the way.

How I employed myself between Epping and Enfield, the poor verses in the front of my paper may inform you, which you may please to christen an "Acrostic in a Cross Road," and which I wish were worthier of the lady they refer to; but I trust you will plead my pardon to her on a subject so delicate as a lady's good *name*. Your candour must acknowledge that they are written straight. And now, dear Madam, I have left myself hardly space to express my sense of the friendly reception I found at Fornham. Mr. Williams will tell you that we had the pleasure of a slight meeting with him on the road, where I could almost have told him, but that it seemed ungracious, that such had been your hospitality, that I scarcely missed the good master of the family at Fornham, though heartily I should have rejoiced to have made a little longer acquaintance with him. I will say nothing of our deeper obligations to both of you, because I think we agreed at Fornham that gratitude may be over-exacted on the part of the obliging, and over-expressed on the part of the obliged person.

My sister and Miss Isola join in respects to Mr. Williams and yourself. Miss Isola will have the pleasure of writing to you next week, and we shall hope at your leisure to hear of your own health, etc.

I am, dear Madam, with great respect, your obliged

CHARLES LAMB.

LETTER CCCCIX.] *Enfield, Good Friday*, 1830.

Dear Madam—I do assure you that your verses gratified me very much, and my sister is quite *proud* of them. For the first time in my life I congratulated myself upon the shortness and meanness of my name. Had it been Schwartzenberg or Esterhazy, it would have put you to some puzzle. I am afraid I shall sicken you of acrostics, but this last was written *to order*. I beg you to have inserted in your country paper something like this advertisement: "To the nobility, gentry, and others, about Bury.—C. Lamb respectfully informs his friends and the public in general, that he is leaving off business in the acrostic line, and he is going into an entirely new line. Rebuses and Charades done as usual, and upon the old terms. Also, Epitaphs to suit the memory of any person deceased."

I thought I had adroitly escaped the rather unpliable name of "Williams," curtailing your poor daughters to their proper surnames; but it seems you would not let me off so easily. If these trifles amuse you, I am paid. Though really 'tis an operation too much like—"A, applepie; B, bit it." To make amends, I request leave to lend you the "Excursion," and to recommend, in particular, the "Churchyard Stories,"—in the seventh book, I think. They will strengthen the tone of your mind after its weak diet on acrostics.

Miss Isola is writing, and will tell you that we are going on very comfortably. Her sister is just come. She blames my last verses, as being more written on Mr. Williams than on yourself; but how should I have parted whom a Superior Power has brought together? I beg you will jointly accept of our best respects, and pardon your obsequious if not troublesome correspondent, C. L.

P.S.—I am the worst folder-up of a letter in the world, except certain Hottentots, in the land of Caffre, who never fold up their letters at all, writing very badly upon skins, etc.

To ROBERT SOUTHEY.

LETTER CCCCX.] *May* 10, 1830.

Dear Southey—My friend Hone, whom you would like *for a friend,* I found deeply impressed with your generous notice of him in your beautiful *Life of Bunyan,* which I am just now full of. He has written to you for leave to publish a certain good-natured letter. I write not this to enforce his request, for we are fully aware that the refusal of such publication would be quite consistent with all that is good in your character. Neither he nor I expect it from you, nor exact it; but if you would consent to it, you would oblige me by it, as well as him. He is just now in a critical situation: kind friends have opened a coffee-house for him in the City, but their means have not extended to the purchase of coffee-pots, credit for Reviews, newspapers, and other paraphernalia. So I am sitting in the skeleton of a possible divan. What right I have to interfere, you best know. Look on me as a dog who went once temporarily insane, and bit you, and now begs for a crust. Will you set your wits to a dog?

Our object is to open a subscription, which my friends of the *Times* are most willing to forward for him, but think that a leave from you to publish would aid it.

But not an atom of respect or kindness will or shall it abate in either of us if you decline it. Have this strongly in your mind.

Those *Every-Day* and *Table* Books will be a treasure a hundred years hence, but they have failed to make Hone's fortune.

Here his wife and all his children are about me, gaping for coffee customers; but how should they come in, seeing no pot boiling!

Enough of Hone. I saw Coleridge a day or two since. He has had some severe attack, not paralytic; but if I had not heard of it I should not have found it out. He looks, and especially speaks, strong. How are all the Wordsworths and all the Southeys? whom I am obliged to you if you have not brought up haters of the name of C. LAMB.

P.S.—I have gone lately into the acrostic line. I find genius (such as I had) declines with me, but I get clever. Do you know anybody that wants charades, or such things, for Albums? I do 'em at so much a sheet. Perhaps an epigram (not a very happy-gram) I did for a schoolboy yesterday may amuse. I pray Jove he may not get a flogging for any false quantity; but 'tis, with one exception, the only Latin verses I have made for forty years; and I did it "to order."

CUIQUE SUUM.

Adsciscit sibi divitias et opes alienas
Fur, rapiens, spolians quod mihi, quodque tibi,
Proprium erat, temnens haec verba, meumque tuumque;
Omne suum est: tandem cuique suum tribuit:
Dat resti collum; vestes, vah! carnifici dat;
Sese Diabolo: sic bene, Cuique suum.

I write from Hone's; therefore Mary cannot send her love to Mrs. Southey, but I do.

Yours ever,   C. L.

To Mr. MOXON.

LETTER CCCCXI.]   *May* 12, 1830.

Dear M.—I dined with your and my Rogers, at Mr. Cary's yesterday. Cary consulted me on the proper bookseller to offer a lady's MS. novel to. I said I would write to *you*. But I wish you would call on the translator of Dante, at the British Museum, and talk with him. He is the pleasantest of clergymen. I told him of all Rogers's handsome behaviour to you, and you are already no stranger. Go! I made Rogers laugh about your Nightingale Sonnet, not having heard one. 'Tis a good sonnet, notwithstanding. You shall have the books shortly.   C. L.

To Dr. ASBURY.

LETTER CCCCXII.]   [*May* 1830.]

Dear Sir—Some draughts and boluses have been brought here which we conjecture were meant for the young lady whom you saw this morning, though they are labelled for

Miss ISOLA LAMB.

No such person is known on the Chase Side, and she is fearful of taking medicines which may have been made up for another patient. She begs me to say that she was born an *Isola* and christened *Emma*. Moreover that she is Italian by birth, and that her ancestors were from Isola Bella (Fair Island) in the kingdom of Naples. She has never changed her name and rather mournfully adds that she has not prospect at present of doing so. She is literally I. SOLA, or single, at present. Therefore she begs that the obnoxious monosyllable may be omitted on future Phials,—an innocent syllable enough, you'll say, but she has no claim to it. It is the bitterest pill of the seven you have sent her. When a lady loses her good *name*, what is to become of her? Well she must swallow it as well as she can, but begs the dose may not be repeated.

Yours faithfully, CHARLES LAMB (not Isola).

To VINCENT NOVELLO.

LETTER CCCCXIII.] *Friday, May* 14, 1830.

Dear Novello—Mary hopes you have not forgot you are to spend a day with us on Wednesday. That it may be a long one, cannot you secure places now for Mrs. Novello, yourself, and the Clarkes? We have just tableroom for four. Five make my good landlady fidgety; six, to begin to fret; seven, to approximate to fever-point. But, seriously, we shall prefer four to two or three. We shall have from half-past ten to six, when the coach goes off, to scent the country. And pray write *now*, to say you do so come, for dear Mrs. Westwood else will be on the tenters of incertitude. C. L.

Vincent Novello, Esq.,
66, Great Queen Street, Lincoln's-Inn Fields.

To MR. HONE.

LFTTER CCCCXIV.] *May* 21, 1830.

Dear Hone—I thought you would be pleased to see this letter. Pray, if you have time, to call on Novello, No. 66, Great Queen St. I am anxious to learn whether he received his Album I sent on Friday by our nine o'clock morning stage. If not, beg him inquire at the *Old Bell*, Holborn.
CHARLES LAMB.

Southey will see in the *Times* all we proposed omitting is omitted.

To VINCENT NOVELLO.

LETTER CCCCXV.] *May* 1830.

Dear N.—Pray write immediately to say "The Book has come safe." I am anxious, not so much for the autographs, as for that bit of the hairbrush. I enclose a cinder which belonged to Shield, when he was poor, and lit his own fires. Any memorial of a great musical genius, I know, is acceptable; and Shield has his merits, though Clementi, in my opinion, is far above him in the Sostenuto. Mr. Westwood desires his compliments, and begs to present you with a nail that came out of Jomelli's coffin, who is buried at Naples. C. LAMB.

To Mrs. HAZLITT.

LETTER CCCCXVI.]   *May 24, 1830.*

Mary's love? Yes. Mary Lamb is quite well.

Enfield, Saturday.

Dear Sarah—I found my way to Northaw on Thursday, and saw a very good woman behind a counter, who says also that you are a very good lady. I did not accept her offered glass of wine (home-made, I take it), but craved a cup of ale, with which I seasoned a slice of cold lamb, from a sandwich box, which I ate in her back-parlour, and proceeded for Berkhampstead, etc.; lost myself over a heath, and had a day's pleasure. I wish you could walk as I do, and as you used to do. I am sorry to find you are so poorly; and, now I have found my way, I wish you back at Goody Tomlinson's. What a pretty village 'tis! I should have come sooner, but was waiting a summons to Bury. Well, it came; and I found the good parson's lady (he was from home) exceedingly hospitable.

Poor Emma, the first moment we were alone, took me into a corner, and said, "Now, pray, don't *drink;* do check yourself after dinner, for my sake, and when we get home to Enfield you shall drink as much as ever you please, and I won't say a word about it." How I behaved, you may guess, when I tell you that Mrs. Williams and I have written acrostics on each other, and she hoped that she should have "no reason to regret Miss Isola's recovery, by its depriving *her* of our begun correspondence." Emma stayed a month with us, and has gone back (in tolerable health) to her long home, for *she* comes not again for a twelvemonth. I amused Mrs. Williams with an occurrence on our road to Enfield. We travelled with one of those troublesome fellow-passengers in a stage coach, that is called a well-inform'd man. For twenty miles we discoursed about the properties of steam, probabilities of carriage by ditto, till all my science, and more than all, was exhausted, and I was thinking of escaping my torment by getting up on the outside, when, getting into Bishops Stortford, my gentleman, spying some farming land, put an unlucky question to me: "What sort of a crop of turnips do you think we shall have this year?" Emma's eyes turned to me, to know what in the world I could have to say; and she burst into a violent fit of laughter, maugre her pale, serious cheeks, when, with the greatest gravity, I replied, that "it depends, I believe, upon boiled legs of mutton." This clenched our conversation; and my gentleman, with a face half wise, half in scorn, troubled us with no more conversation, scientific or philosophical, for the remainder of our journey. Ayrton was here yesterday, and as *learned* to the full as my fellow-traveller. What a pity that he will spoil a wit and a devilish pleasant fellow (as he is) by wisdom. He talked on music, and by having read Hawkins and Burney recently, I was enabled to talk of names, and show more knowledge than he had suspected I possessed; and in the end he begged me to shape my thoughts upon paper, which I did after he was gone, and sent him.

FREE THOUGHTS ON SOME EMINENT COMPOSERS.

> Some cry up Haydn, some Mozart,
> Just as the whim bites. For my part,
> I do not care a farthing candle
> For either of them, or for Handel, etc.

Martin Burney is as good and as odd as ever. We had a dispute about the word "heir," which I contended was pronounced like "air." He said that might be in common parlance; or that we might so use it, speaking of the "Heir at Law," a comedy; but that in the law courts it was necessary to give it a full aspiration, and to say *Hayer;* he thought it might even vitiate a cause, if a counsel pronounced it otherwise. In conclusion, he "would consult Serjeant Wilde;" who gave it against him. Sometimes he falleth into the water; sometimes into the fire. He came down here, and insisted on reading Virgil's "Eneid" all through with me (which he did,) because a Counsel must know Latin. Another time he read out all the Gospel of St. John, because Biblical quotations are very emphatic in a Court of Justice. A third time he would carve a fowl, which he did very ill-favouredly, because "we did not know how indispensable it was for a barrister to do all those things well—those little things were of more consequence than we supposed." So he goes on, harassing about the way to prosperity, and losing it; with a long head, but somewhat a wrong one —harum-scarum. Why does not his guardian angel look to him? He deserves one: may be, he has tired him out.

I am tired with this long scrawl, but I thought in your exile you might like a letter. Commend me to all the wonders in Derbyshire; and tell the devil I humbly kiss my—hand to him.

Yours ever,   C. LAMB.

London, May 24, 1830.

Mrs. Hazlitt,
    Mr. Broomhead's,
        St. Anne's Square, Buxton.

LETTER CCCCXVII.]   *June 3, 1830.*

Dear Sarah—I named your thought about William to his father, who expressed such horror and aversion to the idea of his singing in public, that I cannot meddle in it directly or indirectly. Ayrton is a kind fellow; and if you chuse to consult him by letter, or otherwise, he will give you the best advice, I am sure, very readily. *I have no doubt that M. Burney's objection to interfering was the same with mine.* With thanks for your pleasant long letter, which is not that of an invalid, and sympathy for your sad sufferings,

I remain, in haste, Yours truly.   [NO SIGNATURE.]

Mary's kindest love.

Mrs. Hazlitt, at Mr. Broomhead's,
   St. Anne's Square, Buxton.

To WILLIAM HONE.

LETTER CCCCXVIII.]   *Enfield, June* 17, 1830.

I hereby impower Mathilda Hone to superintend daily the putting into the twopenny post the *Times* newspaper of the day before, directed "Mr. Lamb, Enfield," which shall be held a *full and sufficient direction;* the said insertion to commence on Monday morning next. And I do engage to pay to William Hone, Coffee and Hotel Man, the quarterly sum of £1, to be paid at the ordinary Quarter days, or thereabout, for the reversion of the said paper, commencing with the 24th inst., or Feast of John the Baptist; the intervening days to be held and considered as nothing.   C. LAMB.

Vivant Coffee, Coffee-potque!

Mr. Hone,
  Coffee-house and Hotel,
    13, Gracechurch Street, London.

To BERNARD BARTON.

LETTER CCCCXIX.]   *June* 28, 1830.

Dear B. B.—Could you dream of my publishing without sending a copy to you? You will find something new to you in the volume, particularly the translations. Moxon will send to you the moment it is out. He is the young poet of *Christmas,* whom the Author of the "Pleasures of Memory" has set up in the book-vending business with a volunteer'd loan of £500. Such munificence is rare to an almost stranger; but Rogers, I am told, has done many good-natured things of this kind.

I need not say how glad to see A. K. and Lucy we should have been,— and still shall be, if it be practicable. Our direction is Mr. Westwood's, Chase Side, Enfield; but alas I know not theirs. We can give them a bed. Coaches come daily from the Bell, Holborn.

You will see that I am worn to the poetical dregs, condescending to acrostics, which are nine fathom beneath album verses; but they were written at the request of the lady where our Emma is, to whom I paid a visit in April to bring home Emma for a change of air after a severe illness, in which she had been treated like a daughter by the good Parson and his whole family. She has since returned to her occupation. I thought on you in Suffolk, but was forty miles from Woodbridge. I heard of you the other day from Mr. Pulham of the India House.

Long live King William the IVth!

S. T. C. says we have had wicked kings, foolish kings, wise kings, good kings (but few), but never till now have we had a blackguard king.

Charles the Second was profligate, but a gentleman.

I have nineteen letters to dispatch this leisure Sabbath for Moxon to send with copies; so you will forgive me short measure, and believe me,

Yours ever,   C. L.

Pray do let us see your Quakeresses if possible.

To WILLIAM HONE.

LETTER CCCCXX.]   *July* 1, 1830.

Pray let Mathilda keep my newspapers till you hear from me, as we are meditating a town residence.   C. LAMB.

Let her keep them as the apple of her eye.

Mr. Hone,
13, Gracechurch Street.

To MRS. RICKMAN.

LETTER CCCCXXI.]   [Undated, and no post-mark.]
                                                              Enfield [1830].

Dear Mrs. Rickman—I beg your acceptance of a little Volume, which may amuse either of your young Ladies. It pretends to no high flights, and may lie about with albums, shells, and such knick nacks. Will you re-give, or *lend* me, by the bearer, the one Volume of Juvenile Poetry? I have tidings of a second at Brighton. If the two tally, we may some day play a hand at old Whist, *who shall have both*.

With best regards to you all, yours ever,   C. LAMB.

Any little commissions in the Book line from Mr. Rickman, or any of your friends, will be most punctually attended to by my friend the Publisher.

To BERNARD BARTON.

LETTER CCCCXXII.]   *August* 30, 1830.

Dear B. B.—My address is 34, Southampton Buildings, Holborn. For God's sake do not let me be pester'd with Annuals. They are all rogues who edit them, and something else who write in them. I am still alone, and very much out of sorts, and cannot spur up my mind to writing. The sight of one of those year books makes me sick. I get nothing by any of 'em, not even a copy.

Thank you for your warm interest about my little volume, for the critics on which I care the five hundred thousandth part of the tythe of a half-farthing. I am too old a Militant for that. How noble, tho', in Robert Southey to come forward for an old friend, who had treated him so unworthily!

Moxon has a shop without customers, I a book without readers. But what a clamour against a poor collection of Album verses, as if we had put forth an Epic! I cannot scribble a long letter: I am, when not on foot, very desolate, and take no interest in anything, scarce hate anything but Annuals. I am in an interregnum of thought and feeling. What a beautiful Autumn morning this is, if it was but with me as in times past when the candle of the Lord shined round me! I cannot even muster enthusiasm to admire the French heroism. In better times I hope we may some day meet, and discuss an old poem or two. But if you'd have me not sick, no more of Annuals.   C. L., Ex-Elia.

Love to Lucy and A. K. always.

To VINCENT NOVELLO.

LETTER CCCCXXIII.]   *November* 8, 1830.

> Tears are for lighter griefs. Man weeps the doom
> That seals a single victim to the tomb.
> But when Death riots, when with whelming sway
> Destruction sweeps a family away;
> When Infancy and Youth, a huddled mass,
> All in an instant to oblivion pass,
> And Parent hopes are crush'd: what lamentation
> Can reach the depth of such a desolation?
> Look upward, Feeble Ones! look up, and trust,
> That He, who lays this mortal frame in dust,
> Still hath the immortal Spirit in His keeping.
> In Jesus' sight they are not dead, but sleeping.

Dear N., will these lines do? I despair of better. Poor Mary is in a deplorable state here at Enfield.

Love to all,   C. LAMB.

To MR. MOXON.

LETTER CCCCXXIV.]   *November* 12, 1830.

Dear Moxon—I have brought my sister to Enfield, being sure that she had no hope of recovery in London. Her state of mind is deplorable beyond any example. I almost fear whether she has strength at her time of life ever to get out of it. Here she must be nursed, and neither see nor hear of anything in the world out of her sick chamber. The mere hearing that Southey had called at our lodgings totally upset her. Pray see him, or hear of him at Mr. Rickman's, and excuse my not writing him. I dare not write or receive a letter in her presence; every little talk so agitates her. Westwood will receive any letter for me, and give it me privately.

Pray assure Southey of my kindliest feelings towards him; and if you do not see him, send this to him.

Kindest remembrances to your sister, and believe me ever yours,

C. LAMB.

Remember me kindly to the Allsops.

To GEORGE DYER.

LETTER CCCCXXV.]   *December 20, 1830.*

Dear Dyer—I should have written before to thank you for your kind letter, written with your own hand. It glads us to see your writing. It will give you pleasure to hear that after so much illness we are in tolerable health and spirits once more. Poor Enfield, that has been so peaceable hitherto, has caught the inflammatory fever; the tokens are upon her; and a great fire was blazing last night in the barns and haystacks of a farmer, about half a mile from us. Where will these things end? There is no doubt of its being the work of some ill-disposed rustic; but how is he to be discovered? They go to work in the dark with strange chemical preparations, unknown to our forefathers. There is not even a dark lantern, to have a chance of detecting these Guy Fauxes. We are past the iron age, and are got into the fiery age, undreamed of by Ovid. You are lucky in Clifford's Inn, where I think you have few ricks or stacks worth the burning. Pray, keep as little corn by you as you can for fear of the worst. It was never good times in England since the poor began to speculate upon their condition. Formerly they jogged on with as little reflection as horses. The whistling ploughman went cheek by jowl with his brother that neighed. Now the biped carries a box of phosphorous in his leather breeches, and in the dead of night the half-illuminated beast steals his magic potion into a cleft in a barn, and half the country is grinning with new fires. Farmer Graystock said something to the touchy rustic, that he did not relish, and he writes his distaste in flames. What a power to intoxicate his crude brains, just muddlingly awake to perceive that something is wrong in the social system,—what a hellish faculty above gunpowder! Now the rich and poor are fairly pitted. We shall see who can hang or burn fastest. It is not always revenge that stimulates these kindlings. There is a love of exerting mischief. Think of a disrespected clod that was trod into earth, that was nothing, on a sudden by damned arts refined into an exterminating angel, devouring the fruits of the earth and their growers in a mass of fire; what a new existence! What a temptation above Lucifer's! Would Clod be anything but a clod if he could resist it? Why, here was a spectacle last night for a whole country, a bonfire visible to London, alarming her guilty towers, and shaking the Monument with an ague fit, all done by a little vial of phosphor in a clown's fob. How he must grin, and shake his empty noddle in clouds! The Vulcanian epicure! Alas! can we ring the bells backward? Can we unlearn the arts that pretend to civilise, and then burn the world? There is a march of science; but who shall beat the drums for its retreat? Who shall persuade the boor that phosphor will not ignite? Seven goodly stacks of hay, with cornbarns proportionable, lie smoking ashes and chaff, which man and beast would sputter out and reject like those apples of asphaltes and bitumen. The food for the inhabitants of earth will quickly disappear. Hot rolls may say, "Fuimus panes, fuit quartern-loaf, et ingens gloria apple-pasty-orum." That the good old munching system may last thy time and mine, good un-incendiary George, is the devout prayer of thine,

To the last crust, C. LAMB.

LETTER CCCCXXVI.] *February* 22, 1831.

Dear Dyer—Mr. Rogers, and Mr. Rogers's friends, are perfectly as-sured that you never intended any harm by an innocent couplet, and that in the revivification of it by blundering Barker you had no hand what-ever. To imagine that at this time of day Rogers broods over a fantastic expression of more than thirty years' standing, would be to suppose him indulging his "Pleasures of Memory" with a vengeance. You never penned a line which for its own sake you need, dying, wish to blot. You mistake your heart if you think you *can* write a lampoon. Your whips are rods of roses. Your spleen has ever had for its object vices, not the vicious; abstract offences, not the concrete sinner. But you are sensitive, and wince as much at the consciousness of having committed a compli-ment, as another man would at the perpetration of an affront. But do not lug me into the same soreness of conscience with yourself. I maintain, and will to the last hour, that I never writ of you but *con amore;* that if any allusion was made to your nearsightedness, it was not for the purpose of mocking an infirmity, but of connecting it with scholar-like habits: for is it not erudite and scholarly to be somewhat near of sight before age naturally brings on the malady? You could not then plead, the *obrepens senectus.* Did I not moreover make it an apology for a certain *absence,* which some of our friends may have experienced, when you have not on a sudden made recognition of them in a casual street-meeting? And did I not strengthen your excuse for this slowness of recognition, but further accounting morally for the present engagement of your mind in worthy objects? Did I not, in your person, make the handsomest apology for ab-sent-of-mind people that was ever made? If these things be not so, I never knew what I wrote, or meant by my writing, and have been penning libels all my life without being aware of it. Does it follow that I should have exprest myself exactly in the same way of those dear old eyes of yours *now*, now that Father Time has conspired with a hard task-master to put a last extinguisher upon them? I should as soon have insulted the Answerer of Salmasius when he awoke up from his ended task and saw no more with mortal vision. But you are many films removed yet from Milton's calamity. You write perfectly intelligibly. Marry, the letters are not all of the same size or tallness; but that only shows your proficiency in the *hands*, text, german-hand, court-hand, sometimes law-hand, and affords variety. You pen better than you did a twelvemonth ago; and if you continue to improve, you bid fair to win the golden pen which is the prize at your young gentlemen's academy. But you must beware of Valpy, and his printing-house, that hazy cave of Trophonius, out of which it was a mercy that you escaped with a glimmer. Beware of MSS. and Variæ Lectiones. Settle the text for once in your mind, and stick to it. You have some years' good sight in you yet, if you do not tamper with it. It is not for you (for *us* I should say) to go poring into Greek contractions, and star-gazing upon slim Hebrew points. We have yet the sight

> Of sun, and moon, and star, throughout the year,
> And man and woman.

You have vision enough to discern Mrs. Dyer from the other comely gentlewoman who lives up at staircase No. 5; or, if you should make a blunder in the twilight, Mrs. Dyer has too much good sense to be jealous for a mere effect of imperfect optics. But don't try to write the Lord's Prayer, Creed, and Ten Commandments in the compass of a half-penny; nor run after a midge, or a mote, to catch it; and leave off hunting for needles in bundles of hay, for all these things strain the eyes. The snow is six feet deep in some parts here. I must put on jack-boots to get at the Post-Office with this. It is not good for weak eyes to pore upon snow too much. It lies in drifts. I wonder what its drift is; only that it makes good pancakes, remind Mrs. Dyer. It turns a pretty green world into a white one. It glares too much for an innocent colour methinks. I wonder why you think I dislike gilt edges. They set off a letter marvellously. Yours, for instance, looks for all the world like a tablet of curious *hieroglyphics* in a gold frame. But don't go and lay this to your eyes. You always wrote hieroglyphically, yet not to come up to the mystical notations and conjuring characters of Dr. Parr. You never wrote what I call a schoolmaster's hand, like Mrs. Clarke; nor a woman's hand, like Southey; nor a missal hand, like Porson; nor an all-of-the-wrong-side sloping hand, like Miss Hayes; nor a dogmatic, Mede-and-Persian, peremptory hand, like Rickman; but you ever wrote what I call a Grecian's hand; what the Grecians write (or used) at Christ's Hospital; such as Whalley would have admired, and Boyer have applauded, but Smith or Atwood (writing-masters) would have horsed you for. Your boy-of-genius hand and your mercantile hand are various. By your flourishes, I should think you never learned to make eagles or corkscrews, or flourish the governors' names in the writing-school; and by the tenour and cut of your letters, I suspect you were never in it at all. By the length of this scrawl you will think I have a design upon your optics; but I have writ as large as I could, out of respect to them; too large, indeed, for beauty. Mine is a sort of deputy Grecian's hand; a little better, and more of a worldly hand, than a Grecian's, but still remote from the mercantile. I don't know how it is, but I keep my rank in fancy still since school-days. I can never forget I was a deputy Grecian! And writing to you, or to Coleridge, besides affection, I feel a reverential deference as to Grecians still. I keep my soaring way above the Great Erasmians, yet far beneath the other. Alas! what am I now? What is a Leadenhall clerk, or India pensioner, to a deputy Grecian? How art thou fallen, O Lucifer! Just room for our loves to Mrs. D., etc.   C. LAMB.

To REV. H. F. CARY.

LETTER CCCCXXVII.]   *April* 13, 1831.

Dear C.—I am *daily* for this week expecting Wordsworth, who will not name a day. I have been expecting him by months and by weeks; but he has reduced the hope within the seven fractions hebdomadal of this hebdoma. Therefore I am sorry I cannot see you on Thursday. I think within a week or two I shall be able to invite myself some day for a day, but we hermits with difficulty poke out of our shells. Within that ostraceous retirement I meditate not unfrequently on you. My sister's kindest remembrances to you both.   C. L.

To BERNARD BARTON.

LETTER CCCCXXVIII.]   *April* 30, 1831.

Vir Bone!—Recepi literas tuas amicissimas, et in mentem venit responsuro mihi, vel raro, vel nunquam, inter nos intercedisse Latinam linguam, organum rescribendi, loquendive. Epistolæ tuæ, Plinianis elegantiis (supra quod TREMULO deceat) refertæ, tam a verbis Plinianis adeo abhorrent, ut ne vocem quamquam (Romanam scilicet) habere videaris, quam "ad canem," ut aiunt, "rejectare possis." Forsan desuetudo Latinissandi ad vernaculam linguam usitandam, plusquam opus sit, coegit. Per adagia quædam nota, et in ore omnium pervulgata, ad Latinitatis perditæ recuperationem revocare te institui.

Felis in abaco est, et ægrè videt.

Omne quod splendet nequaquam aurum putes.

Imponas equo mendicum, equitabit idem ad diabolum.

Fur commodè a fure prenditur.

O MARIA, MARIA, valdé CONTRARIA, quomodo crescit hortulus tuus? Nunc majora canamus.

Thomas, Thomas, de Islington, uxorem duxit die nuperâ Dominicâ. Reduxit domum posterâ. Succedenti baculum emit. Postridie ferit illam. Ægrescit illa subsequenti. Proximâ (nempe Veneris) est mortua. Plurimum gestiit Thomas, quòd appropinquanti Sabbato efferenda sit.

Horner quidam Johannulus in angulo sedebat, artocreas quasdam deglutiens. Inseruit pollices, pruna nana evellens, et magnâ voce exclamavit "Dii boni, quàm bonus puer fio!"

Diddle-diddle-dumkins! menus unicus filius Johannes cubitum ivit, integris braccis, caligâ unâ tantūm, indutus. Diddle-diddle, etc. DA CAPO.

Hic adsum saltans Joannula. Cum nemo adsit mihi, semper resto sola.

Ænigma mihi hoc solvas, et Œdipus fies.
Quâ ratione assimulandus sit equus TREMULO?
Quippe cui tota communicatio sit per HAY et NEIGH, juxta consilium illud Dominicum, "Fiat omnis communicatio vestra YEA et NAY."

In his nugis caram diem consumo, dum invigilo valetudini carioris nostræ Emmæ, quæ apud nos jamdudum ægrotat. Salvere vos jubet mecum Maria mea, ipsa integrâ valetudine.   ELIA.

Ab agro Enfeldiense datum, Aprilis nescio quibus Calendis—Davus sum, non Calendarius.

P.S.—Perdita in toto est Billa Reformatura.

To REV. H. F. CARY.

Datum ab agro Enfeldiensi,
LETTER CCCCXXIX.]   *Maii die sextâ,* 1831.

Assidens est mihi bona soror, Euripiden evolvens, donum vestrum, carissime Cary, pro quo gratias agimus, lecturi atque iterum lecturi idem. Pergratus est liber ambobus, nempe "Sacerdotis Commiserationis," sacrum opus a te ipso Humanissimæ Religionis Sacerdote dono datum. Lachrymantes gavisuri sumus; est ubi dolor fiat voluptas; nec semper dulce mihi est ridere; aliquando commutandum est he! he! he! cum heu! heu! heu!

A Musis Tragicis me non penitus abhorruisse testis sit Carmen Calamitosum, nescio quo autore linguâ prius vernaculâ scriptum et nuperrimè a me ipso Latine versum scilicet, "Tom Tom of Islington." Tenuistine?

> "Thomas Thomas de Islington,
> Uxorem duxit Die quâdam Solis,
> Abduxit domum sequenti die,
> Emit baculum subsequenti,
> Vapulat illa posterâ,
> Ægrotat succedenti, Mortua fit crastinâ."

Et miro gaudio afficitur Thomas luce posterâ quod subsequenti (nempe, Dominicâ) uxor sit efferenda.

> "En Iliades Domesticas!
> En circulum calamitatum!
> Planè hebdomadalem tragœdiam."

I nunc et confer Euripiden vestrum his luctibus, hâc morte uxoriâ; confer Alcesten! Hecuben! quas non antiquas Heroinas Dolorosas.

Suffundor genas lachrymis tantas strages revolvens. Quid restat nisi quod Tecum Tuam Caram salutemus ambosque valere jubeamus, nosmet ipsi bene valentes. ELIA.

To JOHN TAYLOR.

LETTER CCCCXXX.] *June* 8, 1831.

Dear Sir—I am extremely sorry to be obliged to decline the article proposed, particularly as I should have been flattered with a Plate accompanying it. In the first place, Midsummer Day is not a topic I could make anything of, I am so pure a Cockney, and little read besides in May games and antiquities; and in the second, I am here at Margate, spoiling my holydays with a Review I have undertaken for a friend, which I shall barely get through before my return, for that sort of work is a hard task to me. If you will excuse the shortness of my first contribution (and I *know* I can promise nothing more for July) I will endeavour a longer article for *our next*. Will you permit me to say that I think Leigh Hunt would do the Article you propose in a masterly manner, if he has not outwrit himself already upon the subject. I do not return the proof to save postage—because it is correct, with *one exception*. In the stanza from Wordsworth you have changed *day* into *air* for rhyme's sake. *Day* is the right reading, and *I implore you to restore it*.

The other passage, which you have queried, is to my ear correct. Pray let it stand.

Dear sir, yours truly, C. LAMB.

Margate.
J. Taylor, Esq.

On second consideration I do enclose the proof.

To Mr. MOXON.

LETTER CCCCXXXI.] *August* 1831.

Dear M.—The *R.A.* here memorised was George Dawe, whom I knew well, and heard many anecdotes of, from DANIELS and WESTALL, at H. Rogers's; *to each of them* it will be well to send a magazine in my name.

It will fly like wildfire among the Royal Academicians and artists. Could you get hold of Procter?—his chambers are in Lincoln's Inn, at Montagu's; or of Janus Weathercock?—both of their *prose* is capital. Don't encourage poetry. The "Peter's Net" does not intend funny things only. All is fish. And leave out the sickening "Elia" at the end. Then it may comprise letters and characters addressed to Peter; but a signature forces it to be all characteristic of the one man Elia, or the one man, Peter, which cramped me formerly. I have agreed *not* for my sister to know the subjects I choose till the magazine comes out; so beware of speaking of 'em, or writing about 'em save generally. Be particular about this warning. Can't you drop in some afternoon, and take a bed? The *Athenæum* has been hoaxed with some exquisite poetry, that was, two or three months ago, in "Hone's Book." I like your first Number capitally. But is it not small? Come and see us, week-day if possible.

Send or bring me Hone's Number for August. The anecdotes of E. and of G. D. are substantially true; what does Elia (or Peter) care for dates? The poem I mean is in "Hone's Book," as far back as April. I do not know who wrote it; but 'tis a poem I envy—*that* and Montgomery's "Last Man:" I envy the writers, because I feel I could have done something like them.   C. L.

LETTER CCCCXXXII.]   *September* 5, 1831.

Dear M.—Your letter's contents pleased me. I am only afraid of taxing you. Yet I want a stimulus, or I think I should drag sadly. I shall keep the moneys in trust, till I see you fairly over the next 1st January: then I shall look upon them as earned. No part of your letter gave me more pleasure (no, not the £10, tho' you may grin) than that you will revisit old Enfield, which I hope will be always a pleasant idea to you.

Yours, very faithfully,   C. L.

LETTER CCCCXXXIII.]   *October* 24, 1831.

To address an abdicated monarch is a nice point of breeding. To give him his lost titles is to mock him; to withhold 'em is to wound him. But his minister, who falls with him, may be gracefully sympathetic. I do honestly feel for your diminution of honours, and regret even the pleasing cares which are part and parcel of greatness. Your magnanimous submission, and the cheerful tone of your renunciation, in a letter which, without flattery, would have made an "ARTICLE," and which, rarely as I keep letters, shall be preserved, comfort me a little. Will it please, or plague you, to say that when your parcel came I damn'd it? for my pen was warming in my hand at a ludicrous description of a Landscape of an R.A., which I calculated upon sending you to-morrow, the last day you gave me. Now any one calling in, or a letter coming, puts an end to my writing for the day. Little did I think that the mandate had gone out, so destructive to my occupation, so relieving to the apprehensions of the whole body of R.A.'s; so you see I had not quitted the ship while a plank was remaining.

To drop metaphors, I am sure you have done wisely. The very spirit of your epistle speaks that you have a weight off your mind. I have one on mine; the cash in hand, which, as —— less truly says, burns in my pocket. I feel queer at returning it (who does not?), you feel awkward at retaking it (who ought not). Is there no middle way of adjusting this fine embarrassment? I think I have hit upon a medium to skin the sore place over, if not quite to heal it. You hinted that there might be something under £10, by and by, accruing to me—*Devil's Money* (you are sanguine, say £7:10s.); that I entirely renounce, and abjure all future interest in: I insist upon it; and "by him I will not name," I won't touch a penny of it. That will split your loss, one half, and leave me conscientious possessor of what I hold. Less than your assent to this, no proposal will I accept of.

The Rev. Mr. ——, whose name you have left illegible (is it *Seagull?*) never sent me any book on Christ's Hospital, by which I could dream that I was indebted to him for a dedication. Did G. D. send his penny tract to me to convert me to Unitarianism? Dear, blundering soul! why I am as old a one-Goddite as himself. Or did he think his cheap publication would bring over the Methodists over the way here? However, I'll give it to the pew-opener, in whom I have a little interest, to hand over to the clerk, whose wife she sometimes drinks tea with, for him to lay before the deacon, who exchanges the civility of the hat with him, for to transmit to the minister, who shakes hands with him out of chapel, and he, in all odds, will —— with it.

I wish very much to see you. I leave it to you to come how you will; we shall be very glad (we need not repeat) to see your sister, or sisters, with you; but for you, individually, I will just hint that a dropping in to tea, unlooked for, about five, stopping bread-and-cheese and gin-and-water, is worth a thousand Sundays. I am naturally miserable on a Sunday; but a week-day evening and supper is like old times. Set out *now*, and give no time to deliberation.

P.S.—The second volume of "Elia" is delightful (ly bound, I mean), and quite cheap. Why, man, 'tis a unique! If I write much more I shall expand into an article, which I cannot afford to let you have so cheap. By the by, to show the perverseness of human will, while I thought I *must* furnish one of those accursed things monthly, it seemed a labour above Hercules's "Twelve" in a year, which were evidently monthly contributions. Now I am emancipated, I feel as if I had a thousand Essays swelling within me. False feelings both!

Your ex-Lampoonist, or Lamb-punnist, from Enfield, October 24, or "last day but one for receiving articles that can be inserted."

LETTER CCCCXXXIV.]   *February* 1832.

Dear Moxon—The snows are ancle-deep, slush, and mire, that 'tis hard to get to the post-office, and cruel to send the maid out. 'Tis a slough of despair, or I should sooner have thanked you for your offer of the *"Li[e,"* which we shall very much like to have, and will return duly. I do not know when I shall be in town, but in a week or two, at farthest, when I will come as far as you, if I can. We are moped to death with confinement within doors. I send you a curiosity of G. Dyer's tender conscience. Between thirty and forty years since, G. published the "Poet's Fate," in which were two very harmless lines about Mr. Rogers; but Mr. R. not quite approving of them, they were left out in a subsequent edition, 1801. But G. has been worrying about them ever since; if I have heard him once, I have heard him a hundred times, express a remorse proportioned to a consciousness of having been guilty of an atrocious libel. As the devil would have it, a fool they call Barker, in his "Parriana," has quoted the identical two lines, as they stood in some obscure edition anterior to 1801, and the withers of poor G. are again wrong. His letter is a gem; with his poor blind eyes it has been laboured out at six sittings. The history of the couplet is in page 3 of this irregular production, in which every variety of shape and size that letters can be twisted into is to be found. Do show *his* part of it to Mr. R. some day. If he has bowels, they must melt at the contrition so queerly charactered of a contrite sinner. G. was born, I verily think, without original sin, but chooses to have a conscience, as every Christian gentleman should have; his dear old face is insusceptible of the twist they call a sneer, yet he is apprehensive of being suspected of that ugly appearance. When he makes a compliment, he thinks he has given an affront,—a name is personality. But show (no hurry) this unique recantation to Mr. R., 'tis like a dirty pocket-handkerchief, mucked with tears of some indigent Magdalen. There is the impress of sincerity in every pot-hook and hanger; and then the gilt frame to such a pauper picture! It should go into the Museum. I am heartily sorry my Devil does not answer. We must try it a little longer; and, after all, I think I must insist on taking a portion of its loss upon myself. It is too much you should lose by two adventures. You do not say how your general business goes on, and I should very much like to talk over it with you here.

Come when the weather will possibly let you; I want to see the Wordsworths, but I do not much like to be all night away. It is dull enough to be here together, but it is duller to leave Mary; in short, it is painful, and in a flying visit I should hardly catch them. I have no beds for them if they came down, and but a sort of a house to receive them in; yet I shall regret their departure unseen; I feel cramped and straitened every way. Where are they?

We have heard from Emma but once, and that a month ago, and are very anxious for another letter.

You say we have forgot your powers of being serviceable to us. *That* we never shall: I do not know what I should do without you when I want a little commission. Now then: there are left at Miss Buffam's, the "Tales of the Castle," and certain volumes of the "Retrospective Review." The first should be conveyed to Novello's, and the Reviews should be taken to Talfourd's office, ground-floor, East side, Elm Court, Middle Temple, to whom I should have written, but my spirits are wretched; it is quite an effort to write this. So, with the *"Life,"* I have cut you out three pieces of service. What can I do for you here, but hope to see you very soon, and think of you with most kindness? I fear to-morrow, between rains and snows, it would be impossible to expect you, but do not let a practicable Sunday pass. We are always at home.

Mary joins in remembrances to your sister, whom we hope to see in any fine-ish weather, when she'll venture.

Remember us to Allsop, and all the dead people; to whom, and to London, we seem dead.

To Dr. J. BADAMS.

LETTER CCCCXXXV.]   *Enfield* (early in 1832).

Dear Badams—I am very, very sorry at my heatedness yesterday, which spoiled the pleasure I should have taken in seeing you better, but I had had a four or five hours' hot walk, with the delicate task of dissuading a friend from a purpose of taking a house here, which friend would have attracted down crowds of literary men, which men would have driven me wild. And in my rage it seemed to me that the person I unjustly fell upon was meditating the same sort of colonisation here. Respects and sincere likings to Mrs. Badams, and the most humble apology C. L. can offer.

To W. S. LANDOR.

LETTER CCCCXXXVI.]   *April* 9, 1832.

Dear Sir—Pray accept a little volume. 'Tis a legacy from Elia, you'll see. Silver and gold had he none, but such as he had left he you. I do not know how to thank you for attending to my request about the Album. I thought you would never remember it. Are not you proud and thankful, Emma? *Yes; very, both.*

[Signed] EMMA ISOLA.

Many things I had to say to you, which there was not time for. One, why should I forget? 'tis for Rose Aylmer, which has a charm I cannot explain. I lived upon it for weeks. Next, I forgot to tell you I knew all your Welsh annoyances, the measureless B.'s. I knew a quarter of a mile of them. Seventeen brothers and sixteen sisters, as they appear to me in memory. There was one of them that used to fix his long legs on my fender, and tell a tale of a shark every night, endless, immortal. How have I grudged the salt-sea ravener not having had his gorge of him! The shortest of the daughters measured five foot eleven without her shoes. Well, some day we may confer about them. But they were tall. Truly, I have discover'd the longitude. Sir, if you can spare a moment, I should be happy to hear from you. That rogue Robinson detained your verses till I call'd for them. Don't entrust a bit of prose to the rogue; but believe me,

Your obliged,   C. L.

W. S. Landor, Esq.

To SAMUEL TAYLOR COLERIDGE.

LETTER CCCCXXXVII.]   *April* 14, 1832.

My dear Coleridge—Not an unkind thought has passed in my brain about you; but I have been wofully neglectful of you; so that I do not deserve to announce to you, that if I do not hear from you before then, I will set out on Wednesday morning to take you by the hand. I would do it this moment, but an unexpected visit might flurry you. I shall take silence for acquiescence, and come. I am glad you could write so long a letter. Old loves to, and hope of kind looks from, the Gillmans when I come.

Yours, *semper idem,*   C. L.

If you ever thought an offence, much more wrote it, against me, it must have been in the times of Noah, and the great waters swept it away. Mary's most kind love, and maybe a wrong prophet of your bodings!— here she is crying for mere love over your letter. I wring out less, but not sincerer showers.

My direction is simply, Enfield.

To MR. MOXON.

LETTER CCCCXXXVIII.]   [1832.]

Thank you for the books. I am ashamed to take tithe thus of your press. I am worse to a publisher than the two Universities and the British Museum. A. C. I will forthwith read. B. C. (I can't get out of the A, B, C) I have more than read. Taken altogether, 'tis too Lovey; but what delicacies! I like most "King Death"; glorious 'bove all, "The Lady with the Hundred Rings"; "The Owl"; "Epistle to What's his Name" (here, may be, I'm partial); "Sit down, Sad Soul"; "The Pauper's Jubilee" (but that's old, and yet 'tis never old); "The Falcon"; "Felon's Wife'; damn "Madame Pasty" (but that is borrowed);

> Apple-pie is very good,
> And so is apple-pasty;
> But ———
> O Lord! 'tis very nasty:

but chiefly the dramatic fragments,—scarce three of which should have escaped my specimens, had an antique name been prefixed. They exceed his first. So much for the nonsense of poetry; now to the serious business of life. Up a court (Blandford Court) in Pall Mall (exactly at the back of Marlborough House), with iron gate in front, and containing two houses, at No. 2, did lately live Leishman, my tailor. He is moved somewhere in the neighbourhood; devil knows where. Pray find him out, and give him the opposite. I am so much better, though my head shakes in writing it, that, after next Sunday, I can well see Forster and you. Can you throw B. C. in? Why tarry the wheels of my "Hogarth"?

CHARLES LAMB.

To LOUISA BADAMS.

LETTER CCCCXXXIX.]   *December* 31, 1832.

Dear Mrs. B.—Mary has not enterprise enough to venture on a *journey* at this dreary time of the year, and 'tis too uncomfortable for us to leave her, for a night even, to the discourteous hospitalities of old frosty Westwood and his thin spouse: types of Christmas turned sour, or the 1st of January born with teeth and wrinkles. Cordial Illcomes, Not Welcomes—"wretched New Years to you": Discompliments of the Season. Spring, and we, will lure her out some fine April day. Instead pray accept of our kindest congratulations.

Besides, I have been not a little disconcerted.

On the night of our murder (an hour or two before it), the maid being busy, I went out to order an additional pint of porter for Moxon who had surprised us with a late visit. Now I never go out quite disinterested upon such occasions. And I begged a half-pint of ale at the bar which our sweet-faced landlady good-humouredly complied with, asking me into the parlour, but a side door was just open that disclosed a more cheerful blaze, and I entered where four people were engaged over Dominoes. One of them, Fare, invited me to join in it, partly out of impudence, I believe; however, not to balk a Christmas frolic, I complied, and played with Danby, but soon gave over, having forgot the game. I was surprised with D. challenging me as having known me in the Temple. He must have been a child then. I did not recognise him, but perfectly remembered his father, who was a hairdresser in the Temple. This was all that passed, as I went away with my beer. Judge my surprise when the next morning I was summoned before Dr. Creswell to say what I knew of the transaction. My examination was conducted with all delicacy, and of course I was soon dismissed. I was afraid of getting into the papers, but I was pleased to find myself only noticed as a "gentleman whose name we could not gather." Poor D.! the few words I spoke to him were to remind him of a trick Jem White played upon his father. The boy was too young to know anything about it. In the *Morning Post* appeared this paragraph: "Yesterday morning, Mr. Danby, the respectable Hairdresser in Pump Court in the Temple, in a fit of delirium threw himself out of a 2 pair stairs window, looking into the passage that leads to Fig-tree Court, and his head was literally smashed to atoms." White went to D.'s to see how it operated and found D. quietly weaving wigs, and the shop full of lawyers that had come to enquire particulars. D. was a man much respected. Indeed hairdressers in the Inns of Court are a superior race of tradesmen. They generally leave off rich, as D. did. Well, poor D. had never heard the story or probably forgotten it—and his company looking on me a little suspiciously, as they do at alehouses when a rather better drest person than themselves attempts to join 'em—(it never answers,—at least it seemed so to me when I heard of the murder)—I went away. One often fancies things afterwards that did not perhaps strike one at the time. However, after all, I have felt queer ever since. It has almost sickened me of the Crown and Horseshoe, and I shan't hastily go into the taproom again. I have made a long letter and can just say good-bye,

C. LAMB.

Mrs. Badams,
11 Old Church Street,
Paddington.

To MR. SERJEANT TALFOURD.

LETTER CCCCXL.]   *February* 1833.

My dear T.—Now cannot I call him *Serjeant;* what is there in a coif? Those canvas sleeves protective from ink, when he was a law-chit—a *Chitty*-ling (let the leathern apron be apocryphal), do more 'specially plead to the Jury Court, of old memory. The costume (will he agnise it?) was as of a desk-fellow, or Socius Plutei. Methought I spied a brother!

That familiarity is extinct for ever. Curse me if I can call him Mr. Serjeant—except, mark me, in *company.* Honour where honour is due; but should he ever visit us (do you think he ever will, Mary?), what a distinction should I keep up between him and our less fortunate friend, H. C. R.! Decent respect shall always be the Crabb's—but, somehow, short of reverence.

Well, of my old friends, I have lived to see two knighted, one made a judge, another in a fair way to it. Why am I restive? why stands my sun upon Gibeon?

Variously, my dear Mrs. Talfourd (I can be more familiar with her!), Mrs. *Serjeant* Talfourd,—my sister prompts me—(these ladies stand upon ceremonies)—has the congratulable news affected the members of our small community. Mary comprehended it at once, and entered into it heartily. Mrs. Westwood was, as usual, perverse; wouldn't, or couldn't, understand it. A Serjeant! She thought Mr. T. was in the law. Didn't know that he ever 'listed.

Emma alone truly sympathised. *She* had a silk gown come home that very day, and has precedence before her learned sisters accordingly.

We are going to drink the health of Mr. and Mrs. Serjeant, with all the young serjeantry; and that is all that I can see that I shall get by the promotion.

Valete, et mementote amici quondam vestri humillimi.

C. L.

To Mr. MOXON.

LETTER CCCCXLI.]   *February* 10, 1833.

I wish you would omit "by the Author of Elia" now, in advertising that damn'd "Devil's Wedding." I had sneaking hopes you would have dropt in to-day, 'tis my poor birthday. Don't stay away so. Give Forster a hint. You are to bring your brother some day—*sisters* in better weather. Pray give me one line to say if you receiv'd and forwarded Emma's pacquet to Miss Adams—and how Dover Street looks. Adieu. Is there no Blackwood this month? What separation will there be between the Friend's preface and THE ESSAYS? Should not "Last Essays," etc. etc., head them? If 'tis too late, don't mind. I don't care a farthing about it.

Mr. Moxon.

To LOUISA BADAMS.

LETTER CCCCXLII.]   *February* 15, 1833.

Dear Mrs. B.—Thanks for your remembrance of your old fellow-prisoners at murderous Enfield. By the way, Cooper, who turned King's evidence, is come back again whitewash'd, has resumed his seat at chapel, and took his sister (a fact!) up the Holt White's lane to shew her the topography of the deed. I intend asking him to supper. They say he is pleasant in conversation. Will you come and meet him?

I don't know how we shall see you. Mary has objections to travelling, and I never stay out the night when I come up. Couldn't Badams and you make a 24 hours' day here? The room is vacant at the Horseshoe where Fare slept last, unless you prefer Johnson's last bed.

Mary, Emma, and I have got thro' the *Inferno* with the help of Cary—and Mary is in for it. She is commencing Tasso. When the Spring is riper, we will spare Emma for a few days, if you'll be kind to her. Triple loves and kind memory to you both.　　　　　　　　C. L.

To WILLIAM HONE.

LETTER CCCCXLIII.]　　　　　　　　　　　　*March* 6, 1833.

Dear Friend—Thee hast sent a Christian epistle to me, and I should not feel dear if I neglected to reply to it, which would have been sooner if that vain young man, to whom thou didst intrust it, had not kept it back. We should rejoice to see thy outward man here, especially on a day which should not be a first day, being liable to wordly callers-in on that day. Our little book is delayed by a heathenish injunction, threatened by the man Taylor. Canst thou copy and send, or bring with thee, a vanity in verse which in my younger days I wrote on friend Aders's pictures? Thou wilt find it in the book, called the *Table Book*.

Tryphena and Tryphosa, whom the world calleth Mary and Emma, greet you with me.　　　　　　　　　　　　　　　Ch. LAMB.

6th of 3rd month, 4th day.
W. Hone, Esq.,
　　Grasshopper Hotel,
　　　　Gracechurch Street.

To Mr. MOXON.

LETTER CCCCXLIV.]　　　　　　　　　　　　*March* 19, 1833.

I shall expect Forster and two Moxons on Sunday, and hope for Procter. I am obliged to be in town next Monday. Could we contrive to make a party (paying or not is immaterial) for Miss Kelly's that night; and can you shelter us after the play—I mean Emma and me. I fear I cannot persuade Mary to join us.

N.B.—I can sleep at a public house. Send an Elia (mind I *insist* on buying it), to T. Manning, Esq., at Sir G. Tuthill's, Cavendish Square. Do write.

E. Moxon.

LETTER CCCCXLV.]　　　　　　　　　　　　*April* 27, 1833.

Dear M.—Mary and I are very poorly. We have had a sick child, who, sleeping or not sleeping, next me, with a pasteboard partition between, killed my sleep. The little bastard is gone. My bedfellows are cough and cramp; we sleep three in a bed. Domestic arrangements (baker, butcher, and all) devolve on Mary. Don't come yet to this house of pest and age! We propose, when you and E. agree on the time, to come up and meet you at the B——'s, say a week hence, but do you make the appointment. Mind, our spirits are good, and we are happy in your happinesses.

C. L.

Our old and ever loves to dear Emma.

To Mrs. HAZLITT.

LETTER CCCCXLVI.]   *Mr. Walden's, Church Street,*
                                     Edmonton, May 31, 1833.

Dear Mrs. Hazlitt—I will assuredly come and find you out when I am better. I am driven from house to house by Mary's illness. I took a sudden resolution to take my sister to Edmonton, where she was under medical treatment last time, and have arranged to board and lodge with the people. Thank God, I have repudiated Enfield. I have got out of hell, despair of heaven, and must sit down contented in a half-way purgatory. Thus ends this strange eventful history. But I am nearer town, and will get up to you somehow before long.

I repent not of my resolutions. 'Tis late, and my hand is unsteady; so good-bye till we meet.

Your old   C. L.

Mrs. Hazlitt,
No. 4, Palace Street, Pimlico.

To WILLIAM WORDSWORTH.

LETTER CCCCXLVII.]   [End of May nearly] 1833.

Dear Wordsworth—Your letter, save in what respects your dear sister's health, cheered me in my new solitude. Mary is ill again. Her illnesses encroach yearly. The last was three months, followed by two of depression most dreadful. I look back upon her earlier attacks with longing: nice little durations of six weeks or so, followed by complete restoration,—shocking as they were to me then. In short, half her life she is dead to me, and the other half is made anxious with fears and lookings forward to the next shock. With such prospects, it seemed to me necessary that she should no longer live with me, and be fluttered with continued removals; so I am come to live with her, at a Mr. Walden's and his wife, who take in patients, and have arranged to lodge and board us only. They have had the care of her before. I see little of her: alas! I too often hear her. *Sunt lachrymæ rerum!* and you and I must bear it.

To lay a little more load on it, a circumstance has happened, *cujus pars magna fui,* and which, at another crisis, I should have more rejoiced in. I am about to lose my old and only walk-companion, whose mirthful spirits were the "youth of our house," Emma Isola. I have her here now for a little while, but she is too nervous, properly to be under such a

roof, so she will make short visits,—be no more an inmate. With my perfect approval, and more than concurrence, she is to be wedded to Moxon,
at the end of August—so "perish the roses and the flowers"—how is it?
Now to the brighter side. I am emancipated from the Westwoods, and
I am with attentive people, and younger. I am three or four miles nearer
the great city; coaches half-price less, and going always, of which I will
avail myself. I have few friends left there, one or two though, most beloved. But London streets and faces cheer me inexpressibly, though not
one known of the latter were remaining.

Thank you for your cordial reception of "Elia." *Inter nos*, the *Ariadne*
is not a darling with me; several incongruous things are in it, but in the
composition it served me as illustrative.

I want you in the "Popular Fallacies" to like the "Home that is no
home," and "Rising with the lark."

I am feeble, but cheerful in this my genial hot weather. Walked sixteen
miles yesterday. I can't read much in summer time.

With my kindest love to all, and prayers for dear Dorothy,
I remain most affectionately yours,   C. LAMB.

At Mr. Walden's, Church Street, Edmonton, Middlesex.

Moxon has introduced Emma to Rogers, and he smiles upon the project. I have given E. my MILTON (will you pardon me) in part of a *portion*. It hangs famously in his Murray-like shop.

To Miss RICKMAN.

Thursday.

LETTER CCCCXLVIII.]   *May 23, 1833.*

Dear Miss Rickman—My being a day in town, and my being moved
from Enfield, made your letter late, and my reply in consequence. I am
glad you like *Elia*. Perhaps, as Miss Kelly is just now in notoriety, it
may amuse you to know that "Barbara S." is *all* of it true of *her*, being
all communicated to me from her own mouth. The "wedding" of course
you found out to be Sally Burney's. As to Mrs. G. I know no reason why
your dear mother should not call upon her. I remember Rickman and
she did *not* return Mr. and Mrs. G.'s congratulatory visit on their wedding. No fresh reason has occurred since to prevent any civilities on their
side. By a sudden illness of my Sister (they now last half the year, in
violence first, and a succeeding dreadful depression) I have come to the
resolution of living with her under it at a place where she is under regular
treatment, and am at Mr. Walden's, Church Street, Edmonton. In a few
weeks, I should like one quiet day among you, but not before. With loves
to father and mother, and your kind-hearted Sister, whose Christian
name I am an heathen if I just now can remember,
Yours sincerely,   C. LAMB.

Mrs. Godwin is a second wife. Mary Wolstoncroft has been dead thirty years!

To Miss Rickman,
  New Palace Yard,
    Westminster.

To MR. MOXON.

LETTER CCCCXLIX.]   *May* 1833.

Dear M.—A thousand thanks for your punctualities. What a cheap book is the last Hogarth you sent me! I am pleased now that Hunt *diddled* me out of the old one. Speaking of this, only think of the new farmer with his thirty acres. There is a portion of land in Lambeth Parish, called Knave's Acre. I wonder he overlook'd it. Don't show this to the firm of D—— and Co. I next want one copy of *Leicester's School,* and wish you to pay Leishman, Taylor, 2, Blandford Place, Pall Mall, opposite the British Institution, £6:10s., for coat and waistcoat, etc. etc., and I vehemently thirst for the fourth No. of Nichols's Hogarth, to bind one up (the two books) as Hogarth and Supplement. But as you know the price, don't stay for its appearance; but come as soon as ever you can with your bill of all demands in full, and as I have none but £5 notes, bring with you sufficient change. Weather is beautiful. I grieve sadly for Miss Wordsworth. We are all well again. Emma is with us, and we all shall be glad of a sight of you. Come on Sunday if you *can*, better if you come before.

Perhaps Rogers would smile at this. A pert, half chemist, half apothecary in our town who smatters of literature, and is immeasurably unlettered, said to me, "Pray, sir, may not Hood be reckon'd the Prince of Wits in the present day?" To which I assenting, he adds, "I had always thought that Rogers had been reckon'd the Prince of Wits, but I suppose that now Mr. Hood has the better title to that appellation." To which I replied, that Mr. R. had wit with much better qualities, but did not aspire to the principality. He had taken all the puns manufactured in John Bull for our friend, in sad and stupid earnest. One more *Album Verses,* please. Adieu.   C. L.

To THOMAS ALLSOP.

LETTER CCCCL.]   *July* 1833.

My dear Allsop—I think it will be impossible for us to come to Highgate in the time you propose. We have friends coming to-morrow, who may stay the week; and we are in a bustle about Emma's leaving us— so we will put off the hope of seeing Mrs. Allsop till we come to Town, after Emma's going, which is in a fortnight and a half, when we mean to spend a time in Town, but shall be happy to see you on Sunday, or any day.

In haste. Hope our little Porter does.

Yours ever, C. L.

To Mr. MOXON.

LETTER CCCCLI.] *July* 24, 1833.

For God's sake give Emma no more watches; *one* has turned her head. She is arrogant and insulting. She said something very unpleasant to our old clock in the passage, as if he did not keep time, and yet he had made her no appointment. She takes it out every instant to look at the moment-hand. She lugs us out into the fields, because there the bird-boys ask you, "Pray, sir, can you tell us what's o'clock?" and she answers them punctually. She loses all her time looking to see "what the time is." I overheard her whispering, "Just so many hours, minutes, etc., to Tuesday; I think St. George's goes too slow." This little present of Time!—why,—'tis Eternity to her!

What can make her so fond of a gingerbread watch?

She has spoiled some of the movements. Between ourselves, she has kissed away "half-past twelve," which I suppose to be the canonical hour in Hanover Square.

Well, if "love me, love my watch" answers, she will keep time to you. It goes right by the Horse Guards.

Dearest M.—Never mind opposite nonsense. She does not love you for the watch, but the watch for you. I will be at the wedding, and keep the 30th July, as long as my poor months last me, as a festival, gloriously.

Yours ever, ELIA.

We have not heard from Cambridge. I will write the moment we do. Edmonton, 24th July, twenty minutes past three by Emma's watch.

LETTER CCCCLII.] [1833.]

Dear M.—Many thanks for the books; but most thanks for one immortal sentence: "If I do not *cheat* him, never *trust* me again." I do not know whether to admire most, the wit or justness of the sentiment. It has my cordial approbation. My sense of *meum* and *tuum* applauds it. I maintain it, the eighth commandment hath a secret special reservation, by which the reptile is exempt from any protection from it. As a dog, or a nigger, he is not a holder of property. Not a ninth of what he detains from the world is his own. "Keep your hands from picking and stealing," is no ways referable to his acquists. I doubt whether bearing false witness against thy neighbour at all contemplated this possible scrub. Could Moses have seen the speck in vision? An *ex post facto* law alone could relieve him; and we are taught to expect no eleventh commandment. The outlaw to the Mosaic dispensation!—unworthy to have seen Moses behind!—to lay his desecrating hands upon Elia! Has the irreverent arktoucher been struck blind, I wonder? The more I think of him, the less I think of him. His meanness is invisible with aid of solar microscope. My moral eye smarts at him. The less flea that bites little fleas! The great BEAST! The beggarly NIT!

More when we meet; mind, you'll come, two of you; and couldn't you go off in the morning, that we may have a day-long curse at him, if curses are not dis-hallowed by descending so low! Amen. Maledicatur in extremis!   C. L.

To LOUISA BADAMS.

LETTER CCCCLIII.]   · *August* 20, 1833.

Dear Mrs. Badams—I was at church as the grave Father, and behaved tolerably well, except at first entrance when Emma in a whisper repressed a nascent giggle. I am not fit for weddings or burials. Both incite a chuckle. Emma looked as pretty as Pamela, and made her responses delicately and firmly. I tripped a little at the altar, was engaged in admiring the altar-piece, but, recalled seasonably by a Parsonic rebuke, "Who gives this woman?" was in time resolutely to reply "I do." Upon the whole the thing went off decently and devoutly. Your dodging post is excellent; I take it, it was at Wilsdon. We shall this week or next dine at Islington. I am writing to know the day, and in that case see you the next day and talk of beds. *My* lodging may be on the cold floor. I long for a *hard fought game* with Badams. With haste and thanks for your *unusually* entertaining letter, yours truly,

CHARLES AND MARY LAMB.

TO MR. AND MRS. MOXON.

LETTER CCCCLIV.]   *August* 1833.

Dear Mr. and Mrs. Moxon—Time very short. I wrote to Miss Fryer, and had the sweetest letter about you, Emma, that ever friendship dictated. "I am full of good wishes, I am crying with good wishes," she says; but you shall see it.

Dear Moxon—I take your writing most kindly, and shall, most kindly, your writing from Paris.

I want to crowd another letter to Miss Fryer into the little time after dinner, before post time. So with twenty thousand congratulations, Yours,   C. L.

I am calm, sober, happy. Turn over for the reason. I got home from Dover Street, by Evans, *half as sober as a judge.* I am turning over a new leaf, as I hope you will now.

[*The turn of the leaf presented the following from Miss Lamb:*]

My dear Emma and Edward Moxon—Accept my sincere congratulations, and imagine more good wishes than my weak nerves will let me put into good set words. The dreary blank of *unanswered questions* which I ventured to ask in vain was cleared up on the wedding-day by Mrs. W. taking a glass of wine, and, with a total change of countenance, begging leave to drink Mr. and Mrs. Moxon's health. It restored me from that moment, as if by an electrical stroke, to the entire possession of my senses. I never felt so calm and quiet after a similar illness as I do now. I feel as if all tears were wiped from my eyes, and all care from my heart.

MARY LAMB.

[*At the foot of this letter is the following by Charles:*]

Wednesday.

Dears, again—Your letter interrupted a seventh game at picquet which *we* were having, after walking to Wright's and purchasing shoes. We pass our time in cards, walks, and reading. We attack Tasso soon.

C. L.

Never was such a calm, or such a recovery. 'Tis her own words undictated.

To REV. H. F. CARY.

LETTER CCCCLV.]   *September 9, 1833.*

Dear Sir—Your packet I have only just received, owing, I suppose, to the absence of Moxon, who is flaunting it about *à la Parisienne*, with his new bride, our Emma, much to his satisfaction, and not a little to our dulness. We shall be quite well by the time you return from Worcestershire, and most, most (observe the repetition) glad to see you here, or anywhere.

I will take my time with Darley's act. I wish poets would write a little plainer; he begins some of his words with a letter which is unknown to the English typography.

Yours, most truly,   C. LAMB.

P.S.—Pray let me know when you return. We are at Mr. Walden's, Church Street, Edmonton; no longer at Enfield. You will be amused to hear that my sister and I have, with the aid of Emma, scrambled through the "Inferno," by the blessed furtherance of your polar-star translation. I think we scarce left anything unmade-out. But our partner has left us, and we have not yet resumed. Mary's chief pride in it was that she should some day brag of it to you. Your *Dante* and Sandys' *Ovid* are the only helpmates of translations. Neither of you shirk a word. Fairfax's *Tasso* is no translation at all. 'Tis better in some places, but it merely observes the number of stanzas; as for images, similes, etc., he finds 'em himself, and never troubles Peter for the matter.

In haste, dear Cary, yours ever,   C. LAMB.

Has M. sent you "Elia," second volume? If not he shall. Taylor and we are at law about it.

To MR. AND MRS. MOXON.

LETTER CCCCLVI.]   *November,* 29, 1833.

Mary is of opinion with me, that two of these sonnets are of a higher grade than any poetry you have done yet. The one to Emma is so pretty! I have only allowed myself to transpose a word in the third line. Sacred shall it be for any intermeddling of mine. But we jointly beg that you will make four lines in the room of the four last. Read "Darby and Joan," in Mrs. Moxon's first album. There you'll see how beautiful in age the looking back to youthful years in an old couple is. But it is a violence to the feelings to anticipate that time in youth. I hope you and Emma will have many a quarrel and many a make-up (and she is beautiful in reconciliation!) before the dark days shall come, in which ye shall say "there is small comfort in them." You have begun a sort of character of Emma in them, very sweetly: carry it on, if you can, through the last lines.

I love the sonnet to my heart, and you *shall* finish it, and I'll be damn'd if I furnish a line towards it. So much for that. The next best is to the Ocean.

> "Ye gallant winds, if e'er your LUSTY CHEEKS
> Blew longing lover to his mistress' side,
> O, puff your loudest, spread the canvas wide,"

is spirited. The last line I altered, and have realtered it as it stood. It is closer. These two are your best. But take a good deal of time in finishing the first. How proud should Emma be of her poets!

Perhaps "O Ocean" (though I like it) is too much of the open vowels which Pope objects to. "Great Oceans!" is obvious. To save sad thoughts I think is better (though not good) than for the mind to save herself. But 'tis a noble sonnet. "St. Cloud" I have no fault to find with.

If I return the sonnets, think it no disrespect, for I look for a printed copy. You have done better than ever. And now for a reason I did not notice 'em earlier. On Wednesday they came, and on Wednesday I was a-gadding. Mary gave me a holiday, and I set off to Snow Hill. From Snow Hill I deliberately was marching down, with noble Holborn before me, framing in mental cogitation a map of the dear London in prospect, thinking to traverse Wardour Street, etc., when diabolically, I was interrupted by

> Heigh-ho!
> Little Barrow!—

(Emma knows him,) and prevailed on by him to spend the day (infinite loss!) at his sister's, a pawnbroker's in Gray's Inn Lane, where was an album, and (O march of intellect!) plenty of literary conversation, and more acquaintance with the state of modern poetry than I could keep up with. I was positively distanced. Knowles's play, which, epilogued by me, lay on the piano, alone made me hold up my head. When I came home I read your letter, and glimpsed at your beautiful sonnet,

"Fair art thou as the morning, my young bride,"

and dwelt upon it in a confused brain, but determined not to open them till next day, being in a state not to be told of at Chatteris. Tell it not in Gath, Emma, lest the daughters triumph! I am at the end of my tether. I wish you would come on Tuesday with your fair bride. Why can't you? Do. We are thankful to your sister for being of the party. Come, and *bring* a sonnet on Mary's birthday. Love to the whole Moxonry, and tell E. I every day love her more, and miss her less. Tell her so, from her loving uncle, as she has let me call myself. I bought a fine embossed card yesterday, and wrote for the Pawnbrokeress's album. She is a Miss Brown, engaged to a Mr. White. One of the lines was (I forget the rest; but she had them at twenty-four hours' notice; she is going out to India with her husband)—

"May your fame
And fortune, Frances, WHITEN with your name!"

Not bad as a pun. I *will* expect you before two on Tuesday. I am well and happy, tell E.

To MR. ROGERS.

LETTER CCCCLVII.]   *December* 1833.

My dear Sir—Your book, by the unremitting punctuality of your publisher, has reached me thus early. I have not opened it, nor will till tomorrow, when I promise myself a thorough reading of it. The "Pleasures of Memory" was the first school present I made to Mrs. Moxon; it has those nice woodcuts, and I believe she keeps it still. Believe me, that all the kindness you have shown to the husband of that excellent person seems done unto myself. I have tried my hand at a sonnet in the *Times;* but the turn I gave it, though I hoped it would not displease you, I thought might not be equally agreeable to your artist. I met that dear old man at poor Henry's, with you, and again at Cary's, and it was sublime to see him sit, deaf, and enjoy all that was going on in mirth with the company. He reposed upon the many graceful, many fantastic images he had created; with them he dined, and took wine. I have ventured at an antagonist copy of verses, in the *Athenæum*, to *him*, in which he is as everything, and you as nothing. He is no lawyer who cannot take two sides. But I am jealous of the combination of the sister arts. Let them sparkle apart. What injury (short of the theatres) did not Boydell's Shakspeare Gallery do me with Shakspeare? to have Opie's Shakspeare, Northcote's Shakspeare, light-headed Fuseli's Shakspeare, heavy-headed Romney's Shakspeare, wooden-headed West's Shakspeare (though he did the best in Lear), deaf-headed Reynolds's Shakspeare, instead of my and everybody's Shakspeare; to be tied down to an authentic face of Juliet; to have Imogen's portrait; to confine the illimitable! I like you and Stothard (you best), but "out upon this half-faced fellowship!" Sir, when I have read the book, I may trouble you, through Moxon, with some faint criticisms. It is not the flatteringest compliment, in a letter to an author, to say you have not read his book yet. But the devil of a reader he must be who prances through it in five minutes; and no longer have I received the parcel. It was a little tantalising to me to receive a letter from Landor, *Gebir* Landor, from Florence, to say he was just sitting down to read my "Elia," just received; but the letter was to go out before the reading. There are calamities in authorship which only authors know. I am going to call on Moxon on Monday, if the throng of carriages in Dover Street, on the morn of publication, do not barricade me out.

With many thanks, and most respectful remembrances to your sister, Yours, C. LAMB.

Have you seen Coleridge's happy exemplification in English of the Ovidian Elegiac metre?

> In the Hexameter rises the fountain's silvery current,
> In the Pentameter aye falling in melody down.

My sister is papering up the book,—careful soul!

To MARY BETHAM.

LETTER CCCCLVIII.]   *Church Street, Edmonton.*

Dear Mary Betham—I received the Bill, and when it is payable, some ten or twelve days hence, will punctually do with the overplus as you direct: I thought you would like to know it came to hand, so I have not waited for the uncertainty of when your nephew sets out. I suppose my receipt will serve, for poor Mary is not in a capacity to sign it. After being well from the end of July to the end of December, she was taken ill almost on the first day of the New Year, and is as bad as poor creature can be. I expect her fever to last 14 or 15 weeks—if she gets well at all, which every successive illness puts me in fear of. She has less and less strength to throw it off, and they leave a dreadful depression after them. She was quite comfortable a few weeks since, when Matilda came down here to see us.

You shall excuse a short letter, for my hand is unsteady. Indeed, the situation I am in with her shakes me sadly. She was quite able to appreciate the kind legacy while she was well. Imagine her kindest love to you, which is but buried awhile, and believe all the good wishes for your restoration to health from   C. LAMB.

  Miss Mary Betham,
    to the care of Sir Wm. Betham,
      Record Tower, Dublin.

To MISS FRYER.

LETTER CCCCLIX.]   *February* 14, 1834.

Dear Miss Fryer—Your letter found me just returned from keeping my birthday (pretty innocent!) at Dover Street. I see them pretty often. I have since had letters of business to write, or should have replied earlier. In one word, be less uneasy about me; I bear my privations very well; I am not in the depths of desolation, as heretofore. Your admonitions are not lost upon me. Your kindness has sunk into my heart. Have faith in me! It is no new thing for me to be left to my sister. When she is not violent, her rambling chat is better to me than the sense and sanity of this world. Her heart is obscured, not buried; it breaks out occasionally; and one can discern a strong mind struggling with the billows that have gone over it. I could be nowhere happier than under the same roof with her. Her memory is unnaturally strong; and from ages past, if we may so call the earliest records of our poor life, she fetches thousands of names and things that never would have dawned upon me again, and thousands from the ten years she lived before me. What took place from early girlhood to her coming of age principally lives again (every important thing, and every trifle) in her brain, with the vividness of real presence. For twelve hours incessantly she will pour out without intermission all her past life, forgetting nothing, pouring out name after name to the Waldens, as a dream; sense and nonsense; truths and errors huddled together; a medley between inspiration and possession. What things we are! I know you will bear with me, talking of these things. It seems to ease me, for I have nobody to tell these things to now. Emma, I see, has got a harp! and is learning to play. She has framed her three Walton pictures, and pretty they look. That is a book you should read; such sweet religion in it, next to Woolman's, though the subject be baits, and hooks, and worms, and fishes. She has my copy at present, to do two more from.

Very, very tired! I began this epistle, having been epistolising all the morning, and very kindly would I end it, could I find adequate expressions to your kindness. We did set our minds on seeing you in Spring. One of us will indubitably. But I am not skilled in almanack learning to know when Spring precisely begins and ends. Pardon my blots; I am glad you like your book. I wish it had been half as worthy of your acceptance as John Woolman. But 'tis a good-natured book.

To WILLIAM WORDSWORTH.

LETTER CCCCLX.]

Church Street, Edmonton,
February 22, 1834.

Dear Wordsworth—I write from a house of mourning. The oldest and best friends I have left are in trouble. A branch of them (and they of the best stock of God's creatures, I believe) is establishing a school at Carlisle. Her name is Louisa Martin; her address, 75, Castle Street, Carlisle; her qualities (and her motives for this exertion) are the most amiable, most upright. For thirty years she has been tried by me, and on her behaviour I would stake my soul. O, if you can recommend her, how would I love you—if I could love you better! Pray, pray, recommend her. She is as good a human creature,—next to my sister, perhaps, the most exemplary female I ever knew. Moxon tells me you would like a letter from me; you shall have one. *This* I cannot mingle up with any non-sense which you usually tolerate from C. Lamb. Need he add loves to wife, sister, and all? Poor Mary is ill again, after a short lucid interval of four or five months. In short, I may call her half dead to me. Good you are to me. Yours with fervour of friendship, for ever.   C. L.

If you want references, the Bishop of Carlisle may be one. Louisa's sister (as good as she, she cannot be better, though she tries,) educated the daughters of the late Earl of Carnarvon, and he settled a handsome annuity on her for life. In short, all the family are a sound rock.

To THOMAS MANNING.

LETTER CCCCLXI.]   *May* 10, 1834.

You made me feel so funny, so happy-like; it was as if I was reading one of your old letters taken out at hazard any time between the last twenty years, 'twas so the same. The unity of place, a garden! The old Dramatis Personæ, a landlady and Daughter. The puns the same in mould. Will nothing change you? 'Tis but a short week since honest Ryle and I were lamenting the gone-by days of Manning and Whist. How savourily did he remember them! Might some great year but bring them back again! This was my exclaim, and R. did not ask for an explanation. I have had a scurvy nine years of it, and am now in the sorry fifth act. Twenty weeks nigh has she been now violent, with but a few sound months before, and these in such dejection that her fever might seem a relief to it. I tried to bring her to town in the winter once or twice, but it failed. Tuthill led me to expect that this illness would lengthen with her years, and it has cruelly—with that new feature of despondency after. I am with her alone now in a proper house. She is, I hope, recovering. We play Picquet, and it is like the old times awhile, then goes off. I struggle to town rarely, and then to see London, with little other motive—for what is left there hardly? The streets and shops entertaining ever, else I feel as in a desert, and get me home to my cave. Save that once a month I pass a day, a gleam in my life, with Cary at the Museum (He is the flower of clergymen) and breakfast next morning with Robinson. I look to this as a treat. It sustains me. C. is a dear fellow, with but two vices, which in any less good than himself would be crimes past redemption. He has no relish for Parson Adams—hints that he might not be a very great Greek scholar after all (does Fielding hint that he was a Parson?)—and prefers "Ye shepherds so cheerful and gay," and "My banks they are furnished with bees," to "The Schoolmistress." I have not seen Wright's, but the faithfulness of C., Mary and I can attest. For last year, in a good interval, I giving some lessons to Emma, now Mrs. Moxon, in the *sense* part of her Italian (I knew no words), Mary pertinaciously undertook, being 69, to read the *Inferno* all thro' with the help of his Translation, and we got thro' it with Dictionaries and Grammars, of course to our satisfaction. Her perseverance was gigantic, almost painful. Her head was over her task, like a sucking bee, morn to night. We were beginning the *Purgatory*, but got on less rapidly, our great authority for grammar, Emma, being fled, but should have proceeded but for this misfortune. Do not come to town without apprising me. We must all three meet somehow and "drink a cup."

Yours,

C. L.

Mary strives and struggles to be content when she *is* well. Last year when we talked of being dull (we had just lost our seven-years-nearly inmate), and Cary's invitation came, she said, "Did not I say something or other would turn up?" In her first walk *out* of the house, she would read every Auction advertisement along the road, and when I would stop her she said, "These are *my* Play-bills." She felt glad to get into the world again, but then follows lowness. She is getting about tho', I very much hope. She is rising, and will claim her morning Picquet. I go to put this in the Post first. I walk 9 or 10 miles a day, alway up the road, dear London-wards. Fields, flowers, birds, and green lanes, I have no heart for. The bare road is cheerful, and almost as good as a street. I saunter to the Red Lion duly, as you used to the Peacock.

T. Manning, Esq.,
Puckeridge, Herts.

To Rev. JAMES GILLMAN.

LETTER CCCCLXII.]

Mr. Walden's, Church Street,
Edmonton, August 5, 1834.

My dear Sir—The sad week being over, I must write to you to say that I was glad of being spared from attending; I have no words to express my feeling with you all. I can only say that when you think a short visit from me would be acceptable, when your father and mother shall be able to see me *with comfort,* I will come to the bereaved house. Express to them my tenderest regards and hopes that they will continue our friends still. We both love and respect them as much as a human being can, and finally thank them with our hearts for what they have been to the poor departed.

God bless you all,   C. LAMB.

To REV. H. F. CARY.

LETTER CCCCLXIII.]   *September* 12, 1834.

"By Cot's plessing we will not be absence at the grace."

Dear C.—We long to see you, and hear account of your peregrinations, of the Tun at Heidelburg, the Clock at Strasburg, the statue at Rotterdam, the dainty Rhenish, and poignant Moselle wines, Westphalian hams, and Botargoes of Altona. But perhaps you have seen, not tasted any of these things.

Yours, very glad to chain you back again to your proper centre, books and Bibliothecæ,

C. and M. LAMB.

I have only got your note just now *per negligentiam periniqui Moxoni.*

To MR. CHILDS.

LETTER CCCCLXIV.]

Monday. Church Street, Edmonton (*not Enfield, as you erroneously direct yours.*) [*September* 15, 1834.]

Dear Sir—The volume which you seem to want is not to be had for love or money. I with difficulty procured a copy for myself. Yours is gone to enlighten the tawny Hindoos. What a supreme felicity to the author (only he is no traveller) on the Ganges or Hydaspes (Indian streams) to meet a smutty Gentoo ready to burst with laughing at the tale of Bo-Bo! for doubtless it hath been translated into all the dialects of the East. I grieve the less, that Europe should want it. I cannot gather from your letter whether you are aware that a second series of the Essays is published by Moxon, in Dover Street, Piccadilly, called "The Last Essays of Elia," and, I am told, is not inferior to the former. Shall I order a copy for you? and will you accept it? Shall I *lend* you, at the same time, my sole copy of the former volume (Oh! return it) for a month or two? In return, you shall favour me with the loan of one of those Norfolk-bred grunters that you laud so highly; I promise not to keep it above a day. What a funny name Bungay is! I never dreamt of a correspondent thence. I used to think of it as some Utopian town, or borough in Gotham land. I now believe in its existence, as part of Merry England!

[*Here are some lines scratched out.*]

The part I have scratched out is the best of the letter. Let me have your commands.

CH. LAMB, alias ELIA.

TO REV. H. F. CARY.

LETTER CCCCLXV.]   [*October* 1834.]

I protest I know not in what words to invest my sense of the shameful violation of hospitality which I was guilty of on that fatal Wednesday. Let it be blotted from the calendar. Had it been committed at a layman's house, say a merchant's or manfacturer's, a cheese-monger's or greengrocer's, or, to go higher, a barrister's, a member of Parliament's, a rich banker's, I should have felt alleviation, a drop of self pity. But to be seen deliberately to go out of the house of a clergyman drunk! a clergyman of the Church of England too! not that alone, but of an expounder of that dark Italian Hierophant, an exposition little short of *his* who dared unfold the Apocalypse: divine riddles both; and, without supernal grace vouchsafed, Arks not to be fingered without present blasting to the touchers. And then, from what house! Not a common glebe or vicarage (which yet had been shameful), but from a kingly repository of sciences, human and divine, with the primate of England for its guardian, arrayed in public majesty, from which the profane vulgar are bid fly. Could all those volumes have taught me nothing better! With feverish eyes on the succeeding dawn I opened upon the faint light, enough to distinguish, in a strange chamber, not immediately to be recognised, garters, hose, waistcoat, neckerchief, arranged in dreadful order and proportion, which I knew was not mine own. 'Tis the common symptom on awaking, I judge my last night's condition from. A tolerable scattering on the floor I hail as being too probably my own, and if the candlestick be not removed I assoil myself. But this finical arrangement, this finding everything in the morning in exact diametrical rectitude, torments me. By whom was I divested? Burning blushes! not by the fair hands of nymphs, the Buffam Graces? Remote whispers suggested that I *coached* it home in triumph. Far be that from working pride in me, for I was unconscious of the locomotion; that a young Mentor accompanied a reprobate old Telemachus; that, the Trojan-like, he bore his charge upon his shoulders, while the wretched incubus, in glimmering sense, hiccuped drunken snatches of flying on the bats' wings after sunset. An aged servitor was also hinted at, to make disgrace more complete, one, to whom my ignominy may offer further occasions of revolt (to which he was before too fondly inclining) from the true faith; for, at the sight of my helplessness, what more was needed to drive him to the advocacy of Independency? Occasion led me through Great

Russell Street yesterday. I gazed at the great knocker. My feeble hands in vain essayed to lift it. I dreaded that Argus Portitor, who doubtless lanterned me out on that prodigious night. I called the Elginian marbles. They were cold to my suit. I shall never again, I said, on the wide gates unfolding, say, without fear of thrusting back, in a light but peremptory air, "I am going to Mr. Cary's." I passed by the walls of Balclutha. I had imaged to myself a zodiac of third Wednesdays irradiating by glimpses the Edmonton dulness. I dreamed of Highmore! I am de-vited to come on Wednesdays. Villanous old age, that, with second childhood, brings linked hand in hand her inseparable twin, new inexperience, which knows not effects of liquor. Where I was to have sate for a sober, middle-aged-and-a-half gentleman, literary too, the neat fingered artist can educe no notions but of a dissolute Silenus, lecturing natural philosophy to a jeering Chromius, or a Mnasilus. Pudet. From the context gather the lost name of ——.

LETTER CCCCLXVI.]   [*October* 18, 1834.]

Dear Sir—The unbounded range of munificence presented to my choice, staggers me. What can twenty votes do for one hundred and two widows! I cast my eyes hopeless among the viduage. *N.B.*—Southey might be ashamed of himself to let his aged mother stand at the top of the list, with his £100 a year and butt of sack. Sometimes I sigh over No. 12, Mrs. Carve-ill, some poor relation of mine, no doubt. No. 15 has my wishes, but then she is a Welsh one. I have Ruth upon No. 21. I'd tug hard for No. 24. No. 25 is an anomaly; there can be no Mrs. Hogg. No. 34 ensnares me. No. 73 should not have met so foolish a person. No. 92 may bob it as she likes, but she catches no cherry of me. So I have even fixed at hap-hazard, as you'll see.

Yours, every third Wednesday,   C. L.

To MRS. DYER.

LETTER CCCCLXVII.]   *December* 22, 1834.

Dear Mrs. Dyer—I am very uneasy about a *Book,* which I either have lost or left at your house on Thursday. It was the book I went out to fetch from Miss Buffam's while the tripe was frying. It is called "Phillip's Theatrum Poetarum," but it is an English book. I think I left it in the parlour. It is Mr. Cary's book, and I would not lose it for the world. Pray, if you find it, book it at the Swan, Snow Hill, by an Edmonton stage immediately, directed to Mr. Lamb, Church Street, Edmonton, or write to say you cannot find it. I am quite anxious about it. If it is lost, I shall never like tripe again.

With kindest love to Mr. Dyer and all, yours truly,   C. LAMB.

NOTES

NOTES

CHAPTER I

1796–1800

The Letters of this period are chiefly addressed to Coleridge, then at Bristol. They relate the sad fortunes of the Lamb family, arising out of the death of the mother in September 1796. They are also largely critical, and deal with Coleridge's first published poems, and the joint volume in which Lamb and Charles Lloyd made their earliest appearance in print.

LETTER I (p. 573).—Southey had just published his *Joan of Arc,* in quarto. He had produced two years before at Bristol, in conjunction with Robert Lovell, *Poems by Bion and Moschus.* Charles Valentine Le Grice, here mentioned, was schoolfellow with Lamb and Coleridge at Christ's Hospital, as also was James White. (For Le Grice, see *Dict. Nat. Biog.*) The latter published his *Original Letters of Sir John Falstaff* in this year. They were dedicated, in a manifestly satirical spirit, to "Master Samuel Irelaunde." The allusions in the letter to Coleridge's "Numbers" are to the weekly issue of his *Watchman,* which first appeared on March 1, 1796, and expired on May 13. *Conciones ad Populum,* or Addresses to the People, appeared in November 1795.

LETTER II (p. 574).—*Poems on Various Subjects,* by S. T. Coleridge, late of Jesus College, Cambridge, was published this year, and it is to this volume, or the proof-sheets of it sent for inspection, that Lamb here refers as "your poems." The volume contained four sonnets signed C. L., and Coleridge's Preface announced that they "were written by Mr. Charles Lamb of the India House." The other sonnets by Lamb here submitted to Coleridge's opinion appeared in the second edition of Coleridge's Poems, in 1797. The story of the preparation of these small volumes of verse may be read, concurrently with these letters, in Joseph Cottle's *Recollections of Coleridge,* vol. i. *Moschus* was Robert Lovell, Southey's brother-in-law, several of whose sonnets were printed by Coleridge in his *Watchman.* He died of fever in this year. The "difference" which Lamb alludes to as having arisen between Coleridge and Southey was the split on the Pantisocratic Scheme which was to have been carried out by the young colonists on the banks of the Susquehanna.

LETTER III (p. 579).—The simile of the Laplander,

> . . . "by Niemi lake,"

is from Coleridge's *Destiny of Nations.* The allusion to the "Monody on Henderson" in this letter needs explanation. John Henderson was a singular genius and precocious scholar, the son of a Bristol schoolmaster, an account of whom will be found in the appendix to the second volume of Cottle's *Recollections of Coleridge*. Cottle was also the author of the "Monody on Henderson" here referred to. It had appeared in a small volume of poems published, without Cottle's name, at Bristol in 1795. Coleridge had evidently forwarded this volume to Lamb for his opinion. The lines criticised by Lamb occur in the following passage:—

> "As o'er thy tomb, my Henderson! I bend,
> Shall I not praise thee? scholar, Christian, friend!
> The tears which o'er a brother's recent grave
> Fond nature sheds, those copious tears I gave;
> But now that Time her softening hues has brought
> And mellowed anguish into pensive thought;
> Since through the varying scenes of life I've passed,
> Comparing still the former with the last,
> I prize thee more! The *great*, the *learn'd* I see,
> Yet memory turns from *little men* to *thee*."

The other "Monody" here criticised is that of Coleridge on Chatterton. The first symptoms of the subsequent coolness between Coleridge and Lamb may here be detected. It had its source in a delicate matter—Coleridge's alterations of Lamb's sonnets. The "Epitaph on an Infant" is the famous one—

> "Ere sin could blight or sorrows fade;"

at which Lamb never tired of laughing, up to the day when he applied it, in his "Essay on Roast Pig," to the infant grunter.

Dr. Foster was a popular corruption of Dr. Faustus in the old rhyme here alluded to:—

> "Dr. Forster was a good man.
> He whipped his scholars now and then,
> And when he whipped them, he made them dance
> Out of Scotland into France,
> Out of France into Spain,
> And then he whipped them back again!"

LETTER IV (p. 586).—*Your part of the "Joan of Arc."* "To the second book Coleridge contributed some four hundred lines, where Platonic philosophy and protests against the Newtonian hypothesis of æther are not very appropriately brought into connection with the shepherd-girl of Domremi. These lines disappeared from all editions after the first."—(Dowden's *Southey*, in the "Men of Letters Series.")

The verses on Lamb's grandmother are those afterwards entitled "The Grandame." See p. 539.

LETTER V (p. 587).—The *Salutation*. The inn near Christ's Hospital where Lamb and Coleridge used occasionally to meet and discuss poetry after Coleridge's departure from school. See Lamb's Preface to the 1818 edition of his works.

As curious a specimen of translation. A copy of this forgotten French novel is in my possession. It is entitled "Sentimental Tablets of the good Pamphile, written in the months of August, September, October, and November 1789, by M. Gorjy. Translated from the French by P. S. Dupuy, of the East India

House, London, 1795." In the list of subscribers at the end of the volume appear many names connected with the India House, familiar to us through Lamb's correspondence, including Mr. Thomas Bye, Mr. Ball (afterwards of Canton), Charles and Frederick Durand, Mr. Evans, Mr. Savory (a brother of "Hester"), and "C. Lamb" himself.

LETTER VI (p. 589).—The Dactyls here parodied were by Southey, one stanza of them only being Coleridge's. They appear in Southey's Collected Poems as "The Soldier's Wife," and begin—

> "Weary way-wanderer! languid and sick at heart,
> Travelling painfully over the rugged road;
> Wild-visaged wanderer! God help thee, wretched one."

It will be remembered as a curious coincidence that the same lines attracted the notice of the writers in the *Anti-Jacobin*, where a very humorous parody of them appears, which may be compared with Lamb's. Another like experiment in Latin metres by Southey was there transmuted into the more famous *Knife-Grinder*.

Your own lines, introductory to your poem on "Self," *run smoothly and pleasurably.* I am inclined to think that the reference is to a Fragment by Coleridge called "Melancholy," and to a poem addressed to Lamb, entitled "To a Friend, together with an Unfinished Poem." I believe that the unfinished poem was the Fragment just mentioned. Both were written as early as 1794, and the Fragment first appeared in the *Morning Chronicle*.

The poem referred to on the "Prince and Princess" was that bearing the title "On a Late Connubial Rupture in High Life," now first submitted to Lamb in manuscript.

Dyer stanza'd him. The first mention in these letters of George Dyer. See notes to "Oxford in the Vacation" (*Essays of Elia*).

LETTER VII (p. 591).—White's *Falstaff Letters* have been already referred to. Dr. Kenrick's *Falstaff's Wedding* was published in 1760. See notes in *Essays of Elia*, to "Oxford in the Vacation." Bürger's *Leonora*, translated by William Taylor of Norwich, first appeared in this year.

The Statute de Contumeliâ. See Coleridge's "Lines composed in a Concert Room." In most editions of Coleridge these lines are dated 1799, but it will be seen that Coleridge submitted them to Lamb three years before.

LETTERS VIII, IX, X, XI (pp. 593-598).—The following letters tell the sad story of the death of Lamb's mother. Whether the Mr. Norris of Christ's Hospital, here mentioned, is the Mr. Randal Norris, afterwards Sub-Treasurer of the Inner Temple, and to the end of his life Lamb's faithful friend, I cannot say. But I believe him to have been the same, and to have been thus designated because Coleridge would best remember Mr. Norris by his frequent visits to Charles Lamb when at Christ's Hospital. See "Christ's Hospital Five and Thirty Years Ago" in *Essays of Elia*.

Write as religious a letter as possible. Coleridge, we might be sure, obeyed this touching behest. In Gillman's unfinished *Life of Coleridge* there is given a letter by Coleridge addressed "To a friend in great anguish of mind on the sudden death of his mother." It is beyond all doubt the one addressed on this occasion to Lamb, for, as will be seen, it cites Lamb's particular request for "a religious letter." It runs as follows:—

"Your letter, my friend, struck me with a mighty horror. It rushed upon me and stupefied my feelings. You bid me write you a religious letter: I am not a man who would attempt to insult the greatness of your anguish by any other consolation. Heaven knows that in the easiest fortunes there is much dissatisfaction and weariness of spirit: much that calls for the exercise of patience and resignation; but in storms like these, that shake the dwelling and make the heart tremble, there is no middle way between despair and the yielding up of the whole spirit unto the guidance of faith. And surely it is a matter of joy that your faith in Jesus has been preserved: the Comforter that should relieve you is not far from you. But, as you are a Christian, in the name of that Saviour who was filled with bitterness and made drunken with wormwood, I conjure you to have recourse in frequent prayer to 'his God and your God,' the God of mercies and Father of all comfort. Your poor father is, I hope, almost senseless of the calamity: the unconscious instrument of Divine Providence knows it not, and your mother is in Heaven. It is sweet to be roused from a frightful dream by the song of birds, and the gladsome rays of the morning. Ah! how infinitely more sweet to be awakened from the blackness and amazement of a sudden horror by the glories of God manifest, and the hallelujahs of angels.

"As to what regards yourself, I approve altogether of your abandoning what you justly call vanities. I look upon you as a man called by sorrow and anguish and a strange desolation of hopes into quietness, and a soul set apart and made peculiar to God: we cannot arrive at any portion of heavenly bliss without, in some measure, imitating Christ. And they arrive at the largest inheritance who imitate the most difficult parts of His character, and, bowed down and crushed under foot, cry in fulness of faith, 'Father, Thy will be done.'

"I wish above measure to have you for a little while here: no visitants shall blow on the nakedness of your feelings; you shall be quiet, and your spirit may be healed. I see no possible objection, unless your father's helplessness prevent you, and unless you are necessary to him. If this be not the case, I charge you write me that you will come.

"I charge you, my dearest friend, not to dare to encourage gloom or despair: you are a temporary sharer in human miseries that you may be an eternal partaker of the Divine Nature. I charge you, if by any means it is possible, come to me" (Gillman's *Life of Coleridge*, vol. i. p. 338). See, afterwards, poor Lamb's comments on the concluding sentences of this letter.

LETTER XII (p. 599).—Lamb begins to find an interest in books once more. William Lisle Bowles's Poem, *Hope,* appeared this year in handsome quarto. *The Pursuits of Literature,* by T. J. Mathias, was also just published in its complete form, but anonymously.

LETTER XIII (p. 600).—Coleridge had removed about Christmas of this year to a cottage at Nether-Stowey near Bristol, in order to be near his friend Thomas Poole. A letter written to Joseph Cottle, shortly after his arrival, tells the same story of deep melancholy as he had also apparently confided to Lamb:—"On the Saturday, the Sunday and ten days after my arrival at Stowey, I felt a depression too dreadful to be described,

'So much I felt my genial spirits droop,
My hopes all flat: Nature within me seemed
In all her functions, weary of herself.'

"Wordsworth's conversation aroused me somewhat, but even now I am not the man I have been, and I think never shall. A sort of calm hopelessness diffuses itself over my heart. Indeed every mode of life which has promised me bread and cheese, has been one after another torn away from me, but God remains."

The rest of Lamb's letter refers to the arrangements in progress for the publication of the second edition (1797) of Coleridge's Poems, with others by Lamb and Lloyd. The sonnet ending "So, for the mother's sake," is that entitled "To a Friend who asked how I felt when the Nurse first presented my Infant to me."

LETTER XIV (p. 602).—Coleridge dedicated the volume of 1797 to his brother, George Coleridge of Ottery St. Mary; but the sonnets contained in the volume were prefaced by one addressed to Bowles, beginning—

"My heart has thanked thee, Bowles;"

and to this sonnet Lamb here alludes. The lines cited by Lamb, beginning—

"When all the vanities of life's brief day,"

are unknown to me. His own motto, from Massinger, is from *A Very Woman, or The Prince of Tarent.* He quoted the scene in which it occurs, twelve years later, in his *Dramatic Specimens.*

LETTER XV (p. 604).—The forthcoming volume of 1797 is here under discussion. The numbers "40, 63," etc., refer to the pages in the first edition of Coleridge's Poems, 1796. "40" is "Absence, A Farewell Ode;" "63" a sonnet, "To the Autumnal Moon;" "84" "An Imitation from Ossian." In spite of Lamb's remonstrances these were omitted from the second edition. Of the "Epitaph on an Infant,"

"Ere sin could blight or sorrow fade,"

Coleridge was indeed showing himself "tenacious." It had already appeared in the *Morning Chronicle,* and the *Watchman.* What lines of Lamb's are referred to, as beginning—

"Laugh all that weep,"

I cannot say. They did not appear in the forthcoming volume. The sonnet on Mrs. Siddons was a joint composition of Lamb and Coleridge.

The lines *"Dear native brook,"* published first in the *Watchman,* are the well-known sonnet "To the River Otter." No. "48" is the sonnet "To Priestley," beginning—

"Tho' roused by that dark Vizir Riot rude;"

"52" the sonnet "To Kosciusko;" and "53" that "To Fayette." *The last five lines of* 50 are those which conclude the sonnet to Sheridan. Sara Coleridge had a share in one poem in the edition of 1796,—that on page 129, here referred to, called "The Production of a Young Lady," on the subject of the loss of a silver thimble.

LETTER XVI (p. 606).—*The "divine chit-chat of Cowper"* was, as we learn from a sentence in the following letter, a phrase of Coleridge's own. Coleridge uses it again in a letter to John Thelwall of December 17:—"But do not let us introduce an Act of Uniformity against poets. I have room enough in *my* brain to admire, aye, and almost equally, the *head* and fancy of Akenside and the *heart* and fancy of Bowles, the solemn lordliness of Milton, and the divine chit-chat of Cowper, and whatever a man's excellence is, that will be likewise his fault" (S. T. C. to J. Thelwall, Bristol, December 17, 1796. Mr. Cosens's MSS.)

LETTER XVII (p. 606).—*"The sainted growing woof,"* etc. I have not traced this and the following quotation to their source. Coleridge's Lines on Burns, here referred to, were printed in a Bristol paper, and afterwards included in the poem, "To a friend who declared his intention of writing no more poetry."

LETTER XVIII (p. 608).—*"The odd coincidence of two young men.* In the joint volume of 1797 Charles Lloyd republished a series of sonnets on the death of his grandmother, Priscilla Farmer. It will be remembered that Lamb's lines, "The Grandame," appeared in the same volume.

LETTER XIX (p. 610).—The lines to his sister were afterwards withdrawn by Lamb from the forthcoming volume, but were printed in the *Monthly Magazine* for October 1797, with the simple heading "Sonnet to a Friend." They will be found on page 4 of the second volume of this series. "David Hartley Coleridge" was now in his second year, having been born September 19, 1796. Priestley's "Examination of the Scotch Doctors" was, I presume, his reply to Dr. Jamieson and others who had criticised his *History of the Corruptions of Christianity.*

LETTER XX (p. 610).—Mention has been already made of Coleridge's contribution to Southey's *Joan of Arc* of certain lines in the second book. Coleridge in later years entirely endorsed his friend Lamb's opinion of the lines. On reading them again he says, "I was really astonished (1) at the schoolboy, wretched, allegoric machinery; (2) at the transmogrification of the fanatic virago into a modern novel-pawing proselyte of the Age of Reason—a Tom Paine in petticoats; (3) at the utter want of all rhythm in the verse, the monotony and dead plumbdown of the pauses, and the absence of all bone, muscle, and sinew in the single lines."

The lines were omitted from all editions of Southey's Poem after the first, but were reprinted by Coleridge under the title of "The Destiny of Nations: a Vision," in his *Sibylline Leaves*, in 1817, and will be found in all complete editions of Coleridge's Poems. Lamb, with characteristic certainty of taste, selects for praise the finest lines of the whole composition—

> "For she had lived in this bad world
> As in a place of tombs,
> And touch'd not the pollutions of the dead."

Montauban dancing with Roubigné's tenants, is an incident in Mackenzie's *Julia de Roubigné*—the story which probably suggested to Lamb to attempt prose fiction.

The poem of Coleridge's here referred to as the "Dream" is that afterwards entitled "The Raven: a Christmas Tale told by a schoolboy to his little brothers and sisters," first printed in the *Morning Post* of March 10, 1798, and afterwards reprinted in *Annual Anthology*, and in *Sibylline Leaves*.

My poor old aunt. See verse on p. 613.

No after friendship e'er can raise—from John Logan's poem "On the death of a young lady."

John Woolman. Readers of the *Essays of Elia* will remember the reference to the writings of John Woolman, the Quaker, in the essay "A Quaker's Meeting."

The poem in Southey's new volume which Lamb calls the "Miniature," was actually called "On my own miniature Picture," the "Robert" being of course Southey himself. "Spirit of Spenser! was the wanderer wrong?" is the last line of the poem.

Flocci-nauci-what-do-you-call-'em-ists! may be deemed worthy of a note. "Flocci, nauci" is the beginning of a rule in the old Latin grammars, containing a list of words signifying "of no account," *floccus* being a lock of wool, and *naucus* a trifle. Lamb was recalling a sentence in one of Shenstone's Letters:— "I loved him for nothing so much as his flocci-nauci-nihili-pili-fication of money."

Mr. Rogers is indebted for his story. In a note to "An Effusion on an Autumnal Evening," in the first edition of his Poems, Coleridge had asserted that the tale of Florio in Rogers's *Pleasures of Memory* was to be found in the *Lochleven* of Bruce. As the fruit of Lamb's remonstrance in this letter Coleridge introduced a handsome apology to Rogers in the next edition (1797), admitting that, on a re-examination of the two poems, he had not found sufficient resemblance to justify the charge.

LETTER XXI (p. 614).—*Did the wand of Merlin wave?* Lamb refers to his sonnet, beginning "Was it some sweet delight of Fairy?" In the 1796 edition of Coleridge's Poems the passage had run thus:—

> "Or did the wizard wand
> Of Merlin wave, impregning vacant air,
> And kindle up the vision of a smile
> In those blue eyes?"

This, it seems, was an alteration of Coleridge's. In accordance with Lamb's instructions in this letter, the passage appeared in the 1797 edition without the "wizard wand of Merlin." *Mr.* Merlin, the conjurer, of Oxford Street, was a well-known person at the end of the eighteenth century.

LETTER XXII (p. 617).—*Those very schoolboy-ish verses.* Refers to the lines "To Sara and her Samuel."

LETTER XXIII (p. 618).—Compare with previous letter of January 5, 1797.

LETTER XXIV (p. 621).—Charles Lloyd, the son of a banker at Birmingham, lived under Coleridge's roof at Bristol, and at Nether-Stowey from the autumn of 1796 to the close of 1797. He was all his life subject to ill-health and persistent melancholia. The "Dedication" to which Lamb refers is the one to his sister, which introduced his portion of the volume of 1797. It ran thus:— "The few following poems, creatures of the Fancy and the Feeling, in life's more *vacant* hours; produced for the most part by Love in Idleness, are, with all a brother's fondness, inscribed to Mary Ann Lamb, the author's best friend and sister."

LETTER XXV (p. 622).—*The above* was Lamb's poem, "A Vision of Repentance," published in an appendix to the volume of 1797. See p. 519.

LETTER XXVI (p. 622).—"Gryll will be Gryll, and keep his hoggish mind." —Spenser, *Faëry Queen.*
Of my last poem. "The Vision of Repentance," mentioned in previous letter. *Riding behind in the basket* alludes to its being relegated to an appendix, with certain others by his two companions.

LETTER XXVII (p. 624).—*Life of John Buncle,* by Amory. See reference to this book, a great favourite of Lamb's, in the Essay on "Imperfect Sympathies."   .

LETTER XXVIII (p. 624).—*Our little book* was the volume of 1797, which now appeared with the following title-page:—"Poems, by S. T. Coleridge. Second edition. To which are now added Poems by Charles Lamb and Charles Lloyd," followed by the Latin motto of Coleridge, from the imaginary Epistles of Groscollias:—"Duplex nobis vinculum, et amicitiae et similium junctarumque Camenarum; quod utinam neque mors solvat, neque temporis longinquitas."
The Richardson referred to in this and other letters was evidently some one in authority at the India House, who controlled the important matter of Lamb's occasional holidays.

LETTER XXIX (p. 625).—Written after Lamb's visit to Coleridge at Nether-Stowey. Talfourd placed this letter in the year 1800, and has been followed by all subsequent editors. Yet, strangely enough, the summer in which it was written is placed beyond all question by the letter itself. The visit to Coleridge of which it tells was for many reasons a memorable one. It was on the evening of Lamb's arrival that Coleridge met with the accident to his leg which prevented his accompanying him on a walk, and drew from him the well-known lines, entitled "This Lime-Tree Bower my Prison," containing the apostrophe to Lamb, "My gentle-hearted Charles," under which Lamb so often affected to wince. An allusion to Coleridge's injured leg, it will be seen, occurs in this letter; and a further allusion to little Hartley cutting his teeth, adds a quite independent corroboration of the date.
That Inscription.—In all probability Wordsworth's lines "Left upon a Seat in a Yew-Tree," printed in the following year in the *Lyrical Ballads.*

LETTER XXX (p. 626).—*A little passage of Beaumont and Fletcher's.* The lines thus altered are from the "Maid's Tragedy" and run thus:—

> "And am prouder
> That I was once your love (though now refused),
> Than to have had another true to me."

When time drives flocks from field to fold. A noteworthy instance of Lamb's random recollections. He has here blended a line of "The Nymph's Reply to the Shepherd" in *England's Helicon,* with another from the song in *Love's Labour's Lost.*

LETTER XXXI (p. 628).—*I had well-nigh quarrelled with Charles Lloyd.* This sentence seems to throw light upon the origin of Lamb's beautiful verses, composed in this very month, "The Old Familiar Faces," and to suggest a different interpretation of them from that usually given. In my Memoir of Lamb ("Men of Letters Series"), I had supposed, in company with many others, that the allusion in the lines—

> "I have a friend, a kinder friend has no man.
> Like an ingrate, I left my friend abruptly—
> Left him, to muse on the old familiar faces"—

was to Coleridge, between whom and Lamb the relations had, as we have seen, for some time been rather strained. But it has been pointed out to me by an obliging correspondent that the reference in the lines just quoted is more probably to this temporary rupture with Lloyd; and that the "Friend of my bosom, thou more than a brother," in the last stanza but one, is addressed to Coleridge. It is pleasant to think that this should be the true explanation, and I gladly accept my correspondent's correction.

Coleridge, as the address at the end of the letter shows, was now at Shrewsbury, on a visit to the Unitarian minister, the Rev. Mr. Rowe, whom he then proposed to succeed in that office.

LETTER XXXII (p. 629).—Lamb had been introduced to Southey by Coleridge, as long back as 1795; but, according to Talfourd, "no intimacy ensued until he accompanied Lloyd in the summer of 1797 to the little village of Burton, near Christ Church in Hampshire, where Southey was then residing, and where they spent a fortnight as the poet's guests."

Sir R. Phillips was the proprietor of the *Monthly Magazine.*

Coleridge, in company with Wordsworth and his sister, left England for Germany in September 1798. Coleridge was absent a little less than a year. It was perhaps well for the future relations between him and Lamb that this temporary separation took place. Poetic rivalry and poetic criticism freely indulged on both sides had left bitterness behind. The whole pitiable story may be read, if it is worth reading, in the pages of Cottle's *Early Recollections of Coleridge.* Cottle tells us that Coleridge forwarded to him Lamb's letter, containing the sarcastic *Theses* here propounded, adding "these young visionaries" (meaning Lamb and Lloyd) "will do each other no good." The *Theses* were prefaced by the following remarks:—"Learned Sir, my friend, presuming on our long habits of friendship, and emboldened further by your late liberal permission to avail myself of your correspondence in case I want any knowledge (which I intend to do, when I have no Encyclopædia or Ladies' Magazine at hand to refer to in any matter of science), I now submit to your inquiries the above theological propositions, to be by you defended or oppugned (or both) in the schools of Germany, whither I am told you are departing, to the utter dissatisfaction of your native Devonshire, and regret of universal England; but to my own individual consolation, if, through the channel of your wished return, learned Sir, my friend, may be transmitted to this our island, from those famous theological wits of Leipsic and Gottingen, any rays of illumination, in vain to be derived from the home growth of our English halls and colleges. Finally wishing, learned Sir, that you may see Schiller, and swing in a wood (*vide* Poems) and sit upon a tun, and eat fat hams of Westphalia,— I remain your friend and docile pupil to instruct, CHAS. LAMB."

LETTER XXXIII (p. 631).—*Rosamund Gray*, by Charles Lamb, was published in this year, 1798.

LETTER XXXIV (p. 631).—The Eclogue here criticised was that entitled *The Ruined Cottage*.

How does your Calendar prosper? There would seem to have been an idea of calling the *Annual Anthology* a Calendar or Almanack of the Muses. Southey thus opens his preface to the first volume of the work:—"Similar collections to the present have long been known in France and Germany under the title of *Almanacks of the Muses*."

LETTER XXXV (p. 633).—The first of a remarkable series of letters to Charles Lloyd's brother, Robert, first printed in *Charles Lamb and the Lloyds*, a volume edited by Mr. E. V. Lucas in 1898. The reader is referred to that volume for full information as to the Lloyd family, and the remarkable discovery of these letters in 1894.

LETTER XXXVIII (p. 636).—Southey, who was now taking Coleridge's place as Lamb's chief literary correspondent, had sent two more Eclogues for his opinion—*The Wedding*, and *The Last of the Family*.

LETTER XXXIX (p. 637).—The *Lyrical Ballads*, the joint production of Wordsworth and Coleridge, had just made its appearance, published by Joseph Cottle, at Bristol. It contained four poems by Coleridge, one being the "Ancient Mariner." Lamb's pre-eminence as a critic, at this early age of three-and-twenty, appears wonderfully in his remarks upon this poem. "That last poem, which is yet one of the finest written," evidently refers to Wordsworth's "Lines written a few miles above Tintern Abbey," which come last in the little duodecimo volume. In the *Critical Review* for October 1798 Southey had reviewed the *Lyrical Ballads*. Of the *Ancient Mariner* he wrote, "We do not sufficiently understand the story to analyse it. It is a Dutch attempt at German sublimity. Genius has here been employed in producing a poem of little merit."

LETTER XLII (p. 640).—The lines entitled "Mystery of God," or "Living without God in the world," originally appeared in the first volume of Cottle's *Annual Anthology*, published this year, edited by Southey. The sonnet referred to would seem to be the one to his sister, already given, "Friend of my earliest years." One of the titles proposed for the *Anthology* was "Gleanings." It was in fact a poetical miscellany to which Coleridge, Southey, Lloyd, and others, including the Cottles, contributed. Two volumes only were published. Pratt, the editor of Pratt's *Gleanings through Wales, Holland, and Westphalia* (1795), was a bookseller at Bath, who published novels and poems, as well as various compilations.

Southey continued to send his poems, as he wrote them, for Lamb's criticisms. The "Witch Ballad" was "The Old Woman of Berkeley," written in this year, as was also "Bishop Bruno." Lamb's "Witch" was the poem originally intended as an episode in *John Woodvil*, but afterwards withdrawn and printed separately. The "Dying Lover" is the young Philip Fairford mentioned in the poem. George Dyer was at this time preparing a volume of poems. The lines criticised by Lamb occur in an ode "addressed to Dr. Robert Anderson" (*Poems*, by George Dyer: Longman and Co., 1801). Dyer did not accept his friend's correction. The line remains—

> "Dark is the poet's eye—but shines his name."

The "two noble Englishmen" were of course Wordsworth and Coleridge. Coleridge, as is well known, parted from Wordsworth and his sister while they were still at Hamburg.

LETTER XLIII (p. 642).—*John May* was a gentleman whose acquaintance Southey had made during his first visit to Portugal, and who was thenceforth one of Southey's most intimate friends and frequent correspondents.

LETTER XLV (p. 644).—Most of Southey's poems here referred to will be found in vols. ii. and vi. of the ten-volume edition, collected by himself, 1837. "The Parody" is the ballad called "The Surgeon's Warning." "Cousin Margaret" is the poem "To Margaret Hill."

LETTER XLVI (p. 646).—See Southey's lines "To a Spider," vol. ii. of the edition just named.
Sam Le Grice. For some amusing particulars concerning him see *Leigh Hunt's Autobiography*, chap. iii. "He was the maddest of all the great boys in my time: clever, full of address, and not hampered by modesty. Remote rumours, not lightly to be heard, fell on our ears respecting pranks of his among the nurses' daughters. He had a fair handsome face, with delicate aquiline nose and twinkling eyes. I remember his astonishing me when I was 'a new boy,' with sending me for a bottle of water, which he proceeded to pour down the back of G., a grave Deputy Grecian. On the master asking him one day why he, of all the boys, had given up no exercise (it was a particular exercise that they were bound to do in the course of a long set of holidays) he said he had had a 'lethargy.'" He must, however, have had a good heart. See the previous letter of Lamb to Coleridge in which he tells of Sam Le Grice giving up every hour of his time to amuse the poor old father, in the sad period following the death of Lamb's mother.

LETTER XLIX (p. 649).—*I am much pleased with his poems in the Anthology.* See C. Lloyd's poem, "Lines to a Brother and Sister" (*Annual Anthology*, vol. i. 192).
A sight of his novel—*Edmund Oliver*, published in 1798.

LETTER L (p. 650).—Lamb had been visiting his old haunts, near Blakesware in Herts. See note to "Blakesmoor in Hertfordshire;" *Essays of Elia*, p. 138.
Gebor is Lamb's spelling of "Gebir"—Landor's poem, which was published in this year.

LETTER LI (p. 650).—Thomas Manning, whose name appears here for the first time as Lamb's correspondent, was so remarkable a man as to warrant my giving a few particulars of his life, taken from the Memoir prefixed to his "Journey to Lhasa," in 1811-12 (*George Bogle and Thomas Manning's Journey to Thibet and Lhasa,* by C. R. Markham, 1876).—"He was the second son of the Rev. William Manning, Rector of Diss in Norfolk, and was born at his father's first living of Broome, in the same county, on the 8th of November 1772. Owing to ill-health in early life he was obliged to forego the advantages of a public school; but under his father's roof he was a close student of both classics and mathematics, and became an eager disciple of the philosophy of Plato. On his recovery he went to Caius College, Cambridge, and studied intensely, especially mathematics. While at Cambridge he published a work on Algebra, and a smaller book on Arithmetic. He passed the final examination, and was expected to be at least second wrangler, but his strong repugnance to oaths and tests debarred him from academic honours and preferments, and he left the university without a degree."

He continued to reside at Cambridge, as a private tutor at Caius, many years after the time when he should have graduated, and was there when Lamb first made his acquaintance, through the introduction of Charles Lloyd, in the autumn of 1799. "After he had lived at Cambridge for some years he began to brood over the mysterious empire of China, and devoted his time to an investigation of the language and arts of the Chinese, and the state of their country. He resolved to enter the Celestial Empire at all hazards, and to prosecute his researches till death stopped him, or until he should return with success. To enable him to undertake this hazardous enterprise he studied the Chinese language under the tuition of Dr. Hagar in France, and afterwards, with the aid of a Chinese, in London. When the English travellers were seized by Napoleon on the breaking out of war in 1803, Manning obtained leave to quit France entirely owing to the respect in which his undertaking was held by the learned men at Paris. His passport was the only one that Napoleon ever signed for an Englishman to go to England after war began."

The rest of Manning's adventures, and the result of his extraordinary expedition to Lhasa in 1811, as well as Manning's own Journal kept during his travels, will be found in Mr. Clements Markham's volume.

Manning was afterwards Chinese Interpreter to Lord Amherst's Embassy in 1817. He then "returned to England, after an absence of nearly twelve years, apparently a disappointed man. He was in Italy from 1827 to 1829, and then went to live in strict retirement at Bexley, whence he removed to a cottage near Dartford, called Orange Grove. He led a very eccentric life. It is said that he never furnished his cottage, but only had a few chairs, one carpet, and a large library of Chinese books. He wore a milky-white beard down to his waist." He died at Bath on the 2nd of May 1840, aged sixty-eight.

The Title of the Play.—Lamb had at first intended to call his play, *John Woodvil,* by a different name—*Pride's Cure.*

CHAPTER II

1800–1809

Letter LIII (p. 653).—*Mr. Wyndham's unhappy composition.* Coleridge's criticism on Wyndham's note, contributed to the *Morning Post* in January 1800, is reprinted in the *Essays on his own Times* (i. 261).

Cottrellian grace. Doubtless an allusion to Sir Charles Cotterell, Master of the Ceremonies at the Court of Charles II.

LETTER LIV (p. 653).—*My Enemy's B*—— is, I am afraid, a variation upon "My enemy's dog" in a well-known speech from *King Lear.*
Mary Hayes. Mary Hayes was an intimate friend of Godwin and his wife, Mary Wollstonecraft. She wrote in the *Monthly Magazine,* also a novel called *Emma Courtenay.* "An uncommon book. Mary Hayes is an agreeable woman and a Godwinite." (Southey, *Life and Correspondence,* i. 305).

LETTER LV (p. 654).—"War, and Nature, and Mr. Pitt." Evidently some popular allegorical print of the day.

LETTER LVI (p. 655).—*Supposed manuscript of Burton.* See "Curious Fragments, extracted from a common-place book which belonged to Robert Burton."
Olivia was Charles Lloyd's sister.

LETTER LVII (p. 656).—*Hetty died on Friday night.* Charles and Mary's one servant.

LETTER LIX (p. 657).—*To lodge with a friend in town.* John Mathew Gutch, a schoolfellow of Lamb's at Christ's Hospital, afterwards the editor of *Felix Farley's Bristol Journal.* He was in partnership with a law-stationer in Southampton Buildings, Holborn. Lamb lodged there occasionally for several years to come. See Letter to Coleridge, later on, p. 668.

LETTER LXII (p. 659).—*Lamb is quite enough.* There was evidently a disposition in the early days of Lamb's friendships to spell his name with a final *e.* I have seen it thus misspelt in magazines of the time.
By terming me gentle-hearted in print. See Coleridge's lines, "This Lime-Tree Bower my Prison," first published in the *Annual Anthology.*
I have hit off the following. See "A Ballad: Noting the Difference of Rich and Poor." See p. 523.
W.'s tragedy. "The Borderers." The second edition of the *Lyrical Ballads* was published this year.

LETTER LXIII (p. 660).—*His friend Frend.* The Rev. William Frend, who was expelled the University of Cambridge for tenets savouring of Unitarianism.
George Dyer. See note to the Elia Essay, "Oxford in the Vacation." *Essays of Elia,* p. 8.

LETTER LXIV (p. 662).—*Dr. Anderson.* James Anderson (1739-1808), writer on Agriculture and Politico-Economical subjects.

LETTER LXVII (p. 664).—The references to poems in this letter are to the second volume of the *Annual Anthology,* just published. "Blenheim" is, of course, Southey's well-known ballad; "Lewti" and the "Raven" are by Coleridge.
Your 141st page refers to the poem " 'This Lime-Tree Bower my Prison,' a poem addressed to Charles Lamb, of the India House, London," in which Lamb was styled, "my gentle-hearted Charles."

LETTER LXIX (p. 668.)—*On a visit to Grattan.* Lamb's own slip of the pen for *Curran.* See Mr. Kegan Paul's *Life of Godwin.*

LETTER LXX (p. 669).—John Mathew Gutch, when Lamb lodged with him in Southampton Buildings, Holborn, was in business there as a law-stationer. He was at the time engaged to a Miss Wheeley, the daughter of a coach-builder at Birmingham, and it was during one of his occasional visits to his fiancée in that city that Lamb played upon him the very harmless practical joke contained in this letter. Gutch married Miss Wheeley in the following year. The letter was kindly placed at my disposal by a niece of Mr. Gutch.

LETTER LXXI (p. 669).—*Helen.* These verses were by Mary Lamb.
Alfred, an epic poem by Joseph Cottle of Bristol, the bookseller and poet.
Hurlothrumbo.—For Samuel Johnson, author of this and other now forgotten extravagances, see *Dict. Nat. Biography.* The work referred to by Lamb is probably "A Vision of Heaven," published in 1738.

LETTER LXXII (p. 671).—*A "Conceit of Diabolic Possession."* See the lines afterwards entitled "Hypochondriacus" (See p. 524).

LETTER LXXVI (p. 675).—*A pleasant hand, one Rickman.* John Rickman (1771-1840), for many years Clerk-Assistant at the Table of the House of Commons, an eminent statistician, and author of the system for taking the population census, besides many other inventions of greater or less utility. He became the intimate friend of Lamb, Southey, and others of that set.
Mr. Crisp was a barber over whose shop Manning lodged, in St. Mary's Passage, Cambridge.
My Play. "John Woodvil."

LETTER LXXIX (p. 679).—*How to abridge the Epilogue.* The epilogue Lamb was writing for Godwin's play, *Antonio.* The next two or three letters deal with the production and the failure of the unfortunate drama. See Mr. Kegan Paul's *Life of Godwin.*

LETTER LXXXIII (p. 683).—*The Preface must be expunged.* In the British Museum is Lamb's copy of Dyer's Poems. It contains the cancelled preface, and on the margin of advertisement, explaining how the book begins at p. lxix. instead of p. i., Lamb has written, "One copy of this cancelled Preface, snatched out of the fire, is prefixed to this volume." The cancelled preface ran to sixty-six pages, not eighty, as Lamb says to Manning. Writing to G. C. Bedford, 22nd March 1817, respecting one of his books then printing, Southey says, "Now, pray, be speedy with the cancels. On such an occasion Lamb gave G. Dyer the title of *Cancellarius Magnus.*" (*Letters of R. S.* i. 428.) For this interesting reference I am indebted to my friend Mr. J. Dykes Campbell.

LETTER LXXXIV (p. 685).—*Miss Wesley.* Daughter of Samuel and niece of John Wesley. "Eccentric but estimable," says H. Crabb Robinson in Diary, 27th May 1812.
One Miss Benjay. Miss Elizabeth Benger, authoress of various poems and histories. See *Dictionary of National Biography,* iv. 221.

Letter LXXXV (p. 687).—*Barbara Lewthwaite*. The little heroine of Wordsworth's poem "The Pet Lamb."

Letter LXXXVI (p. 688).—The "second volume" that Lamb had borrowed was the second volume of the *Lyrical Ballads*, then just published. The "Song of Lucy" is clearly the famous lyric beginning—

"She dwelt among the untrodden ways."

Lamb's criticism on the second title of the "Ancient Mariner" proved effectual in the end, but the title was retained until the publication of the *Sibylline Leaves* in 1817. The stanzas referred to by Lamb as "The Mad Mother," are those beginning with the words, "Her eyes are wild." Wordsworth in later editions dropped the original title.

I totally differ from your idea. Wordsworth had appended a note to the second edition of the *Lyrical Ballads* (vol. i.), expressing his opinion on the *Ancient Mariner*, and the probable causes of its failure to please. The note is of such singular interest, and so little known, that I make no apology for giving it in full.

"Note to the Ancient Mariner, p. 155.—I cannot refuse myself the gratification of informing such Readers as may have been pleased with this Poem, or with any part of it, that they owe their pleasure in some sort to me; as the Author was himself very desirous that it should be suppressed. This wish had arisen from a consciousness of the defects of the Poem, and from a knowledge that many persons had been much displeased with it. The Poem of my Friend has indeed grave defects; first, that the principal person has no distinct character, either in his profession of mariner, or as a human being who, having been long under the control of supernatural impressions, might be supposed himself to partake of something supernatural; secondly, that he does not act, but is continually acted upon; thirdly, that the events, having no necessary connection, do not produce each other; and, lastly, that the imagery is somewhat too laboriously accumulated. Yet the Poem contains many delicate touches of passion, and indeed the passion is everywhere true to nature; a great number of the stanzas present beautiful images, and are expressed with unusual felicity of language; and the versification, though the metre is itself unfit for long poems, is harmonious and artfully varied, exhibiting the utmost powers of that metre, and every variety of which it is capable. It therefore appeared to me that these several merits (the first of which, namely, that of the passion, is of the highest kind) gave to the Poem a value which is not often possessed by better Poems. On this account I requested of my friend to permit me to republish it."

The coarse epithet of "pin-point." In the first version of the *Poet's Epitaph*, the line to which we are now accustomed—

"Thy ever-dwindling soul away,"

ran thus:—

"Thy pin-point of a soul away."

Letter LXXXVIII (p. 691).—The greater portion of this letter was in earlier editions printed in the Notes. It is now included in the Text, and a delightful paragraph about George Dyer is now restored.

Letter LXXXIX (p. 693).—*George Dyer's Poems:* Longman and Rees, 1801. The passage about Shakspeare from the long poem called "Poetic Sympathies" in this volume, beginning—

> "Yet, muse of Shakspeare, whither wouldst thou fly
> With hurried step, and dove-like, trembling eye?"

is hardly worth quoting further, but may be referred to by the curious.

John Stoddart, Esq. John, afterwards Sir John, Stoddart, was the brother of Mrs. William Hazlitt (the *first* W. H.). He was a writer in the *Times*—quarrelled with Walter, and set up the *New Times,* a short-lived venture, and went to Malta, where he was Chief Justice. While there he invited S. T. Coleridge to visit him, and the invitation was accepted.

My back tingles from the northern castigation. This alludes, of course, to the letter from Wordsworth referred to in the letter to Manning of Feb. 15, 1801.

I am going to change my lodgings. The Lambs were now about to leave Southampton Buildings (see Letter LXIX) for Mitre Court Buildings, in the Temple, destined to be their home for the next eight years.

Letter XCI (p. 696).—Baron Maseres, Cursitor Baron of the Exchequer. See the Elia Essay, "The Old Benchers of the Inner Temple."

Letter XCV (p. 700).—*Walter Wilson,* bookseller, and afterwards writer, best known as the author of the *Memoirs of Defoe,* to which Lamb was later to contribute some interesting critical matter.

Letter XCVI (p. 700).—See Lamb's Essay on "Newspapers Thirty-five Years Ago," and the note upon it in this edition. He there tells us that this epigram gave the unfortunate *Albion* its *coup de grâce.*

Letter XCVIII (p. 703).—*Your story.* The story of Godwin's later play of *Faulkener* would seem to be indicated here. That play was built upon Defoe's *Roxana,* and Lamb here suggests that the strange history of Richard Savage's parentage might advantageously be borrowed. *Faulkener* was not produced till 1807, and then unsuccessfully. A subsequent letter (No. C.) evidently refers to the plot of the same proposed drama.

Letter XCIX (p. 704).—The first of a series of letters to Rickman here printed for the first time. Rickman had gone to Dublin as secretary to Charles Abbot (afterwards Lord Colchester) who was made Chief Secretary for Ireland this year. Abbot held the office for only six months, being elected to the Speakership of the House of Commons in January 1802. Rickman remained his secretary after the return to London, and rose to being First Clerk Assistant at the House of Commons.

George Burnett. The son of a farmer in Somersetshire. He was sent to Balliol College, Oxford, and there made the acquaintance of Southey, who was at the same college. He subsequently joined Southey and Coleridge in their "Pantisocracy" scheme. Through these two friends he made the acquaintance of Lamb. He figures largely in these letters to Rickman, where he is commonly styled George the Second, in distinction from Dyer, George the First.

The Professor is courting. Godwin married Mrs. Clairmont in December of this year. She was a widow with two children. The daughter came to play an important part in the lives of Shelley and Byron. *Abbas, King of Persia,* was the title of Godwin's second tragedy, which was not destined to be performed.

LETTER CIV (p. 711).—*The Goul and Gouless* are Godwin and his new wife. "So am not I, said the foolish fat scullion."—*Tristram Shandy.*

LETTER CV (p. 713).—*Letter with the broad seal.* Rickman was Deputy Keeper of the Privy Seal at the Castle.
Earl of Buchan was only sixty years of age at this date. This eccentric nobleman, it will be remembered, was the owner of Dryburgh Abbey, and bestowed its sepulchral aisle upon Walter Scott in order that he might be there buried with his Haliburton ancestors.

LETTER CVII (p. 715).—*Lord Stanhope.* George Burnett had been chosen as tutor to Lord Stanhope's two sons.

LETTER CVIII (p. 716).—*The sweet girl.* See Note to Letter CXXVI. The young lady's name was Mary Druitt.
His two young lords. This would seem to be a fairly accurate account of what happened. After the *escapade* of the two sons, Lord Stanhope paid Burnett a year's salary. Burnett did not long remain an inmate of Lord Stanhope's house, and became later a regimental surgeon.

LETTER CXI (p. 719).—*My Play,* "John Woodvil." The copy sent to Manning, mainly in the handwriting of Mary Lamb, with various omissions marked and corrections added in the handwriting of Charles, is before me, kindly lent by Mr. C. R. Manning of Diss. In the inside cover of the MS. is pasted a sheet of paper, on which Lamb has written as follows:—
Mind this goes for a letter. (Acknowledge it *directly,* if only in ten words.)
Dear Manning—(I shall want to hear this comes safe.) I have scratched out a good deal, as you will see. Generally, what I have rejected was either *false in feeling,* or a violation of character—mostly of the first sort. I will here just instance in the concluding few lines of the "Dying Lover's Story," which completely contradicted his character of *silent* and *unreproachful.* I hesitated a good deal what copy to send you, and at last resolved to send the worst, because you are familiar with it, and can make it out; and a stranger would find so much difficulty in doing it, that it would give him more pain than pleasure.
This is compounded precisely of the two persons' hands you requested it should be.—Yours sincerely, C. LAMB.
I will now transcribe the "Londoner." I have printed this letter, with the accompanying note by Talfourd, but in point of fact the "Londoner" was never published in the *Reflector.* See p. 375.

LETTER CXIV (p. 721).—This letter is written to Coleridge on the return of Charles and Mary from paying him a holiday visit at Keswick. Thomas Clarkson was then residing in a cottage on Ulswater. See following letter to Manning.

LETTER CXVI (p. 722).—*Fenwick is a ruined man.* See *Elia Essays,* "The Two Races of Men," and "Newspapers Thirty-five Years Ago."
Fell, my other drunken companion. Mr. Ralph Fell, author of a *Tour through the Batavian Republic*—according to Southey, a "dull book."

LETTER CXVII (p. 724).—The first of several letters in this correspondence written in Latin; and in the present instance, as would appear, in reply to a challenge from Coleridge. The letter as hitherto printed is full of certain mistakes for which Lamb is clearly not responsible. These I have ventured to correct, but I have not thought it desirable to amend the Latinity otherwise in passages where it is certainly not immaculate. The grammar and idiom are frequently so lax as to jeopardise the writer's meaning, but with the assistance of my friend Dr. Calvert of Shrewsbury, I hope I have disentangled most of Lamb's somewhat involved allusions. The letter is interesting as bearing reference to several events of interest in the lives of both Coleridge and Wordsworth. It bears date October 9, 1802. A few days earlier, on October 2, Wordsworth had been married to Mary Hutchinson. On the same day (possibly by mere coincidence) Coleridge had printed in the *Morning Post* the first version of his splendid Ode, entitled "Dejection." In this version the person addressed throughout is a certain "Edmund," and not, as in the later revision of the poem, the "Lady," addressed in the often quoted lines—

> "O Lady, we receive but what we give,
> And in *our* Life alone does Nature live."

That "Edmund," the writer's dearest friend and a great poet, could be no other than Wordsworth we might be sure from internal evidence, even if we had not in this letter a curious confirmation. The *Carmina Chamouniana* refer to Coleridge's "Hymn before Sunrise, in the Vale of Chamouni," then recently printed for the first time in the *Morning Post*. Lamb's allusions will be intelligible to those who recall the passage beginning—

> "Who bade the sun
> Clothe you with rainbows? Who with living flowers
> Of loveliest blue, spread garlands at your feet?
> God! God! the torrents, like a shout of nations,
> Utter! the ice-plain bursts, and answers God!"

Although hitherto printed by Lamb's editors, *Tod, Tod,* the reading, I am convinced, should be *Dodd, Dodd.* There is a mountain near Skiddaw called *Skiddaw Dodd,* which Lamb doubtless remembered. Furthermore, the crime and punishment of "the unhappy Doctor," bearing the same name, was fresh in the memory of many persons then living.

The comparisons of the First Consul with the Roman Emperors refer to a series of Essays then recently published by Coleridge in the *Morning Post.* They are reprinted in the *Essays on his own Times:* Pickering, 1850 (vol. ii. pp. 478-514). The allusion to the *Ludus Americanus* must perhaps remain unsolved. The "Flying Opossum" was little Derwent Coleridge, then just entering his third year. The child's vain attempts to pronounce the name of this creature in his picture-book, to which he never attained nearer than "Pi-pos," had fastened this nickname upon the little fellow. "Pi-pos" will recur in many of the succeeding letters.

I append a translation, partly paraphrased, of the entire letter:—

My very dear Friend—"Pay the post, and go to——" you say; *i. e.* to Tartarus. Nay! but have *you* not rather caught a Tartar? Here have I, for all these years, used my vernacular with (for a writing-clerk) passable elegance; and yet you are bent on goading me on with your neat and masterly letter, to yelp an answer in such dog-Latin as I may. However, I will try, though afraid my outlandish and far-fetched barbarisms will bring disgrace upon Christ's Hospital, the school still so proud of its learned Barnes and Markland, where in days gone by a wrong-headed master perseveringly drenched me with classical lore. But I must go on as best I can. Come then at my call, all ye troops of conjugations or declensions! horrible spectres! and come first and foremost thou—mightiest shadow and image of the Rod—now thank Heaven a thing of the past, the thought of which makes me howl as though I were a boy again!

Your lines written at Chamouni I certainly think very noble, but your English rendering of the echo among the Grisons (*God! God!*) rather jars upon me. I cannot forget that in your own Cumbrian mountains I heard you rouse the echo (Dodd! Dodd!) of the unfortunate Doctor's name, a sound by no means divine! As to the rest, I entirely approve.

Your comparisons also I recognise fully as witty and wise. But how about their truth? I find you asserting in one breath quite inconsistently, merely for comparison's sake, that the First Consul is endowed with the "irritable mind" of Julius Cæsar, as well as with a "constitutional coolness and politic craft" more appropriate to Augustus: and then in the third place you have taken much trouble to extract a resemblance to Tiberius. Why deal with one or two Cæsars when the whole Twelve are only too ready to offer you their services for comparison? Besides I respect antiquity too much not to detest unfair parallels.

I am wonderfully pleased to have your account of the marriage of Wordsworth, or perhaps I should say of a certain "Edmund" of yours. All blessings rest on thee, Mary! too happy in thy lot. . . . I wish thee also joy in this new alliance, Dorothy—truly so named, that other "gift of God."

The American "Ludus" of which you prattle so much, Coleridge, I pass over, as utterly abhorrent from a "Ludus" (as such things go). For tell me, what "fun" is there in estranging from ourselves, sprung from the same stock (for the sake of one miserable *jeu d'esprit*), the whole of the Columbian nation. I ask you for a subject for something "Sportive," and you offer me "Bloody Wars."

To wind up, good-bye, and let me know what you think of my Latin style; and wish for me all health and beauty to my "Flying Opossum," or as you prefer to call him the "Odd Fish." Best greetings to your wife and my good Hartley. We are well, self and sister, who desires her best wishes. No more at present. My time is not my own.

I had almost forgotten to tell you that I have two volumes of John Milton's Latin Works, which (*D.V.*) I will have sent with the rest of your books sooner or later by Mary. You know, however, that in such matters I am by no means in the habit of hurrying; and I plead guilty. I have only to say further that they are handsome volumes, containing all J. M.'s Latin works. I am just now myself engaged and deeply interested in his every spirited Apology for the People of England.

I will carefully observe your instructions about Stuart. Good-bye, once more; and O remember me.

LETTER CXVIII (p. 725).—*Your offer about the German poems.* Coleridge was to translate some of the best German lyrics into literal prose, and Lamb was then to turn them into verse. One experiment of the kind is Lamb's version of Thekla's Song in "Wallenstein."

Your "Epigram on the Sun and Moon." An epigram of Coleridge's contributed this month to the *Morning Post:*—"On the curious circumstance that in the German language the sun is feminine and the moon masculine."

Allen. The schoolfellow of Coleridge and Lamb at Christ's Hospital. Robert Allen went to University College, Oxford, in 1792—the year after Coleridge went to Jesus College, Cambridge. Coleridge visited Allen at Oxford in June 1794, and was introduced by him to Southey. Allen was one of the original Pantisocrats. He was very handsome. See anecdote of him in the Elia Essay, "Christ's Hospital five and thirty years ago."

LETTER CXIX (p. 726).—*"Once a Jacobin."* An essay of Coleridge's in the *Morning Post* for October 1802. "Once a Jacobin, always a Jacobin." *Essays on his own Times,* ii. p. 542.

Sam Le Grice. Lamb's schoolfellow at Christ's Hospital. See Elia Essay, "Christ's Hospital five and thirty years ago."

LETTER CXX (p. 728).—S. T. C.'s first letter to Mr. Fox was published in the *Morning Post* of Thursday, November 4, 1802. A second followed on November 9. Both are included in the *Essays on his own Times,* vol. ii.

LETTER CXXI (p. 729).—Joseph Cottle, the bookseller and publisher, was also, like his brother Amos, a poet. He produced *Malvern Hills* in 1798. *Alfred,* an epic poem, in 1801.

LETTER CXXII (p. 730).—*A merry natural captain.* Captain, afterwards Admiral Burney, who sailed with Captain Cook in two of his voyages.

LETTER CXXIII (p. 732).—*On the death of a young Quaker.* See the beautiful verses entitled "Hester" (See *Poems,* p. 511.) Miss Emma Savory of Blackheath, a niece of Hester Savory, has kindly supplied me with a few biographical details. "She (Hester) was the eldest sister of my father, A. B. Savory, and lived with him and his sisters, Anna and Martha, at Pentonville. She married Charles Stoke Dudley, and died, eight months after her marriage, of fever. I possess a miniature portrait of her which I greatly value. My mother used to say that her beauty consisted more in expression than in regularity of features." I may add that I have seen this miniature which, even after reading Lamb's tender and beautiful lyric, is anything but disappointing. It is a bright-eyed gypsy face such as we know so well from the canvas of Reynolds. Miss Savory adds, "I do not think our mother was aware of Charles Lamb's attachment to Hester Savory. Perhaps she did not know it herself."

LETTER CXXIV (p. 732).—This letter refers to the third edition (1803) of Coleridge's Poems, which he had placed in Lamb's hands for revision. The poem called "The Silver Thimble" is that already referred to, in which Sara Coleridge had some small share. The verses on "Flicker and Flicker's Wife" were entitled simply, "Written after a Walk before Supper." They open thus—

"Tho' much averse, dear Jack, to flicker,
To find a likeness for friend V—ker,
I've made this Earth and air and sea
A voyage of Discovery!
And let me add (to ward off strife),
For V—ker, and for V—ker's wife."

Lamb's habitual inaccuracy comes out here also. As for the omission of this *jeu d'esprit* in the forthcoming edition, no one will be found to dissent from his judgment.

LETTER CXXVI (p. 734).—This letter is addressed to "Mr. T. Manning, Maison Magnan, No. 342 Boulevard Italien, Paris."

An epitaph scribbled upon a poor girl. Written upon a young lady of the name of Mary Druitt, at Wimborne, Dorsetshire. This was done at the request of John Rickman. Lamb was not personally acquainted with the girl, but wrote the lines on Rickman's description. The late Mr. J. P. Collier gives a slightly different version of the lines in his "Old Man's Diary" (privately printed). Mr. Collier says that the girl died at the age of nineteen, of smallpox, and that the lines were engraved upon the tomb; but I learn from members of the Druitt family still living at Wimborne that this latter statement is not correct. (See Letter CVIII.)

LETTER CXXXI (p. 739).—Lamb's animadversions upon Godwin's lengthy *Life of Chaucer* are as usual admirably just. The work consisted of four-fifths ingenious guessing to one-fifth of material having any historic basis.

Schoolboy copy of verses for Merchant Taylors' boys. The boys were allowed to get help from outside in the composition of their weekly epigrams. In later years we find him making some for the late Archdeacon Hessey and his brother, when at that school.

LETTER CXXXVIII (p. 746).—*Farewell to my "Friendly Traitress."* The "Farewell to Tobacco." First published in Leigh Hunt's *Reflector* in 1811, and afterwards in Lamb's collected works in 1818. See *Poems*, p. 525.

LETTER CXXXIX (p. 747).—*Mr. Dawe.* See the paper by Lamb, written long afterwards, "Recollections of a late Royal Academician." (*Mrs. Leicester's School*, etc., p. 307.)

Lord Nelson, died October 21, 1805.

Luck to Ned Search. The light of Nature, by Edward Search, Esq., was a work by Abraham Tucker, which Hazlitt was at this time engaged in abridging and editing. His abridgment appeared in 1807.

The American Farmer. Letters from an American Farmer, Philadephia, 1774, by Hector St. John Crevecœur.

LETTER CXLI (p. 749).—*Life of Fawcett.* "Report was rife that a life of the Rev. Joseph Fawcett, Mr. Hazlitt's early friend, might be expected from the same quarter; but such was not the fact" (*Memoir of Hazlitt*, by his Grandson). Fawcett was a dissenting minister at Walthamstow, who published various *Sermons, Poems,* etc.

LETTER CXLVI (p. 753).—Addressed:—"Mr. Manning, Passenger on Board the *Thames*, East Indiaman, Portsmouth." A short postscript to this letter was omitted by Talfourd:—"One thing more, when you get to Canton you will most likely see a young friend of mine, Inspector of Teas, named Ball. He is a very good fellow, and I should like to have my name talked of in China. Give my kind remembrances to the same Ball."

LETTER CXLVIII (p. 755).—*The good news of Mrs. W.* Wordsworth's son Thomas was born on the 16th of June 1806.

Mr. H—See p. 403.

A young gentleman of my office. We shall have occasion hereafter to mention this fellow-clerk of Lamb's. For an account of Coleridge's early passion for Evans' sister Mary, see Gillman's *Life of Coleridge* and Cottle's *Reminiscences*.

LETTER CLIII (p. 762).—*The Tales from Shakspeare.* The plates referred to by Lamb were designed (as is believed) by William Mulready, then a young man of twenty, and engraved by William Blake. The "bad Baby" was a familiar nickname for Mrs. Godwin. The subject from the *Merchant of Venice* was lettered, "Gratiano and Nerissa desire to be married;" the illustration to the *Midsummer Night's Dream* bore for title "Nic Bottom and the Fairies." In spite of Lamb's objection to this latter, it is by far the best of all the illustrations, both in design and drawing, and indicates very clearly the hand of Blake. The "giants and giantesses" of whom Lamb complains are certainly too frequent in these illustrations.

LETTER CLIV (p. 763).—The story of William Hazlitt's disappearance, which caused anxiety to his family, will be found in the *Memoir of Hazlitt*, by his grandson (chapter xi.).

LETTER CLV (p. 763).—Talfourd omitted a few sentences from this letter, which may as well be restored. "Godwin keeps a shop in Skinner Street, Cornhill; he is termed children's bookseller, and sells penny, twopenny, threepenny, and fourpenny books. Sometimes he gets an order for the dearer sort of books (mind, all that I tell you in this letter is true)."

As the boys followed Tom the Piper. Edward FitzGerald, in a letter to Mr. Aldis Wright of March 1878, writes, apropos of this passage: "I had not thought who Tom was: rather acquiesced in some idea of the 'pied Piper of Hamelin'; and not half an hour after, chancing to take down Browne's *Britannia's Pastorals*, found Tom against the Maypole with a ring of Dancers about him. I suppose Tom survived in folk-lore till dear Lamb's time; but how he, a Cockney, knew of it, I don't know."

LETTER CLVI (p. 766).—The passage about the "giant's vomit" was from the story of Polyphemus in Lamb's version of the *Odyssey*.

LETTER CLVIII (p. 767).—Coleridge's *Friend* made its first appearance on the 1st of June 1809, and its last on March 15, 1810.

CHAPTER III

1809–1816

LETTER CLX. (p. 769).—*Mrs. Clarke.* The mistress of the Duke of York, second son of George III., and Commander-in-Chief of the Forces. "It was established beyond the possibility of doubt that the Duke had permitted Mrs. Clarke to interfere in military promotions; that he had given commissions at her recommendation; and that she had taken money for the recommendations." In consequence of the public excitement and indignation on the subject, the Duke resigned his office on the 20th of March of this year.

Godwin's little book. Godwin, *On Sepulchres.*

LETTER CLXI (p. 771).—*Wordsworth's book.* The Convention of Cintra. "Concerning the relations of Great Britain, Spain, and Portugal to each other, and to the common enemy at this crisis, and specifically as affected by the Convention of Cintra," etc. etc., by W. Wordsworth. Longmans. May 20, 1809.

Daniel, enriched with manuscript notes. These are printed in *Notes and Queries,* 1st Series, vi. 117.

Two volumes of Juvenile Poetry. "Poetry for Children, entirely original." By the Author of *Mrs. Leicester's School.* In two volumes. London. Printed for M. J. Godwin at the Juvenile Library, No. 44, Skinner Street. 1809.

Cœlebs. "Cœlebs in Search of a Wife," by Hannah More, published in 1809.

LETTER CLXII (p. 773).—For full information about Charles Lloyd, the father of Lamb's friends, Charles and Robert Lloyd, see Mr. E. V. Lucas's *Charles Lamb and the Lloyds.*

LETTER CLXIII (p. 774).—*The rich Auditors in Albemarle Street.* The audience at the Lectures by Coleridge, given at the Royal Institution the year before.

My admiration of the pamphlet. Evidently refers to Wordsworth's pamphlet on the Convention of Cintra, mentioned in a preceding letter (No. CLXI).

LETTER CLXV (p. 775).—*Dr. Tuthill,* afterwards Sir George L. Tuthill, M. D., Physician to Bethlehem, Bridewell, and Westminster Hospitals.

Hazlitt has written a grammar. "A new and improved grammar of the English tongue for the use of schools . . . to which is added a new guide to the English tongue, in a letter to Mr. W. F. Mylius, author of the School Dictionary, by Edward Baldwin, Esq. (Godwin)." 1810.

LETTER CLXVII (p. 778).—See Lamb's Essay "On the Poetical Works of George Wither" (*Essays,* p. 323). The annotated volume is now in the possession of Mr. A. C. Swinburne, who has published a full and very interesting account of it (see *Nineteenth Century,* Jan. 1886).

LETTER CLXVIII (p. 779).—*Winterslow, near Sarum.* The residence of William Hazlitt, on the border of Salisbury Plain. Charles and Mary Lamb spent their summer holiday with Mr. and Mrs. Hazlitt this year. Basil Montagu had written to Lamb suggesting to him to revise a MS. treatise on the subject of Capital Punishment.

LETTER CLXIX (p. 779).—*H. Robinson.* Henry Crabb Robinson. See his delightful *Diaries* for frequent mention of Charles and Mary Lamb.

LETTER CLXX (p. 780).—*Cram monsters in the voids of the maps.* Lamb was thinking of Swift's lines (in the "Ode to Poetry") about the geographers who—

"On Afric downs

Place elephants for want of towns."

LETTER CLXXI (p. 780).—*Your continuation of the Essay on Epitaphs.* Wordsworth had published the first part of this essay in Coleridge's *Friend,* February 22, 1810. He published it later in separate form with additions. The "turgid epitaph" referred to was one from a churchyard in Westmoreland, of the year 1693, of which Wordsworth thought it worth while to compose a simpler version in prose.

LETTER CLXXIII (p. 782).—*Your reply to the Edinburgh Review.* "Reformist's reply to the Edinburgh Review," 1810. "A pamphlet," says Hunt in his *Autobiography,* "which I wrote in defence of the *Review's* own reforming principles, which it had lately taken into its head to renounce as impracticable."

LETTER CLXXIV (p. 783).—John Lamb's brochure has at length come to light, and an account of it was first published by Mr. L. S. Livingston in the New York *Bookman* for January 1899. It is entitled, "A Letter to the Right Hon. William Windham on his opposition to Lord Erskine's Bill for the Prevention of Cruelty to Animals, London, 1810." Mr. Windham had taken the line, in the House of Commons, that the subject was one not fitted for legislation. John Lamb, in his protest, expressly insists on man's cruelty to *eels,* and dilates on the theme with much rhetorical effusiveness.

LETTER CLXXV (p. 783).—The letter congratulates William Hazlitt on the birth of his first child, or at least the first which survived.
H. Bunbury, Esq. (1750-1811). The caricaturist, friend of Johnson, Goldsmith, and Garrick.
Martin and the card-boys. Martin Burney and the rest of the little whistcoterie.

LETTER CLXXVI (p. 784).—*To give your vote to-morrow.* H. Crabb Robinson, under date, March 16, 1811, writes: "C. Lamb stepped in to announce Dr. Tuthill's defeat as candidate for the post of physician to St. Luke's Hospital." The contest, Mrs. Procter informed me, was very severe, and many friends of the candidates bought governorships at £50 for the sake of votes. Basil Montagu bought one for Lamb.

LETTER CLXXVII (p. 785).—*The Well-bred Scholar.* I do not find any work of this name assigned to W. F. Mylius, who was a diligent compiler of schoolbooks. He was a master at Christ's Hospital. Dr. Southey was a brother of the poet.
Going to eat turbot. At the annual dinner of old Christ's Hospital boys.

LETTER CLXXVIII (p. 786).—*The noblest conversational poem.* Wordsworth's *Excursion,* just published.
The whole surface of Hyde Park is dry crumbling sand. Early in August 1814, the three London Parks were thrown open to the public, in celebration of the Peace between England and France. There were fireworks and illuminations; Chinese Pagodas and "Temples of Concord" were erected; and the Parks were, in fact, converted into a vast Fair. It was two years before they recovered their usual verdure.

"At the coming of the milder day." See Wordsworth's Poem, "Hart-Leap
Well"—

> "She leaves these objects to a slow decay,
> That what we are, and have been, may be known;
> But at the coming of the milder day
> These monuments shall all be overgrown."

LETTER CLXXIX (p. 788).—*"Remorse."* Coleridge's tragedy, which, owing
to the good offices of Lord Byron, had been brought out at Drury Lane, January 23, 1813, with a Prologue by Lamb. It ran twenty nights.
Old Jimmy Boyer. Rev. James Boyer, the former Head-Master of Christ's
Hospital, while Lamb and Coleridge were at the school.

LETTER CLXXX (p. 789).—*Time enough for the Quarterly.* Lamb's forthcoming Review of the *Excursion.* See the Review, and notes thereupon, in
Mrs. Leicester's School and other Writings, etc., pp. 210 and 395.

LETTER CLXXXI (p. 791).—*Your experience about tailors.* Wordsworth
may have told Lamb a story of some tailor in his neighbourhood who had
thrown himself over a precipice. If so, it is possible that James Hogg, in his
volume of Parodies (the *Poetic Mirror*), published a year or more later, having
heard the same story, called his Parody of the *Excursion,* the "Flying Tailor."
Another explanation is possible. Lamb may already have seen Hogg's Parody
in MS., and in this case the opening paragraph of this letter may be simple, and
rather mischievous, *badinage.* The reference to Burton is obviously to Lamb's
paper "On the Melancholy of Tailors," signed "Burton Junior," which appeared first in the *Champion,* Dec. 4, 1814.
W. H. is William Hazlitt, who had lately reviewed Wordsworth's *Excursion*
in the *Examiner.* This Review was partially reprinted by Hazlitt in the *Round
Table,* 1817.
The melancholy Jew. A Jew of the name of Levi had lately flung himself
from the monument in Fish Street Hill.
Another Hylas. "An interesting little love-adventure which he (Hazlitt) met
with down at the Lakes while he was on his first experimental trip in search of
sitters, is so distinctly alluded to in a letter from Lamb to Wordsworth, that I
shall just give what Lamb says about it, premising that Patmore had heard in
his time of some story of my grandfather being struck by the charms of a village beauty in Wordsworth's neighbourhood, and of having narrowly escaped
being ducked by the swains for his ill-appreciated attentions. Wordsworth had
evidently described the whole affair in a letter to Lamb" (*Memoirs of William
Hazlitt,* by W. C. Hazlitt, i. 105, 106).

LETTER CLXXXII (p. 792).—*I have read "It won't do."* The first words of
Jeffrey's famous Review of the *Excursion* in the *Edinburgh,* November 1814,
"This will never do!"

LETTER CLXXXIII (p. 793).—*Your successive book presents.* In 1815
Wordsworth published a New Edition of his Poems with the following title:—
*Poems by William Wordsworth: including Lyrical Ballads, and the Miscel-
laneous Pieces of the Author. With Additional Poems, a new Preface, and a
Supplementary Essay. In two Volumes.* Among the poems that appeared for

the first time in this edition were "Yarrow Visited," "The Force of Prayer; or, The Founding of Bolton Abbey," "The Farmer of Tilsbury Vale," "Laodamia," "Yew Trees," "A Night Piece," and others. It was naturally on these that Lamb made his comments. He also refers to the various changes of text made since the appearance of the previous edition in 1807. Some of the former readings were restored in later editions, perhaps in consequence of Lamb's remonstrances. The admirable line—

"The stone-chat and the glancing sand-piper"

(as Lamb truly says, "a line quite alive") is one of these. It occurs in the beautiful poem "Lines left upon a Seat in a Yewtree," and in the 1815 edition had given place to the far inferior—

"The stone-chat, or the sand-lark, restless Bird,
Piping along the margin of the lake."

The "substitution of a shell" to which Lamb alludes was in the poem "The blind Highland Boy," where the vessel in which the poor boy embarked was originally a washing-tub, but which was now exchanged (at the request of friends whose self-respect was wounded) for a turtle-shell.

The Preface is noble. The allusion in the words that follow is to a mention Wordsworth had made of Lamb, in citing a sentence from his Essay on Hogarth. He there speaks of Lamb as one of his "most esteemed friends." The "printed extracts from those first poems" refers to the extracts from an "Evening Walk" and "Descriptive Sketches," early poems first published in 1793.

The poems "by a female friend" were by Dorothy Wordsworth. "Three short pieces (now first published)," we read in the Preface, "are the work of a Female Friend, and the Reader to whom they may be acceptable is indebted to me for his pleasure."

An undoubtable picture of Milton. This picture, which came into Charles Lamb's possession after his brother's death, was given by him to Emma Isola.

The Latin Poems of V. Bourne. Cowper's friend, and Master at Westminster School. Lamb, as well as Cowper, wrote and printed various translations from Bourne's Latin Poems.

"To them each evening had its glittering star"—from the *Excursion,* Book V. "The man and his consort" are the matron and her husband on whose industrious lives these lines are a comment.

LETTER CLXXXIV (p. 795).—*"Yarrow Visited."* The lovely stanza referred to I would almost hope there is no need to cite, but it is a pleasure to repeat it:—

"But thou that didst appear so fair
To fond imagination,
Dost rival in the light of day
Her delicate creation."

The poem called by Lamb the "Boy-builders" is that better known as "Rural Architecture." It was first printed in 1800, and had a final stanza, omitted in 1815, ending with the lines—

"Then, light-hearted boys, to the top of the crag,
And I'll build up a giant with you."

I don't often go out a "may"ing;—"must" is the tense with me now. It is interesting to remember that Hood uses this antithesis with exquisite effect in his "Ode to Melancholy":—

> "Even as the blossoms of the *May,*
> Whose fragrance ends in *must.*"

"What is good for a bootless bene?" The first line of the poem on Bolton Abbey:—

> " 'What is good for a bootless bene?'
> With these dark words begins my tale;
> And their meaning is, whence can comfort spring
> When Prayer is of no avail?"

Who looked over your proof-sheets and left "ordebo" in that line of Virgil? Wordsworth had cited in his preface Virgil's lines in the first Eclogue about the shepherd and the goats:—

> "Non ego vos posthac viridi projectus in antro
> Dumosa pendere procul de rupe *videbo.*"

LETTER CLXXXV (p. 798).—Southey's *Roderick, The Last of the Goths,* was published in quarto, in 1814.

LETTER CLXXXVI (p. 799).—*Hartley's intellectuals.* Hartley Coleridge, now just nineteen years of age, was at Oxford.
Spend a week at Poole's. Thomas Poole, a gentleman whose name has occurred already as the friend of Coleridge and Lamb. Poole succeeded to his father's business as a tanner at Nether-Stowey. Coleridge made his acquaintance, through friends in Bristol, as early as 1794; and it was to be near Poole that he went to live at Stowey in the winter of 1796-97. It was thus that Nether-Stowey became, as Mrs. Henry Sandford, Poole's relative, truly says, "a centre of the leading intellectual impulses of the time." Among other friends of Poole's were Sir Humphry Davy, the Wedgwood brothers, and John Rickman; and in a less intimate degree Wordsworth, Southey, and Clarkson. Poole retired from business about the year 1804, and thenceforth devoted himself to the interests of his native place, and to all questions affecting the welfare of the labouring classes. He died in 1837. An admirable memoir of Poole has been written by Mrs. Henry Sandford in her book *Thomas Poole and his Friends* (Macmillan and Co.).

LETTER CLXXXVII (p. 800).—*Alsager.* Thomas Massa Alsager. For twenty-eight years attached to the *Times* newspaper, in which he wrote the city and money articles. He further controlled the musical department of the paper. He did more than perhaps any man of his time to promote the study and performance of classical chamber music, especially Beethoven's Quartettes. Hence Lamb's allusion to the propriety of varying the spelling of his name. He died in 1846.
Heautontimorumenos. "The Self-tormentor," the title of a comedy of Terence.
Capell Lofft (1751-1824). The Whig lawyer, writer on legal and political subjects, and poet. He was a native of Bury St. Edmunds, and brought into

notice the Suffolk poet, Bloomfield. He sometimes printed sonnets with his initials C. L., to the disgust of Lamb, who bore the same.

The juvenile Talfourd. This first mention of one who was afterwards to be Lamb's biographer deserves a word of comment. He was at this time a young man of twenty, living in chambers in Inner Temple Lane, and reading with Mr. Joseph Chitty, the Special Pleader. Talfourd had just before this been introduced to Lamb at the house of Mr. William Evans, of the India House, and editor of the Pamphleteer. I shall have occasion hereafter to mention this latter gentleman in connection with Lamb and Joseph Cottle.

LETTER CLXXXVIII (p. 802).—Miss Hutchinson, Mrs. Wordsworth's sister.

LETTER CXCI (p. 806).—The Political Sonnets and Ode. The ode was evidently Wordsworth's Thanksgiving Ode, composed on the morning of the day appointed for a General Thanksgiving, January 18, 1816.

The Covent Garden Manager has declined accepting his Tragedy. Coleridge's play Zapolya. Though Byron's good offices were ineffectual in getting this second tragedy accepted by the managers, Byron introduced Coleridge to John Murray, which was the means (according to Moore) of its publication as A Christmas Tale a year later.

At a Chemist's Laboratory in Norfolk Street. This was probably Lamb's joke. He assumes that Coleridge would naturally choose a chemist's laboratory as being handy for opium purchases.

LETTER CXCII (p. 807).—The revise of the poems and letter. The letter referred to was Wordsworth's Letter to a Friend of Burns, London, 1816. Wordsworth had been consulted by a friend of Burns as to the best mode of vindicating the reputation of the poet which, it was alleged, had been much injured by the publication of Dr. Currie's Life and Correspondence of Burns.

Morgan is with us every day. John Morgan, Coleridge's old Bristol friend, and through life one of his kindest and staunchest supporters. He had a house at Calne, in Wiltshire, where Coleridge lived with him for many months at a time. Lamb was in all probability staying with Morgan when he wrote the letter that follows, dated from that town.

LETTER CXCIII (p. 808).—Marie. Miss Betham's "Lay of Marie" (1816).

LETTER CXCIV (p. 809). Henry Dodwell was a fellow-clerk of Lamb's in the India House. This exquisite letter was first printed by me in the Eversley Edition. I quoted a portion of it in the Notes to a previous volume of this edition. The "Cobbetts" are of course the "Political Registers."

LETTER CXCV (p. 810).—The unhappy lady. Matilda Betham, who painted miniatures as well as writing poems and compiling histories. "Her knightly brother" was Sir William Betham, at this time in Ireland, Deputy to the Ulster King of Arms.

G. Dyer, Executor to a Nobleman. Dyer was one of Lord Stanhope's ten executors. In company with his colleagues he was bequeathed a share of the Earl's disposable property.

CHAPTER IV

1817–1823

LETTER CXCVI (p. 812).—William Ayrton (1777-1858), Director of the Music at the King's Theatre in 1816. Famous as an impresario and as a musical critic. He edited Charles Knight's *Musical Library,* which did so much to popularise the best composers in this country. He was the first to produce *Don Giovanni* in England, in April of this year.

The late Mr..Mellish. Mr. Mellish, of Enfield, for many years M.P. for Middlesex. He made a large fortune as an army contractor. Whether he ever committed himself to opinions on poetical matters I do not know.

LETTER CXCVII (p. 814).—Mr. Barron Field; born 23rd October 1786; practised at the Bar for some years, going the Oxford Circuit. In 1816 he married and went out to New South Wales as Judge of the Supreme Court at Sydney. He returned to England in 1824, having resigned his post, and was afterwards appointed Chief-Justice of Gibraltar. See the Elia Essay, "Distant Correspondents." "Botany Bay" is now so much a matter of history that Lamb's allusions to the criminal population, among whom he pictures his old friend as living, almost require explanation.

> "So thievish 'tis, that the eighth commandment itself
> Scarce seemeth there to be"

is of course a parody of Coleridge's lines in the "Ancient Mariner"—

> "So lonely 'twas that God Himself
> Scarce seemèd there to be."

The reader will not have much difficulty in separating the "lies," to which Lamb pleads guilty in the various pieces of intelligence here transmitted, from the truths. If the Mitchell mentioned was Thomas Mitchell, the translator of Aristophanes, he did not die till many years later, and Mr. Thomas Barnes became the famous editor of the *Times* instead of going to Demerara or Essequibo. George Dyer, on the other hand, was actually one of the six executors and residuary legatees under the will of Lord Stanhope. "Mr. Lawrey" was the Rev. Walter Lawry, a Wesleyan minister (*Bibliotheca Cornub.* vols. i. and iii.).

LETTER CXCVIII (p. 815).—*We have left the Temple.* Lamb and his sister had lived for about nine years in Mitre Court Buildings, and for about the same period in Inner Temple Lane.

LETTER CC (p. 817).—*The Garden of England,* Covent Garden.
Southey's curse. The *Curse of Kehama.*
Coleridge's state and affairs. The new course of lectures, here spoken of as contemplated by Coleridge, were delivered early in the year following at a lecture-room in Flower de Luce Court, Fleet Street.

LETTER CCI (p. 818).—This brief note is worth printing, because it led to the remarkable evening at Haydon's, when Lamb met Keats, Wordsworth, and the Comptroller of Stamps. See Haydon's *Diaries,* or my *Memoir of Lamb* (Men of Letters Series), p. 86.

LETTER CCII (p. 818).—*W. H. goes on lecturing against W. W.* Hazlitt's Lectures on the English Poets, delivered at the Surrey Institution.

LETTER CCIII (p. 821).—The "books" here referred to are the collected edition of Lamb's works in two volumes, published in 1818 by the Olliers. The letter to Southey that follows is also on the subject of the new publication.

LETTER CCV (p. 822).—The "ticket" here mentioned was apparently for two courses of lectures delivered by Coleridge in December 1818 at the Crown and Anchor Tavern in the Strand.

LETTER CCVI (p. 823).—*To John Chambers.* Mr. Chambers was a fellow-clerk with Lamb in the India House, and one of his most intimate friends in the office. This letter, formerly in the possession of the late Mr. George Bentley, of New Burlington Street, was first printed by me with his most kind permission. The circumstances under which this tissue of audacious invention and wildest humour was penned are not hard to divine. Mr. Chambers was clearly kept away from business by an attack of eczema, or some kindred affection of the skin, and Lamb, after a fashion of which there are many other instances, sits down to amuse the absent invalid by supplying him with material for a hearty laugh. The "intelligence" forwarded is of course the simplest romance, grounded in each case, we may suppose, on certain bodily or mental peculiarities in the office clerks respectively named. The anecdote of Mr. Bye's sonnets and their resemblance to Petrarch has been so often quoted from this letter, though unpublished, as to have become already historical. The few notes that follow are taken from some memoranda supplied by the late Mr. H. G. Bohn, from whose collection the letter passed into the hands of Mr. Bentley.

The letter is addressed to Mr. John Chambers, Leamington, Warwick.

As Venn would say. Mr. Venn was an auctioneer.

As D—— does before 12 *o'Clock.* "Mr. Dowley, who was clerk and office-assistant to Mr. Chambers."

Wadd and Plumley. Wadd was son of a Rev. Dr. Wadd; Plumley was the son of a silversmith on Ludgate Hill. *Hyde* was a clerk in the same office, familiarly called Old Jemmy Hyde. He claimed to be descended from Lord-Chancellor Hyde. *Friend* "eventually became chief clerk when the Company passed into the hands of the Government." *Bye,* "another clerk in the same office, and held to be very stupid; got into debt and was dismissed." See Letter to Manning of 28th May 1819. Mr. Bonn adds that "this letter is evidently complete although it ends abruptly and is not signed."

LETTER CCVII (p. 824).—*A copy of "Peter Bell."* The verses to which Lamb here refers were those which J. Hamilton Reynolds wrote and published a few days in advance of Wordsworth's "Peter Bell," in ridicule of the poet. The squib, issued from the publishing house of Taylor and Hessey, bore on its title-page, *Peter Bell: A Lyrical Ballad.* "I do affirm that I am the *real* Simon Pure." It consists of some fifty stanzas, roughly imitated from the actual metre of Wordsworth's poem. It was furnished with a prose Preface and Appendix. The opening lines of the former may be cited as giving some idea of the insolent spirit in which the whole *jeu d'esprit* was conceived:—"It is now a period of one-and-twenty years since I first wrote some of the most perfect compositions (except certain pieces I have written in my later days) that ever dropped from poetical pen. My heart hath been right and powerful all its years. I never thought an evil or a weak thought in my life. It has been my aim and my achievement to deduce moral thunder from buttercups, daisies, celandines, and (as a poet, scarcely inferior to myself, hath it) 'such small deer,' " etc. etc. etc. The verses that follow are composed by stringing together allusions to Alice Fell, Betty Foy, Harry Gill, and other names from Wordsworth's best-known ballads, with phrases and mannerisms borrowed from the more mawkish of his earlier poems. It may be added that it was the publication of this *first* "Peter Bell," to which Wordsworth's came *second,* that explains Shelley writing a "Peter Bell the *Third.*"

Rogers has been re-writing your Poem of the Strid. Rogers wrote a poem on the same incident as that of Wordsworth's "Force of Prayer: or, The Founding of Bolton Priory." Rogers's poem was called "The Boy of Egremond," and the first two lines of it—

> " 'Say what remains when Hope is fled?'
> She answered, 'Endless weeping.' "

were, in some later editions of Wordsworth's poems, prefixed as a motto to his "Force of Prayer."

How do you like my way of writing with two inks? This letter was actually so written, in lines of black and red ink alternately.

Letter CCVIII (p. 826).—*The Gladness of Wheathamstead.*Lamb had relations in Hertfordshire, where his grandmother, Mrs. Field, resided so long. See the Essay, "Mackery End in H——shire."

Tommy Bye. See preceding letter to Mr. Chambers. Mrs. Gold was the married name of Miss Burrell, the actress. Manning was now once more in England after his long absence in China. This letter was addressed to him at Ware in Hertfordshire.

Letter CCIX (p. 827).—*How proud we are here of the dedication.* Wordsworth had just published his early poem "The Waggoner," in compliance with Lamb's request made in a former letter. It appeared, with a few shorter poems, in 1819, with the following dedication to Lamb:—

"My dear Friend—When I sent you, a few weeks ago, 'The Tale of Peter Bell,' you asked 'Why "The Waggoner" was not added?' To say the truth, from the higher tone of imagination, and the deeper touches of passion aimed at in the former, I apprehended this little piece could not accompany it without disadvantage. In the year 1806, if I am not mistaken, 'The Waggoner' was read to you in manuscript, and as you have remembered it for so long a time, I am the more encouraged to hope that, since the localities on which the poem partly depends did not prevent its being interesting to you, it may prove acceptable to others. Being, therefore, in some measure the cause of its present appearance, you must allow me the gratification of inscribing it to you, in acknowledgment of the pleasure I have derived from your writings, and of the high esteem with which

"I am very truly yours,

"WILLIAM WORDSWORTH."

Benjamin is the waggoner's name.

Mary Sabilla Novello. The wife of Vincent Novello, the eminent composer and organist.

LETTER CCX (p. 829).—This letter to Lamb's old friend Joseph Cottle, publisher and poet of Bristol, has, I venture to think, an interesting history attached to it. This and the following two letters were first printed by Cottle in his *Early Recollections of Coleridge,* published in 1837. Cottle gave the date of the first two correctly (1819), but by some oversight dated the last of the three 1829. Recent editors have made the error complete by dating them all 1829. Accordingly, in the autumn of 1886, when engaged in arranging the Letters for the present edition, I was perplexed by this confusion of dates, and could discover no internal evidence in the Letters themselves to resolve my doubts. A recent editor of Lamb's Correspondence had confidently announced that the Collection of Likenesses of British Bards was a certain work called *Effigies Poeticæ,* being a set of portraits of distinguished English Poets, with short notices of their lives and works, which was not in fact issued till the year 1824. This work (the letterpress of which, issued anonymously, was by Barry Cornwall) only included poets already deceased, and therefore did not contain any portrait or notice of Joseph Cottle. When I had given up hope of finding any clue to the mystery, the actual volume indicated by Lamb came to light. It proved to be a copy of Byron's *English Bards and Scotch Reviewers,* profusely illustrated with engravings and drawings of the various poets and other literary characters occurring in the famous satire. My attention was called to the copy by its containing, as its solitary water-colour drawing, a hitherto unknown portrait of Charles Lamb, by Mr. Joseph, A.R.A.; but on examining the book further, I found that it contained also a pencil drawing of Joseph Cottle, evidently copied from a miniature. The date of the compilation, as given on a special title-page, was 1819, and the person by whom it was compiled, one William Evans. By inquiring from the latest possessor of the volume, I discovered that this Mr. Evans was Lamb's old friend of that name, a colleague in the India House, to whom Lamb owed his first introduction to Talfourd. Here then was beyond doubt the "particular friend" who was making a selection of the "Likenesses of Living Bards." That Lamb was perfectly well aware of the use Mr. Evans proposed to make of the portraits in question we cannot doubt; and we can imagine with what characteristic equanimity he was allowing his own portrait to appear in illustration of lines by Byron quite as scornful as those in which poor Cottle was described. As Joseph Cottle, however, might not have received the intelligence with the same philosophic calm, Lamb did not think it necessary to inform his old friend of the precise destination of his portrait. Since I made known these facts in the columns of the *Athenæum,* Mr. Evans's volume has passed into the keeping of the British Museum.

LETTER CCXI (p. 829).—*A daughter of Joseph's, R. A.* The name of Mr. Joseph's daughter is appended to several of the drawings in Mr. Evans's volume, but by some oversight not to the likeness of Joseph Cottle, which was a copy from a miniature by Branwhite of Bristol. Mr. Joseph was an associate only of the Royal Academy. He never attained the full rank of R.A.

Your better favour, the "Messiah." "In consequence of this application," Cottle tells us, referring to the preceding letter of Lamb's, "I sent C. Lamb a portrait by Branwhite, and enclosed for his acceptance the second part of my *Messiah.*" Cottle had published the first part of this Epic, "in twenty-four books," four years earlier. Lamb, as usual, hits with unerring skill one of the few lines in the dreary waste of commonplace that have some felicity of diction. Cottle had ruined the effect of the musical couplet—

> "The willowy brook was there, but that sweet sound—
> When to be heard again on earthly ground?"

by adding the feeble lines—

> "(While sorrow gave th' involuntary tear),
> Had ceased to vibrate on our listening ear."

LETTER CCXII (p. 830).—Cottle's *Fall of Cambria,* in twenty-four books, was published in 1811.

Anything you should write against Lord Byron. Cottle had evidently informed Lamb of his "Expostulatory Epistle to Lord Byron"—composed and published after the publication of the first two cantos of *Don Juan.* Of this effusion, in rhymed couplets, the following few lines may be given as a fair sample:—

> "Sunk, but not lost, from dreams of death arise!
> No longer tempt the patience of the skies!
> Confess, with tears of blood, to frowning Heaven
> The foul perversion of *His* talents given!
> Retrace thy footsteps! Ere the wish be vain
> Bring back the erring thousands in thy train!
> Let none, at death, despairing charge on thee
> Their blasted peace, in shuddering agony!
> Their prop, their heart's last solace, rent away
> That one *long night* might quench their *Perfect Day.*"

LETTER CCXIII (p. 831).—Talfourd assigned this note to the year 1829, but it certainly belongs to the year 1819, for Coleridge's sonnet referred to, "Fancy in Nubibus: or the Poet in the Clouds," was first printed in *Blackwood's Magazine* in November 1819, and this copy was evidently sent to Lamb in manuscript and before publication. For the better enjoyment of this humorous letter I make no apology for reprinting the poem:—

> "O! it is pleasant, with a heart at ease,
>   Just after sunset, or by moonlight skies,
> To make the shifting clouds be what you please,
>   Or let the easily persuaded eyes
> Own each quaint likeness issuing from the mould
>   Of a friend's fancy; or with head bent low
> And cheek aslant see rivers flow of gold
>   'Twixt crimson banks; and then a traveller, go
> From mount to mount through Cloudland, gorgeous land!
>   Or, listening to the tide, with closèd sight,
> Be that blind bard, who on the Chian strand,

> By those deep sounds possessed with inward light,
> Beheld the Iliad and the Odyssee
> Rise to the swelling of the voiceful sea."

LETTER CCXIV (p. 831).—William Wordsworth, the third son of the poet, had just come to the school of the Charter House in London, and on this Wednesday half-holiday the Lambs had asked him to dinner.

A certain preface about imagination. The allusion is to Wordsworth's own lines in "The Leech-Gatherer," cited by him in the Preface to the 1815 edition of his Poems:—

> "Like a sea-beast crawled forth, that on a shelf
> Of rock or sand reposeth, there to sun itself."

It is perhaps impertinent to point out the exquisite allusion to the poet having "ever been on Westminster Bridge."

LETTER CCXV (p. 832).—*Some of Lloyd's lines on you.* The "Stanzas addressed to * * *," in Lloyd's *Desultory Thoughts in London*, written this year.

Capel Lofft's. A sonnet dated from Manchester and signed C. L. had just appeared in a newspaper.

Your marine sonnet was Coleridge's sonnet, "Fancy in Nubibus—a sonnet composed on the sea-coast," which appeared in *Blackwood's Magazine* of November 1819. In the same number there is a note on Sir Thomas Browne by Coleridge, but not contributed by him. It is signed G. J.

LETTER CCXVI (p. 833).—I have included this fragment of a letter because all Lamb's opinions of contemporary poetry are worth preserving. Wordsworth's "Duddon" sonnets had been published this year, and with them "Dion," "Artegal and Elidure," "The Pass of Kirkstone," "The Longest Day," and others.

LETTER CCXVIII and CCXIX (p. 834).—These letters were first printed in Mrs. Mathews's Memoir of her Husband in 1839 (vol. iii. p. 192). As they imply, Charles and Mary Lamb had been invited to meet Charles Mathews, the elder, and his wife at the Gillmans'. Mrs. Mathews gives an account of the dinner, from which the following sketch of Lamb's outward man is worth preserving:—"Mr. Lamb's first approach was not pre-possessing. His figure was small and mean; and no man certainly was ever less beholden to his tailor. His 'bran' new suit of black cloth (in which he affected several times during the day to take great pride, and to cherish as a novelty that he had long looked for and wanted) was drolly contrasted with his very rusty silk stockings, shown from his knees, and his much too large *thick* shoes without polish. His shirt rejoiced in a wide ill-plaited frill, and his very small, tight, white neckcloth was hemmed to a fine point at the ends that formed part of the little bow. His hair was black and sleek, but not formal, and his face the gravest I ever saw, but indicating great intellect, and resembling very much the portraits of King Charles I. Mr. Coleridge was very anxious about his *pet* Lamb's first impression upon my husband, which I believe his friend saw; and guessing that he had been extolled, he mischievously resolved to thwart his panegyrist, disappoint the strangers, and altogether to upset the suspected plan of showing him off."

Master Mathew, a character in Ben Jonson's *Every man in his Humour.*

LETTER CCXX (p. 834).—Mr. Collier had published in 1820 his "Poetical Decameron: or, Ten Conversations on English Poets and Poetry, particularly of the reigns of Elizabeth and James I."; and this is the work now acknowledged by Lamb. The discoveries about *Twelfth Night* were only as to the origin of the plot being found in a novel by Barnaby Rich. The reference to the comedy and its performance at the Temple in Manningham's *Diary,* had not as yet been discovered by Mr. Collier. Lamb's allusion to *Osrades* is very curious. I feel no doubt that this is what he wrote in the letter, and that it was his imperfect recollection of the actual name, Rosader, the character corresponding to Shakspeare's Orlando in Lodge's *Rosalind,* the novel on which Shakspeare built his *As You Like It.* The speech of Rosader in addressing the Duke and company in the forest is one of those cited by Mr. Collier (vol. ii. p. 174). It begins, "Whatsoever thou be that art maister of these lustie squires I salute thee as graciously as a man in extreme distresse may: knowe that I and a fellow friend of mine are here famished in the forrest for want of food: perish we must, unless relieved by thy favours."

The character of the Ass. A sixteenth century tract entitled "The Nobleness of the Ass," discussed by Mr. Collier's three "Friends in Council," is here referred to (i. 168). Lamb contributed a short notice of it to his friend Hone's *Every-Day Book.* See *Mrs. Leicester's School,* etc., p. 298.

The line you cannot appropriate. The line was—

"And weep the more because I weep in vain";

from Gray's sonnet on the death of his friend West.

You will find last poem but one. Morton, one of the speakers in Mr. Collier's *Decameron,* instances Sir P. Sidney and an epitaph written on him by Sir Walter Raleigh, in which, according to Harrington, he is called "The Scipio and the Petrarke of our time."

LETTER CCXXI (p. 835).—The "beautiful lines" here referred to were a copy of verses published in the *London Magazine* for August 1821, signed "Olen." They were entitled "Epistle to Elia: suggested by his Essay "Molle atque facetum' on New Year's Eve." Lamb's essay had appeared in the number of the Magazine for the preceding January. The poem was a grave protest against the despondent and sceptical tone of Lamb's speculations on a future state of being. It is too long to give in its entirety, extending to nearly two hundred lines, but an extract may be cited in proof of the eloquent earnestness of the remonstrance. Speaking of the vagueness of Lamb's imaginings of the life to come, the writer goes on:—

"No! never dream it:
If thou but think this error, O redeem it.
The same that shadowed the green, leafy dells,
And gave them music sweeter than *thy bells,*
Has furnished out thy Heaven by the sweet name
Of *Paradise.* And thou, too, art the same:
The soul that revelled in thy Burton's page
Shall be alive with thee; the bard and sage
Thou lovedst here, they wait but thy arrival;
Thy death shall be a sleep, a self-survival.
Yea, thou shalt stand in pause when thou hast set
Thy foot upon heaven's threshold, and beget

> Effaced remembrances of forms and times,
> Greetings and partings in these earthly climes:
> And there shall come a rush upon thy brain
> Of recollected voices, a sweet pain
> Of sudden recognition; gentle stealings
> Of wakened memory—deep, voluptuous feelings,
> Pressures and kisses, that shall make thee start
> At thy own consciousness, and own, *Thou art.*"

Lamb, it will be seen, conjectured that the lines might be by James Montgomery. They were by the late Sir Charles Elton, of Clevedon Court, a frequent contributor at that time to the *London Magazine,* and were included by him in a volume, *Boyhood, and other Poems,* published in 1835.

This letter is doubly interesting, as revealing the origin of Lamb's famous signature. There is no sufficient reason for supposing the explanation fictitious; and Mr. Lowell's conjecture that Lamb owed it to the *Epistolæ Ho-Elianæ* of James Howell cannot seriously be entertained.

LETTER CCXXII (p. 836).—The first of a series of letters to Cowden Clarke, which Mrs. Cowden Clarke most kindly placed at my disposal. It need hardly be explained that Mrs. Clarke was a daughter of Vincent Novello. Lamb was living just now in country lodgings at Dalston, and was not within easy reach of Leigh Hunt at Hampstead.

LETTER CCXXIV (p. 837).—The first sketch of the famous "Roast Pig" Essay, which appeared in the *London Magazine* of the following September.

LETTER CCXXV (p. 838).—*Poor John's loss.* Lamb's elder brother, John, had died in November of the previous year. Captain Burney died in the same month.

The foul enchanter——"letters four do form his name." The quotation is from Coleridge's poem, "Fire, Famine, and Slaughter," where it is a paraphrase for Pitt. Here it is certainly intended for Joseph Hume, who had already established his fame as an Economical Reformer, and who the year before had cut down the salaries of the Distributors of Stamps, which directly affected Wordsworth.

Busirane is the name of an enchanter in the *Fairy Queen.* Hume was engaged in attacking the salaries, pensions, and superannuation allowances of the public service generally.

Milton hangs over my fireside. The portrait of Milton had come into Lamb's possession through the death of his brother John.

My meeting with Dodd. See the Essay on "Some of the Old Actors," then just printed in the *London.* The fortunes of this magazine were already waning.

LETTER CCXXVI (p. 840).—*The Numberer of the People.* Mr. Rickman first organised the machinery for taking the decennial census.

LETTER CCXXVIII (p. 840).—John Clare (1793-1864), the son of an agricultural labourer in Northamptonshire. He had published, through Taylor and Hessey, *Poems, descriptive of Rural Life and Scenery;* and later in the same year (1821), *The Village Minstrel, and other Poems.* These are the volumes, doubtless, which are acknowledged in this letter. Clare's verse appeared from time to time in the *London Magazine,* through which association he and Lamb had become acquainted.

The "sonnet" in the *London* for August referred to by Lamb was unsigned. *Since I saw you I have been in France.* Charles and Mary Lamb left London in the middle of June 1822 for a holiday in Paris. They were for a while the guests of James Kenney, the dramatist, at Versailles. From an entry in Crabb Robinson's *Diary* we learn that they travelled in company with a French gentleman, and a nurse for Miss Lamb, in readiness for any return of her frequent illness. Charles Lamb was absent a month, but Mary Lamb remained at the Kenneys' some time longer, returning to England on the 10th of September. See subsequent letters to Mrs. Kenney and to Barron Field.

LETTER CCXXIX (p. 841).—*Bernard Barton.* This is the earliest of the interesting series of letters to the Quaker poet, of Woodbridge, in Suffolk. Mr. Barton was clerk in the Bank of the Messrs. Alexander in that town. He was a contributor to the *London Magazine,* and Lamb had first met him at the hospitable table of the publishers, Messrs. Taylor and Hessey, who were in the habit of gathering their staff together at periodical dinners. On one of these occasions Lamb had spoken playfully of the inconsistency of a member of the Society of Friends writing poetry, and out of a friendly remonstrance in reply there arose a correspondence, long carried on with the greatest satisfaction to both. For fuller information about Mr. Barton, I would refer to the short biography of him prefixed to a selection of his poems published after his death in 1849. The memoir, a model in style and feeling of what such a thing should be, is by the late Edward FitzGerald, who married Mr. Barton's only daughter and child. "Napoleon," with other poems, was the third volume of verse published by Mr. Barton. It had just before appeared. The sonnet here quoted is of course Lamb's own.

LETTER CCXXX (p. 842).—The original of this letter is in the possession of my friend, Mr. W. J. Jefferson of Folkestone, whose mother was the *Sophy* of the letter. Mary Lamb had apparently been asked to bring home a stray waistcoat of Crabb Robinson's that he had left behind him in Paris. The allusions to the cow and the canary bird are to certain disturbers of Lamb's sleep that existed at his Dalston lodgings. Little Sophy, a daughter of the Kenneys, was one of twin-sisters; Lamb called her his "little wife." The allusion to the sixpence is surely to the old nursery rhyme:—

> "I love a sixpence, pretty, pretty sixpence,
> I love a sixpence dearer than my life—"

LETTER CCXXXI (p. 843).—The following independent account of the visit to Talma was supplied to me by the late Mr. Edward FitzGerald:—"Lamb was staying at Paris with Kenney, when Talma invited them with Howard Payne, to come and see an original picture of Shakspeare on an old pair of bellows which he had purchased for a thousand francs, and which proved to be a well-known imposture, of which the great tragedian had recently become the victim. After admiring his supposed acquisition, the party announced their intention of seeing him that evening in the play of *Regulus,* and invited him to sup with them afterwards, to which he assented. Lamb, however, could not at all enter into the spirit of French acting, and in his general distaste made no exception in favour of his intended guest. This, however, did not prevent their mutual and high relish of each other's character and conversation, nor was any allusion made to the performance, till, on rising to go, Talma inquired 'how he liked it?' Lamb shook his head and smiled. 'Ah!' said Talma, 'I was not very happy to-night; you must see me in *Sylla*.'—'Incidit in Scyllam,' said Lamb, 'qui vult vitare Charybdim.'—'Ah! you are a rogue—a great rogue,' said Talma, shaking him cordially by the hand as they parted." The Shakspeare portrait imposture is exposed in an article in *Chambers's Journal* of 27th September 1856, "The Apocryphal in Portraiture."

Lamb's description of Paris in this letter may well be supplemented by a few notes written for his sister's guidance after his own return to England. He advises her to walk along the "Borough-side of the Seine," where she would find a mile and a half of printshops and bookstalls. "Then there is a place where the Paris people put all their dead people, and bring them flowers and dolls and gingerbread-nuts and sonnets and such trifles; and that is all I think, worth seeing as sights, except that the streets and shops of Paris are themselves the best sight."

LETTER CCXXXII (p. 844).—*Your letter and poem*. The poem sent was Bernard Barton's "Verses on the Death of Percy Bysshe Shelley," just issued in pamphlet shape. Shelley had perished on the 8th of July in this year. The line taken in the poem was naturally one of solemn lamentation over the unhappy principles of the late poet.

LETTER CCXXXIII (p. 845).—*Poor Godwin*. "The pecuniary troubles already mentioned assumed no serious form till the year 1821, nor did any real crisis arrive till the year 1822. The title to the proprietorship of the house in Skinner Street, of which Godwin held a long lease, was disputed, and an action for ejectment was brought against him. After considerable litigation the suit was finally decided adversely to Godwin's interests. The results were an enforced move from Skinner Street, a claim for arrears of rent, which was wholly unlooked for, the disorganisation of the whole of the business which had been carried on with considerable and increasing success, and finally Godwin became bankrupt."—(Kegan Paul's *William Godwin, his Friends and Contemporaries*.)

LETTER CCXXXV (p. 845).—The first of a short series of letters to John Howard Payne, the American actor and playwright. These letters appeared first, with comments by Mr. R. S. Chilton, in the *Century Magazine* for October 1882. To Mr. Chilton and the Editor I am indebted for their kind permission to use them. Mr. Payne lived much in Paris, where presumably Lamb made his acquaintance during his recent visit. Payne had a career of great poverty and struggle, but later in life was made United States Consul at Tunis, where he died in 1852. Among his many dramas was *Clari, the Maid of Milan*, in which occurs the famous "Home, sweet Home," set by Bishop. Lamb's letters to him deal chiefly with some of Payne's dramas then being performed in London. The "little wife" at Versailles in the following letter is the Sophy Kenney of a preceding letter to Mrs. Kenney.

LETTER CCXXXVII (p. 847).—The proposed Dedication was for the first collected edition of the *Elia Essays*, published early in the following year. It was, in accordance with Lamb's "second thoughts" here explained, not ultimately used. The "sort of Preface" which appeared in the forthcoming number was the "Character of the late Elia," by a Friend.

LETTER CCXXXVIII (p. 848).—Mr. Walter Wilson, an early friend of Lamb's, was engaged upon a Life of De Foe, and had written to Lamb for guidance. Wilson's *Memoirs of the Life and Times of Daniel De Foe* appeared in 1829. Lamb supplied to the work an "Estimate of De Foe's Secondary Novels," which is, in fact, an expanded version of the criticism contained in this letter. See *Mrs. Leicester's School*, etc. etc., p. 304.

LETTER CCXL (p. 850).—This letter was written to Miss Wordsworth, then on a visit to her brother, the Master of Trinity, at Cambridge.

My new year's speculations. The memorable Essay on "New Year's Eve." Whether the reference to the author of the *Pleasures of Hope* means that Lamb now believed the lines signed "Olen" to have been by the poet Campbell, is uncertain. Possibly it is only a playful allusion to his having himself *not* indulged in these "Pleasures" in the essay in question.

Mrs. Paris, our Cambridge friend. Mrs. Paris, mother of the eminent physician of that name, was the sister of Lamb's friend Ayrton. It was at her house that the Lambs first made their acquaintance of Emma Isola.

LETTER CCXLI (p. 851).—The first of a series of letters to Mr. John Bates Dibdin, now for the first time printed. Mr. Dibdin was born in 1798, and died on May 11, 1828. He was the eldest son of Charles Dibdin the Younger, author of *Young Arthur,* and of innumerable plays, poems, songs, etc., and a grandson of Charles Dibdin, the nautical song-writer and composer. John Bates Dibdin held a clerkship in the office of Messrs. Railton, Rankin, and Co., Merchants, in the Old Jewry. He for several years edited the *European Magazine.* He went to Madeira in the hope of re-establishing his health, but shortly after his return to England died of consumption. I am indebted for this information to his nephew, Mr. Robert W. Dibdin, who has most kindly placed the original letters in his possession at my disposal. To him I am further obliged for the following interesting account of Lamb's introduction to his uncle. The account is mainly in the words of a sister of John Bates Dibdin who survived him till quite recently. It fully explains the allusions in the present letter. Miss Dibdin (Mrs. Tonna), after mentioning that she had visited Lamb at Islington, writes:—"My brother, who took me there, had become very intimate with him, after a previously somewhat long acquaintance. He was himself engaged in the city, and had constant occasion to conduct the giving or taking of cheques, as it might be, at the India House. There he always selected the 'little clever man' in preference to the other clerks. At that time the *Elia Essays* were appearing in print. No one had the slightest conception who 'Elia' was. He was talked of everywhere, and everybody was trying to find him out, but without success. At last, from the style and manner of conveying his ideas and opinions on different subjects, my brother began to suspect that Lamb was the individual so widely sought for, and wrote some lines to him, anonymously, sending them by post to his residence, with the hope of sifting him on the subject. Although Lamb could not *know* who sent him the lines, yet he looked very hard at the writer of them the next time they met, when he walked up, as usual, to Lamb's desk in the most unconcerned manner, to transact the necessary business. Shortly after, when they were again in conversation, something dropped from Lamb's lips which convinced his hearer, beyond a doubt, that his suspicions were correct. He therefore wrote some more lines (anonymously, as before), beginning—

'I've found thee out, O Elia!'

and sent them to Colebrook Row. The consequence was that at their next meeting Lamb produced the lines, and after much laughing, confessed himself to be *Elia*. This led to a warm friendship between them."

The present letter was evidently written by Lamb on the occasion of this mutual disclosure. Mr. Dibdin had signed his poetic appeals to Elia with only the letter "D." Lamb's assumption that his new friend's Christian name was Timothy is, of course, purely gratuitous.

LETTER CCXLII (p. 852).—Mr. Bruton was a farmer in Hertfordshire, and a distant connection by marriage of Lamb. See letter of Lamb to Manning, May 1819, "How are my cousins, the Gladmans of Wheathamstead, and farmer Bruton? Mrs. Bruton is a glorious woman." These presents of pig were among the first-fruits of Lamb's famous essay in the *London* of September 1822.

LETTER CCXLIII (p. 853).—"While Mr. Barton's poetical labours affected his health, the first success of them for a time disconcerted him with his clerkship; though neither injured health, nor hope deferred, ever overshadowed his social good-humour, or discovered themselves in repining: nay, he even thought of quitting the bank and Woodbridge altogether, and trusting to his pen for subsistence; an unwise scheme in all men, most unwise in one who had so little authorly tact as himself. From this, however, he was fortunately diverted by all the friends to whom he communicated his design" (*Memoir*, by Edward FitzGerald).

LETTER CCXLV (p. 855).—*Sewell.* W. Sewell's *History of the Quakers,* 1725.

Abbeypony History. Sara Coleridge published in 1822 a translation of Martin Dobrizhoffer's Latin *Account of the Abipones,* a performance, in her father's judgment, "unsurpassed for pure mother English by anything I have read for a long time."

Mr. Mitford's place. The Rev. John Mitford, Rector of Benhall, Suffolk, poet and editor of poets, a neighbour and intimate friend of Bernard Barton.

LETTER CCXLVII (p. 857).—*An edition of "Roxana."* In the Prologue that Lamb wrote to Godwin's play of *Faulkener* in 1807, he alluded to the circumstance of Godwin being indebted to De Foe's *Roxana.* See *Mrs. Leicester's School,* etc., p. 371, and Kegan Paul's *Life of Godwin,* ii. 162.

Who wrote "Quarl." The authorship of *Philip Quarl* is still, I believe, undetermined.

LETTER CCXLVIII (p. 858).—*"A Letter to an Old Gentleman whose education had been neglected."* This *jeu d'esprit* of Lamb's was ultimately published in the *London Magazine* of January 1825. See *Mrs. Leicester's School,* etc., p. 250.

I took up Scott. Critical Essays on the English Poets, by John Scott, the Quaker poet of Amwell.

I dined in Parnassus. An account of this dinner is given by Thomas Moore in his *Journals.* Moore gives April 4 as the date of the dinner, so Lamb's date is one of his not uncommon slips. Moore writes:—"Dined at Monkhouse's, a gentleman I had never seen before, on Wordsworth's invitation, who lives there when he comes to town. A singular party—Coleridge, Wordsworth and wife, Rogers, Charles Lamb (the hero at present of the *London Magazine*), and his sister (the poor woman who went mad with him in the Diligence on the way to Paris), and a Mr. Robinson, one of the *minora sidera* of the constellation of the Lakes. . . . Charles Lamb, a clever fellow certainly, but full of villainous and abortive puns, which he miscarries of every minute" (Moore's *Journals*, iv. 51).

LETTER CCXLIX (p. 859).—*My little book*. The first series of *Elia* (1823)
The Quaker incident. See Essay on "Imperfect Sympathies" (*Elia*, p. 51)
The discovery of roasting pigs. See p. 108.
His friend Naylor. James Naylor, one of the most fanatical of the disciples of George Fox; shamefully persecuted by order of the Parliament in 1656.
How did you like Hartley's sonnets? Hartley Coleridge had published in the *London Magazine* for February his earliest sonnets, those addressed to his friend Robert Jameson. The first of these, here referred to, is the one beginning—

"When we were idlers with the loitering rills."

See Hartley Coleridge's *Poems*, i. 5.
I borrowed a seal of a friend. The friend was Barron Field. The letter to the "great man" was to Walter Scott, on occasion of the appeal in behalf of Godwin.

LETTER CCLII (p. 861).—*Your precious present*. A miniature of Pope, which Procter had sent him.
I have dined with T. Moore. See preceding letter, No. CCXLVIII, p. 858.

LETTER CCLIII (p. 862).—Written to Miss Hutchinson (Mrs. Wordsworth's sister), who was taking charge of an invalid relative, Mrs. Monkhouse, at Ramsgate. Lamb's grave accusations against his sister's penmanship are merely playful. Note the delightful strokes of humour in this and the following letter—" 'Time' (as was said of one of us) 'toils after us in vain.' " Johnson's line on Shakspeare—"Panting Time toiled after him in vain."
Mr. Gruvellegan would appear to be Lamb's facetious attempt to reproduce the name of Edward Quillinan, afterwards Wordsworth's son-in-law. Lee Priory was the seat of Sir S. E. Brydges, the father of Quillinan's first wife.

LETTER CCLIV (p. 863).—*My letter to the old gentleman*. The parody on De Quincey's *Letters to a Young Man whose Education has been Neglected*. See previous letter to Barton of 5th March.
I miss Janus. "Janus Weathercock," the now notorious Thomas Griffiths Wainewright (the forger and poisoner), had been on the regular staff of the *London Magazine*.

LETTER CCLVII (p. 865).—This fragment of a letter to Charles Lloyd was first printed in the volume of Barton's Letters and Poems already referred to. Lamb's letter was written to Lloyd on occasion of receiving from him a fresh volume of his poetry: *Poems,* by Charles Lloyd: London, 1823. Among them are "Lines, written Feb. 6, 1822, on the death of Mary Lloyd, Mother of the Author"; "Stanzas on the Death of Mary Braithwaite, the third Sister of the Author"; and others.

LETTER CCLVIII (p. 865).—*I abused Hastings.* The Elia Essay "The Old Margate Hoy" was written during Lamb's sojourn at Hastings, and published in the *London Magazine* of this very month, July 1823. In the course of that essay he had, as he says, "abused Hastings." Readers of *Elia* will remember the passage about "this detestable Cinque Port." But, as will be seen, Lamb came to change his opinion of its merits. The small country church, here described, is the little church of Hollington, a mile or two out of Hastings. It evidently inspired Lamb's fancy in a wonderful degree. He recurs to the subject in more than one letter of this period.

Southey has attacked "Elia." See chap. vii. of my *Memoir of Lamb* in the Men of Letters Series. Southey's article appeared in the Quarterly for January 1823. The Elia Essay "On Witches and other Night Fears" was the one specially chosen by Southey to point his moral.

LETTER CCLX (p. 867).—*Your kind sonnet.* What sonnet this could have been I do not know. Barton had published a sonnet to Elia in the *London* of the previous February, beginning—

"Delightful author! unto whom I owe
Moments and moods of fancy and of feeling."

Barton included it in his volume *Poetic Vigils* in 1824. It embodies some discriminating criticism.

Mr. Cary, the Dante-man—The first mention in these letters of the Rev. H. F. Cary, the translator of Dante, and a frequent contributor to the *London Magazine*. He had a residence at the British Museum as Assistant-Keeper of Printed Books.

LETTER CCLXI (p. 868).—Hood was at this time on a visit to Hastings for his health. Lamb, who had himself been there lately, writes to instruct his friend as to seeing the lions, among which the little church at Hollington again appears. The reference to Standgate Street is simply a practical joke. There is no such street in Hastings, and though great changes have been made in the nomenclature of streets and roads in that town, the oldest inhabitant can recall no such name.

"He sang in meads." Quoted incorrectly from Landor's *Gebir*, Book iv.—

"In smiling meads how sweet the brook's repose
To the rough ocean, and red restless sands."

Tom Woodgate was a boatman at Hastings, under whose care Hood often enjoyed a sail. See the "Literary Reminiscences" in *Hood's Own*. "Old Lignum Janua" in the opening of this letter would appear to be a Latin alternative for him.

LETTER CCLXIII (p. 869).—*Your "Stanzas on Bloomfield."* This poem had been sent to Lamb, on its appearance in the columns of a local paper, and when it was next printed in Barton's *Poetic Vigils* (1824) it was with certain modifications. That word "Horkey," for instance, which is the Suffolk name for the Harvest Supper, had disappeared (probably in deference to Lamb's objections), and the stanza in which it occurred was recast so as to admit of "Harvest-Home" instead.

How happily you have brought in his subjects.—

> "Circling the *Old Oak Table* round,
>   Whose moral worth thy measure **owns,**
> Heroes and heroines yet are found
>   Like *Abner and the Widow Jones.*
> There *Gilbert Meldrum's* sterner tones
>   In virtue's cause are bold and free,
> And ev'n the patient sufferer's moans
>   In pain and sorrow plead for thee."

I meditate a letter to S. in the "London." The famous letter to Southey appeared in the following month.

LETTER CCLXVI (p. 870).—Mr. Dibdin had sent Lamb a sucking pig (yet another result of the memorable essay), and with it a miniature semblance of a pig worked in satin and straw.
Sir!—as I say to Southey. A reference to the solemn and formal opening of his letter to Southey in the current number of the *London Magazine.*

LETTER CCLXVII (p. 871).—*The kindness of your note.* Southey's letter is published by me for the first time in the notes to "Lamb's Letter to Southey in the *London Magazine,*" in a previous volume of this edition. The "Confessions of a Drunkard" was a paper of Lamb's contributed some years before to a compilation by Basil Montagu, called "Some Enquiries into the Effects of Fermented Liquors. By a Water Drinker." In the *Quarterly* for April 1822 appeared an article on Dr. Reid's treatise on "Hypochondriasis and other Nervous Affections." These "Confessions of a Drunkard" were there referred to as "a fearful picture of the consequences of intemperance," which the reviewer went on to say "we have reason to know is a true tale."

LETTER CCLXVIII (p. 872).—*Thou wilt see a funny passage.* See the Elia Essay "Amicus Redivivus," in *Elia,* p. 186.

LETTER CCLXX (p. 874).—Mr. W. Harrison Ainsworth, the future novelist, is here addressed. He must have lent Lamb the works of William Warner, the Elizabethan poet, author of *Albion's England.* The only English version of Goethe's *Faust* then accessible was Hayward's.
Ainsworth, a youth of eighteen, was as yet residing at Manchester, where his father was a solicitor. He came up to London in the following year.

CHAPTER V

1824–1827

LETTER CCLXXII (p. 876).—Thurtell, the notorious murderer of Mr. William Weare, "who lived in Lyon's Inn," was executed at Hertford on this day. It will be remembered that at his trial one of the witnesses enunciated the famous definition of Respectability. See Carlyle's Works, *passim.*

LETTER CCLXXIII (p. 877).—*Your friend Taylor.* The Rev. C. B. Taylor, curate of Hadleigh, Suffolk, author of various religious stories, now forgotten. *Your account of my black-balling.* It had been proposed to admit *Elia* for circulation in a Book Club in Woodbridge, to which Barton and other Friends belonged, with the result here mentioned.

> "*I have been merry once or twice ere now.*"
—Master Silence, in *Henry IV.* Part II.

Coleridge's book. Aids to Reflection, published in 1825. It consists largely, as will be remembered, of passages from Leighton's writings with Coleridge's comments.

The decision against Hunt. The Liberal: Verse and Prose from the South, edited by Leigh Hunt in Italy, contained in its opening number Byron's "Vision of Judgment." The Constitutional Association filed a criminal information in the King's Bench for libel against John Hunt, the publisher. The case came on January 15, 1824, and the defendant was ultimately fined £100, and required to give security for good behaviour for five years.

LETTER CCLXXIV (p. 878).—"*Inesilla, or the Tempter,*" a story by one of the brothers Ollier, who had published Lamb's collected works in 1818.

LETTER CCLXXV (p. 878).—"*Poetic Vigils.*" A volume of verse by Bernard Barton, then in preparation. The motto finally chosen for the title-page was a stanza of Henry Vaughan, the Silurist—

> "Dear night! this world's defeat."

LETTER CCLXXVI (p. 879).—In 1824, Mr. FitzGerald tells us, Barton "received a handsome addition to his income from another quarter. A few members of his Society, including some of the wealthier of his own family, raised £1200 among them for his benefit. . . . It seems that he felt some delicacy at first in accepting the munificent testimony which his own people offered to his talents." Lamb's letter is in reply to one from Barton, consulting him on this matter. Lamb, it will be seen, overstates the amount contributed.

LETTER CCLXXVIII (p. 881). This interesting letter is printed from the original in the possession of Mr. B. M'George of Glasgow, who kindly placed it at my disposal. The letter arose out of the following circumstances. James Montgomery, the poet, had this year edited a volume of original prose and verse, setting forth the wrongs and sufferings of the little chimney-sweepers, for whose relief a Society had been for some time labouring. The volume was entitled, *The Chimney-Sweeper's Friend, and Climbing-Boy's Album.* Lamb had been invited to contribute a poem, but not finding time or inspiration, sent instead Blake's verses, "The Chimney-Sweeper," then all but unknown to the ordinary reader of poetry. They appeared in Montgomery's volume with this heading, "Communicated by Mr. Charles Lamb from a very rare and curious little work," the very rare work being Blake's *Songs of Innocence.* Bernard Barton, himself a contributor to Montgomery's *Album,* had there discovered these verses of Blake's, and had written to Lamb to ask questions concerning the writer of them. "Is Blake a real name?" was evidently his wonder. It will be seen that even Lamb did not know Blake's Christian name.

Your recent acquisitions of the Picture and the Letter. Barton had received from some relatives at Carlisle a portrait of his father, which had greatly pleased him. Barton describes it in a letter to his friend Taylor, included in Mr. FitzGerald's *Memoir.* The picture of Lamb's father, here referred to, has been engraved in Mr. Procter's *Memoir of Lamb.*

His poems have been sold hitherto only in Manuscript. Lamb obviously means that the *Songs of Innocence* were not printed, but etched in writing-hand on the same plates as the drawings that illustrate them. As usual, Lamb was one of the first to recognise genius where the world in general only saw insanity.

The Society with the affected name. "The Society for Ameliorating the Condition of Infant Chimney-Sweepers" is the name of one Society, mentioned in Montgomery's book, having this philanthropic object.

With the exception of an Epilogue. This was an epilogue to Shakspeare's *Richard II.,* performed by the family of Lamb's friend, Barron Field. By the kindness of the late Miss M. L. Field of Hastings, I possess a copy of this epilogue, which will be found in its place, printed (I believe) for the first time, in *Mrs. Leicester's School,* etc. See note in that volume.

So we have lost another Poet. Byron had died at Missolonghi on the 19th of April.

LETTER CCLXXIX (p. 882).—*Your very pretty volume. Poetic Vigils,* now at last published (1824).

You have done Woolman injustice. In some lines headed "A Memorial of John Woolman, a Minister of the Gospel among the Quakers," written in anapæstic verse.

The piece on Nayler. "A Memorial of James Nayler, the Reproach and Glory of Quakerism."

LETTER CCLXXX (p. 883).—*Young Arthur.* A story in verse by Mr. Dibdin's father, Charles Dibdin the Younger. Many of the interspersed lyrics are thoroughly graceful and musical.

Just returned from Botany Bay. Barron Field had this year resigned his post of Judge of the Supreme Court at Sydney, and returned to England.

LETTER CCLXXXI (p. 883).—Mr. Cary had sent Lamb his translation of the *Birds* of Aristophanes.

LETTER CCLXXXII (p. 884).—*On getting a house over your head.* "Now, too, after having long lived in a house that was just big enough to eat and sleep in, while he was obliged to board with the ladies of a Quaker School over the way, he obtained a convenient house of his own, where he got his pictures and books about him" (FitzGerald's *Memoir*).

The album shall be attended to. The album of Lucy Barton, to which the poem given in the succeeding letter was contributed.

The "Prometheus," unbound. Mr. Mitford, Barton's neighbour and friend, had written to a local bookseller for a copy of Shelley's *Prometheus Unbound,* and after some delay had received the answer that he was sorry the work was not to be obtained "in sheets."

A sonnet conceived and expressed with a witty delicacy. Shelley's lines hardly constitute a sonnet. Lamb refers to his "Lines to a Reviewer," beginning—

> "Alas! good friend, what profit can you see
> In hating such a hateless thing as me?
> There is no sport in hate where all the rage
> Is on one side."

A futile effort in the next Number. The beautiful Essay, "Blakesmoor in Hertfordshire," was in the *London Magazine* for September 1824.

LETTER CCLXXXIII (p. 885).—These verses were headed, when sent in this letter, "In the Album of *Hannah* Barton." Lamb explains why he had assumed that Christian name.

LETTER CCLXXXV (p. 887).—Mr. Procter (Barry Cornwall) was married to Miss Anne Skepper, the step-daughter of Basil Montagu, in October 1824.

LETTER CCLXXXVI (p. 887).—Mr. Monkhouse, a cousin of Mrs. Wordsworth's, was threatened with consumption, and had been ordered by his physicians to winter in Devonshire. Miss Hutchinson was staying at Torquay with the Monkhouses. He died early in the following year.

LETTER CCLXXXVII (p. 888).—One of Mr. Mitford's vases, which were actually made in China and sent home, is now, through the friendly offices of Mr. John Loder of Woodbridge, in the Editor's possession.

Fauntleroy, the memorable banker and forger, was executed on November 30, 1824.

LETTER CCLXXXVIII (p. 890).—The book, transformed by the servant-maid into "Luster's Tables," was (as will easily be guessed) *Luther's Tabletalk*.

LETTER CCLXXXIX (p. 891).—Leigh Hunt was still with his family in Genoa. See the allusion in the last sentences of the letter. He did not return to England till late in the following year, 1825.

Vincentio is Vincent Novello. Lamb probably wrote *Isabella,* but Mrs. Novello's name was *Mary Sabilla; Mr. Clark* was Charles Cowden Clarke, her son-in-law. The various details respecting the Novello family are pure romance. The reference to the quite recent marriage of Procter (in October 1824) further fixes the date of the letter.

Irving has dedicated a book to S. T. C. Irving's "Anniversary Sermon of the London Missionary Society," preached at Whitfield's Tabernacle in May 1824, and published with a Dedication to Coleridge. The following is an extract from this Dedication: "——When I state the reason to be that you have been more profitable to my faith in orthodox doctrine, to my spiritual understanding of the Word of God, and to my right conception of the Christian Church, than any or all of the men with whom I have entertained friendship and conversation, it will perhaps still more astonish the mind and stagger the belief of those who have adopted, as once I did myself, the misrepresentations which are purchased for hire and vended for a price concerning your character and works." See Mrs. Oliphant's *Life of Irving,* vol. i. chap. ix.

LETTER CCXCI (p. 892).—*The Chessiad*, a mock-heroic poem, by Charles Dibdin the Younger. The simile of the charwoman is a fair specimen of the whole, but (*pace* Lamb) is hardly up to the level of Hudibras. The volume sent was *Comic Tales and Lyrical Fancies;* including *The Chessiad*, a mock-heroic, in five cantos, etc. etc. (London, 1825.)

LETTER CCXCII (p. 893).—*De Quincey's* "Parody." Lamb's "Letter to an Old Gentleman," etc., already more than once referred to as a parody of De Quincey's *Letter to a Young Man whose Education has been Neglected.*

The "Horns." A paper of Lamb's, entitled "A Vision of Horns," rather poor and forced, and on a dubious subject, was printed in the *London Magazine* for this month.

The Memoir of Liston. See *Mrs. Leicester's School,* etc., p. 253. It appeared, as did also the parody on De Quincey, in the *London Magazine* for January 1825.

In the next Number I figure as a Theologian! Lamb published a short paper, "Unitarian Protests," directed against the conformity to Church ceremonies by his old friends the Unitarians.

I have lately picked up an epigram. The epigram in question was by Henry Man, one of the clerks in the South-Sea House, when Lamb first knew that Institution. The two noble earls were Lord Spencer and Lord Sandwich. Lamb refers to the two "forgotten volumes" by Man, in his Elia Essay, "Recollections of the South-Sea House." The volumes were published in 1802: *Miscellaneous Works in Verse and Prose of the late Henry Man.* The epigram is there given. Man was Deputy-Secretary of the South-Sea House in 1793.

LETTER CCXCIV (p. 894).—*That ugly paper,* the "Vision of Horns" before mentioned.

"Dream on J. Bunyan." Refers possibly to some lines by Barton on seeing a portrait of John Bunyan, which were printed some time after in Major's edition of the *Pilgrim's Progress,* with Southey's Biography of the author.

The second Number. Of the *London Magazine,* New Series.

The queen of the East Angles. Barton's daughter, Lucy.

LETTER CCXCV (p. 895).—*I saw Tuthill yesternight.* Lamb had been taking medical advice as to his qualifications to retire from the India House, on the score of ill-health.

LETTER CCXCVII (p. 896).—See Lamb's Elia Essay, "The Superannuated Man," p. 172, *The Last Essays of Elia.* The final release from his slavery came about on the last Tuesday in March. Two medical men, Tuthill, and Coleridge's friend, Gillman of Highgate, gave him the necessary certificates.

LETTER CCXCVIII (p. 898).—

> *"The little bird that wings the sky."*

A random shot at Lovelace's—

> *"The birds that wanton in the air*
> *Know no such liberty."*

Tell me how you like "Barbara S." See *The Last Essays of Elia* (p. 180). It appeared in the *London* for this month. The actual heroine of the story was Fanny Kelly.

LETTER CCC (p. 899).—*Coleridge has just finished his Prize Essay.* Refers to a paper by Coleridge, on the *Prometheus* of Æschylus, read before the Royal Society of Literature on the 18th of May 1825.

My "hiatus crumenæ." What Falstaff calls this "consumption of the purse." Lamb had retired upon two-thirds of his salary; hence the reference to his missing "thirds."

LETTER CCCI (p. 900).—*My poor pittance in the "London."* The allusion is to the Elia Essay, "The Convalescent," in the *London Magazine* for this month.

Your book. Barton had sent Lamb his volume, *Poems*, by Bernard Barton, 1820. It contains "Meditations in Great Bealings Churchyard," and the other pieces referred to by Lamb. It is dedicated in some prefatory lines to Maria Hack, and the volume itself opens with "Verses supposed to be written in a Burial-ground belonging to the Society of Friends," in which the "baldness" of the ground, as regards "sculptured monuments," is apologised for.

Anne Knight. Mrs. Knight, a member of the Society of Friends, who kept a school at Woodbridge, was a dear and intimate friend of Bernard Barton and his daughter.

LETTER CCCII (p. 901).—This letter is in reply to one from Coleridge, first printed in the "Literary Reminiscences" in *Hood's Own.* Coleridge had met with the *Odes and Addresses to Great People*, by Hood and his brother-in-law, J. H. Reynolds, but published anonymously, and had conjectured from internal evidence that the volume was by Lamb. He wrote accordingly to tax Lamb with it. "Yes, Master Charles," he writes, "you are discovered"; and he adds, "the puns are nine out of ten good, the 'Newgatory,' transcendent."

LETTER CCCIX (p. 903).—Southey had sent Lamb his *Book of the Church* (1824), and his poem, the *Tale of Paraguay*, just published (1825). The poem was founded upon incidents in Dobrizhoffer's *History of the Abipones*, translated from the Latin by Sara Coleridge three years before. Hence the "compliment to the translatress" referred to by Lamb. In the third canto of the poem, Southey, in describing Dobrizhoffer, proceeds thus:—

> "But of his native speech because well-nigh
> Disuse in him forgetfulness had wrought,
> In Latin he composed his history;
> A garrulous, but a lively tale, and fraught
> With matter of delight and food for thought.
> And if he could in Merlin's glass have seen
> By whom his tomes to speak our tongue were taught,
> The old man would have felt as pleased, I ween,
> As when he won the ear of that great Empress Queen."

Southey's poem was prefaced with a poetical dedication to his little daughter, Edith May Southey, beginning—

> "Edith! ten years are numbered since the day
> Which ushers in the cheerful month of May,
> To us by thy dear birth, my daughter dear,
> Was blest."

The poem itself opens with an apostrophe to the discoverer of vaccination—

"Jenner! forever shall thy honoured name."

I have a one-act farce going to be acted at the Haymarket. Probably the *Pawnbroker's Daughter*, which happily was not destined to be performed.

G. Dyer is in the height of an uxorious paradise. According to Crabb Robinson, he married a laundress in Clifford's Inn.

LETTER CCCV (p. 905).—*You have come off triumphant with Bartholomew Fair.* In the Number of the *Every-Day Book* for September 5, 1825, there is a long account of a personal visit to Bartholomew Fair, by Hone himself.

LETTER CCCVI (p. 905).—This playful note was printed by me for the first time. The allusion to "flame-coloured" hose would seem to arise out of an indistinct association with Sir Andrew Aguecheek.

LETTER CCCVII (p. 905).—Lamb was at this time contributing to the new *Monthly Magazine* his "Popular Fallacies." They appeared between January and September in this year, and are the "Proverbs" referred to. See also the following letter.

LETTER CCCIX (p. 906).—*I got your book.* Barton's last volume of poems, *Devotional Verses: founded on, and illustrative of, Select Texts of Scripture* (London, 1826.)

Uniform as they are, and untristorify'd. This last word is certainly as Lamb wrote it, but what he meant by it, and from what he formed it, I must leave to the critics to determine.

The "Spiritual Law" is a short poem on the text "But the word is very nigh thee, in thy mouth and in thy heart, that thou may'st do it."

Whipping the Greek drama upon the back of Genesis. In some verses on Abraham's willingness to sacrifice Isaac, Barton had written—

> "Brief colloquy, yet more sublime
> To every feeling heart
> Than all the boast of classic time
> Or Drama's proudest art;
> Far, far beyond the Grecian stage,
> Or Poesy's most glowing page."

LETTER CCCX (p. 907).—*"The Religion of the Actors."* A little paper by Lamb, printed in the new *Monthly Magazine* for May of this year.

LETTER CCCXI (p. 908).—*Your nephew's pleasant book.* Henry Nelson Coleridge published this year with John Murray, *Six Months in the West Indies in 1825,* the narrative of a journey taken by the young man in company with his uncle for the benefit of his health. It contains pleasant and graphic descriptions of the various places visited, and is written throughout in a witty vein, and in a tone of rather ostentatious Epicureanism, which no doubt led to Coleridge's strictures on its morality. The style is curiously unlike Lamb's, but exhibits many signs of the influence of the *Sentimental Journey,* as Lamb truly remarks. But the little volume "saddens into excellent sense" towards the end, in a serious discussion of the then burning question of West Indian Slavery.

F. K. Fanny Kelly.

LETTER CCCXV (p. 910).—*The likeness which accompanies this letter* was obviously the well-known etching on copper by Mr. Brook Pulham. This portrait was taken in 1825, and is now in the possession of the India Office.

LETTER CCCXVI (p. 910).—Mr. Dibdin was staying at Hastings, as his delicate health often obliged him to do, and was lodging at a baker's, to which fact allusions will be discovered in this and the following letters. The theme of the little church at Hollington is again the subject of infinite variations. "Blucher Row" is a thing of the past, and has merged into a thoroughfare bearing a quite other name.
Peter Fin. The name of a personage in a poem of Thomas Hood's.

LETTER CCCXVIII (p. 912).—Lamb and his friend Dibdin were given to exchanging letters in rhyme. The "Dibdin Muse" seems to have favoured, in various degree, all members of the family, and we find Lamb retorting that he too came of a poetical stock, and adducing his father, old John Lamb, the *Lovel* of the Essay on "The Old Benchers of the Inner Temple." See that Essay, and my notes upon it. Poor Dibdin had apparently allowed "plan, sir" to rhyme to "stanza" in the effusion which called forth this reply. "Small Bohemia," or "Little Bohemia," remains to this day, I believe, the name of a district outside Hastings.

LETTER CCCXIX (p. 914).—*The Quotidian.* Hone's *Every-Day Book.* Lamb had published some "Quatrains" to Hone in the *London Magazine,* which were reprinted in the *Every-Day Book* of July 9, 1826. Hone appended to them a poetical reply in the same number, headed "Quatorzians." For Lamb's verses, see *Poems,* p. 553. They begin—

"I like you and your book, ingenious Hone!"

LETTER CCCXX (p. 915).—Another of those wild and grotesque effusions, written to amuse the invalid during his enforced loneliness at a watering-place. Mr. Dibdin's nephew informs me that his uncle was remarkable for his genuine piety and religious habits, which makes the banter even more extravagant. "Old Ranking" was, of course, one of the firm in the Old Jewry, young Dibdin's employers.

LETTER CCCXXI (p. 916).—*The Garrick plays.* Lamb was laboriously going through this collection, bequeathed by Garrick to the nation, for the purpose of publishing selections from them in his friend Hone's *Table Book.* I may just refer to Lamb's expression, *"dross matters,"*—matters, that is, touching *money.* In previous editions of Lamb's Letters, readings have varied curiously from "these matters" to "dress matters."

LETTER CCCXXII (p. 917).—*Sacred Specimens.* Mr. Mitford published this year his *Sacred Specimens: Selected from Early English Poets.*
Hood's book is mighty clever. Whims and Oddities. Second Series.

LETTER CCCXXIII (p. 918).—Talfourd misdated this letter by a year, placing it in 1826. "Poor Norris" was Randal Norris, Sub-Treasurer of the Inner Temple, and one of the earliest and most loyal friends of Lamb and his parents. He died this month, and was buried in the Temple churchyard. Norris was connected through his wife with the Hertfordshire village of Widford, which Lamb knew so well. It adjoined Blakesware. It is worth noting that in the Second Series of *Elia,* published in Lamb's lifetime, in 1833, this letter to Talfourd, with a few variations and the substitution of changed initials for the real names, was included as an essay, under the title of "A Death Bed. In a Letter to R. H., Esq., of B———." In the essay, Norris appears as "N. R.": poor deaf Richard as "deaf Robert"; and Charley (Lamb himself) as "Jimmie." In the concluding sentences, a more explicit account is given of the family's necessities. "They are left almost provisionless. Some life assurance there is; but I fear not exceeding———. Their hopes must be from your Corporation, which their father has served for fifty years."

The essay was withdrawn after the first edition of the Second Series. Probably the wife and daughters of Randal Norris objected (and not without reason) to have their family circumstances disclosed, under so very slender a disguise.

We'll still make 'em run. The old song referred to is the original version of *Hearts of Oak.* It was published in the *Universal Magazine* for March 1760, entitled "A new Song, sung by Mr. Champness in *Harlequin's Invasion.*"

> "They swear they'll invade us, those terrible foes
> They frighten our women, our children, and beaus;
> But should their flat-bottoms in darkness get o'er,
> Still Britons they'll find to receive them on shore."

The song was written under the inspiration of the year (1759) of Pitt's greatest triumphs—the year of Minden and Quebec. See *Notes and Queries,* 7th series, vii. 18.

LETTER CCCXXV (p. 919).—This letter was clearly written for publication and appeared in Hone's *Table Book* (i. 3). It served as preface to the selections which thenceforth were given weekly.

LETTER CCCXXVII (p. 920).—*The last Extract.* See *Table Book,* i. 357. In the passage from Porter's "Two angry Women of Abingdon" the printer had given the line referred to—

> "Blush forth golden hair and glorious red,"

ruining at once sense and metre.

LETTER CCCXXVIII (p. 921).—*Your picture.* Haydon's "Alexander," exhibited in the Royal Academy this year. See Haydon's *Diary,* ii. 149.

The *two lordlike Bucks* were, according to Haydon, who first printed this note of Lamb's, the Duke of Devonshire and Agar Ellis.

LETTER CCCXXIX (p. 921).—This letter was addressed to Novello in the pages of Hone's *Table Book* (i. 514). It followed the publication (in the "Garrick" Series) of the beautiful lyric from George Peele's *Arraignment of Paris,* beginning—

> "Fair and fair and twice so fair,
> As fair as any may be."

Lamb headed his letter "To my esteemed friend and excellent musician, V. N., Esq."

LETTER CCCXXX (p. 922).—*A correspondent in your last number.* See *Table Book,* i. 803. This letter was signed "The Veiled Spirit." Lamb's reply appeared in the next number (ii. 10).

LETTER CCCXXXI (p. 922).—This letter was first printed by me in its entirety from the original manuscript. The first paragraph, hitherto omitted, tells an amusing and characteristic story of Lamb and Thomas Hood.

The picture verses were some lines written by Lamb to accompany the gift to Barton of a coloured print, in a frame. The lines were afterwards published in his *Album Verses,* 1830.

Bernard Barton delighted to cover his walls with such pictures as he could afford, respecting which a pleasant passage will be found in Edward Fitz-Gerald's *Memoir.* Lamb had somewhere picked up a coloured print representing a little boy learning to read at his mother's knee, and showing many obvious signs of childish obstinacy. For this picture Lamb had borrowed from Thomas Hood an old frame, considerably too large for it; but by carefully coating the superfluous margin of glass with cobbler's-wax, he and his friend Hood had succeeded in giving the whole a reputable appearance. It was on suggesting the use of this frame that Hood observed that Barton would be "sure to like it, because it was *broad-brimmed.*" In writing his verses Lamb, remembering the jest, ended as follows:—

> "For the Frame—
> 'Tis not ill-suited to the same;
> Oak-carved, not gilt, for fear of falling;
> Old-fashioned, plain, yet not appalling;
> And broad-brimmed, as the Owner's Calling."

The last line, Lamb here requests Bernard Barton to expunge. When he printed the poem three years afterwards in *Album Verses,* he retained the line, but with a modification—

> "And *sober,* as the Owner's Calling."

The print, in its ill-fitting frame, hung over the mantelpiece in the late Mrs. FitzGerald's (Lucy Barton's) drawing-room. The original manuscript, with the last line carefully erased with Barton's "best ivory-handled," is, by her generous kindness, in the possession of the editor. The picture has yet one more poetic association. It forms the subject of some pretty verses by Barton, in his *New Year's Eve, and other Poems,* 1828, entitled "Fireside Quatrains to Charles Lamb."

LETTER CCCXXXII (p. 923).—In Hone's *Table Book* (ii. 55) appeared a sonnet of Lamb's addressed to Miss Kelly, "on her excellent Performance of Blindness in the revived opera of *Arthur and Emmeline.*" Hence this letter.

LETTER CCCXXXIII (p. 924).—First printed by Mr. P. G. Patmore in *My Friends and Acquaintance* (1854).

Dash was a dog that had been given to Lamb by Thomas Hood. Mr. Patmore has much to tell of this roving animal, who ultimately was transferred to Mr. Patmore's keeping. See *My Friends and Acquaintance*, vol. i. p. 29.

> *"If he bring but a relict away,*
> *He is happy, nor heard to complain."*

See Shenstone's Pastoral Ballad, "Absence"—

> "The pilgrim that journeys all day
> To visit some far-distant shrine,
> If he bear but a relique away
> Is happy, nor heard to repine."

LETTER CCCXXXIV (p. 925).—*I am busy with a farce in two acts. The Intruding Widow*, a dramatic poem founded on Mr. Crabbe's tale of *The Confidant. (The Wife's Trial.)* Ultimately published in *Blackwood's Magazine*.

LETTER CCCXXXV (p. 926).—Sir John Stoddart, Chief-Justice at Malta. See Letter LXXXIX.
Fearn's "Anti-Tooke." Anti Tooke or, an Analysis of Language. (London, 1824.)

LETTER CCCXXXVI (p. 927).—*My engraving.* The etching on copper by Brook Pulham.
I had my Blakesware. See Essay, "Blakesmoor in Hertfordshire," p. 138, *The Last Essays of Elia*, in this edition. The essay was first published in the *London Magazine*.

LETTER CCCXXXVII (p. 928).—The reference here is to Lamb's contributions to the *Table Book* of extracts from the Garrick plays. Hone felt deeply the kindness of Lamb and his sister during his struggling career. In dedicating to them his *Every-Day Book*, he says:—"How can I forget your and Miss Lamb's sympathy and kindness when glooms overmastered me, and that your pen sparkled in the book when my mind was in clouds and darkness. These 'trifles,' as each of you would call them, are benefits scored upon my heart."

LETTER CCCXXXVIII (p. 928).—Barton had been sending verses for Emma Isola's album. Respecting Mr. Fraser's projected album, see note to Letter CCCLII.
"Future Lord Byrons and sweet L. E. L.'s." This is a line from some verses on albums, which have been attributed, I think on insufficient grounds, to Lamb himself.
My tragi-comedy. The Intruding Widow.
Your Drummonds. Lamb uses the name of one famous firm of bankers to indicate Barton's employers, the Alexanders.
En passant. I despair of interpreting Lamb's attempts at the French language. Talfourd, equally hopeless, omitted the last sentence, but I restore it from the original manuscript.

LETTER CCCXXXIX (p. 930).—See *Table Book*, ii. 287, "Past, Present, and Future. Extemporaneous Lines, written to oblige a young Friend who suggested the Topic." Hone signed his own contributions with a *. In the poem occur these lines, to which Lamb specially refers:—

> "Time, that faithful tutor,
> Were I but teachable, might show the Future
> As the Present is; and yet I paint it
> Teeming with joy."

LETTER CCCXLII (p. 931).—*Mr. Watts.* Alaric A. Watts, the editor of various albums and keepsakes.

> *"Lord, what good hours do we keep!"*

—From a poem by Charles Cotton, quoted in the *Complete Angler.*

A feeble counter-action thro' the Table Book of last Saturday. We must suppose there had been some critical attacks upon Hood's "Plea of the Midsummer Fairies" (1827), for Lamb contributed to the *Table Book* a prose version of a portion of that poem, under the title, "The Defeat of Time: or a Tale of the Fairies" (*Table Book*, ii. 335). After paraphrasing the earlier part of the poem, Lamb breaks off with the following postscript:—"What particular endearments passed between the Fairies and their Poet passes my pencil to delineate; but if you are curious to be informed, I must refer you, gentle reader, to the 'Plea of the Fairies,' a most agreeable poem lately put forth by my friend Thomas Hood; of the first half of which the above is nothing but a meagre and a harsh prose abstract. Farewell. (Elia.) *The words of Mercury are harsh after the songs of Apollo."*

LETTER CCCXLIV (p. 933).—*Mr. Moxon.* The earliest mention, save in a letter of the June preceding, of one afterwards to be Lamb's friend and publisher, and the husband of Emma Isola. He was then a young man of six-and-twenty.

LETTER CCCXLV (p. 933).—Dash had been made over to the care of the Patmores, having been found by the Lambs "intractable and wild."

I've sent him two poems. One of these was the poem, "On an infant dying as soon as born," written at the request of Mrs. Hood on the death of her first child. See *Poems*, p. 534.

LETTER CCCXLVIII (p. 935).—This letter was first printed in Mrs. Mathews's Memoirs of her husband (iii. 596). It was there given *à propos* of the suggestion that had been made to Lamb, through Barron Field, that he should write an elaborate description of the pictures in Mathews's famous Theatrical Portrait Gallery.

An imitator of me. Rejected Articles was a collection of parodies of various prose writers, by Mr. P. G. Patmore (1826), one of the many *jeux d'esprit* suggested by the success of the more famous *Rejected Addresses.* The first article in the volume was a paper purporting to be by Elia, entitled "An Un-Sentimental Journey." It was no more successful than many other attempts to imitate a style essentially inimitable.

LETTER CCCXLIX (p. 936).—The original of this letter is in the possession of the family of my friend, Mr. George Loveday of Wardington, Banbury. Mr. Dodwell (it will be remembered) was a fellow-clerk of Lamb's in the India

House. The names indicated by initials were other colleagues of Lamb and his correspondent.

LETTER CCCLII (p. 939).—*The kind "knitter in the sun!"* Lamb is thinking of the line in *Twelfth Night*—

> *"The spinsters and the knitters in the sun."*

A Bijoux. So Lamb wrote, and French was not his strong point. The *Bijou* for 1828, published by Pickering, was edited by W. Fraser, afterwards editor of the *Foreign Quarterly Review.* Besides the Royal contributions referred to in Lamb's letter to Barton of 28th August 1827, the *Bijou* contained one of Lamb's ("Fresh clad from Heaven, an angel bright"); three poems of Coleridge's—"Youth and Age," "Work without Hope," "The Two Founts"; and here, moreover, was first printed Blanco White's immortal sonnet, beginning "Mysterious Night!"

LETTER CCCLIII (p. 939).—Leigh Hunt would appear to have desired a portrait of Lamb, as one of certain projected illustrations for the work he had in preparation, *Lord Byron and some of his Contemporaries: with Recollections of the Author's Life and of his Visit to Italy.* 1828. The book ultimately appeared, however, without the portraits. Both the likenesses of Lamb, here mentioned, have been since engraved. The one by Hazlitt "in a queer dress" represents Lamb in a nondescript costume, with a ruff.

LETTER CCCLVI (p. 940).—*Your welcome present. The Widow's Tale, and Other Poems,* by Bernard Barton, 1827. The author prefixes a note to the "Widow's Tale," stating that the incidents are taken from the painful but interesting "Account of the loss of five Wesleyan missionaries and others in the *Maria* mail-boat off the Island of Antigua, by Mrs. Jones, the only survivor on that mournful occasion." A woodcut on the title-page, representing three shipwrecked travellers *in extremis* on a raft at sea, is, as Lamb remarks, "a rueful *lignum mortis.*" All the poems or passages indicated by Lamb with approval are given in the memorial volume on Barton already referred to. The "third stanza, at p. 108," that made Lamb long to see Van Balen, was from a poem describing a picture by that artist, representing some angel children leading up a lamb to the infant Saviour in His mother's lap. The stanza, containing a simile that Lamb thought exquisite, may well be quoted here. It is from the "Grandsire's Tale," in which the old man relates the early death of his grandchild:—

> "Though some might deem her pensive, if not sad,
>   Yet those that knew her better, best could tell
> How calmly happy, and how meekly glad
>   Her quiet heart in its own depths did dwell:
> Like to the waters of some crystal well,
>   In which the stars of heaven at noon are seen,
> Fancy might deem on her young spirit fell
>   Glimpses of light more glorious and serene
> Than that of life's brief day, so heavenly was her mien."

An artist who painted me lately. Henry Meyer, referred to in the letter to Leigh Hunt of November 1827.

CHAPTER VI

1828–1834

LETTER CCCLVIII (p. 943).—*Hunt's Lord B.* Leigh Hunt's *Lord Byron and some of his Contemporaries,* etc. etc. 1828.

Hazlitt's speculative episodes. In his *Life of Napoleon Buonaparte,* four volumes. 1828.

The "Companion." One of Leight Hunt's numerous ventures of the periodical sort. It began on January 9, and was discontinued on July 23, of this year 1828. A glance at the list of contents in Mr. Alexander Ireland's valuable Bibliography supports Lamb's complaint that there was too much in it of Madame Pasta. One article in the *Companion* was "Walks home by night in bad weather—Watchmen."

One Clarke a schoolmaster. The father of Cowden Clarke, the Rev. John Clarke, was a schoolmaster at Enfield. Keats, it will be remembered, was one of his pupils.

Holmes. Edward Holmes, author of the *Life of Mozart* and other musical works, was also at Mr. Clarke's school. He contributed at this time articles on musical subjects to the *Atlas* newspaper.

Victoria. Mary Victoria Novello, afterwards Mrs. Cowden Clarke. The Novellos lived for a while at Shacklewell Green, near Dalston. Cowden Clarke, it should be added, was in early life a teacher in his father's school, which explains Lamb's allusion to the "schoolmaster text hand."

Thurtell. Not the murderer, but his brother Thomas, who kept the Cock Tavern in the Haymarket.

LETTER CCCLIX (p. 945).—*The things which Pickering has.* Certain verses of Lamb's offered to Mr. Pickering for his *Bijou,* if not used, were promised to Thomas Hood, who was editing another annual called the *Gem.*

LETTER CCCLXI (p. 945).—*Mitford tells you of H.'s book.* Lamb apparently refers to William Hazlitt's *Spirit of the Age; or, Contemporary Portraits,* published in 1825, in which his own was one of the Portraits sketched. See Letter to Bernard Barton of February 10, 1825.

The author of "May you like it." The Rev. C. B. Tayler, the vicar of Hadleigh, Suffolk, Barton's neighbour and friend.

LETTER CCCLXIII (p. 946).—Moxon was at this time with Mr. Hurst, the publisher, in St. Paul's Churchyard.

Poor John Scott's Second, on occasion of the duel with Christie in 1821, in which Scott was killed.

LETTER CCCLXV (p. 947).—In 1828 a project was formed for erecting a monument to Thomas Clarkson, on the hill above Wade's Mill on the Buntingford Road, in Hertfordshire, this being the spot where the resolution of devoting his life to the abolition of the Slave Trade first took possession of him. This was in Clarkson's lifetime, for he survived till 1846. The scheme was abandoned for the time, but has been revived and carried out within the last few years.

Upon a hillock at Forty Hill. Forty Hill is a district of Enfield.

LETTER CCCLXVI (p. 948).—*Your Chairing the Member.* One of two pictures that Haydon had just painted, the subjects taken from certain frolics that he had witnessed when in the King's Bench Prison. The other was "The Mock Election," purchased for five hundred guineas by King George IV. "Chairing the Member" was exhibited by Haydon, with other of his pictures, in August of this year, at the Western Bazaar in Bond Street. "Besides the new picture, the Exhibition included 'Solomon,' 'Christ's Entry into Jerusalem,' and the drawings for the two prison pictures. 'The Mock Election' was not there, as it had before this been removed to Windsor." (*Tom Taylor's Life of B. R. Haydon.*)

LETTER CCCLXVIII (p. 949).—*How are all the little orphans?* The allusion requires some explanation. The key to it will be found in Lamb's letter to Procter of January 29, 1829. Lamb there relates how Miss Holcroft, daughter of Thomas Holcroft, the dramatist, during a visit to Enfield in the summer of 1828 had kindly interested herself in the infant child of a man who had just been apprehended for sheep-stealing, and had worked it a cap. More than once after this incident Lamb playfully assumes that Miss Holcroft's interest in the fatherless is unabated, and that in fact her home in London, where she lived with her stepfather, James Kenney, was swarming with these orphan protégés. See, again, Letter to the same lady, of December 5, 1828.

LETTER CCCLXX (p. 952).—The *Edition de Luxe* here spoken of as in preparation was published in 1830, with a Prefatory Memoir of Bunyan by Southey. It was illustrated by Martin, and published by Barton's friend, John Major. Macaulay's review of this edition will be remembered. His observations on Martin's unfitness for this kind of illustration bear a strong resemblance to Lamb's.

The Gem. The *Gem* for 1829 was edited by Thomas Hood. In the volume for that year appeared Lamb's verses "On an infant dying as soon as born," written at the request of Mrs. Hood, on the death of her infant child.

LETTER CCCLXXI (p. 953).—The note which Lamb wrote to Hood, on discovering in the *Gem*, the practical joke referred to in a letter to Procter of January 22, 1829. He indicates the temporary exchange of names by the opening and concluding words of his communication. Bridget, it will be remembered, is the name by which his sister is always described in the *Essays of Elia*.

LETTER CCCLXXII (p. 954).—*When you lurked at the Greyhound.* Cowden Clarke and his bride spent their quiet honeymoon at the Inn at Enfield, as Mrs. Cowden Clarke tells us. They were married on the 5th of July of this year.

LETTER CCCLXXIII (p. 954).—The "Epithalamium" referred to in the former letter was, on second thoughts, despatched to Vincent Novello. Mrs. Cowden Clarke, who first printed this parody upon the school of Dryden in the *Gentleman's Magazine* for December 1873, dwells with just appreciation upon the admirable fooling of the entire letter.

LETTER CCCLXXIV (p. 957).—Laman Blanchard published this year a little volume of Poems, *Lyric Offerings,* dedicated to Lamb.

LETTER CCCLXXV (p. 957).—Barton had sent Lamb his latest volume, *A New Year's Eve, and other Poems.* (London, 1828.) It was dedicated "to Charles Richard Sumner, Bishop of Winchester, in memorial of his courtesy and kindness," and had for frontispiece an engraving of a drawing by Martin, of Christ walking on the sea. Lamb, in applauding the picture, refers to certain strictures upon Martin contained in a previous letter to Barton. "Power and Gentleness, or the Cataract and the Streamlet," is perhaps as charming a lyric as Barton ever wrote. It contains the stanza about the streamlet, which was a favourite with that admirable judge, Edward FitzGerald:—

> "More gaily now it sweeps
> By the small schoolhouse, in the sunshine bright;
> And o'er the pebbles leaps
> Like happy hearts by holiday made light."

The full title of the "Lady Russell" poem was, "Lady Rachel Russell: or, a Roman Hero and an English Heroine compared." The "stanzas to 'Chalon'" were "On a Portrait by A. E. Chalon, R.A."—the portrait being one of Clarkson, the Abolitionist.

As Sh—— says of Religion. It is hardly necessary to point out that the allusion is to Hamlet's—

> "And fair Religion make
> A rhapsody of words."

I much like the "Heron." "Syr Heron. Inscribed to my ingenious friend, John Major, on receiving from him a seal bearing the impress of that bird."

"Fludyer." "To Sir Samuel Fludyer, on the devastation effected on his Marine Villa at Felixstowe by the encroachments of the Sea." The answer to the enigma is clearly, as Mrs. FitzGerald has pointed out to me, *an auctioneer's hammer.*

LETTER CCCLXXVI (p. 958).—Lamb here again makes humorous capital over Miss Holcroft's imaginary home for orphans. (See previous letter of October 2, 1828.) He now assumes that the measles are probably current among them. Miss Holcroft was at this time shortly to be married to Carlyle's friend, Dr. John Badams.

LETTER CCCLXXVIII (p. 960).—As Procter had tried a practical joke upon Lamb, the latter seems to have thought it a good opportunity to return the compliment. In the details that follow, concerning the case that "fretted him to death," the element of truth was that John Lamb had, shortly before his death, married a widow, who had a married daughter, Elizabeth Dowden. This, I have ascertained, was a fact. Lamb, as his brother's executor, had some trouble in administering the estate; but the elaborate and impossible farrago of details here built upon the simple foundation is, of course, the wildest nonsense. The serious reference to the 170th chapter of "Fearne's Contingent Remainders" (a classic work, divided, I believe, into some dozen or fifteen chapters) is delightfully conceived. Talfourd adds that the alleged coolness between Lamb and his legal friends was part of the fiction.

A few lines of verse for a young friend's album. It was for Emma Isola's album that the verses were asked.

Barry C—— is Barry Cornwall, Mr. Procter's poetical "Alias."

LETTER CCCLXXIX (p. 962).—I have revised previous texts of this letter
from the original in Mrs. Procter's possession, and restored one or two characteristic sentences hitherto omitted.

The anti-Capulets. The Montagus (Basil Montagu and his wife).

Miss Holcroft. Louisa Holcroft, daughter of the dramatist, married Mr.
Badams, Carlyle's friend. See Carlyle's *Reminiscences.*

Burke's case. Burke and Hare, the Edinburgh resurrection men. Burke was
hanged on the 28th of this January. "A shot" was explained in evidence to be a
slang word used by the gang for a "subject to be murdered."

A sonnet of mine. "The Gipsy's Malison." See the next letter to Procter, in
which the sonnet is given.

'Twas written for the "Gem." Edited this year by Hood.

They published the "Widow" instead. The "Widow" was a short essay, accompanying a steel engraving of a sentimental picture by Leslie, of a kind
common in annuals and keepsakes, bearing the same title. Hood wrote this
paper in imitation of Lamb's style, and boldly appended to it the signature,
"C. Lamb." The imitation is only tolerably successful. It opens thus:—

A WIDOW

hath always been a mark for mockery—a standing butt for wit to level at. Jest
after jest hath been huddled upon her close cap, and stuck, like burrs, upon
her weeds. Her sables are a perpetual "Black Joke."

Satirists—prose and verse—have made merry with her bereavements. She
is a stock character on the stake. Farce bottleth up her crocodile tears, or la-
belleth her empty lachrymatories. Comedy mocketh her precocious flirtations,
and, twitteth her with "the funeral baked meats coldly furnishing forth the
marriage tables."

I confess, when I called the other day on my kinswoman G.— then in the
second week of her widowhood—and saw her sitting, her young boy by her side,
in her recent sables, I felt unable to reconcile her estate with any risible associations. The lady with a skeleton moiety—in the old print in Bowles's old
shop-window—seemed but a type of her condition, etc. etc.

LETTER CCCLXXX (p. 963).—See preceding letter to Procter, of 22nd
January.

Abactor, we may conclude, is the Latin equivalent for sheep-stealer given
in Ainsworth's *Dictionary.*

LETTER CCCLXXXI (p. 964).—Mr. Procter was a solicitor, "incipient," but
not precisely a "conveyancer."

O thou above the Painter. James Barry, the historical painter.

Giraldus Cambrensis, the historian, otherwise known as Giraldus de *Barri.*

Thy most ingenious and golden cadences. The verses that Procter had sent
for Emma Isola's album, in reply to Lamb's invitation. They turned upon the
coincidence of the young lady's name with that of the lovely island in the
Lago Maggiore, so well known to all sojourners at Baveno. The lines ended—

"Isola Bella, whom all poets love!"

The "fairest hands in Cambridge" were Emma Isola's, who had many friends
in the University town. She was then preparing to accept a situation as gover-

ness in the family of Mr. Williams, Rector of Fornham, near Bury St. Edmunds.

Unsphinx this riddle for me. It is perhaps impertinent to point out that the flippant allusions that follow are to the disastrous family history of one who had dealings with a notable propounder of riddles.

LETTER CCCLXXXII (p. 965).—I append a translation:—

"Most eloquent Poet! although epithets of that sort, I am well aware, apply to orators rather than poets—for all that, most eloquent!

"There has been now for some time staying with us in the Enfield country a future attorney, the most illustrious Martin Burney, who is taking his holiday —escaped, for a while, from business so called, and an office without clients. He begs and implores you (Martin does, I mean), if by blessed fortune a tardy client should turn up in his absence, that you will let him know by letter addressed here. Do you understand? or ought I to write in a tongue so barbarous as English to you, prince of scholars? C. LAMB.

"If an estate in freehold is granted to a grandfather, and if in the same deed it is granted mediately or immediately to the heir or heirs of the body of the said grandfather, these last are words of Limitation, not Perquisition. This is my ruling."

The postscript to this letter is supplementary to the legal fiction elaborated in the previous letter of 19th January.

LETTER CCCLXXXIII (p. 965).—*Astrea.* D'Urfé's famous Pastoral Romance.

Inconstant, yet fair. This sentence and the following sum up, with exquisite skill, the euphuistic style of Sidney's *Arcadia.*

Cowden with the Tuft. A description formed from analogy with the hero of the fairy tale, *Riquet with the Tuft.* Mr. Clarke, as his wife informs us, had a bald head fringed with rather demonstrative tufts of hair.

LETTER CCCLXXXIV (p. 965).—Talfourd tells us that Crabb Robinson sent Lamb a copy of *Pamela,* under a mistaken belief that he had borrowed a previous copy and not returned it.

LETTER CCCLXXXV (p. 966).—*Darley's very poetical poem. Sylvia: or, the May Queen.* 1827.

"Christmas." By Edward Moxon.

Field's Appendix. "Geographical Memoirs on New South Wales, by various hands," etc. etc. Edited by Barron Field, Esq., F.L.S., 1825. In the Appendix is printed "First Fruits of Australian Poetry," originally printed privately in New South Wales. See Lamb's notice of these poems, *Mrs. Leicester's School,* etc., p. 235.

I have writ in the old Hamlet. A reprint of the first quarto (1603) of *Hamlet,* then lately discovered.

The copy thus sent was retained by Barton, in accordance with the permission given in this letter, and is now, through the kindness of Mrs. Edward Fitz-Gerald, in the Editor's collection. On the fly-leaf, in Lamb's handwriting, is the inscription:—"Present this to Mr. Mitford in my name, if he has not got it.—C. L."

By being "woefully below our editions of it," Lamb means, of course, that the quarto of 1603 is but a first sketch, unless it be an unauthorised and garbled version of the play as we know it

LETTER CCCLXXXVII (p. 967).—*The report of thy torments*. Crabb Robinson, in his *Diary*, quotes a letter of his own to Wordsworth of 22nd April, describing this attack:—"Went to bed at two, and in the morning found my left knee as crooked as the politics of the Ministry are, by the anti-Catholics, represented to be. After using leeches, poultices, etc., for three weeks, I went down to Brighton, and again, in a most unchristian spirit, put myself under the hands of the Mahomedan Mahomet—was stewed in his vapour-baths, and shampooed under his pagan paws."

LETTER CCCLXXXIX (p. 969).—This, and a subsequent letter of 15th November, are on the subject of Mr. Walter Wilson's *Life and Times of De Foe*, then in preparation. The ode here referred to is Lamb's "Ode to the Treadmill," written in imitation of De Foe's "Ode to the Pillory." See *Poems*, p. 542.

LETTER CCCXCI (p. 969).—*Our young friend Emma*. Emma Isola, who was at this time governess to the Williamses at Fornham.
His name was Dibdin. The young man, Lamb's letters to whom were first printed in this edition. He returned from Madeira, as Lamb relates, and died of his "long disease" on May 11, 1828.
Southey's Dialogues. Sir Thomas More: or, Colloquies on the Progress and Prospects of Society. 1829.
In acknowledgment of a sonnet I sent him. See the sonnet, "To Samuel Rogers, Esq.," p. 564.

LETTER CCCXCII (p. 970).—*Your kind inquisitive Eliza*. Eliza Barton, Bernard Barton's sister.
An old rejected farce of mine. The Pawnbroker's Daughter.

LETTER CCCXCIV (p. 972). This letter is printed by the kind permission of Sir Edmund Elton of Clevedon Court. It was written to his grandfather, Sir Charles A. Elton, who succeeded to the baronetcy in 1842. Sir Charles (at the date of this letter, Mr. C. A. Elton) was a classical scholar and poet, who contributed largely to the *London Magazine*, a circumstance which first brought him and Lamb together. It will be remembered that he there wrote the lines signed "Olen," which had greatly pleased and touched Lamb. In the present instance he had evidently sent Lamb a present of several of his published volumes, including his "Specimens of the Classical Poets translated into English verse" (1814), and his "Remains of Hesiod," similarly translated (1815). Lamb's criticisms apply mainly to these two volumes. The reference to the "tenderest parts in your own little volume," is certainly to the pathetic poem "The Brothers, a Monody," written by Elton on the death of his two sons by drowning in 1819, and published in the following year.

LETTER CCCXCV (p. 973).—Talfourd had christened his latest child, Charles Lamb Talfourd. The father adds this note: "The child who bore the name so honoured by his parents survived his godfather only a year, dying at Brighton, whither he had been taken in the vain hope of restoration, on the 3rd of December 1835."

LETTER CCCXCVI (p. 974).—*An honest couple our neighbours*. A Mr. and Mrs. Thomas Westwood. Mr. Westwood was a retired tradesman, and agent to the *Phœnix* Assurance Office.

LETTER CCCXCVIII (p. 975).—Wilson's work on De Foe was just published. Lamb had contributed to it his "Estimate of De Foe's Secondary Novels." See *Mrs. Leicester's School*, etc., p. 304. Lamb had written a letter to Wilson seven years (not fifteen) before, containing some remarks upon these novels, which Wilson also makes use of in his work on De Foe. Much of what he wrote in the friendly letter naturally reappeared in the more formal essay. Hence Lamb's allusion to the "two papers" puzzling the reader, "being so akin." Hazlitt reviewed Wilson's *Life and Times of De Foe* in the *Edinburgh* of January 1830.

LETTER CCCXCIX (p. 976).—*The excursionists.* Mr. Westwood, Lamb's landlord, had driven Mary Lamb over to Highgate to see the Gilmans and Coleridge. The note that follows this would appear to refer to a later excursion, conducted by the same "Son of Nimshi." But Lamb's habit of not dating letters confuses matters sadly.

LETTER CCCCII (p. 979).—*Hazlitt has just been defrauded.* By the failure of the publishers of his *Life of Napoleon*.

LETTER CCCCIII (p. 980).—Wordsworth's letter to Lamb, to which this is the reply, is given in Bishop Wordsworth's Memoirs of the Poet (ii. 223). It bears date 10th January of this year, and begins: "A whole twelvemonth have I been a letter in your debt, for which fault I have been sufficiently punished by self-reproach." The letter tells of the dangerous illness of Dorothy Wordsworth, and of Wordsworth's own weakened eyesight.
Henry Crabb is Henry Crabb Robinson.
Can I cram loves enough to you all in this little O? Those who know their Shakspeare will take the allusion to a line in the Chorus to Henry V.

LETTER CCCCIV (p. 983).—*To furnish A. C. with the scrap.* A. C. is Allan Cunningham, who was preparing his *Lives of the Painters*, and wanted that portion of Lamb's letter to Barton of May 15, 1824, which referred to William Blake. The letter was sent to Cunningham, in accordance with the permission here given, but the "scrap" was apparently crowded out, for it did not appear in the first edition of Cunningham's work in the Family Library. It was, however, preserved among the Cunningham papers, and is given in the latest edition of the work in Bohn's Series.
That Joseph Paice. See Lamb's Elia Essay, "Modern Gallantry." In the *Athenæum* for the year 1841 (See p. 75), will be found some interesting particulars of Mr. Paice, by the late Miss Anne Manning.

LETTER CCCCV (p. 983).—*Your hopes about Dick Norris.* Richard Norris, the son of Lamb's old friend, Randal Norris, Sub-Treasurer of the Inner Temple. Mrs. Hazlitt had noticed that *a* Mr. Norris was Treasurer of the Inn this year, and had too hastily inferred that young Norris had succeeded to his late father's post.

LETTER CCCCVI (p. 984).—The Rev. James Gillman was the son of Mr. Gillman of Highgate. Lamb's information concerning the Norwich people is, of course, what would in his day have been called "raillery," and in our day "chaff." Who Mr. Battin was, I know not. Talfourd assumes that this letter was to the elder Gillman, but the allusion to his correspondent having something "professionally" to say to the Revelations in Greek, seems to point to his being in holy orders. The friends in Spitalfields are, I presume, the weavers.

LETTER CCCCVII (p. 985).—*Phillips (not the Colonel)*. "Edward Phillips, Esq., Secretary to the Right Hon. Charles Abbott, Speaker of the House of Commons. The 'Colonel' alluded to was the Lieutenant of Marines who accompanied Captain Cook on his last voyage, and on shore with that great man when he fell a victim to his humanity" (Talfourd).

Mrs. B——'s. Obviously Mrs. Burney. An ingenious editor of Lamb's Letters has filled up the blank with Mrs. *Battle's* name! John Murray had proposed to Lamb to publish a supplementary volume of specimens from the old dramatists.

LETTER CCCCVIII (p. 986).—This letter was written after Lamb's return to London from a visit to the Williamses at Fornham. He had taken Miss Isola, now convalescent after a severe attack of brain fever, back with him to Enfield. Two of the acrostics that Lamb wrote for the amusement of Mrs. Williams and her family were afterwards included by Lamb in his *Album Verses*, published this year. One is an acrostic epitaph on Mrs. Williams, her name being Grace Joanna Williams; the other on her youngest daughter, Louisa Clare.

LETTER CCCCIX (p. 987).—Mrs. Williams seems also to have been fond of writing acrostics, and had composed one on Mary Lamb.

She blames my last verses. This acrostic was not included by Lamb in his next volume of *Album Verses*:—

> "Go little Poem, and present
> Respectful terms of compliment;
> A gentle lady bids thee speak!
> Courteous is *she*, tho' thou be weak—
> Evoke from Heaven as thick as manna

> "Joy after joy on Grace Joanna:
> On Fornham's Glebe and Pasture land
> A blessing pray. Long, long may stand,
> Not touched by Time, the Rectory blithe;
> No grudging churl dispute his Tithe;
> At Easter be the offerings due

> "With cheerful spirit paid; each pew
> In decent order filled; no noise
> Loud intervene to drown the voice,
> Learning, or wisdom of the Teacher;
> Impressive be the Sacred Preacher,
> And strict his notes on holy page;
> May young and old from age to age
> Salute, and still point out, 'The good man's Parsonage!'"

LETTER CCCCX (p. 988).—*My friend Hone*. Hone was at this time established by the help of friends in the *Grasshopper* Coffee House in Gracechurch Street.

An epigram I did for a schoolboy. This schoolboy was the late Archdeacon Hessey, who published in the *Taylorian* (a periodical supported by the Merchant Taylors' boys) an account of his father taking him to see Lamb at Colebrook Cottage in 1825. Archdeacon Hessey informs us that the subject of the epigram was suggested by "the grim satisfaction which had recently been expressed by the public at the capture and execution of several notorious highwaymen."

LETTER CCCCXI (p. 989).—*Rogers's handsome behaviour to you.* The poet had advanced Moxon £500 wherewith to set up in business as publisher. Moxon had published more than one volume of verse, including a book of sonnets of his own.

LETTER CCCCXII (p. 989).—This delightful letter was first printed in the *Athenæum* a few years since, and is here given by the kind permission of the editor. Lamb adopts Procter's conceit of the island in Maggiore.

LETTER CCCCXVI (p. 991).—*Ayrton was here yesterday.* Lamb elsewhere gives a quite different account of the origin of his verses on the Eminent Composers. In a letter to Ayrton, Lamb represents them as having been written at the request of Novello, who had desired Lamb "to give him my real opinion respecting the distinct grades of excellence in all the eminent composers of the Italian, German, and English schools." I am afraid we cannot absolve Lamb from the charge of fibbing in one or other of these statements. Martin Burney, who was originally a solicitor, had been lately called to the Bar. The step did not prove a success.

LETTER CCCCXVII (p. 992).—There had been a suggestion that William Hazlitt's son, who was endowed with a fine voice, should adopt music as a profession. Ayrton, as a well-known authority on music, and impresario, would be naturally resorted to for counsel.

LETTER CCCCXVIII (p. 993).—The scheme for establishing Hone in a coffee-house business had been carried into effect, and Lamb, with characteristic helpfulness, arranges to have his newspaper at second-hand from the establishment in Gracechurch Street.

LETTER CCCCXIX (p. 993).—Lamb had just published, with Moxon, his *Album Verses.* The translations referred to are those from the Latin of Vincent Bourne.

LETTER CCCCXXII (p. 994).—The little volume of *Album Verses* was rather rudely handled by the reviewers, notably by the *Literary Gazette.* This review, Talfourd tells us, provoked some verses from Southey, which were inserted in the *Times,* and of which the following, as evincing his unchanged friendship, may not unfitly be inserted here:—

> "Charles Lamb! to those who know thee justly dear
>   For rarest genius, and for sterling worth,
> Unchanging friendship, warmth of heart sincere,
>   And wit that never gave an ill thought birth,
>   Nor ever in its sport infixed a sting;
>   To us who have admired and loved thee long,
> It is a proud as well as pleasant thing
>   To hear thy good report, now borne along

" 'Diddle, diddle, dumkins! my son John
　　Went to bed with his breeches on;
　　One shoe off and the other shoe on,
　　Diddle, diddle,' etc.　(Da Capo.)

" 'Here am I, jumping Joan;
　　When no one is by, I'm here alone.'

"Solve me this Riddle, and you will be an Œdipus. Why is a horse like a Quaker? Because his whole communication is by 'Hay and Neigh,' in accordance with the Scriptural injunction ('Yea and Nay').

"With these trifles I get through the precious day, while watching by the sick-bed of our more precious Emma, who has been at home with us ill, now for a long time. Mary joins me in best greetings; she is quite well.
　　　　　　　　　　　　　　　　　　　　　　　　　　　ELIA.'

"Given at Enfield on one or other of the Calends of April. 'I am Davus, not' —almanack maker!

"*P.S.*—The Reform Bill is thrown out for good."

LETTER CCCCXXIX (p. 1000).—I append a free translation of the letter:—
　　　　　　　　　　　　　　　　　　　　　　　　"*Enfield, May* 6, 1831.

"My good sister is sitting by me, turning the leaves of the *Euripides,* your present, dearest Cary, for which we thank you, and mean to read it again and again. The book is doubly acceptable to us both, as the sacred work of the 'Priest of Compassion,' and as the gift of one, himself a Priest of the most humane Religion in the world.

"When in tears, we are on the eve of joy: there are times when sorrow becomes gladness; laughter is not always sweet; we must sometimes exchange He! He! He! for. Heu! Heu! Heu! That the Tragic Muse is not wholly repugnant to me, witness this Song of Disaster, originally written by some unknown author in the vernacular, but lately turned by me into Latin—I mean, 'Tom of Islington.' Do you take? . . . . And finally Tom is filled with joy that on the following day (Sunday, to wit) his spouse must be carried out to burial. Lo! a domestic Iliad! A cycle of calamity! A seven-days' Tragedy!

"Go now and compare your vaunted *Euripides* with griefs like these! Such a death of wives as this! Where is your Alcestis now? your Hecuba? your other Dolorous Heroines of antiquity?

"My cheeks are bathed in tears as I muse upon these tragedies! What remains but to greet you and your own dear spouse, and to wish you as good health as we ourselves are enjoying.　　　　　　　　　　　　ELIA."

LETTER CCCCXXX (p. 1001).—Although the date of this letter has been hitherto given 1831, I believe that it should be 1821. The letter is evidently written to Mr. Taylor, the publisher of the *London*, at the time Lamb was contributing to that magazine his *Essays of Elia.* In the number for July, 1821, appeared the essay "Mackery End in Hertfordshire," and it is in this essay that the stanza from Wordsworth occurs to which reference is obviously made:—

　　　　　"But thou, that didst appear so fair
　　　　　　　To fond Imagination,
　　　　　Dost rival in the light of *day*
　　　　　　　Her delicate creation!"

> Upon the honest breath of public praise:
> We know that with the elder sons of song,
> In honouring whom thou hast delighted still,
> Thy name shall keep its course to after days."

There were some further lines, very severe upon Lamb's recent critics.

LETTER CCCCXXIII (p. 995).—These lines were written, Mrs. Cowden Clarke tells us, "at the request of Vincent Novello, in memory of four sons and two daughters of John and Ann Rigg, of York. All six, respectively aged 19, 18, 17, 16, 7, and 6, were drowned at once by their boat being run down on the river Ouse, near York, August 19, 1830."

LETTER CCCCXXIV (p. 995).—This note had been hitherto placed out of its order. After their two months' stay in London, Lamb had to take his sister back to Enfield. Southey came to London on a visit to John Rickman, at the House of Commons, on the 1st of November.

LETTER CCCCXXVI (p. 997).—From a later letter to Moxon we gain further particulars of George Dyer and his sensitive conscience. As far back as the end of the preceding century Dyer had written a couplet in his poem "The Poet's Fate," in which occurred some slighting mention of Rogers. A Mr. Barker, in his *Parriana*, had recently quoted and so revived the unfortunate couplet—hence Dyer's apprehensions.

Great Erasmians. Two forms at Christ's Hospital were nicknamed "Great Erasmus" and "Little Erasmus," probably from the fact that the *Colloquies* and other works of Erasmus were read in these forms. Grecian and Deputy-Grecian are also well-known grades of distinction in the nomenclature of Christ's Hospital.

LETTER CCCCXXVIII (p. 999).—"Good man!—I have received your most friendly letter, and it occurred to me as I was about to answer it that the Latin Tongue has seldom or never been exchanged by us, as a medium for corresponding or speaking. Your letters, replete with Plinian elegancies (rather more than is seemly in a Quaker), are so remote from the language of Pliny that you do not appear to have a single word (a Roman word, of course, I mean) to 'throw to a dog,' as the saying is. Possibly a long disuse of writing Latin has driven you to the use of your vernacular tongue unnecessarily. I have resolved, therefore, to recall you to the recovery of your lost Latinity by means of certain familiar and generally well-known proverbs:—

" 'The cat's in the cupboard, and she can't see.'
" 'All that glitters is not gold.'
" 'Put a beggar on horseback and he will ride to the Devil.'
" 'Set a thief to catch a thief.'
" 'Mary, Mary, quite contrary, how does your garden grow?'
"Now let us sing of weightier themes!—
" 'Tom, Tom, of Islington, married a wife on Sunday. He brought her home on Monday; Bought a stick on Tuesday; Beat her well on Wednesday; Sick was she on Thursday; Dead was she on Friday; Glad was Tom on Saturday night, to bury his wife on Sunday.'
" 'Little Jack Horner sat in a corner,' etc. etc. etc.

Taylor's proposed improvement of the stanza by the substitution of "air" for "day" is sufficiently amusing.

LETTER CCCCXXXI (p. 1001).—Lamb contributed to the *Englishman's Magazine* of September 1831 a paper entitled "Recollections of a late Royal Academician" (see *Mrs. Leicester's School*, etc., p. 307, and notes). This was Lamb's first contribution to the magazine after Moxon became its publisher. It was arranged that Lamb should furnish miscellaneous papers under the general heading of *Peter's Net*.

Janus Weathercock. The afterwards notorious Wainwright, the forger and poisoner.

The Athenæum has been hoaxed. The poem in question had appeared in Hone's *Year Book* (1831) under the date 30th April. It was entitled "The Meadows in Spring," and was thus prefaced by its author, who signed himself "Epsilon":—"These verses are in the old style; rather homely in expression; but I honestly profess to stick more to the simplicity of the old poets than the moderns, and to love the philosophical good-humour of our old writers more than the sickly melancholy of the Byronian wits. If my verses be not good, they are good-humoured, and that is something." The verses, as Lamb points out, were again published, as a novelty, in the *Athenæum* of a few months later. The editor of the *Athenæum* (July 9, 1831) appended to them the following note:—"We have a suspicion that we could name the writer; if so, we are sure his name would grace our pages as much as his verses." It is Lamb that is here pointed to, and accordingly he now disowns the authorship. I am glad to be able, on the authority of my friend Mr. W. Aldis Wright, to clear up the mystery. The verses were certainly by the late Edward FitzGerald, then a young man of only one-and-twenty. Mr. Aldis Wright thus tells the story:—"In the year 1873 Edward FitzGerald told a correspondent of mine that when he was a lad, or rather more than a lad, he sent some verses to Hone, which were afterwards copied into the *Athenæum* of the time. These were ascribed to Charles Lamb, who wrote to say *he* did not write them—he wished he had." It is obvious that these are the verses referred to, signed with the first letter (Epsilon) of FitzGerald's favourite signature, E. F. G. The lines, which open thus—

> "'Tis a dull sight
> To see the year dying,
> When autumn's last wind
> Sets the yellow wood sighing,
> Sighing, oh sighing."—

are very beautiful, in the style of the seventeenth-century poets, and we cannot wonder at Lamb envying the unknown author.

The Anecdotes of E. and of G. D. E. is Elliston, anecdotes of whom Lamb had contributed to the *Englishman's Magazine* in the August number, under the heading *Ellistoniana*. G. D. is, of course the George Dawe just before named.

Montgomery's "Last Man." Was Lamb confusing Montgomery and Campbell, or was he thinking of Montgomery's "Common Lot," which we know to have been a favourite with him?

LETTER CCCCXXXIII (p. 1002).—Moxon had just resolved to abandon his unsuccessful venture, the *Englishman's Magazine*.

Devil's Money. The sum paid by Moxon for Lamb's poetical squib, *Satan in Search of a Wife*, published this year in a thin volume, with illustrations (see *Mrs. Leicester's School*, etc., p. 381).

Any book on Christ's Hospital. J. I. Wilson's *History of Christ's Hospital* (1821). Several editions of this book contained quotations from Lamb and tributes to his genius. Mr. "Seagull" was perhaps Rev. John Seager.

LETTER CCCCXXXV (p. 1005).The date of this note is uncertain, but was probably about the time given above. Carlyle's friend from Birmingham, Dr. Badams the chemist, had married Louisa Holcroft in 1828, and about two years before Badams' death in 1834, had taken a house in Enfield, where they occasionally resided. Carlyle in his *Reminiscences* (Froude's Edition, ii. 164) relates how "Badams with his wife was living out at Enfield, in a big old rambling sherd of a house among waste gardens; thither I twice or thrice went, much liking the man, but never getting any good of him." It was on one of these occasions that Carlyle met Charles and Mary Lamb, "a very sorry pair of phenomena," as he goes on to describe. It would appear from this note that Lamb had been somewhat irritated at the Badams couple meditating a residence so near him. Perhaps Carlyle was one of those who justifies Lamb's presentiment.

LETTER CCCCXXXVI (p. 1005).—Lamb sends Landor one of his volumes, probably the unfortunate *Satan in Search of a Wife*. Landor had sent some verses for Emma Isola's album.

Rose Aylmer. I may be pardoned for quoting once more Landor's lovely poem. The charm that Lamb could not explain lies partly perhaps in the singular beauty of the lady's name, and its repetition in the second stanza:—

> "Ah! what avails the sceptre Race
> And what the form divine?
> What every virtue, every grace?
> Rose Aylmer, all were thine!

> "Rose Aylmer, whom these wakeful eyes
> May weep, but never see,
> A night of memories and of sighs
> I consecrate to thee."

Separate fragments of this letter are given in Forster's *Life of Landor*. There we also learn that the "measureless B.'s" were the family of Mr. Charles Betham, a tenant of Landor's at Llanthony. He was the brother of Miss Matilda Betham, whose name has occurred more than once in Lamb's correspondence. See Forster's *Walter Savage Landor, a Biography*, i. 382-386.

LETTER CCCCXXXVIII (p. 1006).—Mr. Moxon had sent Lamb his last two poetical publications. A. C. (Allan Cunningham) had brought out his *Maid of Elvar*, and B. C. (Barry Cornwall) a volume of songs and ballads. The poems whose titles follow are from the latter volume. "Epistle to What's his Name" is Procter's "Epistle to Charles Lamb on his Retirement from the India House," a tender and discriminating tribute.

LETTER CCCCXXXIX (p. 1007).—Another of Lamb's elaborate fictions, though in this instance a fiction founded upon fact. A singularly brutal murder had been committed in Enfield on the night of December 19th in this year. The victim, a man of the name of Danby, then recently returned from India and supposed to have money about him, was drinking that evening in the parlour of the Crown and Horseshoe, in company with three men of the names of Johnson, Fare, and Cooper. Johnson and Cooper, when the hour for closing arrived, took Danby up a lane called Holt White's Hill, and there the murder was committed. All three men were arrested on the following morning. They were tried at the Old Bailey in January following. Fare was acquitted, Cooper turned king's evidence, but Johnson was convicted, and was hanged four days later.

The whole story of Lamb's accidental association with the accused men in the public-house parlour is, of course, a joke. Probably there may have been a wig-maker of the name of Danby in the Temple when Lamb was a child, which gave him the opportunity for an additional experiment on his correspondent's credulity. A full account of the murder will be found in the *Annual Register* for 1833.

LETTER CCCCXL (p. 1008).—Talfourd had just been made a serjeant. Lamb remembered him, fifteen years back, when he was a "Chitty-ling," or pupil of Joseph Chitty.

H. C. R. Henry Crabb Robinson, who never proceeded to the higher ranks of the advocate's profession.

LETTER CCCCXLI (p. 1009).—Moxon was just about to publish the *Last Essays of Elia* in a volume. The "Friend's Preface" is the well-known preface written by Lamb himself, but purporting to be by "a friend of the late Elia."

LETTER CCCCXLIII (p. 1010).—William Hone, in his latter years, reverted to the religious and dissenting associations of his youth, and became an occasional and very earnest preacher. Lamb playfully adapts his style to his friend's new vocation. The verses of Lamb's, which he inquires for, will be found in Hone's *Year Book* (*not* his *Table Book*), March 19, 1831. They are headed "To C. Aders, Esq., on his Collection of Paintings by the old German Masters." The lines are, to say the truth, not very good.

LETTER CCCCXLVI (p. 1011).—Charles and Mary had just made what was destined to be their last change of residence, from Enfield to the neighbouring village of Edmonton. They now arranged to board and lodge with a Mr. and Mrs. Walden at Bay Cottage, in Church Street. The name has been of late years changed, in honour of its distinguished occupants, to *Lamb's* Cottage. It is within a stone's throw of the parish church and of Lamb's grave.

LETTER CCCCXLVII (p. 1011).—The *Last Essays of Elia* were just published in a volume by Moxon. They included one on the "Barrenness of the Imaginative Faculty in the Productions of Modern Art." The "Ariadne" of Titian in the National Gallery is there described and criticised, and it is to this that Lamb refers in the present letter. The "Popular Fallacies" were also reprinted in this volume from the *New Monthly Magazine.*

LETTER CCCCLII (p. 1014).—This very fierce letter appears to refer to the lawsuit between Moxon and Taylor respecting the copyright in the essays forming the second series of *Elia.*

LETTER CCCCLIII (p. 1015).—This charming little note pleasantly completes the story of Emma Isola's courtship by Edward Moxon. Mrs. Moxon died at Brighton on the 2nd of February 1891, at the age of eighty-two. She was accordingly twenty-four at the time of her marriage.

LETTER CCCCLVI (p. 1017).—Edward Moxon was preparing a new collection of sonnets, afterwards published in a slender octavo, dedicated to Wordsworth, in 1835. It included several inspired by his "young Bride." Moxon accepted one at least of Lamb's corrections; for the fifth sonnet, when printed, opened thus—

> "Four days, wild Ocean, on thy troubled breast
> A wanderer I have been!"

Knowles's play, epilogued by me.—"The Wife."

LETTER CCCCLVII (p. 1018).—An early copy of Rogers's volume of poems, with illustrations by Turner and Stothard, published in 1834, had been sent to Lamb.

A sonnet in the "Times." The sonnet which I now append, appeared in the *Times* of December 13, 1833:—

> *"To Samuel Rogers, Esq., on the new Edition of his
> 'Pleasures of Memory.'*
>
> "When thy gay book hath paid its proud devoirs,
> Poetic friend, and fed with luxury
> The eye of pampered aristocracy
> In flittering drawing-rooms and gilt boudoirs,
> O'erlaid with comments of pictorial art
> However rich or rare, yet nothing leaving
> Of healthful action to the soul-conceiving
> Of the true reader—yet a nobler part
> Awaits thy work, already classic styled.
> Cheap-clad, accessible, in homeliest show
> The modest beauty thro' the land shall go
> From year to year, and render life more mild;
> Refinement to the poor man's hearth shall give
> And in the moral heart of England live."

Your artist. Thomas Stothard. He died within a few months of this mention of him, in April 1834, at the age of seventy-nine. The verses, published in the *Athenæum*, beginning—

> "Consummate artist, whose undying name
> With classic Rogers shall go down to fame,"

will be found in *Mrs. Leicester's School*, etc. p. 373.

Poor Henry's. Henry Rogers, brother of the poet.

Coleridge's happy exemplification. Lamb, after his custom, does not quote the lines correctly, nor does he appear to have been aware that they were translated from Schiller—

> "In the Hexameter rises the fountain's silvery column;
> In the Pentameter aye, falling in melody back"

Coleridge's version was first printed in *Friendship's Offering*, 1834.

LETTER CCCCLVIII (p. 1019).—This letter was first printed by me from the original in the possession of B. MacGeorge, Esq., of Glasgow. It is worthy of preservation, if only for the beautiful thought in the last sentence. *The kind legacy* refers to a legacy of £30 from Anne Betham to Mary Lamb.

LETTER CCCCLIX (p. 1020).—Miss Fryer, of Chatteris in Cambridge-shire, was an old schoolfellow of Emma Isola. Dover Street was now the home of the Edward Moxons, and was to achieve a deservedly high name in as-sociation with poets and poetry.

LETTER CCCCLX (p. 1021).—Louisa Martin was an old friend of Lamb and his sister. She bore the nickname of "Monkey," and some verses addressed to her will be found in *Poems*, p. 556.

LETTER CCCCLXI (p. 1021).—This interesting and touching letter was first printed by me from the original in Rev. C. R. Manning's possession. *Wright's* is, of course, meant for Wright's translation of Dante, and the *faithfulness of C. for* Cary's.

LETTER CCCCLXII (p. 1022).—Samuel Taylor Coleridge died at Mr. Gill-man's, Highgate, on the 25th of July 1834. "Shortly after," Talfourd tells us, "assured that his presence would be welcome, Lamb went to Highgate. There he asked leave to see the nurse who had attended upon Coleridge; and being struck and affected by the feeling she manifested towards his friend, insisted on her receiving five guineas from him."

LETTER CCCCLXIII (p. 1023).—Mr. Cary had just returned from a tour through Normandy and the South of France. It was in the previous year that he had visited Holland and Germany. This note is in answer to an invitation to the resumed monthly dinners at the Museum.

LETTER CCCCLXIV (p. 1023).—"In December 1834 Mr. Lamb received a letter from a gentleman, a stranger to him—Mr. Childs of Bungay, whose copy of *Elia* had been sent on an Oriental voyage, and who, in order to replace it, applied to Mr. Lamb." (Talfourd.)

LETTER CCCCLXV (p. 1024).—Mr. Cary's son, in his Memoir of his father, does not print this letter, though he gives other letters of Lamb's. Talfourd gives it without any date. It has been hitherto assumed to belong to the pre-ceding year, but there are reasons why I think this unlikely.

LETTER CCCCLXVI (p. 1025).—"The following notelet is in answer to a letter inclosing a list of candidates for a Widow's Fund Society, for which he was entitled to vote. A Mrs. Southey headed the inclosed list." (Talfourd.)

LETTER CCCCLXVII (p. 1025).—The Rev. Henry Cary, in the Memoir of his father, after quoting Lamb's short note of 12th September, adds:—"Not many weeks after, Lamb died. He had borrowed of my father Phillips's *Thea-*

trum Poetarum Anglicanorum, which was returned by Lamb's friend, Mr. Moxon, with the leaf folded down at the account of Sir Philip Sydney." Mr. Cary acknowledged the receipt of the book by the following

LINES TO THE MEMORY OF CHARLES LAMB

"So should it be, my gentle friend;
Thy leaf last closed at Sydney's end.
Thou, too, like Sydney, wouldst have given
The water, thirsting and near heaven;
Nay, were it wine, filled to the brim,
Thou hadst look'd hard, but given, like him.

"And art thou mingled then among
Those famous sons of ancient song?
And do they gather round, and praise
Thy relish of their nobler lays?
Waxing in mirth to hear thee tell
With what strange mortals thou didst dwell!
At thy quaint sallies more delighted,
Than any's long among them lighted!

"'Tis done: and thou hast joined a crew
To whom thy soul was justly due;
And yet, I think, where'er thou be,
They'll scarcely love thee more than we."

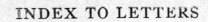

INDEX TO LETTERS